Tax Formula for Corporate Taxpayers

Income *(from whatever source)*	$ xxx,xxx
Less: Exclusions from gross income	− xx,xxx
Gross Income	$ xxx,xxx
Less: Deductions	− xx,xxx
Taxable Income	$ xxx,xxx
Applicable tax rates	× xx%
Gross Tax	$ xx,xxx
Less: Tax credits and prepayments	− x,xxx
Tax Due *(or refund)*	$ xx,xxx

Students – Get Study Help Now for Your Tax Course

Do you need more help studying for your taxation class?
Order the Study Guide to this textbook and get up-to-date help fast!

- **Study Highlights** – an outline of key topics for each chapter.
- **Key Terms** used in the chapter.
- **Self-Quizzing** with helpful, annotated answers.

Check with your bookstore. Ask for ISBN 0-324-66166-5.

Or Order Online Now. Go to **academic.cengage.com/taxation/SWFT**. Select your text from the titles listed. At the Student Resources page for your text, select Book Supplements. Click on the link for Study Guide and add it to the shopping cart.

Test Drive the Study Guide with Free Sample Chapter. Go to **academic.cengage.com/taxation/SWFT**, select your text from the titles listed, go to the Student Resources page, and click on the Sample Study Guide Chapter link to download a chapter.

Get Even More Help – *Ask Your Instructor* about Assigning These Practice Sets

- *For Individual Taxation:*
  Practice Sets for South-Western Federal Taxation: Individual Income Taxes, 2009 Edition. These practice sets, by Raymond Wacker (Southern Illinois University), are comprehensive and designed to be completed near the end of the course using tax preparation software such as TaxCut®. ISBN: 0-324-66120-7
- *For Corporations, S Corporations, and Partnerships:*
  Practice Sets for South-Western Federal Taxation: Corporations, Partnerships, Estates & Trusts, 2009 Edition. These practice sets, by Don Trippeer (SUNY College at Oneonta), allow you to put your corporations and partnerships knowledge to use, ensuring proper understanding of concepts and procedures using TaxCut® or other tax preparation software. ISBN: 0-324-66165-7

Practice sets work with the latest tax forms and are available for purchase online by visiting **academic.cengage.com/taxation/SWFT**

Check with your instructor before buying practice sets. Solutions are available to instructors only in a separate volume.

TaxCut. More than software.

Put the experience
of H&R Block
tax professionals
on your side.

- Step-by-step interview guides you through a customized process.

- Accurate Calculations and 100% Satisfaction—Guaranteed.*

- Worry-free Audit Support™ when you e-file and access to tax advice

  from an H&R Block tax professional.

H&R BLOCK®

You got people™

SOUTH-WESTERN
FEDERAL TAXATION

Corporations, Partnerships, Estates & Trusts

EDITION 2009

General Editors

William H. Hoffman, Jr.
J.D., Ph.D., CPA

William A. Raabe
Ph.D., CPA

James E. Smith
Ph.D., CPA

David M. Maloney
Ph.D., CPA

Contributing Authors

James H. Boyd
Ph.D., CPA
Arizona State University

D. Larry Crumbley
Ph.D., CPA
Louisiana State University

Jon S. Davis
Ph.D., CPA
University of Wisconsin-Madison

Steven C. Dilley
J.D., Ph.D., CPA
Michigan State University

William H. Hoffman, Jr.
J.D., Ph.D., CPA
University of Houston

David M. Maloney
Ph.D., CPA
University of Virginia

Gary A. McGill
Ph.D., CPA
University of Florida

Mark B. Persellin
Ph.D., CPA, CFP®
St. Mary's University

William A. Raabe
Ph.D., CPA
The Ohio State University

Boyd C. Randall
J.D., Ph.D.
Brigham Young University

Debra L. Sanders
Ph.D., CPA
Washington State University

W. Eugene Seago
J.D., Ph.D., CPA
Virginia Polytechnic
Institute and State University

James E. Smith
Ph.D., CPA
College of William and Mary

Eugene Willis
Ph.D., CPA
University of Illinois,
Urbana-Champaign

SOUTH-WESTERN
CENGAGE Learning™

Australia • Brazil • Japan • Korea • Mexico • Singapore • Spain • United Kingdom • United States

SOUTH-WESTERN
CENGAGE Learning

South-Western Federal Taxation: Corporations, Partnerships, Estates & Trusts, 2009 Edition

William H. Hoffman, Jr., William A. Raabe, James E. Smith, David M. Maloney

Vice President of Editorial, Business: Jack W. Calhoun

Editor-in-Chief: Rob Dewey

Senior Developmental Editor: Craig Avery

Marketing Manager: Kristen Hurd

Marketing Communications Manager: Libby Shipp

Senior Content Project Manager: Tim Bailey

Media Editor: Robin Browning

Website Project Manager: Brian Courter

Senior Frontlist Buyer: Doug Wilke

Production Service: LEAP Publishing Services, Inc.

Compositor: Cadmus Communications

Senior Art Director: Michelle Kunkler

Internal Designer: Diane Gliebe/Design Matters

Cover Designer: Craig Ramsdell

Cover Image: © Getty Images, Inc.

For product information and technology assistance, contact us at **Cengage Learning Academic Resource Center, 1-800-423-0563**

For permission to use material from this text or product, submit all requests online at **www.cengage.com/permissions** Further permissions questions can be emailed to **permissionrequest@cengage.com**

Exam*View*® is a registered trademark of eInstruction Corp. Windows is a registered trademark of the Microsoft Corporation used herein under license.

Cengage Learning WebTutor™ is a trademark of Cengage Learning.

Student Edition ISBN 13: 978-0-324-66017-3
Student Edition ISBN 10: 0-324-66017-0
Student Edition with CD ISBN 13: 978-0-324-66021-0
Student Edition with CD ISBN 10: 0-324-66021-9
Instructor's Edition with CD ISBN 13: 978-0-324-66183-5
Instructor's Edition with CD ISBN 10: 0-324-66183-5
Loose Leaf Edition with CD ISBN 13: 978-0-324-66163-7
Loose Leaf Edition with CD ISBN 10: 0-324-66163-0

ISSN: 0270-5265
2009 Annual Edition

South-Western Cengage Learning
5191 Natorp Boulevard
Mason, OH 45040
USA

Cengage Learning products are represented in Canada by Nelson Education, Ltd.

For your course and learning solutions, visit **academic.cengage.com**

Purchase any of our products at your local college store or at our preferred online store **www.ichapters.com**

Printed in the United States of America
1 2 3 4 5 6 7 12 11 10 09 08

To the Student

The Leadership You Trust—The Innovation You Expect—The Service You Deserve

◆

South-Western Federal Taxation is the most trusted and largest selling brand in college taxation. We are focused exclusively on providing the most useful, comprehensive, and up-to-date tax texts, online study aids, tax preparation tools, and print study guides to help you succeed in your tax courses and beyond.

◆

More than just a textbook, *Corporations, Partnerships, Estates & Trusts, 2009 Edition* provides a dynamic learning experience in and out of the classroom. Built around the areas students have identified as the most important, our complete study system will offer you options in the way you learn.

Online Resources and Study Tools

TaxCut® software automatically comes with this textbook to provide you with an additional tax preparation tool!

TaxCut. More than software. Put the experience of H&R Block tax professionals on your side.

Thomson/RIA's Checkpoint® Student Edition is an **optional item** your instructor may have ordered, offering six-month access to a leading online tax research database.

3 Simple Ways Checkpoint® Helps You Make Sense of All Those Taxes:

- Intuitive Web-based design makes it fast and simple to find what you need.
- A comprehensive collection of primary tax law, cases, and rulings along with analytical insight you simply can't find anywhere else.
- Checkpoint® has built-in productivity tools such as calculators to make research more efficient—a resource more tax pros use than any other.

Book Companion Web Site—academic.cengage.com/taxation/swft—contains updates, quizzes, and a rich array of **free learning aids**:

- **Free interactive quizzes.** These short, self-graded quizzes help you brush up on chapter topics. Many more self-quizzes are available in the Study Guide—see below.
- **Flashcards** use chapter terms and definitions to aid you in learning tax terminology for each chapter.
- **Online glossary** for each chapter provides terms and definitions from the text in alphabetical order for easy reference.
- **Learning objectives** are downloadable for each chapter to keep you on track.
- **Tax Tips for the Recent Graduate** introduce the college graduate to some common tax considerations that could be beneficial in reducing the dreaded "tax-bite."
- **Tax Updates** provide the most recent tax information and major changes to the tax law.
- **Tax tables** used in the textbook are downloadable for reference.
- **Download a Study Guide Chapter FREE Before You Buy!** Get one chapter of the print Study Guide free online. The Study Guide contains questions and problems with solutions for self-study, as well as chapter highlights that point you to the right place in the text for further study. Order it from your bookstore (**ISBN 0-324-66166-5**) or buy it online by chapter at **ichapters.com**.

iChapters.com

Visit **iChapters.com** to receive 25 percent off on more than 10,000 print, digital, and audio study tools that allow you to:

- **Practice, review, and master course concepts** ... *by purchasing the study guide or practice sets that work hand-in-hand with this textbook.*
- **Join the thousands of students who've benefited from iChapters.com**. Just search by author, title, or ISBN; then filter the results by "Study Tools" and select the format best suited for you.

Additional Student Resources

Study Guide, ISBN 0-324-66166-5
Do you need more help studying for your taxation class? Order the Study Guide to receive:

- Study Highlights—an outline of key topics for each chapter.
- Key Terms used in the chapter.
- Self-Quizzing with helpful, annotated answers that are keyed to pages in the 2009 Edition.

Check with your bookstore or order on **iChapters.com**.

Corporations, S Corporations, and Partnerships Practice Sets ISBN 0-324-66165-7
Ask your instructor about assigning these practice sets.
Written specifically for **Corporations, Partnerships, Estates & Trusts, 2009 Edition,** these practice sets are comprehensive and designed to be completed near the end of the course using tax preparation software such as TaxCut®.

Check with your instructor before ordering practice sets—solutions are available to instructors only in a separate volume.

For over 30 years, the **South-Western Federal Taxation** Series has guided more than 1.5 million students through the ever-changing field of Federal taxation.

With commitment to leadership, innovation, and service, we have a stake in your success both now and in the future.

About the Editors

William H. Hoffman Jr. earned B.A. and J.D. degrees from the University of Michigan and M.B.A. and Ph.D. degrees from the University of Texas. He is a licensed CPA and attorney in Texas. His teaching experience includes: the University of Texas (1957–1961), Louisiana State University (1961–1967), and the University of Houston (1967–1999). Professor Hoffman has addressed many tax institutes and conferences and has published extensively in academic and professional journals. His articles appear in *The Journal of Taxation, The Tax Adviser, Taxes— The Tax Magazine, The Journal of Accountancy, The Accounting Review,* and *Taxation for Accountants.*

William A. Raabe teaches tax courses in the Fisher College of Business at the Ohio State University. A graduate of Carroll College (WI) and the University of Illinois, Dr. Raabe's teaching and research interests include international and multistate taxation, technology in tax education, personal financial planning, and the economic impact of sports teams and fine arts groups. Professor Raabe also writes *Federal Tax Research* and the PricewaterhouseCoopers Tax Case Studies. He has written extensively about book-tax differences in financial reporting, including a book about the corporate Schedule M–3 and articles and cases addressing FIN 48 issues. Dr. Raabe has been a visiting tax faculty member for a number of public accounting firms, bar associations, and CPA societies. He has received numerous teaching awards, including the Accounting Educator of the Year award from the Wisconsin Institute of CPAs.

James E. Smith is the John S. Quinn Professor of Accounting at the College of William and Mary. He has been a member of the Accounting Faculty for over 30 years. He received his Ph.D. degree from the University of Arizona. Professor Smith has served as a discussion leader for Continuing Professional Education programs for the AICPA, Federal Tax Workshops, and various state CPA societies. He has conducted programs in more than 40 states for approximately 25,000 CPAs. He has been the recipient of the AICPA's Outstanding Discussion Leader Award and the American Taxation Association/Arthur Andersen Teaching Innovation Award. Among his other awards are the Virginia Society of CPAs' Outstanding Accounting Educator Award and the James Madison University's Outstanding Accounting Educator Award. He was the President of the Administrators of Accounting Programs Group (AAPG) in 1991–1992. He was the faculty adviser for the William and Mary teams that received first place in the Andersen Tax Challenge in 1994, 1995, 1997, 2000, and 2001 and in the Deloitte Tax Case Study Competition in 2002, 2004, 2005, and 2006.

David M. Maloney, Ph.D., CPA, is the Carman G. Blough Professor of Accounting at the University of Virginia's McIntire School of Commerce. He completed his undergraduate work at the University of Richmond and his graduate work at the University of Illinois at Urbana-Champaign. Since joining the Virginia faculty in January 1984, Professor Maloney has taught Federal taxation in the graduate and undergraduate programs and has received major research grants from the Ernst & Young and KPMG Foundations. In addition, his work has been published in numerous professional journals, including *Journal of Taxation, The Tax Adviser, Tax Notes, Corporate Taxation, Accounting Horizons, Journal of Taxation of Investments,* and *Journal of Accountancy.* He is a member of several professional organizations, including the American Accounting Association and the American Taxation Association.

CONTENTS IN BRIEF

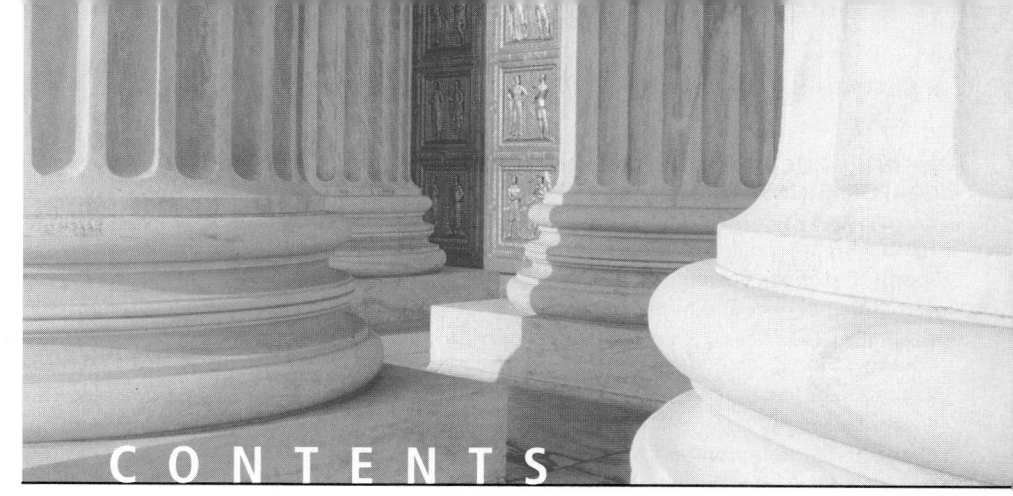

CONTENTS

PART 3: FLOW-THROUGH ENTITIES

PART 4: ADVANCED TAX PRACTICE CONSIDERATIONS

PART 5: FAMILY TAX PLANNING

APPENDIXES

PART 1

Introduction

The Federal law is an unbelievably complex set of rules. In working with these rules, however, it is helpful to understand why they came about. Also necessary is the ability to locate the sources of these rules. Part I, therefore, is devoted to the "whys" of the tax law and the applications of the tax research process.

CHAPTER 1
Understanding and Working with the
Federal Tax Law

CHAPTER 1

Understanding and Working with the Federal Tax Law

LEARNING OBJECTIVES

After completing Chapter 1, you should be able to:

LO.1
Realize the importance of revenue needs as an objective of Federal tax law.

LO.2
Appreciate the influence of economic, social, equity, and political considerations on the development of the tax law.

LO.3
Understand how the IRS, as the protector of the revenue, has affected tax law.

LO.4
Recognize the role of the courts in interpreting and shaping tax law.

LO.5
Identify tax law sources—statutory, administrative, and judicial.

LO.6
Locate tax law sources.

LO.7
Be able to carry out tax research.

LO.8
Assess the validity and weight of tax law sources.

LO.9
Make use of various tax planning procedures.

LO.10
Be aware of the role of taxation on the CPA examination.

The Whys of the Tax Law

The Federal tax law is a mixture of statutory provisions, administrative pronouncements, and court decisions. Anyone who has attempted to work with this body of knowledge is familiar with its complexity. Commenting on his 48-page tax return, the author James Michener said, "It is unimaginable in that I graduated from one of America's better colleges, yet I am totally incapable of understanding tax returns." For the person who has to wade through rule upon rule to find the solution to a tax problem, it may be of some consolation to know that the law's complexity can be explained. There is a reason for the formulation of every rule. Knowing these reasons, therefore, is a considerable step toward understanding the Federal tax law.

The major objective of the Federal tax law is the raising of revenue. Despite the importance of the fiscal needs of the government, however, other considerations explain certain portions of the law. In particular, economic, social, equity, and political factors play a significant role. Added to these factors is the marked impact the Internal Revenue Service (IRS) and the courts have had and will continue to have on the evolution of Federal tax law. These matters are treated in the first part of this chapter. Wherever appropriate, the discussion is related to subjects covered later in the text.

LO.1

Realize the importance of revenue needs as an objective of Federal tax law.

Revenue Needs

The foundation of any tax system has to be the raising of revenue to absorb the cost of government operations. Ideally, annual outlays should not exceed anticipated revenues. This situation leads to a balanced budget with no deficit. Many states have achieved this objective by passing laws or constitutional amendments precluding deficit spending. Unfortunately, the Federal government has no such prohibition, and the national debt has grown, reaching $9 trillion, or more than $30,000 per citizen, in late 2007. Concern about the rising debt has caused Congress to become more deficit-conscious when enacting tax legislation.

TAX *in the News* — REVENUE NEUTRALITY IN CURRENT PERSPECTIVE

During the Bush administration, the major thrust of tax legislation has been to reduce taxes. The first legislation (the Tax Relief Reconciliation Act of 2001) attempted to reduce taxes while avoiding significant *immediate* revenue loss. Consequently, many changes were to be phased in over periods of up to 10 years. Follow-up legislation (including major bills in 2002, 2003, and 2004) made further reductions and accelerated the phase-in of many of the changes already scheduled.

As these tax reductions were intended to "jump-start" the economy, they were not cushioned by revenue offsets. Instead, revenue neutrality is achieved over the long run through the use of "sunset provisions." Simply stated, a sunset provision is a built-in time machine that reinstates the law that existed before the tax reduction went into effect. Like the tax reduction phase-ins, however, the sunset provisions do not take effect at the same time. Furthermore, what is to preclude Congress from revoking a particular sunset provision, thereby making the tax reduction permanent? Needless to say, the end result is a Federal tax system that is highly unstable, largely unpredictable, and hardly revenue neutral.

The current Democrat-led Congress has a "pay-as-you-go" approach to tax legislation. The Democrats' emphasis on revenue offsets to their spending plans may affect many of the sunset provisions. By allowing a sunset provision to take effect, they can avoid the stigma associated with *directly* raising taxes, yet accomplish the same result.

When enacting tax legislation, Congress often is guided by the concept of **revenue neutrality** so that any changes neither increase nor decrease the net revenues raised under the prior rules. Revenue neutrality does not mean that any one taxpayer's tax liability remains the same. Since this liability depends upon the circumstances involved, one taxpayer's increased tax liability could be another's tax saving. Revenue-neutral tax reform does not reduce deficits, but at least it does not aggravate the problem.

Economic Considerations

LO.2

Appreciate the influence of economic, social, equity, and political considerations on the development of the tax law.

Using the tax system to attempt to accomplish economic objectives has become increasingly popular in recent years. Generally, this process involves amending the Internal Revenue Code[1] through tax legislation and emphasizes measures designed to help control the economy or encourage certain activities and businesses.

Control of the Economy. Congress has made use of depreciation write-offs as a means of controlling the economy. Theoretically, shorter asset lives and accelerated methods should encourage additional investments in depreciable property acquired for business use. Conversely, longer class lives and the required use of the straight-line method of depreciation dampen the tax incentive for capital outlays.

Another approach that utilizes depreciation as a means of controlling capital investment is the amount of write-off allowed upon the acquisition of assets. This approach is followed by the § 179 election to immediately expense assets (up to $128,000 in 2008). It also was the approach used by Congress in various prior provisions that permitted up to 50 percent additional first-year depreciation.

A change in the tax rate structure has a more immediate impact on the economy. When tax rates are lowered, taxpayers are able to obtain additional spendable funds. In the interest of revenue neutrality, however, rate decreases may be accompanied by a reduction or elimination of deductions or credits. Thus, lower rates do not always mean lower taxes.

Encouragement of Certain Activities. Without passing judgment on the wisdom of any such choices, it is quite clear that the tax law does encourage certain

---

[1]The Internal Revenue Code is a compilation of Federal tax legislation that appears in Title 26 of the U.S. Code.

types of economic activity or segments of the economy. For example, the desire to foster technological progress helps explain the favorable treatment accorded to research and development expenditures. Under the tax law, such expenditures can be deducted in the year incurred or, alternatively, capitalized and amortized over a period of 60 months or more. In terms of timing the tax saving, such options usually are preferable to a capitalization of the cost with a write-off over the estimated useful life of the asset created.[2]

The encouragement of technological progress can also explain why the tax law places the inventor in a special position. Not only can patents qualify as capital assets, but under certain conditions their disposition automatically carries long-term capital gain treatment.[3]

Are ecological considerations a desirable objective? If they are, it explains why the tax law permits a 60-month amortization period for costs incurred in the installation of pollution control facilities.

With a view toward conserving and developing national energy resources, in 2005 Congress enacted legislation that provides tax incentives to encourage certain activities. Not only are various tax credits made available for home energy conservation expenditures but favorable tax treatment is extended to the purchase of "clean fuel" vehicles. Further, the law provides significant tax incentives to encourage the development of more efficient and reliable energy infrastructure (i.e., power grids).

Does stimulating the development and rehabilitation of low-income rental housing benefit the economy? The tax law definitely favors these activities by allowing generous tax credits to taxpayers incurring such costs.

Is saving desirable for the economy? Saving leads to capital formation and thus makes funds available to finance home construction and industrial expansion. The tax law provides incentives to encourage saving by giving private retirement plans preferential treatment. Not only are contributions to Keogh (H.R. 10) plans and certain Individual Retirement Accounts (IRAs) deductible, but income from such contributions accumulates on a tax-free basis. As noted in a following section, the encouragement of private-sector pension plans can be justified under social considerations as well.

Encouragement of Certain Industries. Who can question the proposition that a sound agricultural base is necessary for a well-balanced national economy? Undoubtedly, this belief can explain why farmers are accorded special treatment under the Federal tax system. Among the benefits are the election to expense rather than capitalize certain expenditures for soil and water conservation and fertilizers and the election to defer the recognition of gain on the receipt of crop insurance proceeds.

The tax law favors the development of natural resources by permitting the use of percentage depletion on the extraction and sale of oil and gas and specified mineral deposits and a write-off (rather than a capitalization) of certain exploration costs. The railroad and banking industries also receive special tax treatment. All of these provisions can be explained, in whole or in part, by economic considerations.

A well-balanced economy should also include a vigorous and dynamic manufacturing industry. To encourage this sector, in 2004 Congress enacted a tax incentive based on profits from manufacturing. Known as the domestic production activities deduction, the benefit is structured in such a manner as to stimulate the creation of jobs.

Encouragement of Small Business. At least in the United States, a consensus exists that what is good for small business is good for the economy as a whole. This assumption has led to a definite bias in the tax law favoring small business.

---

[2]If the asset developed has no estimated useful life, no write-off would be available without the two options allowed by the tax law.

[3]A long-term capital gain has a favorable tax advantage for individuals.

TAX *in the News*   **CAN TAXES CHANGE BEHAVIOR?**

Peter the Great, the ruler of Russia from 1682 to 1725, imposed a tax on beards (except for the clergy) because he felt that beards were "unnecessary, uncivilized, and ridiculous." If an individual did not pay the tax, a tax official would scrape off the beard. Without warning Peter himself would take a straight razor to the faces of bearded men appearing before him. When Peter attended a ceremony or banquet, anyone arriving with a beard would depart without it.

Source: *Adapted from Erik Jensen, "Taxation of Beards," Tax Notes (January 5, 2000), pp. 153–157.*

In the corporate tax area, several provisions can be explained by the desire to benefit small business. One provision enables a shareholder in a small business corporation to obtain an ordinary deduction for any loss recognized on a stock investment. Normally, such a loss would receive the less attractive capital loss treatment. The point of this favoritism is to encourage additional equity investments in small business corporations.[4] Another provision permits the shareholders of a small business corporation to make a special election that generally will avoid the imposition of the corporate income tax.[5] Furthermore, such an election enables the corporation to pass through to its shareholders any of its operating losses.[6]

The tax rates applicable to corporations tend to favor small business in that size is relative to the amount of taxable income generated in any one year. Since a corporate tax rate of 34 percent applies only to taxable income in excess of $75,000, corporations that stay within this limit are subject to lower average tax rates.

EXAMPLE 1

For calendar year 2008, Brown Corporation has taxable income of $75,000, and Red Corporation has taxable income of $100,000. Based on this information, the corporate income tax is $13,750 for Brown Corporation and $22,250 for Red Corporation (see Chapter 2). Brown Corporation is subject to an average tax rate of 18.33% ($13,750/$75,000), while Red Corporation is subject to an average rate of 22.25% ($22,250/$100,000). ■

If a corporation has taxable income in excess of $100,000, the benefits of the lower brackets are phased out until all income is taxed at the maximum rate of 34 percent. Once taxable income reaches $10 million, the rate becomes 35 percent.

One of the justifications for the enactment of the tax law governing corporate reorganizations (see Chapter 7) was the economic benefit it would provide for small businesses. By allowing corporations to combine without adverse tax consequences, small corporations would be in a position to compete more effectively with larger concerns.

Social Considerations

Some of the tax laws, especially those related to the Federal income tax of individuals, can be explained by social considerations. Rather than using loans, grants, and other programs to reach desired goals, Congress often uses the Tax Code to provide incentives and benefits (e.g., the higher education incentives). The following are some notable examples:

---

[4]Known as Section 1244 stock, this subject is covered in Chapter 4.

[5]Known as the S corporation election, the subject is discussed extensively in Chapter 12.

[6]In general, an operating loss can benefit only the corporation incurring the loss through a carryback or carryover to profitable years. Consequently, the shareholders of the corporation usually cannot take advantage of any such loss.

- The refundable earned income tax credit. As Congress has deemed it socially desirable to reduce the number of people on the welfare rolls and to cut funding for welfare programs, this credit has come to replace some welfare programs.
- The nontaxability of certain benefits provided to employees through accident and health plans financed by employers. It is socially desirable to encourage such plans, since they provide medical benefits in the event of an employee's illness or injury.
- The nontaxability to the employee of some of the premiums paid by an employer for group term insurance covering the life of the employee. These arrangements can be justified in that they provide funds to help the family unit adjust to the loss of wages caused by the employee's death.
- The tax treatment to the employee of contributions made by an employer to qualified pension or profit sharing plans. The contribution and any income it earns are not taxed to the employee until the funds are distributed. Private retirement plans are encouraged because they supplement the subsistence income level the employee would otherwise have under the Social Security system.[7]
- The deduction allowed for contributions to qualified charitable organizations. The deduction attempts to shift some of the financial and administrative burden of socially desirable programs from the public (the government) to the private (the citizens) sector.
- Various tax credits, deductions, and exclusions that are designed to encourage taxpayers to obtain additional education (e.g., HOPE scholarship credit, lifetime learning credit, and the Coverdell Education Savings Account).[8]
- The credit allowed for amounts spent to furnish care for certain minor or disabled dependents to enable the taxpayer to seek or maintain gainful employment. Who could deny the social desirability of encouraging taxpayers to provide care for their children while they work?
- The disallowance of a tax deduction for certain expenditures that are deemed to be contrary to public policy. This disallowance extends to such items as fines, penalties, illegal kickbacks, and bribes to government officials. Public policy considerations also have been used to disallow gambling losses in excess of gambling gains and political campaign expenditures in excess of campaign contributions. Social considerations dictate that the tax law should not encourage these activities by permitting a deduction.
- The adoption tax credit of up to $11,650 in 2008 ($11,390 in 2007) to cover expenses incurred by individuals who adopt or attempt to adopt a child.

Many other examples could be included, but the conclusion would be unchanged: social considerations do explain a significant part of the Federal tax law.

Equity Considerations

The concept of equity is relative. Reasonable persons can, and often do, disagree about what is fair or unfair. In the tax area, moreover, equity is generally tied to a particular taxpayer's personal situation. To illustrate, Ms. Jones may have difficulty understanding why none of the rent she pays on her apartment is deductible, while her brother, Mr. Jones, is able to deduct a large portion of the monthly payments he makes on his personal residence in the form of interest and taxes.[9]

---

[7]The same rationale explains the availability of similar arrangements for self-employed persons (the H.R. 10 or Keogh plan).

[8]These provisions can also be justified under the category of economic considerations. No one can take issue with the conclusion that a better educated workforce carries a positive economic impact.

[9]The encouragement of home ownership can be justified on both economic and social grounds. In this regard, it is interesting to note that some state income tax laws allow a form of relief (e.g., tax credit) to the taxpayer who rents his or her personal residence.

TAX *in the News*   **TREATING EVERYONE THE SAME**

As noted in the text, the justification for allowing a Federal income tax deduction for state and local income taxes paid is to mitigate the effect of having the same income be taxed twice. But what if instead of imposing an income tax a state derives comparable amounts of revenue from a general sales tax? Is it fair to deny a deduction to taxpayers in that state just because the tax the state levies is imposed on sales rather than on income?

Congress, in the American Jobs Creation Act of 2004, resolved this purported inequity by allowing a Federal income tax deduction for state and local general sales taxes. However, a taxpayer who is subject to both state income and sales taxes must make a choice. One or the other, but not both, can be claimed as a deduction.

In the same vein, compare the tax treatment of a corporation with that of a partnership. Two businesses may be of equal size, similarly situated, and competitors in the production of goods or services, but they are not comparably treated under the tax law. The corporation is subject to a separate Federal income tax; the partnership is not. Whether the differences in tax treatment can be logically justified in terms of equity is beside the point. The tax law can and does make a distinction between these business forms.

Equity, then, is not what appears fair or unfair to any one taxpayer or group of taxpayers. It is, instead, what the tax law recognizes. Some recognition of equity does exist, however, and explains part of the law. The concept of equity appears in tax provisions that alleviate the effect of multiple taxation and postpone the recognition of gain when the taxpayer lacks the ability or wherewithal to pay the tax. Equity also helps mitigate the effect of the application of the annual accounting period concept and helps taxpayers cope with the eroding result of inflation.

Alleviating the Effect of Multiple Taxation. The same income earned by a taxpayer may be subject to taxes imposed by different taxing authorities. If, for example, the taxpayer is a resident of New York City, income might generate Federal, New York State, and New York City income taxes. To compensate for this inequity, the Federal tax law allows a taxpayer to claim a deduction for state and local income taxes. The deduction, however, does not neutralize the effect of multiple taxation since the benefit derived depends on the taxpayer's Federal income tax rate.[10]

Equity considerations can explain the Federal tax treatment of certain income from foreign sources. Since double taxation results when the same income is subject to both foreign and U.S. income taxes, the tax law permits the taxpayer to choose either a credit or a deduction for the foreign taxes paid.

The imposition of a separate income tax on corporations leads to multiple taxation of the same income.

EXAMPLE 2

During the current year, Gray Corporation has net income of $100,000, of which $5,000 was received as dividends from stock it owns in IBM Corporation. Assume Gray Corporation distributes the after-tax income to its shareholders (all individuals). At a minimum, the distribution received by the shareholders will be subject to two income taxes: the corporate income

---

[10]A tax credit, rather than a deduction, would eliminate the effects of multiple taxation on the same income.

tax when the income is earned by Gray Corporation and the individual income tax when the balance is distributed to the shareholders as a dividend. The $5,000 Gray receives from IBM Corporation fares even worse. Because it is paid from income earned by IBM, it has been subjected to a third income tax (the corporate income tax imposed on IBM).[11] ∎

For corporate shareholders, for whom triple taxation is possible, the law provides a deduction for dividends received from certain domestic corporations. The deduction, usually 70 percent of the dividends, would be allowed to Gray Corporation for the $5,000 it received from IBM Corporation. (See the discussion in Chapter 2.) For the individual shareholder, legislation has reduced the tax on qualified dividends to 15 percent (0 percent for lower-bracket shareholders). By allowing a preferential lower tax rate, the approach is to *mitigate* (not *eliminate*) the effect of multiple taxation. (See the discussion in Chapter 5.)

In the area of the Federal estate tax, several provisions reflect attempts to mitigate the effect of multiple taxation. Some degree of equity is achieved, for example, by allowing a limited credit against the estate tax for foreign death taxes imposed on the same transfer. Other estate tax credits are available and can be explained on the same grounds.[12]

The Wherewithal to Pay Concept. The wherewithal to pay concept recognizes the inequity of taxing a transaction when the taxpayer lacks the means with which to pay the tax. It is particularly suited to situations when the taxpayer's economic position has not changed significantly as a result of a transaction.

EXAMPLE 3	White Corporation holds unimproved land as an investment. The land has a basis to White of $60,000 and a fair market value of $100,000. The land is exchanged for a building (worth $100,000) that White will use in its business.[13] ∎

EXAMPLE 4	White Corporation owns a warehouse that it uses in its business. At a time when the warehouse has an adjusted basis of $60,000, it is destroyed by fire. White collects the insurance proceeds of $100,000 and, within two years of the end of the year in which the fire occurred, uses all of the proceeds to purchase a new warehouse.[14] ∎

EXAMPLE 5	Tom, a sole proprietor, decides to incorporate his business. In exchange for the business's assets (adjusted basis of $60,000 and a fair market value of $100,000), Tom receives all of the stock of Azure Corporation, a newly created corporation.[15] The Azure stock is worth $100,000. ∎

EXAMPLE 6	Rose, Sam, and Tom want to develop unimproved land owned by Tom. The land has a basis to Tom of $60,000 and a fair market value of $100,000. The RST Partnership is formed with the following investments: land worth $100,000 transferred by Tom, $100,000 cash by Rose, and $100,000 cash by Sam. Each party receives a one-third interest in the RST Partnership.[16] ∎

---

[11]This result materializes because under the tax law a corporation is not allowed a deduction for the dividend distributions it makes.

[12]See Chapter 17.

[13]The nontaxability of like-kind exchanges applies to the exchange of property held for investment or used in a trade or business for property to be similarly held or used.

[14]The nontaxability of gains realized from involuntary conversions applies when the proceeds received by the taxpayer are reinvested within a prescribed period of time in property similar or related in service or use to that converted. Involuntary conversions take place as a result of casualty losses, theft losses, and condemnations by a public authority.

[15]Transfers of property to controlled corporations are discussed in Chapter 4.

[16]The formation of a partnership is discussed in Chapter 10.

EXAMPLE 7

Amber Corporation and Crimson Corporation decide to consolidate to form Aqua Corporation.[17] Pursuant to the plan of reorganization, Tera exchanges her stock in Amber Corporation (basis of $60,000 and fair market value of $100,000) for stock in Aqua Corporation worth $100,000. ∎

In all of the preceding examples, White Corporation, Tom, or Tera had a realized gain of $40,000 [$100,000 (fair market value of the property received) − $60,000 (basis of the property given up)].[18] It seems inequitable to force the taxpayer to recognize any of this gain for two reasons. First, without disposing of the property or interest acquired, the taxpayer would be hard-pressed to pay the tax.[19] Second, the taxpayer's economic situation has not changed significantly. To illustrate by referring to Example 5, can it be said that Tom's position as sole shareholder of Azure Corporation is much different from his prior status as owner of a sole proprietorship?

Several warnings are in order concerning the application of the wherewithal to pay concept. Recognized gain is merely postponed and not necessarily avoided. Because of the basis carryover to the new property or interest acquired in these nontaxable transactions, the gain element is still present and might be recognized upon a subsequent taxable disposition. Referring to Example 5, suppose Tom later sold the stock in Azure Corporation for $100,000. Tom's basis in the stock is $60,000 (the same basis as in the assets transferred), and the sale results in a recognized gain of $40,000. Also, many of the provisions previously illustrated prevent the recognition of realized losses. Since such provisions are automatic in application (not elective with the taxpayer), they could operate to the detriment of a taxpayer who wishes to obtain a deduction for a loss. The notable exception involves involuntary conversions (Example 4). Here, nonrecognition treatment is elective with the taxpayer and will not apply to a realized loss if it is otherwise deductible.

The wherewithal to pay concept has definitely served as a guideline in shaping part of the tax law. Nevertheless, it is not a hard and fast principle that is followed in every case. Only when the tax law specifically provides for no tax consequences will this result materialize.

EXAMPLE 8

Mary Jo exchanges stock in Green Corporation (basis of $60,000 and fair market value of $100,000) for stock in Purple Corporation (fair market value of $100,000). The exchange is not pursuant to a reorganization. Under these circumstances, Mary Jo's realized gain of $40,000 is recognized for Federal income tax purposes.[20] ∎

The result reached in Example 8 seems harsh in that the exchange does not place Mary Jo in a position to pay the tax on the $40,000 gain. How can this result be reconciled with that reached in Example 7 when the exchange was nontaxable? In other words, why does the tax law apply the wherewithal to pay concept to the exchange of stock pursuant to a corporate reorganization (Example 7) but not to certain other stock exchanges (Example 8)?

Recall that the wherewithal to pay concept is particularly suited to situations in which the taxpayer's economic position has not changed significantly as a result of a transaction. In Example 7, Tera's stock investment in Amber Corporation really continues in the form of the Aqua Corporation stock since Aqua was formed

---

[17]Corporate reorganizations are discussed in Chapter 7.

[18]Realized gain can be likened to economic gain. However, the Federal income tax is imposed only on that portion of realized gain considered to be recognized under the law. Generally, recognized (or taxable) gain can never exceed realized gain.

[19]If the taxpayer ends up with other property (boot) as part of the transfer, gain may be recognized to this extent. The presence of boot, however, helps solve the wherewithal to pay problem, since it provides property (other than the property or interest central to the transaction) with which to pay the tax.

[20]The exchange of stock does not qualify for nontaxable treatment as a like-kind exchange (refer to Example 3).

through a consolidation of Amber and Crimson Corporations.[21] In Example 8, however, the investment has not continued. Here Mary Jo's ownership in Green Corporation has ceased, and an investment in an entirely different corporation has been substituted.

Mitigating the Effect of the Annual Accounting Period Concept.

For purposes of effective administration of the tax law, all taxpayers must report to and settle with the Federal government at periodic intervals. Otherwise, taxpayers would remain uncertain as to their tax liabilities, and the government would have difficulty judging revenues and budgeting expenditures. The period selected for final settlement of most tax liabilities is one year. At the close of each year, a taxpayer's position becomes complete for that particular year. Referred to as the annual accounting period concept, the effect is to divide each taxpayer's life into equal annual intervals for tax purposes.

The finality of the annual accounting period concept can lead to dissimilar tax treatment for taxpayers who are, from a long-range standpoint, in the same economic position.

EXAMPLE 9

Rena and Samuel are both sole proprietors and have experienced the following results during the past three years:

	Profit (or Loss)	
Year	Rena	Samuel
2006	$50,000	$150,000
2007	60,000	60,000
2008	60,000	(40,000)

Although Rena and Samuel have the same profit of $170,000 over the period 2006–2008, the finality of the annual accounting period concept places Samuel at a definite disadvantage for tax purposes. The net operating loss procedure offers Samuel some relief by allowing him to apply some or all of his 2008 loss to the earliest profitable years (in this case 2006). Thus, Samuel, with a net operating loss carryback, is placed in a position to obtain a refund for some of the taxes he paid on the $150,000 profit reported for 2006. ■

The same reasoning used to support the deduction of net operating losses can be applied to explain the special treatment excess capital losses and excess charitable contributions receive. Carryback and carryover procedures help mitigate the effect of limiting a loss or a deduction to the accounting period in which it is realized. With such procedures, a taxpayer may be able to salvage a loss or a deduction that might otherwise be wasted.

The installment method of recognizing gain on the sale of property allows a taxpayer to spread tax consequences over the payout period.[22] The harsh effect of taxing all the gain in the year of sale is avoided. The installment method can also be explained by the wherewithal to pay concept since recognition of gain is tied to the collection of the installment notes received from the sale of the property. Tax consequences tend to correspond to the seller's ability to pay the tax.

EXAMPLE 10

In 2006, Tim sold unimproved real estate (cost of $40,000) for $100,000. Under the terms of the sale, Tim receives two notes from the purchaser, each for $50,000 (plus interest).

---

[21]This continuation is known as the continuity of interest concept, which forms the foundation for all nontaxable corporate reorganizations. The concept is discussed at length in Chapter 7.

[22]Under the installment method, each payment received by the seller represents a return of basis (the nontaxable portion) and profit from the sale (the taxable portion).

One note is payable in 2007 and the other note in 2008. Without the installment method, Tim would have to recognize and pay a tax on the gain of $60,000 for the year of the sale (2006). This result is harsh, since none of the sale proceeds will be received until 2007 and 2008. With the installment method, and presuming the notes are paid when each comes due, Tim recognizes half of the gain ($30,000) in 2007 and the remaining half in 2008. ∎

The annual accounting period concept has been modified to apply to situations in which taxpayers may have difficulty accurately assessing their tax positions by year-end. In many such cases, the law permits taxpayers to treat transactions taking place in the next year as having occurred in the prior year.

EXAMPLE 11

Monica, a calendar year taxpayer, is a participant in an H.R. 10 (Keogh) retirement plan. (See Appendix C for a definition of a Keogh plan.) Under the plan, Monica contributes 20% of her net self-employment income, such amount being deductible for Federal income tax purposes. On April 10, 2008, Monica determines that her net self-employment income for calendar year 2007 was $80,000. Consequently, she contributes $16,000 (20% × $80,000) to the plan. Even though the $16,000 contribution was made in 2008, the law permits Monica to claim it as a deduction for tax year 2007. Requiring Monica to make the contribution by December 31, 2007, in order to obtain the deduction for that year would force her to arrive at an accurate determination of net self-employment income long before her income tax return must be prepared and filed. ∎

Similar exceptions to the annual accounting period concept cover certain charitable contributions by accrual basis corporations (Chapter 2), and the dividend distributions by S corporations (Chapter 12).

Coping with Inflation. During periods of inflation, bracket creep has plagued the working person. Because of the progressive nature of the income tax, any wage adjustment to compensate for inflation can increase the income tax bracket of the recipient. The overall impact is an erosion of purchasing power. Congress recognized this problem and began to adjust various income tax components (the **indexation** procedure) in 1985, based upon the rise in the consumer price index over the prior year. For example, due to the inflation factor, the amount of a personal and dependency exemption has been increased over the years. Indexation also applies to dollar amounts of other components, including the tax brackets and the standard deduction.

Political Considerations

A large segment of the Federal tax law is made up of statutory provisions. Since these statutes are enacted by Congress, is it any surprise that political considerations influence tax law? For purposes of discussion, the effect of political considerations on the tax law is divided into the following topics: special interest legislation, political expediency, and state and local influences.

Special Interest Legislation. Unquestionably, certain provisions of the tax law can be explained largely by looking to the political influence some pressure groups have exerted on Congress. For example, is there any other reason why prepaid subscription and dues income is not taxed until earned while prepaid rents are taxed to the landlord in the year received? These exceptions came about because certain organizations (e.g., the American Automobile Association) convinced Congress that special tax treatment was needed to cover income received from multiyear dues and subscriptions.

Special interest legislation is not necessarily to be condemned if it can be justified on economic or social grounds. At any rate, it is an inevitable product of our political system.

Political Expediency. Various tax reform proposals rise and fall in favor, depending upon the shifting moods of the American public. That Congress is sensitive to popular feeling is an accepted fact. Therefore, certain provisions of the tax law can be explained on the basis of the political climate at the time of enactment. Once the general public became aware that certain large and profitable corporations were able to avoid the corporate income tax, Congress responded with an alternative minimum tax. Since a portion of a corporation's adjusted current earnings has been made a tax preference item, many large corporations no longer escape taxation (see Chapter 3).

Measures that deter more affluent taxpayers from obtaining so-called preferential tax treatment have always had popular appeal and, consequently, the support of Congress. Provisions such as the alternative minimum tax, the imputed interest rules, and the limitation on the deductibility of interest on investment indebtedness can be explained on this basis. In the same vein are the provisions imposing penalty taxes on corporations that unreasonably accumulate earnings or are classified as personal holding companies (see Chapter 3).

The provisions raising income tax rates on more affluent taxpayers and increasing the amount of the earned income credit are also at least partially attributable to political expediency.

State and Local Influences. Political considerations have played a major role in the exclusion from gross income of interest received on state and local obligations. In view of the furor that has been raised by state and local political figures every time repeal of this tax provision has been proposed, one might well regard it as sacred.

Somewhat less apparent has been the influence state law has had in shaping our present Federal tax law. Of prime importance in this regard has been the effect of the community property system employed in some states.[23] At one time, the tax position of the residents of these states was so advantageous that many common law states actually adopted community property systems.[24] The political pressure placed on Congress to correct the disparity in tax treatment was considerable. To a large extent, this was accomplished in the Revenue Act of 1948, which extended many of the community property tax advantages to residents of common law jurisdictions.[25] Thus, common law states avoided the trauma of discarding the time-honored legal system familiar to everyone. The impact of community property law on the Federal estate and gift taxes is further explored in Chapters 17 and 18.

<table>
<tr><td>

LO.3

Understand how the IRS, as the protector of the revenue, has affected tax law.

</td></tr>
</table>

Influence of the Internal Revenue Service

The IRS has been influential in many areas beyond its role in issuing administrative pronouncements. In its capacity as the protector of the national revenue, the IRS has been instrumental in securing the passage of much legislation designed to curtail the most flagrant tax avoidance practices (closing tax loopholes). In its capacity as the administrator of the tax laws, the IRS has sought and obtained legislation to make its job easier (administrative feasibility).

---

[23]The states with community property systems are Louisiana, Texas, New Mexico, Arizona, California, Washington, Idaho, Nevada, Wisconsin, and (if elected by the spouses) Alaska. The rest of the states are classified as common law jurisdictions. The difference between common law and community property systems centers around the property rights possessed by married persons. In a common law system, each spouse owns whatever he or she earns. Under a community property system, one-half of the earnings of each spouse is considered owned by the other spouse. Assume, for example, Harold and Ruth are husband and wife, and their only income is the $40,000 annual salary Harold receives. If they live in New York (a common law state), the $40,000 salary belongs to Harold. If, however, they live in Texas (a community property state), the $40,000 salary is divided equally, in terms of ownership, between Harold and Ruth.

[24]Such states included Michigan, Oklahoma, and Pennsylvania.

[25]The major advantage extended was the provision allowing married taxpayers to file joint returns and compute the tax liability as if the income had been earned one-half by each spouse. This result is automatic in a community property state since half of the income earned by one spouse belongs to the other spouse. The income-splitting benefits of a joint return are now incorporated as part of the tax rates applicable to married taxpayers.

TAX *in the News* — THE NONCOMPLIANCE RATE INCREASES

In spite of the IRS's efforts as the protector of the revenue and notwithstanding the compliance provisions of the tax law, the United States has a tax gap of approximately $345 billion (gross amount in 2001). According to IRS estimates, individuals report only about 57 percent of their business income, down from 70 percent in 1988. Farmers' noncompliance rate is a staggering 72 percent. The IRS estimates the noncompliance rates and the dollars lost as follows:

	Noncompliance Rate	Amount Lost (Billions of $)
Capital gains	12%	$11
Partnerships, S corporations	18%	22
Rents and royalties	51%	13
Sole proprietor income	57%	68
Farm income	72%	6

Source: *Adapted from Janet Novack, "The Evader Next Door," Forbes, April 23, 2007, pp. 34–37.*

The IRS as Protector of the Revenue. Innumerable examples can be given of provisions in the tax law that have stemmed from the direct efforts of the IRS to prevent taxpayers from exploiting a loophole. Working within the letter of existing law, ingenious taxpayers and their advisers devise techniques that accomplish indirectly what cannot be accomplished directly. As a consequence, legislation is enacted to close the loophole that taxpayers have located and exploited. The following examples can be explained in this fashion and are discussed in more detail in the chapters to follow:

- The use of a fiscal year by personal service corporations, partnerships, S corporations, and trusts to defer income recognition to the owners (see Chapters 2, 10, 12, and 19).
- The use of the cash basis method of accounting by certain large corporations (see Chapter 2).
- The deduction of passive investment losses and expenses against other income (see Chapters 2 and 10).
- The shifting of income to lower-bracket taxpayers through the use of reversionary trusts (see Chapter 19).

In addition, the IRS has secured from Congress legislation of a more general nature that enables it to make adjustments based upon the substance, rather than the formal construction, of what a taxpayer has done. One provision, for example, authorizes the IRS to establish guidelines on the thin capitalization issue. This question involves when corporate debt will be recognized as debt for tax purposes and when it will be reclassified as equity or stock (see the discussion of thin capitalization in Chapter 4). Another provision permits the IRS to make adjustments to a taxpayer's method of accounting when the method used by the taxpayer does not clearly reflect income. The IRS has also been granted the authority to allocate income and deductions among businesses owned or controlled by the same interests when the allocation is necessary to prevent the evasion of taxes or to reflect the income of each business clearly.

EXAMPLE 12

Gold Corporation and Silver Corporation are brother-sister corporations (the stock of each is owned by the same shareholders), and both use the calendar year for tax purposes. For the current tax year, each has taxable income as follows: $335,000 for Gold Corporation and $50,000 for Silver Corporation. Not included in Gold Corporation's taxable income, however, is $10,000 of rent income usually charged Silver Corporation for the use of some property owned by Gold. Since the parties have not clearly reflected the taxable income of each business, the IRS can allocate $10,000 of rent income to Gold Corporation. After the allocation, Gold Corporation has taxable income of $345,000, and Silver Corporation has taxable income of $40,000.[26] ■

Also of a general nature is the authority Congress has given the IRS to prevent taxpayers from acquiring corporations to obtain a tax advantage when the principal purpose of the acquisition is the evasion or avoidance of the Federal income tax. The provision of the tax law that provides this authority is discussed briefly in Chapter 7.

Administrative Feasibility. Some of the tax law is justified on the grounds that it simplifies the task of the IRS in collecting the revenue and administering the law. With regard to collecting the revenue, the IRS long ago realized the importance of placing taxpayers on a pay-as-you-go basis. Elaborate withholding procedures apply to wages, while the tax on other types of income may have to be paid at periodic intervals throughout the year. The IRS has been instrumental in convincing the courts that accrual basis taxpayers should pay taxes on prepaid income in the year received and not when earned. This approach may be contrary to generally accepted accounting principles, but it is consistent with the wherewithal to pay concept.

Of considerable aid to the IRS in collecting revenue are the numerous provisions that impose interest and penalties on taxpayers for noncompliance with the tax law. These provisions include penalties for failure to pay a tax or to file a return that is due and the negligence penalty for intentional disregard of rules and regulations. Various penalties for civil and criminal fraud also serve as deterrents to taxpayer noncompliance. This aspect of the tax law is discussed in Chapter 16.

One of the keys to the effective administration of our tax system is the audit process conducted by the IRS. To carry out this function, the IRS is aided by provisions that reduce the chance of taxpayer error or manipulation and therefore simplify the audit effort that is necessary. An increase in the amount of the standard deduction reduces the number of individual taxpayers who will be in a position to claim itemized deductions. With fewer deductions to check, the audit function is simplified.[27] The same objective can be used to explain the $345,800 unified gift tax credit in 2008 and the $12,000 annual gift tax exclusion (see Chapter 17). These provisions decrease the number of tax returns that must be filed (as well as reduce the taxes paid) and thereby save audit effort.[28]

LO.4

Recognize the role of the courts in interpreting and shaping tax law.

Influence of the Courts

In addition to interpreting statutory provisions and the administrative pronouncements issued by the IRS, the Federal courts have influenced tax law in two other respects.[29] First, the courts have formulated certain judicial concepts that serve as guides in the application of various tax provisions. Second, certain key decisions have led to changes in the Internal Revenue Code. Understanding this influence helps explain some of our tax laws.

Judicial Concepts Relating to Tax Law. Although ranking the tax concepts developed by the courts in order of importance is difficult, the concept of substance over form would almost certainly be near the top of any list. Variously described as the

---

[26]By shifting $10,000 of income to Gold Corporation (which is in the 34% bracket), the IRS gains $3,400 in taxes. Allowing the $10,000 deduction to Silver Corporation (which is in the 15% bracket) costs the IRS only $1,500. See Chapter 2 for a further discussion of the income tax rates applicable to corporations.

[27]The IRS gave the same justification when it proposed to Congress the $100 per event limitation on personal casualty and theft losses. Imposition of the limitation eliminated many casualty and theft loss deductions and, as a consequence, saved the IRS considerable audit time. Also, an additional limitation equal to 10% of adjusted gross income applies to the total of nonbusiness losses after reduction by the floor of $100 for each loss.

[28]Particularly in the case of nominal gifts among family members, taxpayer compliance in reporting and paying a tax on such transfers would be questionable. The absence of the $12,000 gift tax exclusion would create a serious enforcement problem for the IRS.

[29]A great deal of case law is devoted to ascertaining congressional intent. The courts, in effect, ask: What did Congress have in mind when it enacted a particular tax provision?

"telescoping" or "collapsing" process or the "step transaction approach," it involves determining the true substance of what occurred. In a transaction involving many steps, any one step may be collapsed (or disregarded) to arrive directly at the result reached.

EXAMPLE 13

In 2008, Mrs. Greer, a widow, wants to give $24,000 to Jean without incurring any gift tax liability.[30] She knows that the law permits her to give up to $12,000 each year per person without any tax consequences (the annual exclusion). With this in mind, the following steps are taken: a gift by Mrs. Greer to Jean of $12,000 (nontaxable because of the $12,000 annual exclusion), a gift by Mrs. Greer to Ben of $12,000 (also nontaxable), and a gift by Ben to Jean of $12,000 (nontaxable because of Ben's annual exclusion). Considering only the form of what Mrs. Greer and Ben have done, all appears well from a tax standpoint. In substance, however, what has happened? By collapsing the steps involving Ben, it is apparent that Mrs. Greer has made a gift of $24,000 to Jean and therefore has not avoided the Federal gift tax. ∎

The substance over form concept plays an important role in transactions involving corporations.

Another leading tax concept developed by the courts deals with the interpretation of statutory tax provisions that operate to benefit taxpayers. The courts have established the rule that these relief provisions are to be narrowly construed against taxpayers if there is any doubt about their application. Suppose, for example, Beige Corporation wants to be treated as an S corporation (see Chapter 12) but has not satisfied the statutory requirements for making the required election. Because S corporation status is a relief provision favoring taxpayers, chances are the courts will deny Beige Corporation this treatment.

Important in the area of corporate-shareholder dealings (see the discussion of constructive dividends in Chapter 5) and in the resolution of valuation problems for estate and gift tax purposes (see Chapters 17 and 18) is the **arm's length concept.** Particularly in dealings between related parties, transactions can be tested by questioning whether the taxpayers acted in an "arm's length" manner. The question to be asked is: Would unrelated parties have handled the transaction in the same way?

EXAMPLE 14

The sole shareholder of a corporation leases property to the corporation for a monthly rental of $50,000. To test whether the corporation should be allowed a rent deduction for this amount, the IRS and the courts will apply the arm's length concept. Would the corporation have paid $50,000 a month in rent if the same property had been leased from an unrelated party (rather than from the sole shareholder)? ∎

The **continuity of interest concept** originated with the courts but has, in many situations, been incorporated into statutory provisions of the tax law. Primarily concerned with business readjustments, the concept permits tax-free treatment only if the taxpayer retains a substantial continuing interest in the property transferred to the new business. Due to the continuing interest retained, the transfer should not have tax consequences because the position of the taxpayer has not changed. This concept applies to transfers to controlled corporations (Chapter 4), corporate reorganizations (Chapter 7), and transfers to partnerships (Chapter 10). The continuity of interest concept helps explain the results reached in Examples 5 through 7 of this chapter. This concept is further discussed in Chapter 7.

Also developed by the courts, the **business purpose concept** principally applies to transactions involving corporations. Under this concept, some sound business reason that motivates the transaction must be present in order for the prescribed tax treatment to result. The avoidance of taxation is not considered to be a sound business purpose.

---

[30]The example assumes that Mrs. Greer has exhausted her unified tax credit. See Chapter 17.

EXAMPLE 15

Beth and Charles are equal shareholders in Brown Corporation. They have recently disagreed about the company's operations and are at an impasse about the future of Brown Corporation. This shareholder disagreement on corporate policy constitutes a sound business purpose and would justify a division of Brown Corporation that will permit Beth and Charles to go their separate ways. Whether the division of Brown would be nontaxable to the parties depends on their compliance with the statutory provisions dealing with corporate reorganizations. The point is, however, that compliance with statutory provisions would not be enough to ensure nontaxability without a business purpose for the transaction. ■

The business purpose concept is discussed further in Chapter 7.

Judicial Influence on Statutory Provisions. Some court decisions have been of such consequence that Congress has incorporated them into statutory tax law. An illustration of this influence appears in Example 16.

EXAMPLE 16

In 1983, Brad claimed a capital loss of $100,000 for Tan Corporation stock that had become worthless during the year. In the absence of any offsetting gains, the capital loss deduction produced no income tax savings for Brad either in 1983 or in future years. In 1986, Brad institutes a lawsuit against the former officers of Tan Corporation for their misconduct that resulted in the corporation's failure and thereby led to Brad's $100,000 loss. In settlement of the suit, the officers pay $50,000 to Brad. The IRS argued that the full $50,000 should be taxed as gain to Brad. The Tan stock was written off in 1983 and had a zero basis for tax purposes. The $50,000 recovery Brad received on the stock was, therefore, all gain. The IRS's position was logical, but not equitable. The court stated that Brad should not be taxed on the recovery of an amount previously deducted unless the deduction produced a tax savings. Since the $100,000 capital loss deduction in 1983 produced no tax benefit, none of the $50,000 received in 1986 results in gain. ■

The decision reached by the courts in Example 16, known as the **tax benefit rule**, is part of the statutory tax law.

Court decisions sometimes create uncertainty about the tax law. Such decisions may reach the right result but do not produce the guidelines necessary to enable taxpayers to comply. In many situations, Congress may be compelled to add certainty to the law by enacting statutory provisions specifying when a particular tax consequence will or will not materialize. The following are examples of this type of judicial "cause" and the statutory "effect":

- When a stock redemption will be treated as an exchange or as a dividend (see Chapter 6).
- What basis a parent corporation will have in the assets received from a subsidiary that is liquidated shortly after its acquisition (see Chapter 6).

Some of the statutory provisions can be explained by a negative reaction by Congress to a particular court decision. One decision, for example, held that the transfer of a liability to a controlled corporation should be treated as boot received by the transferor (see Chapter 4). Congress apparently disagreed with this treatment and promptly enacted legislation to change the result.

Summary

In addition to its revenue-raising objective, the Federal tax law has developed in response to several other factors:

- *Economic considerations.* Here, the emphasis is on tax provisions that help regulate the economy and encourage certain activities and types of businesses.
- *Social considerations.* Some tax provisions are designed to encourage or discourage certain socially desirable or undesirable practices.
- *Equity considerations.* Of principal concern in this area are tax provisions that alleviate the effect of multiple taxation, recognize the wherewithal to pay

concept, mitigate the effect of the annual accounting period concept, and recognize the eroding effect of inflation.

- *Political considerations.* Of significance in this regard are tax provisions that represent special interest legislation, reflect political expediency, and illustrate the effect of state law.
- *Influence of the IRS.* Many tax provisions are intended to aid the IRS in collecting revenue and administering the tax law.
- *Influence of the courts.* Court decisions have established a body of judicial concepts relating to tax law and have, on occasion, led Congress to enact statutory provisions that either clarify or negate their effect.

These factors explain various tax provisions and thereby help in understanding why the tax law developed to its present state. The next step involves learning to work with the tax law.

Working with the Tax Law—Tax Sources

Understanding taxation requires a mastery of the sources of tax law. These sources include not only the legislative provisions in the Internal Revenue Code, but also congressional Committee Reports, Regulations, Treasury Department pronouncements, and court decisions. Thus, the primary sources of tax information are the pronouncements of the three branches of government: legislative, executive, and judicial.

The law is of little significance, however, until it is applied to a set of facts and circumstances. A tax researcher must not only be able to read and interpret the sources of the law but must also understand the relative weight of authority within the rules of law. Learning to work with the tax law involves three basic steps:

1. Familiarity with the sources of the law.
2. Application of research techniques.
3. Effective use of planning procedures.

The remainder of this chapter introduces the sources of tax law and explains how the law is applied to problems and conditions of individual and business transactions. Statutory, administrative, and judicial sources of the tax law are considered first.

Statutory Sources of the Tax Law

LO.5
Identify tax law sources—statutory, administrative, and judicial.

Origin of the Internal Revenue Code. Before 1939, the statutory provisions relating to taxation were contained in the individual revenue acts enacted by Congress. The inconvenience and confusion that resulted from dealing with many separate acts led Congress to codify all of the Federal tax laws. Known as the Internal Revenue Code of 1939, the codification arranged all Federal tax provisions in a logical sequence and placed them in a separate part of the Federal statutes. A further rearrangement took place in 1954 and resulted in the Internal Revenue Code of 1954.

Perhaps to emphasize the magnitude of the changes made by the Tax Reform Act (TRA) of 1986, Congress redesignated the Internal Revenue Code of 1954 as the Internal Revenue Code of 1986. This change is somewhat deceiving since the tax law was not recodified in 1986, as it had been in 1954. TRA of 1986 merely amended, deleted, or added provisions to the Internal Revenue Code of 1954. For example, before TRA of 1986, § 336 provided the general rule that no gain or loss would be recognized by a corporation when it distributed assets in kind to its shareholders in complete liquidation. After the effective date of TRA of 1986, § 336 provides that gain or loss will be recognized upon the same distributions (see Chapter 6).

TAX *in the News*	**THE 67,204-PAGE GORILLA**

Few will dispute that our tax laws are extremely complex. Almost 60 percent of tax filers pay a professional to calculate their taxes, and individuals and businesses pay about $300 billion in tax preparation costs, according to the Tax Foundation. That's a 20 percent surcharge on top of the $1.5 trillion in taxes actually paid.

Even tax professionals cannot agree on the taxes owed by a typical taxpayer with a complex tax return. Of course, much of the problem is the tangle of deductions, credits, and exceptions that are found in the 67,204-page Internal Revenue Code. Since simplification would require taking away many tax breaks, do not expect the 67,204-page gorilla to go away.

The following observations will help clarify the significance of the three Codes:

- Neither the 1939, the 1954, nor the 1986 Code changed all of the tax law existing on the date of enactment. Much of the 1939 Code, for example, was incorporated into the 1954 Code. The same can be said for the transition from the 1954 to the 1986 Code. This point is important in assessing judicial and administrative decisions interpreting provisions under prior Codes. For example, a decision interpreting § 61 of the Internal Revenue Code of 1954 will have continuing validity since this provision carried over unchanged to the Internal Revenue Code of 1986.
- Statutory amendments to the tax law are integrated into the existing Code. Thus, the Work Opportunity Tax Act of 2007 became part of the Internal Revenue Code of 1986.

Do not conclude, however, that the codification and recodification process has made the Internal Revenue Code a simplistic body of laws. To a large extent, the complexity of our current Code can be attributed to its growth.

The Legislative Process. Federal tax legislation generally originates in the House of Representatives, where it is first considered by the House Ways and Means Committee. Tax bills originate in the Senate when they are attached as riders to other legislative proposals.[31] If acceptable to the House Ways and Means Committee, the proposed bill is referred to the entire House of Representatives for approval or disapproval. Approved bills are sent to the Senate, where they are referred to the Senate Finance Committee for further consideration.

In the next step, the bill is referred from the Senate Finance Committee to the whole Senate. Assuming no disagreement between the House and the Senate, a bill passed by the Senate is referred to the President for approval or veto. If the bill is approved or if the President's veto is overridden, the bill becomes law and part of the Internal Revenue Code.

When the Senate version of the bill differs from that passed by the House, the Joint Conference Committee resolves these differences. The Joint Conference Committee includes members of the House Ways and Means Committee and the Senate Finance Committee.

Referrals from the House Ways and Means Committee, the Senate Finance Committee, and the Joint Conference Committee are usually accompanied by Committee Reports. These Committee Reports often explain the provisions of the proposed legislation and are therefore a valuable source in ascertaining the *intent*

---

[31]The Tax Equity and Fiscal Responsibility Act of 1982 originated in the Senate; its constitutionality was unsuccessfully challenged in the courts. The Senate version of the Deficit Reduction Act of 1984 was attached as an amendment to the Federal Boat Safety Act.

of Congress. What Congress has in mind when it considers and enacts tax legislation is, of course, the key to interpreting that legislation. Since Regulations normally are not issued immediately after a statute is enacted, taxpayers often look to Committee Reports to ascertain congressional intent.

The typical legislative process dealing with tax bills can be summarized as follows:

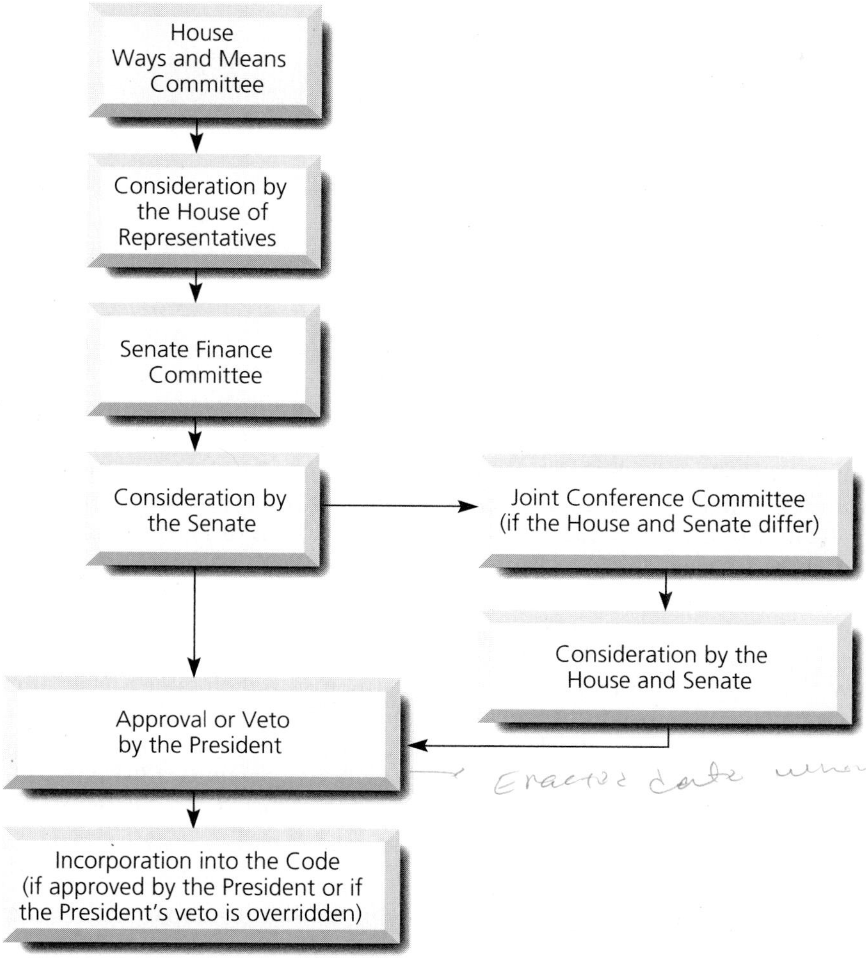

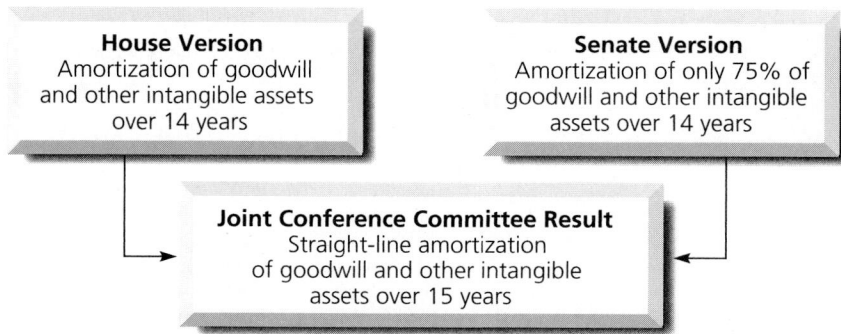

The role of the Joint Conference Committee indicates the importance of compromise in the legislative process. The practical effect of the compromise process can be illustrated by reviewing what happened in the Revenue Reconciliation Act (RRA) of 1993 (H.R. 2264) with respect to the amortization of acquired goodwill:

Some tax provisions are commonly referred to by the number the bill received in the House when first proposed or by the name of the member of Congress sponsoring the legislation. For example, the Self-Employed Individuals Tax Retirement Act of 1962 is popularly known as H.R. 10 (the House of Representatives Bill No. 10) or as the Keogh Act (Keogh being one of the members of Congress sponsoring the bill).

Arrangement of the Code. In working with the Code, it helps to understand the format. Note the following partial table of contents:

Subtitle A. Income Taxes
 Chapter 1. Normal Taxes and Surtaxes
  Subchapter A. Determination of Tax Liability
   Part I. Tax on Individuals
    Sections 1–5
   Part II. Tax on Corporations
    Sections 11–12

* * *

In referring to a provision of the Code, the *key* is usually the Section number. In citing Section 2(a) (dealing with the status of a surviving spouse), for example, it is unnecessary to include Subtitle A, Chapter 1, Subchapter A, Part I. Merely mentioning Section 2(a) will suffice since the Section numbers run consecutively and do not begin again with each new Subtitle, Chapter, Subchapter, or Part. Not all Code Section numbers are used, however. Note that Part I ends with Section 5 and Part II starts with Section 11 (at present there are no Sections 6, 7, 8, 9, and 10).[32]

Tax practitioners commonly refer to a specific area of income taxation by Subchapter designation. Some of the more common Subchapter designations include Subchapter C (Corporate Distributions and Adjustments), Subchapter K (Partners and Partnerships), and Subchapter S (Tax Treatment of S Corporations and Their Shareholders). Particularly in the last situation, it is much more convenient to describe the subject of the applicable Code provisions (Sections 1361 through 1379) as S corporation status rather than as the "Tax Treatment of S Corporations and Their Shareholders."

Citing the Code. Code Sections often are broken down into subparts.[33] Section 2(a)(1)(A) serves as an example.

§ 2 (a) (1) (A)

              ▶ Abbreviation for "Section"
              ▶ Section number
              ▶ Subsection number[34]
              ▶ Paragraph designation
              ▶ Subparagraph designation

---

[32]When the 1954 Code was drafted, Section numbers were intentionally omitted. This omission provided flexibility to incorporate later changes into the Code without disrupting its organization. When Congress does not leave enough space, subsequent Code Sections are given A, B, C, etc., designations. A good example is the treatment of §§ 280A through 280H.

[33]Some Code Sections do not have subparts. See, for example, § 482.

[34]Some Code Sections omit the subsection designation and use, instead, the paragraph designation as the first subpart. See, for example, §§ 212(1) and 1221(1).

Broken down as to content, § 2(a)(1)(A) becomes:

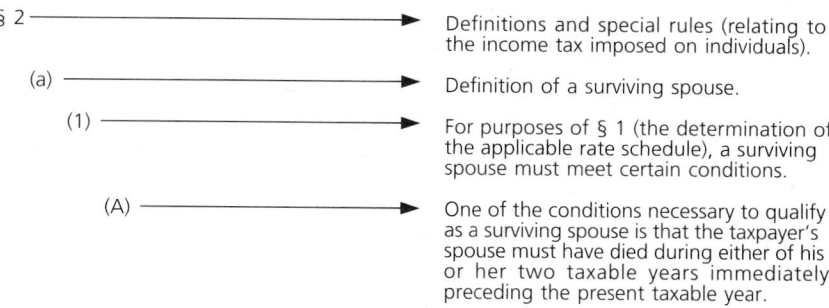

§ 2 ——————————————————→ Definitions and special rules (relating to the income tax imposed on individuals).

(a) ——————————————→ Definition of a surviving spouse.

(1) ——————————————→ For purposes of § 1 (the determination of the applicable rate schedule), a surviving spouse must meet certain conditions.

(A) ——————————→ One of the conditions necessary to qualify as a surviving spouse is that the taxpayer's spouse must have died during either of his or her two taxable years immediately preceding the present taxable year.

Throughout this text, references to Code Sections are in the form just given. The symbols "§" and "§§" are used in place of "Section" and "Sections." Unless otherwise stated, all Code references are to the Internal Revenue Code of 1986. The format followed in the remainder of the text is summarized as follows:

Complete Reference	Text Reference
Section 2(a)(1)(A) of the Internal Revenue Code of 1986	§ 2(a)(1)(A)
Sections 1 and 2 of the Internal Revenue Code of 1986	§§ 1 and 2
Section 2 of the Internal Revenue Code of 1954	§ 2 of the Internal Revenue Code of 1954
Section 12(d) of the Internal Revenue Code of 1939[35]	§ 12(d) of the Internal Revenue Code of 1939

Administrative Sources of the Tax Law

The administrative sources of the Federal tax law can be grouped as follows: Treasury Department Regulations, Revenue Rulings and Procedures, and various other administrative pronouncements. All are issued either by the U.S. Treasury Department or the IRS. The role played by the IRS in this process is considered in greater depth in Chapter 16.

Treasury Department Regulations. Regulations are issued by the U.S. Treasury Department under authority granted by Congress. Interpretative by nature, they provide taxpayers with considerable guidance on the meaning and application of the Code. Although not issued by Congress, Regulations do carry considerable weight. They are an important factor to consider in complying with the tax law. Anyone taking a position contrary to a finalized Regulation must disclose that fact on Form 8275 or Form 8275–R in order to avoid costly penalties.

Since Regulations interpret the Code, they are arranged in the same sequence. Regulations are, however, prefixed by a number that indicates the type of tax or administrative, procedural, or definitional matter to which they relate. For example, the prefix 1 designates the Regulations under the income tax law. Thus, the Regulations under Code § 2 would be cited as Reg. § 1.2, with subparts added for further identification. The numbering of these subparts often has no correlation with the Code subsections. The prefix 20 designates estate tax Regulations; 25 covers gift tax Regulations; 31 relates to employment taxes; and 301 refers to Regulations dealing with procedure and administration. This listing is not all-inclusive.

---

[35]Section 12(d) of the Internal Revenue Code of 1939 is the predecessor to § 2 of the Internal Revenue Code of 1954. Keep in mind that the 1954 Code superseded the 1939 Code.

New Regulations and changes in existing Regulations usually are issued in proposed form before they are finalized. The time interval between the proposal of a Regulation and its finalization permits taxpayers and other interested parties to comment on the propriety of the proposal. **Proposed Regulations** under Code § 2, for example, would be cited as Prop.Reg. § 1.2.

Sometimes the Treasury Department issues **Temporary Regulations** relating to elections and other matters where immediate guidance is critical. Temporary Regulations often are needed for recent legislation that takes effect immediately. Temporary Regulations have the same authoritative value as final Regulations and may be cited as precedent for three years. Temporary Regulations also are issued as Proposed Regulations and automatically expire within three years after the date of issuance. Temporary Regulations and the simultaneously issued Proposed Regulations carry more weight than traditional Proposed Regulations. An example of a Temporary Regulation is Temp.Reg. § 1.199–8T, which covers computer software for purposes of the domestic production activities deduction.

Proposed, final, and Temporary Regulations are published in the *Federal Register* and are reproduced in major tax services. Final Regulations are issued as Treasury Decisions (TDs).

Revenue Rulings and Revenue Procedures.

Revenue Rulings are official pronouncements of the National Office of the IRS. Like Regulations, Revenue Rulings are designed to provide interpretation of the tax law. However, they do not carry the same legal force and effect as Regulations and usually deal with more restricted problems.

A Revenue Ruling often results from a specific taxpayer's request for a letter ruling. If the IRS believes that a taxpayer's request for a letter ruling deserves official publication due to its widespread impact, the holding will be converted into a Revenue Ruling. In making this conversion, names, identifying facts, and money amounts are changed to disguise the identity of the requesting taxpayer. The IRS then issues what would have been a letter ruling as a Revenue Ruling.

Revenue Procedures are issued in the same manner as Revenue Rulings, but deal with the internal management practices and procedures of the IRS. Familiarity with these procedures increases taxpayer compliance and helps make the administration of the tax laws more efficient. Revenue Procedures often involve mechanical rules, but sometimes substantive positions are embedded in them as well. Revenue Rulings and Revenue Procedures serve an important function in that they provide guidance to both IRS personnel and taxpayers in handling routine tax matters.

Both Revenue Rulings and Revenue Procedures are published weekly by the U.S. Government in the *Internal Revenue Bulletin* (I.R.B.). Semiannually, the bulletins for a six-month period are gathered together and published in a bound volume called the *Cumulative Bulletin* (C.B.).[36] The proper form for citing Rulings and Procedures depends on whether the item has been published in the *Cumulative Bulletin* or is available in I.R.B. form. Consider, for example, the following transition:

Temporary Citation
$\begin{cases}$ Rev.Rul. 2007–49, I.R.B. No. 31, 237.
Explanation: Revenue Ruling Number 49, appearing on page 237
of the 31st weekly issue of the *Internal Revenue Bulletin* for 2007. $\end{cases}$

Permanent Citation
$\begin{cases}$ Rev.Rul. 2007–49, 2007–2 C.B. 237.
Explanation: Revenue Ruling Number 49, appearing on page 237
of volume 2 of the *Cumulative Bulletin* for 2007. $\end{cases}$

Note that the page reference of 237 is the same for both the I.R.B. (temporary) and the C.B. (permanent) versions of the Ruling. The IRS numbers the pages of the

---

[36]Generally, only two volumes of the *Cumulative Bulletin* are published each year. The I.R.B.s are available at **http://www.irs.gov**. Another excellent online source for finding the I.R.B.s is Tax Almanac (**http://www.taxalmanac.org**).

I.R.B.s consecutively for each six-month period to facilitate their conversion to C.B. form.

Revenue Procedures are cited in the same manner, except that "Rev.Proc." is substituted for "Rev.Rul." Procedures, like Rulings, are published in the *Internal Revenue Bulletin* (the temporary source) and later transferred to the *Cumulative Bulletin* (the permanent source).

Other Administrative Pronouncements.
Treasury Decisions (TDs) are issued by the Treasury Department to promulgate new Regulations, to amend or otherwise change existing Regulations, or to announce the position of the Government on selected court decisions. Like Revenue Rulings and Revenue Procedures, TDs are published in the *Internal Revenue Bulletin* and subsequently transferred to the *Cumulative Bulletin.*

Technical Information Releases (TIRs) are usually issued to announce the publication of various IRS pronouncements (e.g., Revenue Rulings, Revenue Procedures).

Letter rulings are issued for a fee by the National Office of the IRS upon a taxpayer's request and describe how the IRS will treat a proposed transaction for tax purposes. In general, they apply only to the taxpayer who asks for and obtains the ruling, but post-1984 rulings may be substantial authority for purposes of avoiding the accuracy-related penalties.[37] Although this procedure may sound like the only real way to carry out effective tax planning, the IRS limits the issuance of letter rulings to restricted, preannounced areas of taxation. Thus, a ruling may not be obtained on many of the problems that are particularly troublesome for taxpayers.[38] For example, the IRS will not issue a ruling as to whether compensation paid to shareholder-employees is reasonable (see Chapter 5) or whether § 269 applies (the acquisition of a corporation to evade or avoid income tax [see Chapter 7]). The main reason the IRS will not rule on such matters is that they involve fact-oriented situations.

The IRS must make letter rulings available for public inspection after identifying details are deleted. Published digests of private letter rulings can be found in *Private Letter Rulings* (published by Research Institute of America), BNA *Daily Tax Reports,* and Tax Analysts & Advocates *Tax Notes. IRS Letter Rulings Reports* (published by Commerce Clearing House) contains both digests and full texts of all letter rulings. *Letter Ruling Review* (Tax Analysts), a monthly publication, selects and discusses the more important of the approximately 200 letter rulings per month.

The National Office of the IRS releases technical advice memoranda (TAMs) weekly. TAMs resemble letter rulings in that they give the IRS's determination of an issue. Letter rulings, however, are responses to requests by taxpayers, whereas TAMs are issued by the National Office of the IRS in response to questions raised by taxpayers or IRS field personnel during audits. TAMs deal with completed rather than proposed transactions and are often requested for questions relating to exempt organizations and employee plans. Although TAMs are not officially published and may not be cited or used as precedent, post-1984 TAMs may be substantial authority for purposes of the accuracy-related penalties. See Chapter 16 for a discussion of these penalties.

Both letter rulings and TAMs are issued with multidigit file numbers. Consider, for example, Ltr.Rul. 200731021, dealing with the exclusion from gross income of certain contributions by an employer to accident and health plans. Broken down by digits, the file number reveals the following information:

---

[37]Notice 90–20, 1990–1 C.B. 328, part V (A).

[38]Rev.Proc. 2008–3, I.R.B. No. 1, 110, contains a listing of areas in which the IRS will not issue advance rulings. From time to time, subsequent Revenue Procedures are issued that modify or amplify Rev.Proc. 2008–3.

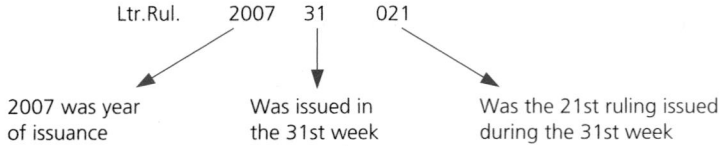

Letter rulings and TAMs issued before 2000 are often cited with only two-digit years (e.g., Ltr.Rul. 9933108).

Like letter rulings, **determination letters** are issued at the request of taxpayers and provide guidance concerning the application of the tax law. They differ from individual rulings in that the issuing source is the Area Director rather than the National Office of the IRS. Also, determination letters usually involve completed (as opposed to proposed) transactions. Determination letters are not published and are made known only to the party making the request.

The following examples illustrate the distinction between individual rulings and determination letters:

EXAMPLE 17	The shareholders of Black Corporation and White Corporation want assurance that the consolidation of the corporations into Gray Corporation will be a nontaxable reorganization (see Chapter 7). The proper approach is to request from the National Office of the IRS an individual ruling concerning the income tax effect of the proposed transaction. ∎

EXAMPLE 18	Gilbert operates a barber shop in which he employs eight barbers. To comply with the rules governing income tax and payroll tax withholdings, Gilbert wants to know whether the barbers working for him are employees or independent contractors. The proper procedure is to request a determination letter on the status of the barbers from the Area Director in Holtsville, New York, or Newport, Vermont, depending on the location of the requesting firm. ∎

Judicial Sources of the Tax Law

The Judicial Process in General. After a taxpayer has exhausted some or all of the remedies available within the IRS (no satisfactory settlement has been reached at the agent or at the conference level discussed in Chapter 16), the dispute can be taken to the Federal courts. The dispute is first considered by a court of original jurisdiction (known as a trial court) with any appeal (either by the taxpayer or the IRS) taken to the appropriate appellate court. In most situations, the taxpayer has a choice of any of four trial courts: a Federal District Court, the U.S. Court of Federal Claims, the Tax Court, or the Small Cases Division of the Tax Court. The trial and appellate court system for Federal tax litigation is illustrated in Figure 1–1.

The broken line between the Tax Court and the Small Cases Division indicates that there is no appeal from the Small Cases Division. Currently, the jurisdiction of the Small Cases Division of the Tax Court is limited to $50,000 or less. The proceedings of the Small Cases Division are informal, and its decisions are not precedents for any other court decision and are not reviewable by any higher court. Proceedings can be more timely and less expensive in the Small Cases Division. Some of these cases can now be found on the U.S. Tax Court Internet site.

American law, following English law, is frequently *made* by judicial decisions. Under the doctrine of *stare decisis*, each case (except in the Small Cases Division) has precedential value for future cases with the same controlling set of facts.

Judges are not required to follow judicial precedent beyond their own jurisdiction. For example, the decisions of an appellate court are binding only on the trial courts within its jurisdiction and not on other trial courts. Different appellate courts may reach different opinions about the same issue. Further, the doctrine of precedential authority requires a court to follow prior cases only where the issues

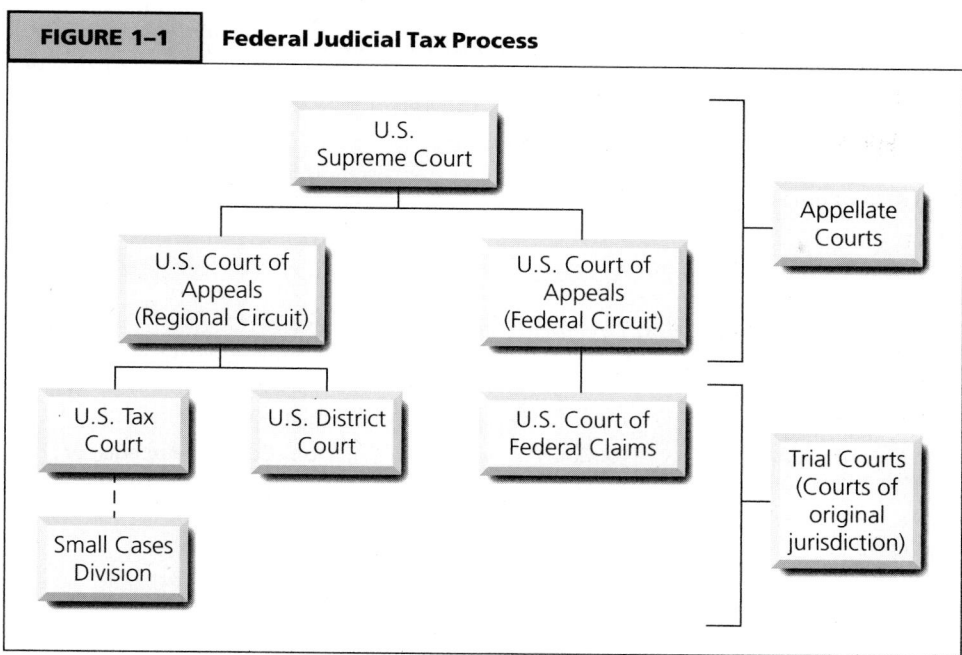

FIGURE 1–1 **Federal Judicial Tax Process**

(handwritten margin note: STARE DECISIS)

and material facts of the current case are essentially the same as those involved in the prior decisions.

Most Federal and state appellate court decisions and some decisions of trial courts are published. More than 6 million judicial opinions have been published in the United States; over 200,000 cases are published each year.[39] Published court decisions are organized by jurisdiction (Federal or state) and level of court (appellate or trial).

Trial Courts. The differences between the various trial courts (courts of original jurisdiction) can be summarized as follows:

- There is only one Court of Federal Claims and only one Tax Court, but there are many Federal District Courts. The taxpayer does not select the District Court that will hear the dispute but must sue in the one that has jurisdiction.
- The U.S. Court of Federal Claims has jurisdiction over any claim against the United States that is based on the Constitution, any Act of Congress, or any regulation of an executive department.
- Each of the 94 District Courts has only one judge, the Court of Federal Claims has 16 judges, and the Tax Court has 19 regular judges. In the case of the Tax Court, the whole court will review a case (the case is sent to court conference) only when more important or novel tax issues are involved. Many cases will be heard and decided by one of the 19 regular judges. If a case is reviewed by the full Tax Court, such an *en banc* decision has compelling authority.
- The Court of Federal Claims meets most often in Washington, D.C., while a District Court meets at a prescribed seat for the particular district. Since each state has at least one District Court and many of the populous states have more, the inconvenience and expense of traveling for the taxpayer and counsel (present with many suits in the Court of Federal Claims) are largely eliminated. The Tax Court is officially based in Washington, D.C., but the various judges travel to different parts of the country and hear cases at predetermined locations and dates. This procedure eases the distance problem for the taxpayer, but it can mean a delay before the case comes to trial and is decided.

[39]Mersky and Dunn, *Fundamentals of Legal Research*, 8th ed. (Westbury, N.Y.: The Foundation Press, 2002).

CONCEPT SUMMARY   1–1

Federal Judicial System

Issue	U.S. Tax Court	U.S. District Court	U.S. Court of Federal Claims
Number of judges per court	19*	1	16
Payment of deficiency before trial	No	Yes	Yes
Jury trial available	No	Yes	No
Types of disputes	Tax cases only	Most criminal/civil cases	Claims against the United States
Jurisdiction	Nationwide	Location of taxpayer	Nationwide
Appeal route	U.S. Court of Appeals	U.S. Court of Appeals	U.S. Court of Appeals for the Federal Circuit

*There are also 14 special trial judges and 9 senior judges.

- The Tax Court hears only tax cases; the Court of Federal Claims and District Courts hear nontax litigation as well. This difference, as well as the fact that many Tax Court justices have been appointed from IRS or Treasury Department positions, has led some to conclude that the Tax Court has more expertise in tax matters.
- The only court in which a taxpayer can obtain a jury trial is a District Court. Juries can decide only questions of fact and not questions of law, however. Therefore, taxpayers who choose the District Court route often do not request a jury trial. In this event, the judge will decide all issues. Note that a District Court decision is controlling only in the district in which the court has jurisdiction.
- Before the Court of Federal Claims or a District Court can have jurisdiction, the taxpayer must pay the tax deficiency assessed by the IRS and then sue for a refund. If the taxpayer wins (assuming no successful appeal by the IRS), the tax paid plus appropriate interest will be recovered. Jurisdiction in the Tax Court, however, is usually obtained without first paying the assessed tax deficiency. In the event the taxpayer loses in the Tax Court (and no appeal is taken or any appeal is unsuccessful), the deficiency must be paid with accrued interest.
- Appeals from a District Court or a Tax Court decision are to the appropriate U.S. Court of Appeals. Appeals from the Court of Federal Claims go to the Court of Appeals for the Federal Circuit.
- Special trial judges hear small tax cases and write summary opinions. The IRS's deficiency recovery rate is higher here than in regular Tax Court decisions. Beginning in 2001, these summary opinions are now posted on the U.S. Tax Court's Internet site; regular decisions have been posted there since 1995.
- Since there are "gray areas" in the tax laws, courts may disagree as to the proper tax treatment of a dispute. With these splits in judicial authority, a taxpayer may have some flexibility to "forum shop"—choose the most favorable route to bring a lawsuit.

Some of the characteristics of the judicial system described above are summarized in Concept Summary 1–1.

Appellate Courts.   An appeal from a trial court goes to the U.S. Court of Appeals of appropriate jurisdiction. Generally, a three-judge panel hears a Court of Appeals case, but occasionally the *full* court will decide more controversial conflicts. A jury trial is not available.

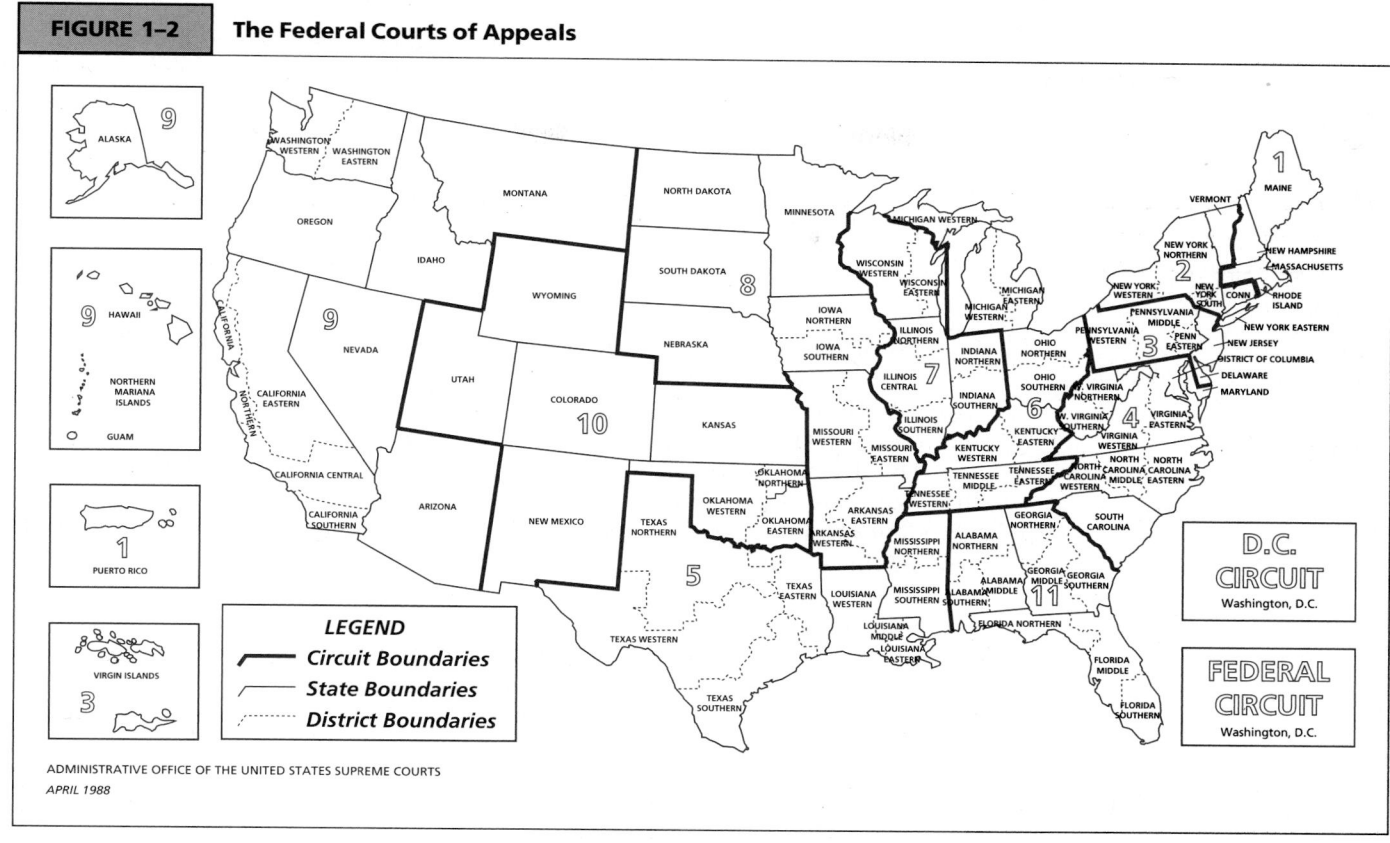

FIGURE 1–2   The Federal Courts of Appeals

LEGEND
— Circuit Boundaries
／ State Boundaries
⋯ District Boundaries

ADMINISTRATIVE OFFICE OF THE UNITED STATES SUPREME COURTS
APRIL 1988

Figure 1–2 shows the geographic area within the jurisdiction of each Federal Court of Appeals.

If the IRS loses at the trial court level (District Court, Tax Court, or Court of Federal Claims), it need not (and frequently does not) appeal. The fact that an appeal is not made, however, does not indicate that the IRS agrees with the result and will not litigate similar issues in the future.

The IRS may decide not to appeal for a number of reasons. First, the current litigation load may be heavy. As a consequence, the IRS may decide that available personnel should be assigned to other, more important cases. Second, the IRS may determine that this is not a good case to appeal. For example, the taxpayer may be in a sympathetic position, or the facts may be particularly strong in his or her favor. In such event, the IRS may wait to test the legal issues involved with a taxpayer who has a much weaker case. Third, if the appeal is from a District Court or the Tax Court, the Court of Appeals of jurisdiction could have some bearing on whether the IRS decides to pursue an appeal. Based on past experience and precedent, the IRS may conclude that the chance for success on a particular issue might be more promising in another Court of Appeals. The IRS will wait for a similar case to arise in a different jurisdiction.

ETHICAL and EQUITABLE *Considerations*

CHOOSING CASES FOR APPEAL

The IRS loses a tax case against a prominent citizen in the U.S. District Court of Iowa. The taxpayer, a minister, had set up three separate trusts for each of his three children (i.e., a total of nine trusts). The IRS argued that under Reg. § 1.641(a)–0(c) these trusts should be consolidated and treated as three trusts to stop the taxpayer from mitigating the progressive tax structure (e.g., the 35 percent top tax bracket).

The IRS has decided to appeal a case in the multiple trust area. As one of the IRS's attorneys, you must choose between the Iowa case and a similar multiple trust conflict in the U.S. District Court of Virginia. Here the taxpayer is a CPA who has established two different trusts for her two children (i.e., a total of four trusts). [See *Estelle Morris Trusts*, 51 T.C. 20 (1968).]

In making your decision, you note that potentially more sympathy may be associated with the minister's profession than with the CPA's. Other considerations are the facts indicating that the attempt at tax avoidance is more egregious in the Iowa case and a colleague's opinion that the Virginia case is winnable. Which case will you select? Comment on whether it is fair for the IRS to select a case to appeal in this fashion.

District Courts, the Tax Court, and the Court of Federal Claims must abide by the precedents set by the Court of Appeals of jurisdiction. A particular Court of Appeals need not follow the decisions of another Court of Appeals. All courts, however, must follow the decisions of the U.S. Supreme Court.

The Tax Court is a national court, meaning that it hears and decides cases from all parts of the country. For many years, the Tax Court followed a policy of deciding cases based on what it thought the result should be, even when its decision might be appealed to a Court of Appeals that had previously decided a similar case differently.

Some years ago, this policy was changed. Now the Tax Court will still decide a case as it feels the law should be applied *only* if the Court of Appeals of appropriate jurisdiction has not yet ruled on the issue or has previously decided a similar case in accordance with the Tax Court's decision. If the Court of Appeals of appropriate jurisdiction has previously held squarely on point otherwise, the Tax Court will conform even though it disagrees with the holding.[40] This policy is known as the *Golsen* rule.

E X A M P L E 19	Gene lives in Texas and sues in the Tax Court on Issue A. The Fifth Circuit Court of Appeals, the appellate court of appropriate jurisdiction, has already decided, in a case involving similar facts but a different taxpayer, that Issue A should be resolved against the IRS. Although the Tax Court feels that the Fifth Circuit Court of Appeals is wrong, under the *Golsen* rule, it will render judgment for Gene. Shortly thereafter, Beth, a resident of New York, in a comparable case, sues in the Tax Court on Issue A. Assume that the Second Circuit Court of Appeals, the appellate court of appropriate jurisdiction, has never expressed itself on Issue A. Presuming the Tax Court has not reconsidered its position on Issue A, it will decide against Beth. Thus, it is entirely possible for two taxpayers suing in the same court to end up with opposite results merely because they live in different parts of the country. ∎

Appeal to the U.S. Supreme Court is by Writ of **Certiorari**. If the Court agrees to hear the case, it will grant the Writ (*cert. granted*). Most often, it will deny jurisdiction (*cert. denied*). For whatever reason or reasons, the Supreme Court rarely hears tax cases. The Court usually grants certiorari to resolve a conflict among the Courts of Appeals (e.g., two or more appellate courts have assumed opposing positions on a particular issue) or when the tax issue is extremely important. The granting of a Writ of Certiorari indicates that at least four members of the Supreme Court believe that the issue is of sufficient importance to be heard by the full Court.

The role of appellate courts is limited to a review of the trial record compiled by the trial courts. Thus, the appellate process usually involves a determination of whether the trial court applied the proper law in arriving at its decision. Usually, an appellate court will not dispute a lower court's fact-finding determination.

An appeal can have any of a number of possible outcomes. The appellate court may approve (affirm) or disapprove (reverse) the lower court's finding, and it may also send the case back for further consideration (remand). When many issues are

---

[40]*Jack E. Golsen*, 54 T.C. 742 (1970); see also *John A. Lardas*, 99 T.C. 490 (1992).

involved, it is not unusual to encounter a mixed result. Thus, the lower court may be affirmed (*aff'd*) on Issue A and reversed (*rev'd*) on Issue B, while Issue C is remanded (*rem'd*) for additional fact finding.

When more than one judge is involved in the decision-making process, disagreement is not uncommon. In addition to the majority view, one or more judges may concur (agree with the result reached but not with some or all of the reasoning) or dissent (disagree with the result). In any one case, the majority view controls. But concurring and dissenting views can have influence on other courts or, at some subsequent date when the composition of the court has changed, even on the same court.

Judicial Citations—General.

Having briefly described the judicial process, it is appropriate to consider the more practical problem of the relationship of case law to tax research. As previously noted, court decisions are an important source of tax law. The ability to cite a case and to locate it is therefore a must in working with the tax law. The usual pattern for a judicial citation is as follows: case name, volume number, reporter series, page or paragraph number, and court (where necessary).

Judicial Citations—The U.S. Tax Court.

A good starting point is the U.S. Tax Court. The Tax Court issues three types of decisions: Regular decisions, Memorandum decisions, and summary opinions. They differ in both substance and form. In terms of substance, Memorandum decisions deal with situations necessitating only the application of already established principles of law. Regular decisions involve novel issues not previously resolved by the Tax Court. In actual practice, this distinction is not always preserved. Not infrequently, Memorandum decisions will be encountered that appear to warrant Regular status and vice versa. At any rate, do not conclude that Memorandum decisions possess no value as precedents. Both Memorandum and Regular decisions represent the position of the Tax Court and, as such, can be relied upon. Summary opinions, on the other hand, are issued in small tax cases and may not be used as precedent in any other case.

Regular decisions are published by the U.S. Government in a series called *Tax Court of the United States Reports* (T.C.). Each volume of these reports covers a six-month period (January 1 through June 30 and July 1 through December 31) and is given a succeeding volume number. But, as was true of the *Cumulative Bulletin*, there is usually a time lag between the date a decision is rendered and the date it appears in bound form. A temporary citation may be necessary to help the researcher locate a recent Regular decision. Consider, for example, the temporary and permanent citations for *CRSO*, a decision filed on April 30, 2007:

Temporary Citation	{	*CRSO*, 128 T.C. ___, No. 12 (2007). *Explanation:* Page number left blank because not yet known.
Permanent Citation	{	*CRSO*, 128 T.C. 153 (2007). *Explanation:* Page number now available.

Both citations tell us that the case ultimately will appear in Volume 128 of the *Tax Court of the United States Reports*. But until this volume is bound and made available to the general public, the page number must be left blank. Instead, the temporary citation identifies the case as being the 12th Regular decision issued by the Tax Court since Volume 127 ended. With this information, the decision can be easily located in either of the special Tax Court services published by Commerce Clearing House (CCH) and by Research Institute of America (RIA—formerly by Prentice-Hall [P-H]). Once Volume 128 is released, the permanent citation can be substituted and the number of the case dropped. Starting in 1995, both Regular and Memorandum decisions are issued on the U.S. Tax Court Web site (**http://www .ustaxcourt.gov/**).

Before 1943, the Tax Court was called the Board of Tax Appeals, and its decisions were published as the *United States Board of Tax Appeals Reports* (B.T.A.). These 47 volumes cover the period from 1924 to 1942. For example, the citation *Karl Pauli* 11 B.T.A. 784 (1928) refers to the 11th volume of the *Board of Tax Appeals Reports*, page 784, issued in 1928.

Memorandum decisions are published by CCH and by RIA (formerly by P-H). Consider, for example, the three different ways that *Walter H. Johnson* can be cited:

> *Walter H. Johnson*, T.C.Memo. 1975–245
> The 245th Memorandum decision issued by the Tax Court in 1975.
>
> *Walter H. Johnson*, 34 TCM 1056
> Page 1056 of Vol. 34 of the CCH *Tax Court Memorandum Decisions.*
>
> *Walter H. Johnson*, P-H T.C.Mem.Dec. ¶75,245
> Paragraph 75,245 of the P-H *T.C. Memorandum Decisions.*

Note that the third citation contains the same information as the first. Thus, ¶75,245 indicates the following information about the case: year 1975, 245th T.C.Memo. decision.[41]

Summary opinions are cited as in the following example for *Edmund T. MacMurray*, filed on May 31, 2007.

> *Edmund T. MacMurray*, T.C. Summary Opinion 2007–118.

Starting in 2001, summary opinions are reported on the U.S. Tax Court Web site.

Judicial Citations—The U.S. District Courts, Claims Court, and Courts of Appeals.

District Court, Claims Court (now Court of Federal Claims), Court of Appeals, and Supreme Court decisions dealing with Federal tax matters are reported in both the CCH *U.S. Tax Cases* (USTC) and the RIA (formerly P-H) *American Federal Tax Reports* (AFTR) series.

Federal District Court decisions, dealing with *both* tax and nontax issues, are also published by West Publishing Company in its *Federal Supplement Second* (F.Supp.2d) series. This series follows the *Federal Supplement* (F.Supp.) series, which concluded in 1998 with Volume 999. The following examples illustrate how a District Court case can be cited in three different forms:

> *Simons-Eastern Co. v. U.S.*, 73–1 USTC ¶9279 (D.Ct.Ga., 1972).
> *Explanation:* Reported in the first volume of the *U.S. Tax Cases* (USTC) published by Commerce Clearing House for calendar year 1973 (73–1) and located at paragraph 9279 (¶9279).
>
> *Simons-Eastern Co. v. U.S.*, 31 AFTR2d 73–640 (D.Ct.Ga., 1972).
> *Explanation:* Reported in the 31st volume of the second series of the *American Federal Tax Reports* (AFTR2d) published by Prentice-Hall (now RIA) and beginning on page 640. The "73" preceding the page number indicates the year the case was published but is a designation used only in recent decisions.
>
> *Simons-Eastern Co. v. U.S.*, 354 F.Supp. 1003 (D.Ct.Ga., 1972).
> *Explanation:* Reported in the 354th volume of the *Federal Supplement* (F.Supp.) series published by West Publishing Company and beginning on page 1003.

In all of the preceding citations, note that the name of the case is the same (Simons-Eastern Co. being the taxpayer), as is the reference to the Federal District Court of Georgia (D.Ct.Ga.) and the year the decision was rendered (1972).[42]

---

[41]In this text, the Research Institute of America (RIA) citation for Memorandum decisions of the U.S. Tax Court is omitted. Thus, *Walter H. Johnson* would be cited as 34 TCM 1056, T.C.Memo. 1975–245.

[42]In this text, the case will be cited in the following form: *Simons-Eastern Co. v. U.S.*, 73–1 USTC ¶9279, 31 AFTR2d 73–640, 354 F.Supp. 1003 (D.Ct.Ga., 1972).

Beginning in October of 1982, decisions of the Claims Court are reported by West Publishing Company in a series designated *Federal Claims Reporter*. Thus, the Claims Court decision in *Recchie v. U.S.* appears as follows:

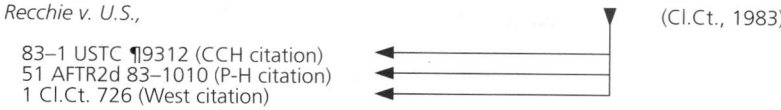

Recchie v. U.S.,   (Cl.Ct., 1983)

   83–1 USTC ¶9312 (CCH citation)
   51 AFTR2d 83–1010 (P-H citation)
   1 Cl.Ct. 726 (West citation)

Beginning on October 30, 1992, the Claims Court underwent a further name change. The new designation, U.S. Court of Federal Claims, began with Volume 27 of the former Cl.Ct. (West citation), now abbreviated as Fed.Cl.

Decisions of the Courts of Appeals are published in a West Publishing Company reporter designated as the *Federal Third* (F.3d) series, which began in October 1993, at the conclusion of the *Federal Second* (F.2d) series. Illustrations of the different forms follow:

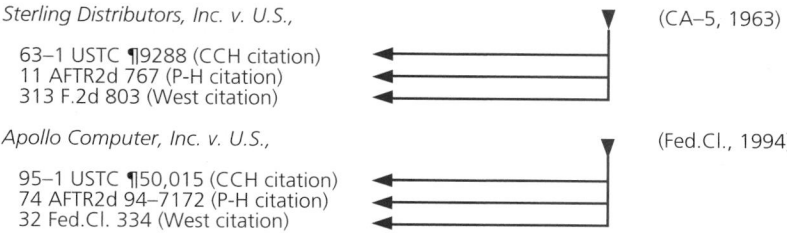

Sterling Distributors, Inc. v. U.S.,   (CA–5, 1963)

   63–1 USTC ¶9288 (CCH citation)
   11 AFTR2d 767 (P-H citation)
   313 F.2d 803 (West citation)

Apollo Computer, Inc. v. U.S.,   (Fed.Cl., 1994)

   95–1 USTC ¶50,015 (CCH citation)
   74 AFTR2d 94–7172 (P-H citation)
   32 Fed.Cl. 334 (West citation)

Note that *Sterling Distributors, Inc. v. U.S.* is a decision rendered by the Fifth Circuit Court of Appeals in 1963 (CA–5, 1963) while *Apollo Computer, Inc. v. U.S.* was rendered in 1994 by the U.S. Court of Federal Claims.

If the IRS loses in a decision, it may indicate whether it agrees or disagrees with the results reached by the court by publishing an **acquiescence** ("A" or "*Acq.*") or **nonacquiescence** ("NA" or "*Nonacq.*"), respectively. The acquiescence or nonacquiescence is published in the *Internal Revenue Bulletin* and the *Cumulative Bulletin* as an *Action on Decision*. The IRS can retroactively revoke an acquiescence or nonacquiescence. Originally, acquiescences and nonacquiescences were published only for Regular U.S. Tax Court decisions, but since 1991 the IRS has expanded its acquiescence program to include other civil tax cases where guidance is helpful.

Judicial Citations—The U.S. Supreme Court.
Like all other Federal tax cases (except those rendered by the U.S. Tax Court), Supreme Court decisions are published by Commerce Clearing House in the USTCs and by Research Institute of America (formerly P-H) in the AFTRs. The U.S. Government Printing Office also publishes these decisions in the *United States Supreme Court Reports* (U.S.) as does West Publishing Company in its *Supreme Court Reporter* (S.Ct.) and the Lawyer's Co-operative Publishing Company in its *United States Reports, Lawyer's Edition* (L.Ed.). The following illustrates the different ways the same decision can be cited:

U.S. v. The Donruss Co.,   (USSC, 1969)

   69–1 USTC ¶9167 (CCH citation)
   23 AFTR2d 69–418 (P-H citation)
   89 S.Ct. 501 (West citation)
   393 U.S. 297 (U.S. Government Printing Office citation)
   21 L.Ed.2d 495 (Lawyer's Co-operative Publishing Co. citation)

The parenthetical reference (USSC, 1969) identifies the decision as having been rendered by the U.S. Supreme Court in 1969. The citations given in this text for Supreme Court decisions will be limited to the CCH (USTC), the RIA or P-H for older volumes (AFTR), and the West (S.Ct.) versions.

ROLLING STONES GATHER LITTLE TAXES

The Rolling Stones—Sir Mick Jagger, Charlie Watts, and Keith Richards—paid tax of only 1.6 percent on their earnings of approximately $455 million over the past 20 years. Not only did they use offshore trusts and companies to obtain tax breaks, but more importantly, they became tax exiles from Great Britain, moving to the Netherlands in 1972. There is no direct tax on royalties under Dutch law. Sir Mick Jagger's fortune is estimated to be approximately $385 million. International tax planning does help a poor soul.

Other Sources of the Tax Law

Other sources of the tax law include tax treaties and tax periodicals.

Effect of Treaties. The United States signs certain tax treaties (sometimes called tax conventions) with foreign countries to render mutual assistance in tax enforcement and to avoid double taxation. The Technical and Miscellaneous Revenue Act of 1988 provided that neither a tax law nor a tax treaty takes general precedence. Thus, when there is a direct conflict, the most recent item will take precedence. More than 34 Sections of the Code contain direct references to treaties [e.g., § 245(a)(10)].

Tax Periodicals. The various tax periodicals provide additional sources of tax information. The easiest way to locate a journal article on a particular tax problem is through online resources like *Federal Tax Articles* (CCH) and *Index to Federal Tax Articles* (Warren, Gorham and Lamont).

The following are some of the more useful tax periodicals with their online addresses (usually preceded by **http://**):

Journal of Taxation
Journal of International Taxation
Practical Tax Strategies
Estate Planning
Corporate Taxation
Business Entities
ria.thomson.com/Journals

The Tax Executive
www.tei.org

The Tax Adviser
aicpa.org/pubs/taxadv

Practical Accountant
webcpa.com/publications.cfm

Tax Law Review
www.law.nyu.edu/programs/tax/review.html

Journal of the American Taxation Association
atasection.org/jata.html

The ATA Journal of Legal Tax Research
aaahq.org/ata/_ATAMenu/ATAPubJLTR.html

Oil, Gas & Energy Quarterly
bookstore.lexis.com/bookstore/product/10462.html

Trusts and Estates
trustsandestates.com

Journal of Passthrough Entities
TAXES—The Tax Magazine
tax.cchgroup.com/Books

National Tax Journal
ntj.tax.org

Tax Notes
taxanalysts.com/TaxNotes

The Tax Lawyer
www.law.georgetown.edu/journals/tax

Working with the Tax Law—Locating Tax Sources

LO.6

Locate tax law sources.

Electronic versus Paper Tax Sources

Computerized tax research tools have replaced paper resources in most tax practices. There are two chief ways to conduct tax research using computer resources: (1) online and CD-ROM subscription services and (2) online free Internet sites.

Accessing tax documents through electronic means offers a number of advantages over a strictly paper-based approach.

- Materials generally are available faster through an electronic system. Online services are updated daily and can be accessed from remote locations.
- Some tax documents (e.g., slip opinions of trial-level court cases, interviews with policymakers) are available only through electronic means.
- Commercial subscriptions to electronic tax services are likely to provide, at little or no cost, additional tax law sources to which the researcher would not have access through stand-alone purchases of traditional material. For example, the full texts of letter rulings are quite costly to acquire in a paper-based format, but electronic publishers may bundle the rulings with other material for a reasonable cost.
- When searching the topical index of a topical or annotated paper tax service, a user is relying on someone else's judgment. The keyword that the researcher needs may or may not be used by the editor. In a computerized tax service, however, the user creates his or her own keywords, and the software index will electronically scan all the files and retrieve whichever documents contain those words.
- A computerized tax service may retrieve documents that are no longer in print and may obtain regularly published documents to which a researcher does not have access.
- Most computerized services allow a user to retrieve documents in order of relevance or listed by database sources.

Computerized tools allow the tax library to reflect the tax law itself, including its dynamic and daily changes. Nevertheless, using electronic means to locate tax law sources cannot substitute for developing and maintaining a thorough knowledge of the tax law or for logical and analytical review in addressing open tax research issues.

Conventional Tax Sources

Tax services are either annotated or topical. However, today with hypertext linking, most of the electronic tax services may be entered using either a Code Section or a topical search. The two major paper annotated services are organized by Internal Revenue Code Sections, whereas most of the services are organized by major topics. The following major services are available:

Standard Federal Tax Reporter, Commerce Clearing House. (annotated)

United States Tax Reporter, Research Institute of America (entitled *Federal Taxes* prior to July 1992). (annotated)

Mertens Law of Federal Income Taxation, West Group. (topical)

Federal Tax Coordinator 2d, Research Institute of America. (topical)

Tax Management Portfolios, Bureau of National Affairs. (topical)

CCH's Tax Research Consultant, Commerce Clearing House. (topical)

Analysis of Federal Taxes: Income, Research Institute of America. (topical)

Working with the Tax Services. In this text, it is not feasible to teach the use of any particular tax service because this knowledge can be obtained only by

EXHIBIT 1–1	Electronic Tax Services

Electronic Tax Service	Description
CCH	Includes the CCH tax service, primary sources including treatises, and other subscription materials. Ten to 20 discs and online.
RIA	Includes the RIA topical *Coordinator* and the annotated tax service formerly provided by Prentice-Hall. The citator has elaborate document-linking features, and major tax treatises are provided. One to 10 discs and online.
WESTLAW	Code, Regulations, *Cumulative Bulletins*, cases, citators, and editorial material. About a dozen discs and online.
Kleinrock's	A single disc with tax statutory, administrative, and judicial law. Another single disc provides tax forms and instructions for Federal and state jurisdictions.

practice. The representatives of the various tax services provide users with printed booklets and individual instruction on the use of the services. However, several important observations about the use of tax services cannot be overemphasized. First, always check for current developments. The main text of any service is revised too infrequently to permit reliance on that portion as the *latest* word on any subject. Where such current developments can be found depends on which service is being used. The CCH service contains a special volume devoted to current matters. Second, when dealing with a tax service synopsis of a Treasury Department pronouncement or a judicial decision, remember there is no substitute for the original source.

To illustrate, do not base a conclusion solely on a tax service's commentary on *Simons-Eastern Co. v. U.S.*[43] If the case is vital to the research, look it up. The facts of the decision may be distinguishable from those in the problem being researched. This is not to say that the case synopsis contained in the tax service is wrong; it might just be misleading or incomplete.

Citators help researchers learn the history of tax decisions and Revenue Rulings and evaluate the strengths of their holdings. The three major multivolume citators are the RIA Citator 2nd Series, the CCH Citator, and Shepard's Federal Tax Citations. Computerized citators can be found in WESTLAW (KeyCite) and LEXIS (Auto-Cite and Shepard's). The RIA and CCH Citators are available through their computerized tax services. The use of the RIA Citator is described later in this chapter.

Electronic Tax Sources

Virtually all of the major commercial tax publishers and most of the primary sources of the law itself, such as the Supreme Court and some of the Courts of Appeals, provide tax materials in electronic formats. Competitive pressures have rewarded tax practitioners who have developed computer literacy skills, and the user-friendliness of the best of the tax research software is of great benefit to both the daily and the occasional user. Exhibit 1–1 summarizes the most popular of the electronic tax services on the market today.

In using these resources, usually, the law is found using one of the following strategies:

- *Search* various databases using keywords that are likely to be found in the underlying documents, as written by Congress, the judiciary, or administrative sources.

---

[43]Cited in Footnote 42.

EXHIBIT 1–2	Online Tax Services

Online Service	Description
LEXIS/NEXIS	Federal and state statutory, administrative, and judicial material. Extensive libraries of newspapers, magazines, patent records, and medical and economic databases, both U.S. and foreign-based.
RIA	Includes the RIA tax services, major tax treatises, Federal and state statutes, administrative documents, and court opinions. Extensive citator access, editorial material, and practitioner aids.
CCH	Includes the CCH tax service, primary sources including treatises, and other subscription materials. Tax and economic news sources, extensive editorial material, and practitioner support tools.
WESTLAW	Federal and state statutes, administrative documents, and court opinions. Extensive citator access, editorial material, and gateways to third-party publications. Extensive government document databases.

- *Link* to tax documents for which all or part of the proper citation is known (e.g., Code Section, court decision).
- *Browse* the tax databases, examining various tables of contents and indexes in a traditional manner or using cross-references in the documents to jump from one tax law source to another.

CD-ROM Services. The CD has been a major source of electronic tax data for about a decade. Data compression techniques continue to allow more tax materials to fit on a single disc every year. CCH, RIA, WESTLAW, and others offer vast tax libraries to the practitioner, often in conjunction with a subscription to traditional paper-based resources or accompanied by newsletters, training seminars, and ongoing technical support.

At its best, a CD-based tax library provides the archival data that make up a permanent, core library of tax documents. For about $300 a year, the tax CD is updated quarterly, providing more comprehensive tax resources than the researcher is ever likely to need. The CD is comparable in scope to a paper-based library of a decade ago costing perhaps $20,000 to establish and $5,000 per year in perpetuity to maintain. If the library is contained on a small number of discs, it also can offer portability through use on notebook computers.

Online Systems. An online research system allows a practitioner to obtain virtually instantaneous use of tax law sources by accessing the computer of the service provider. Online services generally employ price-per-search cost structures, which can be as much as $200 per hour, significantly higher than the cost of CD materials. Thus, unless a practitioner can pass along related costs to clients or others, online searching generally is limited to the most important issues and to the researchers with the most experience and training in search techniques.

Perhaps the best combination of electronic tax resources is to conduct day-to-day work on a CD system, so that the budget for the related work is known in advance, and augment the CD search with online access where it is judged to be critical. Exhibit 1–2 provides details on the contents of the most commonly used commercial online tax services.

EXHIBIT 1–3	The IRS's *Digital Daily*

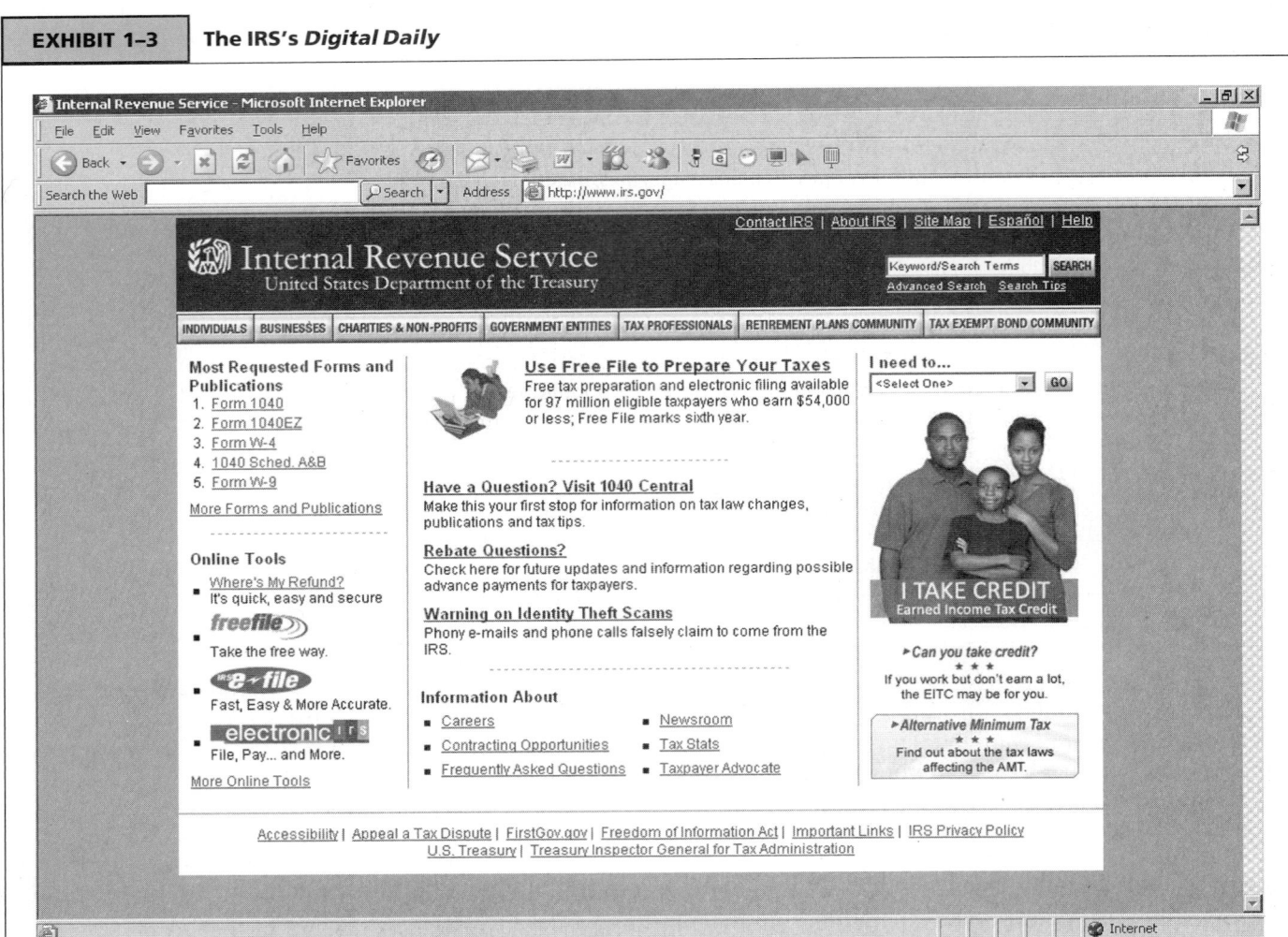

The Internet. The Internet provides a wealth of tax information in several popular forms, sometimes at no direct cost to the researcher. Using so-called browser software that often is distributed with new computer systems and their communication devices, the tax professional can access information provided around the world that can aid the research process.

- *Home pages (sites) on the World Wide Web (WWW)* are provided by accounting and consulting firms, publishers, tax academics and libraries, and governmental bodies as a means of making information widely available or of soliciting subscriptions or consulting engagements. The best sites offer links to other sites and direct contact to the site providers. One of the best sites available to the tax practitioner is the Internal Revenue Service's *Digital Daily*, illustrated in Exhibit 1–3. This site offers downloadable forms and instructions, "plain English" versions of Regulations, and news update items. Exhibit 1–4 lists some of the Web sites that may be most useful to tax researchers and their Internet addresses as of press date.
- *Newsgroups* provide a means by which information related to the tax law can be exchanged among taxpayers, tax professionals, and others who subscribe to the group's services. Newsgroup members can read the exchanges among other members and offer replies and suggestions to inquiries as desired.

EXHIBIT 1–4 | **Tax-Related Web Sites**

Web Site	WWW Address at Press Date (Usually preceded by http://www.)	Description
Internal Revenue Service	**irs.gov/**	News releases, downloadable forms and instructions, tables, and e-mail
Court opinions	The site at **law.emory.edu/caselaw** allows the researcher to link to the site of the jurisdiction (other than the Tax Court) that is the subject of the query.	
Tax Analysts	**taxanalysts.com**	Policy-oriented readings on the tax law and proposals to change it, moderated bulletins on various tax subjects
Tax Sites Directory	**taxsites.com**	References and links to tax sites on the Internet, including state and Federal tax sites, academic and professional pages, tax forms, and software
Tax laws online	Regulations are at **cfr.law.cornell.edu/cfr/** and the Code is at **uscode.house.gov/ search/criteria.shtml** and **www4.law.cornell.edu/uscode/**	
Commercial tax publishers	For instance, **tax.com** and **cch.com**	Information about products and services available for subscription and newsletter excerpts
Large accounting firms and professional organizations	For instance, the AICPA's page is at **aicpa.org**, Ernst & Young is at **ey.com/**, and KPMG is at **kpmg.com**	Tax planning newsletters, descriptions of services offered and career opportunities, and exchange of data with clients and subscribers
Cengage Learning South-Western	**academic.cengage.com/taxation/SWFT**	Informational updates, newsletters, support materials for students and adopters, and continuing education
U.S. Tax Court decisions	**ustaxcourt.gov**	Recent U.S. Tax Court decisions

NOTE: Caution: addresses change frequently.

Discussions address the interpretation and application of existing law, analysis of proposals and new pronouncements, and reviews of tax software.

- *E-mail capabilities* are available to most tax professionals through an employer's equipment or by a subscription providing Internet access at a low and usually fixed cost for the period. E-mail allows for virtually instantaneous sending and receiving of messages, letters, tax returns and supporting data, spreadsheets, and other documents necessary to solve tax problems.

Working with the Tax Law—Tax Research

LO.7

Be able to carry out tax research.

Tax research is the method used to determine the best available solution to a situation that possesses tax consequences. In other words, it is the process of finding a competent and professional conclusion to a tax problem. The problem may originate from either completed or proposed transactions. In the case of a completed transaction, the objective of the research is to determine the tax result of what has already taken place. For example, is the expenditure incurred by the taxpayer deductible or not deductible for tax purposes? When dealing with proposed

(handwritten: $/62 Reprint Memberlumple)

(handwritten top margin: more Facts issues)

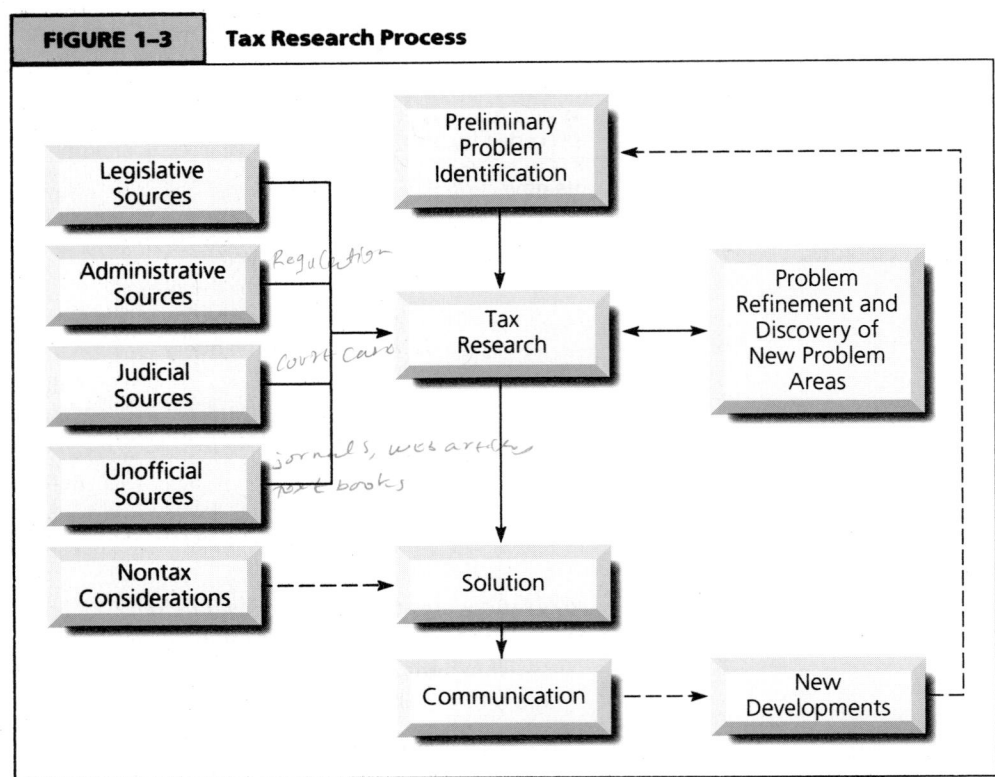

(handwritten annotations on figure: "Regulation", "Court Case", "journals, web articles, text books")

transactions, the tax research process is concerned with the determination of possible alternative tax consequences. To the extent that tax research leads to a choice of alternatives or otherwise influences the future actions of the taxpayer, it becomes the key to effective tax planning.

Tax research involves the following procedures:

- Identifying and refining the problem.
- Locating the appropriate tax law sources.
- Assessing the validity of the tax law sources.
- Arriving at the solution or at alternative solutions while giving due consideration to nontax factors.
- Effectively communicating the solution to the taxpayer or the taxpayer's representative.
- Following up on the solution (where appropriate) in light of new developments.

This process is depicted schematically in Figure 1–3. The broken lines indicate steps of particular interest when tax research is directed toward proposed, rather than completed, transactions.

Identifying the Problem

Problem identification starts with a compilation of the relevant facts involved. In this regard, *all* of the facts that might have a bearing on the problem must be gathered as any omission could modify the solution reached. To illustrate, consider what appears to be a very simple problem.

EXAMPLE 20

Dana Pehrson advances $52,000 to her nephew in 2001 to enable him to attend a private college. Seven years later, she claims a bad debt deduction for $42,000 that the nephew has not repaid. The problem: Is Dana entitled to a bad debt deduction? ∎

Refining the Problem. Before a bad debt deduction can arise, it must be established that a debt really existed. In a related-party setting (e.g., aunt and nephew), the IRS may contend that the original advance was not a loan but, in reality, a gift. Of key significance in this regard would be whether the lender (the aunt) had an honest and real expectation of payment by the borrower (the nephew).[44] Indicative of this repayment expectation is whether the parties preserved the formalities of a loan, including the following:

- The borrower issued a written instrument evidencing the obligation.
- The loan arrangement provided for interest.
- The note specified a set due date.
- Collateral was available to the lender in the event of default by the borrower.[45]

The presence of some or all of these formalities does not, however, guarantee that a bona fide loan will be found. By the same token, the absence of some or all of the formalities does not make the advance a gift. Applying the formalities criteria to Example 20 is not possible since key facts (e.g., the presence or absence of a written note) are not given. Nevertheless, several inferences might be made that lead to a loan interpretation:

- It appears that the nephew has repaid at least $10,000 of the $52,000 that he borrowed. If the parties intended a gift of the full amount of the loan, why was partial repayment made?
- Although one would not expect a nephew on his way to college to have assets to serve as collateral for a loan, the fact that he was obtaining additional education could reinforce any expectation of repayment. In most situations, a person with a college education will possess a higher earning potential than one without such education. This education would improve the nephew's financial ability to repay the loan.

Further Refinement of the Problem. It may be impossible to determine whether the advance constitutes a loan or a gift with any degree of certainty. In either event, however, the tax consequences of each possibility must be ascertained.

If the advance is determined to be a gift, it is subject to the Federal gift tax.[46] Whether or not a gift tax results depends upon how much of the unified tax credit the aunt has available to absorb the gift tax on $42,000 [$52,000 (total gift) − $10,000 (annual exclusion in 2001)].[47] Whether the transfer results in a gift tax or not, it must be reported on Form 709 (United States Gift Tax Return) since the amount of the gift exceeds the annual exclusion.

Even if it is assumed that Dana made a gift to her nephew in 2001, does not the intervention of seven years preclude the IRS from assessing any gift tax that might be due as a result of the transfer?[48] Further research indicates that the statute of limitations on assessments does not begin to run when a tax return is not filed.[49]

To complete the picture, what are the tax consequences if the advance is treated as a loan? Aside from the bad debt deduction aspects (covered later in the chapter), the tax law provides more immediate tax ramifications:[50]

---

[44]*William F. Mercil,* 24 T.C. 1150 (1955), and *Evans Clark,* 18 T.C. 780 (1952), *aff'd* 53–2 USTC ¶9452, 44 AFTR 70, 205 F.2d 353 (CA–2, 1953).

[45]*Arthur T. Davidson,* 37 TCM 725, T.C.Memo. 1978–167.

[46]The transfer does not come within the unlimited gift tax exclusion of § 2503(e)(2)(A) since the aunt did not pay the amount directly to an educational institution. Besides, the exclusion covers only tuition payments and not other costs attendant on going to college (e.g., room and board).

[47]The tax, in turn, depends upon the amount of taxable gifts the aunt has made in the past. For a discussion of the mechanics of the Federal gift tax, see Chapter 17.

[48]Throughout the discussion of Example 20, the assumption has been made that if a gift occurred, it took place in 2001. That assumption need not be the case. Depending upon the aunt's intent, she could have decided to make a gift of the unpaid balance anytime after the loan was made (e.g., 2002, 2003, etc.).

[49]See § 6501(c)(3) and the discussion of the statute of limitations in Chapter 16.

[50]§ 7872.

- If interest is not provided for, it is imputed with the following effect:
  a. The lender (the aunt) must recognize interest income as to the imputed value.
  b. Since the lender has not received the interest, she is deemed to have made a gift of the interest to the borrower.
  c. The borrower (nephew) may be entitled to deduct (as an itemized expense) in some tax years a portion of the amount of interest deemed paid to the lender (aunt).
- If interest is provided for but the rate is lower than market (as determined by the yield on certain U.S. government securities), the differential is treated as noted above.
- For gift loans of $100,000 or less, the imputed element cannot exceed the net investment income of the borrower.

Locating the Appropriate Tax Law Sources

Once the problem is clearly defined, what is the next step? Although the next step is a matter of individual judgment, most tax research begins with the index volume of the tax service or a keyword search on an online tax service (see the earlier discussion of Electronic Tax Sources). If the problem is not complex, the researcher may bypass the tax service and turn directly to the Internal Revenue Code and the Treasury Regulations. For the beginner, this latter procedure saves time and will solve many of the more basic problems. If the researcher does not have a personal copy of the Code or Regulations, resorting to the appropriate volume(s) of a tax service or a CD-ROM may be necessary. Several of the major tax services publish paperback editions of the Code and Treasury Regulations that can be purchased at modest prices. These editions are usually revised twice each year.

Assessing the Validity of Tax Law Sources

LO.8
Assess the validity and weight of tax law sources.

After a source has been located, the next step is to assess the source in light of the problem at hand. Proper assessment involves careful interpretation of the tax law and consideration of the law's relevance and validity.

Interpreting the Internal Revenue Code. The language of the Code often is extremely difficult to comprehend. For example, a former subsection [§ 341(e)] relating to collapsible corporations contained *one* sentence of more than 450 words (twice as many as in the Gettysburg Address). Within this same subsection was another sentence of 300 words.

The Code must be read carefully for restrictive language such as "*at least* 80 percent" and "*more than* 80 percent" or "*less than* 50 percent" and "*exceeds* 50 percent." It also makes a great deal of difference, for example, whether two or more clauses are connected by "*or*" or by "*and.*"

If an answer is not in the Code, it may be necessary to resort to the Regulations and judicial decisions. In 1969, Congress directed the Treasury Department to promulgate Regulations under § 385 to distinguish corporate debt from corporate equity. As of yet, there are no Regulations under § 385. The researcher, therefore, must resort to past judicial decisions for a definition of debt.

Sometimes the Code directs the researcher elsewhere for the answer. For example, § 162(c) refers to the Foreign Corrupt Practices Act for purposes of determining when payments to foreign officials are deductible.

Cross-referencing between Code Sections is often poor or nonexistent. Code Sections are enacted at different times by Congresses that are operating under stringent deadlines. Consequently, a certain lack of integration within the Code is frequently apparent.

Definitions vary from one Code Section to another. For example, § 267 disallows losses between related parties and includes brothers and sisters in the definition of related parties. Not so with § 318, which deals with the definition of related parties as to certain stock redemptions.

Assessing the Validity of a Treasury Regulation.

Treasury Regulations are often said to have the force and effect of law. This statement is certainly true for most Regulations, but some judicial decisions have held a Regulation or a portion thereof invalid. Usually, this is done on the grounds that the Regulation is contrary to the intent of Congress.

Keep the following observations in mind when assessing the validity of a Regulation:

- In a challenge, the burden of proof is on the taxpayer to show that the Regulation is wrong. However, a court may invalidate a Regulation that varies from the language of the statute and has no support in the Committee Reports.
- If the taxpayer loses the challenge, the negligence penalty may be imposed. This accuracy-related provision deals with the "intentional disregard of rules and regulations" on the part of the taxpayer and is explained further in Chapter 16.
- Some Regulations merely reprint or rephrase what Congress has stated in its Committee Reports issued in connection with the enactment of tax legislation. Such Regulations are "hard and solid" and almost impossible to overturn because they clearly reflect the intent of Congress.
- In some Code Sections, Congress has given to the "Secretary or his delegate" the authority to prescribe Regulations to carry out the details of administration or to otherwise complete the operating rules. Under such circumstances, it could almost be said that Congress is delegating its legislative powers to the Treasury Department. The Congressional Research Service found that Congress delegated regulatory authority to the Treasury on more than 240 occasions from 1992 through 2000, an average of more than 26 delegations per year. Regulations issued pursuant to this type of authority truly possess the force and effect of law and are often called "legislative" Regulations. They are to be distinguished from "interpretative" Regulations, which purport to explain the meaning of a particular Code Section. Examples of legislative Regulations are those dealing with consolidated returns issued under §§ 1501 through 1505. As a further example, note the authority granted to the Treasury Department by § 385 to issue Regulations setting forth guidelines on when corporate debt can be reclassified as equity (see Chapter 4).

Assessing the Validity of Other Administrative Sources of the Tax Law.

Revenue Rulings issued by the IRS carry less weight than Treasury Department Regulations. Rulings are important, however, in that they reflect the position of the IRS on tax matters. In any dispute with the IRS on the interpretation of tax law, taxpayers should expect agents to follow the results reached in any applicable rulings.

Actions on Decisions further tell the taxpayer the IRS's reaction to certain court decisions. Recall that the IRS follows a practice of either acquiescing (agreeing) or nonacquiescing (not agreeing) with court decisions where guidance may be helpful. This practice does not mean that a particular decision has no value if the IRS has nonacquiesced in the result. It does, however, indicate that the IRS will continue to litigate the issue involved.

The validity of individual letter rulings issued by the IRS is discussed in Chapter 16.

Assessing the Validity of Judicial Sources of the Tax Law.

The judicial process as it relates to the formulation of tax law has been described. How much reliance can be placed on a particular decision depends upon the following variables:

- The level of the court. A decision rendered by a trial court (e.g., a Federal District Court) carries less weight than one issued by an appellate court (e.g., the Fifth Circuit Court of Appeals). Unless Congress changes the Code, decisions by the U.S. Supreme Court represent the last word on any tax issue.
- The legal residence of the taxpayer. If, for example, a taxpayer lives in Texas, a decision of the Fifth Circuit Court of Appeals means more than one rendered by the Second Circuit Court of Appeals. This is true because any appeal from a U.S. District Court or the U.S. Tax Court would be to the Fifth Circuit Court of Appeals and not to the Second Circuit Court of Appeals.
- Whether the decision represents the weight of authority on the issue. In other words, is it supported by the results reached by other courts?
- The outcome or status of the decision on appeal. For example, was the decision appealed and, if so, with what result?

In connection with the last two variables, the use of a manual citator or a computer search is invaluable to tax research.[51] The use of a manual citator is described in a later section of this chapter.

Assessing the Validity of Other Sources.

Primary sources of tax law include the Constitution, legislative history materials, statutes, treaties, Treasury Regulations, IRS pronouncements, and judicial decisions. The IRS regards only primary sources as substantial authority. However, reference to secondary materials such as legal periodicals, treatises, legal opinions, general counsel memoranda, technical advice memoranda, and written determinations can be useful. In general, secondary sources are not authority.

Although the statement that the IRS regards only primary sources as substantial authority is generally true, there is one exception. For purposes of the accuracy-related penalty in § 6662, the IRS has expanded the list of substantial authority to include a number of secondary materials (e.g., letter rulings, general counsel and technical advice memoranda, and the "Blue Book").[52] The "Blue Book" is the general explanation of tax legislation prepared by the Joint Committee on Taxation of the U.S. Congress.

As under former § 6661, "authority" does not include conclusions reached in treatises, legal periodicals, and opinions rendered by tax professionals.

Arriving at the Solution or at Alternative Solutions

Returning to Example 20, assume the parties decide that the loan approach can be justified from the factual situation involved. Does this assumption lead to a bad debt deduction for the aunt? Before this question can be resolved, the loan needs to be classified as either a business or a nonbusiness debt. One of the reasons the classification is important is that a nonbusiness bad debt cannot be deducted until it becomes entirely worthless. Unlike a business debt, no deduction for partial worthlessness is allowed.[53]

It is very likely that the loan the aunt made in 2001 falls into the nonbusiness category. Unless exceptional circumstances exist (e.g., the lender was in the trade or business of lending money), loans in a related-party setting are treated as nonbusiness. The probability is high that the aunt would be relegated to nonbusiness bad debt status.

The aunt has the burden of proving that the remaining unpaid balance of $42,000 is *entirely* worthless.[54] In this connection, what collection effort, if any, has

---

[51]The major manual citators are published by Commerce Clearing House, RIA, and Shepard's Citations, Inc. See the prior comments under Working with the Tax Services.

[52]Notice 90–20, 1990–1 C.B. 328, part V (A).

[53]See § 166 and the discussion of Investor Losses in Chapter 4.

[54]Compare *John K. Sexton*, 48 TCM 512, T.C.Memo. 1984–360, with *Stewart T. Oatman*, 45 TCM 214, T.C.Memo. 1982–684.

the aunt made? But would any such collection effort be fruitless? Perhaps the nephew is insolvent, ill, or unemployed, or has departed for parts unknown.

Even if the debt is entirely worthless, one further issue remains to be resolved. In what year did the worthlessness occur? It could be, for example, that worthlessness took place in a year before it was claimed.[55]

A clear-cut answer may not be possible as to a bad debt deduction for the aunt in year 2008 (seven years after the advance was made). This uncertainty does not detract from the value of the research. Often a guarded judgment is the best possible solution to a tax problem.

Communicating Tax Research

Once the problem has been researched adequately, a memo, letter, or spoken presentation setting forth the result may be required. The form such a communication takes could depend on a number of considerations. For example, is any particular procedure or format for communicating tax research recommended by either an employer or an instructor? Are the research results to be given directly to the client, or will they first pass to the preparer's employer? If an oral presentation is required, who will be the audience? How long should you talk?[56] Whatever form it takes, a good tax research communication should contain the following elements:

- A clear statement of the issue.
- In more complex situations, a short review of the factual pattern that raises the issue.
- A review of the pertinent tax law sources (e.g., Code, Regulations, rulings, judicial authority).
- Any assumptions made in arriving at the solution.
- The solution recommended and the logic or reasoning in its support.
- The references consulted in the research process.

Figures 1–4, 1–5, and 1–6 present a sample client letter and memoranda for the tax files.

Working with the Tax Law—Tax Planning

| LO.9 |
| Make use of various tax planning procedures. |

Tax research and tax planning are inseparable. The main purpose of effective tax planning is to reduce the taxpayer's total tax bill. This reduction does not mean that the course of action selected must produce the lowest possible tax under the circumstances. The minimization of tax payments must be considered in the context of the legitimate business goals of the taxpayer.

Nontax Considerations

There is a danger that tax motivations may take on a significance that does not conform to the true values involved. In other words, tax considerations can operate to impair the exercise of sound business judgment. Thus, the tax planning process can lead to ends that are socially and economically objectionable. Unfortunately, a tendency exists for planning to move toward the opposing extremes of either not enough or too much emphasis on tax considerations. The happy medium is a balance that recognizes the significance of taxes, but not beyond the point at which planning detracts from the exercise of good business judgment.

---

[55]*Ruth Wertheim Smith*, 34 TCM 1474, T.C.Memo. 1975–339.

[56]For more on crafting oral presentations, see W. A. Raabe and G. E. Whittenburg, "Talking Tax: How to Make a Tax Presentation," *Tax Adviser*, March 1997, pp. 179–182.

FIGURE 1–4	Client Letter

Hoffman, Raabe, Smith, & Maloney, CPAs
5191 Natorp Boulevard
Mason, OH 45040

August 25, 2008

Homer Lynch
111 Avenue G
Lakeway, OH 45232

Dear Mr. Lynch:

This letter is in response to your request that we review the tax result of a gift made in 1976 and determine the unified tax credit available upon Sonya's death in 2008. Our conclusions are based upon the facts as outlined in your letter of August 14.

The gift of $66,000 made to your son on October 1, 1976, did not result in any Federal gift tax for several reasons. First, your wife, Sonya, elected to split the gift with you. Second, both of you chose to use the $30,000 specific exemption that was in effect at that time. As a consequence, the transfer was treated as follows:

	Homer	Sonya
Amount of gift made	$ 33,000	$ 33,000
Annual exclusion available in 1976	(3,000)	(3,000)
Specific exemption used	(30,000)	(30,000)
Taxable gift	$ –0–	$ –0–

When the specific exemption is used after September 8, 1976, an adjustment must be made to the unified transfer tax credit. The adjustment requires that the credit be reduced by 20 percent of the exemption used.

When Sonya died in 2008, the credit available to her estate was not the standard $780,800 for 2008. Because of the adjustment required, the credit must be reduced by $6,000 (20% × $30,000 specific exemption previously used). Her credit, then, is $774,800 ($780,800 − $6,000).

Should you desire more information or a further clarification of our conclusions, do not hesitate to contact me.

Sincerely,

James Randolph, CPA
Partner

The remark is often made that a good rule to follow is to refrain from pursuing any course of action that would not be followed were it not for certain tax considerations. This statement is not entirely correct, but it does illustrate the desirability of preventing business logic from being "sacrificed at the altar of tax planning."

Components of Tax Planning

Popular perception of tax planning often is restricted to the adage "defer income and accelerate deductions." Although this timing approach does hold true and is important, meaningful tax planning involves considerably more.

Preferable to deferring income is complete *avoidance*. Consider, for example, the corporate employee who chooses nontaxable fringe benefits over a fully taxable future pay increase.[57] Complete avoidance of gain recognition also occurs when the owner of appreciated property transfers it by death. Presuming a step-up in basis occurs, the built-in appreciation forever escapes the income tax.[58]

---

[57]See Example 10 in Chapter 13.

[58]See Example 19 in Chapter 18.

FIGURE 1–5	Tax File Memorandum

August 18, 2008

TAX FILE MEMORANDUM

FROM: James Randolph

SUBJECT: Homer Lynch
            Engagement Issues

Today, I talked to Homer Lynch with regard to his letter of August 14, 2008.

On October 1, 1976, Homer made a gift of $66,000 to his son. Homer's wife, Sonya, elected to split the gift, and each elected to use the full $30,000 specific exemption. Sonya died this year, and Homer is the executor of her estate.

ISSUE: Was any gift tax due on the 1976 transfer? How much unified transfer tax credit can Homer claim when he files a Form 706 for Sonya's estate? I told Homer that we would have the answers to these questions within a month.

FIGURE 1–6	Tax File Memorandum

August 28, 2008

TAX FILE MEMORANDUM

FROM: James Randolph

SUBJECT: Homer Lynch
            Engagement Conclusions

Homer made a gift of $66,000 to his son on October 1, 1976. No gift tax resulted because Homer's wife, Sonya, elected (under § 2513) to split the gift. This election made two annual exclusions available ($3,000 each) and allowed the use of the specific exemptions ($30,000 each). As neither spouse had a taxable gift ($33,000 − $3,000 − $30,000 = $0), no gift tax resulted.

What is the unified tax credit available to Sonya's estate when she dies in 2008? Section 2010(b) requires that the credit be reduced by 20 percent of the specific exemption used after September 8, 1976. Does this adjustment apply to a nonowner donor spouse such as Sonya? *Estate of James O. Gawne*, 80 T.C. 478 (1983), makes clear that it does.

If the recognition of income cannot be avoided, its deferral will postpone income tax consequences. *Deferral* of income can take many forms. Besides like-kind exchanges and involuntary conversions, most retirement plans put off income tax consequences until the payout period. Deferral of gain recognition can also occur when appreciated property is transferred to a newly formed corporation or partnership.[59]

A corollary to the deferral of income is the acceleration of deductions. For example, an accrual basis, calendar year corporation desires an additional charitable deduction for 2008 but has a cash-flow problem. If the corporation authorizes the contribution in 2008 and pays it on or before March 17, 2009, the deduction can be claimed for 2008.[60] Taxes can be saved by *shifting* income to lower-bracket taxpayers. Gifts of appreciated property to lower-bracket family members can reduce the applicable capital gain rate on a later sale by 15 percentage points (from 15 percent to 0 percent).[61]

---

[59]See Example 1 in Chapter 4 and Example 8 in Chapter 10.
[60]See Example 16 in Chapter 2.

[61]See Example 34 in Chapter 18.

TAX *in the News* | **TAX AVOIDANCE AND TAX EVASION**

There is a fine line between legal tax planning and illegal tax planning—tax avoidance versus tax evasion. Though both aim to eliminate or reduce taxes, tax evasion implies the use of subterfuge and fraud as a means to this end. The IRS believes that through tax evasion taxpayers shortchanged the government by a staggering $345 billion in 2001. This gross tax gap is the annual difference between Federal taxes owed and those timely paid.

Tax avoidance, however, is merely tax minimization through legal techniques. In this sense, tax avoidance becomes the proper objective of all tax planning. Perhaps because common goals are involved, popular usage has blurred the distinction between tax avoidance and tax evasion. Consequently, the association of the two concepts has

kept some taxpayers from properly taking advantage of planning possibilities. The now-classic words of Judge Learned Hand in *Commissioner v. Newman** reflect the true values a taxpayer should have:

> Over and over again courts have said that there is nothing sinister in so arranging one's affairs as to keep taxes as low as possible. Everybody does so, rich or poor; and all do right, for nobody owes any public duty to pay more than the law demands: taxes are enforced extractions, not voluntary contributions. To demand more in the name of morals is mere cant.

*47–1 USTC ¶9175, 35 AFTR 857, 159 F.2d 848 (CA–2, 1947).

If income cannot be avoided, deferred, or shifted, the nature of the gain can be *converted*. By changing the classification of property, income taxes can be reduced. Thus, the taxpayer who transfers appreciated inventory to a controlled corporation has converted ordinary income property to a capital asset. When the stock is later sold, preferential capital gain rates apply.[62]

The conversion approach can also work in tax planning for losses. Properly structured, a loan to a corporation that becomes worthless can be an ordinary loss rather than the less desirable capital loss. Likewise, planning with § 1244 permits an investor in qualified small business stock to convert what would be a capital loss into an ordinary loss.[63]

Effective tax planning requires that careful consideration be given to the *choice of entity* used for conducting a business. The corporate form results in double taxation but permits shareholder-employees to be covered by fringe benefit programs. Partnerships and S corporations allow a pass-through of losses and other tax attributes, but transferring ownership interests as gifts to family members may be difficult.[64]

Although the substance of a transaction, rather than its form, generally controls, this rule is not always the case with tax planning. *Preserving formalities* often is crucial to the result. Is an advance to a corporation a loan or a contribution to capital? The answer may well depend on the existence of a note. Along with preserving formalities, the taxpayer should keep records that support a transaction. Returning to the issue of loan versus contribution to capital, how is the advance listed on the books of the borrower? What do the corporate minutes say about the advance?[65]

Lastly, effective tax planning requires *consistency* on the part of taxpayers. A shareholder who treats a corporate distribution as a return of capital cannot later avoid a stock basis adjustment by contending that the distribution was really a dividend.[66]

In summary, the key components of tax planning include the following:

- *Avoid* the recognition of income (usually by resorting to a nontaxable source or nontaxable event).
- *Defer* the recognition of income (or accelerate deductions).

---

[62]See Concept Summary 13–1 in Chapter 13.
[63]See Examples 30 and 31 in Chapter 4.
[64]See Example 43 in Chapter 11 and Example 48 in Chapter 12

[65]See Example 28 in Chapter 4.
[66]See the Ethical and Equitable Considerations on page 5–22 in Chapter 5.

- *Convert* the classification of income (or deductions) to a more advantageous form (e.g., ordinary income into capital gain).
- *Choose* the business *entity* with the desired tax attributes.
- Preserve *formalities* by generating and maintaining supporting documentation.
- Act in a manner *consistent* with the intended objective.

Tax Planning—A Practical Application

Returning to the facts in Example 20, what should be done to help protect the aunt's bad debt deduction?

- All formalities of a loan should be present (e.g., written instrument, definite and realistic due date).
- Upon default, the lender (aunt) should make a reasonable effort to collect from the borrower (nephew). If not, the aunt should be in a position to explain why any such effort would be to no avail.
- If interest is provided for, it should be paid.
- Any interest paid (or imputed under § 7872) should be recognized as income by the aunt.
- Because of the annual exclusion of $10,000 in 2001 (now $12,000), it appears doubtful that actual (or imputed) interest would necessitate the filing of a Federal gift tax return by the aunt. But should one be due, it should be filed.
- If § 7872 applies (not enough or no interest is provided for), the nephew should keep track of his net investment income. This record keeping is important since the income the aunt must recognize may be limited by this amount.

In terms of the components of tax planning (see prior discussion beginning on page 1–44), what do these suggestions entail? Note the emphasis on the formalities—written instrument, definite and realistic due date. Also, much is done to provide the needed documentation—gift tax returns, if necessary, are filed, and the nephew keeps track of his investment income. Most important, however, is that the aunt will have been *consistent* in her actions—recognizing actual (or imputed) interest income and making a reasonable effort to collect on the loan.

Throughout this text, each chapter concludes with observations on Tax Planning Considerations. Such observations are not all-inclusive but are intended to illustrate some of the ways in which the material in the chapter can be effectively used to minimize taxes.

Follow-Up Procedures

Tax planning usually involves a proposed (as opposed to a completed) transaction and is based upon the continuing validity of the advice resulting from tax research. A change in the tax law (either legislative, administrative, or judicial) could alter the original conclusion. Additional research may be necessary to test the solution in light of current developments.

Under what circumstances does a tax practitioner have an obligation to inform a client as to changes in the tax law? The legal and ethical aspects of this question are discussed in Chapter 16.

Use of the RIA Citator

The *Federal Tax Citator* is a separate multivolume service with monthly supplements that may be used to determine the status of tax decisions, Revenue Rulings, and Revenue Procedures. A similar citation process is available with the online research system. Cases that are traced by the *Citator* are divided into the issues involved. Since the researcher may be interested in only one issue, only those cases involving that issue need to be checked.

FIGURE 1–7	RIA Citator Symbols for Court Decisions

Judicial History of the Case		Syllabus of the Cited Case	
a	affirmed (by decision of a higher court)	**iv**	four (on all fours with the cited case)
d	dismissed (appeal to a higher court dismissed)	**f**	followed (the cited case followed)
m	modified (decision modified by a higher court, or on rehearing)	**e**	explained (comment generally favorable, but not to a degree that indicates the cited case is followed)
r	reversed (by a decision of a higher court)	**k**	reconciled (the cited case reconciled)
s	same case (e.g., on rehearing)	**n**	dissenting opinion (cited in a dissenting opinion)
rc	related case (companion cases and other cases arising out of the same subject matter are so designated)	**g**	distinguished (the cited case distinguished either in law or on the facts)
x	certiorari denied (by the Supreme Court of the United States)	**l**	limited (the cited case limited to its facts. Used when an appellate court so limits a prior decision, or a lower court states that in its opinion the cited case should be so limited)
(C or G)	The Commissioner or Solicitor General has made the appeal		
(T)	Taxpayer has made the appeal	**c**	criticized (adverse comment on the cited case)
(A)	Tax Court's decision acquiesced in by Commissioner	**q**	questioned (the cited case not only criticized, but its correctness questioned)
(NA)	Tax Court's decision nonacquiesced in by Commissioner	**o**	overruled
sa	same case affirmed (by the cited case)		
sd	same case dismissed (by the cited case)		
sm	same case modified (by the cited case)		
sr	same case reversed (by the cited case)		
sx	same case—certiorari denied		

Reprinted from RIA *Citator 2nd Series* Volume 1 © 1992, Thomson/RIA. Reprinted with permission.

The volumes of the *Federal Tax Citator* and the period of time covered by each are as follows:

- Volume 1 (1863–1941).
- Volume 2 (1942–1948).
- Volume 3 (1948–1954).
- Volume 1, Second Series (1954–1977).
- Volume 2, Second Series (1978–1989).
- Volume 3, Second Series (1990–1996).
- Volume 4, Second Series (1997–2002).
- Volume 5, Second Series (2003–2005).
- Annual and monthly cumulative paperback supplements.

Through the use of symbols, the *Citator* indicates whether a decision is followed, explained, criticized, questioned, or overruled by a later court decision. These symbols are reproduced in Figure 1–7.

EXAMPLE 21

Determine the background and validity of *Adda v. Comm.*, 49 USTC ¶9109, 37 AFTR 654, 171 F.2d 457 (CA–4, 1948). ■

The headnote for *Adda* summarizes the holding of the court and lists the two main issues involved (designated "1" and "2") in the case. As noted previously, the issue designation procedure facilitates the use of the *Citator*.

| FIGURE 1–8 | Excerpt from Volume 3, First Series |

> **ADAMSTON FLAT GLASS CO.** v **COMM.**,
> 162 F(2d) 875, 35 AFTR 1579 (CCA 6)
> 4—Forrest Hotel Corp. v. Fly, 112 F Supp
> 789, 43 AFTR 1080, 1953 P.-H. page 72,856
> (DC Miss)
> **ADDA** v **COMM.**, 171 F(2d) 457, 37 AFTR 654,
> 1948 P.-H. ¶ 72,655 (CCA 4, Dec 3, 1948)
> Cert. filed, March 1, 1949 (T)
> No cert. (G) 1949 P-H ¶ 71,050
> x—Adda v Comm., 336 US 952, 69 S Ct 883,
> 93 L Ed 1107, April 18, 1949 (T)
> sa—Adda, Fernand C. A., 10 TC 273 (No.
> 33), ¶ 10.33 P.-H. TC 1948
> iv—Milner Hotels, Inc., N. Y., 173 F (2d)
> 567, 37 AFTR 1170, 1949 P.-H. page 72,528
> (CCA 6)
> 1—Nubar; Comm. v, 185 F(2d) 588, 39 AFTR
> 1315, 1950 P.-H. page 73,423 (CCA 4)
> g-1—Scottish Amer. Invest. Co., Ltd.,
> The, 12 TC 59, 12-1949 P.-H. TC 32
> g-1—Nubar, Zareh, 13 TC 579, 13-1949
> P.-H. TC 318

Reprinted from *RIA Citator 1st Series* Volume 3
©1955, Thomson/RIA. Reprinted with permission.

| FIGURE 1–9 | Excerpt from Volume 1, Second Series |

> **ADCO SERVICE, INC., ASSIGNEE** v **GRAPHIC COLOR PLATE, INC.**, 36 AFTR2d 75-6342 (NJ) (See Adco Service, Inc., Assignee v Graphic Color Plate)
> **ADDA** v **COMM.**, 171 F2d 457, 37 AFTR 654 (USCA 4)
> Rev. Rul. 56-145, 1956-1 CB 613
> 1—Balanovski; U.S. v, 236 F2d 304, 49 AFTR 2013 (USCA 2)
> 1—Liang, Chang Hsiao, 23 TC 1045, 23-1955 P-H TC 624
> f-1—Asthmanefrin Co., Inc., 25 TC 1141, 25-1956 P-H TC 639
> g-1—de Vegvar, Edward A. Neuman, 28 TC 1061, 28-1957 P-H TC 599
> g-1—Purvis, Ralph E. & Patricia Lee, 1974 P-H TC Memo 74-669
> k-1—deKrause, Piedad Alvarado, 1974 P-H TC Memo 74-1291
> 1—Rev. Rul. 56-392, 1956-2 CB 971

Reprinted from *RIA Citator 2nd Series* Volume 1
©1992, Thomson/RIA. Reprinted with permission.

Refer to Volume 3 for the AFTR Series (covering the period from October 7, 1948, through July 29, 1954) of the *Federal Tax Citator*. Information about the case is located in the excerpt reproduced in Figure 1–8.

Correlating the symbols in Figure 1–7 with the shaded portion of Figure 1–8 reveals the following information about *Adda v. Comm.*:

- Application for certiorari (appeal to the U.S. Supreme Court) filed by the taxpayer (T) on March 1, 1949.
- Certiorari was denied (x) by the U.S. Supreme Court on April 18, 1949.
- The trial court decision is reported in 10 T.C. 273 and was affirmed on appeal (sa) to the Fourth Court of Appeals.
- During the time frame of Volume 3 of the *Citator* (October 7, 1948, through July 29, 1954), one decision (*Milner Hotels, Inc.*) has agreed "on all fours with the cited case" (iv). One decision (*Comm. v. Nubar*) has limited the cited case to its facts (l), and two decisions (*The Scottish American Investment Co., Ltd.* and *Zareh Nubar*) have distinguished the cited case on issue 1 (g–1).

The portion of Volume 1 of the *Citator* Second Series (covering the period from 1954 through 1977) dealing with *Adda v. Comm.* is reproduced in Figure 1–9.

Correlating the symbols in Figure 1–7 with the shaded portion of Figure 1–9 reveals the following additional information about *Adda v. Comm.*:

- The case was cited without comment in two rulings and two decisions: Rev.Rul. 56–145 and Rev.Rul. 56–392, *Balanovski* and *Liang*.
- It was followed in *Asthmanefrin Co.* (f–1).
- It was distinguished in *de Vegvar* and *Purvis* (g–1).
- It was reconciled in *deKrause* (k–1).

Reference to the "Court Decisions" section of Volume 2, Second Series of the *Citator* covering the period from 1978 through 1989 (not reproduced here) shows that *Adda v. Comm.* was cited in *Robert E. Cleveland* and *Judith C. Connelly*, each case limited to its facts (l).

The *Citator* includes a cumulative supplement, and each month there is a cumulative paperback supplement. Be sure to refer to these monthly supplements, or very recent citations might be overlooked.

Except as otherwise noted, it would appear that *Adda v. Comm.* has withstood the test of time.

LO.10
Be aware of the role of taxation on the CPA examination.

Taxation on the CPA Examination

The CPA examination has changed from a paper-and-pencil exam to a computer-based exam with increased emphasis on information technology and general business knowledge. The 14-hour exam has four sections, and taxation is included in the 3-hour Regulation section. The taxation part of the Regulation section covers:

- Federal tax procedures and accounting issues.
- Federal taxation of property transactions.
- Federal taxation—individuals.
- Federal taxation—entities.

Each exam section includes both multiple-choice questions and case studies called simulations. The multiple-choice part consists of three sequential testlets, each containing 24 to 30 questions. These testlets are groups of questions prepared to appear together. In addition, each exam section includes a testlet that consists of two simulations. A candidate may review and change answers within each testlet but cannot go back after exiting a testlet. Candidates take different, but equivalent exams.

Simulations are small case studies designed to test a candidate's tax knowledge and skills using real-life work-related situations. The simulations range from 30 to 50 minutes in length and complement the multiple-choice questions. Simulations include a four-function pop-up calculator, a blank spreadsheet with some elementary functionality, and authoritative literature appropriate to the subject matter. The taxation database includes authoritative excerpts (e.g., Internal Revenue Code and Federal tax forms) that are necessary to complete the tax case study simulations. Examples of such simulations follow.

EXAMPLE 22

The *tax citation type* simulation requires the candidate to research the Internal Revenue Code and enter a Code Section and subsection. For example, Amber Company is considering using the simplified dollar-value method of pricing its inventory for purposes of the LIFO method that is available to certain small businesses. What Code Section is the relevant authority in the Internal Revenue Code to which you should turn to determine whether the taxpayer is eligible to use this method? To be successful, the candidate needs to find § 474. ■

EXAMPLE 23

A *tax form completion* simulation requires the candidate to fill out a portion of a tax form. For example, Green Company is a limited liability company (LLC) for tax purposes. Complete the income section of the 2007 IRS Form 1065 for Green Company using the values found and calculated on previous tabs along with the following data:

Ordinary income from other partnerships	$ 5,200
Net gain (loss) from Form 4797	2,400
Management fee income	12,000

The candidate is provided with page 1 of Form 1065 on which to record the appropriate amounts. ■

Candidates can learn more about the CPA examination at **http://www.cpa-exam.org**. This online tutorial site reviews the exam's format, navigation functions, and tools. A 30- to 60-minute sample examination will familiarize a candidate with the type of questions on the exam.

KEY TERMS

Acquiescence, 1–31

Arm's length concept, 1–15

Business purpose concept, 1–15

Certiorari, 1–28

Continuity of interest concept, 1–15

Determination letters, 1–24

Indexation, 1–11

Letter rulings, 1–23

Nonacquiescence, 1–31

Proposed Regulations, 1–22

Revenue neutrality, 1–3

Revenue Procedures, 1–22

Revenue Rulings, 1–22

Tax benefit rule, 1–16

Temporary Regulations, 1–22

Wherewithal to pay, 1–8

PROBLEM MATERIALS

DISCUSSION QUESTIONS

1. Other than raising revenue, what considerations explain various provisions in our tax laws?

2. What is meant by *revenue neutrality?* pay as U go

3. What was the overall justification for the § 179 election to immediately expense assets?

4. Give some examples of tax provisions that foster technological progress.

5. Explain how the following tax provisions encourage small business:
   a. The nature of a shareholder's loss on a stock investment.
   b. The tax rates applicable to corporations.
   c. Nontaxable corporate divisive reorganizations.

6. What purpose is served by the refundable earned income credit?

7. What purposes are served by the favorable tax treatment of pension contributions?

8. What is the reason for a provision that allows an adoption tax credit?

9. What is meant by *equity considerations?*

10. What is the justification for the various credits, deductions, and exclusions that are designed to encourage taxpayers to obtain additional education?

11. In mitigating the effect of the double taxation of income at the Federal level, what relief does a deduction for state income taxes paid provide? Would a credit be preferable?

12. Some states that impose a state income tax allow the taxpayer a deduction for any Federal income taxes paid. What is the justification for such an approach?

Issue ID

13. A provision of the Code allows a taxpayer a deduction for Federal income tax purposes for state and local income taxes paid. Does this provision eliminate the effect of multiple taxation of the same income? Why or why not? In this connection, consider the following:
    a. Taxpayer, an individual, has itemized deductions that are less than the standard deduction.
    b. Taxpayer is in the 10% tax bracket for Federal income tax purposes. The 33% tax bracket.

14. Yvonne operates a profitable sole proprietorship. Because the business is expanding, she would like to transfer it to a newly created corporation. Yvonne is concerned, however, over the possible tax consequences that would result from incorporating. Please comment.

Issue ID

15. Assume the same facts as in Question 14. Yvonne is also worried that once she incorporates, the business will be subject to the Federal corporate income tax. Any suggestions?

16. In regard to situations in which the tax law recognizes the wherewithal to pay concept, discuss the effect of the following:
    a. The basis to the transferor of property received in a nontaxable exchange.
    b. The recognition by the transferor of any realized loss on the transfer.
    c. The receipt of boot or other property by the transferor.

17. Does the wherewithal to pay concept enable a transferor to permanently avoid the recognition of any gain or loss? Give an example in the law permanently forgiving the recognition of gain or loss.

18. Brenda exchanges 600 shares of Veritex Corporation stock for a one-fourth interest in the Blue Partnership. Since this exchange is not pursuant to a nontaxable reorganization, does the wherewithal to pay concept shield Brenda from the recognition of gain or loss? Why?

19. Give some exceptions to the annual accounting period concept.

20. Mel, a calendar year cash basis taxpayer, is a participant in an H.R. 10 (Keogh) retirement plan for self-employed persons. To get the deduction for 2008, Mel makes his contribution on December 30, 2008.
    a. Why was there an element of urgency in Mel's action?
    b. Was Mel misinformed about the tax law? Explain.

21. What is the justification for the indexation of various tax provisions?

22. Should special interest legislation be condemned? Explain.

23. Illustrate how state laws have influenced Federal tax laws.

24. Give some examples of tax provisions that resulted from efforts by the IRS to prevent taxpayers from exploiting loopholes.

25. Describe how the IRS achieves administrative feasibility through each of the following tax provisions:
    a. The standard deduction allowed to individual taxpayers.
    b. The $345,800 unified tax credit allowed for gift tax purposes in 2008.
    c. The $12,000 annual exclusion allowed for gift tax purposes.

26. What is the arm's length concept? *limitation to deduction b/t related e...*

27. Explain the business purpose concept.

Issue ID

28. White Corporation lends $404,000 to Red Corporation with no provision for interest. White Corporation and Red Corporation are owned by the same shareholders. How might the IRS restructure this transaction with adverse tax consequences?

29. Under what circumstances can court decisions lead to changes in the Code?

30. In 1986, Congress codified the then-existing Federal tax provisions, and this compilation became the Internal Revenue Code of 1986. Discuss the validity of this statement.

31. Federal tax legislation originates in the Senate Finance Committee. Comment as to the validity of this statement.

32. What happens when the Senate version of a tax bill differs from that passed by the House?

33. Determine the subparts of § 108(a)(1)(A).

34. Is § 1221(1) a proper Code Section citation?

35. Why are certain Code Section numbers missing from the Internal Revenue Code (e.g., §§ 6, 7, 8, 9, 10)?

36. Where can a researcher find newly issued Proposed, final, and Temporary Regulations?

37. Interpret each of the following citations:
    a. Ltr.Rul. 200019007.
    b. Rev.Proc. 93–27, 1993–2 C.B. 343.
    c. Rev.Rul. 91–26, 1991–1 C.B. 184.
    d. Notice 88–99, 1988–2 C.B. 422.
    e. TAM 199901004.

38. Cy Young calls you requesting an explanation of the fact-finding determination of a Federal Court of Appeals. Prepare a letter to be sent to Cy answering this query. His address is 1072 Richmond Lane, Keene, NH 01720.

Communications

39. Milt Pappas calls you with respect to a tax issue. He has found a tax case in the U.S. District Court of South Carolina that is in favor of his position. The IRS lost and did not appeal the case. Over the phone, you explain to Milt the significance of the failure to appeal. Prepare a tax file memorandum outlining your remarks to Milt.

Communications

40. In assessing the validity of a court decision, discuss the significance of the following:
    a. The decision was rendered by the U.S. District Court of Wyoming. Taxpayer lives in Wyoming.
    b. The decision was rendered by the U.S. Court of Federal Claims. Taxpayer lives in Wyoming.
    c. The decision was rendered by the Second Circuit Court of Appeals. Taxpayer lives in California.
    d. The decision was rendered by the U.S. Supreme Court.
    e. The decision was rendered by the U.S. Tax Court. The IRS has acquiesced in the result.
    f. Same as (e) except that the IRS has issued a nonacquiescence as to the result.

41. Which court issued these decisions?
    a. *Carpenter v. U.S.*, 484 U.S. 19 (1987).
    b. *U.S. v. Olis*, 429 F.3d 540 (CA–5, 2005).
    c. *Stephen G. Sherman*, 36 TCM 1191.
    d. *E. T. Pratt*, 64 T.C. 203 (1975).
    e. *J. R. Parks v. U.S.*, 434 F.Supp. 206 (D.Ct.Tex., 1977).
    f. Rev.Rul. 92–29, 1992–1 C.B. 20.

42. Refer to Figure 1–7 illustrating the use of the RIA *Federal Tax Citator*. Explain the following abbreviations:
    a. sx
    b. NA
    c. r
    d. a
    e. f
    f. e
    g. k
    h. c
    i. q
    j. o

43. Kenny Rogers needs to learn quickly about corporate liquidations. How should Kenny approach his research?

Decision Making

44. Determine whether the following items are primary sources or secondary sources for the purpose of substantial authority.

a. Revenue Ruling.
b. Article written by a judge in *Tax Notes*.
c. Memorandum Tax Court decision.
d. The "Blue Book."
e. A letter ruling.

45. How can a citator help a researcher?

PROBLEMS

46. Thelma owns some real estate (basis of $120,000 and fair market value of $65,000) that she would like to sell to her son, Sandy, for $65,000. Thelma is aware, however, that losses on sales between certain related parties are disallowed for Federal income tax purposes [§ 267(a)(1)]. Thelma therefore sells the property to Paul (an unrelated party) for $65,000. On the next day, Paul sells the property to Sandy for the same amount. Is Thelma's realized loss of $55,000 deductible? Explain.

47. Bart exchanges some real estate (basis of $800,000 and fair market value of $1 million) for other real estate owned by Roland (basis of $1.2 million and fair market value of $900,000) and $100,000 in cash. The real estate involved is unimproved and is held by Bart and Roland, before and after the exchange, as investment property.
   a. What is Bart's realized gain on the exchange? Recognized gain?
   b. What is Roland's realized loss? Recognized loss?
   c. Support your results to (a) and (b) under the wherewithal to pay concept as applied to like-kind exchanges (§ 1031).

48. Using the legend provided, classify the overall objective of the particular tax provision:

Legend	
CE = Control of the economy	W = Wherewithal to pay concept
EA = Encouragement of certain activities	AF = Administrative feasibility
EI = Encouragement of certain industries	ESB = Encouragement of small business
SC = Social considerations	

   a. Like-kind exchange treatment.
   b. An increase in the individual tax rate.
   c. The S corporation election.
   d. Adoption expense credit.
   e. Percentage depletion.
   f. Unified estate tax credit.
   g. Charitable contribution deduction.

49. Determine whether the following states are community property or common law states:
   a. Texas.
   b. Vermont.
   c. Arizona.
   d. North Carolina.
   e. Alaska.
   f. California.

50. Troy sells property (basis of $35,000) to Beige Corporation for $50,000. Based on the following conditions, how could the IRS challenge this transaction?
   a. Troy is the sole shareholder of Beige Corporation.
   b. Troy is the son of the sole shareholder of Beige Corporation.
   c. Troy is neither a shareholder in Beige Corporation nor related to any of Beige's shareholders.

51. a. What are letter rulings?
    b. What are technical advice memoranda (TAMs)?

52. Explain what is meant by these citations:

    a.   Rev.Proc. 2002–37, 2002–22 I.R.B. 1030.

    b.   Rev.Rul. 67–269, 1967–2 C.B. 298.

    c.   Notice 88–37, 1988–1 C.B. 522.

53. Using the legend provided, classify each of the following citations as to the location. There may be more than one answer for a citation.

Legend	
IRC = Internal Revenue Code	FR = *Federal Register*
IRB = *Internal Revenue Bulletin*	NA = Not applicable
CB = *Cumulative Bulletin*	

    a.   Rev.Rul. 65–34, 1965–1 C.B. 86.

    b.   § 7482(a).

    c.   *Jack E. Golsen,* 54 T.C. 742 (1970).

    d.   TD 8875.

    e.   Reg. § 1.6081–4.

    f.   Ltr.Rul. 200530003.

    g.   Temp.Reg. § 1.861–9T(g)(3)(i).

54. To which U.S. Court of Appeals would a person living in each of the following states appeal from the U.S. Tax Court?

    a.   Louisiana.

    b.   Utah.

    c.   Georgia.

    d.   Idaho.

    e.   Vermont.

55. Using the legend provided, classify each of the following citations as to the court:

Legend	
T = U.S. Tax Court	D = U.S. District Court
C = U.S. Court of Federal Claims	A = U.S. Court of Appeals
U = U.S. Supreme Court	N = None of the above

    a.   Ltr.Rul. 9331012.

    b.   237 F.Supp. 80 (D.Ct.Conn., 1964).

    c.   90 T.C. 460 (1988).

    d.   9 B.T.A. 502 (1927).

    e.   26 TCM 339 (1967).

    f.   112 F.Supp. 164 (Ct.Cls., 1953).

    g.   312 U.S. 212 (1941).

    h.   298 F.2d 784 (CA–3, 1962).

56. Locate the following tax services in your library and indicate the name of the publisher and whether the service is organized by topic or by Code Section:

    a.   *United States Tax Reporter.*

    b.   *Standard Federal Tax Reporter.*

    c.   *Federal Tax Coordinator 2d.*

    d.   *Mertens Law of Federal Income Taxation.*

    e.   *Tax Management Portfolios.*

    f.   *CCH's Tax Research Consultant.*

57. Using the legend provided, classify each of the following tax sources:

Legend	
P = Primary tax source	B = Both
S = Secondary tax source	N = Neither

  a. Sixteenth Amendment to the Constitution.
  b. Tax treaty between the United States and China.
  c. Temporary Regulations.
  d. Revenue Procedure.
  e. General Counsel Memoranda (1988).
  f. Tax Court Memorandum decision.
  g. *Tax Notes* article.
  h. Legislative Regulations.
  i. Letter ruling (before 1985).
  j. District Court decision.
  k. Small Cases Division of U.S. Tax Court decision.
  l. Senate Finance Committee Report.
  m. Technical advice memorandum (1991).

58. Rank these items according to their reliability:
  a. Letter ruling.
  b. Legislative Regulation.
  c. Code Section.
  d. Revenue Ruling.
  e. Proposed Regulation.
  f. Interpretative Regulation.
  g. Recent Temporary Regulation.

59. Using the legend provided, classify each of the following decisions or statements in regard to the RIA *Federal Tax Citator*.

Legend			
a	= affirmed	g	= distinguished
d	= dismissed	c	= criticized
r	= reversed	f	= followed
o	= overruled	x	= certiorari denied
(A)	= Acquiesced	remg	= remanding

  a. *Casey v. Comm.*, 56 T.C. 477 (1971), *aff'd* 460 F.2d 1259 (CA–4, 1972), *cert. denied.*
  b. *Deputy v. DuPont*, 308 U.S. 488 (1940), *rev'g* 103 F.2d 257 (CA–3, 1939), *rem'g* 22 F.Supp. 589 (D.Ct.Del., 1938).
  c. f-2. *Linda M. Liberi Toner*, 71 T.C. 778.
  d. *58th St. Plaza Theatre, Inc.*, 16 T.C. 469 (1951), *aff'd* 195 F.2d 724 (CA–2, 1952), *cert. denied*, 344 U.S. 820 (1952), *acq.* 1952–1 C.B. 4.
  e. g-1. *Ralph E. Purvis*, 1974 P-H T.C.Memo. 74–164.

RESEARCH PROBLEMS

Note: Solutions to Research Problems can be prepared by using the **RIA Checkpoint®Student Edition** online research product, which is available to accompany this text. It is also possible to prepare solutions to the Research Problems by using tax research materials found in a standard tax library.

Research Problem 1. Locate the following cited items and give a brief description of the topic or opinion in the item:
  a. § 301(b)(1).
  b. § 337(a).
  c. § 706(b)(3).

Research Problem 2. Determine whether the IRS agreed or disagreed with the results of these court decisions.
  a. *Moore v. Comm.*, T.C.Memo. 2006–171.
  b. *Pacific Gas and Electric Co. v. U.S.*, 417 F.3d 1375 (Fed.Cir., 2005).
  c. *Estate of Mitchell v. Comm.*, 250 F.3d 696 (CA–9, 2001).

    d. *IRS v. Donald Snyder*, 343 F.3d 1171 (CA–9, 2003).
    e. *Paul Pekar*, 113 T.C. 158 (1999).

Research Problem 3. Determine the disposition of the following decisions at the appellate level.
    a. *Black Hills Corp.*, 102 T.C. 505 (1994).
    b. *Bilar Tool & Die Corp.*, 62 T.C. 213 (1974).
    c. *Ira L. Patrick*, 36 TCM 655 (1977).
    d. *American Bemberg Corp.*, 10 T.C. 361 (1948).
    e. *Deputy v. DuPont*, 103 F.2d 257 (CA–3, 1939).
    f. *Dahood v. U.S.*, 585 F.Supp. 93 (D.Ct.N.H., 1984).
    g. *Edwards & Sons, E.W. v. U.S.*, 162 F.Supp. 97 (D.Ct.N.Y., 1957).

Research Problem 4. Determine the disposition of the following decisions at the Supreme Court level or on rehearing:
    a. *Durovic v. Comm.*, 487 F.2d 36 (CA–7, 1973).
    b. *Fuller Estate v. Comm.*, 171 F.2d 704 (CA–3, 1948).
    c. *Houston Chronicle Publishing Co. v. U.S.*, 481 F.2d 1240 (CA–5, 1973).
    d. *Johnson v. Johnson*, 495 F.2d 1079 (CA–6, 1974).
    e. *Love Box Co., Inc. v. Comm.*, 842 F.2d 1213 (CA–10, 1988).

Research Problem 5. A taxpayer has an unpaid tax of $29,343 not *including* interest and penalties of $61,842. Can the taxpayer file in the Small Cases Division of the U.S. Tax Court? Show support for your answer in a tax memorandum.

Communications

Partial list of research aids:
§ 7463(f)(1).

Research Problem 6. Complete the following citations:
    a. *Betty R. Carraway*, T.C.Memo. 1994–____.
    b. *Robert E. Imel*, 61 T.C. ____ (1973).
    c. *Higgins v. Comm.*, 312 U.S. 212 (____).
    d. Rev.Rul. 68–378, 1968–____ C.B. ____.
    e. *Dye v. U.S.*, 121 F.3d 1399 (____, 1997).
    f. Rev.Proc. 2003–85, ____ C.B. 1184.
    g. *Talen v. U.S.*, 355 F.Supp.2d 22 (D.Ct.D.C., ____).

Research Problem 7. A 21-year-old single college student, a New York Mets fan, comes to your office after catching Barry Bonds's record-setting home run ball on August 7, 2007. Assume the baseball was worth about $600,000 on the day after the student caught the ball. He indicates that he plans to keep 51% of the proceeds from the sale of the ball and give the remainder to his friend who went to the game with him. Outline any tax consequences of these transactions to the student who went to the game during a layover from a flight to Australia.

Communications

Use the tax resources of the Internet to address the following questions. Do not restrict your search to the World Wide Web, but include a review of newsgroups and general reference materials, practitioner sites and resources, primary sources of the tax law, chat rooms and discussion groups, and other opportunities.

Internet
Activity

Research Problem 8. Go to each of the following Internet locations:
    a. Several primary sources of the tax law, including the U.S. Supreme Court, a Court of Appeals, the Internal Revenue Service, the U.S. Tax Court, and final Regulations.
    b. Sources of proposed Federal tax legislation.
    c. A collection of tax rules for your state.

Research Problem 9. Who is Lee Sheppard? Using the Internet, find several of her columns. Does she tend to be pro-government or anti-government?

PART 2

Corporations

Corporations are separate entities for Federal income tax purposes. Subchapter C of the Code is devoted to the tax treatment of regular corporations. Part II deals mainly with the operating rules contained in Subchapter C that apply to regular corporations and with the effects of various capital transactions on the C corporation and its shareholders.

CHAPTER 2

Corporations: Introduction and Operating Rules

LEARNING OBJECTIVES

After completing Chapter 2, you should be able to:

LO.1
Summarize the various forms of conducting a business.

LO.2
Compare the taxation of individuals and corporations.

LO.3
Discuss the tax rules unique to corporations.

LO.4
Compute the corporate income tax.

LO.5
Explain the rules unique to computing the tax of multiple corporations.

LO.6
Describe the reporting process for corporations.

LO.7
Understand the impact of tax return positions on financial statements.

LO.8
Evaluate corporations as an entity form for conducting a business.

LO.1
Summarize the various forms of conducting a business.

Tax Treatment of Various Business Forms

Business operations can be conducted in a number of different forms. Among the various possibilities are the following:

- Sole proprietorships.
- Partnerships.
- Trusts and estates.
- S corporations (also known as Subchapter S or S corporations).
- Regular corporations (also called Subchapter C or C corporations).

For Federal income tax purposes, the distinctions among these forms of business organization are very important. The following discussion of the tax treatment of sole proprietorships, partnerships, and regular corporations highlights these distinctions. Trusts and estates are covered in Chapter 19, and S corporations are discussed in Chapter 12.

Sole Proprietorships

A sole proprietorship is not a taxable entity separate from the individual who owns the proprietorship. The owner of a sole proprietorship reports all business income and expenses of the proprietorship on Schedule C of Form 1040. The net profit or loss from the proprietorship is then transferred from Schedule C to Form 1040, which is used by the taxpayer to report taxable income. The proprietor reports all of the net profit from the business, regardless of the amount actually withdrawn during the year.

Income and expenses of the proprietorship retain their character when reported by the proprietor. For example, ordinary income of the proprietorship is treated as ordinary income when reported by the proprietor, and capital gain is treated as capital gain.

EXAMPLE 1

George is the sole proprietor of George's Music Shop. Gross income of the business for the year is $200,000, and operating expenses are $110,000. George also sells a capital asset held by the business for a $10,000 long-term capital gain. During the year, he withdraws $60,000 from the business for living expenses. George reports the income and expenses of the business on Schedule C, resulting in net profit (ordinary income) of $90,000. Even though he withdrew only $60,000, George reports all of the $90,000 net profit from the business on Form 1040, where he computes taxable income for the year. He also reports a $10,000 long-term capital gain on Schedule D of Form 1040. ■

Partnerships

Partnerships are not subject to the income tax. However, a partnership is required to file Form 1065, which reports the results of the partnership's business activities. Most income and expense items are aggregated in computing the net profit of the partnership on Form 1065. Any income and expense items that are not aggregated in computing the partnership's net income are reported separately to the partners. Some examples of separately reported income items are interest income, dividend income, and long-term capital gain. Examples of separately reported expenses include charitable contributions and expenses related to interest and dividend income. Partnership reporting is discussed in detail in Chapter 10.

The partnership net profit (loss) and the separately reported items are allocated to each partner according to the partnership's profit sharing agreement, and the partners receive separate K–1 schedules from the partnership. Schedule K–1 reports each partner's share of the partnership net profit and separately reported income and expense items. Each partner reports these items on his or her own tax return.

Jim and Bob are equal partners in Canary Enterprises, a calendar year partnership. During the year, Canary Enterprises had $500,000 gross income and $350,000 operating expenses. In addition, the partnership sold land that had been held for investment purposes for a long-term capital gain of $60,000. During the year, Jim withdrew $40,000 from the partnership, and Bob withdrew $45,000. The partnership's Form 1065 reports net profit of $150,000 ($500,000 income − $350,000 expenses). The partnership also reports the $60,000 long-term capital gain as a separately stated item on Form 1065. Jim and Bob each receive a Schedule K–1 reporting net profit of $75,000 and separately stated long-term capital gain of $30,000. Each partner reports net profit of $75,000 and long-term capital gain of $30,000 on his own return. ■

Corporations

Corporations are governed by Subchapter C or Subchapter S of the Internal Revenue Code. Those governed by Subchapter C are referred to as **C corporations** or **regular corporations**. Corporations governed by Subchapter S are referred to as **S corporations**.

S corporations, which do not pay Federal income tax, are similar to partnerships in that net profit or loss flows through to the shareholders to be reported on their separate returns. Also like partnerships, S corporations do not aggregate all income and expense items in computing net profit or loss. Certain items flow through to the shareholders and retain their separate character when reported on the shareholders' returns. See Chapter 12 for detailed coverage of S corporations.

Unlike proprietorships, partnerships, and S corporations, C corporations are taxpaying entities. This results in what is known as a *double taxation* effect. A C corporation reports its income and expenses on Form 1120. The corporation computes tax on the net income reported on the corporate tax return using the rate schedule applicable to corporations (see Exhibit 2–1 later in this section). When a corporation distributes its income, the corporation's shareholders report dividend income on their own tax returns. Thus, income that has already been taxed at the corporate level is also taxed at the shareholder level. The effects of double taxation (disregarding the effect of payroll and self-employment taxes) are illustrated in Examples 3 and 4.

E X A M P L E 3	Lavender Corporation earns net profit of $100,000 in 2008. It pays corporate tax of $22,250 (refer to Exhibit 2–1 on page 2–5). This leaves $77,750, all of which is distributed as a dividend to Mike, a 43-year-old single individual and the corporation's sole shareholder. Mike has taxable income of $68,800 ($77,750 − $5,450 standard deduction − $3,500 personal exemption). He pays tax at the preferential rate applicable to dividends received by individuals. His tax is $5,438 [($32,550 × 0%) + ($36,250 × 15%)]. The combined tax on the corporation's net profit is $27,688 ($22,250 paid by the corporation + $5,438 paid by the shareholder). ∎

E X A M P L E 4	Assume the same facts as in Example 3, except that the business is organized as a sole proprietorship. Mike reports the $100,000 net profit from the business on his tax return. He has taxable income of $91,050 ($100,000 − $5,450 standard deduction − $3,500 personal exemption) and pays tax of $19,472. Therefore, operating the business as a sole proprietorship results in a tax *savings* of $8,216 in 2008 ($27,688 from Example 3 − $19,472). ∎

Examples 3 and 4 deal with a specific set of facts. The conclusions reached in this situation cannot be extended to all decisions about a form of business organization. Each specific set of facts and circumstances requires a thorough analysis of the tax factors. In many cases, the tax burden will be greater if the business is operated as a corporation (as in Example 3), but sometimes operating as a corporation can result in tax savings, as illustrated in Examples 5 and 6.

E X A M P L E 5	In 2008, Tan Corporation files Form 1120 reporting net profit of $100,000. The corporation pays tax of $22,250 and distributes the remaining $77,750 as a dividend to Carla, the sole shareholder of the corporation. Carla has income from other sources and is in the top individual tax bracket of 35% in 2008. As a result, she pays tax of $11,663 ($77,750 × 15% rate on dividends) on the distribution. The combined tax on the corporation's net profit is $33,913 ($22,250 paid by the corporation + $11,663 paid by the shareholder). ∎

E X A M P L E 6	Assume the same facts as in Example 5, except that the business is a sole proprietorship. Carla reports the $100,000 net profit from the business on her tax return and pays tax of $35,000 ($100,000 net profit × 35% marginal rate). Therefore, operating the business as a sole proprietorship results in a tax *cost* of $1,087 in 2008 ($35,000 − $33,913 tax from Example 5). ∎

Taxation of Dividends. As noted earlier, the income of a C corporation is subject to double taxation—once at the corporate level when it is earned and again at the shareholder level when it is distributed as dividends. Double taxation stems, in part, from the fact that dividend distributions are not deductible by the corporation. Shareholders of closely held corporations frequently attempt to circumvent this disallowance by disguising a dividend distribution as some other purported transaction. One of the more common ways of disguising dividend distributions is to pay excessive compensation to shareholder-employees of a closely held corporation. The IRS scrutinizes compensation and other economic transactions (e.g., loans, leases, sales) between shareholders and closely held corporations to ensure that payments are reasonable in amount. (See Chapter 5 for more discussion on disguised dividends.)

Double taxation also stems from the fact that dividend distributions are taxable to the shareholders. Historically, dividend income has been taxed at the same rates as ordinary income. However, to alleviate some of the double taxation effect, Congress reduced the tax rate applicable to dividend income of individuals for years after 2002. Qualified dividend income is currently taxed at the same preferential rate as long-term capital gains—15 percent (0 percent for taxpayers in the bottom two tax brackets). The preferential rate on dividend income is set to expire for years after 2010.

EXHIBIT 2–1	Corporate Income Tax Rates

Taxable Income		Tax Is:	
Over—	But Not Over—		Of the Amount Over—
$ 0	$ 50,000	15%	$ 0
50,000	75,000	$ 7,500 + 25%	50,000
75,000	100,000	13,750 + 34%	75,000
100,000	335,000	22,250 + 39%	100,000
335,000	10,000,000	113,900 + 34%	335,000
10,000,000	15,000,000	3,400,000 + 35%	10,000,000
15,000,000	18,333,333	5,150,000 + 38%	15,000,000
18,333,333	—	35%	0

[Handwritten margin notes:]
DiVidend
< 20% = 70%
> 20% = 80%
If DRD Credit or?
NOL exception Kice
If U consolidet
you don't need to file
Schedule C. in tax
return.

Comparison of Corporations and Other Forms of Doing Business.

Chapter 13 presents a detailed comparison of sole proprietorships, partnerships, S corporations, and C corporations as forms of doing business. However, it is appropriate at this point to consider some of the tax and nontax factors that favor corporations over proprietorships.

Consideration of tax factors requires an examination of the corporate rate structure. The income tax rate schedule applicable to corporations is reproduced in Exhibit 2–1. As this schedule shows, the marginal rates for corporations range from 15 percent to 39 percent. In comparison, the marginal rates for individuals range from 10 percent to 35 percent. The corporate form of doing business presents tax savings opportunities when the applicable corporate marginal rate is lower than the applicable individual marginal rate.

EXAMPLE 7

Susanna, an individual taxpayer in the 35% marginal tax rate bracket, can generate $100,000 of additional taxable income in the current year. If the income is taxed to Susanna, the associated tax is $35,000 ($100,000 × 35%). If, however, Susanna is able to shift the income to a newly created corporation, the corporate tax is $22,250 (see Exhibit 2–1). Thus, by taking advantage of the lower corporate marginal tax rates, a tax *savings* of $12,750 ($35,000 − $22,250) is achieved. ∎

Any attempt to arbitrage the difference between the corporate and individual marginal tax rates also must consider the double taxation effect. When the preferential rate for dividend income is considered, however, tax savings opportunities still exist.

EXAMPLE 8

Assume in Example 7 that the corporation distributes all of its after-tax earnings to Susanna as a dividend. The dividend results in tax of $11,663 [($100,000 − $22,250) × 15%] to Susanna. Thus, even when the double taxation effect is considered, the combined tax burden of $33,913 ($22,250 paid by the corporation + $11,663 paid by the shareholder) represents a tax *savings* of $1,087 when compared to the $35,000 of tax that results when the $100,000 of income is subject to Susanna's 35% marginal rate. ∎

Examples 7 and 8 ignore other tax considerations that also must be considered in selecting the proper form of doing business, but they illustrate the tax savings that can be achieved by taking advantage of rate differentials. Some of the other tax

GLOBAL *Tax Issues*

COUNTRIES CUT CORPORATE TAX RATES TO ATTRACT CAPITAL INVESTMENT

Recent cuts in corporate tax rates by Germany and other major European countries are illustrative of the growing competition among countries to attract and retain capital investment. These countries are responding to the success that some smaller European countries (e.g., Ireland) have had in stimulating economic growth with tax cuts. In addition to retaining existing capital investment, another goal of the tax cuts is to enable a country to attract new foreign investment.

In determining the best tax environment for its operations, a corporation must consider a country's income tax rates, but other tax provisions (e.g., depreciation allowances) also are important. Often, when countries have reduced their corporate tax rates, they have simultaneously made other tax provisions less favorable; thus, for some corporations, the net result may be no real tax savings. Also, nontax considerations, such as a country's infrastructure, labor costs, employment laws, and access to target markets, may play a bigger role in attracting capital investment than tax policy.

considerations that could affect the selection of a business form include the character of business income, the expectation of business losses, and payroll taxes.

All income and expense items of a proprietorship retain their character when reported on the proprietor's tax return. In the case of a partnership or S corporation, several separately reported items (e.g., charitable contributions and long-term capital gains) retain their character when passed through to the partners or shareholders, respectively. However, the tax attributes of income and expense items of a C corporation do not pass through the corporate entity to the shareholders. As a result, if the business is expected to generate tax-favored income (e.g., tax-exempt income or long-term capital gains), one of the other (non-C corporation) forms of business may be desirable.

Losses of a C corporation are treated differently than losses of a proprietorship, partnership, or S corporation. A loss incurred by a proprietorship may be deductible by the owner, because all income and expense items are reported by the proprietor. Partnership losses are passed through the partnership entity and may be deductible by the partners, and S corporation losses are passed through to the shareholders. C corporation losses, however, have no effect on the taxable income of the shareholders. Therefore, one of the non-C corporation forms of business may be desirable if business losses are anticipated.

EXAMPLE 9

Franco plans to start a business this year. He expects the business will incur operating losses for the first three years and then become highly profitable. Franco decides to operate as an S corporation during the loss period, because the losses will flow through and be deductible on his personal return. When the business becomes profitable, he intends to switch to C corporation status. ■

The net income of a proprietorship is subject to the self-employment tax, as are some partnership allocations of income to partners. In the alternative, wages paid to a shareholder-employee of a corporation (C or S) are subject to payroll taxes. The combined corporation-employee payroll tax burden should be compared with the self-employment tax associated with the proprietorship and partnership forms of business. This analysis should include the benefit of the deduction available to a corporation for payroll taxes paid.

Nontax Considerations. Nontax considerations will sometimes override tax considerations and lead to the conclusion that a business should be operated as a corporation. The following are some of the more important nontax considerations:

- Sole proprietors and general partners in partnerships face the danger of *unlimited liability*. That is, creditors of the business may file claims not only against the assets of the business but also against the personal assets of proprietors or general partners. Shareholders are protected from claims against their personal assets by state corporate law.
- The corporate form of business organization can provide a vehicle for raising large amounts of capital through widespread stock ownership. Most major businesses in the United States are operated as corporations.
- Shares of stock in a corporation are freely transferable, whereas a partner's sale of his or her partnership interest is subject to approval by the other partners.
- Shareholders may come and go, but a corporation can continue to exist. Death or withdrawal of a partner, on the other hand, may terminate the existing partnership and cause financial difficulties that result in dissolution of the entity. This *continuity of life* is a distinct advantage of the corporate form of doing business.
- Corporations have *centralized management*. All management responsibility is assigned to a board of directors, who appoint officers to carry out the corporation's business. Partnerships, by contrast, may have decentralized management, in which every owner has a right to participate in the organization's business decisions. **Limited partnerships**, though, may have centralized management. Centralized management is essential for the smooth operation of a widely held business.

Limited Liability Companies

The **limited liability company (LLC)** has proliferated greatly in recent years, particularly since 1988 when the IRS first ruled that it would treat qualifying LLCs as partnerships for tax purposes. All 50 states and the District of Columbia have passed laws that allow LLCs, and thousands of companies have chosen LLC status. As with a corporation, operating as an LLC allows its owners to avoid unlimited liability, which is a primary *nontax* consideration in choosing the form of business organization. The tax advantage of LLCs is that qualifying businesses may be treated as partnerships for tax purposes, thereby avoiding the problem of double taxation associated with regular corporations.

Some states allow an LLC to have centralized management, but not continuity of life or free transferability of interests. Other states allow LLCs to adopt any or all of the corporate characteristics of centralized management, continuity of life, and free transferability of interests. The comparison of business entities in Chapter 13 includes a discussion of LLCs.

Entity Classification

Can an organization not qualifying as a corporation under state law still be treated as such for Federal income tax purposes? Unfortunately, the tax law defines a corporation as including "associations, joint stock companies, and insurance companies."[1] As the Code contains no definition of what constitutes an *association*, the issue became the subject of frequent litigation.

It was finally determined that an entity would be treated as a corporation if it had a majority of characteristics common to corporations. For this purpose, relevant characteristics are:

- Continuity of life.
- Centralized management.
- Limited liability.
- Free transferability of interests.

---

[1]§ 7701(a)(3).

These criteria did not resolve all of the problems that continued to arise over corporate classification. When a new type of business entity—the limited liability company—was developed, the IRS was deluged with inquiries regarding its tax status. As LLCs became increasingly popular with professional groups, all states enacted statutes allowing some form of this entity. Invariably, the statutes permitted the corporate characteristic of limited liability and, often, that of centralized management. Because continuity of life and free transferability of interests are absent, partnership classification was hoped for. This treatment avoided the double taxation inherent in the corporate form.

In late 1996, the IRS eased the entity classification problem by issuing the **check-the-box Regulations**.[2] Effective beginning in 1997, the Regulations enable taxpayers to choose the tax status of a business entity without regard to its corporate (or noncorporate) characteristics. These rules have simplified tax administration considerably and should eliminate the type of litigation that arose with regard to the association (i.e., corporation) status.

Under the check-the-box rules, entities with more than one owner can elect to be classified as either a partnership or a corporation. An entity with only one owner can elect to be classified as a corporation or as a sole proprietorship. In the event of default (i.e., no election is made), multi-owner entities are classified as partnerships and single-person businesses as sole proprietorships.

The election is not available to entities that are actually incorporated under state law or to entities that are required to be corporations under Federal law (e.g., certain publicly traded partnerships). Otherwise, LLCs are not treated as being incorporated under state law. Consequently, they can elect either corporation or partnership status.

Eligible entities make the election as to tax status by filing Form 8832 (Entity Classification Election).

<table>
<tr><td>**LO.2**</td></tr>
<tr><td>Compare the taxation of individuals and corporations.</td></tr>
</table>

An Introduction to the Income Taxation of Corporations

An Overview of Corporate versus Individual Income Tax Treatment

In a discussion of how corporations are treated under the Federal income tax, a useful approach is to compare their treatment with that applicable to individual taxpayers.

Similarities. Gross income of a corporation is determined in much the same manner as it is for individuals. Thus, gross income includes compensation for services rendered, income derived from a business, gains from dealings in property, interest, rents, royalties, dividends—to name only a few items. Both individuals and corporations are entitled to exclusions from gross income. However, corporate taxpayers are allowed fewer exclusions. Interest on municipal bonds is one exclusion that is applicable to both individual and corporate taxpayers.

Gains and losses from property transactions are handled similarly. For example, whether a gain or loss is capital or ordinary depends upon the nature of the asset in the hands of the taxpayer making the taxable disposition. In defining what is not a capital asset, § 1221 makes no distinction between corporate and noncorporate taxpayers.

In the area of nontaxable exchanges, corporations are like individuals in that they do not recognize gain or loss on a like-kind exchange and may defer recognized gain on an involuntary conversion of property. The exclusion of gain provisions dealing with the sale of a personal residence do not apply to corporations. Both

---

[2]Reg. §§ 301.7701–1 through –4, and –7.

corporations and individuals are vulnerable to the disallowance of losses on sales of property to related parties or on wash sales of securities. The wash sales rules do not apply to individuals who are traders or dealers in securities or to corporations that are dealers if the securities are sold in the ordinary course of the corporation's business. Upon the sale or other taxable disposition of depreciable property, the recapture rules generally make no distinction between corporate and noncorporate taxpayers.[3]

The business deductions of corporations also parallel those available to individuals. Deductions are allowed for all ordinary and necessary expenses paid or incurred in carrying on a trade or business. Specific provision is made for the deductibility of interest, certain taxes, losses, bad debts, accelerated cost recovery, charitable contributions, net operating losses, research and experimental expenditures, and other less common deductions. There is no distinction between business and nonbusiness interest or business and nonbusiness bad debts for corporations. Thus, these amounts are deductible in full as ordinary deductions by corporations. No deduction is permitted for interest paid or incurred on amounts borrowed to purchase or carry tax-exempt securities. The same holds true for expenses contrary to public policy and certain unpaid expenses and interest between related parties.

Some of the tax credits available to individuals can also be claimed by corporations. This is the case with the foreign tax credit. Not available to corporations are certain credits that are personal in nature, such as the child care credit, the credit for elderly or disabled taxpayers, and the earned income credit.

Dissimilarities. The income taxation of corporations and individuals also differs significantly. As noted earlier, different tax rates apply to corporations and to individuals. Corporate tax rates are discussed in more detail later in the chapter (see Examples 28 and 29).

All allowable corporate deductions are treated as business deductions. Thus, the determination of adjusted gross income (AGI), so essential for individual taxpayers, has no relevance to corporations. Taxable income is computed simply by subtracting from gross income all allowable deductions and losses. Corporations need not be concerned with itemized deductions or the standard deduction. The deduction for personal and dependency exemptions is not available to corporations.

The $100 floor on the deductible portion of personal casualty and theft losses applicable to individuals does not apply to corporations. Also inapplicable is the provision limiting the deductibility of nonbusiness casualty losses to the amount in excess of 10 percent of AGI.

Specific Provisions Compared

A comparison of the income taxation of individuals and corporations appears in Concept Summary 2–1 located at the end of this chapter. However, in making this comparison, the following areas warrant special discussion:

- Accounting periods and methods.
- Capital gains and losses.
- Passive losses.
- Charitable contributions.
- Domestic production activities deduction.
- Net operating losses.
- Special deductions available only to corporations.

Accounting Periods and Methods

Accounting Periods. Corporations generally have the same choices of accounting periods as do individual taxpayers. Like an individual, a corporation may choose

---

[3]§§ 1245 and 1250, but see § 291(a).

| **TAX** *in the News* | **DOES U.S. CORPORATE TAX POLICY HURT THE COUNTRY'S GLOBAL COMPETITIVENESS?** |

The Treasury Department recently reported that U.S. corporations are subject to the second highest average tax rate (a combined Federal and state income tax rate of 39 percent) among industrialized countries, and many experts are concerned about the effect on U.S. competitiveness in global markets. The department also observed that the extensive use of deductions and credits in U.S. tax policy is detrimental to global competitiveness. By encouraging tax-based decisions instead of economic-based decisions, these preferences distort the flow of capital and thereby adversely affect economic growth and job creation in the United States. Some argue that U.S. competitiveness in global markets would improve if corporate tax rates and preferences were cut. According to the Treasury, a reduction in the top corporate tax rate to 27 percent (from 35 percent) could be combined with the elimination of many major tax preferences (e.g., domestic production activities deduction, municipal bond interest exemption, research activities credit) at no revenue loss to the Federal government. Given the current political environment and large Federal budget deficits, any legislative proposal for substantive change in U.S. corporate tax policy would have to be both revenue-neutral and backed by much of the business community if it is to have any chance of success.

a calendar year or a fiscal year for reporting purposes. Corporations, however, enjoy greater flexibility in the selection of a tax year. For example, corporations usually can have different tax years from those of their shareholders. Also, newly formed corporations (as new taxpayers) usually have a choice of any approved accounting period without having to obtain the consent of the IRS. **Personal service corporations (PSCs)** and S corporations, however, are subject to severe restrictions in the use of a fiscal year. The rules applicable to S corporations are discussed in Chapter 12.

A PSC has as its principal activity the performance of personal services, and such services are substantially performed by shareholder-employees. The performance of services must be in the fields of health, law, engineering, architecture, accounting, actuarial science, performing arts, or consulting.[4] Because placing a PSC on a fiscal year and retaining a calendar year for the shareholder-employee can result in a significant deferral of income, a PSC must generally use a calendar year.[5] However, a PSC can *elect* a fiscal year under any of the following conditions:

- A business purpose for the year can be demonstrated.
- The PSC year results in a deferral of not more than three months' income. The corporation must pay the shareholder-employee's salary during the portion of the calendar year after the close of the fiscal year. Furthermore, the salary for that period must be at least proportionate to the employee's salary received for the fiscal year.
- The PSC retains the same year that was used for its fiscal year ending 1987, provided the latter two requirements applicable to the preceding condition are satisfied.

| EXAMPLE 10 | Valdez & Vance is a professional association of public accountants. Because it receives over 40% of its gross receipts in March and April of each year from the preparation of tax returns, Valdez & Vance has a May 1 to April 30 fiscal year. Under these circumstances, the IRS might permit Valdez & Vance to continue to use the fiscal year chosen since it reflects a natural business cycle (the end of the tax season). Valdez & Vance has a business purpose for using a fiscal year. ■ |

| EXAMPLE 11 | Beige Corporation, a PSC, paid Burke $120,000 in salary during its fiscal year ending September 30, 2008. The corporation cannot satisfy the business purpose test for a fiscal year. However, the corporation can continue to use its fiscal year without any negative tax effects, |

provided that Burke receives at least $30,000 [(3 months/12 months) × $120,000] as salary during the period October 1 through December 31, 2008. ■

Accounting Methods. As a general rule, the cash method of accounting is unavailable to *regular* corporations.[6] However, several substantive exceptions apply in the case of the following types of corporations:

- S corporations.
- Corporations engaged in the trade or business of farming and timber.
- Qualified PSCs.
- Corporations with average annual gross receipts of $5 million or less. (In applying the $5 million-or-less test, the corporation uses the average of the three prior taxable years.)

Most individuals and corporations that maintain inventory for sale to customers are required to use the accrual method of accounting for determining sales and cost of goods sold. However, as a matter of administrative convenience, the IRS will permit any entity with average annual gross receipts of not more than $1 million for the most recent three-year period to use the cash method. This applies even if the taxpayer is buying and selling inventory. Also as a matter of administrative convenience, the IRS will permit certain entities with average annual gross receipts greater than $1 million but not more than $10 million for the most recent three-year period to use the cash method.

A corporation that uses the accrual method of accounting must observe a special rule in dealing with related parties. If the corporation has an accrual outstanding at the end of any taxable year, it cannot claim a deduction until the recipient reports the amount as income.[7] This rule is most often encountered when a corporation deals with a person who owns more than 50 percent of the corporation's stock.

E X A M P L E   12

Teal, Inc., an accrual method corporation, uses the calendar year for tax purposes. Bob, a cash method taxpayer, owns more than 50% of the corporation's stock at the end of 2008. On December 31, 2008, Teal has accrued $25,000 of salary to Bob. Bob receives the salary in 2009 and reports it on his 2009 tax return. Teal cannot claim a deduction for the $25,000 until 2009. ■

Capital Gains and Losses

Capital gains and losses result from the taxable sales or exchanges of capital assets.[8] Whether these gains and losses are long term or short term depends upon the holding period of the assets sold or exchanged. Each year, a taxpayer's long-term capital gains and losses are combined, and the result is either a *net* long-term capital gain or a *net* long-term capital loss. A similar aggregation is made with short-term capital gains and losses, the result being a *net* short-term capital gain or a *net* short-term capital loss. The following combinations and results are possible:

1. A net long-term capital gain and a net short-term capital loss. These are combined, and the result is either a net capital gain or a net capital loss.
2. A net long-term capital gain and a net short-term capital gain. No further combination is made.
3. A net long-term capital loss and a net short-term capital gain. These are combined, and the result is either a net capital gain or a net capital loss.
4. A net long-term capital loss and a net short-term capital loss. No further combination is made.

---

[6]§ 448.
[7]§ 267(a)(2).

[8]See Chapter 16 of *South-Western Federal Taxation: Individual Income Taxes* (2009 Edition) for a detailed discussion of capital gains and losses.

Capital Gains. Individuals generally pay tax on net (long-term) capital gains at a maximum rate of 15 percent.[9] Corporations, by contrast, receive no favorable rate on capital gains and must include the net capital gain, in full, as part of taxable income.

Capital Losses. Net capital losses (refer to combinations 3 and 4 and, possibly, to combination 1) of corporate and individual taxpayers receive different income tax treatment. Generally, individual taxpayers can deduct up to $3,000 of such net losses against other income. Any remaining capital losses can be carried forward to future years until absorbed by capital gains or by the $3,000 deduction.[10] Loss carryovers retain their identity as either long term or short term.

EXAMPLE 13

Robin, an individual, incurs a net long-term capital loss of $7,500 for calendar year 2008. Assuming adequate taxable income, Robin may deduct $3,000 of this loss on his 2008 return. The remaining $4,500 ($7,500 − $3,000) of the loss is carried to 2009 and years thereafter until completely deducted. The $4,500 will be carried forward as a long-term capital loss. ∎

Unlike individuals, corporate taxpayers are not permitted to claim any net capital losses as a deduction against ordinary income. Capital losses, therefore, can be used only as an offset against capital gains. Corporations may, however, carry back net capital losses to three preceding years, applying them first to the earliest year in point of time. Carryforwards are allowed for a period of five years from the year of the loss. When carried back or forward, a long-term capital loss is treated as a short-term capital loss.

EXAMPLE 14

Assume the same facts as in Example 13, except that Robin is a corporation. None of the $7,500 long-term capital loss incurred in 2008 can be deducted in that year. Robin Corporation may, however, carry back the loss to years 2005, 2006, and 2007 (in this order) and offset it against any capital gains recognized in these years. If the carryback does not exhaust the loss, it may be carried forward to calendar years 2009, 2010, 2011, 2012, and 2013 (in this order). Either a carryback or a carryforward of the long-term capital loss converts the loss to a short-term capital loss. ∎

Passive Losses

The **passive loss** rules apply to individual taxpayers and to closely held C corporations and personal service corporations (PSCs).[11] For S corporations and partnerships, passive income or loss flows through to the owners, and the passive loss rules are applied at the owner level. The passive loss rules are applied to closely held C corporations and to PSCs to prevent taxpayers from incorporating to avoid the passive loss limitation.

A corporation is closely held if, at any time during the taxable year, more than 50 percent of the value of the corporation's outstanding stock is owned, directly or indirectly, by or for not more than five individuals. A corporation is classified as a PSC if it meets the following requirements:

- The principal activity of the corporation is the performance of personal services.
- The services are substantially performed by shareholder-employees.
- More than 10 percent of the stock (in value) is held by shareholder-employees. *Any* stock held by an employee on *any* one day causes the employee to be an shareholder-employee.

The general passive activity loss rules apply to PSCs. Passive activity losses cannot be offset against either active income or portfolio income. The application of

---

[9]A 0% rate applies to individual taxpayers in the 10% and 15% brackets.
[10]§ 1212.

[11]§ 469(a).

the passive activity rules is not as harsh for closely held C corporations. They may offset passive losses against active income, but not against portfolio income.

EXAMPLE **15**

Brown, a closely held C corporation that is not a PSC, has $300,000 of passive losses from a rental activity, $200,000 of active business income, and $100,000 of portfolio income. The corporation may offset $200,000 of the $300,000 passive loss against the $200,000 active business income, but may not offset the remainder against the $100,000 of portfolio income. If Brown is a PSC, then none of the $300,000 of passive losses is deductible in the current year. ■

Subject to certain exceptions, individual taxpayers are not allowed to offset passive losses against *either* active or portfolio income.

Charitable Contributions

Both corporate and individual taxpayers may deduct charitable contributions if the recipient is a qualified charitable organization. Generally, a deduction will be allowed only for the year in which the payment is made. However, an important exception is made for *accrual basis corporations*. They may claim the deduction in the year preceding payment if two requirements are met. First, the contribution must be authorized by the board of directors by the end of that year. Second, it must be paid on or before the fifteenth day of the third month of the next year.

EXAMPLE **16**

On December 29, 2008, Blue Company, a calendar year, accrual basis taxpayer, authorizes a $5,000 donation to the Atlanta Symphony Association (a qualified charitable organization). The donation is made on March 13, 2009. If Blue Company is a partnership, the contribution can be deducted only in 2009.[12] However, if Blue Company is a corporation and the December 29, 2008 authorization was made by its board of directors, Blue may claim the $5,000 donation as a deduction for calendar year 2008. ■

Property Contributions. The amount that can be deducted for a noncash charitable contribution depends on the type of property contributed. Property must be identified as long-term capital gain property or ordinary income property. *Capital gain property* is property that, if sold, would result in long-term capital gain or § 1231 gain for the taxpayer. Such property generally must be a capital asset and must be held for the long-term holding period (more than 12 months).

The deduction for a charitable contribution of capital gain property is generally measured by fair market value.

EXAMPLE **17**

During the current year, Mallard Corporation donates a parcel of land (a capital asset) to Oakland Community College. Mallard acquired the land in 1988 for $60,000, and the fair market value on the date of the contribution is $100,000. The corporation's charitable contribution deduction (subject to a percentage limitation discussed later) is measured by the asset's fair market value of $100,000, even though the $40,000 appreciation on the land has never been included in income. ■

In two situations, a charitable contribution of capital gain property is measured by the basis of the property, rather than fair market value. If the corporation contributes *tangible personal property* and the charitable organization puts the property to an unrelated use, the appreciation on the property is not deductible. Unrelated use is defined as use that is not related to the purpose or function that qualifies the organization for exempt status.

---

[12]Each calendar year partner will report an allocable portion of the charitable contribution deduction as of December 31, 2009 (the end of the partnership's tax year). See Chapter 10.

EXAMPLE 18

White Corporation donates a painting worth $200,000 to Western States Art Museum (a qualified organization), which exhibits the painting. White had acquired the painting in 1980 for $90,000. Because the museum put the painting to a related use, White is allowed to deduct $200,000, the fair market value of the painting. ■

EXAMPLE 19

Assume the same facts as in the previous example, except that White Corporation donates the painting to the American Cancer Society, which sells the painting and deposits the $200,000 proceeds in the organization's general fund. White's deduction is limited to the $90,000 basis because it contributed tangible personal property that was put to an unrelated use by the charitable organization. ■

The deduction for charitable contributions of capital gain property to certain private nonoperating foundations is also limited to the basis of the property.

ETHICAL and EQUITABLE *Considerations*

IS IT BETTER NOT TO KNOW?

Puffin Corporation, your client, donated a painting to Tri-City Art Museum. The painting, which had been displayed in the corporate offices for several years, had a basis of $20,000 and a fair market value of $100,000. Puffin deducted a charitable contribution of $100,000 on its tax return.

You have learned that Tri-City Art Museum, also a client of yours, did not display the painting because it did not fit well with the museum's collection. Instead, Tri-City sold the painting for $100,000 and placed the funds in its operating budget. What action, if any, should you take?

Ordinary income property is property that, if sold, would *not* result in long-term capital gain or § 1231 gain for the taxpayer. Examples of ordinary income property include inventory and capital assets that have not been held long term. In addition, § 1231 property (depreciable property used in a trade or business) is treated as ordinary income property to the extent of any ordinary income recaptured under § 1245 or § 1250. As a general rule, the deduction for a contribution of ordinary income property is limited to the basis of the property. On certain contributions of inventory by *corporations*, however, the amount of the deduction is equal to the lesser of (1) the sum of the property's basis plus 50 percent of the appreciation on the property or (2) twice the property's basis. The following contributions of inventory qualify for this increased contribution amount.

- A contribution of property to a charitable organization for use that is related to the organization's exempt function and such use is solely for the care of the ill, needy, or infants. (Individual taxpayers also qualify for this exception if the property is "wholesome food.")
- A contribution of books to a public school (K through 12) that uses the books in its educational programs.
- A contribution of tangible personal research property constructed by the corporation to a qualified educational or scientific organization that uses the property for research or experimentation, or research training. (The property must be contributed within two years from the date of its construction by the donor, and its original use must begin with the donee.)
- A contribution of computer equipment and software to a qualified educational organization or public library that uses the property for educational purposes. (The property must be contributed within three years from the date of its acquisition or construction by the donor, and its original use must begin with the donor or donee.)[13]

---

[13]These conditions are set forth in §§ 170(e)(3), (4), and (6). At the time of this writing, the enhanced deduction associated with the contribution of food, book, and computer equipment inventory is available only for contributions made by December 31, 2007. However, the general consensus is that Congress will extend some or all of these provisions.

Lark Corporation, a clothing retailer, donates children's clothing to the Salvation Army to be used to attire homeless children. Lark's basis in the clothes is $2,000, and the fair market value is $3,000. Lark's deduction is $2,500 [$2,000 basis + 50%($3,000 − $2,000)]. If, instead, the fair market value is $7,000, Lark's deduction is $4,000 (2 × $2,000 basis). ■

Limitations Imposed on Charitable Contribution Deductions. Like individuals, corporations are subject to percentage limits on the charitable contribution deduction.[14] For any one year, a corporate taxpayer's contribution deduction is limited to 10 percent of taxable income. For this purpose, taxable income is computed without regard to the charitable contribution deduction, any net operating loss carryback or capital loss carryback, dividends received deduction, and domestic production activities deduction. Any contributions in excess of the 10 percent limitation may be carried forward to the five succeeding tax years. Any carryforward must be added to subsequent contributions and will be subject to the 10 percent limitation. In applying this limitation, the current year's contributions must be deducted first, with excess deductions from previous years deducted in order of time.[15]

During 2008, Orange Corporation (a calendar year taxpayer) had the following income and expenses:

Income from operations	$140,000
Expenses from operations	110,000
Dividends received	10,000
Charitable contributions made in May 2008	5,000

For purposes of the 10% limitation *only*, Orange Corporation's taxable income is $40,000 ($140,000 − $110,000 + $10,000). Consequently, the allowable charitable deduction for 2008 is $4,000 (10% × $40,000). The $1,000 unused portion of the contribution can be carried forward to 2009, 2010, 2011, 2012, and 2013 (in that order) until exhausted. ■

Assume the same facts as in Example 21. In 2009, Orange Corporation has taxable income (for purposes of the 10% limitation) of $50,000 and makes a charitable contribution of $4,500. The maximum deduction allowed for 2009 is $5,000 (10% × $50,000). The first $4,500 of the allowed deduction must be allocated to the contribution made in 2009, and $500 of the balance is carried over from 2008. The remaining $500 of the 2008 contribution may be carried over to 2010, etc. ■

Domestic Production Activities Deduction

One important purpose of the American Jobs Creation Act of 2004 was to replace certain tax provisions that our world trading partners regarded as allowing unfair advantage to U.S. exports. Among other changes, the Act created a deduction based on the income from manufacturing activities (designated as *domestic production activities*). For 2008 and 2009, the **domestic production activities deduction**[16] is 6 percent of the lower of:

- qualified production activities income, or
- taxable income (adjusted gross income in the case of individuals).

The deduction, however, cannot exceed 50 percent of an employer's W–2 wages related to qualified production activities income.

---

[14]The percentage limitations applicable to individuals and corporations are set forth in § 170(b).

[15]The carryover rules relating to all taxpayers are in § 170(d).
[16]§ 199.

EXAMPLE 23

Elk Corporation, a calendar year taxpayer, manufactures golf equipment. For 2008, Elk had taxable income of $360,000 and qualified production activities income of $380,000. Elk's deduction is $21,600 [6% × $360,000 (the lesser of $380,000 or $360,000)]. Elk's W–2 wages related to qualified production activities income were $50,000, so the W–2 wage limitation ($50,000 × 50% = $25,000) does not apply. ■

A phase-in provision increases the rate to 9 percent for 2010 and thereafter. See Chapter 3 for a detailed discussion of the domestic production activities deduction.

Net Operating Losses

Like the net operating loss (NOL) of an individual, the NOL of a corporation may be carried back 2 years and forward 20 to offset taxable income for those years. Similarly, corporations also may elect to forgo the carryback period and just carry forward an NOL. A corporation does not adjust its tax loss for the year for capital losses as do individual taxpayers, because a corporation is not permitted a deduction for net capital losses. Nor does a corporation make adjustments for any non-business deductions as do individual taxpayers. Further, a corporation is allowed to include the dividends received deduction (discussed below) in computing its NOL.[17]

EXAMPLE 24

In 2008, Green Corporation has gross income (including dividends) of $200,000 and deductions of $300,000 excluding the dividends received deduction. Green Corporation had received taxable dividends of $100,000 from Fox, Inc. stock. Green has an NOL computed as follows:

Gross income (including dividends)		$ 200,000
Less:		
Business deductions	$300,000	
Dividends received deduction (70% of $100,000)	70,000	(370,000)
Taxable income (or loss)		($ 170,000)

The NOL is carried back two years to 2006. (Green Corporation may forgo the carryback option and elect instead to carry forward the loss.) Assume Green had taxable income of $40,000 in 2006. The carryover to 2007 is computed as follows:

Taxable income for 2006	$ 40,000
Less NOL carryback	(170,000)
Taxable income for 2006 after NOL carryback (carryover to 2007)	($ 130,000)

■

LO.3

Discuss the tax rules unique to corporations.

Deductions Available Only to Corporations

Dividends Received Deduction. The purpose of the **dividends received deduction** is to mitigate triple taxation. Without the deduction, income paid to a corporation in the form of a dividend would be taxed to the recipient corporation with no corresponding deduction to the distributing corporation. Later, when the recipient corporation paid the income to its individual shareholders, the income would again be subject to taxation with no corresponding deduction to the corporation. The dividends received deduction alleviates this inequity by causing only some or none of the dividend income to be taxable to the recipient corporation.

---

[17]The modifications required to arrive at the amount of NOL that can be carried back or forward are in § 172(d).

As the following table illustrates, the amount of the dividends received deduction depends upon the percentage of ownership (voting power and value) the recipient corporate shareholder holds in a domestic corporation making the dividend distribution.[18]

Percentage of Ownership by Corporate Shareholder	Deduction Percentage
Less than 20%	70%
20% or more (but less than 80%)	80%
80% or more*	100%

* The payor corporation must be a member of an affiliated group with the recipient corporation.

DRD

The dividends received deduction is limited to a percentage of the taxable income of a corporation. For this purpose, taxable income is computed without regard to the NOL, the domestic production activities deduction, the dividends received deduction, and any capital loss carryback to the current tax year. The percentage of taxable income limitation corresponds to the deduction percentage. Thus, if a corporate shareholder owns less than 20 percent of the stock in the distributing corporation, the dividends received deduction is limited to 70 percent of taxable income. However, the taxable income limitation does not apply if the corporation has an NOL for the current taxable year.[19]

The following steps are useful in applying these rules.

1. Multiply the dividends received by the deduction percentage.
2. Multiply the taxable income by the deduction percentage.
3. The deduction is limited to the lesser of Step 1 or Step 2, unless subtracting the amount derived in Step 1 from 100 percent of taxable income *generates* an NOL. If so, the amount derived in Step 1 should be used. This is referred to as the NOL rule.

Red, White, and Blue Corporations, three unrelated calendar year corporations, have the following transactions for the year:

EXAMPLE 25

	Red Corporation	White Corporation	Blue Corporation
Gross income from operations	$ 400,000	$ 320,000	$ 260,000
Expenses from operations	(340,000)	(340,000)	(340,000)
Dividends received from domestic corporations (less than 20% ownership)	200,000	200,000	200,000
Taxable income before the dividends received deduction	$ 260,000	$ 180,000	$ 120,000

In determining the dividends received deduction, use the three-step procedure described above:

	Red	White	Blue
Step 1 (70% × $200,000)	$140,000	$140,000	$140,000
Step 2			
70% × $260,000 (taxable income)	$182,000		
70% × $180,000 (taxable income)		$126,000	
70% × $120,000 (taxable income)			$84,000
Step 3			
Lesser of Step 1 or Step 2	$140,000	$126,000	
Deduction generates an NOL			$140,000

White Corporation is subject to the 70 percent of taxable income limitation. It does not qualify for NOL rule treatment since subtracting $140,000 (Step 1) from $180,000 (100 percent of taxable income) does not yield a negative figure. Blue Corporation does qualify for NOL rule treatment because subtracting $140,000 (Step 1) from $120,000 (100 percent of taxable income) yields a negative figure. In summary, each corporation has a dividends received deduction for the year as follows: $140,000 for Red Corporation, $126,000 for White Corporation, and $140,000 for Blue Corporation.

No dividends received deduction is allowed unless the corporation has held the stock for more than 45 days.[20] This restriction was enacted to close a tax loophole involving dividends on stock that is held only transitorily. When stock is purchased shortly before a dividend record date and soon thereafter sold ex-dividend, a capital loss corresponding to the amount of the dividend often results (ignoring other market valuation changes). If the dividends received deduction was allowed in such cases, the capital loss resulting from the stock sale would exceed the related dividend income.

EXAMPLE 26

On October 3, 2008, Pink Corporation (5 million shares outstanding) declares a $1 per share dividend for shareholders of record as of November 3, 2008, and payable on December 3, 2008. Black Corporation purchases 10,000 shares of Pink stock on October 28, 2008, for $25,000, and sells those 10,000 shares ex-dividend on November 5, 2008, for $15,000. (It is assumed that there is no fluctuation in the market price of the Pink stock other than the dividend element.) The sale results in a short-term capital loss of $10,000 ($15,000 amount realized − $25,000 basis). On December 3, Black receives a $10,000 dividend from Pink. Without the holding period restriction, Black Corporation would recognize a $10,000 deduction (subject to the capital loss limitation) but only $3,000 of income [$10,000 dividend − $7,000 dividends received deduction ($10,000 × 70%)], or a $7,000 net loss. However, since Black did not hold the Pink stock for more than 45 days, no dividends received deduction is allowed. ■

Another restriction applies to the dividends received deduction when the underlying stock is debt financed. Like the holding period restriction, this provision also was enacted to close a tax loophole. A corporation that finances the purchase of dividend-paying stock receives an interest expense deduction from such financing, but would report only a small amount of the related income if the dividends received deduction was allowed unabated. In general, the debt-financed stock restriction reduces the dividends received deduction with respect to any dividend-paying stock by the percentage of the investment in the stock that is debt financed.[21] For instance, if a stock purchase is financed 50 percent by debt, the dividends received deduction for dividends on such stock is reduced by 50 percent. However, the reduction in the dividends received deduction cannot exceed the amount of the interest deduction allocable to the dividend.

ETHICAL and EQUITABLE *Considerations*

MAXIMIZING THE DIVIDENDS RECEIVED DEDUCTION

As of December 30, 2008, Robin Corporation (a calendar year taxpayer) has gross income from operations of $497,000, expenses from operations of $556,000, and dividends received from domestic corporations (less than 20 percent ownership) of $200,000. Currently, Robin does not expect any more income or expenses to be realized by year-end.

However, Robin's tax department has suggested that the corporation incur another $1,001 of deductible expenditures before year-end. What is the motivation behind the tax department's recommendation, and is such year-end tax planning ethical?

---

[20]The stock must be held more than 45 days during the 91-day period beginning on the date that is 45 days before the ex-dividend date (or, in the case of preferred stock, more than 90 days during the 181-day period beginning on the date that is 90 days before the ex-dividend date). § 246(c).

[21]§ 246A.

Organizational Expenditures Deduction.

Expenses incurred in connection with the organization of a corporation normally are chargeable to a capital account. That they benefit the corporation during its existence seems clear. But how can they be amortized when most corporations possess unlimited life? The lack of a determinable and limited estimated useful life would therefore preclude any tax write-off. Section 248 was enacted to solve this problem.

Under § 248, a corporation may elect to amortize **organizational expenditures** over the 180-month period beginning with the month in which the corporation begins business.[22] Organizational expenditures *subject to the election* include the following:

- Legal services incident to organization (e.g., drafting the corporate charter, bylaws, minutes of organizational meetings, terms of original stock certificates).
- Necessary accounting services.
- Expenses of temporary directors and of organizational meetings of directors or shareholders.
- Fees paid to the state of incorporation.

Expenditures that *do not qualify* include those connected with issuing or selling shares of stock or other securities (e.g., commissions, professional fees, and printing costs) or with the transfer of assets to a corporation. These expenditures reduce the amount of capital raised and are not deductible at all.

The first $5,000 of organizational costs can be immediately expensed, with any remaining amount of organizational costs amortized over a 180-month period. However, this $5,000 expensing amount is phased out on a dollar-for-dollar basis when these costs exceed $50,000. For example, a corporation with $52,000 of organizational costs would expense $3,000 [$5,000 − ($52,000 − $50,000)] of this amount and amortize the $49,000 balance ($52,000 − $3,000) over 180 months.

To qualify for the election, the expenditure must be *incurred* before the end of the taxable year in which the corporation begins business. In this regard, the corporation's method of accounting is of no consequence. Thus, an expense incurred by a cash basis corporation in its first tax year qualifies even though the expense is not paid until a subsequent year.

The election is made in a statement attached to the corporation's return for its first taxable year. The return and statement must be filed no later than the due date of the return (including any extensions).

If the election is *not* made on a timely basis, organizational expenditures cannot be deducted until the corporation ceases to do business and liquidates. These expenditures will be deductible if the corporate charter limits the life of the corporation.

EXAMPLE 27

Black Corporation, an accrual basis taxpayer, was formed and began operations on May 1, 2008. The following expenses were incurred during its first year of operations (May 1–December 31, 2008):

Expenses of temporary directors and of organizational meetings	$15,000
Fee paid to the state of incorporation	2,000
Accounting services incident to organization	18,000
Legal services for drafting the corporate charter and bylaws	32,000
Expenses incident to the printing and sale of stock certificates	48,000

Black Corporation elects to amortize organizational costs under § 248. Because of the dollar cap (i.e., dollar-for-dollar reduction for amounts in excess of $50,000), no immediate expensing under the $5,000 rule is available. The monthly amortization is $372 [($15,000 +

---

[22]The month in which a corporation begins business may not be immediately apparent. See Reg. § 1.248–1(a)(3). For a similar problem in the Subchapter S area, see Chapter 12.

$2,000 + $18,000 + $32,000) ÷ 180 months], and $2,976 ($372 × 8 months) is deductible for tax year 2008. Note that the $48,000 of expenses incident to the printing and sale of stock certificates does not qualify for the election. These expenses cannot be deducted at all but reduce the amount of the capital realized from the sale of stock. ■

Organizational expenditures are distinguished from *startup expenditures.*[23] Startup expenditures include various investigation expenses involved in entering a new business, whether incurred by a corporate or an individual taxpayer. Startup expenses also include operating expenses, such as rent and payroll, that are incurred by a corporation before it actually begins to produce any gross income. At the election of the taxpayer, such expenditures (e.g., travel, market surveys, financial audits, legal fees) are deductible in the same manner as organizational expenditures. Thus, up to $5,000 can be immediately expensed (subject to the excess-of-$50,000 phaseout) and any remaining amounts amortized over a period of 180 months.

LO.4
Compute the corporate income tax.

Determining the Corporate Income Tax Liability

Corporate Income Tax Rates

Corporate income tax rates have fluctuated widely over past years. Refer to Exhibit 2–1 for a schedule of current corporate income tax rates. Unlike the individual income tax rate brackets, the corporate income tax rate brackets are not indexed for inflation.

EXAMPLE 28

Gold Corporation, a calendar year taxpayer, has taxable income of $90,000 for 2008. Its income tax liability is $18,850, determined as follows:

Tax on $75,000	$13,750
Tax on $15,000 × 34%	5,100
Tax liability	$18,850

■

For a corporation that has taxable income in excess of $100,000 for any tax year, the amount of the tax is increased by the lesser of (1) 5 percent of the excess or (2) $11,750. In effect, the additional tax means a 39 percent rate for every dollar of taxable income from $100,000 to $335,000.

EXAMPLE 29

Silver Corporation, a calendar year taxpayer, has taxable income of $335,000 for 2008. Its income tax liability is $113,900, determined as follows:

Tax on $100,000	$ 22,250
Tax on $235,000 × 39%	91,650
Tax liability	$113,900

Note that the tax liability of $113,900 is 34% of $335,000. Thus, due to the 39% rate (34% normal rate + 5% additional tax on taxable income between $100,000 and $335,000), the benefit of the lower rates on the first $75,000 of taxable income completely phases out at $335,000. The normal rate drops back to 34% on taxable income between $335,000 and $10 million. ■

Under § 11(b), personal service corporations are taxed at a flat 35 percent rate on all taxable income. Thus, PSCs do not enjoy the tax savings of being in the 15 to 34 percent brackets applicable to other corporations. For this purpose, a PSC is a

---

[23]§ 195.

corporation that is substantially employee owned. Also, it must engage in one of the following activities: health, law, engineering, architecture, accounting, actuarial science, performing arts, or consulting.

Alternative Minimum Tax

Corporations are subject to an alternative minimum tax (AMT) that is similar to the AMT applicable to individuals.[24] The AMT for corporations, as for individuals, involves a broader tax base than does the regular tax. Like an individual, a corporation is required to apply a minimum tax rate to the expanded base and pay the difference between the AMT tax liability and the regular tax. Many of the adjustments and tax preference items necessary to arrive at alternative minimum taxable income (AMTI) are the same for individuals and corporations.

Although the objective of the AMT is the same for individual and corporate taxpayers, the rate and exemptions are different. Computation of the AMT for corporations is discussed in Chapter 3.

Tax Liability of Related Corporations

Related corporations are subject to special rules for computing the income tax, the accumulated earnings credit, and the AMT exemption.[25] If these restrictions did not exist, the shareholders of a corporation could gain significant tax advantages by splitting a single corporation into *multiple* corporations. The next two examples illustrate the potential *income tax* advantage of multiple corporations.

> **LO.5**
>
> Explain the rules unique to computing the tax of multiple corporations.

EXAMPLE 30

Gray Corporation annually yields taxable income of $300,000. The corporate tax on $300,000 is $100,250, computed as follows:

Tax on $100,000	$ 22,250
Tax on $200,000 × 39%	78,000
Tax liability	$100,250

■

EXAMPLE 31

Assume that Gray Corporation in the previous example is divided equally into four corporations. Each corporation would have taxable income of $75,000, and the tax for each (absent the special provisions for related corporations) would be computed as follows:

Tax on $50,000	$ 7,500
Tax on $25,000 × 25%	6,250
Tax liability	$13,750

The total liability for the four corporations would be $55,000 ($13,750 × 4). The savings would be $45,250 ($100,250 − $55,000). ■

A comparison of Examples 30 and 31 reveals that the income tax savings that could be achieved by using multiple corporations result from having more of the total income taxed at lower rates. To close this potential loophole, the law limits a controlled group's taxable income in the tax brackets below 35 percent to the amount the corporations in the group would have if they were one corporation. Thus, in Example 31, under the controlled corporation rules, only $12,500 (one-fourth of the first $50,000 of taxable income) for each of the four related corporations would be taxed at the 15 percent rate. The 25 percent rate would apply to the next $6,250 (one-fourth of the next $25,000) of taxable income of each corporation. This equal allocation of the $50,000 and $25,000 amounts is required unless

---

[24]Small corporations are not subject to the alternative minimum tax.   [25]§ 1561(a).

all members of the controlled group consent to an apportionment plan providing for an unequal allocation. Controlled groups include parent-subsidiary groups, brother-sister groups, combined groups, and certain insurance companies.

Similar limitations apply to the $250,000 accumulated earnings credit for controlled groups and to the $40,000 exemption amount for purposes of computing the AMT. Both the accumulated earnings tax and the AMT are discussed in Chapter 3. Controlled groups are discussed in detail in Chapter 8.

LO.6

Describe the reporting process for corporations.

Procedural Matters

Filing Requirements for Corporations

A corporation must file a Federal income tax return whether or not it has taxable income.[26] A corporation that was not in existence throughout an entire annual accounting period is required to file a return for the portion of the year during which it was in existence. In addition, a corporation must file a return even though it has ceased to do business if it has valuable claims for which it will bring suit. A corporation is relieved of filing income tax returns only when it ceases to do business and retains no assets.

The corporate return is filed on Form 1120. [Note: The shorter Form 1120-A was discontinued for tax years beginning in 2007.]

Corporations electing under Subchapter S (see Chapter 12) file on Form 1120S. Forms 1120 and 1120S are reproduced in Appendix B.

The return must be filed on or before the fifteenth day of the third month following the close of a corporation's tax year. As noted previously, a regular corporation, other than a PSC, can use either a calendar or a fiscal year to report its taxable income. The tax year of the shareholders has no effect on the corporation's tax year.

Corporations can receive an automatic extension of six months for filing the corporate return by filing Form 7004 by the due date for the return.[27] However, the IRS may terminate the extension by mailing a 10-day notice to the taxpayer corporation. A Form 7004 must be accompanied by the corporation's estimated tax liability.

Estimated Tax Payments

A corporation must make payments of estimated tax unless its tax liability can reasonably be expected to be less than $500. The required annual payment (which includes any estimated AMT liability) is the *lesser* of (1) 100 percent of the corporation's final tax or (2) 100 percent of the tax for the preceding year (if that was a 12-month tax year and the return filed showed a tax liability).[28] Estimated payments can be made in four installments due on or before the fifteenth day of the fourth month, the sixth month, the ninth month, and the twelfth month of the corporate taxable year. The full amount of the unpaid tax is due on the due date of the return. For a calendar year corporation, the payment dates are as follows:

> April 15
> June 15
> September 15
> December 15

A corporation failing to pay its required estimated tax payments will be subjected to a nondeductible penalty on the amount by which the installments are less than the tax due. However, the underpayment penalty will not be imposed if the estimated payments are timely and are equal to the tax liability of the corporation for the prior year or equal to the tax due computed on an annualized basis. If the

---

[26]§ 6012(a)(2).
[27]§ 6081.

[28]§§ 6655(d) and (e).

annualized method is used for one installment and the corporation does not use this method for a subsequent installment, any shortfall from using the annualized method for a prior payment(s) must be made up in the subsequent installment payment. The penalty is imposed on each installment; that is, a corporation must pay one-fourth of its required annual payment by the due date of each installment.

A *large* corporation cannot base its installment payments on its previous year's tax liability except for its first installment payment. A corporation is considered large if it had taxable income of $1 million or more in any of its three preceding years.

Schedule M–1—Reconciliation of Taxable Income and Financial Net Income

Schedule M–1 of Form 1120 is used to *reconcile* net income as computed for financial accounting purposes with taxable income reported on the corporation's income tax return (commonly referred to as book/tax differences). Schedule M–1 is required of corporations with less than $10 million of total assets.

The starting point on Schedule M–1 is net income per books (financial accounting net income). Additions and subtractions are entered for items that affect net income per books and taxable income differently. The following items are entered as additions (see lines 2 through 5 of Schedule M–1):

- Federal income tax liability (deducted in computing net income per books but not deductible in computing taxable income).
- The excess of capital losses over capital gains (deducted for financial accounting purposes but not deductible by corporations for income tax purposes).
- Income that is reported in the current year for tax purposes but is not reported in computing net income per books (e.g., prepaid income).
- Various expenses that are deducted in computing net income per books but are not allowed in computing taxable income (e.g., charitable contributions in excess of the 10 percent ceiling applicable to corporations).

The following subtractions are entered on lines 7 and 8 of Schedule M–1:

- Income reported for financial accounting purposes but not included in taxable income (e.g., tax-exempt interest).
- Expenses deducted on the tax return but not deducted in computing net income per books (e.g., a charitable contributions carryover deducted in a prior year for financial accounting purposes but deductible in the current year for tax purposes).

The result is taxable income (before the NOL deduction and the dividends received deduction).

E X A M P L E   32

During the current year, Tern Corporation had the following transactions:

Net income per books (after tax)	$92,400
Taxable income	50,000
Federal income tax liability (15% × $50,000)	7,500
Interest income from tax-exempt bonds	5,000
Interest paid on loan, the proceeds of which were used to purchase the tax-exempt bonds	500
Life insurance proceeds received as a result of the death of a key employee	50,000
Premiums paid on key employee life insurance policy	2,600
Excess of capital losses over capital gains	2,000

For book and tax purposes, Tern Corporation determines depreciation under the straight-line method. Tern's Schedule M–1 for the current year is as follows:

Schedule M-1	Reconciliation of Income (Loss) per Books With Income per Return					
	Note: Schedule M-3 required instead of Schedule M-1 if total assets are $10 million or more—see instructions					
1	Net income (loss) per books . . .	92,400		7	Income recorded on books this year not included on this return (itemize):	
2	Federal income tax per books . .	7,500				
3	Excess of capital losses over capital gains .	2,000			Tax-exempt interest $ 5,000 _ _ _ _ _ _	
4	Income subject to tax not recorded on books				Life insurance proceeds 50,000	
	this year (itemize): _ _ _ _ _ _ _ _ _ _ _ _ _				_ _ _ _ _ _ _ _ _ _ _ _ _ _ _ _ _ _ _ _	55,000
	_ _			8	Deductions on this return not charged against book income this year (itemize):	
5	Expenses recorded on books this year not deducted on this return (itemize):				a Depreciation . . $ _ _ _ _ _ _	
a	Depreciation . . $ _ _ _ _ _ _ _				b Charitable contributions $ _ _ _ _ _ _	
b	Charitable contributions $ _ _ _ _ _ _ _ _				_ _ _ _ _ _ _ _ _ _ _ _ _ _ _ _ _ _ _ _	
c	Travel and entertainment $ _ _ _ _ _ _ _					
	Prem.–life ins. $2,600; Int.– state bonds $500	3,100		9	Add lines 7 and 8	55,000
6	Add lines 1 through 5	105,000		10	Income (page 1, line 28)—line 6 less line 9	50,000

Schedule M–2 reconciles unappropriated retained earnings at the beginning of the year with unappropriated retained earnings at year-end. Beginning balance plus net income per books, as entered on line 1 of Schedule M–1, less dividend distributions during the year equals ending retained earnings. Other sources of increases or decreases in retained earnings are also listed on Schedule M–2.

EXAMPLE 33

Assume the same facts as in Example 32. Tern Corporation's beginning balance in unappropriated retained earnings is $125,000. During the year, Tern distributed a cash dividend of $30,000 to its shareholders. Based on these further assumptions, Tern's Schedule M–2 for the current year is as follows:

Schedule M-2	Analysis of Unappropriated Retained Earnings per Books (Line 25, Schedule L)					
1	Balance at beginning of year . . .	125,000		5	Distributions: a Cash . . .	30,000
2	Net income (loss) per books . . .	92,400			b Stock . . .	
3	Other increases (itemize): _ _ _ _ _ _ _ _ _				c Property . .	
	_ _			6	Other decreases (itemize): _ _ _ _ _ _ _ _	
	_ _			7	Add lines 5 and 6	30,000
4	Add lines 1, 2, and 3	217,400		8	Balance at end of year (line 4 less line 7)	187,400

Corporations with less than $250,000 of gross receipts and less than $250,000 in assets do not have to complete Schedule L (balance sheet) and Schedules M–1 and M–2 of Form 1120. Similar rules apply to Form 1120S. These rules are intended to ease the compliance burden on small business.

Schedule M–3—Net Income (Loss) Reconciliation for Corporations with Total Assets of $10 Million or More

Corporate taxpayers with total assets of $10 million or more are required to report much greater detail relative to differences between income (loss) reported for financial purposes and income (loss) reported for tax purposes. This expanded reconciliation of book and tax income (loss) is reported on **Schedule M–3**. Corporations that are not required to file Schedule M–3 may do so voluntarily. Any corporation that files Schedule M–3 is not allowed to file Schedule M–1. Comparison of Schedule M–3 with Schedule M–1 (illustrated in Example 32) reveals the significantly greater disclosure requirements. Schedule M–3 is reproduced in Appendix B of this text.

Schedule M–3 is a response, at least in part, to recent financial reporting scandals, including Enron, WorldCom, and others. One objective of Schedule M–3 is to create greater transparency between corporate financial statements and tax returns. Another objective is to identify corporations that engage in aggressive tax practices by requiring that transactions that create book/tax differences be disclosed on corporate tax returns. The increase in transparency and disclosure comes at a cost, however, as the IRS estimates that, on average, almost 85 hours are needed to complete and file a Schedule M–3, and many tax professionals believe that estimate is too low.

Total assets for purposes of the $10 million test are determined from the taxpayer's financial reports. If the taxpayer files Form 10–K with the Securities and Exchange Commission (SEC), that statement is used. If no 10–K is filed, information from another financial source is used, in the following order: certified financial statements, prepared income statements, or the taxpayer's books and records.

Part I—Financial Information and Net Income (Loss) Reconciliation. Part I requires the following financial information about the corporation.

- The source of the financial net income (loss) amount used in the reconciliation—SEC Form 10–K, audited financial statements, prepared financial statements, or the corporation's books and records.
- Any restatements of the corporation's income statement for the filing period, as well as any restatements for the past five filing periods.
- Any required adjustments to the net income (loss) amount referred to above (see Part I, lines 5 through 10).

The adjusted net income (loss) amount must be reconciled with the amount of taxable income reported on the corporation's Form 1120.

Because of Schedule M–3's complexity, the coverage in this chapter will be limited to some of the more important concepts underlying the schedule. A series of examples adapted from the instructions for Schedule M–3 will be used to illustrate these concepts.

EXAMPLE 34

Southwest Sportsman's Corporation (SSC) sells hunting and fishing equipment to sportsmen. SSC has several stores in Texas, New Mexico, and Arizona. It also has a subsidiary in Mexico, which is organized as a Mexican corporation. SSC, which does not file a Form 10–K with the SEC, reports income from its Mexican subsidiary on its audited financial statements, which show net income of $45 million in 2008. The Mexican corporation, which is not consolidated by SSC for tax purposes and is therefore not an includible corporation, had net income of $7 million. SSC must enter $7 million on Part I, line 5a of Schedule M–3, resulting in net income per income statement of includible corporations of $38 million. ■

A situation similar to that described in Example 34 could result in additional entries in Part I of Schedule M–3. For example, if SSC engaged in transactions with its nonincludible Mexican subsidiary, an entry would be required on line 8 (adjustment to eliminations of transactions between includible corporations and nonincludible entities).

Part II—Reconciliation of Net Income (Loss) of Includible Corporations with Taxable Income per Return. Part II reconciles income and loss items of includible corporations, while Part III reconciles expenses and deductions. As indicated in Example 34, corporations included in a financial reporting group may differ from corporations in a tax reporting group. Corporations may also be partners in a partnership, which is a flow-through entity. The following example illustrates the adjustments that are required in this situation.

EXAMPLE 35

Southwest Sportsman's Corporation also owns an interest in a U.S. partnership, Southwest Hunting Lodges (SHL). On its audited financial statements, SSC reported net income of $10 million as its distributive share from SHL. SSC's Schedule K–1 from SHL reports the following amounts:

Ordinary income	$5,000,000
Long-term capital gain	7,000,000
Charitable contributions	4,000,000
Section 179 expense	100,000

In order to adjust for the flow-through items from the partnership, SSC must report these items on Schedule M–3, Part II, line 9 [Income (loss) from U.S. partnerships]. The corporation reports $10 million (book income) on line 9, column (a). SSC reports income per tax return of $7.9 million ($5,000,000 + $7,000,000 − $4,000,000 − $100,000) in column (d) of line 9, and a permanent difference of $2.1 million in column (c). ■

Part III—Reconciliation of Expense/Deduction Items. Part III lists 35 reconciling items relating to expenses and deductions. For these items, taxpayers must reconcile differences between income statement amounts (column a) and tax return

amounts (column d), then classify these differences as temporary (column b) or permanent (column c) differences. The totals of the reconciling items from Part III are transferred to Part II, line 27, and are included with other items required to reconcile financial statement net income (loss) to tax return net income (loss).

EXAMPLE 36

Southwest Sportsman's Corporation acquired intellectual property in 2008 and deducted amortization of $20,000 on its financial statements, which were prepared according to GAAP. For Federal income tax purposes, SSC deducted $30,000. The corporation must report the amortization on line 28, Part III as follows: $20,000 book amortization in column (a), $10,000 temporary difference in column (b), and $30,000 tax return amortization in column (d). ∎

EXAMPLE 37

In January 2008, Southwest Sportsman's Corporation established an allowance for uncollectible accounts (bad debt reserve) of $35,000 on its books and increased the allowance by $65,000 during the year. As a result of a client's bankruptcy, SSC decreased the allowance by $25,000 in November 2008. The corporation deducted the $100,000 of increases to the allowance on its 2008 income statement but was not allowed to deduct that amount on its tax return. On its 2008 tax return, the corporation was allowed to deduct the $25,000 actual loss sustained because of its client's bankruptcy. On its financial statements, SSC treated the $100,000 increase in the bad debt reserve as an expense that gave rise to a temporary difference. On its 2008 tax return, SSC took a $25,000 deduction for bad debt expense. These amounts must be reported on line 32, Part III as follows: $100,000 book bad debt expense in column (a), $75,000 temporary difference in column (b), and $25,000 tax return bad debt expense in column (d). ∎

Example 36 illustrates the Schedule M–3 reporting when book expenses are less than tax return deductions. Example 37 illustrates reporting procedures when book expenses are greater than tax return deductions. Both examples illustrate the reporting of temporary differences. The amounts from both examples are included in the totals derived in Part III and are carried to Part II, line 27. The reconciliation of book income and taxable income occurs in lines 26 through 30. The reconciled amount of net income derived on Part II, line 30, column (a) must be equal to the taxable income reported on corporate Form 1120.

Financial Accounting Considerations

LO.7

Understand the impact of tax return positions on financial statements.

A review of the Schedule M–1 (or Schedule M–3) adjustments to Form 1120 (see prior discussion) reveals considerable differences in the tax and financial accounting treatment of certain transactions. These differences can be *permanent* and appear on the tax return *or* the financial statements but not on both. Some examples of permanent differences include interest income on municipal bonds, the dividends received deduction, the domestic production activities deduction, and fines and penalties. Other differences are *temporary* and appear on both the tax return *and* the financial statements but in different periods. Here, the variation is due to timing as to when (or how much of) the transaction is taken into account. Some examples of temporary differences include depreciation, depletion, unearned income, reserves for bad debts and product warranties, NOLs, and excess capital losses and charitable contributions.

Other differences between the information reported on the tax return and that reflected on the financial statements can arise in parent-subsidiary situations. For financial accounting purposes, a parent corporation must include the earnings of all subsidiaries (both domestic and some foreign) in which it owns 50 percent or more of the voting stock.[29] For Federal income tax purposes, however, a consolidated return includes only those domestic subsidiaries where the stock ownership is 80 percent or more, while foreign subsidiaries are not eligible for inclusion.[30]

---

[29]Under Accounting Principles Board Opinion No. 23 (*Accounting for Income Taxes—Special Areas*), some or all of the earnings of a foreign subsidiary are not included if they will not be repatriated (i.e., are permanently reinvested overseas).

[30]§§ 1504(a) and (b). Consolidated returns are discussed in Chapter 8.

The accounting treatment for the differences between tax and financial accounting concepts is handled in FAS 109 as supplemented by FIN 48.

FAS 109. Issued by the Financial Accounting Standards Board (FASB) in 1992, FAS 109 (*Accounting for Income Taxes*) prescribes the rules governing the determination of the current income tax expense reported on the income statement and for deferred taxes shown on the balance sheet. Current income tax expense for book purposes is determined by adjusting net income (before tax) for permanent differences (e.g., interest income on municipal bonds) and applying the applicable tax rate to the balance. Deferred taxes are based on temporary differences between tax and financial accounting treatment and are accounted for through the use of deferred tax liability and asset accounts. A deferred tax liability results when the book basis of an item exceeds its tax basis (e.g., the excess of MACRS over straight-line depreciation). A deferred tax asset results when the book basis of an item is less than its tax basis (e.g., accrual for product warranty expense).

Recording a deferred tax asset is appropriate only if it is "more likely than not" that the future tax benefit will materialize. If this threshold cannot be met, a valuation account must be established that properly measures the value of the expected benefit. Valuation accounts are contra accounts and often arise in situations involving carryovers (e.g., NOLs, excess charitable contributions and capital losses). FAS 109 provides examples of negative evidence (e.g., expected future losses) and positive evidence (e.g., unrealized appreciation in assets) that can be utilized in determining the amount of a valuation allowance.

For financial statement purposes, deferred tax liabilities and assets must be classified as either current or noncurrent. Most often the classification will depend on the nature of the asset or liability to which each relates. Thus, a deferred tax liability for excess depreciation will be noncurrent as it relates to fixed assets, while a deferred tax asset for bad debts will be current as accounts receivable are involved. For balance sheet presentation purposes, the asset and liability accounts are offset against each other to arrive at net current and net noncurrent (asset or liability) amounts.

Additional disclosures in the financial statements or notes thereto may require allocations of income tax expense to discontinued operations, extraordinary items, prior-year adjustments, and the overall effect of accounting changes. Footnote comments can provide an in-depth analysis of the provisions for income tax expense (both current and deferred) as well as pending tax controversies with Federal, state, and foreign jurisdictions.

FIN 48. Prior to **FIN 48**, many taxpayers established reserves for uncertain income tax positions. Some of these reserves were intended to "cushion" the effect on financial statements of adverse tax consequences resulting from unfavorable IRS audits or the negative resolution of pending litigation. Such reserves were created under the guidelines outlined in FAS 5 (*Accounting for Contingencies*). Unfortunately, however, these reserves were often used as a "cookie jar" to shift earnings from one period to another.

To add clarity to this area, the FASB issued Interpretation No. 48 (*Accounting for Uncertain Income Taxes*) in July 2006. FIN 48 is applicable to all entities (including nonprofit organizations and pass-through entities) that issue financial statements in conformance with generally accepted accounting principles (GAAP). It is generally effective for fiscal years beginning after December 15, 2006.

Certain tax *positions* that have *material* financial statement implications might be taken in conducting the operations of an entity. Examples of such tax positions include:

- No return is filed.[31]
- Income or expense is allocated between jurisdictions.[32]

---

[31]This could be the case where the entity maintains that no "nexus" exists. See Chapter 15, page 15–8.

[32]Intercompany pricing can cause this result. See the discussion of § 482 and APAs in Chapter 9.

- Expenditures are deducted rather than capitalized.[33]
- Income is excluded from the return.[34]
- A transaction or an entity is classified as tax-exempt.[35]

FIN 48 states that a tax position must be recognized when it has a "more-likely-than-not" probability (i.e., a more than 50 percent chance) of *being sustained* on examination. Being sustained presumes that an audit will occur (i.e., no reliance on the "audit lottery" omission is allowed) and that the taxing authority will have full knowledge of all facts and circumstances. Being sustained also entails going through all levels of appeal—both administrative and judicial. Consequently, being sustained may require an assessment of legal authority (i.e., court cases, administrative rulings). In this regard, the respective statutes of limitations should be taken into account. If no return was filed, however, there may be no limit to the number of open years. When the "more-likely-than-not" threshold is not met, then the tax position cannot be considered, and any tax benefit resulting therefrom must be discarded.

The following examples illustrate some of the basic provisions of FIN 48.

EXAMPLE 38

In the current year, Purple Corporation identifies two tax positions requiring the application of FIN 48: tax position 1, which relates to a tax benefit of $100,000; and tax position 2, which relates to a tax benefit of $200,000. In applying the recognition criterion of FIN 48, Purple has determined that tax position 1 does not satisfy the "more-likely-than-not" threshold, but that tax position 2 does satisfy the threshold. As a result, the tax benefit of position 2 qualifies for recognition and should be measured, but the tax benefit of position 1 does not qualify for recognition. ■

Once the uncertain tax position is recognized, it must be measured. The intent is to show the largest amount of tax benefit that has a more than 50 percent chance of being realized upon ultimate settlement. To compute the amount of the benefit that results requires the use of probability analysis—see Appendix A of FIN 48 for various probability methodologies that can be applied.

EXAMPLE 39

Assume in Example 38 that Purple has determined the amounts and the probabilities of the possible estimated outcomes regarding tax position 2.

Possible Estimated Outcome	Individual Probability of Occurring (%)	Cumulative Probability of Occurring (%)
$200,000	10	10
150,000	25	35
100,000	35	70
50,000	30	100

Because $100,000 is the largest amount of benefit that has a greater than 50% likelihood of being realized upon ultimate settlement, Purple recognizes a financial statement benefit of $100,000 related to tax position 2. ■

FIN 48 also necessitates consideration of the interest and penalties that will be assessed under relevant tax law if the uncertain position taken is not successful. For financial statement purposes, interest begins to accrue at the same time as under applicable tax law.

Since FIN 48 is an interpretation of FAS 109, the results of its application are incorporated into the various components of the income tax accrual process. Thus, the current income tax expense amount as well as the balances of the deferred tax asset and liability accounts may be affected. FIN 48 requires several additional

---

[33]This result often occurs with self-constructed fixed assets.

[34]A frequent omission by the debtor when debt is forgiven.

[35]See Chapter 14, pages 14–3 and 14–15.

TAX *in the News*   **WILL THE IRS REQUEST FIN 48 WORKPAPERS?**

Compliance with FIN 48 requires taxpayers to substantiate uncertain tax positions. The records and documentation (FIN 48 workpapers) needed for this process likely will contain sensitive information regarding a firm's analysis of its tax positions. Taxpayers concerned about how aggressive the IRS will be in requesting FIN 48 workpapers have received some favorable news. The IRS's Chief Counsel recently concluded that FIN 48 workpapers are considered tax accrual workpapers (TAWs) [GLAM 2007-0012 (3/22/07)]. Currently, the IRS practices a "policy of restraint" when it comes to requesting TAWs from taxpayers. Under this policy, the IRS limits its requests for TAWs to situations involving listed transactions (as defined under Regulation § 1.6011–4) or in unusual circumstances and where factual data required to support the return are not in the taxpayer's records. Though a policy of restraint is music to the ears of taxpayers, the song may be short lived. A more recent IRS memorandum instructed examiners to scrutinize tax footnotes and other FIN 48 disclosures in financial statements to garner information about questionable tax positions. Further, the IRS indicates that it is reviewing its TAW policy to "ensure that it is still appropriate in today's environment" [LMSB-04-0507-044(5/10/07)].

qualitative and quantitative disclosures. One is a reconciliation of unrecognized tax benefits at the beginning and end of the period including any decreases due to settlements with tax authorities (or court actions) and lapse of the statute of limitations. Further, the entity must show the amount of unrecognized tax benefits that would have an impact on the effective tax rate if the benefits were recognized.

Like Schedule M–3, FIN 48 follows a trend toward increased scrutiny in accounting for income taxes. The additional transparency that results from disclosing uncertain tax positions will be of considerable assistance to taxing authorities in carrying out their audit function. In this regard, it may serve as a deterrent to aggressive tax planning procedures (e.g., use of tax shelters) and could even dampen more conservative approaches to tax deferral. In some cases, the threat of financial statement disclosure could compel some entities to prematurely settle pending tax disputes.

FIN 48 is intended to increase the comparability of financial statements by standardizing certain accounting practices. Its proper implementation, however, will require significant compliance effort and cost. Only time will tell whether the additional comparability that results warrants the expenditure involved.

Form 1120 Illustrated

To provide an example on the use of the corporate income tax return, a Form 1120 has been completed, for Swift Corporation (see below). Due to the $10 million test, Swift Corporation does not require the use of Schedule M–3.

Swift Corporation was formed on January 10, 1985, by James Brown and Martha Swift to sell men's clothing. Pertinent information regarding Swift is summarized as follows:

- The business address is 6210 Norman Street, Buffalo, TX 79330.
- The employer identification number is 75–3284680; the principal business activity code is 448110.
- James Brown and Martha Swift each own one-half of the outstanding common stock; no other class of stock is authorized. James Brown is president of the company, and Martha Swift is secretary-treasurer. Both are full-time employees of the corporation, and each receives a salary of $70,000. James's Social Security number is 299-50-2594; Martha's Social Security number is 400-40-6680.
- The corporation uses the accrual method of accounting and reports on a calendar basis. The specific chargeoff method is used in handling bad debt losses, and inventories are determined using the lower of cost or market method. For book and tax purposes, the straight-line method of depreciation is used.
- During 2007, the corporation distributed a cash dividend of $35,000. Selected portions of Swift's profit and loss statement reflect the following debits and credits:

Account	Debit	Credit
Gross sales		$1,040,000
Sales returns and allowances	$ 50,000	
Purchases	506,000	
Dividends received from stock investments in less-than-20%-owned U.S. corporations		60,000
Interest income		
State bonds	$ 9,000	
Certificates of deposit	11,000	20,000
Premiums on term life insurance policies on the lives of James Brown and Martha Swift; Swift Corporation is the designated beneficiary	8,000	
Salaries—officers	140,000	
Salaries—clerical and sales	100,000	
Taxes (state, local, and payroll)	35,000	
Repairs	20,000	
Interest expense		
Loan to purchase state bonds	$ 4,000	
Other business loans	10,000	14,000
Advertising	8,000	
Rental expense	24,000	
Depreciation	16,000	
Other deductions	21,000	

A comparative balance sheet for Swift Corporation reveals the following information:

Assets	January 1, 2007	December 31, 2007
Cash	$ 240,000	$ 163,850
Trade notes and accounts receivable	104,200	142,300
Inventories	300,000	356,000
Federal bonds	50,000	50,000
State bonds	100,000	100,000
Prepaid Federal tax	—	1,700
Stock investment	300,000	400,000
Buildings and other depreciable assets	120,000	120,000
Accumulated depreciation	(44,400)	(60,400)
Land	10,000	10,000
Other assets	1,800	1,000
Total assets	$1,181,600	$1,284,450
Liabilities and Equity		
Accounts payable	$ 150,000	$ 125,000
Other current liabilities	40,150	33,300
Mortgages	105,000	100,000
Capital stock	250,000	250,000
Retained earnings	636,450	776,150
Total liabilities and equity	$1,181,600	$1,284,450

Net income per books (before any income tax accrual) is $234,000. During 2007, Swift Corporation made estimated tax payments to the IRS of $61,000. Swift Corporation's Form 1120 for 2007 is reproduced on the following pages.

Form **1120**		**U.S. Corporation Income Tax Return**			OMB No. 1545-0123	
Department of the Treasury Internal Revenue Service		For calendar year 2007 or tax year beginning .... , 2007, ending .... , 20 .... ▶ See separate instructions.			**2007**	

A Check if:		Use IRS label. Otherwise, print or type.	Name	B Employer identification number	
1a Consolidated return (attach Form 851) .	☐		*Swift Corporation*	75 ┊ 3284680	
b Life/nonlife consolidated return .	☐		Number, street, and room or suite no. If a P.O. box, see instructions.	C Date incorporated	
2 Personal holding co. (attach Sch. PH) .	☐		*6210 Norman Street*	*1-10-85*	
3 Personal service corp. (see instructions) .	☐		City or town, state, and ZIP code *Buffalo, TX 79330*	D Total assets (see instructions)	
				$ *1,284,450*	*00*

4 Schedule M-3 attached ☐	**E** Check if: **(1)** ☐ Initial return **(2)** ☐ Final return **(3)** ☐ Name change **(4)** ☐ Address change

	1a	Gross receipts or sales	*1,040,000* ┊ *00*	**b** Less returns and allowances *50,000* ┊ *00* **c** Bal ▶	**1c**	*990,000*	*00*
	2	Cost of goods sold (Schedule A, line 8) .			**2**	*450,000*	*00*
	3	Gross profit. Subtract line 2 from line 1c			**3**	*540,000*	*00*
	4	Dividends (Schedule C, line 19) .			**4**	*60,000*	*00*
Income	**5**	Interest .			**5**	*11,000*	*00*
	6	Gross rents .			**6**		
	7	Gross royalties .			**7**		
	8	Capital gain net income (attach Schedule D (Form 1120)) .			**8**		
	9	Net gain or (loss) from Form 4797, Part II, line 17 (attach Form 4797)			**9**		
	10	Other income (see instructions—attach schedule) .			**10**		
	11	**Total income.** Add lines 3 through 10 . ▶			**11**	*611,000*	*00*

	12	Compensation of officers (Schedule E, line 4) .		**12**	*140,000*	*00*
	13	Salaries and wages (less employment credits) .		**13**	*100,000*	*00*
	14	Repairs and maintenance .		**14**	*20,000*	*00*
	15	Bad debts .		**15**		
	16	Rents .		**16**	*24,000*	*00*
Deductions (See instructions for limitations on deductions.)	**17**	Taxes and licenses .		**17**	*35,000*	*00*
	18	Interest .		**18**	*10,000*	*00*
	19	Charitable contributions .		**19**		
	20	Depreciation from Form 4562 not claimed on Schedule A or elsewhere on return (attach Form 4562) .		**20**	*16,000*	*00*
	21	Depletion .		**21**		
	22	Advertising .		**22**	*8,000*	*00*
	23	Pension, profit-sharing, etc., plans .		**23**		
	24	Employee benefit programs .		**24**		
	25	Domestic production activities deduction (attach Form 8903) .		**25**		
	26	Other deductions (attach schedule) .		**26**	*21,000*	*00*
	27	**Total deductions.** Add lines 12 through 26 . ▶		**27**	*374,000*	*00*
	28	Taxable income before net operating loss deduction and special deductions. Subtract line 27 from line 11		**28**	*237,000*	*00*
	29	**Less: a** Net operating loss deduction (see instructions). **29a**				
		b Special deductions (Schedule C, line 20) . **29b** *42,000* ┊ *00*		**29c**	*42,000*	*00*

	30	**Taxable income.** Subtract line 29c from line 28 (see instructions) .		**30**	*195,000*	*00*
	31	**Total tax** (Schedule J, line 10) .		**31**	*59,300*	*00*
Tax and Payments	**32 a**	2006 overpayment credited to 2007 . **32a**				
	b	2007 estimated tax payments . . **32b** *61,000* ┊ *00*				
	c	2007 refund applied for on Form 4466 **32c** ( ) **d** Bal ▶ **32d** *61,000* ┊ *00*				
	e	Tax deposited with Form 7004 . **32e**				
	f	Credits: **(1)** Form 2439_____ **(2)** Form 4136_____ **32f**		**32g**	*61,000*	*00*
	33	Estimated tax penalty (see instructions). Check if Form 2220 is attached . ▶ ☐		**33**		
	34	**Amount owed.** If line 32g is smaller than the total of lines 31 and 33, enter amount owed .		**34**		
	35	**Overpayment.** If line 32g is larger than the total of lines 31 and 33, enter amount overpaid . .		**35**	*1,700*	*00*
	36	Enter amount from line 35 you want: **Credited to 2008 estimated tax** ▶ **Refunded** ▶		**36**	*1,700*	*00*

Sign Here

Under penalties of perjury, I declare that I have examined this return, including accompanying schedules and statements, and to the best of my knowledge and belief, it is true, correct, and complete. Declaration of preparer (other than taxpayer) is based on all information of which preparer has any knowledge.

▶ _____ _____ ▶ _____

Signature of officer   Date   Title

May the IRS discuss this return with the preparer shown below (see instructions)? ☐ **Yes** ☐ **No**

Paid Preparer's Use Only	Preparer's signature ▶		Date	Check if self-employed ☐	Preparer's SSN or PTIN
	Firm's name (or yours if self-employed), address, and ZIP code ▶			EIN ┊	
				Phone no. ( )	

For Privacy Act and Paperwork Reduction Act Notice, see separate instructions.   Cat. No. 11450Q   Form **1120** (2007)

Form 1120 (2007)   Page **2**

Schedule A Cost of Goods Sold (see instructions)

1	Inventory at beginning of year	300,000
2	Purchases.	506,000
3	Cost of labor.	
4	Additional section 263A costs (attach schedule)	
5	Other costs (attach schedule).	
6	**Total.** Add lines 1 through 5	806,000
7	Inventory at end of year	356,000
8	**Cost of goods sold.** Subtract line 7 from line 6. Enter here and on page 1, line 2	450,000

9a Check all methods used for valuing closing inventory:

   (i) ☐ Cost

   (ii) ☒ Lower of cost or market

   (iii) ☐ Other (Specify method used and attach explanation.) ▶ --

  b Check if there was a writedown of subnormal goods . . . . ▶ ☐

  c Check if the LIFO inventory method was adopted this tax year for any goods (if checked, attach Form 970) . . . . . ▶ ☐

  d If the LIFO inventory method was used for this tax year, enter percentage (or amounts) of closing inventory computed under LIFO **9d**

  e If property is produced or acquired for resale, do the rules of section 263A apply to the corporation? . . . . ☐ Yes ☒ No

  f Was there any change in determining quantities, cost, or valuations between opening and closing inventory? If "Yes," attach explanation . . . . ☐ Yes ☒ No

Schedule C Dividends and Special Deductions (see instructions)

		(a) Dividends received	(b) %	(c) Special deductions (a) × (b)
1	Dividends from less-than-20%-owned domestic corporations (other than debt-financed stock) . . .	60,000	70	42,000
2	Dividends from 20%-or-more-owned domestic corporations (other than debt-financed stock) . . .		80	
3	Dividends on debt-financed stock of domestic and foreign corporations		see instructions	
4	Dividends on certain preferred stock of less-than-20%-owned public utilities . .		42	
5	Dividends on certain preferred stock of 20%-or-more-owned public utilities . . .		48	
6	Dividends from less-than-20%-owned foreign corporations and certain FSCs . .		70	
7	Dividends from 20%-or-more-owned foreign corporations and certain FSCs . . .		80	
8	Dividends from wholly owned foreign subsidiaries		100	
9	**Total.** Add lines 1 through 8. See instructions for limitation			42,000
10	Dividends from domestic corporations received by a small business investment company operating under the Small Business Investment Act of 1958 . . .		100	
11	Dividends from affiliated group members		100	
12	Dividends from certain FSCs		100	
13	Dividends from foreign corporations not included on lines 3, 6, 7, 8, 11, or 12 . .			
14	Income from controlled foreign corporations under subpart F (attach Form(s) 5471) .			
15	Foreign dividend gross-up			
16	IC-DISC and former DISC dividends not included on lines 1, 2, or 3			
17	Other dividends			
18	Deduction for dividends paid on certain preferred stock of public utilities			
19	**Total dividends.** Add lines 1 through 17. Enter here and on page 1, line 4 . . ▶	60,000		
20	**Total special deductions.** Add lines 9, 10, 11, 12, and 18. Enter here and on page 1, line 29b . . . . . ▶			42,000

Schedule E Compensation of Officers (see instructions for page 1, line 12)

Note: Complete Schedule E only if total receipts (line 1a plus lines 4 through 10 on page 1) are $500,000 or more.

	(a) Name of officer	(b) Social security number	(c) Percent of time devoted to business	(d) Common	(e) Preferred	(f) Amount of compensation
1	James Brown	299-50-2594	100 %	50 %	%	70,000
	Martha Swift	400-40-6680	100 %	50 %	%	70,000
			%	%	%	
			%	%	%	
			%	%	%	

2	Total compensation of officers	140,000
3	Compensation of officers claimed on Schedule A and elsewhere on return	
4	Subtract line 3 from line 2. Enter the result here and on page 1, line 12	140,000

Form **1120** (2007)

Form 1120 (2007)   Page **3**

Schedule J   Tax Computation (see instructions)

1	Check if the corporation is a member of a controlled group (attach Schedule O (Form 1120)) ▶ ☐		
2	Income tax. Check if a qualified personal service corporation (see instructions) ▶ ☐	2	59,300 00
3	Alternative minimum tax (attach Form 4626)	3	
4	Add lines 2 and 3	4	59,300 00
5a	Foreign tax credit (attach Form 1118)	5a	
b	Credits from Forms 5735 and 8834	5b	
c	General business credit. Check applicable box(es): ☐ Form 3800 ☐ Form 5884 ☐ Form 6478 ☐ Form 8835, Section B ☐ Form 8844 ☐ Form 8846	5c	
d	Credit for prior year minimum tax (attach Form 8827)	5d	
e	Bond credits from: ☐ Form 8860 ☐ Form 8912	5e	
6	**Total credits.** Add lines 5a through 5e	6	
7	Subtract line 6 from line 4	7	59,300 00
8	Personal holding company tax (attach Schedule PH (Form 1120))	8	
9	Other taxes. Check if from: ☐ Form 4255 ☐ Form 8611 ☐ Form 8697 ☐ Form 8866 ☐ Form 8902 ☐ Other (attach schedule)	9	
10	**Total tax.** Add lines 7 through 9. Enter here and on page 1, line 31	10	59,300 00

Schedule K   Other Information (see instructions)

		Yes	No
1	Check accounting method: **a** ☐ Cash **b** ☒ Accrual **c** ☐ Other (specify) ▶ _____		
2	See the instructions and enter the:		
a	Business activity code no. ▶ *448110*		
b	Business activity ▶ *Retail sales*		
c	Product or service ▶ *Men's clothing*		
3	At the end of the tax year, did the corporation own, directly or indirectly, 50% or more of the voting stock of a domestic corporation? (For rules of attribution, see section 267(c).)		X
	If "Yes," attach a schedule showing: (a) name and employer identification number (EIN), (b) percentage owned, and (c) taxable income or (loss) before NOL and special deduction of such corporation for the tax year ending with or within your tax year.		
4	Is the corporation a subsidiary in an affiliated group or a parent-subsidiary controlled group?		X
	If "Yes," enter name and EIN of the parent corporation ▶ _____		
5	At the end of the tax year, did any individual, partnership, corporation, estate, or trust own, directly or indirectly, 50% or more of the corporation's voting stock? (For rules of attribution, see section 267(c).)	X	
	If "Yes," attach a schedule showing name and identifying number. (Do not include any information already entered in 4 above.) Enter percentage owned ▶ _____		
6	During this tax year, did the corporation pay dividends (other than stock dividends and distributions in exchange for stock) in excess of the corporation's current and accumulated earnings and profits? (See sections 301 and 316.)		X
	If "Yes," file **Form 5452,** Corporate Report of Nondividend Distributions.		
	If this is a consolidated return, answer here for the parent corporation and on **Form 851,** Affiliations Schedule, for each subsidiary.		

		Yes	No
7	At any time during the tax year, did one foreign person own, directly or indirectly, at least 25% of (a) the total voting power of all classes of stock of the corporation entitled to vote or (b) the total value of all classes of stock of the corporation?		X
	If "Yes," enter: (a) Percentage owned ▶ _____ and (b) Owner's country ▶ _____		
c	The corporation may have to file **Form 5472,** Information Return of a 25% Foreign-Owned U.S. Corporation or a Foreign Corporation Engaged in a U.S. Trade or Business. Enter number of Forms 5472 attached ▶ _____		
8	Check this box if the corporation issued publicly offered debt instruments with original issue discount. ▶ ☐		
	If checked, the corporation may have to file **Form 8281,** Information Return for Publicly Offered Original Issue Discount Instruments.		
9	Enter the amount of tax-exempt interest received or accrued during the tax year ▶ $ *9,000*		
10	Enter the number of shareholders at the end of the tax year (if 100 or fewer) ▶ *2*		
11	If the corporation has an NOL for the tax year and is electing to forego the carryback period, check here ▶ ☐		
	If the corporation is filing a consolidated return, the statement required by Regulations section 1.1502-21(b)(3) must be attached or the election will not be valid.		
12	Enter the available NOL carryover from prior tax years (Do not reduce it by any deduction on line 29a.) ▶ $ _____		
13	Are the corporation's total receipts (line 1a plus lines 4 through 10 on page 1) for the tax year **and** its total assets at the end of the tax year less than $250,000?		X
	If "Yes," the corporation is not required to complete Schedules L, M-1, and M-2 on page 4. Instead, enter the total amount of cash distributions and the book value of property distributions (other than cash) made during the tax year. ▶ $ _____		

Form **1120** (2007)

Form 1120 (2007)   Page **4**

Schedule L	Balance Sheets per Books	Beginning of tax year		End of tax year	
	Assets	**(a)**	**(b)**	**(c)**	**(d)**
1	Cash		240,000		163,850
2a	Trade notes and accounts receivable .	104,200		142,300	
b	Less allowance for bad debts	( )	104,200	( )	142,300
3	Inventories		300,000		356,000
4	U.S. government obligations		50,000		50,000
5	Tax-exempt securities (see instructions) .		100,000		100,000
6	Other current assets (attach schedule) .				1,700
7	Loans to shareholders				
8	Mortgage and real estate loans . . .				
9	Other investments (attach schedule) . .		300,000		400,000
10a	Buildings and other depreciable assets .	120,000		120,000	
b	Less accumulated depreciation . . .	(44,400)	75,600	(60,400)	59,600
11a	Depletable assets				
b	Less accumulated depletion	( )		( )	
12	Land (net of any amortization) . . .		10,000		10,000
13a	Intangible assets (amortizable only) . .				
b	Less accumulated amortization . . .	( )		( )	
14	Other assets (attach schedule) . . .		1,800		1,000
15	Total assets		1,181,600		1,284,450
	Liabilities and Shareholders' Equity				
16	Accounts payable		150,000		125,000
17	Mortgages, notes, bonds payable in less than 1 year				
18	Other current liabilities (attach schedule) .		40,150		33,300
19	Loans from shareholders				
20	Mortgages, notes, bonds payable in 1 year or more		105,000		100,000
21	Other liabilities (attach schedule) . . .				
22	Capital stock: a Preferred stock . .				
	b Common stock . .	250,000	250,000	250,000	250,000
23	Additional paid-in capital				
24	Retained earnings—Appropriated (attach schedule)				
25	Retained earnings—Unappropriated . .		636,450		776,150
26	Adjustments to shareholders' equity (attach schedule)				
27	Less cost of treasury stock		( )		( )
28	Total liabilities and shareholders' equity .		1,181,600		1,284,450

Schedule M-1	Reconciliation of Income (Loss) per Books With Income per Return

Note: Schedule M-3 required instead of Schedule M-1 if total assets are $10 million or more—see instructions

1	Net income (loss) per books	174,700	7	Income recorded on books this year not included on this return (itemize):	
2	Federal income tax per books . . .	59,300		Tax-exempt interest $ 9,000	
3	Excess of capital losses over capital gains .			-----------------------------	
4	Income subject to tax not recorded on books this year (itemize): ------------------			-----------------------------	9,000
	-----------------------------------		8	Deductions on this return not charged against book income this year (itemize):	
5	Expenses recorded on books this year not deducted on this return (itemize):		a	Depreciation . . . $ ----------	
a	Depreciation . . . $ --------------		b	Charitable contributions $ ----------	
b	Charitable contributions $ --------------			-----------------------------	
c	Travel and entertainment $ --------------			-----------------------------	
	Prem.–life ins. $8,000; Int.– state bonds $4,000	12,000	9	Add lines 7 and 8	9,000
6	Add lines 1 through 5	246,000	10	Income (page 1, line 28)—line 6 less line 9	237,000

Schedule M-2	Analysis of Unappropriated Retained Earnings per Books (Line 25, Schedule L)

1	Balance at beginning of year	636,450	5	Distributions: a Cash	35,000
2	Net income (loss) per books	174,700		b Stock	
3	Other increases (itemize): -------------			c Property . . .	
	-----------------------------------		6	Other decreases (itemize): -----------	
			7	Add lines 5 and 6	35,000
4	Add lines 1, 2, and 3	811,150	8	Balance at end of year (line 4 less line 7)	776,150

Form **1120** (2007)

Although most of the entries on Form 1120 for Swift Corporation are self-explanatory, the following comments may be helpful:

- In order to arrive at the cost of goods sold amount (line 2 on page 1), Schedule A (page 2) must be completed.
- Reporting of dividends requires the completion of Schedule C (page 2). Gross dividends are shown on line 4 (page 1), and the dividends received deduction appears on line 29b (page 1). Separating the dividend from the deduction facilitates the application of the 80 percent and 70 percent of taxable income exception (which did not apply in Swift's case).
- Income tax liability is $59,300, computed as follows:

Tax on $100,000	$22,250
Tax on $95,000 at 39%	37,050
	$59,300

The result is transferred to line 2 of Schedule J and ultimately is listed on line 31 (page 1). Because the estimated tax payment of $61,000 is more than the tax liability of $59,300, Swift will receive a tax refund of $1,700.

- In completing Schedule M–1 (page 4), the net income per books (line 1) is net of the Federal income tax ($234,000 − $59,300). The left side of Schedule M–1 (lines 2–5) represents positive adjustments to net income per books. After the negative adjustments are made (line 9), the result is taxable income before NOLs and special deductions (line 28, page 1).
- In completing Schedule M–2 (page 4), the beginning retained earnings figure of $636,450 is added to the net income per books as entered on Schedule M–1 (line 1). The dividends distributed in the amount of $35,000 are entered on line 5 and subtracted to arrive at the ending balance in unappropriated retained earnings of $776,150.
- Because this example lacks certain details, supporting schedules that would be attached to Form 1120 have not been included. For example, a Form 4562 would be included to verify the depreciation deduction (line 20, page 1), and other deductions (line 26, page 1) would be supported by a schedule.

Consolidated Returns

Corporations that are members of a parent-subsidiary affiliated group may be able to file a consolidated income tax return for a taxable year. Consolidated returns are discussed in Chapter 8.

Corporate versus Noncorporate Forms of Business Organization

The decision to use the corporate form in conducting a trade or business must be weighed carefully. Besides the nontax considerations of the corporate form (limited liability, continuity of life, free transferability of interests, and centralized management), tax ramifications will play an important role in any such decision. Close attention should be paid to the following:

1. Operating as a regular corporate entity (C corporation) results in the imposition of the corporate income tax. Corporate taxable income will be taxed twice—once as earned by the corporation and again when distributed to the shareholders. Since dividends are not deductible, a closely held corporation may have a strong incentive to structure corporate distributions in a

LO.8
Evaluate corporations as an entity form for conducting a business.

TAX PLANNING
Considerations

deductible form. Before JGTRRA lowered the rate on qualified dividends to 15 percent, shareholders had a tax incentive to bail out profits in the form of salaries, interest, or rent.[36] With the 15 percent rate on qualified dividends, shareholders may save taxes by having the corporation pay dividends rather than salaries, rent, or interest, which could be taxed at an individual marginal rate as high as 35 percent. The decision should be made only after comparing the tax cost of the two alternatives. The window of opportunity for reaping the benefit of the preferential tax rate on dividend income is set to close by 2011, however, and this must be considered in the analysis.

2. The differences in Federal tax brackets between an individual and a corporation may not be substantial. Furthermore, several state and local governments impose higher taxes on corporations than on individuals. In these jurisdictions, the combined Federal, state, and local tax rates on the two types of taxpayers are practically identical. Consequently, the tax ramifications of incorporating can be determined *only* on a case-by-case basis.

3. Corporate-source income loses its identity as it passes through the corporation to the shareholders. Thus, items that normally receive preferential tax treatment (e.g., interest on municipal bonds) are not taxed as such to the shareholders.

4. As noted in Chapter 5, it may be difficult for shareholders to recover some or all of their investment in the corporation without an ordinary income result. Most corporate distributions are treated as dividends to the extent of the corporation's earnings and profits. However, with the 15 percent rate on qualified dividends, dividends are taxed at the same rate as net capital gains.

5. Corporate losses cannot be passed through to the shareholders.[37]

6. The liquidation of a corporation will normally generate tax consequences to both the corporation and its shareholders (see Chapter 6).

7. The corporate form provides shareholders with the opportunity to be treated as employees for tax purposes if the shareholders render services to the corporation. Such status makes a number of attractive tax-sheltered fringe benefits available. They include, but are not limited to, group term life insurance and excludible meals and lodging. One of the most attractive benefits of incorporation is the ability of the business to provide accident and health insurance to its employees, including shareholders. Such benefits are not included in the employee's gross income. Similar rules apply to other medical costs paid by the employer. These benefits are not available to partners and sole proprietors.

Operating the Corporation

Tax planning to reduce corporate income taxes should occur before the end of the tax year. Effective planning can cause income to be shifted to the next tax year and can produce large deductions by incurring expenses before year-end. Particular attention should be focused on the following.

Charitable Contributions. Recall that accrual basis corporations may claim a deduction for charitable contributions in the year preceding payment. The contribution must be authorized by the board of directors by the end of the tax year and paid on or before the fifteenth day of the third month of the following year. It might be useful to authorize a contribution even though it may not ultimately be made. A deduction cannot be thrown back to the previous year (even if paid within the two and one-half months) if it has not been authorized.

---

[36]Such procedures lead to a multitude of problems, one of which, the reclassification of debt as equity, is discussed in Chapter 4. The problems of unreasonable salaries and rents are covered in Chapter 5 in the discussion of constructive dividends.

[37]Points 1, 2, and 5 could be resolved through a Subchapter S election (see Chapter 12), assuming the corporation qualifies for such an election. In part, the same can be said for point 3.

Timing of Capital Gains and Losses. A corporation should consider offsetting profits on the sale of capital assets by selling some of the depreciated securities in the corporate portfolio. In addition, any already realized capital losses should be carefully monitored. Recall that corporate taxpayers are not permitted to claim any net capital losses as deductions against ordinary income. Capital losses can be used only as an offset against capital gains. Further, net capital losses can only be carried back three years and forward five. Gains from the sales of capital assets should be timed to offset any capital losses. The expiration of the carryover period for any net capital losses should be watched carefully so that sales of appreciated capital assets occur before that date.

Net Operating Losses. In some situations, electing to forgo an NOL carryback and utilizing the carryforward option may generate greater tax savings.

EXAMPLE 40

Ruby Corporation incurred a $50,000 NOL in 2008. Ruby, which was in the 15% bracket in 2006 and 2007, has developed a new product that management predicts will push the corporation into the 34% bracket in 2009. If Ruby carries the NOL back, the tax savings will be $7,500 ($50,000 × 15%). However, if Ruby elects to carry the NOL forward, assuming management's prediction is accurate, the tax savings will be $17,000 ($50,000 × 34%). ■

When deciding whether to forgo the carryback option, several factors should be considered. First, the time value of the tax refund that is lost by not using the carryback procedure should be calculated. Second, the election to forgo an NOL carryback is irrevocable. Thus, one cannot later choose to change if the predicted high profits do not materialize. Third, consider the future increases (or decreases) in corporate income tax rates that can reasonably be anticipated. This last consideration is the most difficult to work with. Although corporate tax rates have remained relatively stable in recent years, taxpayers have little assurance that future rates will remain constant.

Dividends Received Deduction. The dividends received deduction normally is limited to the lesser of 70 percent of the qualifying dividends or 70 percent of taxable income. The deduction limits are raised to 80 percent for a dividend received from a corporation in which the recipient owns 20 percent or more of the stock. An exception to the taxable income limitation is made when the full deduction yields an NOL. In close situations, therefore, the proper timing of income or deductions to generate an NOL may yield a larger dividends received deduction.

Organizational Expenditures. To qualify for the 180-month amortization procedure of § 248, only organizational expenditures incurred in the first taxable year of the corporation can be considered. This rule could prove to be an unfortunate trap for corporations formed late in the year.

EXAMPLE 41

Thrush Corporation is formed in December 2008. Qualified organizational expenditures are incurred as follows: $62,000 in December 2008 and $30,000 in January 2009. If Thrush uses the calendar year for tax purposes, only $62,000 of the organizational expenditures can be written off over a period of 180 months. ■

The solution to the problem posed by Example 41 is for Thrush Corporation to adopt a fiscal year that ends on or beyond January 31. All organizational expenditures will then have been incurred before the close of the first taxable year.

Shareholder-Employee Payment of Corporate Expenses. In a closely held corporate setting, shareholder-employees often pay corporate expenses (e.g., travel and entertainment) for which they are not reimbursed by the corporation. The IRS often disallows the deduction of these expenses by the shareholder-employee, since the payments are voluntary on his or her part. If the deduction is more beneficial at the shareholder-employee level, a corporate policy against reimbursement of such expenses should be established. Proper planning in this regard would be to decide before the beginning of each tax year where the deduction would do the most good. Corporate policy on reimbursement of such expenses could be modified on a year-to-year basis depending upon the circumstances.

In deciding whether corporate expenses should be kept at the corporate level or shifted to the shareholder-employee, the treatment of unreimbursed employee expenses must be considered. First, since employee expenses are itemized deductions, they will be of no benefit to the taxpayer who chooses the standard deduction option. Second, these expenses will be subject to the 2 percent-of-AGI floor. No such limitation will be imposed if the corporation claims the expenses.

CONCEPT SUMMARY 2–1

Income Taxation of Individuals and Corporations Compared

	Individuals	Corporations
Computation of gross income	§ 61.	§ 61.
Computation of taxable income	§§ 62, 63 (b) through (h).	§ 63 (a). Concept of AGI has no relevance.
Deductions	Trade or business (§ 162); nonbusiness (§ 212); some personal and employee expenses (generally deductible as itemized deductions).	Trade or business (§ 162).
Charitable contributions	Limited in any tax year to 50% of AGI; 30% for long-term capital gain property unless election is made to reduce fair market value of gift.	Limited in any tax year to 10% of taxable income computed without regard to the charitable contribution deduction, NOL carryback, capital loss carryback, dividends received deduction, and domestic production activities deduction.
	Excess charitable contributions carried over for five years.	Same as for individuals.
	Amount of contribution is the fair market value of long-term capital gain property; ordinary income property is limited to adjusted basis; capital gain property is treated as ordinary income property if certain tangible personalty is donated to a nonuse charity or a private nonoperating foundation is the donee.	Same as for individuals, but exceptions allowed for certain inventory and for scientific property where one-half of the appreciation is allowed as a deduction.
	Time of deduction—year in which payment is made.	Time of deduction—year in which payment is made unless accrual basis taxpayer. Accrual basis corporation can take deduction in year preceding payment if contribution was authorized by board of directors by end of year and contribution is paid by fifteenth day of third month of following year.
Casualty losses	$100 floor on personal casualty and theft losses; personal casualty losses deductible only to extent losses exceed 10% of AGI.	Deductible in full.

Income Taxation of Individuals and Corporations Compared—Continued

	Individuals	Corporations
Net operating loss	Adjusted for several items, including nonbusiness deductions over nonbusiness income and personal exemptions.	Generally no adjustments.
	Carryback period is 2 years while carryforward period is 20 years.	Same as for individuals.
Dividends received deduction	None.	70%, 80%, or 100% of dividends received depending on percentage of ownership by corporate shareholder.
Net capital gains	Taxed in full. Tax rate generally cannot exceed 15% on net long-term capital gains.	Taxed in full.
Capital losses	Only $3,000 of capital loss per year can offset ordinary income; unused loss is carried forward indefinitely to offset capital gains or ordinary income up to $3,000; short-term and long-term carryovers retain their character.	Can offset only capital gains; unused loss is carried back three years and forward five; carryovers and carrybacks are characterized as short-term losses.
Passive losses	In general, passive activity losses cannot offset either active income or portfolio income.	Passive loss rules apply to closely held C corporations and personal service corporations.
		For personal service corporations, passive losses cannot offset either active income or portfolio income.
		For closely held C corporations, passive losses may offset active income but not portfolio income.
Domestic production activities deduction	Based on 6% of the lesser of qualified production activities income (QPAI) *or* modified AGI.	Based on 6% of the lesser of qualified production activities income (QPAI) *or* taxable income.
Tax rates	Progressive with six rates (10%, 15%, 25%, 28%, 33%, 35%).	Progressive with four rates (15%, 25%, 34%, 35%). Two lowest brackets phased out between $100,000 and $335,000 of taxable income, and additional tax imposed between $15,000,000 and $18,333,333 of taxable income.
Alternative minimum tax	Applied at a graduated rate schedule of 26% and 28%. Exemption allowed depending on filing status (e.g., $66,250 in 2007 for married filing jointly); phaseout begins when AMTI reaches a certain amount (e.g., $150,000 for married filing jointly).	Applied at a 20% rate on AMTI less exemption; $40,000 exemption allowed but phaseout begins when AMTI reaches $150,000; adjustments and tax preference items are similar to those applicable to individuals but also include 75% adjusted current earnings. Small corporations (gross receipts of $5 million or less) are not subject to AMT.

KEY TERMS

C corporations, 2–3	FIN 48, 2–27	Personal service corporations (PSCs), 2–10
Check-the-box Regulations, 2–8	Limited liability company (LLC), 2–7	Regular corporations, 2–3
Dividends received deduction, 2–16	Limited partnerships, 2–7	Related corporations, 2–21
Domestic production activities deduction, 2–15	Organizational expenditures, 2–19	S corporations, 2–3
FAS 109, 2–27	Passive loss, 2–12	Schedule M–1, 2–23
		Schedule M–3, 2–24

PROBLEM MATERIALS

DISCUSSION QUESTIONS

1. Jennifer and Jamie are starting a business and have asked you for advice about whether they should form a partnership, a corporation, or some other type of entity. Prepare a list of questions you would ask in helping them decide which type of entity they should choose. Explain your reasons for asking each of the questions.

2. Arnold owns 35% of the stock of Yellow Corporation (a C corporation), which earns $140,000 during 2008. He also owns a 35% interest in Pastel Partnership, which earns $140,000 during 2008. During 2008, Yellow does not pay any dividends, and Pastel does not make any distributions. Discuss Arnold's tax consequences as a result of the above information.

Decision Making

3. Art, an executive with Azure Corporation, plans to start a part-time business selling products on the Internet. He will devote about 15 hours each week to running the business. Art's salary from Azure places him in the 35% tax bracket. He projects substantial losses from the new business in each of the first three years and expects sizable profits thereafter. Art plans to leave the profits in the business for several years, sell the business, and retire. Would you advise Art to incorporate the business or operate it as a sole proprietorship?

4. Lucille owns a sole proprietorship, and Mabel is the sole shareholder of a C (regular) corporation. Each business sustained a $20,000 operating loss and a $7,000 capital loss for the year. How will these losses affect the taxable income of the two owners?

5. Conner is the sole owner of Service Enterprises (SE). SE earned net operating income of $120,000 during the year and had a long-term capital loss of $5,000. Conner withdrew $80,000 of the profit from SE. How should Conner report this information on his individual tax return for 2008 if SE is:
   a. A proprietorship?
   b. A C corporation?
   c. An S corporation?

Issue ID

6. Tanesha is the sole shareholder of Egret Corporation. Egret's sales have doubled in the last four years, and Tanesha has determined that the business needs a new warehouse. Tanesha has asked your advice as to whether she should (1) have the corporation acquire the warehouse or (2) acquire the warehouse herself and rent it to the corporation. What are the relevant tax issues that you will discuss with Tanesha?

7. Vivian, the sole shareholder of Dolphin Corporation, has the corporation pay her $400,000 in 2008. In addition to the $400,000, Vivian has other sources of income and is in the 35% tax bracket. Discuss the tax results for Vivian and Dolphin if the corporation:

   a.   Treats the $400,000 as salary.
   b.   Treats the $400,000 as a dividend.
   c.   Treats the $400,000 as salary and the IRS determines that $100,000 of that amount is unreasonable compensation.

8.   Al is a 25% shareholder and the president of ABC, Inc. The board of directors of ABC has decided to pay him an additional $20,000 for the year based on outstanding performance and will pay the $20,000 as a dividend. Jay is a 25% shareholder and the president of JKL, Inc. The board of directors of JKL has decided to pay him an additional $20,000 for the year based on outstanding performance and will pay the $20,000 as salary. Both Al and Jay are in the 35% bracket as individual taxpayers. Discuss how these payments will affect the tax liabilities of Al, Jay, and the corporations.

9.   Explain how limited liability companies (LLCs) are classified for Federal tax purposes.

10.   Erica has chosen to operate her new business as a single member LLC. Discuss the tax and nontax advantages of Erica's choice.

11.   C corporations generally can elect tax years that are different from those of their shareholders, but the use of a fiscal tax year is limited in some cases. Discuss these limitations.

12.   Which of the following C corporations will be allowed to use the cash method of accounting? Explain your answers.
   a.   Red Corporation, which had gross receipts of $4 million in 2005, $7 million in 2006, and $13 million in 2007.
   b.   White Corporation, which had gross receipts of $2 million in 2005, $4 million in 2006, and $6 million in 2007.

13.   Jeong, a cash basis taxpayer, is the sole shareholder of Porpoise, Inc., a calendar year, accrual basis C corporation. During 2008, she rented a warehouse that she owned to the corporation for $10,000 per month. Because Porpoise was short of cash, it did not pay rent for November and December. Instead it accrued $20,000 of rent expense on December 31, 2008. It plans to pay the rent to Jeong on April 1, 2009. In which year can Porpoise deduct the rent? When must Jeong report the rent income?

14.   A taxpayer recognized a net long-term capital gain of $10,000 for the current year. How is the gain treated if the taxpayer is a corporation? An individual?

15.   Kathy owns all of the stock in Eagle Corporation. During 2008, Kathy incurs a $25,000 long-term capital loss, and Eagle Corporation also incurs a $25,000 long-term capital loss. Compare the treatment of these transactions on the tax returns of Kathy and Eagle.

16.   Osprey Corporation, a closely held corporation, has $180,000 of active income, $108,000 of portfolio income, and a $270,000 loss from a passive activity.
   a.   How much of the passive loss can Osprey deduct if it is a personal service corporation (PSC)?
   b.   If it is not a PSC?

17.   Hummingbird Corporation, a closely held corporation that is not a PSC, has $70,000 of active income, $25,000 of portfolio income, and a $90,000 loss from a passive activity. How much of the passive loss can Hummingbird deduct?

18.   On December 30, 2008, Andrea, a sole proprietor, pledged to make a $20,000 charitable contribution on or before March 15, 2009. Aqua Corporation made a similar pledge on the same date, and the contribution was authorized by Aqua's board of directors. Assuming both contributions are made in January 2009, when can Andrea and Aqua Corporation, both calendar year taxpayers, deduct the contributions?

19.   Phoenix Corporation, a retailer of children's clothing, donates clothing to the Red Cross to be used to clothe poor children. Phoenix's charitable deduction for this gift will be limited to the corporation's basis in the inventory contributed. Assess the validity of this statement.

20.   The board of directors of Orange Corporation, a calendar year taxpayer, is holding its year-end meeting on December 28, 2008. One topic on the board's agenda is the

Issue ID

approval of a $25,000 gift to a qualified charitable organization. Orange has a $20,000 charitable contribution carryover to 2008 from a prior year. Identify the tax issues the board should consider regarding the proposed contribution.

21. For 2008, the domestic production activities deduction for a corporation is 6% of the taxpayer's qualified production activities income. Assess the validity of this statement.

Issue ID

22. Finch Corporation, organized in 2007, had profits in 2007 and 2008. In 2009, the corporation has a loss from operations, receives dividends from another corporation, and incurs a long-term capital loss. Identify the tax issues.

23. Marmot Corporation pays a dividend of $800,000 in 2008. Otter Corporation, which is in the 25% marginal bracket, owns 30% of Marmot's stock. Gerald, an individual taxpayer in the 25% marginal bracket, also owns 30% of Marmot's stock. Compare and contrast the treatment of the dividend by Otter Corporation and Gerald.

24. In connection with organizational expenditures, comment on the following:
    a. Those that qualify for amortization.
    b. Those that do not qualify for amortization.
    c. The period over which amortization can take place.
    d. Expenses incurred but not paid by a cash basis corporation.
    e. The special election that allows limited immediate expensing.
    f. The timing of the election to amortize.

25. Teal, Inc., a calendar year corporation, incorporates in January 2008 and incurs $12,000 of rent and payroll expense before it opens its store for business in March. How much, if any, of the $12,000 is deductible in 2008?

26. George is the sole shareholder of Palmetto Corporation, which has annual taxable income of approximately $75,000. He decides to form two new corporations and transfer one-third of the Palmetto assets to Poplar Corporation and one-third to Spruce Corporation. This will result in each of the three corporations having approximately $25,000 taxable income each year. George believes this plan will reduce overall corporate income taxes. Will George's plan work? Discuss.

27. Schedule M–1 of Form 1120 is used to reconcile financial net income with taxable income reported on the corporation's income tax return as follows: net income per books + additions − subtractions = taxable income. Classify the following items as additions or subtractions in the Schedule M–1 reconciliation.
    a. Charitable contributions carryover from previous year.
    b. Travel and entertainment expenses in excess of deductible limits.
    c. Book depreciation in excess of allowable tax depreciation.
    d. Federal income tax per books.
    e. Charitable contributions in excess of deductible limits.
    f. Premiums paid on life insurance policy on key employee.
    g. Proceeds of life insurance paid on death of key employee.
    h. Tax-exempt interest.
    i. Interest incurred to carry tax-exempt bonds.

28. For years ending after December 31, 2004, corporate taxpayers with total assets of $10 million or more are required to report much greater detail relative to differences between book and tax income (loss). What were the government's objectives in creating this reporting requirement?

29. Wolf Corporation owns a 40% interest in Fox Enterprises, a partnership. Fox has ordinary income and a short-term capital gain in 2008. In addition, Fox makes charitable contributions during the year. How are these items reported on Wolf's Schedule M–3?

30. Briefly discuss how deferred tax assets and liabilities arise under FAS 109.

31. The requirements of FIN 48 apply only to corporations having assets of $10 million or more. Assess the validity of this statement.

PROBLEMS

32. Emu Company, which was formed in 2008, had operating income of $100,000 and operating expenses of $80,000 in 2008. In addition, Emu had a long-term capital loss of $5,000. How does Andrew, the owner of Emu Company, report this information on his individual tax return under the following assumptions?
    a. Emu Company is a proprietorship, and Andrew does not withdraw any funds from Emu during the year.
    b. Emu Company is a C corporation and pays no dividends during the year.

33. Ellie and Linda are equal owners in Otter Enterprises, a calendar year business. During the year, Otter Enterprises has $500,000 of gross income and $300,000 of operating expenses. In addition, Otter sells assets that had been held as an investment for a long-term capital gain of $60,000 and makes distributions to Ellie and Linda of $40,000 each. Discuss the impact of this information on the taxable income of Otter, Ellie, and Linda if Otter is:
    a. A partnership.
    b. An S corporation.
    c. A C corporation.

34. Mesquite Corporation had a $150,000 net profit from operations in 2008 and paid Sheryl, its sole shareholder, a dividend of $108,250 ($150,000 net profit − $41,750 corporate tax). Sheryl has a large amount of income from other sources and is in the 35% marginal tax bracket. Would Sheryl's tax situation be better or worse if Mesquite Corporation were a proprietorship and Sheryl withdrew $108,250 from the business during the year?

35. Chris owns 100% of Orange Company, which had an NOL of $150,000 ($400,000 operating income − $550,000 operating expenses) in 2008. Chris was a material participant in the activities of the business during the year. Orange Company also had a long-term capital loss of $20,000. Chris has sufficient income from other activities to be in the 35% marginal tax bracket before considering results from Orange Company. He has no recognized capital gains in 2008. Explain the tax treatment if Orange Company is:
    a. A corporation.
    b. An LLC.

36. Johnson Company had revenue of $200,000 and incurred business expenses of $110,000 in 2008. Ed Johnson, owner of the company, is single and has no dependents. He uses the $5,450 standard deduction in computing taxable income for 2008. The personal exemption amount for 2008 is $3,500. Johnson Company is Ed's only source of income. Compute Ed's after-tax income if:
    a. Johnson Company is a sole proprietorship, and Ed withdraws $70,000 for living expenses during the year.
    b. Johnson Company is a corporation, Ed is the sole shareholder, and the corporation pays out all of its after-tax income as a dividend to Ed.
    c. Johnson Company is a corporation, Ed is the sole shareholder, and the corporation pays Ed a salary of $71,150. Assume this will increase the corporation's business expenses to $181,150.

37. Wilson Enterprises, a calendar year taxpayer, suffers a casualty loss of $112,500. How much of the casualty loss will be a tax deduction to Wilson under the following circumstances?
    a. Wilson is an individual proprietor and has AGI of $165,000. The casualty loss was a personal loss, and the insurance recovered was $45,000.
    b. Wilson is a corporation, and the insurance recovered was $45,000.

38. Benton Company (BC) has one owner, who is in the 35% Federal income tax bracket. BC's gross income is $200,000, and its ordinary trade or business deductions are $97,000. Compute the tax liability on BC's income for 2008 under the following assumptions:

Decision Making

Communications

a. BC is operated as a proprietorship, and the owner withdraws $70,000 for personal use.

b. BC is operated as a corporation, pays out $70,000 as salary, and pays no dividends to its shareholder.

c. BC is operated as a corporation and pays out no salary or dividends to its shareholder.

d. BC is operated as a corporation, pays out $70,000 as salary, and pays out the remainder of its earnings as dividends.

e. Assume Robert Benton of 1121 Monroe Street, Ironton, OH 45638 is the owner of BC, which was operated as a proprietorship in 2008. Robert is thinking about incorporating the business in 2009 and asks your advice. He expects about the same amounts of income and expenses in 2009 and plans to take $70,000 per year out of the company whether he incorporates or not. Write a letter to Robert [based on your analysis in (a) and (b) above] containing your recommendations.

39. Herbert, a physician, is the sole shareholder of Dove Corporation, a professional association. The corporation paid Herbert a salary of $240,000 during its fiscal year ending September 30, 2008.

a. How much salary must Dove Corporation pay Herbert during the period October 1 through December 31, 2008, to permit the corporation to continue to use its fiscal year without negative tax effects?

b. Dove Corporation had net profit of $70,000 for the year ending September 30, 2008. Compute the corporation's tax liability for the year.

40. Pelican Corporation, a calendar year taxpayer, has two unrelated, cash method shareholders: Charles owns 55% of the stock, and Lucinda owns the remaining 45%. As executives of Pelican, Charles and Lucinda each receive a year-end bonus that is based on the profitability of the corporation. The bonuses for 2008 amount to $100,000 for Charles and $110,000 for Lucinda. The bonuses are paid to both individuals on January 30, 2009. How much of the $210,000 of bonuses is deductible by Pelican in 2008 if the corporation is:

a. A cash method taxpayer?

b. An accrual method taxpayer?

41. Ramona Chadwick owns 100% of Violet Company. In 2008, Violet recognizes a long-term capital gain of $100,000 and no other income (or loss). Ramona is in the 35% tax bracket and has no recognized capital gains (or losses) before considering her ownership interest in Violet. How much 2008 income tax results from the $100,000 long-term capital gain if Violet is:

a. A corporation?

b. A proprietorship?

42. During the year, Loon Corporation has the following transactions: $600,000 operating income, $525,000 operating expenses, $65,000 municipal bond interest, $45,000 long-term capital gain, and $78,000 short-term capital loss.

a. Compute Loon's taxable income for the year.

b. Assume the same facts except that Loon's long-term capital gain is $96,000 (instead of $45,000). Compute Loon's taxable income for the year.

43. In 2008, a business sells a capital asset, which it had held for two years, at a loss of $24,000. How much of the capital loss may be deducted in 2008, and how much is carried back or forward under the following circumstances?

a. The business was a sole proprietorship owned by Joe. Joe had a short-term capital gain of $9,000 in 2008 and a long-term capital gain of $6,000. Joe had ordinary net income from the proprietorship of $50,000.

b. The business is incorporated. The corporation had a short-term capital gain of $9,000 and a long-term capital gain of $6,000. Its ordinary net income from the business was $50,000.

44. During 2008, Gorilla Corporation has net short-term capital gains of $90,000, net long-term capital losses of $570,000, and taxable income from other sources of $1.5 million. Prior years' transactions included the following:

2004 Net short-term capital gains	$300,000
2005 Net long-term capital gains	120,000
2006 Net short-term capital gains	90,000
2007 Net long-term capital gains	210,000

   a. How are the capital gains and losses treated on Gorilla's 2008 tax return?
   b. Determine the amount of the 2008 capital loss that is carried back to each of the previous years.
   c. Compute the amount of capital loss carryover, if any, and indicate the years to which the loss may be carried.
   d. If Gorilla is a sole proprietorship, rather than a corporation, how would Leslie (the owner) report these transactions on her 2008 tax return?

45. In 2008, Condor Corporation, a closely held C corporation that is not a PSC, has $80,000 of active business income, $25,000 of portfolio income, and a $90,000 passive loss from a rental activity. How much of the passive loss can Condor deduct in 2008? Would your answer differ if Condor were a PSC?

46. In the current year, Robin Corporation, a computer manufacturer, contributes 100 laptop computers (fair market value of $70,000) to a qualified charitable organization. The computers were manufactured earlier this year by Robin at a cost of $30,000. Determine the amount of Robin Corporation's charitable deduction for each of the following situations. (Ignore the taxable income limitation.)
   a. The qualified organization is a local church that will sell the computers and use the proceeds for an addition to its day care facility.
   b. The qualified organization is a local university that will use the computers in its student computer lab.
   c. Assume the same facts as in (b), except that the computers are worth $100,000 on the date of the contribution.

47. Joseph Thompson is president and sole shareholder of Jay Corporation. In December 2008, Joe asks your advice regarding a charitable contribution he plans to have the corporation make to the University of Maine, a qualified public charity. Joe is considering the following alternatives as charitable contributions in December 2008:

Decision Making

Communications

	Fair Market Value
(1) Cash donation	$120,000
(2) Unimproved land held for six years ($20,000 basis)	120,000
(3) Maize Corporation stock held for eight months ($20,000 basis)	120,000
(4) Brown Corporation stock held for two years ($170,000 basis)	120,000

   Joe has asked you to help him decide which of these potential contributions will be most advantageous taxwise. Jay's taxable income is $3.5 million before considering the contribution. Rank the four alternatives and write a letter to Joe communicating your advice. The corporation's address is 1442 Main Street, Freeport, ME 04032.

48. Leopard, Inc., a calendar year C corporation, had the following income and expenses in 2008:

Income from operations	$500,000
Expenses from operations	240,000
Dividends received (less than 20% ownership)	30,000
Domestic production activities deduction	10,000
Charitable contribution	35,000

   a. What is Leopard's charitable deduction for 2008?
   b. What happens to the portion of the contribution that is not deductible in 2008?

49. Dan Simms is the president and sole shareholder of Simms Corporation, 1121 Madison Street, Seattle, WA 98121. Dan plans for the corporation to make a charitable contribution to the University of Washington, a qualified public charity. He will have the corporation donate Jaybird Corporation stock, held for five years, with a basis of $8,000 and a fair market value of $20,000. Dan projects a $200,000 net profit for Simms Corporation in 2008 and a $100,000 net profit in 2009. Dan calls you on December 1, 2008, and asks whether he should make the contribution in 2008 or 2009. Write a letter advising Dan about the timing of the contribution.

50. Cheetah, Inc., a calendar year C corporation, manufactures kitchen cabinets. For 2008, Cheetah had taxable income of $600,000, qualified production activities income of $750,000, and W–2 wages of $75,000.
    a. How much is Cheetah's domestic production activities deduction for 2008?
    b. Assume the same amounts for 2010. How much is Cheetah's domestic production activities deduction for 2010?

51. During the year, Ruby Corporation, a calendar year taxpayer, has the following transactions:

Income from operations	$400,000
Expenses from operations	540,000
Dividends (less than 20% ownership)	80,000

    a. Determine Ruby's NOL for the year.
    b. What are Ruby's options as to the carryover of the NOL?

52. In each of the following independent situations, determine the dividends received deduction. Assume that none of the corporate shareholders owns 20% or more of the stock in the corporations paying the dividends.

	Green Corporation	Orange Corporation	Yellow Corporation
Income from operations	$ 700,000	$ 800,000	$ 700,000
Expenses from operations	(600,000)	(900,000)	(740,000)
Qualifying dividends	100,000	200,000	200,000

53. Owl Corporation was formed on December 1, 2008. Qualifying organizational expenses were incurred and paid as follows:

Incurred and paid in December 2008	$12,000
Incurred in December 2008 but paid in January 2009	6,000
Incurred and paid in February 2009	3,600

    Assuming that Owl Corporation makes a timely election under § 248 to expense and amortize organizational expenditures, what amount may be deducted in the corporation's first tax year under each of the following assumptions?
    a. Owl Corporation adopts a calendar year and the cash basis of accounting for tax purposes.
    b. Same as (a), except that Owl Corporation chooses a fiscal year of December 1– November 30.
    c. Owl Corporation adopts a calendar year and the accrual basis of accounting for tax purposes.
    d. Same as (c), except that Owl Corporation chooses a fiscal year of December 1– November 30.

54. Hummingbird Corporation, an accrual basis taxpayer, was formed and began operations on July 1, 2008. The following expenses were incurred during the first tax year (July 1 to December 31, 2008) of operations:

Expenses of temporary directors and of organizational meetings	$14,000
Fee paid to the state of incorporation	2,000
Accounting services incident to organization	10,000
Legal services for drafting the corporate charter and bylaws	27,000
Expenses incident to the printing and sale of stock certificates	16,000
	$69,000

Assume Hummingbird Corporation makes an appropriate and timely election under § 248 and the related Regulations. What is the maximum organizational expense Hummingbird may write off for tax year 2008?

55. In each of the following independent situations, determine the corporation's income tax liability. Assume that all corporations use a calendar year for tax purposes and that the tax year involved is 2008.

	Taxable Income
Purple Corporation	$ 48,000
Azul Corporation	320,000
Pink Corporation	335,000
Turquoise Corporation	6,700,000
Teal Corporation	22,600,000

56. The following information for 2008 relates to Pine Corporation, a calendar year, accrual method taxpayer. You are to determine the amount of Pine's taxable income for the year using this information. You may use Schedule M–1, which is available on the IRS Web site.

Net income per books (after-tax)	$209,710
Federal income tax expense	30,050
Interest income from tax-exempt bonds	32,000
Interest paid on loan incurred to purchase tax-exempt bonds	2,650
Life insurance proceeds received as a result of death of corporation president	100,000
Premiums paid on policy on the life of corporation president	4,040
Excess of capital losses over capital gains	5,550

57. The following information for 2008 relates to Sparrow Corporation, a calendar year, accrual method taxpayer.

Net income per books (after-tax)	$134,700
Federal income tax liability	59,300
Tax-exempt interest income	6,000
MACRS depreciation in excess of straight-line depreciation used for financial purposes	8,000
Charitable contribution in excess of taxable income limitation	7,000
Premiums paid on life insurance policy on the president (Sparrow is beneficiary of policy)	5,000
Interest on loan to purchase tax-exempt bonds	3,000

Based on the above information, use Schedule M–1 of Form 1120, which is available on the IRS Web site, to determine Sparrow's taxable income for 2008.

58. Pro Golf Warehouse, Inc. (PGW), sells golf equipment throughout the United States. PGW also sells golf equipment in Canada through its subsidiary, Canadian Golf Warehouse (CGW), which is organized as a Canadian corporation. In addition, PGW has an American subsidiary, Tennis Supplies, Inc. (TSI). PGW includes income (loss) from both subsidiaries on its audited financial statements, which show net income of $97 million in 2008. CGW, which is not consolidated by PGW for U.S. tax purposes, had

net income of $31 million. TSI, which is consolidated for U.S. tax purposes, had a loss of $16 million. How is this information reported on Schedule M–3?

59. PGW (refer to Problem 58) also owns an interest in a U.S. partnership, Pro Practice Ranges (PPR). On its audited financial statements, PGW reported net income of $4.5 million as its distributive share from PPR. PGW's Schedule K–1 from PPR reflects the following amounts:

Ordinary income	$3,500,000
Section 179 expense	100,000
Charitable contributions	1,000,000
Long-term capital gain	1,500,000

How is this information reported on Schedule M–3?

60. PGW acquired intellectual property in 2008 and deducted amortization of $35,000 on its financial statements, which were prepared according to GAAP. For Federal income tax purposes, PGW deducted $65,000. How is this information reported on Schedule M–3?

61. In January 2008, PGW established an allowance for uncollectible accounts (bad debt reserve) of $90,000 on its books and increased the allowance by $125,000 during the year. As a result of a client's bankruptcy, PGW decreased the allowance by $60,000 in November 2008. PGW deducted the $215,000 of increases to the allowance on its 2008 income statement but was not allowed to deduct that amount on its tax return. On its 2008 tax return, the corporation was allowed to deduct the $60,000 actual loss sustained because of its client's bankruptcy. On its financial statements, PGW treated the $215,000 increase in the bad debt reserve as an expense that gave rise to a temporary difference. On its 2008 tax return, PGW took a $60,000 deduction for bad debt expense. How is this information reported on Schedule M–3?

62. In the current year, Concord Corporation identifies one tax position, with a related tax benefit of $150,000, which requires the application of FIN 48. In applying the recognition criterion of FIN 48, Concord has determined that this tax position has a 60% probability of being sustained on examination. Concord has determined the amounts and the probabilities of the possible estimated outcomes regarding the tax position as follows.

Possible Estimated Outcome	Individual Probability of Occurring (%)	Cumulative Probability of Occurring (%)
$150,000	20	20
100,000	25	45
75,000	30	75
25,000	25	100

Based on the above information, should Concord recognize a financial statement benefit for the tax position, and, if so, how much is the recognized benefit?

Issue ID

63. In January, Don and Steve each invested $100,000 cash to form a corporation to conduct business as a retail golf equipment store. On January 3, they paid Bill, an attorney, to draft the corporate charter, file the necessary forms with the state, and write the bylaws. They leased a store building and began to acquire inventory, furniture, display equipment, and office equipment in February. They hired a sales staff and clerical personnel in March and conducted training sessions during the month. They had a successful opening on April 1, and sales increased steadily throughout the summer. The weather turned cold in October, and all local golf courses closed by October 15, which resulted in a drastic decline in sales. Don and Steve expect business to be very good during the Christmas season and then to taper off significantly from January 1 through the end of February. The corporation accrued bonuses to Don and Steve on December 31, payable on April 15 of the following year. The corporation made timely estimated tax payments throughout the year. The corporation hired a bookkeeper in February, but he does not know much about taxation. Don and Steve have retained you as a tax consultant and have asked you to identify the tax issues that they should consider.

TAX RETURN PROBLEMS

1. Timothy Patton and Ann Terry each own 50% of the common stock of Builder's Software, Inc. (BSI). No other class of stock is authorized. On January 4, 1999, they formed BSI to develop and market accounting software for construction entities. Pertinent information regarding BSI is summarized as follows:

    *   BSI's business address is 1600 Chicago Avenue, Minneapolis, MN 55404; its telephone number is (612) 555-1217; and its e-mail address is bsi@bsi.com.
    *   The employer identification number is 54–3044456, and the principal business activity code is 541519.
    *   Timothy is president of the company, and Ann is vice president.
    *   Both Timothy and Ann are full-time employees of BSI. Timothy's Social Security number is 527–22–1111, and Ann's Social Security number is 431–55–4224.
    *   BSI is an accrual method, calendar year taxpayer. Inventories are determined using FIFO and the lower of cost or market method. BSI uses the straight-line method of depreciation for both book and tax purposes.
    *   During 2007, the corporation distributed cash dividends of $50,000.
    *   The domestic production activities deduction for 2007 is $4,698. You are not provided enough detailed data to complete a Form 8903 (domestic production activities deduction). If you solve this problem using TaxCut, enter the amount of the DPAD on line 25 of Form 1120.

    BSI's financial statements for 2007 are shown below.

Income Statement

Operating Income

Gross sales		$1,526,000
Sales returns and allowances		(43,110)
Net sales		$1,482,890
Cost of goods sold		
Beginning inventory	$221,000	
Cost of labor	121,000	
Additional § 263A costs	186,600	
Other costs	135,320	
Cost of goods available for sale	$663,920	
Ending inventory	(118,320)	(545,600)
Gross profit from operations		$937,290

Operating Expenses

Salaries—officers:		
Timothy Patton	$120,000	
Ann Terry	120,000	$240,000
Salaries—clerical and sales		226,190
Taxes:		
Property	$ 22,869	
Payroll	52,239	
State income	11,796	
Other miscellaneous	11,642	98,546
Repairs and maintenance		24,816
Meals and entertainment		7,220
Travel		14,770
Charitable contributions		7,000
Fine paid to City of Minneapolis for building code violation		2,683

Operating Expenses

Interest expense on business loans	$12,068
Advertising	40,151
Rental expense	33,233
Depreciation*	41,948
Contributions to pension plans	38,587
Employee benefit programs	21,025
Accounting services	18,000
Dues and subscriptions	2,867
Insurance	24,321
Legal and professional services	9,199
Miscellaneous expenses	5,874
Telephone	3,248
Premiums on term life insurance policies on the lives of Timothy and Ann; BSI is the designated beneficiary	8,000

Total expenses	(879,746)
Net operating income	$ 57,544

Other Income

Dividends received from stock investments in less-than-20%-owned U.S. corporations		10,000
Interest income:		
State of Minnesota bonds	$ 4,037	
Certificates of deposit	3,462	7,499

Other Expense

Interest expense to purchase state bonds	(2,266)
Net income before Federal income taxes	$ 72,777
Federal income tax	(13,400)
Net income per books	$ 59,377

*You are not provided enough detailed data to complete a Form 4562 (depreciation). If you solve this problem using TaxCut, enter the amount of depreciation on line 20 of Form 1120.

Balance Sheet

Assets	January 1, 2007	December 31, 2007
Cash	$ 58,856	$ 55,889
Trade notes and accounts receivable	70,385	96,264
Inventories	221,000	118,320
State bonds	121,500	121,500
Certificates of deposit	60,075	60,880
Stock investment	146,198	146,198
Buildings and other depreciable assets	349,077	349,077
Accumulated depreciation	(79,925)	(121,873)
Land	125,550	168,580
Other assets	7,117	12,628
Total assets	1,079,833	$1,007,463

Liabilities and Equity	January 1, 2007	December 31, 2007
Accounts payable	$ 155,673	$ 129,047
Other current liabilities	53,436	38,664
Mortgages	220,114	179,765
Capital stock	125,000	125,000
Retained earnings	525,610	534,987
Total liabilities and equity	$1,079,833	$1,007,463

During 2007, BSI made estimated tax payments of $3,500 each quarter to the IRS. Prepare a Form 1120 for BSI for tax year 2007. Suggested software: TaxCut.

2. Tammy Adams and Fernando Hernandez each own 50% of Custom Designs, Inc. (CDI). No other class of stock is authorized. On May 6, 2003, they formed CDI to provide architectural services. Pertinent information regarding CDI is summarized as follows:

- CDI's business address is 2120 Adobe Drive, Las Cruces, NM 88011; its telephone number is (575) 541-1122; and its e-mail address is cdi@cdi.com.
- The employer identification number is 75–3392241, and the principal business activity code is 541310.
- Tammy is president of the company, and Fernando is vice president.
- Tammy and Fernando are the only full-time architects employed by CDI, and they perform all of the professional architectural services of the corporation. Tammy's Social Security number is 399–55–6543, and Fernando's Social Security number is 400–55–9876.
- CDI is a cash method, calendar year taxpayer. CDI uses the straight-line method of depreciation for both book and tax purposes. The corporation does not maintain any inventory.
- During 2007, the corporation distributed cash dividends of $20,000.
- The domestic production activities deduction for 2007 is $1,147. You are not provided enough detailed data to complete a Form 8903 (domestic production activities deduction). If you solve this problem using TaxCut, enter the amount of the DPAD on line 25 of Form 1120.

CDI's financial statements for 2007 are shown below.

Income Statement

Income		
Professional fees		$896,000
Interest income (certificates of deposit)		3,600
Total income		$899,600

Expenses		
Salaries—officers:		
Tammy Adams	$260,000	
Fernando Hernandez	260,000	$520,000
Salaries—clerical		42,000
Taxes:		
Property	26,810	
Payroll	28,280	
State income	3,140	
Other miscellaneous	7,390	65,620
Repairs and maintenance		16,340
Meals and entertainment		8,460
Travel		5,600
Charitable contributions		1,200
Interest expense on business loans		31,100

Expenses

Advertising	$23,250
Rental expense	14,650
Depreciation*	28,910
Contributions to pension plans	45,000
Employee benefit programs	21,170
Accounting services	12,500
Dues and subscriptions	5,100
Insurance	20,750
Legal and professional services	11,000
Miscellaneous expenses	4,360
Telephone	7,700

Total expenses	(884,710)
Net income before taxes	$ 14,890
Federal income tax	(6,291)
Net income per books	$ 8,599

*You are not provided enough detailed data to complete a Form 4562 (depreciation). If you solve this problem using TaxCut, enter the amount of depreciation on line 20 of Form 1120.

Balance Sheet

Assets	January 1, 2007	December 31, 2007
Cash	$ 21,610	$ 22,580
Trade notes and accounts receivable	41,100	33,300
Certificates of deposit	144,000	137,000
Buildings and other depreciable assets	210,922	221,488
Accumulated depreciation	(47,520)	(76,430)
Land	42,000	42,000
Other assets	3,638	2,490
Total assets	$415,750	$382,428

Liabilities and Equity	January 1, 2007	December 31, 2007
Accounts payable	$ 21,000	$ 16,036
Other current liabilities	17,110	11,853
Mortgages	126,000	114,300
Capital stock	200,000	200,000
Retained earnings	51,640	40,239
Total liabilities and equity	$415,750	$382,428

During 2007, CDI made estimated tax payments of $1,600 each quarter to the IRS. Prepare a Form 1120 for CDI for tax year 2007. Suggested software: TaxCut.

RESEARCH PROBLEMS

THOMSON

RIA

Communications

Note: Solutions to Research Problems can be prepared by using the **RIA Checkpoint® Student Edition** online research product, which is available to accompany this text. It is also possible to prepare solutions to the Research Problems by using tax research materials found in a standard tax library.

Research Problem 1. In 2004, Stephanie Contour formed a single-member LLC in the state of Florida through which she operated a business until November 2005. Stephanie did not elect, under the "check-the-box" Regulations, to have the LLC treated as a corporation for Federal tax purposes. Instead, Stephanie reported the income and deductions of the LLC on Schedule C of her Forms 1040 for 2004 and 2005. During the time the LLC was in existence, the business employed anywhere from three to seven individuals. However, neither the LLC nor Stephanie paid any employment taxes with respect to the employees. In the current year, the IRS assessed Stephanie for the unpaid employment taxes of $25,000 and placed a lien on her property. Stephanie believes the unpaid employment taxes are a liability of the LLC and that the Florida LLC law shields her from liabilities of the LLC. She has asked your assistance in responding to the employment tax assessment. Prepare a memo for the client file documenting the results of your research.

Research Problem 2. Jackal Corporation declared a dividend of $4 per share on September 15, 2005. The date of record was October 17 and the date of payment was October 24. The stock exchange on which the Jackal Corporation stock is traded set an ex-dividend date of October 24. On October 20, Coyote Corporation sold 1,000 shares of Jackal Corporation stock to Fox Corporation through the exchange for $75 per share. As required by exchange rules, Coyote signed an agreement that Fox was entitled to the dividend that was to be paid on October 24.

Coyote Corporation, which had paid $45 per share for the Jackal Corporation stock in 2003, reported a long-term gain of $30,000 [($75 − $45) × 1,000)] on its 2005 Federal tax return. Fox Corporation reported dividend income of $4,000 ($4 per share × 1,000 shares) and took a 70% dividends received deduction. Have Coyote Corporation and Fox Corporation reported these transactions properly?

Research Problem 3. Jared Hamilton, a singer/guitarist, travels around the country performing solo concerts on college campuses. He has two employees who make up his road crew. The road crew sets up his equipment and sells Hamilton memorabilia (CDs, T-shirts, posters, etc.) during intermissions and after the concerts. For the last several years, Hamilton has operated his business as Hamilton Entertainment, Inc. (HEI). HEI, a C corporation with Hamilton as the sole shareholder, has generated about 75% of its income from ticket sales and about 25% from memorabilia sales.

In January 2007, Hamilton sets up a second corporation, Hamilton Memorabilia, Inc. (HMI). The new corporation (HMI) handles all memorabilia sales, while HEI now handles only the concert arrangements and concert ticket sales. The two road crew employees continue to perform the same duties as before and continue to be paid by HEI. (HMI is billed for the salaries paid on its behalf.) Hamilton spends about 80% of his time on HEI activities and the remainder on HMI. He set up HMI in order to sell the memorabilia business and concentrate on his career as a performer.

Upon audit, the IRS advises Hamilton that the new arrangement causes HEI to be classified as a qualified personal service corporation. Write a memorandum to the files evaluating the merits of the position taken by the IRS.

Communications

Use the tax resources of the Internet to address the following questions. Do not restrict your search to the World Wide Web, but include a review of newsgroups and general reference materials, practitioner sites and resources, primary sources of the tax law, chat rooms and discussion groups, and other opportunities.

Internet
Activity

Research Problem 4. Using the Internet, refer to page 2 of the Instructions for Schedule M–3 (Form 1120) and answer the question posed by the following example:

A Corporation (U.S.) owns subsidiary corporations B (U.S.) and F (foreign). On its consolidated financial balance sheet with B and F, A Corporation reports assets of $12 million. On its consolidated U.S. Federal income tax return with B, A Corporation lists assets of $8 million.

Must a Schedule M–3 be completed and filed?

Research Problem 5. Download the forms used to compute a corporation's estimated tax payments and to transmit the payment to an approved bank. Complete the forms for a corporation that must make quarterly estimated payments of $11,000 this year.

Research Problem 6. To minimize the application of FIN 48, a taxpayer may seek an expedited resolution of uncertain tax positions from the IRS. Using only the Internet for your research, explain why an expedited resolution might be useful and how such a resolution is obtained from the IRS.

Corporations: Special Situations

LEARNING OBJECTIVES

After completing Chapter 3, you should be able to:

LO.1

Understand the reasons for the domestic production activities deduction (DPAD).

LO.2

Identify the components of the domestic production activities deduction (DPAD).

LO.3

Recognize and work with the different types of domestic production gross receipts (DPGR).

LO.4

Make the necessary adjustments to DPGR to arrive at qualified production activities income (QPAI).

LO.5

Cope with the collateral problems associated with the domestic production activities deduction (DPAD).

LO.6

Explain the reason for the alternative minimum tax.

LO.7

Calculate the alternative minimum tax applicable to corporations.

LO.8

Understand the function of adjusted current earnings (ACE).

LO.9

Evaluate the current status of the penalty taxes on corporate accumulations.

LO.10

Understand the accumulated earnings tax.

LO.11

Understand the personal holding company tax.

When a business is operated as a C corporation, situations are encountered that require the application of specialized tax rules. This chapter discusses these situations, which involve the following provisions of the tax law:

- The domestic production activities deduction (DPAD) of § 199.
- The alternative minimum tax (AMT) of § 55.
- The penalty taxes of § 531 and § 541.

The DPAD (also known as the "manufacturers' deduction") is not limited to C corporations and is available to other types of entities as well. Nevertheless, the DPAD is more apt to be found among corporations (either C or S types) than among individuals. The reason is that manufacturing activities require capital, which is easily raised through the use of a corporate entity. Moreover, the DPAD presents unique problems for C corporations, particularly when extended affiliated group members are involved.

Like the DPAD, the AMT is not limited to C corporations and applies to other types of entities as well. Fewer corporations may be subject to the AMT than to the DPAD, however, due to the exemption for small corporations. An ACE adjustment relates only to certain corporations and is not required of other taxpayers.

The penalty taxes of § 531 and § 541 are unique to C corporations. The taxes are characteristically imposed on closely held corporations that accumulate profits to avoid dividend distributions. As dividends are no longer fully taxed as ordinary income (before 2009), these penalty taxes can easily be avoided. Nevertheless, an awareness of their potential danger is necessary to preclude an inadvertent miscue. This awareness is particularly needed with the penalty tax on personal holding companies (i.e., § 541) since its imposition is not dependent on the existence of a tax avoidance motive.

LO.1

Understand the reasons for the domestic production activities deduction (DPAD).

Domestic Production Activities Deduction

To improve the balance of trade and mitigate the effect of its relatively high corporate tax rates, the United States has had a number of export incentives—the last of which was the extraterritorial income (ETI) regime. The ETI regime provided the benefit of an exclusion from income for certain foreign sales. Consequently, it is not surprising that the World Trade Organization found the ETI provisions to be an illegal export subsidy.

The American Jobs Creation Act of 2004 repealed the ETI exclusion but did not replace it with a comparable tax benefit for U.S. exporters. Instead, a new broad-based "domestic production activities deduction" for U.S. manufacturers was enacted.[1] Certain domestic producers can claim a deduction equal to 9 percent of **qualified production activities income (QPAI)** subject to several limitations. To curtail revenue loss, the deduction is phased in as follows: 3 percent for tax years

---

[1] Section 101 of the American Jobs Creation Act of 2004, as modified by § 513(b) of the Tax Increase Prevention and Reconciliation Act of 2005 (TIPRA).

| TABLE 3–1 | Maximum DPAD Savings for C Corporations (Years 2007–2009) |

Taxable Income Range	Marginal Tax Rate*	Maximum Tax Savings**
$1–$50,000	15%	$450
$50,001–$75,000	25%	$1,125
$75,001–$100,000	35%	$2,100
$100,001–$335,000	39%	$7,839
$335,001–$10,000,000	34%	$204,000
$10,000,001–$15,000,000	35%	$315,000
$15,000,001–$18,333,333	35%	$385,000
>$18,333,333	35%	>$385,000

*Assumptions: corporate tax rates remain the same for 2008 as in 2007, and the § 199 deduction does not reduce taxable income sufficiently to reduce the marginal tax rate.

**Taxable income × 0.06 × marginal tax rate.

Source: Adapted from S. C. Dilley and Fred Jacobs, "The Qualified Production Activities Deduction: Some Planning Tools," *Tax Notes*, July 4, 2005, p. 95.

beginning in 2005 or 2006, 6 percent for tax years beginning in 2007 to 2009, and 9 percent for tax years thereafter.[2] A fiscal year taxpayer was not eligible to claim the deduction until its tax year ended in 2006.

The domestic production activities deduction, as a replacement for ETI, no longer presents an "international tax" issue—the deduction does not require exporting or any other activity outside the United States. Also, the deduction is not limited to the taxpayers that benefited from the ETI provisions and provides benefits to more businesses than just those considered manufacturers. When fully phased in (at the 9% allowance amount), the deduction will reduce the corporate tax rate by about 3 percentage points.

There is an important limitation on the amount of the deduction. The **domestic production activities deduction (DPAD)** cannot exceed 50 percent of the **W–2 wages** paid by the taxpayer during the tax year. The purpose of this limitation is to preserve U.S. manufacturing jobs and discourage their outsourcing.

The deduction is available to a variety of taxpayers including individuals, partnerships, S corporations, cooperatives, estates, and trusts. For a pass-through entity (e.g., partnerships, S corporations), the deduction flows through to the individual owners. In the case of a sole proprietor, a deduction *for* adjusted gross income (AGI) results and is claimed on Form 1040, line 35, page 1. A Form 8903 must be attached to support the deduction. The Joint Committee on Taxation estimates that about 25 percent of the total benefit will accrue to 45,000 S corporations, 15,000 partnerships, and 50,000 sole proprietorships. Table 3–1 reflects the present savings that this provision will offer for C corporations.

The DPAD is designed to provide a tax benefit in a somewhat unique manner. Unlike other deductions, the DPAD does not result from a direct expenditure or other outlay. Instead, it is a deduction based on the net income earned from a specified source. A manufacturing concern, therefore, will determine its DPAD on the profit from the sale of the item produced, not on the cost of production. Thus, the DPAD is a deduction based on income!

Since the DPAD requires no additional outlay, the overall tax effect is similar to that of a rate reduction or a tax credit. The DPAD should not directly reduce earnings and profits, and FASB requires this benefit to be reported as a special charge (e.g., similar to a tax credit).[3]

---

[2]§ 199(a)(2).

[3]FASB Staff Position No. FAS 109-1. **http://www.fasb.org/fasb_staff_positions/ fsp_fas109-1.pdf.**

> **EXHIBIT 3–1** **Some Common § 199 Acronyms**
>
> CGS = cost of goods sold
> DPAD = domestic production activities deduction
> DPGR = domestic production gross receipts
> EAG = expanded affiliated group
> MPGE = manufactured, produced, grown, or extracted
> QPAI = qualified production activities income
> QPP = qualified production property
> TPP = tangible personal property

The DPAD rules introduce a number of terms and related acronyms. To help clarify the discussion that follows, Exhibit 3–1 lists some of the more common acronyms found in § 199.

LO.2

Identify the components of the domestic production activities deduction (DPAD).

important

Components of the Deduction

The domestic production activities deduction (DPAD) is based on the following formula in 2008–2009.[4]

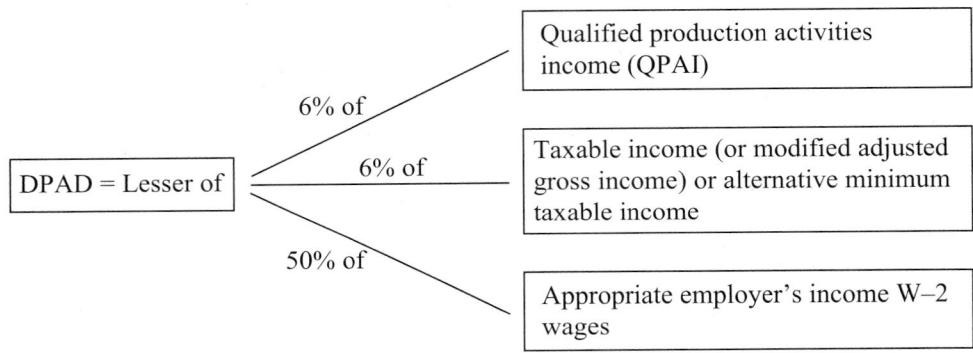

Taxable income is determined without regard to the DPAD. In the case of an individual (sole proprietor or an owner of a flow-through entity), modified AGI is substituted for taxable income.[5]

The taxable income limitation is determined after the application of any net operating loss (NOL) deduction for the tax year. Thus, a company with an NOL carryforward for a tax year is ineligible for the DPAD if such carryforward eliminates current taxable income. Further, a taxpayer may lose part or all of the DPAD benefit if there is an NOL carryback for that year. As taxable income is reduced by the NOL carryback, there is a corresponding reduction in the DPAD. If QPAI cannot be used in a particular year due to the taxable income limitation (see the above formula), it is lost forever.

EXAMPLE 1

Opal, Inc., manufactures and sells costume jewelry. It also sells costume jewelry purchased from other manufacturers. During 2008, Opal had a *profit* of $200,000 (QPAI) from the sale of its own manufactured jewelry and a *loss* of $50,000 from the sale of the purchased jewelry. Based on this information, Opal's QPAI is $200,000, and its taxable income (TI) is $150,000 ($200,000 − $50,000). Opal's DPAD becomes $9,000 [6% of the lesser of $200,000 (QPAI) or $150,000 (TI)]. ■

---

[4]The 6% rate becomes 9% after 2009.
[5]§ 199(d)(2). Modified AGI means AGI without any DPAD allowance and
determined in accordance with the instructions to Form 8903.

WHY CAN'T THE UNITED STATES LEARN FROM OTHERS?

Congress enacted the domestic production activities deduction in 2004 as part of the American Jobs Creation Act. In a somewhat novel approach to providing a tax benefit, a deduction is allowed based on the profit derived from certain activities. For the most part, the activities that qualify must involve production, processing, or manufacturing. Profit from performance of services generally will not qualify for the deduction.

Although a producers' deduction is new to the United States, it is not a stranger elsewhere. Canada wrestled with a similar provision for over two decades and recently scrapped it as being too controversial. During its existence, taxpayers' efforts to qualify for the deduction led to some bizarre situations. A ski resort claimed that it qualified because it manufactured artificial snow when the weather failed to cooperate. A radiologist claimed he was "processing" X-rays in reaching a diagnosis. The *coup de grâce* came when Burger King successfully contended that the assembling of salads and the broiling of burgers constituted "manufacturing."

Is there any reason to believe that the U.S. experiment with a producers' deduction will not result in the same fanciful and creative manipulation that characterized the Canadian version? To say that the new producers' deduction will not be manipulated is to underestimate the imagination and resourcefulness of the U.S. taxpayer.

Perhaps Congress should have paid more attention to the experience of our neighbor to the north before enacting the producers' deduction.

EXAMPLE 2

Assume the same facts as in Example 1, except that Opal also has an NOL carryover of $300,000 from 2007. As taxable income for 2008 is zero ($200,000 − $50,000 − $300,000), there is no DPAD. ■

The DPAD is further limited by 50 percent of an employer's W–2 wages, including the sum of the aggregate amount of wages and elective deferrals, required to be included on the W–2 wage statements for the employees during the employer's taxable year. W–2 wages do not include any amount that is not properly included in a return filed with the Social Security Administration on or before the sixtieth day after the due date (including extensions) for such return. After May 17, 2006, *only those wages that are properly allocable to domestic production gross receipts (DPGR)* may be used. On or before this date, the source of the W–2 wages did not matter.[6]

EXAMPLE 3

In 2008, Red, Inc., has QPAI of $2 million and taxable income of $2.1 million. Since Red outsources much of its work to independent contractors, its W–2 wage base that relates entirely to domestic production activities is $80,000. Although Red's DPAD normally would be $120,000 [6% of the lesser of $2 million (QPAI) or $2.1 million (TI)], it is limited to $40,000 [50% of $80,000 (W–2 wages)]. ■

EXAMPLE 4

Assume the same facts as in Example 3, except that Red also pays salaries of $50,000 that relate to its *nonproduction activities.* On or before May 17, 2006, the wage limitation could be $65,000 [50% of $130,000 ($80,000 + $50,000)]. After this date, however, the $50,000 is not available, and the wage limitation is $40,000. ■

The IRS provides various alternative methods (including some safe harbors) for calculating the W–2 wage amount.

---

[6]§§ 199(b)(2)(B) and (C). The change in the W-2 wage limitation was made by TIPRA, which explains the transitional date of May 17, 2006. Proposed Regulations applicable to the change were released by T.D. 9293 and appear in the *Federal Register* for October 19, 2006.

There are two safe harbors for calculating the W–2 wage amount:

1. With a wage-expense method, the employer multiplies the W–2 wages by the ratio of the wage expenses used to determine QPAI to the total wage expenses used to determine taxable income for the tax year.
2. Under a small business simplified overall method, W–2 wages are charged against DPGR in the same proportion as DPGR bears to total gross receipts.

Presuming the taxable income and W–2 wage limitations are not applicable, the DPAD is a percentage of qualified production activities income (QPAI). QPAI is the excess of **domestic production gross receipts (DPGR)** over the sum of cost of goods sold (CGS) and other deductions and a ratable portion of deductions not directly allocable to such receipts.[7]

Domestic Production Gross Receipts

LO.3

Recognize and work with the different types of domestic production gross receipts (DPGR).

These five specific categories of domestic production gross receipts (DPGR) qualify for the DPAD:

- Lease, rental, license, sale, exchange, or other disposition of qualified production property (QPP) that was manufactured, produced, grown, or extracted (MPGE) in the United States.
- Qualified films largely created in the United States.
- Production of electricity, natural gas, or potable water.
- Construction (but not self-construction) performed in the United States.
- Engineering and architectural services for domestic construction.

The operation of these categories is illustrated in Figure 3–1. In general, DPGR does not include any gross receipts derived from property leased, licensed, or rented for use by a related person.

The sale of food and beverages prepared by a taxpayer at a retail establishment and the transmission or distribution of electricity, natural gas, or potable water are specifically excluded from the definition of DPGR.

Gross Receipts That Qualify.

In many cases, a taxpayer must determine the portion of its total gross receipts that is DPGR. For example, suppose a taxpayer produces a product in the United States that qualifies for the deduction and also produces the same product at a facility outside the United States. Does the taxpayer's accounting system reflect the portion of the gross receipts that is attributable to the U.S. production and the portion attributable to production outside the United States? In order to determine DPGR, an apportionment will be necessary. The IRS indicates that a taxpayer must use a reasonable method that accurately identifies DPGR and non-DPGR based on all of the information available.[8] If a taxpayer uses a

[7]Final Regulations for § 199 were issued in May 2006 (see T.D. 9263 and Rev.Proc. 2006–22) and are effective for taxable years after May 31, 2006. For taxable years beginning on or before this date, however, taxpayers may rely on Notice 2004–14 (2005–1 C.B. 498) *or* the Temporary Regulations (2005–47, I.R.B. 987).

[8]Reg. § 1.199–1(d)(2) and Notice 2005–14. The Notice also mentions the factors the IRS will consider in determining if the taxpayer's allocation method is reasonable.

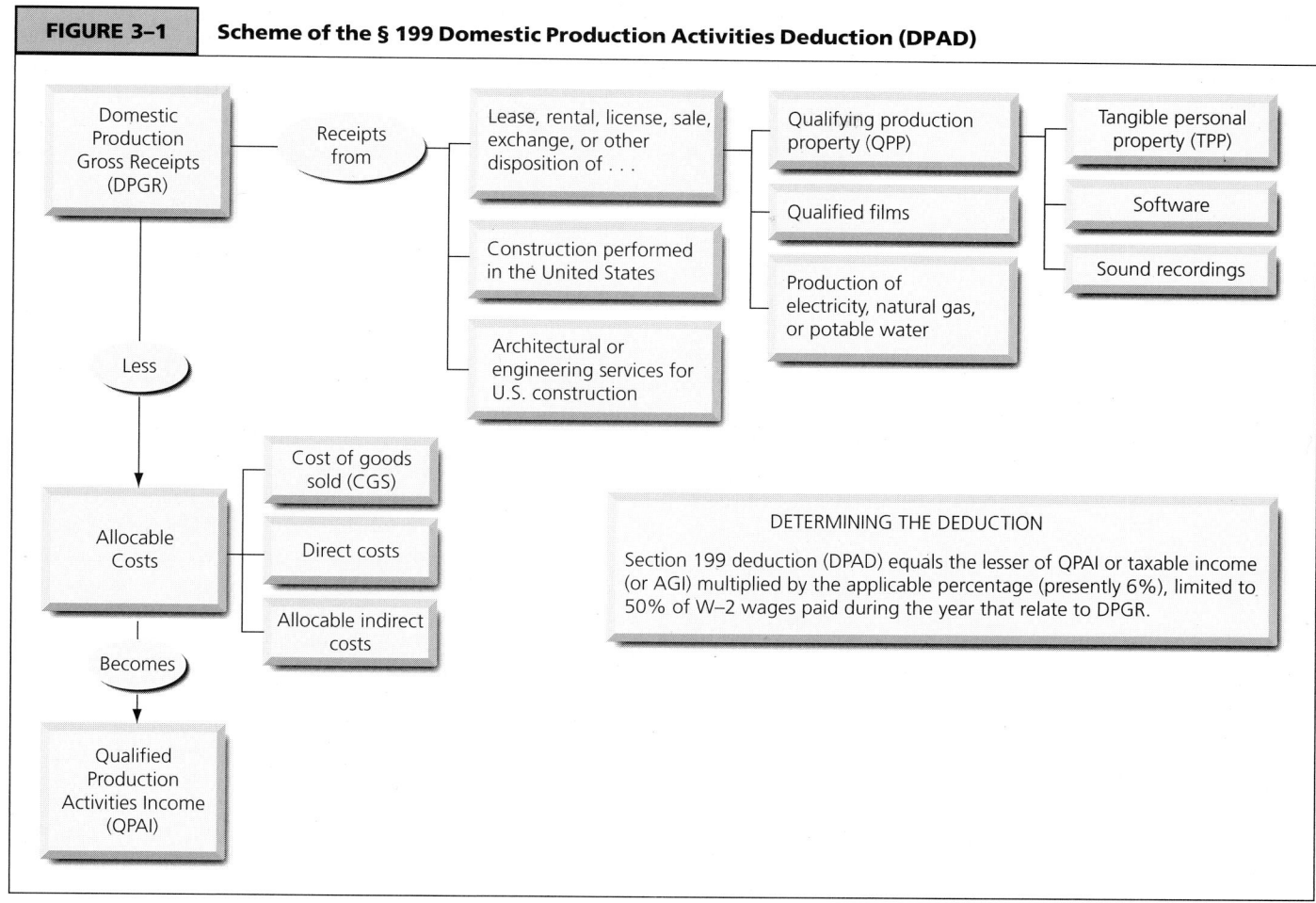

FIGURE 3-1 **Scheme of the § 199 Domestic Production Activities Deduction (DPAD)**

specific identification method (e.g., specifically identifies where the product was MPGE) for any other purpose, the same method must be used to determine DPGR.

An overall *de minimis* safe-harbor test is applicable when small amounts of non-DPGR are present. A taxpayer with less than 5 percent of total gross receipts from non-DPGR may treat all gross receipts as DPGR and is not required to allocate.

EXAMPLE 5

Orange, Inc., produces a product in both the United States and Mexico. Gross receipts derived are $2.2 million for the United States and $900,000 for Mexico. Only the $2.2 million qualifies as DPGR. ■

EXAMPLE 6

Assume the same facts as in Example 5, except that the production in Mexico yields only $100,000 (rather than $900,000) in gross receipts. Now, the safe-harbor test is met since 4.3% ($100,000/$2,300,000) is less than 5%. Consequently, the full $2.3 million ($2.2 million + $100,000) is DPGR. ■

For some taxpayers, the benefits to be derived from § 199 are so minimal that the costs of compliance are not worth the tax saving that will result. For such cases, a reverse *de minimis* safe harbor exists. Under this provision, a taxpayer can treat all of its receipts as non-DPGR if less than 5 percent of the total are DPGR.[9]

---

[9]Reg. §§ 1.199(d)(3)(ii) and (d)(4).

EXAMPLE 7	Garnet Corporation refines and sells gasoline in the United States. Of the gasoline it sells, 4% is refined in Texas, and 96% is purchased from a nonrelated source in Kuwait. Garnet can treat all of its receipts as non-DPGR and thereby avoid the application of § 199. ■

Gross receipts for the tax year are those that are properly recognized under the taxpayer's method of accounting utilized for Federal tax purposes. Gross receipts include total sales (net of returns and allowances), amounts received from services, and income from investments such as dividends, rents, interest, royalties, and annuities. Items that *do not qualify* as gross receipts include repayment of loans, nonrecognition transactions, and sales taxes collected and remitted.

Gross receipts derived from the performance of services do not qualify as DPGR. Thus, the lease, rental, license, sale, exchange, or other disposition of property that contains a service element (called an embedded service) requires an allocation of the gross receipts and costs attributable to the embedded services. A service is treated as embedded when the price of the service is included in the amount charged by the taxpayer for the property. Examples of embedded services include product warranties, maintenance agreements, training in product use, and customer call-in help assistance. The portion of the gross receipts that is considered for DPAD purposes may not exceed the selling price of the property without the service element. Allocation is not required, however, for a service component that meets a 5 percent *de minimis* test (i.e., is worth less than 5 percent of the selling price of the product). A further exception allows service receipts to be treated as DPGR when the cost is included in the price charged for the property and the service is neither separately offered by the producer nor separately bargained for with a customer.

EXAMPLE 8	Amber Company manufactures and sells televisions. The sale price of every set includes a 90-day warranty. For an extra 4% of the selling price, the customer can extend the warranty to one year, while 20% will cover five years. Proceeds attributable to the 90-day and one-year warranties qualify as DPGR, but those relating to the five-year coverage do not. ■

Qualified Production Property. One of the components of DPGR is the lease, rental, license, sale, exchange, or other disposition of qualified production property. Qualified production property (QPP) includes tangible personal property (TPP), computer software, and sound recordings (see Figure 3–1).[10] Local law is not controlling for purposes of determining whether property is considered tangible personal property. Tangible personal property does not include land, buildings, structural components of buildings, or intangible property such as patents, copyrights, and subscription lists.

Tangible personal property does include the following:

- Automobiles.
- Books.
- Videocassettes.
- Computer diskettes.
- Magazines.
- Newspapers.
- Food.
- Goods.
- Clothing.
- Printing presses.
- Production machinery.

- Transportation equipment.
- Office equipment.
- Refrigerators and stoves.
- Grocery counters.
- Display racks and shelves.
- Testing equipment.
- Gasoline pumps.
- Neon and other signs.
- Vending machines.
- Car lifts.

[10]Reg. § 1.48–1(c). The definition of tangible personal property is derived from the investment tax credit rules.

For example, advertising income attributable to the sale or other disposition of newspapers and magazines qualifies for the deduction.

Machinery and equipment that are not inherently permanent structures are tangible personal property. An inherently permanent structural component of a building is real property. Real property also includes swimming pools, paved parking lots, water systems, railroad spurs, communication facilities, sewers, sidewalks, walls, doors, plumbing, pipes and ducts, elevators and escalators, central air conditioning and heating systems, oil and gas wells, cable, wiring, and inherently permanent oil and gas platforms.[11]

In order to qualify as DPGR, QPP must be manufactured, produced, grown, or extracted (MPGE) *in whole or in significant part* within the United States. Included in this MPGE definition is the making of QPP out of salvage, scrap, or junk materials, or by the use of new or raw materials. "Making" can involve processing, manipulating, refining, or changing the form of an article or combining or assembling two or more articles. Cultivating soil, raising livestock, fishing, and mining minerals fall under MPGE.

The "in whole or in significant part" requirement is satisfied if the employer's MPGE activity is substantial in nature. The substantial in nature requirement is relevant in deciding whether the MPGE activity (already determined to have occurred) was performed in whole or in significant part by the taxpayer in the United States. The requirement is applied by taking into account all of the facts and circumstances. This substantial in nature test is a facts and circumstances test, and a taxpayer cannot use the analogous authorities under the Subpart F Regulations (dealing with controlled foreign corporations—see Chapter 9) in applying this standard. There is a safe harbor if an employer incurs conversion costs (direct labor and related factory burden) related to MPGE of the property within the United States and the costs account for 20 percent or more of the property's cost of goods sold.[12]

Ecru, Inc., pays $75 to purchase a small motor and other parts and materials from related suppliers in Mexico. Ecru incurs $25 in labor costs at its factory in the United States to fabricate a plastic tank body from the materials and to assemble a toy tank. It also incurs packaging, selling, and other costs of $2 and sells the toy tank for $112. The toy tank will be treated as manufactured by the employer "in significant part" because Ecru's labor costs are substantial—they are more than 20% of the taxpayer's total cost for the toy tank [$25/($25 + $75) = 25%]. As a result, Ecru's DPGR is $112, and the full $10 in profit ($112 − $75 − $25 − $2) is QPAI. ∎	*EXAMPLE 9*

Assume the same facts as in Example 9, except that Ecru incurred only $15 (instead of $25) in labor costs. Now, the "significant part" requirement is not met because Ecru's MPGE activity is not substantial under the safe-harbor provision: 16.7% [$15/($15 + $75)] is less than 20%. Therefore, none of the profit is DPGR, and there is no producers' deduction (DPAD). ∎	*EXAMPLE 10*

Only one producer may claim the DPAD. The taxpayer that has the benefits and burdens of ownership under the Federal income tax system during the period the qualifying activity occurs may claim the deduction.

Crimson, Inc., enters into an agreement to have an unrelated supplier, Gray, Inc., manufacture items for Crimson. Only one of the taxpayers is treated as having MPGE the items for purposes of the DPAD. Crimson may obtain the deduction only if it bears the benefits and burdens of ownership.[13] ∎	*EXAMPLE 11*

---

[11]Reg. § 1.48–1(c); Notice 2005–14, § 3.04(11)(c).
[12]Reg. § 1.199–3(g)(3).

[13]There is much dissatisfaction with this "one owner" rule as to contract manufacturing, which often takes place on a consignment basis.

Barring a special agreement establishing ownership, the result in Example 11 will usually favor Gray, Inc. Most often the party providing the manufacturing facility will have title to the goods being manufactured. In many situations, moreover, title may change as a product moves through the manufacturing process.

EXAMPLE 12

Crimson manufactures and sells lawn mowers. The lawn mowers are powered by motors that Crimson purchases from Gray, an unrelated domestic producer. Assuming no arrangement to the contrary, Gray has DPGR from the sale of the motors, while Crimson has DPGR from the sale of the lawn mowers. Gray has title to the motors while they are being manufactured, and Crimson owns the rest of the mower it produces. Crimson will not have a double DPAD because it will have to deduct what it paid for the motors (part of cost of goods sold) in arriving at QPAI (see Figure 3–1). ■

Qualified Films. A qualified film includes any motion picture film or videotape, as well as live or delayed television programming, if not less than 50 percent of the total compensation relating to the production of the property is compensation for services performed in the United States by actors, production personnel, directors, and producers. A taxpayer that MPGE a qualified film may treat the tangible medium to which the qualified film is affixed (e.g., DVD and videocassette) as part of the qualified film, even if the taxpayer purchased the tangible medium. A taxpayer may subcontract the affixing of the film onto a tangible medium. Ticket sales for viewing qualified films do not constitute DPGR. Merely writing a screenplay or other similar material does not result in qualified gross receipts.

EXAMPLE 13

Maize, Inc., produces a qualified film and contracts with Magenta, Inc., an unrelated party, to duplicate the film onto DVDs. Magenta manufactures blank DVDs and duplicates Maize's film onto the DVDs within the United States. It sells the DVDs with the qualified film to Maize, which then sells them to customers. Magenta's gross receipts from manufacturing the DVDs and duplicating the film onto the DVDs are DPGR (assuming all the other requirements are met). Maize's gross receipts from the sale of the DVDs to customers are DPGR (assuming all the other requirements are met). ■

Construction Projects. The DPAD is available to a taxpayer who is involved in the trade or business of construction and performs a qualifying construction activity with respect to U.S. real property. The deduction is not available for taxpayers who self-construct real property. The term "construction" includes most activities that are typically performed in connection with the erection or substantial renovation of real property.

Real property includes residential and commercial buildings (including structural components), inherently permanent structures (but not machinery), and inherently permanent land improvements and infrastructure. Appliances, furniture, and fixtures sold as part of a construction site are not considered to be real property. If, however, more than 95 percent of the total gross receipts derived by a taxpayer from a construction project are attributable to real property, the total gross receipts are DPGR from construction.

Tangential services such as the hauling of trash and debris and the delivery of materials are excluded from DPGR, unless the taxpayer is performing such services in connection with a construction project. Also, proceeds attributable to the disposition of land are not considered gross receipts derived from construction. Further, DPGR does not include gross receipts from the lease or rental of constructed real property.

With respect to land, there is a safe harbor for allocating gross receipts between the proceeds from the sale, exchange, or other disposition of real property constructed by the taxpayer, which qualify for DPGR, and the gross receipts attributable to the sale, exchange, or other disposition of land (which do not qualify). The taxpayer is able to reduce its DPGR costs by certain land costs plus a percentage based on the number of months that lapse between the date the taxpayer acquires the land and the date the taxpayer sells each item of rental property on the land (e.g., 5% for land held not more than 60 months).[14]

Gross receipts attributable to the sale or other disposition of land (including zoning, planning, and entitlement costs) are considered gross receipts attributable to the land, and not to a qualifying construction activity, and therefore are non-DPGR. Costs incurred for cleaning, grading, and demolition in connection with a construction project are now construction activities under the Final Regulations. Any income stream (e.g., rent) from renting apartments in a building prior to its sale is not DPGR.

EXAMPLE 14

Gold Construction Company purchases five residential lots in a new subdivision for $500,000. On these lots it builds five residences that it sells for $4 million. Because the proceeds attributable to the sale of the land cannot qualify, Gold has DPGR of only $3.5 million ($4,000,000 − $500,000). ∎

EXAMPLE 15

A business owner (not engaged in construction activities) retains a general contractor to oversee a substantial renovation of a building, and the general contractor hires a subcontractor to install an electrical system as part of the substantial renovation. Here, both the amount the general contractor receives from the building owner and the amount the subcontractor receives from the general contractor qualify as DPGR from construction. However, the amount from the sale received by the building owner upon the disposition of the building does not qualify as DPGR because the owner was not involved in qualified construction activity with respect to the building.[15] ∎

Construction activities need not satisfy the legal title restrictions that are applicable under the QPP rules to the manufacture of tangible personal property (see the discussion in connection with Examples 11 and 12 above). In Example 15, for instance, note that neither the general contractor nor the subcontractor owned the building they were working on, yet their income qualified for DPGR treatment.

Substantial renovation refers to the renovation of a major component or substantial structural part of real property that materially increases the value of the property, substantially prolongs the useful life of the property, or adapts the property to a new or different use. Thus, cosmetic changes such as painting and replacing shingles would not qualify.

Production of Electricity, Natural Gas, and Potable Water.

DPGR includes gross receipts derived from any lease, rental, license, sale, exchange, or other disposition of electricity, natural gas, or potable water produced in the United States (see Figure 3–1). It does not include those receipts derived from the transmission or distribution of these items to final customers. An integrated taxpayer that carries out all of these functions must allocate the gross receipts among production, transmission, and delivery.

EXAMPLE 16

PowerCo generates electricity that it sells to TransmissionCo. TransmissionCo sells the electricity to ElectricCo, which, in turn, retails it to user-customers. Only PowerCo's gross receipts qualify as DPGR. ∎

EXAMPLE 17

Assume the same facts as in Example 16, except that PowerCo is an integrated producer that generates electricity and delivers it to end users. The gross receipts attributable to the transmission of electricity from the generating facility to a point of local distribution and any gross

---

[14]Reg. § 1.199–3(m)(6)(iv)(A). Ten percent for land held more than 60 months but not more than 120 months, 15% for land held more than 120 months but not more than 180 months. Land held more than 180 months is not eligible.

[15]Reg. § 1.199–3(m).

receipts attributable to the distribution of electricity to final customers are not qualified DPGR. ■

The term "natural gas" includes only natural gas extracted from a natural deposit, not methane gas extracted from a landfill. Natural gas production includes all activities involved in extracting natural gas from the ground and processing the gas into pipeline-quality gas. Gross receipts from the transmission of pipeline-quality gas from a natural gas field or plant to a local distribution company are not DPGR. Further, gross receipts from the transmission from the local gas distribution company to local customers do not qualify.

Production activities with respect to potable water include the acquisition, collection, and storage of untreated water, transportation of such water to a water treatment facility, and treatment of untreated water at such a facility. Potable water refers to unbottled drinking water. DPGR does not include gross receipts derived from the storage of potable water (after completion of treatment) or the delivery of potable water to customers. The IRS believes this provision applies to water utilities and not to taxpayers engaged in the trade or business of producing bottled water. Thus, bottled water companies are to be treated as the producers of tangible personal property.

LO.4
Make the necessary adjustments to DPGR to arrive at qualified production activities income (QPAI).

Adjustments in Arriving at QPAI

Once DPGR is determined, certain adjustments must be made to arrive at qualified production activities income (QPAI). Recall that it is usually 6 percent of QPAI that yields the DPAD. The adjustments that are necessary are listed in Figure 3–1 and include the following:

1. Cost of goods sold (CGS)
2. Direct costs
3. Allocable indirect costs

CGS is equal to beginning inventory plus purchases and production costs and less ending inventory. If a taxpayer can identify from its books and records the CGS allocable to DPGR, that amount is allocable to DPGR. If identification is not possible, a taxpayer must use a reasonable method, but it may not use a different allocation method than it used to allocate gross receipts between DPGR and non-DPGR. Reasonable methods may include those based on gross receipts, number of units sold, number of units produced, or total production costs.

The second category of expenses (direct costs) includes selling and marketing expenses. The third category (allocable indirect costs) is further removed and includes, for example, general and administrative expenses attributable to the selling and marketing expenses.

The second and third categories of expenses (i.e., direct allocable and indirect allocable) may be allocated by one of three methods:

- The *§ 861 Regulation method* may be used by *all* taxpayers but *must* be used by those taxpayers with average annual gross receipts of more than $100 million. Essentially, certain deductions incurred by a U.S. taxpayer must be allocated to various classes of gross income and apportioned between foreign sources and domestic sources. Although time-consuming, the § 861 Regulation method is the most accurate. Unfortunately, for those concerns without international operations, the use of this method will necessitate a resort to unfamiliar rules. The mechanics of the § 861 Regulations are explained and illustrated in Chapter 9 under the heading Allocation and Apportionment of Deductions.
- For employers with average annual gross receipts of $100 million or less or total assets at the end of the taxable year of $10 million or less, a *simplified deduction method* based on relative gross receipts is available. The deductions

are apportioned to DPGR in the same proportion as DPGR bears to total gross receipts.

- For taxpayers that have average gross receipts of $5 million or less or are eligible to use the cash method, a *small business simplified overall method* is available. This method is the same as the previous method except that it can also be used to arrive at CGS.

EXAMPLE 18

Brown, Inc., a qualifying small taxpayer,[16] has total gross receipts of $4.3 million, DPGR of $3.1 million, CGS of $1.3 million, and advertising, selling, and administrative expenses of $500,000. Under the small business simplified overall method, CGS and deductions are apportioned to DPGR in the same proportion as DPGR bears to total gross receipts.

Thus, Brown's QPAI is computed as follows:

DPGR	$3,100,000
Less allowable CGS:	
[($3.1 million/$4.3 million) × $1.3 million]	(937,209)
Less allocable expenses:	
[($3.1 million/$4.3 million) × $500,000]	(360,465)
QPAI	$1,802,326

Presuming the taxable income and W–2 wage limitations do not intervene, Brown's DPAD for 2008 is $108,140 (6% × $1,802,326). ∎

To determine if one of the simplified methods may be used, the average annual gross receipts must be determined at the expanded affiliated group level (discussed later). Also, a member of the expanded affiliated group that qualifies to use one of the simplified methods may do so only if all members of the group elect to use that method.

Collateral Problems

LO.5

Cope with the collateral problems associated with the domestic production activities deduction (DPAD).

Disallowed Production Activities—Preparation of Food and Beverages. DPGR does not include gross receipts from the sale of food and beverages prepared by a taxpayer at a retail establishment.[17] A retail establishment includes real property leased, occupied, or otherwise used by a taxpayer in its trade or business of selling food or beverages to the public and at which the taxpayer makes retail sales. A facility is not a retail establishment if the employer uses the facility only to prepare food or beverages for wholesale sale. There is a 5 percent *de minimis* safe harbor.

EXAMPLE 19

Silver Company buys coffee beans that it roasts and packages at a special facility. The company sells the roasted coffee through a variety of unrelated third-party vendors and also sells roasted coffee at its own retail establishments. These receipts are qualified DPGR.

At Silver's retail establishments, it prepares and sells brewed coffee and food. These receipts are not DPGR. Nevertheless, part of the receipts from the sale of the brewed coffee may be allocated to DPGR to the extent of the value of the roasted beans used to brew the coffee. The amount to be allocated is determined by the price Silver receives from the sale of the roasted beans. ∎

EXAMPLE 20

Rose Company produces donuts that it sells to restaurants and food stores. Rose also operates a snack shop at its manufacturing facility where it sells donuts and coffee to the general

---

[16]As defined in Reg. § 1.199–4(f)(2).   [17]§ 199(c)(4)(B)(i).

public. Rose has gross receipts of $2 million from the wholesale sale of its donuts and $100,000 from the operation of the snack shop. The full $2.1 million is DPGR because the $100,000 falls under the *de minimis* safe-harbor exception [$100,000 is less than 5% of $2.1 million ($2 million + $100,000)]. ∎

The prohibition against the retail sale of prepared food cannot be avoided by restricting sales to take-out orders. The prohibition does not, however, apply to the sale of prepared meals to others for resale.

EXAMPLE 21

Beige Brothers operates a food service business that prepares meals. Some of the meals are served to diners at a café it owns adjacent to the plant, some are sold to customers on a take-out basis, and some are frozen and sold to supermarkets for resale. Only the proceeds from the latter operation will qualify as DPGR. ∎

The prepared food restrictions may have been motivated by the trauma experienced by Canada before it rescinded its producers' deduction—see the discussion in Global Tax Issues earlier in this chapter. As a result, the broiling and assembly of hamburgers and salads by Burger King will not qualify under the U.S. version of the producers' deduction.

Expanded Affiliated Group Rules. Special rules apply to corporations that are members of an **expanded affiliated group (EAG)**. An EAG is an affiliated group as defined for purposes of the consolidated return rules, except that the stock ownership requirement is reduced to more than 50 percent (from 80 percent) and insurance companies and possession credit corporations are not excluded from the group.[18]

In the case of corporations that are members of an EAG, the DPAD is determined by treating the group as a single taxpayer. In effect, therefore, each member of the group is treated as being engaged in the same activities as every other member. The deduction is then allocated among the members in proportion to each member's respective amount of QPAI.

EXAMPLE 22

Red Corporation and Blue Corporation are members of an EAG but do not file a consolidated return. Red manufactures a machine at a cost of $3,000, which it then sells to Blue for $5,000. Blue incurs additional costs of $1,000 on marketing, then sells the machine to an unrelated customer for $7,000. QPAI is $3,000 ($7,000 − $3,000 − $1,000) even though Blue did not perform any manufacturing. Note that this is the same result that would be reached if Blue had not been involved and Red had conducted its own marketing function. ∎

EXAMPLE 23

Assume the same facts as in Example 22, except that the parties are not related. Under these circumstances, Red Corporation has QPAI of $2,000 ($5,000 − $3,000), and Blue Corporation has none. Blue's activities when considered alone are not QPAI since they involve marketing and not production. ∎

If all of the members of an EAG are members of the same consolidated group, the consolidated group's DPAD is calculated based on the group's consolidated taxable income or loss, and not the separate taxable income or loss of its members. The DPAD of a consolidated group must be allocated to the group's members in proportion to each member's QPAI (if any), regardless of whether the member has separate taxable income or loss for the tax year and whether the member has W–2 wages for the tax year.

---

[18]§ 199(d)(4).

Pass-Through Entities Provisions. In the case of pass-through entities (i.e., partnerships, S corporations, trusts, and estates), special rules apply for handling DPADs. Because the deduction is determined at the owner level, each partner or shareholder must make the computation separately.[19] Consequently, the entity allocates to each owner his or her share of QPAI. The QPAI allocated is then combined with the domestic production activities the owner may have from other sources (e.g., a partner also conducts a manufacturing activity of his or her own).

In working with the wage limitation in a pass-through setting, an allocable portion of W–2 wages of the pass-through entity is passed through to the owner, but only those wages properly allocable to DPGR. The partner or shareholder, however, may add any wages separately paid to the amount allocated from the entity. In the case of a partnership, guaranteed payments are not regarded as W–2 wages. Also, if QPAI (computed taking into account only partnership items allocated to the partner for the tax year) is not greater than zero, a partner cannot use any partnership W–2 wages in calculating the DPAD.[20] The wage limitation applies to non-grantor trusts and estates in the same way it applies to partnerships and S corporations.

Generally, the DPAD is determined at the owner level in a pass-through entity situation. In some instances, however, the pass-through of the data needed to make this determination can be cumbersome and burdensome. To simplify matters, therefore, the IRS allows eligible partnerships and S corporations to calculate QPAI and W–2 wages for some or all of the owners at the entity level.[21]

The DPAD has no effect on an S shareholder's stock basis because the deduction is not listed in § 1367(a). Further, an S corporation or partnership that is a qualified small taxpayer may use the small business simplified overall method to apportion cost of goods sold and deductions between DPGR and non-DPGR at the entity level. Also, the IRS may permit a partnership or an S corporation to calculate a shareholder's share of QPAI at the entity level, which is then combined with the shareholder's QPAI.[22] The owner is not allowed to use another cost allocation method to reallocate the costs of the pass-through entity regardless of the method used by the owner to allocate or apportion costs.

The pass-through information is reported by the entity on its Schedule K–1 of Form 1065 (partnership) or Form 1120S (S corporation). Owners include their share of QPAI and W–2 wages on Lines 7 and 14 of Form 8903 (Domestic Production Activities Deduction).

When an entity uses a different tax year than its owners, the pass-through of DPAD attributes may be delayed. As new § 199 took effect for tax years beginning after December 31, 2004, coverage for a fiscal year entity could begin only in 2005.

EXAMPLE 24

John, a calendar year taxpayer, is a partner in Crimson Partnership, which uses a July 1–June 30 fiscal year. John will not be able to pick up any of the partnership's 2008–2009 QPAI until his 2009 individual return (the June 30, 2009 pass-through on Crimson's 2008–2009 fiscal year), which he will file in 2010! ∎

Coordination with the AMT. The DPAD is allowed for purposes of the alternative minimum tax (AMT), except that the deduction is equal to 6 percent (in 2007–2009) of the smaller of (1) QPAI or (2) alternative minimum taxable income (without considering the DPAD) for the tax year. In the case of an individual, modified AGI (ignoring the DPAD) is substituted for AMTI.[23]

---

[19] § 199(d)(1)(A).
[20] Reg. § 1.199–9(b)(3).
[21] Rev.Proc. 2007–34, I.R.B. 2007–23, page 1345 (June 4, 2007).

[22] Reg. §§ 1.199–9(b)(1)(ii) and 1.199–9(c)(1)(ii).
[23] § 199(d)(6).

Alternative Minimum Tax (indirectly) separate tax

LO.6

Explain the reason for the alternative minimum tax.

The perception that many large corporations were not paying their fair share of Federal income tax was especially widespread in the early 1980s. A study released in 1986 reported that 130 of the 250 largest corporations in the United States paid zero or less in Federal taxes in at least one year between 1981 and 1985 (e.g., Reynolds Metals, General Dynamics, Georgia Pacific, and Texas Commerce Bankshares).

Political pressure subsequently led to the adoption of an alternative minimum tax to ensure that corporations with substantial economic income pay a minimum amount of Federal taxes. Corporations are now less able to use exclusions, deductions, and credits available under the law to pay no taxes. A separate tax system with a quasi-flat tax rate is applied each year to a corporation's economic income. If the tentative alternative minimum tax is greater than the regular corporate income tax under § 11, then the corporation must pay the regular tax plus this excess, the **alternative minimum tax (AMT)**.

In general, a corporation is likely to pay an AMT for one or more of three reasons:

- A high level of investment in assets such as equipment and structures.
- Low taxable income due to a cyclical downturn, strong international competition, a low-margin industry, or other factors.
- Investment at low real interest rates, which increases the company's deductions for depreciation relative to those for interest payments.

The 20 percent AMT applicable to many regular corporations is similar to the AMT applicable to individuals.[24] Many of the adjustments and tax preference items necessary to arrive at **alternative minimum taxable income (AMTI)** are the same. The rates and exemptions are different, but the objective is identical—to force taxpayers who are more profitable than their taxable income reflects to pay additional income taxes.

As the AMT is in addition to the regular corporate tax, it is computed somewhat differently. Separate and independent calculations of the amount and character of all items affecting the computation of the AMT are required. The Code itself mandates the treatment of many items affecting the computation of the AMT. Regulations provide broad rules governing the treatment of other items for AMT purposes. However, the Code and Regulations do not provide guidance for many items.

The formula for determining the AMT liability of corporate taxpayers appears in Figure 3–2 and follows the format of Form 4626 (Alternative Minimum Tax—Corporations).

Small Corporation Exemption

For tax years beginning after December 31, 1997, many smaller corporations are not subject to the AMT. Certain corporations that meet several gross receipts tests are exempted from the AMT as long as they remain "small corporations." A corporation initially qualifies as a "small corporation" if it had *average* gross receipts of $5 million or less in the preceding three-year period. If a corporation is not in existence for the entire three-year period, the $5 million test is applied on the basis of the period during which the corporation is in existence.[25]

| EXAMPLE 25 | Swan Corporation had gross receipts of $3.7 million, $4.8 million, and $4.6 million, respectively, for tax years 2005, 2006, and 2007 for an average of $4.37 million. For 2008 AMT purposes, Swan is considered to be a small corporation. ∎ |

---

[24]The AMT provisions for both corporate and noncorporate taxpayers are contained in §§ 55 through 59. The individual AMT rates are 26%/28%.

[25]§ 55(e).

FIGURE 3–2	AMT Formula for Corporations

Regular taxable income before NOL deduction

Plus/minus:		AMT adjustments (except ACE adjustment)
Plus:		Tax preferences
	Equals:	AMTI before AMT NOL deduction and ACE adjustment
Plus/minus:		ACE adjustment
	Equals:	AMTI before AMT NOL deduction
Minus:		AMT NOL deduction (limited to 90%)
	Equals:	Alternative minimum taxable income (AMTI)
Minus:		Exemption
	Equals:	Tentative minimum tax base
Times:		20% rate
	Equals:	Tentative minimum tax before AMT foreign tax credit
Minus:		AMT foreign tax credit
	Equals:	Tentative minimum tax
Minus:		Regular tax liability before credits minus regular foreign tax credit
	Equals:	Alternative minimum tax (AMT)

[Handwritten margin notes: "↑ yur AMT Tax" next to Tax preferences. "Adjstmet + Privae Activit bond eg Volsewagon ore Noon Taxable in Reg Tax but taxable in AMT"]

A corporation that passes the $5 million average gross receipts test will continue to be treated as a small corporation as long as its *average* gross receipts for the three-year period preceding the taxable year do not exceed $7.5 million. For both the $7.5 million and the $5 million test, certain aggregating rules apply to related taxpayers. Once a corporation loses its small corporation protection, the corporation is then liable for the AMT for that year and future years. However, many of the AMT and adjusted current earnings adjustments are modified so that they pertain only to transactions and investments that were entered into *after* the corporation lost its small corporation status (e.g., property placed into service in or after the change year).

EXAMPLE 26

In 2008, Swan Corporation determines that its average gross receipts for the three-year period of 2005, 2006, and 2007 were $8.7 million. Thus, Swan must calculate its AMT liability for 2008, but only on the transactions and investments that it entered into after the start of the year 2008 (e.g., mining exploration and development costs paid or incurred on or after January 1, 2008). ■

AMT Adjustments

LO.7

Calculate the alternative minimum tax applicable to corporations.

As Figure 3–2 indicates, the starting point for computing AMTI is the taxable income of the corporation before any NOL deduction. Certain adjustments must be made to this amount. Unlike tax preference items, which are always additions, the adjustments may either increase or decrease taxable income. For example, the deduction for domestic manufacturing activities (DPAD) is available for purposes of computing minimum taxable income (as well as adjusted current earnings). However, the deduction is limited to the smaller of the qualified production income as determined for the § 11 tax (the regular corporate income tax) or the AMTI without regard to the manufacturing deduction.

The positive adjustments arise as a result of timing differences and are added back to the taxable income in computing AMTI. Since most adjustments only defer taxes, a corporation may recoup AMT paid on these adjustments when the deferral of regular tax created by the adjustment is reversed and the regular tax is due. Once

AMT adjustments reverse themselves, they are deducted from taxable income to arrive at AMTI. This mechanism is called the *netting process.*

Although NOLs are separately stated in Figure 3–2, they are actually negative adjustments. They are separately stated in Figure 3–2 and on Form 4626 because they may not exceed 90 percent of AMTI. Thus, such adjustments cannot be determined until all other adjustments and tax preference items are considered.

Other adjustments to regular taxable income include the following:

- A portion of depreciation on property placed in service after 1986. For realty placed in service before 1999, the adjustment amount is the difference between depreciation for regular tax purposes and ADS depreciation using a 40-year life. For personalty placed in service before 1999, the adjustment is the excess of accelerated depreciation over the amount determined using the 150 percent declining-balance method switching to straight-line. Thus, the depreciation allowances for purposes of the AMT are generally much less favorable than for the regular corporate income tax. For property placed into service after December 31, 1998, this adjustment applies only to MACRS 3-, 5-, 7-, and 10-year property that is depreciated using the 200 percent declining-balance method. Also, the adjustment is only the difference between the depreciation claimed for regular tax purposes and the depreciation using the 150 percent declining-balance method over the property's shorter regular MACRS recovery period.

EXAMPLE 27

Purple Corporation placed an asset costing $10,000 in service on March 15, 2007. Based upon a three-year recovery class life, this personalty has the following effect upon AMTI:

Year	Tax Deduction 200%	AMT Deduction 150%	Increase or (Decrease) AMT Adjustment
2007	$3,333	$2,500	$ 833
2008	4,445	3,750	695
2009	1,481	2,500	(1,019)
2010	741	1,250	(509)

■

- Since different depreciation methods are used for AMT and regular tax purposes especially before 1999, the adjusted bases for these depreciable assets are affected. When the bases are different and the asset is disposed of, a basis adjustment is necessary to reflect the difference in the AMT gain or loss *and* the regular tax gain or loss.

EXAMPLE 28

Assume the same facts as in Example 27, except that the asset is sold at the end of the second year for $4,000. For regular tax purposes, the basis is $2,222 ($10,000 − $3,333 − $4,445), and the basis for AMT purposes is $3,750 ($10,000 − $2,500 − $3,750). Thus, the regular tax gain is $1,778 ($4,000 − $2,222), and the AMT gain is $250 ($4,000 − $3,750). Consequently, a $1,528 negative basis adjustment is required when computing AMT ($1,778 − $250). ■

- Passive activity losses of certain closely held corporations and personal service corporations.
- The excess of mining exploration and development costs deducted over what would have resulted if the costs had been capitalized and written off over 10 years.
- The difference between completed contract and percentage of completion reporting on long-term construction contracts, for some contracts reported under the completed contract method. The percentage of completion method must be used for AMTI purposes for contracts entered into after March 1, 1986.

- Amortization claimed on certified pollution control facilities.
- The difference between installment and total gain, for dealers using the installment method to account for sales. The installment method is not allowed for AMTI purposes.
- A portion of the difference between **adjusted current earnings (ACE)** and unadjusted AMTI (post-1989).

Tax Preferences

AMTI includes designated **tax preference items**. In many cases, this inclusion has the effect of subjecting nontaxable income to the AMT. Some of the most common tax preferences include the following:

- Accelerated depreciation on real property in excess of straight-line (placed in service before 1987).
- Tax-exempt interest on state and local bonds where the generated funds are not used for an essential function of the government.
- Percentage depletion claimed in excess of the adjusted basis of property.
- For integrated oil companies (ExxonMobil, Chevron), the excess of intangible drilling costs over 10-year amortization if in excess of 65 percent of net oil and gas income. This item is not a tax preference for independent oil and gas producers and royalty owners.

Computing Alternative Minimum Taxable Income

The various modifications needed to arrive at the AMTI of a corporation are set forth in Concept Summary 3–1. The Concept Summary shows the effect of the different adjustments and preferences as applied to the taxable income of a C corporation. Some of the items included in the Concept Summary are not discussed in the text. Refer to the instructions to Form 4626 for further coverage of these items.

The following example illustrates the effect of tax preferences and adjustments in arriving at AMTI.

For 2008, Tan Corporation (a calendar year, integrated oil company) had the following transactions:

EXAMPLE 29

Taxable income	$6,000,000
Mining exploration costs	500,000
Percentage depletion claimed (the property has a zero adjusted basis)	700,000
Donation of land held since 1980 as an investment (basis of $400,000 and fair market value of $500,000) to a qualified charity	500,000
Interest on City of Elmira (Michigan) bonds. The proceeds were used for nongovernmental purposes	300,000

Tan Corporation's AMTI for 2008 is determined as follows:

Taxable income		$6,000,000
Adjustments:		
Excess mining exploration costs [$500,000 (amount expensed) − $50,000 (amount allowed over a 10-year amortization period)]		450,000
Tax preferences:		
Excess depletion	$700,000	
Interest on bonds	300,000	1,000,000
AMTI		$7,450,000 ∎

CONCEPT SUMMARY $3-1$

AMT Adjustments and Preferences for Corporations

Adjustments	Positive	Negative	Both[1]
Depreciation of post-1986 real property			X
Depreciation of post-1986 personal property			X
Pollution control facilities			X
Mining exploration and development costs			X
Circulation expenditures (PHC only)			X
Completed contract method			X
Adjusted gain or loss			X
Passive activity losses[2,3]			X
Alternative minimum tax NOL deduction		X	
Loss limitation			X
Nondealer installment sales			X
Adjusted current earnings adjustment			X
Domestic production activities deduction			X
Income from alcohol, biodiesel, and renewable diesel fuels credit		X	
Cooperative's deduction for patronage dividends			X
Income limitation adjustments			X
Income as the beneficiary of an estate/ trust			X
Preferences	**Positive**	**Negative**	**Both[1]**
Percentage depletion in excess of adjusted basis	X		
Accelerated depreciation on pre-1987 real property	X		
Intangible drilling costs[4]	X		
Private activity bond interest income[5]	X		
Merchant Marine Capital Construction Funds	X		
Tax shelter farm activities[3]	X		
Section 833(b) deduction[6]	X		

[1] Timing difference.
[2] Closely held corporations.
[3] Personal service corporations.
[4] Integrated oil companies only.
[5] Does not include Gulf Opportunity Zone bonds.
[6] Blue Cross, Blue Shield, and similar types of organizations.

LO.8

Understand the function of adjusted current earnings (ACE).

Adjusted Current Earnings (ACE)

The purpose of the ACE adjustment is to ensure that the mismatching of earnings and profits (E & P) and taxable income will not produce inequitable results. The calculation of ACE is similar to the calculation of E & P (which is similar to the economic concept of income). S corporations, real estate investment trusts, regulated investment companies, and real estate mortgage investment conduits are not subject to the ACE provisions.

| FIGURE 3–3 | Determining the ACE Adjustment |

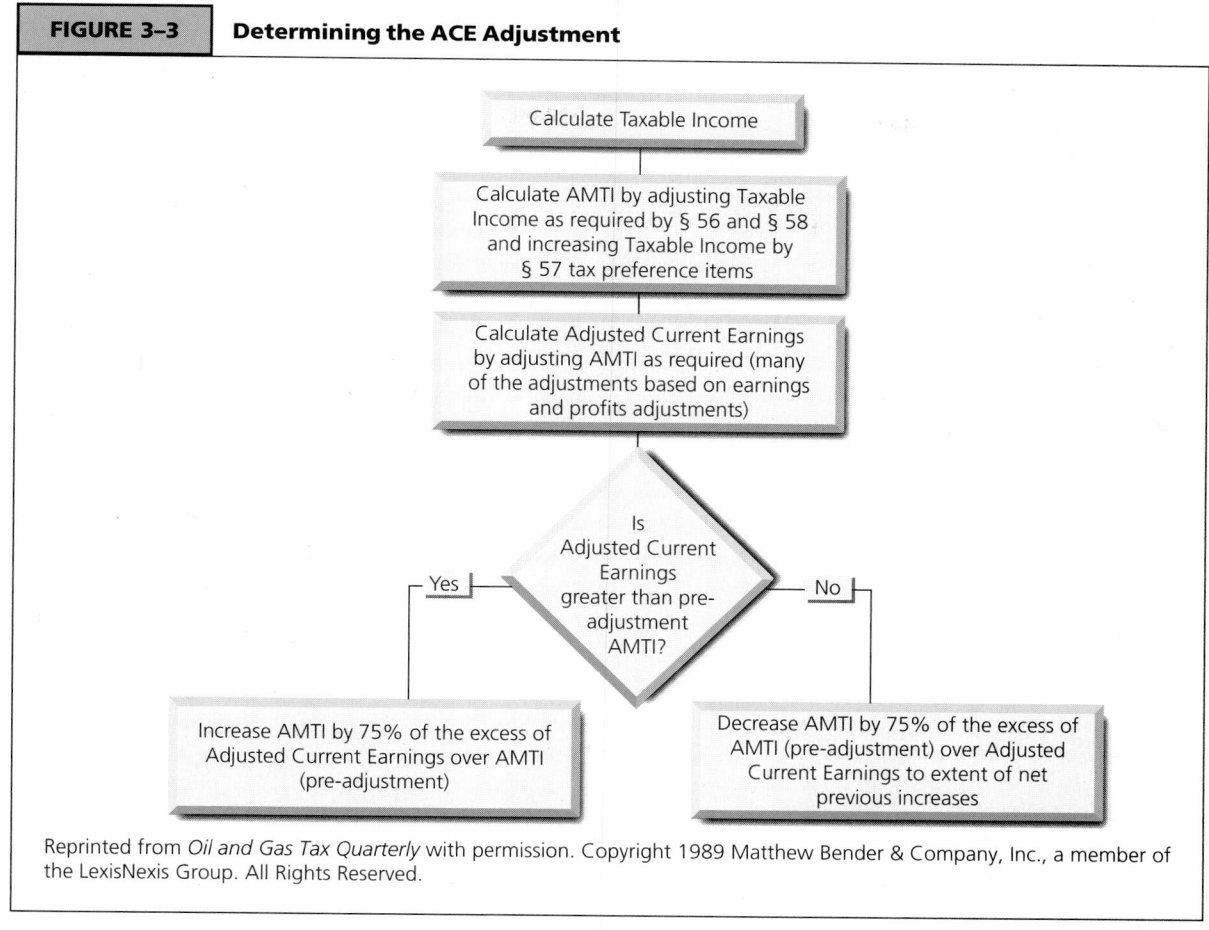

Reprinted from *Oil and Gas Tax Quarterly* with permission. Copyright 1989 Matthew Bender & Company, Inc., a member of the LexisNexis Group. All Rights Reserved.

The ACE adjustment is tax-based and can be a negative amount. AMTI is increased by 75 percent of the excess of ACE over unadjusted AMTI. Or, AMTI is reduced by 75 percent of the excess of unadjusted AMTI over ACE. This negative adjustment is limited to the aggregate of the positive adjustments under ACE for prior years reduced by the previously claimed negative adjustments (see Figure 3–3). Thus, the ordering of the timing differences is crucial because any unused negative adjustment is lost forever. Unadjusted AMTI is AMTI without the ACE adjustment or the AMT NOL.

A calendar year corporation has the following data:

EXAMPLE 30

	2007	2008	2009
Unadjusted AMTI	$6,000,000	$6,000,000	$6,100,000
Adjusted current earnings	7,000,000	6,000,000	5,000,000

In 2007, since ACE exceeds unadjusted AMTI by $1 million, $750,000 (75% × $1,000,000) is included as a positive adjustment to AMTI. No adjustment is necessary for 2008. Unadjusted AMTI exceeds ACE by $1.1 million in 2009, so there is a potential negative adjustment to AMTI of $825,000. Since the total increases to AMTI for prior years equal $750,000 (and there are no negative adjustments), only $750,000 of the potential negative adjustment will reduce AMTI for 2009. Further, $75,000 of the negative amount is lost forever ($825,000 − $750,000). Prior book income adjustments are ignored for limitation purposes. ■

CONCEPT SUMMARY $3-2$

Impact of Various Transactions on ACE

	Effect on Unadjusted AMTI in Arriving at ACE
Tax-exempt income (net of expenses)	Add
Federal income tax	No effect
Dividends received deduction (80% and 100% rules)	No effect
Dividends received deduction (70% rule)	Add
Exemption amount of $40,000	No effect
Key employee insurance proceeds	Add
Excess charitable contribution	No effect
Excess capital losses	No effect
Disallowed travel and entertainment expenses	No effect
Penalties and fines	No effect
Intangible drilling costs deducted currently	Add
Deferred gain on installment sales	Add
Realized (not recognized) gain (e.g., involuntary conversion, like-kind exchanges)	No effect
Loss on sale between related parties	No effect
Gift received	No effect
Net buildup on life insurance policy	Add

ACE should not be confused with current E & P. Many items are treated in the same manner, but certain items that are deductible in computing E & P (but are not deductible in calculating taxable income) generally are not deductible in computing ACE (e.g., Federal income taxes). The impact of various transactions on ACE are shown in Concept Summary 3–2, while the rules relating to E & P and its determination are discussed at length in Chapter 5.

The starting point for computing ACE is AMTI, which is defined as regular taxable income after AMT adjustments (other than the NOL and ACE adjustments) and after tax preferences.[26] The resulting figure is adjusted for the following items in order to determine ACE:

- *Exclusion items.* These are income items (net of related expenses) that will never be included in regular taxable income or AMTI (except on liquidation or disposal of a business). In essence, items that are permanently excluded from unadjusted AMTI are therefore included in ACE (e.g., life insurance proceeds, interest on tax-exempt bonds, and tax benefit exclusions).
- *Depreciation.* For property placed in service before 1994, the depreciation is calculated using the alternative depreciation system outlined in § 168(g). Thus, depreciation is based on acquisition costs using the straight-line method without regard to salvage value. For property placed in service after 1993, the ACE adjustment is eliminated. This change will speed up the depreciation allowance for capital-intensive industries. But computing the prior ACE depreciation adjustment for pre-1994 assets remains complex.
- *Disallowed items.* The NOL deduction is not allowed. However, since the starting point for ACE is AMTI before the NOL, no adjustment is necessary for the NOL. A deduction *is not allowed* for the dividends received deduction of

---

[26]The tax rules pertaining to the ACE adjustment are contained in § 56(g).

70 percent (less than 20 percent ownership). But a deduction *is allowed* for the dividends received deduction of 80 percent (20 percent but less than 80 percent ownership) and 100 percent (80 percent or more ownership).

- *Other adjustments.* Adjustments for the following items are necessary: intangible drilling costs, circulation expenditures, organization expense amortization, LIFO inventory adjustments, and installment sales.
- *Both AMTI and ACE.* Certain deductible items do not reduce ACE: excess charitable contributions, excess capital losses, disallowed travel and entertainment expenses, penalties, fines, bribes, and golden parachute payments.
- *Lessee improvements.* The value of improvements made by a lessee to a lessor's property that is excluded from the lessor's income is excluded from both unadjusted AMTI and ACE.
- *LIFO recapture adjustments.* An increase or decrease in the LIFO recapture amount will result in a corresponding increase or decrease in ACE.

Crimson Corporation makes the ACE adjustment calculation as follows:

EXAMPLE 31

AMTI		$ 5,780,000
Plus:		
Municipal bond interest	$210,000	
Installment gain	140,000	
70% dividends received deduction	300,000	
Income element in cash surrender life insurance	60,000	
Organization expense amortization	70,000	780,000
		$ 6,560,000
Less:		
ACE depreciation in excess of amount allowed for AMTI (property placed in service before 1994)	$230,000	
Life insurance expense	10,000	240,000
Adjusted current earnings		$ 6,320,000
AMTI		−5,780,000
Base amount		$ 540,000
Times		.75
ACE adjustment (positive)		$ 405,000 ■

Exemption

The AMT is 20 percent of AMTI that exceeds the exemption amount. The exemption amount for a corporation is $40,000 reduced by 25 percent of the amount by which AMTI exceeds $150,000.[27]

EXAMPLE 32

Beige Corporation has lost its small corporation status and has AMTI of $180,000. Since the exemption amount is reduced by $7,500 [25% × ($180,000 − $150,000)], the amount remaining is $32,500 ($40,000 − $7,500). Thus, Beige Corporation's alternative minimum tax base (refer to Figure 3–2) is $147,500 ($180,000 − $32,500). ■

Note that the exemption phases out entirely when AMTI reaches $310,000. With the $5 million small corporation exception, this exemption is less important to profitable corporations.

[27] § 55(d)(2).

Minimum Tax Credit

The AMT is a separate tax system that is computed side-by-side with the regular tax. Along with the "netting concept," a **minimum tax credit** is available to eliminate the possibility of double taxation.[28] Essentially, the AMT paid in one tax year may be carried forward indefinitely and used as a credit against the corporation's future *regular* tax liability that exceeds its tentative minimum tax. The minimum tax credit may not be carried back and may not be offset against any future *minimum* tax liability. The credit can be used to reduce regular tax liability in future years (but not below the tentative AMT).

Unfortunately, the law does not cover the reverse situation (a preference item generates a regular tax in one year and results in an AMT in a later year). An example could be unearned income that is taxed in the year of receipt but is not recognized for book income purposes until the year earned. Consequently, it is entirely possible that the same income could be taxed twice.

EXAMPLE 33

Returning to the facts of Example 29, Tan Corporation's AMTI exceeds $310,000, so there is no exemption amount. The tentative minimum tax is $1,490,000 (20% of $7,450,000). Assuming the regular tax liability in 2008 is $1,400,000, the AMT liability is $90,000 ($1,490,000 − $1,400,000). The amount of the minimum tax credit carryover is $90,000, which is all of the current year's AMT. ■

Since the tentative minimum tax of a small corporation will be zero, a small corporation with unused minimum tax credits after 1997 may use them up to the amount of the corporation's regular tax liability (after other credits) *less* 25 percent of the excess, if any, of the regular tax liability over $25,000. This will accelerate a small corporation's ability to use any available tax credits.

EXAMPLE 34

Purple Corporation, a small company, has a significant amount of minimum tax credits, but no AMT liability in 2008. The corporation's regular tax liability (less other credits) for 2008 is $75,000. Purple's allowable minimum tax credit for 2008 is limited to $62,500 [$75,000 − .25($75,000 − $25,000)]. ■

Other Aspects of the AMT

In addition to paying their regular tax liability, corporations have to make estimated tax payments of the AMT liability. Even corporations that prepare quarterly financial statements may find this requirement adds to compliance costs. Unfortunately, the estimated tax payment dates will not coincide with the dates of the financial statements. Accordingly, estimating book income accurately for AMT purposes from the information usually available may be difficult.

The only credit that can be used to offset the AMT is the foreign tax credit (FTC). The general business credit and other credits are unavailable in AMT years.

The AMT can be computed and reported by completing Form 4626.

LO.9

Evaluate the current status of the penalty taxes on corporate accumulations.

Penalty Taxes on Corporate Accumulations

When dividends were taxed as ordinary income, avoiding corporate distributions often proved desirable. In closely held settings where a few high-bracket shareholders controlled corporate policy, the following approach would be taken:

- Accumulate earnings within the corporation. Distribute dividends, if at all, only when the shareholders are in a favorable tax position (e.g., are in low brackets or have offsetting losses).

---

[28]§ 53.

- The accumulations will cause the stock to appreciate in value.
- The shareholders ultimately can recognize this appreciation in value at favorable capital gain rates by selling the stock. Or, if the stock is transferred by death, no gain is ever recognized due to the step-up in basis under § 1014 (see Chapter 18).

Consequently, by not paying dividends (before 2009), a tax rate of 15 percent (i.e., maximum rate on capital gains) has been substituted for 35 percent (i.e., maximum rate on ordinary income). Equally beneficial, recognition of gain has been deferred (to the date of sale) or completely avoided (transfer by death).

Due to the tax avoidance that was occurring through corporate accumulations, the penalty taxes of § 531 (**accumulated earnings tax**) and § 541 (**personal holding company tax**) were enacted. These provisions imposed a penalty tax equal to the highest rate applicable to individuals on corporations used to avoid taxes on shareholders. Prior to the Jobs and Growth Tax Relief Reconciliation Act (JGTRRA) of 2003, the penalty tax rate was 39.6 percent. The penalty tax was imposed in addition to the regular corporate income tax of § 11.

JGTRRA of 2003 reduced the motivation to accumulate at the corporate level with two changes. First, dividends are no longer taxed as ordinary income but are subject to a top rate of 15 percent (before 2009). Second, the penalty tax rate under § 531 and § 541 was reduced to 15 percent (before 2009).

Corporate accumulations may still occur, however, so a brief overview of the penalty taxes that may be imposed is included here.

Accumulated Earnings Tax (§§ 531–537)

The § 531 tax of 15 percent is imposed on **accumulated taxable income (ATI)**, determined as follows:[29]

$$\text{ATI} = \text{Taxable income} \pm \text{Adjustments} - \text{Dividends paid}$$
$$- \text{Accumulated earnings credit}$$

Taxable income is determined in the same manner as in the case of the regular corporate income tax. The adjustments to taxable income generally pertain to a corporation's ability to pay a dividend. Thus, deductions include the corporate income tax and excess charitable contributions, while additions include the NOL and dividends received deductions.

The **accumulated earnings credit** is the greater of the minimum credit of $250,000 ($150,000 for personal service corporations) or the current E & P for the year needed to meet the **reasonable needs of the business**. In determining the minimum credit or the current E & P required to meet the reasonable needs of the business, the balance of past (i.e., accumulated) E & P must be considered. This balance, once it reaches $250,000, also eliminates the use of the minimum credit.

LO.10
Understand the accumulated earnings tax.

EXAMPLE 35

Hazel, a calendar year C corporation, has accumulated E & P of $3.1 million as of January 1, 2008. Its current E & P for 2008 is $500,000, and it has reasonable business needs of $3.5 million. Hazel Corporation's accumulated earnings credit is $400,000 [$3.5 million (reasonable needs) – $3.1 million (accumulated E & P)]. Presuming that Hazel Corporation's current E & P is the same as taxable income as adjusted (see above formula), its ATI for 2008 is $100,000 [$500,000 (taxable income as adjusted) – $400,000 (accumulated earnings credit)]. ∎

EXAMPLE 36

Assume the same facts as in Example 35, except that Hazel Corporation distributes a cash dividend of $100,000 to its shareholders during 2008. Hazel's ATI for 2008 now becomes $0 [$500,000 (taxable income as adjusted) – $400,000 (accumulated earnings credit) – $100,000 (dividends paid)]. ∎

[29]§ 535.

In most cases, ATI and vulnerability to the § 531 penalty tax are avoided by resorting to the accumulated earnings credit. Hence, it is important to recognize what constitutes the reasonable needs of the business. These include expansion of the business, replacement of plant and equipment, working capital needs, product liability losses, debt retirement, self-insurance, and loans to suppliers and customers.[30] Reasonable needs do not include loans to shareholders, investments in unrelated properties or businesses, and unrealistic hazards and contingencies.[31] Finally, if the accumulated earnings credit does not suffice, dividend payments will reduce or eliminate ATI (see Example 36 above).

LO.11

Understand the personal holding company tax.

Personal Holding Company Tax (§§ 541–547)

Often referred to as the tax on "incorporated pocketbooks," the § 541 tax is aimed at the use of the corporate form to shelter investment income. As was true of the § 531 tax, the assumption is that the income will be taxed, if at all,[32] at a lower rate in the hands of a corporate investor than in the case of an individual.

Before the § 541 tax can apply, the corporation must be a personal holding company (PHC). To be a PHC, both the stock ownership and the gross income tests must be satisfied.[33] Under the stock ownership test, more than 50 percent of the value of the outstanding stock must be owned by five or fewer individuals at any time during the last half of the taxable year. Under the gross income test, 60 percent or more of gross income (as adjusted) must consist of personal holding company income (PHCI).

Under the stock ownership test, constructive ownership is taken into account to cover indirect interests. Broad stock attribution rules apply for both family and entity ownership.[34] Closely held family corporations will find the stock ownership test difficult to avoid.

Regarding the gross income test, gross income is adjusted by subtracting capital and § 1231 gains and certain other expenses.[35] PHCI consists of passive types of income such as dividends, interest, rents, and royalties. Rents *or* royalties may be excluded if they are significant in amount (i.e., comprise more than 50 percent of the adjusted gross income). In limited situations, income from personal service contracts performed by a shareholder-employee may be PHCI.[36]

If the PHC definition is satisfied, the penalty tax of 15 percent is imposed on **undistributed PHCI**.[37] Undistributed PHCI is taxable income plus or minus various adjustments and less the dividends paid deduction.[38] The adjustments are similar to those made in arriving at ATI (for purposes of the § 531 tax) and largely reflect the corporation's financial capacity to pay dividends. Thus, the dividends received and NOL deductions are added back, and the corporate income tax and excess charitable contributions (i.e., in excess of the 10 percent limitation) are subtracted.

Note that dividend payments *reduce* both ATI and undistributed PHCI. As these are the bases on which the § 531 tax or the § 541 tax is imposed, either tax can be completely avoided by paying sufficient dividends. This escape hatch is consistent with the reason for these penalty taxes—to punish the use of corporations that improperly accumulate surplus (by not paying dividends).

Both the § 531 tax and the § 541 tax cannot be imposed in the same situation. If a corporation could be subject to both taxes, the § 541 tax predominates.[39]

---

[30]§ 537 and Reg. § 1.537–1.

[31]Reg. § 1.537–2(c).

[32]Although capital gains are subject to the corporate income tax, they are not taxed under either the § 531 or § 541 penalty taxes.

[33]§ 542(a).

[34]§ 544.

[35]As prescribed by § 543(b)(2).

[36]§ 543(a).

[37]§ 541.

[38]§ 545.

[39]§ 532(b)(1).

Domestic Production Activities Deduction

In most states, one problem to be faced with the producers' deduction is its status under local law. Even in those states that do not impose an income tax on individuals, an income tax on corporations may exist. Also, the franchise tax levied on corporations may possess some of the characteristics of an income tax. Do these state taxes allow the DPAD? Due to revenue constraints, many states are decoupling from the Federal rules and are not permitting the deduction for state income tax purposes. Further, any decoupling trend will become more pronounced as the DPAD rate progresses from 6 percent to 9 percent. Any decoupling from the DPAD will add to the discrepancy that exists between the Federal and state tax treatment of income and deductions. For taxpayers with multistate operations, however, it could mean a shifting of some operations to the more tax-friendly jurisdictions (see Tax Planning Considerations in Chapter 15).

The DPAD will compel taxpayers to use extreme care in structuring business transactions. As an illustration, how should the cost of embedded services be treated? Should the cost of a warranty be included as part of the price of the product, or should it be accounted for separately? The answer may depend on what the taxpayer does in the normal course of business. If the warranty is not separately bargained for and is customarily included in the price of the product, then the embedded service qualifies for the DPAD and requires no unbundling (i.e., separation). Also, the *de minimis* rule can avoid the embedded service hurdle if properly used (see Example 8 in this chapter).

When contract manufacturing is involved, the key to the availability of the DPAD depends on the incidents of ownership. Here, advance planning becomes crucial. The parties should decide beforehand who is to receive the deduction. Legal title to the property being produced should then be placed in conformance with this decision (see Examples 11 and 12 in this chapter). But see the discussion of the W–2 wage hurdle in the Tax in the News on page 3–28.

If the production process includes offshore activity, recall that § 199 requires that a "significant part" be performed in the United States. According to the IRS, "significant" means "substantial," and this condition can be satisfied by meeting a 20 percent safe-harbor rule (see Examples 9 and 10 in this chapter). In cases where compliance with this safe-harbor rule is questionable, a ready solution would be to shift some of the offshore production to the United States.

Particularly with a DPAD rate of 6 percent (and a prospective 9 percent) of QPAI, many shareholders of C corporations may prefer a pass-through of the deduction. In such cases, making an S election becomes a viable course of action.

Pass-through entities should consider these approaches:

- An S corporation or partnership that is a qualified small taxpayer may use the small business simplified method to apportion CGS and deductions between DPGR and non-DPGR at the entity level.
- The IRS permits a partnership or an S corporation to calculate the pass-through portions of QPAI at the entity level, which then can be combined with the owner's QPAI.

In order to avoid the W–2 wage limitation imposed on the DPAD, the following observations should be considered:

- For sole proprietors, the self-employment tax does not qualify. In some cases, family members may need to be placed on the payroll to meet the W–2 wage limitation.
- Wages paid and not reported cannot be counted.
- Amounts paid to independent contractors do not qualify.
- Guaranteed payments made to a partner do not qualify.
- Taxpayers that have both qualifying and nonqualifying sales must keep careful records to allocate their W–2 wages.

- A taxpayer's payments to employees for domestic services in a private home are not included in W–2 wages for purposes of the DPAD.
- An individual filing as part of a joint return may take into account wages paid to employees of his or her spouse, provided that the wages are paid in a trade or business (and other requirements are met). This is not true if a taxpayer and spouse file separate returns.

If the taxpayer wants to avoid the allocation and apportionment procedures prescribed by the IRS, complete accounting records that identify the relevant receipts and expenses are essential. For example, the records should reflect what portion of gross receipts qualifies as DPGR and what part does not. In arriving at QPAI, what expenses (including CGS) should be allocated to DPGR and which should not? When based on specific identification, the results reached by a taxpayer should weather any IRS challenge. This type of sophisticated accounting system, however, will generate considerable compliance costs for many taxpayers.

Alternative Minimum Tax

Planning for the AMT is complicated by the fact that many of the procedures recommended run counter to what is done to reduce the regular corporate income tax. Further, the AMT has the perverse effect of increasing a company's effective tax rate during economic slowdowns.

Avoiding Preferences and Adjustments.
Investments in state and local bonds are attractive for income tax purposes because the interest is not included in gross income. Some of these bonds are issued to generate funds that are not used for an essential function of the government. The interest on such bonds is a tax preference item and could lead to the imposition of the AMT. When the AMT applies, an investment in regular tax-exempt bonds or even fully taxed private-sector bonds might yield a higher after-tax rate of return.

For a corporation anticipating AMT problems, capitalizing rather than expensing certain costs can avoid generating preferences and adjustments. The decision should be based on the present discounted value of after-tax cash flows under the available alternatives. Costs that may be capitalized and amortized, rather than expensed, include circulation expenditures, mining exploration and development costs, and research and experimentation expenditures.

Controlling the Timing of Preferences and Adjustments.
In many situations, smaller corporations may be able to avoid the AMT by making use of the exemption. To maximize the exemption, taxpayers should attempt to avoid bunching positive adjustments and tax preferences in any one year. When the expenditure is largely within the control of the taxpayer, timing to avoid bunching is more easily accomplished.

Optimum Use of the AMT and Regular Corporate Income Tax Rate Difference. A corporation that cannot avoid the AMT in a particular year can often save taxes by taking advantage of the difference between the AMT and the regular tax rates. In general, a corporation that expects to be subject to the AMT should accelerate income and defer deductions for the remainder of the year. Since the difference between the regular tax and the AMT may be as much as 14 or 15 percentage points, this strategy results in the income being taxed at less than it would be if reported in the next year. There is always the risk that the regular corporate rates may increase in future years. If the same corporation expects to be subject to the AMT for the next year (or years), this technique must be reversed. The corporation should defer income and accelerate deductions. The strategy delays the date the corporation has to pay the tax.

EXAMPLE 37

Falcon Corporation expects to be in the 34% tax bracket in 2009 but is subject to the AMT in 2008. In late 2008, Falcon is contemplating selling a tract of unimproved land (basis of $200,000 and fair market value of $1 million). Under these circumstances, it is preferable to sell the land in 2008. The gain of $800,000 ($1,000,000 − $200,000) generates a tax of $160,000 [$800,000 (recognized gain) × 20% (AMT rate)]. However, if the land is sold in 2009, the resulting tax is $272,000 [$800,000 (recognized gain) × 34% (regular corporate income tax rate)]. A savings of $112,000 ($272,000 − $160,000) materializes by making the sale in 2008. ■

The S Corporation Option. Corporations that make the S election will not be subject to the corporate AMT. As noted in Chapter 12, however, various AMT adjustments and preferences pass through to the individual shareholders. But one troublesome adjustment, the one involving the ACE adjustment, is eliminated since it does not apply to individual taxpayers. Similarly, the accumulated earnings and personal holding company taxes cannot be imposed on an S corporation.

KEY TERMS

Accumulated earnings credit, 3–25	Alternative minimum taxable income (AMTI), 3–16	Personal holding company tax, 3–25
Accumulated earnings tax, 3–25	Domestic production activities deduction (DPAD), 3–3	Qualified production activities income (QPAI), 3–2
Accumulated taxable income (ATI), 3–25	Domestic production gross receipts (DPGR), 3–6	Reasonable needs of the business, 3–25
Adjusted current earnings (ACE), 3–19	Expanded affiliated group (EAG), 3–14	Tax preference items, 3–19
Alternative minimum tax (AMT), 3–16	Minimum tax credit, 3–24	Undistributed PHCI, 3–26
		W–2 wages, 3–3

PROBLEM MATERIALS

DISCUSSION QUESTIONS

1. Who can claim the manufacturers' deduction? Which taxpayers are more likely to use it?

2. What position does FASB take with respect to the treatment of the DPAD?

3. Explain the relationship between the following items:
   a. DPAD and QPAI.
   b. DPAD and W–2 wages.

    c.   DPAD and TI.

    d.   DPGR and QPAI.

    e.   EAG and DPAD.

    f.   DPAD and AMT.

4. Is the taxable income limitation determined before or after any NOL deduction for the year?

5. Heather, a calendar year taxpayer, is a partner in Sand Company, a profitable fiscal year manufacturing company. When will Heather be able to use the fiscal year 2007–2008 QPAI pass-through from Sand Company?

Issue ID

6. Brad is independently wealthy and does not work. Except for household servants, he has no employees. Due to the phaseout of itemized deductions, Brad claims the standard deduction when he files his Form 1040. Is it possible that Brad might be able to claim a DPAD? Explain.

7. Alicia operates a chain of Tex-Mex fast-food outlets. She also wholesales frozen prepared meals to grocery stores.
    a.   Can Alicia claim a DPAD? Explain.
    b.   Would it matter if all of the fast-food sales are on a take-out basis as the retail outlets have no dining facilities?

8. Maroon Company manufactures a product and sells it with an embedded service.
    a.   What does this mean?
    b.   Give some examples of embedded services.
    c.   Under what circumstances can the amount attributable to an embedded service be part of DPGR?

9. In order to qualify as DPGR, QPP must be MPGE in whole or in significant part within the United States.
    a.   Interpret this statement.
    b.   What does "significant" mean?
    c.   In what context does this problem arise?

10. Only one producer may claim the DPAD. Explain.
    a.   Why is this rule important in the area of contract manufacturing?
    b.   Does the rule present any planning opportunities?

11. Comment on whether or not the following *independent* situations can constitute DPGR:
    a.   Taxpayer performs engineering services in connection with a resort hotel being constructed in Cancún, Mexico.
    b.   Taxpayer contracts to spray paint golf carts manufactured and sold by another.
    c.   Taxpayer, the owner and operator of a hardware store, builds a vacation home in his spare time. The home, including the land, is sold at a profit on eBay.
    d.   Taxpayer, an electrician, subcontracts the electrical work on new homes being constructed by a real estate developer.
    e.   Taxpayer, a utility, generates, transmits, and sells electric power to residential and commercial customers.

Issue ID

12. CSIH, Inc., produces two live television programs and licenses the first program to Clear, Inc., a television station. CSIH licenses the second television program to Zebra's television station, which broadcasts the program on its channel. Both programs contain product placements and advertising for which CSIH receives compensation. CSIH and Clear are unrelated parties and are not members of an EAG. Discuss the DPGR tax result.

Issue ID

13. Jack and Kathleen are equal partners in Red Partnership. For the year, they receive a pass-through of the same amount of QPAI and W–2 wages from Red. Jack, however, is able to claim a larger DPAD on his income tax return than Kathleen. Why?

14. What is the purpose of the ACE adjustment?

15. What factors may make a corporation subject to the AMT?

16. Most of the adjustments and tax preference items necessary to arrive at AMTI are different for corporations and individuals. Assess the validity of this statement.

17. Explain the small corporation exemption for AMT purposes.

18. Regular taxable income – AMT adjustments (except ACE) + Tax preferences = Tentative AMTI – ACE adjustment = AMTI before NOL deduction. Please comment.

19. In arriving at AMTI, why are NOLs stated separately instead of being included with other adjustments?

AMT 90% to warypend

20. Using the legend provided, classify the impact each of the following items has upon unadjusted AMTI in arriving at ACE:

Legend
I = Increase in AMTI
D = Decrease in AMTI
E = Either an increase or a decrease in AMTI
N = No impact

   a. Loss on sale of a piece of equipment to a related party.
   b. Currently deducted intangible drilling costs.
   c. Purchase of raw materials.
   d. Nondeductible transportation fines.
   e. Proceeds from a key employee insurance policy.
   f. Dividends received deduction for a 15%-owned business.
   g. Tax-exempt interest.

21. Using the legend provided, classify the impact each of the following items has upon taxable income or loss for purposes of determining AMTI:

Legend
I = Increase in taxable income
D = Decrease in taxable income
E = Either an increase or a decrease in taxable income
N = No impact

   a. Amortization claimed on certified pollution control facilities.
   b. Adjusted current earnings (ACE) adjustment.
   c. Excess mining exploration and development costs.
   d. AMT net operating loss deduction.
   e. Statutory AMT exemption.
   f. Accelerated depreciation on post-1986 property acquisitions.
   g. Tax-exempt interest on private activity bonds.
   h. LIFO inventory.
   i. Excess percentage depletion of an integrated oil company.

22. Robert Barrack calls you to ask whether his company will have to make estimated tax payments of its AMT liability of approximately $102,200. Prepare a tax file memo indicating what you told Mr. Barrack.

Communications

23. A regular corporation is anticipating AMT problems during 2008. Point out some strategies available to help this corporation avoid or minimize the AMT.

Issue ID

24. Explain the minimum tax credit. What is its purpose?

25. Is the DPAD (§ 199 deduction) allowed for AMT purposes? In this connection, does it matter whether the taxpayer is an individual or a corporation? Explain.

26. ATI = Taxable income + Adjustments + Dividends paid – Accumulated earnings credit. Assess the validity of this formula.

27. What is considered to be personal holding company income?

28. What impact does the S corporation election have on the AMT, the accumulated earnings tax, and the personal holding company tax?

PROBLEMS

29. Wells, Inc., has $12 million of taxable income in 2010. What is the maximum DPAD tax savings for this C corporation? $12 M \times .9 \times .35$

30. In each of the following *independent* situations, determine the DPAD for 2008 for the corporation involved.

	Taxpayer	QPAI	TI	W–2 Wages
a.	Hawk	$400,000	$500,000	$ 20,000
b.	Falcon	800,000	600,000	100,000
c.	Harrier	700,000	900,000	200,000
d.	Peregrine	900,000	900,000*	300,000
e.	Raven	900,000	900,000	200,000**

*Does not include a $100,000 NOL carryover from the previous year.

**Only $50,000 relates directly to manufacturing activities.

31. Kingfisher Corporation produces and sells refrigerators for outdoor use (e.g., patios, porches, verandas). Its major manufacturing facility is in Georgia, but it also has a smaller plant in Honduras. Gross receipts for the current year are derived as follows: $4.1 million from Georgia and $1 million from Honduras.
    a. What is Kingfisher's DPGR for the current year?
    b. What if the gross receipts from the Honduras plant are only $200,000 (not $1 million)?

32. Azure Corporation manufactures and sells climate-controlled wine cabinets. Its most popular model sells for $2,000 and comes with a basic 90-day warranty. For an extra $100, this warranty will be extended to 3 years and for $200 to 10 years. Though the basic warranty is not separately priced, the company estimates its cost as being $20.
    a. If a customer buys a wine cabinet with the basic warranty, how much of the $2,000 paid represents DPGR to Azure?
    b. Assume a customer pays $2,100 to include the extended 3-year warranty. How much of this amount is DPGR?
    c. Assume $2,200 is paid to include the extended 10-year warranty. How much is DPGR?
    d. Could the sales agreement be modified so as to increase the amount qualifying as DPGR? Explain.

33. Swallow Corporation sells portable air filtration systems by means of the Internet and direct mail orders. Most of the components are purchased from foreign suppliers at a cost of $800. Swallow supplies the remaining components and assembles the final product at a cost of $200. Swallow's marketing, packaging, and shipping expenses total $20 per unit. Each unit is sold for $1,400.
    a. What is Swallow's DPGR per unit?
    b. Its QPAI?

34. Assume the same facts as in Problem 33, except that Swallow incurred only $170 (not $200) in production costs.
    a. What is Swallow's DPGR per unit? Its QPAI?
    b. How could this result have been avoided?

Issue ID

35. Robert is the owner of a large apartment complex that was built 30 years ago. As the complex is in serious need of renovation, Robert pays Cardinal Construction Corporation $2.8 million to do the work. Robert also pays an architect $400,000 to draw up plans for the project. Because the rewiring requirements are so extensive, Cardinal pays Dove Electric Company $500,000 to handle this part of the renovation. At all times title to the apartment complex remains with Robert. Who has DPGR and in what amount?

36. Flamingo Corporation, a calendar year taxpayer, sells lawn furniture through big box stores. It manufactures some of the furniture and imports some from unrelated

foreign producers. For tax year 2008, Flamingo's records reveal the following information:

| | Furniture Sold | |
	Manufactured	Imported
Gross receipts	$2,500,000	$1,500,000
CGS	1,000,000	750,000

Flamingo also has selling and marketing expenses of $600,000 and administrative expenses of $200,000. Under the simplified deduction method, what is Flamingo's:
a. DPGR?
b. QPAI?
c. DPAD?

37. Assume the same facts as in Problem 36, except that Flamingo's records do not identify its CGS (as between manufactured and imported furniture) but reflect an unallocated amount of $1,750,000. Further assume that Flamingo is qualified to (and does) use the small business simplified method of allocating CGS and other expenses. What is Flamingo's:
a. QPAI?
b. DPAD?

38. Indigo Corporation, a calendar year taxpayer, manufactures yogurt that it wholesales to grocery stores and other food outlets. It also operates a yogurt shop near its factory where it sells directly to the general public. For tax years 2007 and 2008, gross receipts are as follows:

| | Gross Receipts | |
	Wholesale	Snack Shop
2007	$4,000,000	$220,000
2008	5,000,000	260,000

What is Indigo's DPGR for:
a. 2007?
b. 2008?

39. Violet Corporation manufactures an exercise machine at a cost of $800 and sells the machine to Scarlet Corporation for $1,000 in 2008. Scarlet incurs TV advertising expenses of $300 and sells the machine by phone order for $1,600. If Violet and Scarlet corporations are not related parties, determine their:
a. DPGR.
b. QPAI.
c. DPAD.

40. The Scarlet Partnership has two equal partners in the 35% marginal tax bracket. If Scarlet has $11 million of taxable income in 2008, what could be the maximum DPAD tax savings for this partnership/partners?

41. The controller for Brown, Inc., calculates these tentative taxes for the year 2008:

Regular tax liability	$232,000
Tentative minimum tax	259,600
Personal holding company tax	47,700
Accumulated earnings tax	52,200

What is Brown's probable tax bill for 2008?

42. In each of the following independent situations, determine whether the corporation is a small corporation:
a. Gold Corporation has gross receipts of $5.5 million, $4.7 million, and $4.6 million in 2005, 2006, and 2007, respectively.
b. Silver Corporation has gross receipts of $4.6 million, $5.5 million, and $4.95 million in 2005, 2006, and 2007, respectively.

c.   Copper Corporation has gross receipts of $4.7 million, $4.9 million, and $5.12 million in 2005, 2006, and 2007, respectively.

43. For 2008, Mallard Corporation (a calendar year integrated oil company) had the following transactions:

Taxable income	$5,000,000
Regular tax depreciation on realty in excess of ADS (placed in service in 1989)	1,700,000
Tax-exempt interest on municipal bonds (funds were used for nongovernmental purposes)	500,000
Percentage depletion in excess of the property's adjusted basis	700,000

Assume no ACE adjustment.

a.   Determine Mallard Corporation's AMTI for 2008.
b.   Determine the tentative minimum tax base (refer to Figure 3–2).
c.   Determine the tentative minimum tax.
d.   What is the amount of the AMT?

44. Purple Corporation, a calendar year taxpayer, has the following pre-adjusted AMTI and ACE for 2006 through 2009:

	Pre-adjusted AMTI	ACE
2006	$80,000,000	$70,000,000
2007	60,000,000	90,000,000
2008	50,000,000	40,000,000
2009	60,000,000	20,000,000

Calculate Purple's positive and negative adjustments, if any, for ACE.

45. Based on the following facts, calculate adjusted current earnings (ACE):

Alternative minimum taxable income (AMTI)	$7,120,000
Municipal bond interest	630,000
Expenses related to municipal bonds	50,000
Key employee life insurance proceeds in excess of cash surrender value	2,000,000
Excess of FIFO over LIFO	160,000
Organization expense amortization	100,000
Cost of goods sold	5,220,000
Advertising expenses	625,000
Loss between related parties	260,000
Life insurance expense	300,000

46. In each of the following independent situations, determine the tentative minimum tax (assume the companies are not in small corporation status):

	AMTI (before the Exemption Amount)
Brant Corporation	$170,000
Tern Corporation	190,000
Snipe Corporation	325,000

47. In each of the following *independent* situations relating to the penalty tax under § 531, determine the dividend that the corporation would have to pay to make its ATI (accumulated taxable income) be $0.

	Corporation	Beginning Balance in Accumulated E & P	Taxable Income (as adjusted)	Reasonable Needs of the Business
a.	Oriole	$3,000,000	$200,000	$3,100,000
b.	Teal	3,900,000	300,000	4,000,000
c.	Wren	4,000,000	300,000	4,400,000
d.	Stork	5,000,000	500,000	5,000,000

48. Calculate the accumulated earnings tax based on the following information:

Taxable income	$522,000
Dividends received deduction	42,000
Accumulated earnings credit	31,100
Excess charitable contributions	27,000
Dividends paid	88,000
Federal income tax	177,480

RESEARCH PROBLEMS

Note: Solutions to Research Problems can be prepared by using the **RIA Checkpoint**® **Student Edition** online research product, which is available to accompany this text. It is also possible to prepare solutions to the Research Problems by using tax research materials found in a standard tax library.

Research Problem 1.   Starling Corporation enters into a lump-sum priced contract with Swift Company whereby it will produce and sell machines to Swift. As part of the arrangement:

- The machines will be delivered to Swift.
- A one-year warranty will be provided.
- Operating and maintenance manuals will be provided with the machines.
- Starling will offer Swift employees 100 hours of training and furnish training manuals.
- Spare parts will be available at a discount.
- A three-year service agreement for the machines is included.

None of the above services or property extras are separately offered or bargained for by Starling in selling its products. According to the pronouncements issued by the IRS, which of the above items will generate DPGR?

Research Problem 2.   A calendar year S corporation, Bell, Inc., is an online software and advertising business. Bell approaches your accounting firm with the following question: Is the use of computer software online by customers a lease, rental, license, sale, exchange, or other disposition of the software? In other words, do gross receipts derived from such customers constitute DPGR?

Research Problem 3.   According to any pronouncement issued by the IRS, will the independent situations listed below generate DPGR?
   a. Addie Corporation manufactures QPP in whole or significant part within the United States and uses the QPP in its business. After several years, Addie sells the QPP that it manufactured to Baker Corporation.
   b. Sammy Corporation manufactures QPP within the United States and sells the QPP to Tom, an unrelated person. Tom leases the QPP for three years to Zebra, Inc., a taxpayer unrelated to both Sammy and Tom. Shortly thereafter, Sammy repurchases the QPP from Tom. At the end of the term of the lease, Zebra purchases the QPP from Sammy.
   c. Gabe, Inc., a cable company, charges subscribers $15 a month for its basic cable television service. Larry, an unrelated person, produces a qualified film and licenses it to Gabe for 10¢ per subscriber per month.

Research Problem 4.   Owl, Inc., was owned entirely by Jeri Bell and Jerry Gore, each owning 620,000 of the 1,240,000 shares of common stock outstanding. On January 1, 2008, Owl established an employee stock ownership plan (ESOP) that later received a favorable determination letter from the IRS.

On February 1, 2008, Bell and Gore each sold 500,000 of their shares to the ESOP, each receiving $2.5 million. To facilitate the transaction, the ESOP borrowed $5 million from a local bank; the loan was guaranteed by Owl. During the year, Owl paid $1.4 million in cash dividends to the ESOP with respect to its stock. The ESOP transferred the cash to the bank as payment of principal and interest under the note.

Jeri Bell calls you and asks if Owl may claim a deduction under § 404(k) for the $1.4 million cash dividends. Does Owl have to include the dividends in its computation of ACE, thus avoiding any AMT? Write a memo for the tax files in response to Ms. Bell.

Research Problem 5.   Kelly Caleb, a motion picture music editor, formed Blair Corporation. Kelly is Blair's sole shareholder, director, and officer. The company contracts with motion picture studios for Kelly's services as a music editor. All of the contracts were memorialized, in part, by a "loan-out agreement" or a "deal memorandum." Each contract with the studios made specific reference to Kelly's music services.

Other than compensation paid to Kelly, the company paid no salary or compensation to other employees. The company reported total income of $222,000 from music editing services and also received $68,000 from rent income. Determine any tax problems.

Internet Activity

Use the tax resources of the Internet to address the following questions. Do not restrict your search to the World Wide Web, but include a review of newsgroups and general reference materials, practitioner sites and resources, primary sources of the tax law, chat rooms and discussion groups, and other opportunities.

Research Problem 6.   Tax professionals have criticized several restrictive positions taken in the finalized Regulations under § 199. What are some of these criticisms?

Research Problem 7.   Bills that would repeal the AMT have been introduced in Congress. Do such measures apply to both corporate and noncorporate taxpayers? What is the justification for repealing the tax for each class of taxpayers?

4

Corporations: Organization and Capital Structure

LEARNING OBJECTIVES

After completing Chapter 4, you should be able to:

LO.1
Identify the tax consequences of incorporating a business.

LO.2
Understand the special rules that apply when liabilities are assumed by a corporation.

LO.3
Recognize the basis issues relevant to the shareholder and the corporation.

LO.4
Appreciate the tax aspects of the capital structure of a corporation.

LO.5
Recognize the tax differences between debt and equity investments.

LO.6
Handle the tax treatment of shareholder debt and stock losses.

LO.7
Identify tax planning opportunities associated with organizing and financing a corporation.

Chapters 2 and 3 dealt with three principal areas fundamental to working with corporations: (1) determination of whether an entity is a corporation for Federal income tax purposes, (2) tax rules applicable to the day-to-day operation of a corporation, (3) filing and reporting procedures, and (4) special situations involving corporations.

Chapter 4 addresses more sophisticated issues involving corporations:

- The tax consequences to the shareholders and the corporation upon the organization of and original transfer of property to the corporation.
- The tax result that ensues when shareholders make transfers of property to a corporation after organization.
- The capital structure of a corporation, including equity and debt financing.
- The tax treatment of investor losses.

LO.1

Identify the tax consequences of incorporating a business.

Organization of and Transfers to Controlled Corporations

In General

Property transactions normally produce tax consequences if a gain or loss is realized. As a result, unless an exception in the Code applies, a transfer of property to a corporation in exchange for stock constitutes a taxable sale or exchange of property. The amount of gain or loss is measured by the difference between the value of the stock received and the tax basis of the property transferred.

When a taxpayer's economic status has not changed and the wherewithal to pay is lacking, however, the Code provides special exceptions to the requirement that realized gain or loss be recognized. One such exception pertains to like-kind exchanges. When a taxpayer exchanges property for other property of a like kind, § 1031 provides that gain (or loss) on the exchange is not recognized because a substantive change in the taxpayer's investment has not occurred. Section 1031 is merely a deferral mechanism and does not authorize the permanent nonrecognition of gain or loss. The deferral mechanism is accomplished by calculating a substituted basis for the like-kind property received. With this substituted basis, the realized gain or loss associated with the property given up is ultimately recognized when the property received in the exchange is sold.

Another exception to the general rule deals with transfers to controlled corporations. Section 351 provides that gain or loss is not recognized upon the transfer of property to a corporation when certain conditions are met. This provision reflects the principle that gain should not be recognized when a taxpayer's

CHOICE OF ORGANIZATIONAL FORM WHEN OPERATING OVERSEAS

When the management of a corporation decides to expand its business by establishing a presence in a foreign market, the new business venture may take one of several organizational forms. As each form comes with its respective advantages and disadvantages, making the best choice can be difficult.

One common approach is to conduct the foreign activity as a *branch* operation of the U.S. corporation. The foreign branch is not a separate legal entity, but a division of the U.S. corporation established overseas. As a result, any gains and losses produced by the foreign unit are included in the corporation's overall financial results.

Another possibility is to organize the foreign operations as a *subsidiary* of the U.S. parent corporation. If this route is chosen, the subsidiary may be either a *domestic* subsidiary (i.e., organized in the United States) or a *foreign* subsidiary (organized under the laws of a foreign country).

One fundamental tax difference between these two approaches is that the gains and losses of a domestic subsidiary may be consolidated with the operations of the U.S. parent, while the operations of a foreign subsidiary cannot. Thus, the use of a domestic subsidiary to conduct foreign operations will generally yield the same final result as the use of a branch. With both approaches, the financial statements of the U.S. parent reflect the results of its worldwide operations.

GLOBAL Tax Issues

investment has not substantively changed. For example, when a business is incorporated, the owner's economic status remains the same; only the *form* of the investment has changed. The investment in the business assets carries over to the investment in corporate stock. Further, if only stock in the corporation is received, the taxpayer is hardly in a position to pay a tax on any realized gain. Thus, this approach also is justified under the wherewithal to pay concept discussed in Chapter 1. As noted later, however, if the taxpayer receives property other than stock (i.e., cash or other "boot") from the corporation, realized gain is recognized.

Finally, § 351 exists because Congress believes that tax rules should not impede the exercise of sound business judgment (e.g., choice of the corporate form of doing business). For example, a taxpayer would think twice about forming a corporation if gain recognition (and the payment of a tax) would always be a consequence.

Therefore, the same principles govern the nonrecognition of gain or loss under § 1031 and § 351. With both provisions, gain or loss is postponed until a substantive change in the taxpayer's investment occurs (e.g., a sale to outsiders).

EXAMPLE 1

Ron is considering incorporating his sole proprietorship in order to obtain the limited liability of the corporate form. Ron realizes that if he incorporates, he will be personally liable only for the debts of the business that he has guaranteed. If Ron incorporates his business, the following assets will be transferred to the corporation:

	Tax Basis	Fair Market Value
Cash	$10,000	$ 10,000
Furniture and fixtures	20,000	60,000
Land and building	40,000	100,000
	$70,000	$170,000

In this change of business form, Ron will receive the corporation's stock worth $170,000 in exchange for the assets he transfers. Without the nonrecognition provisions of § 351, Ron would recognize a taxable gain of $100,000 on the transfer ($170,000 value of the stock received — $70,000 basis of the assets transferred). Under § 351, however, Ron does not recognize any gain because his economic status has not really changed. Ron's investment in the assets of his sole proprietorship is now represented by his ownership of stock in the corporation. Thus, § 351 provides for tax neutrality on the incorporation decision. ∎

In a like-kind exchange, the recognition of gain is avoided only to the extent that the taxpayer receives like-kind property. However, the taxpayer must recognize some or all of the realized gain when receiving "boot" (i.e., property of an unlike kind, such as cash). For example, if a taxpayer exchanges a truck used in a business for another truck to be used in the business and also receives cash, the taxpayer has the wherewithal to pay an income tax on the cash involved. Further, the taxpayer's economic status has changed to the extent that cash is received. Thus, realized gain on the exchange is recognized to the extent of the cash received. In like manner, if a taxpayer transfers property to a corporation and receives cash or property other than stock, gain (but not loss) is recognized to the extent of the lesser of the gain realized or the boot received (i.e., the amount of cash and the fair market value of other property received). Any gain recognized is classified (e.g., ordinary, capital) according to the type of assets transferred.[1] As discussed later, the nonrecognition of gain or loss is accompanied by a substituted basis in the shareholder's stock.[2]

EXAMPLE 2

Amanda and Calvin form Quail Corporation. Amanda transfers property with an adjusted basis of $30,000, fair market value of $60,000, for 50% of the stock, worth $60,000. Calvin transfers property with an adjusted basis of $70,000, fair market value of $60,000, for the remaining 50% of the stock. The transfer qualifies under § 351. Amanda has an unrecognized gain of $30,000, and Calvin has an unrecognized loss of $10,000. Both have a substituted basis in the stock in Quail Corporation. Amanda has a basis of $30,000 in her stock, and Calvin has a basis of $70,000 in his stock. Therefore, if either Amanda or Calvin later disposes of the Quail stock in a taxable transaction (e.g., a sale), this deferred gain/loss will then be fully recognized—a $30,000 gain to Amanda and a $10,000 loss to Calvin. ∎

Section 351 is *mandatory* if a transaction satisfies the provision's requirements. The three requirements for nonrecognition of gain or loss under § 351 are that (1) *property* is transferred (2) in exchange for *stock* and (3) the property transferors are in *control* of the corporation after the exchange. Therefore, if recognition of gain or loss is *desired*, the taxpayer must plan to fail to meet at least one of these requirements.

Property Defined

Questions have arisen concerning what constitutes **property** for purposes of § 351. In general, the definition of property is comprehensive. For example, along with plant and equipment, unrealized receivables of a cash basis taxpayer and installment obligations are considered property.[3] Although the disposition of an installment note receivable normally triggers deferred gain, its transfer under § 351 is not treated as a disposition. Thus, gain is not recognized to the transferor. Secret processes and formulas, as well as secret information in the general nature of a patentable invention, also qualify as property under § 351.[4]

However, the Code specifically excludes services rendered from the definition of property. Services are not considered to be property under § 351 for a critical reason. A taxpayer must report as income the fair market value of any consideration received as compensation for services rendered.[5] Consequently, when a taxpayer receives stock in a corporation as consideration for rendering services to the corporation, taxable income results. In this case, the amount of income recognized by

---

[1]§ 351(b) and Rev.Rul. 68–55, 1968–1 C.B. 140.

[2]§ 358(a). See the discussion preceding Example 19.

[3]*Hempt Brothers, Inc. v. U.S.*, 74–1 USTC ¶9188, 33 AFTR2d 74–570, 490 F.2d 1172 (CA–3, 1974), and Reg. § 1.453–9(c)(2).

[4]Rev.Rul. 64–56, 1964–1 C.B. 133; Rev.Rul. 71–564, 1971–2 C.B. 179.

[5]§§ 61 and 83.

the taxpayer is equal to the fair market value of the stock received. The taxpayer's basis in the stock received is its fair market value.

Ann and Bob form Olive Corporation with the transfer of the following consideration:

EXAMPLE 3

	Consideration Transferred		
	Basis to Transferor	Fair Market Value	Number of Shares Issued
From Ann:			
Personal services rendered to Olive Corporation	$ –0–	$20,000	200
From Bob:			
Installment obligation	5,000	40,000	
Inventory	10,000	30,000	800
Secret process	–0–	10,000	

The value of each share in Olive Corporation is $100.[6] Ann has income of $20,000 on the transfer because services do not qualify as "property." She has a basis of $20,000 in her 200 shares of Olive. Bob has no recognized gain on the receipt of stock because all of the consideration he transfers to Olive qualifies as "property" and he has "control" of Olive after the transfer; see the discussion concerning control that follows. Bob has a substituted basis of $15,000 in the Olive stock. ■

Stock Transferred

Nonrecognition of gain occurs only when the shareholder receives stock. Stock includes both common and most preferred. However, it does not include "non-qualified preferred stock," which possesses many of the attributes of debt. In addition, the Regulations state that the term "stock" does not include stock rights and stock warrants. Otherwise, the term "stock" generally needs no clarification.[7]

Thus, any corporate debt or **securities** (e.g., long-term debt such as bonds) received are treated as boot because they do not qualify as stock. Therefore, the receipt of debt in exchange for the transfer of appreciated property to a controlled corporation causes recognition of gain.

Control of the Corporation

For the transaction to qualify as nontaxable under § 351, the property transferors must be in **control** of the corporation immediately after the exchange. Control means that the person or persons transferring the property must have at least an 80 percent stock ownership in the corporation. More specifically, the property transferors must own stock possessing at least 80 percent of the total combined *voting power* of all classes of stock entitled to vote *and* at least 80 percent of the total *number of shares* of all other classes of stock.[8]

Control Immediately after the Transfer. Immediately after the exchange, the property transferors must control the corporation. Control can apply to a single

---

[6]The value of closely held stock normally is presumed to be equal to the value of the property transferred.

[7]§ 351(g). Examples of nonqualified preferred stock include preferred stock that is redeemable within 20 years of issuance and whose dividend rate is based on factors other than corporate performance. Therefore, gain is recognized up to the fair market value of the nonqualified preferred stock

received. Loss may be recognized when the transferor receives *only* nonqualified preferred stock (or nonqualified preferred stock and other boot) in exchange for property. See also Reg. § 1.351–1(a)(1)(ii).

[8]§ 368(c). Nonqualified preferred stock is treated as stock, and not boot, for purposes of this control test.

person or to several taxpayers if they are all parties to an integrated transaction. When more than one person is involved, the exchange does not necessarily require simultaneous exchanges by those persons. However, the rights of those transferring property to the corporation must be previously set out and determined. Also, the agreement to transfer property should be executed "with an expedition consistent with orderly procedure."[9] Therefore, if two or more persons transfer property to a corporation for stock and want to defer gain, it is helpful if the transfers occur close together in time and are made in accordance with an agreement among the parties.

| EXAMPLE 4 | Jack exchanges property, basis of $60,000 and fair market value of $100,000, for 70% of the stock of Gray Corporation. The other 30% of the stock is owned by Jane, who acquired it several years ago. The fair market value of Jack's stock is $100,000. Jack recognizes a taxable gain of $40,000 on the transfer because he does not have control of the corporation after his transfer and his transaction cannot be integrated with Jane's for purposes of the control requirement. ■ |

| EXAMPLE 5 | Rebecca, Daryl, and Paige incorporate their businesses by forming Green Corporation. Rebecca exchanges her property for 300 shares in Green on January 8, 2008. Daryl exchanges his property for 400 shares of Green Corporation stock on January 14, 2008, and Paige exchanges her property for 300 shares in Green on March 6, 2008. Because the three exchanges are part of a prearranged plan and the control test is met, the nonrecognition provisions of § 351 apply to all of the exchanges. ■ |

Stock need not be issued to the property transferors in the same proportion as the relative value of the property transferred by each. However, when stock received is not proportionate to the value of the property transferred, the actual effect of the transactions must be properly characterized. For example, in such situations one transferor may actually be making a gift of valuable consideration to another transferor.

| EXAMPLE 6 | Ron and Shelia, father and daughter, form Oak Corporation. Ron transfers property worth $50,000 in exchange for 100 shares of stock, while Shelia transfers property worth $50,000 for 400 shares of stock. The transfers qualify under § 351 because Ron and Shelia have control of the Oak stock immediately after the transfers of property. However, the implicit gift by Ron to Shelia must be recognized and appropriately characterized. As such, the value of the gift might be subject to the gift tax (see Chapter 17). ■ |

Once control has been achieved, it is not necessarily lost if stock received by shareholders is sold or given to persons who are not parties to the exchange shortly after the transaction. However, a different result might materialize if a *plan* for the ultimate disposition of the stock existed *before* the exchange.[10]

| EXAMPLE 7 | Naomi and Eric form Eagle Corporation. They transfer appreciated property to the corporation with each receiving 50 shares of the stock. Shortly after the formation, Naomi gives 25 shares to her son. Because Naomi was not committed to make the gift, she is considered to own her original shares of Eagle Corporation stock and, along with Eric, to control Eagle "immediately after the exchange." Therefore, the requirements of § 351 are met, and neither Naomi nor Eric is taxed on the exchange. Alternatively, had Naomi immediately given 25 shares to a business associate pursuant to a plan to satisfy an outstanding obligation, the formation of Eagle would be taxable to Naomi and Eric because of their lack of control (i.e., Naomi and Eric, the property transferors, would own only 75% of the stock). ■ |

---

[9]Reg. § 1.351–1(a)(1).

[10]*Wilgard Realty Co. v. Comm.*, 42–1 USTC ¶9452, 29 AFTR 325, 127 F.2d 514 (CA–2, 1942).

ETHICAL and EQUITABLE *Considerations*

A PROFESSIONAL-FREE INCORPORATION

Allen and Beth agree to form Jay Corporation. Allen, who has a reputation for being extremely frugal, decides to follow instructions for incorporating a business that he has found on a free Internet site. Based on his plan, Allen transfers appreciated property to Jay Corporation in exchange for 75 percent of its stock. Beth agrees to provide services to the business for 25 percent of the stock.

Several months later, Allen learns that he has made a terrible blunder. To avoid paying tax on the transfer of his appreciated property, he should have received 80 percent, not 75 percent, of the stock. To correct the problem, Allen convinces Beth to transfer to him 5 percent of the corporation's stock. In return, Allen will give Beth some antiques he has collected. Allen tells Beth that this is a better deal for her because now she will have to report the value of only 20 percent of the corporation's stock as income (instead of 25 percent). Further, she receives the antiques as a tax-free gift.

How do you react to Allen's actions?

Transfers for Property and Services. Nonrecognition treatment for the property transferors may be lost if "too much" stock is transferred to persons who did not contribute property.

EXAMPLE 8

Kate transfers property with a value of $60,000 and a basis of $5,000 for 60% of the stock in newly formed Wren Corporation. Rodney receives 40% of the stock in Wren for services worth $40,000 rendered to the corporation. Both Kate and Rodney have taxable gain on the transaction. Rodney has taxable income of $40,000 because he does not transfer property in exchange for stock. Kate has a taxable gain of $55,000 [$60,000 (fair market value of the stock in Wren Corporation) − $5,000 (basis in the transferred property)] because she, as the sole property transferor, receives only 60% of the stock in Wren Corporation. ■

A person who receives stock both in exchange for services and for property transferred may be treated as a member of the transferring group for purposes of the control test. When this is the case, the person is taxed on the value of the stock issued for services but not on the stock issued for property, assuming the property transferors control the corporation. In this case, all the stock received by the person transferring both property and services is counted in determining whether the transferors acquired control of the corporation.[11]

EXAMPLE 9

Assume the same facts as in Example 8 except that Rodney transfers property worth $30,000 (basis of $3,000) in addition to services rendered to the corporation (valued at $10,000). Now Rodney becomes a part of the control group. Kate and Rodney, as property transferors, together receive 100% of the stock in Wren Corporation. Consequently, § 351 is applicable to the exchanges. As a result, Kate has no recognized gain. Rodney does not recognize gain on the transfer of the property, but he has taxable income to the extent of the value of the shares issued for services rendered. Rodney has current taxable income of $10,000. ■

Transfers for Services and Nominal Property. To be a member of the group and aid in qualifying all transferors under the 80 percent control test, the person contributing services must transfer property having more than a "relatively small value" compared to the services performed. The Regulations provide that stock issued for property whose value is relatively small compared to the value of the stock already owned (or to be received for services rendered) will not be treated as issued in return for property. This will be the result when the primary purpose of the transfer is to qualify the transaction under § 351 for concurrent transferors.[12]

---

[11]Reg. § 1.351–1(a)(2), Ex. 3.

[12]Reg. § 1.351–1(a)(1)(ii).

E X A M P L E 10	Rosalyn and Mark transfer property to Redbird Corporation, each in exchange for one-third of the stock. Reed receives the other one-third of the stock for services rendered. The transaction does not qualify under § 351 because Reed is not a member of the group transferring property and Rosalyn and Mark, as the sole property transferors, together receive only 66²/₃% of the stock. As a result, the post-transfer control requirement is not met.

Assume instead that Reed also transfers a substantial amount of property. Then he is a member of the group, and the transaction qualifies under § 351. Reed is taxed on the value of the stock issued for services, but the remainder of the transaction does not trigger gain or loss recognition. However, if the property transferred by Reed is of a relatively small value in comparison to the stock he receives for his services, and the primary purpose for transferring the property is to cause the transaction to be tax-free for Rosalyn and Mark, the exchange does not qualify under § 351 for any of the taxpayers. ∎ |

Exactly when a taxpayer who renders services and transfers property is included in the control group is often subject to question. However, the IRS has stated that such a transferor can be included in the control group if the value of the property transferred is at least 10 percent of the value of the services provided.[13] If the value of the property transferred is less than this amount, the IRS will not issue an advance ruling that the exchange meets the requirements of § 351.

E X A M P L E 11	Sara and Rick form Grouse Corporation. Sara transfers land (worth $100,000, basis of $20,000) for 50% of the stock in Grouse. Rick transfers equipment (worth $50,000, adjusted basis of $10,000) and provides services worth $50,000 for 50% of the stock. Because the value of the property Rick transfers is not small relative to the value of the services he renders, his stock in Grouse Corporation is counted in determining control for purposes of § 351; thus, the transferors own 100% of the stock in Grouse. In addition, all of Rick's stock, not just the shares received for the equipment, is counted in determining control. As a result, Sara does not recognize gain on the transfer of the land. Rick, however, must recognize income of $50,000 on the transfer of services. Even though the transfer of the equipment qualifies under § 351, his transfer of services for stock does not.

Alternatively, had the value of Rick's property been small relative to the value of his services, the transaction would be fully taxable to both Sara and Rick. In that situation, Sara, the sole property transferor, would not have at least 80% control of Grouse Corporation following the transfer. As a result, she would fully recognize her realized gain. Further, because Rick would not be treated as having transferred property, the § 351 deferral would not be available to him either. ∎ |

Transfers to Existing Corporations. Once a corporation is in operation, § 351 also applies to any later transfers of property for stock by either new or existing shareholders.

E X A M P L E 12	Tyrone and Seth formed Blue Corporation three years ago. Both Tyrone and Seth transferred appreciated property to Blue in exchange for 50 shares each in the corporation. The original transfers qualified under § 351, and neither Tyrone nor Seth was taxed on the exchange. In the current year, Tyrone transfers property (worth $90,000, adjusted basis of $5,000) for 50 additional Blue shares. Tyrone has a taxable gain of $85,000 on the transfer. The exchange does not qualify under § 351 because Tyrone does not have 80% control of Blue Corporation immediately after the transfer—he owns 100 shares of the 150 shares outstanding, or a 66²/₃% interest. ∎

See the Tax Planning Considerations portion of this chapter for additional discussion of this issue.

---

[13]Rev.Proc. 77–37, 1977–2 C.B. 568.

Assumption of Liabilities—§ 357

LO.2

Understand the special rules that apply when liabilities are assumed by a corporation.

Without a provision to the contrary, the transfer of mortgaged property to a controlled corporation could trigger gain to the property transferor if the corporation took over the mortgage. This would be consistent with the treatment given in like-kind exchanges under § 1031. Generally, when liabilities are assumed by another party, the party who is relieved of the debt is treated as having received cash or boot. Section 357(a) provides, however, that when the acquiring corporation assumes a liability in a § 351 transaction, the liability is not treated as boot received for gain recognition purposes. Nevertheless, liabilities assumed by the transferee corporation are treated as boot in determining the basis of the stock received by the shareholder. As a result, the basis of the stock received is reduced by the amount of the liabilities assumed by the corporation. See the more complete discussion of basis computations later.

EXAMPLE 13

Vera transfers property with an adjusted basis of $60,000, fair market value of $100,000, to Oriole Corporation for 100% of the stock in Oriole. The property is subject to a liability of $25,000 that Oriole Corporation assumes. The exchange is tax-free under § 351 because the release of a liability is not treated as boot under § 357(a). However, the basis to Vera of the Oriole stock is $35,000 [$60,000 (basis of property transferred) − $25,000 (amount of the liability assumed by Oriole)]. ■

The general rule of § 357(a) has two exceptions: (1) § 357(b) provides that if the principal purpose of the assumption of the liabilities is to avoid tax *or* if there is no bona fide business purpose behind the exchange, the liabilities are treated as boot; and (2) § 357(c) provides that if the sum of the liabilities exceeds the adjusted basis of the properties transferred, the excess is taxable gain.

Exception (1): Tax Avoidance or No Bona Fide Business Purpose. Unless liabilities are incurred shortly before incorporation, § 357(b) generally poses few problems. A tax avoidance purpose for transferring liabilities to a controlled corporation normally is not a concern in view of the basis adjustment as noted above. Since the liabilities transferred reduce the basis of the stock received, any realized gain merely is deferred and not completely eliminated. Any postponed gain is recognized when and if the stock is disposed of in a taxable sale or exchange.

Satisfying the bona fide business purpose requirement is not difficult if the liabilities were incurred in connection with the transferor's normal course of conducting a trade or business. But this requirement can cause difficulty if the liability is taken out shortly before the property is transferred and the proceeds are utilized for personal purposes.[14] This type of situation is analogous to a cash distribution by the corporation to the shareholder, which is taxed as boot.

EXAMPLE 14

Dan transfers real estate (basis of $40,000 and fair market value of $90,000) to a controlled corporation in return for stock in the corporation. However, shortly before the transfer, Dan mortgages the real estate and uses the $20,000 proceeds to meet personal obligations. Thus, along with the real estate, the mortgage is transferred to the corporation. In this case, the assumption of the mortgage lacks a bona fide business purpose. Consequently, the release of the liability is treated as boot received, and Dan has a taxable gain on the transfer of $20,000.[15]

---

[14]See, for example, *Campbell, Jr. v. Wheeler,* 65–1 USTC ¶9294, 15 AFTR2d 578, 342 F.2d 837 (CA–5, 1965).

[15]§ 351(b).

Amount realized:	
Stock	$ 70,000
Release of liability—treated as boot	20,000
Total amount realized	$ 90,000
Less: Basis of real estate	(40,000)
Realized gain	$ 50,000
Recognized gain	$ 20,000

     ■

The effect of the application of § 357(b) is to taint *all* liabilities transferred even if some are supported by a bona fide business purpose.

EXAMPLE 15

Tim, an accrual basis taxpayer, incorporates his sole proprietorship. Among the liabilities transferred to the new corporation are trade accounts payable of $100,000 and a credit card bill of $5,000. Tim had used the credit card to purchase a wedding anniversary gift for his wife. Under these circumstances, *all* of the $105,000 liabilities are treated as boot and trigger the recognition of gain to the extent gain is realized. ■

Exception (2): Liabilities in Excess of Basis.

The second exception, § 357(c), provides that if the amount of the liabilities assumed exceeds the total of the adjusted bases of the properties transferred, the excess is taxable gain. Without this provision, when **liabilities exceed the basis** in property exchanged, a taxpayer would have a negative basis in the stock received in the controlled corporation.[16] Section 357(c) precludes the negative basis possibility by treating the excess over basis as gain to the transferor.

EXAMPLE 16

Andre transfers land and equipment with adjusted bases of $35,000 and $5,000, respectively, to a newly formed corporation in exchange for 100% of the stock. The corporation assumes the liability on the transferred land in the amount of $50,000. Without § 357(c), Andre's basis in the stock of the new corporation would be a negative $10,000 [$40,000 (bases of properties transferred) + $0 (gain recognized) − $0 (boot received) − $50,000 (liability assumed)]. Section 357(c), however, requires Andre to recognize a gain of $10,000 ($50,000 liability assumed − $40,000 bases of assets transferred). As a result, the stock has a zero basis in Andre's hands, determined as follows:

Bases in the properties transferred ($35,000 + $5,000)	$ 40,000
Plus: Gain recognized	10,000
Less: Boot received	–0–
Less: Liability assumed	(50,000)
Basis in the stock received	$ –0–

Thus, Andre recognizes $10,000 of gain, and a negative stock basis is avoided. ■

The definition of liabilities under § 357(c) excludes obligations that would have been deductible to the transferor had those obligations been paid before the transfer. Therefore, accounts payable of a cash basis taxpayer are not considered to be liabilities for purposes of § 357(c). In addition, they are not considered in the computation of the shareholder's stock basis.

EXAMPLE 17

Tina, a cash basis taxpayer, incorporates her sole proprietorship. In return for all of the stock of the new corporation, she transfers the following items:

---

[16]*Jack L. Easson,* 33 T.C. 963 (1960), *rev'd* in 61–2 USTC ¶9654, 8 AFTR2d 5448, 294 F.2d 653 (CA–9, 1961).

	Adjusted Basis	Fair Market Value
Cash	$10,000	$10,000
Unrealized accounts receivable (amounts due to Tina but not yet received by her)	–0–	40,000
Trade accounts payable	–0–	30,000
Note payable	5,000	5,000

Because the unrealized accounts receivable and trade accounts payable have a zero basis under the cash method of accounting, no income is recognized until the receivables are collected, and no deduction materializes until the payables are satisfied. The note payable has a basis because it was issued for consideration received.

In this situation, the trade accounts payable are disregarded for gain recognition purposes and in determining Tina's stock basis. Thus, for purposes of § 357(c), because the balance of the note payable does not exceed the basis of the assets transferred, Tina does not have a problem of liabilities in excess of basis (i.e., the note payable of $5,000 does not exceed the aggregate basis in the cash and accounts receivable of $10,000). ∎

Conceivably, a situation could arise where both §§ 357(b) and (c) apply in the same transfer. In such a situation, § 357(b) predominates.[17] This could be significant because § 357(b) does not create gain on the transfer, as does § 357(c), but merely converts the liability to boot. Thus, the realized gain limitation continues to apply to § 357(b) transactions.

EXAMPLE 18

Chris forms Robin Corporation by transferring land with a basis of $100,000, fair market value of $1 million. The land is subject to a mortgage of $300,000. One month prior to incorporating Robin, Chris borrows $200,000 for personal purposes and gives the lender a second mortgage on the land. Therefore, on the incorporation, Robin issues stock worth $500,000 to Chris and assumes the two mortgages on the land. Section 357(c) seems to apply to the transfer, given that the mortgages on the property ($500,000) exceed the basis of the property ($100,000). Thus, Chris would have a gain of $400,000 under § 357(c). Section 357(b), however, also applies to the transfer because Chris borrowed $200,000 just prior to the transfer and used the loan proceeds for personal purposes. Thus, under § 357(b), Chris has boot of $500,000 in the amount of the liabilities. Note that *all* of the liabilities are treated as boot, not just the tainted $200,000 liability. Consequently, he has realized gain of $900,000 [$1,000,000 (stock of $500,000 and assumption of liabilities of $500,000) − $100,000 (basis in the land)], and gain is recognized to the extent of the boot of $500,000. Unfortunately for Chris, the relatively more onerous rule of § 357(b) predominates over § 357(c). ∎

Basis Determination and Related Issues

LO.3

Recognize the basis issues relevant to the shareholder and the corporation.

Recall that § 351(a) postpones gain or loss until the transferor-shareholder disposes of the stock in a taxable transaction. The postponement of shareholder gain or loss has a corollary effect on the basis of the stock received by the shareholder and the basis of the property received by the corporation. This procedure ensures that any gain or loss postponed under § 351 ultimately will be recognized when the affected asset is disposed of in a taxable transaction.

Basis of Stock to Shareholder. For a taxpayer transferring property to a corporation in a § 351 transaction, the *stock* received in the transaction is given a substituted basis. Essentially, the stock's basis is the same as the basis the taxpayer had in the property transferred, increased by any gain recognized on the exchange and decreased by boot received. Recall that for basis purposes, boot received includes liabilities transferred by the shareholder to the corporation. Also note that if the

---

[17]§ 357(c)(2)(A).

FIGURE 4–1	Shareholder's Basis in Stock Received
Adjusted basis of property transferred	$xx,xxx
Plus: Gain recognized	xxx
Minus: Boot received (including any liabilities transferred)	(xxx)
Minus: Adjustment for loss property (if elected)	(xxx)
Equals: Basis of stock received	$xx,xxx

shareholder receives *other property* (i.e., boot) along with the stock, it takes a basis equal to its fair market value.[18] See Figure 4–1 and the discussion that follows relating to an elective stock basis reduction that may be made when a shareholder contributes property with a net built-in loss.

Basis of Property to Corporation. The basis of *property* received by the corporation generally is determined under a carryover basis rule. This rule provides that the property's basis to the corporation is equal to the basis in the hands of the transferor increased by the amount of any gain recognized by the transferor-shareholder.[19]

These basis rules are illustrated in Examples 19 and 20.

EXAMPLE 19

Kesha and Ned form Brown Corporation. Kesha transfers land (basis of $30,000 and fair market value of $70,000); Ned invests cash ($60,000). They each receive 50 shares in Brown Corporation, worth $60,000, but Kesha also receives $10,000 in cash from Brown. The transfers of property, the realized and recognized gain on the transfers, and the basis of the stock in Brown Corporation to Kesha and Ned are as follows:

	A	B	C	D	E	F
	Basis of Property Transferred	FMV of Stock Received	Boot Received	Realized Gain (B + C − A)	Recognized Gain (Lesser of C or D)	Basis of Stock in Brown (A − C + E)
From Kesha:						
Land	$30,000	$60,000	$10,000	$40,000	$10,000	$30,000
From Ned:						
Cash	60,000	60,000	–0–	–0–	–0–	60,000

Brown Corporation has a basis of $40,000 in the land (Kesha's basis of $30,000 plus her recognized gain of $10,000). ■

EXAMPLE 20

Assume the same facts as in Example 19 except that Kesha's basis in the land is $68,000 (instead of $30,000). Because recognized gain cannot exceed realized gain, the transfer generates only $2,000 of gain to Kesha. The realized and recognized gain and the basis of the stock in Brown Corporation to Kesha are as follows:

	A	B	C	D	E	F
	Basis of Property Transferred	FMV of Stock Received	Boot Received	Realized Gain (B + C − A)	Recognized Gain (Lesser of C or D)	Basis of Stock in Brown (A − C + E)
Land	$68,000	$60,000	$10,000	$2,000	$2,000	$60,000

Brown's basis in the land is $70,000 ($68,000 basis to Kesha + $2,000 gain recognized by Kesha). ■

[18]§ 358(a).   [19]§ 362(a).

FIGURE 4–2	Corporation's Basis in Property Received	
Adjusted basis of property transferred		$xx,xxx
Plus: Gain recognized by transferor-shareholder		xxx
Minus: Adjustment for loss property (if required)		(xxx)
Equals: Basis of property to corporation		$xx,xxx

Figure 4–2 summarizes the basis calculation for property received by a corporation. Concept Summary 4–1 shows the shareholder and corporate consequences of a transfer of property to a corporation for stock, with and without the application of § 351. The facts applicable to shareholder Kesha's transfer in Example 19 are used to illustrate the differences between the transaction being tax deferred and taxable.

Basis Adjustment for Loss Property. As noted above, when a corporation receives property in a § 351 transaction, the basis for that property is carried over from the shareholder. As a result, the corporation's basis for the property has no correlation to its fair market value. However, in certain situations when **built-in loss property** is contributed to a corporation, its aggregate basis in the property may have to be stepped down so that the basis does not exceed the fair market value of the property transferred. This basis adjustment is necessary to prevent the parties from obtaining a double benefit from the losses involved.

The anti-loss duplication rule applies when the aggregate basis of the assets transferred by a shareholder exceeds their fair market value. When this built-in loss situation exists, the basis in the loss properties is stepped down. The step-down in basis is allocated proportionately among the assets with the built-in loss.[20]

In a transaction qualifying under § 351, Charles transfers the following assets to Gold Corporation in exchange for all of its stock:

EXAMPLE 21

	Tax Basis	Fair Market Value	Built-in Gain/ (Loss)
Equipment	$100,000	$ 90,000	($10,000)
Land	200,000	230,000	30,000
Building	150,000	100,000	(50,000)
	$450,000	$420,000	($30,000)

Charles's stock basis is $450,000 [$450,000 (basis of the property transferred) + $0 (gain recognized) − $0 (boot received)]. However, Gold's basis for the loss assets transferred must be reduced by the amount of the net built-in loss ($30,000) in proportion to each asset's share of the loss.

---

[20]§ 362(e)(2). This adjustment is determined separately with respect to each property transferor. In addition, this adjustment also is required in the case of a contribution to capital by a shareholder.

CONCEPT SUMMARY 4–1

Tax Consequences to the Shareholders and Corporation: With and Without the Application of § 351 (Based on the Facts of Example 19)

	With § 351			Without § 351		
Shareholder	Gain/Loss Recognized	Stock Basis	Other Property Basis	Gain/Loss Recognized	Stock Basis	Other Property Basis
Kesha	Realized gain recognized to extent of boot received; loss not recognized.	Substituted (see Figure 4–1).	FMV	All realized gain or loss recognized.	FMV	FMV
	$10,000	$30,000	$10,000	$40,000	$60,000	$10,000

	With § 351		Without § 351	
Corporation	Gain/Loss Recognized	Property Basis	Gain/Loss Recognized	Property Basis
Brown	No gain or loss recognized on the transfer of corporate stock for property.	Carryover (see Figure 4–2).	No gain or loss recognized on the transfer of corporate stock for property.	FMV
	$0	$40,000	$0	$70,000

Note that the benefit to Kesha of deferring $30,000 of gain under § 351 comes with a cost: her stock basis is $30,000 (rather than $60,000), and the corporation's basis in the property received is $40,000 (rather than $70,000).

	Unadjusted Tax Basis	Adjustment	Adjusted Tax Basis
Equipment	$100,000	($ 5,000)*	$ 95,000
Land	200,000		200,000
Building	150,000	(25,000)**	125,000
	$450,000	($30,000)	$420,000

$$*\frac{\$10,000 \text{ (loss attributable to equipment)}}{\$60,000 \text{ (total built-in loss)}} \times \$30,000 \text{ (net built-in loss)}$$
= $5,000 (adjustment to basis in equipment).

$$**\frac{\$50,000 \text{ (loss attributable to building)}}{\$60,000 \text{ (total built-in loss)}} \times \$30,000 \text{ (net built-in loss)}$$
= $25,000 (adjustment to basis in building). ∎

Note the end result of Example 21:

- Charles still has a built-in loss in his stock basis. Thus, if he sells the Gold Corporation stock, he will recognize a loss of $30,000 [$420,000 (selling price based on presumed value of the stock) − $450,000 (basis in the stock)].

- Gold Corporation can no longer recognize any loss on the sale of *all* of its assets [$420,000 (selling price based on value of assets) − $420,000 (adjusted basis in assets) = $0 (gain or loss)].

In the event a corporation is subject to the built-in loss adjustment, an alternative approach is available. If the shareholder and the corporation both elect, the basis reduction can be made to the shareholder's stock rather than to the corporation's property.

EXAMPLE 22

Assume the same facts as in the previous example. If Charles and Gold elect, Charles can reduce his stock basis to $420,000 ($450,000 − $30,000). As a result, Gold's aggregate basis in the assets it receives is $450,000. If Charles has no intention of selling his stock, this election could be desirable as it benefits Gold by giving the corporation a higher depreciable basis in the equipment and building. ■

Note the end result of Example 22:

- Charles has no built-in loss. Thus, if he sells the Gold Corporation stock, he will recognize no gain or loss [$420,000 (presumed value of the stock) − $420,000 (basis in the stock)].
- Gold Corporation has a built-in loss. Thus, if it sells *all* of its assets [$420,000 (selling price based on value of assets) − $450,000 (basis in assets)], it recognizes a loss of $30,000.

Consequently, the built-in loss adjustment places the loss with either the shareholder or the corporation but not both (compare Examples 21 and 22).

Stock Issued for Services Rendered. A transfer of stock for services is not a taxable transaction to a corporation.[21] But another issue arises: Can a corporation deduct the fair market value of the stock it issues in consideration of services as a business expense? Yes, unless the services are such that the payment is characterized as a capital expenditure.[22]

EXAMPLE 23

Esther and Carl form White Corporation. Esther transfers cash of $500,000 for 100 shares of White Corporation stock. Carl transfers property worth $400,000 (basis of $90,000) and agrees to serve as manager of the corporation for one year; in return, Carl receives 100 shares of stock in White. The value of Carl's services to White Corporation is $100,000. Esther's and Carl's transfers qualify under § 351. Neither Esther nor Carl is taxed on the transfer of their property. However, Carl has income of $100,000, the value of the stock received for the services he will render to White Corporation. White has a basis of $90,000 in the property it acquired from Carl, and it may claim a compensation expense deduction under § 162 for $100,000. Carl's stock basis is $190,000 ($90,000 + $100,000). ■

EXAMPLE 24

Assume the same facts as in Example 23 except that Carl provides legal services (instead of management services) in organizing the corporation. The value of Carl's legal services is $100,000. Carl has no gain on the transfer of the property but has income of $100,000 for the value of the stock received for the services rendered. White Corporation has a basis of $90,000 in the property it acquired from Carl and must capitalize the $100,000 as an organizational expenditure. Carl's stock basis is $190,000 ($90,000 + $100,000). ■

Holding Period for Shareholder and Transferee Corporation. In a § 351 transfer, the shareholder's holding period for stock received in exchange for a capital asset or § 1231 property includes the holding period of the property transferred to the corporation. That is, the holding period of the property is "tacked on" to the holding period of the stock. The holding period for stock received for any other property (e.g.,

---

[21]Reg. § 1.1032–1(a).

[22]Rev.Rul. 62–217, 1962–2 C.B. 59, modified by Rev.Rul. 74–503, 1974–2 C.B. 117.

GLOBAL *Tax Issues*

DOES § 351 COVER THE INCORPORATION OF A FOREIGN BUSINESS?

When a taxpayer wishes to incorporate a business overseas by moving assets across U.S. borders, the deferral mechanism of § 351 applies in certain situations, but not in others. In general, § 351 is available to defer gain recognition when starting up a new corporation outside the United States unless so-called tainted assets are involved. Under § 367, tainted assets, which include assets such as inventory and accounts receivable, are treated as having been sold by the taxpayer prior to the corporate formation; therefore, their transfer results in the current recognition of gain. The presence of tainted assets triggers gain because Congress does not want taxpayers to be able to shift the gain outside the U.S. jurisdiction. The gain recognized is ordinary or capital, depending on the nature of the asset involved.

inventory) begins on the day after the exchange. The corporation's holding period for property acquired in a § 351 transfer is the holding period of the transferor-shareholder, regardless of the character of the property in the transferor's hands.[23]

Recapture Considerations. In a § 351(a) transfer where no gain is recognized, the depreciation recapture rules do not apply.[24] However, any recapture potential associated with the property carries over to the corporation as it steps into the shoes of the transferor-shareholder for purposes of basis determination.

EXAMPLE 25

Paul transfers equipment (adjusted basis of $30,000, original cost of $120,000, and fair market value of $100,000) to a controlled corporation in return for stock. If Paul had sold the equipment, it would have yielded a gain of $70,000, all of which would be recaptured as ordinary income under § 1245. Because the transfer comes within § 351(a), Paul has no recognized gain and no depreciation to recapture. However, if the corporation later disposes of the equipment in a taxable transaction, it must take into account the § 1245 recapture potential originating with Paul. ■

LO.4

Appreciate the tax aspects of the capital structure of a corporation.

Capital Structure of a Corporation

Capital Contributions

When a corporation receives money or property in exchange for capital stock (including treasury stock), neither gain nor loss is recognized by the corporation.[25] Nor does a corporation's gross income include shareholders' contributions of money or property to the capital of the corporation. Moreover, additional money or property received from shareholders through voluntary pro rata transfers also is not income to the corporation. This is the case even though there is no increase in the outstanding shares of stock of the corporation. The contributions represent an additional price paid for the shares held by the shareholders and are treated as additions to the operating capital of the corporation.[26]

Contributions by nonshareholders, such as land contributed to a corporation by a civic group or a governmental group to induce the corporation to locate in a particular community, are also excluded from the gross income of a corporation.[27]

---

[23]§§ 1223(1) and (2).
[24]§§ 1245(b)(3) and 1250(d)(3).
[25]§ 1032.

[26]§ 118 and Reg. § 1.118–1.
[27]See *Edwards v. Cuba Railroad Co.*, 1 USTC ¶139, 5 AFTR 5398, 45 S.Ct. 614 (USSC, 1925).

However, if the property is transferred to a corporation by a nonshareholder in exchange for goods or services, then the corporation must recognize income.[28]

EXAMPLE 26

A cable television company charges its customers an initial fee to hook up to a new cable system installed in the area. These payments are used to finance the total cost of constructing the cable facilities. In addition, the customers will make monthly payments for the cable service. The initial payments are used for capital expenditures, but they represent payments for services to be rendered by the cable company. As such, they are taxable income to the cable company and not contributions to capital by nonshareholders. ■

The basis of property received by a corporation from a shareholder as a **capital contribution** is equal to the basis of the property in the hands of the shareholder, although the basis is subject to a downward adjustment when loss property is contributed. The basis of property transferred to a corporation by a nonshareholder as a contribution to capital is zero.

If a corporation receives *money* as a contribution to capital from a nonshareholder, a special rule applies. The basis of any property acquired with the money during a 12-month period beginning on the day the contribution was received is reduced by the amount of the contribution. The excess of money received over the cost of new property reduces the basis of other property held by the corporation and is applied in the following order:

- Depreciable property.
- Property subject to amortization.
- Property subject to depletion.
- All other remaining properties.

The basis of property within each category is reduced in proportion to the relative bases of the properties.[29]

EXAMPLE 27

A city donates land to Teal Corporation as an inducement for Teal to locate in the city. The receipt of the land produces no taxable income to Teal, and the land's basis to the corporation is zero. If, in addition, the city gives the corporation $100,000 in cash, the money is not taxable income to the corporation. However, if the corporation purchases property with the $100,000 within the next 12 months, the basis of the acquired property is reduced by $100,000. Any excess cash not used is handled according to the ordering rules noted above. ■

---

[28]Reg. § 1.118–1. See also *Teleservice Co. of Wyoming Valley*, 27 T.C. 722 (1957), *aff'd* in 58–1 USTC ¶9383, 1 AFTR2d 1249, 254 F.2d 105 (CA–3, 1958), *cert. den.* 78 S.Ct. 1360 (USSC, 1958).

[29]§ 362(a) and Reg. § 1.362–2(b).

LO.5
Recognize the tax differences between debt and equity investments.

Debt in the Capital Structure

Advantages of Debt. Significant tax differences exist between debt and equity in the capital structure. The advantages of issuing long-term debt instead of stock are numerous. Interest on debt is deductible by the corporation, while dividend payments are not. Further, loan repayments are not taxable to investors unless the repayments exceed basis. A shareholder's receipt of property from a corporation, however, cannot be tax-free as long as the corporation has earnings and profits (see Chapter 5). Such distributions will be taxed as dividends to the extent of earnings and profits of the distributing corporation.

Currently, another distinction between debt and equity relates to the taxation of dividend and interest income. Dividend income on equity holdings is taxed to individual investors at low capital gains rates, while interest income on debt is taxed at higher ordinary income rates.

EXAMPLE 28

Wade transfers cash of $100,000 to a newly formed corporation for 100% of the stock. In its initial year, the corporation has net income of $40,000. The income is credited to the earnings and profits account of the corporation. If the corporation distributes $9,500 to Wade, the distribution is a taxable dividend to Wade with no corresponding deduction to the corporation. Assume, instead, that Wade transfers to the corporation cash of $50,000 for stock and cash of $50,000 for a note of the same amount. The note is payable in equal annual installments of $5,000 and bears interest at the rate of 9%. At the end of the year, the corporation pays Wade interest of $4,500 ($50,000 × 9%) and a note repayment of $5,000. The interest payment is deductible to the corporation and taxable to Wade. The $5,000 principal repayment on the note is neither deducted by the corporation nor taxed to Wade. The after-tax impact to Wade and the corporation under each alternative is illustrated below.

	If the Distribution Is	
	$9,500 Dividend	**$5,000 Note Repayment and $4,500 Interest**
After-tax benefit to Wade*		
[$9,500 × (1 − 15%)]	$8,075	
{$5,000 + [$4,500 × (1 − 35%)]}		$7,925
After-tax cost to corporation**		
No deduction to corporation	9,500	
{$5,000 + [$4,500 × (1 − 35%)]}		7,925

*Assumes Wade's dividend income is taxed at the 15% capital gains rate and his interest income is taxed at the 35% ordinary income rate.
**Assumes the corporation is in the 35% marginal tax bracket.   ∎

Reclassification of Debt as Equity (Thin Capitalization Problem). In situations where the corporation is said to be thinly capitalized, the IRS contends that debt is really an equity interest and denies the corporation the tax advantages of debt financing. If the debt instrument has too many features of stock, it may be treated for tax purposes as stock. In that case, the principal and interest payments are considered dividends. In the current environment, however, the IRS may be less inclined to raise the thin capitalization issue because the conversion of interest income to dividend income would produce a tax benefit to individual investors.

Section 385 lists several factors that *may* be used to determine whether a debtor-creditor relationship or a shareholder-corporation relationship exists. The section authorizes the Treasury to prescribe Regulations that provide more definitive guidelines. To date, the Treasury has not drafted acceptable Regulations.

TAX *in the News*	IS THE DEDUCTIBILITY OF INTEREST ERODING THE FEDERAL CORPORATE TAX BASE?

The Federal corporate tax structure has long had a bias favoring debt financing over equity financing. Some have argued that this "uneven playing field" should be eliminated by allowing dividend payments to be deducted in the same way as interest payments. Proponents of this position won a partial victory in 2003 when the tax rate on dividend income was reduced to a maximum rate of 15 percent (see the relevant discussion in Chapter 5); previously, dividends had been taxed at the relatively higher ordinary income tax rates. Nonetheless, our tax structure still has a bias toward debt financing.

Now, with the current wave of corporate buyouts, some argue that allowing the deduction of interest expense could be contributing to a further erosion of the corporate tax base. When private equity firms take companies public, they often load up the corporations with debt. Because the interest payments on the debt are deductible, the corporation's profits are reduced or eliminated. As a result, the corporation pays little or no corporate income tax. As additional evidence that the interest deduction may be having a negative impact on the corporate tax base, the Brookings Institution reports that even though the United States has the "second-highest corporate tax rate among the 30 countries in the Organization for Economic Cooperation and Development, ... [it] ranks fourth-lowest in terms of corporate tax revenue as a share of gross domestic product—in large part because of the tax benefits afforded to debt financing."

Source: *Adapted from Anita Raghavan, "Debt and the Corporate Tax Base,"* Wall Street Journal, *June 16/17, 2007, p. A5.*

Consequently, taxpayers must rely on judicial decisions to determine whether a true debtor-creditor relationship exists.

For the most part, the principles used to classify debt as equity developed in connection with closely held corporations. Here, the holders of the debt are also shareholders. Consequently, the rules have often proved inadequate for dealing with such problems in large, publicly traded corporations.

Together, Congress, through § 385, and the courts have identified the following factors to be considered in resolving the **thin capitalization** issue:

- Whether the debt instrument is in proper form. An open account advance is more easily characterized as a contribution to capital than a loan evidenced by a properly written note.[30]
- Whether the debt instrument bears a reasonable rate of interest and has a definite maturity date. When a shareholder advance does not provide for interest, the return expected may appear to be a share of the profits or an increase in the value of the shares.[31] Likewise, a lender unrelated to the corporation will usually be unwilling to commit funds to the corporation without a definite due date.
- Whether the debt is paid on a timely basis. A lender's failure to insist upon timely repayment or satisfactory renegotiation indicates that the return sought does not depend upon interest income and the repayment of principal.
- Whether payment is contingent upon earnings. A lender ordinarily will not advance funds that are likely to be repaid only if the venture is successful.
- Whether the debt is subordinated to other liabilities. Subordination tends to eliminate a significant characteristic of the creditor-debtor relationship. Creditors should have the right to share with other general creditors in the event of the corporation's dissolution or liquidation. Subordination also destroys another basic attribute of creditor status—the power to demand payment at a fixed maturity date.[32]

---

[30]*Estate of Mixon, Jr. v. U.S.,* 72–2 USTC ¶9537, 30 AFTR2d 72–5094, 464 F.2d 394 (CA–5, 1972).

[31]*Slappey Drive Industrial Park v. U.S.,* 77–2 USTC ¶9696, 40 AFTR2d 77–5940, 561 F.2d 572 (CA–5, 1977).

[32]*Fin Hay Realty Co. v. U.S.,* 68–2 USTC ¶9438, 22 AFTR2d 5004, 398 F.2d 694 (CA–3, 1968).

- Whether holdings of debt and stock are proportionate (e.g., each shareholder owns the same percentage of debt as stock). When debt and equity obligations are held in the same proportion, shareholders are, apart from tax considerations, indifferent as to whether corporate distributions are in the form of interest or dividends.
- Whether funds loaned to the corporation are used to finance initial operations or capital asset acquisitions. Funds used to finance initial operations or to acquire capital assets the corporation needs are generally obtained through equity investments.
- Whether the corporation has a high ratio of shareholder debt to shareholder equity. Thin capitalization occurs when shareholder debt is high relative to shareholder equity. This indicates the corporation lacks reserves to pay interest and principal on debt when corporate income is insufficient to meet current needs.[33] In determining a corporation's debt-equity ratio, courts look at the relation of the debt both to the book value of the corporation's assets and to their actual fair market value.[34]

Under § 385, the IRS also has the authority to classify an instrument either as *wholly* debt or equity or as *part* debt and *part* equity. This flexible approach is important because some instruments cannot readily be classified either wholly as stock or wholly as debt. It may also provide an avenue for the IRS to address problems in publicly traded corporations.

<table>
<tr><td>**LO.6**</td></tr>
<tr><td>Handle the tax treatment of shareholder debt and stock losses.</td></tr>
</table>

Investor Losses

The difference between equity and debt financing involves a consideration of the tax treatment of worthless stock and securities versus that applicable to bad debts.

Stock and Security Losses

If stocks and bonds are capital assets in their owner's hands, losses from their worthlessness are governed by § 165(g)(1). Under this provision, a capital loss materializes as of the last day of the taxable year in which the stocks or bonds become worthless. No deduction is allowed for a mere decline in value. The burden of proving complete worthlessness is on the taxpayer claiming the loss. One way to recognize partial

---

[33]A court held that a debt-equity ratio of approximately 14.6:1 was not excessive. See *Tomlinson v. 1661 Corp.*, 67–1 USTC ¶9438, 19 AFTR2d 1413, 377 F.2d 291 (CA–5, 1967). A 26:1 ratio was found acceptable in *Delta Plastics, Inc.*, 85 TCM 940, T.C.Memo. 2003–54.

[34]In *Bauer v. Comm.*, 84–2 USTC ¶9996, 55 AFTR2d 85–433, 748 F.2d 1365 (CA–9, 1984), a debt-equity ratio of 92:1 resulted when book value was used. But the ratio ranged from 2:1 to 8:1 when equity included both paid-in capital and accumulated earnings.

worthlessness is to dispose of the stocks or bonds in a taxable sale or exchange.[35] But even then, the **investor loss** is disallowed if the sale or exchange is to a related party.

ETHICAL and EQUITABLE *Considerations*

CAN A LOSS PRODUCE A DOUBLE BENEFIT?

In the late 1990s, Sam invested $100,000 in TechCo, a startup high-technology venture. Although he had great expectations of financial reward, TechCo's efforts were not well received in the market, and the value of Sam's stock investment plummeted. Four years ago, TechCo declared bankruptcy, and Sam wrote off his $100,000 in worthless securities as a long-term capital loss.

To Sam's surprise, this year he receives $40,000 from the bankruptcy trustee in final settlement of TechCo's affairs.

Sam now realizes that he probably should not have claimed the loss four years ago because the deduction is allowed only if the stock is *completely* worthless. The $40,000 recovery indicates that the stock was not completely worthless. Because the three-year statute of limitations has passed, he does not plan to amend his tax return from four years ago. He also decides that the $40,000 is not income in the current year because he is merely recouping some of his original investment. How do you react to Sam's assumptions?

When the stocks or bonds are not capital assets, worthlessness yields an ordinary loss.[36] For example, if the stocks or bonds are held by a broker for resale to customers in the normal course of business, they are not capital assets. Usually, however, stocks and bonds are held as investments and, as a result, are capital assets.

Under certain circumstances involving stocks and bonds of affiliated corporations, an ordinary loss is allowed upon worthlessness.[37] A corporation is an affiliate of another corporation if the corporate shareholder owns at least 80 percent of the voting power of all classes of stock entitled to vote and 80 percent of each class of nonvoting stock. Further, to be considered affiliated, the corporation must have derived more than 90 percent of its aggregate gross receipts for all taxable years from sources other than passive income. Passive income for this purpose includes such items as rents, royalties, dividends, and interest.

Business versus Nonbusiness Bad Debts

In addition to worthlessness of stocks and bonds, the financial demise of a corporation can result in bad debt deductions to those who have extended credit to the corporation. These deductions can be either business bad debts or **nonbusiness bad debts**. The distinction between the two types of deductions is important for tax purposes in the following respects:

- Business bad debts are deducted as ordinary losses while nonbusiness bad debts are treated as short-term capital losses.[38] A business bad debt can generate a net operating loss, but a nonbusiness bad debt cannot.[39]
- A deduction is allowed for the partial worthlessness of a business debt, but nonbusiness debts can be written off only when they become entirely worthless.[40]
- Nonbusiness bad debt treatment is limited to noncorporate taxpayers. However, all of the bad debts of a corporation qualify as business bad debts.[41]

---

[35]Reg. § 1.165–4(a).

[36]§ 165(a) and Reg. § 1.165–5(b).

[37]§ 165(g)(3).

[38]Compare § 166(a) with § 166(d)(1)(B).

[39]Note the modification required by § 172(d)(2).

[40]Compare § 166(a)(2) with § 166(d)(1)(A).

[41]§ 166(d)(1).

When is a debt business or nonbusiness? Unfortunately, since the Code sheds little light on the matter, the distinction has been left to the courts.[42] In a leading decision, the Supreme Court somewhat clarified the picture when it held that if individual shareholders lend money to a corporation in their capacity as investors, any resulting bad debt is classified as nonbusiness.[43] Nevertheless, the Court did not preclude the possibility of a shareholder-creditor incurring a business bad debt.

If a loan is made in some capacity that qualifies as a trade or business, nonbusiness bad debt treatment is avoided. For example, if an employee, who is also a shareholder, makes a loan to preserve employment status, the loan qualifies for business bad debt treatment.[44] Shareholders also receive business bad debt treatment if they are in the trade or business of lending money or of buying, promoting, and selling corporations. If the shareholder has multiple motives for making the loan, according to the Supreme Court, the "dominant" or "primary" motive for making the loan controls the classification of the loss.[45]

| EXAMPLE 29 | Norman owns 48% of the stock of Lark Corporation, which he acquired several years ago at a cost of $200,000. Norman is also employed by the corporation at an annual salary of $80,000. At a time when Lark Corporation is experiencing financial problems, Norman lends it $100,000. Subsequently, the corporation becomes bankrupt, and both Norman's stock investment and his loan become worthless. ∎ |

Norman's stock investment is treated as a long-term capital loss (assuming § 1244 does not apply, as discussed below). But how is the bad debt classified? If Norman can prove that his dominant or primary reason for making the loan was to protect his salary, a business bad debt deduction results. If not, it is assumed that Norman was trying to protect his stock investment, and nonbusiness bad debt treatment results. Factors to be considered in resolving this matter include the following:

- A comparison of the amount of the stock investment with the trade or business benefit derived. In Example 29, the stock investment of $200,000 is compared with the annual salary of $80,000. In this regard, the salary should be considered as a recurring item and not viewed in isolation. A salary of $80,000 each year means a great deal to a person who has no other means of support and may have difficulty obtaining similar employment elsewhere.
- A comparison of the amount of the loan with the stock investment and the trade or business benefit derived.
- The percentage of ownership held by the shareholder. A minority shareholder, for example, is under more compulsion to lend the corporation money to protect a job than one who is in control of corporate policy.

In summary, it is impossible to conclude whether Norman in Example 29 suffered a business or nonbusiness bad debt without additional facts. Even with such facts, the guidelines are vague. Recall that a taxpayer's intent or motivation is at issue. For this reason, the problem is frequently the subject of litigation.[46]

[42]For definitional purposes, § 166(d)(2) is almost as worthless as the debt it purports to describe.

[43]*Whipple v. Comm.*, 63–1 USTC ¶9466, 11 AFTR2d 1454, 83 S.Ct. 1168 (USSC, 1963).

[44]*Trent v. Comm.*, 61–2 USTC ¶9506, 7 AFTR2d 1599, 291 F.2d 669 (CA–2, 1961).

[45]*U.S. v. Generes*, 72–1 USTC ¶9259, 29 AFTR2d 72–609, 92 S.Ct. 827 (USSC, 1972).

[46]See, for example, *Kelson v. U.S.*, 74–2 USTC ¶9714, 34 AFTR2d 74–6007, 503 F.2d 1291 (CA–10, 1974) and *Kenneth W. Graves*, 87 TCM 1409, T.C.Memo. 2004–140.

Section 1244 Stock

1M Stock Equit

In an exception to the capital treatment that generally results, § 1244 permits ordinary loss treatment for losses on the sale or worthlessness of stock of so-called small business corporations. By placing shareholders on a more nearly equal basis with proprietors and partners in terms of the tax treatment of losses, the provision encourages investment of capital in small corporations. Gain on the sale of § 1244 stock remains capital. Consequently, the shareholder has nothing to lose and everything to gain by complying with § 1244.

§ 1252= 50Mil Gross tosses
Hold Stock 5years

Qualification for § 1244.

Only a *small business corporation* can issue qualifying **§ 1244 stock**. To be a small business corporation, the total amount of stock that can be offered under the plan to issue § 1244 stock cannot exceed $1 million. For these purposes, property received in exchange for stock is valued at its adjusted basis, reduced by any liabilities assumed by the corporation or to which the property is subject. The fair market value of the property is not considered. The $1 million limitation is determined on the date the stock is issued. Consequently, even though a corporation fails to meet these requirements when the stock later is disposed of by the shareholder, the stock can still qualify as § 1244 stock if the requirements were met on the date the stock was issued.

Mechanics of the Loss Deduction.

The amount of ordinary loss deductible in any one year from the disposition of § 1244 stock is limited to $50,000 (or $100,000 for spouses filing a joint return). If the amount of the loss sustained in the taxable year exceeds these amounts, the remainder is considered a capital loss.

EXAMPLE 30

Harvey acquires § 1244 stock at a cost of $100,000. He sells the stock for $10,000 in the current year. He has an ordinary loss of $50,000 and a capital loss of $40,000. Alternatively, on a joint return, the entire $90,000 loss is ordinary. ■

Only the original holder of § 1244 stock, whether an individual or a partnership, qualifies for ordinary loss treatment. If the stock is sold or donated, it loses its § 1244 status.

Special treatment applies if § 1244 stock is issued by a corporation in exchange for property that has an adjusted basis above its fair market value immediately before the exchange. For purposes of determining ordinary loss upon a subsequent sale, the stock basis is reduced to the fair market value of the property on the date of the exchange.

EXAMPLE 31

Dana transfers property with a basis of $10,000 and a fair market value of $5,000 to a corporation in exchange for shares of § 1244 stock. Assuming the transfer qualifies under § 351, the basis of the stock under the general rule is $10,000, the same as Dana's basis in the property. However, for purposes of § 1244 and measuring the amount of ordinary loss, the stock basis is only $5,000. If the stock is later sold for $3,000, the total loss sustained is $7,000 ($3,000 − $10,000); however, only $2,000 of the loss is ordinary ($3,000 − $5,000). The remaining portion of the loss, $5,000, is a capital loss. ■

Recall the advantages of issuing some debt to shareholders in exchange for cash contributions to a corporation. A disadvantage of issuing debt is that it does not qualify under § 1244. Should the debt become worthless, the taxpayer generally has a short-term capital loss rather than the ordinary loss for § 1244 stock.

Gain from Qualified Small Business Stock

Shareholders are given special tax relief for gains recognized on the sale or exchange of stock acquired in a **qualified small business corporation**. The holder of **qualified small business stock** may exclude 50 percent of any gain from the sale or exchange of such stock.[47] To qualify for the exclusion, the taxpayer must have held the stock for more than five years and must have acquired the stock as part of an original issue.[48] Only noncorporate shareholders qualify for the exclusion.

A qualified small business corporation is a C corporation whose aggregate gross assets did not exceed $50 million on the date the stock was issued.[49] The corporation must be actively involved in a trade or business. This means that at least 80 percent of the corporation's assets must be used in the active conduct of one or more qualified trades or businesses.

A shareholder can apply the 50 percent exclusion to the greater of (1) $10 million or (2) 10 times the shareholder's aggregate adjusted basis in the qualified stock disposed of during a taxable year.[50]

Working with § 351

Effective tax planning with transfers of property to corporations requires a clear understanding of § 351 and its related Code provisions. The most important question in planning is simply: Does the desired tax result come from complying with § 351 or from avoiding it?

TAX PLANNING
Considerations

Utilizing § 351. If the tax-free treatment of § 351 is desired, ensure that the parties transferring property (which includes cash) receive control of the corporation. Simultaneous transfers are not necessary, but a long period of time between transfers could be disastrous if the transfers are not properly documented as part of a single plan. The parties should document and preserve evidence of their intentions. Also, it is helpful to have some reasonable explanation for any delay in the transfers.

To meet the requirements of § 351, mere momentary control on the part of the transferor may not suffice if loss of control is compelled by a prearranged agreement.[51]

EXAMPLE 32

For many years, Paula operated a business as a sole proprietor employing Brooke as manager. To dissuade Brooke from quitting and going out on her own, Paula promised her a 30% interest in the business. To fulfill this promise, Paula transfers the business to newly formed Green Corporation in return for all its stock. Immediately thereafter, Paula transfers 30% of the stock to Brooke. Section 351 probably does not apply to Paula's transfer to Green Corporation because it appears that Paula was under an obligation to relinquish control. If this preexisting obligation exists, § 351 will not be available to Paula because, as the sole property transferor, she does not have control of Green Corporation. However, if there is no obligation and the loss of control was voluntary on Paula's part, momentary control would suffice.[52] ■

Be sure that later transfers of property to an existing corporation satisfy the control requirement if recognition of gain is to be avoided. In this connection, another transferor's interest cannot be counted if the value of stock received is relatively small compared with the value of stock already owned and the primary purpose of the transfer is to qualify other transferors for § 351 treatment.[53]

Avoiding § 351. Because § 351 provides for the nonrecognition of gain on transfers to controlled corporations, it is often regarded as a favorable relief provision.

[47]§ 1202. The 0% and 15% capital gains rates do not apply. Thus, the maximum effective tax rate on the sale of qualified small business stock is 14% (28% × 50%).

[48]The stock must have been issued after August 10, 1993, which is the effective date of § 1202.

[49]§ 1202(d). Its aggregate assets may not exceed this amount at any time between August 10, 1993, and the date the stock was issued.

[50]§ 1202(b). The amount is $5 million for married taxpayers filing separately.

[51]Rev.Rul. 54–96, 1954–1 C.B. 111.

[52]Compare *Fahs v. Florida Machine and Foundry Co.*, 48–2 USTC ¶9329, 36 AFTR 1161, 168 F.2d 957 (CA–5, 1948), with *John C. O'Connor*, 16 TCM 213, T.C.Memo. 1957–50, *aff'd* in 58–2 USTC ¶9913, 2 AFTR2d 6011, 260 F.2d 358 (CA–6, 1958).

[53]Reg. § 1.351–1(a)(1)(ii).

In some situations, however, avoiding § 351 may produce a more advantageous tax result. The transferors might prefer to recognize gain on the transfer of property if they cannot be particularly harmed by the gain. For example, they may be in low tax brackets, or the gain may be a capital gain from which substantial capital losses can be offset. The corporation will then have a stepped-up basis in the transferred property.

A transferor might also prefer to avoid § 351 to allow for immediate recognition of a loss. Recall that § 351 provides for the nonrecognition of both gains and losses. A transferor who wishes to recognize loss has several alternatives:

- Sell the property to the corporation for its stock. The IRS could attempt to collapse the "sale," however, by taking the approach that the transfer really falls under § 351.[54] If the sale is disregarded, the transferor ends up with a realized, but unrecognized, loss.
- Sell the property to the corporation for other property or boot. Because the transferor receives no stock, § 351 is inapplicable.
- Transfer the property to the corporation in return for securities or nonqualified preferred stock. Recall that § 351 does not apply to a transferor who receives securities or nonqualified preferred stock. In both this and the previous alternatives, watch for the possible disallowance of the loss under the related-party rules.

Suppose the loss property is to be transferred to the corporation and no loss is recognized by the transferor due to § 351. This could present an interesting problem in terms of assessing the economic realities involved.

EXAMPLE 33

Iris and Lamont form Wren Corporation with the following investments: property by Iris (basis of $40,000 and fair market value of $50,000) and property by Lamont (basis of $60,000 and fair market value of $50,000). Each receives 50% of the Wren stock. Has Lamont acted wisely in settling for only 50% of the stock? At first, it would appear so, since Iris and Lamont each invested property of the same value ($50,000). But what about tax considerations? By applying the general carryover basis rules, the corporation now has a basis of $40,000 in Iris's property and $60,000 in Lamont's property. In essence, Iris has shifted a possible $10,000 gain to the corporation while Lamont has transferred a $10,000 potential loss. With this in mind, an equitable allocation of the Wren stock would call for Lamont to receive a greater percentage interest than Iris. This issue is further complicated by the special basis adjustment required when a shareholder, such as Lamont, contributes property with a built-in loss to a corporation. In this situation, if Wren is to take a carryover basis in Lamont's property, Lamont must reduce his stock basis by the $10,000 built-in loss. This reduced stock basis, of course, could lead to a greater tax burden on Lamont when he sells the Wren stock. This may suggest additional support for Lamont having a greater percentage interest than Iris. ∎

Selecting Assets to Transfer

When a business is incorporated, the organizers must determine which assets and liabilities should be transferred to the corporation. A transfer of assets that produce passive income (rents, royalties, dividends, and interest) can cause the corporation to be a personal holding company in a tax year when operating income is low. Thus, the corporation could be subject to the personal holding company penalty tax (see the discussion in Chapter 3) in addition to the regular income tax.

Leasing property to the corporation may be a more attractive alternative than transferring ownership. Leasing provides the taxpayer with the opportunity to withdraw money from the corporation in a deductible form without the payment being characterized as a nondeductible dividend. If the property is given to a family

---

[54]*U.S. v. Hertwig*, 68–2 USTC ¶9495, 22 AFTR2d 5249, 398 F.2d 452 (CA–5, 1968).

member in a lower tax bracket, the lease income can be shifted as well. If the depreciation and other deductions available in connection with the property are larger than the lease income, the taxpayer would retain the property until the income exceeds the deductions.

When an existing cash basis business is incorporated, an important issue to consider is whether the business's accounts receivable and accounts payable will be transferred to the new corporation or be retained by the owner of the unincorporated business. Depending on the approach taken, either the new corporation or the owner of the old unincorporated business will recognize the income associated with the cash basis receivables when they are collected. The cash basis accounts payable raise the corresponding issue of who will claim the deduction.

Another way to shift income to other taxpayers is by the use of corporate debt. Shareholder debt in a corporation can be given to family members in a lower tax bracket. This technique also causes income to be shifted without a loss of control of the corporation.

Debt in the Capital Structure

The advantages and disadvantages of debt as opposed to equity have previously been noted. To increase debt without incurring the thin capitalization problem, consider the following:

- Preserve the formalities of the debt. This includes providing for written instruments, realistic interest rates, and specified due dates.
- If possible, have the corporation repay the debt when it becomes due. If this is not possible, have the parties renegotiate the arrangement. Try to proceed as a nonshareholder creditor would. It is not unusual, for example, for bondholders of publicly held corporations to extend due dates when default occurs. The alternative is to foreclose and perhaps seriously impair the amount the creditors will recover.
- Avoid provisions in the debt instrument that make the debt convertible to equity in the event of default. These provisions are standard practice when nonshareholder creditors are involved. They serve no purpose if the shareholders are also the creditors and hold debt in proportion to ownership shares.

EXAMPLE 34

Gail, Cliff, and Ruth are equal shareholders in Magenta Corporation. Each transfers cash of $100,000 to Magenta in return for its bonds. The bond agreement provides that the holders will receive additional voting rights in the event Magenta Corporation defaults on its bonds. The voting rights provision is worthless and merely raises the issue of thin capitalization. Gail, Cliff, and Ruth already control Magenta Corporation, so what purpose is served by increasing their voting rights? The parties probably used a "boilerplate" bond agreement that was designed for third-party lenders (e.g., banks and other financial institutions). ■

- Pro rata holding of debt is difficult to avoid. For example, if each of the shareholders owns one-third of the stock, then each will want one-third of the debt. Nevertheless, some variation is possible.

EXAMPLE 35

Assume the same facts as Example 34 except that only Gail and Cliff acquire the bonds. Ruth leases property to Magenta Corporation at an annual rent that approximates the yield on the bonds. Presuming the rent passes the arm's length test (i.e., what unrelated parties would charge), all parties reach the desired result. Gail and Cliff withdraw corporate profits in the form of interest income, and Ruth is provided for with rent income. Magenta Corporation can deduct both the interest and the rent payments. ■

- Try to keep the debt-equity ratio within reasonable proportions. A problem frequently arises when the parties form the corporation. Often the amount invested in capital stock is the minimum required by state law. For example, if the state of incorporation permits a minimum of $1,000, limiting the investment to this amount does not provide much safety for later debt financing by the shareholders.

- Stressing the fair market value of the assets rather than their tax basis to the corporation can be helpful in preparing to defend debt-equity ratios.

EXAMPLE 36

Emily, Josh, and Miles form Black Corporation with the following capital investments: cash of $200,000 from Emily; land worth $200,000 (basis of $20,000) from Josh; and a patent worth $200,000 (basis of $0) from Miles. To state that the equity of Black Corporation is $220,000 (the tax basis to the corporation) does not reflect reality. The equity account is more properly stated at $600,000 ($200,000 + $200,000 + $200,000). ∎

- The nature of the business can have an effect on what is an acceptable debt-equity ratio. Capital-intensive industries (e.g., manufacturing, transportation) characteristically rely heavily on debt financing. Consequently, larger debt should be tolerated.

What if a corporation's efforts to avoid the thin capitalization problem fail and the IRS raises the issue on audit? What steps should the shareholders take? They should hedge their position by filing a protective claim for refund claiming dividend treatment on the previously reported interest income. In such an event, ordinary income would be converted to preferential dividend income treatment. Otherwise, the IRS could ultimately invoke the statute of limitations and achieve the best of all possible worlds—the shareholders would have been taxed on the interest income at the ordinary income rates while the corporation would receive no deduction for what is now reclassified as a dividend. By filing the claim for refund, the shareholders have kept the statute of limitations from running until the thin capitalization issue is resolved at the corporate level.

Investor Losses

Be aware of the danger of losing § 1244 attributes. Only the original holder of § 1244 stock is entitled to ordinary loss treatment. If, after a corporation is formed, the owner transfers shares of stock to family members to shift income within the family group, the benefits of § 1244 are lost.

EXAMPLE 37

Norm incorporates his business by transferring property with a basis of $100,000 for 100 shares of stock. The stock qualifies as § 1244 stock. Norm later gives 50 shares each to his children, Susan and Paul. Eventually, the business fails, and the shares of stock become worthless. If Norm had retained the stock, he would have had an ordinary loss deduction of $100,000 (assuming he filed a joint return). Susan and Paul, however, have a capital loss of $50,000 each because the § 1244 attributes are lost as a result of the gift (i.e., neither Susan nor Paul was an original holder of the stock). ∎

KEY TERMS

Built-in loss property, 4–13	Nonbusiness bad debts, 4–21	Section 1244 stock, 4–23
Capital contribution, 4–17	Property, 4–4	Securities, 4–5
Control, 4–5	Qualified small business corporation, 4–23	Thin capitalization, 4–19
Investor loss, 4–21		
Liabilities in excess of basis, 4–10	Qualified small business stock, 4–24	

PROBLEM MATERIALS

DISCUSSION QUESTIONS

1. In terms of justification and effect, § 351 (transfer to a controlled corporation) and § 1031 (like-kind exchange) are much alike. Explain.

2. Under what circumstances will gain and/or loss be recognized on a § 351 transfer?

3. What does "property" include for purposes of § 351?

4. Does "stock" include stock rights and stock warrants under § 351? Does it include preferred stock?

5. Does the receipt of securities in exchange for the transfer of appreciated property to a controlled corporation cause recognition of gain?

6. What is the control requirement of § 351? Describe the effect of the following in satisfying this requirement:
   a. A shareholder renders only services to the corporation for stock.
   b. A shareholder both renders services and transfers property to the corporation for stock.
   c. A shareholder has only momentary control after the transfer.
   d. A long period of time elapses between the transfers of property by different shareholders.

Issue ID

7. Kate transfers appreciated property to Crow Corporation in exchange for 50% of its stock, while Kevin transfers a secret process and services for the remainder of Crow's stock. Kevin's services relate to expertise he will provide in corporate operations *after* Crow's formation. What are the tax issues?

Issue ID

Decision Making

8. Several entrepreneurs plan to form a corporation for purposes of constructing a housing project. Randall will be contributing the land for the project and wants more security than shareholder status provides. He is contemplating two possibilities: receive corporate bonds for his land, or take out a mortgage on the land before transferring it to the corporation. Comment on the choices Randall is considering. What alternatives can you suggest?

9. Marvin and June form Warbler Corporation by transferring appreciated property to the corporation in exchange for shares of Warbler stock. If Marvin donates his shares to a charity immediately after the exchange, are the exchanges taxable?

10. May a transferor who receives stock for both property and services be included in the control group in determining whether an exchange meets the requirements of § 351?

Issue ID

11. At a point when Robin Corporation has been in existence for six years, shareholder Ted transfers real estate (adjusted basis of $20,000 and fair market value of $100,000) to the corporation for additional stock. At the same time, Peggy, the other shareholder, acquires one share of stock for cash. After the two transfers, the percentages of stock ownership are as follows: 79% by Ted and 21% by Peggy.
   a. What were the parties trying to accomplish?
   b. Will it work? Explain.

12. Does the transfer of mortgaged property to a controlled corporation trigger gain to the extent of the mortgage? Explain.

13. Before incorporating her apartment rental business, Libbie takes out second mortgages on several of the units. She uses the mortgage proceeds to make capital improvements to the units. Along with all of the rental units, Libbie transfers the mortgages to the

newly formed corporation in return for all of its stock. Discuss the tax consequences of these procedures.

14. If both § 357(b) and § 357(c) apply to a transfer of property to a corporation under § 351, which provision takes precedence?

15. Discuss how each of the following affects the calculation of the basis of stock received by a shareholder in a § 351 transfer:
    a. The receipt of "other property" (i.e., boot) in addition to stock.
    b. The transfer of a liability to the corporation along with property.
    c. The basis in the property transferred to the corporation.
    d. Property transferred has built-in losses.

16. Identify a situation when a corporation can deduct the value of the stock it issues for the rendition of services. Identify a situation when a deduction is not available.

17. Pursuant to a § 351 transfer, Ernesto transfers property to Mallard Corporation in exchange for Mallard stock. What is Mallard's holding period for the property it receives from Ernesto? What is Ernesto's holding period for the Mallard stock? *Carry over*

18. A corporation acquires property as a contribution to capital from a shareholder and from a nonshareholder. Are the rules pertaining to the property's basis the same? Explain.

19. In structuring the capitalization of a corporation, what are the advantages and disadvantages of utilizing debt rather than equity?

20. In determining whether debt of a corporation should be reclassified as stock, comment on the relevance of the following:
    a. The loan is on open account.
    b. The loan is a demand loan.
    c. The corporation does not make timely repayments of the loan.
    d. Payments on the loan are contingent upon earnings.
    e. The loans are in the same proportion as the shareholdings. The corporation uses the loans to purchase a new building.
    f. The corporation has a debt-equity ratio of 5:1.

21. Assuming § 1244 does not apply, what is the tax treatment of stock that has become worthless?

22. Under what circumstances, if any, may a shareholder deduct a business bad debt on a loan made to the corporation?

23. Three years ago, Ralph purchased stock in White Corporation for $40,000. The stock has a current value of $5,000. Ralph needs to decide which of the following alternatives to pursue. Determine the tax effect of each. *Decision Making*
    a. Without selling the stock, Ralph deducts $35,000 for the partial worthlessness of the White Corporation investment.
    b. Ralph sells the stock to his mother for $5,000 and deducts a $35,000 long-term capital loss.
    c. Ralph sells the stock to a third party and deducts a $35,000 long-term capital loss.
    d. Ralph sells the stock to his aunt for $5,000 and deducts a $35,000 long-term capital loss.
    e. Ralph sells the stock to a third party and deducts an ordinary loss.

24. Keith's sole proprietorship holds assets that, if sold, would yield a gain of $100,000. It also owns assets that would yield a loss of $30,000. Keith incorporates his business using only the gain assets. Two days later, Keith sells the loss assets to the newly formed corporation. What is Keith trying to accomplish? Will he be successful? *Issue ID*

25. Emily incorporates her sole proprietorship, but does not transfer the building the business uses to the corporation. Subsequently, the building is leased to the corporation for an annual rent. What tax reasons might Emily have for not transferring the building to the corporation when the business was incorporated? *Issue ID*

PROBLEMS

26. Elizabeth, Rod, June, and Whit form Zelcova Corporation with the following consideration:

	Consideration Transferred		Number of Shares Issued
	Basis to Transferor	Fair Market Value	
From Elizabeth—			
Personal services rendered to Zelcova Corporation	$ 0	$ 30,000	30
From Rod—			
Equipment	345,000	300,000	300
From June—			
Cash	60,000	60,000	
Unrealized accounts receivable	0	90,000	130*
From Whit—			
Land and building	210,000	450,000	
Mortgage on land and building	300,000	300,000	150

* June receives $20,000 in cash in addition to the 130 shares.

Zelcova Corporation assumes the mortgage transferred by Whit. The value of each share of Zelcova stock is $1,000. As to these transactions, provide the following information:

a. Elizabeth's recognized gain or loss. Identify the treatment given to any such gain or loss.
b. Elizabeth's basis in the Zelcova stock.
c. Rod's recognized gain or loss. Identify the treatment given to any such gain or loss.
d. Rod's basis in the Zelcova stock. What election may Rod consider making as to his stock basis since the property he contributes to Zelcova has a built-in loss?
e. Zelcova Corporation's basis in the equipment. What is the impact to Zelcova if Rod makes the election noted in part (d) above?
f. June's recognized gain or loss. Identify the treatment given to any such gain or loss.
g. June's basis in the Zelcova stock.
h. Zelcova Corporation's basis in the unrealized receivables.
i. Whit's recognized gain or loss. Identify the treatment given to any such gain or loss.
j. Whit's basis in the Zelcova stock.
k. Zelcova Corporation's basis in the land and building.

27. Mark and Gail form Maple Corporation with the following consideration:

	Consideration Transferred		Number of Shares Issued
	Basis to Transferor	Fair Market Value	
From Mark—			
Cash	$ 40,000	$ 40,000	
Installment obligation /R	140,000	360,000	40
From Gail—			
Cash	140,000	140,000	
Equipment	120,000	180,000	
Patent	4,000	280,000	60

The installment obligation has a face amount of $360,000 and was acquired last year from the sale of land held for investment purposes (adjusted basis of $140,000). As to these transactions, provide the following information:

a. Mark's recognized gain or loss.
b. Mark's basis in the Maple Corporation stock. *180*
c. Maple Corporation's basis in the installment obligation.
d. Gail's recognized gain or loss. *0*
e. Gail's basis in the Maple Corporation stock.
f. Maple Corporation's basis in the equipment and the patent.
g. How would your answers to the preceding questions change if Mark received common stock and Gail received preferred stock? *non*
h. How would your answers change if Gail was a partnership?

28. Jane, Jon, and Clyde incorporate their respective businesses and form Starling Corporation. On March 1 of the current year, Jane exchanges her property (basis of $50,000 and value of $150,000) for 150 shares in Starling Corporation. On April 15, Jon exchanges his property (basis of $70,000 and value of $500,000) for 500 shares in Starling. On May 10, Clyde transfers his property (basis of $90,000 and value of $350,000) for 350 shares in Starling.

Decision Making

a. If the three exchanges are part of a prearranged plan, what gain will each of the parties recognize on the exchanges?
b. Assume Jane and Jon exchanged their property for stock four years ago while Clyde transfers his property for 350 shares in the current year. Clyde's transfer is not part of a prearranged plan with Jane and Jon to incorporate their businesses. What gain will Clyde recognize on the transfer?
c. Returning to the original facts, if the property that Clyde contributes has a basis of $490,000 (instead of $90,000), how might the parties otherwise structure the transaction?

29. Ken Henderson (1635 Maple Street, Syracuse, NY 13201) exchanges property, basis of $30,000 and fair market value of $600,000, for 60% of the stock of Red Corporation. The other 40% is owned by Joy Perry, who acquired her stock several years ago. You represent Ken, who asks whether he must report gain on the transfer. Prepare a letter to Ken and a memorandum for the tax files documenting your response.

Communications

30. Dan and Vera form Crane Corporation. Dan transfers land (worth $200,000, basis of $60,000) for 50% of the stock in Crane. Vera transfers machinery (worth $150,000, adjusted basis of $30,000) and provides services worth $50,000 for 50% of the stock.
a. Will the transfers qualify under § 351?
b. What are the tax consequences to Dan and Vera?
c. What is Crane Corporation's basis in the land and the machinery?

31. Three years ago, Irene and Julie formed Hummingbird Corporation. Each transferred property to Hummingbird in exchange for 50 shares of its stock. In the current year, Jaime transfers property worth $600,000 (basis of $90,000) for 50 shares (a one-third interest) in Hummingbird Corporation. What are the tax consequences to Jaime and to Hummingbird on the transfer in the current year?

32. Ann and Bob form Robin Corporation. Ann transfers property worth $420,000 (basis of $150,000) for 70 shares in Robin Corporation. Bob receives 30 shares for property worth $165,000 (basis of $30,000) and for legal services in organizing the corporation; the services are worth $15,000.
a. What gain, if any, will the parties recognize on the transfer?
b. What basis do Ann and Bob have in the stock in Robin Corporation?
c. What is Robin Corporation's basis in the property and services it received from Ann and Bob?

33. Assume in Problem 32 that the property Bob transfers to Robin Corporation is worth $15,000 (basis of $3,000) and his services in organizing the corporation are worth $165,000. What are the tax consequences to Ann, Bob, and Robin Corporation?

34. Kim is an employee of Azure Corporation. In the current year, she receives a salary of $30,000 and is also given 10 shares of Azure stock for services she renders to the corporation. The shares in Azure Corporation are worth $1,000 each. How will the transfer of the 10 shares to Kim be handled for tax purposes by Kim and by Azure Corporation?

35. Rhonda Johnson owns 50% of the stock of Peach Corporation. She and the other 50% shareholder, Rachel Powell, have decided that additional contributions of capital are

Decision Making

needed if Peach is to remain successful in its competitive industry. The two shareholders have agreed that Rhonda will contribute assets having a value of $200,000 (adjusted basis of $15,000) in exchange for additional shares of stock. After the transaction, Rhonda will hold 75% of Peach Corporation and Rachel's interest will fall to 25%.

a. What gain is realized on the transaction? How much of the gain will be recognized?

b. Rhonda is not satisfied with the transaction as proposed. How would the consequences change if Rachel agrees to transfer $1,000 of cash in exchange for additional stock? In this case, Rhonda will own slightly less than 75% of Peach and Rachel's interest will be slightly more than 25%.

c. If Rhonda still is not satisfied with the result, what should be done to avoid any gain recognition?

36. Paul transfers property with an adjusted basis of $50,000, fair market value of $400,000, to Swift Corporation for 90% of the stock. The property is subject to a liability of $60,000, which Swift assumes. What is the basis of the Swift stock to Paul? What is the basis of the property to Swift Corporation?

Issue ID

37. Four years ago, Gene exchanged commercial real estate worth $1.5 million (basis of $300,000) and subject to a mortgage of $200,000, for land worth $1.15 million, subject to a mortgage of $150,000, and cash of $300,000. In the current year, Gene transfers the land that he received in the exchange to newly formed Bronze Corporation for all of its stock. Bronze Corporation assumes the original mortgage on the land, current face amount of $100,000, and a second mortgage, face amount of $20,000. Gene had placed the second mortgage on the land to secure the purchase of some equipment that he used in this business. What are the tax issues?

38. David organizes White Corporation with a transfer of land (basis of $200,000, fair market value of $600,000) that is subject to a mortgage of $150,000. A month before incorporation, David borrowed $100,000 for personal purposes and gave the bank a lien on the land. White Corporation issues stock worth $350,000 to David and assumes the mortgage of $150,000 and the personal loan of $100,000. What are the tax consequences of the incorporation to David and to White Corporation?

Decision Making

39. Michael transfers the following assets to Peach Corporation in exchange for all of its stock. [Assume neither Michael nor Peach plans to make any special tax elections at the time of incorporation.]

Assets	Michael's Adjusted Basis	Fair Market Value
Inventory	$ 60,000	$ 90,000
Delivery vehicles	150,000	100,000
Shelving	80,000	70,000

a. What is Michael's recognized gain or loss?

b. What is Michael's basis in the stock?

c. What is Peach's basis in the inventory, delivery vehicles, and shelving?

d. If Michael has no intentions of selling his Peach stock for at least 15 years, what action would you recommend that Michael and Peach Corporation consider? How does this change the previous answers?

40. Fay, a sole proprietor, is engaged in a cash basis, service business. In the current year, she incorporates the business to form Robin Corporation. She transfers assets with a basis of $400,000 (fair market value of $1.2 million), a bank loan of $360,000 (which Robin assumes), and $80,000 in trade payables in return for all of Robin's stock. What are the tax consequences of the incorporation of the business?

41. Sara and Jane form Wren Corporation. Sara transfers property, basis of $25,000 and value of $200,000, for 50 shares in Wren Corporation. Jane transfers property, basis of $10,000 and value of $185,000, and agrees to serve as manager of Wren for one year; in return, Jane receives 50 shares in Wren. The value of Jane's services to Wren is $15,000.

a. What gain do Sara and Jane recognize on the exchange?

b. What is Wren Corporation's basis in the property transferred by Sara and Jane? How does Wren treat the value of the services Jane renders?

42. Assume in Problem 41 that Jane receives the 50 shares of Wren Corporation stock in consideration for the appreciated property and for providing legal services in organizing the corporation. The value of Jane's services is $15,000.
    a. What gain does Jane recognize?
    b. What is Wren Corporation's basis in the property transferred by Jane? How does Wren treat the value of the services Jane renders?

43. On January 10, 2008, Carol transferred machinery worth $100,000 (basis of $20,000) to a controlled corporation, Lark, in a transfer that qualified under § 351. Carol had deducted depreciation on the machinery in the amount of $85,000 when she held the machinery for use in her proprietorship. On November 14, 2008, Lark Corporation sells the machinery for $95,000. What are the tax consequences to Carol and to Lark Corporation on the sale of the machinery?

44. RetailMart Corporation desires to set up a distribution facility in a midwestern state. After considerable negotiations with a small town in Indiana, RetailMart accepts the following offer: land and building (fair market value of $4 million) and cash of $1.5 million.
    a. How much gain, if any, must RetailMart Corporation recognize?
    b. What basis will RetailMart Corporation have in the land and building?
    c. Within one year of the contribution, RetailMart renovates the building for $800,000 and purchases inventory for $300,000. What basis will RetailMart Corporation have in each of these assets?
    d. What is the treatment of the $400,000 in cash that RetailMart received from the town but did not use?

45. Emily Patrick (36 Paradise Road, Northampton, MA 01060) formed Teal Corporation a number of years ago with an investment of $200,000 cash, for which she received $20,000 in stock and $180,000 in bonds bearing interest of 8% and maturing in nine years. Several years later, Emily lent the corporation an additional $50,000 on open account. In the current year, Teal Corporation becomes insolvent and is declared bankrupt. During the corporation's existence, Emily was paid an annual salary of $60,000. Write a letter to Emily in which you explain how she would treat her losses for tax purposes.

Communications

46. Stock in Jaybird Corporation (555 Industry Lane, Pueblo, CO 81001) is held equally by Vera, Wade, and Wes. Jaybird seeks additional capital in the amount of $900,000 to construct a building. Vera, Wade, and Wes each propose to lend Jaybird Corporation $300,000, taking from Jaybird a $300,000 four-year note with interest payable annually at two points below the prime rate. Jaybird Corporation has current taxable income of $2 million. You represent Jaybird Corporation. Jaybird's president, Steve Ferguson, asks you how the payments on the notes might be treated for tax purposes. Prepare a letter to Ferguson and a memo to your tax files where you document your conclusions.

Communications

47. Sam, a single taxpayer, acquired stock in a corporation that qualified as a small business corporation under § 1244, at a cost of $100,000 three years ago. He sells the stock for $10,000 in the current tax year.
    a. How will the loss be treated for tax purposes?
    b. Assume instead that Sam sold the stock to his sister, Kara, a few months after it was acquired for $100,000 (its fair market value). If Kara sells the stock for $60,000 in the current year, how should she treat the loss for tax purposes?

48. Mac Williams is married and files a joint return. Three years ago, at a cost of $30,000 he acquired stock in a corporation that qualified as a small business corporation under § 1244. A few months after the stock was acquired and when it was still worth $30,000, he gave it to his brother, Bob Williams. Bob, who is married and files a joint return, sells the stock for $10,000 in the current year. Bob is your client and wants to know the tax treatment regarding the sale of the stock. Prepare a letter to this effect and a memo to the file. Bob's address is 10 Hunt Wood Drive, Hadley, PA 16130.

Communications

49. Susan transfers property (basis of $50,000 and fair market value of $25,000) to Thrush Corporation in exchange for shares of § 1244 stock. (Assume the transfer qualifies under § 351.)
    a. What is the basis of the stock to Susan? (Susan and Thrush do not make an election to reduce her stock basis.)

b. What is the basis of the stock to Susan for purposes of § 1244?

c. If Susan sells the stock for $20,000 two years later, how will the loss be treated for tax purposes?

Decision Making

50. Frank, Cora, and Mitch are equal shareholders in Purple Corporation. The corporation's assets have a tax basis of $50,000 and a fair market value of $600,000. In the current year, Frank and Cora each loan Purple Corporation $150,000. The notes to Frank and Cora bear interest of 8% per annum. Mitch leases equipment to Purple Corporation for an annual rental of $12,000. Discuss whether the shareholder loans from Frank and Cora might be reclassified as equity. Consider in your discussion whether Purple Corporation has an acceptable debt-equity ratio.

RESEARCH PROBLEMS

Note: Solutions to Research Problems can be prepared by using the **RIA Checkpoint**® **Student Edition** online research product, which is available to accompany this text. It is also possible to prepare solutions to the Research Problems by using tax research materials found in a standard tax library.

Research Problem 1. A cash basis partnership is incorporated, and the newly formed corporation also chooses to use the cash method of accounting. The partnership transfers $30,000 of accounts receivable along with equipment, land, and cash to the corporation. The corporation agrees to pay accounts payable of the partnership in the amount of $40,000. When the corporation files its tax return for its first year of operation, it does not report as income the $30,000 collected on the accounts receivable. It does, however, deduct the $40,000 it paid on the partnership's accounts payable. The IRS disallows the $40,000 deduction and increases the corporation's taxable income by $30,000. What is the result?

Decision Making

Communications

Research Problem 2. Lynn Jones, Shawn, Walt, and Donna are trying to decide whether they should organize a corporation and transfer their shares of stock in several corporations to this new corporation. All their shares are listed on the New York Stock Exchange and are readily marketable. Lynn would transfer shares in Brown Corporation; Shawn would transfer stock in Rust Corporation; Walt would transfer stock in White Corporation; and Donna would transfer stock in several corporations. The stock would be held by the newly formed corporation for investment purposes. Lynn asks you, her tax adviser, if she would have gain on the transfer of her substantially appreciated shares in Brown Corporation if she transfers the shares to a newly formed corporation. She also asks whether there will be tax consequences if she, Shawn, Walt, and Donna form a partnership, rather than a corporation, to which they would transfer their readily marketable stock. Your input will be critical as they make their decision. Prepare a letter to the client, Lynn Jones, and a memo for the firm's files. Lynn's address is 1540 Maxwell Avenue, Highland, KY 41099.

Research Problem 3. Joel has operated his business as a sole proprietorship for many years but has decided to incorporate the business in order to limit his exposure to personal liability. The balance sheet of his business is as follows:

	Adjusted Basis	Fair Market Value
Assets:		
Cash	$ 50,000	$ 50,000
Accounts receivable	40,000	40,000
Inventory	30,000	60,000
Fixed assets	10,000	200,000
	$130,000	$350,000
Liabilities:		
Trade accounts payable	$ 25,000	$ 25,000
Notes payable	175,000	175,000
Owner's equity	(70,000)	150,000
	$130,000	$350,000

One problem with this plan is that the liabilities of his sole proprietorship exceed the basis of the assets to be transferred to the corporation by $70,000 ($200,000 − $130,000). Therefore, Joel would be required to recognize a gain of $70,000. He is not pleased with this result and asks you about the effect of drawing up a $70,000 note that he would transfer to the corporation. Would the note, which promises a future payment to the corporation of $70,000, enable Joel to avoid recognition of the gain?

Partial list of research aids:
§ 357(c).

Research Problem 4.   Susan is the sole owner of Bluegill Corporation. The basis and value of her stock investment in Bluegill are approximately $100,000. In addition, she manages Bluegill's operations on a full-time basis and pays herself an annual salary of $40,000. Because of a recent downturn in business, she needs to put an additional $80,000 into her corporation to help meet short-term cash-flow needs (e.g., inventory costs, salaries, administrative expenses). Susan believes that the $80,000 transfer can be structured in one of three ways: as a capital contribution, as a loan made to protect her stock investment, or as a loan intended to protect her job. From a tax perspective, which alternative would be preferable in the event that Bluegill's economic slide worsens and bankruptcy results?

Decision Making

Partial list of research aids:
Kenneth W. Graves, 87 TCM 1409, T.C.Memo. 2004–140.

Use the tax resources of the Internet to address the following questions. Do not restrict your search to the World Wide Web, but include a review of newsgroups and general reference materials, practitioner sites and resources, primary sources of the tax law, chat rooms and discussion groups, and other opportunities.

Internet *Activity*

Research Problem 5.   Fundamental differences exist in the attributes underlying common stock and preferred stock. For example, preferred stock generally pays dividends at a higher rate than common stock. This makes preferred stock an attractive investment choice given the current preferential income tax rate applicable to dividend income. However, some preferred stock is treated for tax purposes as long-term debt that generates interest rather than as stock that produces dividends.
a.   What is the current IRS position regarding the factors used to distinguish preferred stock that is treated as stock from preferred stock that is treated as debt?
b.   What are some planning guidelines offered by various investment houses that may be relevant when making preferred stock investments?

Research Problem 6.   Limited liability company (LLC) status has become a very popular form of operating a business over the past several years. Investigate how the growth of LLC status has affected the relative number of new businesses that have chosen to operate as a corporation.

Research Problem 7.   In 2006, how many new businesses organized in the United States chose the corporate form?
a.   How has that number changed from five years earlier?
b.   What percentage of the newly formed corporations are publicly traded?

CHAPTER 5

Corporations: Earnings & Profits and Dividend Distributions

Chapter 4 examined the tax consequences of corporate formation. In Chapters 5 and 6, the focus shifts to the tax treatment of corporate distributions, a topic that plays a leading role in tax planning. The importance of corporate distributions derives from the variety of tax treatments that may apply. From the shareholder's perspective, distributions received from the corporation may be treated as ordinary income, preferentially taxed dividend income, capital gain, or a nontaxable recovery of capital. From the corporation's perspective, distributions made to shareholders are generally not deductible. However, a corporation may recognize losses in liquidating distributions (see Chapter 6), and gains may be recognized at the corporate level on distributions of appreciated property. In the most common scenario, a distribution triggers dividend income to the shareholder and provides no deduction to the paying corporation, resulting in a double tax (at both the corporate and the shareholder level). This double tax may be mitigated by a variety of factors including the corporate dividends received deduction and preferential tax rates on qualifying dividends paid to individuals.

As will become apparent in the subsequent discussion, the tax treatment of corporate distributions can be affected by a number of considerations:

- The availability of earnings to be distributed.
- The basis of the shareholder's stock.
- The character of the property being distributed.
- Whether the shareholder gives up ownership in return for the distribution.
- Whether the distribution is liquidating or nonliquidating.
- Whether the distribution is a "qualifying dividend."
- Whether the shareholder is an individual or another kind of taxpaying entity.

This chapter discusses the tax rules related to nonliquidating distributions of cash and property. Distributions of stock and stock rights are also addressed. Chapter 6 extends the discussion to the tax treatment of stock redemptions and corporate liquidations.

Corporate Distributions—Overview

LO.1

Understand the role that earnings and profits play in determining the tax treatment of distributions.

To the extent that a distribution is made from corporate earnings and profits (E & P), the shareholder is deemed to receive a dividend, taxed as ordinary income or as preferentially taxed dividend income.[1] Generally, corporate distributions are presumed to be paid out of E & P (defined later in this chapter) and are treated as dividends *unless* the parties to the transaction can show otherwise. Distributions not treated as dividends (because of insufficient E & P) are nontaxable to the extent of the shareholder's stock basis, which is reduced accordingly. The excess of the

---

[1]§§ 301(c)(1), 316, and 1(h)(11).

distribution over the shareholder's basis is treated as a gain from sale or exchange of the stock.[2]

EXAMPLE 1

At the beginning of the year, Amber Corporation (a calendar year taxpayer) has E & P of $15,000. The corporation generates no additional E & P during the year. On July 1, the corporation distributes $20,000 to its sole shareholder, Bonnie, whose stock basis is $4,000. In this situation, Bonnie recognizes dividend income of $15,000 (the amount of E & P distributed). In addition, she reduces her stock basis from $4,000 to zero, and she recognizes a taxable gain of $1,000 (the excess of the distribution over the stock basis). ■

Earnings and Profits (E & P)—§ 312

The notion of **earnings and profits** is similar in many respects to the accounting concept of retained earnings. Both are measures of the firm's accumulated capital (E & P includes both the accumulated E & P of the corporation since February 28, 1913, and the current year's E & P). A difference exists, however, in the way these figures are calculated. The computation of retained earnings is based on financial accounting rules while E & P is determined using rules specified in the tax law.

E & P fixes the upper limit on the amount of dividend income that shareholders must recognize as a result of a distribution by the corporation. In this sense, E & P represents the corporation's economic ability to pay a dividend without impairing its capital. Thus, the effect of a specific transaction on E & P can often be determined by assessing whether the transaction increases or decreases the corporation's capacity to pay a dividend.

Computation of E & P

The Code does not explicitly define the term *earnings and profits*. Instead, a series of adjustments to taxable income are identified to provide a measure of the corporation's economic income. Both cash basis and accrual basis corporations use the same approach when determining E & P.[3]

Additions to Taxable Income. To determine current E & P, it is necessary to add *all* previously excluded income items back to taxable income. Included among these positive adjustments are interest on municipal bonds, excluded life insurance proceeds (in excess of cash surrender value), and Federal income tax refunds from tax paid in prior years.

EXAMPLE 2

A corporation collects $100,000 on a key employee life insurance policy (the corporation is the owner and beneficiary of the policy). At the time the policy matured on the death of the insured employee, it possessed a cash surrender value of $30,000. None of the $100,000 is included in the corporation's taxable income, but $70,000 is added to taxable income when computing current E & P. The distribution of the $30,000 cash surrender value does not increase E & P because it does not reflect an increase in the corporation's dividend-paying capacity. Instead, it represents a shift in the corporation's assets from life insurance to cash. ■

In addition to excluded income items, the dividends received deduction and the domestic production activities deduction are added back to taxable income to determine E & P. Neither of these deductions decreases the corporation's assets.

---

[2]§§ 301(c)(2) and (3).

[3]Section 312 describes many of the adjustments to taxable income necessary to determine E & P. Regulation § 1.312–6 addresses the effect of accounting methods on E & P.

Instead, they are partial exclusions for specific types of income (dividend income and income from domestic production activities). Since they do not impair the corporation's ability to pay dividends, they do not reduce E & P.

Subtractions from Taxable Income. When calculating E & P, it is also necessary to subtract certain nondeductible expenses from taxable income. These negative adjustments include the nondeductible portion of meal and entertainment expenses, related-party losses, expenses incurred to produce tax-exempt income, Federal income taxes paid, nondeductible key employee life insurance premiums (net of increases in cash surrender value), nondeductible fines, penalties, and lobbying expenses.

EXAMPLE 3

A corporation sells property with a basis of $10,000 to its sole shareholder for $8,000. Because of § 267 (disallowance of losses on sales between related parties), the $2,000 loss cannot be deducted when calculating the corporation's taxable income. However, since the overall economic effect of the transaction is a decrease in the corporation's assets by $2,000, the loss reduces the current E & P for the year of sale. ∎

EXAMPLE 4

A corporation pays a $10,000 premium on a key employee life insurance policy covering the life of its president. As a result of the payment, the cash surrender value of the policy is increased by $7,000. Although none of the $10,000 premium is deductible for tax purposes, current E & P is reduced by $3,000. The $7,000 increase in cash surrender value is not subtracted because it does not represent a decrease in the corporation's ability to pay a dividend. Instead, it is a change in the corporation's assets, from cash to life insurance. ∎

Timing Adjustments. Some E & P adjustments shift the effect of a transaction from the year of its inclusion in or deduction from taxable income to the year in which it has an economic effect on the corporation. Charitable contributions, net operating losses, and capital losses all necessitate this kind of adjustment.

EXAMPLE 5

During 2008, a corporation makes charitable contributions, $12,000 of which cannot be deducted when calculating the taxable income for the year because of the 10% taxable income limitation. Consequently, the $12,000 is carried forward to 2009 and fully deducted in that year. The excess charitable contribution reduces the corporation's current E & P for 2008 by $12,000 and increases its current E & P for 2009 (when the deduction is allowed) by the same amount. The increase in E & P in 2009 is necessary because the charitable contribution carryover reduces the taxable income for that year (the starting point for computing E & P) and already has been taken into account in determining the E & P for 2008. ∎

Gains and losses from property transactions generally affect the determination of E & P only to the extent that they are recognized for tax purposes. Thus, gains and losses deferred under the like-kind exchange provision and deferred involuntary conversion gains do not affect E & P until recognized. Accordingly, no timing adjustment is required for these items.

Accounting Method Adjustments. In addition to the above adjustments, accounting methods used for determining E & P are generally more conservative than those allowed for calculating income tax. For example, the installment method is not permitted for E & P purposes.[4] Thus, an adjustment is required for the deferred gain from property sales made during the year under the installment method. All principal payments are treated as having been received in the year of sale.

---

[4]§ 312(n)(5).

In 2008, Cardinal Corporation, a calendar year taxpayer, sells unimproved real estate with a basis of $20,000 for $100,000. Under the terms of the sale, Cardinal will receive two annual payments of $50,000 beginning in 2009, each with interest of 9%. Cardinal Corporation does not elect out of the installment method. Since Cardinal's taxable income for 2008 will not reflect any of the gain from the sale, the corporation must make an $80,000 positive adjustment for 2008 (the deferred gain from the sale). Similarly, $40,000 negative adjustments will be required in 2009 and 2010 when the deferred gain is recognized under the installment method. ■

EXAMPLE 6

The alternative depreciation system (ADS) must be used for purposes of computing E & P.[5] This method requires straight-line depreciation over a recovery period equal to the Asset Depreciation Range (ADR) midpoint life.[6] Also, ADS prohibits additional first-year depreciation.[7] If MACRS cost recovery is used for income tax purposes, a positive or negative adjustment equal to the difference between MACRS and ADS must be made each year. Likewise, when assets are disposed of, an additional adjustment to taxable income is required to allow for the difference in gain or loss caused by the gap between income tax basis and E & P basis.[8] The adjustments arising from depreciation are illustrated in the following example.

On January 2, 2006, White Corporation paid $30,000 to purchase equipment with an ADR midpoint life of 10 years and a MACRS class life of 7 years. The equipment was depreciated under MACRS. The asset was sold on July 2, 2008, for $27,000. For purposes of determining taxable income and E & P, cost recovery claimed on the equipment is summarized below.

EXAMPLE 7

Year	Cost Recovery Computation	MACRS	ADS	Adjustment Amount
2006	$30,000 × 14.29%	$ 4,287		
	$30,000 ÷ 10-year ADR recovery period × ½ (half-year for first year of service)		$1,500	$2,787
2007	$30,000 × 24.49%	7,347		
	$30,000 ÷ 10-year ADR recovery period		3,000	4,347
2008	$30,000 × 17.49% × ½ (half-year for year of disposal)	2,624		
	$30,000 ÷ 10-year ADR recovery period × ½ (half-year for year of disposal)		1,500	1,124
Total cost recovery		$14,258	$6,000	$8,258

Each year White Corporation will increase taxable income by the adjustment amount indicated above to determine E & P. Additionally, when computing E & P for 2008, White will reduce taxable income by $8,258 to account for the excess gain recognized for income tax purposes, as shown below.

---

[5]§ 312(k)(3)(A).

[6]See § 168(g)(2). The ADR midpoint lives for most assets are set out in Rev.Proc. 87–56, 1987–2 C.B. 674. The recovery period is 5 years for automobiles and light-duty trucks and 40 years for real property. For assets with no class life, the recovery period is 12 years.

[7]§ 168(k)(2)(D). A special additional first-year cost recovery allowance was allowed for certain property placed in service prior to 2005.

[8]§ 312(f)(1).

GLOBAL Tax Issues

E & P IN CONTROLLED FOREIGN CORPORATIONS

U.S. multinational companies often conduct business overseas using foreign subsidiaries known as "controlled foreign corporations," or CFCs. This organizational structure would seem to be ideal for income tax avoidance if the CFC is incorporated in a low-tax jurisdiction (a tax haven country). In the absence of any rules to the contrary, the higher U.S. tax on foreign earnings could be deferred until the earnings are repatriated to the United States through dividends paid to the U.S. parent.

To prevent this deferral, the tax law compels a U.S. parent corporation to recognize some of the unrepatriated earnings of the CFC as income. The foreign corporation's E & P is used to determine the amount of income that is recognized annually by the U.S. parent corporation. Determining the CFC's E & P is no easy task. Foreign corporations (including CFCs) typically compute their book income using foreign generally accepted accounting principles (GAAP). Since the starting point for computing E & P for foreign corporations is U.S. GAAP book income rather than taxable income, an extra layer of complexity is introduced. First, the foreign company's book income must be converted to a U.S. GAAP basis, and then a series of adjustments must be made (similar to the adjustments reflected in Concept Summary 5–1) to U.S. book income to determine E & P.

	Income Tax	E & P
Amount realized	$27,000	$ 27,000
Adjusted basis for income tax ($30,000 cost − $14,258 MACRS)	(15,742)	
Adjusted basis for E & P ($30,000 cost − $6,000 ADS)		(24,000)
Gain on sale	$11,258	$ 3,000
Adjustment amount ($3,000 − $11,258)	($ 8,258)	

In addition to more conservative depreciation methods, the E & P rules impose limitations on the deductibility of § 179 expense. In particular, this expense must be deducted over a period of five years.[9] Thus, in any year that § 179 is elected, 80 percent of the resulting expense must be added back to taxable income to determine current E & P. In each of the following four years, a negative adjustment equal to 20 percent of the § 179 expense must be made.

The E & P rules also require specific accounting methods in various situations, making adjustments necessary when different methods are used for income tax purposes. For example, E & P requires cost depletion rather than percentage depletion. When accounting for long-term contracts, E & P rules specify the percentage of completion method rather than the completed contract method.[10] As the E & P determination does not allow for the amortization of organizational expenses, any such expense deducted when computing taxable income must be added back to determine E & P.[11] To account for income deferral under the LIFO inventory method, the E & P computation requires an adjustment for changes in the LIFO recapture amount (the excess of FIFO over LIFO inventory value) during the year. Increases in LIFO recapture are added to taxable income and decreases are subtracted.[12] E & P rules also specify that intangible drilling costs and mine exploration and development costs be amortized over a period of 60 months and 120

---

[9]§ 312(k)(3)(B).
[10]§ 312(n)(6).

[11]§ 312(n)(3).
[12]§ 312(n)(4).

CONCEPT SUMMARY 5–1

E & P Adjustments

Nature of the Transaction	Adjustment to Taxable Income to Determine Current E & P	
	Addition	Subtraction
Tax-exempt income	X	
Dividends received deduction	X	
Domestic production activities deduction	X	
Collection of proceeds from insurance policy on life of corporate officer (in excess of cash surrender value)	X	
Deferred gain on installment sale (all gain is added to E & P in year of sale)	X	
Future recognition of installment sale gross profit		X
Excess capital loss and excess charitable contribution (over 10% limitation) in year incurred		X
Deduction of charitable contribution, NOL, or capital loss carryovers in succeeding taxable year (increase E & P because deduction reduces taxable income while E & P was reduced in a prior year)	X	
Federal income taxes paid		X
Federal income tax refund	X	
Loss on sale between related parties		X
Nondeductible fines, penalties, and lobbying expenses		X
Nondeductible meal and entertainment expenses		X
Payment of premiums on insurance policy on life of corporate officer (in excess of increase in cash surrender value of policy)		X
Realized gain (not recognized) on an involuntary conversion	No effect	
Realized gain or loss (not recognized) on a like-kind exchange	No effect	
Percentage depletion (only cost depletion can reduce E & P)	X	
Accelerated depreciation (E & P is reduced only by straight-line, units-of-production, or machine hours depreciation)	X	X
Additional 30% or 50% first-year depreciation	X	
Section 179 expense in year elected (80%)	X	
Section 179 expense in four years following election (20% each year)		X
Increase (decrease) in LIFO recapture amount	X	X
Intangible drilling costs deducted currently (reduce E & P in future years by amortizing costs over 60 months)	X	
Mine exploration and development costs (reduce E & P in future years by amortizing costs over 120 months)	X	

Gain on installment from prior yr. added
Interest income from bonds are +
excess MACRS is added

months, respectively. For income tax purposes, however, these costs can be deducted in the current year.[13]

Circulation expens
you can Expense them imed
ally. It do have to
capitalize.

Summary of E & P Adjustments

E & P serves as a measure of a corporation's earnings that are available for distribution as taxable dividends to the shareholders. Current E & P is determined by making a series of adjustments to the corporation's taxable income that are outlined in Concept Summary 5–1. Other items that affect E & P, such as property dividends, are covered later in the chapter. The effect of stock redemptions on E & P is covered in Chapter 6.

CONCEPT SUMMARY 5–2

Allocating E & P to Distributions

1. Current E & P is allocated first to distributions on a pro rata basis; then, accumulated E & P is applied (as necessary) in chronological order beginning with the earliest distribution. See Example 8.
2. Until the parties can show otherwise, it is presumed that current E & P covers all distributions. See Example 9.
3. When a deficit exists in accumulated E & P and a positive balance exists in current E & P, distributions are regarded as dividends to the extent of current E & P. See Example 10.

4. When a deficit exists in current E & P and a positive balance exists in accumulated E & P, the two accounts are netted at the date of distribution. If the resulting balance is zero or a deficit, the distribution is treated as a return of capital, first reducing the basis of the stock to zero, then generating taxable gain. If a positive balance results, the distribution is a dividend to the extent of the balance. Any loss in current E & P is allocated ratably during the year unless the corporation can show otherwise. See Example 11.

[Handwritten margin notes:]
Accu E&P = <40,000> net when you have less current E&P
Cur Loss = +10,000
apply first 10,000 TXBL DIV
10,000 ROC
AE&P 40,000
CE&n <10,50> Met them
*   30,00*
Dist 20K

Current versus Accumulated E & P

Accumulated E & P is the total of all previous years' current E & P (since February 28, 1913) as computed on the first day of each tax year, reduced by distributions made from E & P. It is important to distinguish between **current E & P** and **accumulated E & P** because the taxability of corporate distributions depends on how these two accounts are allocated to each distribution made during the year. A complex set of rules governs the allocation process.[14] These rules are described in the following section and summarized in Concept Summary 5–2.

LO.3

Apply the rules for allocating earnings and profits to distributions.

Allocating E & P to Distributions

When a positive balance exists in both the current and the accumulated E & P accounts, corporate distributions are deemed to be made first from current E & P and then from accumulated E & P. When distributions exceed the amount of current E & P, it becomes necessary to allocate current and accumulated E & P to each distribution made during the year. Current E & P is allocated on a pro rata basis to each distribution. Accumulated E & P is applied in chronological order, beginning with the earliest distribution. As seen in the following example, this allocation is important if any shareholder sells stock during the year.

EXAMPLE 8

As of January 1 of the current year, Black Corporation has accumulated E & P of $10,000. Current E & P for the year amounts to $30,000. Megan and Matt are sole *equal* shareholders of Black from January 1 to July 31. On August 1, Megan sells all of her stock to Helen. Black makes two distributions to shareholders during the year: $40,000 to Megan and Matt ($20,000 to each) on July 1, and $40,000 to Matt and Helen ($20,000 to each) on December 1. Current and accumulated E & P are allocated to the two distributions as follows:

	Source of Distribution		
	Current E & P	Accumulated E & P	Return of Capital
July 1 distribution ($40,000)	$15,000	$10,000	$15,000
December 1 distribution ($40,000)	15,000	—	25,000

Since 50% of the total distributions are made on July 1 and December 1, respectively, one-half of current E & P is allocated to each of the two distributions. Accumulated E & P is

---

[14]Regulations relating to the source of a distribution are at Reg. § 1.316–2.

applied in chronological order, so the entire amount is applied to the July 1 distribution. The tax consequences to the shareholders are presented below.

	Shareholder		
	Megan	Matt	Helen
July distribution ($40,000)			
Dividend income—			
From current E & P ($15,000)	$ 7,500	$ 7,500	$ –0–
From accumulated E & P ($10,000)	5,000	5,000	–0–
Return of capital ($15,000)	7,500	7,500	–0–
December distribution ($40,000)			
Dividend income—			
From current E & P ($15,000)	–0–	7,500	7,500
From accumulated E & P ($0)	–0–	–0–	–0–
Return of capital ($25,000)	–0–	12,500	12,500
Total dividend income	$12,500	$20,000	$ 7,500
Nontaxable return of capital (assuming sufficient basis in the stock investment)	$ 7,500	$20,000	$12,500

Because the balance in the accumulated E & P account is exhausted when it is applied to the July 1 distribution, Megan has more dividend income than Helen, even though both receive equal distributions during the year. In addition, each shareholder's basis is reduced by the nontaxable return of capital; any excess over basis results in taxable gain. ∎

When the tax years of the corporation and its shareholders are not the same, it may be impossible to determine the amount of current E & P on a timely basis. For example, if shareholders use a calendar year and the corporation uses a fiscal year, then current E & P may not be ascertainable until after the shareholders' returns have been filed. To address this timing issue, the allocation rules presume that current E & P is sufficient to cover every distribution made during the year until the parties can show otherwise.

E X A M P L E   9

Green Corporation uses the fiscal year of July 1 through June 30 for tax purposes. Carol, Green's only shareholder, uses a calendar year. As of July 1, 2008, Green Corporation has a zero balance in its accumulated E & P account. For fiscal year 2008–2009, the corporation suffers a $5,000 deficit in current E & P. On August 1, 2008, Green distributed $10,000 to Carol. The distribution is dividend income to Carol and is reported when she files her income tax return for the 2008 calendar year, on or before April 15, 2009. Because Carol cannot prove until June 30, 2009, that the corporation has a deficit for the 2008–2009 fiscal year, she must assume the $10,000 distribution is fully covered by current E & P. When Carol learns of the deficit, she can file an amended return for 2008 showing the $10,000 as a return of capital. ∎

Additional difficulties arise when either the current or the accumulated E & P account has a deficit balance. In particular, when current E & P is positive and accumulated E & P has a deficit balance, accumulated E & P is *not* netted against current E & P. Instead, the distribution is deemed to be a taxable dividend to the extent of the positive current E & P balance.

E X A M P L E   10

At the beginning of the current year, Brown Corporation has a deficit of $30,000 in accumulated E & P. For the year, it has current E & P of $10,000 and distributes $5,000 to its shareholders. The $5,000 distribution is treated as a taxable dividend since it is deemed to have been made from current E & P even though Brown Corporation still has a deficit in accumulated E & P at the end of the year. ∎

ETHICAL and EQUITABLE *Considerations*   SHIFTING E & P

Ten years ago, Joe began a new business venture with his best friend and college roommate, Frankie. Joe owns 60 percent of the outstanding stock, and Frankie owns 40 percent. The business has had some difficult times, but things are starting to look up.

Yesterday, on December 1, Frankie told Joe that he wants a change of career and is planning to sell all of his stock to Joe's sister, Cindy, at the beginning of the following year. He would sell immediately, but he wants to wait until after the company pays out the current-year shareholder distribution (which is expected to be about $100,000). Cindy has been a longtime employee of the business and has often expressed an interest in becoming more involved. Joe is looking forward to working with his sister, but he now faces a terrible dilemma.

The corporation has a $350,000 deficit in accumulated E & P and only a small amount of current E & P to date (about $20,000). Within the next six weeks, however, Joe expects to sign a major deal with a very large client. If Joe signs the contract this month, the corporation will experience a $300,000 increase in current E & P for the year, causing the forthcoming dividend to be fully taxable to Frankie. As a result, most of next year's distribution would be treated as a tax-free return of capital for Cindy. Alternatively, if Joe waits until January, both he and Frankie will receive a nontaxable distribution this year, but next year's annual distribution will be taxable as a dividend to his sister. What should Joe do?

In contrast to the previous rule, when a deficit exists in current E & P and a positive balance exists in accumulated E & P, the accounts are netted at the date of distribution. If the resulting balance is zero or negative, the distribution is a return of capital. If a positive balance results, the distribution is a dividend to the extent of the balance. Any current E & P is allocated ratably during the year unless the parties can show otherwise.

EXAMPLE 11

At the beginning of the current year, Gray Corporation (a calendar year taxpayer) has accumulated E & P of $10,000. During the year, the corporation incurs a $15,000 deficit in current E & P that accrues ratably. On July 1, Gray Corporation distributes $6,000 in cash to Hal, its sole shareholder. To determine how much of the $6,000 cash distribution represents dividend income to Hal, the balances of both accumulated and current E & P as of July 1 are determined and netted. This is necessary because of the deficit in current E & P.

	Source of Distribution	
	Current E & P	Accumulated E & P
January 1		$10,000
July 1 (½ of $15,000 net loss)	($7,500)	2,500
July 1 distribution of $6,000:		
Dividend income: $2,500		
Return of capital: $3,500		

The balance in E & P on July 1 is $2,500. Thus, of the $6,000 distribution, $2,500 is taxed as a dividend, and $3,500 represents a return of capital. ■

Dividends

As noted earlier, distributions by a corporation from its E & P are treated as dividends. The tax treatment of dividends varies, depending on whether the shareholder receiving them is a corporation or another kind of taxpaying entity. All corporations treat dividends as ordinary income and are permitted a dividends received deduction (see Chapter 2). In contrast, individuals receive reduced tax rates on qualified dividend income while nonqualified dividends are taxed as ordinary income.

Rationale for Reduced Tax Rates on Dividends

The double tax on corporate income has always been controversial. Reformers have argued that taxing corporations twice creates several distortions in the economy, including the following:

- An incentive to invest in noncorporate rather than corporate businesses.
- An incentive for corporations to finance operations with debt rather than new equity because interest payments are deductible.
- An incentive for corporations to retain earnings and to structure distributions of profits to avoid the double tax.

Collectively, these distortions raise the cost of capital for corporate investments and increase the vulnerability of corporations in economic downturns due to excessive debt financing. Reformers argue that eliminating the double tax would remove these distortions, stimulate the economy (with estimated gains of up to $25 billion annually), and increase capital stock in the corporate sector by as much as $500 billion.[15] They also argue that elimination of the double tax would make the United States more internationally competitive because the majority of our trading partners assess only one tax on corporate income. In contrast, supporters of the double tax argue that a double tax is appropriate because of the concentration of economic power held by publicly traded corporations, especially since income tax is based on ability to pay and notions of fairness. They also argue that many of the distortions can already be avoided through the use of deductible payments by closely held C corporations and through partnerships, limited liability companies, and Subchapter S corporations. Finally, supporters of the double tax suggest that the benefits from its repeal would flow disproportionately to the wealthy.[16]

From an international perspective, the double taxation of dividends is unusual. Most countries have adopted a policy of corporate integration, which imposes a single tax on corporate profits. Corporate integration takes several forms. One popular approach is to impose a tax at the corporate level, but allow shareholders to claim a credit for corporate-level taxes paid when dividends are received. A second alternative is to allow a corporate-level deduction for dividends paid to shareholders. A third approach is to allow shareholders to exclude corporate dividends from income. A fourth alternative suggested in the past by the U.S. Treasury is the "comprehensive business income tax," which excludes both dividend and interest income while disallowing deductions for interest expense.

Facing trade-offs between equity and the economic distortions introduced by the double tax and the prevalence of corporate integration throughout the world, the United States continues to struggle with the issue of how corporate distributions should be taxed. Corporate integration has been a recurring suggestion since the Treasury advanced the idea in 1992. The current reduced tax rate on dividends began as a proposal by President Bush in 2003 to exempt **qualified dividends** from tax. However, because estimates indicated that the proposed dividend exclusion would result in a loss of revenue in excess of $600 billion, the process of political compromise eventually led to a reduced tax rate instead of a complete exemption from tax. Most recently, in 2005, the President's Advisory Panel on Federal Tax

---

[15]Integration of Individual and Corporate Tax Systems, Report of the Department of the Treasury (January 1992).

[16]The Urban Institute–Brookings Institution Tax Policy Center estimates that more than one-half—53%—of the benefits from the reduced tax rate on dividends go to the 0.2% of households with incomes over $1 million.

Reform again proposed excluding dividends from tax at the individual level, together with a reduction of capital gains tax rates to 8.25 percent.

Qualified Dividends

Qualified Dividends—Application and Effect. Under current law, dividends that meet certain requirements are subject to a 15 percent tax rate for most individual taxpayers from 2003 through 2010. Individuals in the 10 or 15 percent rate brackets were subject to a 5 percent rate on dividends paid from 2003 through 2007. Beginning in 2008, dividends are exempt from tax for these lower-income taxpayers.[17] After 2010, unless new legislation is enacted, qualified dividends will once again be taxed as ordinary income as they were prior to 2003. Notably, the lower rates on dividend income apply to both the regular income tax and the alternative minimum tax.

Qualified Dividends—Requirements. To be taxed at the lower rates, dividends must be paid by either domestic or certain qualified foreign corporations. Qualified foreign corporations include those traded on a U.S. stock exchange or any corporation located in a country that (1) has a comprehensive income tax treaty with the United States, (2) has an information-sharing agreement with the United States, and (3) is approved by the Treasury.[18]

Two other requirements must be met for dividends to qualify for the favorable rates. First, dividends paid to shareholders who hold both long and short positions in the stock do not qualify. Second, the stock on which the dividend is paid must be held for more than 60 days during the 121-day period beginning 60 days before the ex-dividend date.[19] To allow for settlement delays, the ex-dividend date is typically 2 days before the date of record on a dividend. This holding period rule parallels the rule applied to corporations that claim the dividends received deduction.[20]

| EXAMPLE 12 | In June of the current year, Green Corporation announces that a dividend of $1.50 will be paid on each share of its common stock to shareholders of record on July 15. Amy and Corey, two unrelated shareholders, own 1,000 shares of the stock on the record date (July 15). Consequently, each receives $1,500 (1,000 shares × $1.50). Assume Amy purchased her stock on January 15 of this year, while Corey purchased her stock on July 1. Both shareholders sell their stock on July 20. To qualify for the lower dividend rate, stock must be held for more than 60 days during the 121-day period beginning 60 days prior to July 13 (the ex-dividend date). The $1,500 Amy receives is subject to preferential 15%/0% treatment. The $1,500 Corey receives, however, is not. Corey did not meet the 60-day holding requirement, so her dividend will be taxed as ordinary income. ■ |

Qualified dividends are not considered investment income for purposes of determining the investment interest expense deduction. Taxpayers can, however, elect to treat qualified dividends as ordinary income (taxed at regular rates) and include them in investment interest income. Thus, taxpayers subject to an investment interest expense limitation must evaluate the relative benefits of taxing qualifying dividends at low rates versus using the dividends as investment income to increase the amount of deductible investment interest expense.

---

[17]See §§ 1(h)(1) and (11).

[18]In Notice 2003–69, 2003–2 C.B. 851, the Treasury identified 51 qualifying countries (among those included in the list are the members of the European Union, the Russian Federation, Canada, and Mexico). Several countries were also specifically identified as nonqualifying. These include most of the former Soviet republics (except Kazakhstan), Bermuda, the Netherland Antilles, and Barbados.

[19]§ 1(h)(11)(B)(iii)(I).

[20]See § 246(c).

TAX *in the News*   **WAS THE DIVIDEND TAX CUT A SUCCESS OR A FAILURE?**

In 2004, 374 companies in the Standard & Poor's 500 stock index paid dividends, up from 351 in 2002 and 370 in 2003. This was the highest rate since 1999. Furthermore, the amount of dividends paid in 2004 was a record $183 billion. According to equity market analysts, the growth in dividend payments was fueled both by larger dividends from companies with an established dividend-paying history (e.g., Wal-Mart Stores, Coca-Cola, and Harley-Davidson) and by first-time dividends from growth companies that hadn't paid dividends in the past (e.g., Staples, Cendant Corporation, and Costco Wholesale Corporation). The biggest dividend standout in 2004, however, was Microsoft, which paid a record onetime dividend of $32 billion and doubled its usual quarterly dividend to boot.

Typically, shares of companies that pay dividends outperform those that don't pay dividends. In the first half of 2004, this trend continued. Stock prices of dividend payers in the S&P 500 fell by only about half a percent, while the stock prices of non-dividend-paying companies declined almost 5 percent.

Recent research into the impact of the tax cut on corporate dividend policies provides a clearer picture of its effectiveness. Economists have offered convincing evidence that dividend payments increased following the reduction in tax rates on dividends, even when onetime dividends are not considered. Other research, however, suggests that corporations did not increase total payments to shareholders but substituted dividend payments for stock buybacks. Thus, the change in the tax law may not have led to the effect that was originally intended.

Property Dividends

Although most corporate distributions are cash, a corporation may distribute a **property dividend** for various reasons. The shareholders could want a particular property that is held by the corporation. Similarly, a corporation with low cash reserves may still wish to distribute a dividend to its shareholders.

Property distributions have the same impact as distributions of cash except for effects attributable to any difference between the basis and the fair market value of the distributed property. In most situations, distributed property is appreciated, so its sale would result in a gain to the corporation. Distributions of property with a basis that differs from fair market value raise several tax questions.

- For the shareholder:
  - What is the amount of the distribution?
  - What is the basis of the property in the shareholder's hands?
- For the corporation:
  - Is a gain or loss recognized as a result of the distribution?
  - What is the effect of the distribution on E & P?

Property Dividends—Effect on the Shareholder.

When a corporation distributes property rather than cash to a shareholder, the amount distributed is measured by the fair market value of the property on the date of distribution.[21] As with a cash distribution, the portion of a property distribution covered by existing E & P is a dividend, and any excess is treated as a return of capital. If the fair market value of the property distributed exceeds the corporation's E & P and the shareholder's basis in the stock investment, a capital gain usually results.

The amount distributed is reduced by any liabilities to which the distributed property is subject immediately before and immediately after the distribution and by any liabilities of the corporation assumed by the shareholder. The basis of the

---

[21]Section 301 describes the tax treatment of corporate distributions to shareholders.

Margin notes (handwritten):

LO.5

Understand the tax impact of property dividends on the recipient shareholder and the corporation making the distribution.

distributed property for the shareholder is the fair market value of the property on the date of the distribution.

EXAMPLE 13

Robin Corporation has E & P of $60,000. It distributes land with a fair market value of $50,000 (adjusted basis of $30,000) to its sole shareholder, Charles. The land is subject to a liability of $10,000, which Charles assumes. Charles has a taxable dividend of $40,000 [$50,000 (fair market value) − $10,000 (liability)]. The basis of the land to Charles is $50,000. ■

EXAMPLE 14

Red Corporation owns 10% of Tan Corporation. Tan has ample E & P to cover any distributions made during the year. One distribution made to Red Corporation consists of a vacant lot with an adjusted basis of $75,000 and a fair market value of $50,000. Red has a taxable dividend of $50,000, and its basis in the lot becomes $50,000. ■

Distributing property that has depreciated in value as a property dividend may reflect poor planning. Note what happens in Example 14. Basis of $25,000 disappears due to the loss (adjusted basis of $75,000, fair market value of $50,000). As an alternative, Tan Corporation could sell the lot and use the loss to reduce its taxes. Then, Tan could distribute the $50,000 of proceeds to shareholders.

Property Dividends—Effect on the Corporation. All distributions of appreciated property generate gain to the distributing corporation.[22] In effect, a corporation that distributes gain property is treated as if it had sold the property to the shareholder for its fair market value. However, the distributing corporation does *not* recognize loss on distributions of property.

EXAMPLE 15

A corporation distributes land (basis of $10,000 and fair market value of $30,000) to a shareholder. The corporation recognizes a gain of $20,000. ■

EXAMPLE 16

Assume the property in Example 15 has a basis of $30,000 and a fair market value of $10,000. The corporation does not recognize a loss on the distribution. ■

If the distributed property is subject to a liability in excess of basis or the shareholder assumes such a liability, a special rule applies. For purposes of determining gain on the distribution, the fair market value of the property is treated as not being less than the amount of the liability.[23]

EXAMPLE 17

Assume the land in Example 15 is subject to a liability of $35,000. The corporation recognizes gain of $25,000 on the distribution. ■

Corporate distributions reduce E & P by the amount of money distributed or by the greater of the fair market value or the adjusted basis of property distributed, less the amount of any liability on the property.[24] E & P is increased by gain recognized on appreciated property distributed as a property dividend.

EXAMPLE 18

Crimson Corporation distributes property (basis of $10,000 and fair market value of $20,000) to Brenda, its shareholder. Crimson Corporation recognizes a gain of $10,000. Crimson's E & P is increased by the $10,000 gain and decreased by the $20,000 fair market value of the distribution. Brenda has dividend income of $20,000 (presuming sufficient E & P). ■

---

[22]Section 311 describes how corporations are taxed on distributions.
[23]§ 311(b)(2).

[24]§§ 312(a), (b), and (c).

TAX *in the News*

THE CASE OF THE DISAPPEARING DIVIDEND TAX

During the last few years, U.S. investment banks and offshore hedge funds have developed a novel technique for avoiding the tax on dividends entirely. The strategy involves the use of financial derivatives. A simple version of the strategy is called a stock swap. In the swap, a U.S. investment bank buys a block of stock from an offshore hedge fund. The investment bank and the hedge fund also enter into a derivatives contract. The contract requires the investment bank to make payments to the hedge fund equal to the total return on the stock (both increases in fair market value and dividends) for a designated time period. These payments equal the income and gain the stock would have provided to the hedge fund if it had continued to own the stock. In exchange for these payments, the hedge fund agrees to pay the investment bank an amount based on some benchmark interest rate. The hedge fund also agrees that it will pay the bank an amount equal to the loss if the fair market value of the stock declines.

After purchasing the stock from the hedge fund, the investment bank receives taxable dividend income. For tax purposes, however, the dividend income is completely offset by the expense of payments made to the hedge fund under the derivatives contract. In return, the investment bank receives compensation from the hedge fund equal to a benchmark interest rate. The overseas hedge fund no longer receives taxable dividend income, and the swap payments received are not subject to U.S. taxation. As a result, taxable dividend income is converted to tax-free income.

Some experts estimate that the strategy has allowed hedge funds to avoid paying more than $1 billion a year in taxes on U.S. dividends. Tax authorities are now seeking information on these strategies as they try to determine whether the technique is actually allowed under current tax laws. One key question is whether the trades associated with the technique are executed for any purpose other than to avoid the tax on dividends.

Source: *Adapted from Anita Raghavan, "How Lehman Sold Plan to Sidestep Tax Man,"* Wall Street Journal, *September 17, 2007, p. A1.*

EXAMPLE 19

Assume the same facts as in Example 18, except that the adjusted basis of the property in the hands of Crimson Corporation is $25,000. Because loss is not recognized and the adjusted basis is greater than fair market value, E & P is reduced by $25,000. Brenda reports dividend income of $20,000. ■

EXAMPLE 20

Assume the same facts as in Example 19, except that the property is subject to a liability of $6,000. E & P is now reduced by $19,000 [$25,000 (adjusted basis) − $6,000 (liability)]. Brenda has a dividend of $14,000 [$20,000 (amount of the distribution) − $6,000 (liability)], and her basis in the property is $20,000. ■

Under no circumstances can a distribution, whether cash or property, either generate a deficit in E & P or add to a deficit in E & P. Deficits can arise only through corporate losses.

EXAMPLE 21

Teal Corporation has accumulated E & P of $10,000 at the beginning of the current tax year. During the year, it has current E & P of $15,000. At the end of the year, it distributes cash of $30,000 to its sole shareholder, Walter. Teal's E & P at the end of the year is zero. The accumulated E & P of $10,000 is increased by current E & P of $15,000 and reduced $25,000 by the dividend distribution. The remaining $5,000 of the distribution to Walter does not reduce E & P because a distribution cannot generate a deficit in E & P. ■

Constructive Dividends

LO.6
Understand the nature and treatment of constructive dividends.

Any measurable economic benefit conveyed by a corporation to its shareholders can be treated as a dividend for Federal income tax purposes even though it is not formally declared or designated as a dividend. Also, it need not be issued pro rata to all shareholders[25] or satisfy the legal requirements of a dividend. Such a benefit, often described as a **constructive dividend**, is distinguishable from actual corporate distributions of cash and property in form only.

For tax purposes, constructive distributions are treated the same as actual distributions.[26] Thus, corporate shareholders are entitled to the dividends received deduction (see Chapter 2), and other shareholders receive preferential tax rates (0 or 15 percent) on qualified constructive dividends. The constructive distribution is taxable as a dividend only to the extent of the corporation's current and accumulated E & P. The burden of proving that the distribution constitutes a return of capital because of inadequate E & P rests with the taxpayer.[27]

Constructive dividend situations usually arise in closely held corporations. Here, the dealings between the parties are less structured, and frequently, formalities are not preserved. The constructive dividend serves as a substitute for actual distributions and is usually intended to accomplish some tax objective not available through the use of direct dividends. The shareholders may be attempting to distribute corporate profits in a form deductible to the corporation.[28] Alternatively, the shareholders may be seeking benefits for themselves while avoiding the recognition of income. Although some constructive dividends are disguised dividends, not all are deliberate attempts to avoid actual and formal dividends; many are inadvertent. Thus, an awareness of the various constructive dividend situations is essential to protect the parties from unanticipated, undesirable tax consequences. The most frequently encountered types of constructive dividends are summarized below.

Shareholder Use of Corporate-Owned Property.

A constructive dividend can occur when a shareholder uses corporation property for personal purposes at no cost. Personal use of corporate-owned automobiles, airplanes, yachts, fishing camps, hunting lodges, and other entertainment facilities is commonplace in some closely held corporations. In these situations, the shareholder has dividend income equal to the fair rental value of the property for the period of its personal use.

Bargain Sale of Corporate Property to a Shareholder.

Shareholders often purchase property from a corporation at a cost below the fair market value. These bargain sales produce dividend income equal to the difference between the property's fair market value on the date of sale and the amount the shareholder paid for the property.[29] These situations might be avoided by appraising the property on or about the date of the sale. The appraised value should become the price paid by the shareholder.

Bargain Rental of Corporate Property.

A bargain rental of corporate property by a shareholder also produces dividend income. Here the measure of the constructive dividend is the excess of the property's fair rental value over the rent actually paid. Again, appraisal data should be used to avoid any questionable situations.

Payments for the Benefit of a Shareholder.

If a corporation pays an obligation of a shareholder, the payment is treated as a constructive dividend. The obligation in question need not be legally binding on the shareholder; it may, in fact, be a moral obligation.[30] Forgiveness of shareholder indebtedness by the corporation creates an identical problem.[31] Also, excessive rentals paid by a corporation for the use of shareholder property are treated as constructive dividends.

---

[25]See *Lengsfield v. Comm.*, 57–1 USTC ¶9437, 50 AFTR 1683, 241 F.2d 508 (CA–5, 1957).

[26]*Simon v. Comm.*, 57–2 USTC ¶9989, 52 AFTR 698, 248 F.2d 869 (CA–8, 1957).

[27]*DiZenzo v. Comm.*, 65–2 USTC ¶9518, 16 AFTR2d 5107, 348 F.2d 122 (CA–2, 1965).

[28]Recall that dividend distributions do not provide the distributing corporation with an income tax deduction, although they do reduce E & P.

[29]Reg. § 1.301–1(j).

[30]*Montgomery Engineering Co. v. U.S.*, 64–2 USTC ¶9618, 13 AFTR2d 1747, 230 F.Supp. 838 (D.Ct. N.J., 1964), *aff'd* in 65–1 USTC ¶9368, 15 AFTR2d 746, 344 F.2d 996 (CA–3, 1965).

[31]Reg. § 1.301–1(m).

Unreasonable Compensation. A salary payment to a shareholder-employee that is deemed to be **unreasonable compensation** is frequently treated as a constructive dividend. As a consequence, it is not deductible by the corporation. In determining the reasonableness of salary payments, the following factors are considered:

- The employee's qualifications.
- A comparison of salaries with dividend distributions.
- The prevailing rates of compensation for comparable positions in comparable business concerns.
- The nature and scope of the employee's work.
- The size and complexity of the business.
- A comparison of salaries paid with both gross and net income.
- The taxpayer's salary policy toward all employees.
- For small corporations with a limited number of officers, the amount of compensation paid to the employee in question in previous years.
- Whether a reasonable shareholder would have agreed to the level of compensation paid.[32]

The last factor above, known as the "reasonable investor test," is a relatively new development in the law on reasonable compensation.[33] Its use by the courts has been inconsistent. In some cases, the Seventh Circuit Court of Appeals has relied solely on the reasonable investor test in determining reasonableness, whereas the Tenth Circuit Court of Appeals has largely ignored this factor. Other Federal circuits have used an approach that considers all of the factors in the list.

Loans to Shareholders. Advances to shareholders that are not bona fide loans are constructive dividends. Whether an advance qualifies as a bona fide loan is a question of fact to be determined in light of the particular circumstances. Factors considered in determining whether the advance is a bona fide loan include the following:[34]

- Whether the advance is on open account or is evidenced by a written instrument.
- Whether the shareholder furnished collateral or other security for the advance.
- How long the advance has been outstanding.
- Whether any repayments have been made.
- The shareholder's ability to repay the advance.
- The shareholder's use of the funds (e.g., payment of routine bills versus non-recurring, extraordinary expenses).
- The regularity of the advances.
- The dividend-paying history of the corporation.

Even when a corporation makes a bona fide loan to a shareholder, a constructive dividend may be triggered, equal to the amount of imputed (forgone) interest on the loan.[35] Imputed interest equals the amount by which the interest paid by the Federal government on new borrowings, compounded semiannually, exceeds the interest charged on the loan. When the imputed interest provision applies, the shareholder is deemed to have made an interest payment to the corporation equal to the amount of imputed interest, and the corporation is deemed to have repaid the imputed interest to the shareholder through a constructive dividend. As a result, the corporation receives interest income and makes a nondeductible dividend payment, and the shareholder has taxable dividend income that might be offset with an interest deduction.

---

[32]All but the final factor in this list are identified in *Mayson Manufacturing Co. v. Comm.*, 49–2 USTC ¶9467, 38 AFTR 1028, 178 F.2d 115 (CA–6, 1949).

[33]For example, see *Alpha Medical, Inc. v. Comm.*, 99–1 USTC ¶50,461, 83 AFTR2d 99–697, 172 F.3d 942 (CA–6, 1999).

[34]*Fin Hay Realty Co. v. U.S.*, 68–2 USTC ¶9438, 22 AFTR2d 5004, 398 F.2d 694 (CA–3, 1968). But see *Nariman Teymourian*, 90 TCM 352, T.C.Memo. 2005–302, for an example of how good planning can avoid constructive dividends in the shareholder loan context.

[35]See § 7872.

EXAMPLE 22

If one shareholder chose cash dividend, the other divid. it would be Taxable

Mallard Corporation lends its principal shareholder, Henry, $100,000 on January 2 of the current year. The loan is interest-free and payable on demand. On December 31, the imputed interest rules are applied. Assuming the Federal rate is 6%, compounded semiannually, the amount of imputed interest is $6,090. This amount is deemed paid by Henry to Mallard in the form of interest. Mallard is then deemed to return the amount to Henry as a constructive dividend. Thus, Henry has dividend income of $6,090, which might be offset with a deduction for the interest paid to Mallard. Mallard has interest income of $6,090 for the interest received, with no offsetting deduction for the dividend payment. ■

Loans to a Corporation by Shareholders. Shareholder loans to a corporation may be reclassified as equity because the debt has too many features of stock. Any interest and principal payments made by the corporation to the shareholder are then treated as constructive dividends. This topic was covered more thoroughly in the discussion of "thin capitalization" in Chapter 4.

Stock Dividends and Stock Rights

LO.7

Distinguish between taxable and nontaxable stock dividends and stock rights.

Stock Dividends—§ 305. Historically, **stock dividends** were excluded from income on the theory that the ownership interest of the shareholder was unchanged as a result of the distribution.[36] Recognizing that some distributions of stock could affect ownership interests, the 1954 Code included a provision (§ 305) taxing stock dividends where (1) the stockholder could elect to receive either stock or property or (2) the stock dividends were in discharge of preference dividends. However, because this provision applied to a narrow range of transactions, corporations were able to develop an assortment of alternative methods that circumvented taxation and still affected shareholders' proportionate interests in the corporation.[37] In response, the scope of § 305 was expanded.

In its current state, the provisions of § 305 are based on the proportionate interest concept. As a general rule, stock dividends are excluded from income if they are pro rata distributions of stock or stock rights, paid on common stock. Five exceptions to this general rule exist. For each of these exceptions, listed below, stock distributions may be taxed.

1. Distributions payable in either stock or property at the election of the shareholder.
2. Distributions of property to some shareholders with a corresponding increase in the proportionate interest of other shareholders in either assets or E & P of the distributing corporation.
3. Distributions of preferred stock to some common shareholders and of common stock to other common shareholders.
4. Distributions of stock to preferred shareholders. However, changes in the conversion ratio of convertible preferred stock to account for a stock dividend or stock split are not taxable in some circumstances.
5. Distributions of convertible preferred stock unless it can be shown that the distribution will not result in a disproportionate distribution.

These exceptions to nontaxability of stock dividends deal with various disproportionate distribution situations.

Holders of convertible securities are considered shareholders. Thus, under the second exception above, when interest is paid on convertible debentures and stock dividends are paid on common stock, the stock dividends are taxable. This result is avoided if the conversion ratio or conversion price is adjusted to reflect the price of the stock dividend.[38]

[36]See *Eisner v. Macomber,* 1 USTC ¶32, 3 AFTR 3020, 40 S.Ct. 189 (USSC, 1920).
[37]See "Stock Dividends," Senate Report 91–552, 1969–3 C.B. 519.

[38]See Reg. § 1.305–3(d) for illustrations on how to compute required adjustments on conversion ratios or prices.

DEEMED DIVIDENDS FROM CONTROLLED FOREIGN CORPORATIONS

As described in the Global Tax Issues feature earlier in this chapter, the tax law requires a U.S. parent corporation to recognize some of the unrepatriated earnings of a controlled foreign corporation (CFC) as income. The U.S. parent's basis in the CFC stock is increased by the amount of the taxed but unrepatriated earnings. Subsequently, when cash or property is actually paid to the U.S. parent (i.e., when taxed earnings are repatriated), no income results. Thus, the CFC rules preclude some deferral but do not lead to double taxation.

In an effort to boost the economy, in 2004 Congress introduced a temporary one-year tax break for CFCs. New § 965 allowed an 85 percent deduction for cash dividends paid from untaxed earnings by CFCs to U.S. corporate shareholders. For many corporations, this provision reduced the tax on repatriated foreign earnings from 35 percent to 5.25 percent. By all accounts, § 965 was a resounding success as an estimated $300 billion additional foreign money flowed into the United States during 2005.

If stock dividends are not taxable, the corporation's E & P is not reduced.[39] If the stock dividends are taxable, the distributing corporation treats the distribution in the same manner as any other taxable property dividend.

If a stock dividend is taxable, the shareholder's basis for the newly received shares is fair market value, and the holding period starts on the date of receipt. If a stock dividend is not taxable, the basis of the stock on which the dividend is distributed is reallocated.[40] If the dividend shares are identical to these formerly held shares, basis for the old stock is reallocated by dividing the taxpayer's cost in the old stock by the total number of shares. If the dividend stock is not identical to the underlying shares (e.g., a stock dividend of preferred on common), basis is determined by allocating the basis of the formerly held shares between the old and new stock according to the fair market value of each. The holding period includes the holding period of the formerly held stock.[41]

EXAMPLE 23

Gail bought 1,000 shares of common stock two years ago for $10,000. In the current tax year, Gail receives 10 shares of common stock as a nontaxable stock dividend. Gail's basis of $10,000 is divided by 1,010. Each share of stock has a basis of $9.90 instead of the pre-dividend $10 basis. ■

EXAMPLE 24

Assume Gail received, instead, a nontaxable preferred stock dividend of 100 shares. The preferred stock has a fair market value of $1,000, and the common stock, on which the preferred is distributed, has a fair market value of $19,000. After the receipt of the stock dividend, the basis of the common stock is $9,500, and the basis of the preferred is $500, computed as follows:

Fair market value of common	$19,000
Fair market value of preferred	1,000
	$20,000
Basis of common: $19/20 \times \$10,000$	$ 9,500
Basis of preferred: $1/20 \times \$10,000$	$ 500

■

Stock Rights. The rules for determining taxability of **stock rights** are identical to those for determining taxability of stock dividends. If the rights are taxable, the recipient has income equal to the fair market value of the rights. The fair market value then becomes the shareholder-distributee's basis in the rights.[42] If the rights are exercised, the holding period for the new stock begins on the date the rights

---

[39]§ 312(d)(1).

[40]§ 307(a).

[41]§ 1223(5).

[42]Reg. § 1.305–1(b).

(whether taxable or nontaxable) are exercised. The basis of the new stock is the basis of the rights plus the amount of any other consideration given.

If stock rights are not taxable and the value of the rights is less than 15 percent of the value of the old stock, the basis of the rights is zero. However, the shareholder may elect to have some of the basis in the formerly held stock allocated to the rights.[43] The election is made by attaching a statement to the shareholder's return for the year in which the rights are received.[44] If the fair market value of the rights is 15 percent or more of the value of the old stock and the rights are exercised or sold, the shareholder *must* allocate some of the basis in the formerly held stock to the rights.

EXAMPLE 25

A corporation with common stock outstanding declares a nontaxable dividend payable in rights to subscribe to common stock. Each right entitles the holder to purchase one share of stock for $90. One right is issued for every two shares of stock owned. Fred owns 400 shares of stock purchased two years ago for $15,000. At the time of the distribution of the rights, the market value of the common stock is $100 per share, and the market value of the rights is $8 per right. Fred receives 200 rights. He exercises 100 rights and sells the remaining 100 rights three months later for $9 per right.

Fred need not allocate the cost of the original stock to the rights because the value of the rights is less than 15% of the value of the stock ($1,600 ÷ $40,000 = 4%). If Fred does not allocate his original stock basis to the rights, the tax consequences are as follows:

- Basis of the new stock is $9,000 [$90 (exercise price) × 100 (shares)]. The holding period of the new stock begins on the date the stock was purchased.
- Sale of the rights produces long-term capital gain of $900 [$9 (sales price) × 100 (rights)]. The holding period of the rights starts with the date the original 400 shares of stock were acquired.

If Fred elects to allocate basis to the rights, the tax consequences are as follows:

- Basis of the stock is $14,423 [$40,000 (value of stock) ÷ $41,600 (value of rights and stock) × $15,000 (cost of stock)].
- Basis of the rights is $577 [$1,600 (value of rights) ÷ $41,600 (value of rights and stock) × $15,000 (cost of stock)].
- When Fred exercises the rights, his basis for the new stock will be $9,288.50 [$9,000 (cost) + $288.50 (basis for 100 rights)].
- Sale of the rights would produce a long-term capital gain of $611.50 [$900 (sales price) − $288.50 (basis in the remaining 100 rights)]. ■

TAX PLANNING
Considerations

Corporate Distributions

The following points are especially important when planning for corporate distributions.

- Because E & P is the pool of funds from which dividends may be distributed, its periodic determination is essential to corporate planning. Thus, an E & P account should be established and maintained, particularly if the possibility exists that a corporate distribution might be a return of capital.
- Accumulated E & P is the sum of all past years' current E & P. Because there is no statute of limitations on the computation of E & P, the IRS can redetermine a corporation's current E & P for a tax year long since passed. Such a change affects accumulated E & P and has a direct impact on the taxability of current distributions to shareholders.
- Distributions can be planned to avoid or minimize dividend exposure.

EXAMPLE 26

Flicker Corporation has accumulated E & P of $100,000 as of January 1 of the current year. During the year, it expects to have earnings from operations of $80,000 and to sell an asset for a loss of $100,000. Thus, it anticipates a current E & P deficit of $20,000. Flicker Corporation also

---

TAX *in the News*   **CABLEVISION SYSTEMS' MOVE PAYS REAL DIVIDEND FOR SHAREHOLDERS**

Sometimes, the tax treatment of corporate distributions can provide big tax benefits to shareholders. When companies post a series of net operating losses over several years, they can wipe out previously accumulated E & P. These companies can then distribute cash to shareholders tax-free as a return of capital to the extent of the stock's tax basis. Some of these loss companies generate large of amounts of cash from operations—their losses are created by noncash deductions (i.e., depreciation). Other loss companies borrow cash for their distributions. This approach provides an added benefit: the interest payments on the loans are deductible.

Recently, Cablevision Systems Corporation paid a $10 per share distribution using borrowed cash. The distribution was equal to more than one-third of the company's share price. According to some security analysts, the distribution was likely to qualify for tax-free treatment.

Return of capital distributions provide an excellent planning opportunity for corporations with a controlling shareholder (such as Cablevision), who can set corporate distribution policies. These distributions have the potential to escape tax completely. In Cablevision's case, the distribution will reduce stock basis and defer any tax until the stock is sold. If the shareholders keep their stock until death, the stock receives a step-up in basis to fair market value. This basis step-up can completely wipe out the effect of the basis reduction (and gain potential) triggered by the distribution. As a result, basis adjustment caused by the return of capital distribution dies with the shareholder.

Source: *Adapted from David Reilly, "A Move that Really Pays Dividends,"* Wall Street Journal, *April 25, 2006, p. C3.*

---

expects to make a cash distribution of $60,000. The best approach is to recognize the loss as soon as possible and, immediately thereafter, make the cash distribution to the shareholders. Suppose these two steps take place on January 1. Because the current E & P has a deficit, the accumulated E & P account must be updated (refer to Example 11 in this chapter). Thus, at the time of the distribution, the combined E & P balance is zero [$100,000 (beginning balance in accumulated E & P) − $100,000 (existing deficit in current E & P)], and the $60,000 distribution to the shareholders constitutes a return of capital. Current deficits are allocated pro rata throughout the year unless the parties can prove otherwise; here, they can. ■

EXAMPLE 27

After several unprofitable years, Darter Corporation has a deficit in accumulated E & P of $100,000 as of January 1, 2008. Starting in 2008, Darter expects to generate annual E & P of $50,000 for the next four years and would like to distribute this amount to its shareholders. The corporation's cash position (for dividend purposes) will correspond to the current E & P generated. Consider the following two distribution schedules:

1. On December 31 of 2008, 2009, 2010, and 2011, Darter Corporation distributes a cash dividend of $50,000.
2. On December 31 of 2009 and 2011, Darter Corporation distributes a cash dividend of $100,000.

The two alternatives are illustrated below.

Year	Accumulated E & P (First of Year)	Current E & P	Distribution	Amount of Dividend
		Alternative 1		
2008	($ 100,000)	$50,000	$ 50,000	$50,000
2009	(100,000)	50,000	50,000	50,000
2010	(100,000)	50,000	50,000	50,000
2011	(100,000)	50,000	50,000	50,000
		Alternative 2		
2008	($ 100,000)	$50,000	$ –0–	$ –0–
2009	(50,000)	50,000	100,000	50,000
2010	(50,000)	50,000	–0–	–0–
2011	–0–	50,000	100,000	50,000

Alternative 1 produces $200,000 of dividend income because each $50,000 distribution is fully covered by current E & P. Alternative 2, however, produces only $100,000 of dividend income for the shareholders. The remaining $100,000 is a return of capital. Why? At the time Darter Corporation made its first distribution of $100,000 on December 31, 2009, it had a deficit of $50,000 in accumulated E & P (the original deficit of $100,000 is reduced by the $50,000 of current E & P from 2008). Consequently, the $100,000 distribution yields a $50,000 dividend (the current E & P for 2009), and $50,000 is treated as a return of capital. As of January 1, 2010, Darter's accumulated E & P now has a deficit balance of $50,000 since a distribution cannot increase a deficit in E & P. After adding the remaining $50,000 of current E & P from 2010, the balance on January 1, 2011, is zero. Thus, the second distribution of $100,000, made on December 31, 2011, also yields $50,000 of dividends (the current E & P for 2011) and a $50,000 return of capital. ■

ETHICAL and EQUITABLE *Considerations*

PLAYING GAMES WITH THE STATUTE OF LIMITATIONS

In 2001, Beige Corporation made a cash distribution to its shareholders, one of whom was Steve Jordan. At that time, the parties involved believed the distribution was a return of capital because Beige had no E & P. Accordingly, none of the shareholders reported dividend income. In Steve's case, he reduced the $200,000 original basis of his stock investment by $40,000, his share of the distribution. In 2008, Steve discovered that E & P had been incorrectly computed. The 2001 distribution was fully covered by E & P and should not have been treated as a return of capital.

In 2009, Steve sells his stock in Beige Corporation for $350,000. He plans to report a gain of $150,000 [$350,000 (selling price) − $200,000 (original basis)] on the sale. Although Steve realizes he should have recognized dividend income of $40,000 for 2001, the statute of limitations has made this a closed year.

Comment on Steve's situation.

Planning for Qualified Dividends

Retirement Plans. The reduced tax rates available to individual taxpayers on net capital gain and qualified dividend income reinforce the inadvisability of funding retirement accounts with stock. Since income in § 401(k) plans and IRAs is not taxed when earned, the benefits of the lower tax rates on these forms of income are lost. Instead, distributions from the plans are taxed at ordinary income tax rates.

Individual Alternative Minimum Tax. The lower rates on dividends and long-term capital gains apply under both the regular income tax and the alternative minimum tax. This increases the exposure of many individuals to the alternative minimum tax, particularly those with significant income from dividends or long-term capital gain. As a result, individual taxpayers who pay the alternative minimum tax should reconsider their investment strategies to manage the mix of ordinary income, dividend income, and capital gain.

Closely Held Corporations. Closely held corporations have considerable discretion regarding their dividend policies. In the past, the double tax result provided strong motivation to avoid the payment of dividends. Instead, the incentive was to bail out corporate profits in a manner that provided tax benefits to the corporation. Hence, liberal use was made of compensation, loan, and lease arrangements because salaries, interest, and rent are deductible. Under current law, however, shareholders prefer dividends because salaries, interest, and rent are fully taxed while dividends receive preferential treatment. Thus, the question becomes this: *Should the corporation or the shareholders benefit?* In general, the best strategy considers the tax consequences to both parties.

Consider a corporation paying tax at the 34% rate and an individual shareholder in the 35% tax bracket. A deductible $10,000 payment to the shareholder will *save* the corporation $3,400 in tax, resulting in an after-tax cost of $6,600. The shareholder will pay $3,500 in tax, resulting in after-tax income of $6,500. This creates a joint tax burden of $100 ($3,500 tax paid by the shareholder − $3,400 tax saved by the corporation). If, instead, the corporation paid a $10,000 qualifying dividend to the shareholder, no tax savings would be realized by the corporation, resulting in an after-tax cost of $10,000. The shareholder would owe $1,500 in taxes, leaving $8,500 of income. Considering both the corporation and the shareholder, a dividend creates $1,400 more tax liability than a deductible payment, so the deductible payment is more tax efficient. ■

In Example 28, when the deductible payment is made, the shareholder bears an increased tax burden of $2,000 ($3,500 tax due from the deductible payment − $1,500 tax due from the dividend) while the corporation saves $3,400 ($3,400 tax saved because of the deductible payment − $0 tax saved because of the dividend). Both parties could actually benefit if the corporation transfers part of its benefit to the shareholder through a larger deductible payment.

Assume the same facts as in Example 28, except that the corporation pays a $14,000 deductible payment. In this case, the corporation will save $4,760 ($14,000 × 34%) in tax, resulting in an after-tax cost of $9,240. From the corporation's perspective, this is preferable to a $10,000 dividend because it costs $760 less after tax ($10,000 dividend cost − $9,240 after-tax cost of a $14,000 deductible payment). The shareholder will pay taxes of $4,900 on the deductible payment, resulting in after-tax income of $9,100. The shareholder will also prefer this payment to a dividend because it generates $600 more after-tax income ($9,100 − $8,500 from a dividend). ■

Thus, if properly structured, deductible payments by the corporation to the shareholder still appear to be preferable to dividends in most situations (unless the corporation faces a low tax rate). The benefit of this strategy will be even greater if the shareholder is paying alternative minimum tax.

Constructive Dividends

Tax planning can be particularly effective in avoiding constructive dividend situations. Shareholders should try to structure their dealings with the corporation on an arm's length basis. For example, reasonable rent should be paid for the use of corporate property, and a fair price should be paid for its purchase. The parties should make every effort to support the amount involved with appraisal data or market information obtained from reliable sources at or near the time of the transaction. Dealings between shareholders and a closely held corporation should be as formal as possible. In the case of loans to shareholders, for example, the parties should provide for an adequate rate of interest and written evidence of the debt. Shareholders also should establish and follow a realistic repayment schedule.

If shareholders wish to bail out corporate profits in a form deductible to the corporation, a balanced mix of the possible alternatives lessens the risk of constructive dividend treatment. Rent for the use of shareholder property, interest on amounts borrowed from shareholders, or salaries for services rendered by shareholders are all feasible substitutes for dividend distributions. Overdoing any one approach, however, may attract the attention of the IRS. Too much interest, for example, may mean the corporation is thinly capitalized, and some of the debt may be reclassified as equity investment.

Much can be done to protect against the disallowance of unreasonable compensation. Example 30 is an illustration, all too common in a family corporation, of what *not* to do.

EXAMPLE 30

Bob Cole wholly owns Eagle Corporation. Corporate employees and annual salaries include Mrs. Cole ($120,000), Cole Jr. ($80,000), Bob Cole ($640,000), and Ed ($320,000). The operation of Eagle Corporation is shared about equally between Bob Cole and Ed, who is an unrelated party. Mrs. Cole performed significant services for Eagle during its formative years, but now merely attends the annual meeting of the board of directors. Cole Jr., Bob Cole's son, is a full-time student and occasionally signs papers for the corporation in his capacity as treasurer. Eagle Corporation has not distributed a dividend for 10 years although it has accumulated substantial E & P. Mrs. Cole, Cole Jr., and Bob Cole run the risk of a finding of unreasonable compensation, based on the following factors:

- Mrs. Cole's salary is vulnerable unless proof is available that some or all of her $120,000 annual salary is payment for services rendered to the corporation in prior years and that she was underpaid for those years.[45]
- Cole Jr.'s salary is also vulnerable; he does not appear to earn the $80,000 paid to him by the corporation. Neither Cole Jr. nor Mrs. Cole is a shareholder, but each one's relationship to Bob Cole is enough of a tie-in to raise the unreasonable compensation issue.
- Bob Cole's salary appears susceptible to challenge. Why is he receiving $320,000 more than Ed when it appears that they share equally in the operation of the corporation?
- The fact that Eagle Corporation has not distributed dividends over the past 10 years, even though it is capable of doing so, increases the likelihood of a constructive dividend. ■

What could have been done to improve the tax position of the parties in Example 30? Mrs. Cole and Cole Jr. are not entitled to a salary as neither seems to be performing any services for the corporation. Paying them a salary simply aggravates the problem. The IRS is more apt to consider *all* the family members' salaries excessive under the circumstances. Bob Cole should probably reduce his compensation to correspond with that paid to Ed. He can then attempt to distribute corporate earnings to himself in some other form.

Paying some dividends to Bob Cole would also help alleviate the problem raised in Example 30. The IRS has been successful in denying a deduction for salary paid to a shareholder-employee, even when the payment was reasonable, in a situation where the corporation had not distributed any dividends.[46] Most courts, however, have not denied deductions for compensation solely because a dividend was not paid. A better approach is to compare an employee's compensation with the level of compensation prevalent in the particular industry.

The corporation can provide *indirect* compensation to Bob Cole by paying expenses that benefit him personally, but are nevertheless deductible to the corporation. For example, premiums paid by the corporation for sickness, accident, and hospitalization insurance for Bob Cole are deductible to the corporation and nontaxable to him.[47] Any payments under the policy are not taxable to Bob Cole unless they exceed his medical expenses.[48] The corporation can also pay for travel and entertainment expenses incurred by Cole on behalf of the corporation. If these expenses are primarily for the benefit of the corporation, Bob Cole will not recognize any taxable income, and the corporation will receive a deduction.[49]

When testing for reasonableness, the IRS looks at the total compensation package, including indirect compensation payments to a shareholder-employee. Thus, indirect payments must not be overlooked.

EXAMPLE 31

Cora, the president and sole shareholder of Willet Corporation, is paid an annual salary of $100,000 by the corporation. Cora would like to draw funds from the corporation, but is

---

[45]See, for example, *R.J. Nicoll Co.*, 59 T.C. 37 (1972).

[46]*McCandless Tile Service v. U.S.*, 70–1 USTC ¶9284, 25 AFTR2d 70–870, 422 F.2d 1336 (Ct.Cls., 1970). The court in *McCandless* concluded that a return on equity of 15% of net profits was reasonable.

[47]Reg. § 1.162–10.

[48]The medical reimbursement plan must meet certain nondiscrimination requirements of § 105(h)(2).

[49]Reg. § 1.62–2(c)(4).

concerned that additional salary payments might cause the IRS to contend her salary is unreasonable. Cora does not want Willet to pay any dividends. She also wishes to donate $50,000 to her alma mater to establish scholarships for needy students. In this situation, Willet Corporation can make the contribution on Cora's behalf. The payment clearly benefits Cora, but she will not be taxed on the amount of the contribution,[50] and Willet can take a charitable contribution deduction for the payment. ■

Assume in Example 31 that Cora has made an individual pledge to the university to provide $50,000 for scholarships for needy students. Willet Corporation satisfies Cora's pledge by paying the $50,000 to the university, but she will be taxed on the amount.[51] In this context, the $50,000 payment to the university may be treated as *indirect* compensation to Cora. In determining whether Cora's salary is unreasonable, both the *direct* payment of $100,000 and the *indirect* $50,000 payment will be considered—a total compensation package of $150,000. ■

EXAMPLE 32

KEY TERMS

Accumulated earnings and profits, 5–8

Constructive dividend, 5–16

Current earnings and profits, 5–8

Earnings and profits (E & P), 5–3

Property dividend, 5–13

Qualified dividends, 5–11

Stock dividends, 5–18

Stock rights, 5–19

Unreasonable compensation, 5–17

PROBLEM MATERIALS

DISCUSSION QUESTIONS

1. What factors affect the tax treatment of corporate distributions?

2. What is meant by the term *earnings and profits*?

3. In determining Purple Corporation's current E & P for 2008, how should taxable income be adjusted as a result of the following transactions?
   a. Interest on municipal bonds received in 2008.
   b. A capital loss carryover from 2007, fully used in 2008.
   c. Gain deferred on a qualified § 1031 like-kind exchange that occurred in 2008.
   d. Loss on a sale between related parties in 2008.
   e. Federal income taxes paid in 2008.
   f. Section 179 expense elected and deducted in 2008.

4. In what ways does the computation of E & P require more conservative accounting than the computation of taxable income?

5. Discuss the impact each of the following has on generating or adding to a deficit in E & P:
   a. A dividend distribution by the corporation.
   b. An operating loss of the corporation.

6. Describe the effect of a distribution in a year when the distributing corporation has:
   a. A deficit in accumulated E & P and a positive amount in current E & P.
   b. A positive amount in accumulated E & P and a deficit in current E & P.

---

[50]*Henry J. Knott*, 67 T.C. 681 (1977).

[51]*Schalk Chemical Co. v. Comm.*, 62–1 USTC ¶9496, 9 AFTR2d 1579, 304 F.2d 48 (CA–9, 1962).

    c. A deficit in both current and accumulated E & P.

    d. A positive amount in both current and accumulated E & P.

7. A calendar year corporation has no accumulated E & P, but expects to earn current E & P for the year. A cash distribution to its shareholders on January 1 should result in a return of capital. Comment on the validity of this statement.

8. Discuss the rationale for the reduced tax rates on dividends paid to individuals.

Issue ID   9. White Corporation distributes $500,000 to each of its three shareholders: Steve, Byron, and Fuchsia Corporation. What factors must be considered when determining how the distribution is treated for tax purposes to both the shareholders and White Corporation?

10. What requirements must be met for a dividend payment to qualify for the reduced 15%/0% tax rates?

11. Why would a corporation distribute a property dividend?

Decision Making   12. Raven Corporation owns three automobiles that it uses in its business. It no longer needs two of these automobiles and is considering distributing them to its two shareholders as a property dividend. All three have a fair market value of $20,000 and a basis as follows: automobile A, $27,000; automobile B, $20,000; and automobile C, $12,000. The corporation has asked you for advice. What do you recommend?

Issue ID   13. A corporation is contemplating a possible property distribution to its shareholders. If appreciated property is to be used, does it matter to the distributing corporation whether the property distributed is a long-term capital asset or depreciable property subject to recapture?

14. How does the distribution of property affect E & P?

15. To be treated as a dividend for tax purposes, must a corporation's distribution to its shareholders meet the legal requirements of a dividend, be formally declared, or be issued pro rata to all shareholders? Discuss.

Issue ID   16. Ashley is the president and sole shareholder of Orange Corporation. She is paid an annual salary of $450,000. Her son, Matt, is the company's chief financial officer and is paid a salary of $275,000. Matt works for Orange on a part-time basis. He spends most of his time training for marathons in order to compete in the Olympics. Orange Corporation also advances $70,000 to Ashley as an interest-free loan. What are the tax issues?

17. Whether compensation paid to a corporate employee is reasonable is a question of fact to be determined from the surrounding circumstances. How would the resolution of this problem be affected by each of the following factors?

    a. The employee owns no stock but is the mother-in-law of the sole shareholder.

    b. The shareholder-employee does not have a college degree.

    c. The shareholder-employee works 40 hours per week for another unrelated employer.

    d. The shareholder-employee was underpaid for services during the formative period of the corporation.

    e. The corporation has never paid a dividend.

    f. Year-end bonuses are paid to all employees, but officer-shareholders receive disproportionately larger bonuses.

Decision Making   18. Sparrow Corporation would like to transfer excess cash to its sole shareholder, Adam, who is also an employee. Adam is in the 28% tax bracket, and Sparrow is in the 34% bracket. Because Adam's contribution to the business is substantial, Sparrow believes that a $25,000 bonus in the current year would be viewed as reasonable compensation and would be deductible by the corporation. However, Sparrow is leaning toward paying Adam a $25,000 dividend because the tax rate on dividends is lower than the tax rate on compensation. Is Sparrow correct in believing that a dividend is the better choice? Why or why not?

19. Pink Corporation has several employees. Their names and salaries are listed below.

Judy	$470,000
Holly (Judy's daughter)	100,000
Terry (Judy's son)	100,000
John (an unrelated third party)	320,000

Holly and Terry are the only shareholders of Pink Corporation. Judy and John share equally in the management of the company's operations. Holly and Terry are both full-time college students at a university 300 miles away. Pink has substantial E & P and has never distributed a dividend. Discuss problems related to Pink's salary arrangement.

20. Condor Corporation pays its president and sole shareholder, Katrina, an annual salary of $500,000. Katrina wishes to avoid dividends because of the double tax result. However, she is concerned that if she were to receive any more salary, the IRS might treat it as unreasonable compensation and a constructive dividend. Instead, Katrina is thinking of having Condor contribute $150,000 to her favorite charity. Would there be a problem if Katrina makes a pledge for this amount and Condor pays it on her behalf? Explain.

21. Your client, Raptor Corporation, declares a dividend permitting its common shareholders to elect to receive 9 shares of cumulative preferred stock or 3 additional shares of Raptor common stock for every 10 shares of common stock held. Raptor has only common stock outstanding (fair market value of $45 per share). One shareholder elects to receive preferred stock while the remaining shareholders choose the common stock. Raptor asks you whether the shareholders have any taxable income on the receipt of the stock. Prepare a letter to Raptor and a memo to the file regarding this matter. Raptor's address is 1812 S. Camino Seco, Tucson, AZ 85710.

Communications

22. Describe the rationale underlying the tax treatment of stock distributions.

23. How are nontaxable and taxable stock rights handled for tax purposes?

PROBLEMS

24. At the start of the current year, Red Corporation (a calendar year taxpayer) has accumulated E & P of $100,000. Red's current E & P is $60,000, and during the year, it distributes $200,000 ($100,000 each) to its equal shareholders, Michele and Wally. Michele's stock has a basis of $11,000, and Wally's stock has a basis of $26,000. How is the distribution treated for tax purposes?

25. Redbird Corporation, a calendar year taxpayer, receives dividend income of $250,000 from a corporation in which it holds a 10% interest. Redbird also receives interest income of $35,000 from municipal bonds. (The municipality used the proceeds from the bond issue to construct a library.) Redbird borrowed funds to purchase the municipal bonds and pays $20,000 of interest on the loan. Excluding the items noted above, Redbird's taxable income is $500,000.
    a. What is Redbird Corporation's taxable income after dividend income, interest from the municipal bonds, and interest paid on the loan have been taken into account?
    b. What is Redbird Corporation's accumulated E & P at the end of the year if the beginning balance is $150,000?

26. On October 1, 2008, Silver Corporation, a calendar year corporation, sold a parcel of land (basis of $400,000) for a note in the amount of $1 million. The note is payable in five installments, the first being on June 15 in the following year. Because Silver did not elect out of the installment method, none of the $600,000 gain is included in taxable income for 2008.

    Silver Corporation had a deficit in accumulated E & P of $300,000 on January 1, 2008. For 2008, before considering the effect of the land sale, Silver had a deficit in current E & P of $50,000.

Olivia, the sole shareholder of Silver, owns stock with a basis of $200,000. If Silver distributes $900,000 to Olivia on December 31, 2008, how much income must she report for tax purposes?

27. Jade Corporation (a calendar year, accrual basis taxpayer) had the following transactions during 2008, its second year of operation.

Taxable income	$330,000
Federal income tax liability paid	112,000
Interest income from tax-exempt payors	5,000
Meals and entertainment expenses (total)	3,000
Premiums paid on key employee life insurance	3,500
Increase in cash surrender value attributable to life insurance premiums	700
Proceeds from key employee life insurance policy	130,000
Cash surrender value of life insurance policy at distribution	20,000
Excess of capital losses over capital gains	13,000
MACRS deduction	26,000
Straight-line depreciation using ADS lives	16,000
Section 179 expense elected during 2007	100,000
Organizational expenses incurred in 2007	14,000
Dividends received from domestic corporations (less than 20% owned)	25,000

Jade uses the LIFO inventory method, and its LIFO recapture amount increased by $10,000 during 2008. In addition, Jade sold property on installment during 2007. The property was sold for $40,000 and had an adjusted basis at sale of $32,000. During 2008, Jade received a $15,000 payment on the installment sale. Finally, assume that Jade elected to amortize qualified organizational expenses in 2007. Compute Jade Corporation's current E & P.

28. In each of the following *independent* situations, indicate the effect on taxable income and E & P, stating the amount of any increase (or decrease) as a result of the transaction. Assume E & P has already been increased by taxable income.

Transaction	Taxable Income Increase (Decrease)	E & P Increase (Decrease)
a. Realized gain of $80,000 on involuntary conversion of building ($10,000 of gain is recognized).	_____	_____
b. Mining exploration costs incurred on May 1 of the current year; $24,000 is deductible from current-year taxable income.	_____	_____
c. Sale of equipment to unrelated third party for $240,000; basis is $120,000 (no election out of installment method; no payments are received in the current year).	_____	_____
d. Dividends of $20,000 received from 5%-owned corporation, together with dividends received deduction (assume taxable income limit does not apply).	_____	_____
e. Domestic production activities deduction of $45,000 claimed in current year.	_____	_____
f. Section 179 expense deduction of $100,000 in current year.	_____	_____
g. Impact of current-year § 179 expense deduction in succeeding year.	_____	_____
h. MACRS depreciation of $80,000. ADS depreciation would have been $90,000.	_____	_____
i. Federal income taxes paid in the current year of $80,000.	_____	_____

29. Yellow Corporation, a calendar year taxpayer, made estimated tax payments of $1,000 per quarter for 2008, for a total of $4,000. Yellow filed its 2008 Federal income tax return in 2009 reflecting a tax liability for 2008 of $1,500. Consequently, Yellow received a $2,500 refund in 2009. What is the impact to Yellow's E & P of the payment of estimated taxes and the receipt of the Federal income tax refund?

30. Blue Corporation is a calendar year taxpayer. At the beginning of the current year, Blue has accumulated E & P of $330,000. The corporation incurs a deficit in current E & P of $460,000 that accrues ratably throughout the year. On June 30, Blue distributes $200,000 to its sole shareholder, Marcella. If Marcella's stock has a basis of $40,000, how is she taxed on this distribution?

31. At the beginning of its taxable year, Teal Corporation had E & P of $225,000. On March 30, Teal sold an asset at a loss of $225,000. For the calendar year, Teal incurred a deficit in current E & P of $305,000, which includes the $225,000 loss on the sale of the asset. If Teal made a distribution of $50,000 to its sole shareholder on April 1, how will the shareholder be taxed?

32. Bunting Corporation (a calendar year taxpayer) had a deficit in accumulated E & P of $250,000 at the beginning of the current year. Its net profit for the period January 1 through September 30 was $300,000, but its E & P for the entire taxable year was only $40,000. If Bunting made a distribution of $60,000 to its sole shareholder on October 1, how will the shareholder be taxed?

33. Woodpecker Corporation and Tim each own 50% of Cormorant Corporation's common stock. On January 1, Cormorant has a deficit in accumulated E & P of $200,000. Its current E & P is $90,000. During the year, Cormorant makes cash distributions of $40,000 each to Woodpecker and Tim.
    a. How are the two shareholders taxed on the distribution?
    b. What is Cormorant Corporation's accumulated E & P at the end of the year?

34. Complete the following schedule for each case. Assume the shareholders have ample basis in the stock investment.

	Accumulated E & P Beginning of Year	Current E & P	Cash Distributions (All on Last Day of Year)	Dividend Income	Return of Capital
a.	($150,000)	$ 70,000	$130,000	$	$
b.	200,000	(60,000)	210,000		
c.	130,000	50,000	150,000		
d.	120,000	(40,000)	130,000		
e.	Same as (d) except the distribution of $130,000 is made on June 30, and the corporation uses the calendar year for tax purposes.				

35. Linfort, the sole shareholder of Brown Corporation, sold his Brown stock to Lamar on July 30 for $270,000. Linfort's basis in the stock was $200,000 at the beginning of the year. Brown had accumulated E & P of $120,000 on January 1 and current E & P of $240,000. During the year, Brown made the following distributions: $450,000 cash to Linfort on July 1 and $150,000 cash to Lamar on December 30. How will Linfort and Lamar be taxed on the distributions? How much gain will Linfort recognize on the sale of his stock to Lamar?

36. Sean, a shareholder of Crimson Corporation, is in the 35% tax bracket. This year, he receives a $7,000 qualified dividend from Crimson. Sean has investment interest expense of $16,000 and net investment income of $9,000 (not including the qualified dividend). Assume that Sean does not expect to have any investment income in the foreseeable future. Should Sean treat the distribution as a qualified dividend (subject to a 15% tax rate) or classify it as net investment income?

Decision Making

37. In November of the current year, Sapphire Corporation declared a dividend of $2 per share (the shareholder record date is December 15). Assume that Sapphire has sufficient current E & P to cover the dividend payment. If Alexis purchases 500 shares of Sapphire stock on December 5 and sells the stock on December 25, how is she taxed on the $1,000 dividend?

38. Kathryn, an individual, owns all of the outstanding stock in Copper Corporation. Kathryn purchased her stock in Copper 11 years ago, and her basis is $18,000. At the beginning of this year, the corporation has $38,000 of accumulated E & P and no current E & P (before considering the effect of the distributions). What are the tax consequences to Kathryn (amount of dividend income and basis in property received) and Copper Corporation (gain or loss and effect on E & P) in each of the following situations?
    a. Copper distributes land to Kathryn. The land was held as an investment and has a fair market value of $28,000 and an adjusted basis of $21,000.
    b. Assume that Copper Corporation has no current or accumulated E & P prior to the distribution. How would your answer to (a) change?
    c. Assume that the land distributed in (a) is subject to a $23,000 mortgage (which Kathryn assumes). How would your answer change?
    d. Assume that the land has a fair market value of $28,000 and an adjusted basis of $31,000 on the date of the distribution. How would your answer to (a) change?
    e. Instead of distributing land, assume that Copper decides to distribute furniture used in its business. The furniture has a $7,000 fair market value, a $600 adjusted basis for income tax purposes, and a $2,600 adjusted basis for E & P purposes. When the furniture was purchased four years ago, its original fair market value was $9,000.

39. Apricot Corporation distributes property ($125,000 basis and $150,000 fair market value) to its sole shareholder, Ella. The property is subject to a liability of $200,000, which Ella assumes. Apricot has E & P of $325,000 prior to the distribution.
    a. What gain, if any, does Apricot recognize on the distribution?
    b. What is the amount of Ella's dividend income on the distribution?

40. Red Corporation, with E & P of $800,000, distributes land worth $275,000, adjusted basis of $300,000, to Andrew, its sole shareholder. The land is subject to a liability of $110,000, which Andrew assumes. What are the tax consequences to Red and to Andrew?

41. At the beginning of the current year, Northern Fulmar Corporation (a calendar year taxpayer) has accumulated E & P of $46,000. During the year, Northern Fulmar incurs a $34,000 loss from operations that accrues ratably. On July 1, Northern Fulmar distributes $38,000 in cash to Adriana, its sole shareholder. How will Adriana be taxed on the distribution?

42. Crane Corporation distributes equipment (adjusted basis of $100,000; fair market value of $70,000) to its shareholder, Meng. What are the tax consequences to Crane Corporation and to Meng?

Issue ID

43. Cerulean Corporation has two equal shareholders, Eloise and Olivia. Eloise acquired her Cerulean stock three years ago by transferring property worth $700,000, basis of $300,000, for 70 shares of the stock. Olivia acquired 70 shares in Cerulean Corporation two years ago by transferring property worth $660,000, basis of $110,000. Cerulean Corporation's accumulated E & P as of January 1 of the current year is $350,000. On March 1 of the current year, the corporation distributed to Eloise property worth $120,000, basis to Cerulean of $50,000. It distributed cash of $220,000 to Olivia. On July 1 of the current year, Olivia sold her stock to Magnus for $820,000. On December 1 of the current year, Cerulean distributed cash of $90,000 each to Magnus and Eloise. What are the tax issues?

Decision Making

44. Purple Corporation has accumulated E & P of $65,000 at the beginning of the year. Its current-year taxable income is $320,000. On December 31, Purple distributed business property (worth $140,000, adjusted basis of $290,000) to Peter, its sole shareholder. Peter assumes an $80,000 liability on the property. Included in the determination of Purple's current taxable income is $16,000 of income recognized from an installment

sale in a previous year. In addition, the corporation incurred a Federal income tax liability of $112,000, paid life insurance premiums of $3,500, and received term life insurance proceeds of $55,000 on the death of an officer.

a.   What is Peter's taxable income?

b.   What is the E & P of Purple Corporation after the property distribution?

c.   What is Peter's tax basis in the property received?

d.   How would your answers to (a) and (b) change if Purple had sold the property at its fair market value, used $80,000 of the proceeds to pay off the liability, and then distributed the remaining cash and any tax savings to Peter?

45. Verdigris Corporation owns 25% of the stock of Rust Corporation. On December 20, Rust Corporation, with E & P of $150,000, distributes land with a fair market value of $60,000 and a basis of $90,000 to Verdigris. The land is subject to a liability of $50,000, which Verdigris assumes.

a.   How is Verdigris Corporation taxed on the distribution?

b.   What is Rust Corporation's E & P after the distribution?

46. Wren Corporation lends its principal shareholder, James, $200,000 on January 3 of the current year. The loan is interest-free. Assume the Federal rate is 10%. What are the tax consequences to Wren Corporation and to James with respect to the interest-free loan?

47. Blackbird Corporation is a closely held company with accumulated E & P of $200,000 and current E & P of $250,000. Dan and Patrick are brothers, and each owns a 50% share in Blackbird. On a day-to-day basis, Dan and Patrick share management responsibilities equally. What are the tax consequences of the following independent transactions involving Blackbird, Dan, and Patrick? How does each transaction affect Blackbird's E & P?

a.   Blackbird sells an office building (adjusted basis of $250,000, fair market value of $200,000) to Dan for $175,000.

b.   Blackbird lends Patrick $150,000 on July 1 of this year. The loan is evidenced by a note and is payable on demand. No interest is charged on the loan (the current applicable Federal interest rate is 8%).

c.   Blackbird owns an airplane that it rents to others for a specified rental rate. Dan and Patrick also use the airplane for personal use and pay no rent. During the year, Dan used the airplane for 80 hours while Patrick used it for 120 hours. The rental value of the airplane is $200 per hour, and its maintenance costs average $40 per hour.

d.   Dan leases equipment to Blackbird for $15,000 per year. The same equipment can be leased from another company for $11,000.

48. Katie purchased 5,000 shares of Grebe Corporation common stock six years ago for $80,000. In the current year, Katie receives a preferred stock dividend of 400 shares, while the other holders of common stock received a common stock dividend. The preferred stock Katie received has a fair market value of $40,000, and her common stock has a fair market value of $120,000. Assume that Grebe has ample E & P to cover any distributions made during the year. What is Katie's basis in the preferred and common stock after the dividend is received? When does her holding period commence for the preferred stock?

49. Julie Swanson bought 5,000 shares of Great Egret Corporation stock two years ago for $12,000. Last year, Julie received a nontaxable stock dividend of 1,000 shares in Great Egret Corporation. In the current tax year, Julie sold all of the stock received as a dividend for $9,000. Prepare a letter to Julie and a memo to the file describing the tax consequences of the stock sale. Julie's address is 3737 Canyon Drive, Minneapolis, MN 55434.

Communications

50. Denim Corporation declares a nontaxable dividend payable in rights to subscribe to common stock. One right and $60 entitle the holder to subscribe to one share of stock. One right is issued for every two shares of stock owned. At the date of distribution of the rights, the market value of the stock is $110 per share, and the market value of the rights is $55 per right. Lauren owns 300 shares of stock that she purchased two years ago for $9,000. Lauren receives 150 rights, of which she exercises 105 to purchase 105 additional shares. She sells the remaining 45 rights for $2,475. What are the tax consequences of this transaction to Lauren?

Decision Making

51. Ivana, the president and a shareholder of Robin Corporation, has earned a salary bonus of $15,000 for the current year. Because of the lower tax rates on qualifying dividends, Robin is considering substituting a dividend for the bonus. Assume the tax rates are 28% for Ivana and 34% for Robin Corporation.
    a. How much better off would Ivana be if she were paid a dividend rather than salary?
    b. How much better off would Robin Corporation be if it paid Ivana salary rather than a dividend?
    c. If Robin Corporation pays Ivana a salary bonus of $20,000 instead of a $15,000 dividend, how would your answers to (a) and (b) change?
    d. What should Robin do?

Communications

52. Diver Corporation has a deficit in accumulated E & P of $200,000 as of January 1. Starting this year, Diver Corporation expects to generate annual E & P of $100,000 for the next four years and would like to distribute this amount to its shareholders. How should Diver Corporation distribute the $400,000 over the four-year period to provide the least amount of dividend income to its shareholders (all individuals)? Prepare a letter to your client, Diver Corporation, and a memo for the file. Diver Corporation's address is 1010 Oak Street, Oldtown, MD 20742.

RESEARCH PROBLEMS

Communications

Note: Solutions to Research Problems can be prepared by using the **RIA Checkpoint®
Student Edition** online research product, which is available to accompany this text. It is also possible to prepare solutions to the Research Problems by using tax research materials found in a standard tax library.

Research Problem 1.   Patrick Zimbrick and his son, Dan, own all of the outstanding stock of Osprey Corporation. Both Dan and Patrick are officers in the corporation and, together with their uncle, John, comprise the entire board of directors. Osprey uses the cash method of accounting and has a calendar year-end. In late 2004, the board of directors adopted the following legally enforceable resolution (agreed to in writing by each of the officers):

> Salary payments made to an officer of the corporation that shall be disallowed in whole or in part as a deductible expense for Federal income tax purposes shall be reimbursed by such officer to the corporation to the full extent of the disallowance. It shall be the duty of the board of directors to enforce payment of each such amount.

In 2005, Osprey paid Patrick $560,000 in compensation. Dan received $400,000. On an audit in late 2008, the IRS found the compensation of both officers to be excessive. It disallowed deductions for $200,000 of the payment to Patrick and $150,000 of the payment to Dan. The IRS recharacterized the disallowed payments as constructive dividends. Complying with the resolution by the board of directors, both Patrick and Dan repaid the disallowed compensation to Osprey Corporation in early 2009. Dan and Patrick have asked you to determine how their repayments should be treated for tax purposes. Dan is still working as a highly compensated executive for Osprey while Patrick is retired and living off his savings. Prepare a memo to your firm's client files describing the results of your research.

Partial list of research aids:
§ 1341.
Vincent E. Oswald, 49 T.C. 645 (1968).

Research Problem 2.   Your client, Purple Corporation, has done well since its formation 20 years ago. This year, it recognized a $50 million capital gain from the sale of a subsidiary. Purple's CEO has contacted you to discuss a proposed transaction to reduce the tax on the capital gain. Under the proposal, Purple will purchase all of the common stock in Yellow Corporation for $200 million. Yellow is a profitable corporation that has $63 million in cash and marketable securities, $137 million in operating assets, and approximately $280 million in E & P. After its acquisition, Yellow will distribute $50 million in cash and marketable securities to Purple. Due to the 100% dividends received deduction, no taxable income results to Purple from the dividend. Purple will then resell Yellow for $150 million. The subsequent sale of Yellow generates a $50 million capital loss [$200 million (stock basis) − $150 million (sale price)]. The loss from the stock sale can then be used to offset the preexisting $50 million capital gain. Will the proposed plan work?

Partial list of research aids:
§ 1059.

Research Problem 3. Canary Corporation wholly owns Parrot Corporation, formed six years ago with the transfer of several assets and a substantial amount of cash. Canary's basis in the Parrot stock is $10.5 million. Since it was formed, Parrot has been a very successful manufacturing company and currently has accumulated E & P of $8 million. The company's principal assets are property, plant, and equipment (worth $10 million) and cash and marketable securities of $8.5 million, for a total fair market value of $18.5 million.

Communications

Canary and Parrot are members of an affiliated group and have made the election under § 243(b) to entitle Canary to a 100% dividends received deduction. From a strategic perspective, Canary is no longer interested in manufacturing and is considering a sale of Parrot. In anticipation of a sale in the next year or two, the management of Canary has contacted you for advice. If Parrot is sold outright, Canary Corporation will have a capital gain of $8 million ($18.5 million fair market value less a basis of $10.5 million). As an alternative, taxes on a future sale would be minimized if Parrot first pays Canary an $8 million dividend equal to its E & P. With the 100% dividends received deduction, the payment would be tax-free to Canary. Subsequent to the dividend payment, Parrot can be sold for its remaining value of $10.5 million ($10 million in property, plant, and equipment plus $500,000 in cash), resulting in no gain or loss to Canary.

a.   Prepare a letter to the president of Canary Corporation describing the results of the proposed plan. The president is Thelma Raisbeck, 1914 Broom Street, Wauwatosa, WI 53786.

b.   Prepare a memo for your firm's client files.

Partial list of research aids:
Waterman Steamship Corp. v. Comm., 70–2 USTC ¶9514, 26 AFTR2d 70–5185, 430 F.2d 1185 (CA–5, 1970).

Research Problem 4. Ruby Corporation is required to change its method of accounting for Federal income tax purposes. The change will require an adjustment to income, which will be made over three tax periods. Camille, the sole shareholder of Ruby Corporation, wants to better understand the implications of this adjustment for E & P, as she anticipates a distribution from Ruby in the current year. Prepare a memo for your firm's client files describing the results of your research.

Communications

Partial list of research aids:
§ 481(a).
Rev.Proc. 97–27, 1997–1 C.B. 680.

Use the tax resources of the Internet to address the following questions. Do not restrict your search to the World Wide Web, but include a review of newsgroups and general reference materials, practitioner sites and resources, primary sources of the tax law, chat rooms and discussion groups, and other opportunities.

Internet
Activity

Research Problem 5. Just how common are dividend distributions? Are dividends concentrated in the companies traded on the New York Stock Exchange, or do closely held corporations pay dividends with the same frequency and at the same rates? Have dividends increased since the reduction in tax rates in 2003? Financial institutions and observers are acutely interested in these issues. Search for comments on such questions at various commercial Web sites as well as one or two academic journals or newsgroups.

Research Problem 6. Some hoped that the reduced tax rate on dividends would be made permanent during President Bush's second term in office. Use the Web to search for evidence about the effects of the dividend tax cut to date. Have dividend-paying stocks experienced any increased demand relative to growth stocks? Have any other economic effects (or lack thereof) been observed by the media or by academics? On the basis of your research, would you label the dividend tax cut a success?

Research Problem 7. Over the last few years, there have been several proposals to reform the Federal income tax. Use the Web to ascertain how these proposals have addressed the tax treatment of corporate distributions.

Corporations: Redemptions and Liquidations

LEARNING OBJECTIVES

After completing Chapter 6, you should be able to:

LO.1

Identify the stock redemptions that qualify for sale or exchange treatment.

LO.2

Understand the tax impact of stock redemptions on the distributing corporation.

LO.3

Recognize the restrictions on sale or exchange treatment for certain redemption-like transactions.

LO.4

Understand the tax consequences of complete liquidations for both the corporation and its shareholders.

LO.5

Understand the tax consequences of subsidiary liquidations for both the parent and the subsidiary corporations.

LO.6

Identify planning opportunities available to minimize the tax impact in stock redemptions and complete liquidations.

OUTLINE

Sandra is the sole shareholder of Mockingbird Corporation, having acquired 1,000 shares in the corporation 10 years ago at a cost of $400,000. Mockingbird has been profitable for most of those years and has earnings and profits (E & P) of $800,000. Currently, the Mockingbird shares are worth $1 million.

Sandra needs to raise $500,000 for an investment opportunity. To obtain the necessary funds, she has considered several possible alternatives involving her ownership interest in Mockingbird:

- Mockingbird could declare a dividend, but Sandra wants to avoid having the entire distribution taxed as a dividend, if possible (see Chapter 5).
- Sandra could sell one-half of her stock to an unrelated third party, but she does not want to give up control of the corporation.
- Sandra could sell one-half of her stock directly to Mockingbird in a stock redemption.

Sandra prefers the stock redemption as she believes it would provide her with the following favorable tax consequences while allowing her to retain sole control of Mockingbird:

- Return of capital treatment to the extent of her basis in the stock sold ($200,000).
- Long-term capital gain treatment on the excess of the amount realized over the basis ($300,000).

These favorable tax outcomes typically apply to sales or exchanges of stock held for the required long-term holding period. For example, Sandra would be taxed in this manner on a sale of the stock to an unrelated third party. In the sale to Mockingbird, however, a key characteristic inherent in typical stock sales—a reduction in ownership interest—is missing. Because Sandra would still own 100 percent of Mockingbird after the proposed stock redemption, the Code treats the transaction as a $500,000 dividend distribution (i.e., a return *from* her investment), not as a sale or exchange. However, current tax law does allow *certain* kinds of stock redemptions to qualify for sale or exchange treatment (i.e., a return *of* the owner's investment). In these transactions, as a general rule, the shareholder's ownership interest must be diminished as a result of the redemption. Additionally, a disposition of stock in a complete liquidation of a corporation will generally produce sale or exchange treatment. This chapter examines the tax implications of corporate distributions that are not dividend distributions.

Stock Redemptions—In General

Under § 317(b), a **stock redemption** occurs when a corporation acquires its stock from a shareholder in exchange for cash or other property. Essentially, in a stock redemption, the shareholder is selling the stock back to the issuing corporation, and it resembles a sale of stock to an unrelated third party. However, while a sale of stock to an outsider invariably results in sale or exchange treatment, only a *qualifying* stock redemption is treated as a sale for tax purposes.

Nonqualified stock redemptions are denied sale or exchange treatment because they are deemed to have the same effect as dividend distributions. For example, if a shareholder owns all the stock of a corporation and sells a portion of that stock to the corporation, the shareholder's ownership interest in the corporation does not change. After the redemption, the shareholder still owns all the outstanding stock of the corporation. In this situation, the stock redemption resembles a dividend distribution and is taxed as such.

Stock redemptions occur for a variety of reasons. Publicly traded corporations often reacquire their shares with the goal of increasing shareholder value. For corporations where the stock is closely held, redemptions frequently occur to accomplish particular shareholder goals. For instance, a redemption might be used to acquire the stock of a deceased shareholder of a closely held corporation. Having the corporation provide the funds to purchase the stock from the decedent's estate relieves the remaining shareholders of the need to use their own money to acquire the stock. Stock redemptions also occur as a result of property settlements in divorce actions. For example, when spouses jointly own 100 percent of a corporation's shares, a divorce decree may require the stock interest of one spouse to be bought out. Using a redemption to buy out that spouse's shares relieves the other spouse from having to use his or her own funds for the transaction.

> **LO.1**
>
> Identify the stock redemptions that qualify for sale or exchange treatment.

Stock Redemptions—Sale or Exchange Treatment

Noncorporate shareholders generally prefer to have a stock redemption treated as a sale or exchange rather than as a dividend distribution. For such taxpayers, the maximum tax rate for long-term capital gains is currently 15 percent (0 percent for taxpayers in the 10 or 15 percent marginal tax bracket). The preference for qualifying stock redemption treatment is based on the fact that such transactions result in (1) the tax-free recovery of the redeemed stock's basis and (2) capital gains that can be offset by capital losses. In a nonqualified stock redemption, the *entire* distribution is taxed as dividend income (assuming adequate E & P), which, although taxed at the same rate as long-term capital gains, cannot be offset by capital losses.

EXAMPLE 1

Abby, an individual in the 35% tax bracket, acquired stock in Quail Corporation four years ago for $300,000. In the current year, Quail Corporation (E & P of $1 million) redeems her shares for $450,000. If the redemption qualifies for sale or exchange treatment, Abby will have a long-term capital gain of $150,000 [$450,000 (redemption amount) − $300,000

TAX *in the News*

CAPITAL RESTRUCTURING BY CHARLES SCHWAB RESULTS IN REDEMPTION OF 102 MILLION SHARES

Flush with cash stemming from the sale of a subsidiary for $3.3 billion, discount stock brokerage firm Charles Schwab Corporation embarked on a restructuring plan that included a special $1.2 billion dividend distribution to shareholders and a redemption of 102 million shares of its stock. The stock buyback included 84 million shares acquired pursuant to a public tender offer and a separate purchase of 18 million shares from the corporation's founder and CEO, Mr. Charles Schwab. Most of the shareholders who tendered their stock will likely qualify for sale or exchange treatment. However,

the number of shares redeemed from Mr. Schwab was dependent on the number of shares purchased in the tender offer and was designed to keep his ownership interest (approximately 18 percent) intact. Since his proportionate ownership interest in the corporation remained unchanged after the redemption, the distribution to Mr. Schwab ($369 million) most likely will be taxed as a dividend. Still, the plan allows Mr. Schwab to reap the benefits of the 15 percent preferential tax rate on dividends, a preference that is set to expire at the end of 2010.

(basis)]. Her tax liability on the $150,000 gain will be $22,500 ($150,000 × 15%). If the stock redemption does not qualify as a sale or exchange, the entire distribution will be treated as a dividend, and her tax liability will be $67,500 ($450,000 × 15%). Thus, Abby will save $45,000 ($67,500 − $22,500) in income taxes if the transaction is a qualifying stock redemption. ■

EXAMPLE 2

Assume in Example 1 that Abby has a capital loss carryover of $100,000 in the current tax year. If the transaction is a qualifying stock redemption, Abby can offset the entire $100,000 capital loss carryover against her $150,000 long-term capital gain. As a result, only $50,000 of the gain will be taxed, and her tax liability will be only $7,500 ($50,000 × 15%). On the other hand, if the transaction does not qualify for sale or exchange treatment, the entire $450,000 will be taxed as a dividend at 15%. In addition, assuming she has no capital gains in the current year, Abby will be able to deduct only $3,000 of the $100,000 capital loss carryover to offset her ordinary income. ■

In contrast, however, *corporate* shareholders normally receive more favorable tax treatment from a dividend distribution than would result from a qualifying stock redemption. Corporate shareholders typically report only a small portion of a dividend distribution as taxable income because of the dividends received deduction (see Chapter 2). Further, the preferential tax rate applicable to dividend and long-term capital gain income is not available to corporations. Consequently, tax planning for stock redemptions must consider the different preferences of corporate and noncorporate shareholders.

EXAMPLE 3

Assume in Example 1 that Abby is a corporation, that the stock represents a 40% ownership interest in Quail Corporation, and that Abby has corporate taxable income of $850,000 before the redemption transaction. If the transaction is a qualifying stock redemption, Abby will have a long-term capital gain of $150,000 that will be subject to tax at 34%, or $51,000. On the other hand, if the $450,000 distribution is treated as a dividend, Abby will have a dividends received deduction of $360,000 ($450,000 × 80%), so only $90,000 of the payment will be taxed. Consequently, Abby's tax liability on the transaction will be only $30,600 ($90,000 × 34%). ■

When a qualifying stock redemption results in a *loss* to the shareholder rather than a gain, § 267 disallows loss recognition if the shareholder owns (directly or indirectly) more than 50 percent of the corporation's stock. A shareholder's basis in property received in a stock redemption, qualifying or nonqualified, generally will be the property's fair market value, determined as of the date of the redemption. Further, the holding period of the property begins on that date.

FOREIGN SHAREHOLDERS PREFER SALE OR EXCHANGE TREATMENT IN STOCK REDEMPTIONS

As a general rule, foreign shareholders are subject to U.S. tax on dividend income from U.S. corporations but not on capital gains from the sale of U.S. stock. In some situations, a nonresident alien is taxed on a capital gain from the disposition of stock in a U.S. corporation, but only if the stock was effectively connected with the conduct of a U.S. trade or business of the individual. Foreign corporations are similarly taxed on gains from the sale of U.S. stock investments. Whether a stock redemption qualifies for sale or exchange treatment therefore takes on added significance for foreign shareholders. If one of the qualifying stock redemption rules can be satisfied, the foreign shareholder typically will avoid U.S. tax on the transaction. If, instead, dividend income is the result, a 30 percent withholding tax typically applies. For further details, see Chapter 9.

GLOBAL *Tax Issues*

The Code establishes the criteria for determining whether a transaction is a qualifying stock redemption for tax purposes. The terminology in an agreement between the parties is not controlling, nor is state law. Section 302(b) provides four types of qualifying stock redemptions. Additionally, certain distributions of property to an estate in exchange for a deceased shareholder's stock are treated as qualifying stock redemptions under § 303.

Historical Background and Overview

Under prior law, the *dividend equivalency rule* was used to determine which stock redemptions qualified for sale or exchange treatment. Under that rule, if the facts and circumstances of a redemption indicated that it was essentially equivalent to a dividend, the redemption did not qualify for sale or exchange treatment. Instead, the entire amount received by the shareholder was taxed as dividend income to the extent of the corporation's E & P.

The uncertainty and subjectivity surrounding the dividend equivalency rule led Congress to enact several objective tests for determining the status of a redemption. Currently, the following five types of stock redemptions qualify for sale or exchange treatment:

- Distributions not essentially equivalent to a dividend ("not essentially equivalent redemptions").
- Distributions substantially disproportionate in terms of shareholder effect ("disproportionate redemptions").
- Distributions in complete termination of a shareholder's interest ("complete termination redemptions").
- Distributions to noncorporate shareholders in partial liquidation of a corporation ("partial liquidations").
- Distributions to pay a shareholder's death taxes ("redemptions to pay death taxes").

Concept Summary 6–1 at the end of this section summarizes the requirements for each of the qualifying stock redemptions.

Stock Attribution Rules

To qualify for sale or exchange treatment, a stock redemption generally must result in a substantial reduction in a shareholder's ownership interest in the corporation. In the absence of this reduction in ownership interest, the redemption proceeds are taxed as dividend income. In determining whether a stock redemption has

EXHIBIT 6–1	Stock Attribution Rules

	Deemed or Constructive Ownership
• Family	An individual is deemed to own the stock owned by his or her spouse, children, grandchildren, and parents (not siblings or grandparents).
• Partnership	A partner is deemed to own the stock owned by a partnership to the extent of the partner's proportionate interest in the partnership.
	Stock owned by a partner is deemed to be owned in full by a partnership.
• Estate or trust	A beneficiary or heir is deemed to own the stock owned by an estate or trust to the extent of the beneficiary or heir's proportionate interest in the estate or trust.
	Stock owned by a beneficiary or heir is deemed to be owned in full by an estate or trust.
• Corporation	Stock owned by a corporation is deemed to be owned proportionately by any shareholder owning 50% or more of the corporation's stock.
	Stock owned by a shareholder who owns 50% or more of a corporation is deemed to be owned in full by the corporation.

sufficiently reduced a shareholder's interest, the stock owned by certain related parties is attributed to the redeeming shareholder.[1] Thus, the stock **attribution** rules must be considered along with the stock redemption provisions. Under these rules, related parties are defined to include the following family members: spouses, children, grandchildren, and parents. Attribution also takes place *from* and *to* partnerships, estates, trusts, and corporations (50 percent or more ownership required in the case of regular corporations). Exhibit 6–1 summarizes the stock attribution rules.

EXAMPLE 4

Larry owns 30% of the stock in Blue Corporation, with the other 70% being held by his children. For purposes of the stock attribution rules, Larry is treated as owning 100% of the stock in Blue Corporation. He owns 30% directly and, because of the family attribution rules, 70% indirectly. ■

EXAMPLE 5

Chris owns 40% of the stock in Gray Corporation. The other 60% is owned by a partnership in which Chris has a 20% interest. Chris is deemed to own 52% of Gray Corporation: 40% directly and, because of the partnership interest, 12% indirectly (20% × 60%). ■

As discussed later, the *family* attribution rules (refer to Example 4) can be waived in the case of some complete termination redemptions. In addition, the stock attribution rules do not apply to partial liquidations or redemptions to pay death taxes.

[1]§ 318.

TAX *in the News*   KETCHUP GIANT SUFFERS DEFEAT IN BASIS SHIFTING CASE

When a redemption fails the qualifying stock redemption provisions by reason of the attribution rules, the basis of the redeemed shares attaches to the basis of the shares actually or constructively owned. The H. J. Heinz Company effected a multistep transaction in an attempt to take advantage of this basis shifting rule. First, Heinz had a subsidiary purchase 3.5 million shares of Heinz common stock in the open market for $131 million. Next, Heinz redeemed 3.375 million of the common shares from the subsidiary in exchange for a subordinated convertible note that had a 0 percent coupon rate and matured in seven years at $197 million. At the option of the holder (the subsidiary), the note was convertible into 3.51 million shares of Heinz common stock at any time three years beyond the redemption date and until maturity. Finally, the subsidiary sold its remaining 175,000 shares of Heinz stock to an unrelated third party for $7 million.

Under the § 318 attribution rules, the holder of an option to acquire stock is deemed to own such stock. By applying this attribution rule to the convertible note, the subsidiary's ownership interest in Heinz actually increased as a result of the redemption. Heinz's intent was that this attri-

bution rule would cause the redemption to fail the qualifying redemption provisions and the distribution would therefore be taxed as a dividend to the subsidiary. The 100 percent dividends received deduction available to members of an affiliated group would eliminate any tax on the dividend, and the basis of the redeemed shares would attach to the basis of the 175,000 shares the subsidiary owned after the redemption. Applying the basis shifting rule, the subsidiary claimed a $124 million capital loss on the sale of the 175,000 shares. Its claims for a refund resulting from the carryback of that loss came before the U.S. Court of Federal Claims [*H. J. Heinz Co.*, 2007–1 USTC ¶50,517, 99 AFTR2d 2940, 76 Fed.Cl. 570 (2007)]. In a sternly worded opinion, the court rejected Heinz's position, ruling instead that the redemption transaction was a tax avoidance sham that lacked any genuine business purpose. Applying the step transaction doctrine, the court found that Heinz had acquired the 3.375 million shares in the open market (via the subsidiary's purchase) and not in a redemption. Without a redemption, there was no basis shifting issue and no capital loss realized on the subsidiary's sale of the 175,000 shares.

Not Essentially Equivalent Redemptions

Under § 302(b)(1), a redemption qualifies for sale or exchange treatment if it is "not essentially equivalent to a dividend." This provision represents a continuation of the dividend equivalency rule applicable under prior law. The earlier redemption language was retained principally for redemptions of preferred stock because shareholders often have no control over when corporations call in such stock.[2] Like its predecessor, the **not essentially equivalent redemption** lacks an objective test. Instead, each case must be resolved on a facts and circumstances basis.[3]

Based upon the Supreme Court's decision in *U.S. v. Davis*,[4] a redemption will qualify as a not essentially equivalent redemption only when the shareholder's interest in the redeeming corporation has been meaningfully reduced. In determining whether the **meaningful reduction test** has been met, the stock attribution rules apply. A decrease in the redeeming shareholder's voting control appears to be the most significant indicator of a meaningful reduction,[5] but reductions in the rights of redeeming shareholders to share in corporate earnings or to receive corporate assets upon liquidation are also considered.[6] The meaningful reduction test is applied whether common stock or preferred stock is being redeemed.

EXAMPLE 6

Pat owns 58% of the common stock of Falcon Corporation. After a redemption of part of Pat's stock, he owns 51% of the Falcon stock. Pat continues to have dominant voting rights in Falcon; thus, the redemption is treated as essentially equivalent to a dividend. As a result, the entire amount of the distribution is taxed as dividend income (assuming adequate E & P). ■

---

[2]See S.Rept. No. 1622, 83d Cong., 2d Sess. 44 (1954).
[3]Reg. § 1.302–2(b)(1).
[4]70–1 USTC ¶9289, 25 AFTR2d 70–827, 90 S.Ct. 1041 (USSC, 1970).

[5]See, for example, *Jack Paparo*, 71 T.C. 692 (1979).
[6]See, for example, *Grabowski Trust*, 58 T.C. 650 (1972).

EXAMPLE 7

Maroon Corporation redeems 2% of its stock from Maria. Before the redemption, Maria owned 10% of Maroon Corporation. In this case, the redemption may qualify as a not essentially equivalent redemption. Maria experiences a reduction in her voting rights, her right to participate in current earnings and accumulated surplus, and her right to share in net assets upon liquidation. ■

When a redemption fails to satisfy any of the qualifying stock redemption rules, the basis of the redeemed shares does not disappear. Typically, the basis will attach to the basis of the redeeming shareholder's remaining shares. If, however, the redeeming shareholder has terminated his or her direct stock ownership and the redemption is nonqualified due to the attribution rules, the basis will attach to the basis of the constructively owned stock.[7] In this manner, a nonqualified stock redemption can result in stock basis being shifted from one taxpayer (the redeeming shareholder) to another taxpayer (the shareholder related under the attribution rules).

EXAMPLE 8

$$\frac{3000}{5000} \times 60\% = 36\%$$

Floyd and Fran, husband and wife, each own 50 shares in Grouse Corporation, representing 100% of the corporation's stock. All the stock was purchased for $50,000. Both Floyd and Fran serve as directors of the corporation. The corporation redeems Floyd's 50 shares, but he continues to serve as a director of the corporation. The redemption is treated as a dividend distribution (assuming adequate E & P) because Floyd constructively owns Fran's stock. Floyd's $25,000 basis in the 50 shares redeemed attaches to Fran's stock; thus, Fran now has a basis of $50,000 in the 50 shares she owns in Grouse. ■

Disproportionate Redemptions

A stock redemption qualifies for sale or exchange treatment under § 302(b)(2) as a **disproportionate redemption** if the following conditions are met:

- After the distribution, the shareholder owns *less than* 80 percent of the interest owned in the corporation before the redemption. For example, if a shareholder owns a 60 percent interest in a corporation that redeems part of the stock, the shareholder's ownership interest after the redemption must be less than 48 percent (80 percent of 60 percent).
- After the distribution, the shareholder owns *less than* 50 percent of the total combined voting power of all classes of stock entitled to vote.

In determining a shareholder's ownership interest before and after a redemption, the attribution rules apply.

EXAMPLE 9

Bob, Carl, and Dan, unrelated individuals, own 30 shares, 30 shares, and 40 shares, respectively, in Wren Corporation. Wren has 100 shares outstanding and E & P of $200,000. The corporation redeems 20 shares of Dan's stock for $30,000. Dan paid $200 a share for the stock two years ago. Dan's ownership in Wren Corporation before and after the redemption is as follows:

	Total Shares	Dan's Ownership	Ownership Percentage	80% of Original Ownership
Before redemption	100	40	40% (40 ÷ 100)	32% (80% × 40%)
After redemption	80	20	25% (20 ÷ 80)*	

*Note that the denominator of the fraction is reduced after the redemption (from 100 to 80).

Dan's 25% ownership after the redemption meets both tests of § 302(b)(2). It is less than 80% of his original ownership and less than 50% of the total voting power. The distribution

---

[7]Reg. § 1.302–2(c).

therefore qualifies as a disproportionate redemption and receives sale or exchange treatment. As a result, Dan has a long-term capital gain of $26,000 [$30,000 − $4,000 (20 shares × $200)]. ∎

Assume that Carl and Dan are father and son. The redemption described above would not qualify for sale or exchange treatment because of the effect of the attribution rules. Dan is deemed to own Carl's stock before and after the redemption. Dan's ownership in Wren Corporation before and after the redemption is as follows:

EXAMPLE 10

	Total Shares	Dan's Direct Ownership	Carl's Ownership	Dan's Direct and Indirect Ownership	Ownership Percentage	80% of Original Ownership
Before redemption	100	40	30	70	70% (70 ÷ 100)	56% (80% × 70%)
After redemption	80	20	30	50	62.5% (50 ÷ 80)	

Dan's direct and indirect ownership of 62.5% fails to meet either of the tests of § 302(b)(2). After the redemption, Dan owns more than 80% of his original ownership and more than 50% of the voting stock. Thus, the redemption does not qualify for sale or exchange treatment and results in a dividend distribution of $30,000 to Dan. The basis in the 20 shares redeemed is added to Dan's basis in his remaining 20 shares. ∎

A redemption that does not qualify as a disproportionate redemption may still qualify as a not essentially equivalent redemption if it meets the meaningful reduction test (see Example 7).

ETHICAL and EQUITABLE *Considerations*

CONVERTIBLE PREFERRED STOCK—CONVERSION OR REDEMPTION?

Four years ago, a corporation that does not sell its stock publicly sold some convertible preferred stock to a small investment group. At the option of the shareholders, the preferred stock can be converted into common stock at any time. The preferred stock also has a call feature, allowing the corporation to call (redeem) the stock at any time during the first several years after its issuance. The corporation recently developed a successful invention that it has not yet publicly disclosed. The board of directors of the corporation expects the corporation to experience significant earnings growth in the future as a result of the invention. The directors, all of whom own common stock in the corporation, would like to call the preferred stock so that those shares cannot be converted into common stock and otherwise share in the corporation's future earnings growth. The call price set forth in the preferred stock indenture provides a premium to the shareholders upon redemption. The board of directors votes to redeem all of the outstanding preferred stock and notifies the preferred shareholders of its decision. Did the board of directors act ethically?

Complete Termination Redemptions

A stock redemption that terminates a shareholder's *entire* stock ownership in a corporation will qualify for sale or exchange treatment under § 302(b)(3). The attribution rules generally apply in determining whether the shareholder's stock ownership has been completely terminated. However, the *family* attribution rules do not apply to a **complete termination redemption** if the following conditions are met:

- The former shareholder has no interest, other than that of a creditor, in the corporation for at least 10 years after the redemption (including an interest as an officer, director, or employee).

- The former shareholder files an agreement to notify the IRS of any prohibited interest acquired within the 10-year postredemption period and to retain all necessary records pertaining to the redemption during this time period.

Acquisition of stock in the corporation by bequest or inheritance will not constitute a prohibited interest. The required agreement should be in the form of a separate statement signed by the former shareholder and attached to the return for the year in which the redemption occurs. The agreement should state that the former shareholder agrees to notify the IRS within 30 days of acquiring a prohibited interest in the corporation within the 10-year postredemption period.[8]

| EXAMPLE 11 | Kevin owns 50% of the stock in Green Corporation, while the remaining interest in Green is held as follows: 40% by Wilma (Kevin's wife) and 10% by Carmen (a key employee). Green redeems all of Kevin's stock for its fair market value. As a result, Wilma and Carmen are the only remaining shareholders, now owning 80% and 20%, respectively. If the requirements for the family attribution waiver are met, the transaction will qualify as a complete termination redemption and result in sale or exchange treatment. If the waiver requirements are not satisfied, Kevin will be deemed to own Wilma's (his wife's) stock, and the entire distribution will be taxed as a dividend (assuming adequate E & P). ■ |

| EXAMPLE 12 | Assume in Example 11 that Kevin qualifies for the family attribution waiver for the redemption. In the year of the redemption, Kevin treats the transaction as a sale or exchange. However, if he purchases Carmen's stock seven years after the redemption, he has acquired a prohibited interest, and the redemption distribution is reclassified as a dividend. Kevin will owe additional taxes due to this revised treatment. ■ |

Partial Liquidations

Under § 302(b)(4), a *noncorporate* shareholder is allowed sale or exchange treatment for a distribution that qualifies as a **partial liquidation**. A partial liquidation is a distribution that (1) is *not essentially equivalent to a dividend* and (2) is both pursuant to a plan and made within the plan year or within the succeeding taxable year. There is no requirement for stock to be redeemed in a partial liquidation. Further, if there is a stock redemption pursuant to a partial liquidation, the redemption may be pro rata with respect to the shareholders.

In determining whether a distribution is not essentially equivalent to a dividend, the effect of the distribution on the *corporation* is examined.[9] Consequently, to qualify as a partial liquidation, the distribution must result in a *genuine contraction* of the business of the corporation.

| EXAMPLE 13 | Dove Corporation owned a building with seven floors. Part of the building was rented, and part was used directly in Dove's business. A fire destroyed the two top floors, and Dove received insurance proceeds in reimbursement for the damage sustained. For business reasons, Dove did not rebuild the two floors and, instead, chose to operate on a smaller scale than before the fire. Pursuant to a plan adopted in the current year, Dove uses the insurance proceeds to redeem some stock from its shareholders. The distribution is not essentially equivalent to a dividend and qualifies as a partial liquidation.[10] ■ |

Applying the genuine contraction of a corporate business concept has proved difficult due to the lack of objective tests. The IRS has ruled that neither the sale of investments nor the sale of excess inventory will satisfy the genuine contraction test.[11]

---

[8]Reg. § 1.302–4(a).
[9]§ 302(e)(1)(A).

[10]See *Joseph W. Imler*, 11 T.C. 836 (1948), *acq.* 1949–1 C.B. 2; and Reg. § 1.346–1(a)(2).
[11]Rev.Rul. 60–322, 1960–2 C.B. 118.

To minimize uncertainty, the genuine contraction test should be relied upon only after obtaining a favorable ruling from the IRS.

Pink Corporation has been selling a single product for eight years. It loses its major customer, and a severe drop in sales results. The corporation reduces its inventory investment and has substantial cash on hand. It distributes the excess cash to its shareholders in a pro rata stock redemption. Lynn, one of Pink's shareholders, receives $10,000 for stock that cost her $5,000 two years ago. Since Lynn's ownership interest in Pink remains unchanged, the redemption does not qualify as a not essentially equivalent redemption, a disproportionate redemption, or a complete termination redemption. Further, the reduction in inventory does not qualify as a general contraction of Pink Corporation's business; thus, the distribution is not a partial liquidation. Therefore, the $10,000 is dividend income to Lynn (assuming adequate E & P). The $5,000 basis in the stock redeemed attaches to the basis of Lynn's remaining shares of Pink. ■

A safe-harbor rule, the *termination of a business* test, will satisfy the not essentially equivalent to a dividend requirement. In contrast to the genuine contraction test, the termination of a business test does follow objective requirements. A distribution will qualify under the termination of a business test if the following conditions are met:

- The corporation has two or more qualified trades or businesses. A qualified trade or business is any trade or business that (1) has been actively conducted for the five-year period ending on the date of the distribution and (2) was not acquired in a taxable transaction during that five-year period.
- The distribution consists of the assets of a qualified trade or business or the proceeds from the sale of such assets.
- The corporation is actively engaged in the conduct of a qualified trade or business immediately after the distribution.

Loon Corporation, the owner and operator of a wholesale grocery business with a substantial amount of excess cash, purchased a freight-hauling concern. Six years later, Loon distributes the freight-hauling assets in kind on a pro rata basis to all its noncorporate shareholders. The distribution satisfies the termination of a business test. Loon had conducted both businesses for at least five years and continues to conduct the wholesale grocery business. Thus, the distribution qualifies as a partial liquidation and is treated as a sale or exchange to the shareholders. ■

Redemptions to Pay Death Taxes

Section 303 provides sale or exchange treatment to a redemption of stock included in, and representing a substantial part of, a decedent's gross estate. The purpose of this provision is to provide an estate with liquidity to pay death-related expenses when a significant portion of the estate consists of stock in a closely held corporation. Often such stock is not easily marketable, and a stock redemption represents the only viable option for its disposition. The redemption might not satisfy any of the other qualifying stock redemption provisions because of the attribution rules (e.g., attribution to estate from beneficiaries). A **redemption to pay death taxes** provides sale or exchange treatment without regard to the attribution rules, but the provision limits this treatment to the sum of the death taxes and funeral and administration expenses. A redemption in excess of these expenses may qualify for sale or exchange treatment under one of the § 302 provisions.

An estate's basis in property acquired from a decedent is generally the property's fair market value on the date of death.[12] Typically, there is little change in the

---

[12]If available and elected, an alternate valuation date would apply. § 1014(a).

fair market value of stock from the date of a decedent's death to the date of a redemption to pay death taxes. As a result, if the redemption price in a redemption to pay death taxes is the same as the estate's basis in the stock, the estate will recognize no gain (or loss) on the transaction.

Section 303 applies only to a distribution made with respect to stock of a corporation that is included in the gross estate of a decedent and whose value *exceeds* 35 percent of the value of the adjusted gross estate. (For a definition of "gross estate" and "adjusted gross estate," see the Glossary of Tax Terms in Appendix C.)

EXAMPLE 16

Juan's adjusted gross estate is $2.1 million. The death taxes and funeral and administration expenses of the estate total $320,000. Included in the gross estate is stock of Yellow Corporation valued at $840,000. Juan had acquired the stock nine years ago at a cost of $100,000. Yellow redeems $320,000 of the stock from Juan's estate. Because the value of the Yellow stock in Juan's estate exceeds the 35% threshold ($840,000 ÷ $2.1 million = 40%), the redemption qualifies under § 303 as a sale or exchange to Juan's estate. Assuming the value of the stock has remained unchanged since the date of Juan's death, there is no recognized gain (or loss) on the redemption [$320,000 (amount realized) − $320,000 (estate's stock basis)]. ■

In determining whether the value of stock of one corporation exceeds 35 percent of the value of the adjusted gross estate, the stock of two or more corporations may be treated as the stock of a single corporation. Stock of corporations in which the decedent held a 20 percent or more interest is treated as stock of a single corporation for this purpose.[13] When this exception applies, the stock redeemed can be that of any of the 20 percent or more shareholder interests.

EXAMPLE 17

The adjusted gross estate of a decedent is $3.3 million. The gross estate includes stock of Owl and Robin Corporations valued at $600,000 and $680,000, respectively. Unless the two corporations are treated as a single corporation, § 303 does not apply to a redemption of the stock of either corporation. Assuming the decedent owned all the stock of Owl Corporation and 80% of the stock of Robin, § 303 applies because the decedent's estate includes a 20% or more interest in the stock of each corporation. The 35% test is met when the stock of Owl and Robin is treated as that of a single corporation [($600,000 + $680,000) ÷ $3.3 million = 38.8%]. The stock of Owl or Robin (or both) can be redeemed under § 303. ■

LO.2

Understand the tax impact of stock redemptions on the distributing corporation.

Effect on the Corporation Redeeming Its Stock

Thus far, the discussion has focused on the tax consequences of stock redemptions to the *shareholder*. There are also several tax issues surrounding the redeeming *corporation* that must be addressed, including the recognition of gain or loss on property distributed pursuant to a redemption, the effect on a corporation's E & P from a distribution that is a qualifying stock redemption, and the deductibility of expenditures incurred in connection with a redemption. These issues are discussed in the following paragraphs.

Recognition of Gain or Loss

Section 311 provides that corporations recognize *gain* on all nonliquidating distributions of appreciated property as if the property had been sold for its fair market value. Distributions in redemption of stock, qualifying or not, are nonliquidating distributions. When distributed property is subject to a corporate liability, the fair

---

[13]§ 303(b)(2)(B).

TAX *in the News*	**DISTRICT COURT RULES § 162(k) DISALLOWS DEDUCTION FOR ESOP REDEMPTIONS**

Section 404(k) allows a corporation a deduction for certain cash dividends made with respect to its stock held by an employee stock ownership plan (ESOP). If a corporation distributes cash in redemption of its stock from an ESOP and the redemption fails to satisfy the qualifying redemption provisions, the distribution qualifies as a dividend for purposes of the § 404(k) deduction. However, expenditures incurred in connection with a stock redemption are nondeductible under § 162(k). Whether the § 162(k) disallowance trumps the § 404(k) deduction is in dispute. In 2003, the Ninth Circuit Court of Appeals ruled that payments made in redemption of ESOP-held stock were deductible under § 404(k) notwithstanding § 162(k) [*Boise Cascade Corp. v. U.S.*, 2003–1 USTC ¶50,472, 91 AFTR2d 2003–2280, 329 F.3d 751 (CA–9, 2003)]. In 2006, the IRS issued Final Regulations under §§ 162(k) and 404(k) providing that payments made in redemption of stock held by an ESOP are not deductible. Recently, the U.S. District Court for the District of New Jersey rejected the Ninth Circuit's "flawed" reasoning in *Boise Cascade* and held, instead, that the § 162(k) disallowance overrode an otherwise allowable deduction under § 404(k) [*Conopco, Inc.*, 2007–2 USTC ¶50,582, 100 AFTR2d 2007–5296 (2007)]. The tax years in dispute in this case preceded the effective date of the Final Regulations issued in 2006. Those Final Regulations and the IRS's position on the ESOP redemption issue will almost certainly be tested in future court disputes.

market value of that property is treated as not being less than the amount of the liability.

Losses are not recognized on nonliquidating distributions of property. Therefore, a corporation should avoid distributing loss property (fair market value less than basis) as consideration in the redemption of a shareholder's stock. However, the corporation could sell the property in a taxable transaction in which it can recognize a loss and then distribute the proceeds.

EXAMPLE 18

To carry out a stock redemption, Blackbird Corporation transfers land (basis of $80,000, fair market value of $300,000) to a shareholder. Blackbird has a recognized gain of $220,000 ($300,000 − $80,000). If the land is subject to a liability of $330,000, Blackbird has a recognized gain of $250,000 ($330,000 − $80,000). If the value of the property distributed was less than its adjusted basis, the realized loss would not be recognized. ■

Effect on Earnings and Profits

In a qualifying stock redemption, the E & P of the distributing corporation is reduced by an amount not in excess of the ratable share of the corporation's E & P attributable to the stock redeemed.[14]

EXAMPLE 19

Navy Corporation has 100 shares of stock outstanding. In a qualifying stock redemption, Navy distributes $100,000 in exchange for 30 of its shares. At the time of the redemption, Navy has paid-in capital of $120,000 and E & P of $150,000. The charge to E & P is limited to 30% of the corporation's E & P ($45,000), and the remainder of the redemption price ($55,000) is a reduction of the Navy paid-in capital account. If, instead, the 30 shares were redeemed for $40,000, the charge to E & P would be limited to $40,000, the amount paid by the corporation to carry out the stock redemption. ■

Redemption Expenditures

In redeeming its shares, a corporation may incur certain expenses such as accounting, brokerage, legal, and loan fees. Section 162(k) specifically denies a deduction for expenditures incurred in connection with a stock redemption.

---

[14]§ 312(n)(7).

CONCEPT SUMMARY   6–1

Summary of the Qualifying Stock Redemption Rules

Type of Redemption	Requirements to Qualify
Not essentially equivalent to a dividend [§ 302(b)(1)]	Meaningful reduction in shareholder's voting interest. Reduction in shareholder's right to share in earnings or in assets upon liquidation also considered.
	• Stock attribution rules apply.
Substantially disproportionate [§ 302(b)(2)]	Shareholder's interest in the corporation, after the redemption, must be less than 80% of interest before the redemption and less than 50% of total combined voting power of all classes of stock entitled to vote.
	• Stock attribution rules apply.
Complete termination [§ 302(b)(3)]	Entire stock ownership terminated.
	In general, stock attribution rules apply. However, *family* attribution rules may be waived. Former shareholder must have no interest, other than as a creditor, in the corporation for at least 10 years and must file an agreement to notify IRS of any prohibited interest acquired during 10-year period. Shareholder must retain all necessary records during 10-year period.
Partial liquidation [§ 302(b)(4)]	Not essentially equivalent to a dividend.
	• Genuine contraction of corporation's business.
	• Termination of a business.
	• Corporation has two or more qualified trades or businesses.
	• Corporation terminates one qualified trade or business while continuing another qualified trade or business.
	Distribution may be in form of cash or property.
	Redemption may be pro rata.
	• Stock attribution rules do not apply.
Redemption to pay death taxes [§ 303]	Value of stock of one corporation in gross estate exceeds 35% of value of adjusted gross estate.
	• Stock of two or more corporations treated as stock of a single corporation in applying the 35% test if decedent held a 20% or more interest in the stock of the corporations.
	Redemption limited to sum of death taxes and funeral and administration expenses.
	Generally tax-free because tax basis of stock is FMV on date of decedent's death and value is unchanged at redemption.
	• Stock attribution rules do not apply.

LO.3

Recognize the restrictions on sale or exchange treatment for certain redemption-like transactions.

Stock Redemptions—Additional Limitations

Stock redemptions that do not fall under any of the qualifying stock redemption provisions are treated as dividend distributions to the extent of the corporation's E & P. Resourceful taxpayers, however, devised ways to circumvent the redemption provisions. Two types of these transactions involved structuring what was, in effect, a stock redemption or a dividend distribution as a sale of the stock. The widespread use of these approaches to obtain sale or exchange treatment led to the enactment of § 306, dealing with preferred stock bailouts, and § 304, dealing with sales of stock to related corporations. These two loophole-closing provisions are explained next. Some corporate divisions resemble stock redemptions, and those distributions are also briefly discussed.

Preferred Stock Bailouts

When a corporation's stock is owned entirely (or predominantly) by a few family members and/or related entities, the attribution rules severely limit the opportunities for effecting a qualifying stock redemption. Nonetheless, clever taxpayers devised a scheme called the **preferred stock bailout** in an attempt to obtain the benefits of a qualifying stock redemption without the attendant limitations.[15] Under this scheme, a corporation issued a nontaxable (nonvoting) preferred stock dividend on common stock,[16] the shareholder assigned a portion of his or her basis in the common stock to the preferred stock,[17] and the preferred stock was sold to a third party. Since the disposition did not take the form of a stock redemption, the related limitations on sale or exchange treatment did not apply. As a result, the sale of the preferred stock was treated like any other capital asset disposition where the sales proceeds were offset by the stock's basis and the gain was taxed using the favorable capital gains rate. Unlike a sale of common shares, however, the sale of the preferred stock did not reduce the shareholder's percentage ownership in the corporation.

The tax avoidance possibilities of the preferred stock bailout led to the enactment of § 306. In the case of a sale of *§ 306 stock* to a third party, the shareholder generally has ordinary income on the sale equal to the fair market value of the preferred stock on the date of the stock dividend.[18] The ordinary income is *treated* as a dividend for purposes of the 15 percent (or 0 percent) maximum tax on dividend income[19] but has no effect on the issuing corporation's E & P. No loss is recognized on the sale of the preferred stock;[20] instead, the unrecovered basis in the preferred stock sold is added to the basis of the shareholder's common stock.[21] If, instead of a sale to a third party, the issuing corporation redeems the preferred stock from the shareholder, the redemption proceeds constitute dividend income to the extent of the corporation's E & P (see Chapter 5).[22]

As of January 1 of the current year, Tern Corporation has E & P of $150,000. Naomi owns all of Tern's common stock (100 shares) with a basis of $60,000. On that date, Tern declares and issues a nontaxable preferred stock dividend of 100 shares. After the stock dividend, the fair market value of one share of common is $2,000, and the fair market value of one share of preferred is $1,000. Two days later, Naomi sells the 100 shares of preferred stock to Emily for $100,000. Section 306 produces the following results:

EXAMPLE 20

- After the distribution and before the sale, the preferred stock has a basis to Naomi of $20,000 [($100,000 value of preferred ÷ $300,000 value of preferred and common) × $60,000 (original basis of common stock)]. At this time, the common stock has a new basis of $40,000.

- The sale of the preferred stock generates $100,000 of ordinary income to Naomi. This is the amount of dividend income Naomi would have recognized had cash been distributed instead of preferred stock (i.e., the § 306 taint). The 15% maximum tax rate on dividend income is applicable to the $100,000.

- The $20,000 basis allocated to the preferred stock is added to the basis of the common stock; thus, the common stock basis is increased back to $60,000.

- Tern Corporation's E & P is unaffected by either the stock dividend or its subsequent sale. ■

---

[15]See, e.g., *Chamberlin v. Comm.*, 53–2 USTC ¶9576, 44 AFTR 494, 207 F.2d 462 (CA–6, 1953), *cert. den.* 74 S.Ct. 516 (USSC, 1954).
[16]See § 305(a).
[17]See § 307(a).
[18]§ 306(a)(1).

[19]§ 306(a)(1)(D).
[20]§ 306(a)(1)(C).
[21]Reg. § 1.306–1(b)(2), Example (2).
[22]See § 306(a)(2).

Section 306 stock is stock other than common that (1) is received as a nontaxable stock dividend, (2) is received tax-free in a corporate reorganization or separation to the extent that either the effect of the transaction was substantially the same as the receipt of a stock dividend or the stock was received in exchange for § 306 stock, or (3) has a basis determined by reference to the basis of § 306 stock (e.g., such as a gift of § 306 stock). (Corporate reorganizations are discussed in Chapter 7.) If a corporation has no E & P on the date of distribution of a nontaxable preferred stock dividend, the stock will not be § 306 stock.[23]

Redemptions through the Use of Related Corporations

A shareholder possessing a controlling interest (i.e., direct or indirect ownership of at least 50 percent)[24] in two or more corporations could, in the absence of any statutory limitation, obtain sale or exchange treatment by having one corporation purchase some of the shareholder's stock in a second related corporation. This result could occur even if the shareholder's ownership interest in the corporation whose stock is sold has not been substantively reduced. Section 304 closes this loophole by treating the sale of stock of one corporation to a related corporation as a stock redemption subject to the rules discussed earlier in this chapter. This provision applies to a transfer involving brother-sister corporations as well as to parent-subsidiary situations (see Chapters 2 and 8).

In general, § 304 requires a redemption through the use of related corporations to result in a reduction of ownership interest that would satisfy one of the qualifying stock redemptions of § 302 (e.g., disproportionate redemption) or § 303.[25] If the redemption does not qualify under those rules, the transaction is characterized as a dividend distribution.[26] When brother-sister corporations are involved, the shareholder increases the basis in the stock of the acquiring corporation by the basis of the stock surrendered in the transaction. Likewise, the acquiring corporation's basis in the stock acquired is equal to the basis the shareholder had in such shares.[27]

Distribution of Stock and Securities of a Controlled Corporation

If one corporation controls another corporation, stock in the subsidiary corporation can be distributed to the shareholders of the parent corporation tax-free under § 355. When a subsidiary is newly formed to perfect a corporate division, this provision applies through the divisive corporate reorganization rules discussed in Chapter 7. When a subsidiary already exists, § 355 alone applies, and the transaction can resemble either a dividend, a stock redemption, or a complete liquidation. The rules surrounding these transactions are covered in detail in Chapter 7.

Liquidations—In General

LO.4

Understand the tax consequences of complete liquidations for both the corporation and its shareholders.

When a corporation makes a nonliquidating distribution (e.g., stock redemption), the entity typically will continue as a going concern. With a complete liquidation, however, corporate existence terminates, as does the shareholder's ownership interest. A complete liquidation, like a qualifying stock redemption, produces sale or exchange treatment to the *shareholder.* However, the tax effects of a liquidation to the

---

[23]§ 306(c).
[24]§ 304(c).
[25]See § 304(a)(1).

[26]The distribution is given dividend income treatment to the extent of the sum of E & P of the two related corporations. § 304(b)(2).
[27]Reg. § 1.304–2(a) and § 362(a).

corporation vary somewhat from those of a redemption. Sale or exchange treatment is the general rule for the liquidating corporation, although some losses are disallowed.

The Liquidation Process

A **corporate liquidation** exists when a corporation ceases to be a going concern. The corporation continues solely to wind up affairs, pay debts, and distribute any remaining assets to its shareholders. Legal dissolution under state law is not required for a liquidation to be complete for tax purposes. A liquidation can exist even if the corporation retains a nominal amount of assets to pay remaining debts and preserve legal status.[28]

Shareholders may decide to liquidate a corporation for one or more reasons, including the following:

- The corporate business has been unsuccessful.
- The shareholders wish to acquire the corporation's assets.
- Another person or corporation wants to purchase the corporation's assets. The purchaser may buy the shareholders' stock and then liquidate the corporation to acquire the assets. Alternatively, the purchaser may buy the assets directly from the corporation. After the assets are sold, the corporation distributes the sales proceeds to its shareholders and liquidates.

As one might expect, the different means used to liquidate a corporation produce varying tax results.

Liquidating and Nonliquidating Distributions Compared

As noted previously, a *nonliquidating* property distribution produces gain (but not loss) to the distributing corporation. For the shareholder, the receipt of cash or property produces dividend income to the extent of the corporation's E & P or, in the case of a qualifying stock redemption, results in sale or exchange treatment.

Like a qualifying stock redemption, a complete *liquidation* produces sale or exchange treatment for the shareholders. Similarly, E & P has no impact on the gain or loss to be recognized by the shareholder in either type of distribution.[29] However, a complete liquidation produces different tax consequences to the liquidating corporation. With certain exceptions, a liquidating corporation recognizes gain *and* loss upon the distribution of its assets.

EXAMPLE 21

Goose Corporation, with E & P of $40,000, makes a cash distribution of $50,000 to its sole shareholder. The shareholder's basis in the Goose stock is $20,000. If the distribution is not a qualifying stock redemption or in complete liquidation, the shareholder recognizes dividend income of $40,000 (the amount of Goose's E & P) and treats the remaining $10,000 of the distribution as a return of capital. If the distribution is a qualifying stock redemption or is pursuant to a complete liquidation, the shareholder has a capital gain of $30,000 ($50,000 distribution − $20,000 stock basis). In the latter case, Goose's E & P is of no consequence to the shareholder's tax result. ■

In the event a corporate distribution results in a *loss* to the shareholder, an important distinction exists between nonliquidating distributions and liquidations. Section 267 disallows recognition of losses between related parties in nonliquidating distributions but not in complete liquidations.

---

[28]Reg. § 1.332–2(c).   [29]§ 331.

EXAMPLE 22

The stock of Orange Corporation is owned equally by three brothers, Rex, Sam, and Ted. When Ted's basis in his stock is $40,000, the corporation distributes $30,000 to him in cancellation of all his shares. If the distribution is a qualifying stock redemption, the $10,000 realized loss is not recognized because Ted and Orange Corporation are related parties. Under § 267, Ted is deemed to own more than 50% in value of the corporation's outstanding stock. Ted's direct ownership is limited to 33⅓%, but through his brothers he owns indirectly another 66⅔% for a total of 100%. On the other hand, if the distribution is pursuant to a complete liquidation, Ted's $10,000 realized loss is recognized. ∎

The rules governing the basis of property received from the corporation are identical for both liquidating and nonliquidating distributions. Section 334(a) specifies that the basis of property received in a complete liquidation is its fair market value on the date of distribution, while § 301(d) provides the same treatment for property received in a nonliquidating distribution.

In the following pages, the tax consequences of a complete liquidation are examined, first from the view of the distributing corporation and then in terms of the shareholder. Because the tax rules differ when a subsidiary corporation is liquidated, the rules relating to the liquidation of a subsidiary corporation are discussed separately.

Liquidations—Effect on the Distributing Corporation

The General Rule

Section 336(a) provides that a corporation recognizes *gain or loss* on the distribution of property in a complete liquidation. The property is treated as if it were sold at its fair market value. This treatment is consistent with the notion of double taxation that is inherent in operating a business as a C corporation—once at the corporate level and again at the shareholder level.

As in the case of a nonliquidating distribution, when property distributed in a complete liquidation is subject to a liability of the liquidating corporation, the fair market value used to calculate gain or loss may not be less than the amount of the liability.

EXAMPLE 23

Pursuant to a complete liquidation, Warbler Corporation distributes to its shareholders land held as an investment (basis of $200,000, fair market value of $300,000). If no liability is involved, Warbler has a gain of $100,000 on the distribution ($300,000 − $200,000). Likewise, if the land is subject to a liability of $250,000, Warbler Corporation has a gain of $100,000. If, instead, the liability were $350,000, Warbler's gain on the distribution would be $150,000 ($350,000 − $200,000). ∎

There are four exceptions to the general rule of gain and loss recognition by a liquidating corporation:

- Losses are not recognized on certain liquidating distributions to related-party shareholders.
- Losses are not recognized on certain sales and liquidating distributions of property that was contributed to the corporation with a built-in loss shortly before the adoption of a plan of liquidation.
- A subsidiary corporation does not recognize gains or losses on liquidating distributions to its parent corporation.
- A subsidiary corporation does not recognize losses on liquidating distributions to its minority shareholders.

The first two exceptions, referred to as the "antistuffing rules," are discussed in detail in the next section and are summarized in Figure 6–1 at the end of the section. The last two exceptions, dealing with the liquidation of a subsidiary corporation, are discussed later in this chapter.

Antistuffing Rules

When property is transferred to a corporation in a § 351 transaction or as a contribution to capital, carryover and substituted basis rules generally apply (see Chapter 4). Generally, the transferee corporation takes a basis in the property equal to that of the transferor-shareholder, and the shareholder takes an equal basis in the stock received in the exchange (or adds such amount to existing stock basis in the case of a capital contribution). Without special limitations, a transfer of loss property (fair market value less than basis) in a carryover basis transaction would present opportunities for the duplication of losses.

EXAMPLE 24

Nora, the sole shareholder of Canary Corporation, transfers property (basis of $100,000, fair market value of $30,000) to the corporation in exchange for additional stock. The exchange qualifies under § 351, and Canary would take a carryover basis of $100,000 in the property, and Nora would take a $100,000 basis in the additional stock. A sale or liquidating distribution of the property by Canary Corporation would result in a $70,000 loss [$30,000 (fair market value of property) − $100,000 (property basis)]. Similarly, a sale by Nora of the stock acquired in the § 351 exchange would also result in a $70,000 loss [$30,000 (fair market value of stock) − $100,000 (stock basis)]. ■

Congress addressed this loss duplication issue in the Tax Reform Act of 1986 by enacting two loss limitation ("antistuffing") rules under § 336(d) that apply to corporations upon liquidation. The effect of these rules is to disallow some or all of a loss realized by a corporation in liquidating distributions (and, in some cases, sales) of certain loss property.

The antistuffing rules limited the duplication of losses realized upon a corporation's liquidation, but loss trafficking was still possible if the corporation sold high-basis property in the normal course of business instead of upon or pursuant to liquidation. As a result, Congress revisited the loss duplication issue and, in the American Jobs Creation Act of 2004, enacted limitations to the general basis rules in § 351 and contribution to capital transactions. Unlike the antistuffing rules that disallow losses, the § 362(e)(2) rules require a corporation to step down the basis of property acquired in a § 351 or contribution to capital transaction by the amount of any net built-in loss embodied in such property. The basis step-down is required when a shareholder transfers properties having an aggregate basis in excess of their aggregate fair market value ("net built-in loss"), and it is allocated proportionately among the properties having built-in losses. Alternatively, the transferor-shareholder can elect to reduce his or her stock basis by the amount of net built-in loss. (See Chapter 4 for further discussion of the basis adjustment rules.) The antistuffing rules of § 336(d) continue to apply in the case of liquidating distributions (and certain sales) of loss property, but their bite has been lessened somewhat by the § 362(e)(2) basis step-down rules.

Related-Party Loss Limitation. Losses are disallowed on distributions to *related parties* in either of the following cases:

- The distribution is *not* pro rata, or
- The property distributed is disqualified property.[30]

---

[30]§ 336(d)(1).

A corporation and a shareholder are considered related if the shareholder owns (directly or indirectly) more than 50 percent in value of the corporation's outstanding stock.[31]

A *pro rata distribution* is one where *each* shareholder receives his or her proportionate share of the corporate asset distributed. *Disqualified property* is property that is acquired by the liquidating corporation in a § 351 or contribution to capital transaction during the five-year period ending on the date of the distribution. The related-party loss limitation can apply even if the property was appreciated (fair market value greater than basis) when it was transferred to the corporation.

EXAMPLE 25

Bluebird Corporation stock is owned by Ana and Sanjay, who are unrelated. Ana owns 80% and Sanjay owns 20% of the stock in the corporation. Bluebird has the following assets (none of which were acquired in a § 351 or contribution to capital transaction) that are distributed in complete liquidation of the corporation:

	Adjusted Basis	Fair Market Value
Cash	$600,000	$600,000
Equipment	150,000	200,000
Building	400,000	200,000

Assume Bluebird Corporation distributes the equipment to Sanjay and the cash and the building to Ana. Bluebird recognizes a gain of $50,000 on the distribution of the equipment. The loss of $200,000 on the building is disallowed because the property is distributed to a related party and the distribution is not pro rata (i.e., the building is not distributed 80% to Ana and 20% to Sanjay). ■

EXAMPLE 26

Assume in Example 25 that Bluebird Corporation distributes the cash and equipment to Ana and the building to Sanjay. Again, Bluebird recognizes the $50,000 gain on the equipment. However, it now recognizes the $200,000 loss on the building because the property is not distributed to a related party (i.e., Sanjay does not own more than 50% of the stock in Bluebird Corporation). ■

EXAMPLE 27

Wren Corporation's stock is held equally by three brothers. Four years before Wren's liquidation, the shareholders transfer jointly owned property (basis of $150,000, fair market value of $200,000) to the corporation in return for stock in a § 351 transaction. When the property is worth $100,000, it is transferred pro rata to the brothers in a liquidating distribution. Because each brother owns directly and indirectly more than 50% (i.e., 100% in this situation) of the stock and disqualified property is involved, none of the $50,000 realized loss [$100,000 (fair market value) − $150,000 (basis)] is recognized by Wren Corporation. ■

EXAMPLE 28

Assume in Example 27 that the property's fair market value is $100,000 at the time of the § 351 transfer and $75,000 at the time of the liquidating distribution to the brothers. As a result of the § 362(e)(2) basis step-down rules, Wren Corporation's basis in the property is $100,000 [$150,000 (basis to brothers) − $50,000 (net built-in loss of property transferred)]. In a liquidating distribution of the property to the brothers, Wren would realize a loss of $25,000 [$75,000 (fair market value of property at distribution) − $100,000 (Wren's stepped-down basis in property)]. Because this is a distribution of disqualified property to related parties, none of the $25,000 loss is recognized by Wren. ■

Built-in Loss Limitation. A second loss limitation applies to sales, exchanges, or distributions of built-in loss property (fair market value less than basis) that is

---

[31]Section 267 provides the definition of a related party for purposes of this provision. The rules are similar to the stock attribution rules discussed earlier in this chapter; one exception, however, is that stock owned by a sibling is treated as owned by the taxpayer under § 267.

transferred to a corporation shortly before the corporation is liquidated. The built-in loss limitation applies when both of the following conditions are met:

- The property was acquired by the corporation in a § 351 or contribution to capital transaction.
- Such acquisition was part of a plan whose principal purpose was to recognize a loss on that property by the liquidating corporation. A tax avoidance purpose is presumed in the case of transfers occurring within two years of the adoption of a plan of liquidation.

This disallowance rule applies only to the extent that a property's built-in loss at transfer is not eliminated by a stepped-down basis. Some built-in losses on property transfers will avoid the basis step-down either because built-in gain properties were also transferred by the shareholder (see Chapter 4, Example 21) or because the shareholder elected to step down the basis of his or her stock instead. Any loss attributable to a decline in a property's value after its transfer to the corporation is not subject to the built-in loss limitation.[32]

EXAMPLE 29

On January 2, 2008, Brown Corporation acquires two properties from a shareholder in a transaction that qualifies under § 351.

	Shareholder's Basis	Fair Market Value	Built-in Gain/(Loss)
Land	$100,000	$50,000	($50,000)
Securities	10,000	35,000	25,000
			($25,000)

The net built-in loss of $25,000 results in a stepped-down basis of $75,000 in the land for Brown Corporation [$100,000 (shareholder's basis) − $25,000 (step-down equal to net built-in loss)]. Brown adopts a plan of liquidation on July 9, 2008, and distributes the land to an unrelated shareholder on November 14, 2008, when the land is worth $30,000. Of the $45,000 loss realized [$30,000 (value of land on date of distribution) − $75,000 (basis in land)] by Brown on the distribution, $25,000 is disallowed by the built-in loss limitation [$50,000 (value of land when acquired by Brown) − $75,000 (stepped-down basis in land)], and $20,000 is recognized (equal to the decline in value occurring after acquisition by Brown). ■

The built-in loss limitation applies to a broader range of transactions than the related-party exception, which disallows losses only on certain distributions to related parties (i.e., more-than-50 percent shareholders). The built-in loss limitation can apply to distributions of property to any shareholder, including an unrelated party, and to a *sale or exchange* of property by a liquidating corporation. However, the limitation is narrower than the related-party exception in that it applies only to property that had a built-in loss upon its acquisition by the corporation and only as to the amount of the built-in loss (as adjusted by the basis step-down rules).

EXAMPLE 30

Assume in Example 29 that the land was worth $120,000 on the date Brown Corporation acquired the property. As there is no net built-in loss on the transfer, Brown will have a basis of $100,000 in the land. If the distribution is to an unrelated shareholder, Brown Corporation will recognize the entire $70,000 loss [$30,000 (fair market value on date of distribution) − $100,000 (basis)]. However, if the distribution is to a related party, Brown cannot recognize any of the loss under the related-party loss limitation because the property is

---

[32]§ 336(d)(2).

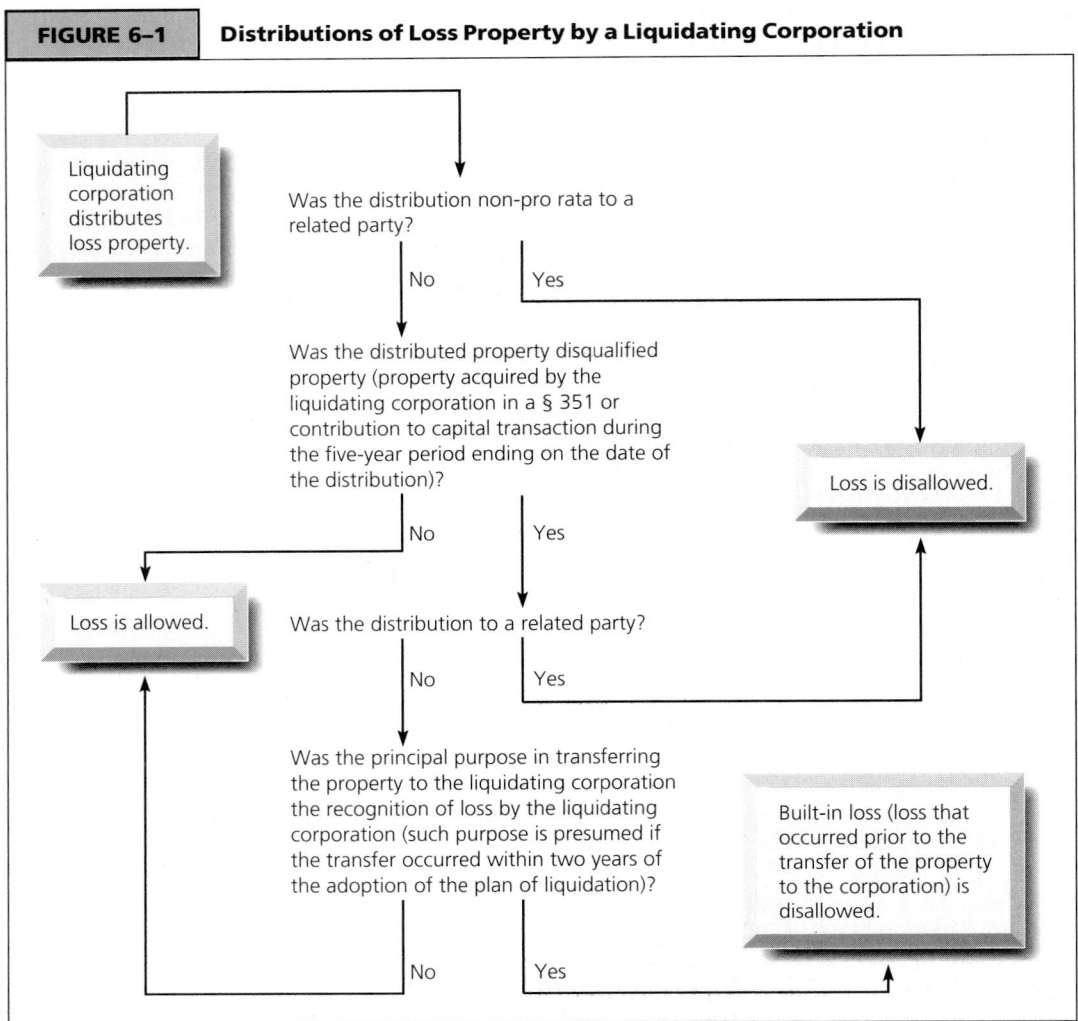

FIGURE 6–1   **Distributions of Loss Property by a Liquidating Corporation**

disqualified property. When the distribution is to a related party, the loss is disallowed even though the entire decline in value occurred during the period the corporation held the property. ∎

The built-in loss limitation will apply only in rare cases if the corporation has held the property more than two years prior to liquidation. The presumption of a tax avoidance purpose for property transferred to a corporation in the two years preceding the liquidation can be rebutted if there is a clear and substantial relationship between the contributed property and the (current or future) business of the corporation. When there was a business reason for the transfer, the built-in loss limitation will not apply.

EXAMPLE 31

Cardinal Corporation's stock is held by two unrelated individuals: 60% by Manuel and 40% by Jack. One year before Cardinal's liquidation, Manuel transfers land (basis of $150,000, fair market value of $100,000) and equipment (basis of $10,000, fair market value of $70,000) to the corporation as a contribution to capital. As there is no net built-in loss on the transfer, Cardinal will have a basis of $150,000 in the land. There is no business reason for the transfer. In liquidation, Cardinal distributes the land (now worth $90,000) to Jack. Even though the distribution is to an unrelated party, the built-in loss of $50,000 is not recognized. However, Cardinal Corporation can recognize the loss of $10,000 ($90,000 − $100,000) that occurred while it held the land. If, instead, the land is distributed to Manuel, a related party, the entire $60,000 loss is disallowed under the related-party loss limitation. ∎

Assume in Example 31 that the land and equipment are transferred to Cardinal Corporation because a bank required the additional capital investment as a condition to making a loan to the corporation. Because there is a business purpose for the transfer, all of the $60,000 loss is recognized if the land is distributed to Jack in liquidation. If, instead, the land is distributed to Manuel, a related party, the entire loss is still disallowed under the related-party loss limitation. ∎

EXAMPLE 32

Tax Paid on Net Gain. To the extent that a corporation pays tax on the net amount of gain recognized as a result of its liquidation, the proceeds available to be distributed to the shareholder are likewise reduced. This reduction for the payment of taxes will reduce the amount realized by the shareholder, which will then reduce the shareholder's gain (or increase the loss) recognized.

Purple Corporation's assets are valued at $2 million after payment of all corporate debts except for $300,000 of taxes payable on net gains it recognized on the liquidation. Therefore, the amount realized by the shareholders is $1.7 million ($2,000,000 − $300,000). As described below, in determining the gain or loss recognized by a shareholder, the amount realized is offset by the stock's adjusted basis. ∎

EXAMPLE 33

ETHICAL and EQUITABLE *Considerations*	**TRANSFEREE LIABILITY FOR TAX DEFICIENCY OF LIQUIDATED CORPORATION**

In 2006, Duckbill Corporation distributed all of its remaining assets to two equal shareholders in a complete liquidation. The two shareholders, Dena Hall and Rosa Garcia, each received a distribution of $100,000 for their stock in Duckbill. In 2008, the IRS audited Duckbill Corporation and assessed additional tax of $80,000 (plus penalties and interest) against the corporation. Since Duckbill was defunct and without assets, the IRS then assessed the entire $80,000 deficiency against Dena Hall, based on transferee liability. The IRS did not attempt to collect any of the deficiency from Rosa Garcia. Is this an equitable solution to the collection of Duckbill's tax liability?

Liquidations—Effect on the Shareholder

The tax consequences to the shareholders of a corporation in the process of liquidation are governed either by the general rule of § 331 or by the exception of § 332 relating to the liquidation of a subsidiary.

The General Rule

In the case of a complete liquidation, § 331(a) provides for sale or exchange treatment for the shareholders. Thus, the difference between the fair market value of the assets received from the corporation and the adjusted basis of the stock surrendered is the gain or loss recognized by the shareholder. Typically, the stock is a capital asset in the hands of the shareholder, and capital gain or loss results. The burden of proof is on the taxpayer to furnish evidence as to the adjusted basis of the stock. In the absence of such evidence, the stock is deemed to have a zero basis, and the full amount of the liquidation proceeds equals the amount of the gain recognized.[33] The basis of property received in a liquidation is the property's fair market value on the date of distribution.[34]

---

[33]*John Calderazzo*, 34 TCM 1, T.C.Memo. 1975–1.   [34]§ 334(a).

Special Rule for Certain Installment Obligations

Corporations often sell assets pursuant to a plan of liquidation, and sometimes these sales are made on the installment basis. If the installment notes are then distributed in liquidation, the corporation recognizes gain (or loss) equal to the difference between the fair market value of the notes and the corporation's basis in the notes.[35] However, shareholders can use the installment method to defer to the point of collection the portion of their gain that is attributable to the notes. This treatment requires the shareholders to allocate their stock basis between the installment notes and the other assets received from the corporation.[36]

EXAMPLE 34

After a plan of complete liquidation has been adopted, Beige Corporation sells its only asset, unimproved land held as an investment. The land has appreciated in value and is sold to Jane (an unrelated party) for $100,000. Under the terms of the sale, Beige Corporation receives cash of $25,000 and Jane's notes for the balance of $75,000. The notes are payable over 10 years ($7,500 per year) and carry an appropriate rate of interest. Immediately after the sale, Beige Corporation distributes the cash and notes to Earl, the sole shareholder. Earl has an adjusted basis of $20,000 in the Beige stock, and the installment notes have a value equal to their face amount ($75,000). These transactions have the following tax results:

- Beige Corporation recognizes gain on the distribution of the installment notes, measured by the difference between the $75,000 fair market value and the basis Beige had in the notes.
- Earl may defer the gain on the receipt of the notes to the point of collection.
- Earl must allocate the adjusted basis in his stock ($20,000) between the cash and the installment notes as follows:

$$\frac{\text{Cash}}{\text{Total receipts}} = \frac{\$25,000}{\$100,000} \times \$20,000 = \$5,000 \text{ basis allocated to the cash}$$

$$\frac{\text{Notes}}{\text{Total receipts}} = \frac{\$75,000}{\$100,000} \times \$20,000 = \$15,000 \text{ basis allocated to the notes}$$

- On the cash portion of the transaction, Earl must recognize $20,000 of gain [$25,000 (cash received) − $5,000 (basis allocated to the cash)] in the year of liquidation.
- Over the next 10 years, Earl must recognize a total gain of $60,000 on the notes, computed as follows:

$$\$75,000 \text{ (fair market value)} - \$15,000 \text{ (basis allocated to the notes)}$$
$$= \$60,000 \text{ (gross profit)}$$

- The gross profit percentage on the notes is 80%, computed as follows:

$$\frac{\$60,000 \text{ (gross profit)}}{\$75,000 \text{ (contract price)}} = 80\%$$

Thus, Earl must report a gain of $6,000 [$7,500 (amount of note) × 80% (gross profit percentage)] on the collection of each note over the next 10 years.
- The interest element is accounted for separately. ∎

LO.5

Understand the tax consequences of subsidiary liquidations for both the parent and the subsidiary corporations.

Liquidations—Parent-Subsidiary Situations

Section 332, an exception to the general rule of § 331, provides that a parent corporation does *not* recognize gain or loss on a liquidation of a subsidiary. In addition,

---

[35]§ 453B(a). Gain is not recognized in the distribution of installment notes by a subsidiary liquidating pursuant to § 332. See the discussion below and §§ 337(a) and 453B(d).

[36]§ 453(h). Installment notes attributable to the sale of inventory qualify only if the inventory was sold in a bulk sale to one person.

the subsidiary corporation recognizes *neither gain nor loss* on distributions of property to its parent.[37]

The requirements for applying § 332 are as follows:

- The parent must own at least 80 percent of the voting stock of the subsidiary and at least 80 percent of the value of the subsidiary's stock.
- The subsidiary must distribute all its property in complete cancellation of all its stock within the taxable year or within three years from the close of the tax year in which the first distribution occurred.
- The subsidiary must be solvent.[38]

If these requirements are met, nonrecognition of gains and losses becomes mandatory. However, if the subsidiary is insolvent, the parent corporation will have an ordinary loss deduction under § 165(g).

When a series of distributions occurs in the liquidation of a subsidiary corporation, the parent corporation must own the required amount of stock (80 percent) on the date the plan of liquidation is adopted. Such ownership must continue at all times until all property has been distributed.[39] If the parent fails the control requirement at any time, the provisions for nonrecognition of gain or loss do not apply to any distribution.[40]

Minority Shareholder Interests

In a § 332 parent-subsidiary liquidation, up to 20 percent of the subsidiary's stock can be owned by minority shareholders. In such liquidations, a distribution of property to a minority shareholder is treated in the same manner as a *nonliquidating* distribution. That is, the subsidiary corporation recognizes gain (but not loss) on the property distributed to the minority shareholder.[41]

EXAMPLE 35

The stock of Tan Corporation is held as follows: 80% by Mustard Corporation and 20% by Arethia. Tan Corporation is liquidated on December 9, 2008, pursuant to a plan adopted on January 10, 2008. At the time of its liquidation, Tan Corporation has assets with a basis of $100,000 and fair market value of $500,000. Tan Corporation distributes the property pro rata to Mustard Corporation and to Arethia. Tan must recognize gain of $80,000 [($500,000 fair market value − $100,000 basis) × 20% minority interest]. Since the corporate tax due in this liquidation relates entirely to the minority shareholder distribution, that amount will most likely be deducted from the $100,000 distribution ($500,000 × 20%) going to Arethia. The remaining gain of $320,000 is not recognized because it is attributable to property being distributed to Mustard, the parent corporation. ∎

A minority shareholder is subject to the general rule requiring the recognition of gain or loss in a liquidation. Accordingly, the difference between the fair market value of the assets received and the basis of the minority shareholder's stock is the amount of gain or loss recognized. Further, the basis of property received by the minority shareholder is the property's fair market value on the date of distribution.[42]

Indebtedness of the Subsidiary to the Parent

If a subsidiary transfers appreciated property to its parent to satisfy a debt, it must recognize gain on the transaction unless the subsidiary is liquidating and the

---

[37]§ 337(a). This is an exception to the general rule of § 336.

[38]§ 332(b) and Reg. §§ 1.332–2(a) and (b).

[39]Establishing the date of the adoption of a plan of complete liquidation could be crucial in determining whether § 332 applies. See, for example, *George L. Riggs, Inc.,* 64 T.C. 474 (1975).

[40]§ 332(b)(3) and Reg. § 1.332–2(a).

[41]§§ 336(a) and (d)(3).

[42]§ 334(a).

conditions of § 332 (discussed above) apply. When § 332 applies, the subsidiary does not recognize gain or loss upon the transfer of properties to the parent in satisfaction of indebtedness.[43]

| EXAMPLE 36 | Eagle Corporation owes its parent, Finch Corporation, $20,000. It satisfies the obligation by transferring land (basis of $8,000, fair market value of $20,000) to Finch. Normally, Eagle would recognize a gain of $12,000 on the transaction. However, if the transfer is made pursuant to a liquidation under § 332, Eagle does not recognize a gain. ∎ |

This nonrecognition provision does not apply to the parent corporation. The parent corporation recognizes gain or loss on the receipt of property in satisfaction of indebtedness, even if the property is received during liquidation of the subsidiary.

| EXAMPLE 37 | Pelican Corporation owns bonds (basis of $95,000) of its subsidiary, Crow Corporation, that were acquired at a discount. Upon liquidation of Crow pursuant to § 332, Pelican receives a distribution of $100,000, the face amount of the bonds. The transaction has no tax effect on Crow. However, Pelican Corporation recognizes gain of $5,000 [$100,000 (amount realized) − $95,000 (basis in bonds)]. ∎ |

Basis of Property Received by the Parent Corporation—The General Rule

Property received in the complete liquidation of a subsidiary has the same basis it had in the hands of the subsidiary.[44] Unless the parent corporation makes a § 338 election (discussed below), this carryover basis in the assets generally will differ significantly from the parent's basis in the stock of the subsidiary. Since the liquidation is a nontaxable exchange, the parent's gain or loss on the difference in basis is not recognized. Further, the parent's basis in the stock of the liquidated subsidiary disappears.

| EXAMPLE 38 | Lark Corporation has a basis of $200,000 in the stock of Heron Corporation, a subsidiary in which it owns 85% of all classes of stock. Lark purchased the Heron stock 10 years ago. In the current year, Lark liquidates Heron Corporation and acquires assets that are worth $500,000 and have a tax basis to Heron of $400,000. Lark Corporation takes a basis of $400,000 in the assets, with a potential gain upon their sale of $100,000. Lark's $200,000 basis in Heron's stock disappears. ∎ |

| EXAMPLE 39 | Indigo Corporation has a basis of $600,000 in the stock of Kackie Corporation, a wholly owned subsidiary acquired 10 years ago. It liquidates Kackie Corporation and receives assets that are worth $500,000 and have a tax basis to Kackie of $400,000. Indigo Corporation takes a basis of $400,000 in the assets it acquires from Kackie. If Indigo sells the assets, it has a gain of $100,000 even though its basis in the Kackie stock was $600,000. Indigo's loss on its stock investment in Kackie will never be recognized. ∎ |

In addition to the parent corporation taking the subsidiary's basis in its assets, the carryover rules of § 381 apply (see Chapter 7). Under that provision, the parent acquires other tax attributes of the subsidiary, including the subsidiary's net operating loss carryover, business credit carryover, capital loss carryover, and E & P.

---

[43]§ 337(b)(1).

[44]§ 334(b)(1) and Reg. § 1.334–1(b). But see § 334(b)(1)(B) (exception for property acquired in some liquidations of foreign subsidiaries).

BASIS RULES FOR LIQUIDATIONS OF FOREIGN SUBSIDIARIES

The basis of property acquired by a parent corporation in the liquidation of a subsidiary corporation is generally equal to the basis the subsidiary had in such property. However, the American Jobs Creation Act of 2004 modified the basis rules regarding property acquired by a U.S. parent in some § 332 liquidations of foreign subsidiaries. In general, if the aggregate basis in a foreign subsidiary's assets exceeds their aggregate fair market value, the U.S. parent will take a fair market value basis in the property acquired. The purpose of this amendment is to deny the importation of built-in losses (excess of basis over fair market value). [See §§ 334(b)(1)(B) and 362(e)(1)(B).]

GLOBAL
Tax Issues

Basis of Property Received by the Parent Corporation—§ 338 Election

Background. As discussed above, the liquidation of a subsidiary generally is a nontaxable transaction, resulting in the nonrecognition of gain or loss for both the parent and the subsidiary corporations and the carryover of the subsidiary's asset bases (and other tax attributes). This treatment reflects the fact that such a liquidation often is merely a change in corporate structure and not a change in substance. This is particularly the case when the parent has owned the stock of the subsidiary since the subsidiary's inception. In such cases, the carried-over bases are comparable to what the parent would have in the subsidiary's assets if the parent, and not the subsidiary, had originally acquired the assets.

The carryover basis rule for § 332 liquidations can result in some inequities when the subsidiary has been in existence for some time prior to the parent's acquisition of the subsidiary's stock. The parent's basis in the stock of the subsidiary will reflect the fair market value of the subsidiary's assets (and goodwill) at the time of the stock purchase. As a result, the parent's basis in the stock of the subsidiary will usually be greater than the subsidiary's basis in its assets. Under the carryover basis rule, a liquidation of the subsidiary would result in the parent taking a basis in the subsidiary's assets that is less than the parent's basis in the stock of the subsidiary. This is the case even if the parent acquired the subsidiary stock solely to obtain the subsidiary's assets.

If the parent corporation could treat the purchase of the subsidiary stock as a purchase of its assets, the parent could take a basis in the assets equal to the acquisition cost of the stock. In most cases, this would mean a higher asset basis and, as a result, larger depreciation deductions and lower gains upon disposition for the parent corporation. To obtain this stock-basis-for-asset-basis result, taxpayers successfully devised stock purchase/subsidiary liquidation transactions that fell outside the purview of § 332.[45] Congress codified this treatment by enacting § 338, which permits the purchase of a controlling interest of stock to be treated as a purchase of the subsidiary's assets.

Requirements for Application. A corporation (the "parent") may *elect* the provisions of § 338 if it acquires stock representing at least 80 percent of the voting power and at least 80 percent of the value of another corporation (the "subsidiary") within a 12-month period ("*qualified stock purchase*"). The stock must be acquired in a taxable transaction (i.e., § 351 and other nonrecognition provisions do not apply). An acquisition of stock by any member of an affiliated group that includes the parent corporation is considered to be an acquisition by the parent.

---

[45]See, e.g., *U.S. v. M.O.J. Corp.*, 60–1 USTC ¶9209, 5 AFTR2d 535, 274 F.2d 713 (CA–5, 1960). See also *Kimbell-Diamond Milling Co.*, 14 T.C. 74 (1950), *aff'd* 51–1 USTC ¶9201, 40 AFTR 328, 187 F.2d 718 (CA–5, 1951), *cert. den.* 72 S.Ct. 50 (USSC, 1951) (IRS argued stock-for-asset basis).

The **§ 338 election** must be made by the fifteenth day of the ninth month beginning after the month in which a qualified stock purchase occurs. If made, the election is irrevocable.

Tax Consequences. Upon a qualified § 338 election, the subsidiary is treated as having sold its assets on the qualified stock purchase date for a value that is determined with reference to the parent's basis in the subsidiary stock plus any liabilities of the subsidiary.[46] The subsidiary is then treated as a new corporation that purchased those assets for a similarly computed amount on the day following the qualified stock purchase date.[47] The deemed sale results in gain (or loss) recognition to the subsidiary, and the deemed purchase results in a stepped-up (or -down) basis for the subsidiary's assets.[48] The subsidiary may, but need not, be liquidated. If the subsidiary is liquidated, the parent will obtain a carryover of the stepped-up (or -down) basis of the subsidiary's assets.

A Comparison of the General Rule and the § 338 Election. Under the general rule of nonrecognition, the liquidation of a subsidiary is tax-free to both the subsidiary (except for any minority interest) and the parent corporation. Under § 338, the subsidiary recognizes gain (or loss) on the deemed disposition of its assets. A liquidation of the subsidiary remains tax-free to the parent. While a carryover basis rule applies in both cases, the subsidiary's assets generally will have a stepped-up basis as a result of the § 338 election, and a liquidation of the subsidiary will result in a carryover of the stepped-up basis to the parent. Further, a liquidation of the subsidiary results in a carryover of its other tax attributes (e.g., E & P) to the parent whether or not a § 338 election is made. However, when the election is made, the subsidiary is treated as a new corporation as of the day following the qualified stock purchase date; as a result, any tax attributes acquired by the parent are likely to be nominal (or zero) in amount.

The holding period of the subsidiary's assets is determined with reference to the substance of the transaction. When the subsidiary is liquidated and there is no § 338 election, the subsidiary's historical holding period in its assets carries over to the parent. This is the typical carryover rule found in other nonrecognition provisions. A § 338 election, however, assumes a sale and repurchase of the subsidiary's assets. As a result of these deemed transactions, the holding period starts anew. If there is a § 338 election and the subsidiary is liquidated, the holding period of the property received by the parent begins on the date of the qualified stock purchase. On the other hand, if there is a § 338 election and the subsidiary is not liquidated, the holding period of the assets begins on the day after the qualified stock acquisition date. The parent-subsidiary liquidation rules are set out in Concept Summary 6–2.

TAX PLANNING
Considerations

Stock Redemptions

Stock redemptions offer several possibilities for tax planning:

- The alternative to a qualifying stock redemption is dividend treatment. The 15 percent (0 percent for taxpayers in the 10 or 15 percent marginal tax bracket) preferential tax rate on dividend income reduces some of the adverse consequences of a nonqualified stock redemption. The preference for dividend income is set to expire at the end of 2010.
- A nonqualified redemption may be preferable to one that produces sale or exchange treatment if the distributing corporation has little or no E & P or the distributee-shareholder is another corporation. In the latter situation,

---

[46]See §§ 338(a)(1) and (b) and Reg. § 1.338–4.
[47]See §§ 338(a)(2) and (b) and Reg. § 1.338–5.

[48]For the rules governing the allocation of the purchase price to the assets, see § 338(b)(5) and Reg. § 1.338–6.

CONCEPT SUMMARY 6–2

Summary of Liquidation Rules

Effect on the Shareholder	Basis of Property Received	Effect on the Corporation
§ 331—The general rule provides for gain or loss treatment on the difference between the FMV of property received and the basis of the stock in the corporation. Gain allocable to installment notes received can be deferred to point of collection.	§ 334(a)—Basis of assets received by the shareholder will be the FMV on the date of distribution (except for installment obligations on which gain is deferred to the point of collection).	§ 336—Gain or loss is recognized for distributions in kind and for sales by the liquidating corporation. Losses are not recognized for distributions to related parties if the distribution is not pro rata or if disqualified property is distributed. Losses may be disallowed on sales and distributions of built-in loss property even if made to unrelated parties.
§ 332—In liquidation of a subsidiary, no gain or loss is recognized to the parent. Subsidiary must distribute all of its property within the taxable year or within three years from the close of the taxable year in which the first distribution occurs. Minority shareholders taxed under general rule of § 331.	§ 334(b)(1)—Property has the same basis as it had in the hands of the subsidiary. Parent's basis in the stock disappears. Carryover rules of § 381 apply. Minority shareholders get FMV basis under § 334(a).	§ 337—No gain or loss is recognized to the subsidiary on distributions to the parent. Gain (but not loss) is recognized on distributions to minority shareholders.
	§ 338—Subsidiary need not be liquidated. If subsidiary is liquidated, parent's basis is new stepped-up (or -down) basis. Parent's basis in the stock disappears. Carryover rules of § 381 apply, but such amounts are likely to be nominal.	§ 338—Gain or loss is recognized to the subsidiary. Subsidiary is treated as a new corporation, and its basis in assets is stepped up (or down) to reflect parent's basis in subsidiary stock plus subsidiary's liabilities. New basis is allocated among various asset classes.

dividend treatment may be preferred due to the availability of the dividends received deduction.

- Stock redemptions are particularly well suited for purchasing the interest of a retiring or deceased shareholder. Rather than the remaining shareholders buying the stock of the retiring or deceased shareholder, the corporation uses its funds to redeem the stock from the retiring shareholder or from the decedent shareholder's estate. The ability to use the corporation's funds to buy out a shareholder's interest is also advantageous in property settlements between divorcing taxpayers. The redeeming corporation need not finance the redemption entirely with cash as it can issue its own notes as consideration in the transaction without adverse tax consequences to the shareholder.

- A third party who wishes to purchase all the stock of a corporation can use a stock redemption to obtain the needed purchase money. This technique is referred to as a "bootstrap acquisition." The third party first purchases a small amount of stock from the shareholders. The corporation then redeems all of its outstanding stock except that of the third party. The third party becomes the sole shareholder of the corporation, but the corporation furnished most of the purchase money.

- A not essentially equivalent redemption provides minimal utility and generally should be relied upon only as a last resort. Instead, the redemption should be

EXCEPTION TO § 332 FOR LIQUIDATIONS OF U.S. SUBSIDIARIES OF FOREIGN CORPORATIONS

When a U.S. subsidiary is liquidated into a U.S. parent, gains (or losses) are not recognized immediately, but rather are deferred as a result of the carryover basis rule. Gains inherent in the transferred assets will be recognized upon their disposition by the parent. Foreign corporations generally are not subject to U.S. taxation, so the liquidation of a U.S. subsidiary into a foreign parent could avoid gain recognition entirely if § 332 were to apply unabated. Section 367(b) overrides § 332 when a U.S. subsidiary is liquidated into a foreign parent, however. Under § 367(b), the subsidiary will recognize gain on the transfer of certain "tainted" assets. Tainted assets include inventory, installment obligations, accounts receivable, and depreciable property (to the extent of depreciation recapture). For further details, see Chapter 9.

structured to satisfy the objective tests required of one of the other qualifying redemptions.

- The timing and sequence of a redemption should be considered carefully as a series of redemptions may have the effect of a dividend distribution. The following example illustrates this point.

EXAMPLE 40

Sparrow Corporation's stock is held as follows: Alma (60 shares), Antonio (20 shares), and Ali (20 shares). Alma, Antonio, and Ali are not related to each other. The corporation redeems 24 of Alma's shares. Shortly thereafter, it redeems 5 of Antonio's shares. Does Alma's redemption qualify as a disproportionate redemption? Taken in isolation, it would appear to meet the 80% and 50% tests. Yet, if the IRS takes into account the later redemption of Antonio's shares, Alma has not satisfied the 50% test; she still owns 36/71 of the corporation after the two redemptions. A greater time lag between the redemptions places Alma in a better position to argue against collapsing the two redemptions as parts of one integrated plan. ■

- For a family corporation in which all of the shareholders are related to each other, the only hope of achieving sale or exchange treatment may lie in the use of a redemption that completely terminates a shareholder's interest or one that follows a shareholder's death. In a complete termination redemption, it is important that the family stock attribution rules be avoided. Here, strict compliance with the requirements for the family attribution waiver (e.g., the withdrawing shareholder does not acquire a prohibited interest in the corporation within 10 years) is crucial.
- In a redemption to pay death taxes, the amount to be sheltered from dividend treatment is limited to the sum of death taxes and funeral and administration expenses. However, a redemption in excess of the limitation does not destroy the applicability of § 303. Further, if the transaction is structured properly, the excess amount can qualify for sale or exchange treatment under one of the other redemption rules.

Disposing of § 306 Stock

Distributing the preferred stock dividend at a time when the corporation has no E & P avoids the § 306 taint altogether. Otherwise, avoiding ordinary income on the disposition of § 306 stock is a difficult feat. Unless the corporation's E & P was nominal at the time of the stock dividend (in the case of a § 306 stock sale) or at the time of the redemption (in the case of a § 306 stock redemption), the disposition of § 306 stock typically produces only ordinary income. The 15 percent (or 0 percent) tax rate applicable to dividend income lessens the bite of such treatment. A gift of § 306 stock does not defeat the ordinary income taint as the taint remains with the stock. However, if the donee is in the 10 or 15 percent marginal tax bracket, the tainted income at disposition would be taxed at the 0 percent tax rate applicable to dividends for the lowest-bracket taxpayers (through 2010). In a charitable contribution of § 306 stock, the deduction is reduced under § 170(e) by the amount of the ordinary income taint.

The sale of § 306 stock in a transaction that terminates the shareholder's entire direct and indirect stock interest (common and preferred) in the corporation will avoid ordinary income treatment, as will a disposition in liquidation of the corporation. Similarly, a redemption of § 306 stock in a complete termination redemption or a partial liquidation avoids the ordinary income result. However, these exceptions are of limited use in the typical disposition of § 306 stock.

Corporate Liquidations

With the exception of parent-subsidiary liquidations, distributions in liquidation are taxed at both the corporate level and the shareholder level. When a corporation liquidates, it can, as a general rule, claim losses on assets that have depreciated in value. These assets should not be distributed in the form of a property dividend or stock redemption because losses are not recognized on nonliquidating distributions.

Shareholders faced with large prospective gains in a liquidation may consider shifting part or all of that gain to other taxpayers. One approach is to donate stock to charity. A charitable contribution of the stock produces a deduction equal to the stock's fair market value (see Chapter 2). Alternatively, the stock may be given to family members. If the family member is in the 10 or 15 percent marginal tax bracket, some or all of the gain on liquidation could be taxed at the 0 percent preferential rate on long-term capital gains. Whether these procedures will be successful in shifting the liquidation-related gain from the taxpayer depends on the timing of the transfer. If the donee of the stock is not in a position to prevent the liquidation of the corporation, the donor may be deemed to have made an anticipatory assignment of income. In such a case, the gain is still taxed to the donor. In addition, possible gift tax issues on the stock transfer must be considered (see Chapter 17). Advance planning of stock transfers therefore is crucial in arriving at the desired tax result.

The installment sale provisions provide some relief from the general rule that a shareholder recognizes all gain upon receiving a liquidating distribution. If the assets of the liquidating corporation are not to be distributed in kind, a sale of the assets in exchange for installment notes should be considered. Shareholders receiving the notes in a liquidation can then report their gain on the installment method as the notes are collected. Gain deferred under the installment method is subject to the tax rates applicable in each year of collection. Under current tax law, the preferential tax rate for long-term capital gains is scheduled to increase to 20 percent (from 15 percent) after 2010. Thus, the deferral of gain on installment obligations received in a liquidation must be weighed against the anticipated 5 percentage point increase in the applicable tax rate for gains deferred beyond 2010.

Parent-Subsidiary Liquidations

The nonrecognition provision applicable to the liquidation of a subsidiary, § 332, is not elective. Nevertheless, some flexibility may be available:

- Whether § 332 applies depends on the 80 percent stock ownership test. A parent corporation may be able to avoid § 332 by reducing its stock ownership in the subsidiary below this percentage to allow for recognition of a loss. On the other hand, the opposite approach may be desirable to avoid gain recognition. A corporate shareholder possessing less than the required 80 percent ownership may want to acquire additional stock to qualify for § 332 treatment.

- Once § 332 becomes effective, less latitude is allowed in determining the parent's basis in the subsidiary's assets. Generally, the subsidiary's existing basis in its assets carries over to the parent. If a timely § 338 election is made, the subsidiary's basis in its assets is stepped up to reflect, in part, the parent's basis in the subsidiary stock. If the subsidiary also is liquidated, the parent obtains assets with the stepped-up basis.
- An election to have the § 338 rules apply should be carefully weighed as the election can be detrimental. The income tax liability on the subsidiary's recognized gain that results from the deemed sale of its assets is the cost under § 338 for obtaining the stepped-up basis. As a result, a § 338 election may be a viable option only when the subsidiary possesses loss and/or credit carryovers that can be used to offset the associated tax.

Asset Purchase versus Stock Purchase

The acquisition of a corporation's assets generally takes one of two forms. In one form, the acquiring corporation purchases the stock of the target corporation, and then the target (subsidiary) is liquidated. In the other form, the acquiring corporation purchases the assets of the target corporation, and then the target distributes the proceeds to its shareholders in liquidation. Nontax considerations may affect the form of acquisition, with each form having both favorable and unfavorable aspects.

An asset purchase requires that title be transferred and that creditors be notified. Further, an asset purchase may not be feasible if valuable nontransferable trademarks, contracts, or licenses are involved. Alternatively, an asset purchase may be preferable to a stock purchase if the target's shareholders refuse to sell their stock. Additionally, an asset purchase avoids the transfer of liabilities (including unknown liabilities) generally inherent in stock acquisitions. An asset purchase also has the advantage of allowing the purchaser to avoid the acquisition of unwanted assets, whereas a stock purchase would involve all of a target's assets.

KEY TERMS

Attribution, 6–6	Meaningful reduction test, 6–7	Redemption to pay death taxes, 6–11
Complete termination redemption, 6–9	Not essentially equivalent redemption, 6–7	Section 338 election, 6–28
Corporate liquidation, 6–17	Partial liquidation, 6–10	Stock redemption, 6–3
Disproportionate redemption, 6–8	Preferred stock bailout, 6–15	

PROBLEM MATERIALS

DISCUSSION QUESTIONS

1. Compare the tax treatment of nonliquidating distributions that are treated as a return *from* a shareholder's investment with the tax treatment of distributions that are treated as a return *of* a shareholder's investment.

2. Why do stock redemptions occur?

3. Would a noncorporate shareholder, such as an individual, prefer a nonqualified or a qualifying stock redemption? Why?

4. Penelope and Haggard, unrelated individuals, own all of the stock in Orange Corporation. In order to finance some unexpected health care costs, Penelope needs to sell her interest in Orange. What issues should be considered in determining whether a redemption of Penelope's stock by Orange Corporation is preferable to a sale of the shares to Haggard or a third party?

   Issue ID

5. During the current year, Flicker, Inc., distributed $80,000 each to Kanisha and Susan in redemption of some of their Flicker stock. The two shareholders are in the 33% tax bracket, and each had a $20,000 basis in her redeemed stock. Kanisha incurred $12,000 of tax on her redemption, but Susan incurred only $9,000 on her redemption. Discuss the likely reason for the difference in their tax liabilities.

6. A shareholder realized a loss in a qualifying stock redemption. Since the redemption qualified for sale or exchange treatment, the loss will be recognized. Assess the validity of this statement.

7. What is the shareholder's basis in property received in a qualifying stock redemption? When does the shareholder's holding period for the property begin? Would your answers differ if the property was distributed in a nonqualified stock redemption?

8. For purposes of the stock attribution rules, what family members are included as "related parties"?

9. How do the § 318 stock attribution rules apply to partnerships and their partners?

10. The § 318 stock attribution rules do not apply in the case of a complete termination redemption. Discuss the validity of this statement.

11. When does a stock redemption qualify as a not essentially equivalent redemption?

12. Bernie owns 600 shares of Robin Corporation, and the remaining 900 shares of Robin are owned by shareholders unrelated to Bernie. If Robin Corporation redeems 200 shares from Bernie, will the redemption qualify for sale or exchange treatment?

13. Two years ago, Jorge transferred property he had used in his sole proprietorship to Flycatcher Corporation, a newly formed corporation, for 50 shares of stock in Flycatcher. The property had an adjusted basis of $300,000 and a fair market value of $800,000. Six months later, Jorge's friend, Polly, transferred property she had used in her sole proprietorship to Flycatcher Corporation for 50 shares of the stock in Flycatcher and cash of $100,000. Her property had an adjusted basis of $150,000 and a value of $900,000. Both Jorge and Polly serve on the board of directors of Flycatcher Corporation. In addition, Polly has a contract with Flycatcher to perform consulting services for the corporation. In the current year, Flycatcher Corporation redeems all of Polly's shares in Flycatcher for property with a value of $1.4 million. What are the tax issues for Polly and Flycatcher?

   Issue ID

14. For purposes of the family attribution waiver in a complete termination redemption, what interest in the corporation, if any, can the redeeming shareholder possess during the 10-year postredemption period?

15. Unlike the other qualifying stock redemption provisions, a distribution can qualify as a partial liquidation even though the shareholder's ownership interest in the corporation remains unchanged. Discuss this statement.

16. Beige Corporation operates several trades or businesses. In the current year, Beige discontinues the operation of one of its businesses and distributes the assets of the discontinued business to its shareholders pursuant to a pro rata stock redemption. What are the tax issues for Beige Corporation and its shareholders?

   Issue ID

17. What are the requirements for a redemption to pay death taxes? What is the tax effect of such a redemption?

18. At the time of her death, Yolanda owned 17% of the outstanding stock of Violet Corporation (basis of $400,000, fair market value of $1.5 million). Yolanda's adjusted gross estate is $4 million, and the death taxes and funeral and administration expenses

total $750,000. Can Yolanda's estate qualify for a redemption to pay death taxes under § 303?

Issue ID

19. Angie and her daughter, Ann, who are the only shareholders of Bluebird Corporation, each paid $100,000 four years ago for their shares in Bluebird. Angie also owns 20% of the stock in Redbird Corporation. The Redbird stock is worth $500,000, and Angie's basis in the stock is $50,000. Angie died in the current year leaving all her property to her husband, Gary, but Ann wants to be the sole shareholder of Bluebird Corporation. Bluebird has assets worth $2 million (basis of $700,000) and E & P of $1 million. Angie's estate is worth approximately $4 million. Angie has made gifts during her lifetime to Ann. What are the tax issues for Angie's estate, Ann, and Bluebird?

Decision Making

20. Indigo Corporation desires to transfer cash of $50,000 or property worth $50,000 to one of its shareholders, Linda, in a redemption transaction that will be treated as a qualifying stock redemption. If Indigo distributes property, the corporation will choose between two assets that are each worth $50,000 and are no longer needed in its business: Property A (basis of $62,000) and Property B (basis of $36,000). Indigo is indifferent as to the form of the distribution, but Linda prefers a cash distribution. Considering the tax consequences to Indigo on the distribution to redeem Linda's shares, what should Indigo distribute?

Issue ID

21. Kackie Corporation (E & P of $1 million) is currently in negotiations to redeem stock from one or more of its shareholders. The form (i.e., cash and/or property) and amount of the distribution(s) to the shareholder(s) are key points of the negotiations. What are the tax issues for Kackie Corporation?

22. A sale of § 306 stock produces harsher tax consequences than those of a normal dividend distribution. Explain.

23. Sally owns a controlling interest (50% or more) in both Almond Corporation and Lark Corporation. In order to avoid the stock redemption provisions, Sally sells some of her shares of stock in Almond to Lark. Since the transaction is not structured as a stock redemption, Sally has succeeded in achieving sale or exchange treatment for the sale. Assess the validity of this statement.

24. When does a corporate liquidation exist for tax purposes?

25. Compare the tax treatment of liquidating (other than parent-subsidiary) and redemption distributions in terms of the following:
    a. Recognition of gain or loss by the shareholder.
    b. Basis of property received by the shareholder.
    c. Recognition of gain or loss by the distributing corporation.
    d. Effect on the distributing corporation's E & P.

26. What is "disqualified property" for purposes of the related-party loss limitation?

27. For the built-in loss limitation to apply, the property must have been acquired by the corporation as part of a plan whose principal purpose was to recognize a loss on the property by the liquidating corporation. Explain this requirement.

28. Explain the tax consequences to a shareholder of a corporation in the process of liquidation under the general rule of § 331. May a shareholder use the installment method to report gain on a complete liquidation?

29. Discuss the stock ownership requirements of the parent corporation for purposes of qualifying a subsidiary liquidation under § 332.

30. Rose Corporation stock is owned 85% by Pheasant Corporation and 15% by Crystal. In a liquidation subject to § 332, Rose distributes assets to Pheasant and Crystal in accordance with their ownership interests. Discuss the tax consequences of the liquidation for Rose, Pheasant, and Crystal.

31. In the context of a § 332 liquidation, does the nonrecognition rule apply to a transfer of property by a subsidiary to a parent in satisfaction of indebtedness? Explain.

32. Condor Corporation pays $1.4 million for 100% of the stock in Dove Corporation. Dove has a basis of $800,000 in its assets and E & P of $210,000. If Condor liquidates Dove and makes no special election, what are the tax consequences to Condor and to Dove?

33. What are the requirements for the application of § 338?

34. What are the tax consequences of a § 338 election to the parent and subsidiary corporations?

PROBLEMS

35. Teal Corporation, with E & P of $1 million, distributes property with a basis of $50,000 and a fair market value of $150,000 to Grace, a 15% shareholder.
    a. What are the tax consequences to Teal Corporation and to Grace if the distribution is a property dividend?
    b. What are the tax consequences in (a) if Grace is a corporation?
    c. What are the tax consequences to Teal Corporation and to Grace if the distribution is a qualifying stock redemption? Assume that half of Grace's stock (basis of $20,000) is redeemed in the transaction.
    d. What are the tax consequences in (c) if Grace is a corporation?
    e. If the parties involved could choose from among the preceding options, which would they choose and why?

    Decision Making

36. Julio is in the 33% tax bracket. He acquired 1,000 shares of stock in Gray Corporation seven years ago at a cost of $90 per share. In the current year, Julio received a payment of $300,000 from Gray Corporation in exchange for 400 of his shares in Gray. Gray has E & P of $1 million. What tax liability would Julio incur on the $300,000 payment in each of the following situations? Assume that Julio has no capital losses.
    a. The payment qualifies for stock redemption (i.e., sale or exchange) treatment.
    b. The payment does not qualify for stock redemption (i.e., sale or exchange treatment is not applicable) treatment.

37. How would your answer to Problem 36 differ if Julio were a corporate shareholder (in the 34% tax bracket) rather than an individual shareholder and the stock ownership in Gray Corporation represented a 15% interest?

38. Assume in Problem 36 that Julio has a capital loss carryover of $70,000 in the current tax year. Julio has no other capital gain transactions during the year. What amount of the capital loss may Julio deduct in the current year in the following situations?
    a. The $300,000 payment from Gray Corporation is a qualifying stock redemption for tax purposes (i.e., receives sale or exchange treatment).
    b. The $300,000 payment from Gray Corporation does not qualify as a stock redemption for tax purposes (i.e., does not receive sale or exchange treatment).
    c. If Julio had the flexibility to structure the transaction as described in either (a) or (b), which form would he choose?

    Decision Making

39. How would your answer to parts (a) and (b) of Problem 38 differ if Julio were a corporate shareholder (in the 34% tax bracket) rather than an individual shareholder and the stock ownership in Gray Corporation represented a 15% interest?

40. Cardinal Corporation has 1,000 shares of common stock outstanding. Hubert owns 400 of the shares, Hubert's father owns 100 shares, Hubert's uncle owns 200 shares, and Redbird Corporation owns 200 shares. Hubert owns 70% of the stock in Redbird Corporation.
    a. Applying the § 318 stock attribution rules, how many shares does Hubert own in Cardinal Corporation?
    b. Assume Hubert owns only 25% of Redbird Corporation. How many shares does Hubert own directly and indirectly in Cardinal Corporation?
    c. Assume the same facts as in (a) above, but in addition, Hubert owns 60% of Yellow Partnership. The partnership owns 100 shares in Cardinal Corporation. How many shares does Hubert own directly and indirectly in Cardinal Corporation?

41. Sheldon owns 600 shares of the 1,000 shares outstanding of Hawk Corporation (E & P of $500,000). The remaining stock in Hawk is owned by several shareholders unrelated to Sheldon. In the current year, Hawk Corporation redeems 75 shares of Sheldon's stock for $75,000. Sheldon had acquired all of his shares 10 years ago at a cost of $100

per share. What are the tax consequences to Sheldon and Hawk Corporation as a result of the stock redemption?

Communications

42. Stork Corporation (E & P of $800,000) has 1,000 shares of common stock outstanding. The shares are owned by the following individuals: Lana Johnson, 250 shares; Lori Johnson (Lana's mother), 250 shares; and Leo Jones (Lana's grandfather), 500 shares. Lana paid $150 per share for the Stork stock eight years ago. Lana is interested in reducing her stock ownership in Stork via a stock redemption for $1,000 per share, the fair market value of the stock. Stork Corporation would distribute cash for the entire redemption transaction. Lana has inquired as to the minimum number of shares that she would have to redeem in order to obtain favorable long-term capital gain treatment and the overall tax consequences of such a redemption to both her and Stork Corporation. Prepare a letter to Lana (1000 Main Street, Oldtown, MN 55166) and a memo for the file in which you explain your conclusions.

43. White Corporation (E & P of $300,000) has 5,000 shares of common stock outstanding. The shares are owned as follows: Belinda Markey, 2,000 shares; Lucian Markey (Belinda's son), 2,000 shares; and Dominic Markey (Belinda's brother), 1,000 shares. In the current year, White redeems all of Belinda's shares. Determine whether the redemption can qualify for sale or exchange treatment under the complete termination redemption rules in each of the following independent circumstances.
    a. Belinda remains as a director of White Corporation.
    b. Belinda resigns as a director of White Corporation; Lucian becomes a director of the corporation to replace Belinda.
    c. Four years after the redemption, Belinda acquires 500 shares in White Corporation as a gift from Dominic.

44. Roberta and Lori, sisters, own all the stock in Swan Corporation (E & P of $700,000). Each has a basis of $25,000 in her 500 shares. Roberta wants to sell her stock for $400,000, the fair market value, but she will continue to serve as controller for Swan Corporation after the sale. Lori would like to purchase Roberta's shares and, thus, become the sole shareholder in Swan, but Lori is short of funds. What are the tax consequences to Roberta, Lori, and Swan Corporation under the following circumstances?
    a. Swan Corporation distributes cash of $400,000 to Lori, and she uses the cash to purchase Roberta's shares.
    b. Swan Corporation redeems all of Roberta's shares for $400,000.

45. Stork Corporation was formed nine years ago to manufacture farm equipment. In addition, Stork began constructing manufactured homes seven years ago. Both businesses have been very profitable, and as a result, Stork has accumulated a sizable investment portfolio of stocks and bonds (fair market value of $600,000, basis of $250,000). Stork Corporation has 2,000 shares of common stock outstanding. Elaine, an individual, owns 1,000 shares (basis of $100,000), and Paisley Corporation owns 1,000 shares (basis of $100,000). For each of the following independent transactions, determine the tax consequences to Stork Corporation, Elaine, and Paisley Corporation. Assume that Stork has E & P of $2 million at the time of each distribution.
    a. The manufactured home business is completely destroyed by fire, and Stork Corporation collects $1.2 million of insurance proceeds. Stork had a basis of $700,000 in the assets of the business. Stork decides to discontinue the business and distributes the insurance proceeds equally to Elaine and Paisley Corporation in redemption of 200 shares of stock from each shareholder.
    b. Stork distributes the assets of the investment portfolio in kind equally to Elaine and Paisley Corporation in redemption of 100 shares of stock from each shareholder.

46. Edward died owning 20% of the total Red Corporation shares outstanding (basis of $600,000), and the Red stock is included in his estate at its date of death value of $1 million. Edward's adjusted gross estate is $2.5 million, and the death taxes and funeral and administration expenses total $500,000. Red Corporation (E & P of $6 million) distributes land (fair market value of $500,000, basis of $340,000) in redemption of one-half of the estate's stock in the corporation. The estate sells the land five months later for $520,000. What are the tax consequences to Red Corporation and to the estate as a result of the redemption and sale?

47. The gross estate of Bridgett, decedent, includes stock of Crane Corporation (E & P of $1 million) and Eagle Corporation (E & P of $700,000) valued at $600,000 and $300,000, respectively. At the time of her death, Bridgett owned 33% of the Crane stock outstanding and 22% of the Eagle stock outstanding. Bridgett had a basis of $97,000 in the Crane stock and $41,000 in the Eagle stock. Bridgett's adjusted gross estate is $2.4 million, and the death taxes and funeral and administration expenses total $300,000. What are the tax consequences to Bridgett's estate if Eagle Corporation redeems all of the Eagle Corporation stock for $300,000?

48. Tan Corporation (E & P of $700,000) has 1,000 shares of stock outstanding owned by two unrelated individuals, Jacob (600 shares) and Julie (400 shares). Both shareholders paid $75 per share for the stock six years ago. In the current year, Tan Corporation redeems 300 shares of Jacob's stock for $320,000.
    a. What are the tax consequences of the stock redemption to Jacob?
    b. What are the tax consequences of the stock redemption to Tan Corporation?

49. Crane Corporation has 4,000 shares of stock outstanding. It redeems 500 shares for $200,000 when it has paid-in capital of $300,000 and E & P of $1.3 million. The redemption qualifies for sale or exchange treatment for the shareholder. Crane incurred $5,000 of accounting and legal fees in connection with the redemption transaction. What is the effect of the distribution on Crane Corporation's E & P? Also, what is the proper tax treatment of the redemption expenditures? Prepare a letter to the president of Crane Corporation (506 Wall Street, Winona, MN 55987) and a memo for the file in which you explain your conclusions.

Communications

50. Ahmad and Cora are the sole shareholders of Blue Corporation. Ahmad and Cora each have a basis of $40,000 in their 500 shares of Blue common stock. When its E & P was $500,000, Blue Corporation issued a preferred stock dividend on the common shares of Ahmad and Cora, giving each 200 shares of preferred stock with a par value of $30 per share. Fair market value of one share of common was $150, and fair market value of one share of preferred was $75.
    a. What are the tax consequences of the distribution to Ahmad and Cora?
    b. What are the tax consequences to Ahmad if he later sells his preferred stock to Adam for $20,000? Adam is not related to Ahmad.
    c. What are the tax consequences if, instead of Ahmad selling the preferred stock to Adam, Blue Corporation redeems the stock from Ahmad for $20,000? Assume Blue's E & P at the time of the redemption is $650,000.

51. Bob owns 1,000 shares of stock in Goose Corporation and 500 shares of stock in Heron Corporation, representing a 100% interest in each corporation. Bob sells 300 shares of Goose stock to Heron Corporation for $80,000. The Goose stock was acquired 10 years ago; the tax basis to Bob of these 300 shares is $10,000. On the date of sale, Goose Corporation and Heron Corporation have E & P of $200,000 and $250,000, respectively. What are the tax consequences of this transaction?

52. The stock of Hawk Corporation is owned equally by three sisters, Michele, Melanie, and Miranda. Hawk owns land (basis of $300,000, fair market value of $280,000) that it has held for investment for eight years. When Michele's basis in her stock is $310,000, Hawk distributes the land to her in exchange for all of her shares. What are the tax consequences for both Hawk and Michele if the distribution is:
    a. A qualifying stock redemption?
    b. A liquidating distribution?

53. Pursuant to a complete liquidation, Oriole Corporation distributes to its shareholders land held for three years as an investment (adjusted basis of $400,000, fair market value of $600,000). The land is subject to a liability of $300,000.
    a. What are the tax consequences to Oriole Corporation on the distribution of the land?
    b. If the land is, instead, subject to a liability of $700,000, what are the tax consequences to Oriole on the distribution?

54. Gray Corporation acquired land in a § 351 transaction in 2006. At that time, the land had a basis of $400,000 and a fair market value of $450,000. Gray has two equal shareholders, Arnold and Beatrice, who are brother and sister. Gray adopts a plan of liquidation in 2008. During that year and pursuant to the liquidation, the corporation distributes the land proportionately to Arnold and Beatrice. The fair market value of

the land at the time of the distribution is $350,000. What amount of loss may Gray Corporation recognize on the 2008 liquidating distribution of the land?

55. On April 12, 2007, Crow Corporation acquired land and equipment in a § 351 transaction. At that time, the land had a basis of $400,000 and a fair market value of $370,000, and the equipment had a basis of $20,000 and a fair market value of $60,000. The land and equipment were transferred to Crow Corporation for use as security for a loan the corporation was in the process of obtaining from a local bank. The bank required the additional capital investment as a condition for making the loan. Crow Corporation adopted a plan of liquidation on October 3, 2008. On December 3, 2008, Crow Corporation distributes the land to Ali, a 35% shareholder. On the date of the distribution, the land had a fair market value of only $150,000. What amount of loss may Crow Corporation recognize on the distribution of the land?

56. On January 5, 2007, Grackle Corporation acquired equipment as a contribution to capital. At that time, the equipment had an adjusted basis of $310,000 and a fair market value of $230,000. This was the only property transferred to Grackle at that time. On July 24, 2008, Grackle Corporation adopted a plan of liquidation. On November 12, 2008, Grackle sold the equipment to Chris, an unrelated party, for its current fair market value of $90,000. Grackle Corporation never used the equipment for any business purpose during the time it owned the equipment. What amount of loss may Grackle Corporation recognize on the sale of the equipment?

Decision Making

57. Pink Corporation acquired land and securities in a § 351 tax-free exchange in 2007. On the date of the transfer, the land had a basis of $1.7 million and a fair market value of $1.9 million, and the securities had a basis of $50,000 and a fair market value of $300,000. Pink Corporation has two shareholders, Maria and Paul, unrelated individuals. Maria owns 70% of the stock in Pink Corporation, and Paul owns 30%. The corporation adopts a plan of liquidation in 2008. On this date, the value of the land has decreased to $700,000. What is the effect of each of the following on Pink Corporation? Which option should be selected?
    a. Distribute all the land to Maria.
    b. Distribute all the land to Paul.
    c. Distribute 70% of the land to Maria and 30% to Paul.
    d. Distribute 50% of the land to Maria and 50% to Paul.
    e. Sell the land and distribute the proceeds of $700,000 proportionately to Maria and to Paul.

Decision Making

58. Assume in Problem 57 that the land had a fair market value of $1.5 million on the date of its transfer to Pink Corporation. On the date of the liquidation, the land's fair market value has decreased to $700,000. How would your answer to Problem 57 change if:
    a. All the land is distributed to Maria?
    b. All the land is distributed to Paul?
    c. The land is distributed 70% to Maria and 30% to Paul?
    d. The land is distributed 50% to Maria and 50% to Paul?
    e. The land is sold and the proceeds of $700,000 are distributed proportionately to Maria and to Paul?

59. After a plan of complete liquidation has been adopted, Purple Corporation sells its only asset, land, to Rex (an unrelated party) for $500,000. Under the terms of the sale, Purple receives cash of $100,000 and Rex's note in the amount of $400,000. The note is payable over five years ($80,000 per year) and carries an appropriate rate of interest. Immediately after the sale, Purple distributes the cash and note to Helen, the sole shareholder of Purple Corporation. Helen has a basis of $50,000 in the Purple stock. What are the tax results to Helen if she wishes to defer as much gain as possible on the transaction? Assume the installment note possesses a value equal to its face amount.

60. The stock of Magenta Corporation is owned by Fuchsia Corporation (95%) and Marta (5%). Magenta is liquidated on September 5, 2008, pursuant to a plan of liquidation adopted earlier in the same year. In the liquidation, Magenta distributes various assets worth $2,375,000 (basis of $1.2 million) to Fuchsia (basis of $1.6 million in Magenta stock) and a parcel of land worth $125,000 (basis of $105,000) to Marta (basis of $40,000 in Magenta stock). Assuming the § 338 election is not made, what are the tax consequences of the liquidation to Magenta, Fuchsia, and Marta?

61. Orange Corporation purchased bonds (basis of $95,000) of its wholly owned subsidiary, Green Corporation, at a discount. Upon liquidation of Green pursuant to § 332, Orange receives payment in the form of land worth $100,000, the face amount of the bonds. Green had a basis of $70,000 in the land. What are the tax consequences of this land transfer to Green Corporation and to Orange Corporation?

62. At the time of its liquidation under § 332, Cardinal Corporation (E & P of $420,000) had the following assets and liabilities: cash ($175,000); marketable securities (fair market value of $310,000, basis of $150,000); unimproved land (fair market value of $510,000, basis of $400,000); unsecured note payable ($50,000); and mortgage on the unimproved land ($350,000). Cardinal also had a general business credit carryover of $25,000. Wren Corporation acquired all the stock of Cardinal seven years ago for $390,000.
    a. How much gain (or loss) will Cardinal Corporation recognize upon the liquidating distribution of its assets and liabilities to Wren Corporation?
    b. How much gain (or loss) will Wren Corporation recognize in the liquidation of Cardinal?
    c. What basis will Wren have in the marketable securities and unimproved land it receives in the liquidation?
    d. What happens to Cardinal's E & P and general business credit carryover?

63. Quail Corporation paid $5.4 million for all the stock of Sparrow Corporation 10 years ago. Sparrow Corporation's balance sheet currently reflects the following fair market values:

Communications

Assets		Liabilities and Shareholder's Equity	
Cash	$ 135,000	Accounts payable	$ 5,400,000
Inventory	405,000	Common stock	5,400,000
Machinery	270,000	Deficit	(7,560,000)
Equipment	1,080,000		
Land	1,350,000		
	$3,240,000		$ 3,240,000

What are the tax consequences to Quail Corporation if it liquidates Sparrow Corporation? Prepare a letter to your client Quail Corporation (1010 Cypress Lane, Community, MN 55166) and a memo for the file in which you explain your conclusions.

64. Falcon Corporation is owned 90% by Canary Corporation. The parent is contemplating a liquidation of Falcon Corporation and the acquisition of its assets. Canary Corporation purchased the Falcon stock from Falcon's two individual shareholders a month ago on January 3, 2008, for $400,000. The financial statements of Falcon Corporation as of January 3, 2008, reflect the following:

	Basis to Falcon Corporation	Fair Market Value
	Assets	
Cash	$ 40,000	$ 40,000
Inventory	80,000	60,000
Accounts receivable	160,000	100,000
Equipment	400,000	320,000
Land	520,000	280,000
	$ 1,200,000	$ 800,000
	Liabilities and Shareholders' Equity	
Accounts payable	$ 120,000	$ 120,000
Mortgages payable	200,000	200,000
Common stock	1,000,000	480,000
Retained earnings	(120,000)	
	$ 1,200,000	$ 800,000

The management of Canary Corporation asks your advice on the feasibility of an election under § 338.

a. Can Canary Corporation make a § 338 election?
b. Assuming Canary can make a § 338 election, is such an election feasible?

RESEARCH PROBLEMS

Communications

Note: Solutions to Research Problems can be prepared by using the **RIA Checkpoint**® **Student Edition** online research product, which is available to accompany this text. It is also possible to prepare solutions to the Research Problems by using tax research materials found in a standard tax library.

Research Problem 1.   Tanya Anderson (4100 E. 6th Street, Tucson, AZ 85711) owns 50% of the common stock of Lavender Corporation. Joseph Hansen, an individual unrelated to Tanya, owns the remaining shares in Lavender. Both shareholders are active in the management of the corporation. Currently, the shareholders do not have an agreement limiting the disposition of either individual's stock interest in Lavender. The two are contemplating a buy-sell agreement that would require a retired or deceased shareholder to sell his or her shares to the other shareholder ("continuing shareholder") at a price fixed by the agreement. The goal is to provide sole ownership of Lavender to the continuing shareholder, but both shareholders have expressed concerns about being able to finance the stock purchase required under the agreement. Lavender Corporation (E & P of $1 million) generates significant profits and positive cash flow annually, and its financial position is excellent. Tanya has contacted you regarding the best way to structure the buy-sell agreement given the shareholders' goals and concerns. Prepare a letter to Tanya and a memo for the file documenting your recommendations.

Research Problem 2.   Samantha Jamison died in February 2008. At the time of her death, Samantha owned 100% of the outstanding stock of Bluebird Corporation (basis of $400,000) and 60% of the outstanding stock of Eagle Corporation (basis of $150,000). Samantha's adjusted gross estate is $8 million, and the death taxes and funeral and administration expenses of the estate total $1.5 million. The gross estate includes the stock of Bluebird and Eagle Corporations valued at the date of death at $3 million and $1 million, respectively. In June 2008, Eagle Corporation (E & P of $800,000) was completely liquidated, and Samantha's estate received a cash distribution of $1 million for the fair market value of the Eagle stock surrendered. In August 2008, Bluebird Corporation (E & P of $2 million) redeemed one-half of the estate's shares in the corporation for the stock's fair market value of $1.5 million. The alternate valuation date is not elected by the estate. What is the proper tax treatment by the estate for the Eagle and Bluebird stock dispositions?

Research Problem 3.   Bethany Padilla formed Green Corporation in 1980, and under her tenure as president and CEO, the corporation was very profitable. To facilitate a transition to a younger management team, Padilla voluntarily relinquished her position as Green's president in 1998. After several disagreements with the new management, Padilla was removed as CEO by the corporation's board of directors in 2000. Padilla remained a director, an employee, and a significant (but not majority) shareholder of Green Corporation; as a result, she continued to exert influence on management decisions. Conflicts between Padilla and other directors arose, and in 2001, the corporation and Padilla entered into an employment contract that provided her with a $150,000 annual salary but no managerial authority. Padilla filed several lawsuits relating to her dismissal as CEO and other claims asserted against Green Corporation. The corporation was concerned about the potential liability associated with these legal claims, as well as the time and cost of defending against them. In 2006, the board of directors entered into a $27 million settlement agreement with Padilla that resulted in the release of all her litigation and employment claims against the corporation (valued at $2 million) and the redemption of all her Green Corporation stock (valued at $25 million). The corporation deducted the $2 million portion of the settlement related to the release of the litigation and employment claims as a § 162(a) trade or business expense. Upon an audit of Green Corporation's 2006 tax return, the IRS disallowed the $2 million deduction, asserting that the entire settlement was incurred in connection with the stock redemption and, therefore, was nondeductible under § 162(k). Determine whether the $2 million is deductible under § 162(a).

Research Problem 4. Bluebonnet Corporation owns 100% of the common stock (basis of $750,000) and preferred stock (basis of $500,000) of Lavender Corporation (E & P of $75,000). Bluebonnet acquired both the common and the preferred stock seven years ago. The preferred stock has a liquidation preference of $200,000. On October 29, 2008, Lavender files a valid Form 8832, Entity Classification Election, changing its classification from a corporation to a disregarded entity for Federal tax purposes effective as of January 1, 2009. On December 31, 2008, Lavender Corporation has assets with a fair market value of $1 million and liabilities of $900,000. Both Lavender and Bluebonnet are calendar year taxpayers. What, if any, are the tax consequences of the Form 8832 election?

Use the tax resources of the Internet to address the following questions. Do not restrict your search to the World Wide Web, but include a review of newsgroups and general reference materials, practitioner sites and resources, primary sources of the tax law, chat rooms and discussion groups, and other opportunities.

Internet
Activity

Research Problem 5. Publicly traded corporations reacquire their own shares for several reasons. Through the use of a tender offer, a corporation can purchase a substantial percentage of the company's stock. Using the Internet as your sole research source, prepare an outline discussing (1) reasons why publicly traded corporations reacquire their own shares and (2) how the tender offer process works for both corporations and shareholders.

Communications

Research Problem 6. Browse the Internet sites of several public accounting firms and find discussions comparing stock purchases with asset purchases when acquiring a business. Based solely on your findings, prepare an outline of the advantages and disadvantages of each form of acquisition.

Communications

7

Corporations: Reorganizations

LEARNING OBJECTIVES

After completing Chapter 7, you should be able to:

LO.1
Understand the general requirements of corporate reorganizations.

LO.2
Determine the tax consequences of a corporate reorganization.

LO.3
Explain the statutory requirements for the different types of reorganizations.

LO.4
Delineate the judicial and administrative conditions for a nontaxable corporate reorganization.

LO.5
Apply the rules pertaining to the carryover of tax attributes in a corporate reorganization.

LO.6
Recognize the role of IRS letter rulings in protecting tax-free treatment for reorganizations.

LO.7
Structure corporate reorganizations to obtain the desired tax consequences.

OUTLINE

One tenet of U.S. tax policy is to encourage business development. To this end, the tax laws allow entities to form without taxation, assuming certain requirements are met. As an extension of this concept, corporate restructurings are also favored with tax-free treatment. Corporations may engage in a variety of acquisitions, combinations, consolidations, and divisions tax-free, as long as the "reorganization" requirements in the Code are met.

Mergers and acquisitions are a popular method of increasing the economic vitality of corporate businesses. The restructuring frenzy peaked in 1999–2000 with more than 20,000 major deals (values greater than $5 million) amounting to almost $2.7 trillion in value. Nine of the largest mergers and acquisitions in the last ten years occurred in the 1998–2000 period (see Exhibit 7–1). Although merger and acquisition activity slowed dramatically after 2000 with the downturn in the U.S. economy and stock market, in recent years the number and dollar values of mergers and acquisitions have been increasing, and the 2006 level surpassed the prior peak in 2000. A new record was set in 2007, and only time will tell what new heights will be reached in the years to come.

Traditionally, when a corporation wanted to dispose of a division, it tried to negotiate a tax-free acquisition by another corporation. A restructuring that is becoming popular with mammoth publicly traded corporations is to distribute these unwanted business units to their shareholders in tax-free transactions. Several of the largest restructuring deals of 2007 were spin-offs. For example, Altria Group distributed its 89 percent ownership of Kraft Foods to its shareholders. This qualifies as one of the largest restructurings since 1998 (see Exhibit 7–1). Other noteworthy spin-offs include Tyco's distribution of its health care (Covidien, Ltd) and electronics (Tyco Electronics, Ltd) businesses, Morgan Stanley's divestiture of its Discover credit card business, Beko Corporation's separation of its newspaper division from its television stations, and SaraLee Corporation's spin-off of Hansbrands, Inc., which is now a separate, publicly traded company.

Another type of restructuring has also seen a dramatic increase in the past few years—mega-bankruptcies. The home mortgage industry has been particularly hard hit as subprime mortgages have seen a substantial increase in homeowner defaults. New Century Financial—the largest independent U.S. lender to individuals with low credit ratings—became a casualty of this lending crisis. Other lenders collapsing into bankruptcy included First Magnus Mortgage, American Home Mortgage, HomeBanc Corporation, NetBank, and People's Choice Financial, to name just a few. New Century makes the list of the largest bankruptcies that have occurred since 1987. Of the mega-bankruptcies listed in Exhibit 7–2, seven

EXHIBIT 7–1   **The Largest Corporate Restructurings in the United States, 1998–2007**

Companies	Year Announced	Total Amount Involved (in $ Billions)
Pfizer and Warner-Lambert	1999	$116.7
AOL and Time Warner	2000	101.0
Exxon and Mobil	1998	81.4
SBC Communications and Ameritech	1998	75.2
BellSouth and AT&T	2006	66.7
Vodafone and AirTouch	1999	62.7
Bell Atlantic and GTE	1998	60.5
Pfizer and Pharmacia	2002	58.3
Procter & Gamble and Gillette	2005	57.9
JPMorgan Chase and Bank One	2004	57.6
British Petroleum and Amoco	1998	56.5
AT&T and Tele-Communications	1998	52.5
Viacom and CBS	1999	48.8
Bank of America and FleetBoston	2003	47.8
Altria and Kraft Foods (spin-off)	2007	46.0

Source: *Mergerstat.com.*

EXHIBIT 7–2   **The Largest Bankruptcies in the United States, 1987–2007**

Company	Year	Total Assets (in $ Billions)
WorldCom, Inc.	2002	$103.9
Enron Corp.	2001	65.5
Conseco	2002	61.4
Pacific Gas and Electric Co.	2001	36.1
Texaco, Inc.	1987	34.9
Financial Corp. of America	1988	33.8
Global Crossing, Ltd.	2002	30.2
Calpine Corp.	2005	27.2
New Century Financial Corp.	2007	26.1
UAL Corp.	2002	25.2
Delta Air Lines	2005	21.8
Adelphia Communications	2002	21.5

Sources: *BankruptcyData.com; New Generation Research, Inc., Boston, Mass.*

occurred in 2001–2002, more than in any other period. Many of these bankruptcies were fueled by the downturn in the economy and financial statement misstatements.

Many mergers are the result of a mutual agreement between the companies involved. Indeed, the current trend is toward friendly mergers, such as Procter & Gamble's acquisition of Gillette, Google's acquisition of YouTube for $1.65 billion

| **TAX** *in the News* | **HISTORICAL PERSPECTIVE ON MERGERS AND ACQUISITIONS** |

Merger and acquisition (M&A) transactions have been an integral part of U.S. business since the 1800s. Historically, M&A activity has experienced peaks and valleys. The following are the peak activity periods.

- **1890–1905.** M&A frenzy involving small firms in similar trades led to a substantial decrease in competition in some industries. The 1890 Sherman Antitrust Act may have started this frenzy because the Act outlawed collusion but not mergers.
- **1915–1929.** The mid-size firms created in the M&A frenzy between 1890 and 1905 now began to merge, leading to oligopolies in which a few large firms dominated an industry. The stock market crash of 1929 put the brakes on the M&A activity.
- **1945–1950.** After World War II, friendly deals in which large corporations acquired privately held companies in similar industries became the M&A fashion.
- **1955–1969.** This era saw the birth of the conglomerate merger. Whereas prior M&A activity had focused on acquisitions in similar industries, now firms were acquiring similar-size businesses in completely unrelated industries. The idea was that diversification would

reduce business risk. This period experienced the longest and most active sustained peak in M&A activity.
- **1976–1979.** When diversification turned out to be less effective than expected, corporations began divesting their unprofitable and unrelated businesses. At the same time, M&As were occurring between huge corporations. Although the number of M&A transactions decreased, the dollar values of the transactions increased.
- **1984–1989.** Mega-mergers, leveraged buyouts, and hostile takeovers became the new M&A strategies. The junk bond market helped finance these deals.
- **1996–2000.** Deregulation of industries and globalization fueled this M&A frenzy. Mega-merger consolidations increased the resulting corporations' market share and created an elite class of market leaders. The 1999–2000 period saw both the largest number of deals and the highest dollar values for M&A transactions. The collapse of the dotcoms in 2001 and numerous corporate scandals burst the M&A bubble, slowing M&A activity to pre-1996 levels.

Source: *Adapted from "Historical Merger and Acquisition Activity,"* Mergerstat Review, *2006.*

in stock, and AT&T's stock-for-stock acquisition of BellSouth, which was approved by 98 percent of the AT&T shares voting on the transaction and 97 percent of the BellSouth shares. Nevertheless, hostile tender offers do occur and are on the rise. The dollar amount of hostile bids in 2005 was just shy of the 2001 level of $110 billion, but was not even close to the all-time record of $665 billion in 1999. The stigma of hostile takeovers is fading—a trend reflected in new, softer terminology. "Hostile" takeover attempts are now known as "unsolicited" or "unilateral" bids, and the term "corporate raiders" has been sanitized to "activists." Corporations, small or large, must be alert to the possibilities of unwanted bids for their company, whether from a competitor or a conglomerate wanting to diversify.

Given the magnitude of the dollar amounts involved in most reorganizations, tax planning strategies play an important role in corporate restructurings. The taxable gain for shareholders is likely to be treated as either a dividend or a capital gain. For individual shareholders, both of these are subject to a maximum tax rate of 15 percent. Corporate shareholders would be allowed a dividends received deduction if the gains are categorized as a dividend. However, since corporations receive no tax rate reduction for capital gains, corporate shareholders and the corporations involved in the restructuring would be taxed at their highest marginal rate on any gains classified as capital. Fortunately, careful planning can reduce or totally eliminate the tax possibilities for both the corporations and their shareholders. Consequently, tax law often dictates the form of the restructuring.

Courts originally concluded that even minor changes in a corporation's structure would produce taxable gains for the shareholders involved.[1] Congress, however, determined that businesses should be allowed to make necessary capital

---

[1]*U.S. v. Phellis*, 1 USTC ¶54, 3 AFTR 3123, 42 S.Ct. 63 (USSC, 1921).

adjustments without being subject to taxation.[2] The theory for nonrecognition in certain corporate restructurings or "reorganizations" is similar to that underlying § 351 treatment and like-kind exchanges. As the Regulations state:

> the new property is substantially a continuation of the old investment . . . and, in the case of reorganizations, . . . the new enterprise, the new corporate structure, and the new property are substantially continuations of the old.[3]

Reorganizations—In General

Although the term **reorganization** is commonly associated with a corporation in financial difficulty, for tax purposes the term refers to any corporate restructuring that may be tax-free under § 368. To qualify as a tax-free reorganization, a corporate restructuring transaction must meet not only the specific requirements of § 368 but also several general requirements. These requirements include the following.

1. There must be a *plan of reorganization*.
2. The reorganization must meet the *continuity of interest* and the *continuity of business enterprise* tests provided in the Regulations.
3. The restructuring must meet the judicial doctrine of having a *sound business purpose*.
4. The court-imposed *step transaction* doctrine should not apply to the reorganization.

All of these concepts are discussed in this chapter. The initial and most important consideration, however, is whether the reorganization qualifies for nonrecognition status under § 368.

Summary of the Different Types of Reorganizations

Section 368(a) specifies seven corporate restructurings or *reorganizations* that will qualify as nontaxable exchanges. If the transaction fails to qualify as a reorganization, it will not receive the special tax-favored treatment. Therefore, a corporation considering a business reorganization must determine in advance if the proposed transaction specifically falls within one of these seven types. In situations involving substantial tax dollars, the parties should obtain a letter ruling from the IRS verifying that the proposed transaction qualifies as a tax-free reorganization under § 368.

The Code states, in § 368(a)(1), that the term *reorganization* applies to any of the following.

A. A statutory merger or consolidation.
B. The acquisition by a corporation of another using solely stock of each corporation (**voting-stock-for-stock exchange**).
C. The acquisition by a corporation of substantially all of the property of another corporation in exchange for voting stock (stock-for-asset exchange).
D. The transfer of all or part of a corporation's assets to another corporation when the original corporation's shareholders are in control of the new corporation immediately after the transfer (divisive exchange, also known as a spin-off, split-off, or split-up).
E. A recapitalization.
F. A mere change in identity, form, or place of organization.
G. A transfer by a corporation of all or a part of its assets to another corporation in a bankruptcy or receivership proceeding.

These seven types of tax-free reorganizations typically are designated by their identifying letters: "Type A," "Type B," "Type C," and so on. Each will be described in more detail later in the chapter.

[2]Reg. § 1.368–1(b). See S.Rept. No. 275, 67th Cong., 1st Sess. (1921), at 1939–1 C.B. 181.

[3]Reg. § 1.1002–1(c).

CONCEPT SUMMARY $7-1$

Gain and Basis Rules for Nontaxable Exchanges

(1) Realized Gain/Loss	(2) Recognized Gain (Not Loss)	(3) Postponed Gain/Loss	(4) Basis of New Asset

Amount realized
– Adjusted basis of
   asset surrendered
	Lesser of boot
	   received or
	   gain realized
		Gain/loss realized (column 1)
		– Gain recognized (column 2)
			FMV of asset (stock) received
			– Postponed gain (column 3) or
			+ Postponed loss (column 3)

Gain/loss realized	Gain recognized	Gain/loss postponed	Adjusted basis in new asset (stock)

LO.2

Determine the tax consequences of a corporate reorganization.

Summary of Tax Consequences in a Tax-Free Reorganization

The tax treatment for the parties involved in a tax-free reorganization almost exactly parallels the treatment under the like-kind exchange provisions of § 1031. In the simplest like-kind exchange, neither gain nor loss is recognized on the exchange of "like-kind" property. When "boot" (defined as non-like-kind property) is involved, gain may be recognized. The four-column template of Concept Summary 7–1 can be used to compute the amount of gain recognized and the adjusted basis in the new asset received in the like-kind exchange.

Unfortunately, the like-kind exchange provisions do not apply to the exchange of stock or securities.[4] Therefore, the general rule is that when an investor exchanges stock in one corporation for stock in another, the exchange is a taxable transaction. If the transaction qualifies as a reorganization under § 368, however, the exchange will be nontaxable. Thus, a § 368 reorganization, in substance, is similar to a nontaxable exchange of like-kind property, and the four-column template of Concept Summary 7–1 is useful for reorganizations as well.

EXAMPLE 1

José holds 1,000 shares of Lotus stock that he purchased for $10,000 several years ago. In a merger of Lotus into Blossom, José exchanges his 1,000 Lotus shares for 1,000 Blossom shares. Both investments are valued at $18 per share. José's realized gain on the exchange is $8,000 [($18 per share × 1,000 shares) − $10,000 basis]. Assuming this exchange qualifies for tax-free treatment under § 368, José's recognized gain is zero. Since his postponed gain is $8,000, José's basis in his new stock is $10,000 [$18,000 (fair market value of new stock) − $8,000 postponed gain]. The exchange of José's stock has no tax consequences for Lotus or Blossom. ■

Gain or Loss. Corporations meeting the § 368 requirements do not recognize gain or loss on a restructuring. There are exceptions to the nonrecognition rule, however. If the acquiring corporation transfers property to the target corporation along with its stock and securities, gain, but not loss, may be recognized. The target may also recognize gain, but not loss, when it fails to distribute the *other property* it receives in the restructuring or distributes its own appreciated property to its shareholders. *Other property* in this case is defined as anything received other than stock or securities and, thus, is treated as boot.[5]

EXAMPLE 2

In a qualifying reorganization, Acquiring Corporation exchanges $80,000 of stock and land with a $20,000 fair market value and a $15,000 basis for all of the assets of Target

---

[4]§ 1031(a)(2)(B). [5]§§ 361(a) and (b).

TAX *in the News*   SARBANES-OXLEY STRENGTHENS THE M&A INDUSTRY

An unintended consequence of the 2002 Sarbanes-Oxley Act (SOX) is the continued delisting of small companies from the national stock markets. The major reason for this behavior by small-capitalization companies may be the added costs of SOX-related compliance. For firms with market capitalization under $1 billion, the costs of SOX compliance in terms of audit fees, legal fees, board compensation, and lost productivity have risen by more than $2.5 million (223 percent), on average, from the pre-SOX amounts. This is a significant burden that many small firms cannot afford.

For firms that cannot afford the SOX compliance burden, a more inviting long-term option than "going dark" is to merge with, or be acquired by, a larger company. In some cases, private firms seeking to enter the public sector are fil-

ing for an initial public offering (IPO) as a signal that they are available for a merger or acquisition. The cost of "going public" has doubled due to SOX. Thus, being acquired provides a quicker and less expensive route to increased capitalization. The SOX requirements are expected to bolster the M&A industry well into the future, as even mid-size companies become overwhelmed by the compliance costs and seek to merge to reduce the burden.

SOX will continue to have measurable effects on corporate business decisions and the accounting profession. While the financial costs stemming from SOX compliance are well documented, the long-term effects of the changes to corporate governance and the financial markets are not yet clear.

Sources: *Adapted from Colleen Marie O' Conner, "Sarbanes-Oxley: Frying the Small Fry,"* Investment Dealers Digest, *June 27, 2005; and Mary Calegari and Howard Turetsky, "Selling to Escape Compliance Costs,"* Mergers and Acquisitions Journal, *September 1, 2006.*

Corporation. Target's assets have a $100,000 fair market value and a $60,000 basis. Due to the *other property* (land) it used in the transfer, Acquiring recognizes a $5,000 gain ($20,000 − $15,000) on the reorganization. If Target distributes the land to its shareholders, it does not recognize gain. If Target retains the land, however, it recognizes gain to the extent of the *other property* received, $20,000. ∎

Generally, the shareholders of corporations involved in a tax-free reorganization do not recognize gain or loss when exchanging their stock unless they receive cash or other property in addition to stock. The cash or other property is considered boot, and the gain recognized by the stockholder is the lesser of the boot received or the realized gain. This is analogous to the treatment of boot in a like-kind exchange.

Kalla, the sole shareholder of Target Corporation in Example 2, has a $70,000 basis in her stock. She exchanges her Target stock for the $80,000 of Acquiring stock plus the land ($20,000) transferred by Acquiring to Target. Kalla has a $30,000 realized gain ($80,000 of stock + $20,000 of land − $70,000 basis in stock given up). Receiving the land (boot) causes her to recognize a $20,000 gain. ∎

E X A M P L E 3

Once the gain is recognized, its character must be determined. The following are the possibilities for gain characterization.

- Dividend to the extent of the shareholder's proportionate share of corporate earnings and profits (E & P). The remaining gain is generally capital gain.
  - The distinction between dividends and long-term capital gain may be less critical now that the tax rate for noncorporate investors is the same for both. However, this distinction is still important when the taxpayer has capital losses to offset or when the capital gain would be classified as short term and therefore not subject to the special tax rates.
- If the requirements of § 302(b) can be met, the transaction will qualify for stock redemption treatment (see Chapter 6).
  - Gains from qualifying stock redemptions are treated as capital gains.

- In computing the shareholder's ownership reduction, shares actually received in the acquiring corporation are compared with the number of shares the shareholder would have received if solely the acquiring corporation's stock had been distributed in the reorganization.[6]

ETHICAL and EQUITABLE *Considerations*

COOL DAYS AND NIGHT FEVERS

CoolDay, a publicly traded corporation, has three plants in Arizona that manufacture commercial air-conditioning systems. The systems have been quite successful in the Southwest because they use 25 percent less energy than conventional air-conditioning systems. Wanting to expand its business into the Northwest, CoolDay is interested in acquiring a manufacturer of home heating units.

After several months of searching, CoolDay identifies a heater manufacturer, Night Fever, that appears to be a promising complement to CoolDay's business line. Night Fever also seems to be in need of some restructuring since it has more production capacity than it currently is using. The problem seems to be with middle management rather than the production line. Night Fever feels that a merger with CoolDay could help with this problem because CoolDay managers would come in to run its plants in Oregon and Colorado.

The acquisition would be structured as a "Type B" reorganization, with Night Fever becoming a subsidiary of CoolDay. Achieving an exchange of CoolDay stock for Night Fever stock will be easy because Night Fever is a closely held corporation with the officers and chief executives holding all of its stock.

The accountants, attorneys, and financial analysts hired as consultants by CoolDay all agree that this merger has great potential. By reducing the middle-management positions by 50 percent due to redundancy, the new company could save millions of dollars in payroll. Since the stock owned by Night Fever's officers and executives will triple in value, several of them will retire after the merger. All remaining officers and executives will be guaranteed their positions for at least five years. The line workers in the manufacturing plants will not be in jeopardy of losing their jobs, although those at the Colorado plant will be asked to relocate to Oregon at their own expense. Although the Colorado plant covers its costs, it is not as profitable as the Oregon plants, so the accountants suggest closing down in Colorado.

What ethical issues does CoolDay's acquisition of Night Fever present?

EXAMPLE 4

Sam acquired a 30% interest in Target five years ago for $80,000. He exchanges his Target stock for $25,000 cash and stock in Acquiring worth $125,000. At the time of the reorganization, Target's E & P is $50,000. Sam has a $70,000 realized gain ($150,000 cash and stock received − $80,000 Target stock basis) and a $25,000 recognized gain (cash boot received). The first $15,000 ($50,000 Target E & P × 30%) is taxable as a dividend, and the remaining $10,000 is treated as capital gain. Both are taxed at a maximum rate of 15%.

Suppose instead that Sam received 10% of the Acquiring stock with a $100,000 fair market value and $50,000 cash. If Sam had received solely stock, he would have received 15% of the Acquiring stock. Since Sam owns less than 80% of the stock he would have owned if solely stock had been distributed (10% ÷ 15% is less than 80%) and less than 50% of Acquiring, he meets the qualifications for sale or exchange treatment under § 302(b)(2). Therefore, Sam's $50,000 recognized gain is a long-term capital gain. ■

Debt security holders receive treatment similar to shareholders. They recognize gain only when the principal amount of the securities received is greater than the principal amount of the securities given up. If securities are received and none are surrendered, gain is also recognized.[7]

The term *security* is not defined in the Code or the Regulations. Generally, however, a debt instrument with a term longer than 10 years (e.g., a bond) is

---

[6] *Comm. v. Clark*, 89–1 USTC ¶9230, 63 AFTR2d 89–860, 109 S.Ct. 1455 (USSC, 1989), and Rev.Rul. 93–61, 1993–2 C.B. 118.

[7] § 354(a)(2)A.

CONCEPT SUMMARY 7–2

Basis Rules for a Tax-Free Reorganization

Basis to Acquiring Corporation of Property Received

Target's basis in property transferred	$xx,xxx
Plus: Gain recognized by Target on the transaction	x,xxx
Equals: Basis of property to Acquiring Corporation	$xx,xxx

Basis to Target Shareholders of Stock and Securities Received

Basis of stock and securities transferred	$xx,xxx
Plus: Gain and dividend income recognized	x,xxx
Minus: Money and fair market value of other property received	(x,xxx)
Equals: Basis of stock and securities received	$xx,xxx

treated as a security, and one with a term of 5 years or less (e.g., a note) is not. An exception to this general rule occurs when the debt instrument issued by the acquiring corporation is exchanged for target securities having the same term and maturity date.[8]

EXAMPLE 5

Alejandra holds a debt instrument from Hibiscus Corporation. The debt's principal value is $10,000, and its maturity date is December 31, 2011. In connection with the merger of Hibiscus and Tea Corporation, Alejandra exchanges her Hibiscus debt for a $10,000 Tea note that matures on December 31, 2011. Even though these notes do not have a term remaining of more than five years, they qualify for tax-free reorganization treatment. ∎

EXAMPLE 6

Assume the same facts as in Example 5, except that in exchange for her $10,000 debt instrument, Alejandra receives a note from Tea with a $15,000 principal value. Alejandra recognizes a $5,000 capital gain on the exchange. ∎

Basis. The assets transferred from the target corporation to the acquiring corporation retain their basis. The acquiring corporation's carryover basis is increased by any gain recognized by the target corporation on the reorganization. Concept Summary 7–2 shows this computation.

EXAMPLE 7

Target exchanges its assets with a $50,000 fair market value and a $30,000 basis for $45,000 of Acquiring stock and $5,000 of land. Target does not distribute the land to its shareholders. Target recognizes a $5,000 gain on the reorganization (due to the other property not being distributed). Acquiring's basis in the assets received from Target is $35,000 [$30,000 (Target's basis) + $5,000 (Target's gain recognized)]. ∎

The tax basis of the stock and securities received by a shareholder pursuant to a tax-free reorganization generally is the same as the basis of those surrendered. This basis is decreased by the fair market value of boot received and increased by the gain and/or dividend income recognized on the transaction. Concept Summary 7–2 provides a summary of these calculations. Another way to compute the basis in the stock and securities received, using the Concept Summary 7–1 template, is to

---

[8]Rev.Rul. 2004–78, I.R.B. 2004–31, July 13, 2004.

CONCEPT SUMMARY 7–3

Tax Consequences of Tax-Free Reorganizations

Treatment is similar to like-kind exchanges.

- No gain or loss is recognized by the acquiring or target corporation unless other property (i.e., boot) is transferred or received by any parties to the reorganization.
- Basis in the assets received by the acquiring corporation is generally carried over from the target corporation.
- The stock received by the target corporation's shareholders takes a substituted basis, derived from their target stock basis.
- Gain, but not loss, may be recognized when boot is transferred by the acquiring corporation.
- Gain, but not loss, may be recognized when the target corporation receives boot and does not distribute the boot to its shareholders.
- Gain, but not loss, may be recognized when target shareholders receive anything other than stock (i.e., boot) in exchange for their target stock.

subtract the gain (or add the loss) postponed from the fair market value of the stock and securities received. This basis computation ensures that the postponed gain or loss will be recognized when the new stock or securities are disposed of in a taxable transaction.

EXAMPLE 8

Quinn exchanges all of his Target Corporation stock for Acquiring Corporation stock plus $3,000 cash. The exchange is pursuant to a tax-free reorganization. Quinn paid $10,000 for the Target stock two years ago. The Acquiring stock received by Quinn has a $12,000 fair market value. Quinn has a $5,000 realized gain ($12,000 stock + $3,000 cash − $10,000 Target stock basis), which is recognized to the extent of the boot received, $3,000. Quinn's basis in the Acquiring stock is $10,000. This can be computed using the template in Concept Summary 7–1 [$12,000 (Acquiring stock value) − $2,000 (postponed gain)] or Concept Summary 7–2 [$10,000 (basis) + $3,000 (gain) − $3,000 (money received)].

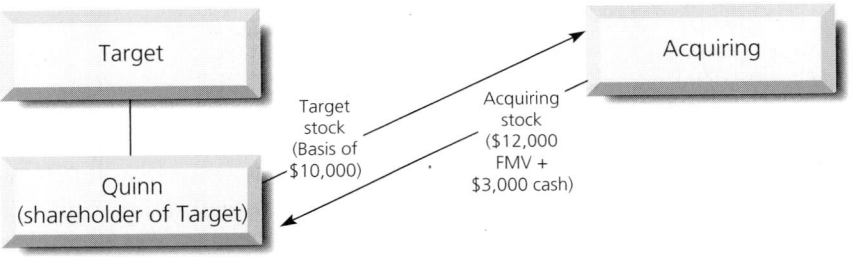

EXAMPLE 9

Assume the same facts as in Example 8, except that Quinn's Target stock basis was $16,000. Quinn realizes a $1,000 loss on the exchange, none of which is recognized. His basis in the Acquiring stock is $13,000 [Concept Summary 7–1: $12,000 (stock received) + $1,000 (loss postponed) or Concept Summary 7–2: $16,000 (basis) − $3,000 (money received)]. ∎

Concept Summary 7–3 furnishes a review of the tax consequences for tax-free reorganizations.

<table>
<tr><td>**LO.3**</td></tr>
<tr><td>Explain the statutory requirements for the different types of reorganizations.</td></tr>
</table>

Types of Tax-Free Reorganizations

Type A

"Type A" reorganizations can be classified as either mergers or consolidations. A **merger** is the union of two or more corporations, with one of the corporations retaining its corporate existence and absorbing the others. The other corporations cease to exist by operation of law. A **consolidation** occurs when a new corporation is created to take the place of two or more corporations. The "Type A" reorganizations are illustrated in Figure 7–1. To qualify as a "Type A" reorganization, mergers and consolidations must comply with the requirements of foreign, state, or Federal statutes.[9]

Acquiring Corporation obtains all the assets of Target Corporation, a French corporation, in exchange for 5,000 shares of Acquiring stock. Target is liquidated by distributing the Acquiring stock to its shareholders in exchange for their shares in Target. All French law requirements are met. This transaction qualifies as a "Type A" statutory merger. ■

EXAMPLE 10

White and Black Corporations are united under state law into new Gray Corporation by transferring all of their assets to Gray in exchange for all of Gray Corporation's stock. White and Black Corporations are then liquidated by distributing Gray stock to their shareholders in exchange for the shareholders' stock in White and Black. This "Type A" reorganization is a consolidation. ■

EXAMPLE 11

Advantages and Disadvantages.

The "Type A" reorganization allows more flexibility than the other types of reorganizations.

- Unlike both "Type B" and "Type C" reorganizations, the acquiring stock transferred to the target need not be voting stock.
- The acquiring corporation can transfer money or other property to the target corporation without destroying tax-free treatment for the stock also exchanged.
  - Money or other property, however, constitutes boot and may cause gain recognition by the acquiring corporation, the target, and/or the target's shareholders.
- When consideration other than stock is given by the acquiring corporation, care must be taken not to run afoul of the **continuity of interest test**.
  - This test, promulgated by the courts, requires that the consideration given by the acquiring corporation be at least 50 percent stock.
- There is no requirement that "substantially all" of the target's assets be transferred to the acquiring corporation as in a "Type C" reorganization.
  - Thus, the target can sell or otherwise dispose of assets not desired by the acquiring corporation without affecting the tax-free nature of the restructuring.

  A "Type A" is not without its disadvantages.

- Each corporation involved in the restructuring must obtain the approval of the majority of its shareholders.
- In almost every state, dissenting shareholders can require that their shares be appraised and purchased.
  - Meeting the demands of objecting shareholders can become so cumbersome and expensive that the parties may be forced to abandon the "Type A" reorganization.
- The acquiring corporation must assume *all* liabilities (including unknown and contingent liabilities) of the target corporation as a matter of state law.

Type B

In a "Type B" reorganization, the acquiring corporation obtains "control" of the target corporation in an exchange involving solely stock. Thus, both corporations survive, and a parent-subsidiary relationship is created. In simple terms, this

---

[9]Reg. § 1.368–2(b)(ii), Example 7–13(ii).

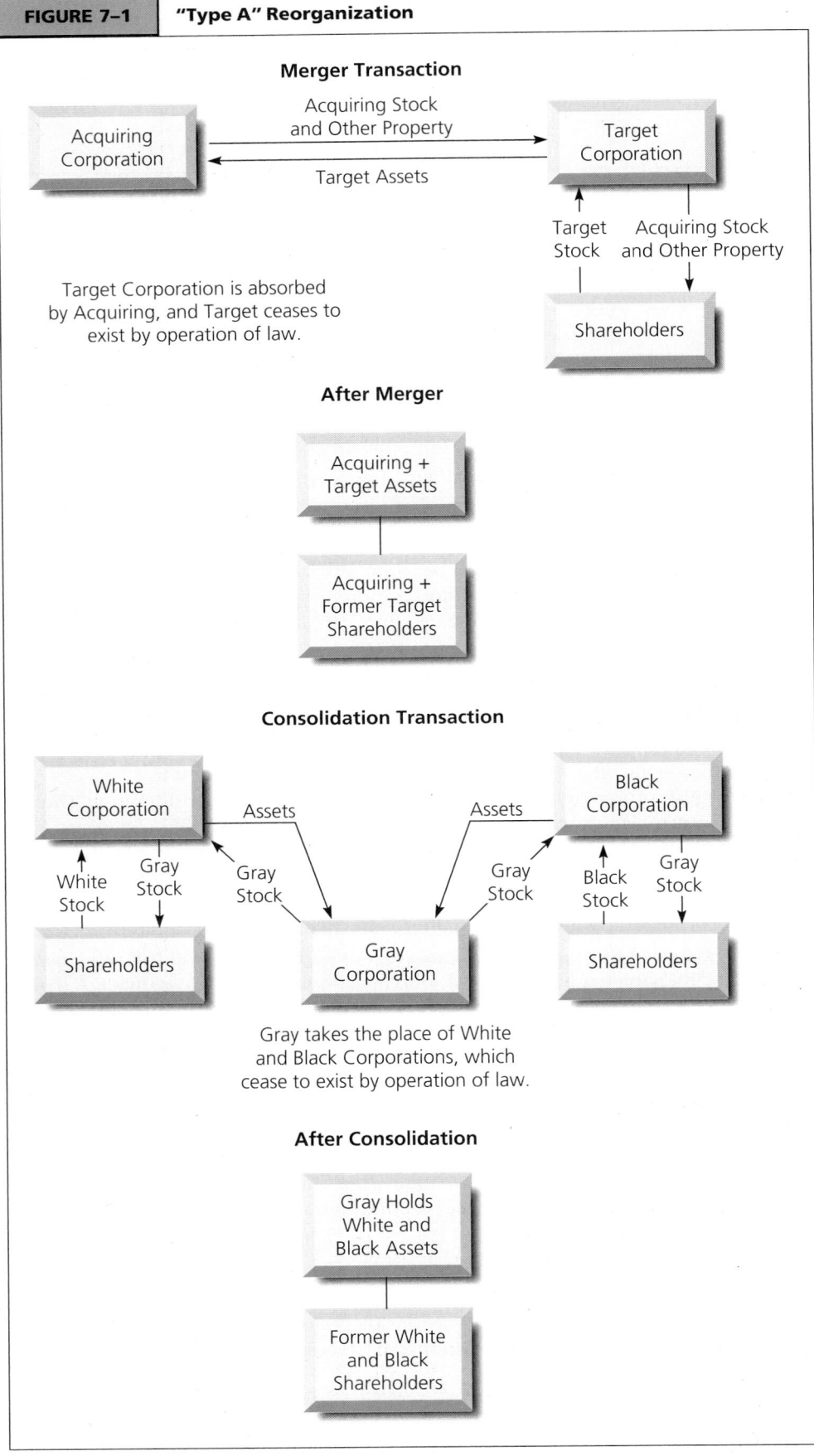

FIGURE 7–1 "Type A" Reorganization

Merger Transaction

Target Corporation is absorbed by Acquiring, and Target ceases to exist by operation of law.

After Merger

Consolidation Transaction

Gray takes the place of White and Black Corporations, which cease to exist by operation of law.

After Consolidation

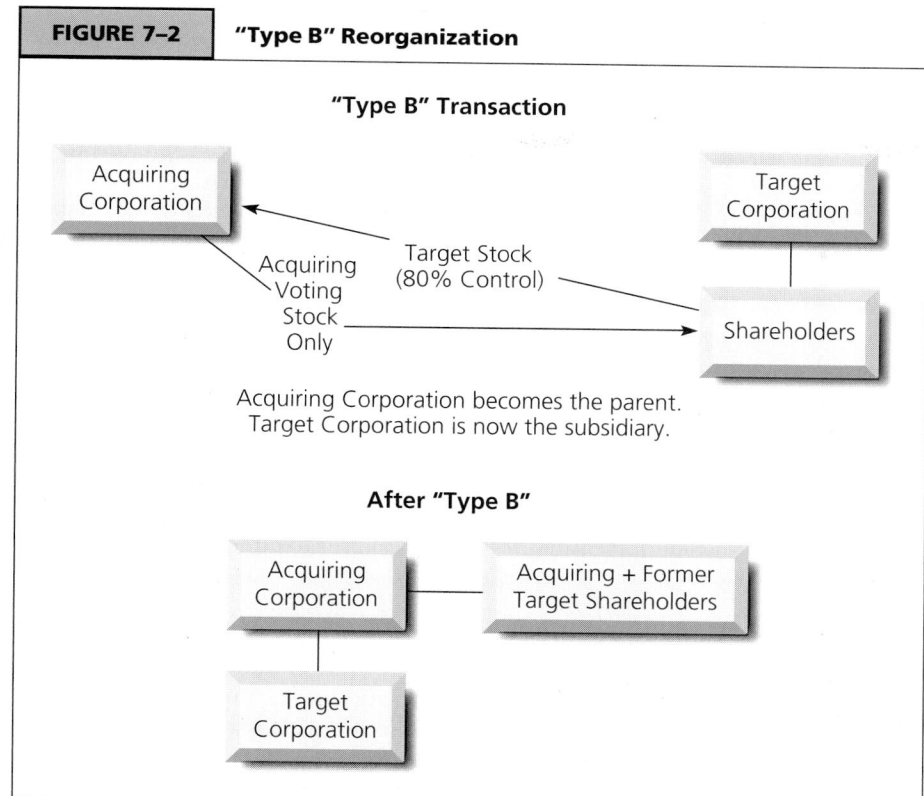

FIGURE 7–2   **"Type B" Reorganization**

§ 381 doesn't apply

"Type B" Transaction

Acquiring Corporation becomes the parent.
Target Corporation is now the subsidiary.

After "Type B"

transaction is an exchange of voting stock for stock. Voting stock must be the *sole* consideration given by the acquiring corporation,[10] a requirement that is strictly construed.[11] The target's stock relinquished in the transaction may be common or preferred, voting or nonvoting.

not used

Since the use of boot is precluded, gain is never recognized in a "Type B" reorganization. An exception to the solely voting stock requirement occurs when the shareholders must receive fractional shares. The target corporation's shareholders may receive cash rather than fractional shares in the acquiring corporation.[12] The "Type B" reorganization is illustrated in Figure 7–2.

EXAMPLE 12

In a transaction between Acquiring Corporation and Target Corporation shareholders, 20% of Acquiring voting stock is exchanged for 80% of all classes of stock in Target Corporation. The exchange qualifies as a "Type B" reorganization. Acquiring becomes the parent of Target. ∎

Control Requirements. The "Type B" reorganization requires that the acquiring corporation be in "control" of the target corporation immediately after the reorganization. **Control** for this purpose requires owning at least 80 percent of all classes of the target corporation's stock. The 80 percent-control-after-reorganization requirement does not mean that all 80 percent must be "acquired" in the restructuring transaction. Stock previously purchased in separate transactions can be counted in determining the 80 percent ownership.[13] Further, the stock may be acquired from the shareholders directly or from the target corporation.

---

[10]The exchange of the acquiring corporation's bonds for the target's bonds may be considered a separate and distinct transaction from a "Type B" reorganization according to Rev.Rul. 98–10, 1998–1 C.B. 643. Consequently, this exchange will not affect an otherwise qualifying "Type B" reorganization.

[11]*A. S. Heverly*, 80–1 USTC ¶9322, 45 AFTR2d 80–1122, 621 F.2d 1227, and *E. S. Chapman*, 80–1 USTC ¶9330, 45 AFTR2d 80–1290, 618 F.2d 856.
[12]Rev.Rul. 66–365, 1966–2 C.B. 116.
[13]Reg. § 1.368–2(c).

EXAMPLE 13

Acquiring Corporation purchased 30% of Target's stock for cash six years ago. It acquires another 60% in the current year by exchanging its voting stock with Target's shareholders. Thus, even though some of the Target shares were acquired with cash, the "Type B" requirements are satisfied through the current 60% exchange.

What if Acquiring Corporation purchased 30% of Target's stock for cash three months ago? Now the acquisition of the additional 60% of Target's stock for voting stock seems to be part of a two-step transaction. The acquisition of the remaining stock for voting stock is probably not tax-free. ■

Disadvantages and Advantages. The solely voting stock consideration requirement is a substantial disadvantage of the "Type B" reorganization. Another disadvantage is that if the acquiring corporation does not obtain 100 percent control of the target corporation, problems may arise with the minority interest remaining in the target.

Nevertheless, the voting-stock-for-stock acquisition has the advantage of simplicity. Generally, the target corporation's shareholders act individually in transferring their stock to the acquiring corporation. Thus, the target corporation itself and the acquiring corporation's shareholders are not directly involved as long as the acquiring corporation has sufficient treasury or unissued shares to effect the transaction.

Type C

In the "Type C" reorganization, the acquiring corporation obtains substantially all of the target corporation's assets in exchange for voting stock and a limited amount of other property. The target corporation must distribute all assets it receives in the reorganization, as well as any of its own property retained. The target corporation then liquidates.[14] Thus, a "Type C" reorganization is essentially an exchange of voting stock for assets followed by liquidation of the target corporation. The exchange is a taxable transaction for the shareholders to the extent that they receive assets other than the acquiring corporation stock. The "Type C" reorganization is illustrated in Figure 7–3.

EXAMPLE 14

Acquiring Corporation transfers voting stock representing a 30% ownership interest to Target Corporation for substantially all of Target's assets. After the exchange, Target's only assets are cash and Acquiring voting stock. Target distributes the Acquiring stock and cash to its shareholders in exchange for their Target stock. The exchange qualifies as a "Type C" reorganization if Target liquidates after the distribution. The exchange is a taxable transaction for the shareholders to the extent that they received cash. ■

"Type A" and "Type C" Reorganizations Compared. A "Type C" reorganization's outcome is similar to that of a "Type A" merger, as can be seen by comparing the diagrams for these reorganizations (Figure 7–3 versus Figure 7–1). However, their requirements differ. A "Type C" has more restrictions regarding the consideration that may be used by the acquiring corporation. Nevertheless, the "Type C" can be preferable to the "Type A," because in the "Type C" the acquiring corporation assumes only the target liabilities that it chooses. It normally is not liable for unknown or contingent liabilities. Further, in some states, only the target corporation's shareholders must approve a "Type C" reorganization.

Consideration in the "Type C" Reorganization. The acquiring corporation's consideration in a "Type C" reorganization normally consists of voting stock. However, there are exceptions to this rule. Cash and other property do not destroy a "Type C" reorganization if at least 80 percent of the fair market value of the target's property is obtained with voting stock.

---

[14]Distributions may be to creditors as well as to shareholders. § 368(a)(2)(G).

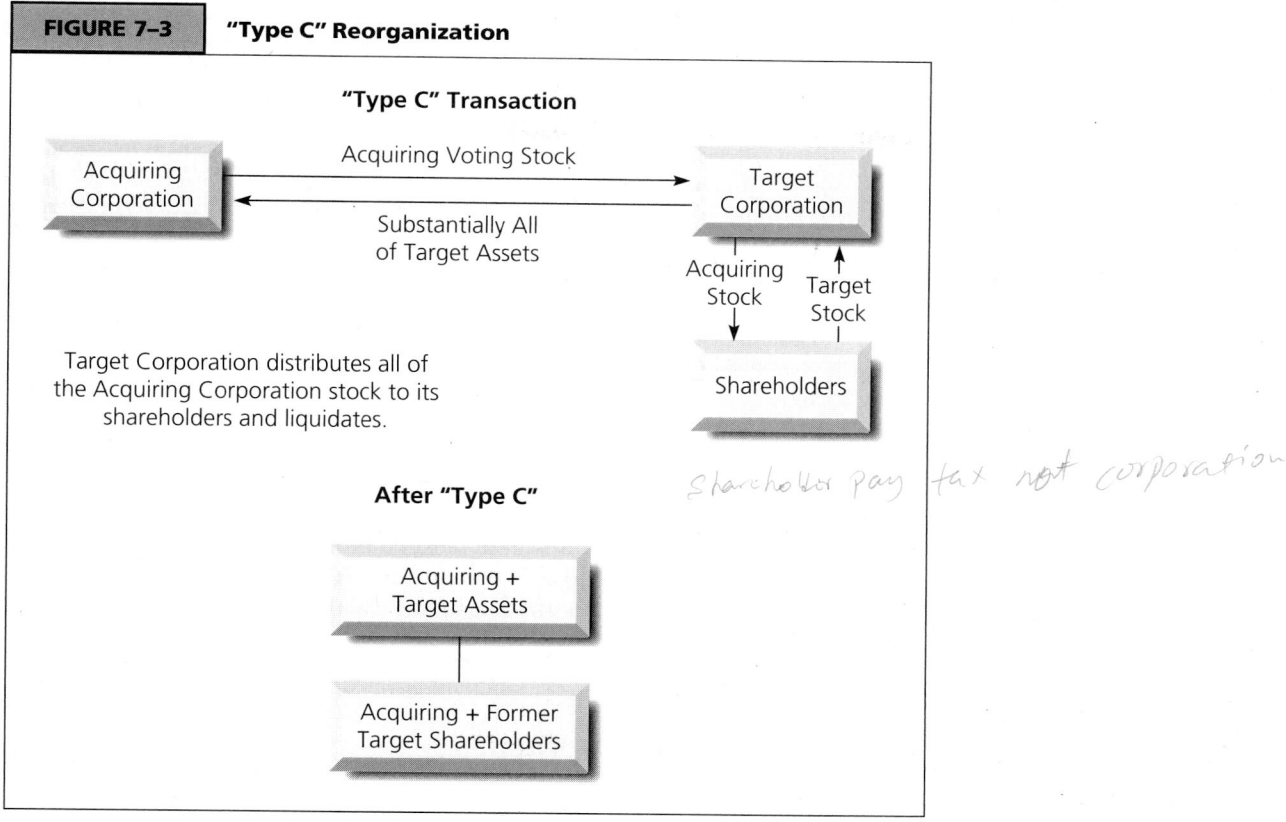

FIGURE 7–3   **"Type C" Reorganization**

Shareholder pay tax not corporation (handwritten)

Although the acquiring corporation has more freedom in the consideration given in a "Type C" than in a "Type B," this freedom is not without a cost. When the acquiring corporation gives solely voting stock for the target corporation's assets, the target corporation's liabilities assumed by the acquiring corporation are not considered *other property* (i.e., boot) in the exchange.[15] The transaction is an exchange of voting stock for assets, and the 80 percent-of-property requirement is met. However, liabilities assumed by the acquiring corporation *are* treated as *other property* if the target corporation receives any property other than voting stock in the reorganization.[16] Liabilities assumed by the acquiring corporation are likely to exceed 20 percent of the fair market value of the assets acquired and, consequently, destroy the "Type C" reorganization.

EXAMPLE 15

Target Corporation exchanges $200,000 assets and a $50,000 liability for Acquiring stock worth $150,000. Target distributes the stock to its shareholders and liquidates. The transaction qualifies as a "Type C" reorganization. The liability is not treated as *other property* received. Acquiring obtained 100% of Target's assets for voting stock. The liability assumed by Acquiring is disregarded as boot in this situation.

Suppose that Target Corporation exchanged its $200,000 assets and $50,000 liability for Acquiring stock worth $140,000 and $10,000 in cash. The liability would be considered *other property* because Target also received cash. *Other property* amounts to $60,000, which exceeds 20% of the fair market value of Target's assets ($200,000 × 20% = $40,000). This transaction would not qualify as a "Type C" reorganization.

If Acquiring had given voting stock worth $170,000 and $30,000 in cash to Target, the transaction would qualify as a "Type C" reorganization. No liabilities are assumed, and the *other property* transferred is less than 20% of the fair market value of the assets ($30,000 < $40,000). ∎

---

[15]§ 368(a)(1)(C).   [16]§ 368(a)(2)(B).

According to Regulation § 1.368–2(d), the acquiring corporation's prior ownership of the target's stock will not prevent the "solely-for-voting-stock" requirement from being met in "Type C" reorganizations. If the acquiring corporation purchased stock in the target corporation in an earlier unrelated transaction, the previously acquired stock will not be considered in determining whether 80 percent of the target's assets were obtained with the acquiring corporation's stock.

EXAMPLE 16

Acquiring Corporation purchased 30% of Target Corporation's stock five years ago. In the current year, the fair market value of Target's assets is $100,000. Acquiring transfers $70,000 of its voting stock to Target in exchange for the 70% of Target's assets that Acquiring currently does not own. This qualifies as a "Type C" reorganization. The previous purchase of Target stock is not considered to be part of the reorganization transaction. Therefore, Acquiring is exchanging voting stock for 100% of Target's assets. ∎

Asset Transfers. The "Type C" reorganization requires that substantially all of the target corporation's assets be transferred to the acquiring corporation. However, there is no statutory definition of "substantially all." To receive a favorable IRS ruling, the target must transfer at least 90 percent of the net asset value or 70 percent of the gross asset value to the acquiring corporation.[17] Smaller percentages may qualify depending on the particular facts and circumstances of the reorganization.[18]

ETHICAL and EQUITABLE Considerations

GIVING VOICE TO ETHICAL VALUES

Through a "Type C" reorganization, Blue I Corporation (a distributor of contact lenses) merged with I Glass Corporation (a distributor of eyeglasses). Blue I acquired all the assets ($1 million) and liabilities ($400,000) of I Glass for $600,000 of Blue I's common voting stock. The transaction was completed on June 1 of the current year. As a staff accountant with the firm preparing the first consolidated tax return for the combined entity, you find a document dated December of last year indicating that, in anticipation of the "Type C" reorganization, Blue I acquired 5 percent of I Glass's stock for cash. The stock was acquired from a shareholder who would have been against the merger. Considering this acquisition as part of the "Type C" reorganization would cause the liabilities to be considered boot, and the 80-percent-of-assets-for-voting-stock requirement would not be met.

You bring your findings to your manager, Joe Fitswaller. Joe has always been a good manager to work for, and you like him. You have been to his house for dinner with his wife and their three children several times. That is why you are surprised when Joe tells you that what you have found is not your concern. Besides, the IRS will never figure out what happened because the stock was acquired in a different tax year. As you discuss this issue with Joe, you realize that he already knew about the transaction before you brought it to his attention. On returning to your work, you find correspondence between Joe and Blue I regarding the December stock acquisition. You also discover that the shareholder from whom the stock was purchased is also named Fitswaller. You suspect that Joe is covering up this issue because he has given advice to Blue I to benefit his relative and has subjected the firm to possible liability for the taxes of Blue I's failed tax-free acquisition of I Glass. Joe will likely lose his job if the partners find out about this.

You know that you must tell the partner on the engagement about what you have found. The risk to the firm is just too great not to divulge this information. What would you write in a memo to the partner about what you have learned and the possible risks to the firm?

Type D

The first three types of tax-free corporate reorganizations are designed for corporate combinations. The "Type D" reorganization is different; it is generally used to

[17]Rev.Rul. 77–37, 1977–2 C.B. 568, amplified by Rev.Proc. 86–42, 1986–2 C.B. 722.

[18]Where 70% of the assets were transferred and 30% were retained to discharge the target's liabilities prior to liquidation, the IRS found that substantially all of the assets were transferred. Rev.Rul. 57–518, 1957–2 C.B. 253.

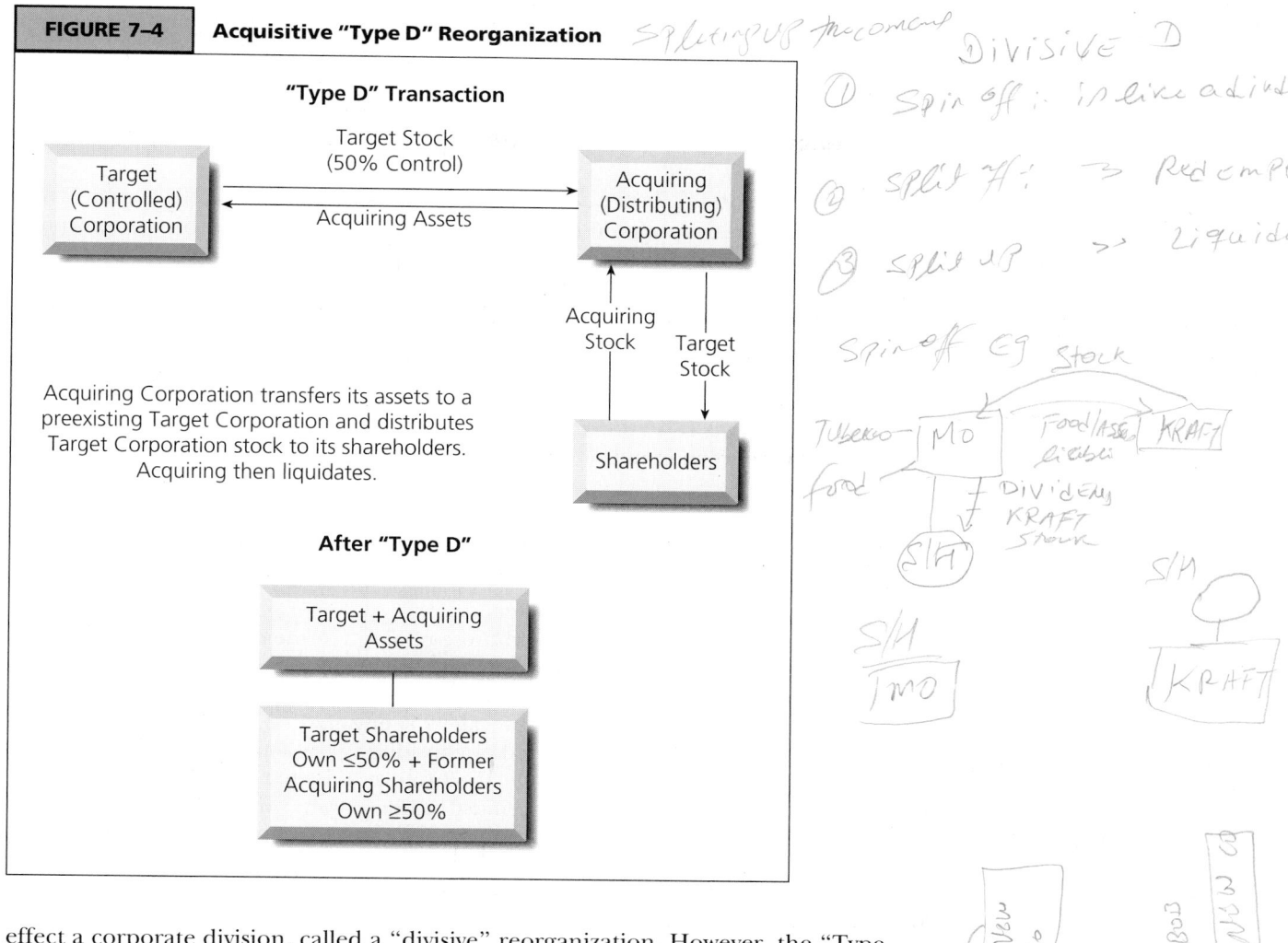

FIGURE 7–4 Acquisitive "Type D" Reorganization

"Type D" Transaction

Target (Controlled) Corporation → Target Stock (50% Control) → Acquiring (Distributing) Corporation

Acquiring (Distributing) Corporation → Acquiring Assets → Target (Controlled) Corporation

Acquiring Stock ↑ | Target Stock ↓

Shareholders

Acquiring Corporation transfers its assets to a preexisting Target Corporation and distributes Target Corporation stock to its shareholders. Acquiring then liquidates.

After "Type D"

Target + Acquiring Assets

Target Shareholders Own ≤50% + Former Acquiring Shareholders Own ≥50%

effect a corporate division, called a "divisive" reorganization. However, the "Type D" can also be used to combine corporations—an "acquisitive" reorganization. In contrast with other restructurings, in the "Type D" acquisitive reorganization, the entity transferring assets is considered the acquiring corporation, and the corporation receiving the property is the target.

Acquisitive "Type D" Reorganization.
If a combination meets the following requirements, it will be treated as a "Type D" reorganization.

- Substantially all of the acquiring corporation's property must be transferred to the target corporation.
- The acquiring corporation must be in control (at least 50 percent) of the target.[19]
- Target stock received by the acquiring corporation, as well as any remaining assets of the acquiring corporation, must be distributed to its shareholders.
- The acquiring corporation must liquidate.

This type of transaction may also meet the "Type C" requirements (from the target's viewpoint). If the transaction can be classified as both a "Type C" and a "Type D" reorganization, it is treated as a "Type D" reorganization.[20] The "Type D" acquisitive reorganization is diagrammed in Figure 7–4. A comparison of Figure 7–4 with Figure 7–3 will illustrate how a "Type D" may also qualify as a "Type C" reorganization.

---

[19]No attribution of ownership is allowed in determining whether there is 50% control. §§ 368(a)(2)(H) and 304(c).

[20]Reg. § 1.368–2(d)(3).

EXAMPLE 17

Acquiring Corporation wishes to control Target Corporation ($300,000 value), but Target holds a nontransferable license. Thus, Target must be the surviving corporation. Acquiring transfers all its assets valued at $700,000 to Target for 70% of Target's stock. Acquiring then distributes all the Target stock to its shareholders in exchange for their Acquiring stock and liquidates. The transaction qualifies as a "Type D" reorganization. ■

Divisive "Type D" Reorganization. Rather than combining, shareholders may wish to split the corporation by distributing its assets among two or more corporations. This might occur for many reasons including antitrust problems, differences of opinion among the shareholders, product liability concerns, increasing shareholder value, or family tax planning. The more typical divisive "Type D" reorganization allows shareholders to accomplish their goals without incurring a current tax liability. In a divisive reorganization, one or more new corporations are formed to receive part or all of the distributing corporation's assets. In exchange for its assets, the distributing corporation must receive stock.

The remaining requirements for a divisive "Type D" reorganization are as follows.

- The stock received by the distributing corporation must constitute control (80 percent) of the new corporation(s).
- The stock of the controlled corporation(s) must be transferred to the distributing corporation's shareholders.
- Both the assets transferred and those retained by the distributing corporation must represent active businesses that have been owned and conducted by the distributing corporation for at least five years before the transfer.
- Whether the distributing corporation is engaged in the active conduct of a trade or business is determined by considering the active businesses of the distributing corporation's consolidated return affiliated group (see Chapter 8). The distributing corporation must be the parent company in the affiliated group.[21] Thus, the distributing parent corporation and all its subsidiaries are treated as one corporation when applying the active business test.
- The stock and securities transfers to the shareholders cannot be principally a device for distributing the earnings and profits of either the distributing corporation or the controlled corporation(s).

EXAMPLE 18

Bell, Inc., is a manufacturing corporation. It also owns investment securities. Bell transfers the investment securities to a newly formed corporation and distributes the stock of the new corporation to its shareholders. The transaction does not qualify as a "Type D" reorganization. Holding investment securities does not constitute a trade or business. The Bell shareholders are taxed on the stock they receive. ■

EXAMPLE 19

Jane and Ivan are the sole shareholders of WM Corporation. WM was organized 10 years ago and is actively engaged in manufacturing two products, widgets and bolts. Considerable friction has developed between Jane and Ivan, who now wish to divide the business. Jane wants the assets used in manufacturing widgets, and Ivan wants to continue manufacturing bolts. The division of the business assets between the shareholders can be accomplished tax-free using one of the divisive "Type D" reorganizations. ■

EXAMPLE 20

CUE, Inc., has manufactured a single product at two plants for the past 10 years. It transfers one plant and related activities to a new corporation, Less, Inc. CUE then distributes the Less stock to its shareholders. Each plant's activities constitute a trade or business. The transaction qualifies as a "Type D" reorganization. ■

---

[21]§ 355(b)(3).

Spin-Offs, Split-Offs, and Split-Ups.

There are three different types of divisive "Type D" reorganizations: spin-offs, split-offs, and split-ups.

- In a **spin-off**, a new corporation is formed to receive some of the distributing corporation's assets in exchange for the new corporation's stock. The distributing corporation's shareholders receive the new corporation's stock without surrendering any of their distributing corporation stock. The shareholders' basis in their distributing corporation stock is allocated between the distributing corporation stock and the new stock, based on the relative fair market value of each.
- A **split-off** resembles a spin-off except that in a split-off the shareholders surrender distributing corporation stock in exchange for stock in the new corporation. Stock basis is computed in the same manner as for a spin-off.
- In a **split-up**, two or more new corporations are formed to receive substantially all of the distributing corporation's assets. The stock of each new corporation is exchanged for the distributing corporation stock. The distributing corporation is then liquidated. The shareholders' basis in the relinquished distributing corporation stock carries over as the basis of stock in the new corporations.

The spin-off and split-off are illustrated in Figure 7–5, and the split-up is illustrated in Figure 7–6.

EXAMPLE 21

Shawnee purchased 10% (500 shares) of DistributingCo eight years ago for $60,000. Before the spin-off reorganization, DistributingCo's stock value was $900,000, and Shawnee's shares were valued at $90,000, or $180 per share ($90,000 ÷ 500 shares). DistributingCo spins off 30% of its business assets into NewCo (fair market value $270,000) and distributes 10,000 shares of NewCo stock to its shareholders. Shawnee's 1,000 NewCo shares are worth $27,000. After the spin-off, the value of DistributingCo is reduced to $630,000, and therefore the value of Shawnee's stock in DistributingCo is $63,000. Shawnee's $60,000 beginning basis in DistributingCo is allocated to the two companies' stock as follows: $18,000 to NewCo stock [$60,000 × ($27,000/$90,000)] and $42,000 to DistributingCo stock [$60,000 × ($63,000/$90,000)]. ∎

EXAMPLE 22

Assume the same facts as in Example 21, except that DistributingCo creates NewCo through a split-off. Shawnee is required to surrender 150 DistributingCo shares to receive the 1,000 NewCo shares. Shawnee's 350 DistributingCo shares (500 − 150) now have a value of $63,000 ($180 × 350), and her NewCo stock is worth $27,000 ($90,000 − $63,000). Shawnee's $60,000 beginning basis in DistributingCo is allocated to the two companies' stock as follows: $42,000 to the DistributingCo stock [$60,000 × ($63,000/$90,000)] and $18,000 to the 1,000 NewCo shares [$60,000 × ($27,000/$90,000)]. ∎

EXAMPLE 23

Gail and Gary are the sole shareholders of Publishers Corporation. Publishers was organized six years ago to publish both books and periodicals. Because of antitrust problems, Publishers wishes to divide its business. Two new corporations are formed, Books and Periodicals. All the assets relating to the book publishing business are transferred to Books. The remaining assets are transferred to Periodicals. Gail exchanges all her Publishers stock for the stock in Books. Gary exchanges all his Publishers stock for the stock in Periodicals. Publishers is liquidated. The transaction qualifies as a "Type D" reorganization split-up. Neither Gail nor Gary recognizes gain on the exchange. Gail's basis in her Publishers stock becomes the basis for her Books stock. Gary's basis in his Publishers stock becomes his basis for his Periodicals stock. ∎

Type E

The "Type E" reorganization is a **recapitalization**—a major change in the character and amount of outstanding capital stock, securities, or paid-in capital of a corporation. The transaction is significant only for the stock- or bondholders who exchange

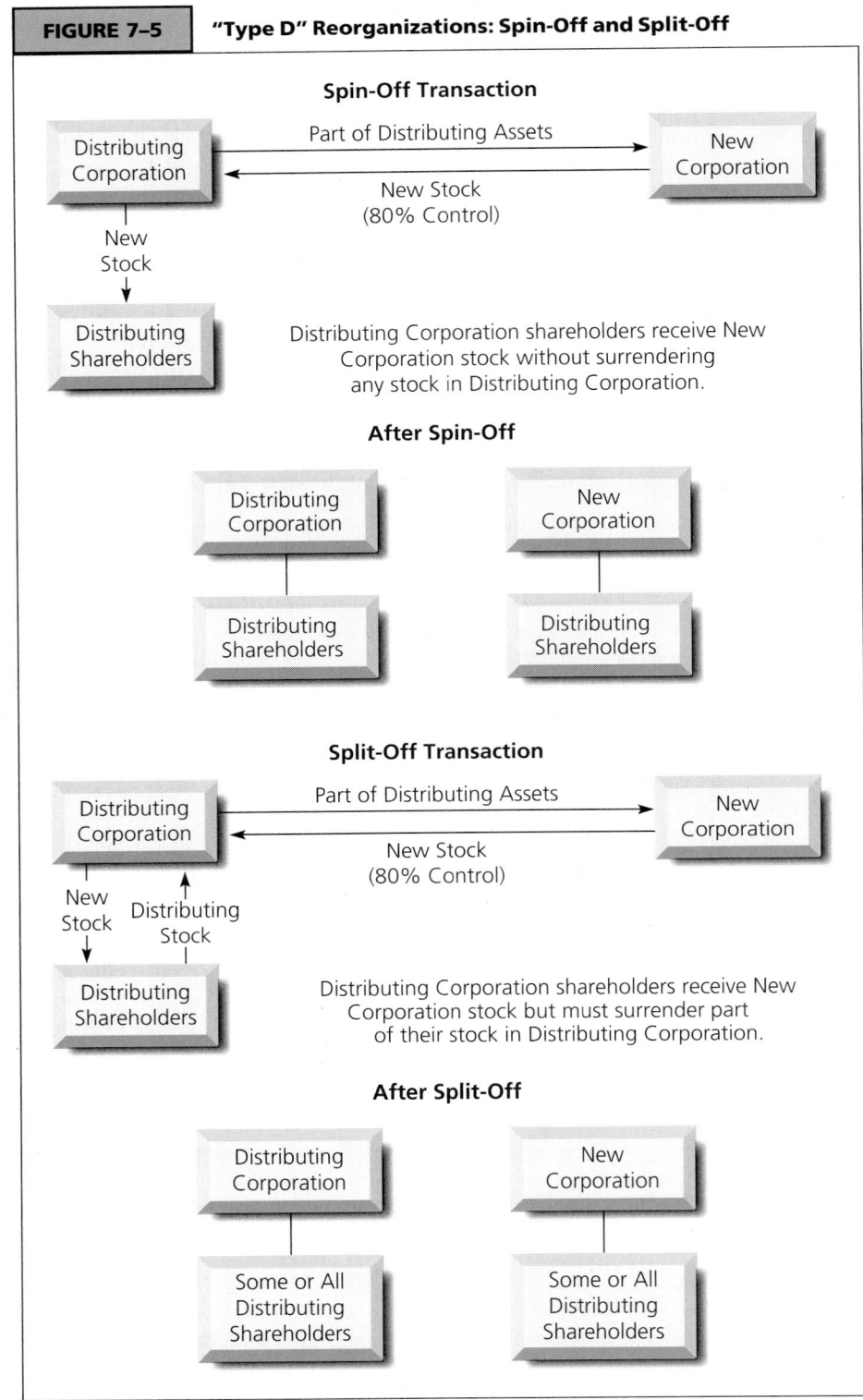

FIGURE 7–5   "Type D" Reorganizations: Spin-Off and Split-Off

their equity or securities. Since no property, stocks, or bonds are exchanged with another corporation, the "Type E" reorganization has no tax implications for the corporation involved. Further, transactions in a corporation's own stock or bonds are not taxable events.[22]

[22]Reg. §§ 1.1032–1(a) and (c).

FIGURE 7–6   "Type D" Reorganization: Split-Up

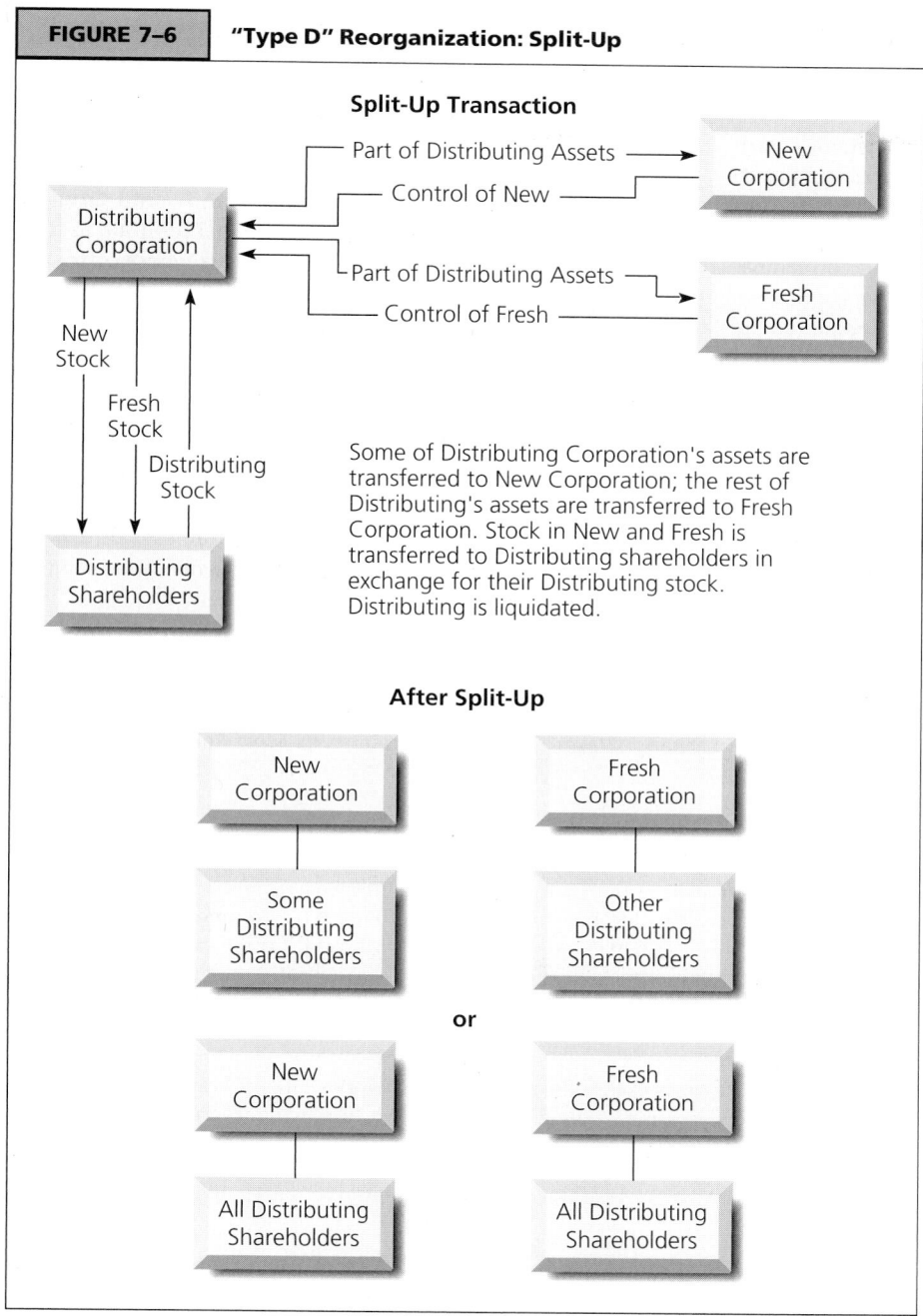

The following types of exchanges qualify for nonrecognition treatment as "Type E" reorganizations: bonds for stock, stock for stock, and bonds for bonds. A corporation can exchange its common stock for preferred stock or its preferred stock for common stock tax-free. The exchange of bonds for other bonds is tax-free when the debt received has a principal amount that is not more than the surrendered debt's principal amount.

EXAMPLE 24

All of Mesquite Corporation's bondholders exchange their $1,000, 6% interest-bearing bonds for $1,000, 8% interest-bearing bonds. This qualifies as a "Type E" reorganization because the surrendered bonds' principal amount is equal to the principal amount of the bonds received. ∎

TAX *in the News*   MERGERS AND CORPORATE SOCIAL RESPONSIBILITY

Many companies are concerned about fulfilling their corporate social responsibility (CSR) as well as with showing a profit. CSR encourages organizations to treat stakeholders in a manner that promotes human rights, protects the environment, and extends beyond the legal requirements imposed on companies. The well-being of employees, local communities, and society in general is furthered when companies take responsibility for the effects of their operational activities on the world.

Concern for CSR can influence mergers and acquisitions. For example, CSR was a factor in Ethos's willingness to be acquired by Starbucks. Both Ethos and Starbucks show a deep sense of social and environmental responsibility. Ethos had made a commitment to help supply clean water to children around the world, and Ethos's founders wanted to ensure that Starbucks would be willing to continue this effort. The founders felt that by becoming part of Starbucks, their potential to help children would be amplified, and this has indeed been the case.

Bayer CropScience is another company exhibiting a social conscience. After acquiring the Indian seed company Proagro as part of its worldwide merger with Aventis CropScience, Bayer started a children's educational program as a way of combating child labor in areas of India where cotton seed is produced. Bayer realized that the Indian farmers were not always adhering to its strict ban on child labor. If farmers ignore the ban, the company responds with a graduated system of sanctions that range from a verbal warning to cancellation of their contract. Bayer provides training and expertise to help the farmers be more productive without the use of child labor. The program is working well. In the 2006–2007 season, Proagro farmers had no children working in the cotton fields, and the farmers were more profitable. Thus, CSR can improve society and the environment while improving the bottom line for the businesses involved.

Sources: *Adapted from "Starbucks Announces Acquisition of Ethos Water and Commitment to Donate More Than $1 Million to Support Clean Water Efforts,"* Business Wire, *April 11, 2005 p. 1; and "Bayer CropScience Presents Its Most Recent News and Research Developments,"* Lab Business Week, *September 16, 2007.*

EXAMPLE 25

Spruce Corporation's stock is owned 80% by Wade and 20% by his children. Wade desires to relinquish his corporate control to his children. He exchanges his common voting stock for nonvoting preferred stock. The exchange qualifies as a "Type E" reorganization. However, any difference in value between stock received and stock surrendered could be treated as compensation or as a gift. ∎

EXAMPLE 26

Cedar Corporation exchanges each of its $1,000 bonds for 10 shares of common stock worth $100 per share. This qualifies as a "Type E" reorganization, and no gain is recognized because the bond value given up is equal to the stock value received ($1,000 = 10 × $100). ∎

Type F

The "Type F" reorganization is "a mere change in identity, form, or place of organization . . . however effected." Since "Type F" reorganizations involve only slight changes to a single operating corporation, the successor corporation is the same corporation as its predecessor.[23] Consequently, the tax characteristics of the predecessor carry over to the successor. A "Type F" reorganization does not jeopardize the status of § 1244 stock, nor will it terminate a valid S corporation election unless that is desired. The IRS has ruled that if a restructuring could qualify as a "Type A," "Type C," or "Type D" as well as a "Type F" reorganization, the "Type F" treatment prevails.[24]

EXAMPLE 27

Conifer Corporation changes its name to Evergreen Corporation. This is a "Type F" reorganization. ∎

---

[23]T.D. 9182.   [24]Rev.Rul. 57–276, 1957–1 C.B. 126.

TAX *in the News* — PROTECTING AGAINST BANKRUPTCY

The bankruptcies of companies such as WorldCom, Enron, and Conseco cost employees, investors, and creditors billions of dollars. Creditors can protect themselves from businesses with bankruptcy potential by learning to recognize "aggressive accounting" practices that are employed on financial statements to mask financial weaknesses and artificially boost net income. Debatable asset valuations, off-balance-sheet liabilities, and manipulation of M&A results are some questionable practices that can signal financial problems ahead.

Firms seeking credit have an incentive to embellish sales revenues at the end of the accounting period when the actual results are lower than projected. Accounting techniques used to enhance revenues include recording sales before they are shipped; treating goods on consignment as sold; underestimating reserves for bad debt and returns; not recognizing current-period credits, returns, or allowances until the next period; and recording premerger revenue of the target as postmerger revenue.

Firms do not have the same revenue recognition incentives for tax purposes as they do for financial accounting. Reading the financial statement footnotes, in particular those regarding book-to-tax differences, can help to untangle the economic reality from the "window dressing" in the formal financial statements. An understanding of FAS 109, which governs the tax provisions on the financial statements, is critical for this task.

For a merger or acquisition to receive tax-favored treatment, there must be a valid business purpose for the transaction. The tax threshold may be too low, however, to determine whether the M&A activity is undertaken primarily to mask financial distress. Examining financial ratios before and after the merger, as well as identifying merger synergies, can reveal the motives for the M&A activity. Additionally, recent and aggressive M&A transactions may be a warning that a more comprehensive analysis is required.

Source: *Adapted from "10 Ways Customers Cook Their Books to Get You to Extend Credit,"* Managing Credit, Receivables & Collections, *July 2006.*

EXAMPLE 28

Orchard Corporation is organized as a Subchapter S corporation. Its shareholders wish to revoke its S election. Changing from an S corporation to a regular C corporation qualifies as a "Type F" reorganization. ■

Type G

Bankruptcy legislation introduced the "Type G" reorganization. In this type of restructuring, all or a part of the debtor corporation's assets are transferred to an acquiring corporation in a bankruptcy or similar proceeding in a Federal or state court. The debtor corporation's creditors must receive the acquiring corporation's voting stock in exchange for debt representing 80 percent or more of the total fair market value of the debtor corporation's liabilities. Since a "Type G" reorganization must proceed according to a plan approved under a bankruptcy proceeding, planning for its use is limited. (See Exhibit 7–3 for a list of the states with the highest business termination rates.)

The acquiring corporation in a "Type G" reorganization must reduce the tax attributes carried over from the bankrupt corporation to the extent of the cancellation-of-debt-income relief. The tax attributes reduced include the following.

- Net operating losses (NOLs).
- General business credits (GBCs).
- Minimum tax credits (MTCs).
- Capital loss carryovers.
- Basis in property.

These attributes are reduced in the order listed above; however, the acquiring corporation may elect to reduce the basis of depreciable property first.[25]

---

[25]Reg. 1.108–7 and T.D. 9127.

EXHIBIT 7–3	Highest Business Termination Rates by State Population, 2006

State	Rank	Business Bankruptcies per 100,000 Population
Colorado	1	14.26
Minnesota	2	12.27
Oregon	3	11.95
Georgia	4	11.63
Texas	5	11.37
Louisiana	6	10.73
Ohio	7	10.04
New Mexico	8	9.64
Oklahoma	9	9.13
Nebraska	10	8.52

Source: *U.S. Small Business Administration, 2007.*

EXAMPLE 29

Worthless Corporation files for Chapter 11 protection when its liabilities exceed its assets by $100,000 (cancellation-of-debt-income relief). Worthless has a $60,000 NOL carryover and a $30,000 capital loss carryover at the time of its restructuring. Through a "Type G" reorganization, NewStart Corporation becomes the successor corporation to Worthless. NewStart must reduce the carryover attributes by $100,000. Consequently, NewStart has no NOL or capital loss carryovers from Worthless, and it must reduce the basis in the assets by $10,000 ($100,000 total carryovers reduction − $60,000 NOL − $30,000 capital losses = $10,000 basis reduction). ■

A summary of the advantages and disadvantages of the various corporate reorganizations described in this chapter is found in Concept Summary 7–4.

LO.4

Delineate the judicial and administrative conditions for a nontaxable corporate reorganization.

Judicial Doctrines

Besides the statutory requirements for reorganizations, several judicially created doctrines have become basic requirements for tax-free treatment. These doctrines include the sound business purpose, continuity of interest, and continuity of business enterprise doctrines. The courts have also formulated the step transaction doctrine to determine the tax status of a reorganization that occurs through a series of related transactions. In addition, a reorganization plan that is consistent with one of the Code reorganizations is required.[26]

Sound Business Purpose

Even if the statutory reorganization requirements are literally followed, a transaction will not be tax-free unless it exhibits a **business purpose**.[27] The business purpose requirement is meant to limit nonrecognition treatment to transactions that are motivated, at least in part, by valid corporate needs. The transaction must have economic consequences germane to the businesses that go beyond mere tax avoidance. Although tax avoidance is not, by itself, considered a business purpose,

[26]Reg. § 1.368–1(c) and *William Hewitt*, 19 B.T.A. 771 (1930). For a definition of a reorganization plan, see Reg. § 1.368–2(g).

[27]Reg. §§ 1.368–1(c) and 1.355–2. See also *Gregory v. Helvering*, 35–1 USTC ¶9043, 14 AFTR 1191, 55 S.Ct. 266 (USSC, 1935). The doctrine as developed in the

Gregory case became a precedent for all transactions that might be shams devised merely for tax avoidance purposes. It brought about the principle of substance over form. All business transactions must have a sound business purpose.

CONCEPT SUMMARY 7–4

Corporate Reorganizations

Reorganization	Type	Advantages	Disadvantages
A	Merger or consolidation	• No requirement that consideration be voting stock. As much as 50% of consideration can be cash and property without tax consequences for the stock received (cash and other property received *are* taxed). 50/50	• All liabilities of target corporation are assumed by acquiring corporation as a matter of law. • Acquiring approval of majority shareholders, dealing with dissenters' rights, and holding shareholder meetings, as required by foreign, state, or Federal law, may present problems.
B	Voting-stock-for-stock exchange	• Stock may be acquired from shareholders. • Procedures to effect reorganization are not complex.	• *Only* voting stock of acquiring corporation may be used. • Must have 80% control of a target corporation. • May have minority interest remaining in target corporation.
C	Stock-for-assets exchange	• Less complex than "Type A"; no foreign, state, or Federal law to follow. • Cash or property consideration for 20% or less of fair market value of property transferred is acceptable. • Acquiring corporation assumes only the target's liabilities that it chooses. 80/20 cash	• *Substantially all* assets of target corporation must be transferred. • Liabilities count as *other property* for 20% rule if any consideration other than stock and liabilities is used. • The target corporation must distribute the stock, securities, and other properties it receives in the reorganization to its shareholders.
D	Corporate division: spin-off, split-off, split-up	• Permits corporate division without tax consequences if no *boot* is involved.	• Control requirements of 50% for an acquisitive reorganization and 80% for a divisive reorganization must be met.
	Acquisitive	• Allows smaller target corporation to retain its existence.	
E	Recapitalization	• Allows for major changes in corporate equity structure.	
F	Change in identity, form, or place of organization	• Survivor is treated as same entity as predecessor; thus, tax attributes of predecessor are retained.	
G	Court-approved reorganization of bankrupt corporation	• Creditors can exchange debts for stock tax-free. • State merger laws need not be followed.	• Planning for use is limited.

the absence of a tax avoidance motive does not establish that there was the requisite business purpose.[28]

Given that a business purpose is required for a tax-free treatment, whose business purpose must it be—the corporation's or the shareholders'? The Regulations indicate that the corporation's business purpose should be paramount. However, the courts have considered both corporate and shareholder purposes because it is sometimes impossible to distinguish between them.[29]

ETHICAL and EQUITABLE Considerations

WHAT IS A SOUND BUSINESS PURPOSE?

Natural Resources, owned and operated by Monica Fairfield, would like to expand by acquiring Metro Publishing. Jay Fairfield, Monica's brother, is the sole shareholder of Metro. Metro's major assets are large net operating losses (NOLs), unused credits, negative accumulated E & P, and antiquated printing equipment. Natural Resources is very profitable and could easily utilize Metro's NOLs and unused credits. As Natural Resources is beginning to have concerns about the accumulated earnings tax, acquiring a corporation with a negative E & P looks very attractive.

Natural Resources wants the acquisition to be treated as a tax-free corporate reorganization, if possible. Upon discussions with Monica and Jay, the acquisition team orchestrating the reorganization learns that Natural Resources is engaged in reclaiming waterways in the proximity of strip mines and that Metro Publishing prints tour guidebooks for major cities. When asked about the business purpose of the merger, Monica says, "Natural Resources needs the NOLs and unused credits to offset its high taxable income. I would also like to help Jay get out from under a failing business. I guess Natural Resources might be able to print environmental pamphlets with Jay's equipment if it not too outdated and if doing that is really necessary."

What ethical issues does the team of acquisition professionals face in structuring the takeover of Metro Publishing by Natural Resources as a tax-free reorganization?

Continuity of Interest

The *continuity of interest* requirement prevents transactions that appear to be sales from qualifying as nontaxable reorganizations. Therefore, the continuity of interest test provides that if a shareholder has substantially the same investment after the restructuring as before, the transaction is not a taxable event. To qualify for tax-favored status, the target corporation shareholders must receive an equity interest in the acquiring corporation.[30]

The Regulations deem that the continuity of interest test is met when the target corporation shareholders receive acquiring corporation stock equal to at least 50 percent of their prior stock ownership in the target. Not all target shareholders need to receive stock in the surviving corporation. The requirement is applied to the aggregate consideration given by the acquiring corporation.

| EXAMPLE 30 | Target Corporation merges into Acquiring Corporation pursuant to state statutes. Under the merger plan, Target's shareholders can elect to receive either cash or stock in Acquiring. The shareholders who hold 40% of Target's outstanding stock elect to receive cash; the remaining 60% of the shareholders elect to receive Acquiring stock. This plan satisfies the |

---

[28]Reg. § 1.355–2(b) and *Marnes Wilson*, 66–1 USTC ¶9103, 16 AFTR2d 6030, 353 F.2d 184 (CA–9, 1966).

[29]*Lewis Trustee v. Comm.*, 49–2 USTC ¶9377, 38 AFTR 377, 176 F.2d 646 (CA–1, 1949); *Estate of Parshelsky v. Comm.*, 62–1 USTC ¶9460, 9 AFTR2d 1382, 303 F.2d 14 (CA–2, 1962).

[30]*Pinellas Ice & Cold Storage v. Comm.*, 3 USTC ¶1023, 11 AFTR 1112, 53 S.Ct. 257 (USSC, 1933), and *LeTulle v. Scofield*, 40–1 USTC ¶9150, 23 AFTR 789, 60 S.Ct. 313 (USSC, 1940). In *LeTulle*, a corporation transferred all its assets to another corporation for cash and bonds. The Court held that the transaction was not a tax-free reorganization if the transferor's only retained interest was that of a creditor. This concept is now in Reg. §§ 1.368–1(b) and (c).

continuity of interest test. The shareholders receiving cash are taxed on the transaction. Those receiving stock are not. ∎

Juanita owns 100% of Target Corporation. Target merges into Acquiring Corporation. Juanita receives 1% of Acquiring's outstanding stock in exchange for all of her Target stock. The continuity of interest test is met; Juanita received only stock for her interest. ∎

EXAMPLE 31

If the continuity of interest requirement is met at the time of the reorganization, a sale of stock to an unrelated party immediately before or after the restructuring will not destroy the continuity of interest. Unrelated parties include individuals, noncorporate entities, and corporations that are not part of either the acquirer's or the target's affiliated group.[31]

Pursuant to a preexisting contract, Juanita, in Example 31, sells all her Acquiring Corporation stock to Ying for its fair market value. This sale occurs one week after the reorganization. Since Ying is not considered a party related to Juanita, the sale to Ying does not affect the continuity of interest test. ∎

EXAMPLE 32

Continuity of Business Enterprise

The **continuity of business enterprise** test ensures that tax-free reorganization treatment is limited to situations where there is a continuing interest in the target's business. Specifically, this test requires the acquiring corporation to either (1) continue the target corporation's historic business (business test) or (2) use a significant portion of the target corporation's assets in its business (asset use test). Continuing one of the target corporation's significant business lines satisfies the business test. Determining whether the acquiring corporation's use of the target's assets is "significant" is based on the relative importance of the assets to the target's former business or their net fair market value.[32] Thus, meeting the asset use test depends on facts and circumstances.

The continuity of interest and business doctrines apply to reorganizations that involve two or more corporations. In these situations, there can be a discontinuance because the transaction may really be a sale rather than a corporate restructuring. When the reorganization involves only one corporation, the continuation of the interest or business is not a concern. Accordingly, these two doctrines do not apply to "Type E" and "Type F" reorganizations.[33]

Step Transaction

The **step transaction** doctrine prevents taxpayers from engaging in a series of transactions for the purpose of obtaining tax benefits that would not be allowed if the transaction was accomplished in a single step. When the steps are so interdependent that the accomplishment of one step would be fruitless without the completion of the series of steps, the transactions may be collapsed into a single step.[34]

The step transaction doctrine presents problems for reorganizations when the acquiring corporation does not want all of the target's assets. For a "Type C" and acquisitive "Type D," the target (acquirer for "Type D") must transfer substantially all of its assets to the acquiring (target for "Type D") corporation. If the target corporation attempts to dispose of its unwanted assets before a reorganization, the step transaction doctrine could ruin the reorganization's tax-favored status. The

---

[31]Reg. § 1.368–1(e)(3).

[32]Reg. § 1.368–1(d).

[33]Reg. § 1.368–1(b); T.D. 9182, 70 Fed.Reg. 9219 (February 25, 2005).

[34]*American Bantam Car Co.*, 11 T.C. 397 (1948), *aff'd* in 49–2 USTC ¶9471, 38 AFTR 820, 177 F.2d 513 (CA–3, 1949), *cert. den.* 70 S.Ct. 622 (USSC, 1950). If the steps have independent economic significance, the doctrine does not apply. See *Esmark, Inc.*, 90 T.C. 171 (1988) and Rev.Rul. 79–250, 1979–2 C.B. 156.

acquiring corporation would have failed to obtain substantially all of the target corporation's assets. Without direct evidence to the contrary, the IRS generally views any transactions occurring within one year of a reorganization as part of the restructuring.[35]

<table>
<tr><td>**LO.5**</td></tr>
<tr><td>Apply the rules pertaining to the carryover of tax attributes in a corporate reorganization.</td></tr>
</table>

Tax Attribute Carryovers

Some target corporation tax features (loss carryovers, tax credits, and E & P deficits) are welcomed by the successor corporation. Others may prove less desirable (positive E & P and assumption of liabilities). The mandatory carryover rules should be carefully considered in every corporate acquisition; they may, in fact, determine the form of the transaction.

Assumption of Liabilities

Since a corporate reorganization must result in some continuation of the previous corporation's business activities, existing liabilities are rarely liquidated (a "Type G" reorganization is the exception). The acquiring corporation either assumes the target corporation's liabilities or takes the target's assets subject to their liabilities. These liabilities are generally not considered boot when determining gain recognition for the corporations involved in the restructuring. Liabilities are problematic only in the "Type C" reorganization, when the acquiring corporation transfers other property to the target as well as stock. In this situation, the liabilities can cause a violation of the 80 percent-of-assets-for-voting-stock requirement.

Allowance of Carryovers

When a corporation acquires a target corporation's property, it also acquires the target's tax attributes. This occurs in the "Type A," "Type C," acquisitive "Type D," and "Type G" reorganizations. Section 381 determines which of the target corporation's tax benefits can be carried over to the successor. The "Type B," "Type E," and "Type F" reorganizations do not fall under the carryover rules of § 381 because the original target corporation remains intact and retains its own tax attributes. In a "Type B" reorganization, the target corporation merely becomes a subsidiary of the acquiring corporation. The "Type E" and "Type F" reorganizations involve only the original corporation; thus, no assets or tax attributes are being acquired. A divisive "Type D" reorganization also is not subject to § 381. In a spin-off or split-off, the old distributing corporation retains its tax attributes, and the new corporation starts fresh with regard to its tax attributes (with the exception of E & P). In a split-up, on the other hand, the tax attributes of the distributing corporation disappear when it liquidates.

Net Operating Loss Carryovers

A target corporation's NOL is one of the beneficial tax attributes (and sometimes its most valuable asset) that may be carried forward to the acquiring corporation. The NOL cannot be carried back to a prior acquiring corporation tax year; it can only be used prospectively. Thus, an NOL is a valuable target corporation asset that an acquiror can desire, because it can offset future income of the combined successor corporation.

---

[35]Reg. § 1.368–2(c), but in Rev.Rul. 69–48, 1969–1 C.B. 106, the IRS applied the step transaction doctrine to transactions that were 22 months apart.

ASIAN M&A ACTIVITY IS HEATING UP

The M&A business has been booming globally for the past two years, and especially in Asia. In 2007, there were almost 8,000 M&A deals in Asia, amounting to nearly $450 billion. The most active Asian sectors were financial services, the computer industry, and miscellaneous services.

Despite being one of the most challenging regulatory and cultural markets, China is leading the pack in Asian M&A activity, and its in-bound deals are expected to gain momentum over the next five years. Market and cultural barriers are less of a drag on M&A activity in China than in the past due to market liberalization and acquiring companies' increased willingness to work with the regulatory authorities over the long haul.

While China is attracting many investors, India is also a hot market for M&A activity. Its M&A volume has doubled in recent years, boosting its contribution to overall Asian M&A activity. India now ranks fifth among Asian nations in the number of cross-border deals annually, and it ranks seventh in the number of acquisitions taking place each year. The increase in activity has occurred even though M&A deals face a lengthy approval process in India's high courts. Legal complexities have long been a deterrent to multinational companies considering M&A activity in India.

In 2006, more than 32,000 M&A deals, with a combined value of almost $4.1 trillion, occurred around the world. The United States and Europe accounted for 81 percent of these transactions. Although Asia is a distant third, contributing 14 percent toward the global value of M&A activity, the Asian M&A business is on the rise and expected to increase dramatically in the next few years.

Sources: *Adapted from Mergerstat, LLC, December 2007;* Financial Times Information, *December 19, 2005, and June 21, 2006; and Oxford Economic Forecasting, Ltd., "The Outlook for M&A Activity," UK Weekly Brief, April 13, 2007.*

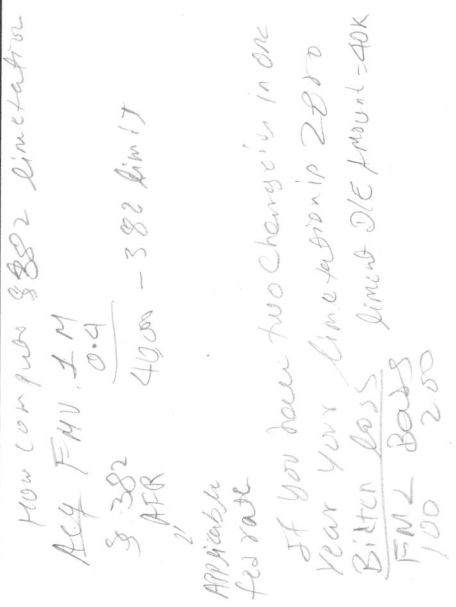

GLOBAL *Tax Issues*

EXAMPLE 33

Target Corporation has accumulated a $3 million NOL prior to its merger with Acquiring Corporation. After the reorganization, the Acquiring/Target successor corporation generates $5 million of taxable income. Target's $3 million NOL carries over to offset the $5 million taxable income, reducing it to $2 million. The successor corporation saves $1,020,000 in Federal income taxes by being able to utilize Target's NOL carryover ($3 million NOL carryover × 34%). Thus, the $3 million NOL is a valuable asset to Target that may be worth as much as $1 million. ■

Ownership Changes. To curtail the tax benefits received from NOL carryovers, § 382 limits the yearly amount of NOL that may be utilized by the successor corporation. The **§ 382 limitation** applies when there is a more than 50-percentage-point ownership change (by value) for the common shareholders of the target (loss) corporation. An **ownership change** takes place on the day (*change date*) that either an *equity structure shift* or an *owner shift* occurs.

- An **equity structure shift** occurs when a tax-free reorganization causes an owner shift. The change date for an equity shift is the date the reorganization takes place. The equity shift limitation is not applicable to "Type F," divisive "Type D," or "Type G" reorganizations.
- An **owner shift** is any change in the common stock ownership of shareholders owning at least 5 percent. Owner shifts can be caused by purchases, stock issuances, redemptions, recapitalizations, and transfers to controlled corporations.

Whether an ownership change has occurred is determined by examining the common stock ownership during a testing period, generally the prior three years.[36]

---

[36]The testing period is the period following the most recent ownership change if that change occurred within the past three years. Further, the testing period cannot begin before the year in which the carryforward being tested occurs. See § 382(i).

Shareholders owning less than a 5 percent interest during the testing period are aggregated and treated as one shareholder for determining an owner shift. Thus, transfers between shareholders who own less than 5 percent do not influence the percentage-point ownership change computation.

andrew mitchel international

EXAMPLE 34

5% S/H public corp to controle

In acustion of there is a boot, it is taken as Dividens

Target Corporation is merged into Acquiring Corporation in a "Type A" reorganization. At the time of the merger, Target had an NOL of $100,000. Pursuant to the merger, Target's shareholders, none of whom own a 5% interest, receive 40% of Acquiring's stock. An equity structure shift has taken place. Since all of Target's shareholders owned less than 5%, they are aggregated in determining the owner shift. As a group, these shareholders owned 100% of the loss corporation prior to the reorganization and only 40% of the successor corporation after the reorganization. A more than 50-percentage-point ownership change has occurred because of the reorganization.

Horizontal Double Dumey

Basis is §351

Orbital

Seibel

New Orbital   *New S*   *§351*

Stock Cash   *S/H*

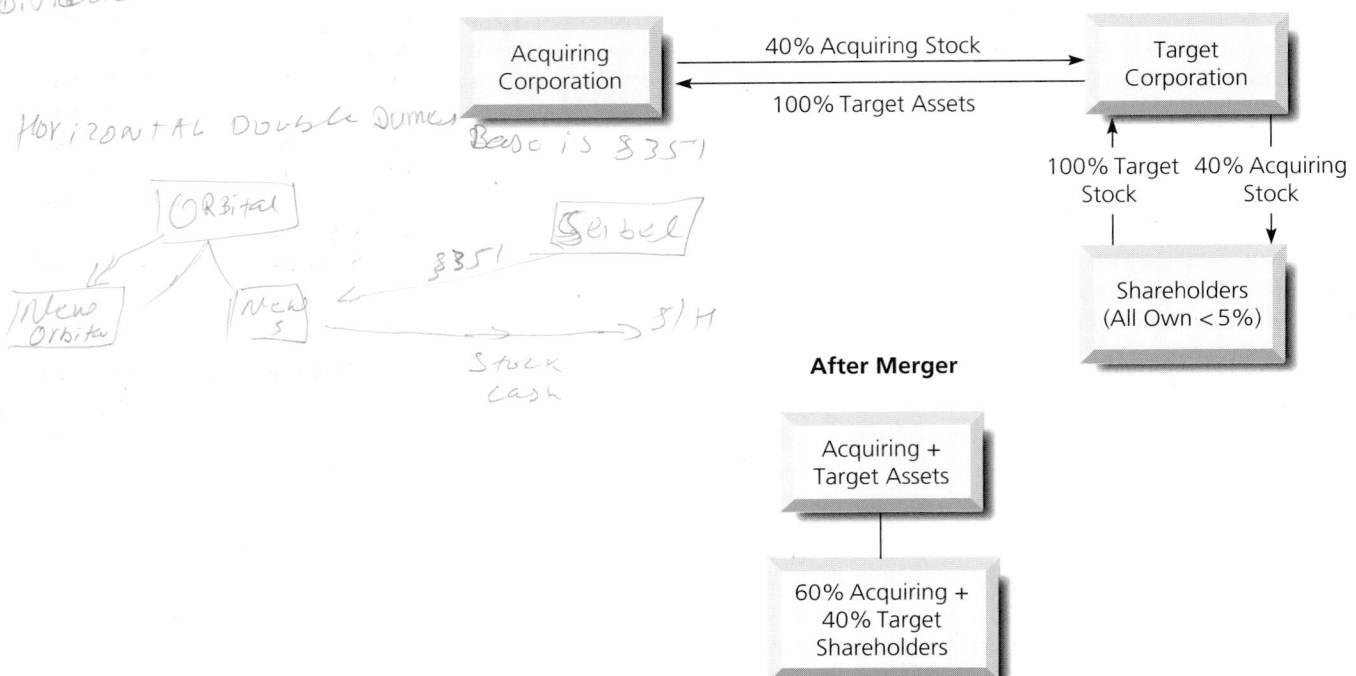

After Merger

When an ownership change occurs, the yearly NOL amount usable by the successor corporation is restricted. The limit is based on the fair market value of the loss corporation's stock (both common and preferred) multiplied by the **long-term tax-exempt rate** (the highest adjusted Federal long-term rate for the prior three-month period).[37] The stock received in a reorganization or the price paid for the loss corporation's stock generally indicates its fair market value.

Since the § 382 limitation is based on the loss corporation's value, there is an incentive to inflate its value prior to the ownership change. This could be accomplished through capital contributions. The so-called anti-stuffing rules prohibit this behavior by disregarding assets contributed within the two years prior to the change date.

---

[37]The determination of value occurs immediately *after* the ownership change in the case of redemptions or other contractions that are associated with the ownership change.

TAX *in the News*   **MERGER MANIA IS A BOARDROOM ILLNESS**

Mergers and acquisitions (M&A) seem to be the current craze in boardrooms across America. Yet research shows that surges in corporate M&A often are poorly timed, appearing just ahead of peaks in the stock market. The M&A activity may help stock market valuations, but only for a while. M&A transactions may extend a bull market a little longer, but at some point the momentum will subside.

While M&A may be good for the market, what is the benefit to the M&A participants themselves? There is little evidence that the acquiring corporation or its shareholders profit from the M&A in the short to medium term. It seems that the investment banks that instigate the M&A are the only real winners. The present boom in M&A appears to be fueled by low yields on debt. As long as the cost of financing is less than the expected cash inflow from the new combined entity, the M&A may appear reasonable, when otherwise it would not. Whether the businesses have synergy and will be profitable in the marketplace is almost beside the point. M&A often fail to be beneficial because the assumptions justifying the combinations are too optimistic and the prices paid are too high. There should be a compelling reason for

the M&A transaction, and the price must be evaluated critically.

M&A that tend to be successful generally involve similar businesses that combine for economies of scale or increased commercial clout. Exxon and Mobil, Nationsbank and Bank of America, and Procter & Gamble and Gillette are examples of these M&A. Another common logic supporting M&A is to combine the producing and distributing facets of a business. Time Warner and AOL, and Travelers and Citibank are examples. These deals may not live up to expectations, however, because the participants overestimate the potential cost reductions and cross-selling.

Some analysts believe that whether an M&A transaction will be profitable depends more on the deal makers than on the deal. If corporate executives are successful in adding value for shareholders generally, any M&A they arrange will also add value. In contrast, seemingly obvious corporate combinations can be disastrous when they are conceived of and orchestrated by executives who manage the M&A transition incompetently.

Source: *Adapted from Conrad De Aenlle, "If It's a Merger, 2nd Thoughts Should Follow," New York Times, April 14, 2007 (Late Edition).*

EXAMPLE 35

Winner Corporation acquires Loser Corporation when Loser has a $250,000 NOL carry-forward. Winner exchanges 30% of its stock valued at $600,000 for all of Loser's stock. The applicable long-term tax-exempt rate at the change date is 5%. Several months before the acquisition by Winner, Loser's shareholders contributed investment assets with a fair market value of $100,000, thus increasing Loser's value from $500,000 to $600,000. The § 382 limitation computation will not include the recent increase in Loser's fair market value. Consequently, the yearly § 382 limitation is $25,000 ($500,000 × 5%). ■

The objective of the § 382 *limitation* is to restrict NOL use to a hypothetical future income stream from the loss corporation. This future income stream is defined as the yield that would be received if the stock was sold and the proceeds were invested in long-term tax-exempt securities. Thus, the formula for computing the § 382 limitation is as follows.

> **Loss corporation's FMV on change date**
> **× Federal long-term tax-exempt rate**
> **= Yearly § 382 limitation**

Section 382 does not disallow an NOL. It merely limits the amount of NOL carryover that the successor corporation can utilize on an annual basis. In some cases, however, due to the § 382 limitation, the NOL may expire before it is utilized fully. Therefore, the § 382 limitation should be considered when determining the tax benefit an acquiring corporation receives from the target corporation's NOL. Since the NOL tax benefit may be the target's most valuable asset, a present value analysis is highly relevant for determining the amount the acquiring corporation is willing to pay for the NOL asset. Tax benefits received in future years are not worth as much as tax benefits received currently. The farther in the future the NOL deduction is available, the less it is worth today. At some point, depending on the discount factor used, the NOL postponed to distant future years may be almost worthless in present value dollar terms.

EXAMPLE 36

MakingIt Corporation acquires WashedUp Corporation in a transaction that subjects WashedUp's $600,000 NOL to a $40,000 per year § 382 limitation. After the acquisition, there are 15 years remaining for deducting the NOL. Given that MakingIt uses a discount factor of 10% for evaluating the benefit of possible transactions, the present value of a $40,000 deduction every year for the next 15 years, assuming a corporate tax rate of 35%, is $106,484. Thus, MakingIt should not pay WashedUp more than $106,484 for the $210,000 NOL tax benefits ($600,000 NOL × 35% tax rate). This means that because of the time value of money the NOL is worth about half of its face value! The present value of the NOL is computed as follows.

> **$40,000 × 35% tax rate = $14,000 tax saving per year × 7.606 (discount factor for present value of annuity for 15 years at a 10% discount rate) = $106,484**

Suppose that the § 382 yearly limitation is $120,000 rather than $40,000. Now the NOL can be fully deducted in 5 years rather than 15 years. Using the same discount factor (10%), the value of the NOL benefit to MakingIt increases to $159,222, computed as follows.

> **$120,000 × 35% tax rate = $42,000 tax savings per year × 3.791(discount factor for present value of annuity for 5 years at a 10% discount rate) = $159,222** ∎

If the successor corporation's current-year taxable income is insufficient to offset the authorized NOL deduction, the amount not utilized may be carried forward and added to the next year's § 382 limitation.

EXAMPLE 37.

Profit Corporation acquires Loss Corporation and its $300,000 NOL in a transaction causing an equity structure shift. Loss's value on the change date is $500,000, and the applicable long-term tax-exempt rate is 5%. Therefore, the yearly § 382 limitation is $25,000 ($500,000 × 5%). During the current year, Profit/Loss successor corporation has $20,000 net income before the NOL deduction. The successor corporation may offset its taxable income by $20,000 of the NOL. Since the § 382 limit is $25,000, the NOL limit for next year will be $30,000 ($25,000 current + $5,000 prior-year carryover) rather than $25,000. ∎

A further limitation on the ability to utilize the NOL carryforward arises in the year that the ownership change occurs (change year). The NOL amount available to the successor corporation in the change year is limited to the percentage of days remaining in the tax year after the change day. The § 382 yearly NOL limitation is multiplied by this percentage.

The formula for this computation is as follows.

> **Yearly § 382 limitation**
> **× Number of days remaining in year/365 (366 in leap year)**
> **= Initial year § 382 limitation**

Lastly, the NOL carryover is disallowed for future taxable years if the successor corporation fails to satisfy the continuity of business enterprise requirement for at least two years following any ownership equity shift. The continuity of business enterprise test is the same as for tax-free reorganizations. That is, a significant historical

CONCEPT SUMMARY 7–5

Summary of Carryover Rules

Tax attributes that carry over from a loss corporation to the successor corporation:

1. Loss carryovers—subject to the § 382 limitation.
   A. Annual limitations on carryover use are evoked when there is an ownership change—a more than 50-percentage-point owner shift or an equity structure shift.
      - Owner shift is a change in the ownership of shareholders owning 5% or more of the corporate stock.
      - Equity shift occurs in tax-free reorganizations, other than a divisive "Type D," a "Type F," or a "Type G."
   B. Annual carryover usage cannot exceed the value of the old loss corporation on the change date (date of transfer) multiplied by the highest long-term tax-exempt Federal rate for the three calendar months prior to the structure change.
   C. Year of transfer. The loss claimed in the year of transfer is limited to the annual limitation multiplied by a percentage representing the remaining days in the year of transfer.
   D. Loss corporation carryovers are applied to the § 382 limitation in this order: built-in capital losses, capital loss carryovers, built-in ordinary losses, NOL carryovers, foreign tax credits, business credit carryovers, and lastly minimum tax credit carryovers.
2. Earnings and profits.
   A. Positive E & P of an acquired corporation carries over.
   B. If either corporation has a deficit in E & P, the successor corporation will have two E & P accounts. One account contains the total positive accumulated E & P as of the date of the transfer. The other contains the total deficit as of the date of the transfer. Future positive E & P may offset the deficit E & P account.
3. Other tax attributes.
   A. Depreciation and cost recovery methods carry over.
   B. The installment method of reporting carries over.

line of the loss corporation's business must be continued, or the successor corporation must use a significant amount of the loss corporation's assets in its business.

EXAMPLE 38

On December 1, Minus transfers all of its assets to Plus (a calendar year corporation) in exchange for 40% of Plus's stock. At the time of the merger, Minus is valued at $900,000 and has an NOL carryover of $200,000. The long-term tax-exempt rate is 5%. Since a more than 50-percentage-point ownership change has occurred for Minus's shareholders, the amount of NOL available for use in the merger year is $3,699 [$900,000 × 5% = $45,000 × (30/365)]. The NOL available to reduce the successor corporation's taxable income in the next year is $45,000. If Minus successor corporation fails to continue Minus's historical business or use substantially all of its assets for a two-year period, the successor corporation is not allowed to use any of Minus's NOL. ■

Earnings and Profits

The E & P of an acquired corporation carries over to a successor corporation.[38] However, the Supreme Court later held that a successor corporation was not permitted to apply the acquired corporation's E & P deficit against its own E & P.[39] The result was confusion in applying these general rules. Earnings and profits of a deficit corporation are now deemed to be received by the successor corporation as of the change date. A deficit may be used only to offset E & P accumulated by the successor corporation after the change date.[40]

---

[38] *Comm. v. Sansome*, 3 USTC ¶978, 11 AFTR 854, 60 F.2d 931 (CA–2, 1931), *cert. den.* 53 S.Ct. 291 (USSC, 1932).

[39] *Comm. v. Phipps*, 49–1 USTC ¶9204, 37 AFTR 827, 69 S.Ct. 616 (USSC, 1949).
[40] § 381(c)(2) and Reg. § 1.381(c)(2)–1(a)(5).

Consequently, the successor corporation must maintain two separate E & P accounts after the change date: one account contains the prior accumulated E & P as of the change date, and the other contains the deficit transferred and E & P accumulated since the change date. The deficit in the post-transfer account may not be used to reduce accumulated E & P in the pre-transfer account.

EXAMPLE 39

Target Corporation is merged into Acquiring Corporation on December 31, 2007. On that date, the E & P balance for Target is a negative $75,000, and for Acquiring it is a positive $400,000. In 2008, current E & P for Acquiring is $50,000. Acquiring now has two E & P balances: pre-2008 $400,000 and post-2007 negative $25,000 ($50,000 − $75,000).

	12/31/2007	E & P 2008	12/31/2008
Post-2007 E & P	($ 75,000)	$50,000	($ 25,000)
Pre-2008 E & P	400,000		400,000

■

Other Carryovers

The capital losses and excess tax credits carried over to the successor corporation are also limited if there is an ownership change for the loss corporation's shareholders.[41] The capital loss carryovers are characterized as short term and are taken before the NOL carryovers in applying the § 382 limitation. Computing the amount of excess credits allowable in the current year is more complicated than determining the capital loss or NOL carryover, as the steps below indicate.

1. Calculate regular tax liability after allowable losses.
2. Compute regular tax liability as if the full § 382 limitation is deductible.
3. Subtract the tax liability in step 2 from the tax liability in step 1. The remainder is the § 382 limitation applicable to excess credits.

EXAMPLE 40

User Corporation acquired $100,000 of general business credits from Idle Corporation. The § 382 limitation for the year is $200,000, and User's taxable income is $800,000 before applying this limitation. If the full deduction allowable by § 382 were utilized, User's taxable income would be $600,000 ($800,000 − $200,000). The amount of general business credit that User may take in the current year is $68,000, computed as follows.

Step 1. Regular tax liability ($800,000 × 34% tax rate):	$272,000
Step 2. Tax liability with full § 382 limitation ($600,000 × 34% tax rate):	204,000
Step 3. Subtract step 2 from step 1:	$ 68,000

■

EXAMPLE 41

Two years ago, Gain Corporation acquired Loss Corporation in a transaction causing an ownership change. The § 382 limitation is $100,000 for the current year. Gain Corporation's taxable income before considering carryovers is $400,000 ordinary income and $100,000 capital gain. The Loss Corporation carryovers to the current year include a $20,000 capital loss, a $60,000 NOL, and $30,000 of excess business credits. The capital loss is utilized first to offset the capital gain, and then the NOL is used against the ordinary income. Taxable income becomes $420,000 ($500,000 − $20,000 − $60,000). If the full § 382 limitation were utilized, taxable income would be $400,000 ($500,000 − $100,000). The amount of excess business credit allowable in the current year is $6,800, computed as follows.

Step 1. Regular tax liability ($420,000 × 34%):	$142,800
Step 2. Tax liability with full § 382 limitation ($400,000 × 34%)	136,000
Step 3. Subtract step 2 from step 1	$ 6,800

■

---

[41]§ 383.

The benefit from all loss corporation carryovers taken in the current year cannot, in total, exceed the calculated yearly § 382 limitation. When a corporation has several types of loss corporation carryovers, they are applied to the § 382 limitation in the following sequence.

1. Built-in capital losses.
2. Capital loss carryovers.
3. Built-in ordinary losses.
4. NOL carryovers.
5. Foreign tax credits.
6. Business credit carryovers.
7. Minimum tax credit carryovers.[42]

Besides the § 382 limitation, the year-of-transfer limitation applies to all of these carryovers.

Disallowance of Carryovers

Irrespective of the carryover rules, the IRS can utilize § 269 to disallow the carryover of tax benefits if a tax avoidance scheme is apparent. Such items are disallowed when a corporation acquires property of another corporation primarily to evade or avoid Federal income tax by securing the benefits that the acquiring corporation would not otherwise enjoy. Whether the principal purpose is tax evasion or avoidance is a question of fact. If the loss corporation's business is promptly discontinued after a corporate reorganization, the IRS may use § 269 to disallow the loss carryovers.

The Role of the Letter Ruling

When feasible, the parties contemplating a corporate reorganization should apply for and obtain from the IRS a letter ruling concerning the income tax effect of the transaction(s). Assuming the parties carry out the transfers as proposed in the ruling request, a favorable ruling provides, in effect, an insurance policy. If the tax implications are significant, as they often are with corporate reorganizations, the advantage of obtaining prior IRS approval is clear. To expedite the letter ruling process, the IRS is now trying to issue the rulings within 10 weeks from the date of the request.[43]

Assessing the Possible Benefits of Restructuring Options

TAX PLANNING
Considerations

Reorganizations are valuable tools in corporate tax-free restructurings. However, it may not be possible to achieve the desired corporate structure by utilizing a single reorganization type. For this reason, reorganizations should not be seen as mutually exclusive transactions; they can be combined with other tax-favored transactions into a comprehensive plan. The tax law allows a series of tax-favored transactions to be recognized as legitimate separate steps when the statutory requirements for each are met.

EXAMPLE 42

Black Corporation operates two businesses, both of which have been in existence for five years. One business is a manufacturing operation; the other is a wholesale distributorship. White Corporation wishes to acquire only the manufacturing business and refuses to purchase all of Black's assets. ■

---

[42]Reg. § 1.383–1(d).   [43]Rev.Proc. 2005–68, 2005–41 I.R.B. 694 (September 14, 2005).

What course of action might be advisable to transfer the manufacturing operation from Black to White with the least, if any, tax costs? Compare the following three possibilities.

1. Black Corporation transfers the manufacturing operation to White Corporation in return for some of the latter's stock.
2. Black Corporation forms Orange Corporation and transfers the manufacturing business to it in return for all of Orange's stock. The Orange stock is then distributed to Black's shareholders. This portion of the arrangement is a nontaxable spin-off. Orange now transfers the manufacturing operation to White Corporation in exchange for some of the latter's stock.
3. Rather than transferring the manufacturing business as described in possibility 2, Black transfers the wholesale distributorship. White exchanges some of its voting stock for the Black stock. Black is now a subsidiary of White.

Possibility 1 probably will not fit within the definition of a "Type C" reorganization, because Black does not transfer substantially all of the assets in return for White stock. The manufacturing operation is transferred, but the wholesale distributorship is not. As a result, Black continues to exist. A "Type C" usually requires that the target corporation liquidate after the reorganization.

Possibility 2 is a spin-off of the assets *desired* by White, followed by a "Type C" reorganization between Orange and White. This approach is acceptable to the IRS even though White does not acquire "substantially all" of Black's assets. The transaction is treated as successfully creating a separate corporation (Orange) through a "Type D" reorganization. The "Type C" is considered to be only between White and Orange. Black is not a party to the latter reorganization.[44]

Possibility 3 follows a different approach. It starts with the spin-off of the *unwanted* assets and concludes with White obtaining the *wanted* assets by exchanging its stock for the Black stock. Taken by itself, this last step satisfies the voting-stock-for-stock requirement of a "Type B" reorganization. If, however, the step transaction doctrine is applied and the spin-off is disregarded, the Orange stock distributed to Black's shareholders might be considered as property *other than voting stock* in White. The IRS has not chosen to take this position and probably will recognize the nontaxability of a spin-off of *unwanted* assets followed by a "Type B" reorganization.[45]

EXAMPLE 43

Major and Minor are unrelated corporations in separate lines of business. For valid business purposes, Major would like to acquire Minor through a nontaxable transaction. Major will continue Minor's line of business after the reorganization and, in light of product liability issues, would like to keep the companies separate. However, there are substantial investment assets in Minor that Major would like to possess. How can Major acquire Minor's investments and still keep Minor as a separate entity? ■

Combining a corporate reorganization with a distribution allows Major to receive the investments and have Minor continue as a corporation. Major exchanges its voting stock for all of Minor's stock. This is accomplished either by a direct exchange with the Minor shareholders, or by Minor recalling its stock and distributing the Major voting stock to its shareholders. Since Major exchanges only voting stock for Minor's stock, the transaction qualifies as a tax-deferred "Type B" reorganization. Minor is now a wholly owned subsidiary of Major. Minor then distributes the investment assets as a dividend to its parent, Major. This distribution qualifies for the 100 percent dividends received deduction. The IRS will not recast this as an acquisition of Minor's assets and stock for voting stock of Major.[46]

---

[44]Rev.Rul. 2003–79, I.R.B. 2003–29.
[45]Rev.Rul. 70–434, 1970–2 C.B. 83.
[46]Rev.Rul. 74–35, 1974–1 C.B. 85.

Carryover Considerations.
Careful consideration of the restructuring alternative can help to preserve desirable tax carryover attributes.

EXAMPLE 44

Acquiring Corporation wants to obtain the assets of Target Corporation. These assets have a $300,000 basis to Target and a $200,000 fair market value. Target has incurred losses in its operations during the past several years and possesses $250,000 in NOLs. Acquiring plans to continue the business conducted by Target, hoping to do so on a profitable basis. ■

To carry out the planned acquisition of Target's assets, Acquiring could consider the following alternatives.

1. Using cash and/or other property, Acquiring purchases the assets directly from Target. Following the purchase, Target liquidates and distributes the cash and/or property to its shareholders.
2. Acquiring purchases for cash and/or other property all of the stock in Target from its shareholders. Shortly thereafter, Acquiring liquidates Target.
3. Utilizing a "Type A" reorganization, Target merges into Acquiring. In exchange for their stock, Target's shareholders receive stock in Acquiring.
4. Under a "Type C" reorganization, Target transfers all of its assets to Acquiring in return for the latter's voting stock. Target distributes the Acquiring stock to its shareholders and liquidates.

A satisfactory solution must center around the preservation of Target Corporation's favorable tax attributes—the high basis in the assets and the NOL carryovers. Alternative 1 is highly unsatisfactory. It will not retain Target's favorable tax attributes. The purchase price (probably $200,000) becomes the basis of the assets in the hands of Acquiring Corporation. Further, any unused NOLs disappear upon Target's liquidation. Target has a realized loss of $100,000 [$300,000 (basis in the assets) − $200,000 (sale proceeds)] from the sale of its assets. Yet the realized loss may generate little, if any, tax savings to Target. In view of Target's unabsorbed NOL carryovers, it appears doubtful that the company will generate much taxable income in the year of sale.

Alternative 2 appears to be a better solution but has a major risk. When a subsidiary is liquidated under § 332, the subsidiary's basis in its assets carries over to the acquiring corporation.[47] Therefore, Target's $300,000 basis in its assets becomes Acquiring's basis in the assets. What Acquiring paid (probably $200,000 plus the net present value of the NOL) for the Target stock becomes irrelevant. Target's NOLs also carry over to Acquiring. However, § 269 (disallowing any deduction or credit when the acquisition was made to evade or avoid income tax) could present a problem. Section 269(b) specifically applies to a liquidation within two years after the acquisition date.

Alternatives 3 and 4 should accomplish the same tax result, but with less tax risk. Presuming Acquiring can establish a business purpose for the "Type A" or "Type C" reorganization, § 269 can be avoided. The preservation of favorable tax attributes, such as the NOL carryover and any built-in loss or credit carryovers, should be considered when acquiring a small corporation.

The alternatives are illustrated in Figure 7–7.

EXAMPLE 45

Cardinal Corporation, worth $200,000, has a $150,000 NOL. The stock in Cardinal is owned by Kevin, 55%, and Fran, 45%. Kevin wants to sell his interest in Cardinal and retire. But what happens to the NOL if Kevin sells his entire interest? There would be a more than 50-percentage-point change in the ownership of Cardinal Corporation. Therefore, the § 382 limitation would be $200,000 times the long-term tax-exempt rate. Assume the rate is 10%. The loss of $150,000 is now limited to $20,000 annually. Can a sale be structured so that the NOL is not so limited?

An owner shift is calculated for the three-year testing period. Kevin could sell 35% of Cardinal stock in Year 1, 5% in Year 2, 5% in Year 3, and 10% in Year 4. None of the three-

---

[47]§ 334(b)(1).

| FIGURE 7-7 | Four Alternatives for Acquiring Corporate Assets |

Alternative 1: Purchase of Target Assets

In a purchase of Target's assets for their fair market value of $200,000, Acquiring Corporation has a $200,000 basis in the assets. Target's higher basis of $300,000 is lost. In addition, its NOL of $250,000 disappears. Although Target recognizes a loss on the liquidation, the loss is not beneficial, as Target does not have taxable income that the loss can offset.

Alternative 2: Purchase of Target Stock—
Liquidation of Target by Acquiring

If Acquiring obtains all of Target's stock from the shareholders and liquidates Target, thereby obtaining all of Target's assets, there is a carryover of Target's basis in its assets. Thus, Acquiring has a basis of $300,000 in the assets. Target's NOL of $250,000 carries over to Acquiring, subject to the § 382 limitation. However, § 269 may be applied to disallow the basis carryover and NOL carryover.

Alternatives 3 and 4: "Type A" or "Type C" Reorganization

In a "Type A" or a "Type C" reorganization, the $300,000 basis in Target's assets will carry over to Acquiring. In addition, the $250,000 NOL carries over to Acquiring, subject to the § 382 limitation. Section 269 is less of a problem than in a subsidiary liquidation under § 332.

---

year testing periods has a more than 50-percentage-point change in the ownership of the corporation. Thus, there is no § 382 limitation. Cardinal can deduct the entire $150,000 NOL sooner rather than later. ■

KEY TERMS

Business purpose, 7–24

Consolidation, 7–11

Continuity of business enterprise, 7–27

Continuity of interest test, 7–11

Control, 7–13

Equity structure shift, 7–29

Long-term tax-exempt rate, 7–30

Merger, 7–10

Owner shift, 7–29

Ownership change, 7–29

Recapitalization, 7–19

Reorganization, 7–5

Section 382 limitation, 7–29

Spin-off, 7–19

Split-off, 7–19

Split-up, 7–19

Step transaction, 7–27

PROBLEM MATERIALS

DISCUSSION QUESTIONS

1. Identify an industry that has seen a dramatic increase in bankruptcies in recent years. Which corporations in this industry made the "largest bankruptcies" list in Exhibit 7–2?

2. Corporate reorganizations can produce taxable gains for the shareholders. Explain whether corporate and individual shareholders prefer the same tax treatment.

3. Briefly list the seven forms of corporate reorganizations that qualify as nontaxable exchanges.

4. Explain how the parties involved in a § 368 corporate reorganization receive treatment similar to that in a like-kind exchange.

5. In what situations can a shareholder's gain caused by a corporate reorganization be treated as a dividend? In what situations could the stock redemption rules apply to a shareholder's gain?

6. Dunn purchased 20,000 shares of stock in Pear Corporation eight years ago. This constituted 20% of Pear's outstanding shares. Last year, Pear redeemed 10,000 shares of Dunn's stock for $100 a share. In the current year, all of Pear's shareholders exchange their stock for an equal number of shares in Plum Corporation plus $5 a share. The cash payment is made because Plum stock is valued at $100 a share and Pear stock is now valued at $105 a share. Plum does not want to issue fractional shares. After the transaction, Pear becomes a subsidiary of Plum. What are the tax issues to be considered in this situation?

Issue ID

7. Explain the stock and control requirements in a "Type B" reorganization. After a "Type B" reorganization, what is the relationship between the corporations participating in the restructuring?

8. What are the stock and asset exchange requirements for a "Type C" reorganization? How do liabilities of the target corporation influence these requirements?

9. Describe the similarities and differences of the "Type A" and "Type C" reorganizations.

10. Compare a "Type B" reorganization with a "Type C" reorganization in terms of consideration.

11. There are four different kinds of "Type D" reorganizations. Briefly describe each type.

12. A "Type E" reorganization is considered to be a recapitalization. What is a recapitalization?

13. "Type F" is a mere change in the identity, form, or place of organization. What constitutes a change in the identity or form of a corporation?

14. The acquiring corporation in a "Type G" reorganization must reduce the tax attributes carried over from the bankrupt corporation. To what extent must the attributes be reduced, and in what order are they reduced?

Issue ID

15. Sun Corporation is considering acquiring Moon Corporation. Sun produces skin care protection products. Moon is a pharmaceutical company that specializes in prescription sleep-enhancing medications. Moon has not been profitable of late and has a sizable NOL and excess business credits. Sun could use these tax attributes, as it is very profitable. If the merger occurs, Sun will exchange 30% of its stock and some cash for most of Moon's assets. Sun is concerned about prescription drug liability issues and, therefore, is considering changing Moon's product line to vitamins. As Sun's adviser, what concerns do you have regarding the proposed merger of Sun and Moon?

16. Star Corporation would like to expand its retail sales business to include small appliances. Rather than try to break into this market, Star would like to acquire a company with a successful appliance sales business. Planet Corporation would fit Star's needs; however, Planet sells commercial as well as small appliances. Since Star has no interest in the commercial appliance market, it asks Planet to sell off this division before the firms enter into a "Type C" reorganization. Provide an analysis of the proposed reorganization.

17. Why does the § 381 limitation not apply to "Type B," "Type E," and "Type F" reorganizations?

18. The amount of NOL that a successor corporation may utilize in any one year is limited by § 382 if there is an ownership change within the testing period for shareholders owning at least 5% of the common stock. How are shareholders that own less than 5% of the stock treated? How long is the testing period?

19. What is the objective of the § 382 limitation?

Communications

20. Emily Arson is the president and sole shareholder of Emar Corporation, a small shoe production company. Though Emar's manufacturing equipment is old and not of much value, Emar's plant has a very favorable location. Mega Tires, Inc., is interested in acquiring Emar solely to obtain the land. Mega Tires would likely junk Emar's manufacturing equipment and demolish the plant so that it could build a new tire retail outlet at the location. The plant and land are 90% of Emar's asset value. Mega Tires has proposed exchanging $1 million of its stock for Emar's assets.

    Emily has heard of the continuity of business enterprise requirement that must be met for a corporate reorganization to receive tax-free treatment. She is concerned that the proposed transaction will not meet this requirement. Write Emily Arson a letter explaining what she must include in her contract with Mega Tires to ensure that the proposed reorganization will satisfy the continuity of business enterprise doctrine. Emily's address is 510 S. Market Street, Alton, MO 65606.

21. Explain the application of the § 382 limitation to tax attributes carried over from a loss corporation to the successor corporation in the year that the corporate reorganization occurs.

22. List the steps in applying the § 382 limitation to excess business credits.

23. How is a target corporation's negative E & P balance treated when it is carried over to the successor corporation?

Communications

24. Ula Washington, CEO of Dove Corporation, is currently working with the corporation's attorneys on the details of a merger involving Dove and Desert Corporation. Counsel has mentioned that receiving a private letter ruling might be good insurance for the merger. If the merger is not treated as tax deferred, Dove, Desert, and their shareholders could pay more than $50 million in Federal taxes. Write a memo to Ula Washington explaining how to view an IRS letter ruling. Discuss how long it will take to receive a letter ruling from the IRS.

25. Pirate Corporation has had financial difficulties for the last three years and has accumulated a $200,000 NOL. Morgan, the majority shareholder and president of Pirate, thinks that Pirate could be successful under new management. Therefore, he would like to

sell his 75% ownership in Pirate and move to Brazil. Xandra would like to purchase Morgan's shares, as she thinks she could manage Pirate back into the black. However, she wants to make sure that the NOL is available, without limitations, to offset the taxable income she expects to generate. Suggest a method for selling Morgan's stock to Xandra that will keep the NOL fully available to offset Pirate's future taxable income.

PROBLEMS

26. What type of reorganization is effected in each of the following transactions?

   Decision Making

   a. Purple Corporation manufactures toys and plastic pots. Due to the possible product liability associated with toys, Purple wants to separate the two divisions. Purple creates two corporations, Blue and Red. It transfers the toy division assets to Blue and the plastic pot division assets to Red in exchange for all of the stock of Blue and Red. Purple then liquidates.

   b. Green Corporation originally was organized as a Subchapter S corporation. It violates the S election requirements and becomes a regular C corporation.

   c. Yellow Corporation and Red Corporation are interested in merging. To indicate to the public that the transaction is not a takeover, a new entity, Orange Corporation, will be formed. Yellow and Red will transfer all of their assets to Orange in exchange for 100% of Orange's common stock worth $500,000 and $600,000 in long-term bonds. The stock and bonds are distributed to the shareholders of Yellow and Red in exchange for their stock. Yellow and Red then liquidate.

   d. Same as (c), except that only Orange stock worth $1.1 million is received and exchanged with the Yellow and Red shareholders.

   e. Amber Corporation has been having financial difficulties and is not able to make the interest payments to its bondholders. Under the guidance of a state court, all of its assets are transferred to New Corporation. New Corporation's voting stock is distributed to all of Amber's bondholders.

   f. Brown Corporation exchanges 25% of its stock and land valued at $100,000 for all of the assets and liabilities of Green Corporation. Green distributes the stock and the land to its shareholders for all of their stock in Green. Green then ceases to exist. The value of Green's assets at the date of the transaction is $350,000.

   g. Black Corporation exchanges 40% of its voting stock for 90% of White's assets worth $900,000 and all of White's liabilities amounting to $200,000. The remaining White assets are distributed to its shareholders. The Black stock is also distributed to the White shareholders in exchange for their stock. White then terminates.

   h. Same as (g), except that Black transfers 40% of its stock and $100,000 in bonds in exchange for all of White's assets and liabilities.

   i. The shareholders of Blue Corporation and Yellow Corporation agree to form Green Corporation. All of the assets of Blue and 60% of the assets of Yellow are transferred to Green in exchange for all of Green's common stock. Some Green stock is distributed to the shareholders of Blue in exchange for all of their Blue stock. Blue then terminates. The Yellow shareholders receive the remaining Green stock and do not have any of their Yellow stock redeemed.

   j. Pink Corporation redeems its 20-year, 5% bonds. The bonds have a face value of $1,000. For each bond, Pink issues 10 shares of preferred stock with $100 par value.

   k. Gray Corporation offers to acquire White stock by exchanging two shares of its voting stock for each share of White stock issued and outstanding. Ninety percent of the White shareholders enter into the exchange with Gray. After the exchange, the White shareholders own 30% of Gray's common stock.

   l. Teal Corporation has been selling and servicing computers for the last 10 years. The shareholders think that it would be wise to separate the company into two corporations for marketing purposes. Aqua Corporation is created. Teal transfers all of the service division (30% of Teal) to Aqua in exchange for all of the stock of Aqua. The stock of Aqua is distributed to the Teal shareholders in exchange for their Teal stock.

27. Atif acquired 55% of Carma Corporation for $400,000 eight years ago. In the current year, Carma merges with Gia Corporation, and Atif receives 7.5% of Gia's stock plus

$300,000 in land. The Gia stock received by Atif is valued at $900,000. At the time of the transaction, Carma's E & P is $450,000, and Gia's E & P is $1.8 million. How should Atif treat this transaction for tax purposes?

28. SapCo is being merged into MapleCo in a transaction qualifying as a "Type A" reorganization. SapCo is equally owned by two shareholders, Latisha and Theo. SapCo transfers its assets worth $800,000 (adjusted basis of $840,000) and $200,000 in liabilities to MapleCo for $100,000 in cash and $500,000 in MapleCo stock. Upon SapCo's liquidation, Latisha and Theo exchange their SapCo stock for equal shares of the cash and stock. Latisha's basis in her stock is $225,000. Theo's adjusted basis in his stock is $330,000.

    Determine the gain or loss that SapCo, MapleCo, Latisha, and Theo recognize from the reorganization. Determine MapleCo's basis in SapCo's assets and Latisha's and Theo's new basis in the MapleCo stock.

29. Assume the same facts as in Problem 28, except that SapCo indicates that its accumulated E & P is $50,000. Latisha has owned her stock for five years. Theo purchased his stock six months ago. Determine the tax consequences for all parties involved in the reorganization.

Decision Making

30. In a transaction qualifying under § 368, the Raven, Inc. bondholders exchange their $10,000 bonds with a 8.4% stated interest rate and a December 31, 2020 maturity date for Quail Corporation $12,000 bonds with a 7% stated interest rate and a June 30, 2025 maturity date. Is this exchange fair to Raven's 20 bondholders? How will this exchange be treated by the bondholders?

31. Quail Corporation was created in 1995 through contributions from Kasha ($700,000) and Fardin ($300,000). In a transaction qualifying as a "Type A" merger reorganization, Quail exchanges all of its assets currently valued at $2.5 million (basis of $1.9 million) for 12,000 shares of Covey Corporation stock plus a $100,000 Covey bond. Quail distributes Covey stock to Fardin in exchange for his Quail stock and distributes Covey stock plus the bond to Kasha for her Quail stock. Quail's current and accumulated E & P before the reorganization amounts to $200,000.
    a. How do Kasha and Fardin treat this transaction for tax purposes?
    b. How do Quail and Covey treat this transaction for tax purposes? What is Covey's basis in the assets it receives from Quail?

32. Rosa owns 60% of Pine Corporation's stock (basis of $100,000), and the other 40% was recently purchased by Arvid (basis of $110,000). Rosa also holds a $50,000 Pine bond. Pine enters into a § 368 reorganization with Lodgepole Corporation, in which Rosa will receive a 12% interest (value of $180,000) in Lodgepole and Arvid will receive a 6% interest (value of $90,000) plus assets worth $30,000. Lodgepole's basis in these assets is $10,000. Rosa will also exchange her $50,000 Pine bond for a $55,000 Lodgepole debenture. The interest rate on the new bond is lower than the rate on Rosa's Pine bond. At the time of the reorganization, Pine's value is $300,000, and Lodgepole's value is $1.2 million.
    a. What are Rosa's and Arvid's bases in their new Lodgepole stock?
    b. What is the amount of gain (loss) recognized by Rosa, Arvid, Pine, and Lodgepole on the reorganization?

33. Lemon Corporation enters into a merger with Lime Corporation. Lemon has assets valued at $900,000 (basis of $980,000) and liabilities of $600,000. Lime transfers its stock for 90% of Lemon's assets and liabilities. Lemon distributes the Lime stock and its remaining asset (value of $90,000, adjusted basis of $80,000) subject to a liability ($60,000) to its shareholder, Lea, in exchange for her Lemon stock. Lea's basis in her Lemon stock is $350,000. Lemon liquidates after collecting all of its stock from Lea.
    a. What is the value of stock transferred from Lime to Lemon?
    b. What is the amount of gain (loss) realized and recognized by Lea from the merger? What is Lea's basis in her Lime stock?
    c. What is the amount of gain (loss) realized and recognized by Lemon and Lime from the merger? What is Lime's basis in Lemon's assets?

Decision Making

34. Stallion Corporation was organized in 1980 by Biped Corporation (55%), Quadruped Corporation (35%), and Slithering Corporation (10%). Stallion has been quite

successful and now has assets worth $12 million (basis of $4.4 million) with liabilities of $2 million. Biped would like to obtain a controlling interest in Stallion by using a "Type B" or "Type C" reorganization. Quadruped is willing to relinquish its interest in Stallion, but Slithering is hesitant because it does not want be a shareholder in Biped. Explain whether Biped can accomplish its acquisition of Stallion by using either a "Type B" or a "Type C" reorganization.

35. Lawn Corporation has just obtained exclusive rights to a new revolutionary fertilizer that is sure to be an instant success in the gardening industry. Unfortunately, Lawn does not have the capital to market the product adequately. Therefore, it is considering joining forces with Garden Corporation, a company with substantial liquid assets and experience in marketing new products. This union, Lawn believes, would give both corporations a competitive edge.

Communications

   Lawn's president, Sheryl Hagen, provides you with the following information and requests your guidance as to what type of reorganization Lawn and Garden should consider.

Corporation	FMV of Assets	Adjusted Basis	Liabilities
Lawn	$600,000	$400,000	$300,000
Garden	800,000	500,000	100,000

Write a letter to Ms. Hagen, explaining the benefits of using a "Type A" consolidation, a "Type C," or an acquisitive "Type D" reorganization. Lawn's address is Route 1, Box 2440, Mason, OH 45040.

36. Sheep Corporation has 10,000 common and 100 preferred shares outstanding that have a net fair market value of $3 million. Goat Corporation would like to acquire Sheep at some time in the future by exchanging its voting stock for the common and preferred Sheep stock outstanding. In discussing this possibility, Sheep's management indicates that the preferred shareholder, Atep, will not agree to a stock-for-stock acquisition by Goat. Rather Atep will want $750,000 in cash for the preferred stock (basis of $700,000). However, management thinks that it can convince the common stock shareholders that the stock-for-stock exchange would be to their benefit. Goat is willing to acquire the preferred stock for cash now and postpone the common stock acquisition until management obtains the common shareholders' consent. Identify the tax issues in the proposed transactions.

Issue ID

37. Frame Corporation, a publicly held entity, has approached Lisa Springs, the CEO of WireCo, regarding the acquisition of its manufacturing plant and equipment contained therein plus any liabilities associated with these assets. Not wanting to recognize a $300,000 gain on the disposition of these assets ($850,000 value − $550,000 basis), Lisa suggests that Frame acquire WireCo using a "Type C" reorganization. However, Frame is not interested in acquiring the building housing WireCo's headquarters that is located adjacent to the plant. The building is valued at $150,000, and its basis is $130,000. WireCo has $200,000 of liabilities associated with the plant and equipment and a $100,000 mortgage on the headquarters building.

Communications

   Lisa Springs requests your advice on whether the transaction can be structured as a "Type C" reorganization if Frame does not acquire the headquarters. WireCo's address is 3443 E. Riverbank Road, Walla Walla, WA 99362. Write a letter to Ms. Springs indicating how to arrange this transaction and meet the requirements of a "Type C" reorganization.

38. Peanut Corporation has three shareholders, Bill, Gene, and Debra. The shareholders purchased their stock in Peanut four years ago at a cost of $300,000 each. For the past eight years, Peanut has been engaged in two lines of business, manufacturing (one plant valued at $800,000) and retail sales (six stores each valued at $300,000). Peanut also has substantial investments ($400,000) that it has held for at least two years.

Issue ID

   To reduce conflicts among the owners, Peanut proposes to transfer the manufacturing assets to PE Corporation, three stores to Nut Corporation, and three stores to Ant Corporation. The investments will be used to equalize the asset values of each of these newly formed corporations. Peanut will distribute all the PE stock to Bill, the Nut stock to Gene, and the Ant stock to Debra in exchange for all of their Peanut stock. Peanut will then dissolve. Discuss the tax consequences of the proposed transaction.

39. Pineapple Company, a manufacturing corporation, has two shareholders, Debra and Erin. They each purchased their stock ten years ago for $500,000. Debra and Erin would like to divide Pineapple by placing its $2.9 million of investment assets ($200,000 basis) into the newly created Pine Corporation in exchange for all of its stock. Debra will exchange her stock in Pineapple for all the stock in Pine. Pineapple will retain the manufacturing assets, and Erin will own 100 percent of Pineapple after the transaction. Discuss the tax consequences of the proposed transaction.

40. Hue and Mian Chow acquired all 5,000 shares of Jade Corporation common stock for $30,000 more than 20 years ago. Their daughter, Deng, owns a $40,000 Jade bond. Hue and Mian think that it is time for Deng to become an equal common stock shareholder in Jade.

   Deng exchanges her bond for 2,000 shares of Jade stock. At the same time, Mian and Hue have 1,000 shares of their common stock exchanged for 100 shares of preferred stock. What are the tax implications of these transactions to Mian, Hue, Deng, and Jade Corporation? Determine the shareholders' bases in their stock.

41. Dewan owns all 2,000 shares of the common voting stock of Palm Corporation ($540,000 value and $40,000 basis). The 1,000 preferred shares are owned by Dewan's niece, Shontal ($300,000 value and $250,000 basis). Dewan has been the president of Palm for the last 20 years. He would now like to retire and let Shontal run the business since she has just graduated from Harvard with an MBA. Shontal will exchange her preferred stock for $300,000 of common stock. Dewan also will exchange his stock; however, he is not sure whether it would be better to receive $540,000 of cumulative preferred stock paying an 8% yearly dividend or bonds of equal value also paying 8% interest. What are the tax consequences of the exchange to Shontal? What advice would you give Dewan?

42. Beach Corporation has just lost a $1.5 million product liability lawsuit. Its assets currently have a value of $2 million, and its outstanding liabilities amount to $800,000 without considering the lawsuit liability. As a result of the lawsuit, Beach's future revenue stream appears to be substantially impaired. Beach's president, Sandy Jones, asks your advice regarding the possibilities of restructuring the corporation. Write Sandy a memo explaining her choices in restructuring Beach.

43. Zucchini Corporation is having financial difficulties and has filed for a "Type G" reorganization under state law. Its liabilities are $800,000, and the fair market value of its assets is $600,000 (adjusted basis of $400,000). A new entity, Squash Corporation, has been created to succeed Zucchini. At the time of the restructuring, Zucchini has a $100,000 NOL carryforward and a $30,000 capital loss carryforward. Explain the tax consequences of the "Type G" reorganization for Squash and Zucchini.

44. Aqua Corporation is a retail operation specializing in pool equipment and furniture. It is very interested in merging with Tara Corporation, which manufactures lamps. Aqua is interested in Tara because Aqua is very profitable and Tara has large business credits that it has not been able to utilize.

   Aqua proposes to exchange 20% of its stock and $200,000 for most of Tara's assets. Those assets that Aqua does not acquire will be distributed to Tara's shareholders. Aqua stock will be distributed to some Tara shareholders, while dissenting Tara shareholders will receive the cash. Aqua is not really interested in the lamp business except for the possibility of making pool lights. It will therefore sell off Tara's assets except those used to manufacture pool lights. What are the tax issues to be considered in these transactions?

45. Timber Corporation is merged into Alpine Corporation on October 20 of the current year. Alpine uses a calendar year for its tax year. At the time of the merger, Timber has a $300,000 NOL. Pursuant to the merger, Timber's shareholders exchanged their stock for 60% of Alpine's stock. Timber's stock is worth $750,000 on the day before the merger, and the Federal long-term tax-exempt rate is 7%. How much of Timber's NOL may offset Alpine's $200,000 taxable income? How is any unused NOL treated?

46. Assume the Timber shareholders in Problem 45 received 30% of Alpine's stock. How much of Timber Corporation's NOL can Alpine utilize under these facts?

47. Fern Corporation has a $200,000 capital loss carryover from last year. On March 1 of the current year, Fern transfers all of its assets (valued at $500,000) to Bulb Corporation for 45% of Bulb's stock. Bulb's taxable income for the current year is $100,000. Its net capital gains (computed without regard to any capital loss carryovers) are $150,000 due to discontinuing Fern's business and selling its assets. How much capital loss carried over from Fern can be used to offset Bulb's capital gains if the Federal long-term tax-exempt rate is 9%?

48. Henri and Simone started Manx Corporation in 2002 by each investing $500,000. Manx develops and manufactures pet toys and supplies. The business has been very profitable (now valued at $5 million) due to Henri's marketing abilities and Simone's knack for inventing toys that pets love. Since Henri and Simone feel that Manx cannot expand further in the pet product industry, they are in the market to acquire another company. *Issue ID*

    Henri hears about LaPerm Corporation from one of their customers. LaPerm is a beauty supply manufacturer. It has a great line of products but has suffered substantial losses due to a lack of strategic marketing and ineffective management. It is a small company with net assets valued at $200,000, but it has a $300,000 NOL and a $100,000 business credit carryover. All the shares of LaPerm are held by Marcel, who started LaPerm 40 years ago. Marcel is 66 and is no longer interested in running the business.

    Before Henri and Simone enter into negotiations with Marcel regarding the acquisition of LaPerm using a tax-deferred reorganization, what issues should be considered?

49. Ruby Corporation completed a restructuring transaction with Gold Corporation on May 31 of the current year. Gold distributed 30% of Ruby's stock to its shareholders in exchange for all of its own stock. Just prior to completion of the reorganization, Gold had assets worth $900,000, liabilities of $350,000, and an NOL carryover of $400,000. The Federal long-term tax-exempt rate was 5%. What is the amount of NOL that Ruby may use in the current year? How much will it be able to utilize in the next tax year?

50. Taipa Corporation is interested in acquiring Kers Corporation through a "Type C" reorganization on January 2 of the current year. Taipa's stock is valued at $10 million and generates $1 million of taxable income yearly. Kers has plant and equipment valued at $780,000 and liabilities of $230,000. It also has a $346,500 NOL with 10 years remaining of the carryover period. If Taipa uses a 12% discount rate for its business investment decisions and the Federal long-term tax-exempt rate is 9%, what percent of its stock should be exchanged for Kers assets? *Decision Making*

51. On December 31, 2007, Tulip Corporation had a capital loss carryforward of $100,000 and excess credits of $30,000. On this day it merged with Lilly Corporation by exchanging all of its assets for $1,750,000 of stock and cash. Tulip then distributed the cash and stock to its shareholders. This caused an ownership change and subjected Lilly to the § 382 limitation. For the year ending December 31, 2008, Lilly computes its taxable income before application of any carryovers to be $500,000. Of this amount, $420,000 is operating income, and $80,000 is capital gains. Determine Lilly's tax liability for 2008 and its carryovers (capital losses and excess credits) to 2009. Assume that the applicable long-term tax-exempt rate is 8%.

52. Disc Corporation is contemplating the acquisition of Density Corporation. Disc is interested in Density because it has a valuable patent used in the process of manufacturing CDs. Density is a young company and has yet to show substantial profits (accumulated E & P of $28,000). However, Disc thinks it can turn Density around by replacing Density's inexperienced managers with a more mature management team. The value of Density is currently estimated at $800,000, and it has a basis in its assets of $500,000. Disc's president asks you to illustrate (with diagrams) the possible tax-free reorganizations of Disc and Density. *Decision Making* *Communications*
    a. Assume that the patent held by Density is transferable.
    b. Assume that the patent held by Density is *not* transferable.

RESEARCH PROBLEMS

Note: Solutions to Research Problems can be prepared by using the **RIA Checkpoint**[R] **Student Edition** online research product, which is available to accompany this text. It is also possible to prepare solutions to the Research Problems by using tax research materials found in a standard tax library.

Research Problem 1. New Gate Corporation desires to acquire Old Post in a nontaxable transaction. Prior to entering into the transaction with New Gate, Old Post issues $800,000 worth of 15-year bonds paying 6% annually. The bonds are purchased by most of Old Post's shareholders and also by many individuals who have no affiliation with Old Post. New Gate makes an offer to the shareholders to exchange two shares of its common voting class A stock for each common share of Old Post and 20 shares of common voting class B stock for each preferred share of Old Post.

Most of the shareholders are reluctant to make the exchange because of the favorable terms of the Old Post bonds they are holding. Consequently, New Gate offers to acquire all of the Old Post outstanding bonds in exchange for New Gate bonds paying 6% interest annually, with an equal principal amount and a 15-year term. All of the Old Post bondholders exchange their debentures, and 90% of the Old Post shareholders exchange their stock. Can these transactions qualify as nontaxable corporate reorganizations? How should these transactions be treated by New Gate, Old Post, and Old Post's shareholders?

Communications

Research Problem 2. Rose Corporation is located in Baton Rouge, Louisiana. It is organized for Federal tax purposes as an S corporation; however, Louisiana does not recognize S corporation status. Therefore, for state legal ease and other valid business reasons, the owners, Liza, Lena, Marian, and Mae, would like to reorganize Rose as either a partnership or a limited liability company (LLC).

The owners' plan is to create a new entity consistent with state laws. Under the check-the-box rules, the new entity would request to be treated as a corporation for Federal tax purposes effective from the date of formation. Once the new entity is created, it will merge with Rose, meeting all state and Federal reorganization requirements. No new ownership interests will be available; thus, Liza, Lena, Marian, and Mae will be the only owners of the new entity and will continue their former ownership percentages and rights.

Can Rose Corporation be converted into a partnership or LLC with a tax-free reorganization? Does Rose lose its S election for Federal tax purposes once the conversion is completed? Write a letter to Mae Miller, the CEO of Rose, answering these questions. Mae's address is 968 N. Live Oak Boulevard, Baton Rouge, LA 70806. Support your conclusions with proper citations.

Research Problem 3. Hawaii Corporation, which is owned equally by two brothers and their younger sister, has been in the business of growing coffee and onions for the last 10 years. Lately, the brothers have been having conflicts regarding the management, operations, and expansion of the business. A professional mediator has suggested that the only way to resolve the issues is to divide the entity. The older brother will retain the coffee business and the Hawaii name. The younger brother and sister will receive stock in a newly formed corporation, Maui Corporation, in exchange for their stock in Hawaii. Maui will continue growing onions, but also will expand into other products.

Hawaii is organized as an S corporation, and Maui will elect S status at the earliest possible date. The transaction will take place as follows. Hawaii will transfer the onion farming assets to Maui in exchange for all of its stock. Hawaii will then exchange all of the younger brother's and sister's stock in Hawaii for all of the stock in Maui. After the transaction, the older brother will own all of Hawaii, and the younger brother and sister will own all of Maui. Both corporations will retain their S status. Will this division of Hawaii qualify as a "Type D" reorganization? Will this division terminate Hawaii's S election or prevent Maui from electing S status?

Research Problem 4. Nye Tools, incorporated in 1995, makes tools and devices for the automotive industry. The original shareholders were Andre (700 shares) and his brother Roscoe (300 shares). In 2000, Andre transferred 100 shares to his wife, and Roscoe sold

50 shares to a business associate. In June 2004, Nye spun off the devices division, creating Nye Devices. In this transaction, Andre exchanged 500 shares of Nye Tools for 500 shares of Nye Devices. Roscoe did not receive any shares of Nye Devices. Wanting to relinquish all ownership of Nye Tools, Andre and his wife sold their remaining 200 shares to Roscoe in 2005.

From 2003 to 2005, Nye Tools accumulated substantial business credits, which it could not fully utilize. Finally, in 2006, Nye Tools had sufficient tax liability to offset all of its business credit carryovers. The IRS audited Nye Tools' 2006 return and is arguing that the business credit carryovers should be limited because there was an ownership change. Roscoe believes that under the stock attribution rules, there has been no ownership change.

Determine whether Roscoe should try to negotiate with the IRS or go to court over the business credit issue. Support your analysis with citations to primary tax sources.

Use the tax resources of the Internet to address the following questions. Do not restrict your search to the World Wide Web, but include a review of newsgroups and general reference materials, practitioner sites and resources, primary sources of the tax law, chat rooms and discussion groups, and other opportunities.

Internet *Activity*

Research Problem 5. The Asian merger and acquisition (M&A) market has become more open in recent years; thus, the M&A activity between U.S. and Asian companies has greatly expanded. Select a country in Asia and review recent M&A activity involving U.S. firms. Create a table listing five U.S. companies recently involved in an Asian merger, the industry classification for the companies, and the dollar amount of stock, cash, and assets exchanged.

Communications

Research Problem 6. The banking industry, and particularly the subprime home mortgage sector, has been hit hard by massive losses that have caused many companies to file for bankruptcy. Investigate this area by finding three articles discussing local financial institutions having problems. Write for your instructor a two-page summary of the articles focusing on the particular companies discussed, and identify the biggest contributing factor leading to their demise.

Communications

Research Problem 7. Merger and acquisition (M&A) activity has picked up momentum again after a lull for a couple of years. Research the M&A activity in an industry of your choice. Create a table, similar to Exhibit 7–1, of the top 10 M&As for the industry. Include your sources in the table.

Communications

Research Problem 8. Find a recent court case or revenue ruling regarding the judicial requirements on mergers or the Code limitations on tax attribute carryovers. Prepare a one-page brief of the case or ruling.

Communications

CHAPTER 8

Consolidated Tax Returns

LEARNING OBJECTIVES

After completing Chapter 8, you should be able to:

LO.1
Apply the fundamental concepts of consolidated tax returns.

LO.2
Identify the sources of the rules for consolidated taxable income.

LO.3
Recognize the major advantages and disadvantages of filing consolidated tax returns.

LO.4
Describe the corporations that are eligible to file on a consolidated basis.

LO.5
Explain the compliance aspects of consolidated returns.

LO.6
Compute a parent's investment basis in a subsidiary.

LO.7
Account for intercompany transactions of a consolidated group.

LO.8
Identify limitations that restrict the use of losses and credits of group members derived in separate return years.

LO.9
Derive deductions and credits on a consolidated basis.

LO.10
Demonstrate tax planning opportunities available to consolidated groups.

Context of the Consolidated Return Rules

To this point, the discussion has centered on the computation of the tax liability of individual corporations under the regular tax calculation, along with specific penalty taxes and the alternative minimum tax. This is an appropriate approach to the study of corporate taxation, as more than 90 percent of the roughly 5.5 million U.S. corporations are closely held (i.e., either by a small group of operators/investors or by members of the same family).

Although some of these family businesses operate in a multiple-corporation environment, the vast majority of the assets held by businesses nationwide are owned by no more than 50,000 large corporate conglomerates. These corporations conduct the bulk of the country's "big business" and generate most of the taxable income earned by corporate taxpayers. In addition, these corporate groups face some special tax rules, which are the subject of this chapter.

Motivations to Consolidate

Corporate conglomerates are present in every aspect of life. The local dairy or bakery is likely to be owned by General Mills or General Foods. Oil and insurance companies own movie-making corporations. Professional sports teams are corporate cousins of the newspapers and television/radio stations that carry their games. The same corporate group that produces night lights for a child's nursery may manufacture control equipment for bombers and other elements of the Defense Department's arsenal.

What brings together these sometimes strange corporate bedfellows? For the most part, nontax motivations provide the strongest incentives for multiple-corporation acquisitions and holdings. Among the many commonly encountered motivations are the following.

- A desire to isolate assets of other group members from the liabilities of specific operating divisions (e.g., to gain limited liability for a tobacco or asbestos company within an operating conglomerate).
- A need to carry out specific estate planning objectives (e.g., by transferring growth or high-risk assets to younger-generation shareholders).
- A wish to isolate the group's exposure to losses and liabilities incurred in joint ventures with "outside" entities (especially when such venturers are not based in the United States).
- A perception that separate divisions/group members will be worth more on the market if they maintain unique identities or otherwise avoid a commingling

of assets and liabilities with other group members (e.g., where a trade name or patent is especially valuable or carries excessive goodwill in the marketplace).
- Conversely, an attempt to shield the identities of a subsidiary's true owners from the public where negative goodwill exists (e.g., with respect to the consequences of a nuclear or industrial accident, or the use of a long-held name of an oil or a tobacco company).

ETHICAL and EQUITABLE *Considerations*

SHELTERING CORPORATE ASSETS

Should corporations be able to shelter their assets from marketplace liabilities through a capital restructuring? The first large corporations to spin off subsidiaries to isolate high-risk assets and their related liabilities from the main business were financial institutions (e.g., risky loans to debtors in exploratory industries or underdeveloped countries) and utilities (e.g., nuclear power facilities). Today, conglomerates involved in developing health care procedures or turning out such products as tobacco and industrial equipment protect the bulk of the entity's assets by isolating product liability risks in subsidiaries.

Given the "deep pockets" mentality of many juries and government agencies, merger or consolidation is a prudent reaction by the corporate community. But shouldn't a society's largest risks be shared among all of its players? And should the tax laws be used to foster the isolation of such risk into shallow and insulated corporate pockets?

In many states, "tort reform" would further limit the business entity's exposure to/accountability for malpractice and product warranty claims. Your state's CPA society asks you to lobby legislators in favor of such a measure. Will you take the assignment?

Although nontax concerns may be the primary reason for the creation of many conglomerates, tax incentives may also play a role. To a large extent, these incentives can be found in the rules that control the filing of **consolidated returns**. In general terms, the IRS allows certain corporate groups to be treated as a single entity for Federal income tax purposes. This enables the group to use available tax exemptions and brackets optimally among its members and to shelter the income of profitable members with the losses of other members. Thus, through the consolidated return rules, corporate taxpayers have an opportunity to manage the combined tax liability of the members of the group.

The consolidated return rules may be available to a taxpayer as a result of various business decisions.

- A consolidated return may result from a merger, acquisition, or other corporate combination (discussed in Chapter 7).

> **LO.1**
>
> Apply the fundamental concepts of consolidated tax returns.

EXAMPLE 1

When Dover Corporation acquires all of the stock of Edwards Corporation, a new corporate group, Dover and Edwards Corporation, is formed. The two group members can elect to file their tax return on a consolidated basis. ■

- A group of business taxpayers may be restructured to comply with changes in regulatory requirements, meet the demands of a competitive environment, or gain economies of scale and operate more efficiently in a larger arrangement. Consequently, an election to file a consolidated return becomes available.

EXAMPLE 2

External Corporation, a retailer, acquires Internal Corporation, a wholesaler, in an effort to control its flow of inventory in unstable economic times. The two group members can elect to file their tax returns on a consolidated basis. ■

- The taxpayers may be seeking to gain tax and other financial advantages that are more readily available to corporate combinations.

TAX *in the News*   DO CONGLOMERATES CREATE CONFLICTS OF INTEREST?

One part of what is now the entertainment giant Time Warner started not long ago as a small UHF station in Atlanta, eventually named WTBS. The Turner Broadcasting System was a small station with a weak signal and no "software" (i.e., programming to fill the broadcast schedule) other than dated reruns of network programs like *The Andy Griffith Show* and low-budget syndicated fare like *Hee Haw*.

With the advent of cable and then satellite television and the demand for all-day news and sports programming, the media company began to emerge from its humble beginnings. Another boost came when Ted Turner became the owner of local professional sports teams—the Braves and the Hawks—and began broadcasting their games. The games filled large blocks of airtime and attracted an audience of great import to advertisers.

But can the disparate members of a conglomerate resist the temptation to act in concert for the good of the entire group? Charges of "soft reporting" among corporate cousins often arise when critical reporting seems lacking. How will an ESPN reporter address the Anaheim Angels infielder whose error cost the team the World Series, given that the Disney Company owns both entities? Given that General Electric owns NBC, will we ever see a *Dateline* segment about how GE bends the rules to obtain Defense Department contracts? Can ABC critics comment negatively on a movie from Disney, the corporate parent?

EXAMPLE 3

Over the next three years, Mary Corporation will be selling a number of its business assets at a loss. If Norbert Corporation acquires all of Mary's stock and the group elects to file its tax returns on a consolidated basis, Norbert will be able to combine its gains from the sale of business property with Mary's losses in computing the group's consolidated § 1231 gain/loss for the year. ■

Source and Philosophy of Consolidated Return Rules

Some form of consolidated corporate tax return has been allowed for Federal purposes since World War I. At that time, the Treasury became suspicious that conglomerates were shifting taxable income to a number of smaller entities to avoid the high marginal rates of the excess profits tax that had been imposed to finance the war effort. Thus, the consolidated return rules can be seen as perhaps the earliest effort of the IRS to limit the tax benefits available to multiple corporations.

EXAMPLE 4

Assume that the marginal Federal income tax rate is 10% on the first $100,000 of taxable income and 15% on any taxable income in excess of $100,000. The additional 5 percentage points constitute a war profits tax, and the revenue raised is used for the war effort.

Further assume that the tax law includes no restrictions on the tax computations of related corporations. A corporation with annual taxable income of $1 million can eliminate its entire exposure to the war profits tax by splitting its business evenly among 10 separate corporations. ■

LO.2

Identify the sources of the rules for consolidated taxable income.

At various times, Congress has modified the pertinent Regulations and imposed a higher tax rate or surcharge on consolidated groups to increase the cost of making the consolidation election. During World War II, when it feared "too much" income of profiteers was being sheltered within consolidated groups, Congress suspended the application of the rules for most taxpayers. On other occasions, including the present, complex limitations were placed on the use and timing of positive tax benefits, such as net operating loss (NOL) carryovers, that were acquired in a corporate consolidation. Congress imposed these limits to discourage profitable corporations from "trafficking" in businesses that had generated net losses.

Currently, Congress has delegated most of its legislative authority involving consolidated returns to the Treasury. As a result, the majority of the rules that affect consolidated groups are found in the Regulations. The Code provisions dealing with consolidated returns are strictly definitional in nature and broad in scope,[1] while the related Regulations dictate the computational and compliance requirements of the group.[2]

As discussed in Chapter 1, "legislative" Regulations of this sort carry the full force and effect of law. Challenges to the content of these Regulations seldom are supported by the courts. Consequently, taxpayers generally participate actively in the hearings process in an effort to have their interpretations included in the final Regulations.

The length and detail of these Regulations make the consolidated return rules among the most complex in the entire Federal income tax law. For the most part, the underlying objective of the rules remains one of organizational neutrality; that is, a group of closely related corporations should have neither a tax advantage nor a disadvantage relative to taxpayers who file separate corporate returns.

ETHICAL and EQUITABLE *Considerations* — DELEGATING AUTHORITY TO THE NONELECTED

In no other area of the tax law has Congress given the Treasury such leeway in crafting both major principles and details as in the area of consolidated returns. Since Treasury staff members are not elected officials, this delegation of authority might appear to be a shirking of congressional duty and a dangerous assignment of legislative power to an isolated group of individuals.

To what extent should Congress delegate its powers over the country's largest businesses (not only the largest players in the global economy but also the largest contributors to campaign and reelection funds)? Can the delegation of congressional powers to Washington-based civil servants, who are virtually immune to the checks and balances of the election process, be healthy for all taxpayers?

You are a member of the House Ways and Means Committee, and your chances of reelection are jeopardized when you must take a position on a consolidated tax return issue: Taxes on old-line manufacturers would increase, while those on more environmentally friendly, high-tech industries would fall. Should you avoid the debate altogether by deferring the issue to the Regulations process?

The derivation of a set of consolidated financial statements for a conglomerate and the computation of its consolidated taxable income correspond only slightly. The equity approach followed for financial accounting purposes has a role in the consolidated return rules, but exceptions to accounting conventions are both critical and numerous. Thus, a knowledge of financial accounting consolidation procedures is not necessarily of great assistance in computing consolidated taxable income, nor is a lack of familiarity with accounting conventions a hindrance.

EXAMPLE 5

Dividends paid by SubCo to its 100% owner, Parent Corporation, are eliminated from the separate taxable income computations of both group members in deriving consolidated taxable income. This treatment parallels the eliminating entry that is made in developing the group's consolidated financial statements.

Later, SubCo sells an asset to its 100% owner, Parent Corporation, at a tax and accounting gain of $100,000. The asset appreciates by another $20,000 before Parent sells it to an unrelated party, Outsider Corporation.

No tax or accounting gain is reported by the group members until the ultimate sale by Parent to Outsider. In constructing the consolidated financial statements, Parent realizes a $120,000 gain. For tax purposes, however, SubCo is assigned $100,000 of the gain, and Parent recognizes only "its" $20,000. ■

---

[1]§§ 1501–1505.
[2]Reg. §§ 1.1501–1, 1.1502–0 through 1.1502–100, 1.1503–1 through 1.1503–2T, and 1.1504–1.

LO.3

Recognize the major advantages
and disadvantages of filing
consolidated tax returns.

Assessing Consolidated Return Status

As Concept Summary 8–1 illustrates, all of the members of a corporate group must meet three broad requirements to be eligible to elect, and maintain the right, to file a consolidated income tax return.

- The corporations must meet the statutory ownership requirements to be classified as an affiliated group.[3]
- The corporations must be eligible to make a consolidation election.[4]
- The group must meet various tax accounting and compliance requirements.[5]

Before making an election to file consolidated tax returns, related taxpayers must weigh the resulting advantages and disadvantages.

The potential advantages of filing consolidated returns are many.

- The operating and capital loss carryovers of one group member may be used to shelter the corresponding income of other group members.
- The taxation of all intercompany dividends may be eliminated.
- Recognition of income from certain intercompany transactions can be deferred.
- Certain deductions and credits may be optimized by using consolidated amounts in computing pertinent limitations (e.g., the deductions for charitable contributions and dividends received, and foreign tax credits).
- The tax basis of investments in the stock of subsidiaries is increased as the members contribute to consolidated taxable income.
- The domestic production activities deduction (§ 199) of a group might be greater than the sum of the deductions for all of the affiliates, as the formula for determining the deduction permits various components to be aggregated.
- The alternative minimum tax (AMT) attributes of all group members can be used in deriving consolidated alternative minimum taxable income (AMTI). This can reduce the adjusted current earnings (ACE) adjustment and optimize other AMT preferences and adjustments.
- The share holdings of all group members can be used in meeting other statutory requirements.[6]

Consolidated returns also have a number of potential disadvantages.

- The election is binding on all subsequent tax years of the group members, unless either the makeup of the affiliated group changes or the IRS consents to a revocation of the election.
- Capital and operating losses of one group member are applied against the corresponding income of the other group members even when assigning the losses to separate return years would produce a greater tax benefit. The benefit might be due, for instance, to rate discounts or changes in tax rates.
- Recognition of losses from certain intercompany transactions is deferred.
- Using consolidated amounts in computing the limitations may decrease the amounts of certain deductions and credits.
- Return elections made by the parent (e.g., to claim a § 901 credit for foreign tax payments rather than a deduction) are binding on all members of the filing group for the year.
- The tax basis of investments in the stock of subsidiaries is decreased when the members generate operating losses and by distributions from members' E & P.
- The requirement that all group members use the parent's tax year creates short tax years for the subsidiaries. As a result, a subsidiary's income may be

---

[3]§§ 1504(a)(1) and (2).
[4]This is a negative definition, rooted in §§ 1504(b) through (f).
[5]See especially Reg. §§ 1.1502–75, –76, and –77.

[6]E.g., for purposes of the § 165(g)(3) ordinary deduction for losses from worthlessness of securities. For the 80% corporate control requirement of § 351, see the discussion in Chapter 4.

CONCEPT SUMMARY 8–1

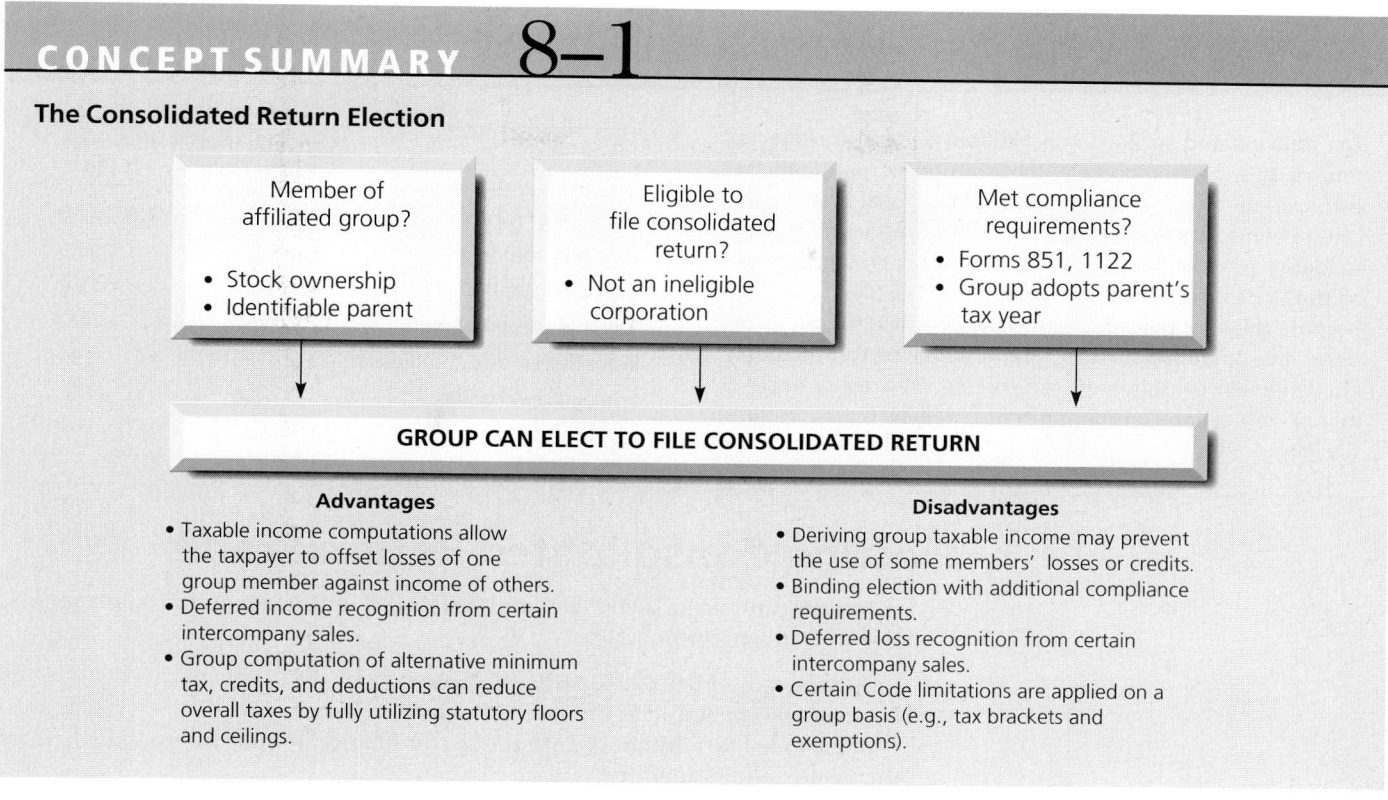

The Consolidated Return Election

Member of affiliated group?	Eligible to file consolidated return?	Met compliance requirements?
• Stock ownership • Identifiable parent	• Not an ineligible corporation	• Forms 851, 1122 • Group adopts parent's tax year

GROUP CAN ELECT TO FILE CONSOLIDATED RETURN

Advantages
- Taxable income computations allow the taxpayer to offset losses of one group member against income of others.
- Deferred income recognition from certain intercompany sales.
- Group computation of alternative minimum tax, credits, and deductions can reduce overall taxes by fully utilizing statutory floors and ceilings.

Disadvantages
- Deriving group taxable income may prevent the use of some members' losses or credits.
- Binding election with additional compliance requirements.
- Deferred loss recognition from certain intercompany sales.
- Certain Code limitations are applied on a group basis (e.g., tax brackets and exemptions).

bunched together needlessly, and one of the years of its charitable contribution and loss carryforward periods may be lost.
- Additional administrative costs may be incurred in complying with the consolidated return Regulations.

The following taxpayers should consider filing consolidated returns.

EXAMPLE 6

- Major Insurance Corporation generates billions of dollars of taxable income every year. Independent Movie Productions, Ltd., is concerned with artistic integrity, and its annual taxable loss totals $10 to $15 million per year. The accumulated losses are of no use to Independent, but Major can use them to effect an immediate tax reduction at its 35% marginal tax rate.

↑TI ↑Tax Losses

- Every year, Parent contributes $1.2 million of its $10 million taxable income to charity. Thus, because of the 10% limitation, it cannot deduct the full amount of the gift in computing taxable income. SubCo generates $3 million of taxable income every year, and it makes no charitable contributions. By filing a consolidated return with SubCo, Parent can deduct its full gift against consolidated taxable income.

↑TI means more CC can be used

On the other hand, certain corporations would make unattractive consolidated return partners.

- Parent sells an asset to SubCo at a $500,000 realized loss. As shown in Example 5, this loss cannot be recognized by the consolidated group until the asset subsequently is sold to Outsider.
- ParentCo holds a large NOL carryforward, and SubCo generates a steady level of taxable income every year. Both corporations are involved in international commerce and make significant tax payments to other countries. SubCo would use these payments to compute a foreign tax credit. But if the corporations file a consolidated return, ParentCo effectively makes the tax accounting elections for the group. It is likely that the ParentCo group will claim the foreign tax credits as deductions against consolidated taxable income, so as to use the NOL carryforward more quickly. ∎

TAX *in the News*   CONSOLIDATED RETURN STATISTICS

Tax data related to 2004 consolidated Federal income tax returns show the important contribution of multinational corporations to U.S. revenues. About 98 percent of all corporate tax revenues are received from corporations filing consolidated returns. Essentially all foreign tax credits allowed by the Code are claimed by consolidated tax filers, probably because they are the most active and profitable of all C corporations operating in the international sector. Yet only about 48,000 consolidated returns are filed every year—a minuscule portion considering that 2 million C corporations file Form 1120.

	Consolidated Returns Only	All Forms 1120
Number of returns	48,000	2,000,000
Assets ($ trillions)	43.4	40.9
Receipts ($ trillions)	14.5	15.9
Taxable income ($ billions)	757	772
Tax after credits ($ billions)	196	199
Foreign tax credits ($ billions)	56	54

Electing Consolidated Return Status

A corporation can join in a consolidated tax return if it meets three requirements, as shown in Concept Summary 8–1.

- It must be a member of an **affiliated group**.
- It cannot be ineligible to file on a consolidated basis.
- It must meet the initial and ongoing compliance requirements specified in the Code and Regulations.

Affiliated Group

An affiliated group exists when one corporation owns at least 80 percent of the voting power and stock value of another corporation.[7] This stock ownership test must be met on every day of the tax year. Multiple tiers and chains of corporations are allowed as long as the group has an identifiable parent corporation (i.e., at least 80 percent of one corporation must be owned by another).

EXAMPLE 7

Two corporate group structures are illustrated below. Both meet the 80% stock ownership test, but the structure on the right is not an affiliated group because there is no identifiable parent entity.

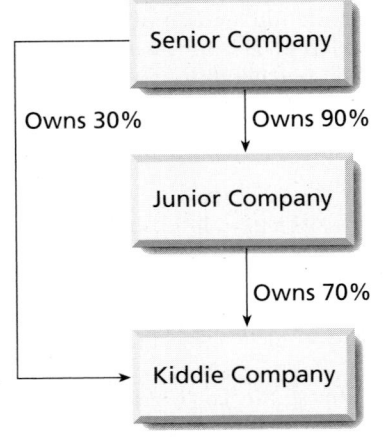
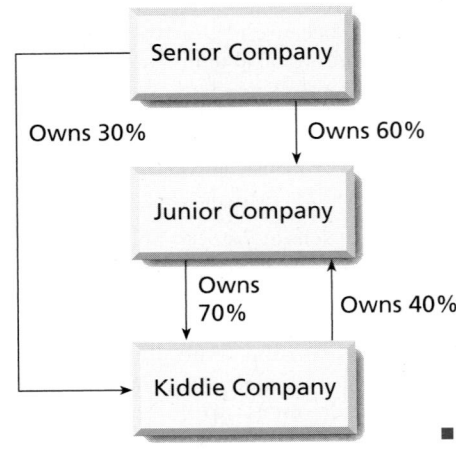

---

[7]§§ 1504(a)(1) and (2).

TABLE 8–1   Comparison of Tax Effects Available to Affiliated Group

Attribute	Treatment If Consolidated Returns Are Filed	Treatment If Separate Returns Are Filed
Tax year	All companies use the parent's tax year.	Companies use various tax years.
Change to common tax year	Required, no IRS permission needed.	Requires IRS permission.
Returns of acquired companies	Separate returns through date of consolidation, then join in consolidated return.	Continue filing for each company's tax year. No extra returns needed.
Intercompany dividend	Eliminated, not taxed.	Include in taxable income, then claim dividends received deduction.
Lower tax brackets	Share one set of rates among the group.	Share one set of rates among the group.
Accumulated earnings credit, $150,000/$250,000 floor	Share one floor among the group.	Share one floor among the group.
Liability for tax	Each company liable for the entire consolidated tax liability.	Each company liable only for its own tax.
Statute of limitations	Extension for one company applies to all in the group.	Each company retains its own statute of limitations.
Accounting methods	Need not conform to parent.	Need not conform to parent.
NOLs, capital gains/losses, § 1231 gains/losses, charitable contribution deductions, § 199 domestic production activities deduction, dividends received deductions, foreign tax credit payments and baskets, etc.	Computed on a consolidated basis.	Computed separately for each company.
Gain/loss on intercompany transactions	Deferred.	Not deferred.
Basis of parent's investment	Changes due to subsidiary operating gain/loss, taxes, and distributions.	No adjustments.

Members of an affiliated group can file tax returns in either of two ways.

- File a separate tax return for each member of the group and claim a 100 percent dividends received deduction for payments passing among them.
- Elect to file income tax returns on a consolidated basis. No 100 percent dividends received deduction is allowed for payments among group members.

Table 8–1 provides additional details as to the tax effects of making a consolidated return election.

A Federal election to form a consolidated group may not be binding for state income tax purposes. Some states allow only separate return filing, and others may define the members of an electing group or tax their income differently than the Federal rules do. See Chapter 15 for additional discussion of the multistate taxation of related corporations.

TAX *in the News*   SOME STATES DON'T ALLOW CONSOLIDATION

Some states have been hesitant to allow a corporate conglomerate doing business within their boundaries to make a consolidation election when computing state taxable income. Perhaps these states question their constitutional ability to tax the income generated by an affiliate that is incorporated elsewhere. Another consideration may be that consolidation would permit losses generated in other states to be applied against taxable income originating within the state.

There is no real consensus among the states as to how to tax a group consolidated for Federal tax purposes. Some states require the group to make a separate election to file on a consolidated basis. Others reserve the right to force the consolidation treatment on a Federal group for state purposes. The diversity that exists is evident in the following table showing a sample of state rules applicable to consolidated returns.

State	Consolidation Allowed?
Alabama	A Federal electing group can make a separate election to file on a consolidated basis for state purposes. With no such election, all must file separate returns.
Alaska	If the group files consolidated returns for Federal purposes, it must do so for state purposes.
Arizona	A Federal electing group can elect to file on a consolidated basis in the state. The state can require a consolidated return to protect its revenues.

State	Consolidation Allowed?
Arkansas	A Federal electing group can elect to file a consolidated return in the state so long as it shows some Arkansas taxable income.
Connecticut	A Federal electing group can elect to file a consolidated return in the state, but it is called a "combined return."
District of Columbia	Consolidation allowed for a Federal electing group only with prior approval of the revenue department. Special rules for high-tech entities.
Louisiana	The state can require a consolidated return, but the taxpayer cannot elect to file one.
Minnesota	No consolidation allowed.
Mississippi	The state can require a consolidated return. The taxpayer can elect to file a consolidated return only with respect to affiliates whose income is generated solely within the state.

Affiliated versus Controlled Group

An affiliated group is similar but not identical to a *parent-subsidiary controlled group*, as discussed in Chapter 2. Members of a controlled group are required to share a number of tax benefits, including the following.

- Discounted marginal tax rates on the first $75,000 of taxable income.[8]
- The $150,000 or $250,000 accumulated earnings credit.[9]
- The $40,000 exemption in computing the alternative minimum tax liability.[10]

In addition, members of a controlled group must defer the recognition of any realized loss on intercompany sales until a sale is made at a gain to a nongroup member.[11] Similarly, any gain on the sale of depreciable property between members of a controlled group is recognized as ordinary income.[12]

A parent-subsidiary controlled group exists when one corporation owns at least 80 percent of the voting power or stock value of another corporation on the last day

---

[8]§§ 11(b)(1) and 1561(a)(1).
[9]§§ 535(c)(2) and 1561(a)(2).
[10]§§ 55(d)(2) and 1561(a)(3).

[11]§§ 267(a)(1), (b)(3), and (f).
[12]§§ 1239(a) and (c).

of the tax year.[13] Multiple tiers of subsidiaries and chains of ownership are allowed, as long as the group has an identifiable parent corporation.

EXAMPLE 8

Aqua Corporation owns 80% of White Corporation. Aqua and White Corporations are members of a parent-subsidiary controlled group. Aqua is the parent corporation, and White is the subsidiary. ■

The parent-subsidiary relationship described in Example 8 is easy to recognize because Aqua Corporation is the direct owner of White Corporation. Real-world business organizations are often much more complex, sometimes including numerous corporations with chains of ownership connecting them. In these complex corporate structures, determining whether the controlled group classification is appropriate becomes more difficult. The ownership requirements can be met through direct ownership (as in Example 8) or through indirect ownership.

EXAMPLE 9

Red Corporation owns 80% of the voting stock of White Corporation, and White Corporation owns 80% of the voting stock of Blue Corporation. Red, White, and Blue Corporations constitute a controlled group in which Red is the common parent and White and Blue are subsidiaries. The same result would occur if Red Corporation, rather than White Corporation, owned the Blue Corporation stock.

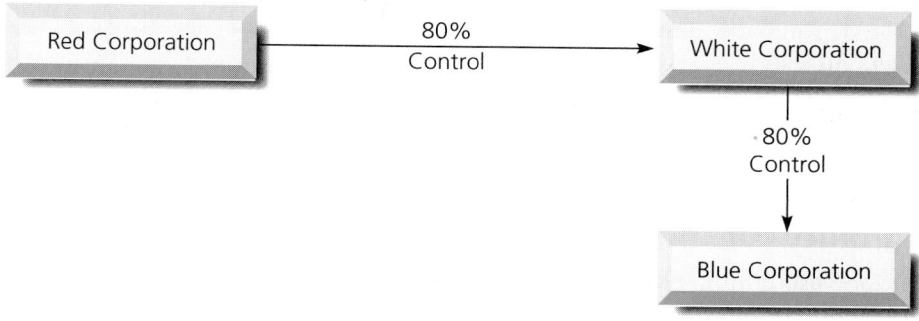

Red is the common parent of a parent-subsidiary
controlled group consisting of Red, White, and Blue Corporations. ■

EXAMPLE 10

Brown Corporation owns 80% of the stock of Green Corporation, which owns 30% of Blue Corporation. Brown also owns 80% of White Corporation, which owns 50% of Blue Corporation. Brown, Green, Blue, and White Corporations constitute a parent-subsidiary controlled group in which Brown is the common parent and Green, Blue, and White are subsidiaries.

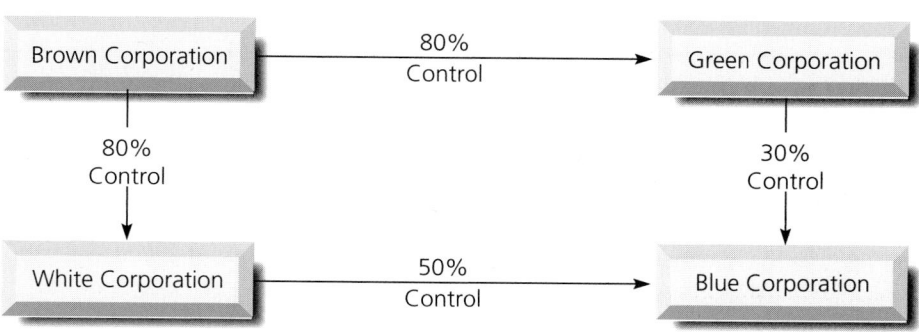

Brown is the common parent of a parent-subsidiary
controlled group consisting of Brown, Green, Blue, and White Corporations. ■

---

[13]§ 1563(a)(1). For this purpose, stock attribution rules apply. In addition, all stock options are considered to be exercised by their holders. §§ 1563(d)(1) and (e)(1) through (3).

The tax effects brought about by electing to file on a consolidated basis include all of the benefit-sharing effects of controlled group membership. In addition, membership in a consolidated group leads to a much more complex set of controlling tax rules, as discussed in the remainder of this chapter.

EXAMPLE 11

ParentCo owns all of the stock of SubCo, and TopCo owns all of the stock of BottomCo. Both pairs of corporations constitute affiliated groups, as well as controlled groups. ParentCo and SubCo elect to file Federal income tax returns on a consolidated basis. TopCo and BottomCo do not so elect. Consequently, they file separate Federal income tax returns.

Both groups share the lower tax rates on the first $75,000 of combined taxable income—ParentCo and SubCo because they file a combined tax return, and TopCo and BottomCo because of the controlled group rules. Neither group can deduct a loss realized on an intercompany sale. But accounting for the taxable income of the consolidated group is much more complex, as indicated by the rules summarized in Table 8–1. ■

The most important differences between an affiliated group and a parent-subsidiary controlled group include the following. In each case, the affiliated group definition is more difficult to meet.

- The stock attribution rules applied in meeting the controlled group stock ownership test are not required for the affiliated group definition. In an affiliated group, the identifiable parent corporation itself must meet the stock ownership test.
- Affiliated group members must meet the stock ownership tests on *every day* of the tax year. The corresponding controlled group tests are applied only on the last day of the year.[14]

L0.4

Describe the corporations that are eligible to file on a consolidated basis.

Eligibility for the Consolidation Election

The Code lists a number of corporations that may *not* use a consolidated return to report their taxable income.[15] Thus, these corporations cannot be used to meet the stock ownership tests, and their taxable incomes cannot be included in a consolidated return. Some of the most frequently encountered entities that are ineligible for consolidated return status include:

- Corporations established outside the United States or in a U.S. possession.
- Tax-exempt (charitable) corporations.[16]
- Insurance companies.
- Partnerships, trusts, estates, limited liability entities, and any other noncorporate entities.[17]

EXAMPLE 12

In the first ownership structure in the accompanying figure, Phillips, Rhesus, Todd, and Valiant form an affiliated group, with Phillips as the parent, under the stock ownership rules. Valiant, a life insurance company, cannot be included in a consolidated return, however, so the consolidation election is available only to Phillips, Rhesus, and Todd. In the second structure, Phillips, Rhesus, and Todd form an affiliated group, and all of them can be included in a properly executed consolidated return. Phillips is the identifiable parent of the group. Rhesus and Todd essentially form a brother-sister group below Phillips.

---

[14]§§ 1501 and 1563(b)(1).

[15]§ 1504(b).

[16]This includes any entity that is exempt from tax under § 501. See Chapter 14 for a discussion of the qualification of organizations for exempt status.

[17]Some less frequently encountered entities also are prohibited from filing on a consolidated basis. These include regulated investment companies (mutual funds) and real estate investment trusts. §§ 1504(b)(4) through (7).

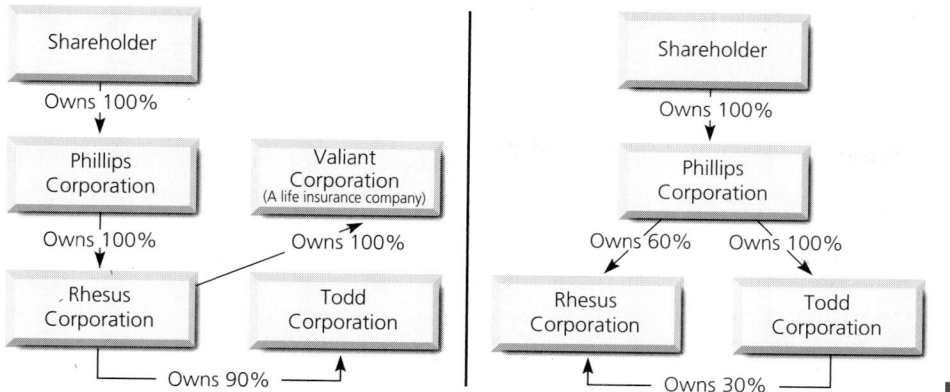

Compliance Requirements

LO.5

Explain the compliance aspects of consolidated returns.

An eligible entity that meets the stock ownership test can be included in a consolidated group if several compliance requirements are met.

The Initial Consolidated Return. The first consolidated tax return must meet certain requirements.

- The Form 1120 for the tax year of the consolidated group should include the taxable results of the operations of all of the members of the consolidated group.[18] This return is filed in lieu of the separate returns of the group members.[19] The identified group then continues to file on a consolidated basis until an eligible group no longer exists or an election to "de-consolidate" is made.[20]
- A Form 1122 should be attached to the first consolidated tax return for each of the subsidiaries included in the group.[21] This form represents a consent by the affiliate to be included in the consolidated group.

The election must be made no later than the extended due date of the parent's return for the year. Only in the case of an inadvertent error can the election to consolidate be rescinded once this extended due date passes.

It is possible for the parent to have negative basis in the subsidiary. See 8–17

Parent Corporation owns 100% of the stock of SubCo. Both corporations use calendar tax years and file separate returns. The entities wish to file on a consolidated basis starting with the tax return for 2008. Parent Corporation does not file to obtain an extended due date for its 2008 return.

If the consolidation election is to be effective, Parent must file a Form 1120 that includes the taxable income of the two corporations by March 15, 2009. SubCo must execute a Form 1122 and attach it to the consolidated Form 1120.

Now assume that Parent Corporation files a complete consolidated Form 1120 on March 3, 2009. On March 6, 2009, the Supreme Court issues a decision that will have a considerable adverse effect on the group's 2011–2014 taxable incomes. If Parent and SubCo file separate

EXAMPLE 13

---

[18]A consolidation election is inferred, even when specific aspects of pertinent forms are completed incorrectly, as long as the members' combined operations are reported on the Form 1120. *American Pacific Whaling Co. v. Comm.,* 35–1 USTC ¶9065, 14 AFTR 887, 74 F.2d 613 (CA–9, 1935).
[19]Reg. § 1.1502–75(a)(1).

[20]Reg. § 1.1502–75(c). The IRS permits such an election only rarely, on the parent's assertion of (1) a good-cause reason to disengage from consolidated status or (2) a substantial change in the tax law that adversely affects the consolidated tax liability.
[21]Reg. § 1.1502–75(b).

2008 returns by March 15, 2009 (or by some later date if an extension to file is obtained in a timely fashion), the IRS will ignore the consolidation election.

If Parent and SubCo fail to file separate returns in this manner, the election to consolidate is in force for all future years, or until the IRS approves Parent's application to revoke it. ■

An application to terminate the consolidation election must be filed at least 90 days prior to the extended due date of the consolidated return.[22] Generally, when a subsidiary leaves an ongoing consolidated group, it must wait five years before it can reenter the group.[23]

Subsequent Consolidated Returns. Each consolidated tax return must include Form 851, Affiliations Schedule. This report identifies all of the corporations in the electing group, summarizes pertinent shareholdings and stock ownership changes that occurred during the tax year, and lists the estimated tax payments made by the group members for the year. Affiliates joining an existing consolidated group need not file a Form 1122, though.

Consolidated tax returns are due on the fifteenth day of the third month following the close of the group's tax year (this is March 15 for a calendar year taxpayer). A six-month extension to file the return can be obtained by executing Form 7004, but an estimated payment of the remaining tax liability for the group must accompany the extension application.

Liability for Taxes. Group members are jointly and severally liable for the entire consolidated tax liability.[24] This rule applies to interest and penalties imposed as a result of audits as well as to tax liabilities. Furthermore, the IRS is not bound to follow internal agreements among group members in apportioning the liability.[25]

EXAMPLE 14

Parent Corporation, a calendar year taxpayer, acquired 100% of the stock of calendar year SubCo on December 20, 2008. The group filed on a consolidated basis from that date until December 31, 2010, when all of the SubCo stock was sold to Foreign Corporation.

An IRS audit determined that Parent owed an additional $10 million in Federal income taxes, relating to a sale it made on December 30, 2008. By mid-2011, however, Parent's cash-flow difficulties had brought it close to bankruptcy and forced it to cease activities.

Due to the consolidation election, the IRS can assess the delinquent taxes from SubCo (and Foreign Corporation). SubCo is liable for the full amount of any consolidated tax liability, even when it is not the source of the income that led to the tax. ■

Starting with the third consolidated return year, estimated tax payments must be made on a consolidated basis.[26] Prior to that year, estimates can be computed and paid on either a separate or a consolidated basis.

Regular tax liability is computed applying the graduated tax rates to consolidated taxable income, following the requirements of controlled group status. In this regard, contributions to the actual payment of the tax liability often are arranged to correspond to contributions to consolidated taxable income.

EXAMPLE 15

Parent Corporation owns 100% of the stock of SubCo, and the two corporations file a consolidated tax return beginning in Year 2. Over the course of a five-year period, the corporations generate the following taxable income/(loss). The low marginal rates that apply to the group's first $75,000 of taxable income might be assigned in various ways.

---

[22]Reg. § 1.1502–75(c)(1)(i).

[23]§ 1504(a)(3); Rev.Proc. 2002–32, 2002–1 C.B. 959.

[24]Reg. § 1.1502–6(a).

[25]Reg. § 1.1502–6(c).

[26]Reg. § 1.1502–5(a)(1).

Year	Parent's Taxable Income	SubCo's Taxable Income	Low Brackets Assigned to Parent	Low Brackets Assigned to SubCo
1	$100,000	($ 10,000)	$37,500	$37,500
2	100,000	(10,000)	75,000	–0–
3	50,000	10,000	65,000	10,000
4	(15,000)	10,000	65,000	10,000
5	100,000	100,000	37,500	37,500

In Year 1, the consolidated group has not yet been formed. Separate returns are filed, and the low tax brackets are apportioned equally between the two entities. Once consolidated returns begin to be filed in Year 2, the indicated elections are made. For Year 2, all of the low brackets are assigned to Parent, rather than wasting any on SubCo, which has a negative taxable income. For Years 3 and 4, the majority of the low brackets are assigned to Parent, because the group believes that Parent's taxable income is more likely to be adjusted upward on an audit. The apportionment is made to create a cushion for Parent in the event that additional tax liability occurs after the initial return is filed. When group members' taxable incomes are close in value and/or exceed $75,000 in total, as in Year 5, a simple equal apportionment of the low brackets is suggested. ∎

Benefits accruing from the graduated corporate tax rates are apportioned equally among the group members unless all members consent to some other method through an annual election. The most commonly used tax-sharing agreements are the *relative taxable income* and *relative tax liability* methods. Under the relative taxable income method,[27] the consolidated tax liability is allocated among the members based on their relative amounts of separate taxable income. When the relative tax liability method is used,[28] the consolidated tax liability is allocated based on the relative hypothetical separate tax liabilities of the members. IRS permission is required for the group to change from one allocation method to another.

The Parent consolidated group reports the following results for the tax year. Assume a 35% marginal tax rate.

EXAMPLE 16

	Parent	SubOne	SubTwo	SubThree	Consolidated
Ordinary income	$400	$100	$–0–	($ 20)	$480
Capital gain/loss	–0–	–0–	100	(25)	75
§ 1231 gain/loss	50	–0–	(50)	–0–	–0–
Separate taxable incomes	$450	$100	$ 50	($ 20)	
				with a $25 capital loss carryover	
Consolidated taxable income					$555
Consolidated tax liability					$194
Foreign tax credit, from SubOne					(19)
Net tax due					$175

---

[27]§ 1552(a)(1); Reg. § 1.1552–1(a)(1).

[28]§ 1552(a)(2); Reg. § 1.1552–1(a)(2).

If the group has consented to the relative taxable income method, the consolidated tax liability is allocated as follows.

	Separate Taxable Income	Allocation Ratio	Allocated Tax Due
Parent	$450	450/600	$131
SubOne	100	100/600	29
SubTwo	50	50/600	15
SubThree	–0–	–0–	–0–
Totals	$600		$175

The results are different if the relative tax liability method is in effect. Specifically, Sub-One gets an immediate tax benefit for the tax credit that it brings to the group. Under neither method, though, does SubThree get any tax benefit from the losses that it brings to the consolidated group.

	Separate Taxable Income	Separate Tax Liability	Allocation Ratio	Allocated Tax Due
Parent	$450	$157.5	157.5/191	$144
SubOne	100	16.0*	16/191	15
SubTwo	50	17.5	17.5/191	16
SubThree	–0–	–0–	–0–	–0–
Totals	$600	$191.0		$175

*After applying foreign tax credit   ∎

Alternative minimum tax (AMT) liability for group members is computed on the basis of consolidated AMTI. The group is allowed only one $40,000 AMT exemption, which is phased out at a rate of 25 percent of the amount by which consolidated AMTI exceeds $150,000. Similarly, the AMT adjustment for adjusted current earnings (ACE), which is 75 percent of the excess of ACE over pre-ACE AMTI, is computed using consolidated amounts.

Tax Accounting Periods and Methods. All the members of a consolidating group must use the parent's tax year.[29] As a result, the group may be required to file a short-year return for the first year a subsidiary is included in the consolidated return, so that the parent's year-end can be adopted.

When a mid-year acquisition occurs, both short years are used in tracking the carryforward period of unused losses and credits. Short-year income and deductions are apportioned between the pre- and post-acquisition periods. The apportionment may be done either on a daily basis or as the items are recorded for financial accounting purposes, at the election of the corporation being acquired.[30]

EXAMPLE 17

All of the stock of calendar year SubCo is acquired by Parent Corporation on July 15, 2008. The corporations elect to file a consolidated return immediately upon the acquisition.

SubCo had generated a long-term capital loss in its 2005 tax year. As of January 1, 2009, only one year remains in the five-year carryforward period for the capital loss.

According to SubCo's financial accounting records, $400,000 of its $1 million accounting and taxable income for the year was generated in 2008 after the acquisition. At SubCo's election, either $400,000 (the "books" apportionment method) or $464,481 [(170 postacquisition

---

[29]Reg. § 1.1502–76(a)(1).   [30]Reg. § 1.1502–76(b)(4).

days/366 days) × $1 million income] (the "daily" method) can be included in the first consolidated return. ■

Members of a consolidated group can continue to use the tax accounting methods that were in place prior to the consolidation election.[31] Thus, the members of a consolidated group may use different accounting methods. On the other hand, because the $5 million gross-receipts test with respect to use of the cash method of accounting is applied on a consolidated basis,[32] some of the group members may need to switch from the cash to the accrual method of tax accounting.

Stock Basis of Subsidiary

Read

LO.6

Compute a parent's investment basis in a subsidiary.

Upon acquiring a subsidiary, the parent corporation records a stock basis on its tax balance sheet equal to the acquisition price. At the end of every consolidated return year, the parent records one or more adjustments to this stock basis, as in the financial accounting "equity" method. This treatment prevents double taxation of gain (or deduction of loss) upon the ultimate disposal of the subsidiary's shares.[33] The adjustments are recorded on the last day of the consolidated return year or on the (earlier) date of the disposal of the shares.[34]

In this regard, positive adjustments to stock basis include:

- An allocable share of consolidated taxable income for the year.
- An allocable share of the consolidated operating or capital loss of a subsidiary that could not utilize the loss through a carryback to a prior year.

Negative adjustments to stock basis include:

- An allocable share of a consolidated taxable loss for the year.
- An allocable share of any carryover operating or capital losses that are deducted on the consolidated return and have not previously reduced stock basis.
- Dividends paid by the subsidiary to the parent out of E & P.

EXAMPLE 18

Parent Corporation acquired all of the stock of SubCo on January 1, 2007, for $1 million. The parties immediately elected to file consolidated tax returns. SubCo had a taxable loss of $100,000 in 2007, but it generated $40,000 taxable income in 2008 and $65,000 in 2009. SubCo paid a $10,000 dividend in mid-2009.

Parent has the following stock bases in SubCo on the last day of each of the indicated years.

| **2007** | $900,000 | **2008** | $940,000 | **2009** | $995,000 | ■ |

When accumulated postacquisition taxable losses of the subsidiary exceed the acquisition price, an **excess loss account** is created.[35] This account (1) allows the consolidated return to recognize the losses of the subsidiary in the current year and (2) enables the group to avoid the need to reflect a negative stock basis on its tax-basis balance sheet. If the subsidiary stock is redeemed or sold to a nongroup member while an excess loss account exists, the seller recognizes the balance of the account as capital gain income.[36]

EXAMPLE 19

Parent Corporation acquired all of the stock of SubCo early in Year 1, for $100,000. As a result of SubCo's operations, the group records the amounts listed.

---

[31]Reg. § 1.1502–17(a).

[32]§§ 448(a)(1) and (c)(2).

[33]This procedure parallels the accounting for tax basis in a partnership or S corporation. See Chapters 10 and 12.

[34]Reg. § 1.1502–32(a). Basis adjustments also are allowed when necessary to determine a tax liability (e.g., when member stock is bought or sold).

[35]Reg. § 1.1502–19.

[36]Reg. §§ 1.1502–19(a)(1) and (2).

Year	Operating Gain/(Loss)	Stock Basis	Excess Loss Account
1	($40,000)	$60,000	$ –0–
2	(80,000)	–0–	20,000
3	30,000	10,000	–0–

If Parent sells the SubCo stock for $50,000 at the end of Year 2, Parent recognizes a $70,000 capital gain ($50,000 amount realized − $0 adjusted basis in stock + $20,000 recovery of excess loss account). If the sale takes place at the end of Year 3, the capital gain is $40,000.[37] ■

To limit the recognition effects of an excess loss account, the group may elect instead to reduce the parent's basis of any remaining stock or indebtedness of the subsidiary that is held after the triggering disposition.[38] After the bases of these other investments have been reduced to zero, the seller recognizes only the balance of the excess loss account.

In a chain of more than one tier of subsidiaries, the computation of the stock basis amounts starts with the lowest-level subsidiary, then proceeds up the ownership structure to the parent's holdings. In this regard, there is no such concept as consolidated E & P. Rather, each entity accounts for its own share of consolidated taxable income on an annual basis, immediately recognizing within E & P any gain or loss on intercompany transactions and reducing E & P by an allocable share of the consolidated tax liability.[39]

Computing Consolidated Taxable Income

When an affiliated group computes its taxable income for the year, it does not simply add together the separate taxable income amounts of its members. Two groups of transactions are removed from the members' tax returns and receive special treatment. Then the special items are recombined with the remaining items of members' taxable incomes to obtain the group's consolidated taxable income for the year. Figure 8–1 illustrates how consolidated taxable income is constructed using this sequential approach.

1. Taxable income is computed for each member on a separate basis.
2. "Group items" and "intercompany items" are isolated and receive special treatment.
3. The remaining separate incomes are combined with the group and intercompany items, resulting in consolidated taxable income.

The Code requires this computational procedure to accomplish several goals.

- Certain transactions are accounted for on a consolidated basis (e.g., charitable contributions and capital gains and losses). This requires that the transactions be isolated from the separate tax returns and computed on a groupwide basis.
- Gains and losses from certain intercompany transactions are deferred until a later tax year. Consequently, they are removed from the tax returns of the members that generated them.
- A few intercompany transactions (e.g., dividend payments) are removed from the taxable income calculation altogether, never to appear in a consolidated return.

---

[37]The Year 3 subsidiary income is first used to eliminate the excess loss account (i.e., before it creates new stock basis). Reg. § 1.1502–32(e)(3).
[38]Reg. § 1.1502–19(a)(6).

[39]Reg. § 1.1502–33(d). In the absence of an election to use some other allocation method, the consolidated tax liability is allocated to each group member according to the relative taxable income method.

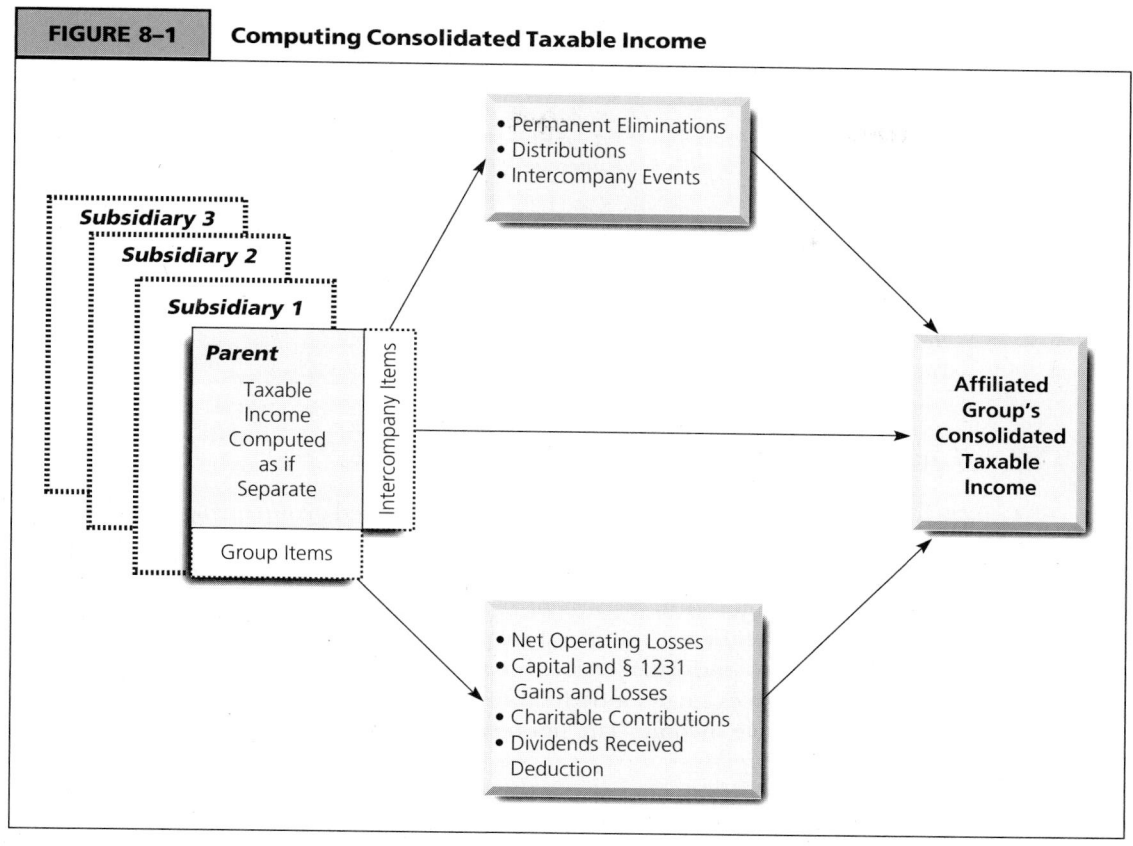

FIGURE 8–1 | **Computing Consolidated Taxable Income**

FIGURE 8–2 | **Consolidated Taxable Income Worksheet**

	Separate Taxable Income	Adjustments	Post-adjustment Amounts
Parent information	_____	_____	_____
Subsidiary information	_____	_____	_____
Group-basis transactions	_____	_____	_____
Intercompany events	_____	_____	_____
Consolidated taxable income	_____	_____	_____
*Permanent eliminations.	**Group-basis transaction.	†Matching rule.

Computational Procedure

The remainder of this chapter will follow the computational procedure suggested in Figure 8–1. Figure 8–2 presents a skeleton worksheet for this computational procedure to be used in examples throughout the remainder of this chapter. Additional information is added to the worksheet for every additional subsidiary. In each case, the starting point for this procedure is the separate taxable incomes of all the group members. Adjustments then are made for group and intercompany items, as indicated in the footnotes to the worksheet.

EXAMPLE 20

Parent Corporation owns 100% of the stock of SubCo. This year, Parent's taxable income amounted to $100,000, while SubCo generated a $40,000 taxable loss. There were no transactions between the two corporations, and they incurred no capital or § 1231 gains/losses, charitable contributions, dividend income, or other items that are accounted for on a group basis. Accordingly, no adjustments are required, and consolidated taxable income is $60,000.

	Separate Taxable Income	Adjustments	Post-adjustment Amounts
Parent information	$100,000		$100,000
SubCo information	(40,000)		(40,000)
Group-basis transactions			
Intercompany events			
Consolidated taxable income			$ 60,000
*Permanent eliminations.	**Group-basis transaction.		†Matching rule.

■

Typical Intercompany Transactions ~~Soc~~

LO.7

Account for intercompany transactions of a consolidated group.

General Rules. When one member of a consolidated group engages in a transaction with another member of the group, an intercompany transaction occurs. In contrast to the financial accounting treatment of most such transactions, the most commonly encountered items *remain in* the members' separate taxable incomes and therefore cancel each other out on a consolidated basis. For instance, when one group member performs services for another member during the year, the purchaser of the services incurs a deductible expenditure, while the service provider generates includible income. The net result is a zero addition to consolidated taxable income.[40]

This two-step procedure prevents the group from avoiding any related-party loss disallowances. Furthermore, when the members involved in the transaction are using different tax accounting methods, the payor's deduction for the expenditure is deferred until the year in which the recipient recognizes the related gross income.[41]

EXAMPLE 21

In the current year, Parent Corporation provided consulting services to its 100%-owned subsidiary, SubCo, under a contract that requires no payments to Parent until next year. Both parties use the accrual method of tax accounting. The services that Parent rendered are valued at $100,000. In addition, Parent purchased $15,000 of supplies from SubCo.

Including these transactions, Parent's taxable income for the year amounted to $500,000. SubCo reported $150,000 of separate taxable income. The group is not required to make any eliminating adjustments. The members' deductions incurred offset the income included by the other party to the intercompany transaction. The consolidated taxable income includes both Parent's $15,000 deduction for supplies and SubCo's $15,000 gross receipts from the sale, so the consolidated taxable income computation *de facto* results in an elimination similar to the kind made in financial accounting. No further adjustment is needed.

	Separate Taxable Income	Adjustments	Post-adjustment Amounts
Parent information	$500,000		$500,000
SubCo information	150,000		150,000
Group-basis transactions			
Intercompany events			
Consolidated taxable income			$650,000
*Permanent eliminations.	**Group-basis transaction.		†Matching rule.

---

[40]Reg. §§ 1.1502–13(a)(1)(i) and (b)(1).   [41]§§ 267(a)(2) and (b)(3); Reg. § 1.1502–13(b)(2).

Assume instead that Parent is a cash basis taxpayer. Since Parent will not recognize the $100,000 of service income earned in the current year until the next tax period, SubCo's related deduction also is deferred until the following year. Thus, the intercompany item—SubCo's deduction—must be eliminated from consolidated taxable income. Additional record keeping is required to keep track of this intercompany transaction (and all others like it), so that the deduction is claimed in the appropriate year.

	Separate Taxable Income	Adjustments	Post-adjustment Amounts
Parent information	$400,000		$400,000
SubCo information	150,000	+ $100,000 due to use of different tax accounting methods	250,000
Group-basis transactions	___	___	
Intercompany events	___	___	
Consolidated taxable income			$650,000
*Permanent eliminations.	**Group-basis transaction.		†Matching rule. ∎

Several other rules also apply to intercompany transactions. Dividends received from other group members are eliminated from the recipients' separate taxable incomes, and no dividends received deduction is allowed.[42] When the distribution consists of noncash assets, the subsidiary payor realizes (but defers recognition of) any gain on the distributed property until the asset leaves the group, and the (eliminated) dividend amount equals the fair market value of the asset.[43]

EXAMPLE 22

Parent Corporation received a $50,000 cash dividend from 100%-owned SubCo in the current year. Including this item, Parent's separate taxable income amounted to $200,000, and SubCo reported $240,000 separate taxable income.

Parent cannot claim a dividends received deduction for this payment, but the dividend is eliminated in computing consolidated taxable income. No elimination is required for SubCo, as dividend payments are nondeductible.

	Separate Taxable Income	Adjustments	Post-adjustment Amounts
Parent information	$200,000	−$50,000 dividend received from SubCo*	$150,000
SubCo information	240,000		240,000
Group-basis transactions	___	___	
Intercompany events	___	___	
Consolidated taxable income			$390,000
*Permanent eliminations.	**Group-basis transaction.		†Matching rule. ∎

LO.8

Identify limitations that restrict the use of losses and credits of group members derived in separate return years.

Members' Net Operating Losses. Often, the election to file consolidated returns is at least partly motivated by the parent corporation's desire to use the positive

---

[42]Reg. § 1.1502–13(f)(2). If the distribution exceeds the payor's E & P, the stock basis of the payor is reduced. When the basis reaches zero, an excess loss account is created. Reg. § 1.1502–19(a). Dividends received from non-group members may result in a dividends received deduction; they constitute a group-basis item (discussed later in the chapter).

[43]§§ 301(b)(1) and (d); § 311(b)(1); Reg. §§ 1.1502–13(c)(7) and (f)(7).

tax attributes of the subsidiary corporation, especially its NOLs. A number of provisions, however, discourage corporate acquisitions that are solely tax motivated.[44]

The usual corporate NOL computations are available for the losses of the consolidated group. Excess losses are carried back 2 years and then forward 20 years, although the parent may elect to forgo the carryback deductions for all members of the group. The NOL is derived after removing any consolidated charitable contribution deduction and capital gain or loss from consolidated taxable income.[45] These items are removed because they have their own carryover periods and rules.[46] The consolidated dividends received deduction remains a part of the consolidated NOL.[47]

EXAMPLE 23

Parent Corporation and SubCo have filed consolidated returns since both entities were incorporated in 2006. Neither group member incurred any capital gain or loss transactions during 2006–2008, nor did they make any charitable contributions. Taxable income computations for the members include the following.

Year	Parent's Taxable Income	SubCo's Taxable Income	Consolidated Taxable Income
2006	$100,000	$ 40,000	$140,000
2007	100,000	(40,000)	60,000
2008	100,000	(140,000)	?
2009	100,000	210,000	?

The 2008 consolidated loss of $40,000 can be carried back to offset 2006 consolidated taxable income. Alternatively, Parent can elect to carry the loss forward to 2009, forgoing any carryback computation. This might be appropriate given an increase in statutory tax rates effective for 2009 or an application of the AMT in 2006 and 2007.

Examine SubCo's 2008 NOL of $140,000. The amount resulted from the following combination of transactions for the year. Unused contributions and capital gain/loss items are subject to their own carryover periods, and they constitute group-basis items, as identified in Figure 8–1.

Operating loss	($140,000)
Net capital gain	15,000
Charitable contributions	20,000
Separate taxable income	(125,000)

■

Complications arise, however, when the corporations enter or depart from a consolidated group, so that members' operating losses are either incurred in a "separate return year" and deducted in a "consolidated return year," or vice versa. A variety of restrictions limit the availability of such deductions to discourage profitable corporations from acquiring unprofitable entities simply to file immediate refund claims based on loss and credit carryforwards. Figure 8–3 summarizes the applicable SRLY (separate return limitation year) limitations.

In any case where the members of a consolidated group change over time, the taxpayer must apportion the consolidated NOL among the group members. When more than one group member generates a loss for the consolidated year, the following formula is used to apportion the loss among the electing group's members.

$$\frac{\text{Member's separate NOL}}{\text{Members' aggregate NOLs}} \;\; \times \;\; \text{Consolidated NOL} \;\; = \;\; \text{Member's apportioned NOL}$$

---

[44]See Chapter 7 and §§ 269, 381, 382, and 482.
[45]Reg. § 1.1502–24(c).
[46]For instance, no election is available that would enable the parent to forgo the net capital loss carryback.

[47]Reg. § 1.1502–21(f).

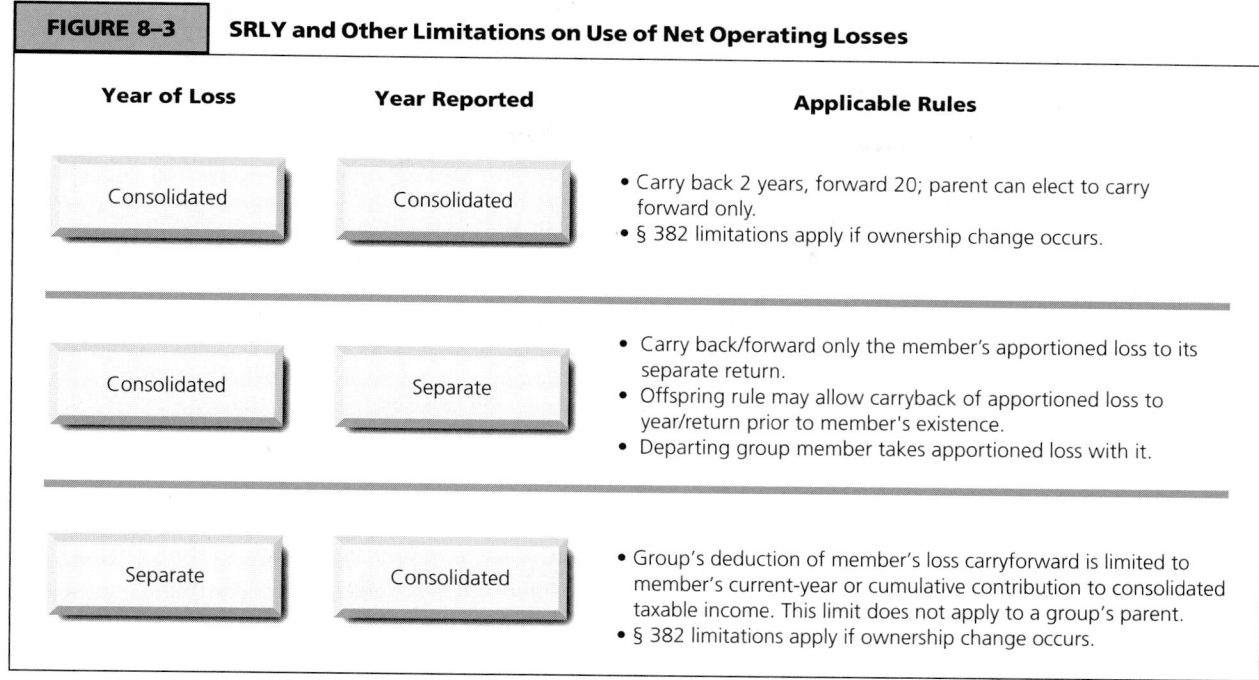

FIGURE 8–3   SRLY and Other Limitations on Use of Net Operating Losses

Year of Loss	Year Reported	Applicable Rules
Consolidated	Consolidated	• Carry back 2 years, forward 20; parent can elect to carry forward only. • § 382 limitations apply if ownership change occurs.
Consolidated	Separate	• Carry back/forward only the member's apportioned loss to its separate return. • Offspring rule may allow carryback of apportioned loss to year/return prior to member's existence. • Departing group member takes apportioned loss with it.
Separate	Consolidated	• Group's deduction of member's loss carryforward is limited to member's current-year or cumulative contribution to consolidated taxable income. This limit does not apply to a group's parent. • § 382 limitations apply if ownership change occurs.

EXAMPLE 24

Parent Corporation and SubCo have filed consolidated returns since 2007. Both entities were incorporated in 2006. Neither group member incurred any capital gain or loss transactions during 2006–2009, nor did they make any charitable contributions. Taxable income computations for the members are listed below.

Year	Parent's Taxable Income	SubCo's Taxable Income	Consolidated Taxable Income
2006*	$100,000	$ 40,000	N/A
2007**	100,000	(40,000)	$60,000
2008**	100,000	(140,000)	?
2009**	100,000	210,000	?

* Separate return year. **Consolidated return year.

In 2008, SubCo can carry back the entire $40,000 consolidated NOL to its separate 2006 tax year, because it is solely responsible for generating the loss. SubCo files for the refund of taxes that result from the carryback, and it alone receives the refund.[48]

Alternatively, Parent could elect to forgo the carryback of the 2008 consolidated loss, thereby preserving the loss deduction for the group's subsequent years. In that case, the 2009 tax reduction from the $40,000 NOL deduction would be claimed merely by filing the 2009 consolidated tax return, and Parent would receive the refund on behalf of the group. ■

In years when a group member files a separate return, only the apportioned NOL may be carried over.

EXAMPLE 25

Parent Corporation, SubOne, and SubTwo have filed consolidated returns since 2007. All of the entities were incorporated in 2006. None of the group members incurred any capital gain or loss transactions during 2006–2009, nor did they make any charitable contributions. Taxable income computations for the members are listed below.

---

[48]Reg. §§ 1.1502–78(b)(1) and (c), Example 4.

Year	Parent's Taxable Income	SubOne's Taxable Income	SubTwo's Taxable Income	Consolidated Taxable Income
2006*	$100,000	$100,000	$ 40,000	N/A
2007**	100,000	100,000	(40,000)	$160,000
2008**	100,000	(60,000)	(120,000)	?
2009**	100,000	100,000	210,000	?

* Separate return year. **Consolidated return year.

If Parent does not elect to forgo the carryback of the 2008 consolidated NOL of $80,000, both subsidiaries can carry losses back to their 2006 separate return years and receive separate refunds. SubOne can carry back a $26,667 loss [(SubOne's NOL $60,000/aggregate NOLs $180,000) × consolidated NOL $80,000], and SubTwo can carry back a $53,333 loss. ∎

Under the so-called offspring rule, the consolidated group can use a carryback loss that is apportioned to a member of the electing group, even though that member was not in existence in the carryback year.[49] If the member joined the group immediately upon its incorporation, but cannot use an apportioned loss in the carryback period because it was not in existence, that loss is still available to the group.[50]

EXAMPLE 26

Parent Corporation, SubOne, and SubTwo have filed consolidated returns since 2007. The first two entities were incorporated and consolidated in 2006, and SubTwo came into existence in 2007 through an asset spin-off from Parent. None of the group members incurred any capital gain or loss transactions during 2006–2009, nor did they make any charitable contributions. Taxable income computations for the members are listed below.

Year	Parent's Taxable Income	SubOne's Taxable Income	SubTwo's Taxable Income	Consolidated Taxable Income
2006*	$100,000	$ 40,000	—	$140,000
2007*	100,000	100,000	($ 40,000)	160,000
2008*	100,000	(60,000)	(120,000)	?
2009*	100,000	100,000	210,000	?

*Consolidated return year.

If Parent does not elect to forgo the carryback of the 2008 consolidated NOL of $80,000, SubOne can carry its $26,667 loss back to 2006. SubTwo's $53,333 share of the loss can also be carried back to 2006 and used by members of the consolidated group. Under the offspring rule, SubTwo is treated as being a member of the group for the entire *group* carryback period because its existence is rooted in Parent's assets. ∎

When a corporation leaves a consolidated group, it takes with it any apportioned share of any unused loss carryforwards, to be used on its subsequent separate returns.

EXAMPLE 27

Parent Corporation, SubOne, and SubTwo have filed consolidated returns since 2006, the year in which all of the entities were incorporated. None of the group members incurred any capital gain or loss transactions during 2006–2009, nor did they make any charitable contributions. Taxable income computations for the members are on the next page.

Parent elects to forgo any loss carryback for the group's 2008 operations. On the first day of the 2009 tax year, a non-U.S. investor purchases all of the stock of SubTwo. On its 2009 separate return, SubTwo can deduct its $53,333 share of the 2008 NOL carryforward.[51]

---

[49]Reg. § 1.1502–79(a)(2).

[50]Reg. § 1.1502–21(b)(2)(ii)(B) restricts the use of this loss to the parent, if the carryback year is a separate return year for the parties.

[51]SubTwo cannot take the entire $120,000 NOL that is attributable to it. Reg. §§ 1.1502–79(a)(1)(ii) and (b)(2)(ii). Losses and carryovers must first be absorbed within the current consolidated return year before any loss apportionment occurs.

CONSOLIDATED RETURNS AND NOLS

Very few countries besides the United States allow the use of consolidated returns. In the view of most countries, tax deductions for operating losses should be used only by those who generated them, not by some sister or other related corporation. This is as much a social principle (the sanctity of the corporate entity) as a revenue-raising provision (NOL deductions mean lower tax collections).

The way European business is conducted makes this result more understandable, as the tax laws of the various countries must ensure that operating losses generated in Tedesco, for instance, are not shifted to Cadenza and converted to deductions there.

This restrictive approach to the trading of operating loss deductions is found in U.S. multistate tax law as well, where tax-oriented border incentives can be especially important. Some states (like Pennsylvania) have, over a specified time period, disallowed the use of loss carryovers of any sort, whereas others (like Ohio) require the taxpayer to deduct only losses assigned to the taxpayer's in-state operations. Multistate tax issues are addressed in Chapter 15.

GLOBAL
Tax Issues

Year	Parent's Taxable Income	SubOne's Taxable Income	SubTwo's Taxable Income	Consolidated Taxable Income
2006*	$100,000	$100,000	$ 40,000	$240,000
2007*	100,000	100,000	(40,000)	160,000
2008*	100,000	(60,000)	(120,000)	?
2009**	100,000	100,000	210,000	N/A

* Consolidated return year. **Separate return year.

■

When an NOL is carried forward from a separate return year onto a consolidated return, another set of limitations, known as the **separate return limitation year (SRLY)** rules, applies.[52] The consolidated return can include an NOL carryforward from the member's SRLY period only to the extent of the lesser of its (1) current-year or (2) cumulative positive contribution to current-year consolidated income.[53]

The SRLY limitations never apply to the electing group's identifiable parent.[54] Nor do they apply to a member that met all of the eligibility and stock ownership tests for consolidated return status, but never was included in a consolidation election.

EXAMPLE 28

Parent Corporation and SubCo have filed consolidated returns since 2007. Both entities were incorporated in 2006. Neither group member incurred any capital gain or loss transactions during 2006–2009, nor did they make any charitable contributions. Taxable income computations for the members are listed below.

Year	Parent's Taxable Income	SubCo's Taxable Income	Consolidated Taxable Income
2006*	$100,000	($40,000)	N/A
2007**	100,000	(10,000)	$90,000
2008**	100,000	15,000	?
2009**	100,000	70,000	?

* Separate return year. **Consolidated return year.

---

[52]Reg. § 1.1502–21(c). The SRLY rules apply to capital loss and credit carryforwards as well.

[53]Reg. § 1.1502–21(c).
[54]Reg. § 1.1502–1(f)(2)(i), known as the "lonely parent" rule.

The thrust of the SRLY rules is to limit Parent's deduction of SubCo's losses from a separate return year against consolidated income. Accordingly, none of SubCo's separate return loss from 2006 can be deducted in computing 2007 consolidated taxable income; the deduction is limited to the lesser of SubCo's current-year (zero) or cumulative (zero) contribution to consolidated taxable income.

In computing 2008 consolidated taxable income, the SubCo SRLY loss deduction is limited to $5,000, the lesser of SubCo's current-year ($15,000) or cumulative ($5,000) contribution to consolidated taxable income. The remaining SRLY deduction reduces consolidated taxable income beginning in 2009. ■

EXAMPLE 29

Parent Corporation and SubCo have filed consolidated returns since 2007. Both entities were incorporated in 2006. Neither group member incurred any capital gain or loss transactions during 2006–2009, nor did they make any charitable contributions. Taxable income computations for the members are listed below.

Year	Parent's Taxable Income	SubCo's Taxable Income	Consolidated Taxable Income
2006*	($ 40,000)	$100,000	N/A
2007**	(100,000)	(10,000)	($110,000)
2008**	20,000	165,000	?
2009**	100,000	70,000	?

* Separate return year. **Consolidated return year.

The 2008 consolidated return can include a deduction for Parent's entire 2006 NOL of $40,000. The deduction is not limited to the lesser of Parent's current-year ($20,000) or cumulative (zero) contribution to consolidated taxable income. SRLY rules do not apply to the group's parent. ■

When both the SRLY rules and a § 382 limitation apply because an ownership change has occurred (see Chapter 7), the § 382 provisions override the SRLY limits.[55]

EXAMPLE 30

The Parent consolidated group includes SubTwo, which was acquired as part of a § 382 ownership change. SubTwo brought with it to the group a $180,000 NOL carryforward, $125,000 of which is available this year under the SRLY rules due to SubTwo's positive contribution to the group's taxable income. The § 382 limitation with respect to SubTwo is $100,000. Accordingly, only $100,000 of the SubTwo NOL can be used to reduce consolidated taxable income this year.

If the § 382 limitation had been $200,000 instead, the full $180,000 NOL deduction would have been allowed. The § 382 rules prevail even with respect to SRLY losses that overlap with the same tax year. ■

LO.9

Derive deductions and credits on a consolidated basis.

Computation of Group Items

Several income and deduction items are derived on a consolidated-group basis. Therefore, statutory limitations and allowances are applied to the group as though it were a single corporation. This computational convention allows group members to match various types of gains and losses and to increase specific limitations, required by the Code, in a manner that optimizes the overall tax benefit.

Specifically, the following items are computed on a group basis with the usual C corporation tax effects applied to the combined group amounts (see Chapter 2).

- Net capital gain/loss.
- Section 1231 gain/loss.

---

[55]Reg. §§ 1.1502–21(g) and –22(g).

- Section 199 domestic production activities deduction.
- Casualty/theft gain/loss.
- Charitable contributions.⚹
- Dividends received deduction.
- Net operating loss.

Following the computational procedure of Figures 8–1 and 8–2, all of the group-basis items are removed from each member's separate taxable income. Then, using the consolidated taxable income figure to that point, statutory limitations are applied to determine group-basis gains, losses, income, and deductions.

EXAMPLE 31

Parent Corporation's current-year taxable income included $300,000 net income from operations and a $50,000 net long-term capital gain. Parent also made a $40,000 contribution to State University. Accordingly, its separate taxable income amounted to $315,000.

Income from operations	$300,000
Capital gain income	+50,000
Charitable contribution (maximum)	−35,000 ⚹
Separate taxable income	$315,000

SubCo generated $170,000 income from operations and incurred a $45,000 short-term capital loss. Thus, its separate taxable income was $170,000, and aggregate separate taxable income for the group amounted to $485,000.

Upon consolidation, a larger amount of Parent's charitable contribution is deductible, and its capital gain is almost fully sheltered from current-year tax.

	Separate Taxable Income	Adjustments	Post-adjustment Amounts
Parent information	$315,000	−$50,000 capital gain income** +$35,000 charitable contribution deduction**	$300,000
SubCo information	170,000	$45,000 short-term capital loss**	170,000
Group-basis transactions		+$5,000 net long-term capital gain −$40,000 charitable contribution deduction (maximum for group is $47,500) ⚹	−35,000
Intercompany events			
Consolidated taxable income			$435,000
*Permanent eliminations.	**Group-basis transaction.		†Matching rule.

∎

Computing these items on a group basis does not always result in a reduction of aggregate group taxable income. Nevertheless, the possibility of using the group-basis computations may affect transactions by group members late in the tax year when it becomes apparent that planning opportunities may be available. It may also encourage the taxpayer to seek out fellow group members that bring complementary tax attributes to the consolidated return.

<table>
<tr><td>*E X A M P L E   32*</td><td></td></tr>
</table>

Parent Corporation owns 15% of the stock of Outsider Corporation throughout the year. Outsider paid a $150,000 dividend to Parent during the year. Parent also generated $400,000 of taxable operating income and sold a § 1231 asset at a $10,000 gain. Parent's separate taxable income is computed below.

Operating income	$ 400,000
Dividend income	+150,000
§ 1231 gain	+10,000
Dividends received deduction (70%)	−105,000
Separate taxable income	$ 455,000

A 10% owner of Outsider, SubCo also received a $100,000 dividend. SubCo's operations produced a $20,000 net taxable loss for the year, and it sold a § 1231 asset at a $4,000 loss. Thus, SubCo's separate taxable income is computed as follows.

Operating income	($ 20,000)
Dividend income	+100,000
§ 1231 loss	−4,000
Dividends received deduction[56]	−53,200
Separate taxable income	$ 22,800

A consolidated return increases the group's dividends received deduction,[57] but it wastes the opportunity to claim SubCo's § 1231 loss as an ordinary deduction.

	Separate Taxable Income	Adjustments	Post-adjustment Amounts
Parent information	$455,000	−$150,000 dividend received from Outsider** −$10,000 § 1231 gain** +$105,000 dividends received deduction**	$400,000
SubCo information	22,800	−$100,000 dividend received from Outsider** +$4,000 § 1231 loss +$53,200 dividends received deduction	(20,000)
Group-basis transactions		+$250,000 dividend received from Outsider −$175,000 dividends received deduction (70% × $250,000) +$6,000 § 1231 gain	+81,000
Intercompany events			
Consolidated taxable income			$461,000
*Permanent eliminations.	**Group-basis transaction.		†Matching rule.

■

---

[56]Limited to 70% of taxable income before the deduction. § 246(b)(1).

[57]The group cannot apply an 80% rate for the dividends received deduction, even though aggregate group ownership in Outsider now exceeds 20%. Reg. § 1.1502–26(a)(1)(i).

The § 199 domestic production activities deduction, or DPAD (see Chapter 3), is allowed for an **expanded affiliated group (EAG)**.[58] If such a group files a Form 1120 as a consolidated group, DPAD is another group item. DPAD is computed on the basis of consolidated taxable income, not the separate taxable income amounts of the members, and the taxable income limitation is applied to this amount. DPAD then is allocated to the group members on the basis of the qualified production activities income (QPAI) of each, regardless of whether the member has a separate taxable gain or loss for the year.[59] If the member's QPAI is negative, it is treated as zero for this purpose.

E X A M P L E   33

Except for the § 199 domestic production activities deduction (DPAD), the members of an electing consolidated group report the following data.

Affiliate	Taxable Income ($ Million)	Qualified Production Activities Income (QPAI) ($ Million)	W–2 Wages ($ Million)
B, parent	50	80	60
C	(20)	40	20
D	10	30	–0–
Totals	40	150	80

The DPAD is computed at the group level, and then it is allocated to the affiliates based on the relative amount of each member's QPAI. Members' separate taxable incomes are recomputed for these amounts, and consolidated taxable income then is determined.

- Member B is allocated 80/150 of the group's DPAD.
- Member C is allocated 40/150 of the group's DPAD.
- Member D is allocated 30/150 of the group's DPAD.

Although member C reported an NOL for the year, it is not separately subject to the taxable income limitation. Further, note that member D separately would not be entitled to any DPAD because of the W–2 wage limitation. These individual limitations are not relevant in the EAG determination of the DPAD. The DPAD is a group item on the consolidated return. ∎

Other items computed on a consolidated basis include all elements of the general business and research credits, any recapture of those credits, the foreign tax credit, the percentage depletion deduction, and all elements of AMTI.

The Matching Rule

A special class of intercompany transactions receives deferral treatment under the Regulations.[60] The gain or loss realized on these transactions is removed from consolidated taxable income until the sold asset leaves the affiliated group. The purpose of this **matching rule** is to prevent group members from accelerating loss deductions that relate to sales of assets within the group. In effect, for purposes of these intercompany transactions the group is treated as a single corporation with multiple operating divisions.

The matching rule applies to sales of assets or the performance of services among group members. The entire deferred gain or loss enters the consolidated

---

[58]An expanded affiliated group includes any group of parent-subsidiary corporations in which more than 50% of each member is owned directly or indirectly by a parent corporation. An EAG can include corporations that are ineligible to elect to file a consolidated return, such as an insurance company. § 199(d)(4)(B).

[59]Intercompany sales among group members are included in qualified production activities income, but receipts from intercompany leases, rentals, and licensing are not. Reg. § 1.199–7(c).

[60]Reg. § 1.1502–13.

taxable income computation when, say, the asset is transferred outside the group through a subsequent sale. Full gain or loss recognition can also be triggered under the "acceleration rule" when the transferor of the property leaves the group or the consolidation election is terminated.[61] The acceleration rule applies when it no longer is possible to produce a proper result under the matching rule.

Generally, the gain or loss on the sale outside the group is recognized in the same manner as it would have been on the initial transfer.[62]

EXAMPLE 34

Parent Corporation sold a plot of land to SubCo in the current year for $100,000. Parent had acquired the land 10 years ago for $40,000. The consolidated return also reflects the operating results of the parties: Parent generated $10,000 income, and SubCo produced a $100,000 gain.

This intercompany transaction triggers the matching rule: Parent's $60,000 realized gain is deferred through an elimination in the computation of consolidated taxable income. The $60,000 gain is recognized by the group when SubCo later sells the land to Outsider Corporation.

	Separate Taxable Income	Adjustments	Post-adjustment Amounts
Parent information	$ 70,000		$ 70,000
SubCo information	100,000		100,000
Group-basis transactions			
Intercompany events		−$60,000 gain on intercompany sale to SubCo†	−60,000
Consolidated taxable income			$110,000
*Permanent eliminations.	**Group-basis transaction.		†Matching rule.

SubCo sold the land to Outsider for $110,000 in a year in which its operating income totaled $60,000 (exclusive of the sale of the land), and Parent's operating income amounted to $170,000.

	Separate Taxable Income	Adjustments	Post-adjustment Amounts
Parent information	$170,000		$170,000
SubCo information	70,000		70,000
Group-basis transactions			
Intercompany events		+$60,000 restored gain on Parent's sale to SubCo†	+60,000
Consolidated taxable income			$300,000
*Permanent eliminations.	**Group-basis transaction.		†Matching rule.

Generally, the matching rule is attractive to the group when intercompany sales take place at a gain. When such sales generate losses, however, the mandatory nature of the rule may become burdensome.

---

[61]Reg. § 1.1502–13(d)(1)(i).

[62]Sections 267 and 1239 may convert other types of gain into ordinary income. See especially Reg. §§ 1.267(f)–1 and 1.1239–1(a) and (b)(3).

Choosing Consolidated Return Partners

LO.10

Demonstrate tax planning opportunities available to consolidated groups.

Taxpayers should optimize their overall tax benefits when choosing consolidated return partners. Within the limitations of the rules discussed earlier in the chapter, attributes of potential target corporations might include some of the following.

TAX PLANNING
Considerations

- Loss and credit carryovers.
- Passive activity income, loss, or credits.
- Gains that can be deferred through intercompany sales.
- Contributions to consolidated ACE adjustments.
- Excess limitation amounts (e.g., with respect to charitable contributions).
- Section 1231 gains, losses, and lookback profiles.

Consolidation versus 100 Percent Dividends Received Deduction

When adequate ownership is held, a 100 percent dividends received deduction is available for payments received from subsidiaries with whom a consolidated return is *not* filed. Thus, this tax benefit is still available when the taxpayer wishes to affiliate with an insurance company, foreign entity, or other ineligible corporation. A taxpayer that cannot find potential group partners with the desired level of complementary tax attributes may also take advantage of this benefit.

Protecting the Group Members' Liability for Tax Payments

Because all group members are responsible for consolidated tax liabilities, interest, and penalties, target subsidiaries and their (present and potential) shareholders should take measures to protect their separate interests.

EXAMPLE 35

Return to the facts of Example 14. Exposure by SubCo and its successive shareholders to tax (and all other) liabilities of Parent Corporation should be minimized by including appropriate clauses in purchase contracts and related documents. For instance, (1) Foreign Corporation could alter its negotiating position so that it pays less to acquire the SubCo stock, or (2) SubCo might attempt to recover any Parent taxes that it pays through courts other than the Tax Court. ∎

A short tax year may be created when a member with a nonmatching tax year joins or leaves the group. When this occurs, the group should consider measures to limit the ensuing negative tax consequences. For instance, additional income can be accelerated into the short year of acquisition. This will reduce any loss carryforwards when the carryover period is effectively shortened due to the takeover. The group should also make suitable income-allocation elections in assigning income to the short year. Finally, group estimated tax payments should be computed using both consolidated and separate liability amounts to determine the more beneficial method. In this way, only the minimum quarterly tax payments are made, and the benefits of the time value of money are maximized.

Documentation Requirements

Adjustments to the basis of subsidiary stock must be fully documented, with detailed workpapers retained by the taxpayer.[63] If a tax understatement results from poor documentation of the subsidiary's stock basis, a penalty is added to the

---

[63]Reg. § 1.1502–32(q). An earlier proposed rule, not adopted, would have required the basis computations to be attached to the consolidated return.

CONCEPT SUMMARY 8–2

The Consolidated Tax Return

1. Groups of corporations form for a variety of tax and nontax reasons. The election to file Federal income tax returns on a consolidated basis allows certain group members to use their positive tax attributes (e.g., loss or credit carryovers) to offset negative tax attributes (e.g., positive taxable income) of other members.

2. Consolidated tax returns are limited to eligible corporations that satisfy stock ownership tests and meet various compliance requirements. For instance, all group members must conform their tax years to that of the parent of the group. Group members may use different tax accounting methods, however.

3. Group members are jointly and severally liable for the overall tax liability of the group. For the most part, computations of estimated tax liabilities must be made on a consolidated basis.

4. The stock basis of a subsidiary is derived from the acquisition price of the stock, increased by the taxable income (or decreased by the losses) of the subsidiary, and decreased by dividend distributions. An excess loss account is created when aggregate losses of the subsidiary exceed both the purchase price and ensuing income amounts. The excess loss account is recaptured as capital gain when the subsidiary stock is disposed of.

5. Under the § 382 or SRLY rules, NOL carryforwards may be deferred when they relate to subsidiaries acquired by the group. When both restrictions apply, the § 382 rules prevail.

6. In computing consolidated taxable income, certain items, such as charitable contributions and § 1231 gains and losses, are computed on a consolidated basis, while other gains and losses are deferred until later tax periods. The group is subject to severe restrictions in using any operating losses of a subsidiary that has been acquired or disposed of.

amount of tax due.[64] Because of the importance of the stock basis computations for this and other reasons, contemporaneous documentation by the parent corporation must be maintained.

KEY TERMS

Affiliated group, 8–8

Consolidated returns, 8–3

Excess loss account, 8–17

Expanded affiliated group (EAG), 8–29

Matching rule, 8–29

Separate return limitation year (SRLY), 8–25

PROBLEM MATERIALS

DISCUSSION QUESTIONS

1. The restructuring of a conglomerate usually occurs for nontax reasons (e.g., to increase market share or stock price). What are some other market-driven reasons to form controlled and affiliated groups?

Decision Making

2. Describe how a corporate entity might be restructured to enable the resulting group to qualify for a consolidation election. [Hint: Recall the corporate changes discussed in Chapter 7, such as the "Type A" reorganization.]

---

[64]The preamble to the Regulation specifies that the penalty applies to misstatements of basis due to negligence and substantial or gross misconduct by the taxpayer. TD 8560, 1994–2 C.B. 200.

3. The consolidated return rules are unique among U.S. income tax laws, in that most of the content of the rules is found in the Regulations, and not the Code. Comment on the desirability of this situation.

4. You are the tax member of a consulting team that is presenting ideas for a possible restructuring to a client. The client has heard that filing consolidated tax returns can produce savings. Prepare for the client an outline on the pros and cons of filing a consolidated return.

Communications

5. The election to consolidate cannot be made unless the affiliates meet three threshold tests. What are those tests? How can the group members satisfy them so that the election can occur?

6. Black, Brown, and Red Corporations are considering a corporate restructuring that would allow them to file Federal income tax returns on a consolidated basis. Black holds significant NOL carryforwards from several years ago. Brown has always been profitable and is projected to remain so. Red has been successful, but its product cycles are mature and operating losses are likely to begin three years from now and last for a decade. What tax issues should the corporations consider before electing to file on a consolidated basis?

Issue ID

7. Continue with the facts presented in Question 6. In addition, assume that Brown Corporation has a history of making large, continuous charitable contributions in its community. In the next three years, Brown's largest investment assets will be priced such that they will be attractive candidates for sale. Modify your list of tax issues to include these considerations.

Issue ID

8. Naming specific entities with which you are familiar, give three examples of operating entities that cannot join a consolidated group.

9. The Flamingo Group cannot decide whether to start to file on a consolidated basis for Federal income tax purposes, effective for its tax year beginning January 1, 2009. Its computational study of the effects of consolidation is taking longer than expected. What is the latest date by which the group must make this critical decision?

10. The Penguin Group cannot decide whether to cease to file on a consolidated basis for Federal income tax purposes, effective for its tax year beginning January 1, 2009. Its computational study of the effects of such a "de-consolidation" is taking longer than expected. What is the latest date by which the group must make this critical decision?

11. Lavender and Azure began to file a calendar year consolidated return for tax year 2006. The group never extends the due date of its tax returns. Lavender acquires all of the stock of Rose on January 1, 2007, and immediately joins the consolidated group. All of the Rose stock is sold to another investor at the end of 2009. Explain the significance of the following dates. Which of your answers can change if the taxpayers so elect?
   a.   March 15, 2007.
   b.   January 1, 2008.
   c.   March 15, 2008.
   d.   January 1, 2015.

Decision Making

12. Large Corporation has just acquired all of the stock of its supplier, LittleCo. Like other affiliates in the Large consolidated return group, LittleCo will be expected to provide cash to its parent corporation to cover an allocable share of the Federal income tax liability that is traceable to LittleCo operations. Describe the major alternative means by which a consolidated group allocates Federal income tax liabilities among its members.

13. Parent Corporation and its wholly owned subsidiary, Child Corporation, file Federal tax returns on a separate basis. Parent manufactures postage meters, and Child provides mail-order services to a cross section of clients in the state.

   Parent uses a calendar tax year, while Child files using an April 30 year-end. Parent's gross receipts for the year total $10 million, and Child's are $2.5 million. Identify some Federal income tax issues as to accounting periods and methods that the group would face if the corporations elect to consolidate.

Issue ID

14. Your firm has assigned you to work with Jeri Byers, the tax director of a small group of corporations. The group qualifies to file on a consolidated basis and plans to make its first election. In a memo to Jeri's tax file, describe some of the more important adjustments that she will need to make in order to keep track of the parent corporation's basis in the stock of each of the subsidiaries.

Communications

Issue ID

15. In December 2008, Parent Corporation renders services worth $250,000 to its wholly owned subsidiary, Child Corporation. Both entities use calendar tax years. Parent uses accrual tax accounting, while Child employs the cash method of accounting. The entities have been filing on a consolidated basis since Child was incorporated many years ago.

    Parent's operations for 2008 resulted in a $2 million loss. Parent sends Child an invoice for the services in December 2008, and Child pays it in January 2009. What tax consequences are the parties trying to accomplish?

16. SubOne Corporation brought a $2 million NOL carryforward into a group of corporations that elected to file on a consolidated basis as of the beginning of this year. Combined results for the year generated $15 million taxable income, $1.5 million of which was attributable to SubOne's activities for the year. Has SubOne been a good consolidation partner?

Decision Making

17. Parent and Child Corporations have filed on a consolidated basis since the mid-1970s. Junior Corporation was formed at the beginning of this year through an asset split-off from Parent. Operations this year resulted in a $2 million operating loss, one-fourth of which can be traced to Junior. Should Junior join the consolidated group this year? Will the group be able to carry back and claim a refund for the $500,000 NOL that is attributable to Junior?

18. Beige owned all of the stock of White when the two corporations were formed a decade ago. The group immediately elected to file on a consolidated basis. The management team of White now has purchased the company from the parent and intends to carry on and expand the business into new markets. When White left the Beige consolidated group, the group held a $3 million NOL carryforward, $800,000 of which was attributable to White operations under formulas used by all of the parties. White will generate $300,000 on each of its first five years' worth of separate returns.

    Advise White as to who "owns" the carryforwards after the corporate division.

19. Congress is concerned that corporations will use the consolidated return rules to "traffic" in NOL carryovers. The Regulations attempt to prevent a parent corporation from acquiring an affiliate simply to use the subsidiary's NOLs accumulated over prior years. Describe the "SRLY" rules and explain how they work to implement congressional intent in this regard.

Communications

20. The computational method of Figure 8–1 indicates that consolidated taxable income includes a number of group items, where limitations are applied on an aggregate basis. In no more than two PowerPoint slides, list as many group items as you can.

Decision Making

21. Intercompany transactions of a consolidated group can be subject to a "matching rule" and an "acceleration rule."
    a. Define both of these terms.
    b. As a tax planner structuring an intercompany transaction, when would it be beneficial to use either rule?

22. Trace the gain/loss recognition by this affiliated group.
    - Year 1: SubCo purchases an asset for $100.
    - Year 3: SubCo sells the asset to Parent for $150.
    - Year 4: Parent sells the asset to Stranger (not an affiliate) for $160.

23. Trace the gain/loss recognition by this affiliated group.
    - Year 1: SubCo purchases an asset for $100.
    - Year 3: SubCo sells the asset to Parent for $50.
    - Year 4: Parent sells the asset to Stranger (not an affiliate) for $40.

Communications

24. Junior was a member of the Rice consolidated group for many years. It left the group effective for the 2008 tax year. In 2005, Junior sold a plot of land to Parent at a $600,000 realized loss. Recognition of that loss by the group was deferred under the matching rule. As a departing group member, does Junior have any right to take the loss with it to be used on its subsequent separate returns? Prepare a memo for the tax research file, outlining the arguments both in Junior's favor and in the remaining group's favor.

25. Consolidated return elections are common among conglomerate groups, but they can be expensive to initiate and maintain. Not all corporate groups make an election to consolidate, even though they qualify to do so. Explain why some groups of affiliates may not make the election to file their Federal income taxes on a consolidated basis.

PROBLEMS

26. Big Corporation and its wholly owned subsidiary, LittleCo, file a consolidated return for Federal income tax purposes. Indicate the financial accounting and tax treatment of the following transactions.
    a. LittleCo pays a $1 million dividend to Big.
    b. LittleCo sells investment land to Big. LittleCo's basis in the land is $400,000. The sale price is $500,000.
    c. Six months after purchasing the land from LittleCo, Big sells the land to Phillips, an unrelated party, for $550,000.

27. Indicate whether each of the following would make good consolidated return partners in computing Federal income tax.
    a. SubCo has a number of appreciated assets that it wants to sell to its parent, Huge Corporation.
    b. SubCo has a number of assets that it wants to sell to its parent, Huge. The assets have declined in market value since SubCo purchased them.
    c. ParentCo has $2 million in suspended foreign tax credits that will expire in two more tax years. Its wholly owned subsidiary, ShortCo, generates $5 million in foreign-source income every year.
    d. This year, ParentCo generated $4 million in taxable income, and its wholly owned subsidiary, Small Corporation, reported a $3 million operating loss. Next year, though, Small is projected to start a four-year period with $20 million total taxable profits.

28. Giant Corporation owns all of the stock of PebbleCo, so they constitute a Federal affiliated group and also a parent-subsidiary controlled group. By completing the following chart, delineate for Giant's tax department some of the effects of an election to file Federal consolidated returns.

Situation	If the Group Files a Consolidated Return	If Separate Tax Returns Continue to Be Filed
a. PebbleCo pays a $1 million cash dividend to Giant.		
b. Taxable income for both group members this year is $50,000.		
c. Giant's tax liability is $65,000, and Pebble's liability totals $75,000.		
d. PebbleCo's manufacturing operations generate $300,000 taxable income for the accumulated earnings tax.		
e. Giant uses a calendar tax year, while PebbleCo's tax year-end is March 31.		
f. Giant uses dollar-value LIFO for its inventory tax accounting, while PebbleCo uses FIFO.		

29. Apply the controlled and affiliated group rules to determine whether a parent-subsidiary controlled group or an affiliated group exists in each of the following independent situations. Circle Y for yes and N for no.

Situation	Parent-Subsidiary Controlled Group?		Affiliated Group?	
a.	Throughout the year, Parent owns 65% of the stock of SubCo.	Y N		Y N	
b.	Parent owns 70% of SubCo. The other 30% of SubCo stock is owned by Senior, a wholly owned subsidiary of Parent.	Y N		Y N	
c.	For 11 months, Parent owns 75% of the stock of SubCo. For the last month of the tax year, Parent owns 100% of the SubCo stock.	Y N		Y N	

30. Senior Corporation owns all of the stock of Junior, Ltd., a corporation that has been declared bankrupt and has no net assets. Junior still owes $1 million to Wholesale, Inc., one of its suppliers, and $2.5 million to the IRS for unpaid Federal income taxes. Senior and Junior have always filed Federal income tax returns on a consolidated basis. What is Senior's exposure concerning Junior's outstanding liabilities?

31. Parent and Sub Corporations file their Federal income tax returns on a consolidated basis. Parent, a calendar year taxpayer, owns all of the outstanding stock of Sub. The consolidation election was effective in January 2006. Both companies are profitable, and tax projections for the future appear below. How much must be remitted to the IRS for estimated payments in each year?

Tax Year	Parent's Federal Tax Estimate	Sub's Federal Tax Estimate
2006	$500,000	$220,000
2007	500,000	200,000
2008	600,000	300,000
2009	650,000	300,000

32. ParentCo owns all of DaughterCo, and the group files its Federal income tax returns on a consolidated basis. Both taxpayers are subject to the AMT this year due to active operations in oil and gas development. No intercompany transactions were incurred this year. If the affiliates filed separate returns, they would report the following amounts.

Company	Adjusted Current Earnings (ACE)	AMT Income before the ACE Adjustment
ParentCo	$1,500,000	$ 800,000
DaughterCo	150,000	400,000
Totals	$1,650,000	$1,200,000

How does the consolidation election affect the overall AMT liability of the group?

33. The Parent consolidated group reports the following results for the tax year. Dollar amounts are listed in millions.

	Parent	SubOne	SubTwo	SubThree	Consolidated
Ordinary income	$700	$200	$ 20	($30)	$ 890
Capital gain/loss	–0–	–0–	60	(25)	35
§ 1231 gain/loss	130	–0–	(55)	–0–	75
Separate taxable incomes	$830	$200	$ 25	($30)	
				with a $25 capital loss carryover	
Consolidated taxable income					$1,000
Consolidated tax liability					$ 350
Energy tax credit, from SubOne					(44)
Net tax due					$ 306

Determine each member's share of the consolidated tax liability, assuming that the members all have consented to use the relative taxable income method. Assume a 35% marginal tax rate.

34. Assume the same facts as in Problem 33, except that the group members have adopted the relative tax liability tax-sharing method.

35. Senior, Ltd., acquires all of the stock of JuniorCo for $30 million at the beginning of 2008. The group immediately elects to file income tax returns on a consolidated basis. Senior's operations generate a $50 million profit every year. In 2009, JuniorCo pays its parent a $9 million dividend. Operating results for JuniorCo are as follows.

2008	$ 4 million
2009	16 million
2010	10 million

   a. Compute Senior's basis in the JuniorCo stock as of the end of 2008, 2009, and 2010.
   b. Same as (a), except that JuniorCo's 2009 tax year produced a $6 million NOL.
   c. Same as (a), except that JuniorCo's 2009 tax year produced a $40 million NOL.

36. Compute consolidated taxable income for the calendar year Teal Group, which elected consolidated status immediately upon creation of the two member corporations in January 2006. All recognized income relates to the consulting services of the firms. No intercompany transactions were completed during the indicated years.

Year	Teal Corporation	Orange Corporation
2006	$250,000	($ 10,000)
2007	250,000	(80,000)
2008	250,000	(200,000)
2009	250,000	10,000

37. Compute consolidated taxable income for the calendar year Moose Group, which elected consolidated status immediately upon the creation of the two member corporations on January 1, 2006. All recognized income is ordinary in nature, and no intercompany transactions were completed during the indicated years.

Year	Moose Corporation	Elk Corporation
2006	$250,000	$ 10,000
2007	250,000	(200,000)
2008	250,000	(440,000)
2009	250,000	75,000

38. Cougar, Jaguar, and Ocelot Corporations have filed on a consolidated, calendar year basis for many years. At the beginning of the 2009 tax year, the group elects to de-consolidate. The group's $4 million NOL carryforward can be traced in the following manner: one-half to Cougar's operations and one-quarter each to Jaguar's and Ocelot's. How will Ocelot treat the NOL on its 2009 separate tax return?

39. The Parent consolidated group includes SubTwo, which was acquired as part of a § 382 ownership change. SubTwo brought with it to the group a large NOL carryforward, $2,500,000 of which is available this year under the SRLY rules due to SubTwo's positive contribution to the group's taxable income. The § 382 limitation with respect to SubTwo is $400,000. How much of SubTwo's NOL can be used this year to reduce consolidated taxable income?

40. Child Corporation joined the Thrust consolidated group in 2008. At the time it joined the group, Child held a $900,000 NOL carryforward. On a consolidated basis, the members of Thrust generated significant profits for many years.

    Child's operating results during the first few consolidated return years were as follows.

    | 2008 | ($100,000) |
    | 2009 | 600,000 |
    | 2010 | 500,000 |

    The § 382 rules do not apply to the group.

    How will Child's NOLs affect consolidated taxable income for these years? Is any refund available with respect to the NOL that Child brought into the group?

41. Parent Corporation sold a plot of undeveloped land to SubCo this year for $100,000. Parent had acquired the land several years ago for $20,000. The consolidated return also reflects the operating results of the parties: Parent generated $130,000 income from operations, and SubCo produced a $20,000 operating loss.
    a. Use the computational worksheet of Figure 8–2 to derive the group members' separate taxable incomes and the group's consolidated taxable income.
    b. Same as (a), except that SubCo sold the land to Outsider Corporation for $110,000 in a subsequent year, when its operating income totaled $30,000 (exclusive of the sale of the land), and Parent's operating income amounted to $90,000.

RESEARCH PROBLEMS

Communications

Note: Solutions to Research Problems can be prepared by using the **RIA Checkpoint®** **Student Edition** online research product, which is available to accompany this text. It is also possible to prepare solutions to the Research Problems by using tax research materials found in a standard tax library.

Research Problem 1.   Your firm's client, UpperCo, owns stock in Lower Corporation. The voting shares and value of the Lower stock owned by Upper are as follows.

- Common stock, 100%.
- Preferred stock, 50%.

    Under Lower's corporate bylaws, the board of directors manages all of the entity's operations and investments. A majority vote of the board is required before any new policy or practice is adopted.

    Board members are elected in the following manner: the common shareholders elect five of the eight board members, and the preferred shareholders separately elect the other three directors.

    Upper would like to file a consolidated tax return with Lower. Is the § 1504 stock ownership test met (i.e., does Upper own 80% of the voting power and value of the Lower stock)? Prepare a memo to your firm's tax research file that addresses this affiliated group issue.

Research Problem 2.   The calendar year Thor Group files its Federal income tax returns on a consolidated basis. The group's members elected to file on a consolidated basis because some of them were generating income, while others were generating losses. To utilize the deductions for the losses, the group began filing a consolidated return.

Now market conditions have changed. Currently, group members are all producing positive Federal taxable incomes. Various groups of shareholders desire to purchase the affiliates of the now-profitable group. If this occurs, the group will no longer meet the ownership requirements for consolidation starting in tax year 2009.

Is it possible to effect a de-consolidation of the group for tax year 2008? Why not just file separate returns for each member of the group for that year? The parent would claim the 100% dividends received deduction on its own return, and this should void the election.

The breakup of the group will take place by the end of June 2009, so no consolidated group will exist for that calendar tax year. But, by using the suggested strategy, the de-consolidation can be effective all the way back to January 2008. Do you agree?

Research Problem 3.   The Cardinal Group had filed on a consolidated basis for several years. Parent Cardinal, Ltd., had a wholly owned subsidiary, Swallow, Inc. The group used a calendar tax year.

Communications

On January 25, 2008, Heron acquired all of the stock of Cardinal, including its ownership in Swallow, an important supplier for Heron's manufacturing process. All parties in the new group intended to file on a consolidated basis immediately and, indeed, used consolidated amounts in filing the 2008 Heron Group return on September 10, 2009.

During the audit of Heron Group's 2008 tax return, the IRS disallowed the use of the consolidated method because no Form 1122s had ever been filed for the affiliates in the new group. In a memo to the tax research file, summarize the possibilities for the Heron Group to be granted an extension to elect consolidated return status.

Use the tax resources of the Internet to address the following questions. Do not restrict your search to the World Wide Web, but include a review of newsgroups and general reference materials, practitioner sites and resources, primary sources of the tax law, chat rooms and discussion groups, and other opportunities.

Internet
Activity

Research Problem 4.   Find a thread in a tax blog involving consolidated returns. Post a question to the site concerning acceptable tax allocation formulas. Write an e-mail to your professor summarizing the following.
a. The text of your posted question.
b. The responses that you received in the first week after posting.
c. The titles of other posters to the group and the type of questions that they are discussing.

Communications

Research Problem 5.   Find an article in a tax or business publication that addresses the way that a consolidated group must organize its information in completing a Schedule M–3 for the consolidated Form 1120. In an e-mail to your professor, diagram a three-tier consolidated group and explain, using material from your article, how many Schedules M–3 the group must file.

Communications

Research Problem 6.   Determine whether the income tax laws of your state, and those of two of its neighbors, allow Federal affiliated groups to use NOL carrybacks. What are the NOL carryback and carryforward periods? What other limitations apply?

Research Problem 7.   Find several journal articles and Web postings addressing the consolidation election. Construct a list titled "Consolidated Returns: Pros and Cons," and submit this document to your instructor. Provide citations for your research.

Communications

Research Problem 8.   Find more details about the evolution and development of the Federal consolidated tax return rules. When were consolidated returns elective? Required? What political forces were at work when the major 1966 and 1995 changes to the Regulations were adopted? When did the Treasury assess a fee or other surcharge for consolidating? Arrange your findings using a timeline and no more than three PowerPoint slides.

Communications

Research Problem 9.   Complete a review of your state's tax laws concerning consolidated returns. Use a format similar to the one described in Research Problem 8.

Communications

CHAPTER 9

Taxation of International Transactions

LEARNING OBJECTIVES

After completing Chapter 9, you should be able to:

LO.1
Understand the framework underlying the U.S. taxation of cross-border transactions.

LO.2
Understand the interaction between Internal Revenue Code provisions and tax treaties.

LO.3
Apply the rules for sourcing income and deductions into U.S. and foreign categories.

LO.4
Explain how foreign currency exchange affects the tax consequences of international transactions.

LO.5
Work with the U.S. tax provisions affecting U.S. persons earning foreign-source income, including the rules relating to cross-border asset transfers, antideferral provisions, and the foreign tax credit.

LO.6
Apply the U.S. tax provisions concerning nonresident alien individuals and foreign corporations.

LO.1

Understand the framework
underlying the U.S. taxation of
cross-border transactions.

Overview of International Taxation

In today's global business environment, most large businesses are truly international in scope. Consider the most recent financial results of three "all-American" companies: Coca-Cola, Ford Motor Company, and Microsoft. Coca-Cola reported that 68 percent of its total net income is from offshore operations, Ford earned $335 million in profits from non-U.S. operations (although it lost money overall), and Microsoft earned $7.2 billion in profits (36 percent of its book net income) from operations outside the United States. Honda, a Japanese company, reported that 64 percent of its sales were in North America; Toyota, another Japanese company, earned 26 percent of its operating income from North America.

Global trade is an integral part of the U.S. economy. In 2006, U.S. exports and imports of goods and services totaled $1.5 trillion and $2.2 trillion, respectively. This international trade creates significant U.S. tax consequences for both U.S. and foreign entities. In the most recent year for which data are available, U.S. corporations reported $166 billion in foreign-source income, paid $41 billion in taxes to foreign governments, and claimed foreign tax credits in excess of $38 billion. Foreign recipients reported $140 billion in U.S.-source income subject to withholding and paid $2.3 billion in U.S. taxes. U.S. corporations controlled by foreign owners reported $102 billion in U.S. taxable income.

Cross-border transactions create the need for special tax considerations for both the United States and its trading partners. From a U.S. perspective, international tax laws should promote the global competitiveness of U.S. enterprises and at the same time protect the tax revenue base of the United States. These two objectives sometimes conflict, however. The need to deal with both contributes to the complexity of the rules governing the U.S. taxation of cross-border transactions.

EXAMPLE 1

U.S. persons engage in activities outside the United States for many different reasons. Consider two U.S. corporations that have established sales subsidiaries in foreign countries. Dedalus, Inc., operates in Germany, a high-tax country, because customers demand local attention from sales agents. Mulligan, Inc., operates in the Cayman Islands, a low-tax country, simply to shift income outside the United States. U.S. tax law must fairly address both situations with the same law. ■

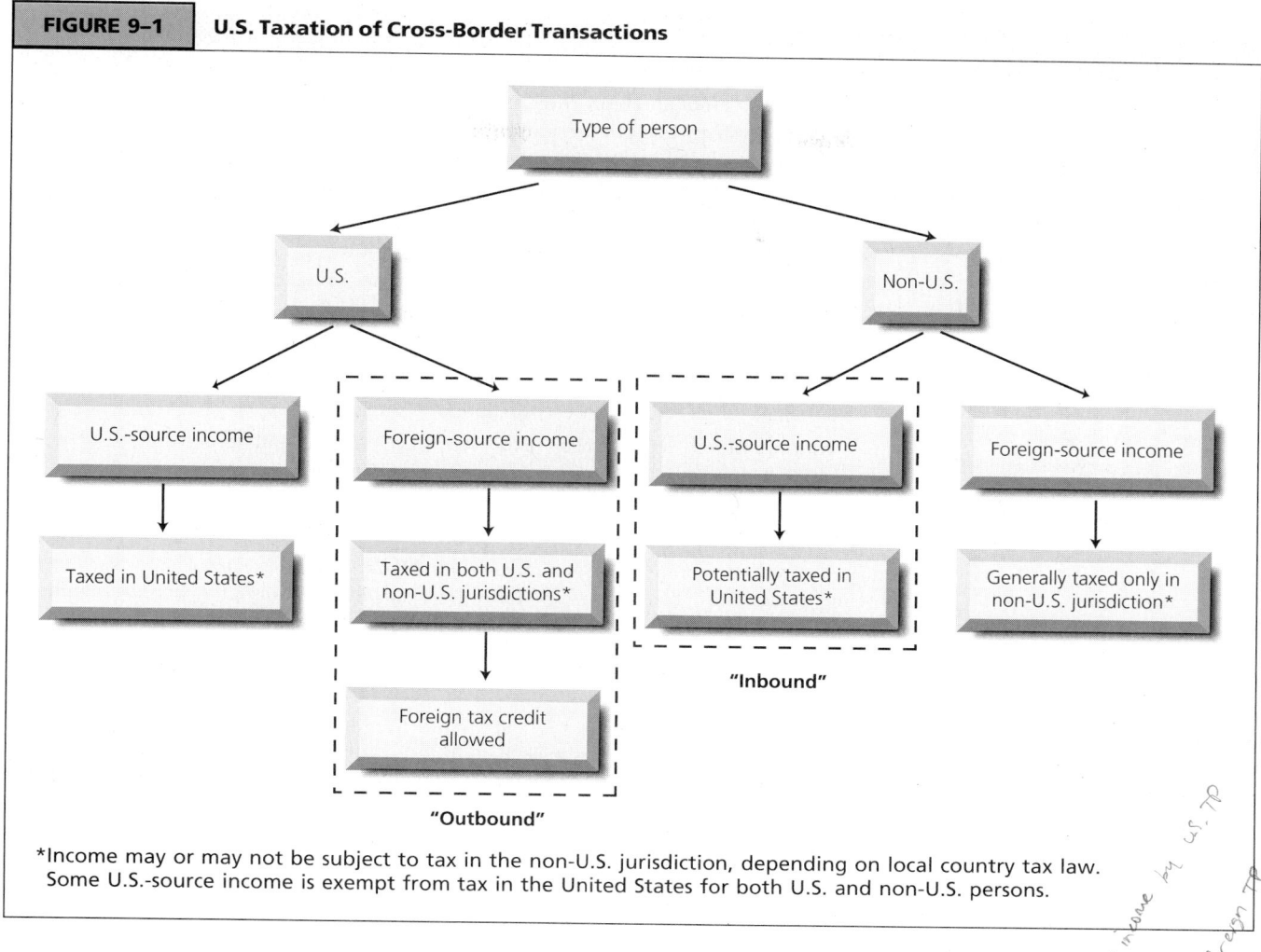

FIGURE 9–1 **U.S. Taxation of Cross-Border Transactions**

*Income may or may not be subject to tax in the non-U.S. jurisdiction, depending on local country tax law. Some U.S.-source income is exempt from tax in the United States for both U.S. and non-U.S. persons.

U.S. international tax provisions are concerned primarily with two types of potential taxpayers: U.S. persons earning foreign-source income and foreign persons earning U.S.-source income.[1] U.S. persons earning U.S.-source income are taxed under the purely domestic provisions of the Internal Revenue Code. Foreign persons earning foreign-source income are not within the taxing jurisdiction of the United States (unless this income is somehow connected to a U.S. trade or business). Figure 9–1 illustrates this categorization.

The United States taxes the worldwide income of U.S. taxpayers. Because foreign governments may also tax some of this income, these taxpayers may be subjected to double taxation. Special provisions such as the foreign tax credit can mitigate this problem. For foreign taxpayers, the United States generally taxes only income earned within its borders. The U.S. taxation of cross-border transactions can be organized in terms of "outbound" and "inbound" taxation. **Outbound taxation** refers to the U.S. taxation of foreign-source income earned by U.S. taxpayers. **Inbound taxation** refers to the U.S. taxation of U.S.-source income earned by foreign taxpayers.

EXAMPLE 2

Gator Enterprises, Inc., a U.S. corporation, operates a manufacturing branch in Italy because of customer demand in Italy, local availability of raw materials, and the high cost of shipping

---

[1]The term "person" includes an individual, corporation, partnership, trust, estate, or association. § 7701(a)(1). The terms "domestic" and "foreign" are defined in §§ 7701(a)(4) and (5).

GLOBAL *Tax Issues*

OTHER COUNTRIES' TAXES ARE STRANGE, TOO

People often complain about the strange provisions or workings of the U.S. Federal income tax system, but other countries can be criticized in the same way. Much of Europe, for example, is less dependent on income taxes than the United States and more dependent on transaction and wealth taxes, and these can take unusual forms. A quick survey of taxes around the globe finds the following.

Australia	68% tax on cigarette purchases
China	80–100% tax on purchase of autos built outside China
Costa Rica	170% tax on purchase of poultry raised outside the country, 96% tax on purchase of foreign dairy products
Japan	1,000% tax on purchase of rice grown outside the country
Sweden	400% tax on purchase of hard liquor
Turkmenistan	100% tax on luxury items, which include mineral water, cotton mittens, saws, blankets, pillows, mattresses

finished goods. This branch income is taxed in the United States as part of Gator's worldwide income, but it is also taxed in Italy. Without the availability of a foreign tax credit to mitigate this double taxation, Gator Enterprises would suffer an excessive tax burden and could not compete with local Italian companies. ■

EXAMPLE 3

Purdie, Ltd., a corporation based in the United Kingdom, operates in the United States. Although not a U.S. person, Purdie is taxed in the United States on its U.S.-source business income. If Purdie, Ltd., could operate free of U.S. tax, its U.S.-based competitors would face a serious disadvantage. ■

LO.2

Understand the interaction between Internal Revenue Code provisions and tax treaties.

Tax Treaties

The U.S. tax rules governing cross-border transactions are based on both the Internal Revenue Code and **tax treaties**. Tax treaties are bilateral agreements between countries that provide tax relief for those persons covered by the treaties. Tax treaty provisions generally override the treatment otherwise called for under the Internal Revenue Code or foreign tax statutes.

More than 50 income tax treaties between the United States and other countries are in effect (see Exhibit 9–1). These treaties generally provide *taxing rights* with regard to the taxable income of residents of one treaty country who have income sourced in the other treaty country. For the most part, neither country is prohibited from taxing the income of its residents. The treaties generally give one country primary taxing rights and require the other country to allow a credit for the taxes paid on the twice-taxed income.

EXAMPLE 4

ForCo, Ltd., a resident of a foreign country with which the United States has an income tax treaty, earns income attributable to a permanent establishment (e.g., place of business) in the United States. Under the treaty, the United States has primary taxing rights with regard to this income. The other country can also require that the income be included in gross income and can subject the income to its income tax, but it must allow a credit for the taxes paid to the United States on the income. ■

Which country receives primary taxing rights usually depends on the residence of the taxpayer or the presence of a permanent establishment in a treaty country to which the income is attributable. Generally, a permanent establishment is a branch, office, factory, workshop, warehouse, or other fixed place of business.

EXHIBIT 9–1	U.S. Income Tax Treaties in Force as of May 2007

Australia	Iceland	Pakistan
Austria	India	Philippines
Barbados	Indonesia	Poland
Belgium	Ireland	Portugal
Canada	Israel	Romania
China	Italy	Russia
Commonwealth of Independent States*	Jamaica	Slovak Republic
	Japan	Slovenia
Cyprus	Kazakhstan	South Africa
Czech Republic	Korea, Republic of	Spain
Denmark	Latvia	Sweden
Egypt	Lithuania	Switzerland
Estonia	Luxembourg	Thailand
Finland	Mexico	Trinidad and Tobago
France	Morocco	Tunisia
Germany	Netherlands	Turkey
Greece	New Zealand	United Kingdom
Hungary	Norway	Venezuela

*The income tax treaty between the United States and the former Soviet Union now applies to the countries of Armenia, Azerbaijan, Belarus, Georgia, Kyrgyzstan, Moldova, Tajikistan, Turkmenistan, Ukraine, and Uzbekistan. The Commonwealth of Independent States is an association of many of the former constituent republics of the Soviet Union.

Most U.S. income tax treaties reduce the withholding tax rate on certain items of investment income, such as interest and dividends. For example, treaties with France and Sweden reduce the withholding on portfolio dividends to 15 percent and on certain interest income to zero. Many new treaties (e.g., with the United Kingdom, Australia, and Japan) provide for no withholding on dividend payments to parent corporations. The United States has developed a Model Income Tax Convention as the starting point for negotiating income tax treaties with other countries.[2]

Sourcing of Income and Deductions

LO.3

Apply the rules for sourcing income and deductions into U.S. and foreign categories.

The sourcing of income and deductions inside or outside the United States has a direct bearing on a number of tax provisions affecting both U.S. and foreign taxpayers. For example, foreign taxpayers generally are taxed only on income sourced inside the United States, and U.S. taxpayers receive relief from double taxation under the foreign tax credit rules based on their foreign-source income. Accordingly, an examination of sourcing rules is often the starting point in addressing international tax issues.

Income Sourced inside the United States

The determination of the source of income depends on the type of income realized (e.g., income from the sale of property versus income for the use of property). This makes the classification of income an important consideration. Section 861

---

[2]Treasury Department Model Income Tax Convention (November 15, 2006).

WHY THE TREATY PROCESS STALLS

The United States has negotiated several income tax treaties that have never been signed or ratified (e.g., with Argentina, Bangladesh, and Brazil). The treaty process sometimes stalls for several reasons.

One is the desire on the part of some less developed countries for a tax-sparing provision in the treaty. In other words, these countries want the United States to allow a foreign tax credit against U.S. taxes even though U.S. companies operating there actually pay no foreign taxes due to local tax reduction agreements (i.e., tax holidays).

Another reason is the exchange of information provision. Some countries, for example, have anonymous bank rules that would preclude the exchange of information. Not long ago, the Parliament of Kazakhstan voted on a provision to eliminate secret bank accounts so that the United States–Kazakhstan income tax treaty could be ratified.

contains source rules for most types of income. Other rules pertaining to the source of income are found in §§ 862–865.

Interest. Interest income received from the U.S. government, from the District of Columbia, and from noncorporate U.S. residents or domestic corporations is sourced inside the United States. There are a few exceptions to this rule. Certain interest received from a U.S. corporation that earned <u>80</u> percent or more of its active business income from foreign sources over the prior three-year period is treated as foreign-source income. Interest received on amounts deposited with a foreign branch of a U.S. corporation is also treated as foreign-source income if the branch is engaged in the commercial banking business.

EXAMPLE 5

John holds a bond issued by Delta, a domestic corporation. For the immediately preceding three tax years, 82% of Delta's gross income has been active foreign business income. The interest income that John receives for the current tax year from Delta is foreign-source income. ∎

Dividends. Dividends received from domestic corporations (other than certain U.S. possessions corporations) are sourced inside the United States. Generally, dividends paid by a foreign corporation are foreign-source income. However, if a foreign corporation earned <u>25</u> percent or more of its gross income from income effectively connected with a U.S. trade or business for the three tax years immediately preceding the year of the dividend payment, that percentage of the dividend is treated as U.S.-source income.[3]

EXAMPLE 6

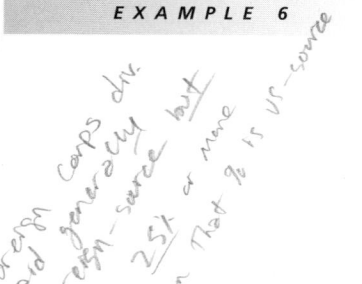

Ann receives dividend income from the following corporations for the current tax year.

Amount	Corporation	Effectively Connected U.S. Income for Past 3 Years	U.S.-Source Income
$500	Green, domestic	85%	$500
600	Brown, domestic	13%	600
300	Orange, foreign	92%	276

[3]For tax years prior to 2004, the U.S.-source portion of a foreign corporation's dividend could be subject to U.S. withholding tax. This provision was repealed for post-2004 tax years. § 871(i)(2)(D).

Because Green Corporation and Brown Corporation are domestic corporations, the dividends they pay are U.S.-source income. Orange Corporation is a foreign corporation that earned 92% of its business income over the prior three years from income effectively connected with a U.S. trade or business. Because Orange meets the 25% threshold, 92% of its dividend is U.S. source. ■

Personal Services Income. The source of income from personal services is determined by the location in which the services are performed (inside or outside the United States). A limited *commercial traveler* exception is available. Under this exception, personal services income must meet all the following requirements to avoid being classified as U.S.-source income.

- The services must be performed by a nonresident alien who is in the United States for 90 days or less during the taxable year.
- The compensation may not exceed $3,000 in total for the services performed in the United States.
- The services must be performed on behalf of:
  - a nonresident alien, foreign partnership, or foreign corporation that is not engaged in a U.S. trade or business or
  - an office or place of business maintained in a foreign country or possession of the United States by an individual who is a citizen or resident of the United States, a domestic partnership, or a domestic corporation.

[handwritten margin note: commercial traveler exception: • 90 days or less • $3,000 or less • on behalf of NRA, foreign]

[handwritten note: → If over then all is U.S.-source income]

Mark, a nonresident alien, is an engineer employed by a foreign oil company. He spent four weeks in the United States arranging the purchase of field equipment for his company. His salary for the four weeks was $3,500. Even though the oil company is not engaged in a U.S. trade or business, and Mark was in the United States for less than 90 days during the taxable year, the income is U.S.-source income because it exceeds $3,000. ■

EXAMPLE 7

The issue of whether income is derived from the performance of personal services is important in determining the income's source. The courts have held that a corporation can perform personal services.[4] In addition, in the absence of capital as an income-producing factor, personal services income can arise even though there is no recipient of the services.[5] If payment is received for services performed partly inside and partly outside the United States, the income must be allocated for source purposes on some reasonable basis that clearly reflects income under the facts and circumstances. The number of days worked in each country is generally acceptable.[6]

[handwritten margin notes: • Corp. may perform personal services • PSI – may arise even w/ no recipient of services • If partially earned it must be allocated]

Rents and Royalties. The source of income received for the use of tangible property is the country in which the property is located. The source of income received for the use of intangible property (e.g., patents, copyrights, secret processes and formulas) is the country in which the property is used.

[handwritten margin notes: Tangible - location   Intangible - used]

Sale or Exchange of Property. Generally, the location of real property determines the source of any income derived from the property. Income from the disposition of U.S. real property interests is U.S.-source income.

The source of income from the sale of personal property (assets other than real property) depends on several factors, including the following.

---

[4]See *British Timken Limited*, 12 T.C. 880 (1949), and Rev.Rul. 60–55, 1960–1 C.B. 270.

[5]See *Robida v. Comm.*, 72–1 USTC ¶9450, 29 AFTR2d 72–1223, 460 F.2d 1172 (CA–9, 1972). The taxpayer was employed in military PXs around the world. He had large slot machine winnings and claimed the foreign earned income

exclusion. The IRS challenged the exclusion on the grounds that the winnings were not earned income because there was no recipient of Robida's services. The court, however, found that, in the absence of capital, the winnings were earned income.

[6]Reg. § 1.861–4(b). See *Stemkowski*, 76 T.C. 252 (1981).

- Whether the property was produced by the seller.
- The type of property sold (e.g., inventory or a capital asset).
- The residence of the seller.

Generally, income, gain, or profit from the sale of personal property is sourced according to the residence of the seller. Income from the sale of purchased inventory, however, is sourced in the country in which the sale takes place.[7]

When the seller has produced the inventory property, the income must be apportioned between the country of production and the country of sale. Gross income is sourced under a 50/50 allocation method unless the taxpayer elects to use the independent factory price (IFP) method or the separate books and records method. The 50/50 method assigns one-half of the inventory profits from export sales to the location of the production assets and one-half to the place of title passage. The IFP method may be elected only where an IFP exists.[8] If the manufacturer or producer regularly sells to wholly independent distributors, this can establish an *independent* factory or production price.

Under § 865, income from the sale of personal property other than inventory is sourced at the residence of the seller unless one of the following exceptions applies.

- Gain on the sale of depreciable personal property is sourced according to prior depreciation deductions to the extent of the deductions. Any excess gain is sourced the same as the sale of inventory.
- Gain on the sale of intangibles is sourced according to prior amortization deductions to the extent of the deductions. Contingent payments, however, are sourced as royalty income.
- Gain attributable to an office or fixed place of business maintained outside the United States by a U.S. resident is foreign-source income.
- Income or gain attributable to an office or fixed place of business maintained in the United States by a nonresident is U.S.-source income.

The sourcing of losses is complicated and depends on the nature of the property. Different rules exist for the disposition of stock versus other personal property.[9]

Transportation and Communication Income. Income from transportation beginning *and* ending in the United States is U.S.-source income. Fifty percent of the income from transportation beginning *or* ending in the United States is U.S.-source income, unless the U.S. point is only an intermediate stop. This rule does not apply to personal services income unless the transportation is between the United States and a possession. Income from space and ocean activities conducted outside the jurisdiction of any country is sourced according to the residence of the person conducting the activity.

International communication income derived by a U.S. person is sourced 50 percent in the United States when transmission is between the United States and a foreign country. International communication income derived by foreign persons is foreign-source income unless it is attributable to an office or other fixed place of business in the United States. In that case, it is U.S.-source income.

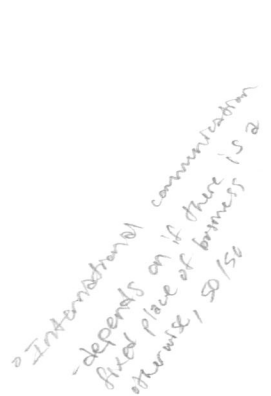

Software Income. Income from the sale or license of software is sourced depending on how the income is classified. Under Regulation § 1.861–18, a transfer of software is classified as either the transfer of a copyright (e.g., the right to the computer program itself) or the transfer of a copyrighted article (the right to use a copy of the computer program). If the transfer is considered a transfer of a

---

[7]§§ 861(a)(6) and 865. The sale is deemed to take place where title passes. See Reg. § 1.861–7(c) regarding title passage. There has been considerable conflict in this area of tax law. See, for example, *Liggett Group, Inc.*, 58 TCM 1167, T.C.Memo. 1990–18.

[8]§ 863(b)(2), Reg. § 1.863–3, and Notice 89–10, 1989–1 C.B. 631.

[9]See Reg. § 1.861–8(e)(7) and Temp.Reg. § 1.865–1T(a)(1). See Reg. §§ 1.865–(2)(a)(1) and (2) regarding the source of losses on the disposition of stock.

TAX *in the News*   **SOURCING INCOME IN CYBERSPACE**

The use of the Internet for more and more consumer and business transactions is posing problems for the taxing authorities. Consumers purchase books, music, clothing, and food from Internet retailers. Businesses negotiate with suppliers via online auctions of products and services. Consultants provide services to their clients over the Web. Very few transactions do not have a counterpart that takes place in cyberspace. The existing income-sourcing rules were developed long before the existence of the Internet, and taxing authorities are finding it challenging to apply these rules to Internet transactions. Where does a sale take place when the Web server is in the Cayman Islands, the seller is in Singapore, and the customer is in Texas? Where is a service performed when all activities take place over the Net? These questions and more will have to be answered by the United States and its trading partners as the Internet economy grows in size and importance.

---

copyright, the income is sourced using the royalty income rules. If the transfer is considered a transfer of a copyrighted article, the income is treated as resulting from a sale of the article and is sourced based on the personal property sales rules.

Income Sourced outside the United States

The provisions for sourcing income outside the United States are not as detailed and specific as those for determining U.S.-source income. Basically, § 862 provides that if interest, dividends, compensation for personal services, income from the use or sale of property, or other income is not U.S.-source income, then it is foreign-source income.

Allocation and Apportionment of Deductions

The United States levies a tax on *taxable income.* Deductions and losses, therefore, must be allocated and apportioned between U.S.- and foreign-source gross income to determine U.S.- and foreign-source taxable income. Deductions directly related to an activity or property are allocated to classes of income. This is followed by apportionment between the statutory and residual groupings (e.g., foreign versus domestic) on some reasonable basis.[10] A deduction not definitely related to any class of gross income is ratably allocated to all classes of gross income and apportioned between U.S.- and foreign-source income.

Ace, Inc., a domestic corporation, has $2 million gross income and a $50,000 expense, all related to real estate activities. The expense is allocated and apportioned using gross income as a basis as follows.

EXAMPLE 8

| | Gross Income | | | Apportionment | |
	Foreign	U.S.	Allocation	Foreign	U.S.
Sales	$1,000,000	$500,000	$37,500*	$25,000	$12,500**
Rentals	400,000	100,000	12,500	10,000	2,500***
			$50,000	$35,000	$15,000

  *$50,000 × ($1,500,000/$2,000,000).

  **$37,500 × ($500,000/$1,500,000).

  ***$12,500 × ($100,000/$500,000).

---

[10]Reg. § 1.861–8.

If Ace could show that $45,000 of the expense was directly related to sales income, the $45,000 would be allocated to that class of gross income, with the remainder allocated and apportioned ratably based on gross income. ∎

Interest expense is allocated and apportioned based on the theory that money is fungible. With limited exceptions, interest expense is attributable to all the activities and property of the taxpayer, regardless of the specific purpose for incurring the debt on which interest is paid.[11] Taxpayers must allocate and apportion interest expense on the basis of assets, using either the fair market value or the tax book value of the assets.[12] Once the fair market value is used, the taxpayer must continue to use this method. Special rules apply in allocating and apportioning interest expense in an affiliated group of corporations.

EXAMPLE 9

Fisher, Inc., a domestic corporation, generates U.S.-source and foreign-source gross income for the current year. Fisher's assets (tax book value) are as follows.

Assets generating U.S.-source income	$18,000,000
Assets generating foreign-source income	5,000,000
	$23,000,000

Fisher incurs interest expense of $800,000 for the current year. Using the tax book value method, interest expense is apportioned to foreign-source income as follows.

$$\frac{\$5,000,000 \text{ (foreign assets)}}{\$23,000,000 \text{ (total assets)}} \times \$800,000 = \underline{\underline{\$173,913}}$$

∎

Specific rules also apply to research and development (R&D) expenditures, certain stewardship expenses, legal and accounting fees and expenses, income taxes, and losses. Although U.S. companies incur about 90 percent of their R&D expenditures at U.S. facilities, several billion dollars are spent on foreign R&D each year. The Regulations provide that a portion of a U.S. company's R&D expenditures must be treated as foreign-source expense if the R&D relates to foreign product sales.

Transfer Pricing

Taxpayers may be tempted to minimize taxation by manipulating the source of income and the allocation of deductions arbitrarily through **transfer pricing**. This manipulation is more easily accomplished between or among related persons. The IRS uses § 482 to counter such actions. The provision gives the IRS the power to reallocate gross income, deductions, credits, or allowances between or among organizations, trades, or businesses owned or controlled directly or indirectly by the same interests. This can be done whenever the IRS determines that reallocation is necessary to prevent the evasion of taxes or to reflect income more clearly. Section 482 is a "one-edged sword" available only to the IRS. The taxpayer generally cannot invoke it to reallocate income and expenses.[13]

EXAMPLE 10

Consider the transaction depicted in Figure 9–2. A U.S. corporation manufactures and sells inventory to an unrelated foreign customer. The sales price for the inventory is $1,000 and the related cost of goods sold (COGS) is $600. The resulting profit of $400 is all taxed to the U.S. corporation, resulting in a $140 U.S. income tax liability ($400 × 35%). If the U.S. corporation has no business presence in the foreign jurisdiction and is merely selling to a customer located there, the foreign government is unlikely to impose any local income tax on

---

[11]Reg. § 1.861–10T(b) describes circumstances in which interest expense can be directly allocated to specific debt. This exception to the fungibility concept is limited to cases in which specific property is purchased or improved with nonrecourse debt.

[12]Reg. § 1.861–9T.

[13]Reg. § 1.482–1(a)(3).

| FIGURE 9–2 | Transfer Pricing Example |

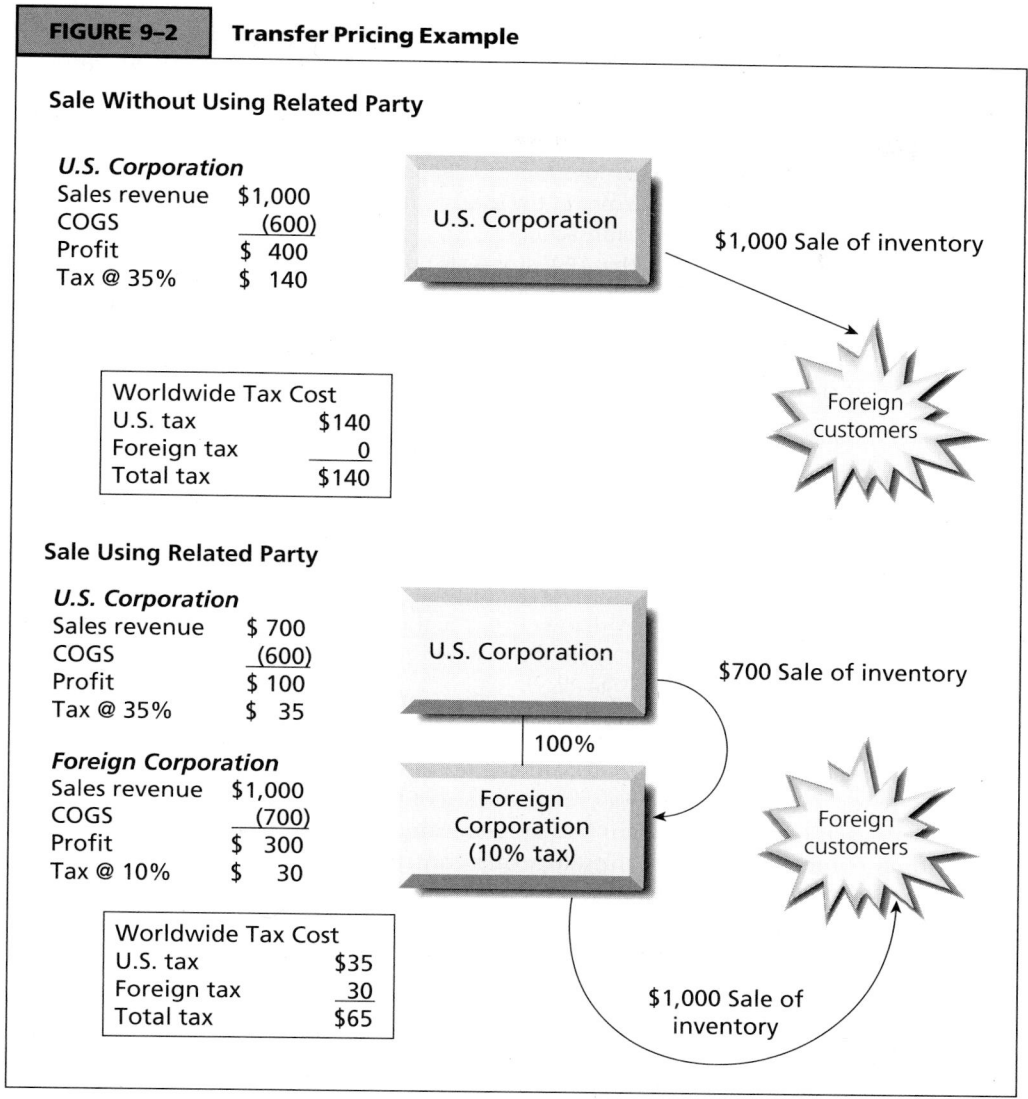

Sale Without Using Related Party

U.S. Corporation

Sales revenue	$1,000
COGS	(600)
Profit	$ 400
Tax @ 35%	$ 140

U.S. Corporation

$1,000 Sale of inventory

Foreign customers

Worldwide Tax Cost	
U.S. tax	$140
Foreign tax	0
Total tax	$140

Sale Using Related Party

U.S. Corporation

Sales revenue	$ 700
COGS	(600)
Profit	$ 100
Tax @ 35%	$ 35

Foreign Corporation

Sales revenue	$1,000
COGS	(700)
Profit	$ 300
Tax @ 10%	$ 30

U.S. Corporation

100%

Foreign Corporation (10% tax)

$700 Sale of inventory

Foreign customers

$1,000 Sale of inventory

Worldwide Tax Cost	
U.S. tax	$35
Foreign tax	30
Total tax	$65

the U.S. corporation. Consequently, the total tax burden imposed on the inventory sale is $140.

Suppose instead that the U.S. corporation attempts to reduce its total tax expense by channeling the inventory sale through a foreign subsidiary in the same country as the foreign customer. In this case, because the U.S. corporation controls the foreign subsidiary, it chooses an intercompany sales price (the transfer price) that moves a portion of the profits from the United States to the foreign country. By selling the inventory it manufactured to its 100%-owned foreign subsidiary for $700, the U.S. corporation reports only $100 of profits and an associated U.S. tax liability of $35. The foreign subsidiary then sells the inventory to the ultimate customer for $1,000 and, with a $700 COGS, earns a $300 profit. In this example, the foreign country imposes only a 10% tax on corporate profits, resulting in a foreign income tax of $30 ($300 × 10%). By using a related foreign entity in a lower-tax jurisdiction, the U.S. corporation has lowered its overall tax liability on the sale from $140 (all U.S.) to $65 ($35 U.S. and $30 foreign).

The critical question is whether the IRS will view the $700 intercompany sales price as the appropriate transfer price. Under § 482, the IRS may question why the foreign corporation deserved to earn $300 of the total $400 profit related to the manufacture and sale of the inventory. In general, the U.S. corporation must document the functions performed by the foreign corporation, the assets it owns that assist in producing the income, or the risks it takes (e.g., credit risk). Without documentation of significant functions, assets, or risks of the foreign subsidiary, the IRS will not consider the $300 profit earned by the foreign

TAX *in the News*

APAs REDUCE UNCERTAINTY IN TRANSFER PRICING DISPUTES

The first Advance Pricing Agreement (APA) was approved in January 1991. The IRS reports that 692 APAs have been executed and 249 others are in negotiation. The taxpayers participating in the APA program come from many different industries. The five most represented industries are financial institutions, computer items and software, chemicals, transportation equipment, and electrical equipment.

Only 10 percent of the largest taxpayers involved in international intercompany transactions have participated in the APA process. However, the volume of intercompany transactions represented by these taxpayers constitutes over 40 percent of the total dollar value of international intercompany transactions.

The APA process is not simple or quick. The IRS reports that the APAs approved in 2006 took an average of 31 months to complete.

Source: *Announcement and Report Concerning Advance Pricing Agreements, February 26, 2007 (Announcement 2007–31).*

corporation to be appropriate, and it will adjust the transfer price upward. If the IRS determines that the transfer price should have been, say, $990, then the U.S. corporation reports a $390 profit (with $136.50 U.S. income tax), and the foreign corporation earns a $10 profit (with $1 in foreign income tax). With this change in transfer price, the U.S. corporation does not succeed in transferring a meaningful portion of its profits to the lower-tax jurisdiction and reduces its tax liability by only $2.50. ∎

The reach of § 482 is quite broad. The IRS takes the position that a corporation and its sole shareholder who works full-time for the corporation can be treated as two separate trades or businesses for purposes of § 482.[14] Two unrelated shareholders who each owned 50 percent of a corporation were held to be acting in concert for their common good and, thus, together controlled the corporation.[15]

In applying § 482, an arm's length price must be determined to assign the correct profits to related entities. Several alternative methods can be used in determining an arm's length price on the sale of tangible or intangible property. The major problem with most pricing methods is that uncontrolled comparable transactions are needed as a benchmark.

An accuracy-related penalty of 20 percent is provided by § 6662 for net § 482 transfer price adjustments (changes in profit allocations by the IRS) for a taxable year that exceed the lesser of $5 million or 10 percent of the taxpayer's gross receipts. In addition, there is a 40 percent penalty for "gross misstatements."

As an aid to reducing pricing disputes, the IRS initiated the Advance Pricing Agreement (APA) program whereby the taxpayer can propose a transfer pricing method for certain international transactions. The taxpayer provides relevant data, which are then evaluated by the IRS. If accepted, the APA provides a safe-harbor transfer pricing method for the taxpayer. Apple Computer, Inc., accomplished the first successful APA submission.

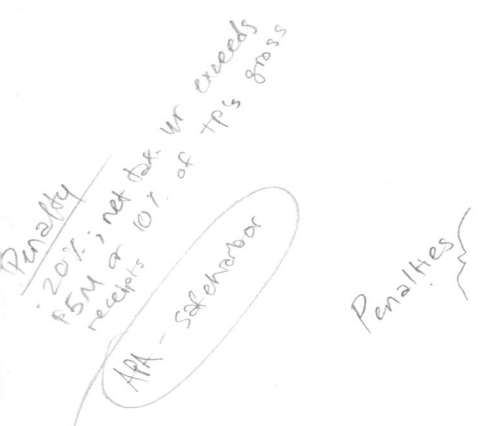

LO.4

Explain how foreign currency exchange affects the tax consequences of international transactions.

Foreign Currency Transactions

The relative value of a foreign currency and the U.S. dollar is described by the foreign exchange rate. Changes in this rate affect the dollar value of foreign property held by the taxpayer, the dollar value of foreign debts, and the dollar amount of gain or loss on a transaction denominated in a foreign currency. Almost every international tax issue requires consideration of currency exchange implications.

[14]Rev.Rul. 88–38, 1988–1 C.B. 246. But see *Foglesong v. Comm.*, 82–2 USTC ¶9650, 50 AFTR2d 82–6016, 691 F.2d 848 (CA–7, 1982), *rev'g* 77 T.C. 1102 (1981).

[15]See *B. Forman Co., Inc. v. Comm.*, 72–1 USTC ¶9182, 29, AFTR2d 72–403, 453 F.2d 1144 (CA–2, 1972).

Dress, Inc., a domestic corporation, purchases merchandise for resale from Fiesta, Inc., a foreign corporation, for 50,000K (a foreign currency). On the date of purchase, 1K is equal to $1 U.S. (1K:$1). At this time, the account payable is $50,000. On the date of payment by Dress (the foreign exchange date), the exchange rate is 1.25K:$1. In other words, the foreign currency has been devalued in relation to the U.S. dollar, and Dress will pay Fiesta 50,000K, which will cost Dress only $40,000. Dress must record the purchase of the merchandise at $50,000 and recognize a foreign currency gain of $10,000 ($50,000 − $40,000). ∎

changes in Foreign exchange rate may cause a foreign currency gain or loss

In recent years, U.S. currency abroad has amounted to more than 50 percent of the U.S. currency in circulation. Taxpayers may find it necessary to translate amounts denominated in foreign currency into U.S. dollars for any of the following purposes.

- Purchase of goods, services, and property.
- Sale of goods, services, and property.
- Collection of foreign receivables.
- Payment of foreign payables.
- Foreign tax credit calculations.
- Recognition of income or loss from foreign branch activities.

The foreign currency exchange rates, however, have no effect on the transactions of a U.S. person who arranges all international transactions in U.S. dollars.

Sellers, Inc., a domestic corporation, purchases goods from Rose, Ltd., a foreign corporation, and pays for these goods in U.S. dollars. Rose then exchanges the U.S. dollars for the currency of the country in which it operates. Sellers has no foreign exchange considerations with which to contend. If instead Rose required Sellers to pay for the goods in a foreign currency, Sellers would have to exchange U.S. dollars to obtain the foreign currency to make payment. If the exchange rate changed from the date of purchase to the date of payment, Sellers would have a foreign currency gain or loss on the currency exchange. ∎

The following concepts are important when dealing with the tax aspects of foreign exchange.

- Foreign currency is treated as property other than money.
- Gain or loss on the exchange of foreign currency is considered separately from the underlying transaction (e.g., the purchase or sale of goods).
- No gain or loss is recognized until a transaction is closed.

Tax Issues

The following major tax issues must be considered when dealing with foreign currency exchange.

- The date of recognition of any gain or loss (see Concept Summary 9–1).
- The source (U.S. or foreign) of the foreign currency gain or loss.
- The character of the gain or loss (ordinary or capital).

Functional Currency

The Code generally adopted FAS 52, the Financial Accounting Standards Board standard on foreign currency translation. FAS 52 introduced the **functional currency** approach. Under this approach, the currency of the economic environment in which the foreign entity operates generally is to be used as the monetary unit to measure gains and losses.

Under § 985, all income tax determinations are to be made in the taxpayer's functional currency. A taxpayer's default functional currency is the U.S. dollar. In most cases, a **qualified business unit (QBU)** operating in a foreign country uses that country's currency as its functional currency. A QBU is a separate and clearly identified

CONCEPT SUMMARY 9–1

Recognition of Foreign Exchange Gain or Loss

Transaction	Date of Recognition
Purchase or sale of inventory or business asset	Date of disposition of foreign currency
Branch profits	Remittance of branch profits
Subpart F income	Receipt of previously taxed income (accumulated E & P)
Dividend from untaxed current or accumulated E & P	No exchange gain or loss to recipient

[handwritten margin note: An individual is not a QBU, but a T or B conducted by an individual may be a QBU]

unit of a taxpayer's trade or business (e.g., a foreign branch). An individual is not a QBU; however, a trade or business conducted by an individual may be a QBU.[16]

Branch Operations

[handwritten margin note: Exchange gain/loss is ordinary]

When a foreign branch (QBU) uses a foreign currency as its functional currency, profit or loss is computed in the foreign currency each year and translated into U.S. dollars for tax purposes. The entire amount of profit or loss, not taking remittances into account, is translated using the average exchange rate for the taxable year. Exchange gain or loss is recognized on remittances from the QBU. The U.S. dollar amount of the remittance at the exchange rate in effect on the date of remittance is compared with the U.S. dollar value (basis pool) of the equity pool of the branch. The rules outline a "foreign exchange exposure pool method" to compute any exchange gain or loss.[17] This exchange gain or loss is ordinary, and it is sourced according to the income to which the remittance is attributable.

Distributions from Foreign Corporations

An actual distribution of E & P from a foreign corporation is included in income by the U.S. recipient at the exchange rate in effect on the date of distribution. Thus, no exchange gain or loss is recognized. Deemed dividend distributions under Subpart F (discussed later in the chapter) are translated at the average exchange rate for the corporation's tax year to which the deemed distribution is attributable. Exchange gain or loss can result when an actual distribution of this previously taxed income is made.

Foreign Taxes

For purposes of the foreign tax credit, foreign taxes accrued generally are translated at the average exchange rate for the tax year to which the taxes relate. Under exceptions to this rule, foreign taxes must be translated at the exchange rate in effect when the foreign taxes were paid.[18] If foreign taxes are paid within two years of accrual, and if they differ from the accrued amount merely because of currency exchange fluctuation, no redetermination is required, even though the actual dollar value paid may differ from the accrued amount. In other cases, when the taxes paid differ from the amount accrued, a redetermination is required.

EXAMPLE 13

Music, Inc., a domestic corporation, has a foreign branch. Foreign taxes attributable to branch income amount to 5,000K (a foreign currency). The taxes are paid within two years

---

[16]Reg. § 1.989(a)–1(b).
[17]Prop.Reg. §§ 1.987–1 and –2.

[18]§§ 986(a)(1)(B) and (C).

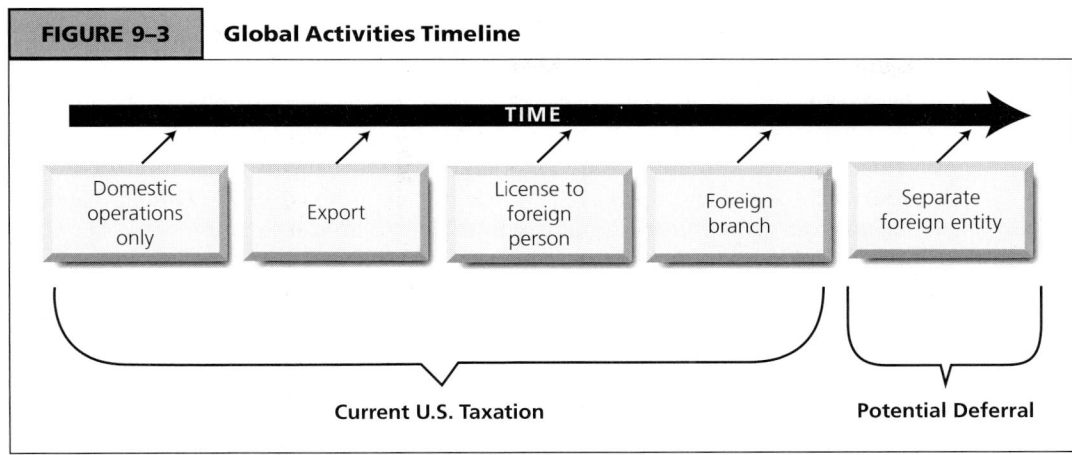

FIGURE 9–3   Global Activities Timeline

of being accrued. The average foreign exchange rate for the tax year to which the foreign taxes relate is .5K:$1. On the date the taxes are paid, the rate is .6K:$1. No redetermination is required, and Music has foreign taxes of $10,000 for purposes of the foreign tax credit. ■

Section 988 Transactions

The disposition of a nonfunctional currency can result in a foreign currency gain or loss under § 988. Section 988 transactions include those in which gain or loss is determined with regard to the value of a nonfunctional currency, such as the following.

- Acquiring (or becoming obligor under) a debt instrument.
- Accruing (or otherwise taking into account) any item of expense or gross income or receipts that is to be paid or received at a later date.
- Entering into or acquiring nearly any forward contract, futures contract, option, or similar investment position.
- Disposing of nonfunctional currency.

Section 988 generally treats exchange gain or loss falling within its provisions as ordinary income or loss. Capital gain or loss treatment may be elected with regard to forward contracts, futures contracts, and options that constitute capital assets in the hands of the taxpayer.

A closed or completed transaction is required. The residence of the taxpayer generally determines the source of a § 988 foreign exchange gain or loss.

U.S. Persons with Foreign Income

U.S. taxpayers often "internationalize" gradually over time. A U.S. business may operate on a strictly domestic basis for several years, then explore foreign markets by exporting its products abroad, and later license its products to a foreign manufacturer or enter into a joint venture with a foreign partner. If its forays into foreign markets are successful, the U.S. business may create a foreign subsidiary and move a portion of its operations abroad by establishing a sales or manufacturing facility. A domestically controlled foreign corporation can have significant U.S. tax consequences for the U.S. owners, and any U.S. taxpayer paying foreign taxes must consider the foreign tax credit provisions. Foreign businesses likewise enter the U.S. market in stages. In either case, each step generates increasingly significant international tax consequences. Figure 9–3 shows a typical timeline for "going global."

LO.5

Work with the U.S. tax provisions affecting U.S. persons earning foreign-source income, including the rules relating to cross-border asset transfers, antideferral provisions, and the foreign tax credit.

Export Property

The easiest way for a U.S. enterprise to engage in global commerce is simply to sell U.S.-produced goods and services abroad. These sales can be conducted with little or no foreign presence and allow the business to explore foreign markets without making costly financial commitments to foreign operations. The U.S. tax consequences of simple export sales are straightforward. All such income is taxed in the United States to the U.S. taxpayer. Whether foreign taxes must be paid on this export income depends on the particular law of the foreign jurisdiction and whether the U.S. taxpayer is deemed to have a foreign business presence there (often called a "permanent establishment"). In many cases, such export income is not taxed by any foreign jurisdiction.

Prior law contained a special tax incentive for U.S. taxpayers exporting goods. This extraterritorial income (ETI) exclusion was repealed by the American Jobs Creation Act of 2004.[19] The Act did not replace the ETI benefit with a new tax benefit for U.S. exporters. Instead, it created a new broad-based "domestic production activities deduction" (DPAD) for U.S. manufacturers and certain other domestic producers equal to 9 percent of the taxpayer's *qualified production activities income* subject to several limitations.[20] The deduction is phased in, with a 3 percent deduction for tax years beginning in 2005 or 2006, a 6 percent deduction for tax years beginning in 2007, 2008, or 2009, and a 9 percent deduction for tax years thereafter. Unlike the earlier ETI exclusion, the DPAD does not require exporting or any other activity outside the United States. The deduction is discussed in Chapter 3.

Cross-Border Asset Transfers

As part of "going international," a U.S. taxpayer may decide to transfer assets outside the United States so that any foreign business will be conducted outside the U.S. tax jurisdiction. To originate investment through, or transfer investment to, a foreign entity, the U.S. taxpayer must make some sort of transfer to the foreign entity. This may take the form of a cash investment or a transfer of assets of a U.S. entity.

In situations where potential taxable income is transferred to a corporation outside the U.S. taxing jurisdiction, the exchange may trigger a tax. The tax result of transferring property to a foreign corporation depends on the nature of the exchange, the assets involved, the income potential of the property, and the character of the property in the hands of the transferor or transferee. Figure 9–4 summarizes the taxation of cross-border asset transfers.

Outbound Transfers. As discussed in Chapters 6 and 7, when assets are exchanged for corporate stock in a domestic transaction, realized gain or loss may be deferred rather than recognized. Similarly, deferral treatment may be available when the following "outbound" capital changes occur, i.e., moving corporate business across country borders and outside the United States.

- A U.S. corporation starts up a new corporation outside the United States (§ 351).
- A U.S. corporation liquidates a U.S. subsidiary into an existing foreign subsidiary (§ 332).
- A U.S. corporation incorporates a non-U.S. branch of a U.S. corporation, forming a new foreign corporation (§ 351).
- A foreign corporation uses a stock swap to acquire a U.S. corporation (Type "B" reorganization).
- A foreign corporation acquires substantially all of a U.S. corporation's net assets (Type "C" reorganization).

---

[19]Section 101 of the American Jobs Creation Act of 2004, P.L. No. 108–357 (October 22, 2004).   [20]§ 199.

FIGURE 9–4	Taxation of Cross-Border Asset Transfers

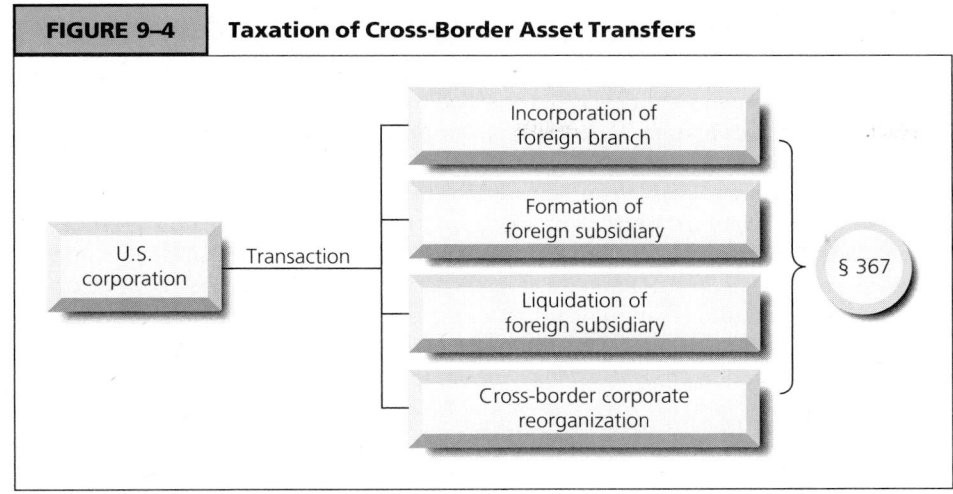

These otherwise tax-deferred transactions may trigger current taxation when foreign corporations are involved. Under § 367, the general rule is that gain deferral is not allowed when assets are leaving the U.S. taxing jurisdiction. However, a major exception allows continued tax deferral for assets transferred to a foreign corporation to be used in a trade or business carried on outside the United States.

The trade or business exception does not apply to certain "tainted" assets, and the transfer of these assets outside the United States triggers immediate gain (but not loss) recognition. The following are "tainted" assets under § 367.

- Inventory (raw goods, work-in-progress, and finished goods).
- Installment obligations and unrealized accounts receivable.
- Foreign currency.
- Property leased by the transferor unless the transferee is the lessee.

[handwritten: tainted assets that trigger immediate gain]

These tainted assets are likely to turn over quickly once the asset transfer is completed, and any appreciation is likely to be recognized outside the U.S. taxing jurisdiction. Consequently, § 367 requires recognition of this gain upon transfer of the asset outside the United States.

EXAMPLE 14

Amelia, Inc., a domestic corporation, incorporates its profitable Irish manufacturing branch and creates a new wholly owned foreign corporation, St. George, Ltd., to engage in manufacturing activities in Ireland. The transfer qualifies as tax deferred under § 351. The branch assets have always been used in Ireland. Amelia transfers the following branch assets to St. George upon its creation.

Asset	Tax Basis	Market Value	Built-in Gain/Loss
Raw materials inventory	$100	$ 400	$ 300
Accounts receivable	200	250	50
Manufacturing equipment	450	925	475
Furniture and fixtures	150	50	(100)
Total	$900	$1,625	$ 725

Although the $725 in realized gain is deferred under § 351, the gain is potentially taxable under § 367 because the assets are leaving the U.S. taxing jurisdiction. The general rule of § 367 is that all the realized gain is recognized by Amelia. However, because St. George will use the transferred assets in the active conduct of a foreign trade or business, the realized

GLOBAL
Tax Issues

BOOM IN CROSS-BORDER MERGERS

Recent years have seen an increase in the number of tax-deferred mergers taking place across national borders. Helen of Troy, the publicly traded cosmetics giant, converted itself from a U.S. corporation into a tax haven corporation without triggering any tax for its shareholders. Once outside the U.S. taxing jurisdiction, the company was free from many of the restrictions imposed by U.S. tax law. U.S. taxing authorities responded to this transaction by issuing new Regulations [Reg. § 1.367(a)–3(c)] to shut down these so-called inversions unless very strict standards were met.

The American Jobs Creation Act of 2004 created even stricter rules in an effort to deter shareholders or partners from turning domestic entities into foreign entities. A domestic corporation or partnership continues to be treated as domestic if:

- A foreign corporation acquires substantially all of its properties after March 4, 2003.
- The former shareholders (or partners) of the U.S. corporation (or partnership) hold 80 percent or more of the foreign corporation's stock after the transaction.
- The foreign corporation does not have substantial business activities in its country of incorporation.

If the former shareholders or partners own at least 60 percent but less than 80 percent of the new corporation, the foreign entity remains foreign, but any corporate-level taxes imposed because of the transfer cannot be offset with net operating losses, foreign tax credits, or certain other tax attributes. In addition, an excise tax is imposed at the maximum capital gains tax rate on the value of certain stock held by insiders at any time during the 12-month period beginning six months before the date of the inversion.

---

gain remains potentially deferred. As the inventory and accounts receivable are "tainted assets," Amelia must recognize $350 of gain upon the transfer ($300 gain attributable to inventory and $50 gain from the accounts receivable). Gain is recognized on an asset-by-asset basis with no offset for losses on other assets. ■

[handwritten margin note: no offset of gain by losses on other assets]

In addition to gain on the tainted assets listed above, any U.S. depreciation (§§ 1245 and 1250) and other types of recapture potential (e.g., §§ 617, 1252, and 1254) in the assets transferred must be recognized to the extent of gain realized. This provision applies only to appreciated assets for which the depreciation or other deduction has resulted in a tax benefit. The U.S. depreciation is the portion of the depreciation attributable to use of the property in the United States. Prior branch losses are also recaptured to the extent that they are not recaptured under the § 904(f) provisions.

The transfer of intangibles is treated separately under § 367(d) as a transfer pursuant to a sale for contingent payments. These amounts are treated as received by the transferor over the life of the intangible and are ordinary income. They are recognized by the transferor and must be commensurate with the income attributable to the intangible. A subsequent disposition by the transferee triggers income recognition to the initial transferor under § 367.

Inbound and Offshore Transfers.

One objective of § 367 is to prevent E & P that has accumulated in U.S.-owned foreign corporations from escaping U.S. taxation. Section 367(b) covers the tax treatment of inbound and offshore transfers with regard to stock of a controlled foreign corporation (CFC). (CFCs are discussed in more detail in a later section.) Examples of inbound transactions include the following.

- The liquidation of a foreign corporation into a domestic parent under § 332.
- The acquisition of the assets of a foreign corporation by a domestic corporation in a Type "C" or Type "D" reorganization.

Offshore transfers include the following.

- A foreign corporation acquisition of a first- or lower-tier foreign corporation in exchange for stock of a non-CFC.
- A foreign corporate Type "B," Type "C," or Type "D" acquisition of a foreign corporation in exchange for CFC stock.
- A foreign § 351 transfer of stock or other property in a foreign corporation having a U.S. shareholder.

U.S. persons that are directly or indirectly parties to an inbound or offshore transfer involving stock of a CFC generally recognize dividend income to the extent of their pro rata share of the previously untaxed E & P of the foreign corporation. In some circumstances, income can be deferred by entering into a gain recognition agreement with the IRS. Special rules apply to the outbound transfer of domestic or foreign shares.

[handwritten margin note: generally recognize dividend income to extent of...]

Tax Havens

Many outbound transfers of assets to foreign corporations are to countries with tax rates higher than or equal to the U.S. rate. Thus, tax avoidance is not the motive for such transfers. Some U.S. corporations, however, make their foreign investment in (or through) a tax haven. A **tax haven** is a country where either locally sourced income or residents are subject to no or low internal taxation. Exhibit 9–2 lists countries classified as tax havens.

One method of potentially avoiding taxation is to invest through a foreign corporation incorporated in a tax haven. Because the foreign corporation is a resident of the tax haven, the income it earns is subject to no or low internal taxes. Tax haven countries may also have provisions limiting the exchange of financial and commercial information.

Figure 9–5 illustrates this use of a tax haven by a U.S. corporation. The U.S. corporation uses a foreign subsidiary corporation in a low- or no-tax country to earn either investment income or a portion of income from business activities (as illustrated previously in the transfer pricing discussion). Because the foreign subsidiary is not consolidated with the domestic parent under U.S. tax law (i.e., the foreign corporation is not a member of the U.S. corporation's affiliated group) and is not itself engaged in any U.S. trade or business, the foreign corporation is not subject to U.S. taxation. Without the application of the transfer pricing rules or the Subpart F rules (discussed later), the foreign corporation's income will escape U.S. taxation until the time that any foreign profits are repatriated back to the U.S. parent as a dividend or similar payment.

A tax haven can also, in effect, be created by an income tax treaty. For example, under an income tax treaty between Country A and Country B, residents of Country A are subject to a withholding tax of only 5 percent on dividend and interest income sourced in Country B. The United States and Country A have a similar treaty. The United States does not have a treaty with Country B, and the withholding tax is 30 percent. A U.S. corporation can create a foreign subsidiary in Country A and use that subsidiary to make investments in Country B. This practice is referred to as **treaty shopping**. If the Country B investment income had been

| EXHIBIT 9–2 | OECD Tax Haven Blacklist |

In 2000, the OECD identified these jurisdictions as tax havens that had not cooperated with its campaign to stop harmful global tax practices. As of 2007, only the countries marked with an asterisk remained on the list.

Andorra*	Maldives
Anguilla	Marshall Islands
Antigua and Barbuda	Monaco*
Aruba	Montserrat
Bahamas	Nauru
Bahrain	Netherlands Antilles
Barbados	Niue
Belize	Panama
British Virgin Islands	Samoa
Cook Island	Seychelles
Dominica	St. Christopher and Nevis
Gibraltar	St. Lucia
Grenada	St. Vincent and the
Guernsey	Grenadines
Isle of Man	Tonga
Jersey	Turks and Caicos Islands
Liberia	U.S. Virgin Islands
Liechtenstein*	Vanuatu

Sources: Organization for Economic Cooperation and Development (OECD), *Towards Global Tax Cooperation: Progress in Identifying and Eliminating Harmful Tax Practices,* 2000; OECD News Release, July 8, 2007; and *The OECD's Project on Harmful Tax Practices: The 2004 Progress Report,* 2006.

earned directly by the U.S. corporation, it would be subject to a 30 percent withholding tax. As a result of investing through the foreign subsidiary created in Country A, the U.S. parent corporation pays only 10 percent in foreign taxes on the income earned, that is, 5 percent to Country B and 5 percent to Country A.

| FIGURE 9–5 | Use of a Tax Haven Corporation |

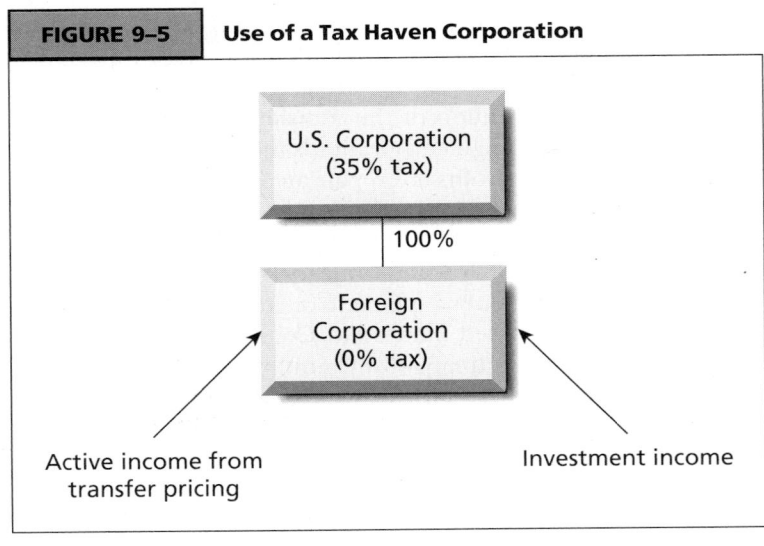

In recent years, many countries have enacted "treaty shopping" provisions. Under the provisions, treaty benefits for withholding taxes are not available to a resident corporation unless a certain percentage of its beneficial interests are owned, directly or indirectly, by one or more individual residents of the country in which the corporation is resident. The most controversial article in the U.S. Model Treaty is Article 22, Limitation on Benefits, which is meant to prevent treaty shopping. Article 22 disallows treaty benefits to an entity unless more than 50 percent of the beneficial interest in the entity is owned, directly or indirectly, by one or more individual residents of the treaty country in which the entity is resident.[21]

Foreign Corporations Controlled by U.S. Persons

To minimize current tax liability, taxpayers often attempt to defer the recognition of taxable income. One way to do this is to shift the income-generating activity to a foreign entity that is not within the U.S. tax jurisdiction. A foreign corporation is the most suitable entity for such an endeavor because, unlike a partnership, it is not a conduit through which income is taxed directly to the owner. Because of the potential for abuse, Congress has enacted various provisions to limit the availability of deferral.

ETHICAL and EQUITABLE *Considerations*

A BOOST TO DOMESTIC INVESTMENT OR A TAX AMNESTY FOR OUTSOURCERS?

The American Jobs Creation Act of 2004 provided a temporary incentive to repatriate foreign profits back to the United States. Section 965 allowed domestic corporations to elect to take a onetime 85 percent dividends received deduction for certain cash dividends received from controlled foreign corporations for either the taxpayer's last tax year that began before October 22, 2004, or the first tax year that began after October 22, 2004. Such dividends had to be reinvested in the United States, and the eligible dividend amount was based on a calculation that considered prior-year average dividends and the amount of earnings considered "permanently reinvested" abroad under financial accounting principles. The intent was to provide a tax benefit only for earnings that would not otherwise have been repatriated to the United States. With an 85 percent dividends received deduction, the effective U.S. corporate tax rate on such dividends was 5.25 percent (35% corporate tax rate × 15% taxable amount).

Supporters of this measure argued that the inflow of cash back to the United States, along with the requirement for reinvestment here, would provide a boost to the domestic economy. The dividend income was lightly taxed but would otherwise never have been taxed in the United States. Critics argued that the tax break was simply a giveaway to U.S. multinational corporations and rewarded outsourcing. They feared that with this precedent, U.S. multinationals may simply outsource more profits to low-tax countries and wait for future tax breaks before repatriating profits. Which argument do you find more convincing? How would you feel if your own company had always repatriated foreign profits back to the United States without the benefit of a special tax break?

Controlled Foreign Corporations. Subpart F, §§ 951–964 of the Code, provides that certain types of income generated by controlled foreign corporations (CFCs) are currently included in gross income by the U.S. shareholders without regard to actual distributions. For Subpart F to apply, the foreign corporation must have been a CFC for an uninterrupted period of 30 days or more during the taxable year. When this is the case, U.S. shareholders must include in gross income their pro rata share of Subpart F income and increase in earnings that the CFC has invested in U.S. property for the tax year. This rule applies to U.S. shareholders who own stock in the corporation on the last day of the tax year or on the last day the foreign corporation is a CFC. The gross income inclusion must be made for their taxable year in which the taxable year of the CFC ends.

---

[21]Additional limitations on the use of treaty benefits are contained in § 894(c).

TAX *in the News*

A MOVE TO THE BEACH FOR U.S. CORPORATIONS SEEKING A VACATION FROM U.S. TAX RULES

A number of U.S.-based companies have decided to cast their lot on the golden shores of Bermuda, reincorporating as Bermuda companies and enjoying Bermuda's low-tax environment. Those with Bermuda headquarters include such well-known companies as Fruit of the Loom, Cooper Industries, Foster Wheeler, and Ingersoll Rand. Even Accenture, formerly Andersen Consulting, established itself in Bermuda.

Many of these companies argue that U.S. international tax policy compromises their ability to compete in the global marketplace. The stock market often rewarded these so-called inversion transactions (i.e., conversion from U.S. to foreign

based) with increased stock prices. Although an inversion transaction often entailed a current tax cost, the long-term tax benefits were considered more important. Many other companies were preparing to invert in 2002 when Congress began developing anti-inversion legislation and the public began reacting negatively to these corporate expatriates. During mid-2002, toolmaker Stanley Works called off its previously announced, and very controversial, inversion plans. Inversion transactions virtually ceased during 2003. Provisions in the American Jobs Creation Act of 2004 further curtailed the benefits of moving offshore.

EXAMPLE 15

Gray, Inc., a calendar year corporation, is a CFC for the entire tax year. Chance Company, a U.S. corporation, owns 60% of Gray's one class of stock for the entire year. Subpart F income is $100,000, and no distributions have been made during the year. Chance, a calendar year taxpayer, includes $60,000 in gross income as a constructive dividend for the tax year. ■

EXAMPLE 16

Gray, Inc., is a CFC until July 1 of the tax year (a calendar year) and earns $100,000 in Subpart F income. Terry, a U.S. citizen, owns 30% of its one class of stock for the entire year. She includes $14,877 [$100,000 × 30% × (181 days/365 days)] in gross income as a constructive dividend for the tax year. ■

A **CFC** is any foreign corporation in which more than 50 percent of the total combined voting power of all classes of stock entitled to vote or the total value of the stock of the corporation is owned by U.S. shareholders on any day during the taxable year of the foreign corporation. The foreign subsidiaries of most multinational U.S. parent corporations are CFCs. For purposes of determining if a foreign corporation is a CFC, a **U.S. shareholder** is defined as a U.S. person who owns, or is considered to own, 10 percent or more of the total combined voting power of all classes of voting stock of the foreign corporation. Stock owned directly, indirectly, and constructively is counted.

Indirect ownership involves stock held through a foreign entity, such as a foreign corporation, foreign partnership, or foreign trust. This stock is considered to be actually owned proportionately by the shareholders, partners, or beneficiaries. Constructive ownership rules, with certain modifications, apply in determining if a U.S. person is a U.S. shareholder, in determining whether a foreign corporation is a CFC, and for certain related-party provisions of Subpart F.[22]

EXAMPLE 17

Shareholders of Foreign Corporation	Voting Power	Classification
Alan	30%	U.S. person
Bill	9%	U.S. person
Carla	40%	Foreign person
Dora	20%	U.S. person
Ed	1%	U.S. person

---

[22]§§ 958 and 318(a).

Bill is Alan's son. Alan, Bill, and Dora are U.S. shareholders. Alan owns 39%, 30% directly and 9% constructively through Bill. Bill also owns 39%, 9% directly and 30% constructively through Alan. Thus, Bill is a U.S. shareholder. Dora owns 20% directly. The corporation is a CFC because U.S. shareholders own 59% of the voting power. Ed, a U.S. person, owns 1% and is not related to any of the other shareholders. Thus, Ed is not a U.S. shareholder and would not have to include any of the Subpart F income in gross income. If Bill were not related to Alan or to any other U.S. persons who were shareholders, Bill would not be a U.S. shareholder, and the corporation would not be a CFC. ■

U.S. shareholders must include their pro rata share of the applicable income in their gross income only to the extent of their actual ownership. Stock held indirectly (but not constructively) is considered actually owned for this purpose.

EXAMPLE 18

Bill, in Example 17, would recognize only 9% of the Subpart F income as a constructive dividend. Alan would recognize 30%, and Dora would recognize 20%. If instead Bill were a foreign corporation wholly owned by Alan, Alan would recognize 39% as a constructive dividend. ■

Subpart F Income. A U.S. shareholder of a CFC does not necessarily lose the ability to defer U.S. taxation of income earned by the CFC. Only certain income earned by the CFC triggers immediate U.S. taxation as a constructive dividend. This tainted income, referred to as Subpart F income, can be characterized as income with little or no economic connection with the CFC's country of incorporation. **Subpart F income** consists of the following.

- Insurance income (§ 953).
- Foreign base company income (§ 954).
- International boycott factor income (§ 999).
- Illegal bribes.
- Income derived from a § 901(j) foreign country.

Subpart F income

Insurance Income. Income attributable to insuring risk of loss outside the country in which the CFC is organized is Subpart F income. This rule precludes U.S. corporations from setting up offshore insurance companies in tax havens to convert expenditures for self-insurance into a deductible insurance premium.

Foreign Base Company Income. Foreign base company income (FBCI) provisions target transactions whereby a CFC earns income that lacks any economic connection to its country of organization. There are five categories of FBCI.

- Foreign personal holding company income.
- Foreign base company sales income.
- Foreign base company services income.
- Foreign base company shipping income (for tax years beginning before 2005 only).
- Foreign base company oil-related income.

FBCI

Foreign personal holding company (FPHC) income consists of the following.

- Dividends, interest, royalties, rents, and annuities.
- Excess gains over losses from the sale or exchange of property (including an interest in a trust or partnership) that gives rise to FPHC income or that does not give rise to any income.
- Excess of foreign currency gains over foreign currency losses (other than any transaction directly related to the business needs of the CFC).
- Income from notional principal contracts.
- Certain payments in lieu of dividends.
- Certain personal service contract income.

| **TAX** *in the News* | **WHO ARE THESE CFCs?** |

The 7,500 largest CFCs accounted for $5.8 trillion of the assets and more than $2.3 trillion of the gross receipts of all CFCs for 2002, the latest year for which complete data are available. These CFCs were engaged primarily in manufacturing (29 percent), services (26 percent) or finance, insurance, or real estate (24 percent). Although these 7,500 CFCs were incorporated in over 100 different countries, CFCs in Europe, Canada, and Japan accounted for over 80 percent of the gross receipts. In 2002, CFCs distributed $97 billion of profits to their U.S. parents and other shareholders. This represented a 2.2 percent increase in distributions over 2000. A "large" CFC is one having $500 million or more in assets.

Source: *Statistics of Income,* **http://www.IRS.gov/pub/irs-soi/02cfcart.pdf.**

Certain FPHC income does not trigger a Subpart F inclusion under exceptions for same-country payments, payments out of non-Subpart F E & P of related CFCs, and active rent and royalty income.

Foreign base company (FBC) sales income is income derived by a CFC where the CFC has very little connection with the process that generates the income and a related party is involved. If the CFC earns income from the sale of property to customers outside the CFC's country of incorporation, and either the supplier or the customer is related to the CFC, such income is FBC sales income.

EXAMPLE 19

Ulysses, Ltd., is a CFC organized in the United Kingdom and owned 100% by Joyce, Inc., a U.S. corporation. Ulysses purchases finished inventory from Joyce and sells the inventory to customers in Hong Kong. This sales income constitutes FBC sales income. ∎

An exception applies to property that is manufactured, produced, grown, or extracted in the country in which the CFC was organized or created and also to property sold for use, consumption, or disposition within that country. In both these situations, the CFC has participated in the economic process that generates the income.

EXAMPLE 20

If Ulysses, from Example 19, purchases raw materials from Joyce and performs substantial manufacturing activity in the United Kingdom before selling the inventory to customers in Hong Kong, the income is not FBC sales income. Even without the manufacturing activity, sales to customers within the United Kingdom would not produce FBC sales income. ∎

Certain income derived by a branch of the CFC in another country can be deemed FBC sales income. This is the case when the effect of using the branch is the same as if the branch were a wholly owned subsidiary.[23]

FBC services income is income derived from the performance of services for or on behalf of a related person and performed outside the country in which the CFC was created or organized. Income from services performed in connection with the sale of property by a CFC that has manufactured, produced, grown, or extracted such property is not FBC services income.

FBC oil-related income is income, other than extraction income, derived in a foreign country by large oil producers in connection with the sale of oil and gas products and sold by the CFC or a related person for use or consumption outside the country in which the oil or gas was extracted.

Subpart F Income Exceptions. A *de minimis* rule provides that if the total amount of a foreign corporation's FBCI and gross insurance income for the taxable year is less than the lesser of 5 percent of gross income or $1 million, none of its gross income

---

[23]§ 954(d)(2).

is treated as FBCI for the tax year. At the other extreme, if a foreign corporation's FBCI and gross insurance income exceed 70 percent of total gross income, all the corporation's gross income for the tax year is treated as Subpart F income.

[handwritten: ★ If FBCI > 70% then all gross income = subpart F income]

FBCI and insurance income subject to high foreign taxes are not included under Subpart F if the taxpayer establishes that the income was subject to an effective rate, imposed by a foreign country, of more than 90 percent of the maximum corporate rate under § 11. For example, the rate must be greater than 31.5 percent (90% × 35%), where 35 percent represents the highest U.S. corporate rate.

Investment in U.S. Property. In addition to Subpart F income, U.S. shareholders must include in gross income their pro rata share of the CFC's increase in investment in U.S. property for the taxable year.[24] U.S. property generally includes: U.S. real property, debt obligations of U.S. persons, and stock in certain related domestic corporations. The CFC must have sufficient E & P to support a deemed dividend.

[handwritten: triggers a constructive dividend but CFC must have sufficient E & P]

---

*[right margin: **EXAMPLE 21**]*

Fleming, Ltd., a CFC, earned no Subpart F income for the taxable year. If Fleming lends $100,000 to Lynn, its sole U.S. shareholder, this debt is considered an investment in U.S. property by Fleming because it now owns a U.S. note receivable. Holding the note triggers a constructive dividend of $100,000 to Lynn, assuming Fleming has sufficient E & P. ∎

Distributions of Previously Taxed Income. Distributions from a CFC are treated as being first from E & P attributable to increases in investment in U.S. property previously taxed as a constructive dividend, second from E & P attributable to previously taxed Subpart F income, and last from other E & P.[25] Thus, distributions of previously taxed income are not taxed again as a dividend but reduce E & P. Any increase in investment in U.S. property is considered attributable first to Subpart F income and thus is not taxed twice.

---

*[right margin: **EXAMPLE 22**]*

In the current year, Jet, Inc., a U.S. shareholder, owns 100% of a CFC, from which Jet receives a $100,000 distribution. The CFC's E & P is composed of the following amounts.

- $50,000 attributable to previously taxed investment in U.S. property.
- $30,000 attributable to previously taxed Subpart F income.
- $40,000 attributable to other E & P.

Jet has a taxable dividend of only $20,000, all attributable to other E & P. The remaining $80,000 is previously taxed income. The CFC's E & P is reduced by $100,000. The remaining $20,000 E & P is all attributable to other E & P. ∎

A U.S. shareholder's basis in CFC stock is increased by constructive dividends and decreased by subsequent distributions of previously taxed income. U.S. corporate shareholders who own at least 10 percent of the voting stock of a foreign corporation are allowed an indirect foreign tax credit for foreign taxes deemed paid on constructive dividends included in gross income under Subpart F. The indirect credit also is available for Subpart F income attributable to certain lower-tier foreign corporations. See the foreign tax credit discussion later in this chapter. The various constructive dividend possibilities for CFC income appear in Concept Summary 9–2.

Dispositions of Stock of a CFC. Under the Subpart F provisions, Subpart F income of a CFC is currently taxed to U.S. shareholders to the extent of their pro rata share. This rule, however, does not reach the earnings of the CFC that are not included in the taxable income of the shareholders under Subpart F (e.g., active trade or business income not involving related persons). Section 1248 prevents the gain from

---

[24]§ 956.

[25]Prior law included another category of previously taxed income related to investment in excess passive assets under § 956A.

CONCEPT SUMMARY 9–2

Income of a CFC That Is Included in Gross Income of a U.S. Shareholder

*Plus all other income, when foreign base company and insurance income exceeds 70% of gross income.
**For pre-2005 CFC tax years only.

the disposition of CFC stock from escaping taxation as ordinary income. This provision requires that gain on the sale or other disposition of stock of a CFC by a U.S. shareholder be treated as dividend income to the extent of the transferor's share of undistributed nonpreviously taxed E & P of the corporation.

Other Antideferral Provision. Congress has enacted another provision to limit the deferral benefits associated with earning investment income through a foreign corporation. The passive foreign investment company (PFIC) rules can trigger constructive dividends to U.S. persons.[26]

A PFIC is similar in theory to a CFC, but the rules are more restrictive. Any level of ownership can subject a U.S. person to taxation under the PFIC provisions if the foreign corporation earns substantial levels of investment income or holds significant investment assets.[27] Foreign mutual funds are often PFICs to their U.S. owners. Income falling under both Subpart F and the PFIC provisions is taxed only under Subpart F to U.S. shareholders of a CFC.

---

[26]Prior to 2005, another antideferral regime, the foreign personal holding company, could also cause immediate U.S. taxation of a foreign corporation's earnings. The 2004 American Jobs Creation Act repealed these rules.

[27]§ 1297.

The Foreign Tax Credit

The United States retains the right to tax its citizens and residents on their total taxable income. This approach can result in double taxation, presenting a potential problem to U.S. persons who invest abroad.

To reduce the possibility of double taxation, Congress enacted the **foreign tax credit (FTC)** provisions. Under these provisions, a qualified taxpayer is allowed a tax credit for foreign income taxes paid. The credit is a dollar-for-dollar reduction of U.S. income tax liability.

For the most recent years data are available, corporations filing U.S. tax returns claimed $42 billion in FTCs and individuals claimed $6.3 billion in FTCs. Corporations claiming FTCs reported worldwide income of $344 billion. Without the benefit of the FTC, much of this income would have been subject to double taxation.

EXAMPLE 23

Ace Tools, Inc., a U.S. corporation, has a branch operation in Mexico, from which it earns taxable income of $750,000 for the current year. Ace pays income tax of $150,000 on these earnings to the Mexican tax authorities. Ace must also include the $750,000 in gross income for U.S. tax purposes. Assume that, before considering the FTC, Ace owes $255,000 in U.S. income taxes on this foreign-source income. Thus, total taxes on the $750,000 could equal $405,000 ($150,000 + $255,000), a 54% effective rate. But Ace takes an FTC of $150,000 against its U.S. tax liability on the foreign-source income. Ace's total taxes on the $750,000 now are $255,000 ($150,000 + $105,000), a 34% effective rate. ■

The FTC is elective for any particular tax year. If the taxpayer does not "choose" to take the FTC, § 164 allows a deduction for foreign taxes paid or incurred. A taxpayer cannot take a credit and a deduction for the same foreign income taxes.[28] However, a taxpayer can take a deduction in the same year as an FTC for foreign taxes that are not creditable (e.g., non-income taxes).

[handwritten margin note: TP can not take a credit AND a deduction]

The Direct Credit. Section 901 provides a direct FTC to U.S. taxpayers that pay or incur a foreign income tax. For purposes of the direct credit, only the taxpayer that bears the legal incidence of the foreign tax is eligible for the credit.

EXAMPLE 24

Snowball, Inc., a U.S. corporation, operates an unincorporated branch manufacturing operation in Australia. On its U.S. tax return, Snowball, Inc., reports $450,000 of taxable income from the Australian branch and $650,000 of taxable income from its U.S. operations. Snowball paid $135,000 in Australian income taxes related to the $450,000 in branch income. This $135,000 is a direct FTC because Snowball directly paid the foreign tax. Snowball's U.S. tax liability after the FTC is determined as follows.

Australian branch income	$ 450,000
U.S. operations income	650,000
Total taxable income	$1,100,000
U.S. tax rate	× 35%
U.S. income tax before FTC	$ 385,000
FTC	(135,000)
Net U.S. tax liability	$ 250,000

[handwritten margin note: b/c foreign rate < Domestic rate FTC is fully creditable w/out limitation]

Because the effective foreign tax rate (30%) is less than the U.S. rate (35%), the $135,000 FTC is fully creditable without limitation (see the discussion under FTC Limitations below). ■

Section 903 provides U.S. taxpayers with a direct FTC for foreign taxes imposed in lieu of an income tax by the foreign government. A credit for withholding tax is

---

[28]§ 275.

the most common example of a § 903 credit. Many governments impose a withholding tax on the gross amount of certain payments of passive income to nonresidents of their countries. This withholding tax also triggers a direct credit. Even though the tax is withheld by the payor of the income, the tax is imposed directly on the recipient.

EXAMPLE 25

Tax w/ holding still qualifies for FTC

MettCo, Inc., a domestic corporation, receives a $5,000 dividend from DeanCo, Ltd., a foreign corporation. The foreign country imposes a 20% withholding tax on dividend payments to nonresidents. Accordingly, DeanCo withholds $1,000 ($5,000 × 20%) from the dividend and remits this tax to the local country tax authorities. DeanCo pays the remaining $4,000 to MettCo.

Although MettCo did not directly pay the $1,000 in foreign tax, the entire amount is allowed as a direct tax to MettCo for FTC purposes. MettCo reports $5,000 in dividend income on its U.S. tax return (the gross amount of the dividend) but receives an FTC against any U.S. tax for the $1,000 in foreign withholding tax. ■

The Indirect Credit. If a U.S. corporation operates in a foreign country through a branch, the direct credit is available for foreign taxes paid. If, however, a U.S. corporation operates in a foreign country through a foreign subsidiary, the direct credit is not available for foreign taxes paid by the foreign corporation. An indirect credit is available to U.S. corporate taxpayers that receive actual or constructive dividends from foreign corporations that have paid foreign income taxes. These foreign taxes are deemed paid by the corporate shareholders in the same proportion as the dividends actually or constructively received bear to the foreign corporation's post-1986 undistributed E & P.

$$\text{Indirect FTC} = \frac{\text{Actual or constructive dividend}}{\text{Post-1986 undistributed E \& P}} \times \text{Post-1986 foreign taxes}$$

Section 78 requires a domestic corporation that chooses the FTC for deemed-paid foreign taxes to *gross up* (add to income) dividend income by the amount of deemed-paid taxes.

EXAMPLE 26

§78 gross-up adjustment

Wren, Inc., a domestic corporation, owns 50% of Finch, Inc., a foreign corporation. Wren receives a dividend of $120,000 from Finch. Finch paid foreign taxes of $500,000 on post-1986 E & P. Finch's post-1986 E & P totals $1.2 million. Wren's deemed-paid foreign taxes for FTC purposes are $50,000.

Cash dividend from Finch	$120,000
Deemed-paid foreign taxes	
$\left(\dfrac{\$120,000}{\$1,200,000} \times \$500,000\right)$	50,000
Gross income to Wren	$170,000

In addition to the $120,000 cash dividend, Wren must include the $50,000 in gross income for the § 78 gross-up adjustment if the FTC is elected. ■

Certain ownership requirements must be met before the indirect credit is available to a domestic corporation. The domestic corporation must own 10 percent or more of the voting stock of the foreign corporation. The credit is also available for deemed-paid foreign taxes of second- and third-tier foreign corporations if the 10 percent ownership requirement is met at the second- and third-tier level. A 5 percent indirect ownership requirement must also be met. The indirect credit is also available for foreign taxes paid by fourth- through sixth-tier foreign corporations if additional requirements are met, including the requirement that these corporations be CFCs. The § 902 ownership requirements are summarized in Figure 9–6.

| FIGURE 9–6 | Section 902 Ownership Requirements |

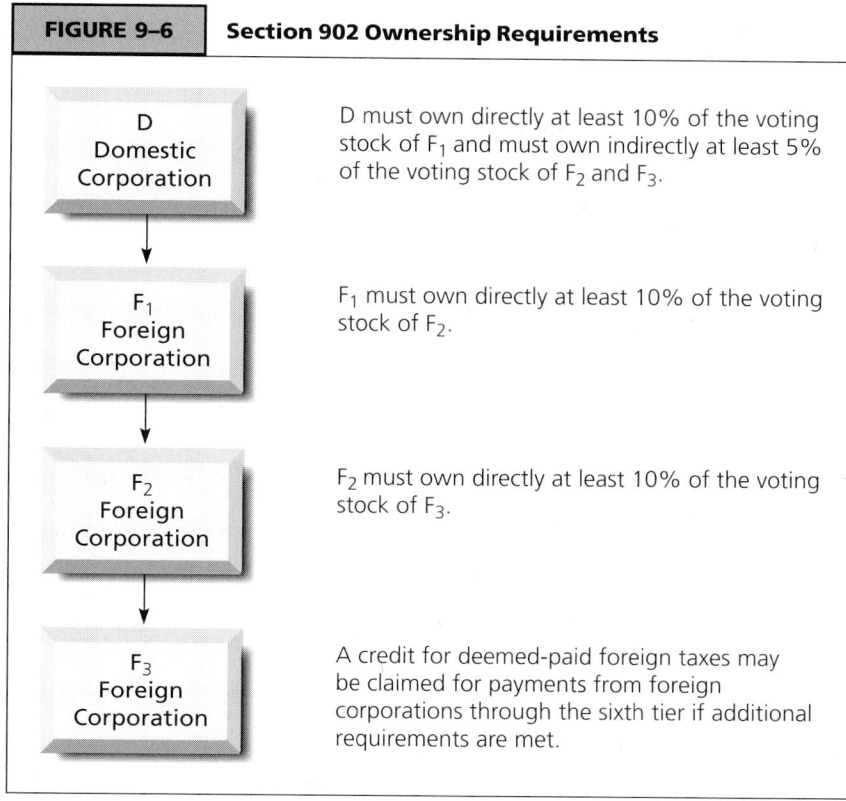

D must own directly at least 10% of the voting stock of F_1 and must own indirectly at least 5% of the voting stock of F_2 and F_3.

F_1 must own directly at least 10% of the voting stock of F_2.

F_2 must own directly at least 10% of the voting stock of F_3.

A credit for deemed-paid foreign taxes may be claimed for payments from foreign corporations through the sixth tier if additional requirements are met.

FTC Limitations. To prevent taxpayers from crediting foreign taxes against U.S. taxes levied on U.S.-source taxable income, the FTC is subject to a limitation. The FTC for any taxable year cannot exceed the lesser of two amounts: (1) the actual foreign taxes paid or accrued or (2) the U.S. taxes (before the FTC) on foreign-source taxable income. The FTC limitation is derived in the following manner.

$$\text{FTC limitation} = \frac{\text{Foreign-source taxable income}}{\text{Total taxable income}^{29}} \times \text{U.S. tax before FTC}$$

MUST KNOW FOR FINAL

EXAMPLE 27

Charlotte, Inc., a domestic corporation that invests in foreign securities, has total taxable income for the tax year of $120,000, consisting of $100,000 in U.S.-source business profits and $20,000 of income from foreign sources. Foreign taxes of $9,500 were withheld by foreign tax authorities. Assume that Charlotte's U.S. tax before the FTC is $42,000. The company's FTC is limited to $7,000 [$42,000 × ($20,000/$120,000)]. Charlotte's net U.S. tax liability is $35,000. ■

42,000
(7,000)
35,000

As Example 27 illustrates, the limitation can prevent the total amount of foreign taxes paid in high-tax jurisdictions from being credited. Taxpayers could overcome this problem by generating additional foreign-source income that is subject to no, or low, foreign taxation.

EXAMPLE 28

Compare Domestic Corporation's FTC situations. In one, the corporation has only $500,000 of highly taxed foreign-source income. In the other, Domestic also has $100,000 of low-taxed foreign-source interest income.

---

[29]For FTC purposes, the taxable income of an individual, estate, or trust is computed without any deduction for personal exemptions. § 904(b)(1).

Foreign Tax Credit: Separate Income Limitations for Tax Years Beginning before 2007

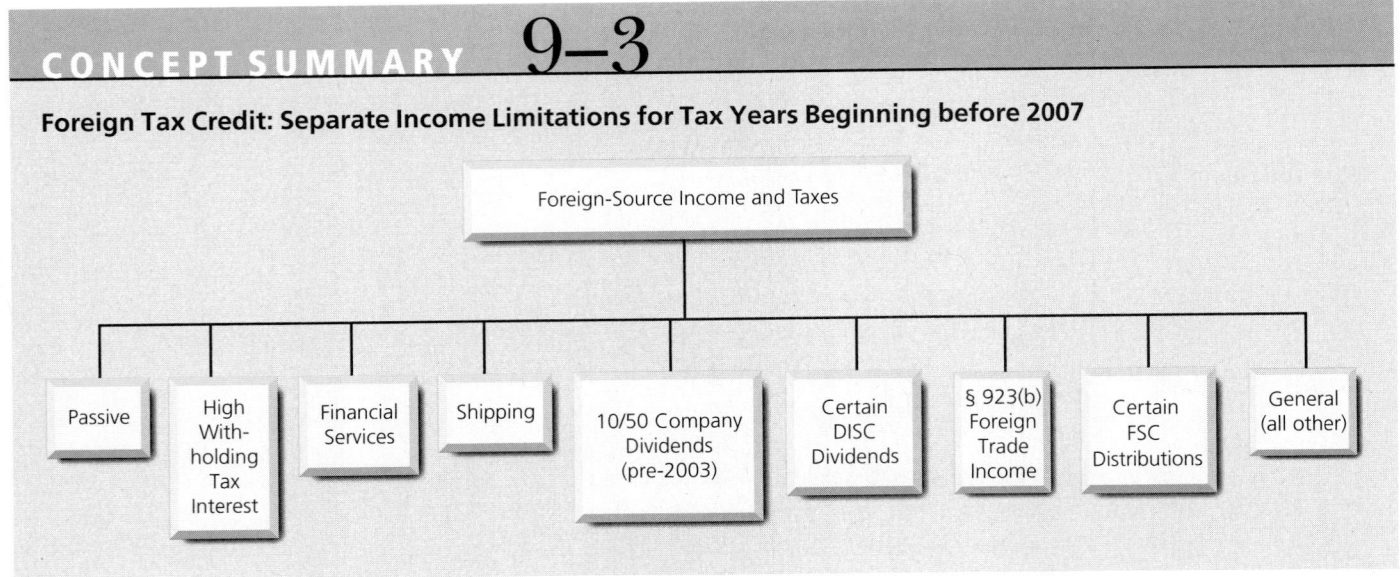

	Only Highly Taxed Income	With Low-Taxed Interest Income
Foreign-source income	$500,000	$600,000
Foreign taxes	275,000	280,000
U.S.-source income	700,000	700,000
U.S. taxes (34%)	408,000	442,000
FTC limitation	170,000*	204,000**

*$408,000 × ($500,000/$1,200,000).

**$442,000 × ($600,000/$1,300,000).

Domestic's foreign taxes increase by only $5,000 ($280,000 − $275,000), but its FTC limitation increases by $34,000 ($204,000 − $170,000). ■

Example 28 illustrates the *cross-crediting* of foreign taxes from high- and low-taxed foreign income. To prevent this practice, the FTC rules require that a separate limitation be calculated for each of certain categories (or baskets) of foreign-source taxable income and the foreign taxes attributable to that income. Section 904(d) provided these income baskets for years beginning before 2007, which still apply to those years if the statute of limitations has not expired.

- Passive income.
- High withholding tax interest.
- Financial services income.
- Shipping income.
- Dividends from a domestic international sales corporation (DISC) or former DISC to the extent they were treated as foreign-source income.
- Taxable income attributable to foreign trade income under § 923(b).
- Distributions from a foreign sales corporation (FSC) or former FSC out of E & P attributable to foreign trade income or qualified interest and carrying charges under § 263(c).

All other foreign-source income was included in a residual (or general) limitation basket. These separate limitations are diagrammed in Concept Summary 9–3. For tax years beginning after 2006, there are only two baskets: passive income and all other (general). Any FTC carryforwards into post-2006 years are assigned to one of these two categories.

EXAMPLE 29

BenCo, Inc., a U.S. corporation, has a foreign branch in France that earns taxable income of $1.5 million from manufacturing operations and $600,000 from passive activities. BenCo pays foreign taxes of $600,000 (40%) and $100,000 (16.67%) respectively, on this foreign-source income. The corporation also earns $4 million of U.S.-source taxable income, resulting in worldwide taxable income of $6.1 million. BenCo's U.S. taxes before the FTC are $2,074,000 (at 34%). The following tabulation illustrates the effect of the separate limitation baskets on cross-crediting.

Foreign Income Category	Net Taxable Amount	Foreign Taxes	U.S. Tax before FTC at 34%	FTC with Separate Limits
General	$1,500,000	$600,000	$510,000	$510,000
Passive	600,000	100,000	204,000	100,000
Total	$2,100,000	$700,000	$714,000	$610,000

Without the separate limitation provisions, the FTC would be the lesser of (1) $700,000 foreign taxes or (2) $714,000 share of U.S. tax [$2,074,000 × ($2,100,000/$6,100,000)]. The separate limitation provisions reduce the FTC by $90,000 ($700,000 − $610,000). The effect of the separate limitation rules is that the foreign-source income taxed at the foreign tax rate of 40% cannot be aggregated with foreign-source income taxed at only 16.67%. ■

In the case of a CFC, the look-through rules classify any dividend (actual or deemed), interest, rent, or royalty income received from the CFC into separate limitation baskets as if such income were earned directly by the U.S. shareholders of the CFC. Dividend income from a foreign corporation at least 10 percent owned but not a CFC (i.e., a 10/50 company) is also subject to the look-through rule.[30] A partner's distributive share of partnership income is also generally categorized in separate limitation baskets based on the character of the partnership's income. Additionally, interest, rent, or royalty payments to certain partners are eligible for look-through treatment.

The limitations can result in unused (noncredited) foreign taxes for the tax year. The carryback period is 1 year, and the carryforward period is 10 years. The taxes can be credited in years when the formula limitation for that year exceeds the foreign taxes attributable to the same tax year. The carryback and carryforward provisions are available only within a specific basket. In other words, excess foreign taxes in one basket cannot be carried over unless there is an excess limitation in the same basket for the carryover year.

Foreign Losses.
Citizens and residents of the United States who hold foreign investments or operations directly (e.g., through a branch operation) or through a conduit entity (e.g., a partnership) have the opportunity to offset foreign losses against U.S.-source income, thereby reducing the U.S. income tax due on U.S.-source income. If the foreign country in which the loss is generated (sourced) taxes subsequent income from these foreign operations, the FTC could reduce or eliminate any U.S. tax on the income.

To prevent this loss of tax revenue to the United States, tax law provides that the overall foreign losses should be recaptured as U.S.-source income for FTC purposes.[31] This is accomplished by reducing the numerator of the FTC limitation

---

[30]Special rules applied to 10/50 company dividends prior to 2003. §§ 904(d)(1)(E),   [31]§ 904(f)(1).
    (d)(2)(E), and (d)(4).

formula. Foreign-source taxable income is reduced by the lesser of (1) the remaining unrecaptured overall foreign loss or (2) 50 percent of foreign-source taxable income for the taxable year (unless the taxpayer elects to recapture a greater percentage). Unrecaptured foreign losses are carried over indefinitely until recaptured.

EXAMPLE 30

Shannon, Inc., a domestic corporation, operates a branch in Japan. The earnings record of the branch is as follows.

Year	Taxable Income (Loss)	Foreign Taxes Paid
2005	($ 15,000)	–0–
2006	(20,000)	–0–
2007	(20,000)	–0–
2008	40,000	$20,000

For 2005–2008, Shannon has U.S.-source taxable income of $300,000 each year. Shannon's 2008 U.S. tax liability before the FTC is $115,600. Its overall foreign loss is $55,000 for 2005–2007. The FTC limitation for 2008 is $6,800 {$115,600 × [$40,000 − (50% × $40,000)]/ $340,000}. ■

A situation may arise in which overall foreign losses have been incurred and the U.S. taxpayer disposes of trade or business property used predominantly outside the United States before any or all of the loss is recaptured. The provisions described above will not necessarily reach such a situation. The statutory solution to this problem is that upon disposal the U.S. taxpayer generates U.S.-source income. The amount of income generated is the lesser of (1) the fair market value of the property less its adjusted basis or (2) the remaining amount of unrecaptured overall foreign losses.[32]

When a taxpayer has a loss for the tax year in one or more foreign-source categories (baskets), the loss must be apportioned pro rata to foreign-source categories with income for the tax year. If there is an overall foreign loss (i.e., foreign losses exceed foreign income in all categories), the overall foreign loss then reduces U.S.-source income. A U.S. loss for the tax year is apportioned pro rata to foreign-source income in each category, but only after the apportionment of any foreign losses to those income categories.

EXAMPLE 31

During 2008, Bloom, Inc., a U.S. corporation, incurred a $10,000 loss in its manufacturing activities and had $25,000 in passive income. The loss in the general basket is apportioned to the passive basket as follows.

Foreign Income Category	Income or Loss	Foreign-Source Taxable Income
General	($10,000)	$ –0–
Passive	25,000	15,000
Total	$15,000	$15,000

In 2009, Bloom earns $25,000 in manufacturing income and $24,000 in passive income. So the previously apportioned loss must be reallocated back to the affected basket as follows.

---

[32]§ 904(f)(3).

Foreign Income Category	Income or Loss	Previously Apportioned Loss	Foreign-Source Taxable Income
General	$25,000	($10,000)	$15,000
Passive	24,000	10,000	34,000
Total	$49,000		$49,000

For tax years beginning after 2006, there is a symmetric treatment for overall domestic losses (U.S.-source losses exceed all foreign-source income). In this case, future U.S.-source income is recharacterized as foreign source.

The Alternative Minimum Tax FTC. For purposes of the alternative minimum tax (AMT), the FTC limitation is calculated by using foreign-source alternative minimum taxable income (AMTI) in the numerator and total AMTI in the denominator of the formula and the tentative minimum tax rather than the regular tax.

$$\text{AMT FTC limitation} = \frac{\text{Foreign-source AMTI}}{\text{Total AMTI}} \times \text{Tentative minimum tax}$$

The taxpayer may elect to use regular foreign-source taxable income in the numerator if it does not exceed total AMTI. The AMT FTC limit must also be determined on a basket-by-basket basis.

Other Considerations. For a foreign levy to qualify for the FTC, it must be a tax, and its predominant character must be that of an income tax in the U.S. sense.[33] A levy is a tax if it is a compulsory payment, rather than a payment for a specific economic benefit such as the right to extract oil. A tax's predominant character is that of an income tax in the U.S. sense if it reaches realized net gain and is not a *soak-up* tax, that is, does not depend on being credited against the income tax of another country. A tax that is levied in lieu of an income tax is also creditable.[34]

EXAMPLE 32

JonesCo, a domestic corporation, generates $2 million of taxable income from operations in Larissa, a foreign country. Larissan law levies a tax on income generated in Larissa by foreign residents only in cases in which the country of residence (such as the United States) allows a tax credit for foreign taxes paid. JonesCo will not be allowed an FTC for taxes paid to Larissa, because the foreign tax is a soak-up tax. ■

For purposes of the FTC, foreign taxes are attributable to the year in which they are paid or accrued. Under § 905, taxpayers using the cash method of accounting for tax purposes may elect to take the FTC in the year in which the foreign taxes accrue. The election is binding on the taxpayer for the year in which it is made and for all subsequent years. Foreign taxes generally must be translated to U.S. dollars at the average exchange rate for the tax year to which the taxes relate.[35]

U.S. Taxation of Nonresident Aliens and Foreign Corporations

LO.6

Apply the U.S. tax provisions concerning nonresident alien individuals and foreign corporations.

Generally, only the U.S.-source income of nonresident alien individuals and foreign corporations is subject to U.S. taxation. This reflects the reach of the U.S. tax jurisdiction. The constraint, however, does not prevent the United States from also taxing the foreign-source income of nonresident alien individuals and foreign

---

[33]Reg. § 1.901–2.
[34]§ 903 and Reg. § 1.903–1.

[35]§ 986(a).

corporations when that income is effectively connected with the conduct of a U.S. trade or business.[36] Concept Summary 9–4 at the end of this section summarizes these tax rules.

Nonresident Alien Individuals

A **nonresident alien (NRA)** individual is an individual who is not a citizen or resident of the United States. For example, Queen Elizabeth is an NRA, because she is not a citizen or resident of the United States. Citizenship is determined under the immigration and naturalization laws of the United States.[37] Basically, the citizenship statutes are broken down into two categories: nationality at birth or through naturalization.

Residency. A person is a resident of the United States for income tax purposes if he or she meets either the green card test or the substantial presence test.[38] If either of these tests is met for the calendar year, the individual is deemed a U.S. resident for the year.

A foreign person issued a green card is considered a U.S. resident on the first day he or she is physically present in the United States after issuance. The green card is Immigration Form I–551. Newly issued cards are now rose colored, but the form is still referred to as the "green card." Status as a U.S. resident remains in effect until the green card has been revoked or the individual has abandoned lawful permanent resident status.

The substantial presence test is applied to an alien without a green card. It is a mathematical test involving physical presence in the United States. An individual who is physically present in the United States for at least 183 days during the calendar year is a U.S. resident for income tax purposes. This 183-day requirement can also be met over a three-year period that includes the two immediately preceding years and the current year, as long as the individual is present in the United States at least 31 days during the current year.[39] For this purpose, each day of the current calendar year is counted as a full day, each day of the first preceding year as one-third day, and each day of the second preceding year as one-sixth day.

| EXAMPLE 33 | Li, a foreign citizen, was present in the United States for 90 days in 2006, 180 days in 2007, and 110 days in 2008. For Federal income tax purposes, Li is a U.S. resident for 2008, because she was physically present for 185 days $[(90 \text{ days} \times \frac{1}{6}) + (180 \text{ days} \times \frac{1}{3}) + (110 \text{ days} \times 1)]$ during the three-year period. ∎ |

Over a 3 yr period [handwritten]

Under the substantial presence test, residence begins the first day the individual is physically present in the United States and ends the last day of physical presence for the calendar year (assuming the substantial presence test is not satisfied for the next calendar year). Nominal presence of 10 days or less can be ignored in determining whether the substantial presence test is met.

The substantial presence test allows for several exceptions. Commuters from Mexico and Canada who are employed in the United States but return home each day are excepted. Also excepted are individuals who are prevented from leaving the United States by medical conditions that arose while the individuals were in the United States. Some individuals are exempt from the substantial presence test, including foreign government-related individuals (e.g., diplomats), qualified teachers, trainees and students, and certain professional athletes.

Exceptions [handwritten]

---

[36]§§ 871, 881, and 882.
[37]Title 8, Aliens and Nationality, *United States Code.*

[38]§ 7701(b).
[39]§ 7701(b)(3)(A).

ETHICAL and EQUITABLE *Considerations*

SHOULD THERE BE SOME "HEART" IN TAX LAW?

In determining whether an alien is a U.S. resident for U.S. income tax purposes under the substantial presence test, days on which a medical condition prevents the person from leaving the United States are not counted as days present in the United States. The medical condition (e.g., illness or injury) must have arisen after the NRA arrived in the United States. In other words, it generally must be an unexpected illness or accident. No such exception is available, however, for a family member or other NRA who is significant to the person who becomes ill or injured. Thus, under this rule, the relative or other significant person may have to either risk being classified as a U.S. resident for the tax year or leave the ill person (or accident victim) alone in the United States. Does this limited exception ignore the human element in illness and recovery?

Nonresident Aliens Not Engaged in a U.S. Trade or Business. Certain U.S.-source income that is *not* effectively connected with the conduct of a U.S. trade or business is subject to a flat 30 percent tax. This income includes dividends, interest, rents, royalties, certain compensation, premiums, annuities, and other fixed, determinable, annual or periodic (FDAP) income. This tax generally is levied by a withholding mechanism that requires the payors of the income to withhold 30 percent of gross amounts.[40] This method eliminates the problems of assuring payment by nonresidents, determining allowable deductions, and, in most instances, the filing of tax returns by nonresidents. Interest received from certain portfolio debt investments, even though U.S.-sourced, is exempt from taxation. Interest earned on deposits with banking institutions is also exempt as long as it is not effectively connected with the conduct of a U.S. trade or business.

Capital gains *not* effectively connected with the conduct of a U.S. trade or business are exempt from tax, as long as the NRA individual was not present in the United States for 183 days or more during the taxable year. If an NRA has not established a taxable year, the calendar year is used. NRAs are not permitted to carry forward capital losses.[41]

Nonresident Aliens Engaged in a U.S. Trade or Business. Two important definitions determine the U.S. tax consequences to NRAs with U.S.-source income: "the conduct of a **U.S. trade or business**" and "**effectively connected income**." Specifically, in order for an NRA's noninvestment income to be subject to U.S. taxation, the NRA must be considered engaged in a U.S. trade or business and must earn income effectively connected with that business.

General criteria for determining if a U.S. trade or business exists include the location of production activities, management, distribution activities, and other business functions. Trading in commodities and securities ordinarily does not constitute a trade or business. Dealers, however, need to avoid maintaining a U.S. trading office and trading for their own accounts. Corporations (other than certain personal holding companies) that are not dealers can trade for their own accounts. There are no restrictions on individuals who are not dealers.

The Code does not explicitly define a U.S. trade or business, but case law has defined the concept as activities carried on in the United States that are regular, substantial, and continuous.[42] Once an NRA is considered engaged in a U.S. trade or business, all U.S.-source income other than FDAP and capital gain income is considered effectively connected to that trade or business and is therefore subject to U.S. taxation.

---

[40]§§ 871 and 1441.

[41]§ 871(a)(2).

[42]See, for example, *Higgins v. Comm.*, 41–1 USTC ¶9233, 25 AFTR 1160, 61 S.Ct. 475 (1941), and *Continental Trading, Inc. v. Comm.*, 59–1 USTC ¶9316, 3 AFTR2d 923, 265 F.2d 40 (CA–9, 1959).

EXAMPLE 34

Vito, an NRA, produces wine for export. During the current year, Vito earns $500,000 from exporting wine to unrelated wholesalers in the United States. The title to the wine passes to the U.S. wholesalers in New York. Vito has no offices or employees in the United States. The income from wine sales is U.S.-source income, but because Vito is not engaged in a U.S. trade or business, the income is not subject to taxation in the United States.

Assume that Vito begins operating a hot dog cart in New York City. This activity constitutes a U.S. trade or business. Consequently, all U.S.-source income other than FDAP or capital gain income will be taxed in the United States as income effectively connected with a U.S. trade or business. Thus, both the hot dog cart profits and the $500,000 in wine income will be taxed in the United States. ■

FDAP and capital gain income may be considered effectively connected income if the assets that generate this income are used in, or held for use in, the trade or business (the asset-use test) or if the activities of the trade or business are a material factor in the production of the income (the business-activities test).[43] As long as FDAP and capital gain income are not effectively connected with a U.S. trade or business, the tax treatment of these income items is the same whether NRAs are engaged in a U.S. trade or business or not.

EXAMPLE 35

Ingrid, an NRA, operates a U.S. business. During the year, cash funds accumulate. Ingrid invests these funds on a short-term basis so that they remain available to meet her business needs. Any income earned from these investments is effectively connected income, under the asset-use test. ■

Effectively connected income is taxed at the same rates that apply to U.S. citizens and residents, and deductions for expenses attributable to that income are allowed. NRAs with effectively connected income are also allowed a deduction for casualty and theft losses related to property located within the United States, a deduction for qualified charitable contributions, and one personal exemption. NRAs with income effectively connected with the conduct of a U.S. trade or business may also be subject to the alternative minimum tax.

Withholding Provisions. The 30 percent U.S. tax on FDAP income is generally administered by requiring the payor of the income to withhold the tax and remit it to the U.S. tax authorities. This assures the government of timely collection and relieves it of jurisdictional problems that could arise if it had to rely on recipients residing outside the United States to pay the tax. In recent years, U.S. payors withheld taxes of $3 billion annually from payments to foreign persons. Japanese recipients received the most U.S.-source income, with recipients from the United Kingdom ranked second. As explained earlier, income tax treaties with other countries provide for reduced withholding on certain types of FDAP income (see Exhibit 9–3 for some examples of withholding rates).

Foreign Corporations

Definition. The classification of an entity as a foreign corporation for U.S. tax purposes is an important consideration. Section 7701(a)(5) defines a foreign corporation as one that is not domestic. A domestic corporation is a corporation that is created or organized in the United States. Thus, though McDonald's is, in reality, a global corporation, it is considered a domestic corporation for U.S. tax purposes, solely because it was organized in the United States.

[43]§ 864(c).

| EXHIBIT 9–3 | Selected Tax Treaty Withholding Rates |

	Interest	Dividends in General	Dividends Paid by U.S. Subsidiary to a Foreign Parent Corporation
Australia	10%	15%	0%
Canada	10	15	5
Ireland	0	15	5
Japan	10	15	0
Mexico	15	15	0
Philippines	15	25	20

Source: IRS Publication 901, *U.S. Tax Treaties.*

Income Not Effectively Connected with a U.S. Trade or Business. U.S.-source FDAP income of foreign corporations is taxed by the United States in the same manner as that of NRA individuals—at a flat 30 percent rate. Generally, foreign corporations qualify for the same exemptions from U.S. taxation for investment income as do NRA individuals. The U.S.-source capital gains of foreign corporations are exempt from the Federal income tax if they are not effectively connected with the conduct of a U.S. trade or business.

Effectively Connected Income. Foreign corporations conducting a trade or business in the United States are subject to Federal income taxation on any U.S.-source income effectively connected with the trade or business. As with NRAs, any FDAP or capital gain income is not considered effectively connected unless the income meets the asset-use or business-activities test.[44] Foreign corporations are subject to the same tax rates on their effectively connected income as domestic corporations.

Branch Profits Tax. The objective of the **branch profits tax** is to afford equal tax treatment to income generated by a domestic corporation controlled by a foreign corporation and to income generated by other U.S. operations controlled by foreign corporations. If the foreign corporation operates through a U.S. subsidiary (a domestic corporation), the income of the subsidiary is taxable by the United States when earned and is also subject to a withholding tax when repatriated (returned as dividends to the foreign parent). Before the branch profits tax was enacted, a foreign corporation with a branch in the United States paid only the initial tax on its U.S. earnings; remittances were not taxed.

In addition to the income tax imposed under § 882 on effectively connected income of a foreign corporation, a tax equal to 30 percent of the **dividend equivalent amount (DEA)** for the taxable year is imposed on any foreign corporation with effectively connected income.[45] The DEA is the foreign corporation's effectively connected earnings for the taxable year, adjusted for increases and decreases in the corporation's U.S. net equity (investment in the U.S. operations). The DEA is limited to current E & P and post-1986 accumulated E & P that is effectively connected, or treated as effectively connected, with the conduct of a U.S. trade or business. U.S. net equity is the sum of money and the aggregate adjusted basis of assets and liabilities directly connected to U.S. operations that generate effectively connected income.

---

[44]§ 864(c).   [45]§ 884.

EXAMPLE 36

Robin, Inc., a foreign corporation, has a U.S. branch operation with the following tax results and other information for the year.

Pretax earnings effectively connected with a U.S. trade or business	$2,000,000
U.S. corporate tax (at 34%)	680,000
Remittance to home office	1,000,000
Increase in U.S. net equity	320,000

Robin's DEA and branch profits tax are computed as follows.

E & P effectively connected with a U.S. trade or business ($2,000,000 − $680,000)	$1,320,000
Less: Increase in U.S. net equity	(320,000)
Dividend equivalent amount	$1,000,000
Branch profits tax rate	× 30%
Branch profits tax	$ 300,000

The 30 percent rate of the branch profits tax may be reduced or eliminated by a treaty provision. If a foreign corporation is subject to the branch profits tax, no other U.S. tax is levied on the dividend actually paid by the corporation during the taxable year.

The Foreign Investment in Real Property Tax Act

Prior to 1980, NRAs and foreign corporations could avoid U.S. taxation on gains from the sale of U.S. real estate if the gains were treated as capital gains and were not effectively connected with the conduct of a U.S. trade or business. In the mid-1970s, midwestern farmers pressured Congress to eliminate what they saw as a tax advantage that would allow nonresidents to bid up the price of farmland. This and other concerns about foreign ownership of U.S. real estate led to the enactment of the Foreign Investment in Real Property Tax Act (FIRPTA) of 1980.

Under **FIRPTA**, gains and losses realized by NRAs and foreign corporations from the sale or other disposition of U.S. real property interests are treated as effectively connected with the conduct of a U.S. trade or business even when those individuals or corporations are not actually so engaged. NRA individuals must pay a tax equal to the lesser of two amounts: (1) 26 (or 28) percent of their alternative minimum taxable income or (2) regular U.S. rates on the net U.S. real property gain for the taxable year.[46] For purposes of this provision, losses are taken into account only to the extent they are deductible as business losses, losses on transactions entered into for profit, or losses from casualties and thefts.

U.S. Real Property Interest (USRPI). Any direct interest in real property situated in the United States and any interest in a domestic corporation (other than solely as a creditor) are U.S. real property interests (USRPIs). This definition applies unless the taxpayer can establish that a domestic corporation was not a U.S. real property holding corporation (USRPHC) during the shorter of two periods: (1) the period during which the taxpayer held an interest in the corporation or (2) the five-year period ending on the date on which the interest was disposed of (the base period). A domestic corporation is not a USRPHC if it holds no USRPIs on the date of disposition of its stock and if any USRPIs held by the corporation during the base period were disposed of in a transaction in which gain, if any, was fully recognized.

---

[46]§ 897.

EXAMPLE 37

From January 1, 2003, through January 1, 2008, Francis (a foreign investor) held shares in Door, Inc., a U.S. corporation. During this period, Door held two parcels of U.S. real estate and stock of Sash, Inc., another U.S. corporation. Sash also owned U.S. real estate. The two parcels of real estate held directly by Door were disposed of on December 15, 2004, in a nontaxable transaction. Sash disposed of its U.S. real estate in a taxable transaction on January 1, 2008.

An interest in Door is treated as a USRPI because Door did not recognize gain on the December 15, 2004 disposition of the USRPIs. If Door's ownership of U.S. real estate had been limited to its indirect ownership through Sash, an interest in Door would not have constituted a USRPI as of January 2, 2008. This result would occur because Sash disposed of its USRPIs in a taxable transaction in which gain was fully recognized. ∎

A USRPHC is any corporation (whether foreign or domestic) where the fair market value of the corporation's USRPIs equals or exceeds 50 percent of the aggregate of fair market value of certain specified assets. These assets are the corporation's USRPIs, its interests in real property located outside the United States, and any other of its assets that are used or held for use in a trade or business. Stock regularly traded on an established securities market is not treated as a USRPI if a person holds no more than 5 percent of the stock.

Gain on a disposition of stock of a foreign real property holding corporation is not subject to tax under FIRPTA. However, gain on a disposition of a USRPI by such a foreign corporation is subject to FIRPTA.

Withholding Provisions.

The FIRPTA withholding provisions require any purchaser or agent acquiring a USRPI from a foreign person to withhold 10 percent of the amount realized on the disposition.[47] A domestic partnership, trust, or estate with a foreign partner, foreign grantor treated as owner, or foreign beneficiary generally must withhold 35 percent of the gain allocable to that person on a disposition of a USRPI. Foreign corporations are also subject to withholding provisions on certain distributions. Without this withholding, NRAs could sell USRPIs, receiving the sales proceeds outside the United States, and jurisdictional issues could make it difficult for the U.S. tax authorities to collect any U.S. tax that might be due on gains. Certain exceptions to FIRPTA withholding are allowed.

Failure to withhold can subject the purchaser or the purchaser's agent to interest on any unpaid amount.[48] A civil penalty of 100 percent of the amount required to be withheld and a criminal penalty of up to $10,000 or five years in prison can be imposed for willful failure to withhold.[49]

Expatriation to Avoid U.S. Taxation

Section 877 provides for U.S. taxation of U.S.-source income earned by individuals who relinquished their U.S. citizenship within 10 years of deriving that income if they gave up their citizenship to avoid U.S. taxation. Furthermore, NRAs who lost U.S. citizenship within a 10-year period immediately preceding the close of the tax year must pay taxes on their U.S.-source income as though they were still U.S. citizens. This provision applies only if the expatriation had as one of its principal purposes the avoidance of U.S. taxes. Individuals are presumed to have a tax avoidance purpose if they meet either of the following criteria.[50]

- Average annual net income tax for the five taxable years ending before the date of loss of U.S. citizenship is more than $139,000 (in 2008).
- Net worth as of that date is at least $2 million.

These provisions also apply to "long-term lawful permanent residents" who cease to be taxed as U.S. residents. A long-term permanent resident is an individual (other than a citizen of the United States) who is a lawful permanent resident of

[47]§ 1445.
[48]§§ 6601, 6621, and 6651.
[49]§§ 6672 and 7202.
[50]§ 877(a)(2). The dollar amounts are adjusted for inflation.

CONCEPT SUMMARY 9–4

U.S. Taxation of NRAs and Foreign Corporations (FCs)

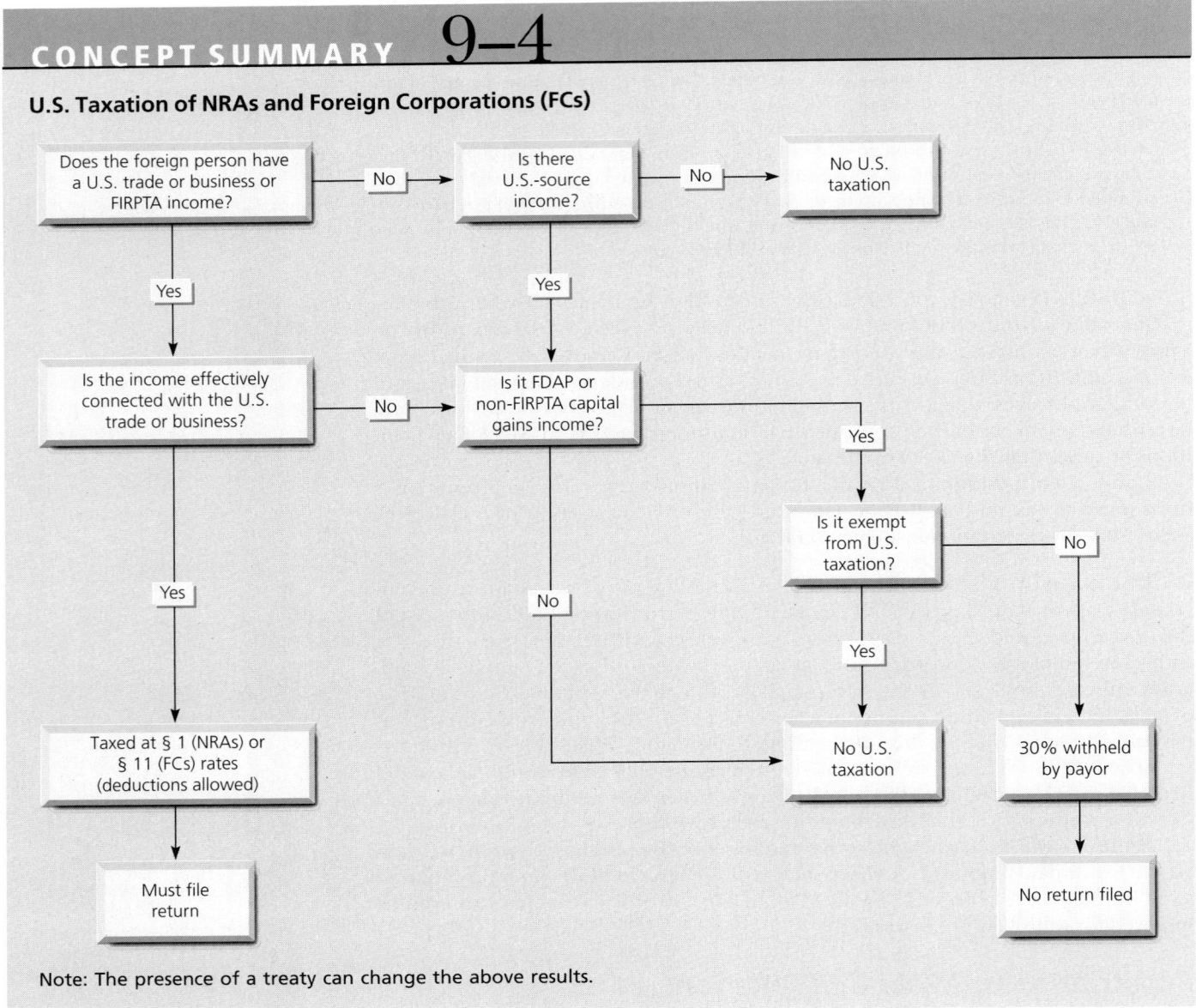

Note: The presence of a treaty can change the above results.

the United States in at least 8 taxable years during the 15-year period ending with the taxable year in which the individual either ceases to be a lawful permanent resident of the United States or begins to be treated as a resident of another country under an income tax treaty between the United States and the other country (and does not waive the benefits of the treaty to residents of that country). An exception applies to certain individuals with dual citizenship.

The United States continues to treat individuals as U.S. citizens or residents until the taxpayers provide required information and an expatriation notice. Expatriates who are subject to the 10-year special tax regime outlined above must file a § 6039G statement annually. Additionally, if an expatriate individual is physically present in the United States for more than 30 days during a calendar year during the 10-year postexpatriation period, the individual is taxed as a U.S. citizen or resident.[51] These expatriation rules, taken as a whole, make it difficult to give up U.S. citizenship or residency simply to avoid U.S. taxation.

---

[51]§ 877(g)(1).

FILING DEADLINES WHEN YOU'RE OVERSEAS

What if you are situated outside the United States when you file a tax return? Working with a non-U.S. postal service can be challenging even on a good day. The established rule still seems to be that the date of the non-U.S. postmark determines whether the return is filed in a timely manner or whether a failure to file penalty will be assessed (Rev.Rul. 80–218).

The IRS seems to be having some trouble digesting this rule, though. In *Pekar*, 113 TC 158, where the non-U.S. postmark indicated that the return had been mailed before its due date, the IRS seemed to be taking a date-received position with the Tax Court. But the Service admitted its mistake in ITA 2000121085, where the reliance-on-postmark test is applied as expected.

No ruling to date has specifically addressed the application of this rule to a private express delivery service like UPS, but neither the Code nor rulings restrict the when-delivered-to-the-carrier rule to domestic shipments, either. Thus, if a U.S. taxpayer living overseas uses a private delivery service, some form of date stamping is a good idea.

Reporting Requirements

The U.S. tax provisions in the international area include numerous reporting requirements. Furthermore, civil and criminal penalties for noncompliance can apply.[52]

A domestic corporation that is 25 percent or more foreign owned must file an information return and maintain certain records where they will be accessible to the IRS.[53] Additionally, any foreign corporation carrying on a trade or business in the United States must file an information return and maintain records in a similar manner.[54]

U.S. shareholders of a CFC must file a Form 5471. The U.S. partners of a controlled foreign partnership must file an information return.[55] A foreign partnership that has gross income that is either U.S.-source or effectively connected with a U.S. trade or business must file a partnership return.[56] Changes in ownership of interests in foreign partnerships (acquisitions or dispositions) must also be reported if a 10 percent or greater interest is involved.[57]

Asset transfers to foreign corporations or partnerships under certain tax-deferred transactions require information returns at the time of the transfer.[58] U.S. taxpayers that control foreign corporations or partnerships must also file annual information returns related to these entities.[59] Creation of, or a transfer to, a foreign trust by a U.S. person necessitates the filing of a Form 3520.[60]

TAX PLANNING *Considerations*

Over time, legislation has tended to reduce the ability to plan transactions and operations in a manner that minimizes tax liability. However, taxpayers who are not limited by the constraints of a particular transaction or operation can use the following suggestions to plan for maximum tax benefits.

The Foreign Tax Credit Limitation and Sourcing Provisions

The FTC limitation is partially based on the amount of foreign-source taxable income in the numerator of the limitation ratio. Consequently, the sourcing of income is

---

[52]See Chapter 16.
[53]§ 6038A.
[54]§ 6038C.
[55]§ 6038.
[56]§ 6031(e).

[57]§ 6046A.
[58]§ 6038B.
[59]§ 6038.
[60]§ 6048.

TAX *in the News*   SO LONG, IT'S BEEN NICE KNOWING YOU

Did you ever wonder who gives up U.S. citizenship? It is easy to find out. Section 877 requires that U.S. citizens and long-term permanent residents inform the IRS of their expatriation on Form 8854, Initial and Annual Expatriation Information Statement, in the year of expatriation and certain years thereafter. Expatriating individuals must also give notice of an expatriating act or termination of residency to the Department of State or the Department of Homeland Security. The government publishes the names of these individuals in the *Federal Register* each quarter. For example, more than 100 people abandoned U.S. citizenship in the second quarter of 2007 alone.

Source: Federal Register, *Vol. 72, No. 90, pp. 26687–26688 (May 10, 2007).*

---

extremely important. Income that is taxed by a foreign tax jurisdiction benefits from the FTC only to the extent that it is classified as foreign-source income under U.S. tax law. Thus, elements that affect the sourcing of income, such as the place of title passage, should be considered carefully before a transaction is undertaken.

It may be possible for a U.S. corporation to alleviate the problem of excess foreign taxes by using the following techniques.

- Generate "same basket" foreign-source income that is subject to a tax rate lower than the U.S. tax rate.
- Reduce highly taxed foreign-source income in favor of foreign-source income that is taxed at a lower rate by shifting operations or intangibles.
- Time the repatriation of foreign-source earnings to coincide with excess limitation years.
- Deduct foreign taxes for years when the deduction benefit would exceed the FTC benefit.

EXAMPLE 38

Della, Inc., a U.S. corporation, has U.S.-source taxable income of $200,000, total taxable income of $300,000, and a U.S. tax liability (before the FTC) of $105,000. Della receives foreign-source taxable income, pays foreign income taxes, and has an FTC as shown.

Basket	Amount	Foreign Taxes	FTC Limitation	Allowed FTC
Passive	$ 80,000	$ 8,000	$28,000	$ 8,000
General	20,000	8,000	7,000	7,000
	$100,000	$16,000		$15,000

If Della can shift $10,000 of passive income into the general basket, the FTC is increased by $1,000. The FTC limitation for the general basket increases to $10,500 [($30,000/$300,000) × $105,000]. This allows all $8,000 of foreign taxes related to the general basket to be credited in the current year. The allowed FTC for the passive basket remains unchanged at $8,000. ■

The Foreign Corporation as a Tax Shelter

An NRA who is able to hold U.S. investments through a foreign corporation can accomplish much in the way of avoiding U.S. taxation. Capital gains (other than dispositions of U.S. real property interests) are not subject to U.S. taxation. This assumes that they are not effectively connected with a U.S. trade or business. The NRA can dispose of the stock of a foreign corporation that holds U.S. real property and not be subject to taxation under § 897 (FIRPTA). Furthermore, the stock of a foreign corporation is not included in the U.S. gross estate of a deceased NRA, even if all the assets of the foreign corporation are located in the United States.

Caution is advised when the foreign corporation may generate income effectively connected with the conduct of a U.S. trade or business. The income may be taxed at a higher rate than if the NRA individually generated the income. The tradeoff between a higher U.S. tax on this income and protection from the U.S. estate tax and § 897 must be weighed.

Planning under Subpart F

The *de minimis* rule allows a CFC to avoid the classification of income as FBC income or insurance income and prevents the U.S. shareholder from having to include it in gross income as a constructive dividend. Thus, a CFC with total FBC income and insurance income in an amount close to the 5 percent or $1 million level should monitor income realization to assure that the *de minimis* rule applies for the tax year. At least as important is avoiding the classification of all the gross income of the CFC as FBC income or insurance income. This happens when the sum of the FBC income and gross insurance income for the taxable year exceeds 70 percent of total gross income.

Careful timing of investment in U.S. property can reduce the potential for constructive dividend income to U.S. shareholders. The gross income of U.S. shareholders attributable to investment in U.S. property is limited to the E & P of the CFC.[61] E & P that is attributable to amounts that have been included in gross income as Subpart F income in either the current year or a prior tax year is not taxed again when invested in U.S. property.

Using the Check-the-Box Regulations

The check-the-box Regulations under § 7701 provide a great deal of flexibility for U.S.-based multinational corporations. Corporations are allowed to organize their branches and subsidiaries around the world in ways that optimize both local country and U.S. taxation. For example, a U.S. corporation may choose to treat its subsidiary in the United Kingdom as a partnership or unincorporated branch for U.S. tax purposes (thus taking advantage of loss flow-throughs) and a corporation under United Kingdom law (where certain tax and liability benefits may exist). The flurry of multinational restructurings since the issuance of the check-the-box Regulations has led to some cries of foul by U.S. taxing authorities who claim that these provisions are being used in inappropriate ways. The Treasury Department and the IRS are currently exploring ways to curb some of these perceived abuses.

Transferring Intangible Assets Offshore

In many industries, a company's intangible assets, such as licenses and patents, produce a relatively large share of total income. For example, the license to use a software program is much more valuable than the actual disk the customer purchases; thus, a large part of the profit from the sale of software accrues to the license holder.

Unlike manufacturing plants, intangible assets can be easily transferred to related entities outside the United States. Congress recognized this potential, and § 367 requires gain to be recognized if intangibles are transferred outside the United States. To avoid this § 367 "toll charge," companies should consider creating their intangibles offshore so that no subsequent transfer is required. Companies may choose to perform their R&D activities within subsidiaries located in tax haven countries in order to create and keep their valuable intangibles in low-tax jurisdictions.

Transfer Pricing

U.S. multinational companies earn income across many different jurisdictions and operate through several different types of entities (e.g., subsidiary corporations, joint ventures, partnerships). With proper planning and documentation, a U.S.

---

[61]§§ 959(a)(1) and (2).

ETHICAL and EQUITABLE *Considerations*

WHEN CAN 1 + 1 = 3?

Pharma, Inc., a U.S. pharmaceutical company, operates in the United States and in Ireland through a wholly owned Irish subsidiary corporation. Pharma manufactures certain aspects of a drug in the United States at a cost of $50 million and sells this product to its Irish subsidiary for $70 million, producing a $20 million profit in the United States. The Irish subsidiary completes the manufacturing of the drug at a cost of $10 million and sells the final product to unrelated customers in Europe for $85 million, producing a $5 million profit in Ireland [$85 million sales price − $70 million cost of goods sold (purchased inventory) − $10 million additional processing costs]. In the aggregate, Pharma and its Irish subsidiary have produced a product at a cost of $60 million and sold it for $85 million, resulting in $25 million in total profits.

What if the IRS decides that the transfer price of $70 million was too low and should have been $74 million? This would indicate that $24 million of the profit should have been in the United States and $1 million in Ireland. Should the tax authorities in Ireland automatically make the transfer pricing adjustment on their side (i.e., reduce the Irish subsidiary's income to $1 million from $5 million)? What if the IRS and the Irish tax authorities disagree and Pharma and its subsidiary end up paying tax on $29 million in profits ($24 million in the United States and $5 million in Ireland) even though only $25 million of economic profits actually exist? Is this fair to the taxpayer? What recourse should Pharma have when it is caught between two governments that disagree?

corporation can organize its intercompany payments for goods and services, interest on debt, and royalties for use of intangible property in such a way as to minimize its worldwide tax burden. For example, a U.S. multinational may choose to borrow in high-tax jurisdictions (where the interest deduction will be more valuable) and earn royalty income in low-tax jurisdictions (where the income escapes heavy taxation).

Such decisions can be made within the legal framework of the tax laws of the United States and other countries. In the United States, § 482 provides the guidelines that must be met to justify and document appropriate transfer pricing. In general, these guidelines require an entity to demonstrate that it deserved to earn its profits based on the functions it performs, the assets it owns, or the risks it takes.

KEY TERMS

Branch profits tax, 9–37	Foreign tax credit (FTC), 9–27	Subpart F, 9–23
CFC (controlled foreign corporation), 9–22	Functional currency, 9–13	Tax haven, 9–19
Dividend equivalent amount (DEA), 9–37	Inbound taxation, 9–3	Tax treaties, 9–4
Effectively connected income, 9–35	Nonresident alien (NRA), 9–34	Transfer pricing, 9–10
	Outbound taxation, 9–3	Treaty shopping, 9–19
FIRPTA, 9–38	Qualified business unit (QBU), 9–13	U.S. shareholder, 9–22
		U.S. trade or business, 9–35

PROBLEM MATERIALS

DISCUSSION QUESTIONS

1. Explain why an income tax treaty can be very favorable to a U.S. person who earns investment income from Germany.

2. Will dividends paid by a foreign corporation be treated as foreign-source income in all cases? Explain.

3. Write a memo outlining the issues that arise when attempting to source income that is earned from Internet-based activities.

Issue ID

Communications

4. Generally, U.S. taxpayers with foreign operations desire to increase foreign-source income and reduce deductions against that foreign-source income in order to increase their FTC limitations. How does § 482 enable the IRS to prevent taxpayers from manipulating the source of income and allocation of deductions? Explain.

5. Explain how a Netherlands branch of a U.S. corporation may use the U.S. dollar as its functional currency.

6. What is a qualified business unit (QBU)? How many QBUs may a single taxpayer have?

7. Describe why the sale of inventory on account in a price denominated in a taxpayer's nonfunctional currency might produce a § 988 currency gain or loss.

8. What are the important concepts to be considered when U.S. assets outside the United States are transferred to foreign persons?

9. Write a memo to a U.S. client explaining why stock of a foreign corporation that it holds may be considered a tax shelter for U.S. tax purposes.

Communications

10. Five unrelated U.S. persons are considering forming a foreign corporation in which they will own equal interests. Will they have to be concerned with the CFC provisions?

Decision Making

11. Joanna owns 5% of Axel, a foreign corporation. Joanna's son, Fred, is considering acquiring 15% of Axel from an NRA. The remainder of Axel is owned 27% by unrelated U.S. persons and 53% by unrelated NRAs. Currently, Fred operates (as a sole proprietorship) a manufacturing business that sells goods to Axel for resale outside the United States and outside Axel's country of residence. Joanna is not concerned about the concentration of investment because she expects to sell her stock in Axel in three years at a significant capital gain. Are there tax issues that Joanna and Fred, both U.S. citizens, need to address?

Issue ID

12. Molly, Inc., a domestic corporation, owns 15% of PJ, Inc., and 12% of Emma, Inc., both foreign corporations. Molly is paid gross dividends of $35,000 and $18,000 from PJ and Emma, respectively. PJ withheld and paid more than $10,500 in foreign taxes on the $35,000 dividend. PJ's country of residence levies a 20% tax on dividends paid to nonresident corporations. However, the tax rate is increased to 30% if the recipient is a resident of a country that provides an FTC. Taxes of $3,600 are withheld on the dividend from Emma. What tax issues must be considered in determining the availability and amount of the FTC allowed to Molly, Inc.?

Issue ID

13. Green, Inc., received a $1,000 dividend from Red, Ltd., a foreign corporation. Red paid $400 in foreign taxes related to this $1,000 of distributed earnings. Explain why Green's gross income related to this dividend is $1,400.

14. Carlos, a nonresident alien, is interested in acquiring U.S. real property as an investment. He knows that he will be taxed in the United States on any gains from the disposition of such property if he holds it directly. Will the result be any different if he acquires the real property within a U.S. corporation?

15. Old Gear, Inc., a foreign corporation, sells vacuum tubes in several countries, including the United States. In fact, currently 18% of Old Gear's sales income is sourced in the United States (through branches in New York and Miami). Old Gear is considering opening additional branches in San Francisco and Houston in order to increase U.S. sales. What tax issues must Old Gear consider before making this move?

Issue ID

16. Write a short memo on the difference between "inbound" and "outbound" activities in the context of U.S. taxation of international income.

Communications

17. If a U.S. taxpayer is subject to U.S. income tax on profits earned outside the United States and such profits are also subject to income tax in the foreign jurisdiction, how does the U.S. taxpayer escape double taxation?

PROBLEMS

18. Madison, a U.S. resident, received the following income items for the current tax year. Identify the source of each income item as either U.S. or foreign.
    a. $2,400 dividend from U.S. Power Company, a U.S. corporation that operates solely in the eastern United States.
    b. $5,200 dividend from Skateworld Corporation, a U.S. corporation that had total gross income of $4 million from the active conduct of a foreign trade or business for the immediately preceding three tax years. Skateworld's total gross income for the same period was $5 million.
    c. $1,500 dividend from International Consolidated, Inc., a foreign corporation that had gross income of $3.4 million effectively connected with the conduct of a U.S. trade or business for the immediately preceding three tax years. International's total gross income for the same period was $6 million.
    d. $600 interest from a savings account at a Florida bank.
    e. $5,000 interest on Warren Corporation bonds. Warren is a U.S. corporation that derived $6 million of its gross income for the immediately preceding three tax years from operation of an active foreign business. Warren's total gross income for this same period was $7.2 million.

Communications

19. Rita, an NRA, is a professional golfer. She played in seven tournaments in the United States in the current year and earned $50,000 in prizes from these tournaments. She deposited the winnings in a bank account she opened in Mexico City after her first tournament win. Rita played a total of 30 tournaments for the year and earned $200,000 in total prize money. She spent 40 days in the United States, 60 days in England, 20 days in Scotland, and the rest of the time in South America. Write a letter to Rita explaining how much U.S.-source income she will generate, if any, from her participation in these tournaments and whether any of her winnings are subject to U.S. taxation. Rita's address is AV Rio Branco, 149-4#, Rio de Janeiro, RJ 22421, Brazil.

20. Determine whether the source of income for the following sales is U.S. or foreign.
    a. Kwaku, an NRA, sells stock in Home Depot, a domestic corporation, through a broker in New York.
    b. Chris sells stock in IBM, a domestic corporation, to his brother, Rich. Both Chris and Rich are NRAs, and the sale takes place outside the United States.
    c. Crows, Inc., sells inventory produced in the United States to customers in Europe. Title passes in the international waters of the Atlantic Ocean. *50% is U.S.*
    d. Jordan, Inc., a domestic corporation, manufactures equipment in Taiwan and sells the equipment to customers in the United States. *50%*

21. Determine whether the source of income in each of the following situations is U.S. or foreign.
    a. Development, Inc., a U.S. corporation, earns $150,000 in royalty income from Far East, Ltd., a foreign corporation, for the use of several patented processes in Far East's manufacturing business, located in Singapore.
    b. Dora, an NRA, is an employee of a foreign corporation. During the tax year, she spends 50 days in the United States purchasing cloth for her employer, a clothing manufacturer. Her yearly salary is $80,000 (translated to U.S. dollars). She spends a total of 250 days working during the year. Her employer has no other business contacts with the United States.
    c. An NRA sells an apartment building to a U.S. resident. The building is located in Chicago. The closing takes place in the NRA's country of residence.
    d. A domestic corporation sells depreciable personal property that it has been using in its foreign branch operations. The property sells for $180,000, has a tax basis of $75,000, and has been depreciated for tax purposes to the extent of $77,000. The property is located in a foreign country but is sold to another domestic corporation. The sales transaction takes place in the United States.

Decision Making

22. Energy, Inc., produces inventory in its foreign manufacturing plants for sale in the United States. Its foreign manufacturing assets have a tax book value of $3 million and a

fair market value of $12 million. Its assets related to the sales activity have a tax book value of $200,000 and a fair market value of $50,000. Energy's interest expense totaled $200,000 for the current year.

a. What amount of interest expense is allocated and apportioned to foreign-source income using the tax book value method? What amount of Energy's interest expense is allocated and apportioned to foreign-source income using the fair market method?

b. If Energy wishes to maximize its FTC, which method should it use?

23. Weight, Inc., a domestic corporation, purchases weight-lifting equipment for resale from HiDisu, a Japanese corporation, for 75 million yen. On the date of purchase, 150 yen is equal to $1 U.S. (¥150:$1). The purchase is made on December 15, 2008, with payment due in 60 days. Weight is a calendar year taxpayer. On December 31, 2008, the foreign exchange rate is ¥140:$1. What amount of foreign currency gain or loss, if any, must Weight recognize for 2008 as a result of this transaction?

24. Table, Inc., a U.S. corporation, operates a manufacturing branch in Mexico and a sales branch in Canada. The Mexican branch uses the peso for all its activities, and the Canadian branch uses the Canadian dollar for all its activities. Provide an explanation to Table's tax director regarding the number of foreign qualified business units the company will have from these activities.

25. Chair, Inc., a U.S. corporation, operates a sales branch in Ireland. Although the operations are located in Ireland, where the euro is the local currency, all the branch's sales are to customers in the United Kingdom. The revenue is collected in British pounds, and the sales branch's employees are paid in British pounds. What functional currency should Chair use for its Irish sales branch?

26. Harold is a citizen and resident of the United States. He pays all of his living expenses in U.S. dollars. He operates an unincorporated trade or business buying and selling rare books over the Internet to Canadian customers. All income and expenses of the rare book business are in Canadian dollars. Explain to Harold the number of qualified business units he has and the related functional currency of the QBUs.

27. Carroll Manufacturing, Inc., a calendar year domestic corporation, operates a branch in Ireland. In the current year, the branch generated 750,000 euros in net profit. On December 31 of the current year, one euro equaled 83 cents. The average exchange rate for the current year between the euro and the dollar was 91 cents. Write a memo to the controller of Carroll explaining (1) how and when the Irish profits will be taxed to Carroll in the United States and (2) under what conditions a foreign currency gain or loss will be recognized.

Issue ID

Communications

28. Green, Inc., a foreign corporation, pays a dividend to its shareholders on November 30. Red, Inc., a U.S. corporation and 9% shareholder in Green, receives a dividend of 5,000K (a foreign currency). Pertinent exchange rates are as follows.

November 30	.9K:$1
Average for year	.7K:$1
December 31	2K:$1

What is the dollar amount of the dividend received by Red, Inc., and does Red have a foreign exchange gain or loss on receipt of the dividend?

29. Explain why the § 367 rules may currently tax corporate transactions that otherwise would be tax deferred.

30. WorldCo, a domestic corporation, is planning to incorporate a branch that it has been operating in a foreign country. WorldCo's branch has a large amount of inventory. Discuss the tax results of transferring this inventory to a newly formed foreign corporation.

31. Beach, Inc., a domestic corporation, operates a branch in Mexico. Over the last 10 years, this branch has generated $50 million in losses. For the last 3 years, however, the branch has been profitable and has earned enough income to entirely offset the prior losses. Most of the assets are fully depreciated, and a net gain would be recognized if

Issue ID

Communications

the assets were sold. The CFO believes that Beach should incorporate the branch now so that this potential gain can be transferred to a foreign corporation, thereby avoiding U.S. tax and, as an added benefit, avoiding U.S. taxes on future income. Draft an outline of a memo to the CFO addressing the tax issues involved in the proposed transaction.

32. McDonald Enterprises, a domestic corporation, owns 100% of OK, Ltd., an Irish corporation. OK's gross income for the year is $10 million. Determine OK's Subpart F income (before any expenses) from the following transactions.
    a.   OK received $600,000 from sales of products purchased from McDonald and sold to customers outside Ireland.
    b.   OK received $1 million from sales of products purchased from McDonald and sold to customers in Ireland.
    c.   OK received $400,000 from sales of products purchased from unrelated suppliers and sold to customers in Germany.
    d.   OK purchased raw materials from McDonald, used these materials to manufacture finished goods, and sold these goods to customers in Italy. OK earned $200,000 from these sales.
    e.   OK received $120,000 for the performance of warranty services on behalf of McDonald. These services were performed in Japan for customers located in Japan.
    f.   OK received $60,000 in dividend income from investments in Canada and Mexico.

33. Round, Inc., a U.S. corporation, owns 80% of the only class of stock of Square, Inc., a CFC. Square is a CFC until June 1 of the current tax year. Round has held the stock since Square was organized and continues to hold it for the entire year. Round and Square are both calendar year taxpayers. Square's Subpart F income for the tax year is $1.3 million, current E & P is $2.9 million, and no distributions have been made for the tax year. What amount, if any, must Round include in gross income under Subpart F for the tax year?

34. Mary Beth Alessio, a U.S. citizen, has placed all her investments in a Cayman Island corporation owned 1% by Mary Beth and 99% by a foreign individual. She pays no income tax in the Cayman Islands on this income. The foreign corporation earns only interest and dividends. Outline a letter informing Mary Beth of the U.S. tax consequences of her foreign investments. Her address is 941 Windom Lane, Hagerstown, MD 21740.

35. Weather, Inc., a domestic corporation, operates in both Mexico and the United States. This year, the business generated taxable income of $600,000 from foreign sources and $800,000 from U.S. sources. All of Weather's foreign-source income is in the general limitation basket. Weather's total taxable income is $1.4 million. Weather pays Mexican taxes of $228,000. What is Weather's FTC for the tax year? Assume a 34% U.S. income tax rate.

36. Rubarb, Inc., a U.S. corporation, earned $500,000 in total taxable income including $80,000 in foreign-source taxable income from its German branch's manufacturing operations and $30,000 in foreign-source taxable income from its Swiss branch's engineering services operations. Rubarb paid $32,000 in German income taxes and $1,500 in Swiss income taxes. Compute Rubarb's U.S. tax liability after any available foreign tax credits. Assume the U.S. tax rate is 34%.

37. Pie, Inc., a U.S. corporation, earned $400,000 in total taxable income, including $50,000 in foreign-source taxable income from its branch manufacturing operations in Brazil and $20,000 in foreign-source income from interest earned on bonds issued by Dutch corporations. Pie paid $25,000 in Brazilian income taxes and $2,000 in Dutch income taxes. Compute Pie's U.S. tax liability after any available foreign tax credits. Assume the U.S. tax rate is 34%.

38. Luck, Inc., a U.S. corporation, earned $800,000 in total taxable income for the current year. This total includes $950,000 in U.S.-source income, $50,000 in foreign-source income in the passive basket, and a $200,000 loss in the general limitation basket. Luck paid $5,000 in foreign income taxes related to the passive basket and incurred no taxes

related to the general limitation basket. What is Luck's allowed foreign tax credit for the current year?

39. Elmwood, Inc., a domestic corporation, owns 15% of Correy, Ltd., a Hong Kong corporation. The remaining 85% of Correy is owned by Fortune Enterprises, a Canadian corporation. At the end of the current year, Correy has $400,000 in post-1986 undistributed E & P and $200,000 in foreign taxes related to this E & P. On the last day of the year, Correy pays a $30,000 dividend to Elmwood. Elmwood's taxable income before inclusion of the dividend is $200,000. What is Elmwood's tax liability after consideration of the dividend and any allowed FTC, assuming a 34% U.S. tax rate?

40. Your client Chips, Inc., is engaged in the cookie production business, with production plants in Florida and Singapore. The U.S. plant has always produced profits, but the Singapore operation has generated $80,000 in losses since inception. This year, the Singapore operation began producing net profits. Draft a brief memo to Sally, the CFO of Chips, explaining why a portion of the current-year foreign-source income must be recharacterized as U.S.-source for FTC limitation purposes.

Communications

41. Brothers, Inc., a U.S. corporation, earns current foreign-source income classified in two different FTC income baskets. It earns $50,000 in passive foreign-source income and suffers a net loss of $40,000 in the general limitation basket. What is the numerator of the FTC limitation formula for the passive basket in the current year? Explain.

42. Hillman, Inc., a U.S. corporation owns 100% of NewGrass, Ltd., a foreign corporation. NewGrass earns only general limitation income. During the current year, NewGrass paid Hillman a $10,000 dividend. The § 902 credit associated with this dividend is $4,000. The foreign jurisdiction requires a withholding tax of 20%, so Hillman received only $8,000 in cash as a result of the dividend. What is Hillman's total U.S. gross income reported as a result of the $8,000 cash dividend?

43. For which of the following foreign income inclusions is a U.S. corporation potentially allowed an indirect FTC under § 902?
    a. Interest income from a 5%-owned foreign corporation.
    b. Interest income from a 60%-owned foreign corporation.
    c. Dividend income from a 5%-owned foreign corporation.
    d. Dividend income from a 60%-owned foreign corporation.

44. Night, Inc., a domestic corporation, earned $300,000 from foreign manufacturing activities on which it paid $90,000 of foreign income taxes. Night's foreign sales income is taxed at a 50% foreign tax rate. What amount of foreign sales income can Night earn without generating any excess FTCs for the current year? Assume a 34% U.S. tax rate.

Decision Making

45. Partin, Inc., a foreign subsidiary of Jones, Inc., a U.S. corporation, has pretax income of 200,000 euros for 2008. Partin accrues 50,000 euros in foreign taxes on this income. The average exchange rate for the tax year to which the taxes relate is .95 euro:$1. None of the income is Subpart F income. If the net earnings of 150,000 euros are distributed when the exchange rate is 1.05 euro:$1, what are the deemed-paid taxes available to Jones? Assume that 2008 is Partin's first year of operation.

46. Collins, Inc., a domestic corporation, operates a manufacturing branch in Singapore. During the current year, the manufacturing branch produces a loss of $300,000. Collins also earns interest income from investments in Europe, where it earns $800,000 in passive income. Collins paid no foreign income taxes related to the Singapore branch, but it paid $64,000 in foreign income taxes related to the passive income. Collins pays U.S. income taxes at the 34% tax rate. What is Collins's allowable FTC for the current year?

47. You are the head tax accountant for the Venture Company, a U.S. corporation. The board of directors is considering expansion overseas and asks you to present a summary of the U.S. tax consequences of investing overseas through a foreign subsidiary. Prepare a detailed outline of the presentation you will make to the board.

Communications

48. Money, Inc., a U.S. corporation, has $500,000 to invest overseas for 2008. For U.S. tax purposes, any additional income earned by Money will be taxed at 34%. Two possibilities for investment are:

Decision Making

Communications

a. Invest the $500,000 in common stock of Exco (a foreign corporation). Exco common stock pays a dividend of $3 per share each year. The $500,000 would purchase 10,000 shares (or 10%) of Exco's only class of stock (voting common). Exco expects to earn $10 million before taxes for 2008 and to be taxed at a flat rate of 40%. Its 2008 E & P before taxes is estimated to be $9.4 million. Exco's government does not withhold on dividends paid to foreign investors.

b. Invest the $500,000 in Exco bonds that pay interest at 7% per year. Assume that the bonds will be acquired at par, or face, value. Exco's government withholds 25% on interest paid to foreign investors.

Analyze these two investment opportunities and determine which would give Money the better return after taxes. Be sure to consider the effect of the FTC. Write a memorandum to Money, Inc., advising the corporation of your findings.

49. IrishCo, a manufacturing corporation resident in Ireland, distributes products through a U.S. office. Current-year taxable income from such sales in the United States is $12 million. IrishCo's U.S. office deposits working capital funds in short-term certificates of deposit with U.S. banks. Current-year interest income from these deposits is $100,000.

   IrishCo also invests in U.S. securities traded on the New York Stock Exchange. This investing is done by the home office. For the current year, IrishCo has realized capital gains of $200,000 and dividend income of $60,000 from these stock investments. Compute IrishCo's U.S. tax liability, assuming that the U.S.-Ireland income tax treaty reduces withholding on dividends to 15% and on interest to 5%. Assume a 34% U.S. tax rate.

50. Vanguard, S.A., a Peruvian corporation, manufactures inventory in Peru. The inventory is sold to independent distributors in the United States, with title passing to the purchaser in the United States. Vanguard has no employees or operations within the United States. All sales activities are conducted through telephone, fax, and Internet communication between Vanguard's home office and its U.S. customers. Explain whether Vanguard has any income effectively connected with a U.S. trade or business.

51. Green, S.A., a Peruvian corporation, manufactures furniture in Peru. It sells the furniture to independent distributors in the United States. Because title to the furniture passes to the purchasers in the United States, Green has $850,000 in U.S.-source income. Green has no employees or operations in the United States related to its furniture business. As a separate line of business, Green buys and sells antique toys. Green has a single employee operating a booth on weekends at a flea market in Waldo, Florida. The antique toy business generated $3,750 in net profits from U.S. sources during the current year. What is Green's effectively connected income for the current year?

52. Palm, Ltd., a foreign corporation, operates a sales branch in the United States that constitutes a U.S. trade or business. Rather than return the profits from the sales branch to the foreign home office, Palm invests the profits in certificates of deposit at U.S. banks. Explain whether the interest earned on these CDs is considered effectively connected with Palm's U.S. trade or business.

Communications

53. Trace, Ltd., a foreign corporation, operates a trade or business in the United States. Trace's U.S.-source income effectively connected with this trade or business is $800,000 for the current year. Trace's current-year E & P is $650,000. Trace's net U.S. equity was $8.2 million at the beginning of the year and $8.6 million at year-end. Trace is a resident in a country that has no income tax treaty with the United States. Briefly outline a memo to Trace's Tax VP reporting Trace's branch profits tax liability for the current year, along with a planning idea for reducing the branch profits tax.

54. Brenda, an NRA individual, owns 30% of the stock of Jeff, Inc., a U.S. corporation. Jeff's balance sheet on the last day of the taxable year is as follows.

		Adjusted Basis	Fair Market Value
Cash (used as working capital)		$ 200,000	$ 200,000
Investment in foreign land		300,000	800,000
Investment in U.S. real estate:			
Land		150,000	400,000
Buildings	$2,300,000		
Less: Depreciation	300,000	2,000,000	5,000,000
		$2,650,000	$6,400,000
Accounts payable		$ 300,000	$ 300,000
Notes payable		500,000	500,000
Capital stock		400,000	4,150,000
Retained earnings		1,450,000	1,450,000
		$2,650,000	$6,400,000

Brenda was in the United States only 40 days in the tax year. She sold all of her stock in Jeff on the last day of the tax year for $6.4 million. Brenda's adjusted basis in the stock sold was $500,000. She sold the stock for cash. What are the U.S. tax consequences, if any, to Brenda?

55. In Problem 54, what are the U.S. tax consequences, if any, to Brenda if Jeff, Inc., is a foreign corporation instead of a domestic corporation?

56. John McPherson is single, an attorney, and a U.S. citizen. He recently attended a seminar where he learned he could give up his U.S. citizenship, move to Bermuda (where he would pay no income tax), and operate his law practice long distance via the Internet with no U.S. tax consequences. Outline a letter informing John of the tax consequences of his proposed actions. His address is 1005 NE 10th Street, Gainesville, GA 32812.

Issue ID

Communications

TAX RETURN PROBLEMS

57. Fleming Products, Inc., a U.S. corporation, has a branch in Canada. The branch earns taxable income of $1 million from manufacturing operations and $500,000 from passive investment. Fleming Products pays Canadian income tax of $400,000 (40%) and $100,000 (20%), respectively, on this foreign-source income. The corporation also earns U.S.-source taxable income from manufacturing operations of $4 million, resulting in worldwide taxable income of $5.5 million. The U.S. taxes before the FTC are $1.87 million (at 34%). Fleming Products (employer ID number 75–2837157) accrues taxes for purposes of the FTC. This information is summarized below.

Income Category	Gross Income	Direct Expenses	Indirect Expenses	Taxable Income	Foreign Taxes
U.S. manufacturing	$ 9,000,000	$4,460,000	$540,000	$4,000,000	NA
Foreign manufacturing	5,000,000	3,700,000	300,000	1,000,000	$400,000
Passive investment	1,000,000	440,000	60,000	500,000	100,000
Total	$15,000,000	$8,600,000	$900,000*	$5,500,000	$500,000

* This $900,000 represents expenses not definitely allocable to any of the corporation's activities. It is allocated and apportioned based on relative gross income.

Complete a Form 1118 to compute Fleming's foreign tax credit in the general limitation income and passive categories. Use the fill-in forms at **http://www.irs.gov**.

58. Cotton Export, Inc., a domestic corporation, has the following taxable income amounts for the 2007 tax year and incurs foreign income taxes as shown.

Type of Income	Source	Amount	Foreign Taxes
Sales	Canada	$ 830,000	$339,000
	U.S.	300,000	–0–
Dividends*	Canada	20,000	5,100**
	U.S.†	25,000	–0–
		$1,175,000	$344,100

U.S. taxes before FTC = $399,500.

*From a portfolio of foreign stocks, all owned less than 1% by vote or value.

**Included in dividend amount (i.e., the $20,000 is before the $5,100 in withholding taxes).

†Net of dividends received deduction.

Gross foreign-source sales income is $1.2 million. Deductions allocable to foreign sales income total $320,000, and the apportioned share of deductions not definitely allocable to foreign sales income is $50,000.

Gross foreign-source dividend income is $21,000. There are no deductions definitely allocable to dividend income. The apportioned share of deductions not definitely allocable to foreign-source dividend income is $1,000.

Determine Cotton's FTC by completing the appropriate Form 1118s. Use the fill-in forms at **http://www.irs.gov**.

RESEARCH PROBLEMS

Communications

Note: Solutions to Research Problems can be prepared by using the **RIA Checkpoint®
Student Edition** online research product, which is available to accompany this text. It is also possible to prepare solutions to the Research Problems by using tax research materials found in a standard tax library.

Research Problem 1.   Jerry Jeff Keen, the CFO of Boots Unlimited, a Texas corporation, has come to you regarding a potential restructuring of business operations. Boots has long manufactured its western boots in plants in Texas and Oklahoma. Recently, Boots has explored the possibility of setting up a manufacturing subsidiary in Ireland, where manufacturing profits are taxed at 10%. Jerry Jeff sees this as a great idea, given that the alternative is to continue all manufacturing in the United States, where profits are taxed at 34%. Boots plans to continue all the cutting, sizing, and hand tooling of leather in its U.S. plants. This material will be shipped to Ireland for final assembly, with the finished product shipped to retail outlets all over Europe and Asia. Your initial concern is whether the income generated by the Irish subsidiary will be considered foreign base company income. Address this issue in a research memo, along with any planning suggestions.

Partial list of research aids:
§ 954(d).
Reg. § 1.954–3(a).
Bausch & Lomb, 71 TCM 2031, T.C.Memo. 1996–57.

Research Problem 2.   A U.S. corporation had the following net taxable income (loss) for the 2006 tax year (when nine separate baskets existed). Its U.S. taxes before the FTC are $600. Determine the FTC limitation for each basket of foreign-source income.

Source (Basket)	Income (Loss)	Foreign Taxes
U.S.-source	($ 68,000)	–0–
Foreign-source passive	70,000	$21,000
Foreign-source oil and gas	30,000	6,000
Foreign-source general	(28,000)	–0–

Partial list of research aids:

§ 904(f)(5).

General Explanation of the Tax Reform Act of 1986 (the Bluebook), Joint Committee on Taxation, pp. 909–912.

Instructions accompanying Form 1118, Foreign Tax Credit—Corporations, Dept. of the Treasury, Internal Revenue Service.

Research Problem 3.   NewCar.com, Inc., an innovative, Internet-based automobile retailer based in Ghana, is beginning to seek customers in the United States. Currently, it has no sales personnel or assets located in the United States, but it makes a few sales to U.S. customers based on orders over its Web site. NewCar.com is considering sending a few sales agents to the United States to set up sales offices in large cities. The offices will have no inventory and will merely provide a place for the sales agents to meet with interested customers. Ghana has no income tax treaty with the United States. How would you advise NewCar.com, Inc., on the tax consequences of its proposed U.S. venture?

Partial list of research aids:

§ 882(a)(1).

Higgins v. Comm., 41–1 USTC ¶9233, 25 AFTR 1160, 61 S.Ct. 475 (1941).

Continental Trading, Inc. v. Comm., 59–1 USTC ¶9316, 3 AFTR2d 923, 265 F.2d 40 (CA–9, 1959).

Piedras Negras Broadcasting Co., 43 BTA 297 (1941), *aff'd* 127 F.2d 260 (CA–5, 1942).

Use the tax resources of the Internet to address the following questions. Do not restrict your search to the World Wide Web, but include a review of newsgroups and general reference materials, practitioner sites and resources, primary sources of the tax law, chat rooms and discussion groups, and other opportunities.

 **Internet** *Activity*

Research Problem 4.   The IRS's Web page at **http://www.irs.gov** contains many useful links to publications, tax forms and instructions, and tax revenue statistics. Locate Web pages for at least three other countries' taxing authorities. Indicate the Web address for each of these pages and describe how these Web pages compare with the IRS's page in terms of content and ease of use.

Research Problem 5.   Locate the most recent annual report (or SEC Form 10K) for three different publicly held U.S. corporations. For each corporation, locate the income tax footnote and determine the percentage of net income before taxes from foreign operations, the current foreign income tax expense (benefit), and the deferred foreign income tax expense (benefit).

Research Problem 6.   Find the text of various tax treaties currently in force in the United States.

a. How does the U.S. income tax treaty with Spain define "business profits" for multinational businesses?

b. How does the U.S. income tax treaty with Japan treat the branch profits tax?

c. List five countries with which the United States has entered into an estate tax treaty.

d. What is the effective date of the latest income tax treaty with Canada?

Research Problem 7.   Locate data on the size of the international economy, including data on international trade, foreign direct investment by U.S. firms, and investment in the United States by foreign firms. Useful Web locations include **http://www.census.gov** and **http://www.bea.gov**. Prepare an analysis of the data for a three-year period using spreadsheet and graphing software, and e-mail the results to your instructor.

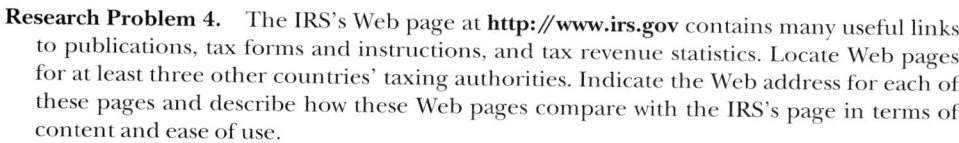

Communications

PART 3

Flow-Through Entities

Unlike C Corporations, some business entities are taxed under the conduit principle. Generally, this means the tax attributes of various transactions are retained as they flow through the entity to the owners. With limited exceptions, no tax is imposed at the entity level. Part III discusses two types of flow-through entities—partnerships and corporations that make the Subchapter S election. Part III also integrates the material on corporations (Part II) with flow-through entities in regard to the decision-making process. By comparing the tax attributes of C corporations, S corporations, and partnerships, the owners are provided with the tools needed to choose the appropriate form for conducting a business.

Partnerships: Formation, Operation, and Basis

LEARNING OBJECTIVES

After completing Chapter 10, you should be able to:

LO.1
Discuss governing principles and theories of partnership taxation.

LO.2
Describe the tax effects of forming a partnership with cash and property contributions.

LO.3
Identify elections available to a partnership, and specify the tax treatment of expenditures of a newly formed partnership.

LO.4
Specify the accounting methods available to a partnership and the methods of determining a partnership's tax year.

LO.5
Calculate partnership taxable income and describe how partnership items affect a partner's income tax return.

LO.6
Determine a partner's basis in the partnership interest.

LO.7
Explain how liabilities affect a partner's basis.

LO.8
Describe the limitations on deducting partnership losses.

LO.9
Describe the treatment of transactions between a partner and the partnership.

LO.10
Provide insights regarding advantageous use of a partnership.

Overview of Partnership Taxation

Forms of Doing Business—Federal Tax Consequences

This chapter and the next two chapters analyze two types of entities that may offer advantages over regular corporations. These entities are partnerships and S corporations, which are called *flow-through* or *pass-through* entities because the owners of the trade or business choose to avoid treating the enterprise as a separate taxable entity. Instead, the owners are taxed on a proportionate share of the entity's taxable income at the end of each of its taxable years.

Often a partnership may provide tax advantages over a C, or regular, corporation. A partnership is subject to only a single level of taxation, while C corporation income is subject to *double taxation*. Corporate income is taxed at the entity level at rates up to 35 percent. Any after-tax income that is distributed to corporate owners as a dividend is taxed again at the owner level. Though partnership income may be subject to high tax rates at the partner level (currently up to about 35 percent for a partner who is an individual), the resulting tax will generally be lower than a combined corporate-level tax and a second tax on a dividend distribution.

In addition, administrative and filing requirements are usually relatively simple for a partnership, and it offers certain planning opportunities not available to other entities. Both C and S corporations are subject to rigorous allocation and distribution requirements. Generally, each income or loss allocation or distribution is proportionate to the ownership interest of each shareholder. A partnership, though, may adjust its allocations of income and cash flow among the partners each year according to their needs, as long as certain standards, discussed later in this chapter, are met. Also, any previously unrealized income of an S or C corporation, such as appreciation of corporate assets, is taxed at the entity level when the corporation liquidates. However, a partnership generally may liquidate tax-free. Finally, many states impose reporting and licensing requirements on corporate entities, including S corporations. These include franchise or capital stock tax returns that may require annual assessments and

TAX *in the News*   PARTNERSHIPS IN THE MOVIES

As movies have become more expensive to produce, many production studios have turned to limited partnerships or limited liability companies (LLCs) as a lucrative source of investment capital. For example, certain well-known studios have sold limited partnership (or LLC) interests in various partnerships formed to produce specific movies.

Often the sponsoring studio injects capital for a small (1–5 percent) general partnership interest, and the investors contribute the remaining capital—often many millions of dollars. The partnership agreement spells out the number and types of films the partnership intends to produce and provides a formula for allocating cash flows to the partners. The partnership agreement includes various benefits for the general partner, the studio, such as a preferred allocation of cash flows. For example, the studio may receive the first $1 million per year, distribution fees for marketing the movies, and/or reimbursement of specified amounts of corporate overhead. Any cash remaining after these expenses is allocated under a fixed formula between the general and limited partners. For example, the limited partners may receive 90 percent of remaining cash flows.

Think about bank financing in comparison, and you will see why the studio finds partnerships so appealing: How many banks would allow the general partner to receive reimbursements and allocations before debt principal and interest are paid?

This capital-raising technique has proved so advantageous to the studios that some related industries, such as movie lighting contractors and special effects companies, have also used limited partnerships (or LLCs) to raise capital. The next time you go to a movie, watch the credits at the end and think about the tremendous number of people who invested cash in the movie, hoping for a blockbuster!

---

costly professional preparation assistance.[1] Partnerships, on the other hand, often have no reporting requirements beyond Federal and state informational tax returns.

For smaller business operations, a partnership enables several owners to combine their resources at low cost. It also offers simple filing requirements, the taxation of income only once, and the ability to discontinue operations relatively inexpensively.

For larger business operations, a partnership offers a unique ability to raise capital with low filing and reporting costs compared to, for example, corporate bond issuances. Special allocations of income and cash-flow items may be used by partnerships to meet the objectives of the owners. The accompanying Tax in the News describes how one industry has used the partnership form as a means of raising capital.

This chapter addresses partnership formation and operations. Chapter 11 focuses on dispositions of partnership interests, partnership distributions, and optional basis adjustments. Chapter 12 discusses the taxation of S corporations.

What Is a Partnership?

A partnership is an association formed by two or more persons to carry on a trade or business, with each contributing money, property, labor, or skill, and with all expecting to share in profits and losses. A "person" can be an individual, trust, estate, corporation, association, or another partnership.[2] For Federal income tax purposes, a partnership includes a syndicate, group, pool, joint venture, or other unincorporated organization through which any business, financial operation, or venture is carried on. The entity must not be otherwise classified as a corporation, trust, or estate.

The types of entities that may be taxed as partnerships include general partnerships, limited liability partnerships, limited partnerships, and limited liability companies. A partnership that conducts a service business, such as accounting, law, or medicine, is usually established as either a **general partnership** or a

---

[1]Certain states treat limited liability companies (LLCs) as corporations for purposes of state franchise taxes.

[2]§§ 7701(a)(1) and (a)(2).

limited liability partnership (LLP). A general partnership consists of two or more general partners. Creditors of a general partnership can collect amounts owed them from both the partnership assets and the personal assets of the owner-partners. A general partner can be bankrupted by a malpractice judgment brought against the partnership, even though the partner was not personally involved in the malpractice.

A limited liability partnership (an "LLP" or "double-LP") is a recently created form of entity. In most states, owners of an LLP are treated much like general partners. The primary difference between an LLP and a general partnership is that an LLP partner is not personally liable for any malpractice committed by other partners. LLPs are discussed in more detail in Chapter 11. The LLP is currently the organizational form of choice for the large accounting firms.

A **limited partnership** is often used for acquiring capital in activities such as real estate development. A limited partnership has at least one general partner and often many limited partners. Typically, only the general partners are personally liable to creditors; each limited partner's risk of loss is restricted to that partner's equity investment in the entity.

An alternative entity form, the **limited liability company (LLC)**, is available in all states and the District of Columbia. An LLC combines the corporate benefit of limited liability for the owners with the benefits of partnership taxation, including the single level of tax and special allocations of income, losses, and cash flows. Owners are technically considered to be "members" rather than partners, but a properly structured LLC is treated as a partnership for all tax purposes. Almost all states permit capital-intensive companies as well as nonprofessional service-oriented businesses and some professional service-providing companies to operate as LLCs. This is highly advantageous to a business entity since the LLC can protect each member's assets from being exposed to the entity's debts. As discussed in Chapter 11, application of the partnership tax rules to an LLC can produce some unusual results.

Elections Related to Partnership Status

The IRS's "check-the-box" Regulations allow most unincorporated business entities—such as general partnerships, limited partnerships, LLPs, and LLCs—to select their Federal tax status.[3] If an unincorporated entity has two or more owners, it generally can choose to be taxed as either a partnership or a C corporation. This provides the entity with flexibility regarding its Federal tax classification. The Regulations, however, do not permit all unincorporated business or investment entities to choose their tax status. Newly formed publicly traded partnerships, for example, must be taxed as corporations.

A partnership generally may elect out of the partnership taxation rules if it is involved in one of the following activities:

- Investment (rather than the active conduct of a trade or business).
- Joint production, extraction, or use of property.
- Underwriting, selling, or distributing a specific security issue.[4]

---

[3] Reg. §§ 301.7701–1 to 301.7701–3.   [4] § 761(a).

If a proper election is made, the partnership is disregarded for Federal tax purposes, and its operations are reported directly on the owners' tax returns.

Partnership Taxation

A partnership is not a taxable entity.[5] Rather, the taxable income or loss of the partnership flows through to the partners at the end of the entity's tax year.[6] Partners report their allocable share of the partnership's income or loss for the year on their tax returns. As a result, the partnership itself pays no Federal income tax on its income; instead, the partners' individual tax liabilities are affected by the activities of the entity.

> **LO.1**
>
> Discuss governing principles and theories of partnership taxation.

> **EXAMPLE 1**
>
> Adam is a 40% partner in the ABC Partnership. Both Adam's and the partnership's tax years end on December 31. In 2008, the partnership generates $200,000 of ordinary taxable income. However, because the partnership needs capital for expansion and debt reduction, Adam makes no cash withdrawals during 2008. He meets his living expenses by reducing his investment portfolio. Adam is taxed on his $80,000 allocable share of the partnership's 2008 income, even though he received no distributions from the entity during 2008. This allocated income is included in Adam's gross income. ■

> **EXAMPLE 2**
>
> Assume the same facts as in Example 1, except the partnership recognizes a 2008 taxable loss of $100,000. Adam's $40,000 proportionate share of the loss flows through to him from the partnership, and he can deduct the loss. (Note: Loss limitation rules discussed later in the chapter may result in some or all of this loss being deducted by Adam in a later year.) ■

Many items of partnership income or expense, gain, or loss retain their identity as they flow through to the partners. This separate flow-through of certain items is required because such **separately stated items** *might* affect any two partners' tax liabilities in different ways. When preparing a personal tax return, a partner takes each of these items into account separately.[7] For example, charitable contributions are separately stated because partners need to compute their own personal limitation on charitable contributions. Some partners are able to deduct the entire amount they are allocated. Others are limited in what they can deduct by the amount of their adjusted gross income (AGI).

> **EXAMPLE 3**
>
> Beth is a 25% partner in the BR Partnership. The cash basis entity collected sales income of $60,000 during 2007 and incurred $15,000 in business expenses. In addition, it sold a corporate bond, in June, for a $9,000 long-term capital gain. Finally, the partnership made a $1,000 contribution to the local Performing Arts Fund drive. The fund is a qualifying charity. BR and all of its partners use a calendar tax year.
>
> For 2007, Beth is allocated ordinary taxable income of $11,250 [($60,000 − $15,000) × 25%] from the partnership. She also is allocated a flow-through of a $2,250 long-term capital gain and a $250 charitable contribution deduction. The ordinary income increases Beth's gross income. The long-term capital gain and charitable contribution are separately stated because they could be treated differently on her tax return from the way they are treated on the tax returns of the other partners. For example, Beth may have capital losses to offset the capital gain or may be subject to a percentage limitation on charitable contribution deductions for 2007. Other partners may have no capital losses or percentage limitations on charitable contribution deductions. ■

The number of items that are separately reported to the partners varies and depends upon whether the partnership is an **electing large partnership**. A partnership qualifies as a large partnership if it had at least 100 partners during its

---

[5]§ 701.
[6]§ 702.

[7]§ 703(a)(1).

immediately preceding taxable year and elects simplified reporting of its taxable items. Such partnerships separately report up to 16 different categories of items to their partners. This means that many items are netted at the partnership level. For example, items such as interest, nonqualifying dividends, and royalty income are combined into one amount, and the electing large partnership reports a share of this amount to each partner. The netting of items at the partnership level makes each partner's tax return easier to complete. Unless otherwise indicated, in this chapter and Chapter 11 assume the partnership is *not* an electing large partnership.

As most partnerships are not electing large partnerships, they may separately report more than 16 categories of items. Some partnership items are netted in these partnerships, but the netting is not as extensive as in electing large partnerships. Pass-through items that are netted in these partnerships include the ordinary income and expenses related to the partnership's trade or business activities. These ordinary income and expense items are netted to produce a single income or loss amount that is passed through to the partners. Most other partnership items are separately stated. For example, net income (loss) from rental real estate activities and net short-term capital gains (losses) are each determined at the partnership level and reported separately to the partners.

Other items that are allocated separately to the partners include recognized gains and losses from property transactions; qualified and ordinary dividend income; tax preferences and adjustments for the alternative minimum tax; expenditures that qualify for the foreign tax credit; information the partner needs to calculate the domestic production activities deduction of § 199; and expenditures that the partners would treat as itemized deductions.

Partnership Reporting

Even though it is not a taxpaying entity, a partnership must file an information tax return, Form 1065. Look at Form 1065 for 2007 in Appendix B, and refer to it during the following discussion. The ordinary income and expense items generated by the partnership's trade or business activities are netted to produce a single income or loss amount. The partnership reports this ordinary income or loss from its trade or business activities on Form 1065, page 1. Schedule K (page 3 of Form 1065) accumulates all items that must be separately reported to the partners, including net trade or business income or loss (from page 1). The amounts on Schedule K are allocated to all the partners. Each partner receives a Schedule K–1, which shows that partner's share of partnership items.

EXAMPLE 4

The BR Partnership in Example 3 reports its $60,000 sales income on Form 1065, page 1, line 1. The $15,000 of business expenses are reported in the appropriate amounts on page 1, line 2 or lines 9–20. Partnership ordinary income of $45,000 is shown on page 1, line 22, and on Schedule K, line 1. The $9,000 net long-term capital gain and the $1,000 charitable contribution are reported only on Schedule K, on lines 9a and 13a, respectively.

Beth receives a Schedule K–1 from the partnership that shows her shares of partnership ordinary income of $11,250, long-term capital gain of $2,250, and charitable contributions of $250 on lines 1, 9a, and 13, respectively.

She combines these amounts with similar items from sources other than BR in her personal tax return. For example, if she has a $5,000 long-term capital loss from a stock transaction during the year, her overall net capital loss calculated on Schedule D of her 1040 is $2,750. She evaluates this net amount to determine the amount she may deduct on her Form 1040. She reports the $250 of charitable contributions on her Schedule A. ■

As this example shows, one must look at both page 1 and Schedule K to get complete information regarding a partnership's operations for the year.

Certain items reported on Schedule K are netted and entered on line 1 of the Analysis of Net Income (Loss) on page 4. The partnership prepares Schedule M–1 or Schedule M–3 to reconcile book and tax net income. Schedule M–3 is required in lieu of Schedule M–1 if, generally, the partnership has $10 million or more in assets at the end of the year. The net taxable income calculated on the Analysis of Net Income (Loss) schedule should agree with the reconciled taxable income on Schedule M–1 (line 9) or the reconciled amount from Schedule M–3, Part II. Schedule L generally shows an accounting-basis balance sheet, and Schedule M–2 reconciles partners' beginning and ending capital accounts.

Partner's Ownership Interest in a Partnership

Each partner typically owns both a **capital interest** and a **profits (loss) interest** in the partnership. A capital interest is measured by a partner's **capital sharing ratio**, which is the partner's percentage ownership of the capital of the partnership. A partner's capital interest can be determined in several ways. The most widely accepted method measures the capital interest as the percentage of net asset value (asset value remaining after payment of all partnership liabilities) a partner would receive on immediate liquidation of the partnership.

A profits (loss) interest is simply the partner's percentage allocation of current partnership operating results. **Profit and loss sharing ratios** are usually specified in the partnership agreement and are used to determine each partner's allocation of partnership ordinary taxable income and separately stated items.[8] The partnership can change its profit and loss allocations at any time simply by amending the partnership agreement.

Each partner's profit, loss, and capital sharing ratios may appear on the partner's Schedule K–1. In many cases, the three ratios are the same. A partner's capital sharing ratio generally equals the partner's profit and loss sharing ratios if all profit and loss allocations, for each year of the partnership's existence, are in the same proportion as the partner's initial contributions to the partnership.

The partnership agreement may, in some cases, provide for a **special allocation** of certain items to specified partners, or it may allocate items in a different proportion from general profit and loss sharing ratios. These items are separately reported to the partner receiving the allocation. For a special allocation to be recognized for tax purposes, it must produce nontax economic consequences to the partners receiving the allocation.[9]

When the George-Helen Partnership was formed, George contributed cash and Helen contributed some City of Iuka bonds that she had held for investment purposes. The partnership agreement allocates all of the tax-exempt interest income from the bonds to Helen as an inducement for her to remain a partner. This is an acceptable special allocation for income tax purposes; it reflects the differing economic circumstances that underlie the partners' contributions to the capital of the entity. Since Helen would have received the exempt income if she had not joined the partnership, she can retain the tax-favored treatment by means of the special allocation. ■	*EXAMPLE 5*

Assume the same facts as in Example 5. Three years after it was formed, the George-Helen Partnership purchased some City of Butte bonds. The municipal bond interest income of $15,000 flows through to the partners as a separately stated item, so it retains its tax-exempt status. The partnership agreement allocates all of this income to George because he is subject to a higher marginal income tax bracket than is Helen. The partnership also allocates $15,000 more of the partnership taxable income to Helen than to George. These allocations are not effective for income tax purposes because they have no purpose other than reduction of the partners' combined income tax liability. ■	*EXAMPLE 6*

---

[8]§ 704(a).   [9]§ 704(b).

A partner has a **basis in the partnership interest**. When income flows through to a partner from the partnership, the partner's basis in the partnership interest increases. When a loss flows through to a partner, basis is reduced.

EXAMPLE 7

Paul contributes $20,000 cash to acquire a 30% capital and profits interest in the Blue Jay Partnership. In its first year of operations, the partnership earns ordinary income of $40,000 and makes no distributions to Paul. Paul's initial basis is the $20,000 he paid for the interest. He reports ordinary income of $12,000 (30% × $40,000 partnership income) on his individual return and increases his basis by the same amount, to $32,000. ■

The Code provides for the increase and decrease in a partner's basis so that the income or loss from partnership operations is taxed only once. In Example 7, if Paul sold his interest at the end of the first year for $32,000, he would have no gain or loss. If the Code did not provide for an adjustment of a partner's basis, Paul's basis would be $20,000, and he would be taxed on the gain of $12,000 in addition to being taxed on his $12,000 share of income. In other words, without the basis adjustment, partnership income would be subject to double taxation.

As the following sections discuss in detail, a partner's basis is important for determining the treatment of distributions from the partnership to the partner, establishing the deductibility of partnership losses, and calculating gain or loss on the partner's disposition of the partnership interest.

A partner's basis is not reflected anywhere on the Schedule K–1. Instead, each partner should maintain a personal record of adjustments to basis. Schedule K–1 does reconcile a partner's **capital account**, but the ending capital account balance is rarely the same amount as the partner's basis. Just as the tax and accounting bases of a specific asset may differ, a partner's capital account and basis in partnership interest may not be equal for a variety of reasons. For example, a partner's basis also includes the partner's share of partnership liabilities. These liabilities are not reported as part of the partner's capital account but are included in the partner's capital account analysis in item M on the partner's Schedule K–1.

Conceptual Basis for Partnership Taxation

The unique tax treatment of partners and partnerships can be traced to two legal concepts that evolved long ago: the **aggregate concept** (or conduit) and the **entity concept**. These concepts influence practically every partnership tax rule.

Aggregate (or Conduit) Concept. The aggregate (or conduit) concept treats the partnership as a channel through which income, credits, deductions, and other items flow to the partners. Under this concept, the partnership is regarded as a collection of taxpayers joined in an agency relationship with one another. The imposition of the income tax on individual partners reflects the influence of this doctrine. The aggregate concept has influenced the tax treatment of other pass-through entities, such as S corporations (Chapter 12) and trusts and estates (Chapter 19).

Entity Concept. The entity concept treats partners and partnerships as separate units and gives the partnership its own tax "personality" by (1) requiring a partnership to file an information tax return and (2) treating partners as separate and distinct from the partnership in certain transactions between a partner and the entity. A partner's recognition of capital gain or loss on the sale of the partnership interest illustrates this doctrine.

Combined Concepts. Some rules governing the formation, operation, and liquidation of a partnership contain a blend of both the entity and aggregate concepts.

Anti-Abuse Provisions

As Chapters 10 and 11 reflect, partnership taxation is often flexible. For example, partnership operating income or losses can sometimes be shifted among partners, and partnership capital gains and losses can sometimes be shifted from one partner to another. The Code contains many provisions designed to thwart unwarranted allocations, but the IRS believes opportunities still abound for tax avoidance. As Chapter 11 notes, the IRS has adopted Regulations that allow it to recharacterize transactions that it considers to be "abusive."[10]

Formation of a Partnership: Tax Effects

Gain or Loss on Contributions to the Partnership

> **LO.2**
>
> Describe the tax effects of forming a partnership with cash and property contributions.

When a taxpayer transfers property to an entity in exchange for valuable consideration, a taxable exchange normally results. Typically, both the taxpayer and the entity realize and recognize gain or loss on the exchange.[11] The gain or loss recognized by the transferor is the difference between the fair market value of the consideration received and the adjusted basis of the property transferred.[12]

In most situations, however, neither the partner nor the partnership recognizes the gain or loss that is realized when a partner contributes property to a partnership in exchange for a partnership interest. Instead, the realized gain or loss is deferred.[13]

There are two reasons for this nonrecognition treatment. First, forming a partnership allows investors to combine their assets toward greater economic goals than could be achieved separately. Only the form of ownership, rather than the amount owned by each investor, has changed. Requiring that gain be recognized on such transfers would make the formation of some partnerships economically unfeasible (e.g., two existing proprietorships are combined to form one larger business). Congress does not want to hinder the creation of valid economic partnerships by requiring gain recognition when a partnership is created. Second, because the partnership interest received is typically not a liquid asset, the partner may not have sufficient cash to pay the tax. Thus, deferral of the gain recognizes the economic realities of the business world and follows the wherewithal to pay principle of taxation.

EXAMPLE 8

Alicia transfers two assets to the Wren Partnership on the day the entity is created, in exchange for a 60% profit and loss interest worth $60,000. She contributes cash of $40,000 and retail display equipment (basis to her as a sole proprietor, $8,000; fair market value, $20,000). Since an exchange has occurred between two parties, Alicia *realizes* a $12,000 gain on this transaction. The gain realized is the fair market value of the partnership interest of $60,000 less the basis of the assets that Alicia surrendered to the partnership [$40,000 (cash) + $8,000 (equipment)].

Under § 721, Alicia *does not recognize* the $12,000 realized gain in the year of contribution. This makes sense, since all she received from the partnership was an illiquid partnership interest; she received no cash with which to pay any resulting tax liability. ■

EXAMPLE 9

Assume the same facts as in Example 8, except that the equipment Alicia contributes to the partnership has an adjusted basis of $25,000. She has a $5,000 *realized* loss [$60,000 − ($40,000 + $25,000)], but she cannot deduct the loss. Realized losses, as well as realized gains, are deferred by § 721.

Unless it was essential that the partnership receive Alicia's display equipment rather than similar equipment purchased from an outside supplier, Alicia should have considered selling the equipment to a third party. This would have allowed her to deduct a $5,000 loss in the year of the sale. Alicia then could have contributed $60,000 cash (including the proceeds

---

[10]Reg. § 1.701–2.
[11]§ 1001(c).

[12]§ 1001(a).
[13]§ 721.

from the sale) for her interest in the partnership, and the partnership would have funds to purchase similar equipment. ∎

EXAMPLE 10

Five years after the Wren Partnership (Examples 8 and 9) was created, Alicia contributes another piece of equipment to the entity. This property has a basis of $35,000 and a fair market value of $50,000. Alicia will defer the recognition of the $15,000 realized gain. Section 721 is effective whenever a partner makes a contribution to the capital of the partnership. ∎

If a partner contributes only capital and § 1231 assets, the partner's holding period in the partnership interest is the same as that partner's holding period for these assets. If cash or other assets that are not capital or § 1231 assets are contributed, the holding period in the partnership interest begins on the date the partnership interest is acquired. If multiple assets are contributed, the partnership interest is apportioned, and a separate holding period applies to each portion.

Exceptions to § 721

The nonrecognition provisions of § 721 do not apply where

- appreciated stocks are contributed to an investment partnership;
- the transaction is essentially a taxable exchange of properties;
- the transaction is a disguised sale of properties; or
- the partnership interest is received in exchange for services rendered to the partnership by the partner.

Investment Partnership. If the transfer consists of appreciated stocks and securities and the partnership is an investment partnership, it is possible that the realized gain on the stocks and securities will be recognized by the contributing partner at the time of contribution.[14] This provision prevents multiple investors from using the partnership form to diversify their investment portfolios on a tax-free basis. A similar provision, § 351(e), applies to corporations (see Chapter 4).

Exchange. If a transaction is essentially a taxable exchange of properties, tax on the gain is not deferred under the nonrecognition provisions of § 721.[15]

EXAMPLE 11

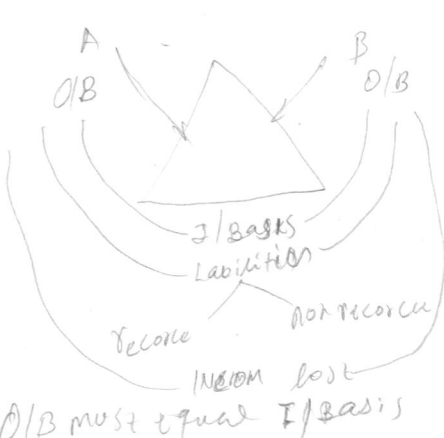

Sara owns land, and Bob owns stock. Sara would like to have Bob's stock, and Bob wants Sara's land. If Sara and Bob both contribute their property to newly formed SB Partnership in exchange for interests in the partnership, the tax on the transaction appears to be deferred under § 721. The tax on a subsequent distribution by the partnership of the land to Bob and the stock to Sara also appears to be deferred under § 731 (discussed in Chapter 11). According to a literal interpretation of the statutes, no taxable exchange has occurred. Sara and Bob will find, however, that this type of tax subterfuge is not permitted. The IRS will disregard the passage of the properties through the partnership and will hold, instead, that Sara and Bob exchanged the land and stock directly. Thus, the transactions will be treated as any other taxable exchange. ∎

Disguised Sale. A similar result occurs in a **disguised sale** of property or of a partnership interest. A disguised sale may occur when a partner contributes appreciated property to a partnership and soon thereafter receives a distribution from the partnership. This distribution may be viewed as a payment by the partnership for purchase of the property.[16]

---

[14]§ 721(b).
[15]Reg. § 1.731–1(c)(3).

[16]§ 707(a)(2)(B).

Kim transfers property to the KLM Partnership. The property has an adjusted basis of $10,000 and a fair market value of $30,000. Two weeks later, the partnership makes a distribution of $30,000 cash to Kim. Under the distribution rules of § 731, the distribution would not be taxable to Kim if the basis for her partnership interest prior to the distribution was greater than the $30,000 cash distributed. However, the transaction appears to be a disguised purchase-sale transaction, rather than a contribution and distribution. Therefore, Kim must recognize gain of $20,000 on transfer of the property, and the partnership is deemed to have purchased the property for $30,000. ∎

A disguised sale of a partnership interest could occur where Partner A contributes property to the partnership and the partnership makes a distribution of the property to Partner B in liquidation of Partner B's interest in the partnership. This transaction may be viewed as a sale of Partner B's partnership interest to Partner A.

Extensive Regulations under § 707 outline situations in which the IRS will presume a disguised sale has occurred. For example, a disguised sale is presumed to exist if both the following occur:

- A contractual agreement requires a contribution by one partner to be followed within two years by a specified distribution from the partnership.
- The distribution is to be made without regard to partnership profits. In other words, the forthcoming distribution is not subject to significant "entrepreneurial risk."

In some cases, assumption of the partner's liabilities by the partnership may be treated as part of the purchase price paid by the partnership. The IRS can also use a facts and circumstances test to treat a transaction as a disguised sale.

The Regulations also outline situations in which a distribution generally will *not* be deemed to be part of a disguised sale. They include a distribution that occurs more than two years after the property is contributed and a distribution that is deemed "reasonable" in relation to the capital invested by the partner and in relation to distributions made to other partners.

Services.
A final exception to the nonrecognition provision of § 721 occurs when a partner receives an interest in the partnership as compensation for services rendered to the partnership. This is not a tax-deferred transaction because services are not treated as "property" that can be transferred to a partnership on a tax-free basis. Instead, the partner performing the services recognizes ordinary compensation income equal to the fair market value of the partnership interest received.[17]

The partnership may deduct the amount included in the service partner's income if the services are of a deductible nature. If the services are not deductible to the partnership, they must be capitalized to an asset account. For example, architectural plans created by a partner are capitalized as part of the structure built with those plans. Alternatively, day-to-day management services performed by a partner for the partnership are usually deductible by the partnership.

Bill, Carl, and Dave form the BCD Partnership, with each receiving a one-third interest in the entity. Dave receives his one-third interest as compensation for tax planning services he will render after the formation of the partnership. The value of a one-third interest in the partnership (for each of the parties) is $20,000. Dave recognizes $20,000 of compensation income, and he has a $20,000 basis in his partnership interest. The same result would occur if the partnership had paid Dave $20,000 for his services and he immediately contributed that amount to the entity for a one-third ownership interest. In either case, the partnership deducts $20,000 in calculating its ordinary business income. ∎

EXAMPLE 12

EXAMPLE 13

---

[17] § 83(a).

Tax Issues Relative to Contributed Property

When a partner makes a tax-deferred contribution of an asset to the capital of a partnership, the tax law assigns a carryover basis to the property.[18] The partnership's basis in the asset is equal to the partner's basis in the property prior to its transfer to the partnership. The partner's basis in the new partnership interest is the same as the partner's basis in the contributed asset. The tax term for this basis concept is *substituted basis.* Thus, two assets are created out of one when a partnership is formed, namely, the property in the hands of the new entity and the new asset (the partnership interest) in the hands of the partner. Both assets are assigned a basis that is derived from the partner's basis in the contributed property.

To understand the logic of these rules, consider what Congress was attempting to accomplish with the deferral approach. Recall that gain or loss is deferred when property is contributed to a partnership in exchange for a partnership interest. The basis amounts are the amounts necessary to allow for recognition of the deferred gain or loss if the property or the partnership interest is subsequently disposed of in a taxable transaction. This treatment is similar to the treatment of assets transferred to a controlled corporation[19] and the treatment of like-kind exchanges.[20]

| EXAMPLE 14 | On June 1, 2008, Luis transfers property to the JKL Partnership in exchange for a one-third interest in the partnership. The property has an adjusted basis to Luis of $10,000 and a fair market value of $30,000 on June 1. Luis has a $20,000 realized gain on the exchange ($30,000 − $10,000), but under § 721, he does not recognize any of the gain. Luis's basis for his partnership interest is the amount necessary to recognize the $20,000 deferred gain if his partnership interest is subsequently sold for its $30,000 fair market value. This amount, $10,000, is referred to as substituted basis. The basis of the property contributed to the partnership is the amount necessary to allow for the recognition of the $20,000 deferred gain if the property is subsequently sold for its $30,000 fair market value. This amount, also $10,000, is referred to as carryover basis. ■ |

The holding period for the contributed asset carries over to the partnership. Thus, the partnership's holding period for the asset includes the period during which the partner owned the asset.

Depreciation Method and Period. If depreciable property is contributed to the partnership, the partnership is usually required to use the same cost recovery method and life used by the partner. The partnership merely "steps into the shoes" of the partner and continues the same cost recovery calculations. The partnership may not elect under § 179 to immediately expense any part of the basis of depreciable property it receives from the transferor partner.

Intangible Assets. If a partner contributes an existing "§ 197" intangible asset to the partnership, the partnership generally will "step into the shoes" of the partner in determining future amortization deductions. Section 197 intangible assets include goodwill, going-concern value, information systems, customer- or supplier-related intangible assets, patents, licenses obtained from a governmental unit, franchises, trademarks, covenants not to compete, and other items.

| EXAMPLE 15 | On September 1, 2006, at a cost of $120,000, James obtained a license to operate a television station from the Federal Communications Commission. The license is effective for 20 years. On January 1, 2008, he contributes the license to the JS Partnership in exchange for a 60% interest. The value of the license is still $120,000 at that time. |

---

[18]§ 723.
[19]§ 351.

[20]§ 1031.

The license is a § 197 asset since it is a license with a term greater than 15 years. The cost is amortized over 15 years. James claims amortization for 4 months in 2006 and 12 months in 2007. Thereafter, the partnership steps into James's shoes in claiming amortization deductions. ∎

Intangible assets that do not fall under the § 197 rules are amortized over their useful life, if any.[21]

Receivables, Inventory, and Losses.

To prevent ordinary income from being converted into capital gain, gain or loss is treated as ordinary when the partnership disposes of either of the following:[22]

- Contributed receivables that were unrealized in the contributing partner's hands at the contribution date. Such receivables include the right to receive payment for goods or services delivered or to be delivered.
- Contributed property that was inventory in the contributor's hands on the contribution date, if the partnership disposes of the property within *five years of the contribution.* For this purpose, inventory includes all tangible property except capital assets and real or depreciable business assets.

Treated as ordinary

EXAMPLE 16

Tyrone operates a cash basis retail electronics and television store as a sole proprietor. Ramon is an enterprising individual who likes to invest in small businesses. On January 2 of the current year, Tyrone and Ramon form the TR Partnership. Their partnership contributions are as follows:

	Adjusted Basis	Fair Market Value
From Tyrone:		
Receivables	$ –0–	$ 2,000
Land used as parking lot*	1,200	5,000
Inventory	2,500	5,000
From Ramon:		
Cash	12,000	12,000

*The parking lot had been held for nine months at the contribution date.

Within 30 days of formation, TR collects the receivables and sells the inventory for $5,000 cash. It uses the land for the next 10 months as a parking lot, then sells it for $3,500 cash. TR realized the following income in the current year from these transactions:

- Ordinary income of $2,000 from collecting receivables.
- Ordinary income of $2,500 from sale of inventory.
- § 1231 gain of $2,300 from sale of land.

Since the land takes a carryover holding period, it is treated as having been held 19 months at the sale date. ∎

A similar rule is designed to prevent a capital loss from being converted into an ordinary loss. Under the rule, if contributed property is disposed of at a loss and the property had a "built-in" capital loss on the contribution date, the loss is treated as a capital loss if the partnership disposes of the property *within five years of the contribution.* The capital loss is limited to the amount of the "built-in" loss on the date of contribution.

---

[21]Reg § 1.167(a)–3.

[22]§ 724. For this purpose, § 724(d)(2) waives the holding period requirement in defining § 1231 property.

CONCEPT SUMMARY 10–1

Partnership Formation and Basis Computation

1. The *entity concept* treats partners and partnerships as separate units. The nature and amount of entity gains and losses and most partnership tax elections are determined at the partnership level.
2. The *aggregate concept* is used to connect partners and partnerships. It allows income, gains, losses, credits, deductions, etc., to flow through to the partners for separate tax reporting.
3. Sometimes both the *aggregate* and the *entity* concepts apply to the same transaction, but one usually dominates.
4. Generally, partners or partnerships do not recognize gain or loss when property is contributed for capital interests.
5. Partners contributing property for partnership interests take the contributed property's adjusted basis for their

outside basis in their partnership interest. The partners are said to take a substituted basis in their partnership interest.
6. The partnership will continue to use the contributing partner's basis for the *inside basis* in property it receives. The contributed property is said to take a carryover basis.
7. The holding period of a partner's interest includes that of contributed property when the property was a § 1231 asset or capital asset in the partner's hands. Otherwise, the holding period starts on the day the interest is acquired. The holding period of an interest acquired by a cash contribution starts at acquisition.
8. The partnership's holding period for contributed property includes the contributing partner's holding period.

EXAMPLE 17

Assume the same facts as Example 16, except for the following:

- Tyrone held the land for investment purposes. It had a fair market value of $800 at the contribution date.
- TR used the land as a parking lot for 10 months and sold it for $650.

TR realizes the following income and loss from the land contribution and sale transactions:

- Capital loss of $400 from sale of the land ($1,200 − $800).
- § 1231 loss of $150 from sale of the land ($800 − $650).

Since the land was sold within five years of the contribution date, the $400 built-in loss is a capital loss. The postcontribution loss of $150 is a § 1231 loss since TR used the property in its business. ∎

Inside and Outside Bases

Throughout these chapters, reference is made to the partnership's inside basis and the partners' outside basis. **Inside basis** refers to the adjusted basis of each partnership asset, as determined from the partnership's tax accounts. **Outside basis** represents each partner's basis in the partnership interest. Each partner "owns" a share of the partnership's inside basis for all its assets, and all partners should maintain a record of their respective outside bases.

In many cases—especially on formation of the partnership—the total of all the partners' outside bases equals the partnership's inside bases for all its assets. Differences between inside and outside basis arise when a partner's interest is sold to another person for more or less than the selling partner's share of the inside basis of partnership assets. The buying partner's outside basis equals the price paid for the interest, but the buyer's share of the partnership's inside basis is the same amount as the seller's share of the inside basis.

Concept Summary 10–1 reviews the rules that apply to partnership asset contribution and basis adjustments.

Tax Accounting Elections

A newly formed partnership must make numerous tax accounting elections. These elections are formal decisions on how a particular transaction or tax attribute should be handled. Most of these elections must be made by the partnership rather than by the partners individually.[23] The *partnership* makes the elections involving the following items:

LO.3

Identify elections available to a partnership, and specify the tax treatment of expenditures of a newly formed partnership.

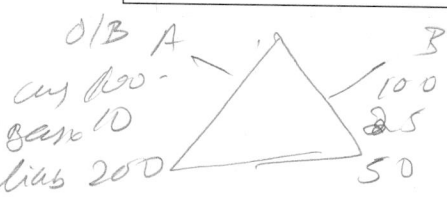

- Inventory method.
- Cost or percentage depletion method, excluding oil and gas wells.
- Accounting method (cash, accrual, or hybrid).
- Cost recovery methods and assumptions.
- Tax year.
- Amortization of organizational costs and amortization period.
- Amortization of startup expenditures and amortization period.
- Method of cost allocation under § 199[24] and, for certain partnerships, determination of "qualified production activities income" (QPAI) and production-related wages.
- Optional basis adjustments for property (§ 754, discussed in Chapter 11).
- Section 179 deductions for certain tangible personal property.
- Nonrecognition treatment for involuntary conversion gains.
- Election out of partnership rules.

Each partner is bound by the decisions made by the partnership relative to the elections. If the partnership fails to make an election, a partner cannot compensate for the error by making the election individually.

Though most elections are made by the partnership, each *partner* individually is required to make a specific election on the following relatively narrow tax issues:

- Whether to reduce the basis of depreciable property first when excluding income from discharge of indebtedness.
- Whether to claim cost or percentage depletion for oil and gas wells.
- Whether to take a deduction or a credit for taxes paid to foreign countries and U.S. possessions.

Initial Costs of a Partnership

In its initial stages, a partnership incurs expenses relating to some or all of the following: forming the partnership (organizational costs), admitting partners to the partnership, marketing and selling partnership units to prospective partners (syndication costs), acquiring assets, starting business operations (startup costs), negotiating contracts, and other items. Many of these expenditures are not currently deductible. However, the Code permits a deduction or ratable amortization (i.e., straight-line) of "organizational" and "startup" costs; acquisition costs for depreciable assets are included in the initial basis of the acquired assets; and costs related to some intangible assets may be amortized. "Syndication costs" may be neither amortized nor deducted.

Organizational Costs. These costs include expenditures that are (1) incident to the creation of the partnership; (2) chargeable to a capital account; and (3) of a character that, if incident to the creation of a partnership with an ascertainable life, would be amortized over that life. Organizational costs include accounting fees and legal fees connected with the partnership's formation. The expenditures must be incurred within a period that starts a reasonable time before the partnership begins business. The period ends with the due date (without extensions) of the tax return for the initial tax year.

---

[23]§ 703(b).

[24]Reg. §§ 1.199–4 and 1.199–5T and Rev.Proc. 2007–34, 2007–1 C.B. 1345.

For organizational costs incurred after October 22, 2004, the partnership may elect to deduct up to $5,000 of the costs in the year in which it begins business. This amount must be reduced, however, by the organizational costs that exceed $50,000. Any organizational costs that cannot be deducted under this provision are amortizable over 180 months beginning with the month in which the partnership begins business.[25] For organizational costs incurred before that date, the taxpayer could elect to amortize the amount over 60 months commencing with the month the taxpayer began business.

For either set of rules, the election to deduct or amortize these amounts must be made by the due date (including extensions) of the partnership return for the year in which it begins business. Failure to make a proper election results in no deduction or amortization of the organizational costs until the partnership is liquidated.

Costs incurred for the following items are not organizational costs:

- Acquiring assets for the partnership.
- Transferring assets to the partnership.
- Admitting partners, other than at formation.
- Removing partners, other than at formation.
- Negotiating operating contracts.
- Syndication costs.

Startup Costs. These costs include operating costs that are incurred after the entity is formed but before it begins business. Such costs include marketing surveys prior to conducting business, pre-operating advertising expenses, costs of establishing an accounting system, costs incurred to train employees before business begins, and salaries paid to executives and employees before the start of business.

The partnership may elect to deduct up to $5,000 of startup costs in the year in which it begins business. This amount must be reduced, however, by the startup costs that exceed $50,000.[26] Costs that are not deductible under this provision are amortizable over 180 months beginning with the month in which the partnership begins business. For startup costs incurred before October 23, 2004, the taxpayer could elect to amortize those costs over 60 months commencing with the month the taxpayer began business.

For each set of rules, the election to deduct and amortize startup costs must be made by the due date (including extensions) of the partnership return for the year it begins business. Failure to make a proper election results in no deduction or amortization of the startup costs until the partnership is liquidated.

EXAMPLE 18	The calendar year Bluejay Partnership was formed on July 1, 2008, and immediately started business. Bluejay incurred $4,000 in legal fees for drafting the partnership agreement and $2,200 in accounting fees for tax advice of an organizational nature. In addition, the partnership incurred $20,000 of pre-opening advertising expenses and $34,000 of salaries and training costs for new employees before opening for business. The partnership selected the accrual method of accounting and made an election to deduct and amortize organizational and startup costs in 2008.

Bluejay incurred $6,200 ($4,000 + $2,200) of organizational costs in 2008. The partnership may deduct $5,040 of these costs on its 2008 tax return. This deduction is the sum of the $5,000 permitted deduction and the $40 ($1,200 × 6/180) amortization deduction for the $1,200 of organizational costs that exceed the $5,000 base amount.

Bluejay incurred $54,000 ($20,000 + $34,000) of startup costs in 2008. The partnership may deduct $2,767 of these costs on its tax return for 2008. This deduction is the sum of

- $5,000 reduced by the $4,000 ($54,000 − $50,000) amount by which the startup costs exceed $50,000.
- $1,767 ($53,000 × 6/180) amortization of the remaining $53,000 ($54,000 − $1,000) of startup costs for 6 months.

---

[25]§ 709.   [26]§ 195.

If Bluejay had failed to make a proper election to deduct or amortize the organizational and startup costs, <u>none</u> of these costs would be deductible until the partnership liquidated. ∎

Thar care

Acquisition Costs of Depreciable Assets.

Expenditures may be incurred in changing the legal title in which certain assets are held from that of the contributing partner to the partnership name. These costs include <u>legal fees</u> incurred to transfer assets and transfer taxes imposed by some states. Such costs are added to the partnership's basis for the depreciable assets and increase the amount the partnership may depreciate. As mentioned earlier, the partnership typically determines its depreciation deductions by "stepping into the shoes" of the contributing partner. If additional costs are incurred, though, the additional basis is treated as a new MACRS asset, placed in service on the date the cost is incurred (e.g., the date the asset is transferred to the partnership).

Syndication Costs.

Syndication costs are capitalized, but no amortization election is available. Syndication costs include the following expenditures incurred for promoting and marketing partnership interests:

- Brokerage fees.
- Registration fees.
- Legal fees paid for security advice or advice on the adequacy of tax disclosures in the prospectus or placement memo for securities law purposes.
- Accounting fees related to offering materials.
- Printing costs of prospectus, placement memos, and other selling materials.

Method of Accounting

Like a sole proprietorship, a newly formed partnership may adopt either the cash or the accrual method of accounting, or a hybrid of these two methods.

However, a few special limitations on cash basis accounting apply to partnerships.[27] The cash method of accounting may not be adopted by a partnership that

- has one or more C corporation partners or
- is a tax shelter.

A C corporation partner does <u>*not*</u> preclude cash basis treatment if

- the partnership meets the $5 million gross receipts test described below,
- the C corporation partner(s) is a qualified personal service corporation, such as an incorporated attorney, or
- the partnership is engaged in the business of farming.

exception

A partnership meets the $5 million gross receipts test if it has not received average annual gross receipts of more than $5 million for all tax years beginning after December 31, 1985. "Average annual gross receipts" is the average of gross receipts for the three tax years ending with the tax period in question. For new partnerships, the period of existence is used. Gross receipts are annualized for short taxable periods. A partnership must change to the accrual method the first year after the year in which its average annual gross receipts exceed $5 million and must use the accrual method thereafter.

A tax shelter is a partnership whose interests have been sold in a registered offering or a partnership in which <u>35 percent of the losses are allocated to limited partners</u>.

Jason and Julia are both attorneys. In 2005, each of them formed a professional personal service corporation to operate their separate law practices. In 2008, the two attorneys decide to form the JJ Partnership, which consists of the two professional corporations. In 2008, JJ's

---

[27]§ 448.

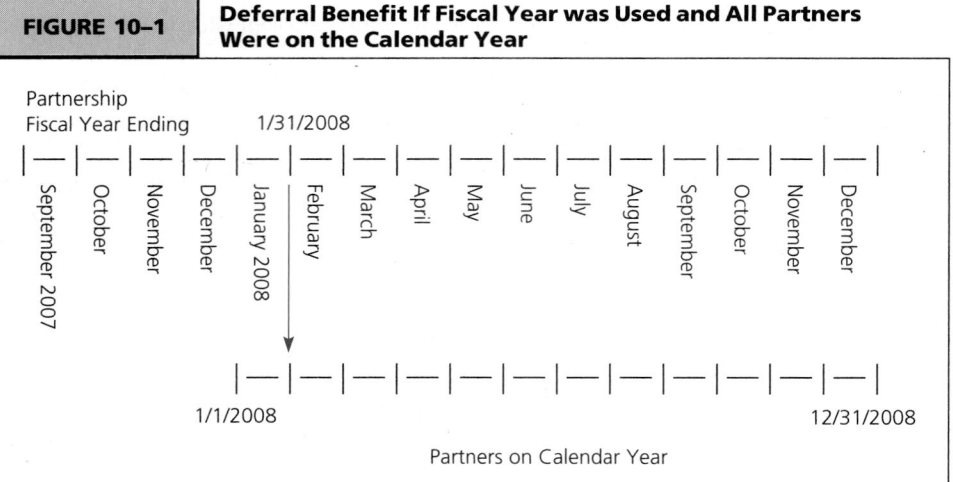

FIGURE 10–1 | **Deferral Benefit If Fiscal Year was Used and All Partners Were on the Calendar Year**

gross receipts are $6 million. JJ may adopt the cash method of accounting, since it is a partnership consisting of qualified personal service corporations. Because JJ has no C corporate partners that are not personal service corporations, the cash method is available even though JJ's average annual gross receipts are greater than $5 million. JJ may also adopt the accrual method of accounting or a hybrid of the cash and accrual methods. ■

Taxable Year of the Partnership

Partnership taxable income (and any separately stated items) flows through to each partner at the end of the *partnership's* taxable year. A *partner's* taxable income, then, includes the distributive share of partnership income for any *partnership* taxable year that ends within the partner's tax year.

When all partners use the calendar year, it would be beneficial in present value terms for a profitable partnership to adopt a fiscal year ending with January 31. Why? As Figure 10–1 illustrates, when the adopted year ends on January 31, the reporting of income from the partnership and payment of related taxes can be deferred for up to 11 months. For instance, income earned by the partnership in September 2007 is not taxable to the partners until January 31, 2008. It is reported in the partner's tax return for the year ended December 31, 2008, which is not due until April 15, 2009. Even though each partner may be required to make quarterly estimated tax payments, some deferral is still possible.

Required Taxable Years. To prevent excessive deferral of taxation of partnership income, Congress and the IRS have adopted a series of rules that prescribe the *required* taxable year an entity must adopt if no alternative tax years (discussed on the next page) are selected. Three rules are presented in Figure 10–2.[28] The partnership must consider each rule in order. The partnership's required taxable year is the taxable year determined under the first rule that applies.

The majority partners' and principal partners' tax year rules in Figure 10–2 are relatively self-explanatory. Under the **least aggregate deferral rule**, the partnership tests the year-ends that are used by the various partners to determine the weighted-average deferral of partnership income. The year-end that offers the least amount of deferral is the *required tax year* under this rule.

---

[28]§ 706(b).

FIGURE 10–2	**Required Tax Year of Partnership**

In Order, Partnership Must Use	Requirements
Majority partners' tax year	• More than 50% of capital *and* profits is owned by partners who have the same taxable year.
Principal partners' tax year	• All partners who own 5% or more of capital *or* profits are principal partners. • All principal partners must have the same tax year.
Year with smallest amount of income deferred	• "Least aggregate deferral rule" (Example 20).

(handwritten annotation: Rules must be considered in order)

EXAMPLE 20

Anne and Bonnie are equal partners in the AB Partnership. Anne uses the calendar year, and Bonnie uses a fiscal year ending August 31. Neither Anne nor Bonnie is a majority partner since neither owns more than 50%. Although Anne and Bonnie are both principal partners, they do not have the same tax year. Therefore, the general rules indicate that the partnership's required tax year must be determined by the "least aggregate deferral rule." The following computations support August 31 as AB's tax year, since the 2.0 product using that year-end is less than the 4.0 product when December 31 is used.

		Test for 12/31 Year-End				
Partner	Year Ends	Profit Interest		Months of Deferral		Product
Anne	12/31	50%	×	–0–	=	0.0
Bonnie	8/31	50%	×	8	=	4.0
Aggregate number of deferral months						4.0

		Test for 8/31 Year-End				
Partner	Year Ends	Profit Interest		Months of Deferral		Product
Anne	12/31	50%	×	4	=	2.0
Bonnie	8/31	50%	×	–0–	=	0.0
Aggregate number of deferral months						2.0

■

Alternative Tax Years. If the required tax year is undesirable to the entity, three other alternative tax years may be available:

• Establish to the IRS's satisfaction that a *business purpose* exists for a different tax year, usually a natural business year at the end of a peak season or shortly thereafter.

• Elect a tax year so that taxes on partnership income are deferred for not more than *three months* from the *required* tax year.[29] Then, have the partnership maintain with the IRS a prepaid, non-interest-bearing deposit of estimated deferred taxes.[30] This alternative may not be desirable since the deposit is based on the highest individual tax rate plus one percentage point, or 36 percent.

• Elect a 52- to 53-week taxable year that ends with reference to the required taxable year or to the taxable year elected under the three-month deferral rule.

---

[29]§ 444.　　　　　　　　　　　　　　　[30]§ 7519.

LO.5

Calculate partnership taxable income and describe how partnership items affect a partner's income tax return.

Operations of the Partnership

An individual, corporation, trust, estate, or another partnership can become a partner in a partnership. Since a partnership is a tax-reporting, rather than a taxpaying, entity for purposes of its Federal (and state) income tax computations, the partnership's income, deductions, credits, and alternative minimum tax (AMT) preferences and adjustments can ultimately be reported and taxed on any of a number of income tax returns (e.g., Forms 1040 [individuals], 1041 [fiduciaries, see Chapter 19], 1120 [C corporations], and 1120S [S corporations]).

A partnership is subject to all other taxes in the same manner as any other business. Thus, the partnership files returns and pays the outstanding amount of pertinent sales taxes, property taxes, and Social Security, unemployment, and other payroll taxes.

Measuring and Reporting Income

The partnership's Form 1065 organizes and reports the transactions of the entity for the tax year. Each of the partnership's tax items is reported on Schedule K of that return. Each partner receives a Schedule K–1 that reports the partner's allocable share of partnership income, credits, and preferences for the year. The IRS also receives a copy of each K–1. Form 1065 is due on the fifteenth day of the fourth month following the close of the partnership's tax year; for a calendar year partnership, this is April 15. The partnership must provide a copy of Schedule K–1 to each partner by this same date. However, partners of an electing large partnership must receive their K–1s one month earlier (March 15 for a calendar year partnership).

Income Measurement. The measurement and reporting of partnership income require a two-step approach. Certain items must be netted at the partnership level, and other items must be segregated and reported separately on the partnership return and each partner's Schedule K–1.

Among the many items passed through separately are the following:

- Net short-term and net long-term capital gains or losses.
- Section 1231 gains and losses.
- Information the partners need to calculate the domestic production activities deduction (§ 199).
- Charitable contributions.
- Portfolio income items (qualified and ordinary dividends, interest, and royalties).
- Expenses related to portfolio income.
- Immediately expensed tangible personal property (§ 179).
- Items allocated among the partners in a different ratio from the general profit and loss ratio.
- Recovery of items previously deducted (tax benefit items).
- AMT preference and adjustment items.
- Self-employment income.
- Passive activity items, such as rental real estate income or loss.
- Intangible drilling and development costs.
- Taxes paid to foreign countries and U.S. possessions.[31]

The reason for separately reporting the preceding items is rooted in the aggregate or conduit concept. These items affect various exclusions, deductions, and credits at the partner level and must pass through without loss of identity so that the proper tax for each partner may be determined.[32]

---

[31]§ 702(a).

[32]§ 702(b).

A partnership is not allowed the following deductions:

- Net operating losses.
- Depletion of oil and gas interests.
- Dividends received deduction.

In addition, items that are only allowed by legislative grace to individuals, such as standard deductions or personal exemptions, are not allowed to the partnership. Also, if a partnership makes a payment on behalf of a partner, such as for alimony, medical expenses, or other items that constitute itemized deductions to individuals, the partnership treats the payment as a distribution or guaranteed payment (discussed later) to the partner, and the partner determines whether to claim the deduction.

This year, the TUV Partnership entered into the following transactions:

EXAMPLE 21

Fees received	$100,000
Salaries paid	30,000
Cost recovery deductions	10,000
Supplies, repairs	3,000
Payroll taxes paid	9,000
Contribution to art museum	6,000
Short-term capital gain	12,000
Passive income (rental operations)	7,500
Qualifying dividends received	1,500
Exempt income (bond interest)	2,100
AMT adjustment (cost recovery)	3,600
Payment of partner Vern's alimony obligations	4,000

The partnership experienced a $20,000 net loss from operations last year, its first year of business.

The partnership's ordinary income is determined as follows:

Nonseparately Stated Items (Ordinary Income)	
Fee income	$100,000
Salaries paid	(30,000)
Cost recovery deductions	(10,000)
Supplies, repairs	(3,000)
Payroll taxes paid	(9,000)
Ordinary income	$ 48,000

The partnership is not allowed a deduction for last year's $20,000 net operating loss—this item was passed through to the partners in the previous year. Moreover, the partnership is not allowed a deduction for payment of Vern's alimony. This payment is probably handled as a distribution to Vern who may claim it as a deduction *for* AGI as if he had paid it himself.

The partnership's separately stated items are:

Separately Stated Items	
Contribution to art museum	$ 6,000
Short-term capital gain	12,000
Passive income (rental operations)	7,500
Qualifying dividends received	1,500
Exempt income (bond interest)	2,100
AMT adjustment (cost recovery)	3,600

[Handwritten notes in right margin: Partnership distribution no gain & loss recognized by the partnership. Distribu liquidation. Monthly distribution = Draw. Gain & loss is only recognized upon distribution of cash. This is true for non-liquidating distribution. Partner basis 5,000 cash distr 7000 — what is gain or loss recognized by the partner & what is his continuing basis (outside base)? ✗ basis become 2000. The only time we recognize gain is if cash exceed the partner('s) basis.]

VARIOUS WITHHOLDING PROCEDURES APPLICABLE TO FOREIGN PARTNERS

A U.S. partnership may have foreign partners, and these partners will be taxed on their U.S. income. Because it might be difficult for the IRS to collect the tax owed by such foreign partners, several Code sections provide for various withholding procedures. The procedures differ depending on whether the income is "effectively connected with a U.S. trade or business," derived from investment property, or related to real estate transactions.

If the partnership purchases real property from a foreign seller, for example, the partnership is required to withhold 10 percent of the purchase price. Further, if the partnership receives "fixed and determinable annual or periodic payments" (FDAP), such as dividends, interest, or rents, it is required to withhold 30 percent of the amounts paid to any foreign person. (The 30 percent withholding rate is often reduced to a lower rate by a tax treaty between the United States and the foreign country.)

Finally, under Regulations issued in 2005, if the partnership has U.S. business income, it must withhold and pay an amount equal to the highest U.S. tax rate applicable to the foreign taxpayer. For a foreign individual or corporate partner, the partnership would withhold 35 percent of any amounts related to a U.S. business.

EXAMPLE 22

Assume the same facts as in Example 21. Tiwanda is a one-third partner in the TUV Partnership. The partnership will give her a Schedule K–1 on which she will be allocated a one-third share of ordinary income and one-third of each of the separately stated items. Thus, in determining her tax liability on her Form 1040, Tiwanda includes $16,000 of ordinary income, a $2,000 charitable deduction, a $4,000 short-term capital gain, $2,500 of passive rent income, $500 of qualifying dividend income, and a $1,200 positive adjustment in computing alternative minimum taxable income. She will disclose her $700 share of tax-exempt interest on the first page of her Form 1040. ■

Domestic Production Activities Deduction (§ 199). As noted in Chapter 3, the conduct of certain businesses, usually manufacturing activities, can yield a domestic production activities deduction (DPAD). To determine the base for the deduction, domestic production gross receipts (DPGR) is first computed and then is reduced by related cost of goods sold and direct and indirect expenses to arrive at qualified production activities income (QPAI). The deduction (or DPAD) is 6 percent (in 2007–2009) of the lesser of QPAI or taxable income.[33] When the taxpayer is not a corporation, modified AGI is substituted for taxable income. In no event, however, may the DPAD exceed 50 percent of the W–2 wages paid that are attributable to domestic production activities.[34]

When pass-through entities are involved (i.e., partnerships, S corporations, estates, and trusts), special rules apply.[35] Specifically, in the case of partnerships, the following rules govern the DPAD computation and allowance:

- Whether an activity qualifies for the DPAD is determined at the entity level.
- For many types of partnerships, QPAI and W–2 wages related to production can be calculated at the entity level.[36] Unless otherwise indicated, assume throughout this chapter that the entity-level calculation applies.

---

[33]§ 199(a). The percentage becomes 9% after 2009.

[34]§ 199(b).

[35]The rules applicable to pass-through entities are contained in § 199(d)(1) and Temp.Reg. § 1.199–5T.

[36]See Rev.Proc. 2007–34, 2007–1 C.B. 1345, generally effective for tax years beginning on or after May 11, 2007 (the taxpayer may elect to apply the Revenue Procedure to tax years beginning on or after May 11, 2006).

- The partnership calculates QPAI by taking into account all separately stated and nonseparately stated items. Income and deduction inclusion and limitations are, for this purpose, determined at the partnership level.
- The Regulations outline specific methods for allocating costs between production-related and non-production-related activities. An "eligible § 861 partnership" must use the § 861 method, as defined. An "eligible widely held pass-through entity" must use the "simplified deduction method." An "eligible small pass-through entity" must use the "small business simplified overall method."
- On Schedule K–1, each partner is allocated his or her share of QPAI and W–2 wages related to domestic production activities. The entity allocates QPAI among the partners using the allocation method used for gross income. The entity allocates W–2 production-related wages among the partners using the allocation method used for allocating wage expense.
- An individual partner will list this pass-through information on Form 8903 (Domestic Production Activities Deduction).
- A partner combines the partnership pass-through items with those from other sources (e.g., a partner has his or her own factory).
- Guaranteed payments made by a partnership to a partner are not considered to be W–2 wages for DPAD purposes.

EXAMPLE 23

For tax year 2008, the BR Partnership had QPAI of $200,000 and W–2 wages related to QPAI of $30,000. Brian is a 40% partner in BR and, as such, is allocated QPAI of $80,000 and W–2 wages of $12,000. If Brian's modified AGI (before the DPAD) is $160,000, his DPAD is determined as follows: 6% × the lesser of $80,000 (QPAI) or $160,000 (MAGI), or $4,800. This amount cannot exceed 50% of Brian's allocable share of W–2 wages, or $6,000 (50% × $12,000). Brian's DPAD, reported as an above-the-line deduction on his Form 1040, is $4,800; the amount is not reduced by the W–2 wages paid limitation. ■

EXAMPLE 24

Assume the same facts as in Example 23, except that part of Brian's income is from a qualified production activity he conducts individually (i.e., apart from the partnership). This activity generates QPAI of $50,000, but there are no W–2 wages—Brian uses contract labor (independent contractors). Now the DPAD calculation is 6% of the lesser of $130,000 ($50,000 + $80,000), or $160,000 (MAGI), or $7,800. But because the wage limitation remains the same (see computation in Example 23), Brian's DPAD is limited to $6,000. ■

Withdrawals. Capital withdrawals by partners during the year do not affect the partnership's income measuring and reporting process. These items usually are treated as distributions made on the last day of the partnership's tax year. Distributions are discussed in Chapter 11.

Penalties. A partner's share of each partnership item should be reported on the partner's tax return in the same manner as presented on the Form 1065. If a partner treats an item differently, the IRS must be notified of the inconsistent treatment.[37] If a partner fails to notify the IRS, a negligence penalty may be added to the tax due.

To encourage the filing of a partnership return, a penalty of $50, per partner, per month (or fraction thereof, but not to exceed five months) is imposed on the partnership for failure to file a complete and timely information return without reasonable cause.[38]

---

[37]§ 6222.

[38]§ 6698.

A partnership with 10 or fewer "natural persons" or corporations as partners, where each partner's share of partnership items is the same for all items, is automatically excluded from these penalties.[39]

<table>
<tr><td>**ETHICAL and EQUITABLE** *Considerations*</td><td>**A PREPARER'S RESPONSIBILITY FOR PARTNERS' TAX RETURNS**</td></tr>
</table>

A partnership's tax return preparer is responsible for accurately presenting information supplied by the partnership in that return. If a flow-through amount is significant to a certain partner, the preparer of the *partnership* return can be treated as the preparer of the *partner's* tax return with respect to that item.

If a preparer misstates an item on a partnership return either by taking a position that is not supportable under current law or by willfully misreporting the item, "preparer penalties" can be assessed. Although these penalties are relatively small, their imposition may lead to the preparer's suspension from practice before the IRS or by a state accountancy board.

As an example, assume Stan, a CPA, knowingly reported a $20,000 deduction for fines and penalties (nondeductible items) in determining the JB Partnership's $30,000 income from operations. This amount is allocated equally to partners Joe and Barb. Joe has other income of $35,000; Barb has other income of $1 million. Stan is treated as the preparer of Joe's tax return with respect to the improper $10,000 flow-through item since the fines and penalties are significant relative to Joe's income. Stan is not the preparer of Barb's return since the fines and penalties are not significant to her income.

In a recent case, the preparer of a partnership return was considered to be the preparer of several partners' returns with respect to partnership items flowing through to the partners. The court reached this decision even though the return preparer never met the individual partners, received no direct fees from the partners, and performed no other services for them.

Do you believe this is a reasonable approach for allocating responsibility for accurate preparation of a partner's tax return? Why or why not?

Partnership Allocations

So far, most examples in this chapter have assumed that the partner has the same percentage interest in capital, profits, and losses. Thus, a partner who owns a 25 percent interest in partnership capital has been assumed to own 25 percent of partnership profits and 25 percent of partnership losses.

Economic Effect. The partnership agreement can provide that any partner may share capital, profits, and losses in different ratios. For example, a partner could have a 25 percent capital sharing ratio, yet be allocated 30 percent of the profits and 20 percent of the losses of the partnership. Such special allocations have, at times, been used in an attempt to manipulate the allocation of tax benefits among partners. The Regulations[40] are designed to prevent unfair use of such manipulation. Although these rules are too complex to discuss in detail, the general outline of one of these rules—the **economic effect test**—can be easily understood.

In general, the economic effect test requires the following:

- An allocation of income or gain to a partner must increase the partner's capital account, and an allocation of deduction or loss must decrease the partner's capital account.
- When the partner's interest is liquidated, the partner must receive net assets that have a fair market value equal to the positive balance in the capital account.

---

[39]§§ 6231(a)(1)(B) and (I). Natural persons for this purpose include individuals who are not nonresident aliens, as well as the estate of a decedent who was not a nonresident alien.

[40]Reg. § 1.704–1(b).

- A partner with a negative capital account must restore that account upon liquidation of the interest. Restoration of a negative capital account can best be envisioned as a contribution of cash to the partnership equal to the negative balance.

These requirements are designed to ensure that a partner bears the economic burden of a loss or deduction allocation and receives the economic benefit of an income or gain allocation.

EXAMPLE 25

Eli and Sanjay each contribute $20,000 cash to the newly formed ES Partnership. The partnership uses the cash to acquire a depreciable asset for $40,000. The partnership agreement provides that the depreciation is allocated 90% to Eli and 10% to Sanjay. Other items of partnership income, gain, loss, or deduction are allocated equally between the partners. Upon liquidation of the partnership, property will be distributed to the partners in accordance with their positive capital account balances. Any partner with a negative capital account must restore the capital account upon liquidation. Assume the first-year depreciation on the equipment is $4,000. Also, assume nothing else happens in the first year that affects the partners' capital accounts.

Eli's capital account is $16,400 ($20,000 − $3,600), and Sanjay's capital account has a balance of $19,600 ($20,000 − $400) after the first year of partnership operations. The Regulations require that a hypothetical sale of the asset for its $36,000 adjusted basis on the last day of the year and an immediate liquidation of the partnership should result in Eli and Sanjay receiving distributions equal to their capital accounts. According to the partnership agreement, Eli would receive $16,400, and Sanjay would receive $19,600 of the cash in a liquidating distribution. Eli, therefore, bears the economic burden of $3,600 depreciation since he contributed $20,000 to the partnership and would receive only $16,400 upon liquidation. Likewise, Sanjay's economic burden is $400 since he would receive only $19,600 of his original $20,000 investment. The agreement, therefore, has economic effect. ■

EXAMPLE 26

Assume the same facts as in Example 25, except that the partnership agreement provides that Eli and Sanjay will receive equal amounts of cash upon liquidation of the partnership. The hypothetical sale of the asset for its $36,000 adjusted basis and the immediate liquidation of the partnership would result in each partner receiving $18,000 cash. Since each partner contributed $20,000 to the partnership and each partner would receive $18,000 upon liquidation, each partner bears the economic burden of $2,000 of depreciation. The original 90%/10% allocation of depreciation to the two partners is defective, and the IRS will require that the depreciation be reallocated equally ($2,000 each) to the two partners to reflect the economic burden borne by each partner. ■

Precontribution Gain or Loss. Certain income, gain, loss, and deductions relative to contributed property may not be allocated under the rules described above. Instead, **precontribution gain or loss** must be allocated among the partners to take into account the variation between the basis of the property and its fair market value on the date of contribution.[41] For nondepreciable property, this means that *built-in* gain or loss on the date of contribution must be allocated to the contributing partner when the property is eventually disposed of by the partnership in a taxable transaction.

EXAMPLE 27

Seth and Tim form the equal profit and loss sharing ST Partnership. Seth contributes cash of $10,000, and Tim contributes land purchased two years ago and held for investment. The land has an adjusted basis of $6,000 and fair market value of $10,000 at the contribution date. For accounting purposes, the partnership records the land at its fair market value of $10,000.

---

[41]§ 704(c)(1)(A).

CONCEPT SUMMARY 10–2

Tax Reporting of Partnership Activities

Event	Partnership Level	Partner Level
1. Compute partnership ordinary income.	Form 1065, line 22, page 1. Schedule K, Form 1065, line 1, page 3.	Schedule K–1 (Form 1065), line 1. Each partner's share is passed through for separate reporting. Each partner's basis is increased.
2. Compute partnership ordinary loss.	Form 1065, line 22, page 1. Schedule K, Form 1065, line 1, page 3.	Schedule K–1 (Form 1065), line 1. Each partner's share is passed through for separate reporting. Each partner's basis is decreased. The amount of a partner's loss deduction may be limited. Losses that may not be deducted are carried forward for use in future years.
3. Separately reported items like portfolio income, capital gain and loss, and § 179 deductions.	Schedule K, Form 1065, various lines, page 3.	Schedule K–1 (Form 1065), various lines. Each partner's share of each item is passed through for separate reporting.
4. Net earnings from self-employment.	Schedule K, Form 1065, line 14, page 3.	Schedule K–1 (Form 1065), line 14.

For tax purposes, the partnership takes a carryover basis of $6,000 in the land. After using the land as a parking lot for five months, ST sells it for $10,600. No other transactions have taken place.

The accounting and tax gain from the land sale are computed as follows:

	Accounting	Tax
Amount realized	$10,600	$10,600
Less: Adjusted basis	10,000	6,000
Gain realized	$ 600	$ 4,600
Built-in gain to Tim	–0–	4,000
Remaining gain (split equally)	$ 600	$ 600

Seth recognizes $300 of the gain ($600 remaining gain ÷ 2), and Tim recognizes $4,300 [$4,000 built-in gain + ($600 remaining gain ÷ 2)]. ∎

If the property is depreciable, Regulations describe allowable methods of allocating depreciation deductions.[42] If contributed property has built-in losses at the contribution date, allocations related to the built-in loss can be made only to the contributing partner. For purposes of allocations to other partners, the partnership's basis in the loss property is treated as being the fair market value of the property at the contribution date.[43]

Concept Summary 10–2 reviews the tax reporting rules for partnership activities.

---

[42]Reg. § 1.704–3.   [43]§ 704(c)(1)(C).

ETHICAL and EQUITABLE *Considerations*	**BUILT-IN APPRECIATION ON CONTRIBUTED PROPERTY**

In the "old days," one partner could contribute cash and another partner could contribute an equal value of appreciated property with no subsequent record-keeping requirements. Future depreciation deductions and gains on sale of the property could be allocated to both partners equally, thereby shifting income from one taxpayer to another. A partner in a lower tax bracket (or with expiring net operating losses and the like) could report the share of the gain on sale of the asset with a relatively low corresponding tax burden.

Section 704(c)(1)(A) was added to the Code to ensure that the partner contributing the property pays tax on any built-in gain. This prevents income shifting among taxpayers and loss of revenue to the IRS.

There is no corresponding provision for S corporations—gains and losses and depreciation expense are allocated among the shareholders without regard to any built-in appreciation on contributed property.

What theory of partnership taxation supports this difference in treatment?

Basis of a Partnership Interest

LO.6

Determine a partner's basis in the partnership interest.

Previously, this chapter discussed how to compute a partner's adjusted basis when the partnership is formed. It was noted that the partner's adjusted basis in the newly formed partnership usually equals (1) the adjusted basis in any property contributed to the partnership plus (2) the fair market value of any services the partner performed for the partnership (i.e., the amount of ordinary income reported by the partner for services rendered to the partnership).

A partnership interest also can be acquired after the partnership has been formed. The method of acquisition controls how the partner's initial basis is computed. If the partnership interest is purchased from another partner, the purchasing partner's basis is the amount paid (cost basis) for the partnership interest. The basis of a partnership interest acquired by gift is the donor's basis for the interest plus, in certain cases, some or all of the transfer (gift) tax paid by the donor. The basis of a partnership interest acquired through inheritance generally is the fair market value of the interest on the date the partner dies.

After the partner is admitted to the partnership, the partner's basis is adjusted for numerous items. The following operating results *increase* a partner's adjusted basis:

- The partner's proportionate share of partnership income (including capital gains and tax-exempt income).
- The partner's proportionate share of any increase in partnership liabilities. (This provision is discussed in the next section.)

The following operating results *decrease* the partner's adjusted basis in the partnership:

- The partner's proportionate share of partnership deductions and losses (including capital losses).
- The partner's proportionate share of nondeductible expenses.
- The partner's proportionate share of any reduction in partnership liabilities.[44]

Under no circumstances can the partner's adjusted basis for the partnership interest be reduced below zero.

Increasing the adjusted basis for the partner's share of partnership taxable income is logical since the partner has already been taxed on the income. By

---

[44]§§ 705 and 752.

increasing the partner's basis, this ensures that the partner is not taxed again on the income when he or she sells the interest or receives a distribution from the partnership.

It is also logical that the tax-exempt income should increase the partner's basis. If the income is exempt in the current period, it should not contribute to the recognition of gain when the partner either sells the interest or receives a distribution from the partnership.

EXAMPLE 28

Yuri is a one-third partner in the XYZ Partnership. His proportionate share of the partnership income during the current year consists of $20,000 of ordinary taxable income and $10,000 of tax-exempt income. None of the income is distributed to Yuri. The adjusted basis of Yuri's partnership interest before adjusting for his share of income is $35,000, and the fair market value of the interest before considering the income items is $50,000.

The unrealized gain inherent in Yuri's investment in the partnership is $15,000 ($50,000 − $35,000) before adjusting for his share of income. Yuri's proportionate share of the income items should increase the fair market value of the interest to $80,000 ($50,000 + $20,000 + $10,000). By increasing the adjusted basis of Yuri's partnership interest to $65,000 ($35,000 + $20,000 + $10,000), this ensures that the unrealized gain inherent in Yuri's partnership investment remains at $15,000. This makes sense because the $20,000 of ordinary taxable income is taxed to Yuri this year and should not be taxed again when Yuri either sells his interest or receives a distribution. Similarly, the exempt income is exempt this year and should not increase Yuri's gain when he either sells his interest or receives a distribution from the partnership. ■

Decreasing the adjusted basis for the partner's share of deductible losses, deductions, and noncapitalizable, nondeductible expenditures is logical for the same reasons. An item that is deductible currently should not contribute to creating a loss when the partnership interest is sold or when a distribution is received from the partnership. Similarly, a noncapitalizable, nondeductible expenditure should never be deductible nor contribute to a loss when a subsequent sale or distribution transaction occurs.

Liability Sharing. A partner's adjusted basis is affected by the partner's share of partnership debt.[45] Partnership debt includes any partnership obligation that creates an asset, results in an expense to the partnership, or results in a nondeductible, noncapitalizable item at the partnership level. This definition includes certain contingent liabilities.[46] The definition also includes most debt that is considered a liability under financial accounting rules except for accounts payable of a cash basis partnership.

Under § 752, an increase in a partner's share of partnership debt is treated as a cash contribution by the partner to the partnership. A partner's share of partnership debt increases as a result of increases in the total amount of partnership debt. A decrease in a partner's share of partnership debt is treated as a cash distribution from the partnership to the partner. A partner's share of partnership debt decreases as a result of (1) decreases in the total amount of partnership debt and (2) assumption of the partner's debt by the partnership.

LO.7

Explain how liabilities affect a partner's basis.

EXAMPLE 29

Jim and Becky contribute property to form the JB Partnership. Jim contributes cash of $30,000. Becky contributes land with an adjusted basis and fair market value of $45,000, subject to a liability of $15,000. The partnership borrows $50,000 to finance construction of a building on the contributed land. At the end of the first year, the accrual basis partnership owes $3,500 in trade accounts payable to various vendors. Assume no other operating activities occurred.

---

[45]§ 752.   [46]Reg. § 1.752–1(a)(4)(ii).

Partnership debt sharing rules are discussed later in this section, but assuming for simplicity that Jim and Becky share equally in liabilities, the partners' bases in their partnership interests are determined as follows:

Jim's Basis		Becky's Basis	
Contributed cash	$30,000	Basis in contributed land	$ 45,000
Share of debt on land (assumed by partnership)	7,500	Less: Debt assumed by partnership	(15,000)
		Share of debt on land (assumed by partnership)	7,500
Initial basis	$37,500	Initial basis	$ 37,500
Share of construction loan	25,000	Share of construction loan	25,000
Share of trade accounts payable	1,750	Share of trade accounts payable	1,750
Basis, end of first year	$64,250	Basis, end of first year	$ 64,250

In this case, it is reasonable that the parties have an equal basis, because each is a 50% owner and they contributed property with identical *net* bases and identical *net* fair market values. ∎

EXAMPLE 30

Assume the same facts as in Example 29. In the second year, the partnership generates $70,000 of taxable income from operations and repays both the $50,000 construction loan and the $3,500 trade accounts payable. The taxable income is allocated equally to each partner and increases each partner's basis by $35,000. The $26,750 ($25,000 + $1,750) reduction of each partner's share of liabilities is treated as a cash distribution to each partner and reduces each partner's adjusted basis by that amount. The $72,500 adjusted basis for each partner at the end of the second year is computed as follows:

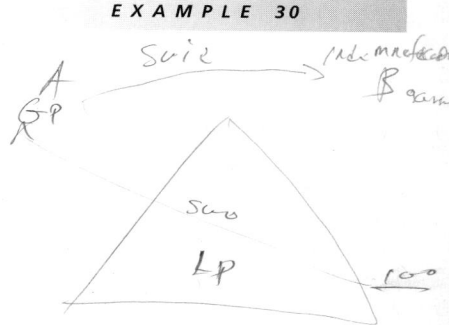

Jim's Basis		Becky's Basis	
Basis, beginning of second year	$ 64,250	Basis, beginning of second year	$ 64,250
Share of taxable income	35,000	Share of taxable income	35,000
Share of construction loan paid	(25,000)	Share of construction loan paid	(25,000)
Share of trade accounts payable paid	(1,750)	Share of trade accounts payable paid	(1,750)
Basis, end of second year	$ 72,500	Basis, end of second year	$ 72,500

∎

Two types of partnership debt exist. **Recourse debt** is partnership debt for which the partnership or at least one of the partners is personally liable. This personal liability can exist, for example, through the operation of state law or through personal guarantees that a partner makes to the creditor. Personal liability of a party related to a partner (under attribution rules) is treated as the personal liability of the partner. **Nonrecourse debt** is debt for which no partner (or party related to a partner) is personally liable. Lenders of nonrecourse debt generally require that collateral be pledged against the loan. Upon default, the lender can claim only the collateral, not the partners' personal assets.

How liabilities are shared among the partners depends upon whether the debt is recourse or nonrecourse and when the liability was incurred. For most debt *created* before January 29, 1989, the rules are relatively straightforward. Recourse debt is shared among the partners in accordance with their loss sharing ratios while non-recourse debt is shared among the partners in accordance with the way they share partnership profits. Although questions arise about the calculation of the profit or loss sharing ratios and the treatment of personal guarantees of debt, the rules for sharing this earlier debt are easy to apply.

The rules for sharing partnership debt created after January 29, 1989, are much more complex. The basic principles of these rules are illustrated below.

Recourse Debt Rules. Recourse debt created after January 29, 1989, is shared in accordance with a **constructive liquidation scenario.**[47]

Under this scenario, the following events are *deemed* to occur at the end of each taxable year of the partnership:

1. Most partnership assets (including cash) become worthless.
2. The worthless assets are sold at fair market value ($0), and losses on the deemed sales are determined.
3. These losses are allocated to the partners according to their loss sharing ratios. These losses reduce the partners' capital accounts.
4. Any partner with a (deemed) negative capital account balance is treated as contributing cash to the partnership to restore that negative balance to zero.
5. The cash deemed contributed by the partners with negative capital balances is used to pay the liabilities of the partnership.
6. The partnership is deemed to be liquidated immediately, and any remaining cash is distributed to partners with positive capital account balances.

The amount of a partner's cash contribution that would be used (in step 5 above) to pay partnership recourse liabilities is that partner's share of these partnership recourse liabilities.

EXAMPLE 31

On January 1 of the current year, Nina and Otis each contribute $20,000 cash to the newly created NO General Partnership. Each partner has a 50% interest in partnership capital, profits, and losses. The first year of partnership operations resulted in the following balance sheet as of December 31:

	Basis	FMV		Basis	FMV
Cash	$12,000	$12,000	Recourse payables	$30,000	$30,000
Receivables	7,000	7,000	Nina, capital	19,500	19,500
Land and buildings	50,000	50,000	Otis, capital	19,500	19,500
	$69,000	$69,000		$69,000	$69,000

The recourse debt is shared in accordance with the constructive liquidation scenario. All of the partnership assets (including cash) are deemed to be worthless and sold for $0. This creates a loss of $69,000 ($12,000 + $7,000 + $50,000), which is allocated equally between the two partners. The $34,500 loss allocated to each partner creates negative capital accounts of $15,000 each for Nina and Otis. If the partnership were actually liquidated, each partner would contribute $15,000 cash to the partnership; the cash would be used to pay the partnership recourse payables; and the partnership would cease to exist. Because each partner would be required to contribute $15,000 to pay the liabilities, each shares in $15,000 of the recourse payables. Accordingly, Nina and Otis will each have an adjusted basis for their partnership interests of $34,500 ($19,500 + $15,000) on December 31. ■

---

[47]Transition rules (beyond the scope of this text) apply to debt created between January 29, 1989, and December 28, 1991.

EXAMPLE 32

Assume the same facts as in Example 31, except that the partners allocate partnership losses 60% to Nina and 40% to Otis. The constructive liquidation scenario results in the $69,000 loss being allocated $41,400 to Nina and $27,600 to Otis. As a consequence, Nina's capital account has a negative balance of $21,900, and Otis's account has a negative balance of $8,100. Each partner is deemed to contribute cash equal to these negative capital accounts, and the cash would be used to pay the recourse liabilities under the liquidation scenario. Accordingly, Nina and Otis share $21,900 and $8,100, respectively, in the recourse debt. Note that the debt allocation percentages (73% to Nina and 27% to Otis) are different from the partners' 60%/40% loss sharing ratios. ■

Nonrecourse Debt Rules. Nonrecourse debt is allocated in three stages. First, an amount of debt equal to the amount of *minimum gain* is allocated to partners who share in minimum gain. The calculation of minimum gain is complex, and details of the calculation are beyond the scope of this text. In general, minimum gain approximates the amount of nonrecourse (mortgage) liability on a property in excess of the "book" basis of the property. Generally, the "book" basis for a property item is the same as the "tax" basis, although sometimes the amounts are different. For example, the "book" basis for contributed property on the date of contribution is its fair market value at that date, not its "tax" basis.

If a lender forecloses on partnership property, the result is treated as a deemed sale of the property for the mortgage balance. Gain is recognized for at least the amount of the liability in excess of the property's "book" basis—hence, minimum gain. Allocation of minimum gain among the partners should be addressed in the partnership agreement.

Second, the amount of nonrecourse debt equal to the remaining *precontribution gain* under § 704(c) is allocated to the partner who contributed the property and debt to the partnership. For this purpose, the remaining precontribution gain is the excess of the current nonrecourse debt balance on the contributed property over the current tax basis of the contributed property.[48] Note that this calculation is only relevant when the "book" and "tax" bases of the contributed property are different.

Third, any remaining nonrecourse debt is allocated to the partners in accordance with one of several different allocation methods. The partnership agreement should specify which allocation method is chosen. Most often, the profit sharing ratio is used.

EXAMPLE 33

Ted contributes a nondepreciable asset to the TK Partnership in exchange for a one-third interest in the capital, profits, and losses of the partnership. The asset has an adjusted tax basis to Ted and the partnership of $24,000 and a fair market value and "book" basis on the contribution date of $50,000. The asset is encumbered by a nonrecourse note (created January 1, 2007) of $35,000. Because the "book" basis exceeds the nonrecourse debt, there is no minimum gain. Under § 704(c) principles, the Regulations provide that the first $11,000 of the nonrecourse debt ($35,000 debt − $24,000 basis) is allocated to Ted. Assume the partnership allocates the remaining $24,000 nonrecourse debt according to the profit sharing ratio, and Ted's share is $8,000. Therefore, Ted shares in $19,000 ($11,000 + $8,000) of the nonrecourse debt.

Ted's basis in his partnership interest is determined as follows:

Substituted basis of contributed property	$ 24,000
Less: Liability assumed by partnership	(35,000)
Plus: Allocation of § 704(c) debt	11,000
Basis before remaining allocation	$ –0–
Plus: Allocation of remaining nonrecourse debt	8,000
Basis in partnership interest	$ 8,000

[48]Reg. § 1.704–3.

The § 704(c) allocation of nonrecourse debt prevents Ted from receiving a deemed distribution ($35,000) in excess of his basis in property he contributed ($24,000). Without this required allocation of nonrecourse debt, in some cases, a contributing partner would be required to recognize gain on a contribution of property encumbered by nonrecourse debt. ∎

Other Factors Affecting Basis Calculations. The partner's basis is also affected by (1) postacquisition contributions of cash or property to the partnership; (2) postacquisition distributions of cash or property from the partnership; and (3) special calculations that are designed to allow the full deduction of percentage depletion for oil and gas wells. Postacquisition contributions of cash or property affect basis in the same manner as contributions made upon the creation of the partnership. Postacquisition distributions of cash or property reduce basis.

EXAMPLE 34

Ryan is a one-third partner in the ERM Partnership. On January 1, 2008, Ryan's basis in his partnership interest was $50,000. During 2008, the calendar year, accrual basis partnership generated ordinary taxable income of $210,000. It also received $60,000 of tax-exempt interest income from City of Buffalo bonds. It paid $3,000 in nondeductible bribes to local law enforcement officials, so that the police would not notify the Federal government about the products that the entity had imported without paying the proper tariffs. On July 1, 2008, Ryan contributed $20,000 cash and a computer (zero basis to him) to the partnership. Ryan's monthly draw from the partnership is $3,000; this is treated as a distribution and not as a guaranteed payment. The only liabilities that the partnership has incurred are trade accounts payable. On January 1, 2008, the trade accounts payable totaled $45,000; this account balance was $21,000 on December 31, 2008. Ryan shares in one-third of the partnership liabilities for basis purposes.

Ryan's basis in the partnership on December 31, 2008, is $115,000, computed as follows:

Beginning balance	$ 50,000
Share of ordinary partnership income	70,000
Share of exempt income	20,000
Share of nondeductible expenditures	(1,000)
Ryan's basis in noncash capital contribution	–0–
Additional cash contributions	20,000
Capital withdrawal ($3,000 × 12)	(36,000)
Share of net decrease in partnership liabilities [1/3 × ($45,000 − $21,000)]	(8,000)
	$115,000

∎

EXAMPLE 35

Assume the same facts as in Example 34. If Ryan withdraws cash of $115,000 from the partnership on January 1, 2009, the withdrawal is tax-free to him and reduces his basis to zero. The distribution is tax-free because Ryan has recognized his share of the partnership's net income throughout his association with the entity via the annual flow-through of his share of the partnership's income and expense items to his personal tax return. Note that the $20,000 cash withdrawal of his share of the municipal bond interest retains its nontaxable character in this distribution. Ryan receives the $20,000 tax-free because his basis was increased in 2008 when the partnership received the interest income. ∎

A partner is required to compute the adjusted basis only when necessary and thus can avoid the inconvenience of making day-to-day calculations of basis. When a partnership interest is sold, exchanged, or retired, however, the partner must compute the adjusted basis as of the date the transaction occurs. Computation of gain or loss requires an accurate calculation of the partner's adjusted basis on the transaction date.

Figure 10–3 summarizes the rules for computing a partner's basis in a partnership interest.

RE 10–3   Partner's Basis in Partnership Interest

Bas is generally adjusted in the following order:

Initial basis. Amount paid for partnership interest, or gift or inherited basis (including share of partnership debt). Amount paid can be amount contributed to the partnership or amount paid to another partner or former partner.

+ Partner's subsequent contributions
+ Since interest acquired, partner's share of the partnership's
  • Debt increase
  • Taxable income items
  • Exempt income items
  • Excess of depletion deductions over adjusted basis of property subject to depletion
– Partner's distributions and withdrawals
– Since interest acquired, partner's share of the partnership's
  • Debt decrease
  • Nondeductible items not chargeable to a capital account
  • Special depletion deduction for oil and gas wells
  • Loss items

★ **The basis of a partner's interest can never be negative.**

Loss Limitations

Partnership losses flow through to the partners for use on their tax returns. However, the amount and nature of the losses allowed in a partner's tax computations may be limited. When limitations apply, all or a portion of the losses are held in suspension until a triggering event occurs. Only then can the losses be used to determine the partner's tax liability. No time limit is imposed on such carryforwards of losses.

Three different limitations may apply to partnership losses that are passed through to a partner:

• The first is the overall limitation contained in § 704(d). This limitation allows the deduction of losses only to the extent the partner has adjusted basis for the partnership interest.
• Losses that are deductible under the overall limitation may then be subject to the at-risk limitation of § 465. Losses are deductible under this provision only to the extent the partner is at risk for the partnership interest.
• Any losses that survive this second limitation may be subject to a third limitation, the passive loss rules of § 469.

Only losses that make it through all these applicable limitations are eligible to be deducted on the partner's tax return.

LO.8

Describe the limitations on deducting partnership losses.

Meg is a partner in a partnership that does not invest in real estate. On January 1, 2008, Meg's adjusted basis for her partnership interest is $50,000, and her at-risk amount is $35,000. Her share of losses from the partnership for 2008 is $60,000, all of which is passive. She has one other passive income-producing investment that produced $25,000 of passive income during 2008.

Meg will be able to deduct $25,000 of partnership losses on her Form 1040 for 2008. Her deductible loss is calculated as follows:

E X A M P L E   36

Applicable Provision	Deductible Loss	Suspended Loss
Overall limitation	$50,000	$10,000
At-risk limitation	35,000	15,000
Passive loss limitation	25,000	10,000

Meg can deduct only $50,000 under the overall limitation. Of this $50,000, only $35,000 is deductible under the at-risk limitation. Under the passive loss limitation, passive losses can be deducted only against passive income. Thus, Meg can deduct only $25,000 on her return in 2008. ∎

Overall Limitation. A partner may only deduct losses flowing through from the partnership to the extent of the partner's adjusted basis in the partnership. A partner's adjusted basis in the partnership is determined at the end of the partnership's taxable year. It is adjusted for distributions and any partnership gains during the year, but it is determined *before considering any losses for the year.*

Losses that cannot be deducted because of this rule are suspended and carried forward (never back) for use against future increases in the partner's adjusted basis. Such increases might result from additional capital contributions, from sharing in additional partnership debts, or from future partnership income.

| EXAMPLE 37 | Carol and Dan do business as the CD Partnership, sharing profits and losses equally. All parties use the calendar year. At the start of the current year, the basis of Carol's partnership interest is $25,000. The partnership sustains an operating loss of $80,000 in the current year. For the current year, only $25,000 of Carol's $40,000 allocable share of the partnership loss can be deducted under the overall limitation. As a result, the basis of Carol's partnership interest is zero as of January 1 of the following year, and Carol must carry forward the remaining $15,000 of partnership losses. ∎ |

| EXAMPLE 38 | Assume the same facts as in Example 37, and that the partnership earns a profit of $70,000 for the next calendar year. Carol reports net partnership income of $20,000 ($35,000 distributive share of income − the $15,000 carryforward loss). The basis of Carol's partnership interest becomes $20,000. ∎ |

At-Risk Limitation. Under the at-risk rules, the partnership losses from business and income-producing activities that individual partners and closely held C corporation partners can deduct are limited to amounts that are economically invested in the partnership. Invested amounts include the adjusted basis of cash and property contributed by the partner and the partner's share of partnership earnings that has not been withdrawn.[49] A closely held C corporation exists when five or fewer individuals own more than 50 percent of the entity's stock under appropriate attribution and ownership rules.

When some or all of the partners are personally liable for partnership recourse debt, that debt is included in the adjusted basis of those partners. Usually, those partners also include the debt in their amount at risk.

No partner, however, carries any financial risk on nonrecourse debt. Therefore, as a general rule, partners cannot include nonrecourse debt in their amount at risk even though that debt is included in the adjusted basis of their partnership interest. This rule has an exception, however, that applies in many cases. Real estate nonrecourse financing provided by a bank, retirement plan, or similar party or by a Federal, state, or local government generally is deemed to be at risk.[50] Such debt is termed **qualified nonrecourse debt**. In summary, although the general rule provides that nonrecourse debt is not at risk, the overriding exception may provide that it is deemed to be at risk.

When determining a partner's loss deduction, the overall limitation rule is invoked first. That is, the deduction is limited to the partner's outside basis at the end of the partnership year. Then, the at-risk provisions are applied to see if the remaining loss is still deductible. Suspended losses are carried forward until a partner has a sufficient amount at risk in the activity to absorb them.[51]

---

[49]§ 465(a).
[50]§ 465(b)(6).

[51]§ 465(a)(2).

E X A M P L E   39

Kelly invests $5,000 in the Kelly Green Limited Partnership as a 5% general partner. Shortly thereafter, the partnership acquires the master recording of a well-known vocalist for $250,000 ($50,000 from the partnership and $200,000 secured from a local bank by means of a *recourse* mortgage). Assume Kelly's share of the recourse debt is $10,000, and her basis in her partnership interest is $15,000 ($5,000 cash investment + $10,000 debt share). Since the debt is recourse, Kelly's at-risk amount is also $15,000. Kelly's share of partnership losses in the first year of operations is $11,000. Kelly is entitled to deduct the full $11,000 of partnership losses under both the overall and the at-risk limitations because this amount is less than both her outside basis and at-risk amount. ■

E X A M P L E   40

Assume the same facts as in Example 39, except that the bank loan is nonrecourse (the partners have no direct liability under the terms of the loan in the case of a default). Kelly's basis in her partnership interest still is $15,000, but she can deduct only $5,000 of the flow-through loss. The amount she has at risk in the partnership does not include the nonrecourse debt. (The debt does not relate to real estate so it is not qualified nonrecourse debt.) ■

Passive Activity Rules.

A partnership loss share may be disallowed under the passive activity rules. These rules apply to partners who are individuals, estates, trusts, closely held C corporations, or personal service corporations. The rules require the partners to separate their interests in partnership activities into three groups:

- *Active.* Earned income, such as salary and wages; income or loss from a trade or business in which the partner materially participates; and guaranteed payments received by the partner for services.
- *Portfolio.* Annuity income, interest, dividends, guaranteed payments from a partnership for interest on capital, royalties not derived in the ordinary course of a trade or business, and gains and losses from disposal of investment assets.
- *Passive.* Income from a trade or business activity in which the partner does not materially participate on a regular, continuous, and substantial basis,[52] or income from many rental activities.

Material participation in an activity is determined annually. The burden is on the partner to prove material participation. The IRS has provided a number of objective tests for determining material participation. In general, these tests require the partner to have substantial involvement in daily operations of the activity. Thus, a Maine vacation resort operator investing in a California grape farm or an electrical engineer employed in Virginia investing in an Iowa corn and hog farm may have difficulty proving material participation in the activities.

Rent income from real or personal property generally is passive income, regardless of the partner's level of participation. Exceptions are made for rent income from activities where substantial services are provided (e.g., certain developers, resorts); from hotels, motels, and other transient lodging; from short-term equipment rentals; and from certain developed real estate.

Usually, passive activity losses can be offset only against passive activity income.[53] In determining the net passive activity loss for a year, losses and income from all passive activities are aggregated. The amount of suspended losses carried forward from a particular activity is determined by the ratio of the net loss from that activity to the aggregate net loss from all passive activities for the year. A special rule for rental real estate (discussed in the following section) allows a limited $25,000 offset against nonpassive income.[54]

A partner making a taxable disposition of an entire interest in a passive activity takes a full deduction for suspended passive activity losses from that activity in the year of disposal.[55] Suspended losses are deductible against income in the following order: income or gain from the passive activity, net income or gain from all passive

---

[52]§§ 469(c)(1) and (2).

[53]§ 469(a)(1).

[54]§ 469(i).

[55]§ 469(g).

activities, and other income. When a passive activity is transferred in a primarily nontaxable exchange (e.g., a like-kind exchange or contribution to a partnership), suspended losses are deductible only to the extent of gains recognized on the transfer. Remaining losses are deducted on disposal of the activity received in the exchange.

EXAMPLE 41

Debra has several investments in passive activities that generate aggregate losses of $10,000 in the current year. Debra wants to deduct all of these losses on her current-year tax return. To assure a loss deduction, she needs to invest in some passive activities that generate income. One of her long-time friends, an entrepreneur in the women's apparel business, is interested in opening a new apparel store in a nearby community. Debra is willing to finance a substantial part of the expansion but does not want to get involved with day-to-day operations. Debra also wants to limit any possible loss to her initial investment.

After substantial discussions, Debra and her friend decide to form a limited partnership, which will own the new store. Debra's friend will be the general partner, and Debra will be a limited partner. Debra invests $100,000, and her friend invests $50,000 and sweat equity (provides managerial skills and know-how). Each has a 50% interest in profits and losses. In the first year of operations, the store generates a profit of $30,000. Since Debra's share of the profit ($15,000) is passive activity income, it can be fully utilized against any of her passive activity losses on other investments. Thus, Debra's share of the apparel store profits enables her to obtain a full deduction of her $10,000 of passive activity losses. ■

Rental Real Estate Losses. In any one year, individuals can offset up to $25,000 of passive losses from rental real estate against active and portfolio income. The $25,000 maximum is reduced by 50 percent of the difference between the taxpayer's modified AGI and $100,000. Thus, when the taxpayer's modified AGI reaches $150,000, the offset is eliminated.

The offset is available to those who actively (rather than materially) participate in rental real estate activities. Active participation is an easier test to meet. Unlike material participation, it does not require regular, continuous, and substantial involvement with the activity. However, the taxpayer must own at least 10 percent of the fair market value of all interests in the rental property and either contribute to the activity's management decisions in a significant and bona fide way or actively participate in arranging for others to make such decisions.

EXAMPLE 42

Raoul invests $10,000 cash in the Sparrow Limited Partnership in the current year for a 10% limited interest in capital and profits. Shortly thereafter, the partnership purchases rental real estate subject to a qualified nonrecourse mortgage of $120,000 obtained from a commercial bank. Raoul has no other passive loss activities during the current year.

Raoul does not participate in any of Sparrow's activities. His share of losses from Sparrow's first year of operations is $27,000. His modified AGI before considering the loss is $60,000. Before considering the loss, Raoul's basis in the partnership interest is $22,000 [$10,000 cash + (10% × $120,000 debt)], and his loss deduction is limited to this amount under the overall limitation. The debt is included in Raoul's amount at risk because it is qualified nonrecourse financing. It may seem that Raoul should be allowed to deduct the $22,000 loss share from portfolio or active income under the rental real estate exception to the passive losses. However, the loss may not be offset against this income because Raoul is not an active participant in the partnership. ■

LO.9
Describe the treatment of transactions between a partner and the partnership.

Transactions between Partner and Partnership

Many types of transactions occur between a partnership and one of its partners. The partner may contribute property to the partnership, perform services for the partnership, or receive distributions from the partnership. The partner may borrow money from or lend money to the partnership. Property may be bought and sold between the partner and the partnership. Several of these transactions were discussed earlier in the chapter. The remaining types of partner-partnership transactions are the focus of this section.

Guaranteed Payments

If a partnership makes a payment to a partner, the payment may be a draw against the partner's share of partnership income; a return of some or all of the partner's original capital contribution; or a guaranteed payment, among other treatments. A **guaranteed payment** is a payment for services performed by the partner or for the use of the partner's capital. The payment may not be determined by reference to partnership income. Guaranteed payments are usually expressed as a fixed-dollar amount or as a percentage of capital that the partner has invested in the partnership. Whether the partnership deducts or capitalizes the guaranteed payment depends on the nature of the payment.

EXAMPLE 43

David, Donald, and Dale formed the accrual basis DDD Partnership in 2008. The partnership and each of the partners are calendar year taxpayers. According to the partnership agreement, David is to manage the partnership and receive a $21,000 distribution from the entity every year, payable in 12 monthly installments. Donald is to receive an amount that is equal to 18% of his capital account, as it is computed by the firm's accountant at the beginning of the year, payable in 12 monthly installments. Dale is the partnership's advertising specialist. He withdraws approximately 3% of the partnership's net income every month for his personal use. David and Donald receive guaranteed payments from the partnership, but Dale does not. ■

Guaranteed payments resemble the salary or interest payments of other businesses and receive somewhat similar income tax treatment.[56] In contrast to the provision that usually applies to withdrawals of assets by partners from their partnerships, guaranteed payments are deductible (or capitalized) by the entity. Deductible guaranteed payments, like any other deductible expenses of a partnership, can create an ordinary loss for the entity. If the partnership distributes appreciated property to pay the guaranteed payment, the partnership must recognize a gain on the transfer.[57]

A partner who receives guaranteed payments during a partnership year must include the payments in income as if they were received on the last day of the partnership year. Guaranteed payments are always taxable as ordinary income to the recipient partner.

EXAMPLE 44

Continue with the situation introduced in Example 43. For calendar year 2008, David receives the $21,000 as provided by the partnership agreement, Donald's guaranteed payment for 2008 is $17,000, and Dale withdraws $20,000. Before considering these amounts, the partnership's ordinary income for 2008 is $650,000.

The partnership can deduct its payments to David and Donald, so the final amount of its 2008 ordinary income is $612,000 ($650,000 − $21,000 − $17,000). Thus, each of the equal partners is allocated $204,000 of ordinary partnership income for their 2008 individual income tax returns ($612,000 ÷ 3). In addition, David reports the $21,000 guaranteed payment as income on his 2008 tax return, and Donald similarly includes the $17,000 guaranteed payment in his 2008 income. Dale's partnership draw is deemed to have come from his allocated $204,000 (or from the accumulated partnership income that was taxed in prior years) and is not taxed separately to him. Dale's basis, though, is reduced by the $20,000 distribution. ■

---

[56]§ 707(c).   [57]Rev.Rul. 2007–40, 2007–1 C.B. 1426.

EXAMPLE 45

Assume the same facts as in Example 44, except that the partnership's tax year ends on March 31, 2009. The total amount of the guaranteed payments is taxable to the partners on that date. Thus, even though David received 9 of his 12 payments for fiscal 2009 in calendar 2008, all of his guaranteed payments are taxable to him in 2009. Similarly, all of Donald's guaranteed payments are taxable to him in 2009 and not when they are received. The deduction for, and the gross income from, guaranteed payments is allowed on the same date that all of the other income and expense items relative to the partnership are allocated to the partners (on the last day of the entity's tax year). ■

Other Transactions between a Partner and a Partnership

Certain transactions between a partner and the partnership are treated as if the partner were an outsider, dealing with the partnership at arm's length.[58] Loan transactions, rental payments, and sales of property between the partner and the partnership are generally treated in this manner. In addition, payments for services are treated this way when the services are short-term technical services that the partner also provides for parties other than the partnership.

EXAMPLE 46

Emilio, a one-third partner in the ABC Partnership, owns a tract of land that the partnership wishes to purchase. The land has a fair market value of $30,000 and an adjusted basis to Emilio of $17,000. If Emilio sells the land to the partnership, he recognizes a $13,000 gain on the sale, and the partnership takes a $30,000 cost basis in the land. If the land has a fair market value of $10,000 on the sale date, Emilio recognizes a $7,000 loss. ■

The time for deducting a payment by an accrual basis partnership to a cash basis service partner depends upon whether the amount is a guaranteed payment or a payment to a partner who is treated as an outsider. A guaranteed payment is includible in the partner's income on the last day of the partnership year when it is properly accrued by the partnership, even though the payment may not be made to the partner until the next taxable year. Conversely, the *partner's* method of accounting controls the timing of the deduction if the payment is treated as made to an outsider. This is because a deduction cannot be claimed for such amounts until the recipient partner is required to include the amount in income under the partner's method of accounting.[59] Thus, a partnership cannot claim a deduction until it actually makes the payment to the cash basis partner, but it could accrue and deduct a payment due to an accrual basis partner even if payment was not yet made.

EXAMPLE 47

Rachel, a cash basis taxpayer, is a partner in the accrual basis RTC Partnership. On December 31, 2008, the partnership accrues but does not pay $10,000 for deductible services that Rachel performed for the partnership during the year. Both Rachel and the partnership are calendar year taxpayers.

If the $10,000 accrual is a guaranteed payment, the partnership deducts the $10,000 in its calendar year ended December 31, 2008, and Rachel includes the $10,000 in her income for the 2008 calendar year. That Rachel is a cash basis taxpayer and does not actually receive the cash in 2008 is irrelevant.

If the payment is classified as a payment to an outsider, the partnership cannot deduct the payment until Rachel actually receives the cash. If, for example, Rachel performs janitorial services (i.e., not in her capacity as a partner) and receives the cash on March 25, 2009, the partnership deducts the payment and Rachel recognizes the income on that date. ■

---

[58]§ 707(a).   [59]§ 267(a)(2).

CONCEPT SUMMARY 10-3

Partner-Partnership Transactions

1. Partners can transact business with their partnerships in a nonpartner capacity. These transactions include the sale and exchange of property, rentals, loans of funds, etc.
2. A payment to a partner may be classified as a guaranteed payment if it is for services or use of the partner's capital and is not based on partnership income. A guaranteed payment may be deductible by the partnership and is included in the partner's income on the last day of the partnership's taxable year.
3. A payment to a partner may be treated as being to an outside (though related) party. Such a payment is deductible or capitalizable by the partnership at the

time it must be included in income under the partner's method of accounting.
4. Guaranteed payments and payments to a partner that are treated as being to an outside party are only deductible if the underlying reason for the payment constitutes an ordinary and necessary (rather than capitalizable) business expense.
5. Losses are disallowed between a partner or related party and a partnership when the partner or related party owns more than a 50% interest in the partnership's capital or profits.
6. When there is income from a related-party sale, it is treated as ordinary income if the property is not a capital asset to both the transferor and the transferee.

Sales of Property. Certain sales of property fall under special rules. No loss is recognized on a sale of property between a person and a partnership when the person owns, directly or indirectly, more than 50 percent of partnership capital or profits.[60] The disallowed loss may not vanish entirely, however. If the transferee eventually sells the property at a gain, the disallowed loss reduces the gain that the transferee would otherwise recognize.

EXAMPLE 48

Barry sells land (adjusted basis to him, $30,000; fair market value, $45,000) to a partnership in which he controls a 60% capital interest. The partnership pays him only $20,000 for the land. Barry cannot deduct his $10,000 realized loss. The sale apparently was not at arm's length, but the taxpayer's intentions are irrelevant. Barry and the partnership are related parties, and the loss is disallowed.

When the partnership sells the land to an outsider at a later date, it receives a sales price of $44,000. The partnership can offset the recognition of its $24,000 realized gain on the subsequent sale ($44,000 sales proceeds − $20,000 adjusted basis) by the amount of the $10,000 prior disallowed loss ($30,000 − $20,000). Thus, the partnership recognizes a $14,000 gain on its sale of the land. ∎

Using a similar rationale, any gain that is realized on a sale or exchange between a partner and a partnership in which the partner controls a capital or profits interest of more than 50 percent must be recognized as ordinary income, unless the asset is a capital asset to both the seller and the purchaser.[61]

EXAMPLE 49

Kristin purchases some land (adjusted basis, $30,000; fair market value, $45,000) for $45,000 from a partnership in which she controls a 90% profits interest. The land was a capital asset to the partnership. If Kristin holds the land as a capital asset, the partnership recognizes a $15,000 capital gain. However, if Kristin is a land developer and the property is not a capital asset to her, the partnership must recognize $15,000 ordinary income from the sale, even though the property was a capital asset to the partnership. ∎

---

[60]§ 707(b).   [61]§ 707(b)(2).

Partners as Employees

A partner usually does not qualify as an employee for tax purposes. Thus, a partner receiving guaranteed payments is not regarded as an employee of the partnership for purposes of withholding taxes. Moreover, since a partner is not an employee, the partnership cannot deduct its payments for the partner's fringe benefits. A general partner's distributive share of ordinary partnership income and guaranteed payments for services are generally subject to the Federal self-employment tax.[62]

Concept Summary 10–3 on the previous page reviews partner-partnership transactions.

LO.10

Provide insights regarding advantageous use of a partnership.

TAX PLANNING
Considerations

Choosing Partnership Taxation

Concept Summary 10–4 enumerates various factors that the owners of a business should consider in deciding whether to use a C corporation, S corporation, or partnership as a means of doing business. The reader should refer back to this list after reading Chapters 11 (advanced partnership topics) and 12 (S corporations). Chapter 13 includes a more elaborate discussion of the tax effects of various forms of conducting business.

Formation and Operation of a Partnership

Potential partners should be cautious in transferring assets to a partnership to ensure that they are not required to recognize any gain upon the creation of the entity. The nonrecognition provisions of § 721 are relatively straightforward and resemble the provisions under § 351, which permit certain tax-free property transfers to corporations. However, any partner can make a tax-deferred contribution of assets to the entity either at the inception of the partnership or later. This possibility is not available to less-than-controlling shareholders in a corporation.

The partners should anticipate the tax benefits and pitfalls that are presented in Subchapter K and should take appropriate actions to resolve any potential problems before they arise. Typically, all that is needed is an appropriate provision in the partnership agreement (e.g., with respect to differing allocation percentages for gains and losses). Recall, however, that a special allocation of income, expense, or credit items in the partnership agreement must satisfy certain requirements before it is acceptable to the IRS.

Basis Considerations and Loss Deduction Limitations

If a partnership incurs a loss for the taxable year, careful planning will help ensure that the partners can claim the deduction.

A partner can contribute capital to the partnership before the end of the tax year. Alternatively, the partnership could incur additional debt. The partner's cash contribution or share of debt increases the partner's basis in the partnership interest. If the loss also meets the "at-risk" and "passive" hurdles, the loss can be deducted.

In the following year, if the partnership is expected to report taxable income, the partner could withdraw cash or pay off debt equal to the income. The partner's cash contribution would have to be invested in the partnership for only a short time. Similarly, the partnership's additional debt would not have to be maintained for a long period of time.

Partnership Reporting Requirements

For most small (under 100 partners) partnerships, the tax return is due by the fifteenth day of the fourth month following the tax year (April 15 for a calendar

---

[62]§ 1402(a).

CONCEPT SUMMARY 10–4

Advantages and Disadvantages of the Partnership Form

The partnership form may be attractive when one or more of the following factors is present:

- The entity is generating net taxable losses and/or valuable tax credits, which will be of use to the owners.
- The owners want to avoid complex corporate administrative and filing requirements.
- Other means of reducing the effects of the double taxation of corporate business income (e.g., compensation to owners, interest, and rental payments) have been exhausted.
- The entity does not generate material amounts of tax preference and adjustment items, which increase the alternative minimum tax liabilities of its owners.
- The entity is generating net passive income, which its owners can use to claim immediate deductions for net passive losses that they have generated from other sources.
- The owners wish to make special allocations of certain income or deduction items that are not possible under the C or S corporation forms.
- The owners anticipate liquidation of the entity within a short period of time. Liquidation of a C or S corporation would generate entity-level recognized gains on appreciated property distributed.
- The owners have adequate bases in their ownership interests to facilitate the deduction of flow-through losses and the assignment of an adequate basis to assets distributed in kind to the owners.

The partnership form may be less attractive when one or more of the following factors is present:

- The tax paid by the individual owners on the entity's income is greater than the tax the entity would pay if it were a C corporation, and the income is not expected to be distributed soon. (If distributed by a C corporation, double taxation would likely occur.)
- The entity is generating net taxable income without distributing any cash to the owners. The owners may not have sufficient cash with which to pay the tax on the entity's earnings.
- The type of income that the entity is generating (e.g., business and portfolio income) is not as attractive to its owners as net passive income would be because the owners could use net passive income to offset the net passive losses that they have generated on their own.
- The entity is in a high-exposure business, and the owners desire protection from personal liability. An LLC, LLP, or LLLP structure may be available, however, to limit personal liability.
- The owners want to avoid Federal self-employment tax.
- Partnership operations are complex (indicating that Form 1065 might not be filed until near the due date for the return), but partners with the same tax year need to file their returns as early as possible for personal reasons (e.g., to meet debt requirements or to receive a tax refund).

year partnership). If all partners and the partnership have the same tax year, the partnership tax return will be due on the same date as the return for any partners who are individual taxpayers. The return will be due one month *after* the due date for the return of a partner that is a Subchapter C or Subchapter S corporation. For example, suppose that a partnership has an individual and a Subchapter S corporation as partners, and all taxpayers use the calendar year. The individual partner's tax return will be due on April 15 (the same date as the partnership's return), but the S corporation's tax return will be due on March 15 (a month earlier).

The partners cannot file an accurate return until they receive the Schedule K–1 from the partnership. A good accountant will pay attention to the partners' status and will attempt to schedule completion of partnership tax returns to accommodate the partners' requirements. Still, in some situations the partners may have to obtain extensions for filing their tax returns because they have not received their Schedule K–1 in time.

In extreme cases, a partner may need to file a return by the original due date (e.g., to meet debt financing requirements or to request a refund of overpaid taxes). In that case, the partner can estimate income from the partnership in the original return and then file an amended return when the Schedule K–1 from the partnership is received.

GLOBAL Tax Issues

PARTNERSHIPS AROUND THE WORLD—AND BEYOND

Technology continues to act as a catalyst—and incentive—for the creation of joint ventures. From Web kiosks at gas stations to global satellite networks, high-tech companies are forging alliances to bring technology to consumers.

Both Microsoft and Time Warner have teamed up with various gas stations, pizza parlors, and numerous other retail outlets to offer programming. These ventures appear to be spurred by a desire to capture larger shares of the ever-expanding advertising market.

Meanwhile, the largest U.S. telecommunications companies are continuing to align themselves with partners in foreign markets: each wants to have the widest possible service coverage area so it can offer efficient communications and computer networking to business clients with a global presence.

Other partnerships have been formed by media and cable companies to offer digital satellite television services on numerous channels to customers for a monthly rental fee. And several partnerships have formed to establish satellite-based Web communications around the world.

Transactions between Partners and Partnerships

Partners should be careful when engaging in transactions with the partnership to ensure that no negative tax results occur. A partner who owns a majority of the partnership generally should not sell property at a loss to the partnership because the loss is disallowed. Similarly, a majority partner should not sell a capital asset to the partnership at a gain, if the asset is to be used by the partnership as other than a capital asset. The gain on this transaction is taxed as ordinary income to the selling partner rather than as capital gain.

As an alternative to selling property to a partnership, the partner should consider a lease arrangement. The partner recognizes rent income, and the partnership has a rent expense. A partner who needs more cash immediately can sell the property to an outside third party; then the third party can lease the property to the partnership for a fair rental.

The timing of the deduction for a payment by an accrual basis partnership to a cash basis partner varies depending on whether the payment is a guaranteed payment or is treated as a payment to an outsider. If the payment is a guaranteed payment, the deduction occurs when the partnership makes the accrual. If the payment is treated as a payment to an outsider, the actual date the payment is made controls the timing of the deduction.

Drafting the Partnership Agreement

Although a written partnership agreement is not required, many rules governing the tax consequences to partners and their partnerships refer to such an agreement. Remember that a partner's distributive share of income, gain, loss, deduction, or credit is determined in accordance with the partnership agreement. Consequently, if taxpayers operating a business in partnership form want a measure of certainty as to the tax consequences of their activities, a carefully drafted partnership agreement is crucial. An agreement that sets forth the obligations, rights, and powers of the partners should prove invaluable in settling controversies among them and provide some degree of certainty as to the tax consequences of the partners' actions.

KEY TERMS

Aggregate concept, 10–8

Basis in the partnership interest, 10–8

Capital account, 10–8

Capital interest, 10–7

Capital sharing ratio, 10–7

Constructive liquidation scenario, 10–30

Disguised sale, 10–10

Economic effect test, 10–24

Electing large partnership, 10–5

Entity concept, 10–8

General partnership, 10–3

Guaranteed payment, 10–37

Inside basis, 10–14

Least aggregate deferral rule, 10–18

Limited liability company (LLC), 10–4

Limited liability limited partnership,10–4

Limited liability partnership (LLP),10–4

Limited partnership, 10–4

Nonrecourse debt, 10–29

Outside basis, 10–14

Precontribution gain or loss, 10–25

Profit and loss sharing ratios, 10–7

Profits (loss) interest, 10–7

Qualified nonrecourse debt, 10–34

Recourse debt, 10–29

Separately stated items, 10–5

Special allocation, 10–7

Syndication costs, 10–17

P R O B L E M   M A T E R I A L S

DISCUSSION QUESTIONS

1. Compare the provision for the nonrecognition of gain or loss on contributions to a partnership (i.e., § 721) with the similar provision related to corporate formation (i.e., § 351). What are the major differences and similarities?

2. Distinguish between the entity concept and the aggregate or conduit concept of partnership taxation.

3. Justin and Tiffany will contribute property to form the equal TJ Partnership. Justin will contribute cash of $20,000 plus land with a fair market value of $80,000 and an adjusted basis of $65,000. Tiffany currently operates a sole proprietorship with assets valued at $100,000 and an adjusted basis of $125,000. Tiffany can either contribute these assets to the partnership or sell them to Sanford Salvage for their fair market value and then contribute the $100,000 cash to the partnership. The partnership needs assets similar to those owned by Tiffany, but it can purchase new assets for $110,000. Describe the tax consequences of the formation to Tiffany, Justin, and the partnership. Be sure to discuss how the results would differ if Tiffany sells the property rather than contributing it.

Issue ID

Decision Making

4. Gerald owns property (basis of $120,000, value of $240,000). He plans to contribute the property to the GMW Partnership in exchange for a one-third interest.
   a. What issues arise if the partnership distributes $60,000 cash to Gerald three months after the property contribution?
   b. What techniques can be used to minimize the risk that these adverse tax consequences might arise?

Issue ID

5. In what situations can the formation of a partnership result in a taxable gain to one or more of the partners?

6. Block, Inc., a calendar year general contractor, and Strauss, Inc., a development corporation with a July 31 year-end, formed the equal SB LLC on January 1 of the current year. Both LLC members are C corporations. The limited liability company was formed to construct and lease shopping centers in Wilmington, Delaware. Block contributed equipment (basis of $650,000, fair market value of $650,000), building permits, and architectural designs created by Block's employees (basis of $0, fair market

Issue ID

value of $100,000). Strauss contributed land (basis of $50,000, fair market value of $250,000) and cash of $500,000. The cash was used as follows:

Legal fees for drafting LLC agreement	$ 10,000
Materials and labor costs for construction in progress on shopping center	400,000
Office expense (utilities, rent, overhead, etc.)	90,000

What issues must the LLC address in preparing its initial tax return?

Issue ID

7. Browne and Red, both C corporations, formed the BR Partnership on January 1, 2006. Neither Browne nor Red is a personal service corporation, and BR is not a tax shelter. BR's gross receipts were $4.6 million, $5 million, $6 million, and $7 million, respectively, for the four tax years ending in 2006, 2007, 2008, and 2009. Describe the methods of accounting available to BR in each tax year.

8. Discuss the adjustments that must be made to a partner's basis in the partnership interest. When are such adjustments made?

9. What is the purpose of the three rules that implement the economic effect test?

Issue ID

Decision Making

10. The BCD Partnership plans to distribute cash of $20,000 to partner Brad at the end of the tax year. The partnership reported a loss for the year, and Brad's share of the loss is $10,000. At the beginning of the tax year, Brad's basis in his partnership interest, including his share of partnership liabilities, was $15,000. The partnership expects to report substantial income in future years.
    a. What rules are used to calculate Brad's ending basis in his partnership interest?
    b. How much gain or loss will Brad report for the tax year?
    c. Will any of the $10,000 loss be deducted?
    d. Could any planning opportunities be used to minimize any negative tax ramifications of the distribution?

11. Describe the three limitations that apply to the deductibility of a loss from a partnership and indicate the order in which these limitations are applied.

12. Discuss situations in which the partnership entity form might be more advantageous (or disadvantageous) than operating as a Subchapter C or S corporation.

13. Comment on the validity of the following statements:
    a. Since a partnership is not a taxable entity, it is not required to file any type of tax return.
    b. Each partner can choose a different method of accounting and depreciation computation in determining the income from the entity.
    c. Generally, a transfer of appreciated property to a partnership results in recognized gain to the contributing partner at the time of the transfer.
    d. A partner can carry forward, for an unlimited period of time, the share of any partnership operating losses that exceed the partner's basis in the entity, provided the partner retains an ownership interest in the partnership.
    e. When a partner renders services to the entity in exchange for an unrestricted interest, that partner does not recognize any gross income.
    f. Losses on sales between a partner and the partnership are never deductible.
    g. A partnership may choose a year that results in the least aggregate deferral of tax to the partners, unless the IRS requires the use of an alternative tax year under the "business purpose" test.
    h. A partner's basis in a partnership interest includes that partner's share of partnership recourse and nonrecourse liabilities.
    i. Built-in loss related to nondepreciable property contributed to a partnership must be allocated to the contributing partner to the extent the loss is eventually recognized by the partnership.
    j. Property that was held as inventory by a contributing partner, but is a capital asset in the hands of the partnership, results in a capital gain if the partnership immediately sells the property.

PROBLEMS

14. Chip and Marty form an equal partnership with a cash contribution of $200,000 from Chip and a property contribution (adjusted basis of $100,000, fair market value of $200,000) from Marty.

    a. How much gain, if any, must Chip recognize on the transfer? Must Marty recognize any gain?
    b. What is Chip's basis in his partnership interest?
    c. What is Marty's basis in his partnership interest?
    d. What basis does the partnership take in the property transferred by Marty?

15. Tom and Liz form an equal partnership with a cash contribution of $60,000 from Tom and a property contribution (adjusted basis of $75,000, fair market value of $60,000) from Liz.

    Decision Making

    a. How much gain or loss, if any, does Liz realize on the transfer? May Liz recognize any gain or loss?
    b. What is Tom's basis in his partnership interest?
    c. What is Liz's basis in her partnership interest?
    d. What basis does the partnership take in the property transferred by Liz?
    e. Are there more effective ways to structure the formation?

16. Kim and Kathy formed the equal K&K Partnership on January 1 of the current year. Kim contributed $50,000 cash and land with a fair market value of $20,000 and an adjusted basis of $15,000. Kathy contributed equipment with a fair market value of $70,000 and an adjusted basis of $50,000. Kathy had previously used the equipment in her sole proprietorship.

    a. How much gain or loss will Kim, Kathy, and the partnership realize?
    b. How much gain or loss will Kim, Kathy, and the partnership recognize?
    c. What bases will Kim and Kathy take in their partnership interests?
    d. What bases will K&K take in the assets it receives?
    e. Are there any differences between inside and outside basis?
    f. How will the partnership depreciate any assets it receives from the partners?

17. Three years after the J&H Partnership is formed, Jamie, a 30% partner, contributes an additional $20,000 cash and land she has held for investment. Jamie's basis in the land is $60,000, and its fair market value is $80,000. Her basis in the partnership interest was $40,000 before this contribution. The partnership uses the land as a parking lot for four years and then sells it for $90,000.

    a. How much gain or loss does Jamie recognize on the contribution?
    b. What is Jamie's basis in her partnership interest immediately following this contribution?
    c. How much gain or loss does J&H recognize on this contribution?
    d. What is J&H's basis in the property it receives from Jamie?
    e. How much gain or loss does the partnership recognize on the later sale of the land, and what is the character of the gain or loss? How much is allocated to Jamie?

18. Beth and Ben are equal partners in the BB Partnership, formed on June 1 of the current year. Ben contributed land that he inherited from his father three years ago. Ben's father purchased the land in 1950 for $6,000. The land was worth $50,000 when Ben's father died. The fair market value of the land was $75,000 at the date it was contributed to the partnership.

    Decision Making

    Beth has significant experience developing real estate. After the partnership is formed, she will prepare a plan for developing the property and secure zoning approvals for the partnership. She would normally bill a third party $25,000 for these efforts. Beth will also contribute $50,000 cash in exchange for her 50% interest in the partnership. The value of her 50% interest is $75,000.

    a. How much gain or income will Ben recognize on his contribution of the land to the partnership? What is the character of any gain or income recognized?
    b. What basis will Ben take in his partnership interest?

   c. How much gain or income will Beth recognize on the formation of the partnership? What is the character of any gain or income recognized?

   d. What basis will Beth take in her partnership interest?

   e. Construct an opening balance sheet for the partnership reflecting the partnership's basis in assets and the fair market value of these assets.

   f. Outline any planning opportunities that may minimize current taxation to any of the parties.

Decision Making

19. Continue with the facts presented in Problem 18. At the end of the first year, the partnership distributes $50,000 cash to Ben. No distribution is made to Beth.

   a. Under general tax rules, how would the payment to Ben be treated?

   b. How much income or gain would Ben recognize as a result of the payment?

   c. Under general tax rules, what basis would the partnership take in the land Ben contributed?

   d. What alternative treatment might the IRS try to impose?

   e. Under the alternative treatment, how much income or gain would Ben recognize?

   f. Under the alternative treatment, what basis would the partnership take in the land contributed by Ben?

   g. How can the transaction be restructured to minimize risk of IRS recharacterization?

20. The MP Partnership was formed to acquire land and subdivide it as residential housing lots. On July 1, 2008, Miranda contributed land valued at $300,000 to the partnership in exchange for a 50% interest. She had purchased the land in 2000 for $140,000 and held it for investment purposes (capital asset). The partnership holds the land as inventory.

     On the same date, Paul contributed land valued at $300,000 that he had purchased in 2001 for $350,000. He also became a 50% owner. Paul is a real estate developer, but he held this land personally for investment purposes. The partnership holds this land as inventory.

     In 2009, the partnership sells the land contributed by Miranda for $340,000. In 2010, the partnership sells half of the subdivided real estate contributed by Paul for $140,000. The other half is finally sold in 2015 for $160,000.

   a. What is each partner's initial basis in his or her partnership interest?

   b. What is the amount of gain or loss recognized on the sale of the land contributed by Miranda? What is the character of this gain or loss?

   c. What is the amount of gain or loss recognized in 2010 and 2015 on the sale of the land contributed by Paul? What is the character of this gain or loss?

21. The partnership agreement for the MP Partnership in Problem 20 provides that all gains and losses are allocated equally between the partners unless otherwise required under the tax law.

   a. How will the gains or losses determined in (b) and (c) in Problem 20 be allocated to each of the partners?

   b. Calculate each partner's basis in his or her partnership interest at December 31, 2015. Assume the partnership has no transactions through the end of the year 2015 other than the transactions described in Problem 20. Why are these balances the same or different?

22. On July 1 of the current year, the R & R Partnership was formed to operate a bed and breakfast inn. The partnership paid $3,000 in legal fees for drafting the partnership agreement and $5,000 for accounting fees related to organizing the entity. It also paid $10,000 in syndication costs to locate and secure investments from limited partners. In addition, before opening the inn for business, the entity paid $15,500 for advertising and $36,000 in costs related to an open house just before the grand opening of the property. The partnership opened the inn for business on October 1.

   a. How are these expenses classified?

   b. How much may the partnership deduct in its initial year of operations?

   c. How are costs treated that are not deducted currently?

   d. What elections must the partnership make in its initial tax return?

23. The Heron Partnership was formed on July 1 of the current year and admitted Carl and Megan as equal partners on that date. The partners contributed $200,000 cash each to establish a children's clothing store in a local shopping mall. The partners spent July and August buying inventory, equipment, supplies, and advertising for their "Grand Opening" on October 1. The partnership will use the accrual method of accounting. The partnership incurred the following costs during its first year of operations:

- Purchased all assets of Granny Newcomb's, Inc., which was going out of business, including:

Inventory	$130,000
Shop fixtures, racks, shelves, etc.	50,000
Trade name and logo	60,000

- Other costs:

Additional inventory	$100,000
Legal fees to form partnership	2,000
Advertising for "Grand Opening"	15,000
Advertising after opening	10,000
Consulting fees for establishing accounting system	5,000
Rent, six months at $2,000/month	12,000
Utilities at $600 per month	3,600
Salaries to sales clerks	30,000
Payments to Carl and Megan for services ($5,000/month each for three months, beginning in October)	30,000
Tax return preparation expense	5,000

- Revenues during the year included the following:

Sales revenues	$325,000
Interest income on bank balances	3,000

- Inventory remaining at the end of the year was valued at $65,000 on a FIFO basis.

a. Determine how each of the above costs and revenues is treated by the partnership, and identify the period over which the costs can be deducted, if any.
b. Calculate the amortization and initial deduction for any organizational or startup costs.
c. Identify any elections the partnership should make on its initial tax return.

24. CourtneyCo, CassandraCo, and ClemCo form the 3Cs Partnership on January 1 of the current year. CourtneyCo is a 50% partner, and CassandraCo and ClemCo are each 25% partners. Each partner and 3Cs use the cash method of accounting. For reporting purposes, CourtneyCo uses a March 31 fiscal year, CassandraCo uses a January 31 fiscal year, and ClemCo uses a February 28/29 fiscal year. What is 3Cs's required tax year under the least aggregate deferral method?

25. Phoebe and Parker are equal members of the Phoenix Partnership. They are real estate investors who formed the partnership several years ago with equal cash contributions. Phoenix then purchased a piece of land.

On January 1 of the current year, to acquire a one-third interest in the entity, Reece contributed to the partnership some land she had held for investment. Reece purchased the land five years ago for $75,000; its fair market value at the contribution date was $90,000. No special allocation agreements were in effect before or after Reece was admitted to the partnership. The Phoenix Partnership holds all land for investment.

Immediately before Reece's property contribution, the balance sheet of the Phoenix Partnership was as follows:

	Basis	FMV		Basis	FMV
Land	$30,000	$180,000	Phoebe, capital	$15,000	$ 90,000
			Parker, capital	15,000	90,000
	$30,000	$180,000		$30,000	$180,000

a. At the contribution date, what is Reece's basis in her interest in the Phoenix Partnership?
b. When does the partnership's holding period begin for the contributed land?

c. On June 30 of the current year, the partnership sold the land contributed by Reece for $90,000. How much is the recognized gain or loss, and how is it allocated among the partners?

d. Prepare a balance sheet reflecting basis and fair market value for the partnership immediately after the land sale described in (c). Assume no other transactions occurred during the tax year.

26. Assume the same facts as in Problem 25, with the following exceptions.

- Reece purchased the land five years ago for $120,000. Its fair market value was $90,000 when it was contributed to the partnership.
- Phoenix sold the land contributed by Reece for $84,000.

a. How much is the recognized gain or loss, and how is it allocated among the partners?

b. Prepare a balance sheet reflecting basis and fair market value for the partnership immediately after the land sale. Also prepare schedules that support the amount in each partner's capital account.

27. Erica and Greg are equal partners in the accrual basis EG Partnership. At the beginning of 2008, Erica's capital account has a balance of $120,000, and the partnership has recourse debts of $80,000 payable to unrelated parties. All partnership recourse debt is shared equally between the partners. The following information about EG's operations for the current year is obtained from the partnership's records:

Taxable income	$140,000
Tax-exempt interest income	2,000
§ 1231 gain	4,000
Long-term capital gain	1,000
Short-term capital loss	3,000
Political contribution	1,000
Charitable contribution to Red Cross	2,000
Cash distribution to Erica	10,000
Payment of Erica's medical expenses	4,000

Assume that year-end partnership debt payable to unrelated parties is $100,000.

a. If all transactions are reflected in her beginning capital and basis in the same manner, what is Erica's basis in the partnership interest at the beginning of the year?

b. If all transactions are reflected in her beginning capital and basis in the same manner, what is Erica's basis in the partnership interest at the end of the year?

28. The RB Partnership is owned equally by Rob and Bob. Bob's basis is $14,000 at the beginning of the tax year. Rob's basis is $9,000 at the beginning of the year. RB reported the following income and expenses for the current tax year:

Sales revenue	$130,000
Cost of sales	45,000
Guaranteed payment to Rob	24,000
Depreciation expense	12,500
Utilities	15,000
Rent expense	16,000
Interest income	3,000
Tax-exempt interest income	4,500
Payment to Mount Vernon Hospital for Bob's medical expenses	10,000

a. Determine the ordinary partnership income and separately stated items for the partnership.

b. Calculate Bob's basis in his partnership interest at the end of the tax year. What items should Bob report on his Federal income tax return?

c. Calculate Rob's basis in his partnership interest at the end of the tax year. What items should Rob report on his Federal income tax return?

29. Assume the same facts as in Problem 28, except that partnership revenues were $90,000 instead of $130,000.
    a. Redetermine the ordinary income and separately stated items for the partnership.
    b. Calculate Bob's basis in his partnership interest at the end of the tax year. How much income or loss should Bob report on his Federal income tax return?
    c. Calculate Rob's basis in his partnership interest at the end of the tax year. How much income or loss should Rob report on his Federal income tax return?

30. As of January 1 of last year, Don's outside basis and at-risk limitation for his 25% interest in the DEF Partnership were $24,000. Don and the partnership use the calendar year for tax purposes. The partnership incurred an operating loss of $120,000 for last year and a profit of $40,000 for the current year. Don is a material participant in the partnership.

    Decision Making

    a. How much loss, if any, may Don recognize for last year?
    b. How much net reportable income must Don recognize for the current year?
    c. What is Don's basis in the partnership as of December 31 of last year?
    d. What is Don's basis in the partnership as of December 31 of the current year?
    e. What year-end tax planning would you suggest to ensure that Don can deduct his share of partnership losses?

31. Fred and Manuel each contribute $100,000 to the newly formed FM Partnership in exchange for a 50% interest. The partnership uses the available funds to acquire equipment costing $160,000 and to fund current operating expenses. The partnership agreement provides that depreciation will be allocated 95% to Fred and 5% to Manuel. All other items of income and loss will be allocated equally between the partners. Upon liquidation of the partnership, property will be distributed to the partners in accordance with their capital account balances. Any partner with a negative capital account must contribute cash in the amount of the negative balance to restore the capital account to $0.

    In its first year, the partnership reported an ordinary loss (before depreciation) of $40,000 and depreciation expense of $32,000. In its second year, operations broke even (no gain or loss), and the partnership reported depreciation expense of $51,200. On the first day of the third year, the partnership sold the equipment for $120,000 and distributed the cash in accordance with the partnership agreement. The partnership was liquidated at this time.

    a. Calculate the partners' bases in their partnership interests at the end of the first and second tax years. Are any losses suspended?
    b. Calculate the partners' bases in their partnership interests after reflecting any gain or loss on disposal of the equipment.
    c. How will partnership cash balances be distributed to the partners on liquidation?
    d. Does the allocation provided in the partnership agreement have economic effect?
    e. What observation can you make regarding the value of a deduction to each partner?

32. Dave and Jeannie each contributed $60,000 cash to the cash basis DJ Partnership. The partnership uses all $120,000 of the cash to purchase a depreciable asset. The partnership agreement provides that depreciation is allocated 60% to Dave and 40% to Jeannie. All other items of partnership income, gain, loss, or deduction are allocated equally between the two partners. During the first year of operations, the partnership produces $20,000 of income before depreciation and deducts $20,000 of depreciation. At the end of the first year, the partnership sells the depreciable asset for its $100,000 book value and liquidates. Assume nothing else happens in the first year that affects the partners' capital accounts.

    a. How much cash is distributed to each partner in the liquidating distribution under the economic effect test?
    b. If the partnership distributes $20,000 cash to Jeannie on June 30 of the current year, how much cash is distributed to each partner in the liquidating distribution under the economic effect test?

33. Your client, the Williams Institute of Technology (WIT), is a 60% partner in the Research Industries Partnership (RIP). WIT is located at 76 Bradford Lane, St. Paul, MN 55164. The controller, Jeanine West, has sent you the following note and a copy of WIT's 2007 Schedule K–1 from the partnership.

    Decision Making

    Communications

Excerpt from client's note:

"RIP expects its 2008 operations to include the following:

Net loss from operations	$200,000
Capital gain from sale of land	100,000

The land was contributed by DASH, the other partner, when its value was $260,000. The partnership sold the land for $300,000. The partnership used this cash to repay all the partnership debt and pay for operating expenditures, which a tax partner in your firm has said RIP can deduct this year. The net loss of $200,000 reflects that deduction.

   We want to be sure we can deduct our full share of this loss, but we do not believe we will have enough basis. We are a material participant in this partnership's activities."

Items Reported on the 2007 Schedule K–1	
WIT's share of partnership recourse liabilities	$90,000
WIT's ending capital account balance	30,000

   Draft a letter to the controller that describes the following:

- WIT's allocation of partnership items.
- WIT's basis in the partnership interest following the allocation.
- Any limitations on loss deductions.
- Any recommendations you have that would allow WIT to claim the full amount of losses in 2008.

Assume WIT's 2007 K–1 accurately reflects the information needed to compute its basis in the partnership interest. Also assume the operating expenditures are fully deductible this year, as the partner said.

   Your client has experience researching issues in the Internal Revenue Code, so you may use some citations. However, be sure the letter is written in layperson's terms and cites are minimized.

34. Lee, Brad, and Rick form the LBR Partnership on January 1 of the current year. In return for a 25% interest, Lee transfers property (basis of $15,000, fair market value of $17,500) subject to a nonrecourse liability of $10,000. The liability is assumed by the partnership. Brad transfers property (basis of $16,000, fair market value of $7,500) for a 25% interest, and Rick transfers cash of $15,000 for the remaining 50% interest. (See Example 29 in the text.) Assume the partnership allocates all "third tier" nonrecourse liabilities in accordance with profit sharing ratios.
    a. How much gain must Lee recognize on the transfer?
    b. What is Lee's basis in his partnership interest?
    c. How much loss may Brad recognize on the transfer?
    d. What is Brad's basis in his partnership interest?
    e. What is Rick's basis in his partnership interest?
    f. What basis does the LBR Partnership take in the property transferred by Lee?
    g. What is the partnership's basis in the property transferred by Brad?

35. Assume the same facts as in Problem 34, except that the property contributed by Lee has a fair market value of $27,500 and is subject to a nonrecourse mortgage of $20,000. (See Example 33 in the text.)
    a. What is Lee's basis in his partnership interest?
    b. How much gain must Lee recognize on the transfer?
    c. What is Brad's basis in his partnership interest?
    d. What is Rick's basis in his partnership interest?
    e. What basis does the LBR Partnership take in the property transferred by Lee?

36. The MGP General Partnership was created on January 1 of the current year by having Melinda, Gabe, and Pat each contribute $10,000 cash to the partnership in exchange for a one-third interest in partnership income, gains, losses, deductions, and credits. On December 31 of the current year, the partnership balance sheet reads as follows:

	Basis	FMV		Basis	FMV
Assets	$60,000	$75,000	Recourse debt	$30,000	$30,000
			Melinda, capital	14,000	19,000
			Gabe, capital	14,000	19,000
			Pat, capital	2,000	7,000
				$60,000	$75,000

Pat's capital account is less than Melinda's and Gabe's capital accounts because Pat has withdrawn more cash than the other partners.

How do the partners share the recourse debt as of December 31 of the current year?

37. Paul and Anna plan to form the PA General Partnership by the end of the current year. The partners will each contribute $80,000 cash, and in addition, the partnership will borrow $240,000 from First State Bank. The $400,000 will be used to buy an investment property. The property will serve as collateral, and both partners will be required to personally guarantee the debt.

Communications

The tentative agreement provides that 60% of operating income, gains, losses, deductions, and credits will be allocated to Paul for the first five years the partnership is in existence. The remaining 40% is allocated to Anna. Thereafter, all partnership items will be allocated equally. The agreement also provides that capital accounts will be properly maintained and that each partner must restore any deficit in the capital account upon the partnership's liquidation.

The partners would like to know, before the end of the tax year, how the $240,000 liability will be allocated for basis purposes. Using the format (1) facts, (2) issues, (3) conclusion, and (4) law and analysis, draft a memo to the tax planning file for the PA Partnership that describes how the debt will be shared between the partners for purposes of computing the adjusted basis of each partnership interest.

38. Chris Elton is a 15% partner in the Cardinal Partnership, which is a lessor of residential rental property. Her share of the partnership's losses for the current year is $70,000. Immediately before considering the deductibility of this loss, Chris's capital account (which, in this case, corresponds to her basis excluding liabilities) reflected a balance of $40,000. Her share of partnership recourse liabilities is $10,000, and her share of the nonrecourse liabilities is $6,000. The nonrecourse liability was obtained from an unrelated bank and is secured solely by the real estate.

Communications

Chris is also a partner in the Bluebird Partnership, which has generated income from long-term (more than 30 days) equipment rental activities. Chris's share of Bluebird's income is $23,000. Chris performs substantial services for Bluebird and spends several hundred hours a year working for the Cardinal Partnership.

Chris's modified adjusted gross income before considering partnership activities is $100,000. Your manager has asked you to determine how much of the $70,000 Cardinal loss Chris can deduct on her current calendar year return. Using the format (1) facts, (2) issues, (3) conclusion, and (4) law and analysis, draft a memo to the client's tax file describing the loss limitations. Be sure to identify the Code sections under which losses are suspended.

39. FredCo and Fran are equal partners in the calendar year F & F Partnership. FredCo uses a fiscal year ending June 30, and Fran uses a calendar year. FredCo receives an annual guaranteed payment of $50,000. F & F's taxable income (after deducting FredCo's guaranteed payment) is $40,000 for 2008 and $50,000 for 2009.
   a. What is the amount of income from the partnership that FredCo must report for its tax year ending June 30, 2009?
   b. What is the amount of income from the partnership that Fran must report for her tax year ending December 31, 2009?
   c. Assume FredCo's annual guaranteed payment is increased to $60,000 starting on January 1, 2009, and the partnership's taxable income for 2008 and 2009 (after deducting FredCo's guaranteed payment) is the same (i.e., $40,000 and $50,000, respectively). What is the amount of income from the partnership that FredCo must report for its tax year ending June 30, 2009?

40. Sonya is a 20% owner of Philadelphia Cheese Treats, Inc., a C corporation that was formed on February 1, 2008. She receives a $5,000 monthly salary from the corporation, and Cheese Treats generates $200,000 of taxable income (after the salary payment) for its tax year ending January 31, 2009.

    a. How do these activities affect Sonya's 2008 adjusted gross income?

    b. Assume, instead, that Cheese Treats is a partnership (January 31 year-end) and that it classifies Sonya's salary as a guaranteed payment. How do these activities affect Sonya's 2008 and 2009 adjusted gross income?

41. Four Lakes Partnership is owned by four sisters. Anne holds a 70% interest; each of the others owns 10%. Anne sells investment property to the partnership for its fair market value of $100,000 (Anne's basis is $150,000).

    a. How much loss, if any, may Anne recognize?

    b. If the partnership later sells the property for $160,000, how much gain must it recognize?

    c. If Anne's basis in the investment property was $20,000 instead of $150,000, how much, if any, gain would she recognize on the sale, and how would the gain be characterized?

TAX RETURN PROBLEMS

1. Craig Howard (623–98–0123), Josh Edwards (410–63–4297), and Dana Prosky (896–49–1235) are equal partners in TDG—the "Tile Doctors Group, LLC"—a limited liability company engaged in residential tile installation in Baton Rouge, Louisiana. TDG's Federal ID number is 42–1234598. The LLC uses the accrual method of accounting and the calendar year for reporting purposes. It began business operations on October 15, 2005. Its current address is 5917 La Rue, Baton Rouge, LA 70825. The 2007 income statement for the LLC reflected net income of $171,000. The following information was taken from the LLC's financial statements for the current year:

Receipts:	
Sales revenues	$975,000
Interest income	3,000
Long-term capital gain	2,400
Short-term capital loss	(600)
Total revenues	$979,800
Cash payments related to cost of goods sold:	
Materials purchases	$280,000
Direct job costs	26,450
Additional § 263A costs	32,950
Contract labor	330,000
Total cash payments—work-in-progress	$669,400
Other cash disbursements (net of additional § 263A costs):	
Rent	$ 10,000
Telephone and utilities	11,000
Contribution to Red Cross	1,500
Meals and entertainment, subject to 50% disallowance	6,000
Guaranteed payment, Dana Prosky, managing LLC member	40,000
Office expense	34,800
Legal fees	3,500
Janitorial services	2,400
Business interest on nonrecourse debt	6,000
Repairs	3,000
Tile cutting equipment	15,000
Total other cash disbursements	$133,200

Noncash expenses:

Amortization	$ 600
Depreciation on equipment owned previously (reported on Schedule A)	16,620

The beginning and ending balance sheets for the LLC were as follows for 2007:

	Beginning	Ending
Cash	$ 20,430	$ 54,630
Inventory (jobs in progress)	63,980	75,000
Long-term investments	46,000	42,000
Equipment	95,000	110,000
Accumulated depreciation	(26,660)	(58,280)
Organizational fees	3,000	3,000
Accumulated amortization	(750)	(1,350)
Total assets	$201,000	$225,000
Nonrecourse debt	$ 96,000	$ 93,000
Capital, Howard	35,000	44,000
Capital, Edwards	35,000	44,000
Capital, Prosky	35,000	44,000
Total liabilities and capital	$201,000	$225,000

The LLC uses the lower of cost or market method for valuing inventory. TDG is subject to § 263A; for simplicity, assume § 263A costs are reflected in the same manner for book and tax purposes. TDG did not change its inventory accounting method during the year. There were no write-downs of inventory items, and TDG does not use the LIFO method.

The LLC claimed $16,620 of depreciation expense for both tax and financial accounting purposes; all $16,620 should be reported on Schedule A. Assume that none of the depreciation creates a tax preference. The LLC will claim a § 179 deduction for the tile cutting equipment purchased during the year.

In order to avoid the cost and compliance burden of being an employer, the LLC uses contract labor. All of its artisans are properly classifed as independent contractors, and the LLC retains several support organizations to provide accounting and janitorial services. The LLC has no W–2 wages.

No guaranteed payments were paid to members other than Dana Prosky. Instead, each member (including Prosky) withdrew $4,000 per month as a distribution (draw) of operating profits. There were no distributions of noncash property.

All debt of the LLC is treated as nonrecourse debt for tax purposes. The members share equally in all LLC liabilities, since all initial contributions and all ongoing allocations and distributions are pro rata. All members are considered "active" for purposes of the passive loss rules.

None of the members sold any portion of their interests in the LLC during 2007. The LLC's operations are entirely restricted to southern Louisiana. All members are U.S. citizens. The LLC had no foreign operations, no foreign bank accounts, and no interest in any foreign trusts or other LLCs. The LLC is not publicly traded and is not a statutory tax shelter. No Forms 8865 are required to be attached to the return.

The IRS's business code for "tile contractors" is 238300. The LLC is not subject to the consolidated audit procedures. The LLC files its tax return in Ogden, Utah. Managing LLC member Dana Prosky lives at 1423 N. Louisiana Boulevard, Baton

Rouge, LA 70823. The capital account reconciliation on Schedule K–1 is prepared on a GAAP basis, which, in this case, corresponds to the tax basis.

a. Prepare pages 1–4 of Form 1065 for TDG. Leave any items blank where insufficient information has been provided. Do not prepare Form 4562 or Schedule D, but prepare other supporting schedules as necessary if adequate information is provided. (You will not be able to prepare a schedule for additional § 263A costs.) *Hint:* Prepare Schedule A first to determine cost of goods sold.

b. Prepare Schedule K–1 for member Dana Prosky.

TaxCut H&R BLOCK

2. Myron M. Fox (297–19–4567), Rhoda R. Fiori (284–74–1234), Cassandra P. Martin (257–62–3395), and Henrietta Q. Pasquale (219–75–4967) are equal partners in FFMP, LLP, a small business consulting services firm (Federal ID number is 67–9580874). The limited liability partnership uses the cash basis and the calendar year and began operations on January 1, 2004. Since that time, it has experienced significant growth each year. Its current address is 2835 Harbor View Drive, Freetown, ME 04469. The following information was taken from the LLP's income statement for the current year:

Revenues		
	Fees collected	$300,000
	Dividend income (all qualified)	3,600
	Taxable business interest	1,400
	Tax-exempt interest	2,600
	Short-term capital loss	(4,000)
	Total revenues	$303,600
Expenses		
	Accounting fees	$ 5,000
	Advertising	5,000
	Contribution to United Fund	2,000
	Depreciation expense	8,119
	Employee salaries	50,000
	Guaranteed payment, Myron M. Fox, office manager	20,000
	Entertainment, subject to 50% disallowance	2,600
	Travel	2,000
	Equipment rental	6,000
	Office rentals paid	24,000
	Interest expense	4,000
	Insurance premiums	2,200
	Office expense	10,481
	Payroll taxes	8,600
	Utilities	5,700
	Total expenses	$155,700

The partnership placed its $65,000 of furniture and fixtures in service on January 1, 2004. This year, it claimed $8,119 of depreciation expense for both tax and financial accounting purposes. The depreciation creates an adjustment of $156 for alternative minimum tax purposes.

On October 15, the partnership sold securities for $44,000; it had purchased the securities for $40,000 on February 3. The firm's activities do not constitute "qualified production activities" for purposes of the § 199 deduction.

Net income per books is $147,900. On January 1, 2007, the partners' capital accounts equaled $60,000 each. No additional capital contributions were made in 2007, and each partner made total withdrawals of $40,000 during the year. The partnership's balance sheet as of December 31, 2007 is as follows:

	Beginning	Ending
Cash	$ 46,577	$?
Tax-exempt securities	52,000	52,000
Marketable securities	160,000	120,000
Office furniture and equipment	65,000	65,000
Accumulated depreciation	(36,577)	?
Total assets	$287,000	$?
Nonrecourse debt payable on equipment	$ 47,000	$ 32,000
Capital, Fox	60,000	?
Capital, Fiori	60,000	?
Capital, Martin	60,000	?
Capital, Pasquale	60,000	?
Total liabilities and capital	$287,000	$?

Assume all debt is shared equally by the partners.

None of the partners, all of whom are U.S. citizens, sold any portion of their interests in FFMP during the year. All of the entity's financial operations are concentrated in Maine although consulting contracts were secured in other states during the year. The partnership had no foreign bank accounts or operations and no interest in any foreign trusts or any other partnerships. The partnership is not publicly traded and is not a statutory tax shelter. The partnership is not subject to consolidated audit procedures and does not have a designated tax matters partner.

The business code for FFMP's operations is 561900. FFMP itself is not a partner in any other partnership. The partnership's Form 1065 is prepared by Fox and is sent to the IRS Service Center in Cincinnati, Ohio. All partners are active in partnership operations.

a. Prepare Form 1065 and Schedule K for FFMP Partnership, leaving blank any items where insufficient information has been provided.
b. Prepare Schedule K–1 for Myron M. Fox, 415 Knight Court, Freetown, ME 04469.

RESEARCH PROBLEMS

Note: Solutions to Research Problems can be prepared by using the **RIA Checkpoint®** **Student Edition** online research product, which is available to accompany this text. It is also possible to prepare solutions to the Research Problems by using tax research materials found in a standard tax library.

Research Problem 1.   Your clients, Mark Henderson and John Burton, each contributed $10,000 cash to form the Realty Management Partnership, a limited partnership. Mark is the general partner, and John is the limited partner. The partnership used the $20,000 cash to make a down payment on a building. The rest of the building's $200,000 purchase price was financed with an interest-only nonrecourse loan of $180,000, which was obtained from an independent third-party bank.

The partnership allocates all partnership items equally between the partners except for the MACRS deductions and building maintenance, which are allocated 70% to John and 30% to Mark. The partnership definitely wishes to satisfy the "economic effect" requirements of Reg. §§ 1.704–1 and 1.704–2 and will reallocate MACRS, if necessary, to satisfy the requirements of the Regulations.

Under the partnership agreement, liquidation distributions will be paid in proportion to the partners' positive capital account balances. Capital accounts are maintained as required in the Regulations. Mark has an unlimited obligation to restore his capital account while John is subject to a qualified income offset provision.

Assume all partnership items, except for MACRS, will net to zero throughout the first three years of the partnership operations. Also, assume that each year's MACRS deduction will be $10,000 (to simplify the calculations).

Communications

Draft a letter to the partnership evaluating the allocation of MACRS in each of the three years under Reg. §§ 1.704–1 and 1.704–2. The partnership's address is 53 East Marsh Ave., Smyrna, GA 30082. Do not address the "substantial" test.

Research Problem 2.   Harrison has considerable experience as a leasing agent for residential rental properties. He feels, though, that his present employer does not adequately compensate him for his work.

Alameda Properties (not a publicly traded partnership) has offered Harrison a position handling leasing activities for a new limited partnership that is being formed to construct and manage three apartment complexes in Southern California. Alameda is willing to hire Harrison for a minimum of two years to lease and manage the properties, but the partnership is unable to pay the $100,000 salary Harrison requires without impairing its ability to make necessary cash distributions to the limited partners.

Alameda is willing to pay Harrison a $60,000 salary for two years, increasing to a market salary thereafter. It is also willing to allow Harrison to purchase a 10% interest in the partnership; unfortunately, Harrison cannot afford the required $25,000 capital contribution.

The partnership expects to have income and cash flows from operations of approximately $200,000 per year. The annual cash flows will be distributed to the partners each year during the estimated seven-year holding period of the properties.

Harrison and Alameda Properties have approached you for assistance in structuring a mutually satisfactory arrangement. You are aware that a partner can be awarded an interest in the future profits of a partnership. Also, you have learned from a colleague that the IRS issued a Notice and Proposed Regulations that outline procedures for structuring such an arrangement so as to avoid current taxation of the expected future profits.

You suggest that, in lieu of requiring Harrison to pay the $25,000 purchase price, Alameda could grant Harrison a 10% interest in Alameda's future profits.

a.   Under Notice 2005–43, what actions must the partnership take to ensure that the profits interest is nontaxable? What is the tax result of receiving a nonforfeitable future profits interest?

b.   Alameda has an interest in making sure that Harrison remains with the company and wants to attach a three-year forfeiture clause to his profits interest. In other words, if Harrison leaves the company within three years, his profits interest is terminated. What additional results arise under Notice 2005–43 if the profits interest is not fully vested?

c.   What are the advantages and disadvantages of the proposed structure to each party?

Research Problem 3.   Fred and Grady formed the FG Partnership as a retail establishment to sell antique household furnishings. Fred is the general partner, and Grady is the limited partner. Both partners contribute $15,000 to form the partnership. The partnership uses the $30,000 contributed by the partners and a recourse loan of $100,000 (obtained from an unrelated third-party lender) to acquire $130,000 of initial inventory.

The partners believe they will have extensive losses in the first year due to advertising and initial cash-flow requirements. Fred and Grady have agreed to share losses equally. To make sure the losses can be allocated to both partners, they have included a provision in the partnership agreement requiring each partner to restore any deficit balance in his partnership capital account upon liquidation of the partnership.

Fred was also willing to include a provision that requires him to make up any deficit balance within 90 days of liquidation of the partnership. As a limited partner, Grady argued that he should not be subject to such a time requirement. The partners compromised and included a provision that requires Grady to restore a deficit balance in his capital account within two years of liquidation of the partnership. No interest will be owed on the deferred restoration payment.

Determine whether FG will be able to allocate the $100,000 recourse debt equally to the two partners to ensure they will be able to deduct their respective shares of partnership losses.

Use the tax resources of the Internet to address the following questions. Do not restrict your search to the World Wide Web, but include a review of newsgroups and general reference materials, practitioner sites and resources, primary sources of the tax law, chat rooms and discussion groups, and other opportunities.

Internet
Activity

Research Problem 4.   Print an article posted by a law firm that comments on pitfalls to avoid in drafting partnership agreements. Ideally, use the home page of a firm that has offices in your state.

Research Problem 5.   Use the search feature on your favorite news site on the Web (e.g, CNN, ABC News, Fox News, etc.) and search for news on partnerships, LLCs, or limited partnerships. What entities did you find that are taking advantage of the partnership entity form? (Be sure these entities are truly legal partnerships. Some entities called "partnerships" by the news media actually involve transfers of stock or formation of a corporation to manage the joint venture.)

Research Problem 6.   Find the home page of a partnership that seems to be soliciting financing from new partners. Comment on the portrayal of the pertinent tax law that is included in the materials, especially with respect to the at-risk rules and the passive activity limitations.

Research Problem 7.   At this writing, partner's one of the IRS's targeted items in its "priority guidance plan" is to issue guidelines related to a partner's receipt of a profits interest or an interest in the future capital of the partnership (also called a "carried interest"). In addition, Congress has considered several proposals for altering taxation of "carried interests." Review the current tax rules and Regulations to determine whether the IRS has acted on this. If so, what is the effect of the new rules on the proposed transaction between Harrison and Alameda in Research Proplem 2?

CHAPTER 11

Partnerships: Distributions, Transfer of Interests, and Terminations

LEARNING OBJECTIVES

After completing Chapter 11, you should be able to:

LO.1
Determine the tax treatment of proportionate nonliquidating distributions from a partnership to a partner.

LO.2
Determine the tax treatment of proportionate distributions that liquidate a partnership.

LO.3
Describe the tax treatment that applies to distributions treated as disguised sales and distributions of marketable securities and precontribution gain property.

LO.4
Describe the general concepts governing tax treatment of disproportionate distributions.

LO.5
Determine the tax treatment under § 736 of payments from a partnership to a retiring or deceased partner.

LO.6
Calculate the selling partner's amount and character of gain or loss on the sale or exchange of a partnership interest.

LO.7
Describe tax issues related to other dispositions of partnership interests.

LO.8
Calculate the optional adjustments to basis under § 754.

LO.9
Outline the methods of terminating a partnership.

LO.10
Describe the special considerations of a family partnership.

LO.11
Describe the application of partnership provisions to limited liability companies (LLCs) and limited liability partnerships (LLPs).

The previous chapter examined the tax effects of partnership formation and operation. Most operating transactions of a partnership present few tax problems; under the aggregate theory of partnership taxation, revenues earned and expenses paid by the partnership flow through to the tax returns of the partners. If the partners are individuals, the transactions are then handled like other individual tax matters.

However, a number of special tax provisions, many of them complex, govern the effects of the following transactions, which are discussed in this chapter:

- Nonliquidating distributions, which in most cases create no recognized gain or loss to the partner receiving the distribution. This treatment contrasts with that of corporate distributions, which may result in dividend income to the shareholder.
- Liquidating distributions, after which the recipient of the distribution is no longer a partner. The general rule here is that gain or loss is not recognized by either the liquidated partner or the partnership. There are exceptions, however, and these may result in gains or losses that are usually capital in nature.
- Sale of a partnership interest to a new or existing partner. This results in the selling partner receiving a return of capital and capital gain or loss. The result follows the entity theory, and the tax treatment is similar to that of a stock sale made by a shareholder in a C or S corporation. Under certain circumstances, however, the aggregate theory may partially govern the results, causing the selling partner to recognize some ordinary income or loss.

This chapter also discusses an optional election a partnership may make concerning adjustments to basis when a partnership interest is sold. Partnership terminations and special problems associated with family partnerships are also explained. The chapter closes with discussions of two specialized business forms, limited liability companies and limited liability partnerships.

Distributions from a Partnership

The tax treatment of distributions from a partnership to a partner was introduced in Chapter 10 in the context of routine cash withdrawals (or "draws") and cash distributions from a continuing partnership to a continuing partner. These draws and distributions reduce the partner's outside basis by the amount of the cash received. The partnership's inside basis in assets is similarly reduced.

Bill is a partner in the BB Partnership. The basis in his partnership interest is $10,000. The partnership distributes $3,000 cash to Bill at the end of the year. Bill does not recognize any gain on the distribution and reduces his basis by $3,000 (the amount of the distribution) to $7,000. Bill's basis in the cash he received is $3,000, and the partnership's inside basis for its assets is reduced by the $3,000 cash distributed. ∎

The result in Example 1 arises whether or not a similar distribution is made to other partners. In a partnership, it is not critical that all partners receive a distribution at the same time as long as capital account balances are maintained appropriately, and final distributions are in accordance with ending capital account balances (see Chapter 10). Capital account maintenance requirements ensure that each partner eventually receives the proper amount, even though current distributions are not in accordance with ownership percentages.

A distribution from the partnership to a partner may consist of cash or partnership property. All distributions, cash and property, fall into two distinct categories:

- Liquidating distributions.
- Nonliquidating distributions.

Whether a distribution is a **liquidating** or **nonliquidating distribution** depends solely on whether the partner remains a partner in the partnership after the distribution is made. A *liquidating* distribution occurs either (1) when a partnership itself liquidates and distributes all of its property to its partners or (2) when an ongoing partnership redeems the interest of one of its partners. This second type of liquidating distribution occurs, for example, when a partner retires from a partnership, or when a deceased partner's interest is liquidated. The two types of liquidating distributions receive differing tax treatment, as later sections of the chapter will explain.

A *nonliquidating* distribution is any other distribution from a continuing partnership to a continuing partner—that is, any distribution that is not a liquidating distribution. Nonliquidating distributions are of two types: draws or partial liquidations. A *draw* is a distribution of a partner's share of current or accumulated partnership profits that have been taxed to the partner in current or prior taxable years of the partnership. A *partial liquidation* is a distribution that reduces the partner's interest in partnership capital but does not liquidate the partner's entire interest in the partnership. The distinction between the two types of nonliquidating distributions is largely semantic, as the basic tax treatment typically does not differ.

Kay joins the calendar year KLM Partnership on January 1, 2008, by contributing $40,000 cash to the partnership in exchange for a one-third interest in partnership capital, profits, and losses. Her distributive share of partnership income for the year is $25,000. If the partnership distributes $65,000 ($25,000 share of partnership profits + $40,000 initial capital contribution) to Kay on December 31, 2008, the distribution is a nonliquidating distribution as long as Kay continues to be a partner in the partnership. This is true even though Kay receives her share of profits plus her entire investment in the partnership. In this case, $25,000 is considered a draw, and the remaining $40,000 is a partial liquidation of Kay's interest. If, instead, the partnership is liquidated or Kay ceases to be a partner in the ongoing partnership, the $65,000 distribution is a liquidating distribution. ∎

A payment from a partnership to a partner is not necessarily treated as a distribution. For example, as discussed in Chapter 10, a partnership may pay interest or rent to a partner for use of the partner's capital or property, make a guaranteed payment to a partner, or purchase property from a partner. If a payment *is* treated as a distribution, it is not necessarily treated under the general tax deferral rules that apply to most partnership distributions. In certain circumstances, the partner may recognize capital gain (or loss) and ordinary income (or loss) when a distribution is received from the partnership.

Finally, a distribution may be either proportionate or disproportionate. In a **proportionate distribution**, a partner receives the appropriate share of certain ordinary income-producing assets of the partnership. A **disproportionate distribution** occurs when the distribution increases or decreases the distributee partner's interest in certain ordinary income-producing assets. The tax treatment of disproportionate distributions is very complex.

The initial discussion and examples in this chapter describe the treatment of proportionate current and liquidating distributions. Special rules related to property distributions are discussed next. Then a brief overview of the rules pertaining to disproportionate distributions is presented.

Proportionate Nonliquidating Distributions

<table>
<tr><td>

LO.1

Determine the tax treatment of proportionate nonliquidating distributions from a partnership to a partner.

</td></tr>
</table>

In general, neither the partner nor the partnership recognizes gain or loss when a proportionate nonliquidating distribution occurs.[1] The partner usually takes a carryover basis for the assets distributed.[2] The distributee partner's outside basis is reduced (but not below zero) by the amount of cash and the adjusted basis of property distributed to the partner by the partnership.[3] The details of the taxation of such distributions are discussed below and are summarized at the end of this section in Concept Summary 11–1. The following examples illustrate the situation and show that a distribution does not change a partner's overall economic position.

EXAMPLE 3

Jay is a one-fourth partner in the SP Partnership. On December 31 of the current tax year, his basis in his partnership interest is $40,000. The fair market value of the interest is $70,000. The partnership distributes $25,000 cash to him on that date. The distribution is not taxable to Jay or the partnership. The distribution reduces Jay's adjusted basis in the partnership to $15,000 ($40,000 − $25,000), and the fair market value of his partnership interest is, arguably, reduced to $45,000 ($70,000 − $25,000). ∎

EXAMPLE 4

Assume the same facts as in Example 3, except that, in addition to the $25,000 cash, the partnership distributes land with an adjusted basis to the partnership of $13,000 and a fair market value of $30,000 on the date of distribution. The distribution is not taxable to Jay or the partnership. Jay reduces his basis in the partnership to $2,000 [$40,000 − ($25,000 + $13,000)] and takes a carryover basis of $13,000 in the land. The fair market value of Jay's remaining interest in the partnership is, arguably, reduced to $15,000 [$70,000 − ($25,000 + $30,000)].

If Jay had sold his partnership interest for $70,000 rather than receiving the distributions, he would have realized and recognized gain of $30,000 ($70,000 selling price − $40,000 outside basis). Because he has not recognized any gain or loss on the distribution of cash and land, he should still have the $30,000 of deferred gain to recognize at some point in the future. This is exactly what will happen. If Jay sells the cash, land, and remaining partnership interest on January 1 of the next year (the day after the distribution), he realizes and recognizes gains of $17,000 ($30,000 − $13,000) on the land and $13,000 ($15,000 − $2,000) on the partnership interest. These gains total $30,000, which is the amount of the original deferred gain. ∎

Note the difference between the tax theory governing distributions from C corporations and partnerships. In a C corporation, a distribution from current or accumulated income (earnings and profits) is taxable as a dividend to the shareholder, and the corporation does not receive a deduction for the amount distributed. This is an example of corporate income being subject to double taxation. In a partnership, a distribution from current or accumulated profits is not taxable because Congress has decided that partnership income should be subject to only a single

---

[1] §§ 731(a) and (b).
[2] § 732(a)(1).

[3] § 733.

level of taxation. Because a partner pays taxes when the share of income is earned by the partnership, this income is not taxed again when distributed.

These results make sense under the entity and aggregate concepts. The entity concept is applicable to corporate dividends, so any amount paid as a dividend is treated as a transfer by the corporate entity to the shareholder and is taxed accordingly. Under the aggregate theory, though, a partner receiving a distribution of partnership income is treated as merely receiving something already owned. Whether the partner chooses to leave the income in the partnership or receive it in a distribution makes no difference.

Gain Recognition. A partner recognizes gain from a proportionate nonliquidating distribution to the extent that the cash received exceeds the outside basis of the partner's interest in the partnership.[4]

EXAMPLE 5

Samantha is a one-third partner in the SMP Partnership. Her basis in this ownership interest is $50,000 on December 31, 2008, after accounting for the calendar year partnership's 2008 operations and for Samantha's 2008 capital contributions. On December 31, 2008, the partnership distributes $60,000 cash to Samantha. She recognizes a $10,000 gain from this distribution ($60,000 cash received − $50,000 basis in her partnership interest). Most likely, this gain is taxed as a capital gain.[5] ■

While distributions *from* current and accumulated earnings are taxed differently to shareholders and partners, cash distributions *in excess* of accumulated profits are taxed similarly for corporate shareholders and partners in partnerships. Both shareholders and partners are allowed to recover the cumulative capital invested in the entity tax-free.

Recall from Chapter 10 that the reduction of a partner's share of partnership debt is treated as a distribution of cash from the partnership to the partner. A reduction of a partner's share of partnership debt, then, first reduces the partner's basis in the partnership. Any reduction of a share of debt in excess of a partner's basis in the partnership is taxable to the partner as a gain.

EXAMPLE 6

Returning to the facts of Example 5, assume that Samantha's $50,000 basis in her partnership interest included a $60,000 share of partnership liabilities. If the partnership repays all of its liabilities, Samantha is treated as receiving a $60,000 distribution from the partnership. The first $50,000 of this distribution reduces her basis to $0. The last $10,000 distributed creates a taxable gain to her of $10,000. ■

A distribution of marketable securities can also be treated as a distribution of cash. Determining the treatment of such distributions is complicated, though, since several exceptions may apply and the basis in the distributed stock must be calculated. Such distributions are discussed later under Property Distributions with Special Tax Treatment: Marketable Securities.

Loss Recognition. The distributee partner cannot recognize a loss on a proportionate nonliquidating distribution. This loss is deferred because tax law typically does not permit losses to be recognized until the loss is certain to occur and the amount is known. After the nonliquidating distribution, the partner still owns the partnership interest, which has an indeterminate future value. Only when a final liquidating distribution is received is the loss certain and known in amount—and potentially deductible.

---

[4]§ 731(a)(1).

[5]§ 731(a). If the partnership holds any "hot assets," however, Samantha will probably recognize some ordinary income. See § 751(b) and the related discussion of ordinary income ("hot") assets and disproportionate distributions later in this chapter.

EXAMPLE 7

Henry has a $50,000 basis in his partnership interest. Assume that on December 31 he receives a distribution of $10,000 cash. As a result of the distribution, his basis in the partnership interest is reduced to $40,000.

Henry knows the partnership has fallen on hard times and that future distributions will probably not amount to more than a few hundred dollars. He does not recognize a loss, even though a loss probably exists. The amount of the loss is not fixed and determinable because he still owns the partnership interest. ■

Property Distributions. In general, a distributee partner does not recognize gain from a property distribution. If the basis of property distributed by a partnership exceeds the partner's basis in the partnership interest, the distributed asset takes a substituted basis. This ensures that the partner does not receive asset basis that is not "paid for."

EXAMPLE 8

Mary has a $50,000 basis in her partnership interest. The partnership distributes land it owns with a basis and a fair market value of $60,000. Mary does not recognize any gain on this distribution because it is a distribution of property. However, Mary should not be allowed to take a carryover basis of $60,000 in the land, when her basis in her partnership interest is only $50,000. Therefore, Mary takes a substituted basis of $50,000 in the land. Her basis in her partnership interest is reduced by the basis she takes in the asset received, or $50,000. Therefore, Mary has a $50,000 basis in the land and a $0 basis in her partnership interest, and she recognizes no gain on this distribution. ■

The rule that no gain or loss is recognized on a property distribution from a partnership has several exceptions. These situations may arise for either a current or a liquidating distribution, so discussion of these exceptions is deferred until all the general rules are discussed (see Property Distributions with Special Tax Treatment later in the chapter).

Ordering Rules. When the inside basis of the distributed assets exceeds the distributee partner's outside basis, the assets are deemed distributed in the following order:

- Cash is distributed first.
- Unrealized receivables and inventory are distributed second.
- All other assets are distributed last.

Unrealized receivables are receivables that have a value to the partnership, but for which the related income has not yet been realized or recognized under the partnership's method of accounting. The term *unrealized receivables* applies only to amounts that will ultimately be realized and recognized as ordinary income. If the partnership uses the cash method of accounting, trade receivables from services or sales are unrealized receivables. If the partnership uses the accrual method, they are not. Unrealized receivables include receivables from sales of ordinary income property and rights to payments for services. For some purposes, unrealized receivables also include ordinary recapture income that would arise if the partnership sold its depreciable assets. Installment gains are unrealized receivables if the gain will be taxed as ordinary income when realized.

Inventory, for purposes of these ordering rules, includes any partnership assets except cash, capital, or § 1231 assets. For example, all accounts receivable are considered to be inventory, although only cash basis receivables are "unrealized receivables."

Because the partner typically does not recognize a gain from a *property* distribution, the Code provides that the partner's basis for property received cannot exceed the partner's basis in the partnership interest immediately before the distribution. For each level of asset distribution, the relevant adjustments are made to the partner's basis in the interest. In other words, after a cash distribution, the partner's basis in the interest is recomputed before determining the effect of a distribution of unrealized receivables or inventory. The basis is again recomputed before determining the effect of a distribution of other assets. If the remaining outside basis at the end of any step is insufficient to cover the entire inside basis of the assets in the next step, that remaining outside basis is allocated among the assets within that class.[6]

EXAMPLE 9

Sally has a $48,000 basis in her partnership interest. On September 10, 2008, the partnership distributes to her cash of $12,000, cash basis receivables with an inside basis of $0 and a fair market value of $10,000, and a parcel of land with a basis to the partnership of $60,000 and a fair market value of $100,000. Sally has a realized gain on the distribution of $74,000 ($12,000 + $10,000 + $100,000 − $48,000). None of that gain is recognized, however, since the $12,000 cash distribution does not exceed her $48,000 adjusted basis for her partnership interest. In determining the basis effects of the distribution, the cash is treated as being distributed first, reducing Sally's adjusted basis to $36,000 ($48,000 − $12,000). The receivables are distributed next, taking a $0 carryover basis to Sally. Her adjusted basis remains at $36,000. The land is distributed last, taking a substituted basis of $36,000 and reducing her adjusted basis for her partnership interest to $0. ∎

When more than one asset in a particular class is distributed, special rules apply. Usually, if the partner's remaining adjusted basis for the partnership interest is less than the partnership's adjusted basis for the distributed assets in the particular class, the partner's adjusted basis for each distributed asset is computed by following three steps:

Step 1 Each distributed asset within the class initially takes a carryover basis.

Step 2 Then, this carryover basis for each of these assets is reduced in proportion to their respective amounts of unrealized depreciation (amount that carryover basis is greater than fair market value). Under no circumstances, however, can the basis of any asset be reduced below its fair market value in step 2.

Step 3 Any remaining decrease in basis is allocated among all the distributed assets in the class in proportion to their respective adjusted bases (as determined in step 2).

EXAMPLE 10

Assume the same facts as in Example 9, except that Sally receives two parcels of land, rather than a single parcel. The partnership's basis for the parcels is $15,000 for Parcel 1 and $45,000 for Parcel 2. Each parcel has a fair market value of $30,000. Sally has a realized gain on the distribution of $34,000 ($12,000 + $10,000 + $60,000 − $48,000). None of that gain is recognized, however, because the $12,000 cash distribution does not exceed her $48,000 adjusted basis.

As in Example 9, Sally takes a $12,000 basis for the cash and a $0 carryover basis for the receivables and has a $36,000 adjusted basis for her partnership interest after these two items are distributed. Because two parcels of land are distributed, and because Sally's remaining $36,000 adjusted basis for her partnership interest is less than the partnership's $60,000 total basis for the two parcels of land, Sally's adjusted basis for each parcel of land is computed by following these steps:

Step 1 She initially takes a carryover basis of $15,000 for Parcel 1 and $45,000 for Parcel 2.

Step 2 She reduces the basis of Parcel 2 to its lower fair market value of $30,000. The basis for Parcel 1 is not adjusted in this step because Parcel 1 has a fair market value greater than its basis.

Step 3 The remaining $9,000 difference between her $36,000 basis for the partnership interest and the $45,000 ($15,000 + $30,000) basis for the land parcels after step 2 is allocated to the two parcels in proportion to their respective bases (as computed in step 2). Therefore, the amount of the step 3 basis reduction allocated to Parcel 1 is:

$$\$9,000 \times \frac{\$15,000}{\$45,000} = \$3,000$$

---

[6]§ 732.

Sally's basis for Parcel 1 is $12,000 ($15,000 − $3,000). The amount of the step 3 basis reduction allocated to Parcel 2 is:

$$\$9,000 \times \frac{\$30,000}{\$45,000} = \$6,000$$

Sally's basis for Parcel 2 is $24,000 ($30,000 − $6,000). ■

EXAMPLE 11

Assume the same facts as in Example 10, and that Sally sells both parcels of land early in 2009 for their fair market values, receiving proceeds of $60,000 ($30,000 + $30,000). She also collects $10,000 from the cash basis receivables. Now she recognizes all of the $34,000 gain that she deferred upon receiving the property from the partnership [$60,000 amount realized − $36,000 basis for the two parcels ($12,000 + $24,000) + $10,000 collected − $0 basis for the receivables]. ■

Review the tax results of Examples 9 and 10. Although Sally does not recognize any of the gain she realizes from the distribution, she has a zero outside basis for her partnership interest. If Sally expects the partnership to generate net losses in the near future, she will *not* find this zero basis attractive. She may be unable to deduct her share of these future losses when they flow through to her on the last day of the partnership's subsequent tax year.

The low basis that Sally has assigned to the parcels of land is of no significant detriment to her if she does not intend to sell the land in the near future. Because land does not generate cost recovery deductions, the substituted basis is used only to determine Sally's gain or loss upon her disposition of the land in a taxable sale or exchange.

Concept Summary 11–1 reviews the general rules that apply to proportionate nonliquidating partnership distributions.

ETHICAL and EQUITABLE *Considerations*

ARRANGING TAX-ADVANTAGED DISTRIBUTIONS

The Sparrow Partnership plans to distribute $200,000 cash to its partners at the end of the year. Marjorie is a 40 percent partner and would receive $80,000. Her basis in the partnership is only $10,000, however, so she would be required to recognize a $70,000 gain if she receives a cash distribution. She has asked the partnership instead to purchase a parcel of land she has found on which she will build her retirement residence. The partnership will then distribute that land to her. Under the partnership distribution rules, Marjorie would take a $10,000 basis in land worth $80,000. Her basis in the partnership would be reduced to $0, and the $70,000 gain is deferred. Do you think this is an appropriate transaction?

LO.2

Determine the tax treatment of proportionate distributions that liquidate a partnership.

Proportionate Liquidating Distributions

Proportionate liquidating distributions consist of a single distribution or a series of distributions that result in the termination of the partner's entire interest in the partnership. If the partnership continues in existence after the partner's interest is liquidated, the rules of § 736 govern the classification of the liquidating payments. These rules are discussed later in the chapter. Other rules apply, however, if the partner's interest is liquidated because the partnership is also liquidating. This section examines the latter type of liquidating distribution.

The partnership itself does not recognize either gain or loss on a proportionate liquidating distribution. The following discussion outlines rules for allocation of basis and possible gain or loss recognition by partners. These rules are summarized in Concept Summary 11–2 at the end of this section.

CONCEPT SUMMARY 11–1

Proportionate Nonliquidating Distributions (General Rules)

1. Neither the distributee partner nor the partnership recognizes any gain or loss on a proportionate non-liquidating distribution. However, if cash distributed exceeds the distributee partner's outside basis, gain is recognized. Property distributions generally do not result in gain recognition.

2. The distributee partner usually takes the same basis in the distributed property that the property had to the partnership (carryover basis). However, where the inside basis of distributed property exceeds the partner's outside basis, the basis assigned to the distributed property cannot exceed that outside basis (substituted basis).

3. Gain recognized by the distributee partner on a proportionate nonliquidating distribution is capital in nature.

4. Loss is never recognized on a proportionate nonliquidating distribution.

Calculations

1. Partner's outside basis.

2. Less: Cash distributed to partner.

3. Gain recognized by partner (excess of Line 2 over Line 1).

4. Partner's remaining outside basis (Line 1 – Line 2). If less than $0, enter $0.

5. Partner's basis in unrealized receivables and inventory distributed (enter lesser of Line 4 or the partnership's inside basis in the unrealized receivables and inventory).

6. Basis available to allocate to other property distributed (Line 4 – Line 5).

7. Partnership's inside basis of other property distributed.

8. Basis to partner of other property distributed (enter lesser of Line 6 or Line 7).

9. Partner's remaining outside basis (Line 6 – Line 8).

Gain Recognition and Ordering Rules. When a partnership liquidates, the liquidating distributions to a partner usually consist of an interest in several or all of the partnership assets. The gain recognition and ordering rules parallel those for nonliquidating distributions, except that the partner's *entire* basis in the partnership interest is allocated to the assets received in the liquidating distribution, unless the partner is required to recognize a loss. A loss may be recognized when *only* cash, unrealized receivables, or inventory is received in the distribution. As a result of the ordering rules, the basis of some assets may be adjusted upward or downward to absorb the partner's remaining outside basis. Unrealized receivables or inventory are never "stepped up," although they may be "stepped down."

The general ordering and gain recognition rules for a proportionate liquidating distribution are summarized as follows:

- Cash is distributed first and results in a capital gain if the amount distributed exceeds the partner's basis in the partnership interest. The cash distributed reduces the liquidated partner's outside basis dollar for dollar. The partner's basis cannot be reduced below zero.
- The partner's remaining outside basis is then allocated to unrealized receivables and inventory up to an amount equal to the partnership's adjusted bases in those properties. If the partnership's bases in the unrealized receivables and inventory exceed the partner's remaining outside basis, the remaining outside basis is allocated to the unrealized receivables and inventory.

- Finally, if the liquidating partner has any outside basis left, that basis is allocated to the other assets received.[7]

EXAMPLE 12

When Tara's basis in her partnership interest is $70,000, she receives cash of $15,000, a proportionate share of inventory, and land in a distribution that liquidates both the partnership and her entire partnership interest. The inventory has a basis to the partnership of $20,000 and a fair market value of $30,000. The land's basis is $8,000, and the fair market value is $12,000. Under these circumstances, Tara recognizes no gain or loss. After reducing Tara's $70,000 basis by the $15,000 cash received, the remaining $55,000 is allocated first to the inventory and then to the land. The basis of the inventory in Tara's hands is $20,000, and the basis of the land is $35,000. ∎

When more than one asset in a particular class is distributed in a proportionate liquidating distribution, special rules may apply. If the partner's remaining basis for the partnership interest is less than the partnership's basis for the distributed assets in the particular class, the partner's basis for each distributed asset is computed as illustrated previously in Example 10. If, however, the partner's remaining basis for the partnership interest is greater than the partnership's basis for the distributed assets in the "other assets" class, the partner's basis for each remaining distributed asset is computed by following three steps:

Step 1 Each distributed asset within the "other assets" class initially takes a carryover basis.

Step 2 Then, this carryover basis for each of these assets is increased in proportion to their respective amounts of unrealized appreciation (amount that fair market value is greater than carryover basis). Under no circumstances, however, can the basis of any asset be increased above its fair market value in step 2.

Step 3 Any remaining increase in basis is allocated among all the distributed assets in the "other assets" class in proportion to their respective fair market values.

EXAMPLE 13

Assume the same facts as in Example 12, except that Tara receives two parcels of land instead of one. The partnership's basis for the parcels is $2,000 for Parcel 1 and $6,000 for Parcel 2. Each parcel has a fair market value of $6,000.

Tara takes a $15,000 basis for the cash and a $20,000 carryover basis for the inventory. She has a $35,000 basis for her partnership interest after these two items are distributed. Because two parcels of land are distributed, and because Tara's remaining $35,000 basis for her partnership interest exceeds the partnership's $8,000 basis for the two parcels of land, Tara's basis for each parcel of land is computed by following these steps:

Step 1 She initially takes a carryover basis of $2,000 for Parcel 1 and $6,000 for Parcel 2.

Step 2 She increases the basis of Parcel 1 by $4,000 to its fair market value of $6,000. The basis for Parcel 2 is not affected in this step because Parcel 2 has a fair market value equal to its basis.

Step 3 Tara's $23,000 ($35,000 − $6,000 − $6,000) remaining basis for her partnership interest is allocated to each land parcel in proportion to each parcel's respective $6,000 fair market value. Therefore, $11,500 [($6,000/$12,000) × $23,000] is allocated to each parcel. Tara's basis in Parcel 1 is $17,500 ($2,000 + $4,000 + $11,500). Her basis in Parcel 2 is also $17,500 ($6,000 + $11,500). ∎

Loss Recognition. The distributee partner recognizes a *loss* on a liquidating distribution if both of the following are true:

---

[7]§§ 731 and 732.

1. The partner receives *only* cash, unrealized receivables, or inventory.
2. The partner's outside basis in the partnership interest exceeds the partnership's inside basis for the assets distributed. This excess amount is the loss recognized by the distributee partner.[8]

The word "only" is important. A distribution of any other property precludes recognition of the loss.

EXAMPLE 14

When Ramon's outside basis is $40,000, he receives a liquidating distribution of $7,000 cash and a proportionate share of inventory having a partnership basis of $3,000 and a fair market value of $10,000. Ramon is not allowed to "step up" the basis in the inventory, so it is allocated a $3,000 carryover basis. Ramon's unutilized outside basis is $30,000 ($40,000 − $7,000 − $3,000). Since he received a liquidating distribution of *only* cash and inventory, he recognizes a capital loss of $30,000 on the liquidation. ∎

EXAMPLE 15

Assume the same facts as in Example 14, except that in addition to the cash and inventory, Ramon receives the desk he used in the partnership. The desk has an adjusted basis of $100 to the partnership. Applying the rules outlined above to this revised fact situation produces the following results:

> *Step 1* Cash of $7,000 is distributed to Ramon and reduces his outside basis to $33,000.
>
> *Step 2* Inventory is distributed to Ramon. He takes a $3,000 carryover basis in the inventory and reduces his outside basis in the partnership to $30,000.
>
> *Step 3* The desk is distributed to Ramon. Since the desk is a § 1231 asset and not cash, an unrealized receivable, or inventory, he cannot recognize a loss. Therefore, Ramon's remaining basis in his partnership interest is allocated to the desk. He takes a $30,000 basis for the desk. ∎

What can Ramon do with a $30,000 desk? If he continues to use it in a trade or business, he can depreciate it. Once he has established his business use of the desk, he could sell it and recognize a large § 1231 loss. If the loss is isolated in the year of the sale, it is an ordinary loss. Thus, with proper planning, no liquidated partner should be forced to recognize a capital loss instead of an ordinary loss.

Gain recognized by the withdrawing partner on the subsequent disposition of inventory is ordinary income unless the disposition occurs more than five years after the distribution.[9] The withdrawing partner's holding period for all other property received in a liquidating distribution includes the partnership's related holding period.

Concept Summary 11–2 outlines the general rules that apply to proportionate liquidating partnership distributions.

Property Distributions with Special Tax Treatment

Recall that a distribution from a partnership to a partner usually does not result in taxable gain. This section discusses three exceptions in which a proportionate distribution, either liquidating or nonliquidating, may result in gain to the partner.

Disguised Sales. As discussed in Chapter 10, a disguised sale is a transaction in which a partner contributes appreciated property to a partnership and soon thereafter receives a distribution of cash or property from the partnership. If the IRS determines the payment is part of a "purchase" of the property, rather than a distribution from the partnership, the usual sale or exchange rules apply. The partner is treated as

> **LO.3**
>
> Describe the tax treatment that applies to distributions treated as disguised sales and distributions of marketable securities and precontribution gain property.

---

[8]§ 731(a)(2).   [9]§ 735(a)(2).

CONCEPT SUMMARY 11–2

Proportionate Liquidating Distributions When the Partnership Also Liquidates (General Rules)

1. Generally, neither the distributee partner nor the partnership recognizes gain or loss when a partnership liquidates. However, a partner recognizes gain if the cash received exceeds the partner's outside basis. A partner recognizes loss when (a) the partner receives only cash, unrealized receivables, or inventory and (b) the partner's outside basis is greater than the partnership's inside basis of the assets distributed.

2. A partner's basis in distributed assets must be determined in a certain order. Cash is distributed first, inventory and unrealized receivables second, and all other assets last. Assets in the last category take a substituted basis equal to the distributee partner's remaining outside basis.

3. Gain or loss recognized by a distributee partner in a distribution that liquidates a partnership is usually capital in nature.

Calculations

1. Partner's outside basis.	_____
2. Less: Cash distributed to partner.	_____
3. Gain recognized by partner (excess of Line 2 over Line 1).	_____
4. Partner's remaining outside basis (Line 1 – Line 2). If less than $0, enter $0.	_____
5. Partner's basis in unrealized receivables and inventory distributed (enter lesser of Line 4 or the inside basis in the unrealized receivables and inventory).	_____
6. Basis to partner of other property distributed (Line 4 – Line 5).	_____
7. Loss recognized by partner (if no other property was distributed, enter amount from Line 6).	_____
8. Partner's remaining outside basis.	$0

having sold the property and must report a gain on the sale. The partnership takes a cost basis in the property purchased. See Chapter 10 for additional discussion.

Marketable Securities. The fair market value of a marketable security distributed to a partner is generally treated as a cash distribution.[10] Some or all of the value of the security over the partner's outside basis prior to the distribution is a taxable gain. The partner must assign a basis to the security received in the distribution, so the distribution ordering rules must be taken into account.

The term *marketable securities* is broadly defined and includes almost any debt or equity interest that is actively traded, including options, futures contracts, and derivatives. Marketable securities are *not* treated as cash if (1) they were originally contributed by the partner to whom they are now distributed (certain exceptions apply to this provision), (2) the property was not a marketable security when acquired by the partnership, or (3) the partner is an eligible partner of an investment partnership, as defined in Chapter 10.

The primary purpose of this rule is to stop the tax avoidance that otherwise would occur if a partnership purchased marketable securities with the intent of immediately distributing them to the partner. As the Ethical and Equitable Considerations earlier in this chapter indicated, a partnership can purchase property desired by a partner, distribute that property to the partner, and allow the partner to defer tax on any appreciation inherent in the partnership interest. This rule prevents a partnership from arranging such a transaction with marketable securities.

---

[10]§ 731(c).

If, on the distribution date, the marketable security is appreciated, it probably was not acquired by the partnership in an effort to assist the distributee partner in reducing the tax on the distribution. The portion of the security value treated as cash is reduced by a proportionate share of the appreciation inherent in the distributed security. The amount of the reduction is the excess of (1) the partner's share of appreciation in this particular security before the distribution over (2) the partner's share of appreciation in the portion of the security retained by the partnership. If the partner's interest in the partnership is liquidated, the gain on the partner's share of the distributed security is deferred. The "reduction" is intended to take into account the partnership's intent, or lack thereof, to reduce the partner's gains.

Assume the A to Z Partnership has the following balance sheet:

	Basis	FMV		Basis	FMV
ZYX Corporation security	$4,000	$10,000	Andy, capital	$ 500	$ 2,000
Land	1,000	10,000	Other partners, capital	4,500	18,000
Total	$5,000	$20,000	Total	$5,000	$20,000

The partnership distributes $2,000 (value) of the ZYX stock to 10% partner Andy in liquidation of his partnership interest. The amount of the distribution treated as cash is the $2,000 fair market value of the stock reduced by Andy's decrease in his share of the inside appreciation in the stock. Before the distribution, Andy's share of appreciation in this stock was $600 [10% × ($10,000 − $4,000)]. *His share* of appreciation in the stock retained by the partnership is $0, because he no longer owns an interest in the partnership. The $2,000 value of the stock is reduced by $600 ($600 appreciation before − $0 after distribution). Andy is treated as if he received a cash distribution of $1,400.

Andy's outside basis was $500 before the distribution. The $1,400 deemed cash distribution triggers gain recognition of $900. ∎

The distributee partner's basis in the security is the sum of (1) the basis in the stock as determined under the regular distribution rules (see the discussion under Ordering Rules above) and (2) the gain recognized on the distribution.

In Example 16, the stock would take a substituted basis of $500 to Andy under the distribution ordering rules. This basis is the lesser of the partnership's inside basis in the stock of $800 (20% × $4,000) or Andy's outside basis of $500 (see Concept Summary 11–2). The recognized gain of $900 increases Andy's basis in the stock to $1,400 ($500 + $900).

This basis determination preserves the inherent built-in gain in Andy's partnership interest. Before the distribution, Andy has $1,500 of appreciation in his interest ($2,000 − $500). After considering the $900 gain on the stock distribution, he should have $600 of untaxed appreciation. The stock value is $2,000, and Andy's basis is $1,400, so the untaxed appreciation is the expected $600 amount. ∎

Unless otherwise indicated, the remaining examples in this chapter assume the partnership is not distributing marketable securities.

Precontribution Gain. Taxable gains may arise on a distribution of property to a partner where precontribution (built-in) gains exist. Specifically, if a partner contributes appreciated property to a partnership, the contributing partner recognizes gain in two situations:

1. If the contributed appreciated property is distributed to another partner within seven years of the contribution date, the contributing partner recognizes the remaining net precontribution gain on the property.[11] The contributing

---
[11]§ 704(c)(1)(B).

partner's basis in the partnership interest is increased by the amount of gain recognized. Also, the basis of the distributed property is increased by this same amount to prevent double taxation of this precontribution gain when the distributee partner later sells the asset.

EXAMPLE 18	In 2008, Rod contributes nondepreciable property with an adjusted basis of $10,000 and a fair market value of $40,000 to the RTCO Partnership in exchange for a one-fourth interest in profits and capital. In 2009, when the property's fair market value is $50,000, the partnership distributes the property to Tom, another one-fourth partner. Since the property was contributed to the partnership within seven years of the date the property was distributed, and precontribution gain of $30,000 ($40,000 − $10,000) was attributable to the property, the built-in gain on the property is taxable to Rod. Therefore, Rod must pay tax on the $30,000 built-in gain in 2009, the year the property was distributed to Tom. Rod increases his basis in his partnership interest by the $30,000 gain recognized. Tom also increases his basis in the property received by $30,000.

Note that if the partnership sells the property to an unrelated third party for $40,000 in 2009, the result is the same for Rod. Under § 704(c)(1)(A), recognized built-in gains must be allocated to the partner who contributed the property, and the partner's outside basis is increased accordingly. ∎

2. The second situation occurs where the partnership distributes *any* property other than cash to a partner within seven years after *that* partner contributes appreciated property to the partnership. In this case, the partner recognizes the lesser of (a) the remaining net precontribution (built-in) gain or (b) the excess of the fair market value of the distributed property over the partner's basis in interest before the distribution.[12] The distributee partner's basis in his or her partnership interest is increased by the amount of gain recognized. To maintain a parity between inside and outside basis, the partnership is allowed to increase its basis in the precontribution gain property remaining in the partnership.

An exception applies if the partner originally contributed the distributed property. The partnership is merely returning property to the original contributor, and the partner is not required to recognize built-in gain. The general rules that govern property distributions apply.

EXAMPLE 19	In 2006, Bill contributes land to the BMC Partnership. His basis in the land was $16,000. The fair market value at the contribution date was $40,000. In 2008, the partnership distributes other property with an adjusted basis of $16,000 and fair market value of $65,000 to Bill. Bill's basis in his partnership interest was $12,000 immediately before the distribution. Since Bill contributed precontribution gain property within seven years of receiving the distribution of other property, he recognizes gain on the distribution. The maximum he must recognize is the net precontribution gain, or $24,000 ($40,000 fair market value − $16,000 adjusted basis of property contributed). He compares this amount to the excess of the fair market value of the distributed property over his basis in his partnership interest, or $53,000 ($65,000 fair market value of property − $12,000 adjusted basis in interest prior to distribution).

Because the $24,000 precontribution gain is less than the $53,000 inherent gain, Bill recognizes gain of $24,000. His basis in his partnership interest increases by the $24,000 gain recognized to $36,000, and the partnership's basis in the "precontribution gain" property Bill originally contributed also increases by $24,000 to $40,000. ∎

EXAMPLE 20	Assume the same facts as in Example 19, except that Bill's basis in his partnership interest was $60,000 before the distribution. In this case, the excess value of the distributed property is only $5,000 ($65,000 − $60,000), so Bill only recognizes gain of $5,000, with corresponding adjustments to the basis of his partnership interest and the partnership's basis in the precontribution gain property.

[12]§ 737.

TAX *in the News*   **SIMPLIFYING PARTNERSHIP TAXATION—A LOSING BATTLE?**

Partnership taxation has become increasingly complex over the past decade. The tax treatment of a distribution differs depending on the type of property being distributed, the appreciation inherent in the property, to whom the property is distributed, and how the partnership originally acquired the property. Liability sharing rules vary depending on the type of liability, the type of partner (general or limited), and when the liability was created. And the "substantial economic effect" rules include numerous pages of guidelines on when and how to allocate income and loss among the partners.

Various parties, including the Joint Committee on Taxation, several members of Congress, and the American Bar Association, have called for simplification of the rules. Even the IRS has presented plans for simplifying some areas (e.g., the disproportionate distribution rules discussed below). Yet none of the recently enacted tax legislation or IRS Regulations have simplified partnership taxation. Also, the IRS is currently considering additional changes to the Regulations that will add considerable complexity to this already difficult area. Pundits speculate that simplification in the partnership area will be slow in coming because most necessary changes would result in a net revenue loss to the government.

The remaining precontribution gain of $19,000 ($24,000 − $5,000) is charged to Bill at some point in the future if the partnership sells the precontribution gain property or distributes it to another partner within seven years of its contribution. Some or all of the remaining precontribution gain may also be recognized if other appreciated property is distributed to Bill within seven years of the original contribution. ■

If the distribution occurs more than seven years after the original contribution, Bill recognizes no gain, and the distribution is handled under the general distribution rules described earlier in this section.

Disproportionate Distributions

LO.4

Describe the general concepts governing tax treatment of disproportionate distributions.

An additional exception to the general gain and loss nonrecognition rule arises when a partnership makes a "disproportionate distribution" of assets. A disproportionate distribution occurs when a partnership makes a distribution of cash or property to a partner and that distribution increases or decreases the distributee partner's proportionate interest in certain of the partnership's ordinary income-producing assets.

These ordinary income-producing assets, called **hot assets**, include substantially **appreciated inventory** and unrealized receivables. Unrealized receivables are rights to receive future amounts that will result in ordinary income when the income is recognized. Inventory, as the term is used here, has a much broader meaning than usual. It includes all assets that are not cash, capital, or § 1231 assets. Substantially appreciated inventory is inventory that has a fair market value in excess of 120 percent of the partnership's adjusted basis for the inventory.

The taxation of disproportionate distributions is based on the aggregate theory of taxation. Under this theory, each partner is deemed to own a proportionate share of the underlying assets of the partnership. In line with this concept, each partner is responsible for recognizing and reporting the proportionate share of ordinary income potential of these assets, such as would arise on the sale of substantially appreciated inventory or on the collection of cash basis receivables.

Section 751(b) maintains each partner's proportionate share of ordinary income by recasting any transaction in which a disproportionate distribution of hot assets is made. If the distributee partner receives less than a proportionate share of hot assets, the transaction is treated as if two separate events occurred: (1) the partnership made a distribution of some of the hot assets to the distributee partner, and (2) that partner immediately sold these hot assets back to the partnership. The partner recognizes ordinary income on the sale of the hot assets, and the partnership takes a cost basis for the hot assets purchased.

EXAMPLE 21

The balance sheet of the AB Partnership is as follows on December 31 of the current tax year:

	Basis	FMV		Basis	FMV
Cash	$26,000	$26,000	Amanda, capital	$13,000	$26,000
Unrealized receivables	–0–	26,000	Bob, capital	13,000	26,000
Total	$26,000	$52,000	Total	$26,000	$52,000

Amanda and Bob are equal partners in the partnership. The partnership makes a liquidating distribution of the unrealized receivables to Amanda and the cash to Bob. Since the unrealized receivables are a hot asset, Amanda has received more than her proportionate share of the hot asset, and Bob has received less than his proportionate share. Section 751 recasts the transaction into two separate events. First, Bob is deemed to receive a current distribution of his 50% share of hot assets (basis = $0; fair market value = $13,000), which he then immediately sells back to the partnership for $13,000 of the cash. Bob recognizes $13,000 ordinary income on the sale, and the partnership takes a $13,000 basis in the receivables purchased. The remaining $13,000 cash received by Bob reduces his adjusted basis for his partnership interest to $0 ($13,000 cash distributed − $13,000 adjusted basis).

Amanda receives both the $13,000 receivables that the partnership purchased from Bob and her share of the remaining $13,000 unrealized receivables. She takes a substituted basis of $13,000 in the receivables and reduces her adjusted basis for her partnership interest to $0. When she collects all $26,000 of the receivables, she will recognize $13,000 of ordinary income ($26,000 cash collected − $13,000 basis for receivables).

Although the mechanical rules of § 751(b) are complicated, the application of the rules in this example has ensured that each partner eventually recognizes his or her $13,000 share of ordinary income. Bob recognizes his share at the time the partnership is liquidated. Amanda's share is recognized when she collects the unrealized receivables. ∎

Although most of the problems and examples in this text involve proportionate distributions, be aware that disproportionate distributions occur frequently in practice. The calculation of ordinary income in disproportionate distributions can become extremely complex. These more difficult calculations are not discussed in this text.

ETHICAL and EQUITABLE *Considerations*

DEFERRING PARTNERS' TAXES BY DELAYING LIQUIDATION

Partnerships often use the liabilities included in a partner's basis to shield losses claimed by the partners. By including a share of the partnership's liabilities in basis, the partner may be able to claim ordinary losses greatly in excess of the capital contributions. When the liabilities are repaid or forgiven, the partner is treated as receiving a distribution of cash and recognizes capital gain treatment on the payment or forgiveness of the debt. This is not a bad planning technique—it provides ordinary losses now and capital gains later!

If the capital gain recognition could be deferred for an extended period, the partners would really be ecstatic. Recently, a large national brokerage firm used such a delaying tactic. Investors originally contributed $200,000 each for an interest in a partnership syndicated by the firm. The partners claimed losses from the partnership far in excess of their original contribution. The property owned by the partnership declined in value, and for various reasons, the partners

sued the brokerage firm. In settlement, the firm agreed to loan the partnership up to $20 million and to continue to manage the property for up to 15 years. The partnership used the cash to distribute about $100,000 to each of the partners and to pay off other existing debt.

The partners will continue to hold their partnership interests during the 15 years the general partner manages the property. Debt still exists, so the partners still have basis in their partnership interests, and the partnership still exists, although the partners' interests in the partnership are virtually worthless. Thus, the partners have received losses and then substantial cash distributions and will be able to defer the capital gain on release of liabilities for another 15 years. Example 7 showed that a partner cannot recognize a loss prior to termination. Now it seems a partner cannot be forced to recognize a gain prior to termination. What do you think of this arrangement?

Liquidating Distributions to Retiring or Deceased Partners

LO.5

Determine the tax treatment under § 736 of payments from a partnership to a retiring or deceased partner.

Payments made by an ongoing partnership in complete liquidation of a retiring partner's interest are classified under § 736 as either *income* or *property* payments. Payments made to a successor to the interest of a deceased partner are similarly classified by § 736.[13] It is critical to observe that § 736 only classifies the payments. Other Code Sections provide the rules for computing the tax effects of these payments. Although these payments can be made in cash, property, or both cash and property, this discussion assumes that all payments are made in cash.

From a practical standpoint, the partnership and the retiring partner negotiate a total buyout package. The retiring partner expects compensation for the partner's proportionate share of the fair market value of each partnership asset. The partner also expects to be compensated for a share of the partnership's going-concern value. *Property* payments [called § 736(b) payments] represent the former type of buyout provision, and *income* payments [§ 736(a) payments] typically represent the latter. Once the total buyout price is determined, § 736 provides rules for determining the allocation between income and property payments, but leaves some room for negotiation between the partner and the partnership over which component of the buyout represents each type of payment.

These paragraphs and Example 22 describe only the general effects of § 736 and do not cover all the nuances of the provision. In general, property payments [§ 736(b) payments] are cash distributions paid by the partnership to the partner in exchange for the partner's interest in partnership assets. The partnership may not deduct these amounts. If the partnership owns no hot assets, the property payment is treated under the normal proportionate distribution rules. If the partnership owns certain hot assets (e.g., depreciation recapture or substantially appreciated inventory), and the retiring partner receives only cash, the distribution is not proportionate. In this case, the property payments to the partner are allocated between cash payments for the partner's share of (1) hot assets and (2) other assets. The hot asset portion is treated as if there is a distribution of the partner's proportionate share of all hot assets and a sale of these hot assets back to the partnership, as illustrated in Example 21. The income recognized in the hot asset sale is ordinary income, and the gain or loss recognized on the rest of the property payments is capital gain or loss.

Income payments [§ 736(a) payments] are treated as a partner's distributive share of partnership income or, alternatively, as a guaranteed payment to the retiring partner. Recall from Chapter 10 that the partner receiving a guaranteed payment recognizes ordinary income. Depending on whether the amount is a distributive share or a guaranteed payment, either (1) the remaining partners report a lesser share of partnership income (distributive share), or (2) the partnership deducts the guaranteed payment.

EXAMPLE 22

Pamela receives cash of $15,000 in liquidation of her partnership interest, in which she has a basis of $10,000. The partnership owns no hot assets. After following all the classification requirements of § 736, $12,000 of this amount is classified as a property payment, and $3,000 is classified as a guaranteed payment. The $12,000 property payment is treated as a distribution from the partnership in exchange for her partnership interest, so Pamela recognizes a $2,000 capital gain on this part of her liquidation proceeds ($12,000 property payment − $10,000 basis in interest). She recognizes $3,000 ordinary income for the guaranteed payment, and the partnership deducts the same amount. ■

---

[13]A successor is typically the estate of the deceased or the party who inherits the decedent's interest.

Property Payments

Cash payments made for the partner's pro rata share of the fair market value of each partnership asset are classified as § 736(b) payments. The following items are not treated as § 736(b) payments, however, if (1) the partnership is primarily a service provider (i.e., "capital is not a material income-producing factor for the partnership") and (2) the retiring or deceased partner was a general partner in the partnership:

- Payments made for the partner's pro rata share of unrealized receivables. For purposes of this rule, unrealized receivables do not include potential depreciation recapture.
- Payments made for the partner's pro rata share of the partnership goodwill, unless the partnership agreement states that the payments are for goodwill. This exception applies only to payments for goodwill that exceed the partner's pro rata share of the partnership's inside basis for goodwill.
- Certain annuities and lump-sum payments made to retiring partners or a deceased partner's successors.

If such payments are made by a service-oriented partnership to a general partner, they are classified as § 736(a) payments.

EXAMPLE 23

The ABC Partnership has the following balance sheet at the end of the current tax year:

	Basis	FMV		Basis	FMV
Cash	$36,000	$36,000	Anne, capital	$15,000	$27,000
Unrealized receivables	–0–	18,000	Bonnie, capital	15,000	27,000
Land	9,000	27,000	Cindy, capital	15,000	27,000
Total	$45,000	$81,000	Total	$45,000	$81,000

Partner Anne is a general partner retiring from the service-oriented partnership. She receives $36,000 cash, none of which is stated to be for goodwill. Because the fair market value of Anne's share of the three recorded assets is only $27,000 ($\frac{1}{3}$ × $81,000), the $9,000 excess payment is for unstated goodwill.

The payment Anne receives for her interest in the cash and land is a § 736(b) property payment. This payment is $21,000, consisting of $12,000 paid for the cash ($\frac{1}{3}$ × $36,000) and $9,000 paid for Anne's share of the fair market value of the land ($\frac{1}{3}$ × $27,000). The remaining cash of $15,000 is for her $6,000 interest in the unrealized receivables and for $9,000 unstated goodwill and is a § 736(a) payment. ■

Section 736(b) payments for "nonhot" assets are treated first as a return of the partner's outside basis in the partnership.[14] Once the entire basis is returned, any additional amounts are taxed to the partner as capital gain. If the cash distributions are not sufficient to return the partner's entire outside basis, the shortfall is taxed to the partner as a capital loss.[15]

EXAMPLE 24

In Example 23, the property payment of $21,000 cash includes amounts for Anne's share of land and cash only, neither of which is a hot asset. If Anne's outside basis is $15,000, she recognizes capital gain of $6,000 [($12,000 + $9,000) − $15,000] on the distribution. However, if Anne's outside basis is $25,000, she recognizes a $4,000 capital loss on the distribution [($12,000 + $9,000) − $25,000]. The partnership cannot deduct any part of the $21,000 property payment. ■

---

[14]§§ 736(b) and 731(a)(1).   [15]§ 731(a)(2).

If part of the property payment is for the partner's share of hot assets, the § 736(b) payment is allocated between the portion related to hot assets and the portion related to other assets. The portion of the payment *not* related to hot assets is treated as described in Example 24. The portion of the payment related to hot assets is treated as discussed earlier under Disproportionate Distributions. Distributions that are disproportionate to the partner's share of hot assets of the partnership are treated as two separate transactions:

- First, the partner's proportionate share of hot assets is deemed to be distributed. A partner cannot step up the basis in hot assets, so on the distribution, the hot assets take the lesser of the partnership's inside basis for the hot assets or the partner's outside basis in the interest.
- Second, these hot assets are deemed to be sold back to the partnership at fair market value. A portion of the § 736(b) payment is allocated to the partnership's deemed purchase of the hot assets.

EXAMPLE 25

If, in Example 23, Anne was a limited partner or the partnership was capital-intensive, the entire payment of $36,000 is a § 736(b) property payment. The $36,000 payment is allocated between hot assets and other assets. The payment for cash and land is a payment for Anne's other assets, as is the payment for partnership goodwill. The payment for the unrealized receivables, however, is a payment for Anne's share of the partnership's hot assets.

The partnership is treated first as distributing Anne's $6,000 proportionate share of unrealized receivables. Anne's carryover basis in the receivables is $0.

Anne then resells the unrealized receivables to the partnership for their $6,000 fair market value. She reports $6,000 of ordinary income on this sale. The partnership now has a basis of $6,000 in its $18,000 of accounts receivable.

The partnership paid Anne $36,000. Of this amount, $6,000 is to "repurchase" her share of receivables; the remaining $30,000 is in exchange for the partnership's other assets ($12,000 for cash + $9,000 for land + $9,000 for goodwill). Anne calculates and reports a $15,000 capital gain ($30,000 payment − $15,000 basis) in addition to the $6,000 ordinary income. ∎

Income Payments

All payments that are not classified as § 736(b) property payments are categorized as § 736(a) income payments. These income payments are further classified into two categories. Payments that are *not* determined by reference to partnership income are treated as guaranteed payments. They are fully taxable as ordinary income to the distributee partner and are fully deductible by the continuing partnership.

Section 736(a) income payments that are determined by reference to partnership income are treated as distributive shares of that income (i.e., an allocation of partnership income for the year). They are taxed to the distributee partner according to their character to the partnership. Thus, for example, they may be taxed as capital gain as well as ordinary income.[16] Since this capital gain and ordinary income are allocated to the liquidated partner, the payments reduce the amount of partnership capital gain and ordinary income allocated to the remaining partners.[17]

EXAMPLE 26

Continue with the same facts as in Example 23 where the partnership is service oriented. The $6,000 cash payment ($18,000 × 1/3) for Anne's pro rata share of the unrealized receivables is classified as a § 736(a) income payment, as is the $9,000 payment for unstated goodwill.

Because the $15,000 § 736(a) income payment ($6,000 + $9,000) is not determined by reference to partnership income, the payment is classified as a guaranteed payment. It is included as ordinary income on Anne's tax return and is deductible by the partnership. ∎

---

[16]§ 702(b).   [17]Reg. § 1.736–1(a)(4).

The following table summarizes the taxation results of Examples 23 through 26, for a partnership where capital is not a material income-producing factor and where it is. In both cases, Anne's basis in her partnership interest was $15,000 before the distribution.

	Tax Character to Anne		Deduction to ABC
Service-oriented partnership:			
§ 736(b) (Example 24)	$ 6,000	capital gain	None
§ 736(a) (Example 26)	15,000	ordinary income	$15,000
Total gain	$21,000		
Capital-intensive partnership:			
§ 736(b) (Example 25)	$15,000	capital gain	None
§ 736(b) (Example 25)	6,000	ordinary income	None
§ 736(a) (Example 25)	–0–	ordinary income	None
Total gain	$21,000		

Has no income payments (handwritten annotation)

As this table illustrates, the characterization under § 736 does not change the overall gain; in both cases Anne recognizes total gain of $21,000. This is appropriate since she receives $36,000 cash against a basis of $15,000.

The character of Anne's income differs solely as a result of the characterization of goodwill. For the service-oriented partnership with unstated goodwill, the payment for goodwill results in ordinary income to the partner. For the capital-intensive partnership, or if the partner is a limited partner, goodwill results in capital gain.

From the partnership's point of view, it is entitled to a deduction for goodwill payments only if it is a service partnership and the retiring partner is a general partner, and then only if the goodwill payment is not stated in the partnership agreement.

The partnership's position also differs as a result of the treatment of unrealized receivables. As a service partnership, it can claim a current deduction for the amount of the distribution related to the receivables. As a capital-intensive partnership, ABC has a cost basis in the receivables when it is deemed to repurchase them from Anne. When the receivables are collected, the partnership's ordinary income is reduced.

Series of Payments

Frequently, the partnership and retiring partner agree that the buyout payment may be made over several years in specified installments. This minimizes the negative cash-flow impact on the partnership and allows the retiring partner to maximize the dollar amount of the buyout arrangement. In certain cases, such as where a retiring partner has been instrumental in developing a business relationship with specific clients, the parties can agree that the buyout payments will be determined by reference to the future income generated by those clients or by reference to overall partnership income, rather than being fixed in amount. If the partners deal at arm's length and specifically agree to the §§ 736(a) and (b) allocation and timing of each class of payment, the agreement normally controls.[18] In the absence of an agreement classifying the payments under § 736, Regulations specify classification rules for each payment. In either situation, certain tax planning opportunities arise that are beyond the scope of this text.

Concept Summary 11–3 reviews the rules for liquidating distributions under § 736.

---

[18]Reg. § 1.736–1(b)(5).

CONCEPT SUMMARY 11–3

Liquidating Distributions of Cash When the Partnership Continues

1. Payments made by an ongoing partnership to a liquidating partner are classified as § 736(a) income payments or as § 736(b) property payments.
2. Section 736(b) property payments are payments made for the liquidated partner's share of partnership assets.
3. If the partnership is a service provider and the partner is a general partner, payments made for the liquidated partner's share of certain unrealized receivables, certain goodwill that is not provided for in the partnership agreement, and certain annuity payments are classified as § 736(a) income payments.
4. Section 736(a) income payments are the payments mentioned in Item 3 above and any other payments that are not classified as § 736(b) property payments.
5. To the extent the § 736(b) property payment is for the partner's share of partnership hot assets, the partner is deemed to have received and sold his or her share of such assets to the partnership. The partner reports ordinary income on this transaction, and the partnership will have a cost basis in the hot asset.
6. To the extent the § 736(b) property payments are classified as a payment for the partner's share of the partnership's "nonhot" assets, the payment is taxed as a return of the partner's outside basis. Any excess cash received over the partner's outside basis is taxed as capital gain.
7. Section 736(a) income payments are further classified as either guaranteed payments or distributive shares. Guaranteed payments are taxable as ordinary income to the partner and are deductible by the partnership. Distributive shares retain the same tax character to the partner as they had to the partnership. Distributive shares paid to the liquidated partner are excludible from the continuing partners' tax returns.

Sale of a Partnership Interest

> **LO.6**
>
> Calculate the selling partner's amount and character of gain or loss on the sale or exchange of a partnership interest.

A partner can sell or exchange a partnership interest, in whole or in part. The transaction can be between the partner and a third party; in this case, it is similar in concept to a sale of corporate stock. Or, as described in the last section, the transaction can be between the partner and the partnership, in which case it is similar in concept to a redemption of corporate stock by the entity. The transfer of a partnership interest produces different results from the transfer of corporate stock because both the entity and aggregate concepts apply to the partnership situation, whereas only the entity concept applies to a sale of stock. The effect of the different rules is that gain or loss resulting from a sale of a partnership interest may be divided into capital gain or loss and ordinary income or loss.

General Rules

Generally, the sale or exchange of a partnership interest results in gain or loss, measured by the difference between the amount realized and the selling partner's adjusted basis in the partnership interest.[19]

Liabilities. In computing the amount realized and the adjusted basis of the interest sold, the selling partner's share of partnership liabilities must be determined, as discussed in Chapter 10. The purchasing partner includes any assumed indebtedness as a part of the consideration paid for the partnership interest.[20]

EXAMPLE 27

Cole originally contributed $50,000 in cash for a one-third interest in the CDE Partnership. During the time Cole was a partner, his share of partnership income was $90,000, and he withdrew $60,000 cash. Cole's capital account balance is now $80,000, and partnership liabilities are $45,000, of which Cole's share is $15,000. Cole's outside basis is $95,000 ($80,000 capital account + $15,000 share of partnership debts).

---

[19]§ 741.

[20]§ 742.

Cole sells his partnership interest to Stephanie for $110,000 cash, with Stephanie assuming Cole's share of partnership liabilities. The total amount realized by Cole is $125,000 ($110,000 cash received + $15,000 of partnership debts transferred to Stephanie). Cole's gain on the sale is $30,000 ($125,000 realized − adjusted basis of $95,000).

Stephanie's adjusted basis for her partnership interest is the purchase price of $125,000 ($110,000 cash paid + $15,000 assumed partnership debt). ■

Income Allocation. When a partner sells an entire interest in the partnership:

- Income for the partnership interest for the tax year is allocated between the buying partner and the selling partner, and
- The partnership's tax year "closes" with respect to the selling partner.

The closing of the tax year causes the selling partner to report the share of income on the sale date rather than at the end of the partnership's tax year.

The selling partner's basis is adjusted for the allocated income or loss before the partner calculates the gain or loss on the sale of the interest.

EXAMPLE 28

On September 30, 2008, Erica sells her 20% interest in the Evergreen Partnership to Jason for $25,000. Erica is a calendar year taxpayer. Evergreen owns no hot assets, and its tax year ends on June 30.

Before the sale, Erica's basis in the partnership interest is $8,000. Her share of current partnership income is $10,000 for the period she owned the partnership interest. Since the partnership's tax year closes with respect to Erica, she must report $10,000 of income on her 2008 tax return. Her basis in the partnership interest is increased to $18,000, and she recognizes a $7,000 capital gain on the sale.

Note that Erica will also report income from Evergreen's tax year ending on June 30, 2008, on her 2008 tax return. ■

There are several acceptable methods of determining the partner's share of income.[21] Under one method, the partnership merely prorates annual income and allocates an amount to the buying and selling partners based on the number of days (or months) in the partnership's tax year in which they were partners. Another method is called the *interim closing of the books* method. As the name implies, the partnership determines its actual income through the date the selling partner sold the interest and allocates a proportionate share of that income to the partner. If partnership earnings are seasonal, the two methods can produce vastly different results.

EXAMPLE 29

Larissa sold her 40% interest in the Owl Partnership to Megan on July 1 of the current tax year. Both Larissa and the partnership report on a calendar year basis. The partnership's income was $60,000 through June 30, and its income for the last half of the year was $2,000. Under the annual proration method, the partnership's income for the year is $62,000, of which 40%, or $24,800, is allocated to the 40% interest. Based on the number of months each was a partner, both Larissa and Megan report income of $12,400 for the current year.

Under the interim closing method, Larissa is allocated 40% of $60,000, or $24,000, and Megan is allocated 40% of $2,000, or $800 of partnership income. ■

 If the partnership uses the cash method for certain items such as interest, taxes, rent, or other amounts that accrue over time, it must allocate these items to each day in the tax year over which they economically accrue and use the interim closing method for these items in determining the amount allocated to a selling partner.[22]

The partnership is not required to issue a Schedule K–1 to the selling partner until the normal filing of its tax return. The partner, though, is required to include the share of partnership income as of the sale date. Consequently, the partner may have to obtain an extension for filing his or her personal return until the

---

[21]§ 706(d)(1) and Regulations thereunder.   [22]§ 706(d)(2).

partnership provides a Schedule K–1. If the partnership uses an IRS-approved fiscal year and the partner uses a calendar year, income bunching may occur, as described in Example 28.

Tax Reporting. Partners who sell or exchange a partnership interest must promptly notify the partnership of the transfers. After notification is received, the partnership may be required to file an information statement with the IRS for the calendar year in which the transfers took place. The statement lists the names and addresses of the transferors and transferees. The partnership provides all parties with a copy of the statement.

Effect of Hot Assets

A major exception to capital gain or loss treatment on the sale or exchange of a partnership interest arises when a partnership has hot assets. As noted previously, *hot assets* are *unrealized receivables* and *inventory*, assets that, when collected or disposed of by the partnership, would cause it to recognize ordinary income or loss. When a partner sells the interest in a partnership, it is as if the partnership had sold its hot assets and allocated to the selling partner the partner's proportionate share of the ordinary income or loss created by the sale. The primary purpose of this rule is to prevent a partner from converting ordinary income into capital gain through the sale of a partnership interest.[23]

Unrealized Receivables. The term "unrealized receivables" generally has the same meaning as in the earlier discussion of disproportionate distributions. As previously noted, unrealized receivables include the accounts receivable of a cash basis partnership and, for sale or exchange purposes, depreciation recapture potential.[24]

E X A M P L E   30

The cash basis Thrush Partnership owns only a $10,000 receivable for rendering health care advice. Its basis in the receivable is zero because no income has been recognized. This item is a hot asset because ordinary income is not generated until Thrush collects on the account.

Jacob, a 50% partner, sells his interest to Mark for $5,000. If Jacob's basis in his partnership interest is $0, his total gain is $5,000. The entire gain is attributable to Jacob's share of the unrealized receivable, so his gain is taxed as ordinary income. ∎

Depreciation recapture represents ordinary income the partnership would recognize if it sold depreciable property. Under the aggregate theory, the selling partner's share of depreciation recapture potential is treated as an unrealized receivable and is taxed to the selling partner as ordinary income, rather than capital gain. (Recall that depreciation recapture is *not* treated as an unrealized receivable for § 736 purposes, discussed previously.)

E X A M P L E   31

Andrew sells his 40% interest in the accrual basis Wren Partnership. The partnership has a depreciable business asset that it originally purchased for $25,000. The asset now has an adjusted basis of $15,000 and a market value of $30,000. Depreciation recapture potential is $10,000 ($25,000 − $15,000). In this case, Wren holds a $10,000 unrealized receivable with a zero basis and a $20,000 ($30,000 − $10,000) nonhot asset with an adjusted basis of $15,000. If Wren sold the asset for $30,000, it would recognize $10,000 of ordinary income and $5,000 of § 1231 gain. Therefore, Andrew recognizes $4,000 ($10,000 × 40%) of ordinary income when he sells his partnership interest. ∎

The effect of the hot asset rule is that a partner selling an interest in a partnership with hot assets must usually recognize both ordinary income (loss) and capital gain (loss).

---

[23]§ 751(a).   [24]§ 751(a)(1).

EXAMPLE 32

Ahmad sells his interest in the equal ABC Partnership to Dave for $17,000 cash. On the sale date, the partnership's cash basis balance sheet reflects the following:

	Basis	FMV		Basis	FMV
Cash	$10,000	$10,000	Liabilities	$ 9,000	$ 9,000
Accounts receivable (for services)	–0–	30,000	Capital accounts		
Nonhot assets	14,000	20,000	Ahmad	5,000	17,000
			Beth	5,000	17,000
			Chris	5,000	17,000
Total	$24,000	$60,000	Total	$24,000	$60,000

The total amount realized by Ahmad is $20,000 ($17,000 cash price + $3,000 of debt assumed by Dave). Since Ahmad's basis for his partnership interest is $8,000 ($5,000 capital account + $3,000 debt share), the total gain recognized on the sale is $12,000 ($20,000 − $8,000).

Because the partnership has an unrealized receivable, the hot asset rule applies. If ABC sold the accounts receivable for $30,000, Ahmad's proportionate share of the ordinary income recognized on this sale would be $10,000 ($30,000 × $^1/_3$). Consequently, $10,000 of the $12,000 recognized gain on the sale relates to Ahmad's interest in the unrealized receivables and is taxed to him as ordinary income. The remaining gain of $2,000 is taxed to him as a capital gain.

Note that under the hot asset rule, Ahmad still reports $12,000 of income or gain; the hot asset rule merely reclassifies part of the gain as ordinary income. The effect of the rule is that the partnership's inherent ordinary income is allocated to the partner who earned it. ∎

EXAMPLE 33

Assume the same facts as in Example 32, except that Ahmad's basis in his partnership interest is $10,000. Under these circumstances, Ahmad's capital gain or loss is zero. Ahmad still has $10,000 of ordinary income because of the unrealized receivables.

If Ahmad's basis in the partnership interest is $11,000 (instead of $10,000), an unusual result occurs. Ahmad has a $9,000 overall gain ($20,000 amount realized − $11,000 basis). The receivables generate $10,000 of ordinary income, and Ahmad recognizes a capital *loss* of $1,000 on the rest of the sale. ∎

Inventory. For a sale or exchange of a partnership interest, the term *inventory* includes all partnership property except money, capital assets, and § 1231 assets. Receivables of an accrual basis partnership are included in the definition of inventory, as they are neither capital assets nor § 1231 assets.[25] This definition also is broad enough to include all items considered to be unrealized receivables.

EXAMPLE 34

Jan sells her one-third interest in the JKL Partnership to Matt for $20,000 cash. On the sale date, the partnership balance sheet reflects the following:

	Basis	FMV		Basis	FMV
Cash	$10,000	$10,000	Jan, capital	$15,000	$20,000
Inventory	21,000	30,000	Kelly, capital	15,000	20,000
Nonhot assets	14,000	20,000	Lynn, capital	15,000	20,000
Total	$45,000	$60,000	Total	$45,000	$60,000

The overall gain on the sale is $5,000 ($20,000 − $15,000). Jan's share of the appreciation in the inventory is $3,000 [($30,000 − $21,000) × $^1/_3$]. Therefore, she recognizes $3,000

---

[25]§ 751(d).

CONCEPT SUMMARY 11–4

Sale of a Partnership Interest

1. A partnership interest is a capital asset and generally results in capital gain or loss on disposal.
2. The outside bases of the selling and buying partners, as well as the pertinent selling price and purchase price, include an appropriate share of partnership debt.
3. Partnership income or loss for the interest is allocated between the selling and buying partners. The selling partner's basis is adjusted before the gain or loss on the sale is calculated.
4. The partnership's tax year closes with respect to the selling partner on the sale date; the seller reports partnership income at that time, and income "bunching" may occur.

5. When hot assets are present, the selling partner's overall gain or loss is reclassified into a capital gain or loss portion and an ordinary income or loss amount related to the partnership's underlying hot assets.
6. Hot assets consist of unrealized receivables and inventory.
7. Unrealized receivables include amounts earned by a cash basis taxpayer from services rendered. They also include depreciation recapture potential that would result if an asset were sold at a gain.
8. Inventory includes all partnership property except cash, capital assets, and § 1231 assets. Inventory also includes unrealized receivables.

of ordinary income because of the inventory and $2,000 of capital gain from the rest of the sale. ■

Concept Summary 11–4 enumerates the rules that apply to sales of partnership interests.

Other Dispositions of Partnership Interests

LO.7

Describe tax issues related to other dispositions of partnership interests.

Partnership interests may be reduced or terminated, and partnerships liquidated, in a variety of other ways, including the following:

- Transfer of the interest to a corporation when the partners control the corporation after the transfer.
- Transfer of the interest to a corporation when the partners *do not* control the corporation after the transfer.
- Like-kind exchanges.
- Death of a partner.
- Gifts.

Transfers to a Corporation

Transfers of a partnership interest to a corporation may take place when one or all partners are ready to retire from the business; they may exchange the partnership interest for stock in an existing corporation and cease to be involved in the day-to-day operations of the business. Alternatively, many partnerships incorporate simply to obtain the protection from liability or other advantages of the corporate form and make no real changes in business operations. Incorporation may occur at a time when the business is expanding and wants to obtain equity capital from issuing shares to outsiders. The corporate form may also provide tax advantages for a successful business that prefers to retain some earnings for internal expansion without having them taxed at the high individual tax rates of the owners.

Recall from Chapter 4 the controlled corporation rules of § 351. These rules provide that gain or loss is not recognized on the transfer of property to a corporation solely in exchange for stock in that corporation if, immediately after the exchange, the stockholders are in control of the corporation.

In many cases, including most of those in which an existing partnership is incorporated and continues to operate, § 351 conditions are met, and the transfer of the partnership interest to the corporation is a nontaxable exchange. If the partners transferring the property do not satisfy the 80 percent control requirements of § 351, they recognize gain or loss on the transfer according to standard rules for sales or exchanges.

If the partnership interest transferred represents 50 percent or more of the total interest in capital or profits, the partnership is terminated. Partnership termination is discussed later in the chapter.

Incorporation Methods. Consider the situation where the partners decide to incorporate an existing partnership by creating a new corporation owned entirely by the partners. At least three alternative methods are available for structuring the incorporation transaction:

- Each partner's interest is transferred to the corporation in exchange for stock under the usual § 351 rules. As a result, the partnership terminates, and the corporation owns all partnership assets and liabilities. The corporation takes a substituted basis for the assets, and the old partners have a substituted basis for the stock.
- The partnership transfers all of its assets to the corporation in exchange for stock and the assumption of partnership liabilities. The stock then is distributed to the partners (generally in a liquidating distribution) in proportion to their partnership interests. The corporation takes a carryover basis for the assets, and the old partners have a substituted basis for the stock.
- The partnership makes a pro rata distribution of all of its assets and liabilities to its partners in complete liquidation. The partners then transfer their undivided interests in the assets and liabilities to the corporation in exchange for stock under § 351. The corporation's basis for the assets is the substituted basis of those assets to the partners. The partners have a substituted basis for the stock.

Assuming that existing partnership debt does not exceed the basis of transferred assets, none of the three incorporation methods generates a recognized gain or loss. They may, however, result in different inside and outside basis amounts. Thus, selecting the appropriate incorporation method is crucial.

Like-Kind Exchanges

The nontaxable like-kind exchange rules do not apply to the exchange of interests in different partnerships.[26] These exchanges are fully taxable under the sale or exchange rules discussed previously. However, an exchange of interests in the same partnership is generally a nontaxable event.[27]

Death of a Partner

If a partner dies, the taxable year of the partnership closes with respect to that partner on the date of death.[28] The deceased partner's share of partnership income or loss is computed to that date and is reported on the partner's final Form 1040.

In professional partnerships, local law may prohibit an estate or other successor from continuing as a partner (beyond a certain time period). In most cases, the remaining partners want to buy out or liquidate the deceased partner's interest in the partnership. The previously discussed rules pertaining to sales and liquidations of partnership interests apply to these transactions.

---

[26]§ 1031(a)(2)(D).
[27]Rev.Rul. 84–52, 1984–1 C.B. 157.

[28]§ 706(c)(2)(A).

Gifts

Generally, the donor of a partnership interest recognizes neither gain nor loss. If the donor's entire interest is transferred, all items of partnership income, loss, deduction, or credit attributable to the interest are prorated between the donor and donee.

The taxable year of the partnership does not close with respect to the donor, however, so the donor reports his or her share of partnership income or loss at the end of the partnership's tax year.

As the following Ethical and Equitable Considerations indicates, the gift of an interest in a partnership owning unrealized receivables can be problematic.

ETHICAL and EQUITABLE *Considerations* | **ASSIGNMENT OF INCOME**

Jim is a partner in a cash basis partnership that specializes in personal injury matters. Cases are accepted on a contingent fee basis. If the client wins, the firm gets 30 percent of the recovery. If the client loses, no fee results. Just before a large judgment is awarded, Jim gives half of his partnership interest to his son, an attorney. The son recognizes as income the portion of the award attributable to the partnership interest he received as a gift. What is Jim trying to accomplish? Will it work?

Optional Adjustments to Property Basis

When a partner purchases a partnership interest, the purchase price reflects what the acquiring partner believes the interest in the partnership is worth. This price reflects, to a large extent, the value the partner places on the partnership assets. Because the value of the assets probably differs from their inside bases, a discrepancy exists between the purchasing partner's outside basis and that partner's share of the inside basis of partnership assets.

If the partnership makes an **optional adjustment election** (**§ 754 election**), the inside basis of the partnership property can be adjusted to reflect the purchase price paid by the partner. If the election is not made, the statute produces some inequitable results.

EXAMPLE 35

A partnership owns a building with an adjusted basis of $450,000 and a fair market value of $900,000. George buys a one-third interest in the partnership for $300,000 (an amount equal to one-third of the value of the building). The partnership does not make an election under § 754. Although the price George paid for the interest was based on fair market value, the building's depreciation continues to be determined on the partnership's related adjusted basis of $450,000, of which George's share is only $150,000. ■

EXAMPLE 36

In contrast, assume that the building in Example 35 had an adjusted basis of $300,000 and a fair market value of $150,000. Assume also that George purchased the one-third interest for $50,000 (an amount equal to one-third of the value of the building). Although the purchase price was based on fair market value, George obtains the benefit of *double* depreciation deductions since these deductions are calculated on the adjusted basis of the depreciable property ($300,000), which is twice the property's market value. ■

A result similar to that in Example 35 can take place when a partnership purchases a retiring partner's interest with a cash payment that is greater than that partner's outside basis for the partnership interest. Without a § 754 election, the partnership cannot increase the adjusted basis of its assets for the excess cash paid to the retiring partner.[29]

---

[29]§§ 743(a) and 734(a), respectively.

An optional adjustment-to-basis election can be made for any year in which a transfer or distribution occurs by attaching a statement to a timely filed partnership return (including extensions).[30] An election is binding for the year for which it is made and for all subsequent years, unless the IRS consents to its revocation. Permission to revoke is granted for business reasons, such as a substantial change in the nature of the business or a significant increase in the frequency of interest transfers. Permission is not granted if it appears the primary purpose is to avoid downward adjustments to basis otherwise required under the election.

In one type of situation, a basis adjustment must generally be made even if the partnership has not made a § 754 election. A basis adjustment is generally *required* if a sale or distribution occurs on or after October 23, 2004, and the partnership has a substantial built-in loss. A substantial built-in loss exists when the partnership's adjusted basis for all partnership property exceeds the fair market value of the property by more than $250,000. If in Example 36, the fair market value of partnership property was less than $50,000 and George purchased the partnership interest on or after October 23, 2004, a basis adjustment is required.

Adjustment: Sale or Exchange of an Interest

If the § 754 optional adjustment-to-basis election is in effect and a partner's interest is sold to or exchanged with a third party, or a partner dies, the partnership adjusts the basis of its assets as illustrated in the following calculation:[31]

Transferee's outside basis in the partnership	$ xxx
Less: Transferee's share of the inside basis of all partnership property	(xxx)
Adjustment	$ xxx

If the amount calculated is positive, the partnership increases the adjusted basis of its assets. If the amount is negative, the basis of the assets is decreased. In either case, the adjustment affects the basis of partnership property with respect to the transferee partner only. When a portion of the optional adjustment results in a step-up of depreciable property, the step-up amount is depreciated as if it were a newly acquired asset. The transferee partner, therefore, shares in the depreciation taken by the partnership on the original asset and, in addition, reports all of the depreciation taken on the step-up basis created by the optional adjustment.

The partner's basis in each property item for which an optional adjustment has been made equals the partner's share of the inside basis for the property item plus or minus the partner's optional basis adjustment that is allocated to that property.

EXAMPLE 37

Keith is a member of the KLM Partnership, and all partners have equal interests in capital and profits. The partnership has made an optional adjustment-to-basis election. Keith's interest is sold to Shawn for $76,000. The balance sheet of the partnership immediately before the sale shows the following:

	Basis	FMV		Basis	FMV
Cash	$ 15,000	$ 15,000	Capital accounts		
Depreciable assets	150,000	213,000	Keith	$ 55,000	$ 76,000
			Leif	55,000	76,000
			Marta	55,000	76,000
Total	$165,000	$228,000	Total	$165,000	$228,000

---

[30]§ 754.   [31]§ 743(b).

The adjustment is the difference between the basis of Shawn's interest in the partnership and his share of the adjusted basis of partnership property. The basis of Shawn's interest is his purchase price, or $76,000. His one-third share of the adjusted basis of partnership property is $55,000 ($165,000 × 1/3). The optional adjustment that is added to the basis of partnership property is $21,000.

Transferee's outside basis in partnership	$76,000
Less: Transferee's share of inside basis of all partnership property	(55,000)
Adjustment	$21,000

The $21,000 basis increase is treated as a new depreciable asset. Depreciation on this asset is allocated to Shawn. If the partnership later sells all the underlying assets, Shawn's share of the gain takes into account the remaining (undepreciated) balance of the $21,000 step-up. ■

Adjustment: Partnership Distributions

Optional adjustments to basis are also available to the partnership when property is distributed to a partner. If a § 754 optional adjustment-to-basis election is in effect, the basis of partnership property is _increased_ by the following:[32]

- Any gain recognized by a distributee partner.
- The excess of the partnership's adjusted basis for any distributed property over the adjusted basis of that property in the hands of the distributee partner.

Conversely, the basis of partnership property is _decreased_ by the following:

- Any loss recognized by a distributee partner.
- In the case of a liquidating distribution, the excess of the distributee partner's adjusted basis of any distributed property over the basis of that property to the partnership.

EXAMPLE 38

Rena has a basis of $50,000 in her partnership interest and receives a building with an adjusted basis to the partnership of $120,000 in termination of her interest. (The partnership has no hot assets.) The building's basis in Rena's hands is $50,000 under the proportionate liquidating distribution rules. If an optional adjustment-to-basis election is in effect, the partnership increases the basis of its remaining property by $70,000.

Partnership's adjusted basis in distributed property	$120,000
Less: Distributee's basis in distributed property	(50,000)
Increase	$ 70,000

■

EXAMPLE 39

Assume the same facts as in Example 38, except the partnership's basis in the building was $40,000. Rena's basis in the building is still $50,000, and the partnership reduces the basis of its remaining property by $10,000.

Distributee's basis in distributed property	$ 50,000
Less: Partnership's adjusted basis in distributed property	(40,000)
Decrease	$ 10,000

■

Although these rules may seem confusing at first reading, understanding the theory on which they are based helps to clarify the situation. Section 734(b) assumes that the inside basis for all partnership assets equals the outside basis for all of the partners' interests immediately before the distribution. When this equality

---

[32]§ 734(b).

exists both before and after a distribution, no adjustment to the basis of partnership property is necessary. However, when the equality does not exist after the distribution, an adjustment can bring the inside and outside bases back into equality. This is the adjustment that is made by the two increases and the two decreases described in the bulleted lists on the previous page.

EXAMPLE 40

Assume the Cardinal Partnership has an inside basis of $12,000 for its assets, which have a fair market value of $15,000. Aaron, Bill, and Carmen each have outside bases of $4,000 for their partnership interests. If the partnership liquidates partner Aaron's interest with a $5,000 cash distribution, the resulting balance sheet is unbalanced as follows:

	Inside (Assets)		Outside (Capital)
Before	$12,000	=	$12,000
Distribution	(5,000)	≠	(4,000)
After	$ 7,000	≠	$ 8,000

This unbalanced situation can be eliminated by adding $1,000 to the inside basis of the formula. Note that this is the same amount as the gain that Aaron recognizes on the distribution ($5,000 cash − $4,000 outside basis = $1,000 gain). Therefore, by adding the amount of Aaron's gain to the inside basis of the partnership assets, the inside basis = outside basis formula is back in balance.

Inside (Assets)		Outside (Capital)
$7,000	≠	$8,000
+1,000		
$8,000	=	$8,000

Note that if the partnership liquidates Aaron's interest with a distribution of land having a $5,000 inside basis, the same unbalanced situation occurs. Although this transaction does not create any recognized gain for Aaron, the $1,000 optional adjustment is the excess of the $5,000 inside basis of the distributed property over the $4,000 substituted basis of that property to Aaron. ■

The two optional adjustment decreases are also explained by this type of analysis.

The basis adjustments created by distributions affect the bases of all remaining partnership properties. Therefore, any depreciation deductions taken on such basis adjustments are allocated to all partners remaining in the partnership after the distribution. The *partnership* also takes these basis adjustments into account in determining any gains or losses on subsequent sales of partnership properties.

Termination of a Partnership

LO.9

Outline the methods of terminating a partnership.

When does a partnership's final tax year end? Technically, it ends when the partnership terminates, which occurs on either of the following events:

- No part of the business continues to be carried on by any of the partners in a partnership.
- Within a 12-month period, there is a sale or exchange of 50 percent or more of the partnership's capital and profits.[33]

---

[33]§ 708(b)(1).

The partnership terminates and its tax year closes when the partnership incorporates or when one partner in a two-party partnership buys out the other partner, thereby creating a sole proprietorship. A termination also occurs when the partnership ceases operations and liquidates.

The partnership taxable year usually does not close upon the death of a partner or upon the liquidation of a partner's interest, unless the liquidation of the interest of one partner in a two-partner partnership effectively terminates the partnership on the liquidation date. However, the partnership year will close in respect to the deceased or liquidated partner.[34] The deceased or liquidated partner's share of partnership income or loss is computed to the date of death or liquidation and reported on the partner's tax return for the year in which the death or liquidation occurs.

The partnership year does not close upon the entry of a new partner to the partnership. It also does not close upon the sale or exchange of an existing partnership interest unless the transaction results in 50 percent or more of the interests in the partnership capital and profits being sold within a 12-month period.

EXAMPLE 41

Partner Olaf, who held a one-third interest in the Oriole Partnership, died on November 20, 2008. The partnership uses an approved fiscal year ending September 30. Olaf used a calendar year. The partnership agreement does not contain a buy-sell provision that is triggered upon the death of a partner. The partnership's tax year does not close with Olaf's death. The partnership tax year does close, however, with respect to Olaf. His share of partnership income or loss for the period from October 1, 2008, to November 20, 2008, is reported on his final Form 1040. The partnership income or loss from November 21, 2008, to September 30, 2009, is taxed to Olaf's estate or other successor. Income from the fiscal year ending September 30, 2008, is reported on Olaf's final income tax return, which covers the period from January 1 to November 20, 2008. The first taxable year for Olaf's estate ends on October 31, 2009.

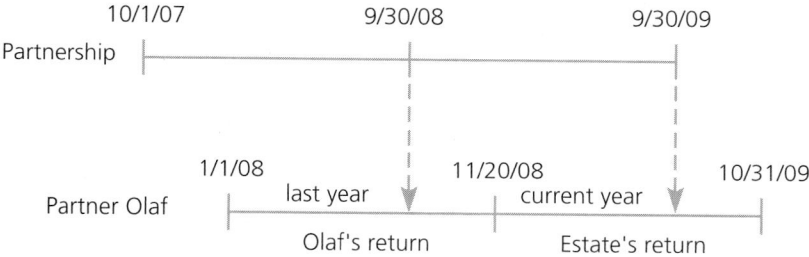

A **technical termination of a partnership** occurs when the partnership business operations continue but the partnership terminates because there has been a sale or exchange of the requisite 50 percent capital and profits interests within 12 months. If the same interest (less than 50 percent) is sold more than once, only one sale is considered in determining whether more than 50 percent has been sold within 12 months. The terminated partnership is deemed to liquidate by transferring its assets and liabilities to a newly formed partnership, which continues its business operations.[35] A technical termination may have numerous consequences, such as creating a different taxable year for the new partnership or modifying the cost recovery methods to be used by the new partnership.

Other Issues

Family Partnerships

LO.10

Describe the special considerations of a family partnership.

Family partnerships are owned and controlled primarily by members of the same family. Such partnerships may be established for a variety of reasons. A daughter may have a particular expertise that, coupled with her parents' abilities, allows

---

[34]§ 706(c)(2)(A).   [35]Reg. § 1.708–1(b).

TAX *in the News*	FAMILY LIMITED PARTNERSHIPS FOR ESTATE PLANNING

One of the most widely used estate planning tools in recent times has been the family limited partnership (FLP). The parents form a partnership with business or other assets and then give their children or grandchildren an interest in the partnership equivalent to the unified credit. Additional tax-free gifts of $12,000 per donee can also be made annually ($24,000 if the parents elect gift splitting).

The appeal of the FLP has increased considerably in recent years since the IRS issued a Revenue Ruling stating that a minority discount could be applied to gifts made by family members. A minority discount allows the nominal fair market value of a business interest to be reduced to account for the fact that the owner would have difficulty selling it for the cash value of the underlying assets because the purchaser would not have management control over these assets. With a minority discount of 30 percent, for example, a gift with a nominal fair market value of $17,142 could be eligible for the full $12,000 annual exclusion. With such a minority discount, a $1 million interest in a partnership could be transferred by a married couple to three children in only about two-thirds of the time it would take to transfer it without the discount. This strategy is particularly useful for assets that are expected to appreciate in value.

In the past couple of years, however, the steep valuation discounts used in FLPs have come under attack by the IRS on the grounds that the partnerships were established primarily for tax avoidance purposes. In some recent cases, the courts have upheld the IRS's position. To avoid this result, an FLP should be established primarily for business reasons (e.g., to facilitate diversification of assets or to transfer ownership to a younger generation). Tax motivations should be a secondary consideration for using an FLP.

them to establish a successful business. Often, however, one primary reason for establishing a family partnership is the desire to save taxes. If the parents are in higher marginal tax brackets than the children, family tax dollars are saved by funneling some of the partnership income to the children.

Valid family partnerships are difficult to establish for tax purposes. A basic tenet of tax law is that income must be taxed to the person who performs the services or owns the capital that generates the income. A parent, therefore, cannot transfer only a profits interest to a child and expect the transfer to be recognized for tax purposes.

Capital versus Services. Because of the concern that family partnerships are established primarily for tax avoidance purposes, a family member is recognized as a partner only in the following cases:

- Capital is a material income-producing factor in the partnership, and the family member's capital interest is acquired in a bona fide transaction (even if by gift or purchase from another family member) in which ownership and control are received.
- Capital is not a material income-producing factor, but the family member contributes substantial or vital services.[36]

If a partnership derives a substantial portion of its gross income from the use of capital, such as inventories or investments in plant, machinery, or equipment, the capital is considered to be a material income-producing factor. Ordinarily, capital is not a material income-producing factor if the partnership's income consists principally of fees, commissions, or other compensation for personal services performed by partners or employees.

Children as Partners. When capital is a material income-producing factor and a partnership interest is transferred by gift or sale to a child who is under age 19 (or a student under age 24), the kiddie tax may apply. Under the kiddie tax, some of the dependent child's distributive share of partnership income may be taxed at the parent's tax rate, unless the income share constitutes earned income. Regardless of

[36]§ 704(e).

age, if the child provides bona fide services to a partnership and the income share constitutes earned income, the parent-partner's tax rate is avoided.

EXAMPLE 42

Karen operates a first-floor-window-washing business in a summer lakeside resort city. Relatively small amounts of capital are required to operate the sole proprietorship (buckets, sponges, squeegees, etc.). During the summer, Karen normally hires middle and high school students to wash windows. Her 17-year-old daughter and 15-year-old son want to work in the business during the summer to earn money for spending and for college. Each obtains the necessary summer work permit. Karen creates the KDS Partnership and gives each child a 5% interest.

Karen figures that if her children were paid an hourly rate, about 5% of KDS's profits would be distributed to them as wages. Karen believes that an ownership interest will help the children learn what running a profitable business entails and prepare them for an active business life after their education is completed.

Since capital is not a material income-producing factor in the business, and the children's profit percentages approximate what they would earn if they were paid an hourly rate, all of the income is classified as earned income. Thus, the kiddie tax is avoided. ■

Gift of Capital Interest. If a family member acquires a capital interest by gift in a family partnership in which capital is a material income-producing factor, only part of the income may be allocated to this interest. First, the donor of the interest is allocated an amount of partnership income that represents reasonable compensation for services to the partnership. Then, the remaining income is divided among the partners in accordance with their capital interests in the partnership. An interest purchased by one family member from another is considered to be created by gift for this purpose.[37]

EXAMPLE 43

A partnership in which a parent transferred a 50% interest by gift to a child generated a profit of $90,000. Capital is a material income-producing factor. The parent performed services valued at $20,000. The child performed no services. Under these circumstances, $20,000 is allocated to the parent as compensation. Of the remaining $70,000 of income attributable to capital, at least 50%, or $35,000, is allocated to the parent. ■

Family LLCs. In recent years, family limited liability companies (LLCs) have been used to achieve the same estate planning goals as family limited partnerships. Because family LLCs often provide more operational flexibility than family limited partnerships, the family LLC may soon be the entity of choice for family estate planning in many jurisdictions.

Limited Liability Companies

Owners of small businesses often wish to combine the limited liability of a corporation with the pass-through provisions of a partnership. S corporations, described in Chapter 12, provide some of these advantages. The limited liability company is a form of entity that goes further in combining partnership taxation with limited personal liability for all owners of the entity. All of the states and the District of Columbia have passed legislation permitting the establishment of LLCs.

Taxation of LLCs. A properly structured LLC with two or more owners is taxed as a partnership. Since none of the LLC members are personally liable for any debts of the entity, the LLC is effectively treated as a limited partnership with no general partners. This may result in unusual application of partnership taxation rules. The IRS has not specifically ruled on many aspects of LLC taxation, so several of the following comments are based on speculation about how a partnership with no general partners would be taxed.

> **LO.11**
>
> Describe the application of partnership provisions to limited liability companies (LLCs) and limited liability partnerships (LLPs).

---

[37]§ 704(e)(3).

- Formation of a new LLC is treated in the same manner as formation of a partnership. Generally, no gain or loss is recognized by the LLC member or the LLC, the member takes a substituted basis in the LLC interest, and the LLC takes a carryover basis in the assets it receives.
- Contributed property with built-in gains or losses is subject to the partnership allocation rules (see the discussion of § 704 under Partnership Allocations in Chapter 10). Also, an LLC member contributing built-in gain property can be subject to tax on certain distributions within seven years of the contribution, as mentioned earlier in this chapter.
- In allocating liabilities to the members for basis purposes, liabilities are generally treated as if they are nonrecourse. This occurs because under the entity's legal structure, generally none of the members individually bears the economic risk of loss for a liability.
- An LLC's income and losses are allocated under § 704. Special allocations are permitted, as long as they meet the requirements outlined in Chapter 10.
- Losses are subject to the three deductibility limitations described in Chapter 10: A loss must meet the basis, at-risk, and passive loss limitations to be currently deductible. Because the debt is generally considered nonrecourse to each of the members, it may not be included in the at-risk limitation unless it qualifies as "qualified nonrecourse financing." Also, the IRS has not issued final guidance as to whether a member is treated as a material or active participant of an LLC for passive loss purposes. Presumably, passive or active status will be based on the time the member spends in LLC activities.
- The available taxable years and initial elections discussed in Chapter 10 are applicable to an LLC.
- Transactions between an LLC and its members are treated as described in Chapter 10.
- The rules described in this chapter for distributions, sales of an interest, and retirement of a member's interest under § 736 all apply to an LLC. An LLC can make an election under § 754 to adjust the inside basis of its assets to reflect changes in the member's outside bases resulting from sales of interests or distributions from the entity. Note that a distribution of appreciated property from a C or an S corporation would result in taxable gain to the entity, whereas such property takes a carryover or substituted basis when distributed from an LLC.
- An LLC member who is an active participant in entity operations may be subject to self-employment taxes on the member's distributive share of the LLC's income (plus the amount of any guaranteed payments for services). Proposed Regulations issued in 1997 indicate that a partner (or LLC member) will not be treated as a limited partner (not subject to self-employment tax) if the partner is personally liable for entity debts, has the ability to contractually obligate the partnership, or works for the partnership for more than 500 hours during the year.

Converting to an LLC. A partnership can convert to an LLC with few, if any, tax ramifications: the old elections of the partnership continue, and the partners retain their bases and ownership interests in the new entity. However, a C or an S corporation that reorganizes as an LLC is treated as having liquidated prior to forming the new entity. The transaction is taxable to both the corporation and the shareholders.

Advantages of an LLC. An LLC offers certain advantages over a limited partnership, including the following:

- Generally, none of the owners of an LLC are personally liable for the entity's debts. General partners in a limited partnership have personal liability for partnership recourse debts.
- Limited partners cannot participate in the management of the partnership. All owners of an LLC have the legal right to participate in the entity's management.

TAX *in the News*   MASTER LIMITED PARTNERSHIPS

With the recent surge in oil and gas prices, investment vehicles that focus on energy-related industries are reporting impressive growth. Such investments had declined in popularity after energy prices crashed at the end of the 1980s. One newly popular investment medium is the oil and gas master limited partnership, or MLP.

In the late 1980s, legislation was enacted permitting formation of energy-related MLPs. Energy companies spun off production and transportation activities into publicly traded MLPs. The cash received from the sale of these limited partnership interests is used to pay down debt or invest in high-growth businesses. With low debt levels, the MLPs produce substantial cash flows, which they distribute to the partners.

As a partnership, an MLP pays no tax on its earnings. Instead, the MLP pays out all earnings as cash distributions to its investors. The MLP issues Schedules K–1 to the investors, who report their share of entity profits directly on their tax returns. Basis calculations are cumbersome, though, because a portion of the distributions may be treated as a return of capital. When the MLP conducts operations in several states, the shareholder must file multiple state income tax returns.

Despite recent price drops, these funds continue to outperform the market—making these extra tax reporting requirements worthwhile. With oil and gas prices continuing to climb, MLPs could continue to be important investment options in coming years.

The advantages of an LLC over an S corporation are discussed in Chapter 13.

Disadvantages of an LLC. The disadvantages of an LLC stem primarily from the entity's relative newness. There is only a limited body of case law interpreting the various state statutes, so the application of some provisions is uncertain. An additional uncertainty for LLCs that operate in more than one jurisdiction is which state's law will prevail and how it will be applied.

Among other factors, statutes differ from state to state as to the type of business an LLC can conduct—particularly as to the extent to which certain service-providing firms can operate as LLCs. A service entity may find it can operate as an LLC in one state but not in another.

Despite these uncertainties, LLCs are being formed at increasing rates.

Limited Liability Partnerships

Although the name is similar, a limited liability partnership (LLP) is quite different from a limited partnership. In 1991, Texas became the first state to allow professionals to organize their practices as registered LLPs. All states now permit LLPs to be formed. Also, about 20 states have adopted legislation authorizing a variation known as a limited liability limited partnership (LLLP).[38] The difference between a general partnership and an LLP is small, but very significant. Recall that general partners are jointly and severally liable for all partnership debts. In some states, partners in a registered LLP are jointly and severally liable for contractual liability (i.e., they are treated as general partners for commercial debt). They are also always personally liable for their own malpractice or other torts. They are not, however, personally liable for the malpractice and torts of their partners. As a result, the exposure of their personal assets to lawsuits filed against other partners and the partnership is considerably reduced.

An LLP must have formal documents of organization and register with the state. Because the LLP is a general partnership in other respects, it does not have to pay any state franchise taxes on its operations—an important difference between LLPs and LLCs in states that impose franchise taxes on LLCs. LLPs are taxed as partnerships under Federal tax statutes.

---

[38]An LLLP is a limited partnership in which the general partners are also protected from entity liabilities. See the Tax in the News on page 10–4 in Chapter 10.

TAX *in the News*   TAX TREATMENT OF "CARRIED INTERESTS"

Limited partnerships are often used as vehicles for raising capital. For example, investors might purchase interests in a limited partnership created to purchase a specific rental real estate property (or properties).

This partnership might be formed by a real estate property management firm using funds loaned by a mortgage banking firm, and with the partnership interests marketed by a brokerage house. The developer, lender, and promoter are often noncorporate firms that accept a "carried interest"—typically, a capital interest in the partnership—in lieu of receiving current compensation for their services. The investment is structured so that there is no value in the carried interest at the time it is awarded—therefore, receipt of the carried interest in exchange for services does not result in current taxation. When the limited partnership is eventually sold or liquidated, these parties receive a gain allocation or a liquidating distribution from the partnership.

For example, say Real Property Developers Group, LLC, accepts a 5 percent interest (at no current cost) in the capital of Rental Property, Ltd. The LLC performs all services entailed in acquiring, managing, and syndicating the limited partnership offering. (Assume the LLC does not receive any allocations of the limited partnership's operating income or expenses.)

When Rental Property, Ltd., is liquidated, the LLC receives a $10 million liquidating distribution. This results in a capital gain because the LLC had no basis in the partnership interest. The arrangement is very attractive as it yields a $10 million capital gain at the end instead of ordinary income when the entity is formed and during the life of the partnership.

Recently, this type of arrangement has come under fire in the financial press. Congress has made several attempts to pass legislation that would result in ordinary income treatment for "carried interests." In recent years, several bills have been proposed that would have adopted this treatment. It may be just a matter of time before one of these bills is passed by both houses of Congress and signed by the President.

The current treatment does have supporters, though. Venture capital firms accept a tremendous amount of risk and incur substantial expenses in forming such ventures, many of which are unsuccessful. The question to be resolved is one of characterization. Should the risk-bearing developer, syndicator, and lender be forced to recognize ordinary income for the performance of services? Or should they be awarded capital gains treatment when the partnership is terminated, reflecting the risk inherent in the venture?

The conversion of a general partnership into a registered LLP is a continuation of the old partnership for tax purposes if all the general partners become LLP partners and hold the same proportionate interests in the LLP that they held in the general partnership. This means that all the old partnership's elections continue in the LLP, including accounting methods, the taxable year-end, and the § 754 election.

Anti-Abuse Regulations

The IRS has issued Regulations that allow it to disregard the form of a partnership transaction when it believes that the transaction (or series of transactions) is abusive.[39] Under the Regulation, a transaction is abusive if it satisfies two tests. First, it must have a principal purpose of substantially reducing the present value of the partners' aggregate Federal tax liability. In addition, the potential tax reduction must be inconsistent with the intent of Subchapter K. If the IRS disregards the form of a transaction, it will recast the transaction in a manner that reflects the transaction's underlying economic arrangement.

It is often difficult to determine whether a proposed transaction will substantially reduce the present value of the partners' aggregate tax liability. Partners may not know their personal tax situations until the transaction occurs and the partner's tax return is completed. Practitioners are concerned that the IRS could try to use "perfect hindsight" to determine if a transaction should be recast. This could make it difficult to anticipate the ultimate tax treatment of many partnership transactions.

---

[39]Reg. § 1.701–2.

The IRS says it will not recast transactions that are bona fide business arrangements and offers several examples in the Regulation. The IRS has also announced that a field examiner cannot invoke the Regulation without approval. Review by a partnership specialty group within the IRS is required before the IRS will challenge a taxpayer's treatment of a transaction under this Regulation.

Sales and Exchanges of Partnership Interests

Delaying Ordinary Income. A partner planning to dispose of a partnership interest in a taxable transaction might consider either an installment sale or a pro rata distribution of hot assets, followed by a sale of the remaining interest in the partnership. Although the partner will have ordinary income when these hot assets are collected or sold, the partner can spread the income over more than one tax year by controlling the collection or disposal dates.

Basis Adjustment for Transferee. If a partnership interest is acquired by purchase, the purchaser may want to condition the acquisition on the partnership's promise to make an election to adjust the basis of partnership assets. Making the election under § 754 results in the basis in the partner's ratable share of partnership assets being adjusted to reflect the purchase price. Failure to do so could result in the loss of future depreciation deductions or could convert ordinary losses into capital losses.

Planning Partnership Distributions

General Guidelines. In planning for any partnership distributions, be alert to the following possibilities:

- When gain recognition is undesirable, ascertain that cash distributions from a partnership, including any debt assumptions or repayments, do not exceed the basis of the receiving partner's interest.
- Distributions of marketable securities may also result in gain, but the current gain can be minimized if the securities *are* appreciated.
- When a partner is to receive a liquidating distribution and the full basis of the interest will not be recovered, the partner's capital loss can be ensured by providing that the only assets received by the partner are cash, unrealized receivables, and inventory. If a capital loss is undesirable, however, the partnership should also distribute a capital or § 1231 asset that will take the partner's remaining basis in the interest. This may result in a more desirable ordinary deduction or loss in the future.
- Current and liquidating distributions may result in ordinary income recognition for either the receiving partner or the partnership if hot assets are present. When such income is undesirable, consider making a distribution of hot assets pro rata to the receiving partner.
- If precontribution gain property is contributed to a partnership, gain to the contributing partner can be further deferred if the partnership waits seven years before (1) distributing the precontribution gain property to another partner or (2) distributing other partnership property to the precontribution gain partner if the value of the other property exceeds the partner's basis in the partnership.
- When the partnership agreement initially is drafted, consider including provisions that govern liquidating distributions of partnership income and property. The specifics of the agreement generally will be followed by the IRS if these and other relevant points are addressed early in the life of the entity.

Valuation Problems. Both the IRS and the courts usually consider the value of a partner's interest or any partnership assets agreed upon by all partners to be correct. Thus, when planning the sale or liquidation of a partnership interest, the results of the bargaining process should be documented. To avoid valuation problems on liquidation, include a formula or agreed-upon valuation procedure in the partnership agreement or in a related buy-sell agreement.

Comparing Sales to Liquidations

When a partner disposes of an entire interest in a partnership for a certain sum, the *before-tax* result of a sale of that interest to another partner or partners is the same as the liquidation of the interest under § 736. In other words, if both transactions result in the partner receiving the same amount of pre-tax dollars, the partner should be ambivalent about which form the transaction takes unless one form offers tax savings that the other does not.

The *after-tax* result of a sale of a partnership interest and a liquidation of a partner's interest by an ongoing partnership may differ considerably. One difference occurs when the payment for that interest is extended over several years. When a partner sells the partnership interest to another partner, the selling partner can postpone the recognition of income under the installment sale rules. These rules are very restrictive and require that gain and income be recognized at least as quickly as the proportionate share of the receivable is collected. However, in a liquidation, more flexibility may be available. Under § 736, the § 736(b) payments for partnership property can be made before the income payments under § 736(a). Furthermore, the § 736(b) payments can be treated as a return of basis first with gain recognized only after the distributee partner has received amounts equal to the basis. This treatment results in a deferral of gain and income recognition under § 736 that is not available under the installment sale provisions.

Payments for Goodwill. The partner who purchases a partnership interest often pays an amount that can be attributed, in part, to partnership goodwill. Purchased goodwill is included in a purchasing partner's outside basis for the partnership interest. The partner cannot amortize the goodwill unless (1) the asset qualifies as a § 197 intangible, amortizable over 15 years, and (2) the partnership makes an election under § 754 to adjust the basis of partnership assets to reflect the purchase price paid. In many cases, the purchasing partner will not obtain a tax benefit from the goodwill until the partnership interest is disposed of.

Under § 736, amounts paid by a service partnership for a general partner's share of partnership goodwill can be treated as a § 736(a) payment. If this payment is a guaranteed payment, it is deductible by the partnership. If it is a distributive share, it is excludible from the income stream of the remaining partners. In effect, this is also like a deduction. If (1) capital is a material income-producing factor of the partnership or (2) the distributee partner was a limited partner, payments for goodwill constitute § 736(b) property payments. These payments are not deductible by the partnership and result in increased capital gain (or decreased capital loss) to the retiring partner.

Termination of Partnership. A partnership terminates if 50 percent or more of the total interest in partnership capital and profits is sold within a 12-month period. A liquidation under § 736, however, is not considered a sale or exchange under this rule. Therefore, a partnership can liquidate a partner's interest without terminating a three-partner partnership, even if the liquidated partner had a 98 percent interest in partnership capital and profits immediately before the liquidating distribution.

A sale and a liquidation of a partnership interest also differ in other respects that are beyond the scope of this text. The point to remember is that differences exist that may result in considerable after-tax savings for the partners. Careful planning can result in a properly structured transaction.

Other Partnership Issues

Choice of Entity. The partnership liquidation rules demonstrate the tax advantages of the partnership form over the C corporation in the final stage of the business's life:

- A service partnership can effectively claim deductions for its payment to a retiring general partner for goodwill.
- The partnership liquidation itself is not a taxable event. Under corporate rules, however, liquidating distributions and sales in preparation for a distribution are fully taxable.
- Tax liability relative to the liquidation is generated at the partner level, but only upon a recognition event (such as receipt of cash in excess of basis, or sale of an asset received in a distribution). The timing of this event is usually under the control of the (ex-)partner. In this manner, the tax obligations can be placed into the most beneficial tax year and rate bracket.

Family Partnerships. If possible, make certain that very young and elderly members of a family partnership contribute services to the entity, so as to justify their income allocations. These services can comprise the most routine facets of the business, including monitoring and operating copy and fax machines and providing ongoing maintenance of the indoor and outdoor landscaping environments. Although no more than a market level of compensation can be assigned for this purpose, the services themselves constitute evidence of the active role that the partner plays in the operations of the entity.

Since there is no equivalent of the kiddie tax for elderly taxpayers, retention of the founding members of the partnership past the nominal retirement age often facilitates the income-shifting goals of the family.

KEY TERMS

Appreciated inventory, 11–15

Disproportionate distribution, 11–4

Hot assets, 11–15

Liquidating distribution, 11–3

Nonliquidating distribution, 11–3

Optional adjustment election, 11–27

Proportionate distribution, 11–4

Section 754 election, 11–27

Technical termination of a partnership, 11–31

Unrealized receivables, 11–6

PROBLEM MATERIALS

DISCUSSION QUESTIONS

1. How is the basis determined for property received in a proportionate liquidating or nonliquidating distribution?

2. Describe the tax treatment of a proportionate nonliquidating distribution of cash, land, and inventory. How are the partner's basis in the property received and the partner's gain or loss on the distribution determined? What are the tax effects to the partnership?

3. The SueBart Partnership distributes the following assets to partner Bart: *Issue ID*

- $10,000 cash.
- An account receivable with a $10,000 value and a $0 basis to the partnership.
- A parcel of land with a $10,000 value and a $2,000 basis to the partnership.

What issues must be considered in determining the tax treatment of the distribution?

4. Describe, in general terms, two types of assets regarded as "hot assets." When is characterization as a "hot asset" relevant?

5. Distinguish between the treatment of § 736 income and property payments. What are the tax consequences of such payments to the retiring partner, the remaining partners, and the partnership?

Issue ID

6. Jody sells her partnership interest to Bill for $10,000. What issues must be addressed by Jody, Bill, and the partnership?

7. Identify amounts that are included in the sales proceeds when a partner sells an interest in the partnership to an unrelated third party. How is the character of the selling partner's gain or loss determined?

8. Who makes the optional adjustment-to-basis election? How is the election made, and what is its effect on future years?

9. Describe the various types of events that can cause a partnership termination. Which of these can cause a "technical" termination?

Issue ID

10. Tiring of the daily grind and uncertainty associated with the home construction industry, Tim is considering selling his partnership interest to Una, who is not a current member of the partnership. Tim, Una, and Tim's partners are concerned about the tax ramifications of the transaction. What potential tax consequences should be called to the attention of all parties involved?

11. Comment on the validity of each of the following statements.
    a. A partner may recognize ordinary income if a proportionate current distribution of cash exceeds the partner's basis in the partnership interest.
    b. A partner may recognize a capital loss in a proportionate current distribution if the only assets received are cash, unrealized receivables, and/or inventory.
    c. In a proportionate liquidating distribution, if a partner receives cash equal to the basis in the partnership interest, any other property received will take a $0 basis.
    d. If a partner contributes property with a precontribution gain and that property is later distributed to that same partner, the partner must recognize a capital gain in the amount of the precontribution gain.
    e. In a disproportionate distribution, either the partnership or the distributee partner might be required to recognize ordinary income.
    f. In a redemption of a partnership interest under § 736, a payment to a general partner in a service partnership for goodwill that is provided for in the partnership agreement is treated as a § 736(b) property payment.
    g. Under § 736 all payments to a retiring partner are either property payments [§ 736(b)] or income payments [§ 736(a)].
    h. In a sale of a partnership interest, the partner will recognize capital gain to the extent that the selling price exceeds the partner's basis in the partnership interest.
    i. A partner may make a § 754 election if gain is recognized on a distribution of cash from the partnership.
    j. A § 754 election might be appropriate if a partner purchases a partnership interest from another partner for substantially more than the partner's share of the underlying basis in partnership assets.

12. What is a family partnership? Under what circumstances can a family member be a partner in such a partnership? What income allocation is required?

13. To what extent are the personal assets of a general partner, limited partner, or member of an LLC subject to (a) contractual liability claims, such as trade accounts payable, and (b) malpractice claims against the entity? Answer the question for partners or members in a general partnership, LLP, nonprofessional LLC, and limited partnership.

Issue ID

14. Jim is retiring from the JSU general services partnership. He is trying to decide whether to sell his 51% interest in the partnership or to liquidate his interest under § 736. Under either scenario, payments would be paid to Jim over several years and would include amounts in exchange for Jim's share of partnership goodwill. Explain why the method selected may make a difference for tax purposes to Jim, JSU, and the other partners.

PROBLEMS

15. Dan's outside basis in his interest in the CDE Partnership is $150,000. In a proportionate nonliquidating distribution, the partnership distributes to him cash of $40,000, inventory (fair market value of $50,000, basis to the partnership of $40,000), and land (fair market value of $60,000, basis to the partnership of $35,000). The partnership continues in existence.
    a.   Does the partnership recognize any gain or loss as a result of this distribution?
    b.   Does Dan recognize any gain or loss as a result of this distribution?
    c.   Calculate Dan's basis in the land, in the inventory, and in his partnership interest immediately following the distribution.

16. When Peggy's outside basis in the NOP Partnership is $180,000, the partnership distributes to her $100,000 cash, an account receivable (fair market value of $80,000, inside basis to the partnership of $0), and a parcel of land (fair market value of $60,000, inside basis to the partnership of $100,000). Peggy remains a partner in the partnership, and the distribution is proportionate to the partners.
    a.   Determine the recognized gain or loss to the partnership as a result of this distribution.
    b.   Determine the recognized gain or loss to Peggy as a result of the distribution.
    c.   Determine Peggy's basis in the land, account receivable, and NOP Partnership after the distribution.

17. In each of the following independent cases in which the partnership owns no hot assets, indicate:

    • Whether the partner recognizes gain or loss.
    • Whether the partnership recognizes gain or loss.
    • The partner's adjusted basis for the property distributed.
    • The partner's outside basis in the partnership after the distribution.

    a.   Pamela receives $60,000 cash in partial liquidation of her interest in the partnership. Pamela's outside basis for her partnership interest immediately before the distribution is $50,000.
    b.   Paul receives $25,000 cash and land with an inside basis to the partnership of $10,000 (value of $12,000) in partial liquidation of his interest. Paul's outside basis for his partnership interest immediately before the distribution is $30,000.
    c.   Assume the same facts as in (b), except that Paul's outside basis for his partnership interest immediately before the distribution is $20,000.
    d.   Perry receives $30,000 cash and an account receivable with a basis of $0 and a fair market value of $25,000 in partial liquidation of his partnership interest. His basis was $20,000 before the distribution. All partners received proportionate distributions.

18. Assume the facts of Problem 17. In each independent case, are additional planning opportunities available to the partnership to maximize its inside basis in its assets? If so, by how much can the basis be increased? What is the effect of any basis increase to the distributee partner or the other partners?

    Decision Making

19. Mark's basis in his partnership interest is $39,000. In a proportionate nonliquidating distribution, Mark receives $30,000 cash and two inventory items with bases of $10,000 each to the partnership. The values of the inventory items are $15,000 and $5,000.
    a.   How much gain or loss, if any, must Mark recognize on the distribution?
    b.   What basis will Mark take in each inventory item?

20. Heloise Hawkins is a 50% partner in the calendar year Hawkins-Henry Partnership. On January 1, 2008, her basis in her partnership interest is $150,000, including her $80,000 share of partnership liabilities. The partnership has no taxable income or loss for the current year. Hawkins-Henry repays all liabilities before the end of 2008 from cash on hand. In a nonliquidating distribution, the partnership distributes $60,000 cash on December 15. It also distributes inventory proportionately to all partners. Heloise

    Communications

receives inventory with a basis of $25,000 and a fair market value of $20,000. In January 2009, Heloise, your client, asks your advice regarding treatment of 2008 operations and distributions. Using the format (1) facts, (2) issues, and (3) conclusion and analysis, draft a letter to Heloise at the Hawkins-Henry Partnership (1622 E. Henry Street, St. Paul, MN 55163) that addresses the following points:

a. How much gain or loss does the partnership recognize as a result of 2008 activities?
b. How much gain or loss must Heloise recognize in 2008?
c. What is Heloise's basis in inventory received?
d. What is Heloise's basis in her partnership interest at the end of 2008?

Issue ID

21. Walden is a 40% partner in the WXY Partnership. He became a partner three years ago when he contributed land with a value of $40,000 and a basis of $20,000 (current value is $90,000). Xavier and Yolanda each contributed $30,000 cash for a 30% interest. Walden's basis in his partnership interest is currently $40,000; the other partners' bases are each $30,000. The partnership has the following assets:

	Basis	FMV
Cash	$ 60,000	$ 60,000
Accounts receivable	–0–	80,000
Marketable securities	20,000	70,000
Land	20,000	90,000
Total	$100,000	$300,000

The partnership will make a distribution of $150,000 in value to the partners before the end of the current year, but the type of property that will be distributed has not been determined. Describe the tax effects on the partners in each of the following independent distribution alternatives:

a. WXY distributes a $45,000 interest in the land each to Yolanda and Xavier and $60,000 of accounts receivable to Walden.
b. WXY distributes $60,000 cash to Walden, $45,000 of marketable securities to Yolanda, and $45,000 of accounts receivable to Xavier.
c. WXY distributes a $36,000 interest in the land and $24,000 of accounts receivable to Walden and $27,000 of cash and $18,000 of accounts receivable each to Xavier and Yolanda.

Issue ID

22. Use the assets and partners' bases from Problem 21. Assume the partnership distributes all its assets in a liquidating distribution. In deciding the allocation of assets, what issues should the partnership consider to minimize each partner's taxable gains?

23. In each of the following independent liquidating distributions in which the partnership also liquidates, determine the amount and character of any gain or loss to be recognized by each partner and the basis of each asset (other than cash) received. In each case, assume distributions of hot assets are proportionate to the partners.

a. Emma has a partnership basis of $40,000 and receives a distribution of $55,000 in cash.
b. Francie has a partnership basis of $60,000 and receives $20,000 cash and a capital asset with a basis to the partnership of $30,000 and a fair market value of $35,000.
c. Georgie has a partnership basis of $72,000 and receives $40,000 cash, inventory with a basis to the partnership of $10,000, and a capital asset with a partnership basis of $16,000. The inventory and capital asset have fair market values of $25,000 and $20,000, respectively.
d. Harris has a partnership basis of $90,000 and receives a distribution of $30,000 cash and an account receivable with a basis of $0 to the partnership (value is $40,000).

Decision Making

24. The basis of Betty's partnership interest is $50,000. Betty receives a pro rata liquidating distribution consisting of $15,000 cash, land with a basis of $20,000 and a fair market value of $26,000, and her proportionate share of inventory with a basis of $22,000 to the partnership and a fair market value of $28,000. Assume the partnership also liquidates.

a. How much gain or loss, if any, must Betty recognize as a result of the distribution?
b. What basis will Betty take in the inventory and land?

c. If the land is sold two years later for $30,000, what are the tax consequences to Betty?

d. What are the tax consequences to the partnership as a result of the liquidating distribution?

e. Is any planning technique available to the partnership to avoid any "lost basis" results?

f. Would your answer to (b) change if this had been a nonliquidating distribution?

25. Assume the same facts as in Problem 24, except that Betty's basis in the partnership is $90,000 instead of $50,000.

a. How much gain or loss, if any, must Betty recognize on the distribution?

b. What basis will Betty take in the inventory and land?

c. What are the tax consequences to the partnership?

d. Would your answer to (a) or (b) change if this had been a nonliquidating distribution?

26. Margaret's basis in her partnership interest is $100,000. In liquidation of her interest, the partnership distributes to Margaret cash of $30,000 and inventory (basis of $40,000 and value of $50,000).

Decision Making

a. How much gain or loss, if any, must Margaret recognize as a result of the distribution?

b. What basis will Margaret take in the inventory?

c. What are the tax consequences to the partnership?

d. Can you recommend an alternative distribution?

e. Would your answer to (a) or (b) change if this had been a nonliquidating distribution?

27. Julie's basis in her partnership interest is $108,000. In a proportionate distribution in liquidation of the partnership, Julie receives $50,000 cash and two parcels of land with bases of $20,000 each to the partnership. The partnership holds both parcels of land for investment, and the parcels have fair market values of $10,000 and $30,000.

a. How much gain or loss, if any, must Julie recognize on the distribution?

b. What basis will Julie take in each parcel?

c. If the land had been held as inventory by the partnership, what effect, if any, would it have on your responses to (a) and (b)?

28. Assume the same facts as in Problem 27, except that Julie receives $50,000 cash and a desk having a basis of $1,200 to the partnership and a fair market value of $2,000.

Decision Making

a. How much loss, if any, may Julie recognize on the distribution?

b. What basis will Julie take in the desk?

c. Suppose Julie's 15-year-old son uses the desk for his personal use for one year before Julie sells it for $1,000. How much loss may Julie recognize on the sale of the desk? What tax planning procedures could have prevented this result?

29. In 2005, Gabriella contributed land with a basis of $16,000 and a fair market value of $25,000 to the Meadowlark Partnership in exchange for a 25% interest in capital and profits. In 2008, the partnership distributes this property to Juanita, also a 25% partner, in a nonliquidating distribution. The fair market value has increased to $30,000 at the time the property is distributed. Juanita's and Gabriella's bases in their partnership interests are each $40,000 at the time of the distribution.

a. How much gain or loss, if any, does Gabriella recognize on the distribution to Juanita? What is Gabriella's basis in her partnership interest following the distribution?

b. What is Juanita's basis in the land she received in the distribution?

c. How much gain or loss, if any, does Juanita recognize on the distribution? What is Juanita's basis in her partnership interest following the distribution?

d. How much gain or loss would Juanita recognize if she later sells the land for its $30,000 fair market value? Is this result equitable?

e. Would your answers to (a) and (b) change if Gabriella originally contributed the property to the partnership in 1998?

30. Winston contributed a tract of undeveloped land to the Nightingale Partnership in 2005. He originally paid $20,000 for the property in 1996, but its value was $70,000 at the date of the contribution. In 2008, the partnership distributes another parcel of land to Winston; the land has a basis to the partnership of $30,000. The fair market value of

the distributed property is $100,000 in 2008. Winston's basis in his partnership interest is $60,000 immediately before the distribution.

    a.   How much gain or loss, if any, does Winston recognize on the distribution?

    b.   What is Winston's basis in his partnership interest following the distribution?

    c.   What is Winston's basis in the property he receives in the distribution?

    d.   After the distribution, what is the partnership's basis in the property originally contributed by Winston?

    e.   Would your answers to (b), (c), and (d) change if Winston originally contributed the property to the partnership in 1998?

31. The FABB Partnership distributes a marketable security to 25% partner Fred in complete liquidation of his interest in the partnership. Use the following facts to answer the questions that follow:

- The partnership's basis in the security is $10,000, and its value is $20,000. The partnership did not own any of this particular security following the distribution.
- Fred's basis in the partnership interest is $5,000 immediately prior to the distribution.
- Fred is a general partner, and capital is a material income-producing factor to the partnership.
- The partnership owns no hot assets.

    a.   How is the security classified under § 736?

    b.   What is the amount of the security distribution that is treated as a cash distribution?

    c.   How much gain does Fred report on the distribution?

    d.   What is Fred's basis in the security he receives in the distribution?

Decision Making

32. Maurice is a 10% general partner in the Chartreuse Partnership, which provides consulting services. The partnership distributes $100,000 cash to Maurice in complete liquidation of his partnership interest. Maurice's share of partnership unrealized receivables immediately before the distribution is $40,000. The partnership has no other hot assets. Assume none of the cash payment is for goodwill. Maurice's basis for his partnership interest immediately before the distribution is $50,000.

    a.   How is the cash payment treated under § 736?

    b.   How much gain or loss must Maurice recognize on the distribution, and what is the character of these amounts?

    c.   How does the partnership treat the distribution to Maurice?

    d.   What planning opportunities might the partnership wish to consider?

    e.   How would your answers to the above questions change if Maurice were a limited partner?

33. DDP Partnership has three equal partners. One of them, Donald, sells his interest to another partner, Paul, for $47,000 cash and the assumption of Donald's share of partnership liabilities. On the sale date, the partnership's cash basis balance sheet reflects the following. Assume that capital accounts reflect the partners' bases in their partnership interests, excluding liabilities.

	Basis	FMV		Basis	FMV
Cash	$51,000	$ 51,000	Note payable	$ 9,000	$ 9,000
Accounts receivable	–0–	60,000	Capital accounts		
Capital assets	9,000	39,000	Donald	17,000	47,000
			David	17,000	47,000
			Paul	17,000	47,000
Total	$60,000	$150,000	Total	$60,000	$150,000

    a.   What is the total amount realized by Donald on the sale?

    b.   How much, if any, ordinary income must Donald recognize on the sale?

    c.   How much capital gain must Donald report?

    d.   What is Paul's basis in the partnership interest acquired?

    e.   If the partnership makes an election to adjust the bases of the partnership assets to reflect the sale, what adjustment is made?

34. Assume in Problem 33 that Donald's partnership interest is not sold to another partner. Instead, the partnership makes a liquidating distribution of $47,000 cash to Donald, and the remaining partners assume his share of the liabilities. How much gain or loss must Donald recognize, and how is it characterized? Assume Donald is a general partner and capital is not a material income-producing factor to the partnership.

35. Hannah, a partner in the cash basis HBA Partnership, has a one-third interest in partnership profits and losses. The partnership's balance sheet at the end of the current year is as follows:

	Basis	FMV		Basis	FMV
Cash	$ 60,000	$ 60,000	Hannah, capital	$ 60,000	$200,000
Receivables	–0–	300,000	Brittney, capital	60,000	200,000
Land	120,000	240,000	Alexis, capital	60,000	200,000
Total	$180,000	$600,000	Total	$180,000	$600,000

Hannah sells her interest in the HBA Partnership to Richard at the end of the current year for cash of $200,000.

a. How much income must Hannah report on her tax return for the current year from the sale, and what is its nature?

b. If the partnership does not make an optional adjustment-to-basis election, what are the type and amount of income that Richard must report in the next year when the receivables are collected?

c. If the partnership did make an optional adjustment-to-basis election, what are the type and amount of income that Richard must report in the next year when the receivables are collected? When the land (which is used in the HBA Partnership's business) is sold for $300,000? Assume no other transactions occurred that year.

36. Dad is the owner of a 60% general partner interest in the Consulting Services Partnership, in which capital is *not* a material income-producing factor. Two unrelated partners each own 20% partnership interests. Dad's basis in his partnership interest is $300,000.

Issue ID

Communications

Dad's son, Dean, worked for the partnership on a part-time basis while he was in college and has shown a strong aptitude for the business. Dad would like to retire and allow Dean to take over the business, but he needs to dispose of his partnership interest for its $600,000 value to do so. The partnership has adequate liquidity to make this distribution.

Dad's share of the partnership's unrealized receivables from services (no depreciation recapture, $0 basis) is $225,000. The partnership has a favorable tax year-end, so the other partners want to make sure the partnership does not terminate. Dean is the beneficiary of a trust fund established by his grandmother. He now receives about $60,000 a year and will control the $750,000 principal amount in four years, when he reaches age 30.

Dad is considering two courses of action:

• Dad can sell his interest to Dean on an installment basis with a balloon payment of the $600,000 principal balance at the end of four years. Dean would pay Dad adequate interest (for purposes of OID and imputed interest rules) on the deferred balance each year. Under this arrangement, the entire 60% interest is deemed to be sold for tax purposes at the time the installment contract is consummated, although gain is deferred until payments are made.

• Dad can allow the partnership to redeem his partnership interest immediately. To structure a transition to the son, the partnership would enter into an employment arrangement with Dean, whereby Dean vests in a 10% interest in the partnership each year for six years in exchange for services rendered to the partnership.

Draft a letter to Dad Thomas (1329 Mesquite Boulevard, Amarillo, TX 79109) addressing the consequences of each proposed alternative. Consider the impact to Dad, the partnership, and Dean.

37. At the end of last year, Ben, a 40% partner in the four-person BBJR Partnership, has an outside basis of $50,000 in the partnership, including a $40,000 share of partnership

debt. Ben's share of the partnership's § 1245 recapture potential is $25,000. All parties use the calendar year. Describe the income tax consequences to Ben in each of the following independent situations that take place in the current year:

a.   On the first day of the tax year, Ben sells his partnership interest to Marilyn for $80,000 cash and the assumption by Marilyn of the appropriate share of partnership liabilities.

b.   Ben dies after a lengthy illness on April 1 of the current year. Ben's brother immediately takes Ben's place in the partnership.

38. Briefly discuss how your responses in Problem 37 would change if the BBJR Partnership had $200,000 of unrealized receivables at the end of the current year, including the § 1245 recapture potential.

39. For each of the following independent fact patterns, indicate whether a termination of the partnership has occurred for tax purposes. Assume no other partnership interests are sold either one year before or one year after the transactions described.

a.   Polly sells her interest in capital and profits of the MPQ Partnership. She owns a 68% interest in capital and a 48% interest in the partnership profits.

b.   Rick and Ron are equal partners in the R & R Partnership. Ron dies on January 15, 2008. Rick purchases Ron's interest from his estate on March 15, 2008. Answer for January 15, 2008.

c.   Answer (b), for March 15, 2008.

d.   Fred, a 58% partner in the profitable F & D Partnership, gives his entire interest to his son on July 1, 2008.

e.   Carol, Cora, and Chris are equal partners in the Canary Partnership. On January 22, 2008, Cora sells her entire interest to Ted. On December 29, 2008, Carol sells a 15% interest to Earl. On January 25, 2009, Chris sells his interest to Frank.

40. Peggy and Cindy, parent and child, operate a local apparel shop as a partnership. The PC Partnership earned a profit of $80,000 in the current year. Cindy's equal partnership interest was acquired by gift from Peggy. Assume that capital is a material income-producing factor and that Peggy manages the day-to-day operations of the shop without any help from Cindy. Reasonable compensation for Peggy's services is $30,000.

a.   How much of the partnership income is allocated to Peggy?

b.   What is the maximum amount of partnership income that can be allocated to Cindy?

c.   Assuming that Cindy is five years old, has no other income, and is claimed as a dependent by Peggy, how is Cindy's income from the partnership taxed?

RESEARCH PROBLEMS

Note: Solutions to Research Problems can be prepared by using the **RIA Checkpoint®️ Student Edition** online research product, which is available to accompany this text. It is also possible to prepare solutions to the Research Problems by using tax research materials found in a standard tax library.

Research Problem 1.   Your client Phil is a one-third general partner in the service-oriented Magpie Partnership. He would like to retire from the partnership at the end of the current year and asks your help in structuring the buyout transaction.

Based on interim financial data and revenue projections for the remainder of the year, the partnership's balance sheet is expected to approximate the following:

	Basis	FMV		Basis	FMV
Cash	$ 60,000	$ 60,000	Maggie, capital	$ 60,000	$150,000
Accounts receivable	–0–	180,000	Phil, capital	60,000	150,000
			Iris, capital	60,000	150,000
Land (capital asset)	120,000	210,000			
Total assets	$180,000	$450,000	Total capital	$180,000	$450,000

Phil's basis in his partnership interest equals his $60,000 capital account balance.

Although the partnership has some current cash, the amount is not sufficient to purchase Phil's entire interest in the current year. The partnership has proposed to pay Phil, in liquidation of his partnership interest, according to the following schedule:

December 31, 2008	$50,000
December 31, 2009	50,000
December 31, 2010	50,000

Phil has agreed to the above payment schedule, but the parties are not sure of the tax consequences of the buyout and have temporarily halted negotiations to consult with their tax advisers. Phil has come to you to discuss the possible income tax ramifications of the buyout and to make sure that he obtains the most advantageous position possible.

a. If the buyout agreement between Phil and Magpie is silent as to the treatment of each payment, how will each payment be treated to Phil and the partnership?

b. As Phil's adviser, what payment schedule should Phil secure to minimize his current tax liability?

c. If you were the tax adviser for the partnership (rather than Phil), what payment schedule would you propose to ensure that the remaining partners receive the earliest possible deductions?

d. What additional planning opportunity might you recommend to the partnership?

Research Problem 2. The accrual basis Four Winds Partnership owned and operated three storage facilities in Milwaukee, Wisconsin. The partnership did not have a § 754 election in effect when partner Suzanne sold her 25% interest to Paul for $250,000. The partnership has no debt. There are no § 197 assets, and no depreciation recapture potential exists on the storage facility buildings.

At the time of the transfer, the partnership's asset bases and fair market values were as follows:

	Basis	Fair Market Value
Cash	$ 50,000	$ 50,000
Accounts receivable	150,000	150,000
Storage facility #1	500,000	200,000
Storage facility #2	400,000	500,000
Storage facility #3	300,000	100,000
Total assets	$1,400,000	$1,000,000

The value of two of the properties is less than the partnership's basis because the properties are in low-income neighborhoods and are not fully leased.

Paul's share of the inside basis of partnership assets is $350,000, and his share of the fair market value of partnership assets is $250,000.

a. What adjustment is required regarding Paul's purchase of the partnership interest? Must a § 754 election be made?

b. Using the basis allocation rules of § 755 and the Regulations thereunder, calculate the amount of the total adjustment to be allocated to each of the partnership's assets.

c. Would an adjustment be required if the partnership was a venture capital firm and, instead of storage facilities, its three primary assets were equity interests owned in target firms? What requirements would have to be satisfied in order to avoid making a basis adjustment?

Research Problem 3. Meg and Tom formed the Golden World Partnership with cash. They immediately executed two "Gift of Limited Partnership Interest" documents transferring a one-fourth interest to each of their two children, David and Mary (ages 7 and 5).

The partnership used the initial contribution to acquire and operate an assisted-living retirement community in Sun Horizon, Arizona. The partnership agreement provides that income will be retained in the business at the discretion of Meg and Tom. Any income that is distributed will be allocated one-fourth to each partner. The children's share of any distributions is placed in trust for their benefit until they reach age 25. Meg and Tom are trustees of the children's trust.

a. Under the Code and Regulations, what factors are taken into account in determining whether a donee is considered a valid member of a partnership for income tax purposes?

b. Are David and Mary valid partners in Golden World? Why or why not?

c. Would the answer to (b) change if David and Mary were ages 28 and 26, personally received their distributions from the partnership, and worked full-time at the retirement community? Support the result with judicial authority.

Internet *Activity*

Use the tax resources of the Internet to address the following questions. Do not restrict your search to the World Wide Web, but include a review of newsgroups and general reference materials, practitioner sites and resources, primary sources of the tax law, chat rooms and discussion groups, and other opportunities.

Communications

Research Problem 4. Print an article written by a tax adviser discussing the merits of the family limited partnership. Write a memo discussing one of the following issues.

a. The effects of Revenue Ruling 93–12 on the use of the entity.

b. The effects of § 704(e) on income computations for the entity.

c. The accuracy of the computations made by the author in the article.

Your memo should include a summary of the findings presented in the article and a summary and discussion of your thoughts. For example, you may wish to address situations in which family limited partnerships may be beneficial or pitfalls in structuring such an entity.

Research Problem 5. On what form or attachment does a partnership report that it has made a § 754 election? Prepare such a form using the facts of Example 38 in the text.

Research Problem 6. Download a copy of the legislation with which your state began to allow the formation of limited liability companies. What types of business activities can an LLC conduct in your state?

CHAPTER 12

S Corporations

L0.1

Explain the tax effects that S corporation status has on shareholders.

[handwritten margin notes: Reasons to be S. Corp (1) No Double taxation (2) Losse early years can be offset by individual on next S. corp No more than 3 Month deferral]

Introduction

The major owners of a minor league baseball team have been operating as a C corporation for four years, incurring significant net operating losses (NOLs). They decide to elect S corporation status to gain immediate deductions for these NOLs. To their surprise, they learn that the NOLs incurred before the S election do not flow through. In effect, the NOLs are locked inside the corporate entity until the S election is terminated. Of course, any "new" NOLs flow through to the owners. Thus, it is clear that one must be careful when selecting the form of business entity under which to operate a business.

An individual establishing a business has a number of choices as to the form of business entity under which to operate. Chapters 2 through 7 outline many of the rules, advantages, and disadvantages of operating as a regular corporation. Chapters 10 and 11 discuss the partnership entity, and Chapter 11 covers the limited liability company (LLC) and limited liability partnership (LLP) forms.

Another alternative, the **S corporation**, provides many of the benefits of partnership taxation and at the same time gives the owners limited liability protection from creditors. The S corporation rules, which are contained in **Subchapter S** of the Internal Revenue Code (§§ 1361–1379), were enacted to allow flexibility in the entity choice that businesspeople face. Thus, S status combines the legal environment of C corporations with taxation similar to that applying to partnerships. S corporation status is obtained through an election by a *qualifying* corporation with the consent of its shareholders.

S corporations are treated as corporations under state law. They are recognized as separate legal entities and generally provide shareholders with the same liability protection afforded by C corporations. For Federal income tax purposes, however, taxation of S corporations resembles that of partnerships. As with partnerships, the income, deductions, and tax credits of an S corporation flow through to shareholders annually, regardless of whether distributions are made. Thus, income is taxed at the shareholder level and not at the corporate level. Payments to S shareholders by the corporation are distributed tax-free to the extent that the distributed earnings were previously taxed. Further, C corporation penalty taxes like the accumulated earnings tax, personal holding company tax, and alternative minimum tax do not apply to an S corporation.

Although the Federal tax treatment of S corporations and partnerships is similar, it is not identical. For instance, liabilities affect an owner's basis differently, and S corporations may incur a tax liability at the corporate level. Furthermore, an S corporation may not allocate income like a partnership, and distributions of appreciated property are taxable in an S corporation situation (see Concept

[handwritten margin note: Differences]

Summary 12–2 later in this chapter). In addition, a variety of C corporation provisions apply to S corporations. For example, the liquidation of C and S corporations is taxed in the same way. As a rule, where the S corporation provisions are silent, C corporation rules apply.

Today, the choice of a flow-through entity is often between an S corporation (a Federal tax entity) and an LLC (a state tax entity). Although an S corporation resembles an LLC, there are differences. A two-or-more-member LLC operates under partnership tax principles, whereas, as just explained, partnership taxation rules do not always apply to an S corporation.

An Overview of S Corporations

Since the inception of S corporations in 1958, their popularity has waxed and waned with changes in the tax law. Before the Tax Reform Act of 1986, their ranks grew slowly. In contrast, in the two years following the 1986 law change, the population of S corporations exploded, increasing by 52 percent. By 1993, more than 1.9 million businesses were filing S corporation returns—48 percent of all corporate returns filed in that year. This rapid growth was driven by a change in the relationship of individual and corporate tax rates. Prior to 1986, maximum individual rates were higher than maximum corporate rates. Following the 1986 tax act, the relationship reversed.

The growth in the number of S corporation elections has continued even though the maximum tax rates are now the same at 35 percent. In 2004, S corporations accounted for 65.7 percent of the 5.35 million corporate tax returns filed, but only 34 percent of the $18.7 billion of total receipts. In 2004, there were 3.5 million S corporations, up from 3.3 million in 2003. Between 1997 and 2004, the number of S corporation tax returns increased by over 1,066,080 or 43.4 percent.

Nearly two-thirds (60 percent) of all S corporations reported positive income. Although only 17 percent of returns were from the wholesale and retail trade sectors, 41.8 percent of the total gross receipts were from this sector in 2004. Since the first S elections were allowed in 1958, the wholesale and retail trade division has dominated key financial measurements.[1] Although the number of S corporation returns increased by 3.7 percent in 2005 over the prior year, other corporate returns declined by 1.8 percent. As the following examples illustrate, S corporations can be advantageous even when the individual tax rate exceeds the corporate tax rate.

E X A M P L E   1

An S corporation earns $300,000 in 2008. The marginal individual tax rate applicable to shareholders is 35% on ordinary income and 15% on dividends. The applicable marginal corporate tax rate is 34%. All after-tax income is distributed currently.

	C Corporation	S Corporation
Earnings	$ 300,000	$ 300,000
Less: Corporate tax	(102,000)	–0–
Available for distribution	$ 198,000	$ 300,000
Less: Tax at owner level	(29,700)	(105,000)
Available after-tax earnings	$ 168,300	$ 195,000

The S corporation generates an extra $26,700 of after-tax earnings ($195,000 − $168,300), when compared with a similar C corporation. The C corporation might be able to reduce this disadvantage, however, by paying out its earnings as compensation, rents, or interest expense. Tax at the owner level can also be deferred or avoided by not distributing after-tax earnings. ■

---

[1]Kelly L. Luttrell, "Wholesale and Retail Trade Division Dominates S Corporations Since 1959," *SOI Bulletin*, Spring 2007.

TAX *in the News* | **THE IRS LAUNCHES AN S CORPORATION RESEARCH PROGRAM**

In August 2005, the IRS announced a plan to study S corporations' reporting compliance. The National Research Program will audit 5,000 randomly selected S corporation tax returns for 2003 and 2004 (an insignificant number considering how many Forms 1120S are filed each year). The IRS last examined S corporation compliance in 1984.

Benson Goldstein, technical manager for the AICPA Tax Division, says that "recent research points to S corporations as a significant source of noncompliance, particularly among high-income individuals." But Tom Ochsenschlager, vice president of taxation for the AICPA, points out that "a lot of the errors made are errors, not malfeasance."

For the first year of the program, Form 1120S audits increased by about 25 percent.

EXAMPLE 2

A new corporation elects S status and incurs an NOL of $300,000. The shareholders may use their proportionate shares of the NOL to offset other taxable income in the current year, providing an immediate tax savings. In contrast, a newly formed C corporation is required to carry the NOL forward for up to 20 years and does not receive any tax benefit in the current year. Hence, an S corporation can accelerate NOL deductions and thereby provide a greater present value for tax savings generated by the loss. ■

When to Elect S Corporation Status

The planner begins by determining the appropriateness of an S election. The following factors should be considered.

- If shareholders have high marginal rates relative to C corporation rates, it may be desirable to avoid S corporation status. Although C corporation earnings can be subject to double taxation, good tax planning mitigates this result, e.g., when the owners take profits out as salary. Likewise, profits of the corporation may be taken out by the shareholders as capital gain income through stock redemptions, liquidations, or sales of stock to others. Alternatively, C corporation profits may be paid out as dividends, subject to a 15 percent maximum tax rate. Any distribution of profits or sale of stock can be deferred to a later year, thereby reducing the present value of shareholder taxes. Finally, potential shareholder-level tax on corporate profits can be eliminated by a step-up in the basis of the stock upon the shareholder's death.

- S corporation status allows shareholders to realize tax benefits from corporate losses immediately—an important consideration in new business enterprises where losses are common. Thus, if corporate NOLs are anticipated and there is unlikely to be corporate income over the near term to offset with the NOLs, S corporation status is advisable. However, the deductibility of the losses to shareholders must also be considered. The at-risk and passive loss limitations apply to losses generated by an S corporation. In addition, as discussed later in this chapter, shareholders may not deduct losses in excess of the basis in their stock. Together these limits may significantly reduce the benefits of an S election in a loss setting.

- If the entity electing S status is currently a C corporation, NOL carryovers from prior years cannot be used in an S corporation year. Even worse, S corporation years reduce the 20-year carryover period. And the corporation may be subject to some corporate-level taxes if it elects S status (see the discussion of the built-in gains tax later in this chapter).

- Because S corporations are flow-through entities, separately stated deduction and income items retain any special tax characteristics when they are reported on shareholders' returns. Whether this consideration favors S status depends upon the character of income and deductions of the S corporation. For instance, it may be an advantage to receive the flow-through of passive income, or the qualified domestic production activities deduction, on the shareholder's tax return, making the S election more attractive. Charitable contributions are not subject to the 10 percent limitation at the corporate level, but an S corporation cannot take advantage of special provisions for contributions of inventory and scientific equipment.

- State and local tax laws also should be considered when making the S election. Although an S corporation usually escapes Federal income tax, it may not be immune from state and local taxes. State taxation of S corporations varies. Some states, including Michigan, treat them the same as C corporations, resulting in a corporate tax liability from an income or franchise tax.
- The choice of S corporation status is affected by a variety of other factors. For example, the corporate alternative minimum tax (see Chapter 3) may be avoided in an S corporation. An in-depth discussion of entity choice is provided in Chapter 13.

Qualifying for S Corporation Status

Definition of a Small Business Corporation

LO.2

Identify corporations that qualify for the S election.

To achieve S corporation status, a corporation *first* must qualify as a **small business corporation**. If each of the following requirements is met, then the entity can elect S corporation status.

- Is a domestic corporation (incorporated and organized in the United States).
- Is an eligible corporation (see below for ineligible types).
- Issues only one class of stock.
- Is limited to a theoretical maximum of 100 shareholders (75 before 2005).
- Has only individuals, estates, and certain trusts and exempt organizations as shareholders.
- Has no nonresident alien shareholder.

Unlike other provisions in the tax law (e.g., § 1244), no maximum or minimum dollar sales or capitalization restrictions apply to small business corporations.

Ineligible Corporations. Small business corporation status is not permitted for non-U.S. corporations, nor for certain banks and insurance companies.

Any domestic corporation that is not an ineligible corporation can be a qualified Subchapter S corporation subsidiary (QSSS), if the S corporation holds 100 percent of its stock and elects to treat the subsidiary as a QSSS.[2] The QSSS is viewed as a division of the parent, so the parent S corporation can own a QSSS through another QSSS. QSSSs have a separate existence for legal purposes, but they exist only within the parent S corporation for tax purposes.

One Class of Stock. A small business corporation may have only one class of stock issued and outstanding.[3] This restriction permits differences in voting rights, but not differences in distribution or liquidation rights.[4] Thus, two classes of common stock that are identical except that one class is voting and the other is nonvoting would be treated as a single class of stock for small business corporation purposes. In contrast, voting common stock and voting preferred stock (with a preference on dividends) would be treated as two classes of stock. Authorized and unissued stock or treasury stock of another class does not disqualify the corporation.

---

[2]§ 1361(b)(3)(B).
[3]§ 1361(b)(1)(D).

[4]§ 1361(c)(4).

Likewise, unexercised stock options, phantom stock, stock appreciation rights, warrants, and convertible debentures usually do not constitute a second class of stock.

The determination of whether stock provides identical rights as to distribution and liquidation proceeds is made based on the provisions governing the operation of the corporation. These *governing provisions* include the corporate charter, articles of incorporation, bylaws, applicable state law, and binding agreements relating to distribution and liquidation proceeds. Employment contracts, loan agreements, and other commercial contracts are *not* considered governing provisions.[5]

EXAMPLE 3

[handwritten: 100% of Shareholder has to elect to become S.Corp]

[handwritten: S.Corp shareholders are taxed either or not they receive income income is taxed as they come as profit]

[handwritten: §1231 unique treatment Gain = Capital Loss = Ordinary Amortized/Depre if owned by the owner > 12 Months. There is recapture]

[handwritten: straight debt]

[handwritten: Y1 Y2 Y3 (10) (20) 50CG 5year lower back 30 ORD income 20 capital Gain]

[handwritten: 1245 PP & 1250 R/E go with §1231 ✓ Gain come as Operating Capital Gain always if NO NOL more if NO 1245, 1250 loss]

Blue, a small business corporation, has two equal shareholders, Smith and Jones. Both shareholders are employed by Blue and have binding employment contracts with the corporation. The compensation paid by Blue to Jones under her employment contract is reasonable. The compensation paid to Smith under his employment contract, however, is excessive, resulting in a constructive dividend. Smith's employment contract was not prepared to circumvent the one-class-of-stock requirement. Because employment contracts are not considered governing provisions, Blue has only one class of stock. ∎

Although the one-class-of-stock requirement seems straightforward, it is possible for debt to be reclassified as stock, resulting in an unexpected loss of S corporation status.[6] To mitigate concern over possible reclassification of debt as a second class of stock, the law provides a set of *safe-harbor provisions.*

First, straight debt *issued in an S corporation year* will not be treated as a second class of stock and will not disqualify the S election.[7] The characteristics of straight debt include the following.

- The debtor is subject to a written, unconditional promise to pay on demand or on a specified date a sum certain in money.
- The interest rate and payment date are not contingent on corporate profits, management discretion, or similar factors.
- The debt is not convertible into stock.
- The debt is held by a creditor who is an individual (other than a nonresident alien), an estate, or a qualified trust.
- Straight debt can be held by creditors actively and regularly engaged in the business of lending money.

In addition to straight debt under the safe-harbor rules, short-term unwritten advances from a shareholder that do not exceed $10,000 in the aggregate at any time during the corporation's taxable year generally are not treated as a second class of stock. Likewise, debt that is held by stockholders in the same proportion as their stock is not treated as a second class of stock, even if it would be reclassified as equity otherwise.[8]

Number of Shareholders.

A small business corporation is limited theoretically to 100 shareholders (75 before 2005). If shares of stock are owned jointly by two individuals, they will generally be treated as separate shareholders.

Family members may be treated as one shareholder for purposes of determining the number of shareholders. The term "members of the family" is defined as the common ancestor, the lineal descendants of the common ancestor, and the spouses (or former spouses) of the lineal descendants or common ancestor.[9] An estate of a family member also may be treated as a family member for purposes of determining the number of shareholders.

---

[5]Reg. § 1.1361–1(l)(2).
[6]Refer to the discussion of debt-versus-equity classification in Chapter 4.
[7]§ 1361(c)(5)(A).
[8]Reg. § 1.1361–1(l)(4).

[9]§§ 1361(c)(1)(A)(ii) and (B)(i). The need for an affirmative election to treat family members as a single shareholder was eliminated in 2005. Notice 2005–91, 2005–51 I.R.B. 1164 provides insight into the determination of who is a family member.

Fred and Wilma (husband and wife) jointly own 10 shares in Marlins, Inc., an S corporation, with the remaining 290 shares outstanding owned by 99 other unrelated shareholders. Fred and Wilma get divorced; pursuant to the property settlement approved by the court, the 10 shares held by Fred and Wilma are divided between them—5 to each. Before the divorce settlement, Marlins had 100 shareholders under the small business corporation rules. After the settlement, it still has 100 shareholders and continues to qualify as a small business corporation. A former spouse is treated as being in the same family as the individual to whom he or she was married. ■

EXAMPLE 4

Type of Shareholder Limitation. Small business corporation shareholders may be resident individuals, estates, certain trusts, and certain tax-exempt organizations.[10] Charitable organizations, employee benefit trusts exempt from taxation, and a one-person LLC classified as a disregarded entity also all can qualify as shareholders of an S corporation. This limitation prevents partnerships, corporations, limited liability partnerships, most LLCs, and most IRAs and Roth IRAs from owning S corporation stock. Partnerships and corporate shareholders could easily circumvent the 100-shareholder limitation as illustrated in the following example.

Saul and 105 of his close friends wish to form an S corporation. Saul reasons that if he and his friends form a partnership, the partnership can then form an S corporation and act as a single shareholder, thereby avoiding the 100-shareholder rule. Saul's plan will not work because partnerships cannot own stock in a small business corporation. ■

EXAMPLE 5

Although partnerships and corporations cannot own small business corporation stock, small business corporations can be partners in a partnership or shareholders in a corporation. This ability allows the 100-shareholder requirement to be bypassed in a limited sense. For example, if two small business corporations, each with 100 shareholders, form a partnership, then the shareholders of both corporations can enjoy the limited liability conferred by S corporation status and a single level of tax on partnership profits.

Nonresident Aliens. Nonresident aliens cannot own stock in a small business corporation.[11] That is, individuals who are not U.S. citizens *must live in the United States* to own S corporation stock. Therefore, shareholders with nonresident alien spouses in community property states[12] cannot own S corporation stock because

---

ETHICAL and EQUITABLE *Considerations*	**EXTORTION PAYMENTS**

Burt is the custodian at Quaker Inn, an S corporation in Grand Isle, Louisiana. Over the years, he has received a total of 276 shares of stock in the corporation through bonus payments.

While listening to a debate on television about a national health care plan, Burt decides that the company's health coverage is unfair. He is concerned about this because his wife is seriously ill.

During the second week in December, Burt informs the president of Quaker that he would like a Christmas bonus of $75,000, or else he will sell 10 shares of his stock to one of his relatives who is a nonresident alien. As a C corporation, Quaker's income tax would be about $136,000.

Can you defend Burt's position?

---

[10]§ 1361(b)(1)(B). Foreign trusts, charitable remainder trusts, and charitable lead trusts cannot be shareholders.
[11]§ 1362(b)(1)(C).

[12]Assets acquired by a married couple are generally considered community property in these states: Louisiana, Texas, New Mexico, Arizona, California, Washington, Idaho, Nevada, Wisconsin, and (if elected by the spouses) Alaska.

the nonresident alien spouse would be treated as owning half of the community property.[13] Similarly, if a resident alien shareholder moves outside the United States, the S election will be terminated.

Making the Election

LO.3

Understand how to make an S election.

To become an S corporation, a *small business corporation* (defined above) must file a valid election with the IRS. The election is made on Form 2553 (see Appendix B). For the election to be valid, it should be filed on a timely basis and all shareholders must consent. For S corporation status to apply in the current tax year, the election must be filed either in the previous year or on or before the fifteenth day of the third month of the current year. An S corporation may obtain a 24-month extension of time to file Form 2553.[14]

EXAMPLE 6

In 2008, a calendar year C corporation in Auburn, Alabama, decides to become an S corporation beginning January 1, 2009. The S corporation election can be made at any time in 2008 or by March 15, 2009. An election after March 15, 2009, will not be effective until the 2010 tax year. ■

Even if the 2½-month deadline is met, a current election is not valid unless the corporation qualifies as a small business corporation for the *entire* tax year. Otherwise, the election will be effective for the following tax year. Late current-year elections, after the 2½-month deadline, may be considered timely if there is reasonable cause for the late filing.

A corporation that does not yet exist cannot make an S corporation election.[15] Thus, for new corporations, a premature election may not be effective. A new corporation's 2½-month election period begins at the earliest occurrence of any of the following events: (1) when the corporation has shareholders, (2) when it acquires assets, or (3) when it begins doing business.[16]

EXAMPLE 7

Several individuals acquire assets on behalf of Rock Corporation on June 29, 2008, and begin doing business on July 3, 2008. They subscribe to shares of stock, file articles of incorporation for Rock, and become shareholders on July 7, 2008. The S election must be filed no later than 2½ months after June 29, 2008 (on or before September 12) to be effective for 2008. ■

The IRS can correct errors in electing S status, where a taxpayer can show that the mistake was inadvertent, the entity otherwise was qualified to be an S corporation, and it acted as if it were an S corporation. Under certain conditions, automatic relief is granted without the need for a letter ruling request and the normal user fee.

Further, the IRS has the authority to honor S elections that were not filed by the deadline. The company must have a reasonable cause for missing the statutory deadline. Sufficient reasonable cause might occur, for example, where both the corporation's accountant and its attorney failed to file the election because each believed the other had done so, or because there was miscommunication as to who was responsible for filing.

An LLC that makes a timely and valid election to be classified as an S corporation is deemed to be classified as an association taxable as a corporation without filing a Form 8832. The LLC must meet all of the other S corporation requirements.

---

[13]See *Ward v. U.S.*, 81–2 USTC ¶9674, 48 AFTR2d 81–5942, 661 F.2d 226 (Ct.Cls., 1981), where the court found that the stock was owned as community property. Since the taxpayer-shareholder (a U.S. citizen) was married to a citizen and resident of Mexico, the nonresident alien prohibition was violated. If the taxpayer-shareholder had held the stock as separate property, the S election would have been valid.

[14]§ 1362(b); Rev. Proc. 2007–62, 2007–41 I.R.B. 786.

[15]See, for example, *T.H. Campbell & Bros., Inc.*, 34 TCM 695, T.C.Memo. 1975–149; Ltr.Rul. 8807070.

[16]Reg. § 1.1372–2(b)(1). Also see, for example, *Nick A. Artukovich*, 61 T.C. 100 (1973).

Shareholder Consent

A qualifying election requires the consent of all of the corporation's shareholders.[17] Consent must be in writing, and it must generally be filed by the election deadline. A consent extension is available only if Form 2553 is filed on a timely basis, reasonable cause is given, and the interests of the government are not jeopardized.[18]

EXAMPLE 8

Vern and Yvonne decide to convert their C corporation into a calendar year S corporation for 2008. At the end of February 2008 (before the election is filed), Yvonne travels to Ukraine and forgets to sign a consent to the election. Yvonne will not return to the United States until June and cannot be reached by fax or e-mail. Vern files the S election on Form 2553 and also requests an extension of time to file Yvonne's consent to the election. Vern indicates that there is a reasonable cause for the extension: a shareholder is out of the country. Since the government's interest is not jeopardized, the IRS probably will grant Yvonne an extension of time to file the consent. Vern must file the election on Form 2553 on or before March 15, 2008, for the election to be effective for the 2008 calendar year. ■

Both husband and wife must consent if they own their stock jointly (as joint tenants, tenants in common, tenants by the entirety, or community property). This requirement has led to considerable taxpayer grief—particularly in community property states where the spouses may not realize that their stock is jointly owned as a community asset.

EXAMPLE 9

Three shareholders, Amy, Monty, and Dianne, incorporate in January and file Form 2553. Amy is married and lives in California. Monty is single and Dianne is married; both live in South Carolina. Because Amy is married and lives in a community property state, her husband also must consent to the S election. South Carolina is not a community property state, so Dianne's husband need not consent. ■

Finally, for current-year S elections, persons who were shareholders during any part of the taxable year before the election date, but were not shareholders when the election was made, must also consent to the election.[19]

EXAMPLE 10

On January 15, 2008, the stock of Columbus Corporation (a calendar year C corporation) was held equally by three individual shareholders: Jim, Sally, and LuEllen. On that date, LuEllen sells her interest to Jim and Sally. On March 14, 2008, Columbus Corporation files Form 2553. Jim and Sally indicate their consent by signing the form. Columbus cannot become an S corporation until 2009 because LuEllen did not indicate consent. Had all three shareholders consented by signing Form 2553, S status would have taken effect as of January 1, 2008. ■

Loss of the Election

An S election remains in force until it is revoked or lost. Election or consent forms are not required for future years. However, an S election can terminate if any of the following occurs.

- Shareholders owning a majority of shares (voting and nonvoting) voluntarily revoke the election.
- A new shareholder owning more than one-half of the stock affirmatively refuses to consent to the election.
- The corporation no longer qualifies as a small business corporation.
- The corporation does not meet the passive investment income limitation.

---

[17]§ 1362(a)(2).

[18]Rev.Rul. 60–183, 1960–1 C.B. 625; *William Pestcoe*, 40 T.C. 195 (1963); Reg. § 1.1362–6(b)(3)(iii).

[19]§ 1362(b)(2)(B)(ii).

Voluntary Revocation. A **voluntary revocation** of the S election requires the consent of shareholders owning a majority of shares on the day that the revocation is to be made.[20] A revocation filed up to and including the fifteenth day of the third month of the tax year is effective for the entire tax year, unless a later date is specified. Similarly, unless an effective date is specified, revocation made after the first 2½ months of the current tax year is effective for the following tax year.

EXAMPLE 11

The shareholders of Petunia Corporation, a calendar year S corporation, voluntarily revoke the S election on January 5, 2008. They do not specify a future effective date in the revocation. Assuming the revocation is properly executed and timely filed, Petunia will be a C corporation for the entire 2008 calendar year. If the election is not made until June 2008, Petunia will remain an S corporation in 2008 and will become a C corporation at the beginning of 2009. ∎

A corporation can revoke its S status *prospectively* by specifying a future date when the revocation is to be effective. A revocation that designates a future effective date splits the corporation's tax year into a short S corporation year and a short C corporation year. The day on which the revocation occurs is treated as the first day of the C corporation year. The corporation allocates income or loss for the entire year on a pro rata basis, based on the number of days in each short year.

EXAMPLE 12

Assume the same facts as in the preceding example, except that Petunia designates July 1, 2008, as the revocation date. Accordingly, June 30, 2008, is the last day of the S corporation's tax year. The C corporation's tax year runs from July 1, 2008, to December 31, 2008. Income or loss for the 12-month period is allocated between the two short years, i.e., 184/366 to the C corporation year. ∎

Rather than using pro rata allocation, the corporation can elect to compute actual income or loss attributable to the two short years. This election requires the consent of everyone who was a shareholder at any time during the S corporation's short year and everyone who owns stock on the first day of the C corporation's year.[21]

Loss of Small Business Corporation Status. If an S corporation fails to qualify as a small business corporation at any time after the election has become effective, its status as an S corporation ends. The termination occurs on the day that the corporation ceases to be a small business corporation.[22] Thus, if the corporation ever has more than 100 shareholders, a second class of stock, or a nonqualifying shareholder, or otherwise fails to meet the definition of a small business corporation, the S election is immediately terminated.

EXAMPLE 13

Peony Corporation has been a calendar year S corporation for three years. On August 13, 2008, one of its 100 shareholders sells *some* of her stock to an outsider. Peony now has 101 shareholders, and it ceases to be a small business corporation. For 2008, Peony is an S corporation through August 12, 2008, and a C corporation from August 13 to December 31, 2008. ∎

Passive Investment Income Limitation. The Code provides a **passive investment income (PII)** limitation for S corporations that were previously C corporations or for S corporations that have merged with C corporations. If an S corporation has C corporation E & P and passive income in excess of 25 percent of its gross receipts

---

[20]§ 1362(d)(1).
[21]§ 1362(e)(3).

[22]§ 1362(d)(2)(B).

for three consecutive taxable years, the S election is terminated as of the beginning of the fourth year.[23]

EXAMPLE 14

For 2005, 2006, and 2007, Diapason Corporation, a calendar year S corporation, received passive income in excess of 25% of its gross receipts. If Diapason holds accumulated E & P from years in which it was a C corporation, its S election is terminated as of January 1, 2008. ∎

PII includes dividends, interest, rents, gains and losses from sales of securities, and royalties net of investment deductions. Rents are not considered PII if the corporation renders significant personal services to the occupant.

EXAMPLE 15

Violet Corporation owns and operates an apartment building. The corporation provides utilities for the building, maintains the lobby, and furnishes trash collection for tenants. These activities are not considered significant personal services, so any rent income earned by the corporation will be considered PII.

Alternatively, if Violet also furnishes maid services to its tenants (personal services beyond what normally would be expected from a landlord in an apartment building), the rent income would no longer be PII. ∎

Reelection after Termination. After an S election has been terminated, the corporation must wait five years before reelecting S corporation status. The five-year waiting period is waived if:

- there is a more-than-50-percent change in ownership of the corporation after the first year for which the termination is applicable, or
- the event causing the termination was not reasonably within the control of the S corporation or its majority shareholders.

Operational Rules

S corporations are treated much like partnerships for tax purposes. With a few exceptions,[24] S corporations generally make tax accounting and other elections at the corporate level. Each year, the S corporation determines nonseparately stated income or loss and separately stated income, deductions, and credits. These items are taxed only once, at the shareholder level. All items are allocated to each shareholder based on average ownership of stock throughout the year. The *flow-through* of each item of income, deduction, and credit from the corporation to the shareholder is illustrated in Figure 12–1.

Computation of Taxable Income

Subchapter S taxable income or loss is determined in a manner similar to the tax rules that apply to partnerships, except that S corporations amortize organizational expenditures under the corporate rules[25] and must recognize gains, *but not losses*, on distributions of appreciated property to shareholders.[26] Other special provisions affecting only the computation of C corporation income, such as the dividends received deduction, do not extend to S corporations.[27] Finally, as with partnerships, certain deductions of individuals are not permitted, including

> **LO.5**
>
> Compute nonseparately stated income and identify separately stated items.

---

[23]§ 1362(d)(3)(A)(ii).

[24]A few elections can be made at the shareholder level (e.g., the choice between a foreign tax deduction or credit).

[25]§§ 248 and 1363(b).

[26]§ 1363(b).

[27]§ 703(a)(2).

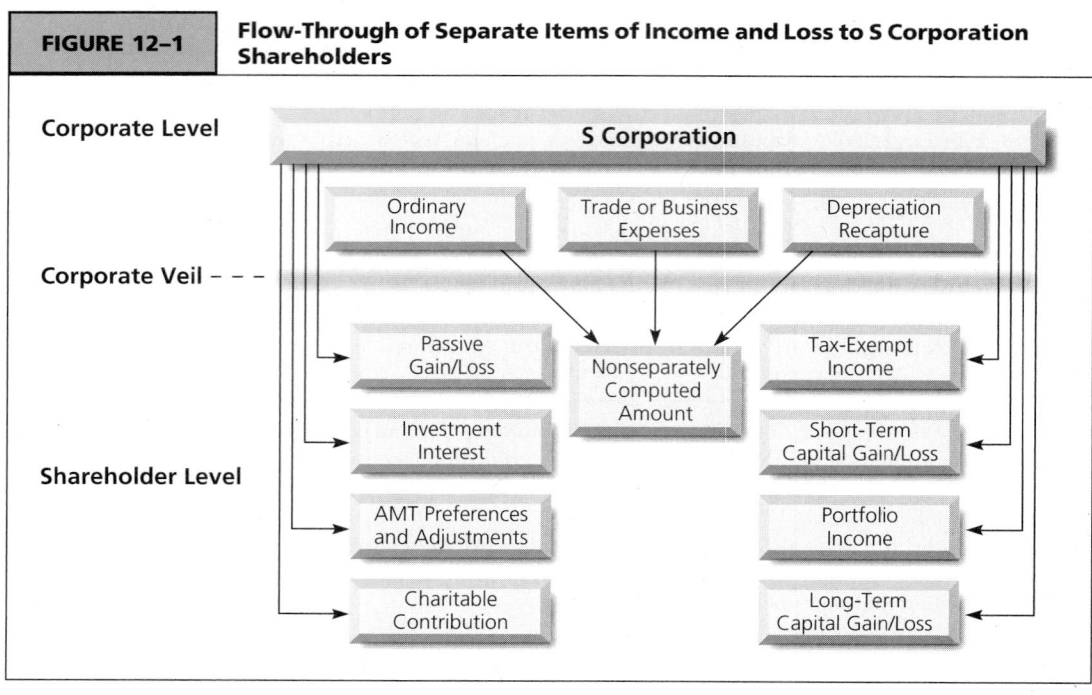

FIGURE 12–1   Flow-Through of Separate Items of Income and Loss to S Corporation Shareholders

alimony payments, personal moving expenses, certain dependent care expenses, the personal exemption, and the standard deduction.

In general, S corporation items are divided into (1) nonseparately stated income or loss and (2) separately stated income, losses, deductions, and credits that could affect the tax liability of any shareholder in a different manner, depending on other factors in the shareholder's tax situation. In essence, nonseparate items are aggregated into an undifferentiated amount that constitutes Subchapter S ordinary income or loss. An S corporation's separately stated items are identical to those separately stated by partnerships. These items retain their tax attributes on the shareholder's return. Separately stated items are listed on Schedule K of the 1120S. They include the following.

- Tax-exempt income.
- Long-term and short-term capital gains and losses.
- Section 1231 gains and losses.
- Charitable contributions (no grace period).
- Passive gains, losses, and credits.
- Certain portfolio income.
- Section 179 expense deduction.
- Domestic production gross receipts and deductions.
- Tax preferences and adjustments for the alternative minimum tax.
- Depletion.
- Foreign income or loss.
- Recoveries of tax benefit items.
- Intangible drilling costs.
- Investment interest, income, and expenses.

EXAMPLE 16

The following is the income statement for Jersey, Inc., an S corporation.

Sales	$ 40,000
Less cost of sales	(23,000)
Gross profit on sales	$ 17,000

Less: Interest expense	$1,200	
Charitable contributions	400	
Advertising expenses	1,500	
Other operating expenses	2,000	(5,100)
		$ 11,900
Add: Tax-exempt interest	$ 300	
Dividend income	200	
Long-term capital gain	500	1,000
Less: Short-term capital loss		(150)
Net income per books		$ 12,750

Subchapter S ordinary income for Jersey is calculated as follows, using net income for book purposes as the starting point.

Net income per books		$ 12,750
Separately stated items		
Deduct: Tax-exempt interest	$ 300	
Dividend income	200	
Long-term capital gain	500	(1,000)
Subtotal		$ 11,750
Add: Charitable contributions	$ 400	
Short-term capital loss	150	550
Subchapter S ordinary income		$ 12,300

The $12,300 of Subchapter S ordinary income, as well as each of the five separately stated items, are divided among the shareholders based upon their stock ownership. ■

└ allocated

Allocation of Income and Loss

LO.6

Allocate income, deductions, and credits to shareholders.

Each shareholder is allocated a pro rata portion of nonseparately stated income or loss and all separately stated items. The pro rata allocation method assigns an equal amount of each of the S items to each day of the year. If a shareholder's stock holding changes during the year, this allocation assigns the shareholder a pro rata share of each item for *each* day the stock is owned. On the date of transfer, the transferor (and not the transferee) is considered to own the stock.[28]

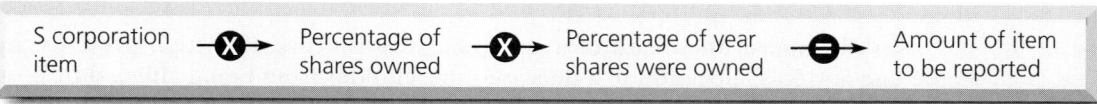

The per-day allocation must be used, unless the shareholder disposes of his or her entire interest in the entity.[29] In case of a complete termination, a short year may result. If a shareholder dies during the year, his or her share of the pro rata items up to the date of death is reported on the final individual income tax return.

E X A M P L E   17

Assume in the previous example that Pat, a shareholder, owned 10% of Jersey's stock for 100 days and 12% for the remaining 265 days. Using the required per-day allocation method, Pat's share of the S corporation items is as follows.

---

[28]Reg. § 1.1377–1(a)(2)(ii).   [29]§§ 1366(a)(1) and 1377(a)(1).

NOL Can be offset by BIG Assets   *10 years recognition*

	Schedule K Totals	Pat's Share		Pat's Schedule K–1 Totals
		10%	12%	
Ordinary income	$12,300	$337	$1,072	$1,409
Tax-exempt interest	300	8	26	34
Dividend income	200	5	17	22
Long-term capital gain	500	14	44	58
Charitable contributions	400	11	35	46
Short-term capital loss	150	4	13	17

Pat's share of the Subchapter S ordinary income is the total of $12,300 \times [0.10 \times (100/365)]$ plus $12,300 \times [0.12 \times (265/365)]$, or $1,409. Each of the Schedule K–1 totals from the right-hand column flows through to the appropriate lines on Pat's individual income tax return (Form 1040). ■

EXAMPLE 18

If Pat in Example 17 dies after owning the stock 100 days, his share of the S corporation items is reported on his final individual income tax return (Form 1040). Thus, only the items in the column labeled 10% in Example 17 are reported on Pat's final tax return. S corporation items that occur after Pat's death most likely would flow through to the income tax return of Pat's estate (Form 1041). ■

The Short-Year Election. If a shareholder's interest is completely terminated by disposition or death during the tax year, all shareholders holding stock during the year and the corporation may elect to treat the S taxable year as two taxable years. The first year ends on the date of the termination. Under this election, an interim closing of the books is undertaken, and the shareholders report their shares of the S corporation items as they occurred during the short tax year.[30]

The short-year election provides an opportunity to shift income, losses, and credits between shareholders. The election is desirable in circumstances where more loss can be allocated to taxpayers with higher marginal rates.

EXAMPLE 19

Alicia, the owner of all of the shares of an S corporation, transfers her stock to Cindy halfway through the tax year. There is a $100,000 NOL for the entire tax year, but $30,000 of the loss occurs during the first half of the year. Without a short-year election, $50,000 of the loss is allocated to Alicia, and $50,000 is allocated to Cindy. If the corporation makes the short-year election, Cindy is allocated $70,000 of the loss. Of course, the sales price of the stock would probably be increased to recognize the tax benefits being transferred from Alicia to Cindy. ■

In the case of the death of a shareholder, a short-year election prevents the income and loss allocation to a deceased shareholder from being affected by post-death events.

EXAMPLE 20

Joey and Karl equally own Rose, Inc., a calendar year S corporation. Joey dies on June 29 of a year that is not a leap year. Rose has income of $250,000 for January 1 through June 29 and $750,000 for the remainder of the year. Without a short-year election, the income is allocated by assigning an equal portion of the annual income of $1 million to each day (or $2,739.73 per day) and allocating the daily portion between the shareholders. Joey is allocated 50% of the daily income for the 180 days from January 1 to June 29, or $246,575.70 [($2,739.73/2) \times 180]. Joey's *estate* is allocated 50% of the income for the 185 days from June 30 to December 31, or $253,425.02 [($2,739.73/2) \times 185].

If the short-year election is made, the income of $250,000 from January 1 to June 29 is divided equally between Joey and Karl, so that each is taxed on $125,000. The income of

---

[30]§ 1377(a)(2).

$750,000 from June 30 to December 31 is divided equally between Joey's estate and Karl, or $375,000 to each. ■

Tax Treatment of Distributions to Shareholders

The amount of any distribution to an S corporation shareholder is equal to the cash plus the fair market value of any other property distributed. How the distribution is taxed depends upon whether the S corporation has C corporation **accumulated earnings and profits** (AEP, described in Chapter 5).

No C Corporation AEP. If the S corporation has never been a C corporation or if it has no C corporation AEP, the distribution is a tax-free recovery of capital to the extent that it does not exceed the shareholder's adjusted basis in the stock of the S corporation. When the amount of the distribution exceeds the adjusted basis of the stock, the excess is treated as a gain from the sale or exchange of property (capital gain in most cases).

EXAMPLE 21

Twirl, Inc., a calendar year S corporation, has no AEP. During the year, Juan, an individual shareholder of the corporation, receives a cash distribution of $12,200 from Twirl. Juan's basis in his stock is $9,700. Juan recognizes a capital gain of $2,500, the excess of the distribution over the stock basis ($12,200 − $9,700). The remaining $9,700 is tax-free, but it reduces Juan's basis in his stock to zero. ■

C Corporation AEP. S corporations with C corporation AEP blend the entity and conduit approaches to taxation. This blending treats distributions of pre-election (C corporation) and postelection (S corporation) earnings differently. Distributions of C corporation AEP are taxed as dividends (0/15% rate), while distributions of previously taxed S corporation earnings are tax-free to the extent of the shareholder's adjusted basis in the stock.

Concept Summary 12–1 outlines the taxation of distributions. These rules are intended to prevent two problems that result when a C corporation has been converted to an S corporation.

- Tax manipulation could result in AEP from the C corporation years being withdrawn without taxation, since S corporation shareholders are taxed on income, not on distributions.
- On the other hand, double taxation could occur. Earnings from the S corporation years might both flow to the shareholders' tax returns as income and be taxed as dividends as if the corporation were a C corporation.

[handwritten margin note: 2 problems that result when a C-corp has been converted to an S-corp.]

A special account is required to track undistributed earnings of an S corporation that have been taxed to shareholders previously. Distributions from this account, known as the **accumulated adjustments account (AAA)**, are tax-free. The AAA begins with a zero balance on the first day of an S corporation's first tax year. Essentially, the AAA is the cumulative total of undistributed nonseparately and separately stated items for S corporation taxable years beginning after 1982. Thus, the account parallels the calculation of C corporation AEP. Calculation of the AAA applies to all S corporations, but the AAA is most important to those that have been C corporations. The AAA provides a mechanism to ensure that the earnings of an S corporation are taxed to shareholders only once.

The AAA is computed by making adjustments in the order specified in Exhibit 12–1. Its balance is determined at the end of each year rather than at the time distributions are made. When more than one distribution occurs in the same year, a pro rata portion of each distribution is treated as having been made out of the AAA.

In calculating the amount in the AAA for purposes of determining the tax treatment of current-year distributions, the net negative adjustments (e.g., the

CONCEPT SUMMARY 12–1

Classification Procedures for Distributions from an S Corporation

Where Earnings and Profits Exist	Where No Earnings and Profits Exist
1. Distributions are tax-free to the extent of the AAA.*	
2. Any previously taxed income (PTI) from pre-1983 tax years can be distributed tax-free.	
3. The remaining distribution constitutes dividend income from AEP.†	
4. Distributions are tax-free to the extent of the other adjustments account (OAA).	
5. Any residual amount is applied as a tax-free reduction in basis of stock.	1. Distributions are nontaxable to the extent of adjusted basis in stock.
6. Excess is treated as gain from a sale or exchange of stock (capital gain in most cases).	2. Excess is treated as gain from a sale or exchange of stock (capital gain in most cases).

*Once stock basis reaches zero, any distribution from the AAA is treated as a gain from the sale or exchange of stock. Thus, basis is an upper limit on what a shareholder may receive tax-free.

†The AAA bypass election is available to pay out AEP before reducing the AAA [§ 1368(e)(3)].

excess of losses and deductions over income) for that tax year are ignored. Tax-exempt income and related expenses (e.g., insurance proceeds and premiums paid for life insurance) do not affect AAA.

A shareholder has a proportionate interest in the AAA, regardless of the size of his or her stock basis.[31] However, since the AAA is a corporate account, no connection exists between the prior accumulated S corporation income and any specific shareholder.[32] Thus, the benefits of the AAA can be shifted from one shareholder to another shareholder. For example, when one S shareholder transfers stock to another shareholder, any AAA on the purchase date may be distributed tax-free to the purchaser. Similarly, issuing additional stock to a new shareholder in an S corporation having AAA dilutes the account relative to the existing shareholders.

The AAA (unlike the stock basis) can have a negative balance. All losses decrease the AAA balance, even those in excess of the shareholder's stock basis. However, *distributions* may not make the AAA negative or increase a negative balance.

Distribution Ordering Rules. A cash distribution from an S corporation with AEP comes first from the AAA (limited to stock basis). The distribution is then deemed to be made from **previously taxed income (PTI)**[33] generated under old S corporation rules (pre-1983). Distributions from the AAA and PTI are tax-free. The remaining distribution is taxed as a dividend to the extent of AEP. After AEP is fully distributed, any residual amount is applied against the shareholder's remaining stock basis. This amount is a tax-free recovery of capital.[34] Any distributions in excess of stock basis are taxed as capital gains.

EXAMPLE 22	Salvia, a calendar year S corporation, distributes $1,300 cash to its only shareholder, Otis, on December 31, 2008. Otis's basis in his stock is $1,400, his AAA is $500, and the corporation has AEP of $750 before the distribution.

---

[31]§ 1368(c).

[32]§ 1368(e)(1)(A).

[33]§§ 1368(c)(1) and (e)(1). Before 1983, an account similar to the AAA was in place, namely, previously taxed income (PTI). Any S corporations in

existence before 1983 may have PTI, which currently may be distributed tax-free.

[34]§ 1368(c).

EXHIBIT 12–1   **Adjustments to the Corporate AAA**

Increase by:

1. Schedule K income items other than tax-exempt income.
2. Nonseparately computed income.
3. Depletion in excess of basis in the property.

Decrease by:

4. Negative Schedule K adjustments other than distributions (e.g., losses, deductions).
5. Any portion of a distribution that is considered to be tax-free from AAA (but not below zero).

Note: When the combination of items 1 through 4 results in a negative number, the AAA is adjusted first for the distribution and then for the adjustments in items 1 through 4.

According to the distribution ordering rules, the first $500 is a tax-free recovery of basis from the AAA. The next $750 is a taxable dividend distribution from AEP. Finally, the remaining $50 of cash is a tax-free recovery of basis. Immediately after the distribution, Salvia has no AAA or AEP, and Otis's stock basis equals $850.

	Corporate AAA	Corporate AEP	Otis's Stock Basis*
Balance, before the distribution	$ 500	$ 750	$1,400
Distribution ($1,300)			
From AAA	(500)		(500)
From AEP		(750)	
From stock basis			(50)
Balance, after the distribution	$ –0–	$ –0–	$ 850

*Details of basis adjustments are discussed later in the chapter.   ■

EXAMPLE 23

Assume the same facts as in the preceding example. During the following year, Salvia has no earnings and distributes $1,000 to Otis. Of the distribution, $850 is a tax-free recovery of basis, and $150 is taxed to Otis as a capital gain. ■

With the consent of all of its shareholders, an S corporation can elect to have a distribution treated as if it were made from AEP rather than from the AAA. This mechanism is known as an AAA **bypass election**. This election may be desirable as a simple means by which to eliminate a small AEP balance. Likewise, a company may make a deemed dividend election or may elect to forgo distributions of PTI.

EXAMPLE 24

Collett, a calendar year S corporation, has AEP of $12,000 and a balance of $20,000 in the AAA. Collett Corporation may elect to distribute the AEP first, creating a $12,000 dividend for its shareholders, before using the AAA. ■

Schedule M-2. S corporations report changes in the AAA on Schedule M-2 of Form 1120S. Schedule M-2 contains a column labeled **Other adjustments account (OAA).** This account includes items that affect basis but not the AAA, such as tax-exempt income and any related nondeductible expenses. For example, life insurance proceeds received and insurance premiums paid are traced through the OAA. Distributions are made from the OAA after AEP and the AAA are depleted to zero. Distributions from the OAA are generally tax-free. Remember, however, that tax-exempt income can cause a taxable dividend if the S corporation has E & P and a distribution occurs.

EXAMPLE 25

During 2008, Sparrow, an S corporation, records the following items.

AAA, beginning of the year	$ 8,500
Previously taxed income, beginning of the year	6,250
Ordinary income	25,000
Tax-exempt interest	4,000
Key employee life insurance proceeds received	5,000
Payroll penalty expense	2,000
Charitable contributions	3,000
Unreasonable compensation	5,000
Premiums on key employee life insurance	2,100
Distributions to shareholders	16,000

Sparrow's Schedule M-2 for the current year appears as follows.

Schedule M-2	**Analysis of Accumulated Adjustments Account, Other Adjustments Account, and Shareholders' Undistributed Taxable Income Previously Taxed**		
	(a) Accumulated adjustments account	**(b)** Other adjustments account	**(c)** Shareholders' undistributed taxable income previously taxed
1 Balance at beginning of tax year . . .	8,500		6,250
2 Ordinary income from page 1, line 21 . .	25,000		
3 Other additions		9,000**	
4 Loss from page 1, line 21	( )		
5 Other reductions	(10,000*)	(2,100)	
6 Combine lines 1 through 5	23,500	6,900	
7 Distributions other than dividend distributions .	16,000		
8 Balance at end of tax year. Subtract line 7 from line 6	7,500	6,900	6,250

*$2,000 (payroll penalty) + $3,000 (charitable contributions) + $5,000 (unreasonable compensation).
**$4,000 (tax-exempt interest) + $5,000 (life insurance proceeds). ■

Schedule M–3: Net Income or Loss Reconciliation.
S corporations that have total assets on Schedule L at the end of the tax year that equal or exceed $10 million must file Schedule M–3 in lieu of Schedule M–1. Schedule M–3 is effective for any tax year ending on or after December 31, 2006. For purposes of measuring total assets at the end of the year, assets may not be netted or offset against liabilities. Total assets may not be reported as a negative number. Total assets must be determined on an overall accrual method of accounting unless both of the following apply: (1) the tax return of the corporation is prepared using an overall cash method of accounting, and (2) no entity includible in the U.S. tax return prepares or is included in financial statements prepared on an accrual basis.

Part I of Schedule M–3 asks certain questions about the corporation's financial statements, and it reconciles financial statement net income or loss to the income or loss per the income statement for the U.S. tax return. Parts II and III reconcile financial statement net income or loss for the U.S. tax return on Schedule M–3, Part I, line 11, to total income or loss on Form 1120S, page 3, Schedule K, line 18.

The Schedule M–3 for S corporations is similar to the Schedule M–3 for a C corporation with some obvious exceptions. Part II of the C corporation Schedule M–3 has 30 lines, versus 26 for the S corporation's Schedule M–3. Moreover, the capital loss limitation and carryforward used do not appear on the S schedule.

Other differences between the C and S schedules include treatment of:

- Foreign withholding taxes.
- Stock option expense.
- Golden parachute payments.
- Compensation with § 162(m) limitation.
- Charitable contribution limitation/carryforward.
- Domestic production activities deduction.

A more complete discussion of Schedule M–3 is found in Chapters 2 and 10.

Effect of Terminating the S Election. Normally, distributions to shareholders from a C corporation are taxed as dividends to the extent of E & P. However, any distribution of *cash* by a corporation to shareholders during a one-year period[35] following S election termination receives special treatment. Such a distribution is treated as a tax-free recovery of stock basis to the extent that it does not exceed the AAA.[36] Since *only* cash distributions reduce the AAA during this *postelection termination period*, a corporation should not make property distributions during this time. Instead, the entity should sell property and distribute the proceeds to shareholders. However, post-termination distributions that are charged against the OAA do not get tax-free treatment. To take advantage of post-termination benefits, an S corporation must know the amount of both the AAA and the OAA as of the date that the election terminates.

EXAMPLE 26

Quinn, the sole shareholder of Roman, Inc., a calendar year S corporation, elects during 2008 to terminate the S election, effective January 1, 2009. As of the end of 2008, Roman has an AAA of $1,300. Quinn can receive a nontaxable distribution of cash during a post-termination period of approximately one year to the extent of Roman's AAA. Although a cash distribution of $1,300 during 2009 would be nontaxable to Quinn, it would reduce the adjusted basis of his stock. ■

Tax Treatment of Property Distributions by the Corporation

<table><tr><td>**LO.7**

Understand how distributions to S corporation shareholders are taxed.</td></tr></table>

An S corporation recognizes a gain on any distribution of appreciated property (other than in a reorganization) in the same manner as if the asset had been sold to the shareholder at its fair market value.[37] The corporate gain is passed through to the shareholders. The character of the gain—capital gain or ordinary income—depends upon the type of asset being distributed. There is an important reason for this gain recognition rule. Without it, property might be distributed tax-free (other than for certain recapture items) and later sold without income recognition to the shareholder because the shareholder's basis equals the asset's fair market value.

The S corporation does not recognize a loss when distributing assets that are worth less than their basis. As with gain property, the shareholder's basis is equal to the asset's fair market value. Thus, the potential loss is postponed until the shareholder sells the stock of the S corporation. Since loss property receives a step-down in basis without any loss recognition by the S corporation, distributions of loss property should be avoided.

EXAMPLE 27

Turnip, Inc., an S corporation for 10 years, distributes a tract of land held as an investment to Chang, its majority shareholder. The land was purchased for $22,000 many years ago and is currently worth $82,000. Turnip recognizes a capital gain of $60,000, which increases the

---

[35]The period is *approximately* one year in length. The post-termination transition period is discussed later in the chapter.

[36]§§ 1371(e) and 1377(b).
[37]§ 311(b).

CONCEPT SUMMARY 12–2

Distribution of Property

	Appreciated Property	Depreciated Property
S corporation	Realized gain is recognized by the corporation, which passes it through to the shareholders. Such gain increases a shareholder's stock basis, generating a basis in the property equal to FMV. On the distribution, the shareholder's stock basis is reduced by the FMV of the property (but not below zero).	Realized loss is not recognized. The shareholder assumes an FMV basis in the property.
C corporation	Realized gain is recognized under § 311(b) and increases E & P (net of tax). The shareholder has a taxable dividend to the extent of E & P and asset basis equals its FMV.	Realized loss is not recognized. The shareholder assumes an FMV basis in the property.
Partnership	No gain to the partnership or partner. The partner takes a carryover basis in the asset, but the asset basis is limited to the partner's basis in the partnership.	Realized loss is not recognized. The partner takes a carryover basis in the asset, but the asset basis is limited to the partner's basis in the partnership.

AAA by $60,000. The gain appears on Turnip's Schedule K, and a proportionate share of it passes through to the shareholders' tax returns. Then the property dividend reduces the AAA by $82,000 (the fair market value). The tax consequences are the same for appreciated property, whether it is distributed to the shareholders and they dispose of it, or the corporation sells the property and distributes the proceeds to the shareholders.

If the land had been purchased for $82,000 and was currently worth $22,000, Chang takes a $22,000 basis in the land. The $60,000 realized loss is not recognized at the corporate level. The loss does not reduce Turnip's AAA. Only when the S corporation sells the asset does it recognize the loss and reduce AAA. ■

EXAMPLE 28

Assume the same facts as in the previous example, except that Turnip is a C corporation ($1 million E & P balance) or a partnership. The partner's basis in the partnership interest is $100,000.

	Appreciated Property		
	S Corporation	C Corporation	Partnership
Entity gain/loss	$60,000	$60,000	$ –0–
Owner's gain/loss/dividend	60,000	82,000	–0–
Owner's basis in land	82,000	82,000	22,000

	Property That Has Declined in Value		
	S Corporation	C Corporation	Partnership
Entity gain/loss	$ –0–	$ –0–	$ –0–
Owner's gain/loss/dividend	–0–	22,000	–0–
Owner's basis in land	22,000	22,000	82,000

■

Shareholder's Basis

LO.8

Calculate a shareholder's basis in S corporation stock.

The calculation of the initial tax basis of stock in an S corporation is similar to that for the basis of stock in a C corporation and depends upon the manner in which the shares are acquired (e.g., gift, inheritance, purchase, exchange under § 351, etc.). Once the initial tax basis is determined, various transactions during the life of the corporation affect the shareholder's basis in the stock. Although each share-holder is required to compute his or her own basis in the S shares, neither Form 1120S nor Schedule K–1 provides a place for deriving this amount.

A shareholder's basis is increased by stock purchases and capital contributions. Operations during the year cause the following upward adjustments to basis.[38]

- Nonseparately computed income.
- Separately stated income items (e.g., nontaxable income).
- Depletion in excess of basis in the property.

Basis then is reduced by distributions not reported as income by the shareholder (e.g., an AAA or PTI distribution). Next, the following items reduce basis (*but not below zero*).

- Nondeductible expenses of the corporation (e.g., fines, penalties, illegal kick-backs).
- Nonseparately computed loss.
- Separately stated loss and deduction items.

As under the partnership rule, basis is first increased by income items; then it is decreased by distributions and finally by losses.[39] Pass-through items (other than distributions) that reduce stock basis are governed by special ordering rules. Noncapital, nondeductible expenditures reduce stock basis before losses or deductible items. A taxpayer may irrevocably elect to have deductible items pass through before any noncapital, nondeductible items. In most cases, this election is advantageous.

EXAMPLE 29

In its first year of operations, Iris, Inc., a calendar year S corporation in Clemson, South Carolina, earns income of $2,000. On February 2 in its second year of operations, Iris dis-tributes $2,000 to Marty, its sole shareholder. During the remainder of the second year, the corporation incurs a $2,000 loss.

Under the S corporation ordering rules, the $2,000 distribution is tax-free AAA to Marty, and the $2,000 loss is *not* passed through because the stock basis cannot be reduced below zero. ∎

A shareholder's basis in the stock can never be reduced below zero. Once stock basis is zero, any additional basis reductions from losses or deductions, but *not* dis-tributions, decrease (but not below zero) the shareholder's basis in loans made to the S corporation. Any excess of losses or deductions over both bases is *suspended* until there are subsequent bases. Once the basis of any debt is reduced, it is later increased (only up to the original amount) by the subsequent *net* increase result-ing from *all* positive and negative basis adjustments. The debt basis is adjusted back to the original amount by any "net increase" before any increase is made in the stock basis.[40] "Net increase" for a year is computed after taking distributions (other than those from AEP) into consideration. A distribution in excess of stock basis does not reduce any debt basis. If a loss and a distribution occur in the same year, the loss reduces the stock basis last, *after* the distribution.

---

[38]§ 1367(a).
[39]Reg. § 1.1367–1(f).

[40]§ 1367(b)(2), Reg. § 1.1367–2(e).

EXAMPLE 30

Stacey, a sole shareholder, has a $7,000 stock basis and a $2,000 basis in a loan that she made to a calendar year S corporation. At the beginning of 2008, the corporation's AAA and OAA balances are $0. Subchapter S ordinary income for 2008 is $8,200. During 2008, the corporation received $2,000 of tax-exempt interest income.

Cash of $17,300 is distributed to Stacey on November 15, 2008. Stacey recognizes only a $100 capital gain.

	Corporate AAA	Corporate OAA	Stacey's Stock Basis	Stacey's Loan Basis
Beginning balance	$ –0–	$ –0–	$ 7,000	$2,000
Ordinary income	8,200		8,200	
Exempt income		2,000	2,000	
Subtotal	$ 8,200	$ 2,000	$17,200	$2,000
Distribution ($17,300)				
From AAA	(8,200)		(8,200)	
From OAA		(2,000)	(2,000)	
From stock basis			(7,000)	
Ending balance	$ –0–	$ –0–	$ –0–	$2,000
Distribution in excess of basis = Capital gain			$ 100	

Pass-through losses can reduce loan basis, but distributions do not. Stock basis cannot be reduced below zero, but the $100 excess distribution does not reduce Stacey's loan basis. ∎

The basis rules for an S corporation are similar to the rules for determining a partner's interest basis in a partnership. However, a partner's basis in the partnership interest includes the partner's direct investment plus a *ratable share* of any partnership liabilities.[41] If a partnership borrows from a partner, the partner receives a basis increase as if the partnership had borrowed from an unrelated third party.[42] In contrast, except for loans from the shareholder to the corporation, corporate borrowing has no effect on S corporation shareholder basis. Loans from a shareholder to the S corporation have a tax basis only for the shareholder making the loan.

The fact that a shareholder has guaranteed a loan made to the corporation by a third party has no effect upon the shareholder's loan basis, unless payments actually have been made as a result of that guarantee.[43] If the corporation defaults on indebtedness and the shareholder makes good on the guarantee, the shareholder's indebtedness basis is increased to that extent.[44]

A flow-through deduction is available for a shareholder loan only where there is clear evidence that the S corporation is liable to the shareholder. A shareholder looking for this result should borrow the money from the bank and then loan the money to the S corporation.

If a loan's basis has been reduced and is not restored, income is recognized when the S corporation repays the shareholder. If the corporation issued a note as evidence of the debt, repayment constitutes an amount received in exchange for a capital asset, and the amount that exceeds the shareholder's basis is entitled to capital gain treatment.[45] However, if the loan is made on open account, the repayment constitutes ordinary income to the extent that it exceeds the shareholder's basis in the loan. Each repayment is prorated

[41]§ 752(a).

[42]Reg. § 1.752–1(e).

[43]See, for example, *Estate of Leavitt*, 90 T.C. 206 (1988), *aff'd* 89–1 USTC ¶9332, 63 AFTR2d 89–1437, 875 F.2d 420 (CA–4, 1989); *Selfe v. U.S.*, 86–1 USTC ¶9115, 57 AFTR2d 86–464, 778 F.2d 769 (CA–11, 1985); *James K. Calcutt*, 91 T.C. 14 (1988).

[44]Rev.Rul. 70–50, 1970–1 C.B. 178.

[45]*Joe M. Smith*, 48 T.C. 872 (1967), *aff'd* and *rev'd* in 70–1 USTC ¶9327, 25 AFTR2d 70–936, 424 F.2d 219 (CA–9, 1970); Rev.Rul. 64–162, 1964–1 C.B. 304.

between the gain portion and the repayment of the debt.[46] Thus, a note should be given to ensure capital gain treatment for the income that results from a loan's repayment.

Sammy is a 57% owner of Falcon, an S corporation in Brooklyn, New York. At the beginning of the year, his stock basis is zero. Sammy's basis in a $12,000 loan made to Falcon and evidenced by Falcon's note has been reduced to $0 by prior losses. At the end of the year, he receives a $13,000 distribution. During the year, his net share of corporate taxable income is $11,000. Because there is no "net increase" (i.e., his share of income is less than the amount of the distribution), Sammy's debt basis is not restored. Instead, his share of income increases his stock basis to $11,000. Therefore, on receipt of the $13,000 distribution, $11,000 is a tax-free recovery of his stock basis, and $2,000 is a capital gain.[47] ■

EXAMPLE 31

Assume in Example 31 that the distribution that Sammy receives is only $8,000. Since the "net increase" is $3,000 ($11,000 income share and $8,000 distribution), the debt basis is restored by $3,000. Accordingly, the remaining income share not used to increase debt basis ($8,000) is used to increase Sammy's stock basis to $8,000. Therefore, on receipt of the $8,000 distribution, all $8,000 is tax-free, reducing the stock basis back to zero. ■

EXAMPLE 32

Treatment of Losses

Net Operating Loss. One major advantage of an S election is the ability to pass through any net operating loss of the corporation directly to the shareholders. A shareholder can deduct an NOL for the year in which the S corporation's tax year ends. The corporation is not entitled to any deduction for the NOL. A shareholder's basis in the stock is reduced to the extent of any pass-through of the NOL, and the shareholder's AAA is reduced by the same deductible amount.[48]

> **LO.9**
>
> Explain the tax effects that losses have on shareholders.

An S corporation in Chapel Hill, North Carolina, incurs a $20,000 NOL for the current year. At all times during the tax year, the stock was owned equally by the same 10 shareholders. Each shareholder is entitled to deduct $2,000 against other income for the tax year in which the corporate tax year ends. ■

EXAMPLE 33

Deductions for an S corporation's NOL pass-through cannot exceed a shareholder's adjusted basis in the stock *plus* the basis of any loans made by the shareholder to the corporation. If a taxpayer is unable to prove the tax basis, the NOL pass-through can be denied.[49] As noted previously, once a shareholder's adjusted stock basis has been eliminated by an NOL, any excess NOL is used to reduce the shareholder's basis for any loans made to the corporation (*but never below zero*). The basis for loans is established by the actual advances made to the corporation, and not by indirect loans.[50] If the shareholder's basis is insufficient to allow a full flow-through and there is more than one type of loss (e.g., in the same year the S corporation incurs both a passive loss and a net capital loss), the flow-through amounts are determined on a pro rata basis.

Ralph is a 50% owner of an S corporation for the entire year. His stock basis is $10,000, and his shares of the various corporate losses are as follows.

Ordinary loss from operations	$8,000
Capital loss	5,000
§ 1231 loss	3,000
Passive loss	2,000

EXAMPLE 34

---

[46]Rev.Rul. 68–537, 1968–2 C.B. 372.
[47]§ 1367(b)(2)(B); Reg. § 1.1367–2(e).
[48]§§ 1368(a)(1)(A) and (e)(1)(A).

[49]See *Donald J. Sauvigne*, 30 TCM 123, T.C.Memo. 1971–30.
[50]*Ruth M. Prashker*, 59 T.C. 172 (1972); *Frederick G. Brown v. U.S.*, 83–1 USTC ¶9364, 52 AFTR2d 82–5080, 706 F.2d 755 (CA–6, 1983).

[handwritten margin notes: The only time U can have negative basis in when its @ cons old sht in Corp. If the loss is based on distributions U cannot Gions U cannot]

Based upon a pro rata approach, the total $10,000 allocable flow-through would be split among the various losses as follows.

$$\text{Ordinary loss} = \frac{\$8,000}{\$18,000} \times \$10,000 = \$\ 4,444.44$$

$$\text{Capital loss} = \frac{\$5,000}{\$18,000} \times \$10,000 = \$\ 2,777.78$$

$$\S\ 1231\ \text{loss} = \frac{\$3,000}{\$18,000} \times \$10,000 = \$\ 1,666.67$$

$$\text{Passive loss} = \frac{\$2,000}{\$18,000} \times \$10,000 = \underline{\$\ 1,111.11}$$

Total allocated loss $\underline{\$10,000.00}$ ∎

The distribution adjustments made by an S corporation during a tax year are taken into account *before* applying the loss limitation for the year. Thus, distributions during a year reduce the adjusted basis for determining the allowable loss for the year, but the loss for the year does *not* reduce the adjusted basis for purposes of determining the tax status of the distributions made during the year.

EXAMPLE 35

[handwritten margin notes: Debt for S. corp has to come from Shareholder. Shareholder has to lend cash for S. corp]

Pylon, Inc., a calendar year S corporation, is partly owned by Doris, who has a beginning stock basis of $10,000. During the year, Doris's share of a long-term capital gain (LTCG) is $2,000, and her share of an ordinary loss is $9,000. If Doris receives a $6,000 distribution, her deductible loss is calculated as follows.

Beginning stock basis	$10,000
Add: LTCG	2,000
Subtotal	$12,000
Less: Distribution	(6,000)
Basis for loss limitation purposes	$ 6,000
Deductible loss	($ 6,000)
Unused loss	($ 3,000)

Doris's stock now has a basis of zero. ∎

A shareholder's share of an NOL may be greater than both stock basis and loan basis. A shareholder is entitled to carry forward a loss to the extent that the loss for the year exceeds basis. Any loss carried forward may be deducted *only* by the *same* shareholder if and when the basis in the stock of or loans to the corporation is restored.[51]

EXAMPLE 36

Dana has a stock basis of $4,000 in an S corporation. He has loaned $2,000 to the corporation and has guaranteed another $4,000 loan made to the corporation by a local bank. Although his share of the S corporation's NOL for the current year is $9,500, Dana may deduct only $6,000 of the NOL on his individual tax return. Dana may carry forward $3,500 of the NOL, to be deducted when the basis in his stock or loan to the corporation is restored. Dana has a zero basis in both the stock and the loan after the flow-through of the $6,000 NOL. ∎

Any loss carryover due to insufficient basis remaining at the end of an approximately one-year post-termination transition period is *lost forever*. The

---

[51]§ 1366(d).

post-termination period includes the 120-day period beginning on the date of any determination pursuant to an audit of a taxpayer that follows the termination of the S corporation's election and that adjusts a Subchapter S item.[52] Thus, if a shareholder has a loss carryover, he or she should increase the stock or loan basis and flow through the loss before disposing of the stock.

Net operating losses from C corporation years cannot be utilized at the corporate level (except with respect to built-in gain, discussed later in this chapter), nor can they be passed through to the shareholders. Further, the carryforward period continues to run during S status.[53] Consequently, the S election may not be appropriate for a C corporation with NOL carryforwards. When a corporation is expecting losses in the future, an S election should be made *before* the loss years.

At-Risk Rules. S corporation shareholders, like partners, are limited in the amount of loss that they may deduct by their "at-risk" amounts. The rules for determining at-risk amounts are similar, but not identical, to the partner at-risk rules. These rules apply to the shareholders, but not to the corporation. An amount at risk is determined separately for each shareholder. The amount of the corporate losses that are passed through and deductible by the shareholders is not affected by the amount the corporation has at risk.

A shareholder usually is considered at risk with respect to an activity to the extent of cash and the adjusted basis of other property contributed to the S corporation, any amount borrowed for use in the activity for which the taxpayer has personal liability for payment from personal assets, and the net fair market value of personal assets that secure nonrecourse borrowing. Any losses that are suspended under the at-risk rules are carried forward and are available during the post-termination transition period. The S stock basis limitations and at-risk limitations are applied before the passive activity limitations.[54]

EXAMPLE 37

Shareholder Ricketts has a basis of $35,000 in his S corporation stock. He takes a $15,000 nonrecourse loan from a local bank and lends the proceeds to the S corporation. Ricketts now has a stock basis of $35,000 and a debt basis of $15,000. However, due to the at-risk limitation, he can deduct only $35,000 of losses from the S corporation. ∎

Passive Losses and Credits. Section 469 provides that net passive losses and credits are not deductible when incurred and must be carried over to a year when there is passive income. Thus, one must be aware of three major classes of income, losses, and credits—active, portfolio, and passive. S corporations are not directly subject to the limits of § 469, but corporate rental activities are inherently passive, and other activities of an S corporation may be passive unless the shareholder(s) materially participate(s) in operating the business. An S corporation may engage in more than one such activity. If the corporate activity is rental or the shareholders do not materially participate, any passive losses or credits flow through. The shareholders are able to apply the losses or credits only against their income from other passive activities.

A shareholder's stock basis is reduced by passive losses that flow through to the shareholder, even though the shareholder may not be entitled to a current deduction due to the passive loss limitations. The existence of material participation is determined at the shareholder level. There are seven tests for material participation, including a need to participate in the activity for more than 500 hours during the taxable year.[55]

---

[52]§ 1377(b)(1).
[53]§ 1371(b).

[54]Reg. § 1.469–2T(d)(6).
[55]Reg. § 1.469–5T(a).

EXAMPLE 38

Heather is a 50% owner of an S corporation engaged in a passive activity. A nonparticipating shareholder, she receives a salary of $6,000 for services as a result of the passive activity. Heather has $6,000 of earned income as a result of the salary. The $6,000 salary creates a $6,000 deduction/passive loss, which flows through to the shareholders. Heather's $3,000 share of the loss may not be deducted against the $6,000 of earned income. Under § 469(e)(3), earned income is not taken into account in computing the income or loss from a passive activity. ∎

LO.10

Compute the built-in gains tax.

Tax on Pre-Election Built-in Gain

Normally, an S corporation does *not* pay an income tax, since all items flow through to the shareholders. But an S corporation that was previously a C corporation may be required to pay a built-in gains tax, a LIFO recapture tax, or a passive investment income tax.

Without the **built-in gains tax** (§ 1374), it would be possible to avoid the corporate double tax on a disposition of appreciated property, by electing S corporation status.

EXAMPLE 39

Zinnia, Inc., a C corporation, owns a single asset with a basis of $100,000 and a fair market value of $500,000. If Zinnia sells this asset and distributes the cash to shareholders, there will be two levels of tax, one at the corporate level and one at the shareholder level. Alternatively, if Zinnia distributes the asset to shareholders, a double tax will still result, since a C corporation is taxed on an implicit gain in the distribution of the appreciated property. The shareholders have a dividend equal to the property's fair market value. In an attempt to avoid the double tax, Zinnia elects S corporation status. It then sells the asset and distributes the proceeds to shareholders. Without the § 1374 tax, the gain would be taxed only once, at the shareholder level. The distribution of the sales proceeds would be a tax-free reduction of stock basis and the AAA. ∎

The § 1374 tax generally applies to C corporations converting to S status after 1986. It is a *corporate-level* tax on any built-in gain recognized when the S corporation disposes of an asset in a taxable disposition within 10 calendar years after the date on which the S election took effect. The 10-year holding period begins on the date of the most recent S election.

General Rules. The base for the § 1374 tax includes any unrealized gain on appreciated assets (e.g., real estate, cash basis receivables, and goodwill) held by a corporation on the day it elects S status. The highest corporate tax rate (currently 35 percent) is applied to the unrealized gain when any of the assets are sold. Furthermore, the gain on the sale (net of the § 1374 tax)[56] passes through as a taxable gain to shareholders.

EXAMPLE 40

Assume the same facts as in the preceding example. Section 1374 imposes a corporate-level tax that must be paid by Zinnia if it sells the asset after electing S status. Upon sale of the asset, the corporation owes a tax of $140,000 ($400,000 × 35%). The shareholders have a $260,000 taxable gain ($400,000 − $140,000). Hence, the built-in gains tax effectively imposes a double tax on Zinnia and its shareholders. ∎

The maximum amount of gain that is recognized over the 10-year period is limited to the *aggregate net* built-in gain of the corporation at the time it converted to S status. Thus, at the time of the S election, unrealized gains of the corporation are offset against unrealized losses. The net amount of gains and losses sets an upper limit on the tax base for the built-in gains tax. Any appreciation after the conversion to S status is subject to the regular S corporation pass-through rules.

[56] § 1366(f)(2).

TAX *in the News*   **S CORPORATIONS DO PAY TAXES**

An S corporation may be subject to four different types of taxes: the built-in gains tax, the excess net passive income tax, the investment recapture tax, and the LIFO recapture tax. The built-in gains tax accounted for about 88.3 percent, or $336.4 million, of all Federal income taxes reported by S corporations in 2003. The excess net passive income tax pulled in only $4.4 million, but the LIFO recapture tax accounted for $39.2 million.

Quadrant, Inc., is a former C corporation whose first S corporation year began on January 1, 2008. At that time, Quadrant had two assets: X, with a value of $1,000 and a basis of $400, and Y, with a value of $400 and a basis of $600. The net unrealized built-in gain as of January 1, 2008, is $400 (i.e., X's $600 gain less Y's $200 loss). If asset X is sold for $1,200 during 2008, and asset Y is retained, the recognized built-in gain is limited to $400. The additional $200 of appreciation after electing S status is not part of the built-in gain. ■

EXAMPLE 41

Loss assets on the date of conversion reduce the maximum built-in gain and any potential tax under § 1374.[57] In addition, built-in losses and built-in gains are netted each year to determine the annual § 1374 tax base. Thus, an incentive exists to contribute loss assets to a corporation before electing S status. However, the IRS indicates that contributions of loss property within two years before the earlier of the date of conversion or the date of filing an S election are presumed to have a tax avoidance motive and will not reduce the corporation's net unrealized built-in gain.

Donna owns all the stock of an S corporation, which in turn owns two assets on the S conversion date: asset 1 (basis of $5,000 and fair market value of $2,500) and asset 2 (basis of $1,000 and fair market value of $5,000). The S corporation has a potential net realized built-in gain of $1,500 (i.e., the built-in gain of $4,000 in asset 2 reduced by the built-in loss of $2,500 in asset 1). However, if Donna contributed the loss asset to the corporation within two years before the S election, the built-in gain potential becomes $4,000; the loss asset cannot be used to reduce built-in gain. ■

EXAMPLE 42

The amount of built-in gain recognized in any year is limited to an "as if" taxable income for the year, computed as if the corporation were a C corporation. Any built-in gain that escapes taxation due to the taxable income limitation is carried forward and recognized in future tax years. Thus, a corporation can defer § 1374 tax liability whenever it has a low or negative taxable income.

Continue with the same facts as in Example 41, but assume that if Quadrant were a C corporation, its taxable income in 2008 would be $300. The amount of built-in gain subject to tax in 2008 is $300. The excess built-in gain of $100 is carried forward and taxed in 2009 (assuming adequate C corporation taxable income in that year). There is no statutory limit on the carryforward period, but the gain would effectively expire at the end of the 10-year recognition period applicable to all built-in gains.[58] ■

EXAMPLE 43

Normally, tax attributes of a C corporation do *not* carry over to a converted S corporation. For purposes of the tax on built-in gain, however, certain carryovers are allowed. In particular, an S corporation can offset built-in gains with unexpired NOLs or capital losses from C corporation years.

---

[57]§§ 1374(c)(2) and (d)(1).

[58]Installment sale gains can be taxed more than 10 years after the S election. § 1374(d)(7); Notice 90–27, 1990–1 C.B. 336.

CONCEPT SUMMARY 12–3

Calculation of the Built-in Gains Tax Liability

Step 1. Select the smaller of built-in gain or taxable income (C corporation rules).*
Step 2. Deduct unexpired NOLs and capital losses from C corporation tax years.
Step 3. Multiply the tax base obtained in step 2 by the top corporate income tax rate.
Step 4. Deduct any business credit carryforwards and AMT credit carryovers arising in a C corporation tax year from the amount obtained in step 3.
Step 5. The corporation pays any tax resulting from step 4.

*Any net recognized built-in gain in excess of taxable income is carried forward to the next year, as long as the next year is within the 10-year recognition period.

EXAMPLE 44

Maple Corporation elects S status, effective for calendar year 2008. Maple has a $10,000 NOL carryover when it elects S status. As of January 1, 2008, one of Maple's capital assets has a basis of $50,000 and a fair market value of $110,000. Early in 2008, the asset is sold for $110,000. Maple recognizes a $60,000 built-in gain when the asset is sold. However, Maple's NOL reduces the built-in gain from $60,000 to $50,000. Thus, only $50,000 is subject to the built-in gains tax. ■

Concept Summary 12–3 summarizes the calculation of the built-in gains tax.

LIFO Recapture Tax. When a corporation uses the FIFO method for its last year before making the S election, any built-in gain is recognized and taxed as the inventory is sold. A LIFO-basis corporation does not recognize this gain unless the corporation invades the LIFO layer during the 10-year recognition period. To preclude deferral of gain recognition under LIFO, any LIFO recapture amount at the time of the S election is subject to a corporate-level tax.

The taxable LIFO recapture amount equals the excess of the inventory's value under FIFO over the LIFO value. No negative adjustment is allowed if the LIFO value is higher than the FIFO value. The resulting tax is payable in four equal installments, with the first payment due on or before the due date for the corporate return for the last C corporation year (without regard to any extensions). The remaining three installments must be paid on or before the due dates of the succeeding corporate returns. No interest is due if payments are made by the due dates, and no estimated taxes are due on the four tax installments. The basis of the LIFO inventory is adjusted to account for this LIFO recapture amount, but the AAA is not decreased by payment of the tax.

Passive Investment Income Penalty Tax

LO.11

Compute the passive investment income penalty tax.

A tax is imposed on the excess passive income of S corporations that possess AEP from C corporation years. The tax rate is the highest corporate rate for the year (35 percent in 2008). The rate is applied to excess net passive income (ENPI), which is determined using the following formula:

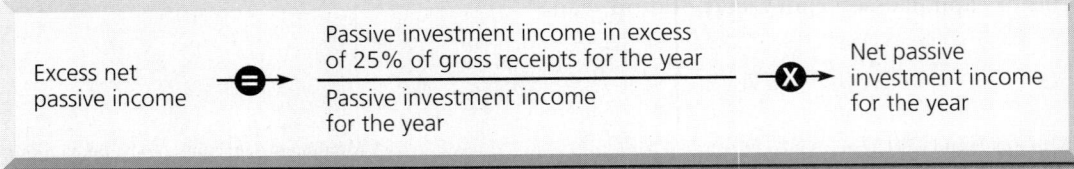

Excess net passive income $=$ $\dfrac{\text{Passive investment income in excess of 25\% of gross receipts for the year}}{\text{Passive investment income for the year}}$ $\times$ Net passive investment income for the year

TAX *in the News*   **THE SELF-EMPLOYMENT INCOME ADVANTAGE**

A significant advantage of an S corporation involves the current definition of self-employment income. Although compensation for services rendered to an S corporation is subject to FICA taxes, a shareholder's share of income from an S corporation is not self-employment income. The ration- ale for this S corporation loophole is that the S shareholder does not personally carry on the entity's trade or business. In contrast, the earned income of a partnership or proprietor- ship is treated as self-employment income to the partner or proprietor.

Passive investment income (PII) includes gross receipts derived from royalties, passive rents, dividends, interest, annuities, and sales and exchanges of stocks and securities (only capital gain from the sale of stocks and securities before May 26, 2007, or 2008 for calendar year taxpayers).[59] Only the net gain from the disposition of capital assets (other than stocks and securities) is taken into account in comput- ing gross receipts. Net passive income is passive income reduced by any deductions directly connected with the production of that income. Any passive income tax reduces the amount the shareholders must take into income.

The excess net passive income cannot exceed the C corporate taxable income for the year before considering any NOL deduction or the special deductions allowed by §§ 241–250 (except the organizational expense deduction of § 248).[60]

Barnhardt Corporation, an S corporation, has gross receipts for the year totaling $264,000 (of which $110,000 is PII). Expenditures directly connected to the production of the PII total $30,000. Therefore, Barnhardt has net PII of $80,000 ($110,000 − $30,000), and its PII for the tax year exceeds 25% of its gross receipts by $44,000 [$110,000 PII − (25% × $264,000)]. Excess net passive income (ENPI) is $32,000, calculated as follows.

EXAMPLE 45

$$\text{ENPI} = \frac{\$44,000}{\$110,000} \times \$80,000 = \$32,000$$

Barnhardt's PII tax is $11,200 ($32,000 × 35%). ■

Other Operational Rules

Several other points may be made about the possible effects of various Code provi- sions on S corporations.

- An S corporation is required to make estimated tax payments with respect to tax exposure because of any recognized built-in gain and excess passive invest- ment income.
- An S corporation may own stock in another corporation, but an S corporation may not have a C corporation shareholder. An S corporation is *not* eligible for a dividends received deduction.
- An S corporation is *not* subject to the 10 percent of taxable income limitation applicable to charitable contributions made by a C corporation.
- Any family member who renders services or furnishes capital to an S corpora- tion must be paid reasonable compensation. Otherwise, the IRS can make adjustments to reflect the value of the services or capital.[61] This rule may make it more difficult for related parties to shift Subchapter S taxable income to children or other family members.

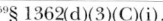

[59]§ 1362(d)(3)(C)(i).
[60]§§ 1374(d)(4) and 1375(a) and (b).

[61]§ 1366(e). In addition, beware of an IRS search for the "real owner" of the stock under Reg. § 1.1373–1(a)(2).

- Although § 1366(a)(1) provides for a flow-through of S items to a shareholder, it does not create self-employment income.[62] This treatment of earned income of S corporations is attractive compared to the treatment of a proprietorship or a partnership whose income is taxed as self-employment income to the owners. Compensation for services rendered to an S corporation is, however, subject to FICA taxes.

EXAMPLE 46

Cody and Dana each own one-third of a fast-food restaurant, and their 14-year-old son owns the other shares. Both parents work full-time in the restaurant operations, but the son works infrequently. Neither parent receives a salary this year, when the taxable income of the S corporation is $160,000. The IRS can require that reasonable compensation be paid to the parents to prevent the full one-third of the $160,000 from being taxed to the son. Otherwise, this would be an effective technique to shift earned income to a family member to reduce the total family tax burden. Furthermore, low or zero salaries can reduce FICA taxes due to the Federal government. ∎

- An S corporation is placed on the cash method of accounting for purposes of deducting business expenses and interest owed to a cash basis related party.[63] Thus, the timing of the shareholder's income and the corporate deduction must match.
- An S corporation may not deduct a payment to one of its shareholders, e.g., a year-end performance bonus, until the payee reports the income.
- The S election is not recognized by the District of Columbia and several states, including Connecticut, Michigan, New Hampshire, and Tennessee. Thus, some or all of the entity's income may be subject to a state-level income tax (e.g., a "sting tax" on large S corporations in Massachusetts).
- If § 1244 stock is issued to an S corporation, the S corporation and its shareholders may not treat losses on such stock as ordinary losses. However, an S corporation may issue § 1244 stock to its shareholders to obtain ordinary loss treatment.
- The § 1202 exclusion of gain on disposition of small business stock is *not* available for S stock.
- Losses may be disallowed due to a lack of a profit motive. If the activities at the corporate level are not profit motivated, the losses may be disallowed under the hobby loss rule of § 183.[64]
- For tax years ending on or after December 31, 2006, S corporations reporting assets of $10 million or more on Schedule L must file Schedule M–3.

ETHICAL and EQUITABLE *Considerations*

AVOIDING SCHEDULE M–3

Your S corporation client has read that a Schedule M–3 is now required for all S corporations with at least $10 million of assets. He says that the new schedule will reveal between 75 to 90 percent of the company's book-tax differences. Although this new schedule will help IRS agents find abusive transactions, he is concerned that it will impose additional compliance burdens. His corporation is approaching $10 million of assets, and he is thinking of either distributing some of the entity's business assets to himself or engaging in a spin-off. Are these techniques ethical?

---

[62]Rev.Rul. 59–221, 1959–1 C.B. 225.
[63]§ 267(b).

[64]*Michael J. Houston*, 69 TCM 2360, T.C.Memo. 1995–159; *Mario G. De Mendoza, III*, 68 TCM 42, T.C.Memo. 1994–314.

When the Election Is Advisable

Effective tax planning with S corporations begins with the determination of whether the election is appropriate. In this context, one should consider the following factors.

- Are losses from the business anticipated? If so, the S election may be highly attractive because these losses pass through to the shareholders.
- What are the tax brackets of the shareholders? If the shareholders are in high individual income tax brackets, it may be desirable to avoid S corporation status and have profits taxed to the corporation at lower C rates (e.g., 15 percent or 25 percent). However, the income still is not in the owners' hands.
- When the shareholders are in low individual income tax brackets, the pass-through of corporate profits is attractive, and reducing the combined income tax becomes the paramount consideration. Under these circumstances, the S election could be an effective tax planning tool. Note, however, that although an S corporation usually escapes Federal taxes, it may not be immune from state and local taxes imposed on corporations, or from several Federal penalty taxes.
- Does a C corporation have an NOL carryover from a prior year? Such a loss cannot be used in an S year (except for purposes of the built-in gains tax). Even worse, S years count in the 20-year carryover limitation. Thus, even if the S election is made, one might consider terminating the election before the carryover limitation expires. Such a termination would permit the loss to be utilized by what is now a C corporation.
- Both individuals and C corporations are subject to the alternative minimum tax. Many of the tax preference and adjustment items are the same, but some apply only to corporate taxpayers while others are limited to individuals. The alternative minimum tax adjustment relating to adjusted current earnings could create havoc with some C corporations (refer to Chapter 3). S corporations themselves are not subject to this tax.
- S corporations and partnerships have limited flexibility in the choice of a tax accounting period.[65]

Making a Proper Election

Once the parties have decided the election is appropriate, it becomes essential to ensure that the election is made properly.

- Make sure all shareholders consent. If any doubt exists concerning the shareholder status of an individual, it would be wise to have that party issue a consent anyway.[66] Too few consents are fatal to the election; the same cannot be said for too many consents.
- Be sure that the election is timely and properly filed. Either hand carry the election to an IRS office or send it by certified or registered mail. The date used to determine timeliness is the postmark date, not the date the IRS receives the election. A copy of the election should become part of the corporation's permanent files.
- Be careful to ascertain when the timely election period begins to run for a newly formed corporation. An election made too soon (before the corporation is in existence) is worse than one made too late. If serious doubts exist as to when this period begins, filing more than one election might be considered a practical means of guaranteeing the desired result.
- It still is beneficial for an S corporation to issue § 1244 stock (refer to Chapter 4). This type of stock allows the original shareholder to obtain an ordinary

---

[65]Entity tax-year constraints are discussed in Chapter 10.   [66]See *William B. Wilson*, 34 TCM 463, T.C.Memo. 1975–92.

TAX *in the News*   **AN ABUSIVE TAX SHELTER?**

During the 2004 presidential campaign, some tax practitioners pointed out that Democratic vice presidential candidate John Edwards had approximately $20 million of legal fees inside his S corporation in 1995. By paying himself a salary of only $360,000, he avoided paying almost $600,000 for the Medicare portion of FICA taxes (imposed at a rate of 2.9 percent).

There was considerable discussion of Edwards's tax situation in the media, and Vice President Dick Cheney mentioned the issue in the vice presidential debate. Reactions tended to follow the party affiliation of the commentator. In general, the $360,000 was probably less than reasonable compensation for Edwards (less than 2 percent of his legal fees), and the IRS could deem any distributions (i.e., recharacterize them) as wages subject to the FICA and FUTA taxes.

Even one of Edwards's defenders said that if these funds were distributed to the senator, he "was making use of an alleged 'tax shelter' and the IRS would be quite justified in treating the distributions as salary." Another commentator said that it was somewhat hypocritical for Edwards to express concern about the solvency of Medicare and Social Security when he had engaged in what seemed to be an attempt to evade the Medicare tax.

---

deduction for a loss on the sale or worthlessness of the stock, rather than long-term capital loss treatment. Shareholders have nothing to lose by complying with § 1244.

Preserving the Election

Recall that an election can be lost intentionally or unintentionally in several ways, and that a five-year waiting period generally is imposed before another S election is available. To preserve an S election, the following points should be kept in mind.

- As a starting point, all parties concerned should be made aware of the various transactions that lead to the loss of an election.
- Watch for possible disqualification of a small business corporation. For example, the death of a shareholder could result in a nonqualifying trust becoming a shareholder. The latter circumstance might be avoided by utilizing a buy-sell agreement or binding the deceased shareholder's estate to turn in the stock to the corporation for redemption or, as an alternative, to sell it to the surviving shareholders.[67]

Planning for the Operation of the Corporation

Operating an S corporation to achieve optimum tax savings for all parties involved requires a great deal of care and, most important, an understanding of the applicable tax rules.

Accumulated Adjustments Account. Although the corporate-level accumulated adjustments account (AAA) is used primarily by an S corporation with accumulated earnings and profits (AEP) from a Subchapter C year, all S corporations should maintain an accurate record of the AAA. Because there is a grace period for distributing the AAA after termination of the S election, the parties must be in a position to determine the balance of the account.

EXAMPLE 47

Nobles, Inc., an S corporation, has no C corporation AEP. Over the years, Nobles made no attempt to maintain an accurate accounting for the AAA. Now, the S election has been

---

[67]See Chapter 18 for a discussion of buy-sell agreements. Most such agreements do not create a second class of S stock. Rev.Rul. 85–161, 1985–2 C.B. 191; *Portage Plastics Co. v. U.S.*, 72–2 USTC ¶9567, 30 AFTR2d 72–5229, 470 F.2d 308 (CA–7, 1973).

terminated, and Nobles has a grace period for distributing the AAA tax-free to its shareholders. A great deal of time and expense may be necessary to reconstruct the AAA balance. ■

When AEP is present, a negative AAA may cause double taxation of S corporation income. With a negative AAA, the recognition of current income restores the negative AAA balance to zero, but a subsequent distribution then is considered to be in excess of AAA and is taxable as a dividend to the extent of AEP. Distributions during the year reduce the stock basis for determining the allowable loss for the year, but the loss does *not* reduce the stock basis for determining the tax status of distributions made during the year. In determining the tax treatment of distributions by an S corporation having AEP, any net adjustments (e.g., excess of losses and deductions over income) for the tax year are ignored.

The AAA bypass election may be used to reduce exposure to the accumulated earnings tax or personal holding company tax in post-S years. This bypass election allows AEP to be distributed instead.

EXAMPLE 48

Zebra, Inc., an S corporation during 2007, has a significant amount in its AEP account. The shareholders expect to terminate the election in 2008, when Zebra will be subject to the lower corporate income tax rates. Since Zebra as a C corporation may be subject to the accumulated earnings penalty tax in 2008, the shareholders may wish to use the AAA bypass election to distribute some or all of the AEP. Of course, any distributions of the AEP account in 2007 would be taxable to the shareholders. ■

A net loss allocated to a shareholder reduces the AAA. This required adjustment should encourage an S corporation to make annual distributions of net income to avoid the reduction of an AAA by a future net loss.

Salary Structure. The amount of salary paid to a shareholder-employee of an S corporation can have varying tax consequences and should be considered carefully. Larger amounts might be advantageous if the maximum contribution allowed for the shareholder-employee under the corporation's retirement plan has not been reached. Smaller amounts may be beneficial if the parties are trying to shift taxable income to lower-bracket shareholders, reduce payroll taxes, curtail a reduction of Social Security benefits, or restrict losses that do not pass through because of the basis limitation.

A strategy of decreasing compensation and correspondingly increasing distributions to shareholder-employees often results in substantial savings in employment taxes. However, a shareholder of an S corporation cannot always perform substantial services and arrange to receive distributions rather than compensation so that the corporation may avoid paying employment taxes. The IRS may deem the shareholder to be an employee, with any distributions recharacterized as wages subject to FICA and FUTA taxes.[68] In effect, the IRS requires that reasonable compensation be paid to shareholder-employees. For planning purposes, some level of compensation should be paid to all shareholder-employees to avoid any recharacterization of nonpassive distributions as deductible salaries—especially in personal service corporations.

The IRS can require that reasonable compensation be paid to family members who render services or provide capital to the S corporation. The IRS also can adjust the items taken into account by family-member shareholders to reflect the value of services or capital they provided. Refer to Example 46.

Unreasonable compensation traditionally has not been a problem for S corporations, but deductible compensation under § 162 reduces an S corporation's

---

[68]Rev.Rul. 74–44, 1974–1 C.B. 287; *Spicer Accounting, Inc. v. U.S.*, 91–1 USTC ¶50,103, 66 AFTR2d 90–5806, 918 F.2d 90 (CA–9, 1990); *Radtke v. U.S.*, 90–1 USTC ¶50,113, 65 AFTR2d 90–1155, 895 F.2d 1196 (CA–7, 1990).

taxable income, which is relevant to the built-in gains tax. Compensation may be one of the larger items that an S corporation can use to reduce taxable income to minimize any built-in gains penalty tax. Thus, IRS agents may attempt to classify compensation as unreasonable to increase the § 1374 tax.

A number of tax-free fringe benefits are denied to a more-than-2 percent shareholder-employee of an S corporation. Such benefits include group term life insurance, medical insurance, and meals and lodging furnished for the convenience of the employer. These items are treated as wages and are subject to most payroll taxes. The employee can take a 100 percent deduction on his or her tax return for medical insurance premiums.

Loss Considerations. A net loss in excess of tax basis may be carried forward and deducted only by the same shareholder in succeeding years. Thus, before disposing of the stock, a shareholder should increase the basis of such stock/loan to flow through the loss. The next shareholder does not obtain the loss carryover.

Any unused loss carryover in existence upon the termination of the S election may be deducted only in the next tax year and is limited to the individual's *stock* basis (not loan basis) in the post-termination year.[69] The shareholder may wish to purchase more stock to increase the tax basis in order to absorb the loss.

The NOL provisions create a need for sound tax planning during the last election year and the post-termination transition period. If it appears that the S corporation is going to sustain an NOL or use up any loss carryover, each shareholder's basis should be analyzed to determine if it can absorb the share of the loss. If basis is insufficient to absorb the loss, further investments should be considered before the end of the post-termination transition year. Such investments can be accomplished through additional stock purchases from the corporation, or from other shareholders, to increase basis. This action ensures the full benefit from the NOL carryover.

EXAMPLE 49

A calendar year C corporation has an NOL of $20,000 in 2007. The corporation makes a valid S election in 2008 and has another $20,000 NOL in that year. At all times during 2008, the stock of the corporation was owned by the same 10 shareholders, each of whom owned 10% of the stock. Tim, one of the 10 shareholders, has an adjusted basis of $1,800 at the beginning of 2008. None of the 2007 NOL may be carried forward into the S year. Although Tim's share of the 2008 NOL is $2,000, the deduction for the loss is limited to $1,800 in 2008 with a $200 carryover. ■

Avoiding the Passive Investment Income Tax. Too much passive investment income (PII) may cause an S corporation to incur a § 1375 penalty tax and/or terminate the S election. Several planning techniques can be used to avoid both of these unfavorable events. Where a small amount of AEP exists, an AAA bypass election may be appropriate to purge the AEP, thereby avoiding the passive income tax altogether. Alternatively, the corporation might reduce taxable income below the excess net passive income; similarly, PII might be accelerated into years in which there is an offsetting NOL. In addition, the tax can be avoided if the corporation manufactures needed gross receipts. By increasing gross receipts without increasing PII, the amount of PII in excess of 25 percent of gross receipts is reduced. Finally, performing significant services or incurring significant costs with respect to rental real estate activities can elevate the rent income to nonpassive.

EXAMPLE 50

An S corporation has paid a passive income penalty tax for two consecutive years. In the next year, the corporation has a large amount of AAA. If the AEP account is small, a bypass election may be appropriate to purge the corporation of the AEP. Without any AEP, no passive investment income tax applies, and the S election is not terminated. Any distribution of AEP to the shareholders constitutes taxable dividends, however.

---

[69]§ 1366(d)(3).

FIGURE 12–2   **Four Alternatives to Reduce Tax Liabilities for Passive-Type C Corporations Electing S Treatment**

Alternative 1: Eliminate AEP before the S election by paying dividends, taxed at the 0/15% rate.
Alternative 2: Liquidate the C corporation and reincorporate as an S corporation. Exposure to the AEP is eliminated.

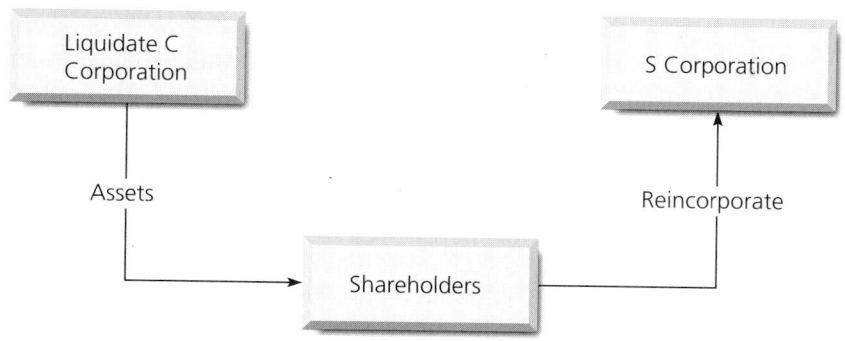

Possible capital gain treatment

Alternative 3: If the AEP amount is small, become an S corporation with possible built-in gains. Use an AAA bypass election to eliminate the AEP by paying a dividend taxed at the 0/15% rate.
Alternative 4: Make an S election, retaining the AEP. Use the following techniques to avoid/reduce the passive investment income tax.
a. Reduce taxable income below excess passive income.
b. Accelerate PII into future years when there is an NOL.
c. Generate more gross receipts.
d. Perform significant services or incur significant costs if a rental type of business.

Another alternative is to manufacture a large amount of gross receipts without increasing PII through an action such as a merger with a grocery store. If the gross receipts from the grocery store are substantial, the amount of the PII in excess of 25% of gross receipts is reduced. ◼

Figure 12–2 shows four alternatives that a C corporation that intends to elect S treatment may use to reduce its tax liability.

Managing the Built-in Gains Tax. The taxable income limitation encourages an S corporation to create deductions or accelerate deductions in the years that built-in gains are recognized. Although the postponed built-in gain is carried forward to future years, the time value of money makes the postponement beneficial. For example, payment of compensation, rather than a distribution, creates a deduction that reduces taxable income and postpones the built-in gains tax.

EXAMPLE 51

Mundy, Inc., an S corporation converted from a C corporation, has built-in gain of $110,000 and taxable income of $120,000 before payment of salaries to its two shareholders. If Mundy pays at least $120,000 in salaries to the shareholders (rather than a distribution), its taxable income drops to zero, and the built-in gains tax is postponed. Thus, Mundy needs to keep the salaries as high as possible to postpone the built-in gains tax in future years and reap a benefit from the time value of money. Of course, paying the salaries may increase the payroll tax burden if the salaries are below FICA and FUTA limits. ◼

Giving built-in gain property to a charitable organization does not trigger the built-in gains tax. To reduce or eliminate the built-in gains tax, built-in *loss* property may be sold in the same year that built-in gain property is sold. Generally, the taxpayer should sell built-in loss property in a year when an equivalent amount of built-in gain property is sold. Otherwise, the built-in loss could be wasted.

EXAMPLE 52

Green Corporation elects S status effective for calendar year 2007. As of January 1, 2007, Green's only asset has a basis of $40,000 and a fair market value of $100,000. If this asset is sold for $120,000 in 2008, Green recognizes an $80,000 gain, of which $60,000 is subject to the corporate built-in gains tax. The other $20,000 of gain is subject to the S corporation pass-through rules and is not subject to the corporate income tax.

Unless the taxpayer can show otherwise, any appreciation existing at the date of the sale or exchange is presumed to be preconversion built-in gain. Therefore, Green incurs a built-in gain of $80,000 unless it can prove that the $20,000 gain developed after the effective date of the election. ■

Controlling Adjustments and Preference Items. The individual alternative minimum tax (AMT) affects more taxpayers than ever before because the tax base has expanded and the difference between regular tax rates and the individual AMT rate has been narrowed. In an S corporation setting, tax preferences flow through proportionately to the shareholders, who, in computing the individual AMT, treat the preferences as if they were directly realized. Thus, the S corporation may not take advantage of the AMT exemption available to a small corporation, but there is no ACE adjustment. Further, if an S corporation has a built-in gain under § 1374, the entity does not pay an AMT on the transaction.

A flow-through of tax preferences can be a tax disaster for a shareholder who is an "almost-AMT taxpayer." Certain steps can be taken to protect such a shareholder from being pushed into the AMT. For example, a large S corporation preference from tax-exempt interest on private activity bonds could adversely affect an "almost-AMT taxpayer." Certain adjustment and preference items are subject to elections that can remove them from a shareholder's AMT computation. Certain positive adjustments can be removed from a shareholder's alternative minimum taxable income base if the S corporation elects to capitalize and amortize certain expenditures over a prescribed period of time. These expenditures include excess intangible drilling and development expenditures, research and experimental costs, mining exploration and development expenditures, and circulation expenses.

Other corporate choices can protect an "almost-AMT shareholder." Using a slower method of cost recovery (rather than a more accelerated method) can be beneficial to certain shareholders. Many of these decisions and elections may generate conflicts of interest, however, with other shareholders who are not so situated and would not suffer from the flow-through of adjustments and tax preference items.

EXAMPLE 53

Tallis, Ltd., an S corporation, is owned equally by Ann, Bob, and Chris. Ann and Bob are subject to a 40% net state and Federal marginal tax rate, while Chris is subject to the AMT. Tallis put the following into service this year.

- Depreciable assets: MACRS deductions per shareholder, $14,290; AMT cost recovery per shareholder, $10,714.
- Mining exploration costs: Regular tax deduction per shareholder, $30,000; AMT deduction per shareholder, $20,000.

Ann and Bob favor the larger regular tax deductions. Chris would like Tallis to elect to use the AMT deduction amounts for regular tax purposes. If the corporation does this, it eliminates the shareholders' related AMT adjustments for the lives of these assets. At the same time, the election does away with Chris's individual-level AMT on these items. Thus, Tallis's tax choice is between:

- Larger deductions at no AMT cost for Ann and Bob.
- Lower deductions and a higher tax base for all shareholders, which would save Chris the related AMT. ■

Allocation of Tax Items. If a shareholder dies or stock is transferred during the taxable year, tax items may be allocated under the pro rata approach or the per-books method. Without the per-books election, a shareholder's pro rata share of tax items is determined by assigning an equal portion of each item to each day of the tax year and then dividing that portion pro rata among the shares outstanding on the transfer day.

With the consent of all affected shareholders and the corporation, an S corporation can elect to allocate tax items according to the permanent records using normal tax accounting rules. The allocation is made as if the taxable year consists of two taxable years. The first portion ends on the date of termination. On the day the shares are transferred, the shares are considered owned by the disposing shareholder. The selected method may be beneficial to the terminating shareholder and harmful to the acquiring shareholder. An election might result in a higher allocation of losses to a taxpayer who is better able to utilize the losses. In the case of the death of a shareholder, a per-books election prevents the income and loss allocation to a deceased shareholder from being affected by postdeath events.

Domestic Production Activities Deduction. The § 199 deduction is determined at the shareholder level. Domestic production gross receipts (DPGR), attributable cost of goods sold (CGS), and allocable deductions earned by the S corporation are passed through to the shareholders. These corporate-level DPGR, CGS, and allocable deductions are combined with any DPGR, CGS, and allocable deductions that the shareholder has from other sources.

An allocable portion of the S corporation's W–2 wages is passed through to the shareholder, but only those wages that are properly allocable to DPGR. Thus, a shareholder is treated as having been paid wages equal to the shareholder's distributable share of wages from the S corporation. See Chapter 3 for the calculation of the qualified domestic production activities deduction.[70]

EXAMPLE 54

An S corporation has $100,000 DPGR and $75,000 of wages, and its qualified production activities income (QPAI) is $25,000. Shareholder Kirby has a 50% interest in the S corporation. All expenses that reduce DPGR are from wages, and all wages paid relate to DPGR.

Kirby is allocated $12,500 of QPAI and $37,500 of wages. Kirby's wage limitation is $18,750 (0.50 × $37,500), but he needs only $750 of wages (6% × $12,500) to cover the QPAI from the S corporation. If Kirby has other QPAI but no wages, the law is not clear as to whether Kirby can use the excess wages of $18,000 for his separate QPAI. ∎

The § 199 deduction has no effect on a shareholder's stock basis. Further, an S corporation may qualify for the small business simplified overall method to apportion cost of goods sold and deductions between DPGR and non-DPGR at the entity level. The IRS may permit an S corporation to calculate a shareholder's share of QPAI at the entity level, to be combined with the shareholder's QPAI. A specific shareholder is not allowed to use another cost allocation method to reallocate the costs of the S corporation, regardless of the method used by the specific shareholder to allocate or apportion costs.

Termination Aspects. It is always advisable to avoid accumulated earnings and profits (AEP) in an S corporation. There is the ever-present danger of terminating the election because of excess passive investment income in three consecutive years. Further, the § 1375 penalty tax is imposed on excess passive net income. Thus, one should try to eliminate such AEP through a dividend distribution or liquidation of the S corporation with a subsequent reincorporation. If the AEP account is small, to eliminate the problem all of the shareholders may consent

---

[70]§ 199(d)(1)(A).

under § 1368(e)(3) to have distributions treated as made first from AEP rather than from the AAA (the AAA bypass election).

Liquidation of an S Corporation. S corporations are subject to many of the same liquidation rules applicable to C corporations (refer to Chapter 6). In general, the distribution of appreciated property to S shareholders in complete liquidation is treated as if the property were sold to the shareholders in a taxable transaction. Unlike a C corporation, however, the S corporation itself incurs no incremental tax on the liquidation gains, because such gains flow through to the shareholders subject only to the built-in gains tax of § 1374. Any corporate gain increases the shareholder's stock basis by a like amount and reduces any gain realized by the shareholder when he or she receives the liquidation proceeds. Thus, an S corporation usually avoids the double tax that is imposed on C corporations. However, when an S corporation liquidates, all of its special tax attributes disappear (e.g., AAA, AEP, PTI, C corporation NOLs, suspended losses).

KEY TERMS

Accumulated adjustments account (AAA), 12–15

Accumulated earnings and profits, 12–15

Built-in gains tax, 12–26

Bypass election, 12–17

Other adjustments account (OAA), 12–17

Passive investment income (PII), 12–10

Previously taxed income (PTI), 12–16

S corporation, 12–2

Small business corporation, 12–5

Subchapter S, 12–2

Voluntary revocation, 12–10

PROBLEM MATERIALS

DISCUSSION QUESTIONS

1. The C corporation penalty taxes such as the accumulated earnings tax, personal holding company tax, and alternative minimum tax apply to the S corporation. Discuss the validity of this statement.

2. Can NOL carryovers from prior C years be used in an S corporation year?

3. Do maximum or minimum dollar sales or capitalization restrictions apply to S corporations? Explain.

4. Which of the following can be a shareholder of an S corporation?
   a. Partnership.
   b. Corporation.
   c. Nonresident alien.
   d. Estate.
   e. Charitable organization exempted from taxation.
   f. IRA.
   g. Minor child.

Issue ID

Communications

5. Bob Roman, the major owner of an S corporation, approaches you for some tax planning help. He would like to exchange some real estate in a like-kind transaction under § 1031 for some real estate that may have some environmental liabilities. Prepare a letter to Bob outlining your suggestion. Bob's address is 8411 Huron Boulevard, West Chester, PA 19382.

Issue ID

6. On March 2, the two 50% shareholders of a calendar year corporation decide to elect S status. One of the shareholders, Terry, purchased her stock from a previous shareholder

(a nonresident alien) on January 18. Identify any potential problems for Terry or the corporation.

7. Define "members of the family" for purposes of the number-of-shareholders requirement for an S corporation.

8. May S corporations be partners in a partnership or shareholders in a corporation?

9. Explain the election process for an S corporation.

10. Elvis Samford calls you and says that his two-person S corporation was involuntarily terminated in February 2007. He asks you if they can make a new S election now, in November 2008. Draft a memo for the file, outlining what you told Elvis.

Communications

11. How is a $120,000 long-term capital gain treated with respect to an S corporation and its 20% shareholder?

12. Using the categories in the following legend, classify each transaction as a plus (+) or minus (−) on Schedule M-2 of Form 1120S. An answer might look like one of these: "+AAA" or "−PTI."

Legend

PTI = Shareholders' undistributed taxable income previously taxed
AAA = Accumulated adjustments account
OAA = Other adjustments account
NA = No direct effect on Schedule M-2

a. Receipt of tax-exempt interest income.
b. Unreasonable compensation determined.
c. Depreciation recapture income.
d. Distribution of nontaxable income (PTI) from 1981.
e. Nontaxable life insurance proceeds.
f. Expenses related to tax-exempt securities.
g. Charitable contributions.
h. Business gifts in excess of $25.
i. Nondeductible fines and penalties.
j. Selling expenses.

13. Collett's S corporation has a small amount of accumulated earnings and profits (AEP), requiring the use of the more complex distribution rules. His accountant tells him that this AEP forces the maintenance of the AAA figure each year. Identify relevant tax issues facing Collett.

Issue ID

14. Caleb Hudson owns 10% of an S corporation. He is confused with respect to his AAA and stock basis. Write a brief memo dated November 1, 2008, to Caleb identifying the key differences between AAA and his stock basis.

Communications

15. What is PTI?

16. For each of the following independent statements, indicate whether the transaction will increase (+), decrease (−), or have no effect (*NE*) on the adjusted basis of a shareholder's stock in an S corporation.
a. Expenses related to tax-exempt income.
b. Long-term capital gain.
c. Nonseparately computed loss.
d. Section 1231 gain.
e. Depletion *not* in excess of basis.
f. Separately computed income.
g. Nontaxable return-of-capital distribution by the corporation.
h. Selling expenses.
i. Business gifts in excess of $25.
j. Depreciation recapture income.
k. Dividends received by the S corporation.

l.   LIFO recapture tax at S election.
m.   Recovery of a bad debt previously deducted.
n.   Short-term capital loss.
o.   Corporate distribution out of AAA.

17. Milton, a 51% owner of an S corporation, has a stock basis of zero at the beginning of the year. Milton's basis in a $30,000 loan made to the S corporation and evidenced by a corporate note has been reduced to zero by pass-through losses. During the year, his net share of corporate ordinary income is $12,000. At the end of the year, Milton receives a $14,000 distribution. Discuss the related income tax consequences.

Issue ID

18. Sheila Jackson is a 50 percent shareholder in Washington, an S corporation. This year, Jackson's share of the Washington loss is $100,000. Jackson has income from several other sources. Identify at least four tax issues that relate to the effects of the S corporation loss on Jackson's tax return.

19. Explain how an S corporation may use unexpired NOLs or capital losses from C corporation years.

Decision Making

20. One of your clients is considering electing S status. Texas, Inc., is a six-year-old company with two equal shareholders, both of whom paid $30,000 for their stock. Going into 2008, Texas has a $110,000 NOL carryforward from prior years. Estimated income is $40,000 for 2008 and $25,000 for each of the next three years. Should Texas make an S election for 2008?

21. A corporation uses the LIFO method for its last year before making an S election. What effect will this have on any built-in gains tax?

22. When AEP is present, how can negative AAA cause double taxation of S corporation income?

23. How do owners of an S corporation treat their own compensation from the entity?

PROBLEMS

24. An S corporation's profit and loss statement shows net profits of $90,000 (book income). The corporation has three equal shareholders. From supplemental data, you obtain the following information about some items that are included in the $90,000.

Selling expenses	($21,200)
Municipal bond interest income	2,000
Dividends received on IBM stock	9,000
§ 1231 gain	6,000
Depreciation recapture income	13,000
Recovery of bad debts	4,000
Long-term capital loss	(9,000)
Salary paid to owners (each)	(11,000)
Cost of goods sold	(97,000)

a.   Determine nonseparately computed income or loss.
b.   What would be the portion of taxable income or loss for Chang, one of the three shareholders?

25. Saul, Inc., a calendar year S corporation, incurred the following items.

Sales	$130,000
Depreciation recapture income	12,000
Short-term capital gain	30,000
Cost of goods sold	(42,000)
Municipal bond interest income	7,000
Administrative expenses	(15,000)
Depreciation expense	(17,000)
Charitable contributions	(14,000)

Calculate Saul's nonseparately computed income.

26. Zebra, Inc., a calendar year S corporation, incurred the following items.

Sales	$100,000
Cost of goods sold	(40,000)
Depreciation expense	(10,000)
Administrative expenses	(5,000)
§ 1231 gain	21,000
Depreciation recapture income	20,000
Short-term capital loss from stock sale	(6,000)
Long-term capital loss from stock sale	(4,000)
Long-term capital gain from stock sale	15,000
Charitable contributions	(4,500)

Sammy is a 40% shareholder throughout the year.
a. Calculate Sammy's share of nonseparately computed income.
b. Calculate Sammy's share of the short-term capital loss.

27. Noon, Inc., a calendar year S corporation, is equally owned by Ralph and Thomas. Thomas dies on April 1 (not a leap year), and his estate selects a March 31 fiscal year. Noon has $400,000 of income for January 1 through March 31 and $600,000 for the remainder of the year.
a. Determine how income is allocated to Ralph and Thomas under the pro rata approach.
b. Determine how income is allocated to Ralph and Thomas under the per-books method.

28. Nashville, Inc., a calendar year S corporation, has an AAA amount of $762,000 at the beginning of 2008. During the year the following items occurred.

Operating income	$216,000
Loss from real estate operations	(4,000)
Insurance proceeds	100,000
Dividend income	17,000
Interest income	3,000
Charitable contributions	(22,000)
§ 179 depreciation expense	(2,500)
Administrative expenses	(35,000)
Premiums paid for life insurance	(3,600)
Cash distributions to shareholders	$ 62,100

Calculate Nashville's ending AAA balance.

29. Goblins, Inc., a calendar year S corporation, has $90,000 of AEP. Tobias, the sole shareholder, has an adjusted basis of $80,000 in his stock with a zero balance in the AAA. Determine the tax aspects if a $90,000 salary is paid to Tobias.

Decision Making

30. Assume the same facts as in Problem 29, except that Goblins pays Tobias a $90,000 dividend from AEP.

Decision Making

31. Trugman, Inc., a calendar year S corporation, is owned equally by four shareholders: Abe, Beth, Charlene, and Don. The company owns a plot of land that was purchased for $120,000 several years ago. On November 4, 2008, when the land is worth $200,000, it is distributed to Don. Assuming Don's basis in the S corporation is $320,000 on the distribution date, what are the tax ramifications?

32. During the year, a calendar year S corporation in Baton Rouge, Louisiana, has a positive AMT adjustment of $65,000 for mining exploration costs, an excess depletion tax preference of $95,000, and a certified pollution control facility positive adjustment of $35,000. The firm's positive ACE adjustment is $130,000. If Marian Callier is a one-fifth shareholder, what effects do these items have on her individual tax return?

Decision Making

Communications

33. In 2008, Ourso, Inc., an S corporation with one shareholder, has a loss of $55,000 and makes a distribution of $70,000 to the shareholder, Bip Wallace. Bip's stock basis at the beginning of the year is $100,000. Write a memo dated October 21, 2008, to your manager discussing any problem that may result and the possible solution.

34. Fabrizius, Inc., an S corporation in Saint Cloud, Minnesota, had a balance in AAA of $100,000 and AEP of $55,000 on December 31, 2008. During 2009, Fabrizius distributes $70,000 to its shareholders, while sustaining a loss of $60,000. Determine any balance in the AAA and the AEP account.

35. At the beginning of the year, Malcolm, a 50% shareholder of a calendar year S corporation, has a stock basis of $22,000. During the year, the corporation has ordinary income of $32,000. The following data are obtained from supplemental sources.

Dividends received from IBM	$12,000
Municipal bond interest income tax exempt int.	18,000
Short-term capital gain	6,000
Depreciation recapture income	10,000
§ 1231 gain	7,000
Charitable contributions	(5,000)
Political contributions	(8,000)
Short-term capital loss	(12,000)
Cash distributions to Malcolm	8,000
Selling expense	(14,000)
Beginning AAA	40,000

   a.   Compute Malcolm's ending stock basis.
   b.   Compute ending AAA.

36. Money, Inc., a calendar year S corporation in Denton, Texas, has two unrelated shareholders, each owning 50% of the stock. Both shareholders have a $400,000 stock basis as of January 1, 2008. At the beginning of 2008, Money has AAA of $300,000 and AEP of $600,000. During 2008, Money has operating income of $100,000. At the end of the year, Money distributes securities worth $1 million, with an adjusted basis of $800,000. Determine the tax effects of these transactions.

37. Assume the same facts as in Problem 36, except that the two shareholders consent to an AAA bypass election.

38. Jeff, a 52% owner of an S corporation, has a stock basis of zero at the beginning of the year. Jeff's basis in a $10,000 loan made to the corporation and evidenced by a corporate note has been reduced to zero by pass-through losses. During the year, his net share of the corporate taxable income is $11,000. At the end of the year, Jeff receives a $15,000 distribution. Discuss the tax effects of the distribution.

39. Assume the same facts as in Problem 38, except that there is no $15,000 distribution, but the corporation repays the loan principal to Jeff. Discuss the tax effects.

40. Assume the same facts as in Problem 38, except that Jeff's share of corporate taxable income is only $8,000, and there is no distribution. However, the corporation repays the $10,000 loan principal to Jeff. Discuss the tax effects. Assume there was no corporate note (i.e., only an account payable). Does this change your answer?

Issue ID

41. Red Dragon, Inc., is an S corporation with a sizable amount of AEP from a C corporation year. The S corporation has $400,000 investment income and $400,000 investment expense in 2008. The company makes cash distributions to enable its sole shareholder to pay her taxes. What are the tax aspects to consider?

42. On January 1, Bobby and Alicia own equally all of the stock of an electing S corporation called Prairie Dirt Delight. The company has a $60,000 loss for the year (not a leap year). On the 219th day of the year, Bobby sells his half of the stock to his son, Bubba. How much of the $60,000 loss, if any, is allocated to Bubba?

43. Flower, Inc., an S corporation, has a $70,000 operating loss during the year (not a leap year). At the beginning of the year, Babe and Sally each own one-half of the stock. On the 219th day of the year, Babe sells her half of the stock to Sammie. How much of the ordinary loss flows through to Babe?

44. A calendar year S corporation has an ordinary loss of $80,000 and a capital loss of $20,000. Ms. Muhammad owns 30% of the corporate stock and has a $24,000 basis in her stock. Determine the amounts of the ordinary loss and capital loss, if any, that flow through to Ms. Muhammad. Prepare a tax memo for the files dated December 3, 2008.

Communications

45. An S corporation reports the following items for 2008.

Built-in gain	$110,000
Taxable income	90,000
NOL carryforward from a C corporation year	12,000
Capital loss carryforward from a C year	8,000
Business credit carryforward from a C year	4,000

Calculate any built-in gains tax liability.

46. Englelage, Inc., converts from a C corporation to an S corporation at the beginning of 2008. The company used the LIFO inventory method in 2007 and reported an ending LIFO inventory value of $110,000 (FIFO value of $190,000). Calculate any tax consequences from this conversion.

47. Savoy, Inc., in Auburn, Alabama, is an accrual basis S corporation with three equal shareholders. The three cash basis shareholders have the following stock basis at the beginning of the year: Andre, $12,000; Crum, $22,000; and Barbara, $28,000. Savoy has the following income and expense items.

Net tax operating loss	($30,000)
Short-term capital gain	37,500
Long-term capital loss	(6,000)
Nondeductible fees and penalties	3,000

The electing corporation distributes $5,000 cash to each of the shareholders during the tax year. Calculate the shareholders' stock bases at the end of the year.

48. Yates Corporation in Cutoff, Louisiana, elects S status, effective for calendar year 2008. Yates' only asset has a basis of $50,200 and a fair market value of $110,400 as of January 1, 2008. The asset is sold at the end of 2008 for $130,800. What are the tax aspects of this transaction for Mark Farris, a 60% owner of the company?

49. Bonnie and Clyde each own one-third of a fast-food restaurant, and their 13-year-old daughter owns the other shares. Both parents work full-time in the restaurant, but the daughter works infrequently. Neither Bonnie nor Clyde receives a salary during the year, when the ordinary income of the S corporation is $180,000. An IRS agent estimates that reasonable salaries for Bonnie, Clyde, and the daughter are $30,000, $35,000, and $10,000, respectively. What adjustments would you expect the IRS to impose upon these taxpayers?

Issue ID

50. Friedman, Inc., an S corporation, holds some highly appreciated land and inventory, and some marketable securities that have declined in value. It anticipates a sale of these assets and a complete liquidation of the company over the next two years. Arnold Schwartz, the CFO, calls you, asking how to treat these transactions. Prepare a tax memo dated June 18, 2008, indicating what you told Arnold over the phone.

Communications

51. Claude Bergeron sold 1,000 shares of Ditta, Inc., an S corporation located in Concord, North Carolina, for $9,000. He has a stock basis of $107,000 in the shares. Assuming that Claude is single and that he is the original owner of these § 1244 stock shares, calculate the appropriate tax treatment of any gain or loss. If he sold the stock for $201,000, could he obtain a 50% exclusion under § 1202 for any gain?

52. Sam, a single individual, is the sole shareholder of an S corporation, which owns a 30% interest in a partnership. In turn, the partnership owns stock in a C corporation, and the stock qualifies as § 1244 stock. The partnership sells the stock at a loss of $120,000. Discuss Sam's current treatment of the loss.

Decision Making

53. Opal is the owner of all of the shares of an S corporation. Opal is considering receiving a salary of $80,000 from the business. She will pay 7.65% FICA taxes on the salary, and the S corporation will pay the same amount of FICA tax. If Opal reduces her salary to $60,000 and takes an additional $20,000 as a distribution, how much total tax could be saved?

54. Blue Corporation elects S status effective for calendar year 2007. As of January 1, 2007, Blue holds two assets.

	Adjusted Basis	Fair Market Value
Land	$50,000	$110,000
IBM Stock	55,000	40,000

Blue sells the land in 2008 for $120,000. Calculate Blue's recognized built-in gain, if any, in 2008.

Decision Making

55. A calendar year C corporation elects S status for 2008. It generates an NOL of $44,000 in 2007 and an NOL of $33,000 in 2008. At all times in 2007 and 2008, the stock of the corporation is owned by the same 10 shareholders, each of whom holds 10% of the stock. Melvin, one of the 10 shareholders, has an adjusted stock basis of $2,300 at the beginning of 2008. Discuss any tax aspects for Melvin.

TAX RETURN PROBLEMS

H&R BLOCK TaxCut

1. Dana Mitchell (243–58–8695) and Deborah Marshall (221–51–8695) are 70% and 30% owners of Dana, Inc. (73–8264911), a candy company located at 145 Avenue A, Dime Box, TX 77823. The company's S corporation election was made on January 15, 2005. The following information was taken from the income statement for 2007.

Tax-exempt income	$ 10,000
Net rent income	50,000
Interest income	100,000
Gross sales receipts	1,100,000
Beginning inventory	9,607
Direct labor	103,102
Direct materials purchased	178,143
Direct other costs	49,356
Ending inventory	3,467
Salaries and wages	42,103
Officers' salaries	50,000
Repairs	16,106
Depreciation	15,254
Interest expense	5,222
Rent expense (operating)	40,000
Taxes	15,101
Charitable contributions (cash)	20,000
Advertising expenses	30,000
Payroll penalties	15,000
Other deductions	49,899
Net income	624,574

A comparative balance sheet appears below.

	January 1, 2007	December 31, 2007
Cash	$ 47,840	$?
Accounts receivable	93,100	123,104
Inventories	9,607	3,467
Prepaid expenses	8,333	17,582
Building and equipment	138,203	185,348
Accumulated depreciation	(84,235)	?
Land	2,000	2,000
Total assets	$ 214,848	$ 764,422
Accounts payable	$ 42,500	$ 72,300
Notes payable (less than 1 year)	4,500	2,100
Notes payable (more than 1 year)	26,700	24,300
Capital stock	30,000	30,000
Retained earnings	111,148	?
Total liabilities and capital	$214,848	$764,422

Dana's accounting firm provides the following additional information.

Distributions to shareholders	$100,000

Using the above information, prepare a complete Form 1120S and a Schedule K–1 for Dana Mitchell, 545 Avenue C, Dime Box, TX 77823. If any information is missing, make realistic assumptions and list them.

2. Jacob Donaldson (234–12–5678) and Ryan Loflin (432–21–8765) are 40% and 60% owners of CD, Inc. (74–1234567), a foundation contractor, located at 10012 Post Oak Boulevard, Houston, Texas 77056. The company's S corporation election was made on April 28, 1994. The following information was taken from the income statement for 2007.

Gross rents	$ 60,000	
Tax-exempt interest	2,000	
Interest income	450	
Gross receipts	800,000	$862,450
Salaries and wages	$200,000	
Repairs	16,000	
Officers' compensation	65,000	
Rent expense (not an operating lease)	54,000	
Taxes	26,000	
Advertising	9,900	
Depreciation	91,800	
Employee benefit programs	1,100	
Other deductions	160,000	623,800
Book income		$238,650

A partially completed comparative balance sheet appears as follows.

	Beginning of the Year	End of the Year
Cash	$ 19,600	$ 41,692
Other investments	161,650	152,580
Buildings & other depreciable assets	711,402	922,112
Accumulated depreciation	(458,313)	(550,113)
Total	$434,339	$566,271
Mortgages, notes, bonds (payable in 1 year or more)	$354,890	$326,891
Capital stock	1,000	1,000
Retained earnings	78,449	?
Total	$434,339	?

The corporation distributed a total of $78,449 to the two shareholders during the year.

From the above information, prepare Form 1120S and Schedule K–1 for Ryan Loflin. If any information is missing, make realistic assumptions.

RESEARCH PROBLEMS

Note: Solutions to Research Problems can be prepared by using the **RIA Checkpoint®** **Student Edition** online research product, which is available to accompany this text. It is also possible to prepare solutions to the Research Problems by using tax research materials found in a standard tax library.

Research Problem 1.   One of your clients has a significant amount of E & P in her S corporation. She asks you what items affect the balance in E & P. The corporation also has some PTI. She is worried about the passive investment income tax and asks you if any elections are available to help her corporation dispose of the E & P.

Communications

Research Problem 2.   Charles, Inc., was a closely held C corporation engaged in the real estate rental business in 2006. The company had $6 million in passive activity losses. In 2007, Charles elected to be taxed as an S corporation, and the company sold a number of rental properties. May these suspended passive activity losses (PAL) be claimed as deductions under § 469(g)(1)(A)?

Recall that an S corporation cannot use carryforwards from a year in which it was a C corporation. If the PAL deductions are disallowed, may Charles readjust its cost basis in the sold property upward? Summarize your findings in a memo to the tax research file of your firm.

Research Problem 3.   Beecher, Inc., is an existing calendar year S corporation. Its accountant approaches you with this question: May an existing S corporation convert to an LLC and elect to be treated as a corporation without losing its S status? Is this a tax-free reorganization, and would the S election terminate?

Communications

Research Problem 4.   May an S corporation issue nonvoting stock in a ratio of 9 shares for every share of voting stock and warrants in a ratio of 10 warrants for every share of nonvoting stock? Thus, if the S corporation has 1,000 shares of voting stock outstanding, the corporation would issue 9,000 shares of nonvoting stock and warrants exercisable into 90,000 shares of nonvoting stock to the original shareholders. The warrants may be exercised at any time over a period of years. The strike price on the warrants is set at a price that is at least equal to 90% of the purported fair market value of the newly issued nonvoting stock on the date the warrants are granted. For this purpose, the fair market value of the nonvoting stock is claimed to be substantially reduced because of the existence of the warrants.

Shortly after the issuance of the nonvoting stock and the warrants, the original shareholders donate the nonvoting stock to an exempt organization. The parties to the transaction claim that, after the donation of the nonvoting stock, the exempt party owns 90% of the stock of the S corporation. The parties further claim that any taxable income allocated on the nonvoting stock to the exempt party is not subject to the unrelated business income tax (UBIT). The original shareholder might also claim a charitable contribution deduction under § 170 for the donation of the nonvoting stock to the exempt party. In some variations of this transaction, the S corporation may issue nonvoting stock directly to the exempt party.

Do you see anything wrong with this strategy? Outline your comments in an e-mail to your instructor.

Use the tax resources of the Internet to address the following questions. Do not restrict your search to the World Wide Web, but include a review of newsgroups and general reference materials, practitioner sites and resources, primary sources of the tax law, chat rooms and discussion groups, and other opportunities.

 **Internet** *Activity*

Research Problem 5. Locate the article by Kelly Luttrell, "S Corporation Returns: 2003," *SOI Bulletin*, Spring 2006. Prepare a graph showing the growth in the number of S corporations versus the decline in the number of all other corporate entities.

Communications

Research Problem 6. Go to the Internet site of a newspaper or business magazine and find a case study of how to start a small business and choose the best tax entity (e.g., C corporation, S corporation, etc.). Summarize your findings in an e-mail to your instructor.

Communications

Research Problem 7. Print out a copy of the S corporation Schedule M–3. Compare it to the partnership Schedule M–3. On one PowerPoint slide, list the four most important differences between the forms.

Research Problem 8. What are the tax consequences if the shareholders liquidate an S corporation? Summarize your findings in a PowerPoint presentation for your classmates.

Communications

Comparative Forms of Doing Business

LEARNING OBJECTIVES

After completing Chapter 13, you should be able to:

LO.1
Identify the principal legal and tax forms for conducting a business.

LO.2
Appreciate the relative importance of nontax factors in making business decisions.

LO.3
Distinguish between the forms for conducting a business according to whether they are subject to single taxation or double taxation.

LO.4
Identify techniques for avoiding double taxation and for controlling the entity tax.

LO.5
Understand the applicability and the effect of the conduit and entity concepts on contributions to the entity, operations of the entity, entity distributions, passive activity loss and at-risk rules, and special allocations.

LO.6
Analyze the effect of the disposition of a business on the owners and the entity for each of the forms for conducting a business.

A variety of factors, both tax and nontax, affect the choice of the form of business entity. The form that is appropriate at one point in the life of an entity and its owners may not be appropriate at a different time.

EXAMPLE 1

Eva is a tax practitioner in Kentwood, the Dairy Center of the South. Many of her clients are dairy farmers. She recently had tax planning discussions with two of her clients, Jesse, a Line Creek dairy farmer, and Larry, a Spring Creek dairy farmer.

Jesse recently purchased his dairy farm. He is 52 years old and just retired after 30 years of service as a chemical engineer at an oil refinery in Baton Rouge. Eva recommended that he incorporate his dairy farm and elect S corporation status for Federal income tax purposes.

Larry has owned his dairy farm since 2002. He inherited it from his father. At that time, Larry retired after 20 years of service in the U.S. Air Force. He has a master's degree in Agricultural Economics from LSU. His farm is incorporated, and shortly after the date of incorporation, Eva had advised him to elect S corporation status. She now advises him to revoke the S election. ■

Example 1 raises a number of interesting questions. Does Eva advise all of her dairy farmer clients to initially elect S corporation status? Why has she advised Larry to revoke his S election? Will she advise Jesse to revoke his S election at some time in the future? Will she advise Larry to make another S election at some time in the future? Why did she not advise Larry to terminate his corporate status? Could Larry and Jesse have achieved the same tax consequences for their dairy farms if they had operated the farms as partnerships instead of incorporating? Does the way the farm is acquired (e.g., purchase versus inheritance) affect the choice of business entity for tax purposes?

This chapter provides the basis for comparatively analyzing the tax consequences of business decisions for five types of tax entities (sole proprietorship, partnership, corporation, S corporation, and limited liability company). Understanding the comparative tax consequences for the different types of entities and being able to apply them effectively to specific fact patterns can lead to effective tax planning, which is exactly what Eva was doing with her two clients. As the following discussion illustrates, a variety of potential answers may exist for each of the questions raised by Eva's advice.

Forms of Doing Business

LO.1

Identify the principal legal and tax forms for conducting a business.

The principal *legal* forms for conducting a business entity are a sole proprietorship, partnership, limited liability company, and corporation.[1] From a *Federal income tax* perspective, these same forms are available with the corporate form being divided into two types (S corporation and C or regular corporation). In most instances, the legal form and the tax form are the same. In some cases, however, the IRS may attempt to tax a business entity as a form different from its legal form. This reclassification normally takes one of two possible approaches:

- The IRS ignores the corporate form and taxes the owners directly (the corporate entity lacks substance).
- The IRS ignores the partnership form and taxes the partnership as if it were a corporation.

The IRS may try to reclassify a corporation for several reasons. One reason is to prevent taxpayers from taking advantage of the potential disparity between the corporate and individual tax rates. Although the highest corporate statutory rate and the highest individual statutory rate are now the same (35 percent), the specific corporate and individual rates applicable to a particular taxpayer may differ. For example, an individual may be in the 35 percent bracket, and the corporation may be in the 15 percent, 25 percent, or 34 percent bracket. Another reason for taxing the owners directly is to make them ineligible for favorable taxation of certain fringe benefits (see the subsequent discussion in Favorable Treatment of Certain Fringe Benefits).

In the case of a partnership, reclassification of a partnership as if it were a corporation can subject the business entity to double taxation. In addition, the resultant loss of conduit status prevents partnership losses from being passed through to the tax returns of the partners.

ETHICAL and EQUITABLE *Considerations*   MARRIED OR SINGLE?

Eagle, Inc., is a calendar year S corporation. Counting married couples as one shareholder, Eagle has 100 shareholders (none of whom are related). Eagle's taxable income is about $2 million, and it normally distributes 80 percent of its earnings to shareholders. Valerie and Gus Sanders each own 5 percent of the stock of Eagle.

After considerable marital discord and the institution of legal proceedings, Valerie and Gus's divorce was finalized on December 5, 2008. On Thanksgiving, however, they began a reconciliation that led to remarriage on December 31, 2008. Even though the divorce meant that there were 101 shareholders for the last 27 days in 2008, Eagle files as an S corporation for 2008. Eagle's accountant justifies the continued S status on the grounds that the remarriage "fixed the tax problem." She concludes that it is unnecessary to get approval from the IRS because in substance Gus and Valerie were always husband and wife.

Evaluate the accountant's conclusion.

The taxpayer generally is bound for tax purposes by the legal form that is selected. A major statutory exception to this is the ability of an S corporation to receive tax treatment similar to that of a partnership.[2] In addition, taxpayers sometimes can control which set of tax rules will apply to their business operations. The "check-the-box" Regulations provide an elective procedure that enables certain entities to be classified as partnerships for Federal income tax purposes even

---

[1] A business entity can also be conducted in the form of a trust or estate. These two forms are not discussed in this chapter. See the discussion of the income taxation of trusts and estates in Chapter 19.

[2] §§ 1361 and 1362.

TAX *in the News*   **PROFESSIONAL SERVICE FIRMS AND ORGANIZATIONAL FORM**

Many professional service firms (e.g., accountants, architects, lawyers) have chosen to become limited liability partnerships (LLPs). In the accounting profession, this includes all of the Big 4 (i.e., Deloitte, Ernst & Young, KPMG, and PricewaterhouseCoopers) and most regional and local accounting firms.

An LLP helps to provide protection for the purely personal assets of the partners. Under the LLP organizational structure, the only partners whose personal assets are at risk to pay a judgment are those actually involved in the negligence or wrongdoing at issue. Note, however, that the entity is still responsible for the full judgment. Thus, the capital of the entity is still at risk.

---

though they have corporate characteristics.[3] These Regulations have greatly simplified the determination of entity classification.

A **limited liability company (LLC)** is a hybrid business form that combines the corporate characteristic of limited liability for the owners with the tax characteristics of a partnership.[4] All of the states now permit this legal form for conducting a business.

The most frequently cited benefit of an LLC is the limited liability of the owners. Compared to the other forms of ownership, LLCs offer additional benefits but also certain disadvantages. Refer to the coverage of the advantages and disadvantages of an LLC in Chapter 11 on pages 11–34 and 11–35.

An individual conducting a sole proprietorship files Schedule C of Form 1040. If more than one trade or business is conducted, a separate Schedule C is filed for each trade or business. A partnership files Form 1065. A corporation files Form 1120, and an S corporation files Form 1120S. An LLC that has elected to be taxed as a partnership files Form 1065.

LO.2

Appreciate the relative importance of nontax factors in making business decisions.

Nontax Factors

Taxes are only one of many factors to consider in making any business decision. Above all, any business decision should make economic sense.

EXAMPLE 2

Albert is considering investing $10,000 in a limited partnership. He projects that he will be able to deduct the $10,000 within the next two years (his share of partnership losses). Since Albert's marginal tax rate is 35%, the deductions will produce a positive cash-flow effect of $3,500 ($10,000 × 35%). However, there is a substantial risk that he will not recover any of his original investment. If this occurs, his negative cash flow from the investment in the limited partnership is $6,500 ($10,000 − $3,500). Albert must decide if the investment makes economic sense. ∎

Capital Formation

The ability of an entity to raise capital is a factor that must be considered. A sole proprietorship is subject to obvious limitations. Compared to the sole proprietorship, the partnership has a greater opportunity to raise funds through the pooling of owner resources.

---

[3]Reg. §§ 301.7701–1 through –4, and –6. Note that if the business has only one owner, the elective procedure enables the entity to be classified as a sole proprietorship.

[4]Depending on state law, an LLC may be organized as a limited liability corporation or a limited liability partnership.

Adam and Beth decide to form a partnership, AB. Adam contributes cash of $200,000, and Beth contributes land with an adjusted basis of $60,000 and a fair market value of $200,000. The partnership is going to construct an apartment building at a cost of $800,000. AB pledges the land and the building to secure a loan of $700,000. ■

EXAMPLE 3

The limited partnership offers even greater potential than the general partnership form because a limited partnership can secure funds from investors (limited partners).

Carol and Dave form a limited partnership, CD. Carol contributes cash of $200,000, and Dave contributes land with an adjusted basis of $60,000 and a fair market value of $200,000. The partnership is going to construct a shopping center at a cost of $5 million. Included in this cost is the purchase price of $800,000 for land adjacent to that contributed by Dave. Thirty limited partnership interests are sold for $100,000 each to raise $3 million. CD also pledges the shopping center (including the land) and obtains nonrecourse creditor financing of $2 million. ■

EXAMPLE 4

Both the § 465 at-risk provision and the § 469 passive activity loss provision have reduced the tax attractiveness of investments in real estate, particularly in the limited partnership form. In effect, the tax consequences have a critical effect on the economic consequences.[5]

Of the different forms of business entities, the corporate form offers the greatest ease and potential for obtaining owner financing because it can issue additional shares of stock. The ultimate examples of this form are the large public companies that are listed on the stock exchanges.

Limited Liability

A corporation offers its owners limited liability under state law. This absence of personal liability on the part of the owners is the most frequently cited advantage of the corporate form.

Ed, Fran, and Gabriella each invest $25,000 for all the shares of stock of Brown Corporation. Brown obtains creditor financing of $100,000. Brown is the defendant in a personal injury suit resulting from an accident involving one of its delivery trucks. The court awards a judgment of $2.5 million to the plaintiff. The award exceeds Brown's insurance coverage by $1.5 million. Even though the judgment will probably result in Brown's bankruptcy, the shareholders will have no personal liability for the unpaid corporate debts. ■

EXAMPLE 5

Limited liability is not available to all corporations. For many years, state laws did not permit professional individuals (e.g., accountants, attorneys, architects, and physicians) to incorporate. Even though professionals are now allowed to incorporate, the statutes do not provide limited liability for the performance of professional services.

Even if state law provides for limited liability, the shareholders of small corporations may have to forgo this benefit. Quite often, such a corporation may be unable to obtain external financing (e.g., a bank loan) unless the shareholders guarantee the loan.

The limited partnership form provides limited liability to the limited partners. Their liability is limited to the amount invested plus any additional amount that they agreed to invest. However, the general partner (or partners) has unlimited liability.

---

[5]See the related discussions in Chapters 10 and 11. For a comprehensive discussion of these provisions, see Chapter 11 in *South-Western Federal Taxation: Individual Income Taxes.*

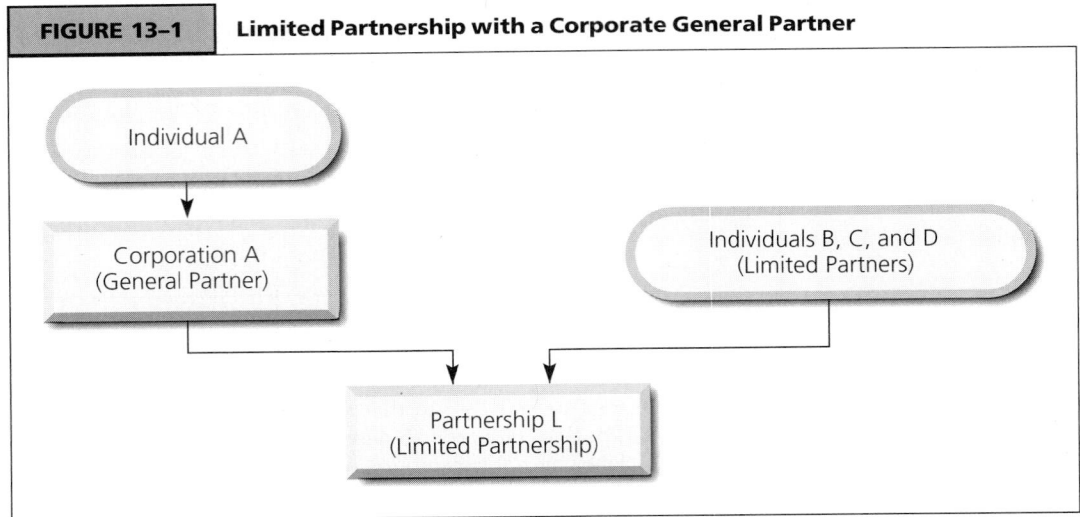

| FIGURE 13–1 | Limited Partnership with a Corporate General Partner |

EXAMPLE 6

Hazel, the general partner, invests $250,000 in HIJ, a limited partnership. Iris and Jane, the limited partners, each invest $50,000. While the potential loss for Iris and Jane is limited to $50,000 each, Hazel's liability is unlimited. ■

Indirectly, it may be possible to provide the general partner with limited liability by having a corporation as the general partner (see Figure 13–1). When the entity is structured this way, the general partner (the corporation) has limited its liability under the corporate statutes. Therefore, individual A is protected from personal liability by being merely the shareholder of Corporation A. Prior to the issuance of the check-the-box Regulations, it was necessary to structure the entity very carefully in order to avoid the limited partnership being classified as an association and taxed as a corporation. With the check-the-box Regulations, the limited partnership depicted in Figure 13–1 can be taxed as a partnership.[6]

Other Factors

Other nontax factors may be significant in selecting an organization form including the following:

- Estimated life of the business.
- Number of owners and their roles in the management of the business.
- Freedom of choice in transferring ownership interests.
- Organizational formality including the related cost and extent of government regulation.

LO.3

Distinguish between the forms for conducting a business according to whether they are subject to single taxation or double taxation.

Single versus Double Taxation

Overall Impact on Entity and Owners

The sole proprietorship, partnership, and LLC are subject to *single* taxation. This result occurs because the owner(s) and the entity generally are not considered separate for tax purposes. Thus, the tax liability is levied at the owner level rather than at the entity level.

---

[6]See the discussions of limited partnerships in Chapter 11. Also see Rev.Proc. 89–12, 1989–1 C.B. 798 and Rev.Rul. 88–76, 1988–2 C.B. 360.

GLOBAL
Tax Issues

TAX RATES AND ECONOMIC ACTIVITY

Tax rates affect economic activity. The corporate income tax rates for selected countries are as follows:

Country	Tax Rate
France (proposed)	25%
Germany	29.8%
Hong Kong	17.5%
Northern Ireland	12.5%
Republic of Ireland	12.5%
Singapore	25%
United States	35%*
Vietnam	25%
Industrial nation's average	29%

*Plus state average of 4.3%.

All of these countries except the United States (and France where a reduction is proposed) have recently reduced their corporate tax rates. The motivation for doing so was to increase the country's attractiveness as a location for foreign investment.

Source: *Adapted from "We're Number One, Alas (Review and Outlook),"* Wall Street Journal, *July 13, p. A12.*

On the other hand, the corporate form is subject to *double* taxation. This is frequently cited as the major tax disadvantage of the corporate form. Under double taxation, the entity is taxed on the earnings of the corporation, and the owners are taxed on distributions to the extent they are made from corporate earnings. If the corporation is a personal service corporation (see Chapter 2), the corporation is subject to a flat tax rate of 35 percent.

The S corporation provides a way to attempt to avoid double taxation and to subject the earnings to a lower tax rate (the actual individual tax rate may be lower than the actual corporate tax rate). However, the ownership structure of an S corporation is restricted in both the number and type of shareholders. In addition, statutory exceptions subject the entity to taxation in certain circumstances. To the extent these exceptions apply, double taxation may result. Finally, the distribution policy of the S corporation may encounter difficulties with the *wherewithal to pay* concept.

EXAMPLE 7

Hawk Corporation has been operating as an S corporation since it began its business two years ago. For both of the prior years, Hawk incurred a tax loss. Hawk has taxable income of $75,000 for 2008 and expects that its earnings will increase each year in the foreseeable future. Part of this earnings increase will result from Hawk's expansion into other communities in the state. Since most of this expansion will be financed internally, no dividend distributions will be made to the shareholders.

Assuming all of Hawk's shareholders are in the 33% tax bracket, their tax liability for 2008 will be $24,750 ($75,000 × 33%). Although the S corporation election will avoid double taxation, the shareholders will have a wherewithal to pay problem. In addition, the actual tax liability for 2008 would have been less if Hawk had not been an S corporation [(15% × $50,000) + (25% × $25,000) = $13,750]. ■

The data in Example 7 can be used to illustrate two additional tax concepts. First, the current wherewithal to pay problem could be resolved by terminating the S corporation election. The tax liability would then be imposed at the corporate level. Since the corporation does not intend to make any dividend distributions, double taxation at the present time would be avoided. Terminating the election will also reduce the overall shareholder-corporation tax liability by $11,000 ($24,750 − $13,750).[7] Second, tax decisions on the form of business organization should consider more than the current taxable year. If the S election is terminated, another election will not be available for five years. If the earnings exceed the expansion needs, Hawk could encounter an accumulated earnings tax problem (at a 15 percent tax rate) if it is a C corporation. Thus, the decision to revoke the election should have at least a five-year time frame. Perhaps a better solution would be to retain the election and distribute enough dividends to the S corporation shareholders to enable them to pay the shareholder tax liability.

Two other variables that relate to the adverse effect of double taxation are the timing and form of corporate distributions. If no distributions are made in the short run, then only single taxation occurs in the short run.[8] To the extent that double taxation does occur in the future, the cash-flow effect should be discounted to the present. Second, when the distribution is made, is it in the form of a dividend or a return of capital (a stock redemption or a complete liquidation)?[9]

EXAMPLE 8	Gray Corporation has taxable income of $100,000 for 2008. Gray's tax liability is $22,250. All of Gray's shareholders are in the 33% bracket. If dividends of $77,750 are distributed in 2008, the shareholders will have a tax liability of $11,663 ($77,750 × 15%), assuming the dividends are qualified dividends. The combined corporation-shareholder tax liability is $33,913 ($22,250 + $11,663) for a combined effective tax rate of 33.9%. ∎

EXAMPLE 9	Assume the same facts as in Example 8, except that the form of the distribution is a stock redemption and the basis for the redeemed shares is $57,750. The shareholders have a recognized gain of $20,000 and a tax liability of $3,000 ($20,000 × 15% beneficial capital gain rate). The combined corporation-shareholder tax liability is $25,250 ($22,250 + $3,000) for a total effective tax rate of 25.25%. ∎

The differences in the tax consequences in Examples 8 and 9 are even more obvious when illustrated in bar graph form (see Figure 13–2).

Alternative Minimum Tax

All of the forms of business are directly or indirectly subject to the alternative minimum tax (AMT).[10] For the sole proprietorship and the C corporation, the effect is direct (the AMT liability calculation is attached to the tax form that reports the entity's taxable income—Form 1040 or Form 1120). For the partnership, LLC, and S corporation, the effect is indirect (the tax preferences and adjustments are passed through from the entity to the owners, and the AMT liability calculation is not attached to the tax form that reports the entity's taxable income—Form 1065 or Form 1120S).

When compared with the other forms of business, the C corporation appears to have a slight advantage. The corporate AMT rate of 20 percent is less than the individual AMT rates of 26 and 28 percent. An even better perspective is provided by comparing the maximum AMT rate with the maximum regular rate for both the individual and the corporation. For the individual, the AMT rate is 80 percent (28%/35%) of the maximum regular rate. The AMT rate for the corporation is 57 percent (20%/35%) of the maximum regular rate. Therefore, on the basis of comparative rates, the C corporation does have an advantage. In addition, as presented below, under certain circumstances, a C corporation is exempt from the AMT.

---

[7]The absence of distributions to shareholders could create an accumulated earnings tax problem under § 531. However, as long as earnings are used to finance expansion, the "reasonable needs" provision will be satisfied, and the corporation will avoid any accumulated earnings tax.

[8]This assumes there is no accumulated earnings tax problem. See the subsequent discussion of distributions in Minimizing Double Taxation.

[9]See the coverage of dividends in Chapter 5 and the coverage of stock redemptions and complete liquidations in Chapter 6.

[10]§ 55.

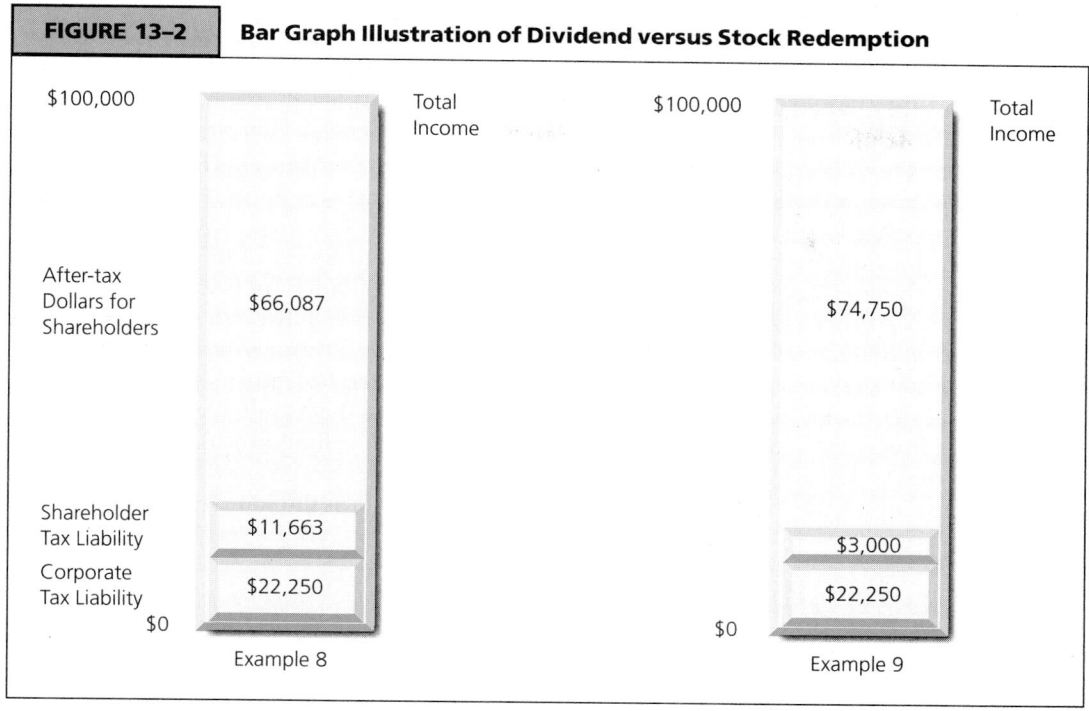

FIGURE 13–2   Bar Graph Illustration of Dividend versus Stock Redemption

The apparent corporate AMT rate advantage may be more than offset by the AMT adjustment that applies only to the C corporation. This is the adjustment for adjusted current earnings (ACE). The amount of the adjustment is 75 percent of the excess of ACE over unadjusted alternative minimum taxable income (AMTI). If unadjusted AMTI exceeds ACE for the tax year, the adjustment is negative.[11]

If the ACE adjustment continually causes the C corporation to be subject to the AMT, the owners should consider electing S corporation status if the eligibility requirements can be satisfied. Since the S corporation does not have this item as an adjustment, it may be possible to reduce the tax liability.

The AMT does not apply to small corporations for tax years beginning after December 31, 1997. For this purpose, a C corporation is classified as a small corporation if it had average annual gross receipts of not more than $5 million for the three-year period beginning after December 1993. A corporation will continue to be classified as a small corporation if its average annual gross receipts for the three-year period preceding the current tax year and any intervening three-year periods do not exceed $7.5 million. Tax legislation enacted in 1998 provided an additional opportunity for a C corporation to be classified as a small corporation. A C corporation automatically is classified as a small corporation in its first year of existence.

If the AMT is going to apply for the taxable year, the entity should consider accelerating income into the current taxable year and delaying deductions so that the resultant increased taxable income will be taxed at the lower AMT rate. For the C corporation, the potential rate differential is 15 percentage points (20 percent AMT rate versus 35 percent regular rate). For the individual taxpayer (i.e., as a sole proprietor, as a partner, or as an S corporation shareholder), the potential tax rate differential is 7 percentage points (28 percent highest AMT rate versus 35 percent regular rate). A present value analysis should be used to assure that the acceleration of income and delaying of deductions do not increase actual tax liabilities.

---

[11]§§ 56(c)(1) and (f). See the discussion of the corporate AMT in Chapter 3.

State Taxation

In selecting a form for doing business, the determination of the tax consequences should not be limited to Federal income taxes. Consideration should also be given to state income taxes and, if applicable, local income taxes.[12]

The S corporation provides a good illustration of this point. Suppose that the forms of business being considered are a limited partnership or a corporation. An operating loss is projected for the next several years. The owners decide to operate the business in the corporate form. The principal nontax criterion for the decision is the limited liability attribute of the corporation. The owners consent to an S corporation election, so the corporate losses can be passed through to the shareholders to deduct on their individual tax returns. However, assume that state law does not permit the S corporation election on the state income tax return. Thus, the owners will not receive the tax benefits of the loss deductions that would have been available on their state income tax returns if they had chosen the limited partnership form. As a result of providing limited liability to the owner who would have been the general partner for the limited partnership, the loss deduction at the state level is forgone.

<table>
<tr><td>**LO.4**</td></tr>
<tr><td>Identify techniques for avoiding double taxation and for controlling the entity tax.</td></tr>
</table>

Controlling the Entity Tax

Of the five forms of business entities, it appears at first glance that only the corporation needs to be concerned with controlling the entity tax. If control is defined in the narrow sense of double taxation, then this issue is restricted to the corporate form. However, from the broader perspective of controlling the tax liability related to the business entity's profits, whether that tax is imposed at the entity or the owner level, all five business forms are encompassed.

Techniques that can be used to minimize the current-period tax liability include the following:

1. Distribution policy.
2. Recognizing the interaction between the regular tax liability and the AMT liability.
3. Utilization of special allocations.
4. Favorable treatment of certain fringe benefits.
5. Minimizing double taxation.

Some of the techniques apply to all five forms of business entities. Others apply to only one of the five forms. Even those that apply to all do not minimize taxes equally for all forms. Since the first three techniques are discussed elsewhere in this chapter, only the last two are discussed here.

Favorable Treatment of Certain Fringe Benefits

Ideally, a fringe benefit produces the following tax consequences:

- Deductible by the entity (employer) that provides the fringe benefit.
- Excludible from the gross income of the taxpayer (employee) who receives the fringe benefit.

From the perspective of the owner or owners of an entity, when the entity provides such favorably taxed fringe benefits to an owner, the benefits are paid for with *before-tax* dollars.

EXAMPLE 10

Rocky, the owner of Rocky's Ranch, a C corporation in the 34% tax bracket, is provided with meals and lodging that qualify for exclusion treatment under § 119. The annual cost

---

[12]See the discussion of multistate corporate taxation in Chapter 15.

of the meals and lodging to Rocky's Ranch is $10,000. Since the cost is deductible in calculating the taxable income of Rocky's Ranch on Form 1120, the after-tax cost to the corporation is only $6,600 [$10,000 − (34% × $10,000)]. Since the $10,000 is excluded in calculating Rocky's gross income, there is no additional tax cost at the owner level. If Rocky had paid for the meals and lodging himself, no deduction would have been permitted because these expenditures are nondeductible personal expenditures. Thus, from Rocky's perspective, the receipt of excludible meals and lodging of $10,000 is equivalent to receiving a distribution from the corporation of $15,385 [$10,000/(100% − 35%)], assuming he is in the 35% tax bracket. ■

Not all favorably taxed fringe benefits receive exclusion treatment. Although not as attractive to the recipient, another approach provided in the Code is deferral treatment (e.g., pension plans and profit sharing plans).

Example 10 illustrates how certain fringe benefits can be used to benefit the owner of an entity and at the same time have a beneficial impact on the combined tax liability of the entity and the owner. In recognition of this, Congress has enacted various nondiscrimination provisions that generally negate favorable tax treatment if the fringe benefit program is discriminatory. In addition, the Code includes several statutory provisions that make the favorably taxed fringe benefit treatment available only to *employees* (e.g., group term life insurance, meal and lodging exclusion).[13]

The IRS defines the term *employee* restrictively. For the owner of a business entity to be treated as an employee, the entity must be a corporation.[14] For this purpose, an S corporation is treated as a partnership, and a greater-than-2 percent shareholder is treated as a partner.[15]

Classification of an owner as a nonemployee produces two negative results. First, the deduction for the cost of the fringe benefit to the entity is disallowed at the entity level. Second, the owner whose fringe benefit has been paid for by the entity must include the cost of the fringe benefit in gross income.

Minimizing Double Taxation

Only the corporate form is potentially subject to double taxation. Several techniques are available for eliminating or at least reducing the second layer of taxation:

- Making distributions to the shareholders that are deductible to the corporation.
- Not making distributions to the shareholders.
- Making distributions that qualify for return of capital treatment at the shareholder level.
- Making the S corporation election.

Note that for distributions made in 2003 and thereafter the availability of the 15%/5% (15%/0% in 2008) rate for qualified dividends reduces the potential negative impact of double taxation (see Chapter 5).

Making Deductible Distributions. Use of the first technique requires careful advance planning. Typical distribution forms that will result in a deduction to the corporation are (1) salary payments to shareholder-employees, (2) lease rental payments to shareholder-lessors, and (3) interest payments to shareholder-creditors.

Recognizing the tax benefit of this technique, the IRS scrutinizes these types of transactions carefully. All three types are evaluated in terms of *reasonableness*.[16] In addition, the interest payments may result in the IRS raising the **thin capitalization**

---

[13]§§ 79 and 119.

[14]Reg. § 1.79–0(b). The IRS has not been completely successful with respect to this position.

[15]§ 1372(a).

[16]§ 162(a)(1). *Mayson Manufacturing Co. v. Comm.,* 49–2 USTC ¶9467, 38 AFTR 1028, 178 F.2d 115 (CA–6, 1949); *Harolds Club v. Comm.,* 65–1 USTC ¶9198, 15 AFTR2d 241, 340 F.2d 861 (CA–9, 1965).

issue and reclassifying some or all of the debt as equity.[17] IRS success with either approach raises the specter of double taxation.

| EXAMPLE 11 | Donna owns all the stock of Green and is also the chief executive officer. Green's taxable income before salary payments to Donna is as follows: |

2006	$ 80,000
2007	50,000
2008	250,000

During the year, Donna receives a monthly salary of $3,000. In December of each year, she reviews the operations for the year and determines the year-end bonus to be paid to the key officers (only Donna for bonus purposes). Donna's yearly bonuses are as follows:

2006	$ 44,000
2007	14,000
2008	214,000

The obvious purpose of Green's bonus program is to reduce the corporate taxable income to zero and thereby avoid double taxation. The examination of Green's tax return by the IRS would likely result in a deduction disallowance for unreasonable compensation. ■

| EXAMPLE 12 | Tom and Vicki each contribute $20,000 to TV Corporation for all the stock of TV. In addition, they each lend $80,000 to TV. The loan is documented by formal notes, the interest rate is 7%, and the maturity date is 10 years from the date of the loan.

The notes provide the opportunity for the corporation to make payments of $5,600 each year to both Tom and Vicki and for the payments not to be subject to double taxation. That is, the interest payments are includible in the gross income of Tom and Vicki, but are deductible by TV in calculating its taxable income. At the time of repayment in 10 years, neither Tom nor Vicki will have any gross income from the repayment since the $80,000 amount realized is equal to the basis for the note of $80,000 (return of capital concept).

If the IRS succeeded in reclassifying the notes as equity, Tom and Vicki's includible gross income of $5,600 each would remain the same (interest income would be reclassified as dividend income that may be taxed at the 15% rate). However, because the dividend payments are not deductible by TV, the corporation's taxable income would increase by $11,200 ($5,600 × 2). To make matters worse, the repayment of the notes in 10 years would not qualify for return of capital treatment and would likely result in dividend income treatment for Tom and Vicki. ■ |

Not Making Distributions. Double taxation will not occur unless the corporation makes (actual or deemed) distributions to the shareholders. A closely held corporation that does not make distributions will eventually encounter an accumulated earnings tax problem unless the reasonable needs requirement is satisfied. When making distribution policy decisions each year, the board of directors should be apprised of any potential accumulated earnings tax problem and take the appropriate steps to eliminate it. The accumulated earnings tax rate of 15 percent in 2008 is the same as the 15 percent rate for qualified dividends for individual taxpayers.[18]

| EXAMPLE 13 | According to an internal calculation made by Dolphin Corporation, its accumulated taxable income is $400,000. The board of directors would prefer not to declare any dividends, but is considering a dividend declaration of $400,000 to avoid the accumulated earnings tax. All of the shareholders are in the 35% bracket.

If a dividend of $400,000 is declared, the tax cost to the shareholders is $60,000 ($400,000 × 15%), assuming the dividends are qualified dividends. If a dividend is not |

---

[17]§ 385; Rev.Rul. 83–98, 1983–2 C.B. 40; *Bauer v. Comm.*, 84–2 USTC ¶9996, 55 AFTR2d 85–433, 748 F.2d 1365 (CA–9, 1984).

[18]§ 531. See the discussion of the accumulated earnings tax in Chapter 3.

declared and the IRS assesses the accumulated earnings tax, the tax cost to the corporation for the accumulated earnings tax also would be $60,000 ($400,000 × 15%).

To make matters worse, Dolphin will have incurred the accumulated earnings tax cost without getting any funds out of the corporation to the shareholders. If the unwise decision were now made to distribute the remaining $340,000 ($400,000 − $60,000) to the shareholders, the additional tax cost at the shareholder level would be $51,000 ($340,000 × 15%). Therefore, the combined shareholder-corporation tax cost would be $111,000 ($60,000 + $51,000). This is 185% ($111,000/$60,000) of the tax cost that would have resulted from an initial dividend distribution of $400,000. ■

The legislation that created the special tax rate of 15 percent for qualified dividends also lowered the accumulated earnings tax rate from 35 percent to 15 percent. This tax rate reduction has substantially lowered the impact of the accumulated earnings tax. In Example 13, the penalty tax at the corporate level prior to the legislative change would have been $140,000 ($400,000 × 35%). Assuming the remaining $260,000 was distributed to the shareholders, the additional tax cost at the shareholder level would have been $91,000 ($260,000 × 35%). Therefore, the combined shareholder-corporation tax cost would have been $231,000 ($140,000 + $91,000) rather than the current $111,000. Thus, by reducing both the tax rate for the accumulated earnings tax and the tax rate on qualified dividends, this legislative change has substantially lowered the tax burden of the accumulated earnings tax.

Assuming that the accumulated earnings tax can be avoided (e.g., a growth company whose reasonable needs justify its no dividend policy), a policy of no distributions to shareholders can avoid the second layer of taxation forever. This will occur if the shares of stock are bequeathed to the taxpayer's beneficiaries. As a result of the step-up in basis rules for inherited property, the basis of the stock for the beneficiaries will be the fair market value at the date of the decedent's death rather than the decedent's basis.

Return of Capital Distributions. The magnitude of the effect of double taxation can be reduced if the corporate distributions to the shareholders can qualify for return of capital rather than dividend treatment. For an ongoing corporation, the stock redemption provisions offer an opportunity to reduce the includible gross income at the shareholder level. The corporate liquidation provisions can be used if the business entity will cease to operate in corporate form. Under redemption and liquidation rules, the distribution may be treated as a sale of some or all of the shareholder's stock resulting in a tax-free recovery of basis and capital gain.

E X A M P L E   14

Copper Corporation makes a distribution of $60,000 to its shareholders. Mark and Kate, two of the shareholders, receive $25,000 and $10,000, respectively. The form of the distribution permits the shareholders to surrender a certain number of shares of stock. The potential exists that the distribution can qualify for stock redemption treatment at the shareholder level. Mark satisfies the requirements for a substantially disproportionate distribution under § 302. Kate does not because she is in control of the corporation after the distribution (she owns 60% of the stock). Assuming Mark's basis for the shares redeemed is $20,000, he has a capital gain of $5,000 ($25,000 − $20,000). Kate has dividend income of $10,000. She must allocate her stock basis among her remaining shares. ■

Electing S Corporation Status. Electing S corporation status generally eliminates double taxation by making the corporation a tax reporter rather than a taxpayer. Therefore, the only tax levy is at the shareholder level. Factors to consider in making this election include the following:

- Are all the shareholders willing to consent to the election?
- Can the qualification requirements under § 1361 be satisfied at the time of the election?

TAX *in the News*   **C CORPORATIONS VERSUS S CORPORATIONS**

Are there more C corporations than S corporations? If you answered yes, you are right, but not by much. According to IRS data, 47 percent of all corporations are S corporations. Most S corporations (81 percent) have only one or two shareholders.

When it comes to share of corporate net income, C corporations win hands down. C corporations report 82 percent of net income.

- Since the qualification requirements become maintenance requirements, can these requirements continue to be satisfied?
- For what period will the conditions that make the election beneficial continue to prevail?
- Will the corporate distribution policy create wherewithal to pay problems at the shareholder level?

EXAMPLE 15

Emerald Corporation commenced business in January 2008. The two shareholders, Diego and Jaime, are both in the 28% tax bracket. The following operating results are projected for the first five years of operations:

2008	($ 50,000)
2009	400,000
2010	600,000
2011	800,000
2012	1,000,000

The corporation plans to expand rapidly. Therefore, no distributions will be made to shareholders. In addition, beginning in 2009, preferred stock will be offered to a substantial number of investors to help finance the expansion.

If the S corporation election is made for 2008, the $50,000 loss can be passed through to Diego's and Jaime's tax returns. Therefore, the cash-flow effect would be $14,000 ($50,000 × 28%). Assume that the election is either revoked or is involuntarily terminated at the beginning of 2009 as a result of the issuance of the preferred stock. The corporate tax liability for 2009 would be $136,000 ($400,000 × 34%).

If the S corporation election is not made for 2008, the $50,000 loss will be a net operating loss. The amount can be carried forward to reduce the 2009 corporate taxable income to $350,000 ($400,000 − $50,000). The resultant tax liability is $119,000 ($350,000 × 34%).

Should the S corporation election be made for just the one-year period? The answer is unclear. With an assumed after-tax rate of return to Diego and Jaime of 10%, the value of the $14,000 one year hence is $15,400 ($14,000 × 110%). Even considering the time value of money, the combined corporation-shareholder negative cash-flow effect of $120,600 ($136,000 − $15,400) in the case of an S election is not significantly different from the $119,000 corporate tax liability that would result for a regular corporation. The differential is even less when related accounting and/or legal fees are considered. ∎

Another benefit of electing S corporation status is that the corporation is not subject to the accumulated earnings or personal holding company taxes.

LO.5

Understand the applicability and the effect of the conduit and entity concepts on contributions to the entity, operations of the entity, entity distributions, passive activity loss and at-risk rules, and special allocations.

Conduit versus Entity Treatment

Under the **conduit concept**, the entity is viewed as merely an extension of the owners. Under the **entity concept**, the entity is regarded as being separate and distinct from its owners. The effects that these different approaches have in the following areas are examined for the partnership (and LLC), C corporation, and S corporation:

- Recognition at time of contribution to the entity.
- Basis of ownership interest.

- Results of operations.
- Recognition at time of distribution.
- Passive activity losses.
- At-risk rules.
- Special allocations.

The sole proprietorship is not analyzed separately because the owner and the business are in essence the same. In one circumstance, however, a tax difference does occur. Recognition does not occur when an owner contributes an asset to a sole proprietorship. Thus, the basis generally is a carryover basis. However, if the asset is a personal use asset, the sole proprietorship's basis is the *lower of* the adjusted basis or the fair market value at the date of contribution. Also note that if a personal use asset is contributed to a partnership or corporation, this *lower of* rule applies.

Effect on Recognition at Time of Contribution to the Entity

Since the conduit approach applies for the partnership and LLC, § 721 provides for no recognition on the contribution of property to the partnership or LLC in exchange for an ownership interest. Section 721 protects both a contribution associated with the formation of the partnership or LLC and later contributions. The partnership or LLC has a carryover basis for the contributed property, and the owners have a carryover basis for their ownership interests.[19]

Since the entity approach applies for the corporation, the transfer of property to a corporation in exchange for its stock is a taxable event. However, if the § 351 control requirement (80 percent) is satisfied, no gain or loss is recognized. In this case, both the corporate property and the shareholders' stock will have a carryover basis.[20] This control requirement makes it more likely that shareholders who contribute appreciated property to the corporation *after* the formation of the corporation will recognize gain.

To the extent that the fair market value of property contributed to the entity at the time of formation is not equal to the property's adjusted basis, it may be desirable to make a special allocation associated with the subsequent sale of the contributed property by the entity. With a special allocation, the owner contributing the property receives the tax benefit or detriment for any recognized gain or loss that subsequently results because of the initial difference between the adjusted basis and the fair market value. For the partnership or LLC, this special allocation treatment is mandatory. No such allocation is available for the C corporation form, since the gain or loss is recognized at the corporation level rather than at the shareholder level. For the S corporation, no such allocation is available. The recognized gain or loss will be reported on the shareholders' tax returns based on their stock ownership.

EXAMPLE 16

Khalid contributes land with an adjusted basis of $10,000 and a fair market value of $50,000 for a 50% ownership interest. At the same time, Tracy contributes cash of $50,000 for the remaining 50% ownership interest. Because the entity is unable to obtain the desired zoning, it subsequently sells the land for $50,000.

If the entity is a C corporation, Khalid has a realized gain of $40,000 ($50,000 − $10,000) and a recognized gain of $0 resulting from the contribution. His basis for his stock is $10,000, and the corporation has a basis for the land of $10,000. The corporation has a realized and recognized gain of $40,000 ($50,000 − $10,000) when it sells the land. Thus, what should have been Khalid's recognized gain becomes the corporation's taxable gain. There is no way that the corporation can directly allocate the recognized gain to Khalid. The corporation could distribute the land to Khalid and let him sell the land, but the distribution may be taxable to Khalid as a dividend, and gain may be recognized at the corporate level on the distribution.

---

[19]See the pertinent discussion in Chapter 10.   [20]See the pertinent discussion in Chapter 4.

If the entity is a partnership or LLC, the tax consequences are the same as in the C corporation illustration except for the $40,000 recognized gain on the sale of the land. The partnership or LLC has a realized and recognized gain of $40,000 ($50,000 − $10,000). However, even though Khalid's share of profits and losses is only 50%, all of the $40,000 recognized gain is allocated to him. If the entity is an S corporation, the tax consequences are the same as in the C corporation illustration except that Khalid reports $20,000 of the recognized gain on his tax return and Tracy reports $20,000 also. ■

Effect on Basis of Ownership Interest

In the case of a partnership or an LLC, the contribution of property to the entity in exchange for an ownership interest is not a taxable event under § 721. Therefore, the owner's basis for the ownership interest is a carryover basis. For C and S corporations, the nontaxable and the related carryover basis results are appropriate only if the 80 percent control requirement of § 351 is satisfied. If the control requirement is not satisfied, any realized gain or loss on the transaction is recognized, and the stock basis is equal to the fair market value of the contributed property.

In a partnership or an LLC, since the owner is the taxpayer, profits and losses of the entity affect the owner's basis in the entity interest. Likewise, the owner's basis is increased by the share of entity liability increases and is decreased by the share of entity liability decreases. This liability effect enables the owner to potentially benefit from the leverage concept. Accordingly, the owner's basis changes frequently.[21]

For the C corporation, the corporation is the taxpayer. Therefore, the shareholder's basis for the stock is not affected by corporate profits and losses or corporate liability increases or decreases.

The treatment of an S corporation shareholder falls in between that of the owner of a partnership or LLC interest and the C corporation shareholder. The S corporation shareholder's stock basis is increased by the share of profits and decreased by the share of losses, but it is not affected by corporate liability increases or decreases. Thus, unlike the owner of a partnership or LLC interest, the S corporation shareholder does not potentially benefit from the leverage concept.

EXAMPLE 17

Peggy contributes cash of $100,000 to an entity for a 30% ownership interest. The entity borrows $50,000 and repays $20,000 of this amount by the end of the taxable year. The profits for the year are $90,000.

If the entity is a partnership or LLC, Peggy's basis at the end of the period is $136,000 ($100,000 investment + $9,000 share of net liability increase + $27,000 share of profits). If Peggy is a C corporation shareholder instead, her stock basis is $100,000 ($100,000 original investment). If the corporation is an S corporation, Peggy's stock basis is $127,000 ($100,000 + $27,000). ■

Effect on Results of Operations

The entity concept is responsible for producing potential double taxation for the C corporation form (the corporation is taxed on its earnings, and the shareholders are taxed on the distribution of earnings). Thus, from the perspective of taxing the results of operations, the entity concept appears to be a disadvantage for the corporation. However, whether the entity concept actually produces disadvantageous results depends on the following:

- Whether the corporation generates positive taxable income.
- The tax rates that apply for the corporation and for the shareholders.
- The distribution policy of the corporation.

---

[21]§§ 705 and 752.

As discussed previously, techniques exist for getting cash out of the corporation to the shareholders without incurring double taxation (e.g., compensation payments to shareholder-employees, lease rental payments to shareholder-lessors, and interest payments to shareholder-creditors). Since these payments are deductible to the corporation, they reduce corporate taxable income. If the payments can be used to reduce corporate taxable income to zero, the corporation will have no tax liability.

The maximum individual tax bracket is the same as the maximum corporate tax bracket (35 percent). However, in a specific situation, the corporate tax rates that apply may be greater than or less than the applicable individual rates. This opportunity for the corporation to be subject to a lower tax rate is less likely to be available for personal service corporations. There, the only rate available is 35 percent.[22]

Double taxation can occur only if distributions (actual or constructive) are made to the shareholders. Thus, if no distributions (actual or constructive) are made and if the entity can avoid the accumulated earnings tax (e.g., based on the statutory credit or the reasonable needs adjustment) and the personal holding company tax (e.g., the corporation primarily generates active income), only one current level of taxation will occur. If distributions do occur in the future with respect to current earnings, the resultant tax liability should be discounted for the interim period. If the distribution can qualify for return of capital treatment (stock redemption or liquidation) rather than dividend treatment, the shareholder tax liability is decreased. Ideally, taxation of the earnings at the shareholder level can be avoided permanently if the stock passes through the decedent shareholder's estate.

Application of the entity concept does result in the earnings components losing their identity when they are passed through to shareholders in the form of dividends. This may produce a negative result for capital gains. Since capital gains lose their identity when passed through in the form of dividends, they cannot be used to offset capital losses at the shareholder level. An even more negative result is produced when dividends are paid out of tax-exempt income. Tax-exempt income is excludible in calculating corporate taxable income, but is included in calculating current earnings and profits. Thus, what should not be subject to taxation (an exclusion) is taxed because of the entity concept.

The partnership, the LLC, and the S corporation use the conduit concept in reporting the results of operations. Any item that is subject to special treatment on the taxpayer-owners' tax return is reported separately to the owners. Other items are netted and reported as taxable income. Thus, taxable income merely represents those income and deduction items that are not subject to special treatment.[23]

Many of the problems that the entity concept may produce for the C corporation form are not present for the partnership, LLC, or S corporation. Included in this category are double taxation, problems with the reasonableness requirement, and loss of identity of the income or expense item at the owner level.

Only the partnership and LLC completely apply the conduit concept in reporting the results of operations. In several circumstances, the S corporation is subject to taxation at the corporate level, including the tax on built-in gains and the tax on certain passive investment income.[24] This limited application of the entity concept necessitates additional planning to attempt to avoid taxation at the corporate level.

Effect on Recognition at Time of Distribution

The application of the conduit concept results in distributions not being taxed to the owners. The application of the entity concept produces the opposite result.

---

[22]§ 11(b)(2).

[23]§§ 701, 702, 1363, and 1366.

[24]§§ 1374 and 1375.

Therefore, distributions can be made to partners, to LLC owners, or to S corporation shareholders tax-free, whereas the same distribution would produce dividend income treatment for C corporation shareholders.

In this regard, a distinction must be made between distributions of earnings and other distributions for the S corporation. The S corporation generally is treated as a conduit with respect to its operations. However, as previously discussed, in several cases the entity concept is applied, and the S corporation becomes a taxpayer rather than merely a tax reporter. In effect, the conduit concept applies to S corporation operations unless otherwise specified in Subchapter S of the Code. Since distributions of earnings are included in the operations category, they are subject to conduit treatment through the application of the accumulated adjustments account (AAA).[25] Distributions in excess of earnings qualify for return of capital treatment.

A combination entity/conduit concept applies to property distributions to S corporation shareholders. As discussed above, the conduit concept applies with respect to the shareholder. However, if the property distributed is appreciated property, § 311(b) provides that the realized gain is recognized at the corporate level (same treatment as a C corporation). This corporate-level gain recognition is an application of the entity concept. Then, however, the conduit concept is applied to the pass-through of the gain to the shareholders.

EXAMPLE 18

Tan, an S corporation, is equally owned by Leif and Matt. Tan distributes two parcels of land to Leif and Matt. Tan has a basis of $10,000 for each parcel. Each parcel has a fair market value of $15,000. The distribution results in a $10,000 ($30,000 − $20,000) recognized gain for Tan. Leif and Matt each report $5,000 of the gain on their individual income tax returns. ■

Stock redemptions and complete liquidations are not covered by the provisions of Subchapter S. Therefore, the tax consequences of an S corporation stock redemption are determined under the C corporation provisions in § 302, while those for a complete liquidation are determined under the C corporation provisions in §§ 331 and 336.

Effect on Passive Activity Losses

The passive activity loss rules apply to the partnership, LLC, and S corporation, but apply to the C corporation only for personal service corporations and closely held corporations. A *closely held corporation* is defined as one that meets the stock ownership requirement under the personal holding company provisions. That is, more than 50 percent of the value of the outstanding stock at any time during the last half of the taxable year is owned by or for not more than five individuals. The definition of a personal service corporation is modified slightly from the standard definition under § 269A. A corporation is classified as a § 469 *personal service corporation* only if the following requirements are satisfied:

- The principal activity of the corporation is the performance of personal services.
- The services are substantially performed by owner-employees.
- Owner-employees own more than 10 percent in value of the stock of the corporation.

The general passive activity loss rules apply to the personal service corporation. Therefore, passive activity losses cannot be offset against either active income or portfolio income. For the closely held corporation, the application of the passive activity rules is less harsh. Although passive activity losses cannot be offset against portfolio income, they can be offset against active income.

[25]§ 1368.

TAX *in the News*   **CERTAIN PARTNERSHIP DISTRIBUTIONS OF APPRECIATED PROPERTY**

Section 311(b) of the Internal Revenue Code, which is applicable to C corporations and S corporations, provides that realized gain on the distribution of appreciated property to a shareholder results in recognized gain to the corporation. There is no similar statutory provision for the distribution of appreciated property made by a partnership to a partner.

However, the IRS recently announced in Revenue Ruling 2007–40 that in one limited circumstance a distribution of appreciated property made by a partnership to a partner results in recognized gain to the partnership. If the appreciated property is distributed to the partner in satisfaction of a guaranteed payment under § 707(c), the distribution is treated as a sale or exchange under § 1001 rather than a distribution under § 731.

The statutory language of § 469(a)(2), which describes the taxpayers subject to the passive activity loss rules, does not mention the partnership, LLC, or S corporation. Instead, it mentions the individual taxpayer. Since the conduit concept applies, the passive activity results are separately stated at the partnership, LLC, or S corporation level and are passed through to the owners with the identity maintained.

Effect of At-Risk Rules

The at-risk rules of § 465 apply to the partnership, LLC, and S corporation. Although the statutory language of § 465(a) mentions none of these, the conduit concept that applies to these entities results in the application of § 465. Section 465 also applies to closely held C corporations (defined the same as under the passive activity loss rules). However, exceptions are available for closely held corporations that are actively engaged in equipment leasing or are defined as qualified C corporations.

The application of the at-risk rules produces a harsher result for the partnership and the LLC than for the S corporation. This occurs because the partnership and the LLC, in the absence of § 465, would have a greater opportunity to use the leveraging concept.

EXAMPLE 19

Walt is the general partner, and Ira and Vera are the limited partners in the WIV limited partnership. Walt contributes land with an adjusted basis of $40,000 and a fair market value of $50,000 for his partnership interest, and Ira and Vera each contribute cash of $100,000 for their partnership interests. They agree to share profits and losses equally. To finance construction of an apartment building, the partnership obtains $600,000 of nonrecourse financing [not qualified nonrecourse financing under § 465(b)(6)] using the land and the building as the pledged assets. Each partner's basis for the partnership interest is as follows:

	Walt	Ira	Vera
Contribution	$ 40,000	$100,000	$100,000
Share of nonrecourse debt	200,000	200,000	200,000
Basis	$240,000	$300,000	$300,000

Without the at-risk rules, Ira and Vera could pass through losses up to $300,000 each even though they invested only $100,000 and have no personal liability for the nonrecourse debt. However, the at-risk rules limit the loss pass-through to the at-risk basis, which is $100,000 for Ira and $100,000 for Vera. Note that the at-risk rules can also affect the general partner. Since Walt is not at risk for the nonrecourse debt, his at-risk basis is $40,000. If the mortgage were recourse debt, his at-risk basis would be $640,000 ($40,000 + $600,000). Thus, as a result of the at-risk rules, leveraging is available only for recourse debt for partners who have potential personal liability. ■

EXAMPLE 20

Assume the same facts as in Example 19, except that the entity is an S corporation and Walt receives 20% of the stock and Ira and Vera each receive 40%. The basis for their stock is as follows:

Walt	$ 40,000
Ira	100,000
Vera	100,000

The nonrecourse debt does not affect the calculation of stock basis. The stock basis for each shareholder would remain the same even if the debt were recourse debt. Only direct loans by the shareholders increase the ceiling on loss pass-through (basis for stock plus basis for loans by shareholders). ■

Effect of Special Allocations

An advantage of the conduit concept over the entity concept is the ability to make special allocations. Special allocations are not permitted for the C corporation form. Indirectly, however, the corporate form may be able to achieve results similar to those produced by special allocations through payments to owners (e.g., salary payments, lease rental payments, and interest payments) and through different classes of stock (e.g., preferred, common). However, even in these cases, the breadth of the treatment and the related flexibility are less than that achievable under the conduit concept.

Although the S corporation is a conduit, it is treated more like a C corporation than a partnership or an LLC with respect to special allocations. This treatment results from the application of the per-share and per-day rule in § 1377(a). Although the S corporation is limited to one class of stock, it can still use the payments to owners procedure. However, the IRS has the authority to reallocate income among members of a family if fair returns are not provided for services rendered or capital invested.[26]

EXAMPLE 21

The stock of an S corporation is owned by Debra (50%), Helen (25%), and Joyce (25%). Helen and Joyce are Debra's adult children. Debra is in the 35% bracket, and Helen and Joyce are in the 15% bracket. Only Debra is an employee of the corporation. She is paid an annual salary of $20,000, whereas employees with similar responsibilities in other corporations earn $100,000. The corporation generates earnings of approximately $200,000 each year.

It appears that the reason Debra is paid a low salary is to enable more of the earnings of the S corporation to be taxed to Helen and Joyce, who are in lower tax brackets. Thus, the IRS could use its statutory authority to allocate a larger salary to Debra. ■

The partnership and LLC have many opportunities to use special allocations, including the following:

---

[26]§ 1366(e).

- The ability to share profits and losses differently from the share in capital.
- The ability to share profits and losses differently.
- The special allocation required under § 704(c) for the difference between the adjusted basis and the fair market value of contributed property.
- The special allocation of any item permitted under § 704(a) if the substantial economic effect rule of § 704(b) is satisfied.
- The optional adjustment to basis permitted under § 754 and calculated under § 734 that results from distributions.
- The optional adjustment to basis permitted under § 754 and calculated under § 743 that results from an acquisition by purchase, taxable exchange, or inheritance.

Disposition of a Business or an Ownership Interest

LO.6

Analyze the effect of the disposition of a business on the owners and the entity for each of the forms for conducting a business.

A key factor in evaluating the tax consequences of disposing of a business is whether the disposition is viewed as the sale of an ownership interest or as a sale of assets. Generally, the tax consequences are more favorable if the transaction is treated as a sale of the ownership interest.

Sole Proprietorship

Regardless of the form of the transaction, the sale of a sole proprietorship is treated as the sale of individual assets. Thus, gains and losses must be calculated separately. Classification as capital gain or ordinary income depends on the nature and holding period of the individual assets. Ordinary income property such as inventory will result in ordinary gains and losses. Section 1231 property such as land, buildings, and machinery used in the business will produce § 1231 gains and losses (subject to depreciation recapture under §§ 1245 and 1250). Capital assets such as investment land and stocks qualify for capital gain or loss treatment.

If the amount realized exceeds the fair market value of the identifiable assets, the excess is attributed to goodwill, which produces capital gain for the seller. If instead the excess payment is attributed to a covenant not to compete, the related gain is classified as ordinary income rather than capital gain. Thus, the seller prefers the excess to be attributed to goodwill.

Unless the legal protection provided by a covenant not to compete is needed, the buyer is neutral as to whether the excess is attributed to goodwill or a covenant. Both goodwill and a covenant are § 197 intangibles and are amortized over a 15-year statutory period.

EXAMPLE 22

Seth, who is in the 35% tax bracket, sells his sole proprietorship to Wilma for $600,000. The identifiable assets are as follows:

	Adjusted Basis	Fair Market Value
Inventory	$ 20,000	$ 25,000
Accounts receivable	40,000	40,000
Machinery and equipment*	125,000	150,000
Buildings**	175,000	250,000
Land	40,000	100,000
	$400,000	$565,000

*Potential § 1245 recapture of $50,000.

**Potential § 1250 recapture of $20,000.

The sale produces the following results for Seth:

	Gain (Loss)	Ordinary Income	§ 1231 Gain	Capital Gain
Inventory	$ 5,000	$ 5,000		
Accounts receivable	–0–			
Machinery and equipment	25,000	25,000		
Buildings	75,000	20,000	$ 55,000	
Land	60,000		60,000	
Goodwill	35,000			$35,000
	$200,000	$50,000	$115,000	$35,000

If the sale is structured this way, Wilma can deduct the $35,000 paid for goodwill over a 15-year period. If instead Wilma paid the $35,000 to Seth for a covenant not to compete for a period of seven years, she still would amortize the $35,000 over a 15-year period. However, this would result in Seth's $35,000 capital gain being reclassified as ordinary income. If the covenant has no legal relevance to Wilma, in exchange for treating the payment as a goodwill payment, she should negotiate for a price reduction that reflects the benefit of the tax on capital gains to Seth. ■

Partnership and Limited Liability Company

The sale of a partnership or LLC can be structured as the sale of assets or as the sale of an ownership interest. If the transaction takes the form of an asset sale, it is treated the same as for a sole proprietorship (described above). The sale of an ownership interest is treated as the sale of a capital asset under § 741 (subject to ordinary income potential under § 751 for unrealized receivables and substantially appreciated inventory). Thus, if capital gain treatment can produce beneficial results for the taxpayer (e.g., has capital losses to offset or has beneficially treated net capital gain), the sale of an ownership interest is preferable.

From the buyers' perspective, the form does not produce different tax consequences. If the transaction is an asset purchase, the basis for the assets is the amount paid for them. Assuming the buyers intend to continue to operate in the partnership or LLC form, the assets can be contributed to the entity under § 721. Therefore, the owners' basis for their entity interest is equal to the purchase price for the assets. Likewise, if ownership interests are purchased, the owners' basis is the purchase price, and the entity's basis for the assets is the purchase price since the original entity will have terminated.[27]

A problem may arise if an individual purchases an entity interest from another partner or limited liability entity owner and the amount paid exceeds the new owner's pro rata share of the entity's basis for the assets. If the new owner does not acquire at least a 50 percent capital and profits interest, the old entity may not terminate.[28]

EXAMPLE 23

Paul purchases Sandra's partnership interest for $100,000. He acquires both a 20% capital interest and a 20% interest in profits and losses. At the purchase date, the assets of the partnership are as follows:

---

[27]§ 708(b)(1)(B).   [28]§§ 708(b)(1)(A) and (B).

TAX *in the News*	A NEW ONE-WAY STREET FOR PARTNERS

Janel paid $800,000 for Waldo's partnership interest in the DWT Partnership. Waldo's outside basis was $600,000, which equaled his share of the partnership's inside basis for the partnership assets. Unless the partnership makes a § 754 election, Janel will eventually pay income taxes on the $200,000 difference between her outside basis of $800,000 and her share of the inside basis of $600,000. However, a § 754 election will activate § 743 and provide her with a special basis adjustment of $200,000. But does she recognize the need for making the § 754 election, and will the other partners cooperate?

Suppose the amounts are reversed (i.e., Janel paid $600,000 for an inside basis of $800,000). In this situation, Janel would prefer to avoid making the § 754 election. Congress in the American Jobs Creation Act of 2004 limited the ability to make this choice. The statutory language of § 743 was modified to require an automatic downward basis adjustment if the partnership has a "substantial built-in loss" at the time of the transfer.

Note that this new § 743 treatment applies only to losses. For built-in gains, an affirmative § 754 election still is necessary in order to receive a § 743 upward basis adjustment.

	Adjusted Basis	Fair Market Value
Cash	$ 10,000	$ 10,000
Inventory	30,000	35,000
Accounts receivable	15,000	15,000
Machinery and equipment	70,000	90,000
Buildings	100,000	150,000
Land	175,000	200,000
	$400,000	$500,000

In effect, Paul paid $100,000 for his 20% share of partnership assets ($500,000 × 20%). His basis for his partnership interest reflects the purchase price of $100,000. However, Paul's proportionate share of the partnership assets is based on the partnership's adjusted basis for the assets of $400,000 (i.e., $400,000 × 20% = $80,000). Since Paul's acquisition of his ownership interest from Sandra did not result in a termination of the partnership, the partnership's adjusted basis for the assets does not change. Therefore, if the partnership were to liquidate all of its assets immediately for $500,000, Paul's share of the recognized gain of $100,000 ($500,000 − $400,000) would be $20,000 ($100,000 × 20%). This result occurs even though Paul paid fair market value for his partnership interest.

The Code does provide an opportunity to rectify this inequity to Paul. If the partnership elects the optional adjustment to basis under § 754, the operational provisions of § 743 will result in Paul having a special additional basis for each of the appreciated partnership assets.

The amount is the excess of the amount Paul effectively paid for each of the assets over his pro rata share of the partnership's basis for the assets.

	Amount Paid (20% Share)	Pro Rata Share of Adjusted Basis	Special Basis Adjustment
Cash	$ 2,000	$ 2,000	$ –0–
Inventory	7,000	6,000	1,000
Accounts receivable	3,000	3,000	–0–
Machinery and equipment	18,000	14,000	4,000
Buildings	30,000	20,000	10,000
Land	40,000	35,000	5,000
	$100,000	$80,000	$20,000

Therefore, if the partnership sells the inventory, Paul's share of the ordinary income is $1,000 ($5,000 × 20%). He then reduces this amount by his special additional basis of $1,000. Thus, the net effect, as it equitably should be, is $0 ($1,000 − $1,000). ∎

As Example 23 illustrates, the optional adjustment-to-basis election under § 754 provides a way to avoid the aforementioned problem. However, four additional factors need to be considered. First, the election must be made by the partnership (or LLC), not just by the acquiring partner. Therefore, the acquiring partner should obtain a written agreement from the other partners indicating they will consent to the § 754 election. Second, the election is a continuing election. Thus, while the election benefits an acquiring partner if the partnership assets are appreciated at the date of acquisition, it produces detrimental consequences (i.e., a negative special basis adjustment) if the adjusted basis exceeds the fair market value of the assets at the acquisition date. Third, the election not only activates the operational provisions of § 743, it also activates the operational provisions of § 734 with respect to partnership distributions. Fourth, if the members of the partnership change frequently, record keeping can become complex.

C Corporation

The sale of the business held by a C corporation can be structured as either an asset sale or a stock sale. The stock sale has the dual advantage to the seller of being less complex both as a legal transaction and as a tax transaction. It also has the advantage of providing a way to avoid double taxation. Finally, the gain or loss on the sale of the stock is a capital gain or loss to the shareholder.

EXAMPLE 24

Jane and Zina each own 50% of the stock of Purple Corporation. They have owned the business for 10 years. Jane's basis for her stock is $40,000, and Zina's basis for her stock is $60,000. They agree to sell the stock to Rex for $300,000. Jane has a long-term capital gain of $110,000 ($150,000 − $40,000), and Zina has a long-term capital gain of $90,000 ($150,000 − $60,000). Rex has a basis for his stock of $300,000. Purple's basis for its assets does not change as a result of the stock sale. ∎

Structuring the sale of the business as a stock sale may produce detrimental tax results for the purchaser. As Example 24 illustrates, the basis of the corporation's assets is not affected by the stock sale. If the fair market value of the stock exceeds the corporation's adjusted basis for its assets, the purchaser is denied the opportunity to step up the basis of the assets to reflect the amount in effect paid for them through the stock acquisition. Note that this is similar to the problem at the partnership (or LLC) level if the § 754 election is not made.

For an asset sale, the seller of the business can be either the corporation or the shareholders. If the seller is the corporation, the corporation sells the business (the assets), pays any debts not transferred, and makes a liquidating distribution to the shareholders. If the sellers are the shareholders, the corporation pays any debts that will not be transferred and makes a liquidating distribution to the shareholders; then the shareholders sell the business.

Regardless of the approach used for an asset sale, double taxation will occur. The corporation is taxed on the actual sale of the assets and is taxed as if it had sold the assets when it makes the liquidating distribution of the assets to the shareholders who then sell the assets. The shareholders are taxed when they receive cash or assets distributed in kind by the corporation.

The asset sale resolves the purchaser's problem of not being able to step up the basis of the assets to their fair market value. The basis for each asset is the amount paid for it. In order to operate in corporate form (assuming the purchaser is not a corporation), the purchaser needs to transfer the property to a corporation in a § 351 transaction.

From the perspective of the seller, the ideal form of the transaction is a stock sale. Conversely, from the purchaser's perspective, the ideal form is an asset purchase. Thus, a conflict exists between the buyer's and the seller's objectives regarding the form of the transaction. Therefore, the bargaining ability of the seller and the purchaser to structure the sale as a stock sale or an asset sale, respectively, has become more critical.

Rather than selling the entire business, an owner may sell his or her ownership interest. Since the form of the transaction is a stock sale, the results for the selling shareholder will be the same as if all the shareholders had sold their stock (i.e., capital gain or capital loss to the shareholder).

ETHICAL and EQUITABLE *Considerations*   **PRACTICE DEVELOPMENT AT ITS WORST!**

Your client, Alan, is the sole shareholder of Green, Inc., a C corporation. Alan formed Green many years ago when he incorporated his landscaping business. One of the assets transferred to Green upon its formation was a tract of unimproved land held by Alan as an investment. The land has since substantially appreciated in value.

Alan would like to sell the business and retire. He has been contacted by Rob, a fishing companion, who is looking for attractive investments. Rob does not intend to operate the landscaping business but is interested in the potential of the unimproved land.

Although Rob knows that Alan is your client, he asks you to represent him as well in consummating the proposed sale. He feels that if a buyer and seller have the same adviser, both time and money can be saved.

You could use the extra fee (and another client), so how do you react to Rob's suggestion?

S Corporation

Since the S corporation is a corporation, it is subject to the provisions for a C corporation discussed previously. Either an asset sale at the corporate level or a liquidating distribution of assets produces recognition at the corporate level. However, under the conduit concept applicable to the S corporation, the recognized amount is taxed at the shareholder level. Therefore, double taxation is avoided directly (only the shareholder is involved) for a stock sale and indirectly (the conduit concept ignores the involvement of the corporation) for an asset sale.

See Concept Summary 13–1 for a summary of the tax consequences of the disposition of a business.

Overall Comparison of Forms of Doing Business

See Concept Summary 13–2 for a detailed comparison of the tax consequences of the following forms of doing business: sole proprietorship, partnership, limited liability company, S corporation, and C corporation.

CONCEPT SUMMARY 13–1

Tax Treatment of Disposition of a Business

Form of Entity	Form of Transaction	Tax Consequences	
		Seller	**Buyer**
Sole proprietorship	Sale of individual assets.	Gain or loss is calculated separately for the individual assets. Classification as capital or ordinary depends on the nature and holding period of the individual assets. If amount realized exceeds the fair market value of the identifiable assets, the excess is allocated to goodwill (except to the extent identified with a covenant not to compete), which is a capital asset.	Basis for individual assets is the allocated cost. Prefers that any excess of purchase price over the fair market value of identifiable assets be identified with a covenant not to compete if the covenant has legal utility. Otherwise, the buyer is neutral since both goodwill and covenants are amortized over a 15-year statutory period.
	Sale of the business.	Treated as if a sale of the individual assets (as above).	Treated as if a purchase of the individual assets (as above).
Partnership and limited liability company	Sale of individual assets.	Treatment is the same as for the sole proprietorship.	Treatment is the same as for the sole proprietorship. If the intent is to operate in partnership or LLC form, the assets can be contributed to a partnership or LLC under § 721.
	Sale of ownership interest.	Entity interest is treated as the sale of a capital asset under § 741 (subject to ordinary income potential under § 751 for unrealized receivables and substantially appreciated inventory).	Basis for new owner's ownership interest is the cost. The new entity's basis for the assets is also the pertinent cost (i.e., contributed to the entity under § 721), since the original entity will have terminated.
C corporation	Sale of corporate assets by corporation (i.e., corporation sells assets, pays debts, and makes liquidating distribution to the shareholders).	Double taxation occurs. Corporation is taxed on the sale of the assets with the gain or loss determination and the classification as capital or ordinary treated the same as for the sole proprietorship. Shareholders calculate gain or loss as the difference between the stock basis and the amount received from the corporation in the liquidating distribution. Capital gain or loss usually results, since stock typically is a capital asset.	Basis for individual assets is the allocated cost. If the intent is to operate in corporate form, the assets can be contributed to a corporation under § 351.
	Sale of corporate assets by the shareholders (i.e., corporation pays debts and makes liquidating distribution to the shareholders).	Double taxation occurs. At the time of the liquidating distribution to the shareholders, the corporation is taxed as if it had sold the assets. Shareholders calculate gain or loss as the difference between the stock basis and the fair market value of the assets received from the corporation in the liquidating distribution. Capital gain or loss usually results, since stock typically is a capital asset.	Same as above.

Tax Treatment of Disposition of a Business—Continued

Form of Entity	Form of Transaction	Tax Consequences	
		Seller	Buyer
	Sale of corporate stock.	Enables double taxation to be avoided. Since the corporation is not a party to the transaction, there are no tax consequences at the corporate level. Shareholders calculate gain or loss as the difference between the stock basis and the amount received for the stock. Capital gain or loss usually results, since stock typically is a capital asset.	Basis for the stock is its cost. The basis for the corporate assets is not affected by the stock purchase.
S corporation	Sale of corporate assets by corporation.	Recognition occurs at the corporate level on the sale of the assets with the gain or loss determination and the classification as capital or ordinary treated the same as for the sole proprietorship. Conduit concept applicable to the S corporation results in the recognized amount being taxed at the shareholder level. Double taxation associated with the asset sale is avoided, because the shareholder's stock basis is increased by the amount of gain recognition and decreased by the amount of loss recognition. Shareholders calculate gain or loss as the difference between the stock basis and the amount received from the corporation in the liquidating distribution. Capital gain or loss usually results, since stock typically is a capital asset.	Basis for individual assets is the allocated cost. If the intent is to operate in corporate form (i.e., as an S corporation), the assets can be contributed to a corporation under § 351.
	Sale of corporate assets by the shareholders.	At the time of the liquidating distribution to the shareholders, recognition occurs at the corporation level as if the corporation had sold the assets. The resultant tax consequences for the shareholders and the corporation are the same as for the sale of corporate assets by the S corporation.	Same as above.
	Sale of corporate stock.	Same as the treatment for the sale of stock of a C corporation.	Same as the treatment for the purchase of stock of a C corporation.

CONCEPT SUMMARY   13–2

Tax Attributes of Different Forms of Business (Assume Partners and Shareholders Are All Individuals)

	Sole Proprietorship	Partnership/Limited Liability Company*	S Corporation**	Regular (C) Corporation***
Restrictions on type or number of owners	One owner. The owner must be an individual.	Must have at least 2 owners.	Only individuals, estates, certain trusts, and certain tax-exempt entities can be owners. Maximum number of shareholders limited to 100.****	None, except some states require a minimum of 2 shareholders.
Incidence of tax	Sole proprietorship's income and deductions are reported on Schedule C of the individual's Form 1040. A separate Schedule C is prepared for each business.	Entity not subject to tax. Owners in their separate capacity subject to tax on their distributive share of income. Entity files Form 1065.	Except for certain built-in gains and passive investment income when earnings and profits are present from C corporation tax years, entity not subject to Federal income tax. S corporation files Form 1120S. Shareholders are subject to tax on income attributable to their stock ownership.	Income subject to double taxation. Entity subject to tax, and shareholder subject to tax on any corporate dividends received. Corporation files Form 1120.
Highest tax rate	35% at individual level.	35% at owner level.	35% at shareholder level.	35% at corporate level plus 15%/0% on any corporate dividends at shareholder level (if qualified dividends; otherwise 35%).
Choice of tax year	Same tax year as owner.	Selection generally restricted to coincide with tax year of majority owners or principal owners, or to tax year determined under the least aggregate deferral method.	Restricted to a calendar year unless IRS approves a different year for business purposes or other exceptions apply.	Unrestricted selection allowed at time of filing first tax return.
Timing of taxation	Based on owner's tax year.	Owners report their share of income in their tax year with or within which the entity's tax year ends. Owners in their separate capacities are subject to payment of estimated taxes.	Shareholders report their shares of income in their tax year with or within which the corporation's tax year ends. Generally, the corporation uses a calendar year, but see "Choice of tax year" above. Shareholders may be subject to payment of estimated taxes. Corporation may be subject to payment of estimated taxes for the taxes imposed at the corporate level.	Corporation subject to tax at close of its tax year. May be subject to payment of estimated taxes. Dividends will be subject to tax at the shareholder level in the tax year received.

Tax Attributes of Different Forms of Business—Continued

	Sole Proprietorship	Partnership/Limited Liability Company*	S Corporation**	Regular (C) Corporation***
Basis for allocating income to owners	Not applicable (only one owner).	Profit and loss sharing agreement. Cash basis items of cash basis entities are allocated on a daily basis. Other entity items are allocated after considering varying interests of owners.	Pro rata share based on stock ownership. Shareholder's pro rata share is determined on a daily basis, according to the number of shares of stock held on each day of the corporation's tax year.	Not applicable.
Contribution of property to the entity	Not a taxable transaction.	Generally not a taxable transaction.	Is a taxable transaction unless the § 351 requirements are satisfied.	Is a taxable transaction unless the § 351 requirements are satisfied.
Character of income taxed to owners	Retains source characteristics.	Conduit—retains source characteristics.	Conduit—retains source characteristics.	All source characteristics are lost when income is distributed to owners.
Basis for allocating a net operating loss to owners	Not applicable (only one owner).	Profit and loss sharing agreement. Cash basis items of cash basis entities are allocated on a daily basis. Other entity items are allocated after considering varying interests of owners.	Prorated among shareholders on a daily basis.	Not applicable.
Limitation on losses deductible by owners	Investment plus liabilities.	Owner's investment plus share of liabilities.	Shareholder's investment plus loans made by shareholder to corporation.	Not applicable.
Subject to at-risk rules	Yes, at the owner level. Indefinite carryover of excess loss.	Yes, at the owner level. Indefinite carryover of excess loss.	Yes, at the shareholder level. Indefinite carryover of excess loss.	Yes, for closely held corporations. Indefinite carryover of excess loss.
Subject to passive activity loss rules	Yes, at the owner level. Indefinite carryover of excess loss.	Yes, at the owner level. Indefinite carryover of excess loss.	Yes, at the shareholder level. Indefinite carryover of excess loss.	Yes, for closely held corporations and personal service corporations. Indefinite carryover of excess loss.
Tax consequences of earnings retained by entity	Taxed to owner when earned and increases his or her investment in the sole proprietorship.	Taxed to owners when earned and increases their respective interests in the entity.	Taxed to shareholders when earned and increases their respective bases in stock.	Taxed to corporation as earned and may be subject to penalty tax if accumulated unreasonably.
Nonliquidating distributions to owners	Not taxable.	Not taxable unless money received exceeds recipient owner's basis in entity interest. Existence of § 751 assets may cause recognition of ordinary income.	Generally not taxable unless the distribution exceeds the shareholder's AAA or stock basis. Existence of accumulated earnings and profits could cause some distributions to be dividends.	Taxable in year of receipt to extent of earnings and profits or if exceeds basis in stock.

Tax Attributes of Different Forms of Business—Continued

	Sole Proprietorship	Partnership/Limited Liability Company*	S Corporation**	Regular (C) Corporation***
Capital gains	Taxed at owner level with opportunity to use alternative tax rate.	Conduit—owners must account for their respective shares.	Conduit, with certain exceptions (a possible penalty tax)—shareholders must account for their respective shares.	Taxed at corporate level with a maximum 35% rate. No other benefits.
Capital losses	Only $3,000 of capital losses can be offset each tax year against ordinary income. Indefinite carryover.	Conduit—owners must account for their respective shares.	Conduit—shareholders must account for their respective shares.	Carried back three years and carried forward five years. Deductible only to the extent of capital gains.
§ 1231 gains and losses	Taxable or deductible at owner level. Five-year lookback rule for § 1231 losses.	Conduit—owners must account for their respective shares.	Conduit—shareholders must account for their respective shares.	Taxable or deductible at corporate level only. Five-year lookback rule for § 1231 losses.
Foreign tax credits	Available at owner level.	Conduit—passed through to owners.	Generally conduit—passed through to shareholders.	Available at corporate level only.
§ 1244 treatment of loss on sale of interest	Not applicable.	Not applicable.	Available.	Available.
Basis treatment of entity liabilities	Includible in interest basis.	Includible in interest basis.	Not includible in stock basis.	Not includible in stock basis.
Built-in gains	Not applicable.	Not applicable.	Possible corporate tax.	Not applicable.
Special allocations to owners	Not applicable (only one owner).	Available if supported by substantial economic effect.	Not available.	Not applicable.
Availability of fringe benefits to owners	None.	None.	None unless a 2%-or-less shareholder.	Available within antidiscrimination rules.
Effect of liquidation/ redemption/ reorganization on basis of entity assets	Not applicable.	Usually carried over from entity to owner unless a § 754 election is made, excessive cash is distributed, or more than 50% of the capital interests are transferred within 12 months.	Taxable step-up to fair market value.	Taxable step-up to fair market value.
Sale of ownership interest	Treated as the sale of individual assets. Classification of recognized gain or loss depends on the nature of the individual assets.	Treated as the sale of an entity interest. Recognized gain or loss is classified as capital under § 741, subject to ordinary income treatment under § 751.	Treated as the sale of corporate stock. Recognized gain is classified as capital gain. Recognized loss is classified as capital loss, subject to ordinary loss treatment under § 1244.	Treated as the sale of corporate stock. Recognized gain is classified as capital gain. Recognized loss is classified as capital loss, subject to ordinary loss treatment under § 1244.

Tax Attributes of Different Forms of Business—Continued

	Sole Proprietorship	Partnership/Limited Liability Company*	S Corporation**	Regular (C) Corporation***
Distribution of appreciated property	Not taxable.	No recognition at the entity level.	Recognition at the corporate level to the extent of the appreciation. Conduit—amount of recognized gain is passed through to shareholders.	Taxable at the corporate level to the extent of the appreciation.
Splitting of income among family members	Not applicable (only one owner).	Difficult—IRS will not recognize a family member as an owner unless certain requirements are met.	Rather easy—gift of stock will transfer tax on a pro rata share of income to the donee. However, IRS can make adjustments to reflect adequate compensation for services.	Same as an S corporation, except that donees will be subject to tax only on earnings actually or constructively distributed to them. Other than unreasonable compensation, IRS generally cannot make adjustments to reflect adequate compensation for services and capital.
Organizational costs	Startup expenditures are eligible for $5,000 limited expensing (subject to phaseout) and amortizing balance over 180 months.	Organization costs are eligible for $5,000 limited expensing (subject to phaseout) and amortizing balance over 180 months.	Same as partnership.	Same as partnership.
Charitable contributions	Limitations apply at owner level.	Conduit—owners are subject to deduction limitations in their own capacities.	Conduit—shareholders are subject to deduction limitations in their own capacities.	Limited to 10% of taxable income before certain deductions.
Alternative minimum tax	Applies at owner level. AMT rates are 26% and 28%.	Applies at the owner level rather than at the entity level. AMT preferences and adjustments are passed through from the entity to the owners.	Applies at the shareholder level rather than at the corporate level. AMT preferences and adjustments are passed through from the S corporation to the shareholders.	Applies at the corporate level. AMT rate is 20%. Exception for small corporations.
ACE adjustment	Does not apply.	Does not apply.	Does not apply.	The adjustment is made in calculating AMTI. The adjustment is 75% of the excess of adjusted current earnings over unadjusted AMTI. If the unadjusted AMTI exceeds adjusted current earnings, the adjustment is negative.

Tax Attributes of Different Forms of Business—Continued

	Sole Proprietorship	Partnership/Limited Liability Company*	S Corporation**	Regular (C) Corporation***
Tax preference items	Apply at owner level in determining AMT.	Conduit—passed through to owners who must account for such items in their separate capacities.	Conduit—passed through to shareholders who must account for such items in their separate capacities.	Subject to AMT at corporate level.

*Refer to Chapters 10 and 11 for additional details on partnerships and limited liability companies.

**Refer to Chapter 12 for additional details on S corporations.

***Refer to Chapters 2 through 9 for additional details on regular (C) corporations.

****Spouses and family members are treated as one shareholder.

TAX PLANNING *Considerations*

The chapter began with an example that illustrated the relationship between tax planning and the choice of business form; it also raised a variety of questions about the advice given by the tax practitioner. By this time, the student should be able to develop various scenarios supporting the tax advice given. The actual fact situations that produced the tax adviser's recommendations were as follows:

- Jesse's experience in the dairy industry consists of raising a few heifers during the last five years he was employed. Eva anticipates that Jesse will have tax losses for the indeterminate future. In choosing between the partnership and the S corporation forms, Jesse indicated that he and his wife must have limited liability associated with the dairy farm.
- Larry was born and raised on his father's dairy farm. Both his education and his Air Force managerial experience provide him with useful tools for managing his business. However, Larry inherited his farm when milk prices were at a low for the modern era. Since none of her dairy farm clients were generating tax profits at that time, Eva anticipated Larry would operate his dairy farm at a loss. Larry, like Jesse, felt that limited liability was imperative. Thus, he incorporated the dairy farm and made the S corporation election.

  For the first two years, Larry's dairy farm produced tax losses. Since then, the dairy farm has produced tax profits large enough to absorb the losses. Larry anticipates that his profits will remain relatively stable in the $50,000 to $75,000 range. Since he is in the 28 percent marginal tax bracket and anticipates no dividend distributions to him from the corporation, his tax liability associated with the dairy farm will be less if he terminates the S corporation election.

As Jesse and Larry's example illustrates, selection of the proper business form can result in both nontax and tax advantages. Both of these factors should be considered in making the selection decision. Furthermore, this choice should be reviewed periodically, since a proper business form at one point in time may not be the proper form at a different time. Note that another business form Eva could have considered for Jesse is the LLC.

In selecting the right entity for conducting any business, tax consequences are important. In looking at the attributes, consideration should be given to the tax consequences of the following:

- Contribution of assets to the entity by the owners at the time the entity is created and at later dates.
- Taxation of the results of operations.
- Distributions to owners.
- Disposition of an ownership interest.
- Termination of the entity.

KEY TERMS

Conduit concept, 13–14

Entity concept, 13–14

Limited liability company (LLC), 13–4

Thin capitalization, 13–11

PROBLEM MATERIALS

DISCUSSION QUESTIONS

1. What are the principal legal forms for conducting a business entity? What are the principal Federal income tax forms for doing so?

2. The legal form of conducting a business entity is not always the same as the form recognized by the IRS for tax purposes. Provide two instances where this variance could occur.

3. Define a limited liability company.

4. The maximum corporate tax rate of 35% is the same as the maximum rate applicable to individuals. Consequently, for any additional taxable income, the corporate tax liability will be the same as the individual tax liability. Do you agree? Why or why not?

5. All of the Big 4 accounting firms changed their ownership form from a general partnership to a limited liability partnership. Discuss the legal and tax ramifications of this modification of ownership form.

6. Several taxpayers would like to conduct a business in partnership form with all of the owners having limited liability. Can a partnership, other than a limited liability partnership, be structured so that this objective is accomplished? If so, are there any tax pitfalls?

7. Compare the partnership and corporate business forms in terms of each of the following nontax factors:
   a. Capital formation.
   b. Limited liability.
   c. Estimated life of the business.
   d. Number of owners and their roles in the management of the business.

8. Gary is an entrepreneur who likes to be actively involved in his business ventures. He is going to invest $400,000 in a business that he projects will produce a tax loss of approximately $75,000 per year in the short run. However, once consumers become aware of the new product being sold by the business and the quality of the service it provides, he is confident the business will generate a profit of at least $100,000 per year. Gary has substantial other income (from both business ventures and investment activities) each year. Advise Gary on the business form he should select for the short run. He will be the sole owner.

   Decision Making

9. Sam is trying to decide whether he should operate his business as a C corporation or as an S corporation. Due to potential environmental hazard problems, it is imperative that the business have limited liability. Sam is leaning toward the S corporation form because it avoids double taxation. However, he is concerned that he may encounter difficulty several years in the future when he may want to issue some preferred stock to his son as a way of motivating him to remain active in the business. Sue, a friend of his, says that he can maintain maximum flexibility by operating as a C corporation. According to her, Sam can avoid double taxation by paying himself a salary equal to the before-tax earnings. As Sam's tax adviser, what is your advice to him?

   Decision Making

10. Can an S corporation's distribution policy generate a *wherewithal to pay* problem for its shareholders? Discuss several ways this problem can be avoided and the tax consequences of doing so.

   Issue ID

11. Is an individual or a C corporation subject to a higher AMT tax rate? What adjustment for AMT purposes applies only to C corporations?

12. All individual taxpayers and C corporations are directly or indirectly subject to the AMT. Evaluate this statement.

Issue ID

13. Nell is going to operate her business as a partnership or as a corporation. If she decides to operate as a corporation, she will elect S corporation status. This will enable her to take advantage of the losses projected for the first two years. Assuming she is going to operate the business in three different states, what question is relevant if she chooses the corporate form but is not relevant if she chooses the partnership form? Assume that Nell satisfies the requirements for the S corporation election.

14. Do different types of favorably taxed fringe benefits yield the same result? Explain.

Issue ID

15. Oscar created Lavender Corporation four years ago. The C corporation has paid Oscar as president a salary of $200,000 each year. Annual earnings after taxes approximate $700,000 each year. Lavender has not paid any dividends nor does it intend to do so in the future. Instead, Oscar wants his heirs to receive the stock with a step-up in stock basis when he dies. Identify the relevant tax issues.

16. What is meant by the term *thin capitalization*? Why is the IRS concerned with the capitalization of corporations?

Decision Making

17. Liane owns land and a building that she has been using in her sole proprietorship. She is going to incorporate her sole proprietorship as a C corporation. Liane is trying to decide whether to contribute the land and building to the corporation or to lease them to the corporation. The net income of the sole proprietorship for the past five years has averaged $200,000. Advise Liane on the tax consequences.

18. Is it possible to permanently avoid double taxation of a C corporation by never making distributions to shareholders (because the stock will appreciate in value and the heirs will receive a step-up in basis on the death of the shareholder)?

19. Orange and Rust have both been in business for approximately nine years. Each corporation has 14 shareholders and taxable income of about $350,000 per year. Neither corporation has made any dividend distributions nor plans to do so in the near future. Explain why Orange may have an accumulated earnings tax problem, while Rust does not.

Decision Making

20. Arnold is going to conduct his business in corporate form. What factors should he consider in deciding whether to operate as a C corporation or as an S corporation?

Issue ID

21. Tammy and Arnold own 40% of the stock of Roadrunner, an S corporation. The other 60% is owned by 99 other shareholders (all are single and unrelated). Tammy and Arnold have agreed to a divorce and are in the process of negotiating a property settlement. Identify the relevant tax issues for Tammy and Arnold.

22. Sabrina is going to contribute an SUV to her wholly owned business. She purchased the SUV three years ago for $58,000 and used it exclusively for personal purposes during this period. The fair market value of the SUV is $40,000. Are the tax consequences different if Sabrina contributes the SUV to an S corporation in which she is a 100% shareholder rather than a C corporation in which she is a 100% shareholder? If the business is a sole proprietorship?

23. Tab and Nora are considering organizing their business either as a partnership or as a corporation. Distinguish between the effects of the conduit and the entity concepts with respect to the recognition of gain or loss at the time of the transfer of assets to the entity. Is it possible to organize the business as a corporation and not have the entity concept apply at that time?

24. Why are special allocations either permitted or required for the partners in a partnership, yet are not permitted for the shareholders in a C corporation or an S corporation?

25. In calculating the basis of a partner's interest in a partnership, the partner's basis is increased by the share of the partnership liabilities. Since an S corporation is taxed

similarly to a partnership, is the same adjustment made in calculating an S corporation shareholder's basis in the stock?

26. Identify the effect of each of the following on a partner's basis for a partnership interest and a shareholder's (both C corporation and S corporation) basis for stock:

- Profits.
- Losses.
- Liability increase.
- Liability decrease.
- Contribution of assets.
- Distribution of assets.

27. The conduit concept applies to an S corporation. Are there any circumstances in which an S corporation is a taxpayer rather than merely a tax reporter?

28. Elk, Inc., an S corporation, has no accumulated earnings and profits or operating income in 2008. If a distribution is made to the shareholders at the end of 2008, how will it affect the basis in their stock?

29. Section 465 does not specifically refer to the at-risk rules as applying to partnerships or S corporations. Consequently, do the at-risk rules apply to these entities?

30. Samuel wants to sell his sole proprietorship, a hair salon, to Eleanor for $250,000.
    a. Does it matter to Samuel whether the form of the transaction is a sale of the business or a sale of the individual assets?
    b. Is the answer in (a) affected by whether the assets have appreciated in value or declined in value?

31. Explain how the tax consequences differ for the complete liquidation of a C corporation and a sale of the stock by the shareholders.

32. Using the legend provided, indicate which form of business entity each of the following characteristics describes. Some of the characteristics may apply to more than one form of business entity.

Legend
SP = Applies to sole proprietorship
P = Applies to partnership
S = Applies to S corporation
C = Applies to C corporation
N = Applies to none

    a. Has limited liability.
    b. Greatest ability to raise capital.
    c. Subject to double taxation.
    d. Not subject to double taxation.
    e. Could be subject to accumulated earnings tax.
    f. Limit on types and number of shareholders.
    g. Has unlimited liability.
    h. Sale of the business can be subject to double taxation.
    i. Profits and losses affect the basis for an ownership interest.
    j. Entity liabilities affect the basis for an ownership interest.
    k. Distributions of earnings are taxed as dividend income to the owners.
    l. Total invested capital cannot exceed $1 million.
    m. AAA is an account that relates to this entity.

33. Using the legend provided, indicate which form of business entity each of the following characteristics describes. Some of the characteristics may apply to more than one form of business entity.

Legend
P = Applies to partnership
S = Applies to S corporation
C = Applies to C corporation

The basis for an ownership interest is:
a. Increased by an investment by the owner.
b. Decreased by a distribution to the owner.
c. Increased by entity profits.
d. Decreased by entity losses.
e. Increased as the entity's liabilities increase.
f. Decreased as the entity's liabilities decrease.

34. Green Partnership, a general partnership, has many opportunities to use special allocations. One of the special allocations available to Green is the optional adjustment-to-basis election under §§ 754 and 743 when a new partner acquires a partnership interest from an existing partner. Discuss the relevant factors that should be considered before making this election.

PROBLEMS

35. A business entity has the following assets and liabilities on its balance sheet:

	Net Book Value	Fair Market Value
Assets	$675,000	$950,000
Liabilities	100,000	100,000

The business entity has just lost a product liability suit with damages of $5 million being awarded to the plaintiff. Although the business entity will appeal the judgment, legal counsel indicates the judgment is highly unlikely to be overturned by the appellate court. The product liability insurance carried by the business has a policy ceiling of $3 million. What is the amount of liability of the entity and its owners if the form of the business entity is:
a. A sole proprietorship?
b. A partnership?
c. A C corporation?
d. An S corporation?

36. Red, White, Blue, and Orange have taxable income as follows:

Corporation	Taxable Income
Red	$ 90,000
White	300,000
Blue	800,000
Orange	30,000,000

a. Calculate the marginal tax rate and the effective tax rate for each of the C corporations.
b. Explain why the marginal tax rate for a C corporation can exceed 35%, but the effective tax rate cannot do so.

Decision Making

Communications

37. Amy and Jeff Barnes are going to operate their florist shop as a partnership or as an S corporation. After paying salaries of $45,000 to each of the owners, the shop's earnings are projected to be about $60,000. The earnings are to be invested in the growth of the

business. Write a letter to Amy and Jeff Barnes (5700 Redmont Highway, Washington, D.C. 20024) advising them as to which of the two entity forms they should select.

38. Jack, an unmarried taxpayer, is going to establish a manufacturing business. He anticipates that the business will be profitable immediately due to a patent that he holds. He anticipates that profits for the first year will be about $200,000 and will increase at a rate of about 20% per year for the foreseeable future. He will be the sole owner of the business. Advise Jack on the form of business entity he should select. Assume Jack will be in the 35% tax bracket.

Decision Making

39. Clay Corporation will begin operations on January 1. Earnings for the next five years are projected to be relatively stable at about $90,000 per year. The shareholders of Clay are in the 33% tax bracket.
    a.   Assume that Clay will reinvest its after-tax earnings in the growth of the company. Should Clay operate as a C corporation or as an S corporation?
    b.   Assume that Clay will distribute its after-tax earnings each year to its shareholders. Should Clay operate as a C corporation or as an S corporation?

Decision Making

40. Mabel and Alan, who are in the 35% tax bracket, recently acquired a fast-food franchise. Each of them will work in the business and receive a salary of $150,000. They anticipate that the annual profits of the business, after deducting salaries, will be approximately $400,000. The entity will distribute enough cash each year to Mabel and Alan to cover their Federal income taxes associated with the franchise.
    a.   What amount will the entity distribute if the franchise operates as a C corporation?
    b.   What amount will the entity distribute if the franchise operates as an S corporation?
    c.   What will be the amount of the combined entity/owner tax liability in (a) and (b)?

41. Parrott is a closely held corporation owned by 10 shareholders (each has 10% of the stock). Selected financial information provided by Parrott follows:

Taxable income	$5,250,000
Positive AMT adjustments (excluding ACE adjustment)	425,000
Negative AMT adjustments	(30,000)
Tax preferences	6,000,000
Retained earnings	850,000
Accumulated E & P	775,000
ACE adjustment	720,000

    a.   Calculate Parrott's tax liability if Parrott is a C corporation.
    b.   Calculate Parrott's tax liability if Parrott is an S corporation.
    c.   How would your answers in (a) and (b) change if Parrott is not closely held (e.g., 5,000 shareholders with no shareholder owning more than 2% of the stock)?

42. Offshore Fishing Corporation, a calendar year taxpayer, is going to sell real estate that it no longer needs. The real estate is located in Corpus Christi, Texas, and has an adjusted basis of $540,000 ($900,000 − $360,000 MACRS straight-line depreciation) and a fair market value of $840,000. (ADS straight-line depreciation would have been $312,000.) The buyer of the real estate would like to close the transaction prior to the end of the calendar year. Offshore Fishing, however, is uncertain whether the tax consequences would be better if it sold the real estate this year or next year. It is considering the following options:

Decision Making

- $840,000 in cash payable on December 31, 2008.
- The sale will be closed on December 31, 2008, with the consideration being a $840,000 note issued by the buyer. The maturity date of the note is January 2, 2009, with the real estate being pledged as security.

Offshore projects its taxable income for 2008 and 2009 to be $900,000 (gross receipts of about $10 million) without the sale of the real estate. Determine the tax consequences to Offshore under each option and recommend the one that should be selected. Consider both the regular income tax and the AMT in making your recommendation.

43. Three unmarried sisters own and operate a dairy farm. They live on the farm and take their meals on the farm for the "convenience of the employer." The fair market value of their lodging is $30,000, and the fair market value of their meals is $18,000. The meals

are prepared for them by the farm cook who prepares their meals along with those of the five other farm employees. Determine the tax consequences of the meals and lodging to the sisters if the farm is:

a. Incorporated.

b. Not incorporated.

44. A business entity's taxable income before the cost of certain fringe benefits paid to owners and other employees is $400,000. The amounts paid for these fringe benefits are as follows:

	Owners	Other Employees
Group term life insurance	$20,000	$40,000
Meals and lodging incurred for the convenience of the employer	50,000	75,000
Pension plan	30,000*	90,000

*H.R. 10 (Keogh) plan for partnership and S corporation.

The business entity is equally owned by four owners.

a. Calculate the taxable income of the business entity if the entity is a partnership, a C corporation, or an S corporation.

b. Determine the effect on the owners for each of the three business forms.

45. Turtle, a C corporation, has taxable income of $400,000 before paying salaries to the three equal shareholder-employees, Britney, Shania, and Alan. Turtle follows a policy of distributing all after-tax earnings to the shareholders.

a. Determine the tax consequences for Turtle, Britney, Shania, and Alan if the corporation pays salaries to Britney, Shania, and Alan as follows:

Option 1		Option 2	
Britney	$180,000	Britney	$67,500
Shania	120,000	Shania	45,000
Alan	100,000	Alan	37,500

b. Is Turtle likely to encounter any tax problems associated with either option?

46. Beaver, a C corporation, is owned by Abner (60%) and Fran (40%). Abner is the president, and Fran is the vice president for sales. Late in 2007, Beaver encounters working capital difficulties. Therefore, Abner loans the corporation $540,000, and Fran loans the corporation $360,000. Each loan is on a 6% note that is due in five years with interest payable annually. Determine the tax consequences to Beaver, Abner, and Fran for 2008 if:

a. The notes are classified as debt.

b. The notes are classified as equity.

Decision Making

47. Marci and Jennifer each own 50% of the stock of Lavender, a C corporation. After paying each of them a "reasonable" salary of $125,000, the taxable income of Lavender is normally around $600,000. The corporation is about to purchase a $2 million shopping mall ($1.5 million allocated to the building and $500,000 allocated to the land). The mall will be rented to tenants at a net rent income (i.e., includes rental commissions, depreciation, etc.) of $500,000 annually. Marci and Jennifer will contribute $1 million each to the corporation to provide the cash required for the acquisition. Their CPA has suggested that Marci and Jennifer purchase the shopping mall as individuals and lease it to Lavender for a fair rental of $300,000. Both Marci and Jennifer are in the 35% tax bracket. The acquisition will occur on January 2, 2008. Determine whether the shopping mall should be acquired by Lavender or by Marci and Jennifer in accordance with their CPA's recommendation. Assume the depreciation on the shopping mall in 2008 is $37,000.

48. Petal, Inc., has taxable income of $625,000 for 2008. It has used up the accumulated earnings credit and has no additional "reasonable needs of the business" for the current tax year. Determine the total potential tax liability for Petal:

a. If it declares no dividends.
b. If it declares and pays dividends equal to the after-tax earnings.
c. In (a) and (b) if Petal is an S corporation.

49. Since Garnet Corporation was formed six years ago, its stock has been held 750 shares by Frank and 250 shares by Grace. Their basis in the stock is $240,000 for Frank and $160,000 for Grace. As part of a stock redemption, Garnet redeems 100 of Frank's shares for $175,000 and 100 of Grace's shares for $175,000.

Decision Making

   a. What are the tax consequences of the stock redemption to Frank and Grace?
   b. How would the tax consequences to Frank and Grace be different if, instead of the redemption, they each sell 100 shares to Chuck (an unrelated party)?
   c. What factors should influence their decision on whether to redeem or sell the 200 shares of stock?

50. Eagle Corporation has been an electing S corporation since its incorporation 10 years ago. During the first three years of operations, it incurred total losses of $250,000. Since then Eagle has generated earnings of approximately $150,000 each year. None of the earnings have been distributed to the three equal shareholders, Claire, Lynn, and Todd, because the corporation has been in an expansion mode. At the beginning of 2008, Claire sells her stock to Nell for $400,000. Nell has reservations about the utility of the S election. Therefore, Lynn, Todd, and Nell are discussing whether the election should be continued. They expect the earnings to remain at approximately $150,000 each year. However, since they perceive that the expansion period is over and Eagle has adequate working capital, they may start distributing the earnings to the shareholders. All of the shareholders are in the 33% tax bracket. Advise the three shareholders on whether the S election should be maintained.

Decision Making

51. Bob Bentz and Carl Pierce each own 50% of the stock of Deer, Inc., a C corporation. When the corporation was organized, Bob contributed cash of $200,000, and Carl contributed land with an adjusted basis of $125,000 and a fair market value of $240,000. Deer assumed Carl's $40,000 mortgage on the land. In addition to the capital contributions, Bob and Carl each loaned the corporation $75,000. The maturity date of the loan is in 10 years, and the interest rate is 8%, the same as the Federal rate.

Communications

   a. Determine the tax consequences to Bob, Carl, and Deer of the initial contribution of assets, the shareholder loans, and the annual interest payments if the loans are classified as debt.
   b. The same as (a) except the loans are reclassified as equity.
   c. You and Bob met over lunch to discuss the tax consequences of the capital contributions and loans he and Carl made to Deer, Inc. Prepare a memo for the files on your discussion.

52. Agnes, Becky, and Carol form a business entity with each contributing the following:

	Adjusted Basis	Fair Market Value	Ownership Percentage
Agnes: Cash	$100,000	$100,000	40%
Becky: Land	60,000	120,000	40%
Carol: Services		50,000	20%

Becky's land has a $20,000 mortgage that is assumed by the entity. Carol, an attorney, receives her ownership interest in exchange for legal services. Determine the recognized gain to the owners, the basis for their ownership interests, and the entity's basis for its assets if the entity is:

   a. A partnership.
   b. A C corporation.
   c. An S corporation.

53. Amber has a 20% ownership interest in an entity for which she initially contributed $100,000. She is one of the original owners of the business. None of the owners are related. During the life of the business, the following have occurred:

- Cumulative losses of $200,000 during the first three years.
- Profits of $150,000 in the next year.
- Distributions to owners of $75,000 at the end of year 3.
- Distribution to Amber of $60,000 that redeems 25% of her ownership interest at the end of year 4. No other owners redeem any of their ownership interest.

Determine the tax consequences to Amber if the entity is:

a. A partnership.
b. An S corporation.
c. A C corporation.

Decision Making

54. On January 1, 2008, John contributes assets (adjusted basis of $40,000; fair market value of $106,000) for a 40% ownership interest in an interior design business. Maria contributes $150,000 cash for a 60% ownership interest. The entity assumes a $6,000 mortgage attributable to one of the assets contributed by John. During 2008, the business earns $100,000 and makes cash distributions of $30,000 to John and $45,000 to Maria. John and Maria are each in the 33% tax bracket.

a. If the business is a C corporation, determine the following:

- Recognized gain to the owners and the business on its creation.
- Original basis for John's and Maria's ownership interests.
- Effect of the earnings to the entity, John, and Maria.
- Effect of the distributions to John and Maria.
- Adjusted basis for John's and Maria's ownership interests at the end of the year.

b. Determine each of the above if the business is an S corporation.
c. If the objective is to minimize the income tax liability, should the business be a C corporation or an S corporation? Assume 2008 is a representative year.

55. A computer retailer has been in existence for five years. Annual profits have been approximately $100,000, and no distributions have been made to the owners. Anita and Hector each own a 50% interest and have the following bases for their ownership interests:

Anita	$200,000
Hector	150,000

The company distributes an undivided interest in investment land (adjusted basis of $280,000; fair market value of $360,000) to Anita and Hector. Determine the tax consequences of the distribution to Anita and Hector if the entity is:

a. A partnership.
b. An S corporation (assume the S election has been in effect for five years).
c. A C corporation.
d. A limited liability company.

56. Beige, Inc., a personal service corporation, has the following types of income and losses for 2008:

Active income	$212,000
Portfolio income	20,000
Passive activity losses	216,000

a. Calculate Beige's taxable income for 2008.
b. Assume that instead of being a personal service corporation, Beige is a closely held corporation. Calculate Beige's taxable income for 2008.

57. Abby and Velma are equal owners of the AV Partnership with Abby investing $75,000 and Velma contributing land and a building (adjusted basis of $50,000; fair market value of $75,000). In addition, the entity borrows $200,000 using recourse financing and $100,000 using nonrecourse financing.

a. What are Abby's and Velma's bases for their partnership interests (i.e., outside bases)?
b. What are Abby's and Velma's at-risk bases?

58. Which of the following special allocations are available to (1) a partnership, (2) a C corporation, and (3) an S corporation?

a. Ability to share profits and losses differently from the share in capital.

b. Ability to share profits and losses differently.

c. The special allocation required under § 704(c) for the difference between the adjusted basis and the fair market value of contributed property.

d. The special allocation of any item permitted under § 704(a) if the substantial economic effect rule of § 704(b) is satisfied.

e. The optional adjustment to basis permitted under § 734 that results from distributions.

f. The optional adjustment to basis permitted under § 743 that results from an acquisition by purchase, taxable exchange, or inheritance.

59. Emily and Freda are negotiating with George to purchase the business that he operates in corporate form (Pelican, Inc.). The assets of Pelican, Inc., a C corporation, are as follows:

Asset	Basis	FMV
Cash	$ 20,000	$ 20,000
Accounts receivable	50,000	50,000
Inventory	100,000	110,000
Furniture and fixtures*	150,000	170,000
Building**	200,000	250,000
Land	40,000	150,000

*Potential depreciation recapture under § 1245 is $45,000.

**The straight-line method was used to depreciate the building. The balance in the accumulated depreciation account is $340,000.

George's basis for the stock of Pelican, Inc., is $560,000. George is in the 35% tax bracket, and Pelican, Inc., is in the 34% tax bracket.

a. Assume that Emily and Freda purchase the stock of Pelican from George and that the purchase price is $908,000. Determine the tax consequences to Emily and Freda, Pelican, and George.

b. Assume that Emily and Freda purchase the assets from Pelican and that the purchase price is $908,000. Determine the tax consequences to Emily and Freda, Pelican, and George.

c. Assume that the purchase price is $550,000 because the fair market value of the building is $150,000, and the fair market value of the land is $50,000. Also, assume that no amount is assigned to goodwill. Emily and Freda purchase the stock of Pelican from George. Determine the tax consequences to Emily and Freda, Pelican, and George.

60. Trey and Willis are purchasing the Copper Partnership from Jan and Gail for $400,000 with Trey and Willis being equal partners. Based on the negotiations, Jan and Gail have succeeded in having the transaction structured as the purchase of the partnership rather than the purchase of the individual assets. The adjusted basis of the individual assets of the Copper Partnership is $350,000.

Decision Making

a. What are Trey's and Willis's bases for their partnership interests (i.e., outside bases)?

b. What is Copper's adjusted basis for its assets after the transaction? Would a § 743 optional adjustment-to-basis election be helpful?

61. Gail and Harry own the GH Partnership, which has conducted business for 10 years. The bases for their partnership interests are $100,000 for Gail and $150,000 for Harry. GH Partnership has the following assets:

Decision Making

Asset	Basis	FMV
Cash	$ 10,000	$ 10,000
Accounts receivable	30,000	28,000
Inventory	25,000	26,000
Building*	100,000	150,000
Land	250,000	400,000

*The straight-line method has been used to depreciate the building. Accumulated depreciation is $70,000.

Gail and Harry sell their partnership interests to Keith and Liz for $307,000 each.

a.   Determine the tax consequences of the sale to Gail, Harry, and GH Partnership.

b.   From a tax perspective, would it matter to Keith and Liz whether they purchase Gail's and Harry's partnership interests or the partnership assets from GH Partnership?

Decision Making

Communications

62. Bill Evans is going to purchase either the stock or the assets of Dane Corporation. All of the Dane stock is owned by Chuck. Bill and Chuck agree that Dane is worth $750,000. The tax basis for Dane's assets is $410,000. Write a letter to Bill advising him on whether he should negotiate to purchase the stock or the assets. Also, prepare a memo for the files. Bill's address is 100 Village Green, Chattanooga, TN 37403.

RESEARCH PROBLEMS

Note: Solutions to Research Problems can be prepared by using the **RIA Checkpoint® Student Edition** online research product, which is available to accompany this text. It is also possible to prepare solutions to the Research Problems by using tax research materials found in a standard tax library.

Research Problem 1.   The stock of Ebony, Inc., is owned as follows:

	Percent Ownership	Basis	FMV
Alma	30	$2,700	$270,000
Ben	30	2,700	270,000
Debbie	20	1,800	180,000
Clyde	20	1,800	180,000

Alma and Ben are the parents of Debbie and Clyde. Managerial positions in Ebony are as follows: Alma is the chief executive officer (CEO), Ben is the chief operating officer (COO), Debbie is the chief financial officer (CFO), and Clyde is the vice president for human resources. Alma and Ben have owned their stock for 30 years, and Debbie and Clyde have owned their stock for 10 years. Alma and Ben are considering disposing of their stock and would like to use the funds to acquire a more lucrative investment. Their initial plan was to have Ebony redeem their stock. However, their accountant has indicated that since they intend to retain their positions as officers, the redemption will not qualify under § 302(b)(3). The accountant suggests that they sell their stock to several outsiders who wish to acquire an interest in Ebony. As Debbie and Clyde expect to move into the CEO and COO positions in a few years, they oppose a sale to outsiders. They are concerned about the loss of family control that would result.

How can this family dilemma be resolved?

Research Problem 2.   Dr. Sanders is a veterinarian who is the sole shareholder of Vet, Inc., an S corporation. The corporation offers consulting and surgical services to other veterinarians that Dr. Sanders provides. Dr. Sanders does not receive regular payments from the corporation but withdraws funds as the need arises. During the current year, he withdraws $118,000, and the net income of the corporation is $225,000. The corporation does not deduct the $118,000 nor does Dr. Sanders include it in his gross income. Dr. Sanders does, however, report the $225,000 in his gross income. Since Dr. Sanders has recognized all of the corporation's income, he sees no need to pay himself a salary. He justifies the treatment by arguing that he is not an employee (i.e., he is the owner) of the corporation, and the Federal income tax consequences are the same. Evaluate the approach taken by Dr. Sanders and Vet, Inc.

Research Problem 3.   Amanda and Paul are equal owners in Talon, Inc., an S corporation, and each has an adjusted basis in the stock of $80,000. In the current year, Talon has a loss of $200,000, and its Schedule K–1s allocate $100,000 to each shareholder.

Amanda and Paul are also equal partners in a partnership. Two years ago, in order to provide additional working capital to Talon, the partnership loaned it $100,000. The loan bore all of the usual attributes of a bona fide loan (i.e., a formal note, market interest rate, payment schedule). The loan was recorded as a note receivable by the partnership and as a note payable on the S corporation accounting records. Formal minutes authorizing the loan stated that the partnership was acting as an agent for Amanda and Paul.

Amanda and Paul each deducted their share (i.e., $100,000) of the S corporation loss. They contend that their combined stock basis and debt basis for § 1366(d) purposes is $130,000 ($80,000 + $50,000). The IRS maintains that the basis of each shareholder is only $80,000 (the basis in the stock). The loan cannot count as part of the shareholder's debt basis as it was not made directly to the S corporation. Evaluate the positions of the taxpayers and the IRS.

Research Problem 4.   Crane is a partner in the Cardinal Partnership. A dispute arose with the partnership regarding his share of current earnings. The partnership contends that the amount is $75,000, while Crane believes his share is $100,000.

Crane ceased being a partner on November 1, 2008. As a result of the dispute, the partnership distributed only $75,000 and placed the disputed $25,000 in escrow. However, Crane's Schedule K–1 from the partnership included the full $100,000. Crane feels that the K–1 should include only the $75,000 that is not in dispute. Is Crane correct?

Use the tax resources of the Internet to address the following questions. Do not restrict your search to the World Wide Web, but include a review of newsgroups and general reference materials, practitioner sites and resources, primary sources of the tax law, chat rooms and discussion groups, and other opportunities.

Internet
Activity

Research Problem 5.   Find an anecdote about a professional consulting firm that recently converted to LLP status. Are the firm and its competition and clients agreeable to the conversion of operating status?

Research Problem 6.   When did your state adopt LLC legislation? When did it receive IRS approval to apply partnership tax law to the entities?

Research Problem 7.   Find an article describing how a specific business put together its employee fringe benefit package in light of the limitations presented by the tax law and its form of operation.

Research Problem 8.   Determine whether your state income tax system permits an S corporation election.

Research Problem 9.   Determine how your state income tax deals with § 199 (domestic production activities deduction).

PART 4

Advanced Tax Practice Considerations

A specialist in taxation must cope with the procedural and ethical aspects of tax practice. Furthermore, the specialist may be confronted with a variety of technical subjects. These include the unique rules applicable to tax-exempt entities and multistate dealings.

Exempt Entities

LEARNING OBJECTIVES

After completing Chapter 14, you should be able to:

LO.1
Identify the different types of exempt organizations.

LO.2
Enumerate the requirements for exempt status.

LO.3
Know the tax consequences of exempt status, including the different consequences for public charities and private foundations.

LO.4
Determine which exempt organizations are classified as private foundations.

LO.5
Recognize the taxes imposed on private foundations and calculate the related initial tax and additional tax amounts.

LO.6
Determine when an exempt organization is subject to the unrelated business income tax and calculate the amount of the tax.

LO.7
List the reports exempt organizations must file with the IRS and the related due dates.

LO.8
Identify tax planning opportunities for exempt organizations.

Ideally, any entity that generates profit would prefer not to be subject to the Federal income tax. All of the types of entities discussed in Chapter 13 are subject to the Federal income tax at one level (e.g., sole proprietorships, partnerships, S corporations, and LLCs generally are subject only to single taxation) or more (e.g., C corporations are subject to double taxation). In contrast, entities classified as **exempt organizations** may be able to escape Federal income taxation altogether.

Churches are among the types of organizations that are exempt from Federal income tax. Nevertheless, one must be careful not to conclude that anything labeled a church will qualify for exempt status.

During the 1970s and 1980s, a popular technique for attempting to avoid Federal income tax was the establishment of so-called mail-order churches. For example, in one scheme, a nurse obtained a certificate of ordination and a church charter from an organization that sold such documents.[1] The articles of incorporation stated that the church was organized exclusively for religious and charitable purposes, including a religious mission of healing the spirit, mind, emotions, and body. The nurse was the church's minister, director, and principal officer. Taking a vow of poverty, she transferred all her assets, including a house and car, to the church. The church assumed all of the nurse's liabilities, including the mortgage on her house and her credit card bills. The nurse continued to work at a hospital and deposited her salary in the church's bank account. The church provided her with a living allowance sufficient to maintain or improve her previous standard of living. She was also permitted to use the house and car for personal purposes.

The IRS declared that such organizations were shams and not bona fide churches. For a church to be tax-exempt under § 501(c)(3), none of its net earnings may be used to the benefit of any private shareholder or individual. In essence, the organization should serve a public rather than a private interest. Though the courts have consistently upheld the IRS position, numerous avoidance schemes such as this have been attempted.

The latest technique being marketed as a way to avoid Federal income taxes is to set up shop as a credit counselor. Credit counselors have an opportunity to qualify for tax-exempt status under § 501(c)(3). Supposedly, such tax-exempt organizations exist to help debt-laden consumers learn to practice sound financial management, become debt-free, and "live the good life." Unfortunately, in reality some credit counseling organizations push consumers into debt repayment schedules with high, poorly disclosed fees that leave the debtor in worse financial shape than before the "counseling." Apparently, the primary motive of such techniques

[1]Rev.Rul. 81–94, 1981–1 C.B. 330.

is to earn profits. These unsavory practices have caused Congress to call for greater IRS scrutiny. The IRS has revoked or is in the process of revoking the tax-exempt status of the 41 credit counselors it has audited. Such credit counselors have earned more than 40 percent of the industry's $1 billion in annual revenues.

As discussed in Chapter 1, the major objective of the Federal tax law is to raise revenue. If revenue raising were the only objective, however, the Code would not contain provisions that permit certain organizations to be either partially or completely exempt from Federal income tax. Social considerations may also affect the tax law. This objective bears directly on the decision by Congress to provide for exempt organization tax status. The House Report on the Revenue Act of 1938 explains:

> The exemption from taxation of money or property devoted to charitable and other purposes is based upon the theory that the Government is compensated for the loss of revenue by its relief from the financial burden which would otherwise have to be met by appropriations from public funds, and by the benefits resulting from the promotion of the general welfare.[2]

Recognizing this social consideration objective, Subchapter F (Exempt Organizations) of the Code (§§ 501–530) provides the authority under which certain organizations are exempt from Federal income tax. Exempt status is not open-ended in that two general limitations exist. First, the nature or scope of the organization may result in it being only partially exempt from tax.[3] Second, the organization may engage in activities that are subject to special taxation.[4]

Types of Exempt Organizations

An organization qualifies for exempt status *only* if it fits into one of the categories provided in the Code. Examples of qualifying exempt organizations and the specific statutory authority for their exempt status are listed in Exhibit 14–1.[5]

Requirements for Exempt Status

Exempt status frequently requires more than mere classification in one of the categories of exempt organizations. Many of the organizations that qualify for exempt status share the following characteristics.

- The organization serves some type of *common good*.[6]
- The organization is *not* a *for-profit* entity.[7]
- *Net earnings* do not benefit the members of the organization.[8]
- The organization does not exert *political influence*.[9]

Serving the Common Good

The underlying rationale for all exempt organizations is that they serve some type of *common good*. However, depending on the type of the exempt organization, the term *common good* may be interpreted broadly or narrowly. If the test is interpreted broadly, the group being served is the general public or some large subgroup thereof. If it is interpreted narrowly, the group is the specific group referred to in the statutory language. One of the factors in classifying an exempt organization as a private foundation is the size of the group it serves.

---

[2]See 1939–1 (Part 2) C.B. 742 for a reprint of H.R. No. 1860, 75th Congress, 3rd Session.

[3]See the subsequent discussion of Unrelated Business Income Tax.

[4]See the subsequent discussions of Prohibited Transactions and Taxes Imposed on Private Foundations.

[5]Section 501(a) provides for exempt status for organizations described in §§ 401 and 501. The orientation of this chapter is toward organizations that

conduct business activities. Therefore, the exempt organizations described in § 401 (qualified pension, profit sharing, and stock bonus trusts) are outside the scope of the chapter and are not discussed.

[6]See, for example, §§ 501(c)(3) and (4).

[7]See, for example, §§ 501(c)(3), (4), (6), (13), and (14).

[8]See, for example, §§ 501(c)(3), (6), (7), (9), (10), (11), and (19).

[9]See, for example, § 501(c)(3).

EXHIBIT 14–1	**Types of Exempt Organizations**

Public & privet foundation
class benefit

Statutory Authority	Brief Description	Examples or Comments
§ 501(c)(1)	Federal and related agencies.	Commodity Credit Corporation, Federal Deposit Insurance Corporation, Federal Land Bank.
§ 501(c)(2)	Corporations holding title to property for and paying income to exempt organizations.	Corporation holding title to college fraternity house.
§ 501(c)(3)	Religious, charitable, educational, scientific, literary, etc., organizations. *they can't lobby & Grass rooting*	Boy Scouts of America, Red Cross, Salvation Army, Episcopal Church, United Fund, University of Richmond. *there is limitation*
§ 501(c)(4)	Civic leagues and employee unions.	Garden club, tenants' association promoting tenants' legal rights in entire community, League of Women Voters.
§ 501(c)(5)	Labor, agricultural, and horticultural organizations.	Teachers' association, organization formed to promote effective agricultural pest control, organization formed to test soil and to educate community members in soil treatment, garden club.
§ 501(c)(6)	Business leagues, chambers of commerce, real estate boards, etc.	Chambers of Commerce, American Plywood Association, National Football League (NFL), Professional Golfers Association (PGA) Tour, medical association peer review board, organization promoting acceptance of women in business and professions.
§ 501(c)(7)	Social clubs.	Country club, rodeo and riding club, press club, bowling club, college fraternities.
§ 501(c)(8)	Fraternal beneficiary societies.	Lodges. Must provide for the payment of life, sickness, accident, or other benefits to members or their dependents.
§ 501(c)(9)	Voluntary employees' beneficiary associations.	Provide for the payment of life, sickness, accident, or other benefits to members, their dependents, or their designated beneficiaries.
§ 501(c)(10)	Domestic fraternal societies.	Lodges. Must not provide for the payment of life, sickness, accident, or other benefits; and must devote the net earnings exclusively to religious, charitable, scientific, literary, educational, and fraternal purposes.
§ 501(c)(11)	Local teachers' retirement fund associations.	Only permitted sources of income are amounts received from (1) public taxation, (2) assessments on teaching salaries of members, and (3) income from investments.
§ 501(c)(12)	Local benevolent life insurance associations, mutual or cooperative telephone companies, etc.	Local cooperative telephone company, local mutual water company, local mutual electric company.
§ 501(c)(13)	Cemetery companies.	Must be operated exclusively for the benefit of lot owners who hold the lots for burial purposes.
§ 501(c)(14)	Credit unions.	Other than credit unions exempt under § 501(c)(1).
§ 501(c)(15)	Mutual insurance companies.	Mutual fire insurance company, mutual automobile insurance company.
§ 501(c)(16)	Corporations organized by farmers' cooperatives for financing crop operations.	Related farmers' cooperative must be exempt from tax under § 521.
§ 501(c)(19)	Armed forces members' posts or organizations.	Veterans of Foreign Wars (VFW), Reserve Officers Association.
§ 501(c)(20)	Group legal service plans.	Provided by a corporation for its employees.
§ 501(d)	Religious and apostolic organizations.	Communal organization. Members must include pro rata share of the net income of the organization in their gross income as dividends.
§ 501(e)	Cooperative hospital service organizations.	Centralized purchasing organization for exempt hospitals.
§ 501(f)	Cooperative service organization of educational institutions.	Organization formed to manage universities' endowment funds.
§ 529	Qualified tuition programs.	Prepaid tuition and educational savings programs.
§ 530	Coverdell Education Savings Accounts.	Qualified education savings accounts.

Property

| TAX *in the News* | **HOW MUCH GETS SPENT FOR CHARITY?** |

How much of what you give to charity goes directly toward the charity's mission and how much goes for overhead costs is something that many donors would like to know. More and more data on this distribution are becoming available, even for small donors. Such knowledge can influence the donor's selection of a charity.

The American Institute of Philanthropy (**charity-watch.org**) grades charities from A+ to F based on financial criteria. One criterion is how much the charity spends to raise $100. The Charity Navigator (**charitynavigator.org**) uses a scale of zero to four stars to rate charities on their financial health, such as how efficiently they use their donations.

Sometimes charities decline contributions because of a potential donor's concern about overhead. Recently, Melissa

Berman, the president of Rockefeller Philanthropy Advisors, turned down the chance to manage a potential client's $90 million contribution to support charities helping children in developing countries. Her reason for declining was the donor's requirement that "not a penny go to operating expenses."

Some charities have undertaken campaigns to convince potential donors that spending money on overhead isn't such a bad thing. Some even seek gifts for the stated purpose of funding overhead. The charities argue that they need overhead funds to get and retain quality staff and to grow. Only time will tell how effective such a sales pitch will be.

Source: *Adapted from Rachel Emma Silverman and Sally Beaty, "Save the Children (But Pay the Bills, Too)," Wall Street Journal, December 26, 2006, p. D1.*

Not-for-Profit Entity

The organization may not be organized or operated for the purpose of making a profit. For some types of exempt organizations, the *for-profit prohibition* appears in the statutory language. For other types, the prohibition is implied.

Net Earnings and Members of the Organization

What uses are appropriate for the net earnings of a tax-exempt organization? The logical answer would seem to be that the earnings should be used for the exempt purpose of the organization. However, where the organization exists for the good of a specific group of members, such an open-ended interpretation could permit net earnings to benefit specific group members. Therefore, the Code specifically prohibits certain types of exempt organizations from using their earnings in this way.

> . . . no part of the net earnings . . . inures to the benefit of any private shareholder or individual.[10]

In other instances, a statutory prohibition is unnecessary because the definition of the exempt organization in the Code effectively prevents such use.

> . . . the net earnings of which are devoted exclusively to religious, charitable, scientific, literary, educational, and fraternal purposes.[11]

Political Influence

Religious, charitable, educational, etc., organizations are generally prohibited from attempting to influence legislation or participate in political campaigns. Participation in political campaigns includes participation both *on behalf of* a candidate and *in opposition to* a candidate.

[10]§ 501(c)(6).   [11]§ 501(c)(10).

TAX *in the News*   **EFFECTS OF SARBANES-OXLEY ON NONPROFIT ENTITIES**

The Sarbanes-Oxley Act does not apply to nonprofit entities. Nevertheless, some nonprofits are voluntarily complying with its provisions. For example, New York's Julliard School and the International Swimming Hall of Fame in Fort Lauderdale have adopted the governance practices, code of ethics, and increased transparency required by Sarbanes-Oxley. Factors contributing to such adoption by nonprofits include the following.

- Accounting firms that audit nonprofits are clamoring for the same financial controls now in place at for-profits.
- Nonprofit trustees are demanding more transparency.
- Nonprofit trustees are concerned that their professional reputations could be hurt if money is misused or the nonprofit falters.

Only in limited circumstances are such exempt organizations permitted to attempt to influence legislation. See the subsequent discussion under Prohibited Transactions.

LO.3

Know the tax consequences of exempt status, including the different consequences for public charities and private foundations.

Tax Consequences of Exempt Status: General

An organization that is appropriately classified as one of the types of exempt organizations is generally exempt from Federal income tax. Four exceptions to this general statement exist, however. An exempt organization that engages in a *prohibited transaction* or is a so-called *feeder organization* is subject to tax. If the organization is classified as a *private foundation*, it may be partially subject to tax. Finally, an exempt organization is subject to tax on its *unrelated business taxable income*.

In addition to being exempt from Federal income tax, an exempt organization may be eligible for other benefits, including the following.

- The organization may be exempt from state income tax, state franchise tax, sales tax, or property tax.
- The organization may receive discounts on postage rates.
- Donors of property to the exempt organization may qualify for charitable contribution deductions on their Federal and state income tax returns. However, *not* all exempt organizations are qualified charitable contribution recipients (e.g., gifts to the National Football League, PGA Tour, and Underwriters Laboratories are not deductible).

Prohibited Transactions

Engaging in a § 503 prohibited transaction can produce three negative results. First, part or all of the organization's income may be subject to Federal income tax. Second and even worse, the organization may forfeit its exempt status. Finally, intermediate sanctions may be imposed on certain exempt organization insiders.

Failure to Continue to Qualify.
Organizations initially qualify for exempt status only if they are organized as indicated in Exhibit 14–1. The initial qualification requirements then effectively become maintenance requirements. Failure to continue to meet the qualification requirements results in the loss of the entity's exempt status.

New Faith, Inc., is an excellent example of an exempt organization that failed to continue to qualify for tax exemption.[12] The stated purposes of the organization

---

[12]*New Faith, Inc.*, 64 TCM 1050, T.C.Memo. 1992–601.

were to feed and shelter the poor. In its application for exempt status, New Faith indicated that it would derive its financial support from donations, bingo games, and raffles. The IRS approved the exempt status.

New Faith's only source of income was the operation of several lunch trucks, which provided food to the general public in exchange for scheduled "donations." Evidence provided by the organization to the Tax Court did not show that the food from the lunch trucks was provided free of charge or at reduced prices. In addition, no evidence was presented to show that the people who received food for free or at below-cost prices were impoverished or needy. The court concluded that the primary purpose of the activity was the conduct of a trade or business. It upheld the IRS's revocation of New Faith's exempt status.

Election Not to Forfeit Exempt Status for Lobbying.
Organizations exempt under § 501(c)(3) (religious, charitable, educational, etc., organizations) are limited in their attempts to influence legislation (lobbying activities) and in participating in political campaigns.[13] Substantial lobbying or political activity can result in the forfeiture of exempt status.

Certain exempt organizations are permitted to engage in lobbying (but not political) activities that are greater than an insubstantial part of their activities, by making a § 501(h) election.[14] Eligible for the election are most § 501(c)(3) organizations (educational institutions, hospitals, and medical research organizations; organizations supporting government schools; organizations publicly supported by charitable contributions; certain organizations that are publicly supported by various sources including admissions, sales, gifts, grants, contributions, or membership fees; and certain organizations that support certain types of public charities).

An eligible § 501(c)(3) organization must make an affirmative election to participate in lobbying activities on a limited basis. The lobbying expenditures of electing organizations are subject to a ceiling. Exceeding the ceiling can lead to the forfeiture of exempt status. Even when the ceiling is not exceeded, a tax may be imposed on some of the lobbying expenditures (as discussed subsequently).

Two terms are key to the calculation of the ceiling amount: **lobbying expenditures** and **grass roots expenditures**. Lobbying expenditures are made for the purpose of influencing legislation through either of the following.

- Attempting to affect the opinions of the general public or any segment thereof.
- Communicating with any legislator or staff member or with any government official or staff member who may participate in the formulation of legislation.

Grass roots expenditures are made for the purpose of influencing legislation by attempting to affect the opinions of the general public or any segment thereof.

The statutory ceiling is imposed on both lobbying expenditures and grass roots expenditures and is computed as follows.

- 150% × Lobbying nontaxable amount = Lobbying expenditures ceiling.
- 150% × Grass roots nontaxable amount = Grass roots expenditures ceiling.

The *lobbying nontaxable amount* is the lesser of (1) $1 million or (2) the amount determined in Figure 14–1.[15] The *grass roots nontaxable amount* is 25 percent of the lobbying nontaxable amount.[16]

---

[13]§ 501(c)(3). In recognition of the influence of technology, even a single Internet link to a partisan political site can taint the exempt entity.

[14]Religious organizations and private foundations cannot make this election.

[15]§ 4911(c)(2).

[16]§ 4911(c)(4).

FIGURE 14–1	Calculation of Lobbying Nontaxable Amount

Exempt Purpose Expenditures	Lobbying Nontaxable Amount Is
Not over $500,000	20% of exempt purpose expenditures*
Over $500,000 but not over $1 million	$100,000 + 15% of the excess of exempt purpose expenditures over $500,000
Over $1 million but not over $1.5 million	$175,000 + 10% of the excess of exempt purpose expenditures over $1 million
Over $1.5 million	$225,000 + 5% of the excess of exempt purpose expenditures over $1.5 million

*Exempt purpose expenditures generally are the amounts paid or incurred for the taxable year to accomplish the following purposes: religious, charitable, scientific, literary, educational, fostering national or international amateur sports competition, or the prevention of cruelty to children or animals.

An electing exempt organization is assessed a tax on **excess lobbying expenditures** as follows.[17]

- 25% × Excess lobbying expenditures = Tax liability.

Excess lobbying expenditures are the greater of the following.[18]

- Excess of the lobbying expenditures for the taxable year over the lobbying nontaxable amount.
- Excess of the grass roots expenditures for the taxable year over the grass roots nontaxable amount.

EXAMPLE 1

Tan, Inc., a qualifying § 501(c)(3) organization, incurs lobbying expenditures of $500,000 for the taxable year and grass roots expenditures of $0. Exempt purpose expenditures for the taxable year are $5 million. Tan elects to be eligible to make lobbying expenditures on a limited basis.

Applying the data in Figure 14–1, the lobbying nontaxable amount is $400,000 [$225,000 + 5%($5,000,000 − $1,500,000)]. The ceiling on lobbying expenditures is $600,000 (150% × $400,000). Therefore, the $500,000 of lobbying expenditures are under the permitted $600,000. However, the election results in the imposition of tax on the excess lobbying expenditures of $100,000 ($500,000 lobbying expenditures − $400,000 lobbying nontaxable amount). The resulting tax liability is $25,000 ($100,000 × 25%). ∎

A § 501(c)(3) organization that makes disqualifying lobbying expenditures is subject to a 5 percent tax on the lobbying expenditures for the taxable year. A 5 percent tax may also be levied on the organization's management. The tax is imposed on management only if the managers knew that making the expenditures was likely to result in the organization no longer qualifying under § 501(c)(3), and if the managers' actions were willful and not due to reasonable cause. The tax does not apply to private foundations (see the subsequent discussion).[19] Concept Summary 14–1 capsulizes the rules on influencing legislation.

Intermediate Sanctions. Prior to 1996, the IRS had only two options available for dealing with exempt organizations (other than private foundations) engaging in prohibited transactions. First, it could attempt to subject part or all of the organization's income to Federal income tax. Second, it could revoke the exempt status

---

[17]§ 4911(a)(1).
[18]§ 4911(b).

[19]§ 4912.

CONCEPT SUMMARY $14-1$

Exempt Organizations and Influencing Legislation

Factor	Tax Result
Entity subject to rule	§ 501(c)(3) organization.
Effect of influencing legislation	Subject to tax on lobbying expenditures under § 4912. Forfeit exempt status under § 501(c)(3). Not eligible for exempt status under § 501(c)(4).
Effect of electing to make lobbying expenditures	Permitted to make limited lobbying expenditures. Subject to tax under § 4911.

of the organization. For private foundations, an additional option was available. The IRS could impose certain taxes on private foundations for engaging in so-called prohibited transactions (see Concept Summary 14–3 later in the chapter).

Tax legislation enacted in 1996 added another option to the IRS toolbox—**intermediate sanctions**—for so-called public charities.[20] The intermediate sanctions take the form of excise taxes imposed on disqualified persons (any individuals who are in a position to exercise substantial influence over the affairs of the organization) who engage in *excess benefit transactions* and on exempt organization managers who participate in such a transaction knowing that it is improper. Such excess benefit transactions include transactions in which a disqualified person engages in a non-fair-market-value transaction with the exempt organization or receives unreasonable compensation.

The excise tax on the disqualified person is imposed at a rate of 25 percent of the excess benefit. For the exempt organization manager, the excise tax is imposed at a rate of 10 percent of the excess benefit (unless such participation is not willful and is due to reasonable cause) with a statutory ceiling of $10,000 for any excess benefit transaction. These excise taxes are referred to as first-level taxes.

A second-level tax is imposed on the disqualified person if the excess benefit transaction is not corrected within the taxable period. This excise tax is imposed at a rate of 200 percent of the excess benefit.

Feeder Organizations

A **feeder organization** carries on a trade or business for the benefit of an exempt organization and remits its profits to the exempt organization. Such organizations are not exempt from Federal income tax. This provision is intended to prevent an entity whose primary purpose is to conduct a trade or business for profit from escaping taxation merely because all of its profits are payable to one or more exempt organizations.[21]

Some income and activities are *not* subject to the feeder organization rules.[22]

- Rent income that would be excluded from the definition of the term *rent* for purposes of the unrelated business income tax (discussed subsequently).
- A trade or business where substantially all the work is performed by volunteers.
- The trade or business of selling merchandise where substantially all the merchandise has been received as contributions or gifts.

---

[20] § 4958.
[21] § 502(a).

[22] § 502(b).

CONCEPT SUMMARY   14–2

Consequences of Exempt Status

General	Exempt from Federal income tax.
	Exempt from most state and local income, franchise, sales, and property taxes.
	Qualify for reductions in postage rates.
	Gifts to the organization often can be deducted by donor.
Exceptions	May be subject to Federal income tax associated with the following.
	• Engaging in a prohibited transaction.
	• Being a feeder organization.
	• Being a private foundation.
	• Generating unrelated business taxable income.

Concept Summary 14–2 highlights the consequences of exempt status.

EXAMPLE 2

Historic Foundation, a § 501(c)(3) organization, operates a museum that depicts life around the time of the Civil War in Georgia and Virginia. Historic receives a Super Burger franchise in a bequest from a wealthy benefactor. Since the franchise is very profitable, Historic's board decides to operate it as a subsidiary, with the profits going to Historic to support its tax-exempt mission. This subsidiary is a taxable entity (a feeder organization) subject to the Federal income tax using the corporate tax rates. ■

LO.4

Determine which exempt organizations are classified as private foundations.

Private Foundations

Tax Consequences of Private Foundation Status

Certain exempt organizations are classified as **private foundations**. This classification produces two negative consequences. First, the classification may have an adverse impact on the contributions received by the donee exempt organization. Contributions may decline because the tax consequences for donors may not be as favorable as if the entity were not a private foundation.[23] Second, the classification may result in taxation at the exempt organization level. The reason for this less beneficial tax treatment is that private foundations define common good more narrowly and therefore are seen as not being supported by, and operated for the good of, the public.

Definition of a Private Foundation. The following § 501(c)(3) organizations are *not* private foundations.[24]

1. Churches; educational institutions; hospitals and medical research organizations; charitable organizations receiving a major portion of their support from the general public or the United States, a state, or a political subdivision thereof that is operated for the benefit of a college or university; and governmental units (favored activities category).
2. Organizations that are broadly supported by the general public (excluding disqualified persons), by governmental units, or by organizations described in (1) above.
3. Entities organized and operated exclusively for the benefit of organizations described in (1) or (2) [a supporting organization].
4. Entities organized and operated exclusively for testing for public safety.

---

[23]§ 170(e)(1)(B)(ii).

[24]§ 509(a).

TAX *in the News*   **RECORD CONTRIBUTIONS TO COLLEGES AND UNIVERSITIES**

Higher education is a major recipient of charitable contributions. Beneficially, such educational institutions are excluded from private foundation status. Although private schools long have depended on donations, public colleges and universities are increasingly looking for gifts, too. A number of states are requiring colleges and universities to fund more of their budgets through tuition and fees, endowment income, and annual giving campaigns.

Donations to higher education amounted to a record $28 billion for the 2005–2006 academic year. This represented a 9.4 percent increase over the prior academic year. Fueling this increase were 80 hefty gifts from corporations, foundations, and individuals ranging from $14 million to $100 million.

The rich schools keep getting richer according to a survey conducted by the Council for Aid to Education, a Rand Group unit. Approximately 20 to 25 percent of the total goes to about 20 universities, with Stanford topping the list with more than $900 million in donations in 2005–2006. The top 10 recipients were:

Stanford
Harvard
Yale
University of Pennsylvania
Cornell
University of Southern California
Columbia
Johns Hopkins
Duke
University of Wisconsin

Source: *Adapted from Joseph Pereira, "Contributors Give Colleges $28 Billion," Wall Street Journal, February 22, 2007, p. D2.*

To meet the broadly supported requirement in (2) above, both the following tests must be satisfied.

- External support test.
- Internal support test.

Under the *external support test*, more than one-third of the organization's support each taxable year *normally* must come from the three groups listed in (2) above, in the following forms.

- Gifts, grants, contributions, and membership fees.
- Gross receipts from admissions, sales of merchandise, performance of services, or the furnishing of facilities in an activity that is not an unrelated trade or business for purposes of the unrelated business income tax (discussed subsequently). However, such gross receipts from any person or governmental agency in excess of the greater of $5,000 or 1 percent of the organization's support for the taxable year are not counted.

The *internal support test* limits the amount of support *normally* received from the following sources to one-third of the organization's support for the taxable year.[25]

- Gross investment income (gross income from interest, dividends, rents, and royalties).
- Unrelated business taxable income (discussed subsequently) minus the related tax.

Lion, Inc., a § 501(c)(3) organization, received the following support during the taxable year.   *EXAMPLE 3*

Governmental unit A for services rendered	$30,000
Governmental unit B for services rendered	20,000
General public for services rendered	20,000

To determine if organization is broadly supported

---

[25]Reg. § 1.509(a)–3(c) generally requires that the external and internal support tests be met in each of the four preceding tax years.

TAX *in the News*   **DONOR-ADVISED FUNDS: A HOT TOPIC**

Suppose that a wealthy taxpayer would like to make a substantial charitable contribution and qualify for the charitable contribution deduction this year. However, he has not yet identified the recipient of the contribution. Or the taxpayer has identified the recipient, but wants the charity to disburse the funds over a number of years. Or the taxpayer wants to make the contribution this year, but be permitted to advise the charitable organization in future years as to the possible use of the donated funds. Can the taxpayer achieve any of these goals and still be eligible for the charitable contribution deduction this year?

There is a way to meet the wealthy taxpayer's objectives. He can make his contribution to a "donor-advised fund." Such funds are components of a qualified charitable organization.

To receive this favorable treatment, however, certain statutory and administrative requirements must be met. Even though the donor may advise how the funds are used, the charitable organization must have ultimate control over their distribution. For any contributions to donor-advised funds made after February 13, 2007, the donor must obtain written acknowledgment from the charitable organization that it has exclusive legal control over the contributed assets.

Recognizing the potential for abuse in this area, both the Senate Finance Committee and the House Ways and Means Committee have identified donor-advised funds as a potential topic for additional legislation.

Gross investment income	$15,000
Contributions from individual substantial contributors (disqualified persons)	15,000

For purposes of the *external support test*, the support from A is counted only to the extent of $5,000 (greater of $5,000 or 1% of $100,000 support). Likewise, for B, only $5,000 is counted as support. Thus, the total countable support is $30,000 ($20,000 from the general public + $5,000 + $5,000), and Lion fails the test for the taxable year ($30,000/$100,000 = 30%; need > 33.3%). The $15,000 received from disqualified persons is excluded from the numerator but is included in the denominator.

In calculating the *internal support test*, only the gross investment income of $15,000 is included in the numerator. Thus, the test is satisfied ($15,000/$100,000 = 15%; cannot > 33%) for the taxable year.

Since Lion did not satisfy both tests, it does not qualify as an organization that is broadly supported. ■

The intent of the two tests is to exclude from private foundation status those § 501(c)(3) organizations that are responsive to the general public rather than to the private interests of a limited number of donors or other persons.

Examples of § 501(c)(3) organizations that would be classified as private foundations, except that they receive broad public support, include the United Fund, the Girl Scouts, university alumni associations, and symphony orchestras.

LO.5

Recognize the taxes imposed on private foundations and calculate the related initial tax and additional tax amounts.

Taxes Imposed on Private Foundations

In general, a private foundation is exempt from Federal income tax. However, because a private foundation is usually not a broadly, publicly supported organization, it may be subject to the following taxes.[26]

- Tax based on investment income.
- Tax on self-dealing.
- Tax on failure to distribute income.
- Tax on excess business holdings.
- Tax on investments that jeopardize charitable purposes.
- Tax on taxable expenditures.

---

[26]§§ 4940–4945.

Need know

CONCEPT SUMMARY 14–3

Taxes Imposed on Private Foundations

Type of Tax	Code Section	Purpose	Private Foundation		Foundation Manager	
			Initial Tax	Additional Tax	Initial Tax	Additional Tax
On investment income	§ 4940	Audit fee to defray IRS expenses.	2%*			
On self-dealing	§ 4941	Engaging in transactions with disqualified persons.	5%**	200%**	2.5%†	50%†
On failure to distribute income	§ 4942	Failing to distribute adequate amount of income for exempt purposes.	15%	100%		
On excess business holdings	§ 4943	Investments that enable the private foundation to control unrelated businesses.	5%	200%		
On jeopardizing investments	§ 4944	Speculative investments that put the private foundation's assets at risk.	5%	25%	5%††	5%†
On taxable expenditures	§ 4945	Expenditures that should not be made by private foundations.	10%	100%	2.5%††	50%†

*May be possible to reduce the tax rate to 1%. In addition, an exempt operating foundation [see §§ 4940(d)(2) and 4942(j)(3)] is not subject to the tax.

**Imposed on the disqualified person rather than the foundation.

† Subject to a statutory ceiling of $10,000.

†† Subject to a statutory ceiling of $5,000.

These taxes restrict the permitted activities of private foundations. Two levels of tax may be imposed on the private foundation and the foundation manager: an initial tax and an additional tax. The initial taxes (first-level), with the exception of the tax based on investment income, are imposed because the private foundation engages in so-called *prohibited transactions*. The additional taxes (second-level) are imposed only if the prohibited transactions are not corrected within a statutory time period.[27] See Concept Summary 14–3 for additional details.

The tax on a failure to distribute income will be used to illustrate how expensive these taxes can be and the related importance of avoiding their imposition. Both an initial (first-level) tax and an additional (second-level) tax may be imposed on a private nonoperating foundation for failure to distribute a sufficient portion of its income. The initial tax is imposed at a rate of 15 percent on the undistributed income for the taxable year that is not distributed by the end of the following taxable year. The initial tax is imposed on such undistributed income for each year until the IRS assesses the tax.

[27]§ 4961.

TAX *in the News*   PRIVATE FOUNDATIONS OF SPORTS CELEBRITIES

Professional sports athletes can make a lot of money. Teams, leagues, agents, and union officials all encourage them to "give back." At least 22 players from the NBA and 37 from the NFL have set up private foundations. While doing good for the community, these foundations boost the athlete's image. Frequently, athletes will grant an interview only on condition that they be allowed to talk about their latest philanthropic work.

Most of these athletes are newcomers to the world of philanthropy. Yet they receive little guidance. As a result, quite often the efficiency ratio (overhead costs versus amounts going to charitable purposes) is out of step with the standard guideline for private foundations of 75 percent spent for charitable purposes. In 2005, for example, one basketball player's foundation spent about $11,000 on charitable programs and more than $101,000 on administrative expenses. A football player's foundation directed only 6.7 percent of its expenses for 2005 to charity.

At the same time, a number of sports celebrities exceed the standard guideline for charitable spending. Foundations in this category for 2005 include the following.

Charity Name	Percentage Spent for Charity
Tiger Woods Foundation	85%
Lance Armstrong Foundation	82%
Andre Agassi Charitable Foundation	88%
Dikembe Mutombo Foundation	81%
Billy Andrade–Brad Faxon Charities	93%
Peyton Manning's Payback Foundation	92%

Source: *Adapted from G. Bruce Knecht, "Big Players in Charity,"* Wall Street Journal, *April 28, 2007, p. P1.*

Inadequate income distribution

The additional tax is imposed at a rate of 100 percent on the amount of the inadequate distribution that is not distributed by the assessment date. The additional tax is effectively waived if the undistributed income is distributed within 90 days after the mailing of the deficiency notice for the additional tax. Extensions of this period may be obtained.

Undistributed income is the excess of the distributable amount (in effect, the amount that should have been distributed) over qualifying distributions made by the entity. The distributable amount is the excess of the minimum investment return over the sum of (1) the unrelated business income tax and (2) the excise tax based on net investment income.[28] The minimum investment return is 5 percent of the excess of the fair market value of the foundation's assets over the unpaid debt associated with acquiring or improving these assets. The foundation's assets employed directly in carrying on the foundation's exempt purpose are not used in making this calculation.

EXAMPLE 4

Gold, Inc., a private foundation, has undistributed income of $80,000 for the taxable year 2005. It distributes $15,000 of this amount during 2006 and an additional $45,000 during 2007. An IRS deficiency notice is mailed to Gold on August 5, 2008. The initial tax is $12,750 [($65,000 × 15%) + ($20,000 × 15%)].

At the date of the deficiency notice, no additional distributions have been made from the 2005 undistributed income. Therefore, since the remaining undistributed income of $20,000 has not been distributed by August 5, 2008, an additional tax of $20,000 ($20,000 × 100%) is imposed.

If Gold distributes the $20,000 of undistributed income for 2005 within 90 days of the deficiency notice, the additional tax is waived. Without this distribution, however, the foundation will owe $32,750 in taxes. ∎

Exhibit 14–2 shows the classifications of exempt organizations and indicates the potential negative consequences of classification as a private foundation.

---

[28]§ 4940.

EXHIBIT 14–2 | **Exempt Organizations: Classification**

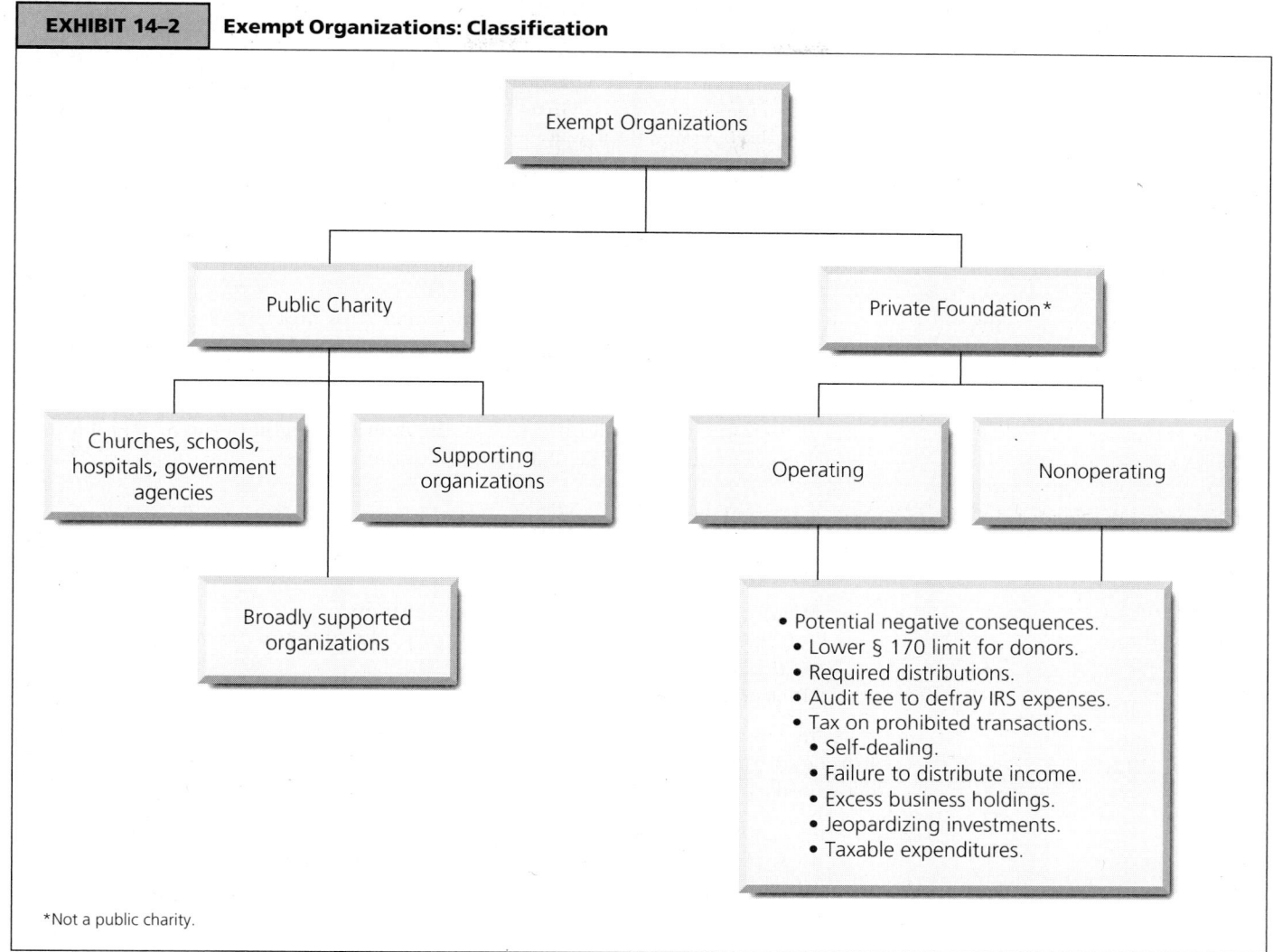

*Not a public charity.

Unrelated Business Income Tax — *excise tax*

As explained in the previous section, private foundations are subject to excise taxes for certain actions. One of these excise taxes penalizes the private foundation for using the foundation to gain control of unrelated businesses (tax on excess business holdings). However, *unrelated business* has different meanings for purposes of that excise tax and for the unrelated business income tax.

The **unrelated business income tax (UBIT)** is designed to treat the entity as if it were subject to the corporate income tax. Thus, the rates that are used are those applicable to a corporate taxpayer.[29] In general, **unrelated business income** is derived from activities not related to the exempt purpose of the exempt organization. The tax is levied because the organization is engaging in substantial commercial activities.[30] Without such a tax, nonexempt organizations (regular taxable business entities) would be at a substantial disadvantage when trying to compete with the exempt organization. Thus, the UBIT is intended to neutralize the exempt entity's tax advantage.[31]

LO.6

Determine when an exempt organization is subject to the unrelated business income tax and calculate the amount of the tax.

---

[29]§ 511(a)(1).
[30]§ 512(a)(1).

[31]Reg. § 1.513–1(b).

EXAMPLE 5

Historic, Inc., is an exempt private foundation. Its exempt activity is to maintain a restoration of eighteenth-century colonial life (houses, public buildings, taverns, businesses, and craft demonstrations) that is visited by more than a million people each year. A fee is charged for admission to the "restored area." In addition to this "museum" activity, Historic operates two hotels and three restaurants that are available to the general public. The earnings from the hotel and restaurant business are used to defray the costs of operating the "museum" activity.

The "museum" activity is not subject to the Federal income tax, except to the extent of any tax liability for any of the aforementioned excise taxes that are levied on private foundations. However, even though the income from the hotel and restaurant business is used for exempt purposes, that income is unrelated business income and is subject to the UBIT. ∎

The UBIT applies to all organizations that are exempt from Federal income tax under § 501(c), except Federal agencies. In addition, the tax applies to state colleges and universities.[32]

A materiality exception generally exempts an entity from being subject to the UBIT if such income is insignificant. See the later discussion of the $1,000 statutory deduction generally available to all exempt organizations.

Unrelated Trade or Business

An exempt organization may be subject to the UBIT in the following circumstances.[33]

- The organization conducts a trade or business.
- The trade or business is not substantially related to the exempt purpose of the organization.
- The trade or business is regularly carried on by the organization.

The Code specifically exempts the following activities from classification as an unrelated trade or business. Thus, even if all of the above factors are present, the activity is not classified as an unrelated trade or business.

- The individuals performing substantially all the work of the trade or business do so without compensation (e.g., an orphanage operates a retail store for sales to the general public, and all the work is done by volunteers).
- The trade or business consists of selling merchandise, and substantially all of the merchandise has been received as gifts or contributions (e.g., thrift shops).
- For § 501(c)(3) organizations and for state colleges or universities, the trade or business is conducted primarily for the convenience of the organization's members, students, patients, officers, or employees (e.g., a laundry operated by the college for laundering dormitory linens and students' clothing, a college bookstore).
- For most employee unions, the trade or business consists of selling to members, at their usual place of employment, work-related clothing and equipment and items normally sold through vending machines, snack bars, or food-dispensing facilities.

Definition of Trade or Business. Trade or business, for this purpose, is broadly defined. It includes any activity conducted for the production of income through the sale of merchandise or the performance of services. An activity need not generate a profit to be treated as a trade or business. The activity may be part of a larger set of activities conducted by the organization, some of which may be related to the exempt purpose. Being included in a larger set does not cause the activity to lose its identity as an unrelated trade or business.[34]

---

[32]§ 511(a)(2) and Reg. § 1.511–2(a)(2).
[33]§ 513(a) and Reg. § 1.513–2(a).

[34]Reg. § 1.513–1(b).

Health, Inc., is an exempt hospital that operates a pharmacy. The pharmacy provides medicines and supplies to the patients in the hospital (i.e., it contributes to the conduct of the hospital's exempt purpose). In addition, the pharmacy sells medicines and supplies to the general public. The activity of selling to the general public constitutes a trade or business for purposes of the UBIT. ■

EXAMPLE 6

Not Substantially Related to the Exempt Purpose.

Exempt organizations frequently conduct unrelated trades or businesses to provide income to help defray the costs of conducting the exempt purpose (like the hotel and restaurant business in Example 5). Providing financial support for the exempt purpose will not prevent an activity from being classified as an unrelated trade or business and thereby being subject to the UBIT.

To be related to the accomplishment of the exempt purpose, the conduct of the business activities must be causally related and contribute importantly to the exempt purpose. Whether a causal relationship exists and the degree of its importance are determined by examining the facts and circumstances. One must consider the size and extent of the activities in relation to the nature and extent of the exempt function that the activities serve.[35]

Art, Inc., an exempt organization, operates a school for training children in the performing arts. As an essential part of that training, the children perform for the general public. The children are paid at the minimum wage for the performances, and Art derives gross income by charging admission to the performances.

The income from admissions is not income from an unrelated trade or business, because the performances by the children contribute importantly to the accomplishment of the exempt purpose of providing training in the performing arts. ■

EXAMPLE 7

Assume the facts are the same as in Example 7, except that four performances are conducted each weekend of the year. Assume that this number of performances far exceeds that required for training the children. Thus, the part of the income derived from admissions for these excess performances is income from an unrelated trade or business. ■

EXAMPLE 8

The trade or business may sell merchandise that has been produced as part of the accomplishment of the exempt purpose. The sale of such merchandise is normally treated as related to the exempt purpose. However, if the merchandise is not sold in substantially the same state it was in at the completion of the exempt purpose, the gross income subsequently derived from the sale of the merchandise is income from an unrelated trade or business.[36]

Help-Self, Inc., an exempt organization, conducts programs for the rehabilitation of the handicapped. One of the programs includes training in radio and television repair. Help-Self derives gross income by selling the repaired items. The income is substantially related to the accomplishment of the exempt purpose. ■

EXAMPLE 9

An asset or facility used in the exempt purpose may also be used in a nonexempt purpose. Income derived from use for a nonexempt purpose is income from an unrelated trade or business.[37]

Civil, Inc., an exempt organization, operates a museum. As part of the exempt purpose of the museum, educational lectures are given in the museum's theater during the operating

EXAMPLE 10

---

[35]Reg. § 1.513–1(d).
[36]Reg. § 1.513–1(d)(4)(ii).

[37]Reg. § 1.513–1(d)(4)(iii) addresses the allocation of expenses to exempt and nonexempt activities.

hours of the museum. In the evening, when the museum is closed, the theater is leased to an individual who operates a movie theater. The lease income received from the individual who operates the movie theater is income from an unrelated trade or business. ∎

ETHICAL and EQUITABLE *Considerations*   **UNRELATED BUSINESS INCOME TAX: SUBSTANTIALLY RELATED**

Mops and More, a § 501(c)(3) organization, makes mops and brooms that it sells to the general public. The exempt organization's mission is to provide short-term employment opportunities and temporary housing for recovering drug addicts during the two-month period they are at a halfway house. Profits from the sales of the mops and brooms are used to support the halfway house. The laborers are paid the minimum wage, with half of this amount going toward their room and board at the halfway house. In prior years, approximately 90 percent of the laborers involved in the production of the mops and brooms were recovering addicts staying at the halfway house. The remaining 10 percent were permanent employees who trained and supervised the recovering addicts.

In prior years, Mops and More has not filed a Form 990–T (Exempt Organization Business Income Tax Return). The treasurer of Mops and More believes that the sale of the mops and brooms does not constitute unrelated business income, because the production of the items is substantially related to the mission of the exempt organization.

For the current tax year, there is a substantial drop in the number of recovering addicts who stay at the halfway house. To meet production quotas, the organization hires foreign workers who are legally in this country on temporary visas. They account for 70 percent of the labor force in the current year.

The treasurer believes that this shift from recovering addicts to foreign workers is temporary in nature. So she does not believe that it is necessary to file a Form 990–T. Has she acted appropriately?

Special Rule for Corporate Sponsorship Payments. The term *unrelated trade or business* does not include the soliciting and receiving of qualified sponsorship payments.[38]

A payment qualifies as a qualified sponsorship payment if it meets the following requirements.

- There is no arrangement or expectation that the trade or business making the payment will receive any substantial benefit other than the use or acknowledgment of its name, logo, or product lines in connection with the activities of the exempt organization.
- Such use or acknowledgment does not include advertising the payor's products or services.
- The payment does not include any payment for which the amount is contingent upon the level of attendance at one or more events, broadcast ratings, or other factors indicating the degree of public exposure to one or more events.

EXAMPLE 11

Pets, Inc., a manufacturer of cat food, contributes $25,000 to Feline Care, Inc., an exempt organization that cares for abandoned cats. In return for the contribution, Feline agrees to put Pets' corporate logo in its monthly newsletter to donors. Under these circumstances, the $25,000 payment is a qualified sponsorship payment and is not subject to the UBIT. ∎

EXAMPLE 12

Assume the same facts as in Example 11, except that Feline agrees to endorse Pets' cat food in its monthly newsletter by stating that it feeds only Pets' cat food to its cats. The $25,000 is not a qualified sponsorship payment and is subject to the UBIT. ∎

---

[38]§ 513(i).

Special Rule for Bingo Games. A special provision applies in determining whether income from bingo games is from an unrelated trade or business. Under this provision, a *qualified bingo game* is not an unrelated trade or business if both of the following requirements are satisfied.[39]

- The bingo game is legal under both state and local law.
- Commercial bingo games (conducted for a profit motive) ordinarily are not permitted in the jurisdiction.

EXAMPLE 13

Play, Inc., an exempt organization, conducts weekly bingo games. The laws of the state and municipality in which Play conducts the games expressly provide that exempt organizations may conduct bingo games, but do not permit profit-oriented entities to do so. Since both of the requirements for bingo games are satisfied, the bingo games conducted by Play are not an unrelated trade or business. ∎

EXAMPLE 14

Game, Inc., an exempt organization, conducts weekly bingo games in City X and City Y. State law expressly permits exempt organizations to conduct bingo games. State law also provides that profit-oriented entities may conduct bingo games in X, which is a resort community. Several businesses regularly conduct bingo games there.

   The bingo games conducted by Game in Y are not an unrelated trade or business. However, the bingo games that Game conducts in X are an unrelated trade or business, because commercial bingo games are regularly permitted to be conducted there. ∎

Special Rule for Distribution of Low-Cost Articles. If an exempt organization distributes low-cost items as an incidental part of its solicitation for charitable contributions, the distributions may not be considered an unrelated trade or business. A low-cost article is one that costs $9.10 (indexed annually) or less for 2008. Examples of such items are pens, stamps, stickers, stationery, and address labels. If more than one item is distributed to a person during the calendar year, the costs of the items are combined.[40]

Special Rule for Rental or Exchange of Membership Lists. If an exempt organization conducts a trade or business that consists of either exchanging with or renting to other exempt organizations the organization's donor or membership list (mailing lists), the activity is not an unrelated trade or business.[41]

Other Special Rules. Other special rules are used in determining whether each of the following activities is an unrelated trade or business.[42]

- Qualified public entertainment activities (e.g., a state fair).
- Qualified convention and trade show activities.
- Certain services provided at cost or less by a hospital to other small hospitals.
- Certain pole rentals by telephone or electric companies.

Unrelated Business Income

Even when an exempt organization conducts an unrelated trade or business, a tax is assessed only if the exempt organization regularly conducts the activity and the business produces unrelated business income.

Regularly Carried on by the Organization. An activity is classified as unrelated business income only if it is regularly carried on by the exempt organization.

---

[39]§ 513(f).
[40]§ 513(h)(1)(A).
[41]§ 513(h)(1)(B).
[42]§§ 513(d), (e), and (g).

This provision assures that only activities that are actually competing with taxable organizations are subject to the UBIT. Accordingly, factors to be considered in applying the *regularly carried on* test include the frequency of the activity, the continuity of the activity, and the manner in which the activity is pursued.[43]

EXAMPLE 15

Silver, Inc., an exempt organization, owns land that is located next to the state fairgrounds. During the 10 days of the state fair, Silver uses the land as a parking lot and charges individuals attending the state fair for parking there. The activity is not regularly carried on. ■

EXAMPLE 16

Black, Inc., an exempt organization, has its offices in the downtown area. It owns a parking lot adjacent to its offices on which its employees park during the week. On Saturdays, it rents the spaces in the parking lot to individuals shopping or working in the downtown area. Black is conducting a business activity on a year-round basis, even though it is only for one day per week. Thus, an activity is regularly being carried on. ■

Unrelated Business Income Defined.   Unrelated business income is generally that derived from the unrelated trade or business, reduced by the deductions directly connected with the conduct of the unrelated trade or business.[44]

Unrelated Business Taxable Income

General Tax Model.   The model for unrelated business taxable income (UBTI) appears in Figure 14–2.

Positive adjustments[45]

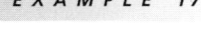
+ CC when they exceed the 10% ceiling (handwritten)

1. A charitable contribution deduction is permitted without regard to whether the charitable contributions are associated with the unrelated trade or business. However, to the extent the charitable contributions deducted in calculating net unrelated business income (see Figure 14–2) exceed 10 percent of UBTI (without regard to the charitable contribution deduction), the excess is treated as a positive adjustment.

EXAMPLE 17

Brown, Inc., an exempt organization, has UBTI of $100,000 (excluding any modifications associated with charitable contributions). Total charitable contributions (all associated with the unrelated trade or business) are $13,000. Assuming that the $13,000 is deducted in calculating net unrelated business income, the excess of $3,000 [$13,000 − 10%($100,000)] is a positive adjustment in calculating UBTI. ■

---

[43]§ 512(a)(1) and Reg. § 1.513–1(c).
[44]§ 512(a)(1).

[45]§§ 512(a)(1) and (b) and Reg. § 1.512(b)–1.

FIGURE 14–2	Tax Formula for Unrelated Business Taxable Income

Gross unrelated business income

− Deductions

= Net unrelated business income

± Modifications

= Unrelated business taxable income

2. Unrelated debt-financed income net of the unrelated debt-financed deductions (see the subsequent discussion of Unrelated Debt-Financed Income).
3. Certain net interest, annuity, royalty, and rent income received by the exempt organization from an organization it controls (80 percent test). This provision overrides the modifications for these types of income (negative adjustment 3).

Negative adjustments

1. Income from dividends, interest, and annuities net of all deductions directly related to producing such income.
2. Royalty income, regardless of whether it is measured by production, gross income, or taxable income from the property, net of all deductions directly related to producing such income.
3. Rent income from real property and from certain personal property net of all deductions directly related to producing such income. Personal property rents are included in the negative adjustment only if the personal property is leased with the real property. In addition, the personal property rent income must be incidental (does not exceed 10 percent of the gross rent income under the lease) to be used in computing the negative adjustment. In both of the following cases, however, none of the rent income is treated as a negative adjustment.
   • More than 50 percent of the rent income under the lease is from personal property.
   • Rent income is calculated using the tenant's profits.

EXAMPLE 18

Beaver, Inc., an exempt organization, leases land and a building (realty) and computers (personalty) housed in the building. Under the lease, $46,000 of the rent is for the land and building, and $4,000 is for the computers. Expenses incurred for the land and building are $10,000. The net rent income from the land and building of $36,000 ($46,000 − $10,000) and the income from the computers of $4,000 are negative adjustments. ∎

EXAMPLE 19

Assume the same facts as in Example 18, except that the rent income is $35,000 from the land and building and $15,000 from the computers. Since the rent income from the computers exceeds $5,000 (10% × $50,000) and is not incidental, it is not a negative adjustment. ∎

EXAMPLE 20

Assume the same facts as in Example 18, except that the rent income is $20,000 from the land and building and $30,000 from the computers. Since more than 50% of the rent income under the lease is from the computers, neither the rent income from the land and building nor that from the computers is a negative adjustment. ∎

If the lessor of real property provides significant services to the lessee, such income, for this purpose, is not rent income.
4. Gains and losses from the sale, exchange, or other disposition of property *except for* inventory.

EXAMPLE 21

Beaver, the owner of the land, building, and computers in Example 18, sells these assets for $450,000. Their adjusted basis is $300,000. Beaver's recognized gain of $150,000 is a negative adjustment. ■

5. Certain research income net of all deductions directly related to producing that income.
6. The charitable contribution deduction is permitted without regard to whether the charitable contributions are associated with the unrelated trade or business. Therefore, to the extent that the charitable contributions exceed those deducted in calculating net unrelated business income (see Figure 14–2), the excess is a negative adjustment in calculating UBTI. In making this calculation, be aware that the 10 percent of UBTI (without regard to the charitable contribution deduction) limit still applies (see positive adjustment 1).

EXAMPLE 22

Canine, Inc., an exempt organization, has UBTI of $100,000 (excluding any modifications associated with charitable contributions). The total charitable contributions are $9,000, of which $7,000 (those associated with the unrelated trade or business) has been deducted in calculating net unrelated business income. Therefore, the remaining $2,000 of charitable contributions is a negative adjustment in calculating UBTI. ■

7. A specific deduction of $1,000 is permitted.

EXAMPLE 23

Petit Care, Inc., an exempt organization, has net unrelated business income of $800. Since Petit will receive a specific deduction of $1,000, its UBTI is $0. Therefore, its income tax liability is $0. ■

After UBTI is determined, that amount is subject to tax using the regular corporate tax rates.

EXAMPLE 24

Patient, Inc., an exempt organization, has UBTI of $500,000. Patient's income tax liability is $170,000 ($500,000 UBTI × 34% corporate tax rate). ■

Unrelated Debt-Financed Income

In the formula for calculating UBTI (see Figure 14–2), unrelated debt-financed income is one of the positive adjustments. Examples of income from debt-financed property include rent income from real estate or tangible personal property, dividends from corporate stock, and gains from the disposition of debt-financed property. Gains from unrelated business income property are also included to the extent the gains are not otherwise treated as unrelated business income.

In terms of the UBIT, the positive adjustment for unrelated debt-financed income is a significant one. Without this provision, a tax-exempt organization could use borrowed funds to acquire unrelated business or investment property and use the untaxed (i.e., exempt) earnings from the acquisition to pay for the property.

Definition of Debt-Financed Income. Debt-financed income is the gross income generated from debt-financed property. *Debt-financed property* is all property of the exempt organization that is held to produce income and on which there is acquisition indebtedness, *except* for the following.[46]

• Property where substantially all (at least 85 percent) of the use is for the achievement of the exempt purpose of the exempt organization.[47]

---

[46]§ 514(b).

[47]Reg. § 1.514(b)–1(b)(1)(ii).

- Property whose gross income is otherwise treated as unrelated business income.
- Property whose gross income is from the following sources and is not otherwise treated as unrelated business income.
  - Income from research performed for the United States or a Federal governmental agency, or a state or a political subdivision thereof.
  - For a college, university, or hospital, income from research.
  - For an organization that performs fundamental (i.e., not applied) research for the benefit of the general public, income from research.
- Property used in an activity that is not an unrelated trade or business.

If the 85 percent test is not satisfied, only the portion of the property that is *not* used for the exempt purpose is debt-financed property.

Deer, Inc., an exempt organization, owns a five-story office building on which there is acquisition indebtedness. Three of the floors are used for Deer's exempt purpose. The two other floors are leased to Purple Corporation. In this case, the *substantially all* test is not satisfied. Therefore, 40% of the office building is debt-financed property, and 60% is not. ■

E X A M P L E   25

Certain land that is acquired by an exempt organization for later exempt use is excluded from debt-financed property if the following requirements are satisfied.[48]

- The principal purpose of acquiring the land is for use (substantially all) in achieving the organization's exempt purpose.
- This use will begin within 10 years of the acquisition date.
- At the date when the land is acquired, it is located in the *neighborhood* of other property of the organization for which substantially all the use is for achieving the organization's exempt purpose.

Even if the third requirement is not satisfied, the land still is excluded from debt-financed property if it is converted to use for achieving the organization's exempt purpose within the 10-year period. Qualification under this provision will result in a refund of taxes previously paid. If the exempt organization is a church, the 10-year period becomes a 15-year period, and the neighborhood requirement is waived.

Definition of Acquisition Indebtedness. Acquisition indebtedness is debt sustained by the exempt organization in association with the acquisition of property. More precisely, *acquisition indebtedness* consists of the unpaid amounts of the following for debt-financed property.[49]

- Debt incurred in acquiring or improving the property.
- Debt incurred before the property was acquired or improved, but which would not have been incurred without the acquisition or improvement.
- Debt incurred after the property was acquired or improved, but which would not have been incurred without the acquisition or improvement.

Red, Inc., an exempt organization, acquires land for $100,000. To finance the acquisition, Red mortgages the land and receives loan proceeds of $80,000. Red leases the land to Duck Corporation. The mortgage is acquisition indebtedness. ■

E X A M P L E   26

---

[48]§ 514(b)(3).

[49]§ 514(c)(1). Educational organizations can exclude certain debt incurred for real property acquisitions from classification as acquisition indebtedness.

EXAMPLE 27

Rose, Inc., an exempt organization, makes improvements to an office building that it rents to Bird Corporation. Excess working capital funds are used to finance the improvements. Rose is later required to mortgage its laboratory building, which it uses for its exempt purpose, to replenish working capital. The mortgage is acquisition indebtedness. ■

Portion of Debt-Financed Income and Deductions Treated as Unrelated Business Taxable Income.

Once the amount of the debt-financed income and deductions is determined, one must ascertain what portion thereof constitutes unrelated debt-financed income and deductions. Unrelated debt-financed income increases UBTI, and unrelated debt-financed deductions decrease UBTI.

The calculation is made for each debt-financed asset. The gross income from the property is multiplied by the following percentage.[50]

$$\frac{\text{Average acquisition indebtedness for the property}}{\text{Average adjusted basis of the property}} = \text{Debt/basis percentage}$$

This percentage cannot exceed 100. If debt-financed property is disposed of during the taxable year at a gain, average acquisition indebtedness in the formula is replaced with highest acquisition indebtedness. *Highest acquisition indebtedness* is the largest amount of acquisition indebtedness for the property during the 12-month period preceding the date of disposition.[51]

Deductions are allowed for expenses directly related to the debt-financed property and the income from it. Cost recovery deductions must apply the straight-line method. Once allowable deductions are determined, this amount is multiplied by the debt/basis percentage.[52]

EXAMPLE 28

White, Inc., an exempt organization, owns an office building that it leases to Squirrel Corporation for $120,000 per year. The average acquisition indebtedness is $300,000, and the average adjusted basis is $500,000. Since the office building is debt-financed property, the gross unrelated debt-financed income is:

$$\frac{\$300,000}{\$500,000} \times \$120,000 = \$72,000.$$

If White's expenses associated with the office building lease (including straight-line cost recovery) equal $50,000, then allowable deductions are:

$$\frac{\$300,000}{\$500,000} \times \$50,000 = \$30,000.$$

Thus, White's net unrelated debt-financed income is $42,000 ($72,000 − $30,000). ■

Average Acquisition Indebtedness.

The *average acquisition indebtedness* for debt-financed property is the average amount of the outstanding debt for the taxable year (ignoring interest) during the portion of the year the property is held by the exempt organization. This amount is calculated by summing the outstanding debt on the first day of each calendar month the property is held by the exempt organization. Then this total is divided by the number of months the property is held by the organization.[53]

EXAMPLE 29

On August 12, Yellow, Inc., an exempt organization, acquires an office building that is debt-financed property for $500,000. The initial mortgage on the property is $400,000. The principal amount of the debt on August 12 and on the first of each subsequent month is as follows.

---

[50]§ 514(a)(1).
[51]§ 514(c)(7).

[52]§ 514(a)(3).
[53]§ 514(c)(7) and Reg. § 1.514(a)–1(a)(3). A partial month is treated as a full month.

CONCEPT SUMMARY 14–4

Unrelated Business Income Tax

Purpose	To tax the entity on unrelated business income as if it were subject to the corporate income tax.
Applicable tax rates	Corporate tax rates.
Exempt organizations to which applicable	All organizations exempt under § 501(c), except Federal agencies.
Entities subject to the tax	The organization conducts a trade or business; the trade or business is not substantially related to the exempt purpose of the organization; and the trade or business is regularly carried on by the organization.
Exceptions to the tax	• All the work is performed by volunteers. • Substantially all of the merchandise being sold has been received by gift. • For § 501(c)(3) organizations, the business is conducted primarily for the benefit of the organization's members, students, patients, officers, or employees. • For most employee unions, the trade or business consists of selling to members work-related clothing and equipment and items normally sold through vending machines, snack bars, or food-dispensing facilities.
$1,000 provision	If the gross income from an unrelated trade or business is less than $1,000, it is not necessary to file a return associated with the unrelated business income tax.

Month	Principal Amount
August 12	$ 400,000
September 1	380,000
October 1	360,000
November 1	340,000
December 1	320,000
Total	$1,800,000

Average acquisition indebtedness is $360,000 ($1,800,000 ÷ 5 months). August is treated as a full month. ∎

Average Adjusted Basis. The *average adjusted basis* of debt-financed property is calculated by summing the adjusted bases of the property on the first and last days during the taxable year the property is held by the exempt organization and then dividing by two.[54]

EXAMPLE 30

Assume the facts are the same as in Example 29. In addition, during the taxable year, depreciation of $5,900 is deducted. The average adjusted basis is $497,050 [($500,000 + $494,100) ÷ 2]. ∎

Concept Summary 14–4 presents the rules concerning the UBIT.

---

[54]§ 514(a)(1) and Reg. § 1.514(a)–1(a)(2).

Reporting Requirements

Obtaining Exempt Organization Status

Not all exempt organizations are required to obtain IRS approval for their exempt status. Among those required by statute to do so are organizations exempt under §§ 501(c)(3), 501(c)(9), and 501(c)(20).[55] Even in these cases, exceptions are provided (e.g., churches).

Even when not required to obtain IRS approval, most exempt organizations do apply for exempt status. Typically, an organization does not want to assume that it qualifies for exempt status and describe itself in that way to the public, only to have the IRS rule later that it does not qualify. Organizations exempt under § 501(c)(3) use Form 1023 [Application for Recognition of Exemption under Section 501(c)(3)]. Form 1024 [Application for Recognition of Exemption under Section 501(a)] is used by most other types of exempt organizations.

If an organization is required to obtain IRS approval for its exempt status and does not do so, it does not qualify as an exempt organization.

ETHICAL and EQUITABLE *Considerations*

FILING FOR EXEMPT STATUS: A CPA's DILEMMA

Waldo is the treasurer of the Alpine Sky Divers Club. In his opinion, the club satisfies all the requirements for exempt status as a social club under § 501(c)(7). When Annette, the club president and an assistant district attorney, asks him if he has completed all the IRS paperwork relating to the club's tax-exempt status, Waldo assures her that he has taken care of everything.

If this were another client, Waldo would have filed a Form 1024 [Application for Recognition of Exemption under Section 501(a)]. He has not done so for Alpine because he has been very busy at work and feels fairly certain that the IRS will never raise the issue of whether the club qualifies for tax-exempt status. He told Annette he had filed the papers with the IRS because she is a stickler for detail and does everything by the book. He also has had several dates with her and does not want to take a chance on spoiling their relationship.

Evaluate Waldo's behavior.

Annual Filing Requirements

Most exempt organizations are required to file an annual information return.[56] The return is filed on Form 990 (Return of Organization Exempt from Income Tax). The following exempt organizations need not file Form 990.[57]

- Federal agencies.
- Churches.
- Organizations whose annual gross receipts do not exceed $25,000.[58]
- Private foundations.

Private foundations are required to file Form 990–PF (Return of Private Foundation). Form 990–PF requires more information than Form 990.

The due date for Form 990 or Form 990–PF is the fifteenth day of the fifth month after the end of the taxable year. These returns are filed with the appropriate IRS Service Center based on the location of the exempt organization's principal office. Requests for extensions on filing are made by filing Form 2758 (Applications for Extension of Time).

---

[55]§§ 505(c), 508(a), and 508(c).
[56]§ 6033(a)(1).
[57]§ 6033(a)(2).

[58]The statutory amount is $5,000. However, under its discretionary authority, the IRS has expanded the exemption amount to $25,000.

TAX *in the News*   **A NEW FORM 990**

Most exempt organizations are required to file an annual information return (Form 990—Return of Organization Exempt from Income Tax). Some major players in the Federal government arena are dissatisfied with the present Form 990.

Both Senator Max Baucus and Senator Chuck Grassley, the ranking and minority members, respectively, of the Sen-

ate Finance Committee, believe that certain vital information is not being provided for hospitals and universities. Perhaps associated with their dissatisfaction, the IRS has initiated a redesign project for Form 990. Draft copies of the new form can be viewed at **irs.gov**.

Source: *Adapted from Tom Herman and Rachel Emma Silverman, "Two Senators Call for Revising IRS Forms by Nonprofit Groups,"* Wall Street Journal, *May 30, 2007, p. D3.*

EXAMPLE 31

Green, Inc., a § 501(c)(3) organization, has a fiscal year that ends June 30, 2008. The due date for the annual return is November 15, 2008. If Green were a calendar year entity, the due date for the 2008 annual return would be May 15, 2009. ∎

Exempt organizations that are subject to the UBIT may be required to file Form 990–T (Exempt Organization Business Income Tax Return). The return must be filed if the organization has gross income of at least $1,000 from an unrelated trade or business. The due date for the return is the fifteenth day of the fifth month after the end of the taxable year.

If an exempt organization is subject to any of the excise taxes imposed on private foundations, Form 4720 (Return of Certain Excise Taxes on Charities and Other Persons) must be filed. The return is filed with the private foundation's Form 990–PF.

EXAMPLE 32

During the year, the First Church of Kentwood receives parishioner contributions of $450,000. Of this amount, $125,000 is designated for the church building fund. First Church is not required to file an annual return (Form 990) because churches are exempt from doing so. In addition, it is not required to file Form 990–T because it has no unrelated business income.

Colonial, Inc., is an exempt private foundation. Gross receipts for the year total $800,000, of which 40% is from admission fees paid by members of the general public who visit Colonial's museum of eighteenth-century life. The balance is endowment income and contributions from the founding donor. Because Colonial is a private foundation, it must file Form 990–PF.

Orange, Inc., is an exempt organization and is not a private foundation. Gross receipts for the year are $20,000. None of this amount is unrelated business income. Orange is not required to file Form 990 because its annual gross receipts do not exceed $25,000.

Restoration, Inc., is an exempt private foundation. Gross receipts for the year are $20,000. None of this amount is unrelated business income. Restoration must file Form 990–PF because private foundations are not eligible for the $25,000 filing exception.

During the year, the Second Church of Port Allen receives parishioner contributions of $300,000. In addition, the church has unrelated business income of $5,000. Second Church is not required to file Form 990 because churches are exempt from doing so. Form 990–T must be filed, however, because churches are not exempt from the UBIT and Second Church has exceeded the $1,000 floor. ∎

Disclosure Requirements

As a result of recent consumer-friendly rules, exempt entities must make more information readily available to the general public.[59] Prior to the issuance of these

---

[59]§ 6104(d), Reg. § 301.6104(d), and T.D. 8818 (April 1999).

rules, the disclosure requirements could be satisfied by making the information available for public inspection during regular business hours at the principal office of the exempt entity.

Copies of the following now must be made available to the general public.[60]

- Form 990.
- Form 1023 (or Form 1024).

Copies of the three most recent returns of the Form 990 must be made available. Private foundations must make Form 990–PF available for public inspection.

If an individual requests the entity's tax form in person, the exempt entity must provide a copy immediately. If the request is received in writing or by e-mail or fax, the copy must be provided within 30 days. The copy must be provided without charge, except for a reasonable fee for reproduction and mailing costs.

If the exempt entity has made the forms widely available to the general public, it is not required to fill individual requests. One technique for making the forms widely available is to put them on the Internet. Individual requests can also be disregarded if the exempt entity can show the request is part of a harassment campaign.

<table>
<tr><td>

LO.8

Identify tax planning opportunities for exempt organizations.

</td></tr>
</table>

TAX PLANNING
Considerations

General

Exempt organization status provides at least two potential tax benefits. First, the entity may be exempt from Federal income tax. Second, contributions to the entity may be deductible by the donor.

An organization that qualifies as an exempt organization may still be subject to certain types of Federal income tax, including the following.

- Tax on prohibited transactions.
- Tax on feeder organizations.
- Tax on private foundations.
- Tax on unrelated business income.

Therefore, classification as an exempt organization should not be interpreted to mean that the organization need not be concerned with any Federal income tax. Such a belief can result in the organization engaging in transactions that produce a substantial tax liability.

An organization is exempt from taxation only if it fits into one of the categories enumerated in the Code. Thus, particular attention must be given to the qualification requirements. These requirements must continue to be satisfied to avoid termination of exempt status (in effect they are now maintenance requirements).

Maintaining Exempt Status

To maintain exempt status, the organization must satisfy both an organizational test and an operational test. The organizational test requires that the entity satisfy the statutory requirements for exempt status on paper. The operational test ensures that the entity does, in fact, satisfy the statutory requirements for exempt status.

King Shipping Consum., Inc. (Zion Coptic Church, Inc.) illustrates that it is usually much easier to satisfy the organizational test than the operational test.[61] Zion's stated purpose was to engage in activities usually and normally associated with churches. Based on this, the IRS approved Zion's exempt status as a § 501(c)(3) organization.

---

[60]An Internet source of Forms 990 and 990–PF and other relevant materials on exempt entities is **http://www.guidestar.com**.

[61]58 TCM 574, T.C.Memo. 1989–593.

Zion's real intent, however, was to smuggle illegal drugs into the country and to distribute them for profit. The church's justification for the drugs was that it used marijuana in its sacrament. During a four-month period, however, the police confiscated 33 tons of marijuana from church members. The IRS calculated that, even assuming the maximum alleged church membership of several thousand, each member would have had to smoke over 33 pounds of marijuana during the four-month confiscation period.

The court concluded that Zion's real purpose was to cloak a large commercial drug smuggling operation. Since this activity was inconsistent with the religious purpose for exempt status, the court upheld the IRS's revocation of Zion's exempt status and the deficiency assessment of approximately $1.6 million.

Private Foundation Status

Exempt organizations that can qualify as public charities receive more beneficial tax treatment than do those that qualify as private foundations. Thus, if possible, the organization should be structured to qualify as a public charity. The following can result when an exempt organization is classified as a private foundation.

- Taxes may be imposed on the private foundation.
  - Tax based on investment income.
  - Tax on self-dealing.
  - Tax on failure to distribute income.
  - Tax on excess business holdings.
  - Tax on investments that jeopardize charitable purposes.
  - Tax on taxable expenditures.
- Donors may receive less favorable tax deduction treatment under § 170 than they would if the exempt organization were not a private foundation.

EXAMPLE 33

David has undeveloped land ($25,000 adjusted basis, $100,000 fair market value) that he is going to contribute to one of the following exempt organizations: Blue, Inc., a public charity, or Teal, Inc., a private nonoperating foundation. David has owned the land for five years.

David asks the manager of each organization to describe the tax benefits of contributing to that organization. He tells them he is in the 35% tax bracket and his AGI exceeds $250,000.

Based on the data provided by the managers, David decides to contribute the land to Blue, Inc. He calculates the amount of the charitable contribution under each option as follows.[62]

Donee	Contribution Deduction	Tax Rate	Contribution Borne by U.S. Government
Blue	$100,000	35%	$35,000
Teal	25,000 ($100,000 − $75,000)	35%	8,750

■

One method of avoiding private foundation status is to have a tax-exempt purpose that results in the organization not being classified as a private foundation (the *organization* approach). If this is not feasible, it may be possible to operate the organization so that it receives broad public support and thereby avoids private foundation status (the *operational* approach).

If the organization is a private foundation, care must be exercised to avoid the assessment of a tax liability on prohibited transactions. This objective can best be achieved by establishing controls that prevent the private foundation from

---

[62]See Chapter 2 of this text and Chapter 10 in *South-Western Federal Taxation: Individual Income Taxes.*

CONCEPT SUMMARY   14–5

Private Foundation Status

	Exempt Organization Is	
	A Private Foundation	**Not a Private Foundation**
Reason for classification	Does not serve the common good because it lacks an approved exempt purpose or does not receive broad public financial support.	Serves the common good
Eligible for exempt status?	Yes	Yes
Most beneficial charitable contribution deduction treatment available to donors?	Depends. No, if the private foundation is classified as a private *nonoperating* foundation.	Yes
Subject to excise taxes levied on prohibited transactions?	Yes	No
Subject to tax on unrelated business income?	Yes	Yes

engaging in transactions that trigger the imposition of the taxes. If an initial tax is assessed, corrective actions should be implemented to avoid the assessment of an additional tax. See Concept Summary 14–5.

Unrelated Business Income Tax

If the exempt organization conducts an unrelated trade or business, it may be subject to tax on the unrelated business income. Worse yet, the unrelated trade or business could result in the loss of exempt status if the IRS determines that the activity is the primary purpose of the organization. Thus, caution and planning should be used to eliminate the latter possibility and to minimize the former.

One approach that can be used to avoid the imposition of the UBIT is to establish a taxable subsidiary to conduct the unrelated trade or business. With a subsidiary, the revenues and expenses of the exempt organization can be separated from those of the unrelated trade or business. When the subsidiary remits its after-tax profits to the exempt organization in the form of dividends, the dividends will not be taxable to the exempt organization. In addition, having a taxable subsidiary conduct the unrelated trade or business avoids the possibility that the IRS will consider the unrelated business income to be an excessive percentage of the total revenues of the exempt organization. Such a view can lead to the IRS's questioning the exempt organization's right to retain its exempt status.

Another approach to avoiding the UBIT is to fail the definition of an unrelated trade or business. This is accomplished by *not* satisfying at least one of the following requirements.

- The organization conducts a trade or business.
- The trade or business is not substantially related to the exempt purpose of the organization.
- The trade or business is regularly carried on by the organization.

Even if the definitional requirements for an unrelated trade or business appear to be satisfied, the negative adjustments in calculating unrelated business taxable income (see Figure 14–2) can be used to minimize the tax liability.

Rental activities best illustrate the necessity of careful planning to avoid including the income from the activity in calculating unrelated business taxable income.

The income from the rental of real property by an exempt organization is not part of unrelated business taxable income. However, leases must be drafted so as to preserve the negative adjustment and avoid the UBIT prevalent in the following circumstances.

- If personal property is leased with real property and more than 50 percent of the rent income under the lease is from personal property, all the rent income is included in calculating unrelated business taxable income.
- If rent income from real property is calculated completely, or in part, based on the profits of the lessee (unless the calculation is based on a fixed percentage of sales or receipts), the rent income is included in calculating unrelated business taxable income.
- If the lessor of real property provides significant services to the lessee, the income is not treated as rent income and thus is included in the computation of unrelated business taxable income.
- If the rent income is received from an organization that the exempt organization controls (80 percent), the income is included in calculating unrelated business taxable income.
- To the extent the rent income is classified as unrelated debt-financed income, it is included in calculating unrelated business taxable income.

KEY TERMS

Debt-financed income, 14–22

Excess lobbying expenditures, 14–8

Exempt organizations, 14–2

Feeder organization, 14–9

Grass roots expenditures, 14–7

Intermediate sanctions, 14–9

Lobbying expenditures, 14–7

Private foundations, 14–10

Unrelated business income, 14–15

Unrelated business income tax (UBIT), 14–15

PROBLEM MATERIALS

DISCUSSION QUESTIONS

1. Are all churches exempt from Federal income tax?

2. Why are certain organizations either partially or completely exempt from Federal income tax?

3. Which of the following organizations qualify for exempt status?
   a. Tulane University.
   b. Virginia Qualified Tuition Program.
   c. Red Cross.
   d. Disneyland.
   e. Ford Foundation.
   f. Jacksonville Chamber of Commerce.
   g. Colonial Williamsburg Foundation.
   h. Professional Golfers Association (PGA) Tour.
   i. Green Bay Packers.
   j. Cleveland Indians.

4. Identify the statutory authority under which each of the following is exempt from Federal income tax.
   a. Kingsmill Country Club.
   b. Shady Lawn Cemetery.

    c.   Amber Credit Union.

    d.   Veterans of Foreign Wars.

    e.   Boy Scouts of America.

    f.   United Fund.

    g.   Federal Deposit Insurance Corporation.

    h.   Bruton Parish Episcopal Church.

    i.   PTA.

    j.   National Press Club.

5. What are the common characteristics shared by many exempt organizations?

6. Adrenna is the treasurer for two exempt organizations. One exempt organization pays no Federal income taxes for 2008, and the other pays Federal income taxes of $100,000 for 2008. Discuss potential reasons for this difference in tax results.

7. Two advantages of exempt organization status are (1) that the entity generally is not subject to Federal income taxes and (2) that donors to such entities are eligible for a charitable contribution deduction. Evaluate this statement.

8. Charity, Inc., a § 501(c)(3) hospital, would like to construct a five-story parking garage that will abut a residential neighborhood. Arnold, a member of the board of directors, has proposed that the board approve a $20,000 contribution to the political campaign of William, a candidate for city council. William privately has indicated his support for the construction of the parking garage. Agnes, his opponent, has publicly opposed the construction next door to the residential neighborhood.

    a.   Are any tax consequences to Charity associated with Arnold's proposal?

    b.   How would your answer differ if Charity were a church?

9. An exempt organization appropriately makes the § 501(h) election to lobby on a limited basis. The amount of its lobbying expenditures is less than its lobbying expenditures ceiling, yet it is subject to a tax at a 25% rate. Explain.

10. Mauve, Inc., a § 501(c)(3) organization, loses its exempt status in 2008 for attempting to influence legislation. Amber, Inc., another § 501(c)(3) organization, also attempts to influence legislation and is in no danger of losing its exempt status. Explain.

11. What are intermediate sanctions, and how are they related to forfeiture of exempt status?

12. Service, Inc., an exempt organization, owns all of the stock of Blue, Inc., a retailer of boating supplies. Blue remits all of its profits to Service. According to a policy adopted by Service's board, 60% of the amount received from Blue is to be spent annually in carrying out Service's tax-exempt mission, and 40% is to be invested in Service's endowment fund. What are the tax consequences to Service and to Blue?

13. Which of the following activities are *not* subject to the tax imposed on feeder organizations?

    a.   Substantially all of the work is performed by volunteers.

    b.   Substantially all of the services are performed by paid employees of the exempt organization.

    c.   Substantially all of the merchandise being sold is used property.

    d.   Substantially all of the merchandise being sold was received as contributions or gifts.

    e.   A building is rented to a tenant who uses the building as a warehouse for her business.

14. What is a private foundation, and what are the disadvantages of an exempt organization being classified as a private foundation?

15. Determine which of the following organizations are *not* private foundations.

    a.   Crestline Baptist Church.

    b.   Girl Scouts.

    c.   League of Women Voters.

    d.   PGA Tour.

    e.   American Institute of CPAs.

    f.   Homewood Middle School PTA.

g.   American Red Cross.

h.   Salvation Army.

i.   Veterans of Foreign Wars.

16.   Describe the external support test and the internal support test for a private foundation.

17.   What types of Federal income taxes that are never imposed on public charities may be imposed on private foundations?

18.   A private foundation engages in a transaction with a disqualified person. What are the tax consequences to the private foundation and to the disqualified person?

19.   At the end of the tax year, a private foundation has excess business holdings of $325,000. This is the first year that the private foundation has had any excess business holdings. What are the tax consequences to the private foundation?

20.   During the tax year, a private foundation makes speculative investments of $640,000 that are classified as jeopardizing investments. What are the tax consequences to the private foundation?

21.   A private foundation has taxable expenditures of $750,000. What are the tax consequences to the private foundation?

22.   Welcome, Inc., a tax-exempt organization, receives 25% of its support from disqualified persons. Another disqualified person has agreed to match this support if Welcome will appoint him to the organization's board of directors. What tax issues are relevant to Welcome as it makes this decision?

Issue ID

23.   Brett recently became the treasurer of Kind, Inc., a § 501(c)(3) organization that feeds the homeless. One of the entity's directors has proposed that Kind purchase and operate a fast-food franchise as part of Kind, Inc., to raise additional revenue to carry out its tax-exempt mission. Since the earnings generated by the fast-food franchise would be tax-exempt, substantial additional revenue would be provided. How should Brett respond?

24.   What circumstances will cause an exempt organization to be subject to the UBIT?

25.   First Church has been selling cards and small books in the church tower. A contribution box is provided in which payments are to be deposited. To increase church revenues, a task force is evaluating setting up a gift shop in the church parish house. What tax issues are relevant to the task force as it makes its decision?

Issue ID

26.   An exempt hospital operates a pharmacy that is staffed by a pharmacist 24 hours per day. The pharmacy serves only hospital patients. Is the pharmacy an unrelated trade or business?

27.   Second Church is going to operate a gift and book shop that will include only religious articles in its inventory. The shop will be staffed by employees who are not church members. Under consideration are two options: (1) organizing the shop as a wholly owned corporate subsidiary and (2) including it within the organizational structure of Second Church. The projected annual profits of $100,000 are to be used in the church's outreach mission. What are the tax consequences of each option? Which should Second Church select?

Decision Making

28.   To which of the following tax-exempt organizations may the UBIT apply?

a.   Red Cross.

b.   Salvation Army.

c.   United Fund.

d.   College of William and Mary.

e.   Rainbow, Inc., a private foundation.

f.   Louisiana State University.

g.   Colonial Williamsburg Foundation.

h.   Federal Land Bank.

29.   Sight, Inc., a tax-exempt organization that trains the visually impaired to restore and tune pianos, receives pianos as contributions. When the number of pianos on hand exceeds 15, Sight sells the excess; the pianos used in the training program the longest are sold first. Is the revenue from the sale of the excess pianos subject to the UBIT?

30. An exempt organization is considering conducting bingo games on Thursday nights as a way of generating additional revenue to support its exempt purpose. Before doing so, however, the president of the organization has come to you for advice regarding the effect on the organization's exempt status and whether the net income from the bingo games will be taxable. Identify the relevant tax issues.

31. When an exempt organization acquires land for later exempt use and there is acquisition indebtedness on the land, what requirements must be satisfied for the land to be excluded from classification as debt-financed property?

32. Tom is the treasurer of the City Garden Club, a new garden club. A friend, who is the treasurer of the garden club in a neighboring community, tells Tom that it is not necessary for the garden club to file a request for exempt status with the IRS. Has Tom received correct advice?

33. Abby recently became the treasurer of First Church. The church has been in existence for three years and has never filed anything with the IRS. Identify any reporting responsibilities Abby might have as church treasurer.

34. The Hope Church, a § 501(c)(3) organization, generates $76,000 of gross receipts this year. White Tail, Inc., a § 501(c)(3) organization, generates $22,000 of gross receipts this year. Must Hope Church or White Tail file an annual information return? If so, what form should be used?

35. Shane and Brittany are treasurers for § 501(c)(3) exempt organizations. Neither exempt organization is a church. Each year Shane's exempt organization files a Form 990 while Brittany's exempt organization files a Form 990–PF. Discuss the public disclosure requirements for each exempt organization.

PROBLEMS

36. Match the following exempt organizations with the statutory authority under which exempt status is granted. The statutory authority may apply to more than one exempt organization.

Exempt Organizations	Statutory Authority
Girl Scouts	§ 501(c)(1)
Catholic Church	§ 501(c)(2)
National Football League (NFL)	§ 501(c)(3)
American Red Cross	§ 501(c)(4)
Salvation Army	§ 501(c)(5)
United Fund	§ 501(c)(6)
Bill and Melinda Gates Foundation	§ 501(c)(7)
University of Richmond	§ 501(c)(8)
Underwriters Laboratories (UL)	§ 501(c)(9)
PGA Tour	§ 501(c)(10)
Veterans of Foreign Wars (VFW)	§ 501(c)(11)
Dallas Rodeo Club	§ 501(c)(12)
PTA	§ 501(c)(13)
Toano Cemetery Association	§ 501(c)(14)
Alpha Chi Omega Sorority	§ 501(c)(15)
Green, Inc., Legal Services Plan	§ 501(c)(16)
National Press Club	§ 501(c)(19)
Federal Deposit Insurance Corporation (FDIC)	§ 501(c)(20)
League of Women Voters	§ 501(d)

37. Teach, Inc., a § 501(c)(3) educational institution, makes lobbying expenditures of $450,000. Teach incurs exempt purpose expenditures of $3.9 million in carrying out its educational mission. Determine the tax consequences to Teach if:

a. It does not elect to be eligible to participate in lobbying activities on a limited basis.

b. It does elect to be eligible to participate in lobbying activities on a limited basis.

38. Choice, Inc., a § 501(c)(3) organization, pays unreasonable compensation to Monica, the treasurer of Choice. Monica's compensation is $400,000. Assume reasonable compensation would be $275,000.

    a. Determine any adverse tax consequences for Choice, Inc.

    b. Determine any adverse tax consequences for Monica.

39. Roadrunner, Inc., is an exempt medical organization. Quail, Inc., a sporting goods retailer, is a wholly owned subsidiary of Roadrunner. Roadrunner inherited the Quail stock last year from a major benefactor of the medical organization. Quail's taxable income is $550,000. Quail will remit all of its earnings, net of any taxes, to Roadrunner to support the exempt purpose of the parent.

    a. Is Quail subject to Federal income tax? If so, calculate the liability.

    b. Arthur Morgan, the treasurer of Roadrunner, has contacted you regarding minimizing or eliminating Quail's tax liability. He would like to know if the tax consequences would be better if Quail were liquidated into Roadrunner. Write a letter to Morgan that contains your advice. Roadrunner's address is 500 Rouse Tower, Rochester, NY 14627.

    c. Would your answer in (a) change if Roadrunner had acquired the Quail stock by purchase or gift rather than by inheritance? Discuss.

    d. How would the tax consequences change if Quail's taxable income was only $100,000 and it remitted only 75% of its earnings, net of taxes, to Roadrunner?

Decision Making

Communications

40. Respond, Inc., a § 501(c)(3) organization, receives the following revenues and incurs the following expenses.

Charitable contributions received	$800,000
Expenses in carrying out its exempt mission	950,000
Net income before taxes of Landscaping, Inc., a wholly owned for-profit subsidiary	200,000

Landscaping, Inc., remits all of its after-tax profits each year to Respond. Calculate the amount of the Federal income tax, if any, for Respond and for Landscaping.

41. Cardinal, Inc., a § 501(c)(3) organization, received support from the following sources.

Governmental unit A for services rendered	$ 7,000
Governmental unit B for services rendered	4,500
General public for services rendered	80,000
Gross investment income	41,000
Contributions from disqualified persons	26,000
Contributions from other than disqualified persons	140,000

Communications

    a. Does Cardinal satisfy the test for receiving broad public support?

    b. Is Cardinal a private foundation?

    c. Arnold Horn, Cardinal's treasurer, has asked you to advise him on whether Cardinal is a private foundation. Write a letter to him in which you address the issue. His address is 250 Bristol Road, Charlottesville, VA 22903.

42. Gray, Inc., a private foundation, has the following items of income and deductions.

Interest income	$24,000
Rent income	60,000
Dividend income	20,000
Royalty income	10,000
Unrelated business income	75,000
Rent expenses	(18,000)
Unrelated business expenses	(10,000)

Gray is not an exempt operating foundation and is not eligible for the 1% tax rate.

    a. Calculate the net investment income.

    b. Calculate the tax on net investment income.

    c. What is the purpose of the tax on net investment income?

43. Eagle, Inc., a private foundation, has been in existence for 10 years. During this period, Eagle has been unable to satisfy the requirements for classification as a private operating foundation. At the end of 2007, it had undistributed income of $280,000. Of this amount, $120,000 was distributed in 2008, and $160,000 was distributed during the first quarter of 2009. The IRS deficiency notice was mailed on August 1, 2010.
    a. Calculate the initial tax for 2007, 2008, and 2009.
    b. Calculate the additional tax for 2010.

Decision Making

44. Otis is the CEO of Rectify, Inc., a private foundation. Otis invests $500,000 (80%) of the foundation's investment portfolio in derivatives. Previously, the $500,000 had been invested in corporate bonds with an AA rating that earned 7% per annum. If the derivatives investment works as Otis's investment adviser claims, the annual earnings could be as high as 20%.
    a. Determine if Rectify is subject to any of the taxes imposed on private foundations.
    b. If so, calculate the amount of the initial tax.
    c. If so, calculate the amount of the additional tax if the act causing the imposition of the tax is not addressed within the correction period.
    d. Are Otis and the foundation better off financially if the prohibited transaction, if any, is addressed within the correction period?

45. The board of directors of Pearl, Inc., a private foundation, consists of Alice, Beth, and Carlos. They vote unanimously to provide a $100,000 grant to Doug, their business associate. The grant is to be used for travel and education and does not qualify as a permitted grant to individuals (i.e., it is a taxable expenditure under § 4945). Each director knows that Doug was selected for the grant because he is a friend of the organization and that the grant is a taxable expenditure.
    a. Calculate the initial tax imposed on the private foundation.
    b. Calculate the initial tax imposed on the foundation manager (i.e., board of directors).

Communications

46. The Open Museum is an exempt organization that operates a gift shop. The museum's annual operations budget is $3.2 million. Gift shop sales generate a profit of $900,000. Another $600,000 of endowment income is generated. Both the income from the gift shop and the endowment income are used to support the exempt purpose of the museum. The balance of $1.7 million required for annual operations is provided through admission fees. Wayne Davis, a new board member, does not understand why the museum is subject to tax at all, particularly since the profits are used in carrying out the mission of the museum. The museum's address is 250 Oak Avenue, Peoria, IL 61625.
    a. Calculate the amount of unrelated business income.
    b. Assume that the endowment income is reinvested rather than being used to support annual operations. Calculate the amount of unrelated business income.
    c. As the museum treasurer, write a letter to Wayne explaining the reason for the tax consequences. Mr. Davis's address is 45 Pine Avenue, Peoria, IL 61625.

47. Safety, Inc., a § 501(c)(3) organization, is located in a building on Nob Hill in San Francisco. The building has underground parking that is used during the week for employee and visitor parking. Since its offices are closed on the weekends, Safety leases the parking space on weekends to Parking, Inc., an independent for-profit company that rents parking spaces for $30 per day to tourists. For the year, Safety receives lease income of $200,000 from Parking, Inc. Parking, Inc.'s profits from the leased underground parking are $150,000. Calculate the amount of unrelated business income for Safety, Inc.

Communications

48. Perch, Inc., an exempt organization, has unrelated business taxable income of $4 million.
    a. Calculate Perch's unrelated business income tax.
    b. Prepare an outline of a presentation you are going to give to the new members of Perch's board on why Perch is subject to the UBIT even though it is an exempt organization.

49. For each of the following organizations, determine the amount of the UBIT.
    a. AIDS, Inc., an exempt charitable organization that provides support for individuals with AIDS, operates a retail medical supply store open to the general public. The net income of the store, before any Federal income taxes, is $325,000.

b. The local Episcopal Church operates a retail gift shop. The inventory consists of the typical items sold by commercial gift shops in the city. The director of the gift shop estimates that 80% of the gift shop sales are to tourists and 20% are to church members. The net income of the gift shop, before the salaries of the three gift shop employees and any Federal income taxes, is $300,000. The salaries of the employees total $80,000.

c. Education, Inc., a private university, has vending machines in the student dormitories and academic buildings on campus. In recognition of recent tuition increases, the university has adopted a policy of merely trying to recover its costs associated with the vending machine activity. For the current year, however, the net income of the activity, before any Federal income taxes, is $75,000.

d. Worn, Inc., an exempt organization, provides food for the homeless. It operates a thrift store that sells used clothing to the general public. The thrift shop is staffed by four salaried employees. All of the clothes it sells are received as contributions. The $100,000 profit generated for the year by the thrift shop is used in Worn's mission of providing food to the homeless.

e. Small, Inc., an exempt organization, has gross unrelated business income of $900 and unrelated business expenses of $400.

50. Serenity, Inc., an exempt organization, has gross unrelated business income of $11,500 and unrelated business expenses of $6,000. Calculate the amount of the UBIT.

51. Falcon Basketball League, an exempt organization, is a youth basketball league for children ages 12 through 14. The league has been in existence for 30 years. In the past, revenue for operations has been provided through community fund-raising and the sale of snacks at the games by the parents. Due to a projected revenue shortfall of approximately $5,000, the governing board has decided to charge admission to the basketball games of $1.00 for adults and $0.50 for children.

    Communications

    a. Will the admission charge affect Falcon's exempt status?

    b. What are the tax consequences to Falcon of the net income from snack sales and the new admission fee?

    c. As the volunteer treasurer of the Falcon League, prepare a memo for the board in which you explain the effect, if any, of the admission fee policy on Falcon's exempt status.

52. Help-Self, Inc., is an exempt organization whose mission is to help the homeless regain their self-image and become productive members of society. One of its programs includes nine months of training as computer repair technicians. After completing the training program, the technicians are employed by Help-Self Computer Repair, a division of Help-Self, Inc., at competitive wages while they search for full-time employment as computer repair technicians (usually two to six months).

    The net income of Help-Self Computer Repair for the current year is $950,000. This amount is used by Help-Self, Inc., in carrying out its mission. All of the other support for Help-Self, Inc., comes from contributions.

    a. Determine the amount, if any, of Help-Self, Inc.'s unrelated business taxable income (UBTI).

    b. Determine the amount, if any, of Help-Self, Inc.'s income tax liability.

53. Port Allen Sugarcane, Inc., contributes $10,000 to the Port Allen Krackers Baseball League, an exempt organization that sponsors summer baseball games for children under age 10. In return for the contribution, Port Allen Krackers includes Sugarcane's corporate logo on the cover of the program it sells at the baseball games.

    a. Determine the effect of the contribution to Port Allen Krackers.

    b. Instead of including the logo on the cover of its programs, Port Allen Krackers endorses Port Allen Sugarcane's sugar by advertising in the program that the mothers of team players use only sugar made by Port Allen Sugarcane for all their baking needs. Determine the effect of the contribution to Port Allen Krackers.

54. Faith Church is exempt from Federal income taxation under § 501(c)(3). To supplement its contribution revenue, it holds bingo games on Saturday nights. It has the licenses and permits required to do so. The net income from the bingo games is $90,000. Of these funds, $60,000 are used to support the ministry of the church. The

balance of $30,000 is invested in Faith's endowment fund for church music. Faith Church is located in a resort city where bingo games can be conducted by churches, charities, and for-profit entities.
  a.   Will conducting the bingo games affect the exempt status of Faith Church?
  b.   Calculate the Federal tax liability, if any, associated with the bingo games.

55. Bluebird, Inc., an exempt organization, has unrelated business taxable income of $200,000 (before any modifications associated with charitable contributions). Charitable contributions made by Bluebird that are associated with the unrelated trade or business are $15,000, and those made that are not associated with the unrelated trade or business are $10,000. Calculate the effect of the charitable contributions on Bluebird's unrelated business taxable income.

56. Comfort, Inc., an exempt hospital, is going to operate a pharmacy that will be classified as an unrelated trade or business. Comfort establishes the pharmacy as a wholly owned subsidiary. During the current year, the subsidiary generates taxable income of $200,000 and pays dividends of $125,000 to Comfort.
  a.   What are the tax consequences to the subsidiary?
  b.   What are the tax consequences to Comfort?

57. Good, Inc., an exempt organization, leases a factory building, machinery, and equipment to Coal Corporation. Under the lease, the annual rent for the building is $150,000, and the rent for the machinery and equipment is $200,000. Depreciation on the building is $5,500, and depreciation on the machinery and equipment is $40,000.
  a.   Calculate the amount of unrelated business taxable income to Good.
  b.   Assume that the rent income from the machinery and equipment is only $20,000 and the related depreciation is $4,000. Calculate the amount of unrelated business taxable income to Good.

58. Kind, Inc., an exempt organization, leases land, a building, and factory equipment to Shirts, Inc. Shirts is a taxable entity that manufactures shirts for distribution through its factory outlet stores. The rent income and the related expenses for Kind are as follows.

	Rent Income	Rent Expenses
Land and building	$100,000	$40,000
Factory equipment	125,000	25,000

  a.   Calculate the amount of Kind's unrelated business taxable income.
  b.   Assume instead that Kind's rent income and expenses are as follows.

	Rent Income	Rent Expenses
Land and building	$100,000	$20,000
Factory equipment	125,000	50,000

Calculate the amount of Kind's unrelated business taxable income.

59. Grouse, Inc., an exempt organization, sells the following assets during the taxable year.

Asset	Gain (Loss)	Use
Building A	$ 43,000	In exempt purposes
Building B	(16,000)	Leased to Tan Corporation
Building C	27,000	In exempt purposes
Inventory	80,000	

Determine the effect of these transactions on Grouse's unrelated business taxable income.

60. Medical, Inc., an exempt organization, has unrelated business taxable income of $450,000 (excluding any modifications associated with charitable contributions). Of total charitable contributions of $44,000 made by Medical, $40,000 are associated with its unrelated trade or business. Determine the effect of the charitable contributions on Medical's unrelated business taxable income.

61. Crow, Inc., an exempt organization, owns a building that cost $600,000. Depreciation of $250,000 has been deducted. The building is mortgaged for $400,000. The mortgage was incurred at the acquisition date. The building contains 10,000 square feet of floor space. Crow uses 7,000 square feet of the building in carrying on its exempt purpose and leases the remaining 3,000 square feet to Uranium Corporation. Is the building debt-financed property?

62. Growth, Inc., an exempt organization, acquires a building for $900,000 on September 1, 2008. The principal amount of the related mortgage on September 1 and on the first day of the following months is as follows.

September	$700,000
October	695,000
November	690,000
December	685,000

Depreciation deducted during 2008 was $6,741. Growth leases the building to Build Corporation.
   a. Calculate the average acquisition indebtedness for the building.
   b. Calculate the average adjusted basis for the building.
   c. Calculate the debt/basis percentage.

63. Rodeo, Inc., is a social club that is exempt under § 501(c)(7). Its annual gross receipts are $312,000. Of this amount, $24,000 is from an unrelated trade or business. Rodeo's fiscal year ends on May 31.
   a. Is Rodeo required to file an annual information return? If so, what form should be used?
   b. Is Rodeo subject to the UBIT? If so, what form should be used?
   c. If tax returns must be filed, what is the due date?

64. Education, Inc., a § 501(c)(3) organization, is a private foundation with a tax year that ends on June 30, 2008. Gross receipts for the fiscal year are $180,000, and the related expenses are $160,000.
   a. Is Education required to file an annual information return?
   b. If so, what form is used?
   c. If so, what is the due date?
   d. How would your answers in (a), (b), and (c) change if Education is an exempt organization that is not a private foundation?

65. Historic Burg is an exempt organization that operates a museum depicting eighteenth-century life. Sally gives the museum an eighteenth-century chest that she has owned for 10 years. Her adjusted basis is $55,000, and the chest's appraised value is $100,000. Sally's adjusted gross income is $300,000. Calculate Sally's charitable contribution deduction if Historic Burg is:
   a. A private operating foundation.
   b. A private nonoperating foundation.

RESEARCH PROBLEMS

Note: Solutions to Research Problems can be prepared by using the **RIA Checkpoint**® **Student Edition** online research product, which is available to accompany this text. It is also possible to prepare solutions to the Research Problems by using tax research materials found in a standard tax library.

Research Problem 1.   Allied Fund, a charitable organization exempt under § 501(c)(3), has branches located in each of the 50 states. Allied is not a private foundation. Rather than having each of the state units file an annual return with the IRS, Allied would like to file a single return that reports the activities of all of its branches. Is this permissible? What is the due date of the return?

Partial list of research aids:
§ 6033.
§ 6072.
Reg. § 1.6033–2(d).

Research Problem 2.   A Native American tribal government issued $1 million of bonds, paying interest at 4.5%. The disclosure document associated with the bonds stated that the bonds were tax-exempt. Is this correct? If so, provide documentation for such classification. Are there any exceptions?

Communications

Research Problem 3.   Wonderful Wilderness, Inc., is a tax-exempt organization. Its mission is to explore, enjoy, and protect the wild places of the earth; practice and promote the responsible use of the earth's ecosystems and resources; educate and enlist humanity to protect and restore the quality of the natural and human environment; and use all lawful means to carry out these objectives.

Lloyd Morgan, the chief financial officer, presents you with the following information. Wonderful Wilderness raises funds to support its mission in a variety of ways including contributions and membership fees. As part of this effort, Wonderful Wilderness develops and maintains mailing lists of its members, donors, catalog purchasers, and other supporters.

Wonderful Wilderness has exclusive ownership rights in its mailing lists. To acquire the names of prospective members and supporters, Wonderful Wilderness occasionally exchanges membership lists with other organizations. In addition, Wonderful Wilderness permits other tax-exempt organizations and commercial entities to pay a fee, as set forth in a fee schedule, to use its mailing lists on a onetime basis per transaction.

Morgan is aware of the UBIT. He is also aware of the § 512(b)(2) provision that excludes royalties from the UBIT. An IRS agent has raised the issue that the revenue from the use of the mailing lists by other entities may be taxable as unrelated business income. Morgan would like you to research this issue for him.

Write a letter to Morgan that contains your findings, and prepare a memo for the tax files. Wonderful Wilderness's address is 100 Wilderness Way, Pocatello, ID 83209.

Communications

Research Problem 4.   City Hospital, a tax-exempt hospital, has purchased a sports and fitness center located about three miles from the hospital. It is a state-of-the-art fitness center that includes an open fitness room with cardiovascular and strength equipment, an indoor track, exercise rooms, racquetball and tennis courts, an aquatic area with two pools, a nutrition center/juice bar, and tanning beds. The hospital's overall goals for the center are to enhance cardiovascular, physical, and psychosocial function, reduce morbidity and mortality, improve quality of life, and promote compliance with a lifelong prevention program.

The membership of the center will consist of three segments of the community: the general public, employees, and former rehabilitation patients. Each group will be charged a monthly fee and an initiation fee with a reduced fee provided for employees. Within each category, the fees vary depending on the member's age and restrictions on availability of the facilities during specific hours. The hospital hired a professional consulting firm to conduct a survey of the community to ensure that the fee structure would achieve its goal of making the center facilities available to an economic cross section of the community.

You have been contacted by Anne Dexter, the chief financial officer for the hospital. She is concerned that some or perhaps all of the revenue from the sports and fitness center will be classified as unrelated business income and therefore be subject to the unrelated business income tax. Write a letter to Ms. Dexter that contains your findings, and prepare a memo for the tax files. City Hospital's address is 1000 Board Street, Billings, MT 59101.

Research Problem 5.   The American Accounting Association holds its regional meetings at seven locations in the spring and its national meeting in August of each year. The meetings include the formal presentation of papers, panel discussions, business sessions, and various committee meetings. In addition, textbook publishers are permitted to display their wares in a publisher's exhibit hall. The book exhibitors must pay a fee to the AAA for the right to do so. Are these fees unrelated business income?

Research Problem 6.   A volunteer fire department located in Green County holds tax-exempt status. As a way of raising funds to support its firefighting activities, the department obtained the permission of the owners of three taverns located in Green County to place "tip jars" in the taverns. A tip jar is a gambling device from which patrons purchase sealed pieces of paper containing numbers, series of numbers, or symbols that may entitle the patron to cash or other prizes. The tip jars are legal under state law and under the county ordinance for tax-exempt organizations.

Under the county ordinance, the tax-exempt organization must receive at least 70% of the net proceeds after the winnings are paid, and the business where the tip jar is located must receive no more than 30%. Under the arrangement with the three taverns, the volunteer fire department received 80%.

The three taverns included the 20% they received in their gross income in calculating their taxable income. Since the volunteer fire department is tax-exempt, it did not pay Federal income taxes on the 80% it received.

The IRS determines that the tip jar income received by the volunteer fire department is unrelated business income and issues a deficiency notice. Evaluate the position of the IRS.

Research Problem 7.   Roger is the pastor at the Third Ecumenical Church in Atlanta. Over lunch with Priscilla, the pastor at another church with whom Roger went to seminary, he learns that another friend's church recently had its tax-exempt status revoked for engaging in political activities. From time to time, certain political figures "give testimony" at Roger's church. Being concerned about his own church's tax-exempt status, he asks you to provide him with the types of activities his church should not engage in or permit.

Communications

Locate a recent Revenue Ruling that you can use to provide Roger with the desired information. Summarize the Ruling with two PowerPoint slides.

Use the tax resources of the Internet to address the following questions. Do not restrict your search to the World Wide Web, but include a review of newsgroups and general reference materials, practitioner sites and resources, primary sources of the tax law, chat rooms and discussion groups, and other opportunities.

 **Internet** *Activity*

Research Problem 8.   Download an application for tax-exempt status that would be filed with the IRS. Write a one-page letter to an organization that is contemplating the filing of such an application. The letter should walk through the application and highlight the information that must be provided and the estimated time required to comply with the directives of the form.

Communications

Research Problem 9.   Locate the Web site of a § 527 organization that supports the Democratic Party and a similar Web site that supports the Republican Party. If possible, determine the amount of money the organization raised and spent associated with the 2006 elections. Chart your findings in a PowerPoint presentation.

Communications

Research Problem 10.   Determine if the Bill and Melinda Gates Foundation is a private foundation. Print a copy of its Form 990 or Form 990–PF.

Research Problem 11.   Verify the exempt status of the symphony orchestra that performs closest to your home. Who are its three highest-paid associates? Send an e-mail to your instructor explaining how you found this information.

Communications

Research Problem 12.   Use Guidestar.org to obtain the following information on the Jamestown Yorktown Foundation, Inc., which is located in Williamsburg, Virginia.

- Locate the foundation's Web site.
- Under what paragraph of § 501(c) is the organization exempt from Federal income tax?
- Use the Form 990 to determine the amount of compensation paid to officers and directors.

CHAPTER 15

Multistate Corporate Taxation

LEARNING OBJECTIVES

After completing Chapter 15, you should be able to:

LO.1
Illustrate the computation of a multistate corporation's state tax liability.

LO.2
Define nexus and explain its role in state income taxation.

LO.3
Distinguish between allocation and apportionment of a multistate corporation's taxable income.

LO.4
Describe the nature and treatment of business and nonbusiness income.

LO.5
Discuss the sales, payroll, and property apportionment factors.

LO.6
Apply the unitary method of state income taxation.

LO.7
Discuss the states' income tax treatment of S corporations, partnerships, and LLCs.

LO.8
Describe other commonly encountered state and local taxes on businesses.

LO.9
Recognize tax planning opportunities available to minimize a corporation's state and local tax liability.

Although most of this text concentrates on the effects of the Federal income tax law upon the computation of a taxpayer's annual tax liability, a variety of tax bases apply to most business taxpayers. For instance, a multinational corporation may be subject to tax in a number of different countries (see Chapter 9). Similarly, the taxpayer may be subject to a county-level wheel tax on its business vehicles, a state sales or use tax on many of its asset purchases, and state and local income or franchise taxes on its net income or on the privilege of doing business in the taxing jurisdiction. Indeed, estimates are that about 40 percent of the tax dollars paid by business taxpayers go to state and local authorities.

Businesses operate in a multistate environment for a variety of reasons. For the most part, nontax motivations drive such location decisions as where to build new plants or distribution centers or whether to move communications and data processing facilities and corporate headquarters. For instance, a business typically wants to be close to its largest markets and to operate in a positive private- and public-sector business climate, where it has access to well-trained and reasonably priced labor, suppliers and support operations, sources of natural resources, communication facilities, and transportation networks.

Many location decisions, though, are motivated by multistate tax considerations.

- The taxpayer's manufacturing, wholesaling, sales, retailing, and credit operations each may be centered in a different state to take advantage of various economic development incentives created by politicians.

- Mail-order and other catalog operations blur the traditional jurisdictional boundaries for buyer and seller alike. Often advertising campaigns boast "no sales tax payable."

- Similarly, the ability to transfer sales and purchase orders, pricing information, and other data via telephone lines, the Internet, and satellite transmissions may tempt the taxpayer to overlook traditional applications of the property and sales tax base. For instance, is computer software tangible (and subject to property tax) or intangible property? Is canned software transferred via the Internet, rather than by disc, subject to sales tax? Which jurisdiction's property tax should apply to a communications satellite?

- In addition to flying over virtually the entire country, the major airlines depart from and land in the majority of the states. Which state's income tax should

---

TAX *in the News*   PAYING THE STATES' BILLS

For 2006, the states collected more than $700 billion in taxes (i.e., more than $2,000 per person). The corporate income tax accounts for only a small portion of the states' revenues— 7 percent in 2006. This percentage is even less than the contribution of the Federal corporate tax to the U.S. government's revenues. Most of the states' property tax collections (2 percent of the total) are received by counties and smaller taxing jurisdictions.

The States' Tax Revenue Sources, 2006

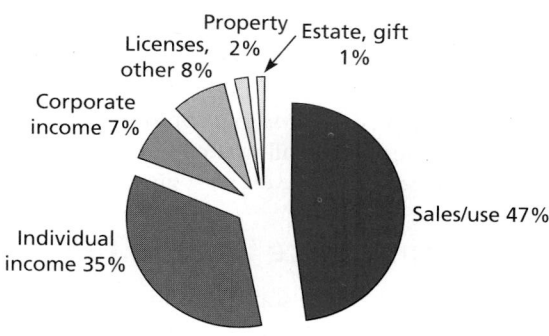

Source: *U.S. Census.*

---

apply to the ticket income? Should sales or income tax apply to sales of movies or liquor while the plane is airborne?

- Local political concerns lead to a multiplicity of tax rules as politicians attempt to serve their constituents by introducing a variety of special tax incentives. This variety can be confusing, however. Taxpayers may have difficulty determining whether they qualify for energy or enterprise zone credits, S corporation status, exemptions from sales tax liability or income tax withholding, or gasoline tax relief at the local level.

- Politicians have a strong incentive to impose new tax burdens on visitors and others who have no direct say in their reelection. Thus, it is increasingly common to see tourist and hotel-bed taxes on convention delegates, city payroll taxes on commuters, and the use of obscure tax formulas that otherwise discriminate against those with limited contact in the area.

- Each jurisdiction in which the entity is subject to tax represents a geometrical increase in compliance responsibilities. For instance, how many tax returns must be filed by a three-shareholder S corporation operating in 15 states?

- Various states and localities have adopted revenue-raising statutes that vary in sophistication and operate on different time schedules. For instance, only a few states have adopted an alternative minimum tax, and states that impose the tax have tended to select different bases. In addition, the aggressiveness with which departments of revenue enforce their tax statutes varies greatly from state to state, even in a context of ongoing pressure to enhance revenues. Accordingly, the taxpayer must deal with a patchwork of germane taxing and enforcement provisions in an environment that is often uncertain.

This chapter reviews the basic tax concepts that are predominant among most states that impose a tax based on net income, and it discusses the major areas in which tax planning can reduce a corporation's overall state tax burden.

Most of this chapter is devoted to a discussion of state taxes that are based on income. Each state is free to identify its corporate tax by a different term. Not all of the states that impose a tax on corporate income call the tax an "income tax." Rather, some states refer to their tax on corporate income as a franchise tax,[1] a business tax, a license tax, or a business profits tax.

Overview of Corporate State Income Taxation

Forty-six states and the District of Columbia impose a tax based on a corporation's taxable income. Since each state is free to create its own tax provisions, the tax practitioner could be faced with 47 entirely different state tax provisions.[2] Fortunately, however, to simplify the filing of tax returns and increase compliance with state tax laws, the majority of states "piggyback" onto the Federal income tax base. This means they have adopted *en masse* part or all of the Federal provisions governing the definition of income and the allowance of various exemptions, exclusions, and deductions. None of the states, however, has piggybacked its tax collections with the IRS.

LO.1

Illustrate the computation of a multistate corporation's state tax liability.

Computing State Income Tax

In more than 40 of the states that impose a corporate income tax, the starting point in computing the tax base is taxable income as reflected on the Federal corporate income tax return (Form 1120). Those states whose computation of state taxable income is not coupled to the Federal tax return have their own state-specific definitions of gross and taxable income. Nonetheless, even these states typically adopt most Federal income and deduction provisions.

Although Federal tax law plays a significant role in the computation of state taxable income, there is a wide disparity in both the methods used to determine a state's taxable income and the tax rates imposed on that income. As only a few states apply more than one or two tax rates to taxable income, there is little progressivity to these tax systems. State tax credits typically are designed to encourage increased hiring and investment in local facilities. Cities and states often use targeted tax credits to entice businesses to expand within their borders. For instance, a state might offer a $10,000 credit for each new job created by the taxpayer or a 15 percent credit for taxpayers who purchase automobiles that were assembled in the state.

The formula used by a multistate corporation to determine its tax liability in a typical state is illustrated in Figure 15–1.

Operational Implications

Generally, the accounting period and methods used by a corporation for state tax purposes must be consistent with those used on the Federal return. States often apply different rules, however, in identifying the members of a group filing a consolidated return and the income of each group member that is subject to tax.

As the starting point for computing state taxable income often is directly related to the Federal taxable income amount, most states also piggyback onto the IRS's audit process. Consequently, virtually all of the states that levy an income tax require notification of the final settlement of a Federal income tax audit. State authorities then adjust the originally calculated state tax liability appropriately.

---

[1] Although a franchise tax in some states is a business privilege tax based on a corporation's capital stock or net worth, several states use that term for the tax that they impose on a corporation's net income.

[2] The District of Columbia operates in much the same manner as a state and imposes a tax based on income. Four states impose no corporate income tax

at all: Nevada, South Dakota, Washington, and Wyoming. Corporations, however, are subject to a business and occupation tax in Washington. Several states base the tax on the entity's gross receipts.

FIGURE 15–1	Computing Corporate State Income Tax Liability

Starting point in computing taxable income*
± State modification items
  State tax base
± Total net allocable income/(loss) *(nonbusiness income)*
  Total apportionable income/(loss) *(business income)*
× State's apportionment percentage
  Income apportioned to the state
± Income/(loss) allocated to the state
  State taxable income/(loss)
× State tax rate
  Gross income tax liability for state
− State's tax credits
  Net income tax liability for the state

*Most states use either line 28 or line 30 of the Federal corporate income tax return (Form 1120). In other states, the corporation is required to identify and report each element of income and deduction on the state return.

State Modifications

Federal taxable income generally is used as the starting point in computing the state's income tax base, but numerous state adjustments or modifications are often made to Federal taxable income to:

- Reflect differences between state and Federal tax statutes.
- Remove income that a state is constitutionally prohibited from taxing.

The required modifications to Federal taxable income vary significantly among the states. Accordingly, this discussion is limited to the most common additions and subtractions that the states require. Exhibit 15–1 lists the most frequently encountered modifications. In computing the taxable income for a given state, only a selected number of these modifications may be applicable.

EXAMPLE 1

Blue Corporation is subject to tax only in State A. The starting point in computing A taxable income is Federal taxable income. Modifications then are made to reflect, among other provisions, the exempt status of interest on A obligations, all dividends received from other U.S. corporations, and the disallowance of a deduction for state income taxes. Blue generated the following income and deductions this year.

Sales	$1,500,000
Interest on Federal obligations	50,000
Interest on municipal obligations of State B	100,000
Dividends received from 50%-owned U.S. corporations	200,000
Total income	$1,850,000
Expenses related to Federal obligations	$ 1,000
Expenses related to municipal obligations	5,000
State income tax expense	50,000
Depreciation allowed for Federal tax purposes (the deduction allowed for state purposes is $300,000)	400,000
Other allowable deductions	1,000,000
Total deductions	$1,456,000

EXHIBIT 15–1	**Common State Modifications**

Addition Modifications

* Interest income received on state and municipal obligations and any other interest income that is exempt from Federal income tax. For this purpose, some states exempt interest earned on their own obligations.

* Expenses deducted in computing Federal taxable income that are directly or indirectly related to U.S. obligations.

* Income-based franchise and income taxes imposed by any state and the District of Columbia that were deducted in computing Federal taxable income.

* The amount by which the Federal deductions for depreciation, amortization, or depletion exceed those permitted by the state.

* The amount by which the state gain or loss from the disposal of assets differs from the Federal gain or loss. Due to the difference in permitted depreciation methods and other adjustments, a corporation's assets may have different Federal and state tax bases. This adjustment is not necessary if the state and Federal basis provisions are identical.

Adjustments required as a result of different elections being made for state and Federal purposes. Examples of such elections include the methods under which income from installment sales or long-term contracts is determined.

Federal net operating loss deduction, if the starting point in the computation of taxable income is Federal taxable income after special deductions.

Subtraction Modifications

* Interest on U.S. obligations or obligations of Federal agencies to the extent included in Federal taxable income but exempt from state income taxes under U.S. law.

* Expenses that are directly or indirectly related to the state and municipal interest that is taxable for state purposes.

* Refunds of franchise and income taxes imposed by any state and the District of Columbia, to the extent included in Federal taxable income.

* The amount by which the state deductions for depreciation, amortization, or depletion exceed the deductions permitted for Federal tax purposes.

Adjustments required as a result of different elections being made for state and Federal purposes, as above.

Dividends received from other U.S. corporations, to the extent included in Federal taxable income.

Net operating loss deduction as determined for state tax purposes.

Federal income tax paid.

*Required by most states.

Blue's taxable income for Federal and state purposes is $139,000 and $295,000, respectively.

Federal Taxable Income	
Sales	$1,500,000
Interest on Federal obligations	50,000
Dividends received from U.S. corporations	200,000
Total income	$1,750,000

Federal Taxable Income

Expenses related to Federal obligations	$ 1,000
State income tax expense	50,000
Depreciation	400,000
Other allowable deductions	1,000,000
Total deductions	$1,451,000
Taxable income before special deductions	$ 299,000
Less: Dividends received deduction (80% × $200,000)	160,000
Federal taxable income	$ 139,000

State A Taxable Income

Federal taxable income	$139,000
Addition Modifications	
Interest on State B obligations	100,000
State income tax expense	50,000
Excess depreciation deduction allowed for Federal purposes ($400,000 − $300,000)	100,000
Expenses related to Federal obligations	1,000
Subtraction Modifications	
Expenses related to State B obligations	(5,000)
Dividends from other corporations, to extent included in Federal taxable income ($200,000 − $160,000)	(40,000)
Interest on Federal obligations	(50,000)
State A taxable income	$295,000

■

EXAMPLE 2

Continue with the facts of Example 1, except that the $100,000 of municipal bond interest was generated from State A obligations. The computation of Federal taxable income is unaffected by this change. Since A exempts interest on its own obligations from taxation, Blue's A taxable income is $200,000.

State A Taxable Income

Federal taxable income	$139,000
Addition Modifications	
State income tax expense	50,000
Excess depreciation deduction allowed for Federal purposes ($400,000 − $300,000)	100,000
Expenses related to Federal obligations	1,000
Subtraction Modifications	
Dividends from other U.S. corporations, to extent included in Federal taxable income ($200,000 − $160,000)	(40,000)
Interest on Federal obligations	(50,000)
State A taxable income	$200,000

■

The UDITPA and the Multistate Tax Commission

The Uniform Division of Income for Tax Purposes Act (**UDITPA**) is a model law relating to the assignment of income among the states for corporations that maintain operations in more than one state (multistate corporations). Many states have adopted the provisions of the UDITPA, either by joining the Multistate Tax Compact or by modeling their laws after the provisions of the UDITPA.

The **Multistate Tax Commission (MTC)** writes regulations and other rules that interpret the UDITPA. When a new MTC rule or regulation is created, the member states propose its adoption to their respective legislatures. The majority of member states adopt the regulations with no exceptions or only minor changes.[3]

Jurisdiction to Impose Tax: Nexus and Public Law 86–272

LO.2

Define nexus and explain its role in state income taxation.

The state in which a business is incorporated has the jurisdiction to tax the corporation, regardless of the volume of its business activity within the state. Whether a state can tax the income of a business that is incorporated in another state usually depends on the relationship between the state and the corporation.

Nexus describes the degree of business activity that must be present before a taxing jurisdiction has the right to impose a tax on an out-of-state entity's income. State law defines the measure of the relationship that is necessary to create nexus. Typically, sufficient nexus is present when a corporation derives income from sources within the state, owns or leases property in the state, employs personnel in the state, or has physical or financial capital there. **Public Law 86–272** limits the states' right to impose an income tax on certain interstate activities.[4] This Federal law prohibits a state from taxing a business whose only connection with the state is to solicit orders for sales of tangible personal property that is sent outside the state for approval or rejection. If approved, the orders must be filled and shipped by the business from a point outside the state.

Only the sales of tangible personal property are immune from taxation under the law, however. Leases, rentals, and other dispositions of tangible personal property are not protected activities. Moreover, dispositions of real property and intangible property, as well as sales of services, are not protected by Public Law 86–272. In this regard, each state constructs its own definition of tangible and intangible property. Thus, since property ownership is not a protected activity, providing company-owned communications, copy, or computer equipment to an out-of-state salesperson may create nexus with a state, even though the salesperson merely solicits sales orders there.

An activity that consists merely of solicitation is immune from taxation. The statute does not define the term *solicitation*, but the Supreme Court has held that *solicitation of orders* includes any explicit verbal request for orders and any speech or conduct that implicitly invites an order.[5] The Court also created a *de minimis* rule, allowing immunity from nexus where a limited amount of solicitation occurs.

Exhibit 15–2 summarizes the activities that the MTC has identified as being directly related to solicitation (protected activities) and activities unrelated to solicitation (which establish income tax nexus for the entity).

Independent Contractors. Public Law 86–272 extends immunity to certain in-state activities conducted by an independent contractor that would not be permitted if performed directly by the taxpayer. Generally, an independent contractor may engage in the following limited activities without establishing nexus for the principal: (1) soliciting sales, (2) making sales, and (3) maintaining a sales office.

---

[3]Many of the states that are not members of the Multistate Tax Compact also model their laws after the UDITPA and the MTC regulations.
[4]15 U.S.C. 381–385.

[5]*Wisconsin Department of Revenue v. William Wrigley, Jr., Co.,* 112 S.Ct. 2447 (1992).

EXHIBIT 15–2	**Common Nexus Definitions under Public Law 86–272**

General rule: P.L. 86–272 immunity from nexus applies where the sales representative's activities are ancillary to the order-solicitation process.

Activities That Usually Do Not Create Nexus

- Advertising campaigns.
- Carrying free samples only for display or distribution.
- Owning or furnishing automobiles to salespersons.
- Passing inquiries or complaints on to the home office.
- Checking customers' inventories for reorder.
- Maintaining a sample or display room for two weeks or less during the year.
- Maintaining an office for an employee, including an office in the home.

Activities Usually Sufficient to Establish Nexus

- Making repairs or providing maintenance.
- Collecting delinquent accounts; investigating creditworthiness.
- Installation or supervision of installation.
- Conducting training classes, seminars, or lectures for persons other than sales personnel.
- Approving or accepting orders.
- Picking up or replacing damaged or returned property.
- Hiring, training, or supervising personnel other than sales employees.
- Providing shipping information and coordinating deliveries.
- Carrying samples for sale, exchange, or distribution in any manner for consideration or other value.
- Owning, leasing, maintaining, or otherwise using any of the following facilities or property in the state: real estate; repair shop; parts department; employment office; purchasing office; warehouse; meeting place for directors, officers, or employees; stock of goods; telephone answering service; or mobile stores (i.e., trucks with driver-salespersons).

Allocation and Apportionment of Income

> **LO.3**
>
> Distinguish between allocation and apportionment of a multistate corporation's taxable income.

A corporation that conducts business activities in more than one state must determine the portion of its net income that is subject to tax by each state. A corporation that has established sufficient nexus with another state generally must both **allocate** and **apportion** its income.

Apportionment is a means by which a corporation's business income is divided among the states in which it conducts business. Under an apportionment procedure, a corporation determines allowable income and deductions for the company as a whole and then apportions some of its net income to a given state, according to an approved formula.

Allocation is a method under which specific components of a corporation's income, net of related expenses, are directly assigned to a certain state. Allocation differs from apportionment in that allocable income is assigned to one state, whereas apportionable income is divided among several states. Nonapportionable (nonbusiness) income generally includes:

- Income or losses derived from the sale of nonbusiness real or tangible property, or
- Income or losses derived from rentals and royalties from nonbusiness real or tangible personal property.

This income normally is allocated to the state where the property that generated the income or loss is located.

TAX *in the News*   SO WHERE DID YOU WORK TODAY?

It is the dream of many intellectual-property employees to work at home with the employer's computer and communications equipment. Not only is the dress code based on the worker's comfort, but the employee can avoid the time and cost of commuting. The employer saves by not having to provide office space.

But what are the tax effects when the employee or independent contractor submits work to an employer located in a different state? The general rule in the past has been that state income taxes fall in full in the state where the work is done. Is this still the rule, or must the employee use the ultimate destination concept and apportion the hours of the day among the various states that receive the work product? If so, on what basis should such apportionment be made? Furthermore, how will the worker avoid potential taxation of the same income by more than one state?

A few states and cities, most notably in New York, are aggressively trying to impose income taxes on the work of telecommuters that enters the state. In these situations, enough nexus purportedly exists to permit the levying of income taxes on telecommuters based in other states. The finding of nexus with New York (both the city and the state) can be an expensive proposition for the worker and employer. Not only do additional taxes result but compliance costs are incurred.

The first round of court cases challenging this extension of nexus has resulted in rulings in favor of the state. Such success may encourage other states (and cities) to impose similar taxes. For now, it will be up to the states considering this form of taxation to decide if the additional revenue is worth the risk of angering the desirable high-tech, information workers who play a large role in our economy.

As Figure 15–1 indicated, total allocable (nonapportionable) income or loss typically is removed from corporate net income before the state's apportionment percentage is applied. The nonapportionable income or loss assigned to a state then is combined with the income apportionable to that state to arrive at total income subject to tax in the state.

EXAMPLE 3

Green Corporation conducts business in States N, O, P, and Q. Green's $900,000 taxable income consists of $800,000 apportionable income and $100,000 allocable income generated from transactions conducted in State Q. Green's sales, property, and payroll are evenly divided among the four states, and the states all employ an identical apportionment formula. Accordingly, $200,000 of Green's income is taxable in each of States N, O, and P. Green is subject to income tax on $300,000 of income in State Q.

Apportionable income	$800,000
Apportionment percentage (apportionable income is divided equally among the four states)	× 25%
Income apportioned to each state	$200,000

	State N	State O	State P	State Q
Income apportioned	$200,000	$200,000	$200,000	$200,000
Income allocated	–0–	–0–	–0–	100,000
Taxable income	$200,000	$200,000	$200,000	$300,000

The Apportionment Procedure

Apportionment assumes that the production of business income is linked to business activity, and the laws of each state define a number of factors believed to indicate the amount of corporate activity conducted within the state. However, apportionment often does not provide a uniform division of an organization's income based on its business activity, because each state is free to choose the type and number of factors that it believes are indicative of the business activity conducted within its borders. Therefore, a corporation may be subject to state income tax on more or less than 100 percent of its income.

An equally incongruous consequence of apportionment may occur when the operations in a state result in a loss.

EXAMPLE 4

Red Corporation's operations include two manufacturing facilities, located in States A and B, respectively. The plant located in A generated $500,000 of income, and the plant located in B generated a loss of $200,000. Therefore, Red's total taxable income is $300,000.

By applying the statutes of each state, Red determines that its apportionment factors for A and B are .65 and .35, respectively. Accordingly, Red's income is apportioned to the states as follows.

$$\text{Income apportioned to State A: } .65 \times \$300,000 = \$195,000$$

$$\text{Income apportioned to State B: } .35 \times \$300,000 = \$105,000$$

Red is subject to tax in B on $105,000 of income, even though the operations conducted in that state resulted in a loss. ■

Business and Nonbusiness Income

Business income is assigned among the states by using an apportionment formula. In contrast, *nonbusiness income* is either apportioned or allocated to the state in which the income-producing asset is located. For instance, income derived from the rental of nonbusiness real property generally is allocated to the state in which the property is located.

LO.4

Describe the nature and treatment of business and nonbusiness income.

EXAMPLE 5

TNT Corporation, a manufacturer of explosive devices, is a multistate taxpayer that has nexus with States P and Q. During the taxable year, TNT's net sales of explosive devices were $900,000; $600,000 of these sales were made in P and $300,000 were made in Q. The corporation also received $90,000 from the rental of nonbusiness real property located in P.

Both states employ a three-factor apportionment formula under which sales, property, and payroll are equally weighted. However, the states do not agree on the definition of apportionable income. Under P's tax provisions, nonbusiness rent income is allocable and business income is apportionable, while Q requires a corporation to apportion all of its (business and nonbusiness) income. The sales factor (the ratio of in-state sales to total sales) for each of the states is computed as follows.

$$\text{State P: } \frac{\$600,000 \text{ (sales in State P)}}{\$900,000 \text{ (total sales)}} = 66.67\%$$

$$\text{State Q: } \frac{\$300,000 \text{ (sales in State Q)}}{\$990,000 \text{ (total sales)}^*} = 30.30\%$$

*Since rent income is treated as business income, rents are included in the denominator of the sales factor. ■

EXAMPLE 6

Continue with the facts of Example 5, except that the rent income was generated from property located in Q, rather than from property located in P. Although the sales factor for P remains the same, the sales factor for Q changes.

$$\text{State P: } \frac{\$600,000 \text{ (sales in State P)}}{\$900,000 \text{ (total sales)}} = 66.67\%$$

$$\text{State Q: } \frac{\$390,000 \text{ (sales in State Q)}}{\$990,000 \text{ (total sales)}} = 39.39\%$$

Due to the composition of the sales factor in the two states, TNT's income never is perfectly apportioned: the aggregate of the sales factors is either more or less than 100%. ■

Business income arises from the taxpayer's regular course of business or constitutes an integral part of the taxpayer's regular business.[6] In determining whether an item of income is (apportionable) business income, state courts have developed a variety of approaches to determine what constitutes a taxpayer's "regular course of business."[7]

A few states, including Connecticut and New Hampshire, fail to distinguish between business and nonbusiness income. In these states, all of a corporation's income is deemed to be business income and subject to apportionment.

EXAMPLE 7

Scarlet Corporation is subject to income tax in several states. Scarlet earned $2.5 million from the sales of its products and $1 million from the sale of assets that were unrelated to its regular business operations.

In the states that distinguish between business and nonbusiness income, $2.5 million of Scarlet's income is apportioned to the state according to the state's apportionment formula. The gain on the sale of the nonbusiness assets is allocated to the state in which the assets were located. In the states that subject a corporation's entire income to apportionment, $3.5 million ($2,500,000 + $1,000,000) is apportioned to the states in which the taxpayer conducts business. ■

Nonbusiness income is "all income other than business income."[8] Usually, nonbusiness income comprises passive and portfolio income, such as dividends, interest, rents, royalties, and certain capital gains. However, passive or portfolio income may be classified as business income when the acquisition, management, and disposition of the underlying property constitute an integral part of the taxpayer's regular business operation.

EXAMPLE 8

Gray Corporation owns and operates two manufacturing facilities, one in State A and the other in State B. Due to a temporary decline in sales, Gray has rented 10% of its A facility to an unaffiliated corporation. Gray generated $100,000 net rent income and $900,000 income from manufacturing.

Both A and B classify such rent income as allocable nonbusiness income. By applying the statutes of each state, as discussed in the next section, Gray determines that its apportionment factors are 0.40 for A and 0.60 for B.

Income Subject to Tax in State A	
Taxable income	$1,000,000
Less: Allocable income	(100,000)
Apportionable income	$ 900,000
Times: Apportionment factor	× 40%
Income apportioned to State A	$ 360,000
Plus: Income allocated to State A	100,000
Income subject to tax in State A	$ 460,000
Income Subject to Tax in State B	
Taxable income	$1,000,000
Less: Allocable income	(100,000)
Apportionable income	$ 900,000
Times: Apportionment factor	× 60%
Income apportioned to State B	$ 540,000
Plus: Income allocated to State B	–0–
Income subject to tax in State B	$ 540,000

■

---

[6]MTC Reg. IV.1.(a).

[7]*Atlantic Richfield Co. v. State of Colorado and Joseph F. Dolan*, 601 P.2d 628 (Colo.S.Ct., 1979); *Appeal of A. Epstein and Sons, Inc.* (Cal.State Bd. of Equalization, 1984).

[8]UDITPA § 1(e).

EXAMPLE 9

Continue with the facts of Example 8, but assume that B does not distinguish between business and nonbusiness income. Thus, all of Gray's income is apportionable.

Gray properly determines that its apportionment factors are 0.40 for A and 0.58 for B. Since the apportionment factors used by the two states are derived differently, Gray's income that is subject to tax does not equal 100%.

Income Subject to Tax in State A	$ 460,000
Income Subject to Tax in State B	
Apportionable income	$1,000,000
Times: Apportionment factor	× 58%
Income apportioned to State B	$ 580,000

Due to differences in the states' definitions of apportionable and allocable income, $1.04 million of Gray's $1 million Federal taxable income is subject to state income taxation. ■

Apportionment Factors: Elements and Planning

LO.5

Discuss the sales, payroll, and property apportionment factors.

Business income is apportioned among the states by determining the appropriate apportionment percentage for each state that has a right to tax the entity. To determine the apportionment percentage for each state, a ratio is established for each of the factors included in the state's apportionment formula. Each ratio is calculated by comparing the level of a specific business activity within a state to the total corporate activity of that type. The ratios then are summed, averaged, and appropriately weighted (if required) to determine the corporation's apportionment percentage for a specific state.

Although apportionment formulas vary among jurisdictions, the traditional three-factor formula equally weights sales, property, and payroll.[9] However, most of the states now use a modified three-factor formula, where the sales factor receives more than a one-third weight. The use of a higher-weighted sales factor tends to pull a larger percentage of an out-of-state corporation's income into the taxing jurisdiction of the state, because the corporation's major activity within the state—the sales of its products—is weighted more heavily than are its payroll and property activities. Overweighting the sales factor, however, provides tax relief for corporations that are domiciled in the state. Those corporations generally own significantly more property and incur more payroll costs (factors that are given less weight in the apportionment formula) within the state than do out-of-state corporations.

EXAMPLE 10

Musk Corporation realized $500,000 of taxable income from the sales of its products in States A and B. Musk's activities in both states establish nexus for income tax purposes. Musk's sales, payroll, and property in the states include the following.

	State A	State B	Total
Sales	$1,250,000	$750,000	$2,000,000
Property	2,500,000	–0–	2,500,000
Payroll	1,500,000	–0–	1,500,000

---

[9]Certain industries, such as financial services institutions, insurance companies, air and motor carriers, pipeline companies, and communications providers, typically are required to use special apportionment formulas.

If State B uses an equally weighted three-factor apportionment formula, $62,500 of Musk's taxable income is apportioned to B.

Sales ($750,000/$2,000,000)	=	37.5%
Property ($0/$2,500,000)	=	–0–
Payroll ($0/$1,500,000)	=	–0–
Sum of apportionment factors		37.5%
Average	÷	3
Apportionment factor for State B		12.5%
Taxable income	×	$500,000
Income apportioned to State B		$ 62,500

If State B uses a double-weighted sales factor in its three-factor apportionment formula, $93,750 of Musk's taxable income is apportioned to B.

Sales ($750,000/$2,000,000)	=	37.5% × 2 =	75%
Property ($0/$2,500,000)	=		–0–
Payroll ($0/$1,500,000)	=		–0–
Sum of apportionment factors			75%
Average		÷	4
Apportionment factor for State B			18.75%
Taxable income		×	$500,000
Income apportioned to State B			$ 93,750

When a state uses a double-weighted sales factor, typically a larger percentage of an out-of-state corporation's income is subject to tax in the state. Here, an additional $31,250 ($93,750 − $62,500) of Musk's income is subject to tax in B. ∎

A single-factor apportionment formula consisting solely of a sales factor is even more detrimental to an out-of-state corporation than an apportionment factor that double weights the sales factor.[10]

EXAMPLE 11

PPR Corporation, a retailer of paper products, owns retail stores in States A, B, and C. A uses a three-factor apportionment formula under which the sales, property, and payroll factors are equally weighted. B uses a three-factor apportionment formula under which sales are double weighted. C employs a single-factor apportionment factor, based solely on sales.

PPR's operations generated $800,000 of apportionable income, and its sales, payroll activity, and average property owned in each of the three states are as follows.

	State A	State B	State C	Total
Sales	$500,000	$400,000	$300,000	$1,200,000
Payroll	100,000	125,000	75,000	300,000
Property	150,000	250,000	100,000	500,000

$280,000 of PPR's apportionable income is assigned to A.

---

[10]Currently, Illinois, Iowa, Maine, Nebraska, Oregon, and Texas require the use of a single-factor apportionment formula.

Sales ($500,000/$1,200,000)	=	41.67%	
Payroll ($100,000/$300,000)	=	33.33%	
Property ($150,000/$500,000)	=	30.00%	
Sum of apportionment factors		105.00%	
Average	÷	3	
Apportionment factor for State A		35.00%	
Apportionable income	×	$800,000	
Income apportioned to State A		$280,000	

$316,640 of PPR's apportionable income is assigned to B.

Sales ($400,000/$1,200,000)	= 33.33% × 2 =	66.66%	
Payroll ($125,000/$300,000)	=	41.67%	
Property ($250,000/$500,000)	=	50.00%	
Sum of apportionment factors		158.33%	
Average	÷	4	
Apportionment factor for State B		39.58%	
Apportionable income	×	$800,000	
Income apportioned to State B		$316,640	

$200,000 of PPR's apportionable income is assigned to C.

Sales ($300,000/$1,200,000)	=	25.00%	
Sum of apportionment factors		25.00%	
Average	÷	1	
Apportionment factor for State C		25.00%	
Apportionable income	×	$800,000	
Income apportioned to State C		$200,000	

Summary

Income apportioned to State A	$280,000
Income apportioned to State B	316,640
Income apportioned to State C	200,000
Total income apportioned	$796,640

Due to the variations in the apportionment formulas employed by the various states, only 99.58% ($796,640/$800,000) of PPR's income is apportioned to the states in which it is subject to tax. ∎

The Sales Factor

The **sales factor** is a fraction, whose numerator is the corporation's total sales in the state during the tax period. The denominator is the corporation's total sales everywhere during the tax period. Gross sales for this purpose generally are net of returns, allowances, and discounts. Moreover, interest income, service charges, and carrying charges are included in the sales factor. Federal and state excise taxes and state sales taxes are included in the factor if these taxes are either passed on to the buyer or included in the selling price of the goods.

Since the sales factor is a component in the formula used to apportion a corporation's business income to a state, only sales that generate business income are includible in the fraction. The "sales" factor actually resembles a "receipts" factor in most states, since it also generally includes business income from the sale of inventory or services, interest, dividends, rentals, royalties, sales of assets, and other business income. Income on Federal obligations, however, is not included in the sales factor.

When the sale involves capital assets, some states require that the gross proceeds, rather than the net gain or loss, be included in the fraction. Most states allow incidental or occasional asset sales and sales of certain intangible assets to be excluded from gross receipts.[11]

In determining the numerator of the sales factor, most states follow the UDITPA's "ultimate destination concept," under which tangible asset sales are assumed to take place at the point of delivery, not at the location at which the shipment originates.

E X A M P L E   12

Olive Corporation, whose only manufacturing plant is located in State A, sells its products to residents of A through its local retail store. Olive also ships its products to customers in States B and C. The products that are sold to residents of A are assigned to A, while the products that are delivered to B and C are assigned to B and C, respectively. ■

Dock Sales. Dock sales occur where a purchaser uses its owned or rented vehicles, or a common carrier with which it has made arrangements, to take delivery of the product at the seller's shipping dock. Most states apply the destination test to dock sales in the same manner as it is applied to other sales. Thus, if the seller makes dock sales to a purchaser that has an out-of-state location to which it returns with the product, the sale is assigned to the purchaser's state.

Throwback Rule. Out-of-state sales that are not subject to tax in the destination state are pulled back into the origination state if that state has adopted a **throwback rule.** About half of the states apply this exception to the destination test.

The throwback rule provides that, when a corporation is not subject to tax in the destination state or the purchaser is the U.S. government, the sales are treated as in-state sales of the origination state, and the actual destination of the product is disregarded. Consequently, when the seller is immune from tax in the destination state under Public Law 86–272, the sales are considered to be in-state sales of the origination state if that state has a throwback provision.

The throwback rule seems inappropriate when the sale is made to a purchaser in another country, where the transaction is subject to a gross receipts tax (but no income tax). In these cases, the taxpayer truly is subject to double taxation, as state taxes increase but no Federal foreign tax credit is available. Nonetheless, most of the throwback states fail to distinguish between U.S. and foreign throwback sales.

E X A M P L E   13

Braun Corporation's entire operations are located in State A. Seventy percent ($700,000) of Braun's sales are made in A, and the remaining 30% ($300,000) are made in State B. Braun's solicitation of sales in B is limited to mailing a monthly catalog to its customers in that state. However, Braun employees do pick up and replace damaged merchandise in State B.

The pickup and replacement of damaged goods establish nexus with A. Braun's activities in B are sufficient (as determined by A's law) to subject Braun to a positive tax, based on its income. Therefore, Braun is permitted to apportion its income between A and B. However, B's definition of activities necessary to create nexus is less strict than that imposed by A; in B, the mere pickup and replacement of damaged goods do not subject a corporation's income to tax.

Braun's taxable income is $900,000. Both A and B impose a 10% corporate income tax and include only the sales factor in their apportionment formulas. If A has not adopted a throwback rule, Braun's effective state income tax rate is 7%.

---

[11]MTC Reg. IV.18.(c).

	Apportionment Factors	Net Income	Tax Rate	Tax
State A	70%	$900,000	10%	$63,000
State B	*	900,000	10%	–0–
Total tax liability				$63,000
Effective state income tax rate: $63,000/$900,000 =				7%

*As determined under B's laws, Braun's income is not apportionable to State B, because of insufficient nexus.

If A has adopted a throwback rule, Braun does not benefit from its lack of nexus with B, because the sales in B are considered to be in-state sales of A. Thus, Braun's effective tax rate is 10%.

	Apportionment Factors	Net Income	Tax Rate	Tax
State A	100%	$900,000	10%	$90,000
State B	–0–	900,000	10%	–0–
Total tax liability				$90,000
Effective state income tax rate: $90,000/$900,000 =				10%
Tax increase due to throwback provision ($90,000 – $63,000)				$27,000

■

The Payroll Factor

The **payroll factor** is determined by comparing the compensation paid for services rendered within a state to the total compensation paid by the corporation. Generally, the payroll factor is a fraction, whose numerator is the total amount that a corporation paid or accrued for compensation in a state during the tax period. The denominator is the total amount paid or accrued by the corporation for compensation during the tax period. For purposes of the payroll factor, compensation includes wages, salaries, commissions, and any other form of remuneration paid or accrued to employees for personal services. Compensation may also include the value of board, rent, housing, lodging, and other benefits or services furnished to employees by the taxpayer in return for personal services, if these amounts constitute Federal gross income.

Payments made to an independent contractor or any other person who is not properly classifiable as an employee generally are excluded from the numerator and denominator of the payroll factor. Some states, including Delaware and New York, exclude from the payroll factor the compensation paid to corporate officers.

More than half of the states provide that earnings paid to a cash or deferred compensation plan, excluded from Federal gross income under § 401(k), are to be included in the numerator and the denominator of the payroll factor. Accordingly, the total compensation that is included in the denominator of a corporation's payroll factor may vary among the states in which the corporation's income is apportioned.

Mice Corporation's sales office and manufacturing plant are located in State A. Mice also maintains a manufacturing plant and sales office in State C. For purposes of apportionment, A defines payroll as all compensation paid to employees, including contributions to § 401(k) deferred compensation plans. Under the statutes of C, neither compensation paid to officers nor contributions to § 401(k) plans are included in the payroll factor. Mice incurred the following personnel costs.

EXAMPLE 14

	State A	State C	Total
Wages and salaries for employees other than officers	$350,000	$250,000	$600,000
Salaries for officers	150,000	100,000	250,000
Contributions to § 401(k) plans	30,000	20,000	50,000
Total	$530,000	$370,000	$900,000

The payroll factor for State A is computed as follows.

$$\frac{\$530,000}{\$900,000} = 58.89\%$$

Since C excludes from the payroll factor any compensation paid to officers and contributions to § 401(k) plans, C's factor is computed as follows.

$$\frac{\$250,000}{\$600,000} = 41.67\%$$

The aggregate of Mice's payroll factors is 100.56% (58.89% + 41.67%). In certain cases, the sum of a corporation's payroll factors may be significantly more or less than 100%. ∎

The compensation of an employee normally is not split between two or more states during the year, unless he or she is transferred or changes positions during the year. Instead, each employee's compensation is allocated to only one state. Under the UDITPA, compensation is treated as paid in the state (it is included in the numerator of the payroll factor) in which the services primarily are performed.

When an employee's services are performed in more than one state, his or her compensation is attributed to the employee's base of operations or, if there is no base of operations in any state in which some part of the service is performed, to the place from which the services are directed or controlled. When no services are performed in the state that serves as the base of operations or the place from which the services are directed, the employee's compensation is attributed to his or her state of residency.[12]

EXAMPLE 15

Geese Corporation has its headquarters and a manufacturing plant in State A. Reggie, a resident of State Y, works at the A manufacturing plant. His compensation is included in the numerator of A's payroll factor, as the service is performed entirely in A. ∎

Only compensation that is related to the production of apportionable income is included in the payroll factor. Accordingly, in those states that distinguish between business and nonbusiness income, compensation related to the operation, maintenance, protection, or supervision of nonbusiness income is not includible in the payroll factor.

EXAMPLE 16

Dog Corporation, a manufacturer of automobile parts, is subject to tax in States X and Y. Dog incurred the following payroll costs.

	State X	State Y	Total
Wages and salaries for officers and personnel of manufacturing facilities	$450,000	$350,000	$800,000
Wages and salaries for personnel involved in nonbusiness rental activities	50,000	–0–	50,000

---

[12]UDITPA § 14.

If both states distinguish between business and nonbusiness income in determining apportionable income and include officers' compensation in the payroll factor, Dog's payroll factors are computed as follows.

$$\text{Payroll factor for State X: } \$450,000/\$800,000 = 56.25\%$$

$$\text{Payroll factor for State Y: } \$350,000/\$800,000 = 43.75\%$$ ∎

EXAMPLE 17

Continue with the facts of Example 16, but assume that Y defines apportionable income as the corporation's total income (business and nonbusiness income). Dog's payroll factor for X remains unchanged, but its payroll factor for Y is reduced.

$$\text{Payroll factor for State X: } \$450,000/\$800,000 = 56.25\%$$

$$\text{Payroll factor for State Y: } \$350,000/\$850,000^* = 41.18\%$$

*$800,000 (compensation related to business income) + $50,000 (compensation related to nonbusiness income). ∎

In deriving the payroll factors, compensation is prorated between business and nonbusiness sources.

EXAMPLE 18

Tall Corporation, a manufacturer of paper products, operates paper mills in States A and B. In addition, the corporation owns nonbusiness rental real property in A. Tall incurred the following compensation expenses.

	State A	State B	Total
Wages and salaries for mill employees	$1,200,000	$1,500,000	$2,700,000
Wages and salaries for administrative staff	600,000	500,000	1,100,000
Compensation of officers	800,000	400,000	1,200,000

Ten percent of the time spent by the administrative staff located in A and 5% of the time spent by officers located in A are devoted to the operation, maintenance, and supervision of the nonbusiness rental property. Both states exclude such rent income from the definition of apportionable income.

Payroll factor for State A

$$\frac{[\$1,200,000 + 90\%(\$600,000) + 95\%(\$800,000)]}{\substack{[\$2,700,000 + 90\%(\$600,000) + \$500,000 \\ + 95\%(\$800,000) + \$400,000]}} = \frac{\$2,500,000}{\$4,900,000} = 51.02\%$$

Payroll factor for State B

$$\frac{[\$1,500,000 + \$500,000 + \$400,000]}{\substack{[\$2,700,000 + 90\%(\$600,000) + \$500,000 \\ + 95\%(\$800,000) + \$400,000]}} = \frac{\$2,400,000}{\$4,900,000} = 48.98\%$$ ∎

The Property Factor

The **property factor** generally is a fraction, whose numerator is the average value of the corporation's real property and its tangible personal property owned and used or rented and used in the state during the taxable year. The denominator is the average value of all of the corporation's real property and its tangible personal property owned or rented and used during the taxable year, wherever it is located. In this manner, a state's property factor reflects the extent of total property usage by the taxpayer in the state.

For this purpose, property includes land, buildings, machinery, inventory, equipment, and other real and tangible personal property, other than coins or currency.[13]

---
[13]MTC Reg. IV.10.(a).

Other types of property that may be included in the factor are construction in progress (even though it does not yet contribute to the production of income), offshore property, outer space property (satellites), and partnership property.

In the case of property that is in transit between locations of the taxpayer or between a buyer and seller, the assets are included in the numerator of the destination state. With respect to mobile or movable property, such as construction equipment, trucks, and leased equipment, which is both in- and outside the state during the tax period, the numerator of a state's property factor generally is determined on the basis of the total time that the property was within the state.

Space satellites used in the communication industry generally are included in the numerator of the property factor based on the ratio of earth stations serviced. For example, if a satellite is being serviced by earth stations located in San Francisco, Chicago, New York, and Houston, 25 percent of the cost of the satellite is included in the numerator of the property factor for each of the four corresponding states.

Property owned by the corporation typically is valued at its average original or historical cost plus the cost of additions and improvements, but without adjusting for depreciation. Some states allow property to be included at net book value or adjusted tax basis. The value of the property usually is determined by averaging the values at the beginning and end of the tax period. Alternatively, some states allow or require the amount to be calculated on a monthly basis if annual computation results in or requires substantial distortions.

EXAMPLE 19

Blond Corporation, a calendar year taxpayer, owns property in States A and B. Both A and B require that the average value of assets be included in the property factor. A requires that the property be valued at its historical cost, and B requires that the property be included in the property factor at its net book value.

	Account Balances at January 1		
	State A	**State B**	**Total**
Inventories	$ 150,000	$ 100,000	$ 250,000
Building and machinery (cost)	200,000	400,000	600,000
Accumulated depreciation for building and machinery	(150,000)	(50,000)	(200,000)
Land	50,000	100,000	150,000
Total	$ 250,000	$ 550,000	$ 800,000

	Account Balances at December 31		
	State A	**State B**	**Total**
Inventories	$ 250,000	$ 200,000	$ 450,000
Building and machinery (cost)	200,000	400,000	600,000
Accumulated depreciation for building and machinery	(175,000)	(100,000)	(275,000)
Land	50,000	100,000	150,000
Total	$ 325,000	$ 600,000	$ 925,000

State A Property Factor			
Historical Cost	**January 1**	**December 31**	**Average**
Property in State A	$ 400,000*	$ 500,000**	$ 450,000
Total property	1,000,000[†]	1,200,000[††]	1,100,000

*$150,000 + $200,000 + $50,000.
**$250,000 + $200,000 + $50,000.
[†]$250,000 + $600,000 + $150,000.
[††]$450,000 + $600,000 + $150,000.

$$\text{Property factor for State A: } \frac{\$450,000}{\$1,100,000} = 40.91\%$$

State B Property Factor			
Net Book Value	**January 1**	**December 31**	**Average**
Property in State B	$550,000	$600,000	$575,000
Total property	800,000	925,000	862,500

$$\text{Property factor for State B: } \frac{\$575,000}{\$862,500} = 66.67\%$$

Due to the variations in the property factors, the aggregate of Blond's property factors equals 107.58%. ■

Leased property, when included in the property factor, is valued at eight times its annual rental. Annual rentals may include payments, such as real estate taxes and insurance, made by the lessee in lieu of rent.

E X A M P L E   20

Jasper Corporation is subject to tax in States D and G. Both states require that leased or rented property be included in the property factor at eight times the annual rental costs, and that the average historical cost be used for other assets. Information regarding Jasper's property and rental expenses follows.

Average Historical Cost	
Property located in State D	$ 750,000
Property located in State G	450,000
Total property	$1,200,000

Lease and Rental Expenses	
State D	$ 50,000
State G	150,000
Total	$ 200,000

Property factor for State D

$$\frac{[\$750,000 + 8(\$50,000)]}{[\$1,200,000 + 8(\$200,000)]} = \frac{\$1,150,000}{\$2,800,000} = 41.07\%$$

Property factor for State G

$$\frac{[\$450,000 + 8(\$150,000)]}{[\$1,200,000 + 8(\$200,000)]} = \frac{\$1,650,000}{\$2,800,000} = 58.93\%$$

■

Only property that is used in the production of apportionable income is includible in the numerator and denominator of the property factor. In this regard, idle property and property that is used in producing nonapportionable income generally are excluded. However, property that is temporarily idle or unused generally remains in the property factor.

<table>
<tr><td>

LO.6

Apply the unitary method of state income taxation.
</td></tr>
</table>

The Unitary Theory

The **unitary theory** developed in response to the early problems that states faced in attributing the income of a multistate business among the states in which the business was conducted. Originally, this theory was applied to justify apportionment of the income of multiple operating divisions within a single company. Over the years, however, the concept has been extended to require the combined reporting of certain affiliated corporations, including those outside the United States.

When two affiliated corporations are subject to tax in different states, each entity must file a return and report its income in the state in which it conducts business. Each entity reports its income separately from that of its affiliated corporations. In an effort to minimize overall state income tax, multistate entities have attempted to separate the parts of the business that are carried on in the various states.

EXAMPLE 21	Arts Corporation owns a chain of retail stores located in several states. To enable each store to file and report the income earned only in that state, each store was organized as a separate subsidiary in the state in which it did business. In this manner, each store is separately subject to tax only in the state in which it is located. ∎

Most states attempt to assign as much of an entity's income to in-state sources as possible, so the *unitary* approach to computing state taxable income is attractive to them. Under this method, a corporation is required to file a "combined return" that includes the results from all of the operations of the related corporations, not just from those that transacted business in the state. In this manner, the unitary method allows a state to apply the apportionment formula to a firm's nationwide or worldwide unitary income. To include the activities of the corporation's subsidiaries in the apportionment formula, the state must determine that the subsidiaries' activities are an integral part of a unitary business and, as a result, are subject to apportionment.

What Is a Unitary Business?

A unitary business operates as a unit and cannot be segregated into independently operating divisions. The operations are integrated, and each division depends on or contributes to the operation of the business as a whole. It is not necessary that each unit operating within a state contribute to the activities of all divisions outside the state. The unitary theory ignores the separate legal existence of the entities and focuses instead on practical business realities. Accordingly, the separate entities are treated as a single business for state income tax purposes, and the apportionment formula is applied to the combined income of the unitary business.

EXAMPLE 22	Continue with the facts of Example 21. Arts manufactured no goods, but conducted central management, purchasing, distributing, advertising, and administrative departments. The subsidiaries carried on a purely intrastate business, and they paid for the goods and services received at the parent company's cost, plus overhead. Arts and the subsidiaries constitute a unitary business due to their unitary operations (purchasing, distributing, advertising, and administrative functions). Accordingly, in states that have adopted the unitary method, the income and apportionment factors of the entire unitary group are combined and apportioned to the states in which at least one member of the group has nexus. ∎

EXAMPLE 23

Crafts Corporation organized its departments as separate corporations on the basis of function: mining copper ore, refining the ore, and fabricating the refined copper into consumer products. Even though the various steps in the process are operated substantially independently of each other with only general supervision from Crafts' executive offices, Crafts is engaged in a single unitary business. Its various divisions are part of a large, vertically structured enterprise, in which each business segment needs the products or raw materials provided by another. The flow of products among the affiliates also provides evidence of functional integration, which generally requires some form of central decision or policy making, another characteristic of a unitary business. ■

Notice that the application of the unitary theory is based on a series of subjective observations about the organization and operation of the taxpayer's businesses, whereas the availability of Federal controlled and affiliated group status (see Chapter 8) is based on objective, mechanical ownership tests. More than half of the states require or allow unitary reporting, a somewhat larger number than in the early 1990s.

Tax Effects of the Unitary Theory

Use of the unitary approach by a state eliminates several of the planning techniques that could be used to shift income between corporate segments to avoid or minimize state taxes. In addition, the unitary approach usually results in a larger portion of the corporation's income being taxable in states where the compensation, property values, and sales prices are high relative to other states. This occurs because the larger in-state costs (numerators in the apportionment formula) include in the tax base a larger portion of the taxable income within the state's taxing jurisdiction. This has an adverse effect upon the corporation's overall state tax burden if the states in which the larger portions are allocated impose a high tax rate relative to the other states in which the business is conducted.

The presence of a unitary business is favorable when losses of unprofitable affiliates may be offset against the earnings of profitable affiliates. It also is favorable when income earned in a high-tax state may be shifted to low-tax states due to the use of combined apportionment factors.

EXAMPLE 24

Rita Corporation owns two subsidiaries, Arts and Crafts. Arts, located in State K, generated taxable income of $700,000. During this same period, Crafts, located in State M, generated a loss of $400,000. If the subsidiaries are independent corporations, Arts is required to pay K tax on $700,000 of income. However, if the corporations constitute a unitary business, the incomes, as well as the apportionment factors, of the two entities are combined. As a result, the combined income of $300,000 ($700,000 − $400,000) is apportioned to unitary states K and M. ■

EXAMPLE 25

Eve Corporation, a wholly owned subsidiary of Dan Corporation, generated $1 million taxable income. Eve's activities and sales are restricted to State P, which imposes a 10% income tax. Dan's income for the taxable period is $1.5 million. Dan's activities and sales are restricted to State Q, which imposes a 5% income tax. Both states use a three-factor apportionment formula that equally weights sales, payroll, and property. Sales, payroll, and average property for each of the corporations are as follows.

	Eve Corporation	Dan Corporation	Total
Sales	$3,000,000	$7,000,000	$10,000,000
Payroll	2,000,000	3,500,000	5,500,000
Property	2,500,000	4,500,000	7,000,000

If the corporations are independent entities, the overall state income tax liability is $175,000.

State P (10% × $1,000,000)	=	$100,000
State Q (5% × $1,500,000)	=	75,000
Total state income tax		$175,000

If the corporations are members of a unitary business, the income and apportionment factors are combined in determining the income tax liability in unitary states P and Q. As a result of the combined reporting, the overall state income tax liability is reduced.

State P Income Tax

Total apportionable income		$2,500,000	
Apportionment formula			
Sales ($3,000,000/$10,000,000)	=	30.00%	
Payroll ($2,000,000/$5,500,000)	=	36.36%	
Property ($2,500,000/$7,000,000)	=	35.71%	
Total		102.07%	
Average (102.07% ÷ 3)		× 34.02%	
State P taxable income		$ 850,500	
Tax rate		× 10%	
State P tax liability			$ 85,050

State Q Income Tax

Total apportionable income		$2,500,000	
Apportionment formula			
Sales ($7,000,000/$10,000,000)	=	70.00%	
Payroll ($3,500,000/$5,500,000)	=	63.64%	
Property ($4,500,000/$7,000,000)	=	64.29%	
Total		197.93%	
Average (197.93% ÷ 3)		× 65.98%	
State Q taxable income		$1,649,500	
Tax rate		× 5%	
State Q tax liability			$ 82,475
Total state income tax, if unitary			$167,525
Total state income tax, if nonunitary			175,000
Tax reduction from unitary combined reporting			$ 7,475

The results of unitary reporting would have been detrimental if Q had imposed a higher rate of tax than P, because a larger percentage of the corporation's income is attributable to Q when the apportionment factors are combined. ∎

By identifying the states that have adopted the unitary method and the criteria under which a particular state defines a unitary business, a taxpayer may reduce its overall state tax by restructuring its corporate relationships to create or guard against a unitary relationship. For instance, an independent business enterprise can be made unitary by exercising day-to-day operational control and by centralizing functions, such as marketing, financing, accounting, and legal services.

WATER'S EDGE IS NOT A DAY AT THE BEACH

As a result of pressure from the business community, the Federal government, and foreign countries, most of the states that impose an income tax on a unitary business's worldwide operations permit a multinational business to elect **water's edge** unitary reporting as an alternative to worldwide unitary filing.

The water's edge provision permits a multinational corporation to elect to limit the reach of the state's taxing jurisdiction over out-of-state affiliates to activities occurring within the boundaries of the United States. The decision to make a water's edge election may have a substantial effect on the tax liability of a multinational corporation. For instance, a water's edge election usually cannot be revoked for a number of years without permission from the appropriate tax authority. Moreover, corporations making this election may be assessed an additional tax or fee for the privilege of excluding out-of-state entities from the combined report.

GLOBAL Tax Issues

Consolidated and Combined Returns

As discussed in Chapter 8, an affiliated group of corporations may file a consolidated return if all members of the group consent. Once such a return has been filed, the group must continue to file on a consolidated basis as long as it remains in existence, or until permission to file separate returns has been obtained. The consolidated return essentially treats the controlled corporations as a single taxable entity. Thus, the affiliated group pays only one tax, based upon the combined income of its members after certain adjustments (e.g., net operating losses) and eliminations (e.g., intercompany dividends and inventory profits).

Several states permit affiliated corporations to file a consolidated return if such a return has been filed for Federal purposes. The filing of a consolidated return is mandatory in only a few states.

Usually, only corporations that are subject to tax in the state can be included in a consolidated return unless specific requirements are met or the state permits the inclusion of corporations without nexus.

Do not confuse elective consolidated returns with required combined returns in unitary states. A combined return is filed in every unitary state in which one or more unitary members have nexus. The computations reflect apportioned and allocated income of the unitary members, resulting in a summary of the taxable income of the entities in each state. The combined method chiefly permits the unitary taxpayer to develop the summary of assigned taxable incomes, which is accepted by (and disclosed to) all of the states.

Taxation of S Corporations

The majority of the 46 states that impose a corporate income tax have special provisions, similar to the Federal law, that govern the taxation of S corporations. As of 2008, only a few states—including Michigan and Tennessee—and the District of Columbia do not provide special (no corporate-level tax) treatment for Federal S corporations. In addition, Massachusetts imposes a corporate-level tax on S corporations that have gross receipts in excess of $6 million. Some states, including Illinois, New York, and California, apply a corporate-level tax, at special rates, on an S corporation.

In the non-S election states, a Federal S corporation generally is subject to tax in the same manner as a regular C corporation. Accordingly, if a multistate S corporation operates in any of these states, it is subject to state income tax and does not realize one of the primary benefits of S status—the avoidance of double taxation.

LO.7

Discuss the states' income tax treatment of S corporations, partnerships, and LLCs.

CONCEPT SUMMARY 15–1

Principles of Multistate Corporate Income Taxation

1. Taxability of an organization's income in a state other than the one in which it is incorporated depends on the laws, regulations, and judicial interpretations of the other state; the nature and level of the corporation's activity in, or contacts with, that state; and, to a limited extent, the application of P.L. 86–272.

2. Each state has adopted its own multistate income tax laws, regulations, methods, and judicial interpretations; consequently, the nonuniformity of state income taxing provisions provides a multitude of planning techniques that allow a multistate corporation to reduce its overall state tax liability legally.

3. The apportionment procedure is used to assign the income of a multistate taxpayer to the various states in which business is conducted. Generally, nonbusiness income is allocated, rather than apportioned, directly to the state in which the nonbusiness income-generating assets are located.

4. The various state apportionment formulas offer planning opportunities in that more or less than 100% of

the taxpayer's income may be subjected to state income tax.

5. Most states employ an equally weighted three-factor apportionment formula. In some states, the sales factor is doubled, and in a few states, only the sales factor is used in apportioning multistate taxable income. Generally, the greater the relative weight assigned to the sales factor, the greater the tax burden on out-of-state taxpayers.

6. The sales factor is based upon the destination concept except where a throwback rule applies. The payroll factor generally includes compensation that is included in Federal gross income, but some states include excludible fringe benefits. An employee's compensation usually is not divided among states. The property factor is derived using the average undepreciated historical costs for the assets and eight times the rental value of the assets.

7. The unitary theory may require the taxpayer to include worldwide activities and holdings in the apportionment factors. A water's edge election can limit these amounts to U.S. transactions.

Other potential tax-related benefits of the S election, including the pass-through of net operating losses and the reduction in the rate of tax imposed on individual and corporate taxpayers, may be curtailed.

EXAMPLE 26

Bryan, an S corporation, has established nexus in States A and B. A recognizes S status, while B does not. Bryan generated $600,000 of ordinary business income and $100,000 of dividends that were received from corporations in which Bryan owns 50% of the stock. Bryan's State B apportionment percentage is 50%.

For B tax purposes, Bryan first computes its income as though it were a C corporation. It then apportions the resulting income to B. Assuming that B has adopted the Federal provisions governing the dividends received deduction, Bryan's income, determined as though it were a C corporation, is $620,000 [$600,000 + (100% − 80%) × $100,000]. Accordingly, Bryan may be subject to B corporate income tax on $310,000 ($620,000 × 50% apportionment percentage) of taxable income. ■

Eligibility

All of the states that recognize S status permit a corporation to be treated as an S corporation for state purposes only if the corporation has a valid Federal S election in place. Generally, the filing of a Federal S election is sufficient to render the corporation an S corporation for state tax purposes. In most states, an entity that is an S corporation for Federal tax purposes automatically is treated as an S corporation for state tax purposes. Wisconsin allows the entity to *elect out* of its S status for state purposes.

Corporate-Level Tax

Although S corporations generally are not taxable entities, Federal income tax liability may arise if the corporation has excess passive investment income or recognized built-in gains. Several states have adopted similar provisions, and, therefore, an S corporation is exempt from the related state income tax only to the extent that it is exempt from corresponding Federal income taxes. In the majority of these states, the imposition of Federal income taxes generates a corporate-level tax for state purposes to the extent that corporate income is allocated or apportioned to the state.

EXAMPLE 27

Amp, an S corporation, has nexus with States X and Y, both of which recognize S status. X imposes a corporate-level tax on S corporations to the extent that the corresponding Federal tax applies. Amp is subject to the § 1374 tax. This year, its Federal excessive passive income is $60,000. The amount of income subject to tax in X depends on Amp's apportionment percentage for X.

If Amp's State X apportionment percentage is 50%, Amp is subject to a corporate-level tax in X on $30,000 of passive income ($60,000 × 50%). ■

A few states deviate from the Federal S corporation provisions and provide that an S corporation is entirely exempt from state income tax only if all of its shareholders are residents of the state. In these states, an S corporation is taxed on the portion of its income that is attributable to nonresident shareholders. Some of these states permit the S corporation to escape corporate-level tax on this income if its nonresident shareholders sign a form, agreeing to pay state tax on their share of the corporation's income. Moreover, about half of the states require the corporation to withhold taxes on the nonresident shareholders' portions of the entity's income.

EXAMPLE 28

ARGO, an S corporation, is subject to income tax only in Vermont. On the last day of its taxable year, 40% of ARGO's stock is held by nonresident shareholders. To the extent that ARGO's stock is held by resident shareholders, the corporation is not subject to income tax. Accordingly, ARGO is not subject to tax on 60% of its income.

The corporation *is* subject to tax on the remaining 40% of its income. ARGO may be able to avoid this corporate-level tax by withholding Vermont income tax for its nonresident shareholders. ■

Composite Tax Return

In an effort to decrease compliance burdens and simplify the filing process for nonresident shareholders of S corporations, several states allow an S corporation to file a single income tax return and pay the resulting tax on behalf of some or all of its nonresident shareholders. State requirements for the filing of a composite or "block" return vary substantially.

Taxation of Partnerships and LLCs

Most states apply income tax provisions to partnerships, limited liability companies (LLCs), and limited liability partnerships (LLPs) in a manner that parallels Federal treatment. The entity is a tax-reporting, not a taxpaying, entity. Income, loss, and credit items are allocated and apportioned among the partners according to the terms of the partnership agreement and state income tax law.

Some states require that the entity make estimated tax payments on behalf of out-of-state partners. This approach helps to assure that nonresident partners file appropriate forms and pay any resulting tax to the state. A few states, including Michigan for partnerships and Texas for LLCs, apply an entity-level tax on operating income. As is the case with S corporations, some states allow composite returns to be filed relative to out-of-state partners.

TAX *in the News* | **WHAT ARE YOU TAXING?**

Taxware.com, an observer of the state and local tax scene, has identified several of the most unusual sales and use tax laws that remain on the books of various states.

- West Virginians may not celebrate Independence Day as vigorously as do those in other states. Sales of sparklers and other novelty items are subject to both the general sales tax and an additional special levy.
- Kentucky horse breeders pay sales tax on "stud fees" related to the breeding of thoroughbred horses.
- North Carolina is a "tax-free zone" for motor sport racing teams. This includes a refund for the sales tax allocated to the fuel used by the aircraft that transport team members to the state.

- Cloth diapers are exempt from sales tax in Wisconsin, but disposables are taxable.
- Ohioans receive a tax break when they die. Makeup applications are exempt from sales tax when they are applied in a mortuary, but not when they occur in a beauty salon.
- Ambulance services in South Dakota are exempt from sales tax when they are provided by a ground vehicle, but not by an airplane.
- Pennsylvania taxes air, in the form of a fee for the vacuum cleaner used at a car wash. No tax applies, though, for air used to inflate tires by a similar machine.

Generally, an in-state partner computes the income tax resulting from all of the flow-through income from the entity. The partner then is allowed a credit for income taxes paid to other states on this income.

Key issues facing partnerships doing business in multiple states include those listed here. Applicable law varies from state to state, and more complex transactions may not yet be addressed by existing law.

- Whether the partnership automatically has nexus with every state in which a partner resides.
- Whether a partner is deemed to have nexus with every state in which the partnership does business.
- How to assign the income/loss of a partner upon retirement or when a liquidating distribution is received.

Other State and Local Taxes

LO.8

Describe other commonly encountered state and local taxes on businesses.

State and Local Sales and Use Taxes

Forty-five states and the District of Columbia impose a consumers' sales tax on retail sales of tangible personal property for use or consumption. In many of these states, in-state localities, including cities, towns, school districts, or counties, also have the power to levy a sales tax. A consumers' sales tax is a tax imposed directly on the purchaser who acquires the asset at retail; the tax is measured by the price of the sale. The vendor or retailer merely acts as a collection agent for the state.

A use tax is designed to complement the sales tax. The use tax has two purposes: to prevent consumers from evading sales tax by purchasing goods outside the state for in-state use, and to provide an equitable sales environment between in-state and out-of-state retailers.

Generally, sales of tangible personal property are subject to tax. In several states, selected services are subject to tax.

A majority of the states exempt sales of certain items from the sales/use tax base. The most common exemptions and exclusions include the following.

- *Sales for resale* are exempt because the purchaser is not the ultimate user of the sold property. For instance, meat purchased by a grocer and a garment purchased by a retailer are not subject to sales/use tax under the resale rule.

- *Casual or occasional sales* that occur infrequently are exempt from the sales/use tax base chiefly for administrative convenience. Most states exclude rummage sales, the transfer of an entire business, sales of used autos, and the like under this rule.
- Most *purchases by exempt organizations* are excluded from taxable sales. Charities, governments and their agencies, and other organizations qualifying for Federal income tax exemption are relieved of sales/use tax liabilities in all of the states.
- *Sales of targeted items* can be exempt to improve the equity of the sales/use tax system. Sales of groceries, medical prescriptions and equipment, and school clothes can fall into this category and become nontaxable. Special exemptions for sales of farm, industrial, and computing equipment might also qualify under this type of exclusion.
- Certain *sales to manufacturers, producers, and processors* may also be exempt. Exemptions usually include one or more of the following.
    - Containers and other packing, packaging, and shipping materials actually used to transfer merchandise to customers of the purchaser.
    - Machines and specific processing equipment and repair parts or replacements exclusively and directly used in manufacturing tangible personal property.

ETHICAL and EQUITABLE *Considerations* — TAXING CLICKS AND BRICKS

Business has convinced Congress to enforce a politically popular "no new taxes on the Internet" pledge through 2008. But does exempting Internet sales from sales/use tax give Internet retailers an unfair advantage over "bricks and mortar" businesses that must collect sales tax on the sales that they make? These retailers have invested in physical stores and merchandise and make up most downtown and shopping mall areas. Why should the law allow a full tax holiday for "clicks and mortar" Internet sellers, which have invested in just-in-time inventories and intangible assets like e-commerce Web software?

Will the next step in the saga look like this? Crate and Barrel sets up computer kiosks in all of its stores so that customers can browse the merchandise in a hands-on manner, then place a sales-tax-free order on one of the terminals.

Comment on the equity of exempting Internet sales from sales/use tax.

A separate set of nexus rules applies in determining whether a seller must collect a sales/use tax from a customer. Strictly, the tax must be collected only if the seller has a physical presence (e.g., a store building but not an Internet Web page) in the state. The regular solicitation of sales by independent brokers establishes sufficient nexus to require a nonresident seller to register and collect the use tax, even though the seller does not have regular employees, agents, and an office or other place of business in the state.[14] As a result, a corporation may be required to collect sales and use taxes in a state even though it is immune from the imposition of an income tax.

Local Property Taxes

Property taxes, a major source of revenue at the city and county level, often are designated as *ad valorem* taxes because they are based on the value of property that is located in the state on a specific date. Generally, that date fixes taxable ownership, situs (location), and the valuation of the property. Nonetheless, to avoid tax

---

[14]*Quill Corp. v. North Dakota,* 112 S.Ct. 1904 (1992); *Scripto, Inc. v. Carson,* 80 S.Ct. 619 (1960).

TAX *in the News* — **COLLECTING THOSE SALES/USE TAX REVENUES**

Today, state and local tax administrators face a major problem: How can governments get their sales/use tax revenues from mail-order, phone, and Internet sales? The problem is that the governments must rely on the seller to collect sales and use taxes, rather than collecting them directly from the purchaser. Consequently, a seller conceivably must deal with thousands of different sales/use taxing jurisdictions, each with its own forms and filing deadlines, rates of applicable tax, and definitions of what is taxable or exempt. Examples of issues on which jurisdictions may disagree include:

- Are snack foods exempt groceries or taxable candy?
- Are therapeutic stockings exempt medical supplies or taxable clothing?
- Which types of software are subject to tax?

Large retailers such as Wal-Mart, Amazon, and Radio Shack can develop software to handle these problems, but smaller businesses cannot afford to create their own software or to purchase someone else's. The result has been a very low level of compliance by sellers with respect to out-of-state sales transactions.

Governments meanwhile have limited resources to enforce tax rules that have long been on the books. Many states ask individuals and businesses to include the unpaid use taxes for Internet, phone, and mail-order purchases on their annual income tax returns, but the number of taxpayers complying is insignificant. This is not a matter of "increasing the taxes on the Internet economy," but rather of collecting revenues that already are due and are desperately needed to balance state budgets.

In an effort to solve these problems, state and local government officials and the Multistate Tax Commission have created the Streamlined Sales Tax Project (SSTP). The goal was to develop model laws that all states could adopt, thereby allowing for more uniform application of the now-disparate sales/use tax rules and more efficient exchange of information among agencies as to sellers and their transactions.

Real change, however, is likely to come only from Congress. The House Ways and Means Committee is considering a bill that would make the SSTP rules uniform law, to some extent, among all the states. In the meantime, legislatures in about two dozen states (mostly the smaller ones) have adopted the SSTP rules.

So far the most popular SSTP rules are those defining what is subject to sales/use tax and what is not. For instance, the rules set out which items of clothing would be subject to tax, but each jurisdiction decides whether to include clothing in the tax base or when to allow amnesties during specific weeks of the tax year. Little interest as yet has been shown in having identical sales/use tax rates among the jurisdictions.

---

evasion, personal property that is temporarily outside the state may be taxed at the domicile of the owner.

Property taxes can take the form of either real property taxes or personal property taxes. States apply different tax rates and means of assessment to the two classes of property. The methods of assessing the value of the real and tangible property also vary in different taxing jurisdictions.

Although a personal property tax may be imposed on both intangible and tangible property, most states limit the tax to tangible property. The distinction between the various items of personal property is important because special rates, computations, or exemptions apply to certain types of property. For instance, inventory constitutes tangible personal property, but is exempt from taxation in most states.

Other Taxes

States may impose a variety of other state and local taxes on corporations, including incorporation or entrance fees or taxes; gross receipt taxes; stock transfer taxes; realty transfer and mortgage recording taxes; license taxes; and franchise taxes based on net worth or capital stock outstanding.

An *incorporation tax* is an excise tax for the corporate privilege conferred on the business. At the time the business is incorporated, the state generally imposes a fee or tax for the privilege of conducting business within the state as a corporation. Similarly, an out-of-state corporation usually must pay an entrance fee or tax before it can transact business in a state other than its state of incorporation.

Some states base the incorporation tax on the par value of the authorized stock. To prevent tax evasion, a few of these states impose a similar fee or tax on subsequent increases in the corporation's authorized stock. Where the incorporation fee or tax is based on the amount of authorized stock, the tax may be based on the total amount of the stock, even though the corporation conducts business in several states.

A *license tax* is an excise tax on the privilege of engaging in a certain business, occupation, or profession. A state may impose business, occupational, or professional license taxes as a means of generating revenue or regulating the activities of the business, occupation, or profession for the public welfare.

Stock and realty transfer and mortgage recording taxes are nonrecurring taxes that are imposed at the time of recording or transfer. *Stock transfer taxes* are imposed on the transfer of shares or certificates of stock of domestic and foreign corporations. The tax typically is based on the number of shares transferred and the par or market value of the stock. Generally, the following stock transfers are exempt from the transfer tax: original issues, deposits of stock as security for a loan, and transfers to a broker for sale or purchase.

The base of the *realty transfer tax* usually is measured by the consideration paid or to be paid for the realty. The *mortgage recording tax* may be based on the actual consideration given, the value of the property, or the debt to be secured by the instrument.

Typically, a *capital stock tax* is an excise tax imposed on a domestic corporation for the privilege of existing as a corporation or imposed on an out-of-state corporation, either for the privilege of doing business or for the actual transaction of business within the state. This annual tax usually is based on the book value of the corporation's net worth, including capital, surplus, and retained earnings. In a few states, a corporation is subject to a *franchise tax* only to the extent that the tax exceeds the corporate income tax, but in the majority of states, the entity is subject to both taxes.

The majority of capital stock taxes are apportioned if the corporation does business or maintains an office in another state. In some states, however, the tax is levied on the entire authorized or issued capital stock of a domestic corporation, even though the corporation may be engaged in business in other states. For corporations based in other states, the tax is imposed only on the capital that is employed in the state as determined by an apportionment formula.

EXAMPLE 29

The balance sheet of Bull, a domestic corporation of State A, at the end of its taxable year is as follows.

Cash	$100,000
Equipment (net of $50,000 accumulated depreciation)	150,000
Building (net of $75,000 accumulated depreciation)	225,000
Land	125,000
Total assets	$600,000
Accounts payable and other short-term liabilities	$100,000
Long-term liabilities	200,000
Capital stock	50,000
Paid-in capital in excess of par value	50,000
Retained earnings	200,000
Total liabilities and equity	$600,000

A imposes a 2% franchise tax based on the entire net worth of a domestic corporation. Bull is subject to a franchise tax in A of $6,000 ($600,000 assets − $300,000 liabilities = $300,000 net worth × 2% rate). ∎

EXAMPLE 30

Continue with the facts of Example 29, except that A subjects a domestic corporation to tax only on the capital that is employed in the state. Bull properly determines its A apportionment percentage as 20%. In this case, Bull's A franchise tax liability is $1,200 ($300,000 net worth × 20% apportionment percentage = $60,000 capital employed in A × 2% rate). ■

ETHICAL and EQUITABLE *Considerations* — ENCOURAGING ECONOMIC DEVELOPMENT THROUGH TAX CONCESSIONS

The tax professional occasionally is in a position to negotiate with a state or city taxing jurisdiction to garner tax relief for a client as an incentive to locate a plant or distribution center in that geographic area. In times when construction budgets are high and interstate competition is fierce, such tax concessions can be significant.

For instance, to encourage a business to build a large distribution center in the area, community leaders might be agreeable to (1) paying for roads, sewer, water, and other improvements through taxpayer bonds; (2) reducing property taxes by 50 percent for the first 10 years of the center's operations; and (3) permanently excluding any distribution-related vehicles and equipment from the personal property tax.

One of the most interesting examples of such incentives was put in place several years ago by Louisiana. Special tax credits are allowed to those making motion pictures in the state, and the credits can be transferred from the filmmakers to silent investors in the productions. As a result, filmmakers spent almost $600 million in the state in 2005, up from just $12 million in 2002. The artistic achievements of the credit have been mixed at best, as the resulting productions include both the award-winning *Ray* and the dubious *Dukes of Haz-*

zard. About a dozen states allow some form of tax credit to filmmakers, with 20 to 25 percent of the total in-state film budget typically qualifying for the credit.

An incentive-granting community provides the concessions even though the influx of new workers will place a great strain on public school facilities and likely necessitate improvements in traffic patterns and other infrastructure. Local residents, even those who obtain jobs at the new facility, and the tax adviser may wonder whether the tax concessions are supportable in light of these changes in the community's quality of life.

Take the position of a large employer that has been located in the area for more than 50 years. By how much should it be willing to absorb the tax increases that result when economic development concessions are used to attract new, perhaps temporary, businesses to the area? Should the employer challenge the constitutionality of the grant of such sizable tax breaks to some, but not all, business taxpayers in the jurisdiction?

Should higher "impact fees" be assessed on new developments? Does your analysis change if the new business competes with the longtime resident for sales? For employees? For political power?

TAX PLANNING *Considerations*

The inconsistencies in the tax laws and rates among the states not only complicate state tax planning, but also provide the nucleus of pertinent planning opportunities. Although several tax planning devices are available to a corporation that does business in only one state, most planning techniques are directed toward corporations that do business or maintain property in more than one state. All suggested tax planning strategies should be reviewed in light of practical business considerations and the additional administrative and other costs that may be incurred, because simply minimizing state taxes may not be prudent from a business perspective.

LO.9

Recognize tax planning opportunities available to minimize a corporation's state and local tax liability.

Selecting the Optimal State in Which to Operate

Because the states employ different definitions of the amount and type of activity necessary to establish nexus, a company has some latitude in selecting the states by which it will be taxed. When a corporation has only a limited connection with a high-tax state, it may abandon that activity by electing an alternative means of accomplishing the same result. For example, if providing a sales representative with a company-owned computer constitutes nexus in an undesired state, the company could eliminate its connection with that state by reimbursing sales personnel for equipment expenses, instead of providing a company computer. Similarly, when nexus is caused by conducting customer training sessions or seminars in the state, the corporation could bypass this connection. This can be done by sending the personnel to a nearby state in which nexus clearly has been established or in which the activity would not constitute nexus.

In addition, when sufficient activity originates from the repair and maintenance of the corporation's products or the activities performed by the sales representatives within the state, the organization could incorporate the service or sales divisions. This would invalidate a nonunitary state's right to tax the parent corporation's income; only the income of the service or sales divisions would be subject to tax. However, this technique is successful only if the incorporated division is a *bona fide* business operation. Therefore, the pricing of any sales or services between the new subsidiary and the parent corporation must be at arm's length, and the operations of the new corporation preferably should result in a profit.

Although planning techniques often are employed to disconnect a corporation's activities from an undesirable state, they can also be utilized to create nexus in a desirable state. For example, when the presence of a company-owned computer creates nexus in a desirable state, the corporation could provide its sales representatives in that state with company-owned equipment, rather than reimbursing or providing increased compensation for equipment costs.

Establishing nexus in a state is advantageous, for instance, when that state has a lower tax rate than the state in which the income currently is taxed, or when losses or credits become available to reduce tax liabilities in the state.

EXAMPLE 31

Bird Corporation generates $500,000 of taxable income from selling goods; specifically, 40% of its product is sold in State A and 60% in State B. Both states levy a corporate income tax and include only the sales factor in their apportionment formulas. The tax rate in A is 10%; B's rate is only 3%. Bird's manufacturing operation is located in A; therefore, the corporation's income is subject to tax in that state. Currently, Bird is immune from tax under Public Law 86–272 in B. Since A has adopted a throwback provision, Bird incurs $50,000 of state income taxes.

	Apportionment Formula	Net Income	Tax Rate	Tax
State A	100/100	$500,000	10%	$50,000
State B	0/100	500,000	3%	–0–
Total tax liability				$50,000

Because B imposes a lower tax rate than A, Bird substantially reduces its state tax liability if sufficient nexus is created with B.

	Apportionment Formula	Net Income	Tax Rate	Tax
State A	40/100	$500,000	10%	$20,000
State B	60/100	500,000	3%	9,000
Total tax liability				$29,000

■

A corporation may benefit by storing inventory in a low- or no-tax state because the average property value in the state in which the manufacturing operation is located is reduced significantly. When the manufacturing operation is located in a high-tax state, the establishment of a distribution center in a low- or no-tax state may reduce the overall state tax liability.

EXAMPLE 32

Trill Corporation realized $200,000 of taxable income from selling its product in States A and B. Trill's manufacturing plant, product distribution center, and warehouses are located in A. The corporation's activities within the two states are as follows.

	State A	State B	Total
Sales	$500,000	$200,000	$700,000
Property	300,000	50,000	350,000
Payroll	100,000	10,000	110,000

Trill is subject to tax in A and B. Both states utilize a three-factor apportionment formula that equally weights sales, property, and payroll; however, A imposes a 10% corporate income tax, while B levies a 3% tax. Trill incurs a total income tax liability of $17,575.

Apportionment Formulas					
	State A			**State B**	
Sales	$500,000/$700,000 =	71.43%	$200,000/$700,000 =	28.57%
Property	$300,000/$350,000 =	85.71%	$50,000/$350,000 =	14.29%
Payroll	$100,000/$110,000 =	90.91%	$10,000/$110,000 =	9.09%
Total		248.05%		51.95%
Apportionment factor (totals/3)		82.68%		17.32%
Income apportioned to the state ($200,000 × apportionment factor)		$165,360		$34,640
Tax rate		× 10%		× 3%
Tax liability		$ 16,536		$ 1,039
Total tax liability			$17,575	

■

EXAMPLE 33

Continue with the facts of Example 32, and further assume that Trill's product distribution center and warehouse operations were acquired for $200,000 and the payroll of these operations is $20,000. Ignoring all nontax considerations, Trill could reduce its tax liability by $3,514 (a 20% reduction) by moving its distribution center, warehouses, and applicable personnel to B.

	State A	State B	Total
Sales	$500,000	$200,000	$700,000
Property	100,000	250,000	350,000
Payroll	80,000	30,000	110,000

Apportionment Formulas					
	State A			**State B**	
Sales	$500,000/$700,000 =	71.43%	$200,000/$700,000 =	28.57%
Property	$100,000/$350,000 =	28.57%	$250,000/$350,000 =	71.43%
Payroll	$80,000/$110,000 =	72.73%	$30,000/$110,000 =	27.27%
Total		172.73%		127.27%
Apportionment factor (totals/3)		57.58%		42.42%

Apportionment Formulas

	State A	State B
Income apportioned to the state ($200,000 × apportionment factor)	$115,160	$ 84,840
Tax rate	× 10%	× 3%
Tax liability	$ 11,516	$ 2,545
Total tax liability	$14,061	
Tax imposed before move to State B	17,575	
Tax reduction due to move	$ 3,514	

■

Restructuring Corporate Entities

One of the major objectives of state tax planning is to design the proper mix of corporate entities. An optimal mix of entities often generates the lowest combined state income tax for the corporation. Ideally, the income from all of the entities will be subject to a low tax rate or no tax at all. However, this generally is not possible. Consequently, the goal of designing a good corporate combination often is to situate the highly profitable entities in states that impose a low (or no) income tax.

Matching Tax Rates and Corporate Income. When the corporation must operate in a high-tax state, divisions that generate losses should also be located there. Alternatively, unprofitable or less profitable operations can be merged into profitable operations to reduce the overall income subject to tax in the state. An ideal candidate for this type of merger may be a research and development subsidiary that is only marginally profitable but is vital to the parent corporation's strategic goals. By using computer simulation models, a variety of different combinations can be tested to determine the optimal corporate structure.

Passive Investment Companies. The creation of a **passive investment company** is another restructuring technique utilized to minimize a corporation's state tax burden. Nonbusiness or passive income generally is allocated to the state in which the income-producing asset is located, rather than apportioned among the states in which the corporation does business. Therefore, significant tax savings may be realized when nonbusiness assets are located in a state that either does not levy an income tax or provides favorable tax treatment for passive income. The corporation need not be domiciled in the state to benefit from these favorable provisions. Instead, the tax savings can be realized by forming a passive investment subsidiary to hold the intangible assets and handle the corporation's investment activities. The passive investment subsidiary technique usually produces the desired result in any no-tax state. Delaware, however, often is selected for this purpose due to its other corporate statutory provisions and favorable political, business, and legal climate.

Delaware does not impose an income tax upon a corporation whose only activity within the state is the maintenance and management of intangible investments and the collection and distribution of income from such investments or from tangible property physically located in another state. Consequently, trademarks, patents, stock, and other intangible property can be transferred to a Delaware corporation whose activity is limited to collecting passive income. The assets can be transferred to the subsidiary without incurring a Federal income tax under § 351 (see Chapter 4).

However, to receive the desired preferential state tax treatment, the holding company's activities within the state must be sufficient to establish nexus in the state. The passive investment company should avoid performing any activity outside the state that may result in establishing nexus with another state. In addition, the formation of the subsidiary must be properly implemented to assure the legal substance of the operation. The passive investment company must have a physical office, and it must function as an independent operation. Ensuring nexus and proper formation is not difficult since numerous consulting organizations are available to furnish new passive investment companies with all of the elements necessary to fulfill these requirements.

Because the subsidiary's activities are confined to Delaware (or some other no- or low-tax state), and its operations generate only passive income, its income will not be taxed in any nonunitary state. Moreover, most states exclude dividends from taxation or otherwise treat them favorably; therefore, the earnings of a passive investment subsidiary can be distributed as a dividend to the parent at a minimal tax cost. If the state in which the parent is located does not levy the full income tax on dividends received, the entire measure of passive income may escape taxation.

Formation of a passive investment subsidiary also may favorably affect the parent corporation's apportionment formula in nonunitary states because the passive income earned by the subsidiary is excluded from the numerator of its sales factor.

EXAMPLE 34

Purple Corporation generates $800,000 of taxable income; $600,000 is income from its manufacturing operations, and $200,000 is dividend income from passive investments. All of Purple's sales are made, and assets are kept, in State A, which imposes a 10% corporate income tax and permits a 100% deduction for dividends received from subsidiaries. The corporation is not subject to tax in any other state. Consequently, Purple incurs $80,000 of income tax (tax base $800,000 × tax rate 10%).

If Purple creates a passive investment subsidiary in State B, which does not impose an income tax upon a corporation whose only activity within the state is the maintenance and management of passive investments, Purple's tax liability is reduced by $20,000 (a 25% decrease). Since passive income is nonbusiness income (which is allocated for state tax purposes to the state in which it is located), the income earned from its passive investments is not subject to tax in A.

	State A (Purple Corporation)	State B (Passive Investment Company)
Taxable income	$600,000	$200,000
Tax rate	× 10%	× –0–*
Tax liability	$ 60,000	$ –0–
Total tax liability		$ 60,000
Tax imposed without restructuring		80,000
Tax reduction due to use of subsidiary		$ 20,000

*B does not impose an income tax on a passive investment corporation.

The income earned by the subsidiary from its passive investments can be distributed to Purple as a dividend without incurring a tax liability because A allows a 100% deduction for dividends that are received from subsidiary corporations. ■

These desired results, however, will not be fully available in states that view the entire corporate operation as being unitary. Since those states require combined

TAX *in the News*

LEAVE THAT GIRAFFE AT HOME!

One of the means by which the states have attacked the use of passive investment subsidiaries is the *Geoffrey* rule. The device is named after Geoffrey the Giraffe, the mascot of Toys 'R Us. Over a decade ago, the Supreme Court of South Carolina held that the presence of intangible assets, including corporate logos and mascots such as Geoffrey, created nexus with the state. Thus, some taxable income could be apportioned to a state where the intangible asset is used. The *Geoffrey* decision came as a surprise to many tax advisers, and the rule now limits some of the planning opportunities formerly available to those operating in nonunitary jurisdictions.

About one-half of the states have attempted, usually through administrative rules, to adopt the *Geoffrey* approach. Other states either have not addressed the issue or purposely have ignored the rule to avoid the appearance of a hostile tax climate that could impede the recruitment of new businesses. Many states want to close this loophole but without seeming unfriendly to business.

The other popular approach used by the states to attack passive investment subsidiaries is to require combined reporting under the unitary theory. Almost a dozen states have adopted required combined reporting, or are considering legislation to do so, in the last few years. These states include New York, Pennsylvania, and Maryland. The unitary tax movement no longer is only a western states phenomenon.

Because the taxes of some taxpayers go up under combined reporting, while the taxes of others decrease, there often is no political force to block the adoption of unitary taxation. In fact, pressure for states to "go unitary" may be fueled by media reports of how well multistate tax planning can work (e.g., how Wal-Mart saves billions in taxes by paying rent for the use of property owned by its affiliates).

Some now are touting unitary tax theories on the basis of fairness. They say that the corporate income tax may be assessed more equitably in today's economy by using the broadest tax base and apportionment data possible.

reporting, the income earned by the passive investment subsidiary is included in the corporation's apportionable or allocable income.

Subjecting the Corporation's Income to Apportionment

When a multistate organization is domiciled in a high-tax state, some of its apportionable income is eliminated from the tax base in that state. In light of the high tax rate, this may result in significant tax savings. Apportioning income will be especially effective where the income that is attributed to the other states is not subject to income tax. The income removed from the taxing jurisdiction of the domicile state entirely escapes state income taxation when the state to which the income is attributed (1) does not levy a corporate income tax; (2) requires a higher level of activity necessary to subject an out-of-state company to taxation than that adopted by the state of domicile; or (3) is prohibited under Public Law 86–272 from taxing the income (assuming that the domicile state has not adopted a throwback provision). Thus, the right to apportion income may provide substantial benefits because the out-of-state sales are excluded from the numerator of the sales factor and may not be taxed in another state.

However, to acquire the right to apportion its income, the organization must have sufficient activities in, or contacts with, one or more other states. Whether the type and amount of activities and/or contacts are considered adequate is determined by the domicile state's nexus rules. Therefore, a corporation should analyze its current activities in, and contacts with, other states to determine which, if any, activities or contacts could be redirected so that the corporation gains the right to apportion its income.

ETHICAL and EQUITABLE Considerations

CAN YOU BE A NOWHERE ADVISER?

The intent of much of today's multistate income tax planning is to create so-called *nowhere sales*, such that the income from the transaction is not subject to tax in any state. Suppose, for instance, that a sale is made from Georgia (a state with no throwback rule) into Nevada (the place of ultimate destination, but a state with no income tax). No state-level income tax liability is generated. Is it ethical for a tax adviser to suggest such a strategy? Could you propose the establishment of a sales office in a nonthrowback state, thereby avoiding state income tax on a transaction that is fully taxable under Federal rules?

Planning with Apportionment Factors

Sales Factor. The sales factor often yields the greatest planning opportunities for a multistate corporation. In-state sales include those to purchasers with a destination point in that state; sales delivered to out-of-state purchasers are included in the numerator of the sales factor of the destination state. However, to be permitted to exclude out-of-state sales from the sales factor of the origination state, the seller generally must substantiate the shipment of goods to an out-of-state location. Therefore, the destinations of sales that a corporation makes and the means by which the goods are shipped must be carefully reviewed. The corporation's overall state tax possibly can be reduced by establishing a better record-keeping system or by manipulating the numerator of the sales factor by changing the delivery location or method.

For example, a corporation may substantially reduce its state tax if the delivery location of its sales is changed from a state in which the company is taxed to one in which it is not. This technique may not benefit the corporation if the state in which the sales originate has adopted the throwback rule.

Property Factor. Because most fixed assets are physically stationary in nature, the property factor is not so easily manipulated. Nonetheless, significant tax savings can be realized by establishing a leasing subsidiary in a low- or no-tax state. If the property is located in a state that does not include leased assets in the property factor, the establishment of a subsidiary from which to lease the property eliminates the assets from the property factor in the parent's state.

Permanently idle property generally is excluded from the property factor. Accordingly, a corporation should identify and remove such assets from the property factor to ensure that the factor is not distorted. It is equally important to identify and remove nonbusiness assets from the property factor in states that distinguish between business and nonbusiness income.

EXAMPLE 35

Quake Corporation's property holdings were as follows.

	State A	Total
Equipment (average historical cost)	$1,200,000	$2,000,000
Accumulated depreciation (average)	800,000	1,000,000

Twenty percent of the equipment in State A is fully depreciated and is idle. Assuming that A includes property in the factor at historical cost, Quake's property factor is 54.55% [($1,200,000 − $240,000 idle property)/($2,000,000 − $240,000)]. If the idle property is not removed from the property factor, Quake's property factor in A is incorrectly computed as 60% ($1,200,000/$2,000,000). ∎

TAX *in the News* — **FINDING NEW REVENUES**

Some states are using "data mining," a form of statistical sampling, to uncover new sources of revenue. Usually, this type of audit strategy involves comparing various state databases (and sometimes even those of neighboring states) to find discrepancies in reporting and to select returns for audit.

For instance, South Carolina expects to capture an extra $100 million in taxes over five years by using motor vehicle records to discover nonfilers of the state personal income tax. Texas finds business nonfilers by searching records of property ownership, and Massachusetts compares its database of income tax filers with those who remit sales/use taxes and the tax on restaurant meals. Another sales/use tax inquiry uses U.S. Customs records to determine whether state residents paid the state use tax when they returned from overseas with newly purchased property.

Other states have witnessed these successes and are considering their own applications of data mining. Several consulting firms provide software that states can use to improve their internal processing capabilities so that they can exploit existing databases.

Payroll Factor. The payroll factor provides planning potential where several corporate employees spend substantial periods of time outside their state of employment, or the corporation is able to relocate highly paid employees to low- or no-tax states.

Use of an independent contractor who works for more than one principal can be beneficial under certain circumstances. Since the commissions paid to independent contractors are excluded from the payroll factor, the taxpayer may reduce its payroll factor in a high-tax state.

EXAMPLE 36

Yellow Corporation's total payroll costs are $1.4 million. Of this amount, $1 million was attributable to State A, a high-tax state. Yellow's payroll factor in A is 71.43% ($1,000,000/ $1,400,000).

Assuming that $200,000 of the A compensation had been paid to sales representatives and that Yellow replaced its sales force with independent contractors, Yellow's payroll factor in A would be reduced to 66.67% [($1,000,000 − $200,000)/($1,400,000 − $200,000)]. ∎

Sales/Use Taxes on Capital Changes

The tax adviser must be aware of the impact that sales and use taxes may have on a transaction that might otherwise be free from income tax. For example, although the transfer of property to a controlled corporation in exchange for its stock generally is not subject to corporate income taxes, several states provide that such transfers constitute taxable sales for sales and use tax purposes. Similarly, a corporate reorganization may be structured to avoid the imposition of income taxes, but under the statutes of several states, such transfers are considered to be taxable sales and, accordingly, are subject to sales and use taxes.

Capital Stock Taxation

Capital stock tax liabilities can be significant for capital-intensive taxpayers to the extent that they reinvest a large portion of retained earnings (the tax base) in productive assets. If all nontax factors are equal, a taxpayer with sizable exposure to a capital stock tax should consider the following techniques.

- Funding expansion with debt, rather than retained earnings.
- Funding subsidiary operations with debt, rather than direct capital contributions.
- Regularly paying dividends to parent companies that are domiciled in tax-favored states, such as Delaware.

KEY TERMS

Allocate, 15–9

Apportion, 15–9

Dock sales, 15–16

Multistate Tax Commission (MTC), 15–8

Nexus, 15–8

Passive investment company, 15–35

Payroll factor, 15–17

Property factor, 15–19

Public Law 86–272, 15–8

Sales factor, 15–15

Throwback rule, 15–16

UDITPA, 15–8

Unitary theory, 15–22

Water's edge, 15–25

PROBLEM MATERIALS

DISCUSSION QUESTIONS

Issue ID

1. As a staff member of the governor of your state, you are charged with bringing new business into the jurisdiction and with keeping the industry and services that are already there. List some of the tax incentives that your Department of Revenue might provide to help meet these goals.

2. Complete the following chart by indicating whether each item is true or false. Explain your answers by reference to the overlap of rules appearing in Federal and most state income tax laws.

Item	True or False
a. Federal taxable income is modified to produce state taxable income.	_____
b. Federal tax accounting methods, such as LIFO inventory and specific write-off of bad debts, are followed for state income tax purposes.	_____
c. State rules as to which entities can join in a consolidated return match those of Federal law.	_____
d. State income tax audits electronically are piggybacked to the Federal process (i.e., taxpayers must notify the state's revenue department when a Federal audit is completed).	_____

3. Describe the Multistate Tax Commission and UDITPA, and comment on their role in state taxation.

4. Many states "outsource" their responsibility to write income tax rules to the Multistate Tax Commission. Evaluate this statement.

Communications

5. In no more than three PowerPoint slides, list some general guidelines that a taxpayer can use to determine if it has an obligation to file an income or sales/use tax return with a particular state. Address the rules for in-state and out-of-state businesses.

6. Sales representative Jones is based in Utah, where the operating plants and corporate headquarters of her employer also are located. She visits customers in Colorado for a day, soliciting orders for the seashells that she sells. The orders are approved in Utah, and the shells are shipped from Oregon within a week. Are these sales subject to the Colorado corporate income tax?

7. Continue with the facts of Question 6. In processing her orders, Jones regularly reviews the credit standing of the customer and decides whether the order should be billed on company credit or sent COD (cash on delivery). Are these sales subject to the Colorado corporate income tax?

8. Describe the key concepts of *allocation* and *apportionment* in the taxation of the net income of a multistate business.

9. The traditional income apportionment formula applied three factors, equally weighted, in determining the taxable income of a business in the state. Now a majority of the states employ a formula in which the sales factor is assigned a greater than one-third weight. Why is such a formula attractive to a state?

Issue ID

10. In computing the corporate income taxes for an Arizona-based client, should a single large sale in July, in which merchandise was shipped to a customer in New Mexico, be included in the Arizona sales factor?

11. Continue with the facts of Question 10. Another large shipment was made to a customer in South Dakota, a state that does not impose any corporate income tax. Is this sale to be included in the Arizona sales factor?

12. About 20 states apply a unitary system of business income taxation.
    a. Explain why these states are attracted to the unitary theory and a combined reporting scheme of multistate income taxation.
    b. Is the application of the unitary theory a help or a detriment to the taxpayer?

13. Name two states that do not allow single-level corporate taxation for Federal S corporations.

14. Comment on special compliance concerns for Federal S corporations in dealing with state income tax systems.

15. Describe two approaches that the states use concerning out-of-state S corporation shareholders.

16. Evaluate this statement: An S corporation can facilitate the meeting of its state income tax filing obligations by developing a common spreadsheet that allocates and apportions income among the states with which it has nexus. This spreadsheet is attached to each of the state returns to be filed. [*Hint*: Use the term "composite return" in your answer.]

17. Describe the typical state income tax system for partners and partnerships.

18. Who remits a sales tax to the taxing state? A use tax?

19. Evaluate this statement: The seller doesn't pay the sales tax—the customer does.

Issue ID

20. Create a PowerPoint outline describing the major exemptions and exclusions from the sales/use tax base of most states. Use your slides to discuss this topic with your accounting students' club.

Communications

21. Give two examples of the sales/use tax occasional sale exemption.

22. What is the Streamlined Sales Tax Project? What tax problems does it address?

23. Your client, Ecru Limited, is considering an expansion of its sales operations, but it fears adverse resulting tax consequences. Write a memo for the tax research file identifying the planning opportunities presented by the ability of a corporation to terminate or create nexus. Be certain to discuss the *Wrigley* case in your analysis.

Communications

24. Your client, Royal Corporation, generates significant interest income from its working capital liquid investments. Write a memo for the tax research file discussing the planning opportunities presented by establishing a passive investment company. Support your memo with a diagram of the resulting flow of assets and income.

Communications

25. Describe the *Geoffrey* rule that has been adopted by some states. Why do the states find this rule attractive?

26. As the director of the multistate tax planning department of a consulting firm, you are developing a brochure to highlight the services it can provide. Part of the brochure is a list of five or so key techniques that clients can use to reduce state income tax liabilities. Develop this list for the brochure.

27. Continuing with Problem 26, provide two or three bullet points containing planning ideas relating to a client's liability for a capital stock tax.

PROBLEMS

28. Use Figure 15–1 to compute Beta Corporation's State F taxable income for the year.

Addition modifications	$12,000
Allocated income (total)	$15,000
Allocated income (State F)	$5,000
Apportionment percentage	28%
Credits	$50
Federal taxable income	$50,000
Subtraction modifications	$11,000
Tax rate	5%

29. Use Figure 15–1 to provide the required information for Warbler Corporation, whose Federal taxable income totals $6 million. Warbler apportions 60% of its business income to State C. Warbler generates $1.2 million of nonbusiness income each year, and 20% of that income is allocated to C. Applying the state income tax modifications, Warbler's business income this year is $5 million.
    a. How much of Warbler's business income does State C tax?
    b. How much of Warbler's nonbusiness income does State C tax?
    c. Explain your results.

30. For each of the following independent cases, indicate whether the circumstances call for an addition modification (A), a subtraction modification (S), or no modification (N) in computing state taxable income. Then indicate the amount of any modification. The starting point in computing State Q taxable income is the year's Federal taxable income.
    a. Q income taxes, deducted on the Federal return as a business expense = $10,000.
    b. State R income taxes, deducted on the Federal return as a business expense = $10,000.
    c. Federal income taxes paid = $30,000.
    d. Refund received from last year's Q income taxes = $3,000.
    e. Local property taxes, deducted on the Federal return as a business expense = $7,000.
    f. Federal cost recovery = $10,000, and Q cost recovery = $15,000.
    g. Federal cost recovery = $15,000, and Q cost recovery = $10,000.
    h. An asset was sold for $18,000; its purchase price was $20,000. Accumulated Federal cost recovery = $11,000, and accumulated Q cost recovery = $8,000.
    i. Federal investment tax credit = $0, and Q investment tax credit = $5,000.
    j. Dividend income received from State R corporation = $10,000, subject to a Federal dividends received deduction of 70%.

31. Perk Corporation is subject to tax only in State A. Perk generated the following income and deductions.

Federal taxable income	$200,000
State A income tax expense	15,000
Refund of State A income tax	3,000
Depreciation allowed for Federal tax purposes	300,000
Depreciation allowed for state tax purposes	180,000

Federal taxable income is the starting point in computing A taxable income. State income taxes are not deductible for A tax purposes. Determine Perk's A taxable income.

32. Flip Corporation is subject to tax only in State X. Flip generated the following income and deductions. State income taxes are not deductible for X income tax purposes.

Sales	$4,000,000
Cost of sales	3,300,000
State X income tax expense	150,000
Depreciation allowed for Federal tax purposes	400,000

Depreciation allowed for state tax purposes	$250,000
Interest income on Federal obligations	20,000
Interest income on X obligations	75,000
Expenses related to X obligations	10,000

a. The starting point in computing the X income tax base is Federal taxable income. Derive this amount.

b. Determine Flip's X taxable income, assuming that interest on X obligations is exempt from X income tax.

c. Determine Flip's X taxable income, assuming that interest on X obligations is subject to X income tax.

33. Jest Corporation owns and operates two facilities that manufacture paper products. One of the facilities is located in State D, and the other is located in State E. Jest generated $2.5 million of taxable income, comprised of $2 million of income from its manufacturing facilities and a $500,000 gain from the sale of nonbusiness property, located in E. E does not distinguish between business and nonbusiness income, but D apportions only business income. Jest's activities within the two states are outlined below.

	State D	State E	Total
Sales of paper products	$4,500,000	$5,800,000	$10,300,000
Property	600,000	1,500,000	2,100,000
Payroll	1,200,000	1,900,000	3,100,000

Both D and E utilize a three-factor apportionment formula, under which sales, property, and payroll are equally weighted. Determine the amount of Jest's income that is subject to income tax by each state.

34. Assume the same facts as Problem 33, except that, under the statutes of both D and E, only business income is subject to apportionment.

35. Millie Corporation has nexus in States A and B. Millie's activities for the year are summarized below.

	State A	State B	Total
Sales	$1,200,000	$ 400,000	$1,600,000
Property			
Average cost	500,000	300,000	800,000
Average accumulated depreciation	(300,000)	(100,000)	(400,000)
Payroll	2,400,000	600,000	3,000,000
Rent expense	10,000	25,000	35,000

Determine the apportionment factors for A and B, assuming that A uses a three-factor apportionment formula under which sales, property (net depreciated basis), and payroll are equally weighted, and B employs a single-factor formula that consists solely of sales. State A has adopted the UDITPA with respect to the inclusion of rent payments in the property factor.

36. Assume the facts of Problem 35, except that A uses a single-factor apportionment formula that consists solely of sales, and B uses a three-factor apportionment formula that equally weights sales, property (at historical cost), and payroll. State B does not include rent payments in the property factor.

37. Assume the facts of Problem 35, except that both states employ a three-factor formula, under which sales are double weighted. The basis of the property factor in A is historical cost, while the basis of this factor in B is the net depreciated basis. Neither A nor B includes rent payments in the property factor.

38. Falcon Corporation operates in two states, as indicated below. This year's operations generated $400,000 of apportionable income.

	State A	State B	Total
Sales	$600,000	$400,000	$1,000,000
Property	300,000	100,000	400,000
Payroll	200,000	50,000	250,000

Compute Falcon's State A taxable income, assuming that State A apportions income based on a:

a. Three-factor formula.

b. Double-weighted sales factor.

c. Sales factor only.

39. Tootie Corporation operates in two states, as indicated below. All goods are manufactured in State A. Determine the sales to be assigned to both states in computing Tootie's sales factor for the year. Both states follow the UDITPA and the MTC regulations in this regard.

Sales shipped to A locations	$200,000
Sales shipped to B locations	490,000
Interest income from Tootie's B business checking accounts	3,000
Rent income from excess space in A warehouse	50,000
Interest income from Treasury bills in Tootie's B brokerage account, holding only idle cash from operations	15,000
Onetime sale of display equipment to B purchaser	75,000
Royalty received from holding patent, licensed to B user	60,000

Decision Making

40. State E applies a throwback rule to sales, while State F does not. State G has not adopted an income tax to date. Orange Corporation, headquartered in E, reported the following sales for the year. All of the goods were shipped from Orange's E manufacturing facilities. Determine its sales factor in those states. Comment on Orange's location strategy, using only your tax computations.

Customer	Customer's Location	This Year's Sales
ShellTell, Inc.	E	$ 75,000,000
Tourists, Ltd.	F	40,000,000
PageToo Corp.	G	55,000,000
U.S. Department of Interior	All 50 states	35,000,000
Total		$205,000,000

Decision Making

41. Aqua Corporation is subject to tax in States G, H, and I. Aqua's compensation expense includes the following.

	State G	State H	State I	Total
Salaries and wages for nonofficers	$200,000	$400,000	$100,000	$700,000
Officers' salaries	–0–	–0–	250,000	250,000
Total				$950,000

Officers' salaries are included in the payroll factor for G and I, but not for H. Compute Aqua's payroll factors for G, H, and I. Comment on your results.

42. Judy, a regional sales manager, has her office in State U. Her region includes several states, as indicated in the sales report below. Judy is compensated through straight commissions on the sales in her region and a fully excludible cafeteria plan conveying various fringe benefits to her. Determine how much of Judy's $150,000 commissions and $40,000 fringe benefit package is assigned to the payroll factor of State U.

State	Sales Generated	Judy's Time Spent There
U	$3,000,000	20%
V	4,000,000	55%
X	5,000,000	25%

43. Justine Corporation operates manufacturing facilities in State G and State H. In addition, the corporation owns nonbusiness rental property in H. Justine incurred the following compensation expenses.

	State G	State H	Total
Manufacturing wages	$475,000	$200,000	$675,000
Administrative wages	200,000	50,000	250,000
Officers' salaries	250,000	50,000	300,000

Thirty percent of the time spent by the administrative staff located in H and 15% of the time spent by officers located in H are devoted to the operation, maintenance, and supervision of the rental property. G includes all income in the definition of apportionable income, while H excludes nonbusiness income from apportionable income. Only G includes officers' compensation in the payroll factor.

Determine Justine's payroll factors for G and H.

44. Kim Corporation, a calendar year taxpayer, has manufacturing facilities in States A and B. A summary of Kim's property holdings follows.

	Beginning of Year		
	State A	State B	Total
Inventory	$ 300,000	$ 200,000	$ 500,000
Plant and equipment	2,500,000	1,500,000	4,000,000
Accumulated depreciation: plant and equipment	(1,200,000)	(500,000)	(1,700,000)
Land	600,000	600,000	1,200,000
Rental property*	900,000	300,000	1,200,000
Accumulated depreciation: rental property	(200,000)	(50,000)	(250,000)

	End of Year		
	State A	State B	Total
Inventory	$ 400,000	$ 150,000	$ 550,000
Plant and equipment	2,500,000	1,200,000	3,700,000
Accumulated depreciation: plant and equipment	(1,500,000)	(450,000)	(1,950,000)
Land	600,000	400,000	1,000,000
Rental property*	950,000	300,000	1,250,000
Accumulated depreciation: rental property	(300,000)	(100,000)	(400,000)

*Unrelated to Kim's regular business operations.

Determine Kim's property factors for the two states, assuming that the statutes of both A and B provide that average historical cost of business property is to be included in the property factor.

45. Assume the facts of Problem 44, except that nonbusiness income is apportionable in B.

Decision Making

46. Crate Corporation, a calendar year taxpayer, has established nexus with numerous states. On December 3, Crate sold one of its two facilities in State X. The cost of this facility was $800,000.

    On January 1, Crate owned property with a cost of $3 million, $1.5 million of which was located in X. On December 31, Crate owned property with a cost of $2.2 million, $600,000 of which was located in X.

    X law allows the use of average annual or monthly amounts in determining the property factor. If Crate wants to minimize the property factor in X, which method should be used to determine the property factor there?

Decision Making

Communications

47. True Corporation, a wholly owned subsidiary of Trumaine Corporation, generated a $400,000 taxable loss in its first year of operations. True's activities and sales are restricted to State A, which imposes an 8% income tax. In the same year, Trumaine's taxable income is $1 million. Trumaine's activities and sales are restricted to State B, which imposes an 11% income tax. Both states use a three-factor apportionment formula that equally weights sales, payroll, and property, and both require a unitary group to file on a combined basis. Sales, payroll, and average property for each corporation are as follows.

	True Corporation	Trumaine Corporation	Total
Sales	$2,500,000	$4,000,000	$6,500,000
Property	1,000,000	2,500,000	3,500,000
Payroll	500,000	1,500,000	2,000,000

    True and Trumaine have been found to be members of a unitary business.
    a. Determine the overall state income tax for the unitary group.
    b. Determine aggregate state income tax for the entities if they were nonunitary.
    c. Incorporate this analysis in a letter to Trumaine's board of directors. Corporate offices are located at 1234 Mulberry Lane, Chartown, AL 35298.

48. Gerald Corporation is part of a three-corporation unitary business. The group has a water's edge election in effect with respect to unitary State Q. State B does not apply the unitary concept with respect to its corporate income tax laws. Nor does Despina, a European country to which Geraldine paid a $4 million value added tax this year.

    Geraldine was organized in Despina and conducts all of its business there. Given the summary of operations that follows, determine Gerald's and Elena's sales factors in B and Q.

Corporation	Customer's Location	Sales
Gerald	B	$20,000,000
	Q	55,000,000
Elena	Q	20,000,000
Geraldine	Despina	25,000,000

Communications

49. Hernandez, which has been an S corporation since inception, is subject to tax in States Y and Z. On Schedule K of its Federal Form 1120S, Hernandez reported ordinary income of $500,000 from its business, taxable interest income of $10,000, capital loss of $30,000, and $40,000 of dividend income from a corporation in which it owns 30%.

    Both states apportion income by use of a three-factor formula that equally weights sales, payroll, and the average cost of property; both states treat interest and dividends as business income. In addition, both Y and Z follow Federal provisions with respect to the determination of taxable income for a corporation. Y recognizes S status, but Z does not. Based on the following information, write a memo to the shareholders of Hernandez, detailing the amount of taxable income on which Hernandez will pay tax in Y and Z. Hernandez corporate offices are located at 5678 Alabaster Circle, Koopville, KY 47697.

	State Y	State Z
Sales	$1,000,000	$800,000
Property (average cost)	500,000	100,000
Payroll	800,000	200,000

50. Using the following information from the books and records of Grande Corporation, determine Grande's total sales that are subject to State C's sales tax. Grande operates a retail hardware store.

Sales to C consumers, general merchandise	$800,000
Sales to C consumers, crutches and other medical supplies	120,000
Sales to consumers in State D, via mail order	80,000
Purchases from suppliers	55,000

51. As a retailer, Granite Corporation sells software programs manufactured and packaged by other parties. Granite also purchases computer parts, assembles them as specified by a customer in a purchase order, and sells them as operating stand-alone computers. All of Granite's operations take place in State F, which levies a 9% sales tax. Results for the current year are as follows.

Sales of software	$2,500,000
Purchases of computer parts	1,700,000
Sales of computer systems	7,500,000
Purchases of office supplies	60,000
Purchases of packaging materials for the computer systems	5,000
Purchases of tools used by computer assemblers	40,000

   a. What is Granite's own sales tax expense for the year?
   b. How much F sales tax must Granite collect and pay over to the state on behalf of other taxpayers subject to the tax?

52. Indicate for each transaction whether a sales (S) or use (U) tax applies or whether the transaction is nontaxable (N). Where the laws vary among states, assume that the most common rules apply. All taxpayers are individuals.
   a. A resident of State A purchases an automobile in A.
   b. A resident of State A purchases groceries in A.
   c. A resident of State B purchases an automobile in A.
   d. A charity purchases office supplies in A.
   e. An A resident purchases in B an item that will be in the inventory of her business.

53. Wayne Corporation is subject to State A's franchise tax. The tax is imposed at a rate of 3% of the corporation's net worth that is apportioned to the state by use of a two-factor (sales and property equally weighted) formula. The property factor includes real and tangible personal property, valued at historical cost as of the end of the taxable year.

   Forty percent of Wayne's sales are attributable to A, and $300,000 of the cost of Wayne's tangible personal property is located in A.

   Determine the A franchise tax payable by Wayne this year, given the following end-of-the-year balance sheet.

Cash		$ 500,000
Equipment	$1,000,000	
Accumulated depreciation	(300,000)	700,000
Furniture and fixtures	$ 200,000	
Accumulated depreciation	(50,000)	150,000
Intangible assets		350,000
Total assets		$1,700,000
Accounts and taxes payable		$ 600,000
Long-term debt		350,000
Common stock		1,000
Additional paid-in capital		249,000
Retained earnings		500,000
Total liabilities and equity		$1,700,000

54. Dread Corporation operates in a high-tax state. The firm asks you for advice on a plan to outsource administrative work done in its home state to independent contractors. This

Decision Making

work now costs the company $750,000 in wages and benefits. Dread's total payroll for the year is $5 million, of which $4 million is for work currently done in the home state.

Issue ID

Communications

55. Prepare a PowerPoint presentation (maximum six slides) entitled "Planning Principles for Our Multistate Clients." The slides will be used to lead a 20-minute discussion with colleagues in the corporate tax department. Keep the outline general, but assume that your colleagues have clients operating in at least 15 states. Address only income tax issues.

RESEARCH PROBLEMS

Internet *Activity*

Use the tax resources of the Internet to address the following questions. Do not restrict your search to the World Wide Web, but include a review of newsgroups and general reference materials, practitioner sites and resources, primary sources of the tax law, chat rooms and discussion groups, and other opportunities.

Communications

Research Problem 1.   Send an e-mail message to the secretary of revenue for your home state, proposing adoption of one of the following provisions that does not currently exist in your state. Justify your proposal with a numerical example.

a. Increase the apportionment weight for the sales factor.

b. Exempt computer and communications technology from the apportionment weight for the property factor.

c. Adopt a throwback rule for the sales factor.

d. Subject advertising expenditures to the sales/use tax.

e. Tax the income of an investment subsidiary set up by a domestic taxpayer.

f. Add a "nexus team" to find the taxpayers operating in your state, but based in Ohio, Illinois, or Arizona.

Communications

Research Problem 2.   For your state and one of its neighbors, determine the following. Place your data in a chart and e-mail your finding to your professor.

a. To what extent does each state follow the rulings of the Multistate Tax Commission?

b. What is each state's apportionment formula, with factors and weightings?

c. Does the state adopt pertinent changes to the Internal Revenue Code? As of what date?

d. Does the state apply entity-level income taxes for S corporations, partnerships, and LLCs? What are the terms of those taxes?

e. What are the requirements for the occasional-sale rule as an exception to the sales/use tax? Who can use this rule?

Research Problem 3.   Does Walmart.com collect use tax when it ships an order into your state? Does Dell.com? Gateway.com? Amazon.com? Crateandbarrel.com? SamGoody.com? (If your state does not have a sales tax law, answer for a neighboring state.)

Communications

Research Problem 4.   Read the "tax footnote" of five publicly traded U.S. corporations. Find the effective state/local income tax rates of each. Create a PowerPoint presentation for your instructor, summarizing the search and reporting the findings.

Communications

Research Problem 5.   Use **http://taxsites.com** or some other index to find a state/local tax organization (e.g., the Committee on State Taxation). Read its current newsletter. In an e-mail to your instructor, summarize a major article at the site. Look especially for articles on one of these topics.

• Adoption of the Streamlined Sales Tax Project provisions at the Federal level or by your home state.

• Legislation applying a physical-presence test as the exclusive definition of nexus at the Federal level or for your state's income or sales/use tax.

• Application of gross receipts taxes on S corporations, partnerships, and LLCs by your home state.

• Limitations on the taxpayer's ability to carry back net operating losses in computing your state's corporate taxable income.

Research Problem 6.   Many states offer a tax credit for expenditures made in-state for new business equipment. For your state and one of its neighbors, summarize in a table three of the tax incentives offered through the income, sales, or property tax structure. In your table, list at least the following.

- Name of the credit, deduction, exemption, etc.
- Who qualifies for the incentive (e.g., corporations, individuals, partnerships).
- Computational base for the incentive (e.g., dollars spent).
- Rate of the credit or deduction.
- Minimums, maximums, and other limitations that apply to the incentive amount.

CHAPTER 16

Tax Practice and Ethics

LEARNING OBJECTIVES

After completing Chapter 16, you should be able to:

LO.1
Describe the organization and structure of the IRS.

LO.2
Identify the various administrative pronouncements issued by the IRS and explain how they can be used in tax practice.

LO.3
Describe the audit process, including how returns are selected for audit and the various types of audits.

LO.4
Explain the taxpayer appeal process, including various settlement options available.

LO.5
Determine the amount of interest on a deficiency or a refund and when it is due.

LO.6
Discuss the various penalties that can be imposed on acts of noncompliance by taxpayers and return preparers.

LO.7
Understand the rules governing the statute of limitations on assessments and on refunds.

LO.8
Summarize the legal and ethical guidelines that apply to those engaged in tax practice.

Few events arouse so much fear in the typical individual or corporation as the receipt of a letter from the Internal Revenue Service (IRS), notifying the taxpayer that prior years' tax returns are to be the subject of an audit. Almost immediately, calls are made to the tax adviser. Advice is sought as to what to reveal (or not reveal) in the course of the audit, how to delay or avoid the audit, and how friendly one should be with the auditor when he or she ultimately arrives.

Indeed, many tax practitioners' reputations with their clients have been made or broken by the way they are observed to behave under the pressure of an audit situation. The strategy and tactics of audits—including such seemingly unimportant issues as whether the tax adviser brings donuts or other refreshments to the audit session, the color of his or her suit and tie, and the most effective negotiation techniques—are the subject of both cocktail party banter and scholarly review.

In actuality, the tax professional can render valuable services to the taxpayer in an audit context, thereby assuring that tax payments for the disputed years are neither under- nor over-reported, as part of an ongoing tax practice. In this regard, the adviser must appreciate the following.

- The elements of the Treasury's tax administration process and opportunities for appeal within the structure of the IRS.
- The extent of the negative sanctions that can be brought to bear against taxpayers whose returns are found to have been inaccurate.
- The ethical and professional constraints on the advice tax advisers can give and the actions they can take on behalf of their clients, within the context of an adversarial relationship with the IRS.

Tax Administration

The Treasury has delegated the administration and enforcement of the tax laws to its subsidiary agency, the IRS. In this process, the Service is responsible for providing adequate information, in the form of publications and forms with instructions, to taxpayers so that they can comply with the laws in an appropriate manner. The IRS also identifies delinquent tax payments and carries out assessment and collection procedures under the restrictions of due process and other constitutional guarantees.

The IRS is the third-largest Federal agency. It employs about 90,000 staff members, and the total agency budget exceeds $11 billion. In meeting its responsibilities, the Service conducts audits of selected tax returns. About 1 percent of all individual tax returns are subjected to audit in a given tax year. However, certain types of both taxpayers and income—including, for instance, high-income individuals (about 1.7 percent for those with income exceeding $100,000, and over 6

TAX *in the News* — HOW BIG IS THE TAX GAP?

Every year the IRS estimates the size of the Federal income "tax gap"—the difference between how much tax *is* collected and how much *should be* collected. The tax gap reflects the taxes not paid by nonfilers, tax cheats, delinquents, and those who interpret or apply the tax laws incorrectly, whether deliberately or innocently.

According to the most recent analysis, the tax gap is a net amount of almost $300 billion annually. More specifically, the underpayments total about $345 billion per year but are offset by $55 billion obtained through IRS enforcement efforts (audits, collection procedures, etc.).

If, by some miracle, the entire tax gap were collected each year, the current Federal budget deficit would be almost eliminated. A complete elimination of the tax gap is unlikely to occur, however.

- Citizens are not likely to tolerate the increased audit activity and data collection necessary for the Treasury to collect all of the tax owed.
- Congress is not likely to adopt the sweeping simplification of the tax law needed to alleviate its complexity, which many see as the underlying cause of the tax gap. Taxpayers who have difficulty understanding the tax law cannot be expected to fully comply with its provisions.

---

percent for those with income exceeding $1 million), cash-oriented businesses, real estate transactions, and estate- and gift-taxable transfers (as high as 25 percent)—are subject to much higher probabilities of audit.

The audit rate for corporations with at least $250 million in assets is about 35 percent, but the rate drops to about 1 percent for businesses with less than $10 million in assets. In the past few years, the IRS has increased its audit and enforcement activities and is currently hiring audit staff at a rate exceeding that of the past decade.

Recently, much of the IRS's effort has been devoted to developing statutory and administrative requirements relative to information reporting and document matching. For instance, when a taxpayer engages in a like-kind exchange or sells a personal residence, various parties to the transaction are required to report the nature and magnitude of the transaction to the IRS. Later the Treasury's computers determine whether the transaction has been reported properly by comparing the information reported by the third parties with the events included on the relevant taxpayers' returns for the year.

In addition, the IRS has been placing increasing pressure on the community of tax advisers. Severe penalties may be assessed on those who have prepared the appropriate return when the Service's interpretation of applicable law conflicts with that of the preparer.

The IRS processes about 135 million individual income tax returns every year, almost 80 million of which are filed electronically. It collects more than $2.25 trillion in tax revenues and pays refunds to about 100 million taxpayers every year. The average refund exceeds $2,200.

Organizational Structure of the IRS

> **LO.1**
>
> Describe the organization and structure of the IRS.

The structure of the IRS is moving toward that illustrated in Figure 16–1. The IRS Commissioner, a presidential appointee, has organized the day-to-day operations of the agency into four divisions, based on the type of tax returns to be processed. Administrative functions, such as those relating to personnel and computer issues, are organized on a shared-services model, managed from the national office. Broader functions, such as litigation, investigations, and taxpayer relations, are managed at the national level as well.

The Chief Counsel, another presidential appointee, is the head legal officer of the IRS. The Chief Counsel's office provides legal advice to the IRS and guidance to the public on matters pertaining to the administration and enforcement of the tax laws. For instance, the Chief Counsel's duties include establishing uniform nationwide interpretative positions on the law, drafting tax guide material

FIGURE 16–1   IRS National Office Organization

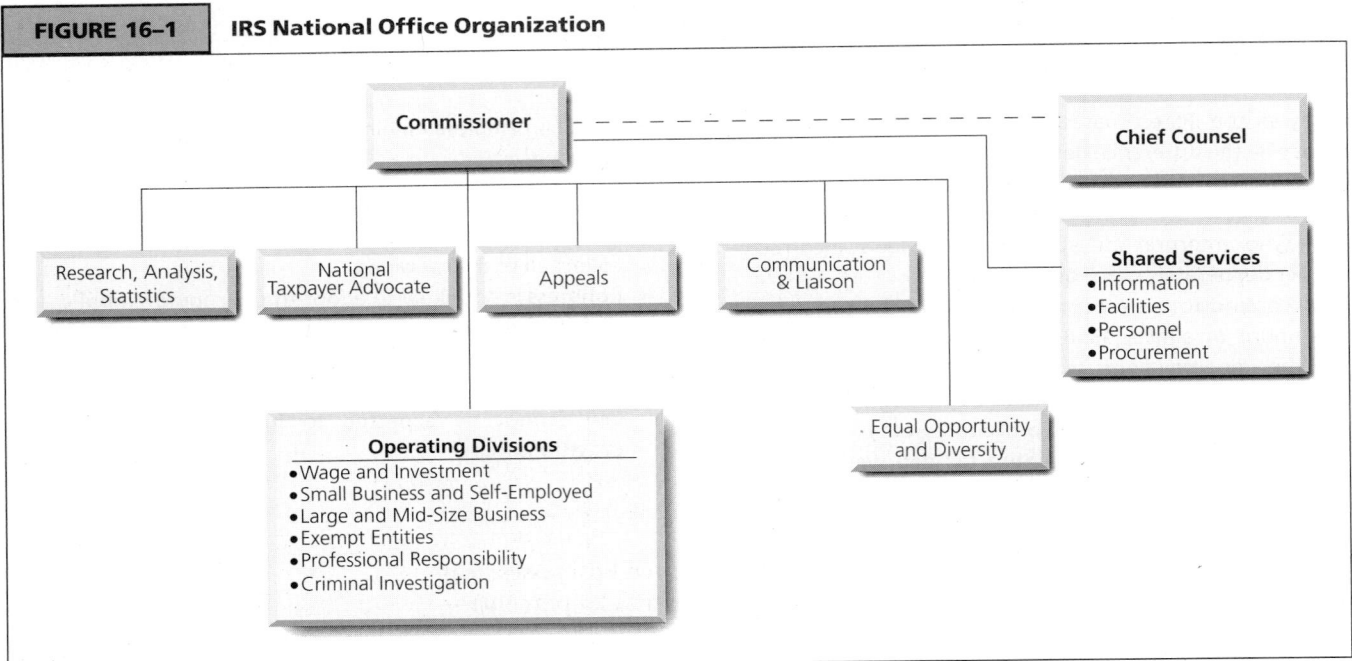

for taxpayers and IRS personnel, issuing technical rulings to taxpayers, and providing advice and technical assistance to IRS personnel. The Chief Counsel represents the IRS in all litigation before the Tax Court.

IRS Procedure—Letter Rulings

LO.2

Identify the various administrative pronouncements issued by the IRS and explain how they can be used in tax practice.

When a tax issue is controversial or a transaction involves considerable tax dollars, the taxpayer often wishes to obtain either assurance or direction from the IRS as to the treatment of the event. The **letter ruling** process is an effective means of dealing directly with the IRS while in the planning stages of a large or otherwise important transaction.

Rulings issued by the National Office provide a written statement of the position of the IRS concerning the tax consequences of a course of action contemplated by the taxpayer. Letter rulings do not have the force and effect of law, but they do provide guidance and support for taxpayers in similar transactions. The IRS issues rulings only on uncompleted, actual (rather than hypothetical) transactions or on transactions that have been completed before the filing of the tax return for the year in question.

In certain circumstances, the IRS will not issue a ruling. It ordinarily will not rule in cases that essentially involve a question of fact.[1] For example, no ruling will be issued to determine whether compensation paid to employees is reasonable in amount and therefore allowable as a deduction.[2]

A letter ruling represents the current opinion of the IRS on the tax consequences of a transaction with a given set of facts. IRS rulings are not unchangeable. They are frequently declared obsolete or are superseded by new rulings in response to tax law changes. However, revocation or modification of a ruling is usually not applied retroactively to the taxpayer who received the ruling, if it was relied on in good faith and if the facts in the ruling request were in agreement with the completed transaction. The IRS may revoke any ruling if, upon subsequent audit, the agent finds a misstatement or omission of facts or substantial discrepancies between the facts in the ruling request and the actual situation.

---

[1] Rev.Proc. 2008–1, I.R.B. No. 1, 1.   [2] Rev.Proc. 2008–3, I.R.B. No. 1, 110.

TAX *in the News* **IRS AUDIT INITIATIVES**

The IRS's current audit initiatives seem to be aimed at chronic and high-risk noncompliance. In an age of shrinking real budget dollars for the Service, this "biggest bang for the buck" strategy may be appropriate. The Service seems to be hunting for annuities of tax dollars, rather than just maximizing current collections. For example, permanently adding a noncompliant taxpayer to the tax rolls can optimize the present value of revenue collections tied to the IRS's efforts.

Announced priority areas for the IRS audit staff include the following.

- Offshore credit card users.
- High-risk, high-income taxpayers.
- Tax shelters, abusive schemes, and their promoters.
- High-income nonfilers.
- Unreported income.

- Transfer pricing involving transactions between U.S. companies and their foreign affiliates.
- Employment taxes.
- Transfers of intangible assets to offshore affiliated companies.
- Executive compensation (particularly stock option transactions).
- Claims of the research credit.
- Abuse of the rules for tax-exempt entities.
- Further research as to audit initiatives.

The agency has stated that it is revising its training materials and case studies to reflect the revised priorities. "Hardball" techniques apparently will be used to deal with the priority issues. Such techniques include issuing summonses, obtaining injunctions, initiating civil audits for shelter participants, and pursuing criminal investigations of shelter promoters.

A ruling may be relied upon only by the taxpayer who requested and received it. It must be attached to the tax return for the year in question.

Letter rulings benefit both the IRS and the taxpayer. Not only do they help promote a uniform application of the tax laws, but they may also reduce the potential for litigation or disputes with IRS agents. In addition, they make the IRS aware of significant transactions being consummated by taxpayers. A $10,000 fee is charged for processing a ruling request; the fee is reduced to $625 if the taxpayer's income is less than $250,000.

IRS Procedure—Other Issuances

In addition to issuing unpublished letter rulings and published rulings and procedures, the IRS issues determination letters and technical advice memoranda.

A **determination letter** relates to a completed transaction when the issue involved is covered by judicial or statutory authority, Regulations, or rulings. Determination letters are issued for various death, gift, income, excise, and employment tax matters.

True Corporation recently opened a car clinic and has employed numerous mechanics. The corporation is not certain whether its educational reimbursement plan is nondiscriminatory. True may request a determination letter. ■

EXAMPLE 1

Assume the same facts as in Example 1. True would like to establish a pension plan that qualifies for the tax advantages of § 401(k). To determine whether the plan qualifies, True should request and obtain a determination letter from the IRS. ■

EXAMPLE 2

A group of physicians plans to form an association to construct and operate a hospital. The determination letter procedure is appropriate to ascertain whether the group is subject to the Federal income tax or is tax-exempt. ■

EXAMPLE 3

A **technical advice memorandum (TAM)** is issued by the National Office to IRS personnel in response to a specific request by an agent, Appellate Conferee, or IRS executive. The taxpayer may request a TAM if an issue in dispute is not treated by the law or precedent and/or published rulings or Regulations. TAMs are also appropriate when there is reason to believe that the IRS is not administering the tax law consistently. For example, a taxpayer may inquire why an agent proposes to disallow a certain expenditure when agents in other districts permit the deduction. Technical advice requests arise from the audit process, whereas ruling requests are issued before any IRS audit.

A technical expedited advice memorandum (TEAM) can be used during an office or field audit. The TEAM is designed to reflect the position of the IRS in a shorter time than a TAM otherwise would take. This quicker response time is possible because the following occur before a TEAM request is submitted.

- The taxpayer and the IRS agree to a set of facts for the case.
- The parties conduct a presubmission conference, with attorneys for both sides in attendance.
- Technology, including e-mails and faxes, is used to gather facts as part of the process.
- The IRS holds an internal strategic planning meeting, discussing potential responses to various holdings that could be issued as part of the TEAM.

Administrative Powers of the IRS

Examination of Records. The IRS can examine the taxpayer's books and records as part of the process of determining the correct amount of tax due. The IRS can also require the persons responsible for the return to appear and to produce any necessary books and records.[3] Taxpayers are required to maintain certain record-keeping procedures and retain the records necessary to facilitate the audit.

Burden of Proof. If the taxpayer meets the record-keeping requirement and substantiates income and deductions properly, the IRS bears the burden of proof in establishing a tax deficiency during litigation. The taxpayer must have cooperated with the IRS regarding reasonable requests for information, documents, meetings, and interviews. For individual taxpayers, the IRS's burden of proof extends to penalties and interest amounts that it assesses in a court proceeding with the taxpayer.[4]

Assessment and Demand. The Code permits the IRS to assess a deficiency and to demand payment for the tax. However, no assessment or effort to collect the tax may be made until 90 days after a statutory notice of a deficiency (a *90-day letter*) is issued. The taxpayer therefore has 90 days to file a petition to the U.S. Tax Court, effectively preventing the deficiency from being assessed or collected pending the outcome of the case.[5]

Following assessment of the tax, the IRS issues a notice and demand for payment. The taxpayer is usually given 30 days after the notice and demand for payment to pay the tax.

If the IRS believes the assessment or collection of a deficiency is in jeopardy, it may assess the deficiency and demand immediate payment.[6] The taxpayer can avoid (*stay*) the collection of the jeopardy assessment by filing a bond for the amount of the tax and interest. This action prevents the IRS from selling any property it has seized.

Collection. If the taxpayer neglects or refuses to pay the tax after receiving the demand for payment, a lien in favor of the IRS is placed on all property (realty and personalty, tangible and intangible) belonging to the taxpayer.

---

[3]§ 7602.
[4]§§ 7491(a)(1), (a)(2)(B), and (c).
[5]§§ 6212 and 6213.

[6]§ 6861. A jeopardy assessment is appropriate, for instance, where the IRS fears that the taxpayer will flee the country or destroy valuable property.

The levy power of the IRS is very broad. It allows the IRS to garnish (*attach*) wages and salary and to seize and sell all nonexempt property by any means. After a 30-day notice period, the IRS can make successive seizures on any property owned by the taxpayer until the levy is satisfied.[7] A taxpayer's principal residence is exempt from the levy process, unless the disputed tax, interest, and penalty exceed $5,000 and a U.S. District Court judge approves of the seizure.[8]

The Audit Process

Selection of Returns for Audit. The IRS utilizes mathematical formulas to select tax returns that are most likely to contain errors and yield substantial amounts of additional tax revenues upon audit. The IRS does not openly disclose all of its audit selection techniques. However, some observations can be made regarding the probability of a return's selection for audit.

> **LO.3**
>
> Describe the audit process, including how returns are selected for audit and the various types of audits.

- Certain groups of taxpayers are subject to audit more frequently than others. These groups include individuals with gross income in excess of $100,000, self-employed individuals with substantial business income and deductions, and cash businesses where the potential for tax evasion is high.

EXAMPLE 4

Tracey owns and operates a liquor store. As nearly all of her sales are for cash, Tracey might be a prime candidate for an audit by the IRS. Cash transactions are easier to conceal than those made on credit. ■

- If a taxpayer has been audited in a past year and the audit led to the assessment of a substantial deficiency, the IRS often makes a return visit.
- An audit might materialize if information returns (e.g., Form W–2, Form 1099) are not in substantial agreement with the income reported on the taxpayer's return. Obvious discrepancies do not necessitate formal audits and usually can be handled by correspondence with the taxpayer.
- If an individual's itemized deductions are in excess of norms established for various income levels, the probability of an audit increases. Certain deductions (e.g., casualty and theft losses, business use of the home, tax-sheltered investments) are sensitive areas, as the IRS realizes that many taxpayers determine the amount of the deduction incorrectly or may not be entitled to the deduction at all.
- The filing of a refund claim by the taxpayer may prompt an audit of the return.
- Some returns are selected because the IRS has targeted a specific industry or type of tax return for in-depth review. This enables examiners to develop special skills and interests applicable to those returns. In the Industry Specialization Program (ISP), returns might be selected from retailers, energy developers, or health care operations for special review. In the Market Segment Specialization Program (MSSP), specialized auditors focus on returns that show passive losses, involve construction activities, or include legal or consulting income.
- Information is often obtained from other sources (e.g., other government agencies, news items, informants). The IRS then applies its own judgment and experience, and it may audit the return to address such questions as, Why did dividend income increase so much this year? Why did mortgage interest payments decrease? How did the taxpayer pay for such a large vacation home, sold this year?

---

[7]The taxpayer can keep certain personal ($7,900) and business ($3,950) property and a minimal amount of his or her income as a subsistence allowance, even if a lien is outstanding. These amounts are indexed for inflation. § 6334.

[8]§§ 6334(a)(13)(A) and (e)(1).

The IRS can pay rewards to persons who provide information that leads to the detection and punishment of those who violate the tax laws. The rewards are paid at the discretion of the IRS. Such a payment usually cannot exceed 15 percent of the taxes, fines, and penalties recovered as a result of such information.[9] About 500 rewards are paid in the typical year. The average reward paid is about $4,500.

Another IRS office, administering the so-called Whistleblower Program, offers special rewards to informants who provide information concerning businesses or high-income (gross income exceeds $200,000) individuals, when more than $2 million of tax, penalty, and interest is at stake. The reward can reach 30 percent of the amount collected by the Treasury and traceable to the whistleblower's information. The reward can be reduced if the whistleblower participated in the original understatement of tax.

The rewards are paid out of the taxes recovered under the informant and whistleblower programs. To claim a reward of this sort, file Form 211 with the IRS.

EXAMPLE 5	Phil reports to the police that burglars broke into his home while he was out of town and took a shoe box containing $25,000 in cash, among other things. A representative of the IRS reading the newspaper account of the burglary might wonder why Phil kept such a large amount of cash in a shoe box at home. ■

EXAMPLE 6	After 15 years, Betty is discharged by her employer, Dr. Franklin. Shortly thereafter, the IRS receives a letter from Betty stating that Franklin keeps two sets of books, one of which substantially understates his cash receipts. ■

The statistical models used by the IRS to select individual tax returns for audit come from random audits of a small number of taxpayers, who are required to document every entry that they made on the Form 1040. The latest round of these National Research Program (NRP) audits took place in late 2007 and resulted in the construction of new Discriminant Inventory Function (DIF) scores that project the amount of revenue that the IRS will gain from pursuing tax returns with various statistical profiles. The higher the DIF score, the better the return to the IRS from pursuing the audit, and the higher the probability of selection for an examination.

These data-seeking audits are controversial and have led to taxpayer complaints to Congress about the stress that they create.[10] But the data from older DIF models no longer reflected the U.S. service-based, information-powered economy. Consequently, more frequent updating of the underlying models is essential for effective enforcement of the tax laws. The IRS believes that, by constantly updating the NRP data through a diligent review of randomly selected tax returns, changes in tax avoidance behaviors will be detected and fewer routine audits will be required.

Many individual taxpayers mistakenly assume that if they do not hear from the IRS within a few weeks after filing their return or if they have received a refund check, no audit will be forthcoming. As a practical matter, most individual returns are examined about two years from the date of filing. If not, they generally remain unaudited. All large corporations, however, are subject to annual audits.

Verification and Audit Procedures. The filed tax return is immediately reviewed for mathematical accuracy. A check is also made for deductions, exclusions, etc., that are clearly erroneous. One obvious error would be the failure to comply with the 7.5 percent limitation on the deduction for medical expenses.

About 5 percent of all paper-filed individual returns show a math error. The math error rate for e-filed returns is only 0.1 percent. When a math or clerical error occurs, the Service Center merely sends the taxpayer revised computations and a

---

[9]§ 7623 and Reg. § 301.7623–1.

[10]On average, the total annual NRP audit sample consists of 13,000 returns. Some of these returns are analyzed without contacting the taxpayer, and other taxpayers are contacted only by mail with queries about one or two items. Only a few returns are subjected to "line-by-line" review. Most of the returns are reviewed for a period of three tax years.

TAX *in the News*   COLLECTING THOSE TAXES DUE

The IRS now uses third-party debt collectors, as do other Federal agencies (e.g., the Department of Education to collect delinquent student loans) and a few state tax departments. The IRS has negotiated a series of contracts with various collection agencies to collect unpaid Federal income and payroll taxes.

These third-party collection efforts will generate over $100 million in delinquent taxes per year. The debt collectors may focus on the more than 75,000 taxpayers who have an outstanding tax bill of more than $100,000. Best estimates are that most of the tax delinquents are not hard-core tax evaders, but individuals and businesses that are experiencing financial problems. Some have negotiated installment payment schedules that are in arrears.

This outsourcing of collection activities has led to some political opposition based on privacy and equity grounds. Can the providers of such services interpret and apply the tax laws as effectively and confidentially as the IRS? Given the level of personnel turnover that is likely to occur, can these third-party collectors ensure that their employees will stay within the boundaries of the law?

Despite these concerns, unpaid tax liabilities are now too large to ignore, especially given the record budget deficit and a more enforcement-oriented IRS. Because private collection agencies can charge a fee of up to 25 percent of the taxes collected, they have an incentive to "close the deal." The result is apt to be much tougher collection tactics than taxpayers are used to.

bill or refund as appropriate. Taxpayers usually are able to settle such matters through a by-mail-only *correspondence audit* with the IRS without the necessity of a formal meeting.

Office audits are conducted in an office of the IRS. Individual returns with few or no items of business income are usually handled through the office audit procedure. In most instances, the taxpayer is required merely to substantiate a deduction, credit, or item of income that appears on the return. The taxpayer presents documentation in the form of canceled checks, invoices, etc., for the items in question.

The *field audit* procedure is commonly used for corporate returns and for returns of individuals engaged in business or professional activities. This type of audit generally involves a more complete examination of a taxpayer's transactions.

A field audit is conducted by IRS agents at the office or home of the taxpayer or at the office of the taxpayer's representative. The agent's work may be facilitated by a review of certain tax workpapers and discussions with the taxpayer's representative about items appearing on the tax return. Table 16–1 summarizes key audit information.

Prior to or at the initial interview, the IRS must provide the taxpayer with an explanation of the audit process that is the subject of the interview and describe the taxpayer's rights under that process. If the taxpayer clearly states at any time during the interview the desire to consult with an attorney, CPA, or enrolled agent or any other person permitted to represent the taxpayer before the IRS, then the IRS representative must suspend the interview.[11]

Any officer or employee of the IRS must, upon advance request, allow a taxpayer to make an audio recording of any in-person interview with the officer or employee concerning the determination and collection of any tax.[12]

Settlement with the Revenue Agent.

Following an audit, the IRS agent may either accept the return as filed or recommend certain adjustments. The **Revenue Agent's Report (RAR)** is reviewed within the IRS. In most instances, the agent's proposed adjustments are approved.

Agents must adhere strictly to IRS policy as reflected in published rulings, Regulations, and other releases. The agent cannot settle an unresolved issue based upon the probability of winning the case in court. Usually, issues involving factual questions can be settled at the agent level, and it may be advantageous for both the

---

[11]§ 7521(b).

[12]§ 7521(a).

TABLE 16–1	IRS Audit Information by Type (Individual Returns Only)	
	Conducted (Number)	Conducted (Percent)
Correspondence audit	581,000	79%
Office audit	68,000	9%
Field audit	86,000	12%

taxpayer and the IRS to reach agreement at the earliest point in the settlement process. For example, it may be to the taxpayer's advantage to reach agreement at the agent level and avoid any further opportunity for the IRS to raise new issues.

If agreement is reached upon the proposed deficiency, the taxpayer signs Form 870 (Waiver of Restrictions on Assessment and Collection of Deficiency in Tax). One advantage to the taxpayer of signing Form 870 at this point is that interest stops accumulating on the deficiency 30 days after the form is filed.[13] When this form is signed, the taxpayer effectively waives the right to receive a statutory notice of deficiency (90-day letter) and to subsequently petition the Tax Court. In addition, it is no longer possible for the taxpayer later to go to the IRS Appeals Division. The signing of Form 870 at the agent level generally closes the case. However, the IRS is not restricted by Form 870 and may assess additional deficiencies if deemed necessary.

The Taxpayer Appeal Process

LO.4

Explain the taxpayer appeal process, including various settlement options available.

If agreement cannot be reached at the agent level, the taxpayer receives a copy of the Revenue Agent's Report and a **30-day letter**. The taxpayer has 30 days to request an administrative appeal. If an appeal is not requested, a **90-day letter** is issued. Figure 16–2 illustrates the taxpayer's alternatives when a disagreement with the IRS persists.

A taxpayer who wishes to appeal must make an appropriate request to the Appeals Division. The request must be accompanied by a written protest except in the following cases.

- The proposed tax deficiency does not exceed $10,000 for any of the tax periods involved in the audit.
- The deficiency resulted from a correspondence or office audit (i.e., not as a result of a field audit).

The Appeals Division is authorized to settle all tax disputes based on the hazards of litigation (the chances of winning in court). Since the Appeals Division has final settlement authority until a 90-day letter has been issued, the taxpayer may be able to negotiate a settlement. In addition, an overall favorable settlement may be reached by "trading" disputed issues. The Appeals Division occasionally may raise new issues if the grounds are substantial and of significant tax impact.

Both the Appeals Division and the taxpayer have the right to request technical advice memoranda from the National Office of the IRS. A TAM that is favorable to the taxpayer is binding on the Appeals Division. Even if the TAM is favorable to the IRS, the Appeals Division may nevertheless settle the case based on the hazards of litigation.

[13]§ 6601(c).

FIGURE 16–2	**Income Tax Appeal Procedure**

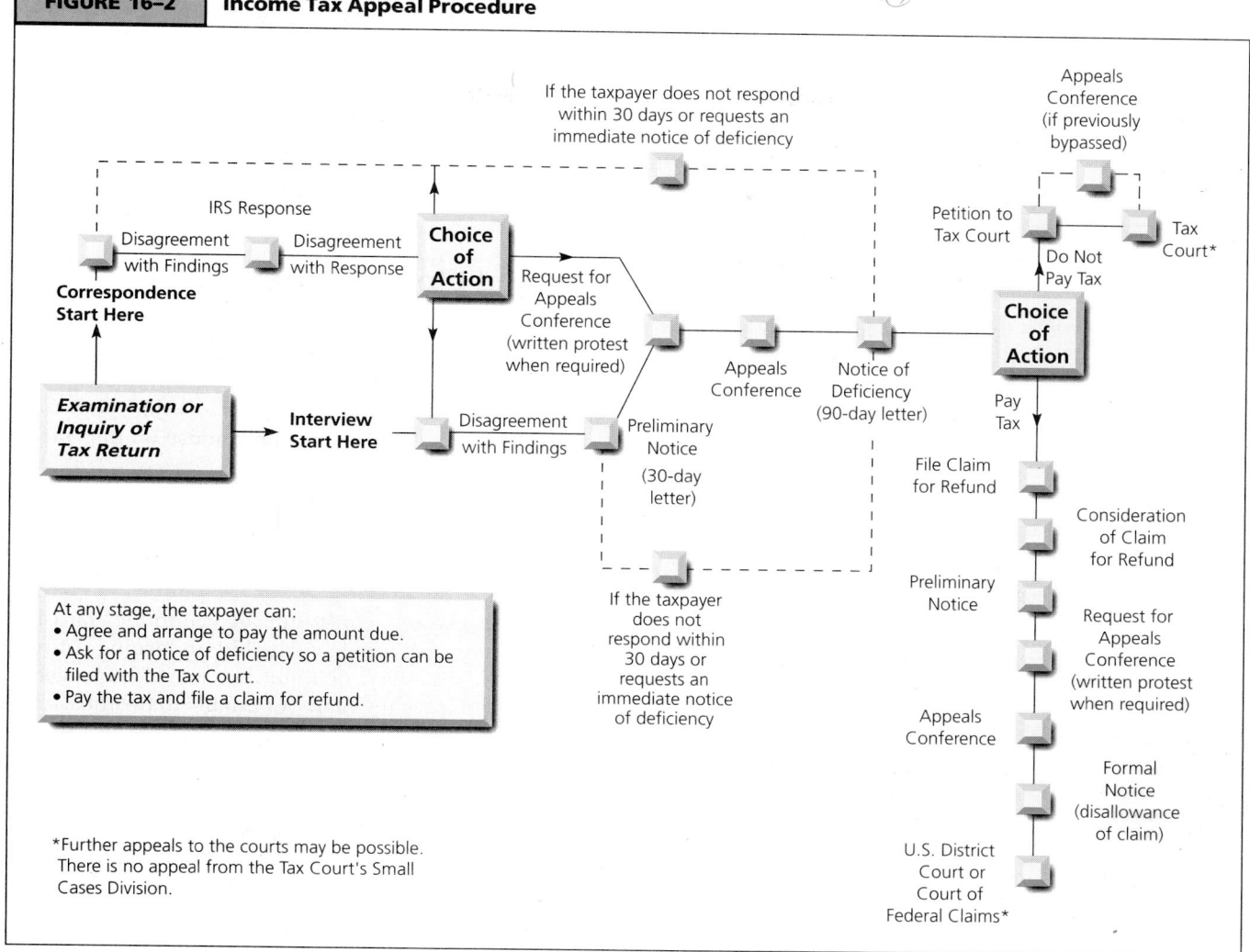

At the time Terri is audited, the corporation that she controls had advances outstanding to her in the amount of $80,000. The IRS field agent held that these advances were constructive dividends to her (refer to the discussion in Chapter 5). Some facts point toward this result (e.g., the corporation is closely held, Terri has made no repayments, and the loan balance has increased over several years). Other facts, however, appear to indicate that these advances are bona fide loans (e.g., a written instrument provides for interest, Terri has the independent means of repayment, and the corporation has a good dividend-paying record).

E X A M P L E   7

The Appeals Division and Terri's representative assess the hazards of litigation as being 50% for each side. Thus, if Terri chooses to take the issue to court, she would have an even chance of winning or losing her case. Based on this assessment, both sides agree to treat $40,000 of the advance as a dividend and $40,000 as a bona fide loan. The agreement enables Terri to avoid $40,000 of dividend income (the loan portion) and saves her the cost of litigating the issue.

Thus, by going to the Appeals Division, Terri obtained a satisfactory settlement otherwise unobtainable from the agent. ■

Taxpayers who file a petition with the U.S. Tax Court have the option of having the case heard before the more informal Small Cases Division if the amount of tax in dispute does not exceed $50,000.[14] If the Small Cases Division is used, neither party may appeal the case.

---

[14]§ 7463(a).

The economic costs of a settlement offer from the Appeals Division should be weighed against the costs of litigation and the probability of winning the case. The taxpayer should also consider the impact of the settlement upon the tax liability for future periods in addition to the years under audit.

If a settlement is reached with the Appeals Division, the taxpayer is required to sign Form 870–AD. Interest stops running on the deficiency when the Appeals Division accepts the Form 870–AD. According to the IRS, this settlement is binding upon both parties unless fraud, malfeasance, concealment, or misrepresentation of material fact has occurred.

Offers in Compromise and Closing Agreements

The IRS can negotiate a compromise if the taxpayer's ability to pay the tax is doubtful. If the taxpayer is financially unable to pay the total amount of the tax, a Form 656 (Offer in Compromise) is filed with the Memphis Internal Revenue Service Center or the Brookhaven Internal Revenue Service Center in Holtsville, New York, depending on the location of the taxpayer. An **offer in compromise** is appropriate in the following circumstances.[15]

- There is doubt as to the taxpayer's liability for the tax (i.e., disputed issues still exist).
- There is doubt as to the collectibility of the tax (i.e., the taxpayer's net worth and earnings capacity are low).
- Payment of the disputed amount would constitute an economic hardship for the taxpayer. For instance, the taxpayer is incapable of earning a living because of a long-term illness or disability, or liquidation of the taxpayer's assets to pay the amount due would leave the taxpayer unable to meet basic living expenses.

The IRS investigates the offer by evaluating the taxpayer's financial ability to pay the tax. In some instances, the compromise settlement includes an agreement for final settlement of the tax through payments of a specified percentage of the taxpayer's future earnings. This settlement procedure usually entails lengthy negotiations with the IRS, but the presumption is that the agency will find terms upon which to enter into a compromise with the taxpayer. A 20 percent current payment is required to set up the compromise offer, and a $150 filing fee is required. Low-income individuals can apply for a waiver of the fee and of the 20 percent lump-sum down payment.[16]

The IRS has statutory authority to enter into a written agreement allowing taxes to be paid on an installment basis if that arrangement facilitates the tax collection. The agency encourages its employees to use installment plans, and an individual who has filed timely tax returns for five years is guaranteed the right to use an installment agreement when the amount in dispute does not exceed $10,000. The taxpayer uses Form 9465 to initiate an installment plan.

The IRS provides an annual statement accounting for the status of the agreement. The agreement may later be modified or terminated because of (1) inadequate information, (2) subsequent change in financial condition, or (3) failure to pay an installment when due or to provide requested information.[17]

A **closing agreement** is binding on both the taxpayer and the IRS except upon a subsequent showing of fraud, malfeasance, or misrepresentation of a material fact.[18] The closing agreement may be used when disputed issues carry over to future years. It may also be employed to dispose of a dispute involving a specific issue for a prior year or a proposed transaction involving future years. If, for

---

[15]§ 7122 and Reg. § 301.7122–1(b).

[16]Reg. § 300.3(b)(1)(ii). "Low-income" is defined as less than 250% of the Federal poverty level.

[17]§ 6159.

[18]§ 7121(b).

example, the IRS is willing to make substantial concessions in the valuation of assets for death tax purposes, it may require a closing agreement from the recipient of the property to establish the income tax basis of the assets.

Interest

LO.5

Determine the amount of interest on a deficiency or a refund and when it is due.

Determination of the Interest Rate. Congress sets the interest rates applicable to Federal tax underpayments (deficiencies) and overpayments (refunds) close to the rates available in financial markets. The Code provides for the rates to be determined quarterly.[19] Thus, the rates that are determined during March are effective for the following April through June.

IRS interest is based on the Federal short-term rates published periodically by the IRS in Revenue Rulings. They are based on the average market yield on outstanding marketable obligations of the United States with remaining maturity of three years or less.

For noncorporate taxpayers, the interest rate applicable to *both* overpayments and underpayments is 7 percent for the first quarter of 2008. For most corporate taxpayers, the rate is 6 percent for overpayments and 7 percent for underpayments. Corporations with large overpayments or underpayments are subject to different rates.

Computation of the Amount of Interest. Interest is compounded daily.[20] Depending on the applicable interest rate, daily compounding doubles the payable amount over a period of five to eight years.

Tables for determining the daily compounded amount are available from the IRS and on the Internet. The tables ease the burden of those who prepare late returns where additional taxes are due.[21]

IRS Deficiency Assessments. Interest usually accrues from the unextended due date of the return until 30 days after the taxpayer agrees to the deficiency by signing Form 870. If the taxpayer does not pay the amount shown on the IRS's notice and demand (tax bill) within 30 days, interest again accrues on the deficiency.

Refund of Taxpayer's Overpayments. If an overpayment is refunded to the taxpayer within 45 days after the date the return is filed or is due, no interest is allowed. When the taxpayer files an amended return or makes a claim for refund of a prior year's tax (e.g., when net operating loss carrybacks result in refunds of a prior year's tax payments), however, interest is authorized from the original due date of the return through the date when the amended return is filed. In general, taxpayers applying for refunds receive interest as follows.

- When a return is filed after the due date, interest on any overpayment accrues from the date of filing. However, no interest is due if the IRS makes the refund within 45 days of the date of filing.

EXAMPLE 8

Naomi, a calendar year taxpayer, files her 2007 return on December 1, 2008. The return reflects an overwithholding of $2,500. On June 8, 2009, Naomi receives a refund of her 2007 overpayment. Interest on the refund began to accrue on December 1, 2008 (not April 15, 2008). ■

EXAMPLE 9

Assume the same facts as in Example 8, except that the refund is paid to Naomi on January 5, 2009 (rather than June 8, 2009). No interest is payable by the IRS, since the refund was made within 45 days of the filing of the return. ■

---

[19]§ 6621.
[20]§ 6622.

[21]Rev.Proc. 95–17, 1995–1 C.B. 556.

- In no event will interest accrue on an overpayment unless the return that is filed is in "processible form." Generally, this means that the return must contain enough information in a readable format to enable the IRS to identify the taxpayer and to determine the tax (and overpayment) involved.
- In the case of a carryback (e.g., net operating loss, capital loss, tax credit), interest on any refund begins to accrue on the due date of the return (disregarding extensions) for the year in which the carryback arises. Even then, however, no interest accrues until a return is filed or, if the return has been filed, if the IRS pays the refund within 45 days.

EXAMPLE 10

Top Corporation, a calendar year taxpayer, incurs a net operating loss during 2007 that it can carry back to tax year 2005 and obtain a refund. On December 26, 2008, Top files a claim for refund. The earliest that interest can begin to accrue in this situation is March 17, 2008, but since the return was not filed until December 26, 2008, the later date controls. If, however, the IRS pays the refund within 45 days of December 26, 2008, no interest need be paid. ■

LO.6

Discuss the various penalties that can be imposed on acts of noncompliance by taxpayers and return preparers.

Taxpayer Penalties

To promote and enforce taxpayer compliance with the U.S. voluntary self-assessment system of taxation, Congress has enacted a comprehensive array of penalties.

Tax penalties may involve both criminal and civil offenses. Criminal tax penalties are imposed only after the usual criminal process, in which the taxpayer is entitled to the same constitutional guarantees as nontax criminal defendants. Normally, a criminal penalty provides for imprisonment. Civil tax penalties are collected in the same manner as other taxes and usually provide only for monetary fines. Criminal and civil penalties are not mutually exclusive; therefore, both types of sanctions may be imposed on a taxpayer.

The Code characterizes tax penalties as additions to tax; thus, they cannot subsequently be deducted by the taxpayer.

Ad valorem penalties are additions to tax that are based upon a percentage of the owed tax. *Assessable penalties*, on the other hand, typically include a flat dollar amount. Assessable penalties are not subject to review by the Tax Court, but ad valorem penalties are subject to the same deficiency procedures that apply to the underlying tax.

Failure to File and Failure to Pay. For a failure to file a tax return by the due date (including extensions), a penalty of 5 percent per month (up to a maximum of 25 percent) is imposed on the amount of tax shown as due on the return, with a minimum penalty amount of $100.[22] If the failure to file is attributable to fraud, the penalty becomes 15 percent per month, to a maximum of 75 percent of the tax.[23]

For a failure to pay the tax due as shown on the return, a penalty of 0.5 percent per month (up to a maximum of 25 percent) is imposed on the amount of the tax. The penalty is doubled if the taxpayer fails to pay the tax after receiving a deficiency assessment.

In all of these cases, a fraction of a month counts as a full month. These penalties relate to the net amount of the tax due.

Obtaining an extension for filing a tax return does not by itself extend the date by which the taxes due must be paid. Thus, an application for an extended due date for a tax return almost always is accompanied by a payment by the taxpayer of a good faith estimate of the taxes that will be owed with the return when it is filed by the extended due date. If the taxpayer does not make such a good faith estimate and payment, the extension itself may be voided by the IRS (e.g., when the return is filed by the extended due date with a much larger amount due than had been estimated).

---

[22]§ 6651(a).

[23]§ 6651(f).

EXAMPLE 11

Conchita uses an automatic six-month extension for the filing of her 2008 tax return. Thus, the return is due on October 15, 2009, not on April 15. Conchita's application for the extension includes a $5,000 check, the amount that she estimates her 2008 return will show as owing for the year when she files it in October. ■

During any month in which both the failure to file penalty and the failure to pay penalty apply, the failure to file penalty is reduced by the amount of the failure to pay penalty.

EXAMPLE 12

Jason files his tax return 10 days after the due date. Along with the return, he remits a check for $3,000, which is the balance of the tax he owes. Disregarding any interest liabilities, Jason's total penalties are as follows.

Failure to pay penalty (0.5% × $3,000)		$ 15
Failure to file penalty (5% × $3,000)	$150	
Less failure to pay penalty for the same period	15	
Failure to file penalty		135
Total penalties		$150

The penalties for one full month are imposed even though Jason was delinquent by only 10 days. Unlike the method used to compute interest, any part of a month is treated as a whole month. ■

These penalties can be avoided if the taxpayer shows that the failure to file and/or failure to pay was due to reasonable cause and not due to willful neglect. The Code is silent on what constitutes reasonable cause, and the Regulations do little to clarify this important concept.[24] Reasonable cause for failure to pay is presumed under the automatic six-month extension (Form 4868) when the additional tax due is not more than 10 percent of the tax liability shown on the return. In addition, the courts have ruled on some aspects of **reasonable cause**.

- Reasonable cause was found where the taxpayer relied on the advice of a competent tax adviser given in good faith, the facts were fully disclosed to the adviser, and he or she considered that the specific question represented reasonable cause.[25] No reasonable cause was found, however, where the taxpayer delegated the filing task to another, even when that person was an accountant or an attorney.[26]
- Among the reasons not qualifying as reasonable cause were lack of information on the due date of the return,[27] illness that did not incapacitate a taxpayer from completing a return,[28] refusal of the taxpayer's spouse to cooperate for a joint return,[29] and ignorance or misunderstanding of the tax law.[30]

Accuracy-Related Penalties. Major civil penalties relating to the accuracy of tax return data, including misstatements stemming from taxpayer negligence and improper valuation of income and deductions, are coordinated under the umbrella term **accuracy-related penalties**.[31] This consolidation of related penalties into a single levy eliminates the possibility that multiple penalties will apply to a single understatement of tax.

---

[24]Reg. § 301.6651–1(c)(1) likens reasonable cause to the exercise of "ordinary business care and prudence" on the part of the taxpayer.

[25]*Estate of Norma S. Bradley,* 33 TCM 70, T.C.Memo. 1974–17.

[26]*U.S. v. Boyle,* 85–1 USTC ¶13,602, 55 AFTR2d 85–1535, 105 S.Ct. 687 (USSC, 1985).

[27]*Beck Chemical Equipment Co.,* 27 T.C. 840 (1957).

[28]*Jacob Gassman,* 26 TCM 213, T.C.Memo. 1967–42, and *Babetta Schmidt,* 28 T.C. 367 (1957). Compare *Estate of Kirchner,* 46 B.T.A. 578 (1942).

[29]*Electric and Neon, Inc.,* 56 T.C. 1324 (1971).

[30]*Stevens Brothers Foundation, Inc.,* 39 T.C. 93 (1965).

[31]§ 6662.

TAX *in the News*   **LOOKING FOR TAX FRAUD**

IRS auditors have found that residents of prisons are filing a sizable number of fraudulent returns. Audits of returns filed by prisoners in 2004 showed $68 million in fraudulent refunds, only $53 million of which were identified by the Service before they were paid. A hearing before the House Ways and Means Oversight Committee found that prisoner tax fraud tends to occur in the following areas.

- False claims under the earned income credit.
- False or improperly prepared Forms W–2.
- False information on a Schedule C.

Investigators believe that prisoners have formed a network to work together, using prison libraries and the Internet, to coordinate this sizable operation.

Only one known conviction involving inmate fraud has occurred. An Arizona man serving a 2.5-year term for forgery added five years to that sentence when he was convicted for

making a fraudulent refund claim of over $200,000 relating to his gambling operations.

The IRS has released the following data showing the scope of the problem for the 2004 filing season.

	Forms 1040 Filed	Fraudulent Refund Claim Included
General population	106,000,000	118,000
Prisoners only	455,000	18,000

The data show that prisoners file only about 0.42 percent of total Forms 1040, yet they account for about 15 percent of all fraudulent refunds. The average refund claimed is $3,755 and most often is assigned to a party "on the outside." It may be that some of these taxpayers just have too much time on their hands!

The accuracy-related penalties each amount to 20 percent of the portion of the tax underpayment that is attributable to one or more of the following infractions.

- Negligence or disregard of rules and regulations.
- Substantial understatement of tax liability.
- Substantial valuation overstatement.
- Substantial valuation understatement.

The penalties apply only where the taxpayer fails to show a *reasonable basis* for the position taken on the return.[32]

Negligence. For purposes of this accuracy-related penalty, **negligence** includes any failure to make a reasonable attempt to comply with the provisions of the tax law. The penalty also applies to any disregard (whether careless, reckless, or intentional) of rules and regulations.[33] The penalty can be avoided upon a showing of reasonable cause and that the taxpayer acted in good faith.[34]

The negligence penalty applies to *all* taxes, except when fraud is involved. A negligence penalty may be assessed when the taxpayer fails to report gross income, overstates deductions, or fails to keep adequate records. When the taxpayer takes a nonnegligent position on the return that is contrary to a judicial precedent or published pronouncement of the IRS, the penalty is waived if the taxpayer has a reasonable basis for the interpretation and has disclosed the disputed position on Form 8275.

Substantial Understatement of Tax Liability. The understatement penalty is designed to strike at middle- and high-income taxpayers who are tempted to play the so-called audit lottery.[35] Some taxpayers take questionable and undisclosed positions on their tax returns in the hope that the return will not be selected for audit. Disclosing the positions would have called attention to the return and increased the probability of audit.

---

[32]Reg. § 1.6662–3(b)(3). Most tax professionals measure this standard as a one-in-four probability of prevailing in court.

[33]§ 6662(c).

[34]§ 6664(c)(1).

[35]§ 6662(b)(2).

A substantial understatement of a tax liability transpires when the understatement exceeds the larger of 10 percent of the tax due or $5,000. For a C corporation, a substantial understatement is the lesser of the following.[36]

- 10 percent of the tax due, but at least $10,000.
- $10 million.

The understatement to which the penalty applies is the difference between the amount of tax required to be shown on the return and the amount of tax actually shown on the return.

The penalty is avoided under any of the following circumstances.[37]

- The taxpayer has **substantial authority** for the treatment.
- The relevant facts affecting the treatment are adequately disclosed in the return by attaching Form 8275.

Penalty for Overvaluation. The objective of the overvaluation penalty is to deter taxpayers from inflating values (or basis), usually of charitable contributions of property, to reduce income taxes.[38]

- The penalty is 20 percent of the additional tax that would have been paid had the correct valuation (or basis) been used.
- The penalty applies only when the valuation (or basis) used by the taxpayer is 150 percent or more of the correct valuation (or basis). The penalty is doubled if the valuation error is *gross* (overstated by 200 percent or more).
- The penalty applies only to the extent that the resulting income tax underpayment exceeds $5,000 ($10,000 for C corporations).

> **EXAMPLE 13**
>
> Gretchen (a calendar year taxpayer) purchased a painting for $10,000. In 2008, when the painting is worth $18,000 (as later determined by the IRS), Gretchen donates the painting to an art museum. Based on the appraisal of a cousin who is an amateur artist, she deducts $40,000 for the donation. Since Gretchen was in the 30% tax bracket, overstating the deduction by $22,000 results in a tax underpayment of $6,600.
>
> Gretchen's penalty for overvaluation is $2,640, or *double* the regular penalty of $1,320 (20% × $6,600 underpayment). ∎

The substantial valuation overstatement penalty is avoided if the taxpayer can show reasonable cause and good faith. However, when the overvaluation involves *charitable deduction property*, the taxpayer must substantiate both of the following.

- The claimed value of the property is based on a qualified appraisal made by a qualified appraiser.
- The taxpayer made a good faith investigation of the value of the contributed property.[39]

Based on these criteria, Gretchen in Example 13 would find it difficult to avoid the penalty. A cousin who is an amateur artist does not meet the definition of a qualified appraiser. Likewise, Gretchen apparently has not made her own good faith investigation of the value of the contributed property.

Penalty for Undervaluation. When attempting to minimize the income tax, it is to the benefit of taxpayers to *overvalue* deductions. When attempting to minimize transfer taxes (estate and gift taxes), however, executors and donors may be inclined to *undervalue* the assets transferred. A lower valuation reduces estate and gift taxes. An accuracy-related penalty is imposed for substantial estate or gift tax

---

[36]§ 6662(d)(1).

[37]§ 6662(d)(2)(B).

[38]§§ 6662(b)(3), (e), and (h).

[39]§§ 6664(c)(2) and (3).

valuation understatements.[40] As with other accuracy-related penalties, reasonable cause and good faith on the part of the taxpayer are a defense.

ETHICAL and EQUITABLE *Considerations*

GOOD FAITH VALUATIONS

When dealing with the undervaluation penalty, the tax adviser may shift from being in adversarial alliance with the taxpayer to being a mediator for the court. Good faith value estimates, especially for family-owned businesses, can easily vary by as much as the 65 percentage points specified for the penalty. Even a gross undervaluation can occur when someone in the business other than the donor or decedent is a particularly talented entrepreneur, an effective sales representative, and/or the founder of the company; similarly, a business may be substantially undervalued when a minority equity interest is involved, or an intangible asset conveys a sizable nominal amount of goodwill to the valuation.

Because most taxpayers are highly averse to incurring any nondeductible penalties, the client may be tempted to compromise on the business valuation "too soon" (i.e., when the return is filed), eliminating any possibility of a more favorable valuation being presented before the Appeals Division or a court. Keeping in mind all of the potential taxpayer and preparer penalties that might apply, the tax professional should stick with a good faith appraisal of the business value, no matter what its nominal amount.

How would you react if your client, a composer, wanted to deduct $100,000 for the contribution of an obscure manuscript to the Symphony Society? What if your (first) appraiser placed the value of the manuscript at $15,000? What course of action would you propose to the client concerning the deduction? Any consequent penalties?

- The penalty is 20 percent of the additional transfer tax that would have been due had the correct valuation been used on Form 706 (estate tax return) or Form 709 (gift and generation-skipping tax return).
- The penalty applies only if the value of the property claimed on the return is 65 percent or less than the amount determined to be correct. The penalty is doubled if the reported valuation error is *gross* (reported value is 40 percent or less than the correct determination).
- The penalty applies only to an additional transfer tax liability in excess of $5,000.

Appraiser's Penalty. When a valuation penalty arises because of the taxpayer's reliance on an appraisal, a further penalty can apply.[41] If the appraiser knew or reasonably should have known that the appraisal would be used as part of a tax or refund computation and that the appraised value more likely than not was improper, then the appraiser pays a penalty equal to the lesser of:

- 10 percent of the tax understatement, but at least $1,000, or
- 125 percent of the gross income received by the appraiser from the engagement (e.g., the appraisal fee collected).

This amount is in addition to the taxpayer's valuation penalty as discussed above.

Penalty for Improper Refund Claim. Whenever a taxpayer files a claim for a tax refund and the refund claim later is found to exceed the final amount allowed by the IRS or a court, a penalty of 20 percent of the disallowed refund results.[42] The penalty is waived if the taxpayer can show a *reasonable basis* for the refund claim (i.e., probably a one-in-four chance that a court would allow the refund). This penalty is

---

[40]§§ 6662(b)(5), (g), and (h).
[41]§ 6695A.

[42]§ 6676.

meant to discourage the taxpayer from overstating the amount of the refund requested from the IRS. It does not apply to claims for the earned income tax credit.

Civil Fraud Penalty. A 75 percent civil penalty is imposed on any underpayment resulting from **fraud** by the taxpayer who has filed a return.[43] For this penalty, the burden of proof *is on the IRS* to show by a preponderance of the evidence that the taxpayer had a specific intent to evade a tax.

Once the IRS has initially established that fraud has occurred, the taxpayer then bears the burden of proof to show by a preponderance of the evidence the portion of the underpayment that is not attributable to fraud.

Although the Code and Regulations do not provide any assistance in ascertaining what constitutes civil fraud, it is clear that mere negligence on the part of the taxpayer (however great) will not suffice. Fraud has been found in cases of manipulation of the books, substantial omissions from income, and erroneous deductions.[44]

Frank underpaid his income tax by $90,000. The IRS can prove that $60,000 of the underpayment was due to fraud. Frank responds by a preponderance of the evidence that $30,000 of the underpayment was not due to fraud. The civil fraud penalty is $45,000 (75% × $60,000). ∎

EXAMPLE 14

If the underpayment of tax is partially attributable to negligence and partially attributable to fraud, the fraud penalty is applied first.

Criminal Penalties. In addition to civil fraud penalties, the Code contains numerous criminal sanctions that carry various monetary fines and/or imprisonment. The difference between civil and criminal fraud is often one of degree. A characteristic of criminal fraud is the presence of willfulness on the part of the taxpayer. Thus, § 7201, dealing with attempts to evade or defeat a tax, contains the following language.

> Any person who *willfully* attempts in any manner to evade or defeat any tax imposed by this title or the payment thereof shall, in addition to other penalties provided by law, be guilty of a felony and, upon conviction thereof, shall be fined not more than $100,000 ($500,000 in the case of a corporation), or imprisoned not more than five years, or both, together with the costs of prosecution. [Emphasis added.]

As to the burden of proof, the IRS must show that the taxpayer was guilty of willful evasion "beyond the shadow of any reasonable doubt."

Failure to Pay Estimated Taxes. A penalty is imposed for a failure to pay estimated income taxes. The penalty applies to individuals and corporations and is based on the rate of interest in effect for deficiency assessments.[45] The penalty also applies to trusts and certain estates that are required to make estimated tax payments. The penalty is not imposed if the tax due for the year (less amounts withheld and credits) is less than $500 for corporations, $1,000 for all others. For employees, an equal part of withholding is deemed paid on each due date.

Quarterly payments are to be made on or before the fifteenth day of the fourth month (April 15 for a calendar year taxpayer), sixth month, ninth month, and the first month of the following year. Corporations must make the last quarterly payment by the twelfth month of the same year.

---

[43]§ 6663. As noted later in the chapter, underpayments traceable to fraudulent acts are not subject to a statute of limitations.

[44]*Dogget v. Comm.*, 60–1 USTC ¶9342, 5 AFTR2d 1034, 275 F.2d 823 (CA–4, 1960); *Harvey Brodsky*, 21 TCM 578, T.C.Memo. 1962–105; and *Lash v. Comm.*, 57–2 USTC ¶9725, 51 AFTR 492, 245 F.2d 20 (CA–1, 1957).

[45]§§ 6655 (corporations) and 6654 (other taxpayers). Other computations can avoid the penalty. See §§ 6654(d)(2) and (k), 6655(e) and (i).

An individual's underpayment of estimated tax is the difference between the estimates that were paid and the least of (1) 90 percent of the current-year tax, (2) 100 percent of the prior-year tax (the tax year must have been a full 12 months, and a return must have been filed), and (3) 90 percent of the tax that would be due on an annualized income computation for the period running through the end of the quarter. When the taxpayer's prior-year adjusted gross income (AGI) exceeds $150,000, the required payment percentage for the prior-year alternative is 110 percent.

A corporation's underpayment of estimated tax is the difference between the estimates that were paid and the least of (1) the current-year tax, (2) the prior-year tax, and (3) the tax on an annualized income computation using one of three methods of computation sanctioned by the Code. For the prior-year alternative, (1) the prior tax year must have been a full 12 months, (2) a nonzero tax amount must have been generated for that year, and (3) large corporations (taxable income of $1 million or more in any of the three immediately preceding tax years) can use the alternative only for the first installment of a year.

In computing the penalty, Form 2210 (Underpayment of Estimated Tax by Individuals) or Form 2220 (Underpayment of Estimated Tax by Corporations) is used.

False Information with Respect to Withholding.

Withholding from wages is an important element of the Federal income tax system, which is based on a pay-as-you-go approach. One way employees might hope to avoid this withholding would be to falsify the information provided to the employer on Form W–4 (Employee Withholding Allowance Certificate). For example, by overstating the number of exemptions, income tax withholdings could be cut or completely eliminated.

To encourage compliance, a civil penalty of $500 applies when a taxpayer claims withholding allowances based on false information. The criminal penalty for willfully failing to supply information or for willfully supplying false or fraudulent information in connection with wage withholding is an additional fine of up to $1,000 and/or up to one year of imprisonment.[46]

Failure to Make Deposits of Taxes and Overstatements of Deposits.

When a business is not doing well or cash-flow problems develop, employers have a great temptation to "borrow" from Uncle Sam. One way this can be done is to fail to pay to the IRS the amounts that have been withheld from the wages of employees for FICA and income tax purposes. The IRS does not appreciate being denied the use of these funds and has a number of weapons at its disposal to discourage the practice.

- A penalty of up to 15 percent of any underdeposited amount not paid, unless the employer can show that the failure is due to reasonable cause and not to willful neglect.[47]
- Various criminal penalties.[48]
- A 100 percent penalty if the employer's actions are willful.[49] The penalty is based on the amount of the tax evaded (i.e., not collected, or not accounted for or paid over). Since the penalty is assessable against the "responsible person" of the business, more than one party may be vulnerable (e.g., the president and treasurer of a corporation). Although the IRS may assess the penalty against several persons, it cannot collect more than the 100 percent due.
- In addition to these penalties, the actual tax due must be remitted. For instance, an employer remains liable for the employees' income and payroll taxes that should have been paid.

---

[46]§§ 6682 and 7205.
[47]§ 6656.

[48]See, for example, § 7202 (willful failure to collect or pay over a tax).
[49]§ 6672.

Failure to Provide Information Regarding Tax Shelters.

The IRS has identified over two dozen transactions that it regards as "tax shelters." These arrangements, often involving leveraged financing and accelerated interest and cost recovery deductions, allegedly are motivated solely by the desire to reduce taxes and have no business or profit-seeking goals. Over the last two decades, the IRS has struggled with numerous means of identifying taxpayers who use such tax shelters.

A tax shelter organizer must register the shelter with the IRS before any sales are made to investors.[50] A penalty of up to $10,000 is assessed if the required information is not filed with the Service. This includes a description of the shelter and the tax benefits that are being used to attract investors. The shelter organizer must maintain a list of identifying information of all its investors. Failure to fully and truthfully maintain the list can result in a penalty of up to $100,000 per investment.

Statutes of Limitations

LO.7

Understand the rules governing the statute of limitations on assessments and on refunds.

A **statute of limitations** defines the period of time during which one party may pursue against another party a cause of action or other suit allowed under the governing law. Failure to satisfy any requirement provides the other party with an absolute defense should the statute be invoked. Inequity would result if no limits were placed on such suits. Permitting an extended period of time to elapse between the initiation of a claim and its pursuit could place the defense at a serious disadvantage. Witnesses may have died or disappeared; records or other evidence may have been discarded or destroyed.

Assessment and the Statute of Limitations.

In general, any tax that is imposed must be assessed within three years of the filing of the return (or, if later, the due date of the return).[51] Some exceptions to this three-year limitation exist.

- If no return is filed or a fraudulent return is filed, assessments can be made at any time. There is, in effect, no statute of limitations in these cases.
- If a taxpayer omits an amount of gross income in excess of 25 percent of the gross income stated on the return, the statute of limitations is increased to six years. The courts have interpreted this rule as including only items affecting income and not the omission of items affecting deductions, operating losses, or cost of sales.[52] In addition, *gross income* here includes capital gains, but not reduced by capital losses.

EXAMPLE 15

During 2003, Jerry had the following income transactions (all of which were duly reported on his timely filed return).

Gross receipts		$480,000
Cost of sales		(400,000)
Net business income		$ 80,000
Capital gains and losses		
Capital gain	$ 36,000	
Capital loss	(12,000)	24,000
Total income		$104,000

Jerry retains your services in 2008 as a tax consultant. It seems that he inadvertently omitted some income on his 2003 return and he wishes to know if he is "safe" under the statute of limitations. The six-year statute of limitations would apply, putting Jerry in a vulnerable position only if he omitted more than $129,000 on his 2003 return [($480,000 + $36,000) × 25%]. ■

---

[50]§ 6111.

[51]§§ 6501(a) and (b)(1).

[52]*The Colony, Inc. v. Comm.*, 58–2 USTC ¶9593, 1 AFTR2d 1894, 78 S.Ct. 1033 (USSC, 1958).

- The statute of limitations may be extended for a fixed period of time by mutual consent of the IRS and the taxpayer. This extension covers a definite period and is made by signing Form 872 (Consent to Extend the Time to Assess Tax). The extension is frequently requested by the IRS when the lapse of the statutory period is imminent and the audit has not been completed. This practice is often applied to audits of corporate taxpayers and explains why many corporations have more than three "open years."

Special rules relating to assessment are applicable in the following situations.

- Taxpayers may request a prompt assessment of the tax, forcing the IRS to examine a return.
- The assessment period for capital loss and net operating loss carrybacks generally relates to the determination of tax in the year of the loss or unused credit rather than in the carryback years.

If the IRS issues a statutory notice of deficiency to the taxpayer, who then files a Tax Court petition, the statute is suspended on both the deficiency assessment and the period of collection until 60 days after the decision of the Tax Court becomes final. The statute is also suspended when the taxpayer is "financially disabled"; that is, the taxpayer has been rendered unable to manage his or her financial affairs by a physical or mental impairment that is likely to last for a year or more or to cause the taxpayer's death. The statute continues to run if another party is authorized to act for the taxpayer in financial matters.[53]

Refund Claims and the Statute of Limitations. To receive a tax refund, the taxpayer is required to file a valid refund claim. The official form for filing a claim is Form 1040X for individuals and Form 1120X for corporations. If the refund claim does not meet certain procedural requirements, the IRS may reject the claim with no consideration of its merit.

- A separate claim must be filed for each taxable period.
- The grounds for the claim must be stated in sufficient detail.
- The statement of facts must be sufficient to permit the IRS to evaluate the merits of the claim.

The refund claim must be filed within three years of the filing of the tax return or within two years following the payment of the tax if this period expires on a later date.[54]

EXAMPLE 16	On March 10, 2006, Louise filed her 2005 income tax return reflecting a tax of $10,500. On July 11, 2006, she filed an amended 2005 return showing an additional $3,000 of tax that was then paid. On May 19, 2009, she filed a claim for refund of $4,500.

Assuming that Louise is correct in claiming a refund, how much tax can she recover? The answer is only $3,000. Because the claim was not filed within the three-year statute of limitations period, Louise is limited to the amount she actually paid during the last two years. ■

Special rules are available for claims relating to bad debts and worthless securities. A seven-year period of limitations applies in lieu of the normal three-year rule.[55] The extended period is provided in recognition of the inherent difficulty of identifying the exact year in which a bad debt or security becomes worthless.

---

[53]"Equitable tolling" or suspension of the statute of limitations has been allowed by some courts when attributable to a taxpayer disability or IRS misconduct. See *Brockamp v. Comm.*, 97–1 USTC ¶50,216, 79 AFTR2d 97–986, 117 S.Ct. 849 (USSC, 1997). §§ 6501(c)(4) and 6511(h).

[54]§§ 6511(a) and 6513(a).
[55]§ 6511(d)(1).

The Tax Profession and Tax Ethics

LO.8

Summarize the legal and ethical guidelines that apply to those engaged in tax practice.

The Tax Practitioner

Who is a tax practitioner? What service does the practitioner perform? To begin defining the term *tax practitioner*, one should consider whether the individual is qualified to practice before the IRS. Generally, practice before the IRS is limited to CPAs, attorneys, and persons who have been enrolled to practice before the IRS (**enrolled agents [EAs]**). In most cases, EAs are admitted to practice only if they pass an examination administered by the IRS. CPAs and attorneys are not required to take this examination and are automatically admitted to practice if they are in good standing with the appropriate licensing board regulating their profession.

Persons other than CPAs, attorneys, and EAs may be allowed to practice before the IRS in limited situations. Circular 230 (entitled "Rules Governing the Practice of Attorneys and Agents Before the Internal Revenue Service") issued by the Treasury Department permits certain notable exceptions.

- A taxpayer may always represent himself or herself. A person may also represent a member of the immediate family if no compensation is received for such services.
- Regular full-time employees may represent their employers.
- Corporations may be represented by any of their bona fide officers.
- Partnerships may be represented by any of the partners.
- Trusts, receiverships, guardianships, or estates may be represented by their trustees, receivers, guardians, or administrators or executors.
- A taxpayer may be represented by whoever prepared the return for the year in question. However, such representation cannot proceed beyond the agent level.

EXAMPLE 17

Joel is currently undergoing audit by the IRS for tax years 2007 and 2008. He prepared the 2007 return himself but paid AddCo, a bookkeeping service, to prepare the 2008 return. AddCo may represent Joel only in matters concerning 2008. However, even for 2008, AddCo would be unable to represent Joel at an Appeals Division proceeding. Joel could, of course, represent himself, or he could retain a CPA, attorney, or EA to represent him in matters concerning both years under examination. ∎

IRS Rules Governing Tax Practice

Circular 230 prescribes the rules governing practice before the IRS. The following are some of the most important rules imposed on CPAs, attorneys, EAs, and all others who prepare tax returns for compensation.

- A prohibition against taking a position on a tax return unless there is a *realistic possibility* of the position being sustained on its merits. Generally, the realistic possibility standard is met when a person knowledgeable in the tax law would conclude that the position has at least a one-in-three probability of prevailing in the court of final jurisdiction.
- A prohibition against taking frivolous tax return positions.
- A requirement that nonfrivolous tax return positions that fail the realistic possibility standard be disclosed in the return (i.e., using Form 8275).
- A requirement to inform clients of penalties likely to apply to return positions and of ways such penalties can be avoided.
- A requirement to make known to a client any error or omission the client may have made on any return or other document submitted to the IRS.
- A duty to submit, in a timely fashion, records or information lawfully requested by the IRS.
- An obligation to exercise due diligence and to use the *best practices* of the tax profession in preparing and filing tax returns accurately.

- A restriction against unreasonably delaying the prompt disposition of any matter before the IRS.
- A restriction against charging the client a contingent fee for preparing an original return, although such a fee can be charged when the tax professional deals with an audited or amended return.
- A restriction against charging the client "an unconscionable fee" for representation before the IRS.
- A restriction against representing clients with conflicting interests.

Anyone can prepare a tax return or render tax advice, regardless of his or her educational background or level of competence. Likewise, nothing prevents the "unlicensed" tax practitioner from advertising his or her specialty, directly soliciting clients, or otherwise violating any of the standards of conduct controlling CPAs, attorneys, and EAs. Nevertheless, some restraints do govern all parties engaged in rendering tax returns for the general public.

- A person who holds himself or herself out to the general public as possessing tax expertise could be liable to the client if services are performed in a negligent manner. At a minimum, the practitioner is liable for any interest and penalties the client incurs because of the practitioner's failure to exercise due care.
- If a practitioner agrees to perform a service (e.g., prepare a tax return) and subsequently fails to do so, the aggrieved party may be in a position to obtain damages for breach of contract.
- The IRS requires all persons who prepare tax returns for a fee to sign as preparer of the return.[56] Failure to comply with this requirement could result in a penalty assessment against the preparer.
- The Code prescribes various penalties for the deliberate filing of false or fraudulent returns. These felonies apply to a tax practitioner who either was aware of the situation or actually perpetrated the false information or the fraud.[57]
- Penalties are prescribed for tax practitioners who disclose to third parties information they have received from clients in connection with the preparation of tax returns or the rendering of tax advice.[58]

EXAMPLE 18

Sarah operates a tax return preparation service. Her brother-in-law, Butch, has just taken a job as a life insurance salesman. To help Butch find contacts, Sarah furnishes him with a list of the names and addresses of all of her clients who report AGI of $50,000 or more. Sarah is subject to the disclosure penalty. ■

- All nonattorney tax practitioners should avoid becoming engaged in activities that constitute the *unauthorized practice of law*. If they engage in this practice (e.g., by drafting legal documents for a third party), action could be instituted against them in the appropriate state court by the local or state bar association. What actions constitute the unauthorized practice of law is largely undefined, though, and such charges are filed only rarely today.

Preparer Penalties

The Code provides penalties to discourage improper actions by tax practitioners.

1. A penalty for understatements due to taking an unreasonable position on a tax return. The penalty is imposed if the tax position:

   - Is not disclosed on the return and there was not a reasonable belief that the position was *more likely than not* (i.e., a greater than 50 percent chance) to be sustained by its merits on a final court review; or

---

[56]Reg. § 1.6065–1(b)(1). Rev.Rul. 84–3, 1984–1 C.B. 264, contains a series of examples illustrating when a person is deemed to be a preparer of the return.

[57]§ 7206.

[58]§ 7216.

| TAX *in the News* | HAVE YOU BEEN DRAFTED BY THE IRS? |

With the accumulation of tax preparer penalties over the years, many tax professionals now feel that they have been "deputized" by the IRS and that, as a consequence, their ability to advise and represent their clients in an aggressive manner is limited. Has the potential for providing effective tax planning diminished as a result of the increased regulation of the tax and accounting profession, the additional disclosures that the tax practitioner must make to the client and to the government, and the severity of preparer penalties?

Not so, according to the IRS. Its objective is to "ensure that attorneys, accountants, and other tax practitioners adhere to professional standards and follow the law." Here are some specific items from the IRS's plan of "best practices" that are designed to raise the level of tax ethics found in tax practice today.

- Strengthen ties with practitioners to achieve the highest level of professional integrity and improve tax compliance.

- Establish and communicate clear, robust, current, and meaningful standards of conduct for tax practitioners.
- Establish and maintain a vigorous, targeted, and effective system of practitioner oversight.
- Establish and administer a fair, diligent, and effective system of sanctions for practitioners who fail to observe standards of conduct.

The IRS plans coordinated actions to address misconduct in the profession. These include assessing preparer penalties, instituting disciplinary actions under Circular 230, suspending e-filing privileges, and using injunctions and criminal penalties where appropriate. Although these ground rules for ethical behavior in the tax profession are not new, the IRS has now stated loudly and clearly that it will pursue their enforcement.

- Is disclosed on the return and there was not a *reasonable basis* (i.e., probably a one-in-four chance) for the position.

Notice that avoiding the preparer penalty requires a higher standard of confidence in the tax position than is needed to avoid the taxpayer penalty for the same position. Avoiding the substantial underpayment penalty on the taxpayer requires that an undisclosed position be supported by *substantial authority* (probably a one-in-three likelihood that a court would allow the position).[59]

The penalty is computed as the greater of $1,000 or one-half of the income of the practitioner that is attributable to the return or claim that violated the conduct standard. The penalty can be avoided by showing reasonable cause and by showing that the preparer acted in good faith.

Josie is the tax return preparer for Hal's Form 1040. The return includes a deduction that has only a 60% chance of being sustained on its merits because it is contrary to an applicable tax Regulation. If a court denies the deduction, Josie is not assessed a § 6694 penalty. ∎

EXAMPLE 19

Josie is the tax return preparer for Hal's Form 1040. The return includes a deduction that has only a 40% chance of being sustained on its merits because it is contrary to an applicable tax Regulation. If a court denies the deduction, Josie is assessed a § 6694 penalty (unless the disputed position was disclosed on the return with a Form 8275-R). The amount of the penalty is the greater of $1,000 or one-half of Josie's fees for preparing Hal's Form 1040. ∎

EXAMPLE 20

Josie is the tax return preparer for Hal's Form 1040. The return includes a deduction that has only a 20% chance of being sustained on its merits because it is contrary to an applicable tax Regulation. If a court denies the deduction, Josie is assessed a § 6694 penalty (even if the

EXAMPLE 21

---

[59]With adequate disclosures to the client, the tax preparer may be subject only to the substantial authority standard. §6694, Notices 2008–11 through –13.

disputed position was disclosed on the return with a Form 8275-R). The amount of the penalty is the greater of $1,000 or one-half of Josie's fees for preparing Hal's Form 1040. ∎

2. A penalty for willful and reckless conduct.[60] The penalty applies if any part of the understatement of a taxpayer's liability on a return or claim for refund is due to:

   - The preparer's willful attempt to understate the taxpayer's tax liability in any manner.
   - Any reckless or intentional disregard of IRS rules or regulations by the preparer.

   The penalty is computed as the greater of $5,000 or one-half of the income of the practitioner that is attributable to the return or claim that violated the conduct standard. Adequate disclosure can avoid the penalty. If both this penalty and the unreasonable position penalty (see item 1 above) apply to the same return, the reckless conduct penalty is reduced by the amount of the penalty for unreasonable positions.

3. A $1,000 ($10,000 for the tax returns of corporations) penalty per return or document is imposed against persons who aid in the preparation of returns or other documents that they know (or have reason to believe) would result in an understatement of the tax liability of another person.[61] Thus, this penalty also applies to those other than the preparer of the actual tax return (e.g., unpaid advisers, attorneys, corporate officers and executives, and tax shelter promoters). Clerical assistance in the return preparation process does not incur the penalty.

   If this penalty applies, neither the unreasonable position penalty (item 1) nor the willful and reckless conduct penalty (item 2) is assessed.

4. A $50 penalty is assessed against the preparer for failure to sign a return or furnish the preparer's identifying number.[62]

5. A $50 penalty is assessed if the preparer fails to furnish a copy of the return or claim for refund to the taxpayer.

6. A $500 penalty may be assessed if a preparer endorses or otherwise negotiates a check for refund of tax issued to the taxpayer.

Privileged Communications

Communications between an attorney and client have long been protected from disclosure to other parties (such as the IRS and the tax courts). A similar privilege of confidentiality extends to tax advice between a taxpayer and tax practitioner, as we used that term above. The privilege is not available for matters involving criminal charges or questions brought by other agencies, such as the Securities and Exchange Commission.[63] Nor is it allowed in matters involving promoting or participating in tax shelters.

A taxpayer likely will want to protect documents such as the tax adviser's research memo detailing the strengths and weaknesses of a tax return position or a conversation about an appeals strategy. The confidentiality privilege should be interpreted in the following manner.

- The privilege often is available when an attorney or CPA completes a tax return for the taxpayer. But some courts have restricted the attorney's privilege in this context on the grounds that the tax professional is conducting accounting work, not offering legal advice. Others assert that the confidentiality privilege is waived when the taxpayer discloses financial data on the tax return. To the

---

[60]§ 6694(b).
[61]§ 6701.

[62]§ 6695.
[63]§ 7525(a)(1).

contrary, if the tax professional is providing traditional legal advice to help the client decide what to disclose on a tax return, the privilege should be available.

- The privilege for CPAs applies only to tax advice. Attorneys still can exercise the privilege concerning advice rendered as a business consultant, estate/financial planner, and so on.
- About a third of the states offer a similar confidentiality privilege for CPAs, but outside the Federal tax appeals process, protection is not yet the norm.
- The privilege is not available for tax accrual workpapers prepared as part of an independent financial audit.

Thus, the CPA needs to exercise care to ensure that the privilege of confidentiality will apply to his or her tax work. Taking the following steps can help.

- Segregate the time spent and documents produced in rendering services for tax compliance from the time and documents devoted to tax advice. Doing this will protect the privilege from being waived as to the tax advice.
- Explain the extent of the privilege to the client—specify what will and will not be protected from the IRS in a dispute.
- Do not inadvertently waive the privilege, say, by telling "too much" to the IRS or to a third party who is not protected by the privilege.
- Indemnify the CPA for time spent protecting and enforcing the privilege once it is challenged.

ETHICAL and EQUITABLE *Considerations* — WHERE DOES MY COST SAVING GO?

As is the case in many other U.S. industries, tax return preparers have been outsourcing some of their operations to lower-cost locations overseas. By some estimates, almost 150,000 state and Federal tax returns are completed in India alone, and all such estimates are probably understated because of a lack of disclosure by tax practitioners.

Circular 230 does not prohibit outsourcing, and the IRS does not even require a disclosure by the tax preparer when it occurs. Tax and consulting firms defend the practice as a cost-saving measure and contend that the confidentiality of taxpayer data is not compromised.

AICPA ethics rules (applying both to tax return preparation and other work) require:

- Notice to the taxpayer before any data are shared with a third-party service provider.
- Acceptance by the practitioner of full responsibility for the third party's work (i.e., as to quality and security).

Should any cost saving that outsourcing provides be passed on to the client in the form of lower fees? Do you expect this will occur?

AICPA Statements on Standards for Tax Services

Tax practitioners who are CPAs, attorneys, or EAs must abide by the codes or canons of professional ethics applicable to their respective professions. The various codes and canons have much in common with and parallel the standards of conduct set forth in Circular 230.[64]

The AICPA has issued a series of Statements on Standards for Tax Services (SSTSs). The Statements are enforceable standards of professional practice for AICPA members working in state or Federal tax practice. The SSTSs comprise part

[64]For an additional discussion of tax ethics, see Raabe, Whittenburg, and Sanders, *Federal Tax Research*, 8th ed. (Cengage Learning/South-Western, 2009), especially Chapters 1 and 14.

of the AICPA's Code of Professional Conduct. Together with the provisions of Circular 230 and the penalty provisions of the Code, the SSTSs make up a set of guidelines for the conduct of the tax practitioner who is also a CPA. Other sources of descriptions of professional ethics are issued by state bar associations and CPA societies, the American Bar Association, and the associations of enrolled agents.

Key provisions of some of the SSTSs are presented below.

Statement No. 1: Tax Return Positions.

Under certain circumstances, a CPA may take a position that is contrary to that taken by the IRS. To do so, however, the CPA must have a good faith belief that the position has a realistic possibility (i.e., probably a one-in-three chance) of being sustained administratively or judicially on its merits if challenged.

The client should be fully advised of the risks involved and the penalties that may result if the position taken by the CPA is not successful. The client should also be informed that disclosure on the return may avoid some or all of these penalties.

In no case, though, should the CPA exploit the audit lottery. That is, the CPA should not take a questionable position based on the probabilities that the client's return will not be chosen by the IRS for audit. Furthermore, the CPA should not "load" the return with questionable items in the hope that they might aid the client in a later settlement negotiation with the IRS.

Statement No. 2: Questions on Returns.

A CPA should make a reasonable effort to obtain from the client, and provide, appropriate answers to all questions on a tax return before signing as preparer. Reasonable grounds may exist for omitting an answer.

- The information is not readily available, and the answer is not significant in amount in computing the tax.
- The meaning of the question as it applies to a particular situation is genuinely uncertain.
- The answer to the question is voluminous.

The fact that an answer to a question could prove disadvantageous to the client does not justify omitting the answer.

Statement No. 3: Procedural Aspects of Preparing Returns.

In preparing a return, a CPA may in good faith rely without verification on information furnished by the client or by third parties. However, the CPA should make reasonable inquiries if the information appears to be incorrect, incomplete, or inconsistent. In this regard, the CPA should refer to the client's returns for prior years whenever appropriate.

EXAMPLE 22

A CPA normally can take a client's word for the validity of dependency exemptions. But suppose a recently divorced client wants to claim his three children as dependents (when he does not have custody and is not awarded the exemptions by the decree). You must act in accordance with § 152(e)(2) in preparing the return, and this will require evidence of a waiver by the custodial parent. Without this waiver, you should not claim the dependency exemptions on your client's tax return. ∎

EXAMPLE 23

While preparing Sunni's income tax return for 2008, you review her income tax return for 2007. In comparing the dividend income reported on the 2007 Schedule B with that received in 2008, you note a significant decrease. Further investigation reveals the variation is due to a stock sale in 2008 that was unknown to you until now. Thus, the review of the 2007 return has unearthed a transaction that should be reported on the 2008 return. ∎

If the Code or Regulations require certain types of verification (as is the case with travel and entertainment expenditures), the CPA must advise the client of these rules. Further, inquiry must be made to ascertain whether the client has complied with the verification requirements.

CONCEPT SUMMARY $16-1$

Tax Administration and Practice

1. The Internal Revenue Service (IRS) enforces the tax laws of the United States. Its size and form of organization reflect its various responsibilities relative to taxpayer interaction, litigation, and collection, as well as its internal functions.

2. The IRS issues various pronouncements in communicating its position on certain tax issues. These pronouncements promote the uniform enforcement of the tax law among taxpayers and among the internal divisions of the IRS. Taxpayers should seek such rulings and memoranda when the nature or magnitude of a pending transaction requires a high degree of certainty in the planning process.

3. IRS audits can take several forms. Taxpayers are selected for audit based on the probable net dollar return to the Treasury from the process. Offers in compromise and closing agreements can be a useful means of completing an audit without resorting to litigation.

4. Certain IRS personnel are empowered to consider the hazards of litigation in developing a settlement with the taxpayer during the audit process.

5. The IRS pays interest to taxpayers on overpaid taxes, starting essentially 45 days after the due date of the return, in amounts tied to the Federal short-term rate.

Interest paid to the IRS on underpayments is similarly based on the Federal rate, starting essentially on the due date of the return. Interest for both purposes is compounded daily.

6. The Treasury assesses penalties when the taxpayer fails to file a required tax return or pay a tax. Penalties also are assessed when an inaccurate return is filed due to negligence or other disregard of IRS rules. Tax preparers are subject to penalties for assisting a taxpayer in filing an inaccurate return, failing to follow IRS rules in an appropriate manner, or mishandling taxpayer data or funds.

7. Statutes of limitations place outer boundaries on the timing and amounts of proposed amendments to completed tax returns that can be made by the taxpayer or the IRS.

8. Tax practitioners must operate under constraints imposed on them by codes of ethics or pertinent professional societies and by Treasury Circular 230. These rules also define the parties who can represent others in an IRS proceeding.

9. A limited privilege of confidentiality exists between the taxpayer and tax preparer.

Statement No. 4: Estimates. A CPA may prepare a tax return using estimates received from a taxpayer if it is impracticable to obtain exact data. The estimates must be reasonable under the facts and circumstances as known to the CPA. When estimates are used, they should be presented in such a manner as to avoid the implication of greater accuracy than exists.

Statement No. 5: Recognition of Administrative Proceeding or Court Decision. As facts may vary from year to year, so may the position taken by a CPA. In these types of situations, the CPA is not bound by an administrative or judicial proceeding involving a prior year.

EXAMPLE 24

Upon audit of Ramon Corporation's income tax return for 2006, the IRS disallowed $78,000 of the $600,000 salary paid to its president and sole shareholder on the grounds that it is unreasonable. You are the CPA who has been engaged to prepare Ramon's income tax return for 2008. Again the corporation paid its president a salary of $600,000 and chose to deduct this amount. Because you are not bound for 2008 by what the IRS deemed reasonable for 2006, the full $600,000 can be claimed as a salary deduction. ■

Other problems that require a CPA to use judgment include reclassification of corporate debt as equity (thin capitalization) and corporate accumulations beyond the reasonable needs of the business (for the penalty tax under § 531).

Statement No. 6: Knowledge of Error. A CPA should promptly advise a client upon learning of an error in a previously filed return or upon learning of a client's failure to file a required return. The advice can be oral or written and should include a recommendation of the corrective measures, if any, to be taken. The error or other omission should not be disclosed to the IRS without the client's consent.

If the past error is material and is not corrected by the client, the CPA may be unable to prepare the current year's tax return. This situation might occur if the error has a carryover effect that prevents the CPA from determining the correct tax liability for the current year.

EXAMPLE 25

In preparing a client's 2008 income tax return, you discover that final inventory for 2007 was materially understated. First, you should advise the client to file an amended return for 2007 reflecting the correct amount in final inventory. Second, if the client refuses to make this adjustment, you should consider whether the error will preclude you from preparing a substantially correct return for 2008. Because this will probably be the case (the final inventory for 2007 becomes the beginning inventory for 2008), you should withdraw from the engagement.

If the client corrects the error, you may proceed with the preparation of the tax return for 2008. You must assure yourself that the error is not repeated. ■

Statement No. 8: Advice to Clients. In providing tax advice to a client, the CPA must use judgment to assure that the advice reflects professional competence and appropriately serves the client's needs. No standard format or guidelines can be established to cover all situations and circumstances involving written or oral advice by the CPA.

The CPA may communicate with the client when subsequent developments affect previous advice on significant matters. However, the CPA cannot be expected to assume responsibility for initiating the communication, unless he or she is assisting a client in implementing procedures or plans associated with the advice. The CPA may undertake this obligation by specific agreement with the client.

TAX PLANNING
Considerations

Strategies in Seeking an Administrative Ruling

Determination Letters. In many instances, the request for an advance ruling or a determination letter from the IRS is a necessary or desirable planning strategy. The receipt of a favorable ruling or determination reduces the risk associated with a transaction when the tax results are in doubt. For example, the initiation or amendment of a qualified pension or profit sharing plan should be accompanied by a determination letter. Otherwise, on subsequent IRS review, the plan may not qualify, and the tax deductibility of contributions to the plan will be disallowed. In some instances, the potential tax effects of a transaction are so numerous and of such consequence that proceeding without a ruling is unwise.

Letter Rulings. In some cases, it may not be necessary or desirable to request an advance ruling. For example, it is generally not desirable to request a ruling if the tax results are doubtful and the company is committed to complete the transaction in any event. If a ruling is requested and negotiations with the IRS indicate that an adverse determination will be forthcoming, it is usually possible to have the ruling request withdrawn. However, the National Office of the IRS may forward its findings, along with a copy of the ruling request, to local IRS personnel. In determining the advisability of a ruling request, the taxpayer should consider the potential exposure of other items in the tax returns of all "open years."

A ruling request may delay the consummation of a transaction if the issues are novel or complex. Frequently, a ruling can be processed within six months, although in some instances a delay of a year or more may be encountered.

Technical Advice Memoranda. A taxpayer in the process of contesting a proposed deficiency with the Appeals Division should consider requesting a technical advice memorandum from the IRS. If the memorandum is favorable to the taxpayer, it is binding on the Appeals Division. The request may be particularly appropriate when the practitioner feels that the agent or Appeals Division has been too literal in interpreting an IRS ruling.

Considerations in Handling an IRS Audit

As a general rule, a taxpayer should attempt to settle disputes at the earliest possible stage of the administrative appeal process. It is usually possible to limit the scope of the examination by furnishing pertinent information requested by the agent. Extraneous information or fortuitous comments may result in the opening of new issues and should be avoided. Agents usually appreciate prompt and efficient responses to inquiries, since their performance may in part be judged by their ability to close or settle assigned cases.

To the extent possible, it is advisable to conduct the investigation of field audits in the practitioner's office, rather than the client's office. This procedure permits greater control over the audit investigation and facilitates the agent's review and prompt closure of the case.

Many practitioners feel that it is generally not advisable to have clients present at the scheduled conferences with the agent, since the client may give emotional or gratuitous comments that impair prompt settlement. If the client is not present, however, he or she should be advised of the status of negotiations. The client makes the final decision on any proposed settlement.

ETHICAL and EQUITABLE *Considerations*   ### SHOULD THE CLIENT ATTEND AN AUDIT?

Whether the client should be present during an audit is a matter of some debate. Certainly, the client's absence tends to slow down the negotiating process because the taxpayer must make all final decisions on settlement terms and is the best source of information for open questions of fact. Nevertheless, most practitioners discourage their clients from attending audits or conferences with the Appeals Division involving an income tax dispute. Ignorance of the law and of the conventions of the audit process can make the taxpayer a "loose cannon" that can do more harm than good if unchecked. All too often, a client will "say too much" in the presence of a government official.

In reality, though, by discouraging clients from attending the audit, practitioners may be interfering with the IRS's function of gathering evidence, depending on what precisely the taxpayer is being prevented from saying. To many practitioners, a "wrong" answer is one that increases taxes, not one that misrepresents the truth. A popular saying among tax advisers is "Don't tell me more than I want to know." Although this philosophy is supportable under various professional codes of conduct, it is hardly defensible in the larger scheme of things.

In your opinion, under what circumstances should the client attend such a session? To what degree should the tax professional "coach" the client as to how to behave in that setting? Or do a taxpayer's rights include the right to increase his or her own tax liability?

Preparing for the Audit. The tax professional must prepare thoroughly for the audit or Appeals proceeding. Practitioners often cite the following steps as critical to such preparations. Carrying out a level of due diligence in preparing for the proceeding is part of the tax professional's responsibility in representing the client.

- Make certain that both sides agree on the issues to be resolved in the audit. The goal here is to limit the agent's list of open issues.
- Identify all of the facts underlying the issues in dispute, including those favorable to the IRS. Gather evidence to support the taxpayer's position, and evaluate the evidence supporting the other side.

- Research current tax law authorities as they bear on the facts and open issues. Remember that the IRS agent is bound only by Supreme Court cases and IRS pronouncements. Determine the degree of discretion that the IRS is likely to have in disposing of the case.
- Prepare a list of points supporting and contradicting the taxpayer's case. Include both minor points bearing little weight and core principles. Short research memos will also be useful in the discussion with the agent. Points favoring the taxpayer should be mentioned during the discussion and "entered into the record."
- Prepare tax and interest computations showing the effects of points that are in dispute, so that the consequences of closing or compromising an issue can be readily determined.
- Determine a "litigation point" (i.e., at which the taxpayer will withdraw from further audit negotiation and pursue the case in the courts). This position should be based on the dollars of tax, interest, and penalty involved, the chances of prevailing in various trial-level courts, and other strategies discussed with the taxpayer. One must have an "end game" strategy for the audit, and thorough tax research is critical in developing that position in this context.

Offers in Compromise. By encouraging the use of offers in compromise to a greater degree than ever before the IRS brings more nonfilers into compliance with the tax system.

Both parties to a tax dispute may find a compromise offer useful because it conclusively settles all of the issues covered by the agreement and may include a favorable payment schedule for the taxpayer.

On the other hand, several attributes of an offer in compromise may work to the detriment of the taxpayer. Just as the IRS no longer can raise new issues as part of the audit proceedings against the taxpayer, he or she cannot contest or appeal any such agreement. As part of the offer process, the taxpayer must disclose all relevant finances and resources, including details he or she might not want the government to know, and an up-front down payment will be due. Furthermore, both parties are bound to the filing positions established by the compromise for five tax years, a level of inflexibility that may work against a taxpayer whose circumstances change over time.

Documentation Issues. The tax practitioner's workpapers should include all research memoranda, and a list of resolved and unresolved issues should be continually updated during the course of the IRS audit. Occasionally, agents request access to excessive amounts of accounting data in order to engage in a so-called fishing expedition. Providing blanket access to working papers should be avoided. Workpapers should be carefully reviewed to minimize opportunities for the agent to raise new issues not otherwise apparent. It is generally advisable to provide the agent with copies of specific workpapers upon request.

In unusual situations, a Special Agent may appear to gather evidence in the investigation of possible criminal fraud. When this occurs, the taxpayer should be advised to seek legal counsel to determine the extent of his or her cooperation in providing information to the agent. Further, it is frequently desirable for the tax adviser to consult his or her own personal legal counsel in such situations. If the taxpayer receives a Revenue Agent's Report, it generally indicates that the IRS has decided not to initiate criminal proceedings. The IRS usually does not take any action on a tax deficiency until the criminal matter has been resolved. If, for whatever reasons, the criminal action is dropped, the 75 percent civil fraud penalty still can be assessed.

Statute of Limitations

Extending the Statute. The IRS requests an extension of the statute of limitations when it finds that there is insufficient time to complete an audit or appellate review. The taxpayer is not compelled to agree to the extension request and may be averse to giving the IRS more time. But adverse consequences can result if the taxpayer denies the IRS request.

Although the statute of limitations governing Thornton's tax return is scheduled to expire in 15 days, the IRS has requested an extension for another 60 days. It wants to complete a more thorough investigation into a disputed $50,000 deduction. If Thornton refuses to agree to the extension, the IRS likely will disallow the entire deduction. However, if Thornton agrees to the extension, all or part of the deduction may be salvaged. ■

A disadvantage of extending the statute is that the IRS sometimes can raise new issues during the extension period. However, the taxpayer can take the following protective measures as a condition to agreeing to the extension.

- Shorten the extension period requested before signing the Form 872. This will reduce the chance that the IRS will find and investigate new issues.
- Restrict the scope of the issues covered by the extension (e.g., extend the period only as to the computation of cost of goods sold).
- Instead of Form 872, use a Form 872–A. This allows for an open-ended termination date of the extension. Consequently, when the examination of a disputed issue is completed, the taxpayer can request that the IRS close off the extension. This reduces the chances that the IRS will find and pursue any new issues.

Prompt Assessment. The "prompt assessment" approach forces the IRS to conduct some sort of an examination of a return. Although most taxpayers are unlikely to volunteer for an audit, the procedure is attractive in several circumstances.

- An estate or trust (Chapters 17–19) is being terminated, and the executor or trustee needs some assurance that the entity's tax affairs are in order.
- A corporation is being liquidated, and the trustee of the liquidating trust wants to protect itself from unanticipated future income tax assessments by the IRS on years open under the statute of limitations.

A request for a prompt assessment is made by filing Form 4810. The IRS has 18 months to complete its review once the taxpayer files the request.[65]

Litigation Considerations

During the process of settlement with the IRS, the taxpayer must assess the economic consequences of possible litigation. Specifically, the probability of winning in court should be weighed against the costs of litigating the dispute (legal, support, and court costs). In some instances, taxpayers become overly emotional and do not adequately consider the economic and psychological costs of litigation.

Signing Form 870 or Form 870–AD precludes the use of the Tax Court as a forum for future litigation. In that event, the taxpayer's only recourse is to pay the taxes and sue for a refund in a different court. The Tax Court was established to provide taxpayers an opportunity to litigate issues without first paying the tax on the deficiency. Some taxpayers, however, prefer to litigate the case in a Federal District Court or the Court of Federal Claims, since the payment of tax effectively stops the running of interest on the deficiency.

In selecting a proper tax forum, consideration should be given to the decisions of the various courts in related cases. The Tax Court follows the decisions of U.S. Courts of Appeals if the court is one to which the taxpayer may appeal.[66] For example, if an individual is in the jurisdiction of the Fifth Circuit Court of Appeals and that court has issued a favorable opinion on the same issue that currently confronts

---

[65]§ 6501(d).

[66]*Jack E. Golsen*, 54 T.C. 742 (1970).

the taxpayer, the Tax Court will follow this opinion in deciding the taxpayer's case, even if previous Tax Court decisions have been adverse.

If the issue involves a question in which equity is needed, strategy may dictate the choice of the Court of Federal Claims, which has frequently given greater weight to equity considerations than to strict legal precedent, or of a Federal District Court, where a jury trial is available.

Penalties

Penalties are imposed upon a taxpayer's failure to file a return or pay a tax when due. These penalties can be avoided if the failure is due to reasonable cause and not due to willful neglect. Reasonable cause, however, has not been liberally interpreted by the courts and should not be relied upon in the routine situation.[67] A safer way to avoid the failure to file penalty is to obtain from the IRS an extension of time for filing the return.

The penalty for failure to pay estimated taxes can become quite severe. Often trapped by the provision are employed taxpayers with outside income. They may forget about the outside income and assume the amount withheld from wages and salaries is adequate to cover their liability. Not only does April 15 provide a real shock (in terms of the additional tax owed) for these persons, but a penalty situation may have evolved. One way for an employee to mitigate this problem (presuming the employer is willing to cooperate) is described in the following example.

EXAMPLE 27

Patty, a calendar year taxpayer, is employed by Finn Corporation and earns (after withholding) a monthly salary of $4,000 payable at the end of each month. Patty also receives income from outside sources (interest, dividends, and consulting fees). After some quick calculations in early October, Patty determines that she has underestimated her tax liability by $7,500 and will be subject to the penalty for the first two quarters of the year and part of the third quarter. Patty, therefore, completes a new Form W–4 in which she arbitrarily raises her income tax withholding by $2,500 a month. Finn accepts the Form W–4, and as a result, an extra $7,500 is paid to the IRS on Patty's account for the payroll period from October through December.

Patty avoids penalties for the underpayment for the first three quarters because withholding of taxes is allocated pro rata over the year involved. Thus, a portion of the additional $7,500 withheld in October–December is assigned to the January 1–April 15 period, the April 16–June 15 period, etc. Had Patty merely paid the IRS an additional $7,500 in October, the penalty would still have been assessed for the earlier quarters. ■

KEY TERMS

Accuracy-related penalty, 16–15	Negligence, 16–16	Substantial authority, 16–17
Closing agreement, 16–12	Ninety-day letter, 16–10	Technical advice memorandum (TAM), 16–5
Determination letter, 16–5	Offer in compromise, 16–12	Thirty-day letter, 16–10
Enrolled agent [EA], 16–23	Reasonable cause, 16–15	
Fraud, 16–19	Revenue Agent's Report (RAR), 16–9	
Letter ruling, 16–4	Statute of limitations, 16–21	

---

[67]*Dustin v. Comm.*, 72–2 USTC ¶9610, 30 AFTR2d 72–5313, 467 F.2d 47 (CA–9, 1972), *aff'g* 53 T.C. 491 (1969).

P R O B L E M   M A T E R I A L S

DISCUSSION QUESTIONS

1. Evaluate this statement: A tax professional must be very familiar with the IRS's operations and organization.

2. What is the IRS? What responsibilities is it charged to carry out?

3. Carol takes some very aggressive positions on her tax return. She maintains, "With the downsizing of the government, my chances of getting caught are virtually zero." Is Carol's approach correct?

4. Recently, a politician was interviewed about fiscal policy, and she mentioned reducing the "tax gap." Explain what this term means. What are some of the pertinent political and economic issues relative to the tax gap? *Issue ID*

5. Describe the current organization, management structure, and operations of the IRS.

6. What are the most important activities that the IRS currently is carrying out in its data collection and audit efforts? Hint: These items often are referred to as IRS Audit Initiatives. They entail targeted programs that are in addition to the usual tax return audit procedures.

7. Your tax supervisor has informed you that the firm has received an unfavorable answer to a ruling request. In a memo to the supervisor, describe the appropriate weight that she should assign to the holding in the ruling. *Communications*

8. While you are representing a client at an audit by the IRS, the IRS agent says, "Since we aren't going to agree on this issue today, let's get tech advice on the matter." What does she mean?

9. What rights does the Internal Revenue Code grant to the IRS concerning a taxpayer's books and records that are maintained to substantiate the annual computation of Federal taxable income?

10. Describe the process that the IRS uses to collect the tax that is found to be due after an audit is completed. Assume that the IRS findings are not appealed but that the taxpayer does not pay the amount due as determined by the audit. Illustrate the process with PowerPoint slides. *Communications*

11. Sarah tells you, "I was worried about getting audited on the tax return I filed two months ago, but I received my refund check today, so the IRS must agree with my figures." Comment.

12. Many tax professionals encourage their clients to pursue tax disputes through the judicial system. But the courts hear only several hundred tax cases in a typical year. Identify some advantages and disadvantages of settling a tax case within IRS channels (i.e., with the auditor or the Appeals Division).

13. Describe the three broad types of IRS audits. Give an example of an issue that each type of audit might address, and indicate how frequently such audits are conducted by the IRS.

14. Which taxpayers should try to settle tax disputes with the Small Cases Division of the U.S. Tax Court? What is the precedential value of a Small Cases decision?

15. The taxpayer has just signed a closing agreement with the IRS. Can the amount of assessed taxes be changed later? Explain.

16. On February 10, 2008, Quon, a calendar year taxpayer, files her 2007 Federal income tax return on which she claims a $1,200 refund. If Quon receives her refund check on May 2, 2008, will it include any interest paid by the Treasury? Explain.

17. For the completion and filing of his 2008 income tax return, Ron retains the services of a CPA. Because of a particularly hectic tax season, the CPA does not complete and file the return until June 2009. Is Ron excused from the failure to file and pay penalties under the reasonable cause exception? Would it make any difference if Ron were entitled to a refund?

18. Which of the valuation penalties is likely to arise when an aggressive taxpayer reports:
    a. A charitable contribution?
    b. An excessive amount for the basis of stock sold in computing a capital gain?
    c. A decedent's taxable estate?

19. Describe how the valuation penalties work. What is the rate of the penalty, and on which amount is it imposed?

20. Give two examples of a taxpayer action that would trigger a civil fraud penalty.

Issue ID

21. In early November, Brad determines that his tax for the year will total $4,000. If his employer is scheduled to withhold only $2,500 in income taxes, what can Brad do to avoid any underpayment penalty?

22. Indicate whether each of the following statements is true or false.
    a. The government never pays a taxpayer interest on an overpayment of tax.
    b. The IRS can compromise on the amount of tax liability if there is doubt as to the taxpayer's ability to pay.
    c. The statute of limitations for assessing a tax never extends beyond three years from the filing of a return.
    d. A taxpayer's claim for a refund is not subject to a statute of limitations.

23. In each of the following cases, distinguish between the terms.
    a. Offer in compromise and closing agreement.
    b. Failure to file and failure to pay.
    c. Ninety-day letter and thirty-day letter.
    d. Negligence and fraud.
    e. Criminal and civil penalties.

24. Special reporting requirements apply to transactions that the IRS has labeled "tax shelters." Describe those requirements.

Issue ID

25. Why should the taxpayer be "let off the hook" and no longer be subject to audit exposure once the applicable statute of limitations has expired? Do statutes of limitations protect the government? Other taxpayers?

Issue ID

26. The disclosures about Enron, Tyco, and WorldCom have changed the regulation of the accounting profession. Who regulates the behavior of tax return preparers? What documents provide the major constraints on the conduct of the tax profession?

27. Lorraine, a vice president of Scott Corporation, prepared and filed the corporate Form 1120 for 2006. This return is being audited by the IRS in 2008.
    a. May Lorraine represent Scott during the audit?
    b. Can Lorraine's representation continue beyond the agent level (e.g., before the Appeals Division)?

28. Give the Circular 230 position concerning each of the following situations sometimes encountered in the tax profession.
    a. Taking an aggressive pro-taxpayer position on a tax return.
    b. Not having a quality review process for a return completed by a partner of the tax firm.
    c. Purposely delaying compliance with a document request received from the IRS.
    d. Not keeping up with changes in the tax law.
    e. Charging $1,500 to complete a Form 1040-EZ.
    f. When representing a taxpayer in a Federal income tax audit, charging a fee equal to one-third of the reduction of the tax proposed by the IRS agent.
    g. Representing both the grantor and the beneficiaries of a trust that is being created.

29. List several of the penalties that can be assessed on tax return preparers, as authorized by the Code.

30. Indicate which codes, canons, and other bodies of ethical statements apply to each of the following tax practitioners.
   a.   CPAs who are members of the AICPA.
   b.   CPAs who are not members of the AICPA.
   c.   Attorneys.
   d.   Enrolled agents.
   e.   Tax preparers who are not CPAs, EAs, or attorneys.

PROBLEMS

31. On March 15, 2008, Gordon paid the $10,000 balance of his Federal income tax three months late. Ignore daily compounding of interest. Determine the interest rate that applies relative to this amount, assuming that:
   a.   Gordon is an individual.
   b.   Gordon is a C corporation.
   c.   The $10,000 is not a tax that is due but is a refund payable by the IRS to Gordon (an individual).
   d.   The $10,000 is not a tax that is due but is a refund payable by the IRS to Gordon (a C corporation).

32. Rita forgot to pay her Federal income tax on time. When she actually filed (without a valid extension), she reported a balance due. Compute Rita's failure to file penalty in each of the following cases.
   a.   One month late, $1,000 additional tax due.
   b.   Four months late, $3,000 additional tax due.
   c.   Six months late, $4,000 additional tax due.
   d.   Four months late due to fraud by Rita, $5,000 additional tax due.

33. Tom filed his Federal income tax return on time but did not remit the balance due. Compute Tom's failure to pay penalty in each of the following cases. The IRS has not issued a deficiency notice.
   a.   Four months late, $3,000 additional tax due.
   b.   Ten months late, $3,000 additional tax due.
   c.   Five years late, $3,000 additional tax due.

34. Compute the failure to pay and failure to file penalties for John, who filed his 2007 income tax return on November 20, 2008, paying the $10,000 amount due at that time. On April 1, 2008, John had received a six-month extension of time in which to file his return. He has no reasonable cause for failing to file his return by October 15 or for failing to pay the tax that was due on April 15, 2008. John's failure to comply with the tax laws was not fraudulent.

35. Olivia, a calendar year taxpayer, does not file her 2007 return until November 29, 2008. At this point, she pays the $25,000 balance due on her 2007 tax liability of $70,000. Olivia did not apply for and obtain any extension of time for filing the 2007 return. When questioned by the IRS on her delinquency, Olivia asserts: "If I was too busy to file my regular tax return, I was too busy to request an extension."
   a.   Is Olivia liable for any penalties for failure to file and for failure to pay?
   b.   If so, compute the penalty amounts.

36. Orville, a cash basis, calendar year taxpayer, filed his income tax return 40 days after the due date. Orville never extended his return, and he paid the taxes that were due when he filed the return. What penalty will Orville incur, and how much will he have to pay if his additional tax is $5,000? Disregard any interest he must pay.

37. Rhoda, a calendar year individual taxpayer, files her 2007 return on December 17, 2008. She did not obtain an extension for filing her return, and the return reflects additional income tax due of $10,000.
   a.   What are Rhoda's penalties for failure to file and to pay?
   b.   Would your answer to (a) change if Rhoda, before the due date of the return, had retained a CPA to prepare the return and it was the CPA's negligence that caused the delay?

38. Dana underpaid her taxes by $250,000. A portion of the underpayment was shown to be attributable to Dana's negligence ($200,000). A court found that a portion of that deficiency constituted civil fraud ($80,000). Compute the total fraud and negligence penalties incurred.

39. Compute the overvaluation penalty for each of the following independent cases involving the taxpayer who filed in 2008 claiming the fair market value of charitable contribution property. In each case, assume a marginal income tax rate of 35%.

	Taxpayer	Corrected IRS Value	Reported Valuation
a.	Individual	$ 40,000	$ 50,000
b.	C corporation	30,000	50,000
c.	S corporation	40,000	50,000
d.	Individual	150,000	200,000
e.	Individual	150,000	250,000
f.	C corporation	150,000	750,000

40. Compute the undervaluation penalty for each of the following independent cases involving the executors who filed in 2008 reporting the value of a closely held business in the decedent's gross estate. In each case, assume a marginal estate tax rate of 45%.

	Reported Value	Corrected IRS Valuation
a.	$ 20,000	$ 25,000
b.	100,000	150,000
c.	150,000	250,000
d.	150,000	500,000

41. Moose, a former professional athlete, now supplements his income by signing autographs at collectors' shows. Unfortunately, Moose has not been conscientious about reporting all of this income on his tax return. Now the IRS has charged him with additional taxes of $80,000 due to negligence in his record keeping and $20,000 due to an intent to defraud the U.S. government of income taxes. No criminal fraud charges are brought against Moose. The District Court finds by a preponderance of the evidence that only half of the $20,000 underpayment was due to Moose's fraudulent action; the remainder was due to mere negligence. Compute the accuracy-related and civil fraud penalties in this matter.

42. Trudy's AGI last year was $200,000. Her Federal income tax came to $40,000, which she paid through a combination of withholding and estimated payments. This year, her AGI will be $300,000, with a projected tax liability of $60,000, all to be paid through estimates. Ignore the annualized income method. Compute Trudy's quarterly estimated payment schedule for this year.

43. Kold Services Corporation estimates that its 2009 taxable income will be $500,000. Thus, it is subject to a flat 34% income tax rate and incurs a $170,000 liability. For each of the following independent cases, compute Kold's minimum quarterly estimated tax payments that will avoid an underpayment penalty.
    a. For 2008, taxable income was ($300,000). Kold carried back all of this loss to prior years and exhausted the entire net operating loss in creating a zero 2008 liability.
    b. For 2008, taxable income was $450,000, and tax liability was $153,000.
    c. For 2007, taxable income was $2 million, and tax liability was $680,000. For 2008, taxable income was $450,000, and tax liability was $153,000.

Decision Making

Communications

44. The Scooter Company, owned equally by Julie (chair of the board of directors) and Jeff (company president), is in very difficult financial straits. Last month, Jeff used the $100,000 withheld from employee paychecks for Federal payroll and income taxes to pay off a creditor who threatened to cut off all supplies. To keep the company afloat, Jeff used these government funds willfully for the operations of the business, but even that effort was

not enough. The company missed the next two payrolls, and today other creditors took action to shut down Scooter altogether. How much will the IRS assess in taxes and penalties in this matter, and from whom? How can you as a tax professional best offer service to Julie, Jeff, and Scooter? Address these matters in a memo for the tax research file.

45. What is the applicable statute of limitations in each of the following independent situations?
    a. No return was filed by the taxpayer.
    b. The taxpayer incurred a bad debt loss that she failed to claim.
    c. A taxpayer inadvertently omitted a large amount of gross income.
    d. Same as (c), except that the omission was deliberate.
    e. A taxpayer innocently overstated her deductions by a large amount.

46. Suzanne (a calendar year taxpayer) had the following transactions, all of which were properly reported on a timely filed return.

Gross receipts		$ 960,000
Cost of sales		(850,000)
Gross profit		$ 110,000
Capital gain	$ 75,000	
Capital loss	(25,000)	50,000
Total income		$ 160,000

    a. Presuming the absence of fraud, how much of an omission from gross income is required before the six-year statute of limitations applies?
    b. Would it matter if cost of sales had been inadvertently overstated by $100,000?
    c. How does the situation change in the context of fraud by Suzanne?

47. On April 2, 2005, Mark filed his 2004 income tax return, which showed a tax due of $50,000. On June 1, 2007, he filed an amended return for 2004 that showed an additional tax of $10,000. Mark paid the additional amount.

Decision Making

    On May 18, 2008, Mark filed a claim for a 2004 refund of $25,000.
    a. If Mark's claim for a refund is correct in amount, how much tax will he recover?
    b. What is the period that government-paid interest runs with respect to Mark's claim for a refund?
    c. How would you have advised him differently?

48. Carol owed $4,000 in Federal income tax when she filed her Form 1040 for 2008. She attached a Post-It note to the 1040 saying, "My inventory computations on last year's (2007) return were wrong so I paid $1,000 too much in tax." Carol then included a check for $3,000 with the Form 1040 for 2008. Write a memo to the tax research file commenting on Carol's actions.

Communications

49. Rod's Federal income tax returns (Form 1040) for the indicated three years were prepared by the following persons.

Year	Preparer
2006	Rod
2007	Ann
2008	Cheryl

    Ann is Rod's next-door neighbor and owns and operates a pharmacy. Cheryl is a licensed CPA and is engaged in private practice. In the event Rod is audited and all three returns are examined, who may represent him before the IRS at the agent level? Who may represent Rod before the Appeals Division?

50. Discuss which penalties, if any, might be imposed on the tax adviser in each of the following independent circumstances. In this regard, assume that the tax adviser:
    a. Suggested to the client various means by which to acquire excludible income.
    b. Suggested to the client various means by which to conceal cash receipts from gross income.
    c. Suggested to the client means by which to improve her cash flow by delaying for six months or more the deposit of the employees' share of Federal employment taxes.
    d. Failed, because of pressing time conflicts, to conduct the usual review of the client's tax return. The IRS later discovered that the return included fraudulent data.

e.   Failed, because of pressing time conflicts, to conduct the usual review of the client's tax return. The IRS later discovered a mathematical error in the computation of the personal exemption.

51. Compute the preparer penalty that the IRS could assess on Gerry in each of the following independent cases.

a.   On March 21, the copy machine was not working, so Gerry gave original returns to her 20 clients that day without providing any duplicates for them. Copies for Gerry's files and for use in preparing state tax returns had been made on March 20.

b.   Because Gerry extended her vacation a few days, she missed the Annual Tax Update seminar that she usually attends. As a result, she was unaware that Congress had changed a law affecting limited partnerships. The change affected the transactions of 25 of Gerry's clients, all of whom understated their tax as a result.

c.   Gerry heard that the IRS was increasing its audits of corporations that hold assets in a foreign trust. As a result, Gerry instructed the intern who prepared the initial drafts of the returns for five corporate clients to leave blank the question about such trusts. Not wanting to lose his position, the intern, a senior accounting major at State University, complied with Gerry's instructions.

Decision Making

52. You are the chair of the Ethics Committee of your state's CPA Licensing Commission. Interpret controlling AICPA authority in addressing the following assertions by your membership.

a.   When a CPA has reasonable grounds for not answering an applicable question on a client's return, a brief explanation of the reason for the omission should not be provided, because it would flag the return for audit by the IRS.

b.   If a CPA discovers during an IRS audit that the client has a material error in the return under examination, he should immediately withdraw from the engagement.

c.   If the client tells you that she paid $500 for office supplies, but has lost the receipts, you should deduct an odd amount on her return (e.g., $499), because an even amount ($500) would indicate to the IRS that her deduction was based on an estimate.

d.   If a CPA knows that the client has a material error in a prior year's return, he should not, without the client's consent, disclose the error to the IRS.

e.   If a CPA's client will not correct a material error in a prior year's return, the CPA should not prepare the current year's return for the client.

RESEARCH PROBLEMS

THOMSON
★
RIA

Note: Solutions to Research Problems can be prepared by using the **RIA Checkpoint®** **Student Edition** online research product, which is available to accompany this text. It is also possible to prepare solutions to the Research Problems by using tax research materials found in a standard tax library.

Communications

Research Problem 1.   You have been assigned the task of preparing a letter ruling request on behalf of one of the firm's clients. As the firm has not prepared a ruling request before, you are to outline the procedure by which the IRS receives and processes such a request. Summarize the more significant points in a memo to the tax file. Provide Code and other citations as needed.

Communications

Research Problem 2.   Blanche Creek (111 Elm Avenue, Patriotville, IN 40123) has engaged your firm because she has been charged with failure to file her 2006 Federal Form 1040. Blanche maintains that the "reasonable cause" exception should apply. During the entire tax filing season in 2007, she was under a great deal of stress at work and in her personal life. As a result, Blanche developed a sleep disorder, which was treated through a combination of pills and counseling.

Your firm ultimately prepared the 2006 tax return for Blanche, but it was filed far beyond the due date. Blanche is willing to pay the delinquent tax and related interest. However, she feels that the failure to pay penalty is unfair as she was ill. Consequently, she could not be expected to keep to the usual deadlines for filing.

Write a letter to Blanche concerning these matters.

Research Problem 3.   Max and Annie are roommates sharing an apartment. Although they know each other well, they have respect for each other's privacy. Thus, when Max's 2006 Form 1040 was audited by the IRS, he made no mention of the audit to Annie.

When Annie was clearing the answering machine that they shared, she heard the following message: "Max, this is Richard, the IRS auditor. My figures show that you owe the government $10,000 in taxes and another $4,500 in penalties and interest."

When Annie brought up the message during dinner conversation that night, Max was furious. How could the IRS be so careless as to broadcast this news to a stranger? Didn't he have any privacy and confidentiality rights? Max calls you to determine whether he might have a case against the IRS or Richard, the agent.

Research Problem 4.   You have just rendered service for a taxpayer as an expert witness in a case heard by the U.S. Tax Court. The taxpayer is requesting reimbursement for your fees and for those amounts paid to her attorney in presenting the case. Your billing rate for this type of engagement is $200 per hour, the market rate for such services in your city, plus out-of-pocket expenses (e.g., auto mileage, computer charges). How much of your fee will the taxpayer recover?

Research Problem 5.   Tax preparer Renee had promised her client Joan Holloway that her tax refund for 2002 would be about $12,000. As Renee completed the return, though, she discovered that the actual refund would be only about one-third of the amount predicted. Worried that Joan would use a different tax firm next filing season, Renee purposely added about $25,000 in fictitious deductions to Joan's Schedule C for her computer consulting business. The return was filed in a timely fashion, and the refund was issued by the IRS at the level that Renee had promised.

In 2008, the IRS conducted a thorough, targeted investigation of the consulting industry and discovered Joan's improper deduction. The auditor issued an assessment of $8,100 additional tax, plus interest, against Joan. The notice of deficiency also included a 20% penalty for a substantial underpayment of tax. Joan and Chester, her new tax adviser, want to dispute the assessment on the grounds that the statute of limitations has expired. Will this defense be successful in relieving Joan of the tax, interest, and penalty due?

Use the tax resources of the Internet to address the following questions. Do not restrict your search to the World Wide Web, but include a review of newsgroups and general reference materials, practitioner sites and resources, primary sources of the tax law, chat rooms and discussion groups, and other opportunities.

Internet *Activity*

Research Problem 6.   Find an article in which a tax professional describes the confidentiality privilege available under the Code for a CPA tax adviser. Then construct a list of "Confidentiality Dos and Don'ts for the CPA." Summarize the article in an e-mail to your professor.

Communications

Research Problem 7.   Corporations with large estimated tax overpayments and underpayments are subject to special interest rates. (a) Find in the Code how these rates are determined. (b) List such rates that have been in effect for the last six calendar quarters.

Research Problem 8.   Prepare a graph illustrating the trends in IRS audit activity over the past decade, and submit it to your instructor. First decide whether you are measuring audited returns, tax dollars recovered by audit, or budget resources dedicated to audit activities. Next decide which types of taxpayers and returns you will be graphing. Then find your data at **http://www.irs.gov.**

Communications

Research Problem 9.   In a PowerPoint presentation for your classmates, describe how the confidentiality privilege applies to a tax shelter's:
a. Investors.
b. Promoters.
c. Tax advisers.

Communications

Research Problem 10.   Every year toward the end of the Form 1040 filing season, newspapers and blogs run articles about how to pay your taxes if you lack the funds to do so. The articles promote filing extensions, installment plans, and credit card payments. Find two articles of this sort that were published in the last 12 months. Summarize the articles, and develop a speech outline and no more than four PowerPoint slides for a presentation you will make to your town's Young Executives Club.

Communications

PART 5

Family Tax Planning

Family tax planning has as its objective the minimization of all taxes imposed on the family unit. Carrying out this objective requires familiarity with the rules applicable to transfers by gift and by death. These rules must then be applied to reduce the transfer tax burden. Also to be considered are the income tax consequences of the transfers made. Finally, entities created as a result of these transfers (trusts and estates) are subject to unique income tax rules.

The Federal Gift and Estate Taxes

LEARNING OBJECTIVES

After completing Chapter 17, you should be able to:

LO.1
Understand the nature of the Federal gift and estate taxes.

LO.2
Work with the Federal gift tax formula.

LO.3
Work with the Federal estate tax formula.

LO.4
Understand the operation of the Federal gift tax.

LO.5
Compute the Federal gift tax.

LO.6
Recognize the components of the gross estate.

LO.7
Describe the components of the taxable estate.

LO.8
Determine the Federal estate tax liability.

LO.9
Appreciate the role of the generation-skipping transfer tax.

Transfer Taxes—In General

Until now, this text has dealt primarily with the various applications of the Federal income tax. Also important in the Federal tax structure are various excise taxes that cover transfers of property. Sometimes called transaction taxes, excise taxes are based on the value of the property transferred, not on the income derived from the property. Two such taxes—the Federal gift tax and the Federal estate tax—are the central focus of Chapters 17 and 18.

The importance of being familiar with rules governing transfer taxes can be shown with a simple illustration.

EXAMPLE 1

After 20 years of marriage to George, Helen decides to elope with Mark, a bachelor and long-time friend. Helen and Mark travel to a country in the Caribbean where Helen obtains a divorce, and she and Mark are married. Fifteen years later in 2008, Helen dies. Her will leaves all of her property (estimated value of $3 million) to Mark. Under the unlimited marital deduction (discussed later in the chapter), Helen's estate has no tax to pay. ■

But the marital deduction applies only to transfers between husband and wife. Suppose the jurisdiction where Helen and Mark live does not recognize the validity of divorces granted by the Caribbean country involved. If this is the case, Helen and Mark are not married because Helen was never legally divorced from George. If Mark is not Helen's spouse, no marital deduction is available. Disregarding any administration expenses, Helen's estate must pay an estate tax of $450,000.

Nature of the Taxes

LO.1

Understand the nature of the Federal gift and estate taxes.

Historical Background. Federal tax law imposes a tax on the gratuitous transfer of property in one of two ways. If the transfer occurs during the owner's life, it is subject to the Federal gift tax. If the property passes by virtue of the death of the owner, the Federal estate tax applies. Originally, the two taxes were governed by different rules including separate sets of tax rates. As Congress felt that lifetime transfers of wealth should be encouraged, the gift tax rates were lower than the estate tax rates.[1]

The Tax Reform Act of 1976 significantly changed the approach taken by the Federal gift and estate taxes. Recognizing that prior rules had not significantly stimulated a preference for lifetime over death transfers, Congress decided that all

---

[1]The estate tax was enacted in 1916. Because the estate tax could be avoided by making transfers just prior to dying (i.e., "deathbed gifts"), a gift tax was added in 1932.

transfers should be <u>taxed the same way</u>. Consequently, much of the distinction between life and death transfers was eliminated. Instead of subjecting these transfers to two separate tax rate schedules, the Act substituted a **unified transfer tax** that covered all gratuitous transfers. Thus, gifts were subject to a gift tax at the same rates as those applicable to transfers at death. In addition, the law eliminated the prior exemptions allowed under each tax and replaced them with a unified tax credit.

The Tax Relief Reconciliation Act of 2001 made further changes. Reacting to general public sentiment, Congress concluded that the Federal estate tax was objectionable because it leads to the breakup of family farms and other closely held businesses. This was not the case with the gift tax, since lifetime transfers are voluntary and within the control of the owner of the property. Thus, by scheduled increases in the unified tax credit applicable to estates, the estate tax will be eliminated by the year 2010, but the gift tax is retained. For budget reasons, all changes made by the 2001 Act are eliminated after December 31, 2010 (referred to as a "<u>sunset</u>" provision). Thus, the estate tax is reincarnated for transfers by death after 2010.

Congressional policy toward transfer taxes over the years is summarized below.

- Prior to the Tax Reform Act of 1976, the lower gift tax rates favored transfers by gift.
- The Tax Reform Act of 1976 took a neutral approach by establishing a unified transfer tax that applied the same tax rates to transfers by gift and transfers by death.
- The Tax Relief Reconciliation Act of 2001 favored transfers by death, as the estate tax was phased out, while the gift tax was retained.
- After 2010, the estate tax will be reinstated and placed on parity with the gift tax by returning to the rules that existed prior to the Tax Relief Reconciliation Act of 2001.

Clearly, Congress has not been consistent in its treatment of lifetime (i.e., gift tax) and death (i.e., estate tax) transfers.

Persons Subject to the Tax.

The Federal gift tax is imposed on the right to transfer property by one person (the donor) to another (the donee) for less than full and adequate consideration. The tax is payable by the donor.[2] If the donor fails to pay the tax when due, the donee may be held liable for the tax to the extent of the value of the property received.[3]

A gift by a corporation is considered a gift by the individual shareholders. A gift to a corporation is generally considered a gift to the individual shareholders. In certain cases, however, a gift to a charitable, public, political, or similar organization may be regarded as a gift to the organization as a single entity.[4]

Upon the death of an individual, the Federal estate tax is imposed on the entire estate.[5] The executor (or administrator) of the estate has the obligation to pay any estate tax that may be due.

If the transferor is a resident or citizen of the United States, then the location of the property transferred is immaterial. Thus, a gift by a U.S. resident of property located in Honduras is subject to the Federal gift tax. For a U.S. citizen, the place of residence at the time of the transfer is not relevant. For these purposes, "United States" includes only the 50 states and the District of Columbia and <u>does not</u> <u>include</u> U.S. possessions or territories.[6]

---

[2] § 2502(c).

[3] § 6324(b). Known as the doctrine of transferee liability, this rule also operates to enable the IRS to enforce the collection of other taxes (e.g., income tax, estate tax).

[4] Reg. §§ 25.0–1(b) and 25.2511–1(h)(1). But note the exemption from the Federal gift tax for certain transfers to political organizations discussed later.

[5] § 2001(a). Subchapter A (§§ 2001 through 2058) covers the estate tax treatment of those who are either residents or citizens.

[6] § 7701(a)(9).

GLOBAL Tax Issues

[handwritten margin notes: Death taxes — Estate — inheritance → some do both]

ARE NRAs SUBJECT TO U.S. TRANSFER TAXES?

For individuals who are neither residents nor citizens of the United States (i.e., non-resident aliens or NRAs), the Federal gift tax applies only to gifts of property situated within the United States. The Code, however, exempts from coverage gifts of intangible assets, such as stocks and bonds [§§ 2501(a)(2) and (3) and § 2511(a)].

For decedents who are NRAs, the Federal estate tax is imposed on the value of any property located within the United States. Special rules apply to the estate taxation of NRAs (§§ 2101 through 2108), and Form 706NA is used for reporting purposes.

Type of Death Tax. Death taxes fall into two categories: estate and inheritance. The U.S. government, some states, and several foreign countries impose estate taxes. Inheritance taxes are imposed by some states and other countries. Some states and countries use <u>both</u> types of taxes.

The Federal estate tax differs in several respects from the typical *inheritance tax.* First, the Federal estate tax is levied on the decedent's entire estate. It is a tax on the right to pass property at death. Inheritance taxes apply to the right to receive property at death and are therefore levied on the heirs. Second, the relationship of the heirs to the decedent usually has a direct bearing on the amount of the inheritance tax. In general, the more closely related the parties, the larger the exemptions and the lower the applicable rates.[7] Except for transfers to surviving spouses that may result in a marital deduction, the relationship of the heirs to the decedent has no effect on the Federal estate tax.

LO.2

Work with the Federal gift tax formula.

Formula for the Gift Tax. Like the income tax, which uses taxable income (not gross income) as a tax base, the gift tax usually does not apply to the full amount of the gift. Deductions and the annual exclusion may be allowed to arrive at an amount called the **taxable gift.** However, unlike the income tax, which does not consider taxable income from prior years, *prior taxable gifts* must be added in arriving at the tax base to which the unified transfer tax rate is applied. Otherwise, the donor could start over again each year with a new set of progressive rates.

EXAMPLE 2

Don makes taxable gifts of $1 million in 1986 and $1 million in 2008. Presuming no other taxable gifts and *before applying the unified tax credit,* Don must pay a tax of $345,800 (see Appendix A, page A–4) on the 1986 transfer and a tax of $780,800 (see Appendix A, page A–7) on the 2008 transfer (using a tax base of $2 million). If the 1986 taxable gift had not been included in the tax base for the 2008 gift, the tax would have been $345,800. The correct tax liability of $780,800 is more than twice $345,800! ∎

Because the gift tax is cumulative in effect, a credit is allowed against the gift taxes paid (or deemed paid) on prior taxable gifts included in the tax base. The deemed paid credit is explained later in the chapter.

EXAMPLE 3

Assume the same facts as in Example 2. Don will be allowed a credit of $345,800 against the gift tax of $780,800. Thus, his gift tax liability for 2008 becomes $435,000 ($780,800 − $345,800). ∎

In 1982, the annual exclusion was increased from $3,000 to $10,000. By allowing larger amounts to be exempt from the gift tax, taxpayer compliance may

---

[7]For example, one state's inheritance tax provides an unlimited exemption for a surviving spouse and charities, $100,000 for Class A heirs (lineal descendants and ascendants), $500 for Class B heirs (collateral heirs), and $100 for Class C (other relatives and strangers). Beginning tax rates applicable to the nonexempt portion range from 2% to 10%, with the top rate applicable to Class C heirs reaching 20%.

FIGURE 17–1	**Formula for the Federal Gift Tax**

Determine whether the transfers are considered gifts by referring to §§ 2511 through 2519; list the fair market value of only the covered transfers		$xxx,xxx
Determine the deductions allowed by § 2522 (charitable) and § 2523 (marital)	$xx,xxx	
Claim the annual exclusion (per donee) under § 2503(b), if available	12,000	xx,xxx
Taxable gifts [as defined by § 2503(a)] for the current period		$ xx,xxx
Add: Taxable gifts from prior years		xx,xxx
Total of current and past taxable gifts		$ xx,xxx
Compute the gift tax on the total of current and past taxable gifts by using the rates in Appendix A		$ x,xxx
Subtract: Gift tax paid or deemed paid on past taxable gifts and the unified tax credit		xxx
Gift tax due on transfers during the current period		$ xxx

improve, as the tax will apply only to larger, planned gifts and not to day-to-day transfers. As noted in Chapter 1, the result is to ease the audit function of the IRS. The annual exclusion is indexed to account for *significant* inflation.[8] Under this provision, the exclusion has been $12,000 since 2006.

The formula for the gift tax is summarized in Figure 17–1.

Formula for the Federal Estate Tax. The Federal unified transfer tax at death, commonly known as the Federal estate tax, is summarized in Figure 17–2.

The reason that post-1976 taxable gifts are added to the taxable estate to arrive at the tax base goes back to the scheme of the unified transfer tax. Starting in 1977, all transfers, whether lifetime or by death, were to be treated the same. Consequently, taxable gifts made after 1976 must be accounted for upon the death of the donor. Note that the possible double tax effect of including these gifts is mitigated by allowing a credit against the estate tax for the gift taxes previously paid or deemed paid.

Role of the Unified Tax Credit. Before the unified transfer tax, the gift tax allowed a $30,000 specific exemption for the lifetime of the donor. A comparable $60,000 exemption was allowed for estate tax purposes. The purpose of these exemptions was to allow donors and decedents to transfer modest amounts of wealth without being subject to the gift and estate taxes. Unfortunately, inflation took its toll, and more taxpayers became subject to these transfer taxes than Congress believed was appropriate. The congressional solution was to rescind the exemptions and replace them with the **unified tax credit**.

Table 17–1 shows the unified tax credit applicable to transfers by gift and by death from 2000 through 2011.[9] The Tax Relief Reconciliation Act of 2001 froze the credit applicable to the gift tax at $345,800 (exclusion amount of $1 million). By increasing the exclusion amount, the estate tax is phased out by 2010. For 2010 only, the maximum gift tax rate drops to 35 percent (for taxable gifts over $500,000), and this change results in a credit of $330,800. For 2011, the sunset provision reinstates the credit status that existed for 2002.

LO.3

Work with the Federal estate tax formula.

[8] § 2503(b)(2).

[9] The unified tax credits prior to 2000 can be found in §§ 2010 and 2505.

FIGURE 17–2	Formula for the Federal Estate Tax		
Gross estate (§§ 2031–2046)			$xxx,xxx
Subtract:			
Expenses, indebtedness, and taxes (§ 2053)		$xx	
Losses (§ 2054)		xx	
Charitable bequests (§ 2055)		xx	
Marital deduction (§§ 2056 and 2056A)		xx	
State death taxes (§ 2058)		xx	x,xxx
Taxable estate (§ 2051)			$ xx,xxx
Add: Post-1976 taxable gifts [§ 2001(b)]			x,xxx
Tax base			$xxx,xxx
Tentative tax on tax base [§ 2001(c)]			$ xx,xxx
Subtract:			
Unified transfer tax on post-1976 taxable gifts (gift taxes paid or deemed paid)		$xx	
Tax credits (including the unified tax credit) (§§ 2010–2016)		xx	x,xxx
Estate tax due			$ xxx

The **exclusion amount** (also termed the **exemption equivalent** and the **bypass amount**) is the amount of the transfer that will pass free of the gift or estate tax by virtue of the credit.

EXAMPLE 4

In 2008, Janet makes a taxable gift of $1 million. Presuming she has made no prior taxable gifts, Janet will not owe any gift tax. Under the tax rate schedules (see Appendix A, page A–7), the tax on $1 million is $345,800, which is the exact amount of the credit allowed.[10] ∎

Valuation for Estate and Gift Tax Purposes

The value of the property on the date of its transfer generally determines the amount that is subject to the gift tax or the estate tax. Under certain conditions, however, an executor can elect to value estate assets on the **alternate valuation date**.[11]

The alternate valuation date election was designed as a relief provision to ease the economic hardship that could result when estate assets decline in value over the six months after the date of death. If the election is made, all assets of the estate are valued six months after death *or* on the date of disposition if this occurs earlier.[12] The election covers *all* assets in the gross estate and cannot be applied to only a portion of the property.

---

[10]The rate schedules are contained in § 2001(c), and *some* are reproduced in Appendix A (pages A–4 to A–7) of this text. Neither the credits nor the rate schedules are subject to indexation for inflation.

[11]The election is made by the executor of the estate and is irrevocable. § 2032(d).

[12]§ 2032(a)(1). For this purpose, the term "disposition" is broadly defined. It includes the transfer of property to an heir to satisfy a bequest and the use of property to fund a testamentary trust. Reg. § 20.2032–1(c).

TABLE 17-1	Partial List of Unified Tax Credits

	Gift Tax		Estate Tax	
Year of Transfer	Credit	Exclusion Amount	Credit	Exclusion Amount
2000 and 2001	$220,550	$ 675,000	$ 220,550	$ 675,000
2002 and 2003	345,800	1,000,000	345,800	1,000,000
2004 and 2005	345,800	1,000,000	555,800	1,500,000
2006, 2007, and 2008	345,800	1,000,000	780,800	2,000,000
2009	345,800	1,000,000	1,455,800	3,500,000
2010	330,800	1,000,000	tax repealed	
2011	345,800	1,000,000	345,800	1,000,000

EXAMPLE 5

Robert's gross estate consists of the following property:

	Value on Date of Death	Value Six Months Later
Land	$1,800,000	$1,840,000
Stock in Brown Corporation	900,000	700,000
Stock in Green Corporation	500,000	460,000
Total	$3,200,000	$3,000,000

If Robert's executor elects the alternate valuation date, the estate must be valued at $3 million. It is not permissible to value the land at its date of death value ($1.8 million) and choose the alternate valuation date for the rest of the gross estate. ■

[handwritten note: Probate = to prove well]

[handwritten note: AVD — applied to all assets]

EXAMPLE 6

Assume the same facts as in Example 5, except that the executor sells the stock in Green Corporation for $480,000 four months after Robert's death. If the alternate valuation date is elected, the estate must be valued at $3,020,000 ($1,840,000 + $700,000 + $480,000). As to the Green stock, the value on its date of disposition controls because that date occurred prior to the six months' alternate valuation date. ■

[handwritten note: •If sold selling price gets computed w/ AVD assets b/c it is FMV.]

The alternate valuation date election is not available unless the estate must file a Form 706 (Estate Tax Return). When an estate is required to file a Form 706 is discussed later in this chapter.

The election of the alternate valuation date must decrease the value of the gross estate *and* decrease the estate tax liability.[13] The reason for this last requirement is that the income tax basis of property acquired from a decedent will be the value used for estate tax purposes (discussed further in Chapter 18).[14] Without a special limitation, the alternate valuation date could be elected solely to add to income tax basis.

[handwritten note: AVD must decreases value of: -gross estate AND -estate tax liability]

EXAMPLE 7

Al's gross estate consists of assets with a date of death value of $3 million and an alternate valuation date value of $3.1 million. Under Al's will, all of his property passes outright to Jean (Al's wife). Because of the marital deduction, no estate tax results regardless of which value is used. But if the alternate valuation date could be elected, Jean would have an income tax basis of $3.1 million in the property acquired from Al. ■

[handwritten note: AVD may not be elected here b/c of 2 things above aren't decreased]

[13]§ 2032(c). [14]§ 1014(a).

TAX *in the News*   **WHAT ARE THE CHANCES?**

Under the Tax Relief Reconciliation Act of 2001, the estate tax is scheduled to be phased out by 2010. Even more fantastic, a "sunset" provision in the Act reincarnates this tax as of January 1, 2011. (The "sunset" provision was mandated due to budget considerations.)

What are the chances that all of these provisions will take effect as scheduled? Hopefully, not very high! The sunset reincarnation is particularly absurd and makes meaningful estate planning impossible. Tax practitioners are placed in the ridiculous posture of advising clients to live at least until 2010 but to be sure and die before 2011.

Numerous bills have been introduced in Congress that would modify the scheduled phaseout and subsequent reinstatement of the estate tax. Some of these bills retained the phaseout but rescinded the sunset provision, while other proposals called for an immediate repeal of the estate tax with no later reinstatement. Such proposals, however, remain problematic. Budget deficits, aggravated by the conflict in Iraq, do not favor any further curtailment of the revenue that transfer taxes yield. Also, there is strong conceptual support for some form of an estate tax. Perhaps an acceptable compromise would be a version that provides a generous exclusion amount and contains relief provisions to help preserve family businesses.

The alternate valuation date cannot be elected in Example 7 for two reasons, either of which would suffice. First, the alternate valuation date will not decrease Al's gross estate. Second, the election will not decrease Al's estate tax liability. Thus, his estate must use the date of death valuation of $3 million. As a result, Jean's income tax basis in the property received from Al is $3 million.

ETHICAL and EQUITABLE *Considerations*   **AN EXECUTOR'S PREROGATIVE**

Denny dies in 2007 and is survived by Mary (Denny's second wife) and Rodney (a son from the first marriage). Under Denny's will his property, largely comprising marketable securities, is equally divided between Mary and Rodney with all estate expenses and taxes assigned to Rodney's portion. The will designates Mary as the executor of the estate.

Denny's gross estate has a date of death value of $5 million and an alternate valuation date value of $4.8 million. Although use of the alternate valuation date would save $46,000 in estate taxes, the election is not made. Why is the election not made? Was the failure to make the election improper?

The election of the alternate valuation date does not take into account any postdeath income earned by the property. Any accrued income, therefore, is limited to that existing as of the date of death.

EXAMPLE 8

So on AVD:
• accrued income not counted
• FMV of property +
prior accrued income
before AVD

At the time of her death, Emma owned, among other assets, an apartment building with a value of $800,000 on which $40,000 of rents had accrued. On the alternate valuation date, the property had a value of $780,000 and accrued rents were $30,000. If the § 2032 election is made, $820,000 ($780,000 + $40,000) as to this property is included in Emma's gross estate. The $30,000 of postdeath income is not part of her gross estate. ■

Another valuation option available for estate tax purposes is the special use valuation method. Election of this method is limited to certain situations involving interests in closely held businesses (usually farms). Special use valuation is discussed in Chapter 18.

Key Property Concepts

When property is transferred either by gift or by death, the form of ownership can have a direct bearing on any transfer tax consequences. Understanding the different forms of ownership is necessary for working with Federal gift and estate taxes.

Undivided Ownership. Assume Dan and Vicky own an undivided but equal interest in a tract of land. Such ownership can fall into any of four categories: joint tenancy, tenancy by the entirety, tenancy in common, or community property.

If Dan and Vicky hold ownership as **joint tenants** or **tenants by the entirety**, the right of survivorship exists. This means that the last tenant to survive receives full ownership of the property. Thus, if Dan predeceases Vicky, the land belongs entirely to Vicky. None of the land will pass to Dan's heirs or will be subject to administration by Dan's executor. A tenancy by the entirety is a joint tenancy between husband and wife.

If Dan and Vicky hold ownership as **tenants in common** or as community property, death does not defeat an owner's interest. Thus, if Dan predeceases Vicky, Dan's one-half interest in the land will pass to his estate or heirs.

Community property interests arise from the marital relationship. Normally, all property acquired after marriage, except by gift or inheritance, by husband and wife residing in a community property state becomes part of the community. The following states have the community property system in effect: Louisiana, Texas, New Mexico, Arizona, California, Washington, Idaho, Nevada, Wisconsin, and (by election of the spouses) Alaska. All other states follow the common law system of ascertaining a spouse's rights to property acquired after marriage.

Partial Interests. Interests in assets can be divided in terms of rights to income and principal. Particularly when property is placed in trust, it is not uncommon to carve out various income interests that must be accounted for separately from the ultimate disposition of the property itself.

> Under Bill's will, a ranch is to be placed in trust, life estate to Sam, Bill's son, with remainder to Sam's children (Bill's grandchildren). Under this arrangement, Sam is the life tenant and, as such, is entitled to the use of the ranch (including any income) during his life. Upon Sam's death, the trust terminates, and its principal passes to his children. Thus, Sam's children receive outright ownership in the ranch when Sam dies. ■

EXAMPLE 9

The Federal Gift Tax

General Considerations

LO.4

Understand the operation of the Federal gift tax.

Requirements for a Gift. For a gift to be complete under state law, the following elements must be present.

- A donor competent to make the gift.
- A donee capable of receiving and possessing the property.
- Donative intent on behalf of the donor.
- Actual or constructive delivery of the property to the donee or the donee's representative.
- Acceptance of the gift by the donee.

Incomplete Transfers. The Federal gift tax does not apply to transfers that are incomplete. Thus, if the transferor retains the right to reclaim the property or has not really parted with the possession of the property, a taxable event has not taken place.

| EXAMPLE 10 | Lesly creates a trust, income payable to Mary for life, remainder to Paul. Under the terms of the trust instrument, Lesly can revoke the trust at any time and repossess the trust principal and the income earned. No gift takes place on the creation of the trust; Lesly has not ceased to have dominion and control over the property. ■ |

| EXAMPLE 11  | Assume the same facts as in Example 10, except that one year after the transfer, Lesly relinquishes his right to terminate the trust. At this point, the transfer becomes complete, and the Federal gift tax applies. ■ |

Business versus Personal Setting. In a business setting, full and adequate consideration is apt to exist. If the parties are acting in a personal setting, however, a gift usually is the result.

| EXAMPLE 12 | Grace loans money to Debby in connection with a business venture. About a year later, Grace forgives part of the loan. Grace probably has not made a gift to Debby if she and Debby are unrelated parties.[15] ■ |

| EXAMPLE 13 | Assume the same facts as in Example 12, except that Grace and Debby are mother and daughter and no business venture is involved. If the loan itself was not actually a disguised gift, the later forgiveness is probably a gift. ■ |

It is the position of the IRS that valuable consideration (such as would preclude a gift result) does not include a payment or transfer based on "love and affection . . . promise of marriage, etc."[16] Consequently, property settlements in consideration of marriage (i.e., pre- or antenuptial agreements) are regarded as gifts.

Do not conclude that the presence of *some* consideration is enough to preclude Federal gift tax consequences. Again, the answer may rest on whether the transfer occurred in a business setting.

| EXAMPLE 14 | Peter sells Bob some real estate for $40,000. Unknown to Peter, the property contains valuable mineral deposits and is really worth $200,000. Peter may have made a bad business deal, but he has not made a gift of $160,000 to Bob. ■ |

| EXAMPLE 15 | Assume the same facts as in Example 14, except that Peter and Bob are father and son. In addition, Peter is very much aware that the property is worth $200,000. Peter has made a gift of $160,000 to Bob. ■ |

ETHICAL and EQUITABLE *Considerations*

WHAT CONSTITUTES SUPPORT?

When Earl's daughter, Clara, turns 40, he gives her a Mercedes convertible as a birthday present. Clara is married and has a family of her own. She is a licensed orthopedic surgeon and maintains a successful practice in the field of sports medicine.

Earl does not regard the transfer as being subject to the gift tax. As a parent, he is merely satisfying his obligation of support. Such obligation includes providing your child with transportation. Is Earl's reasoning sound?

---

[15]The forgiveness could result in taxable income to Debby under § 61(a)(12).   [16]Reg. § 25.2512–8.

Certain Excluded Transfers. Transfers to political organizations are exempt from the application of the Federal gift tax.[17] This provision in the Code made unnecessary the previous practice whereby candidates for public office established multiple campaign committees to maximize the number of annual exclusions available to their contributors. As noted later, an annual exclusion of $12,000 for each donee passes free of the Federal gift tax.

The Federal gift tax does not apply to tuition payments made to an educational organization (e.g., a college) on another's behalf. Nor does it apply to amounts paid on another's behalf for medical care.[18] In this regard, the law is realistic since it is unlikely that most donors would recognize these items as transfers subject to the gift tax. The payments, however, must be made directly to the provider (e.g., doctor, hospital, college). There is no requirement that the beneficiary of the service (e.g., patient, student) qualify as a dependent of the person making the payment.

Satisfying an obligation of support is not subject to the gift tax. Thus, no gift takes place when parents pay for their children's education because one of the obligations of parents is to educate their children. What constitutes an obligation of support is determined by applicable state law. In many states, for example, adult children may have an obligation of support with respect to providing for indigent parents.

Lifetime versus Death Transfers. Be careful to distinguish between lifetime *(inter vivos)* and death (testamentary) transfers.

EXAMPLE 16

Dudley buys a 12-month certificate of deposit (CD) from State Bank and lists ownership as follows: "Dudley, payable on proof of death to Faye." Nine months later, Dudley dies. When the CD matures, Faye collects the proceeds from State Bank. No gift takes place when Dudley invests in the CD; Faye has received a mere expectancy (i.e., to obtain ownership of the CD upon Dudley's death). At any time before his death, Dudley may withdraw the funds or delete Faye's name from the account, thereby cutting off her expectancy. Furthermore, no gift occurs upon Dudley's death as the CD passes to Faye by testamentary disposition. As noted later, the CD will be included in Dudley's gross estate as property in which the decedent had an interest (§ 2033). ∎

The payable on death designation used in Example 16 is a form of ownership frequently used in a family setting when investments are involved (e.g., stocks and bonds, savings accounts). Also known as a **Totten trust**, it is very similar in effect to a revocable trust (see Example 10 above). Both carry the advantage of avoiding the probate estate (see Chapter 18). A Totten trust, however, is simpler to use in the case of bank accounts and securities, and it avoids the need of having to create a formal trust.

Transfers Subject to the Gift Tax

Whether a transfer is subject to the Federal gift tax depends upon the application of §§ 2511 through 2519 and the applicable Regulations.

Gift Loans. Loans between related parties are quite common. Such loans are frequently made to help pay for a college education or to finance a new business owned by a family member. Presuming that the advance is a bona fide loan at the outset (i.e., a gift is not intended), the absence of a provision for adequate interest can generate a multitude of tax consequences.

EXAMPLE 17

Harold lends his daughter Venetia $400,000 to start a dental practice. The loan is payable on demand, and no interest is provided for. Assuming a Federal interest rate of 10%, *each year* the loan is outstanding, the following tax consequences ensue.

---

[17]§ 2501(a)(5).

[18]§ 2503(e).

- *Gift tax.* Harold makes a gift to Venetia of $40,000 (10% × $400,000). The annual exclusion is available to offset part of this transfer.
- *Income tax.* Harold has interest income of $40,000, and Venetia has an interest deduction of a like amount.[19] Because it relates to her trade or business, Venetia has a deduction *for* adjusted gross income. ∎

The Code defines a gift loan as "any below-market loan where the foregoing [sic] of interest is in the nature of a gift."[20] Unless tax avoidance was one of the principal purposes of the loan, special limitations apply if the gift loan does not exceed $100,000. In such a case, the interest element may not exceed the borrower's net investment income.[21] Furthermore, if the net investment income does not exceed $1,000, it is treated as zero. Under a $1,000 *de minimis* rule, the interest element is disregarded.

Certain Property Settlements (§ 2516).
Normally, the settlement of certain marital rights is not regarded as being for consideration and is subject to the Federal gift tax.[22] As a special exception to this general approach, Congress enacted § 2516. By this provision, transfers of property interests made under the terms of a written agreement between spouses in settlement of their marital or property rights are deemed to be for adequate consideration. These transfers are exempt from the Federal gift tax if a final decree of divorce is obtained within the three-year period beginning on the date one year before the parties entered into the agreement. Likewise excluded are transfers to provide a reasonable allowance for the support of minor children (including legally adopted children) of a marriage. The agreement need not be approved by the divorce decree.

Disclaimers (§ 2518).
A disclaimer is a refusal by a person to accept property that is designated to pass to him or her. The effect of the disclaimer is to pass the property to someone else.

EXAMPLE 18

Earl dies without a will and is survived by a son, Andy, and a grandson, Jay. At the time of his death, Earl owned real estate that, under the applicable state law, passes to the closest lineal descendant, Andy in this case. If, however, Andy disclaims his interest in the real estate, state law provides that the property passes to Jay. At the time of Earl's death, Andy has considerable property of his own, and Jay has none. ∎

Why might Andy want to consider disclaiming his inheritance and have the property pass directly from Earl to Jay? By doing so, an extra transfer tax may be avoided. If the disclaimer does not take place (i.e., Andy accepts the inheritance) and the property eventually passes to Jay (either by gift or by death), the later transfer is subject to the application of either the gift tax or the estate tax.

The Federal gift tax can also be avoided in cases of a partial disclaimer of an undivided interest.

EXAMPLE 19

Assume the same facts as in Example 18, except that Andy wishes to retain half of the real estate for himself. If Andy makes a timely disclaimer of an undivided one-half interest in the property, the Federal gift tax does not apply to the portion passing to Jay. ∎

To be effective, the disclaimer must be timely made. Generally, this means no later than nine months after the right to the property arose. Furthermore, the

---

[19]Example 20 in Chapter 1 deals with a similar situation and also covers any nonbusiness bad debt deduction the creditor might have if the loan is not repaid.
[20]§ 7872(f)(3).

[21]Net investment income has the same meaning given to the term by § 163(d). Generally, net investment income is investment income (e.g., interest, dividends) less related expenses.
[22]Reg. § 25.2512–8.

person making the disclaimer must not have accepted any benefits or interest in the property.

Other Transfers Subject to Gift Tax. Other transfers that may carry gift tax consequences (e.g., the exercise of a power of appointment, the creation of joint ownership) are discussed and illustrated in connection with the Federal estate tax.

Income Tax Considerations. Generally, a donor has no income tax consequences on making a gift.[23] A donee recognizes no income on the receipt of a gift.[24] A donee's income tax basis in the property received depends on a number of factors (e.g., donor's basis, year of gift, gift tax incurred by donor) and is discussed elsewhere in this text.[25]

Annual Exclusion

In General. The first $12,000 ($11,000 prior to 2006) of gifts made to any one person during any calendar year (except gifts of future interests in property) is excluded in determining the total amount of gifts for the year.[26] The **annual exclusion** applies to all gifts of a present interest made during the calendar year in the order in which they are made until the $12,000 exclusion per donee is exhausted. For a gift in trust, each beneficiary of the trust is treated as a separate person for purposes of the exclusion.

A **future interest** is defined as one that will come into being (as to use, possession, or enjoyment) at some future date. Examples of future interests include such rights as remainder interests that are commonly encountered when property is transferred to a trust. A *present interest* is an unrestricted right to the immediate use, possession, or enjoyment of property or of the income.

During 2008, Laura makes the following cash gifts: $8,000 to Rita and $13,000 to Maureen. Laura may claim an annual exclusion of $8,000 with respect to Rita and $12,000 with respect to Maureen. ∎	*EXAMPLE 20*

By a lifetime gift, Ron transfers property to a trust with a life estate (with income payable annually) to June and remainder upon June's death to Albert. Ron has made two gifts: one to June of a life estate and one to Albert of a remainder interest. (The valuation of each of these gifts is discussed in Chapter 18.) The life estate is a present interest and qualifies for the annual exclusion. The remainder interest granted to Albert is a future interest and does not qualify for the exclusion. Note that Albert's interest does not come into being until some future date (on the death of June). ∎	*EXAMPLE 21*

Although Example 21 indicates that the gift of an income interest is a present interest, this is not always the case. If a possibility exists that the income beneficiary may not receive the immediate enjoyment of the property, the transfer is of a future interest.

Assume the same facts as in Example 21, except that the income from the trust need not be payable annually to June. It may, at the trustee's discretion, be accumulated and added to the principal. Since June's right to receive the income from the trust is conditioned on the trustee's discretion, it is not a present interest. No annual exclusion is allowed. The mere possibility of diversion is enough. It would not matter if the trustee never exercised the discretion to accumulate and did, in fact, distribute the trust income to June annually. ∎	*EXAMPLE 22*

---

[23]For situations where recognition can occur, see Chapter 18, page 18–23.
[24]Both gifts and inheritances are excluded from income under § 103.

[25]Section 1015 is discussed and illustrated in Chapter 18, pages 18–12 to 18–14.
[26]§ 2503(b).

[handwritten margin note: "If 21 or under, interests passed to that person are present"]

Trust for Minors. Section 2503(c) offers an important exception to the future interest rules just discussed. Under this provision, a transfer for the benefit of a person who has not attained the age of 21 years on the date of the gift may be considered a gift of a present interest. This is true even though the minor is not given the unrestricted right to the immediate use, possession, or enjoyment of the property. For the exception to apply, the following conditions must be satisfied.

- Both the property and its income may be expended by or for the benefit of the minor before the minor attains the age of 21.
- Any portion of the property or its income not expended by the time the minor reaches the age of 21 shall pass to the minor at that time.
- If the minor dies before attaining the age of 21, the property and its income will be payable either to the minor's estate or as the minor may designate under a general power of appointment (discussed later in the chapter).

The exception allows a trustee to accumulate income on behalf of a minor beneficiary without converting the income interest to a future interest.

EXAMPLE 23	Bret places property in trust, income payable to Billy until he reaches 21, remainder to Billy or Billy's estate. Under the terms of the trust instrument, the trustee is empowered to accumulate the trust income or apply it toward Billy's benefit. In either event, the accumulated income and principal must be paid to Billy whenever he reaches 21 years of age or to whomever Billy designates in his will if he dies before reaching that age. The conditions of § 2503(c) are satisfied, and Bret's transfer qualifies for the annual exclusion. Billy's interest is a present interest. ∎

From a nontax standpoint, the § 2503(c) exception makes good sense. After all, it avoids making trustees distribute income to a minor just to obtain an annual exclusion. In many situations, providing the minor with more than modest sums may be unwise.

Contributions to Qualified Tuition Programs. For income tax purposes, § 529 plans have become the best of all possible worlds. Although no up-front deduction is allowed,[27] income earned by the fund accumulates free of income tax, and distributions are not taxed if they are used for higher education purposes. A special provision allows a donor to enjoy a gift tax advantage by using five years of annual exclusions.[28]

EXAMPLE 24	Trevor and Audrey would like to start building a college education fund for their 10-year-old granddaughter, Loni. In 2008, Trevor contributes $120,000 to the designated carrier of their state's § 529 plan. By electing to split the gift and using five annual exclusions [2 (number of donors) × $12,000 (annual exclusion) × 5 years = $120,000], no taxable gift results. (The gift-splitting election is discussed in detail later in this chapter.) ∎

Making the five-year election precludes Trevor and Audrey from using any annual exclusion on gifts to Loni for the next four years.[29] If either donor dies before the period is up, the annual exclusions are allocated pro rata in computing the gross estate.

---

[27]Depending on the taxpayer's home state, some (or all) of the deduction may be allowed for *state* income tax purposes.

[28]Section 529(c)(2)(A) protects against future interest treatment.

[29]Trevor and Audrey could resort to § 2503(e)(2)(A) to avoid any gift at all. As mentioned earlier, a *direct* payment of tuition to certain educational institutions is exempt from the gift tax. But this rule does not help to build an education fund for future use, as § 529 does. Recall that Loni, the granddaughter, is 10 years old.

The election does not, however, impair the availability of the annual exclusion as to gifts to *other* donees.

Section 529(c)(4) provides that these college plans are not to be included in the gross estate of the transferor. This preferential treatment is needed because § 529 plans are incomplete transfers (some or all of the funds may be returned if college is not attended). As noted later, incomplete transfers are invariably subject to the estate tax.

Deductions

In arriving at taxable gifts, a deduction is allowed for transfers to certain qualified charitable organizations. On transfers between spouses, a marital deduction may be available. Since both the charitable and marital deductions apply in determining the Federal estate tax, these deductions are discussed later in the chapter.

Computing the Federal Gift Tax

> **LO.5**
>
> Compute the Federal gift tax.

The Unified Transfer Tax Rate Schedule.

The top rates of the unified transfer tax rate schedule originally reached as high as 70 percent. Over the years, these top rates were reduced to 55 percent. Under the Tax Relief Reconciliation Act of 2001, the top rate was reduced to 45 percent in 2007 (46 percent in 2006, 47 percent in 2005, 48 percent in 2004, and 49 percent in 2003).[30] Keep in mind that the unified transfer tax rate schedule applies to all transfers (by gift or death) after 1976 and before 2010. Different rate schedules apply for pre-1977 gifts and pre-1977 deaths.

The Deemed Paid Adjustment.

Review the formula for the gift tax in Figure 17–1, and note that the tax base for a current gift includes *all* past taxable gifts. The effect of the inclusion is to force the current taxable gift into a higher bracket due to the progressive nature of the unified transfer tax rates (refer to Example 2). To mitigate such double taxation, the donor is allowed a credit for any gift tax previously paid or deemed paid (refer to Example 3).

Limiting the donor to a credit for the gift tax *actually paid* on pre-1977 taxable gifts would be unfair. Pre-1977 taxable gifts were subject to a lower set of rates than those in the unified transfer tax rate schedule. As a consequence, the donor is allowed a *deemed paid* credit on pre-1977 taxable gifts. This is the amount that would have been due under the unified transfer tax rate schedule had it been applicable. *Post-1976* taxable gifts *also* are subject to the deemed paid adjustment since the same rate schedule may not be involved in all gifts. Compare the variation in rates in Appendix A, pages A–4 through A–7. For post-1976 taxable gifts, it is entirely possible that the deemed paid credit allowed could be *less* than the gift tax that was actually paid.

EXAMPLE 25

In 2000, Carla made a taxable gift of $3 million, which resulted in a Federal gift tax of $1,070,250* (see Appendix A, page A–4). In 2008, Carla makes another taxable gift of $3 million. The tax on the 2008 gift is determined as follows.

Taxable gift made in 2008	$3,000,000
Add taxable gift made in 2000	3,000,000
Total of current and past taxable gifts	$6,000,000

---

[30]§ 2001(c)(2)(B). Note the drop in the top rate from 50% to 45% in the rate schedules for 2002 through 2007, reproduced in Appendix A (pages A–5, A–6, and A–7). The rates for 2008 are on page A–7 and on the inside of the back cover of the text.

Unified transfer tax on $6,000,000 per Appendix A, page A–7 [$555,800 + 45%($6,000,000 − $1,500,000)]		$2,580,800
Subtract:		
Deemed paid tax on 2000 gift—use Appendix A, page A-7 [$555,800 + 45%($3,000,000 − $1,500,000)]	$1,010,250*	
Unified credit for 2008	345,800	(1,356,050)
Gift tax due on the 2008 gift		$1,224,750

* Adjusted for the $220,550 unified credit available for year 2000 (see Table 17–1).

Note that Carla's deemed paid credit allowed is $60,000 *less* than was originally paid ($1,070,250 − $1,010,250). As previously mentioned, the variance is due to the tax rate changes that have taken place since 2000. ∎

The Election to Split Gifts by Married Persons.
To understand the reason for the gift-splitting election of § 2513, consider the following situations:

EXAMPLE 26

Dick and Margaret are husband and wife and reside in Michigan, a common law state. Dick has been the only breadwinner in the family, and Margaret has no significant property of her own. Neither has made any prior taxable gifts or has used the $30,000 specific exemption previously available for pre-1977 gifts. In 2008, Dick makes a gift to Leslie of $2,024,000. Presuming the election to split gifts did not exist, Dick's gift tax is as follows.

Amount of gift	$2,024,000
Subtract: Annual exclusion	(12,000)
Taxable gift	$2,012,000
Gift tax on $2,012,000 per Appendix A, page A–7 [$780,800 + (45% × $12,000)]	$ 786,200
Subtract: Unified transfer tax credit for 2008	(345,800)
Gift tax due on the 2008 taxable gift	$ 440,400

∎

EXAMPLE 27

Assume the same facts as in Example 26, except that Dick and Margaret always have resided in California (a community property state). Even though Dick is the sole breadwinner, income from personal services generally is community property. Consequently, the gift to Leslie probably involves community property. If this is the case, the gift tax is as follows.

	Dick	Margaret
Amount of gift	$1,012,000	$1,012,000
Subtract: Annual exclusion	12,000	12,000
Taxable gift	$1,000,000	$1,000,000
Gift tax on $1,000,000 per Appendix A, page A–7	$ 345,800	$ 345,800
Subtract: Unified transfer tax credit for 2008	345,800	345,800
Gift tax due on the 2008 taxable gift	$ –0–	$ –0–

∎

As the results of Examples 26 and 27 indicate, married donors residing in community property jurisdictions possessed a significant gift tax advantage over those residing in common law states. To rectify this inequity, the Revenue Act of 1948 incorporated into the Code the predecessor to § 2513. Under this provision, a gift made by a person to someone other than his or her spouse may be considered, for

Federal gift tax purposes, as having been made one-half by each spouse. Returning to Example 26, Dick and Margaret could treat the gift passing to Leslie as being made one-half by each of them. They may do this even though the cash belonged to Dick. As a result, the parties are able to achieve the same tax consequence as in Example 27.

To split gifts, the spouses must be legally married to each other at the time of the gift. If they are divorced later in the calendar year, they may still split the gift if neither marries anyone else during that year. They both must indicate on their separate gift tax returns their consent to have all gifts made in that calendar year split between them. In addition, both must be citizens or residents of the United States on the date of the gift. A gift from one spouse to the other spouse cannot be split. Such a gift might, however, be eligible for the marital deduction.

The election to split gifts is not necessary when husband and wife transfer community property to a third party. It is available, however, if the gift consists of the separate property of one of the spouses. Generally, separate property is property acquired before marriage and property acquired after marriage by gift or inheritance. The election, then, is not limited to residents of common law states.

Procedural Matters

Having determined which transfers are subject to the Federal gift tax and the various deductions and exclusions available to the donor, the procedural aspects of the tax should be considered. The following section discusses the return itself, the due dates for filing and paying the tax, and other related matters.

The Federal Gift Tax Return. For transfers by gift, a Form 709 (U.S. Gift Tax Return) must be filed whenever the gifts for any one calendar year exceed the annual exclusion or involve a gift of a future interest. A Form 709 need not be filed, however, for transfers between spouses that are offset by the unlimited marital deduction regardless of the amount of the transfer.[31]

In 2008, Larry makes five gifts, each in the amount of $12,000, to his five children. If the gifts do not involve future interests, a Form 709 need not be filed to report the transfers. ∎

EXAMPLE 28

During 2008, Esther makes a gift of $24,000 cash of her separate property to her daughter. To double the amount of the annual exclusion allowed, Jerry (Esther's husband) is willing to split the gift. Since the § 2513 election can be made only on a gift tax return, a Form 709 must be filed even though no gift tax will be due as a result of the transfer. ∎

EXAMPLE 29

In Example 29, no gift tax return would be necessary if the transfer consisted of community property. Since two donors are now involved, the cap for filing becomes more than $24,000, rather than more than $12,000.

Presuming a gift tax return is due, it must be filed on or before the fifteenth day of April following the year of the gift.[32] As is the case with other Federal taxes, when the due date falls on Saturday, Sunday, or a legal holiday, the date for filing the return is the next business day. Note that the filing requirements for Form 709 have no correlation to the accounting year used by a donor for Federal income tax purposes. Thus, a fiscal year taxpayer must follow the April 15 rule for any reportable gifts. If sufficient reason is shown, the IRS is authorized to grant reasonable extensions of time for filing the return.[33]

---

[31] § 6019(a)(2).
[32] § 6075(b)(1).

[33] § 6081. Under § 6075(b)(2), an extension of time granted to a calendar year taxpayer for filing an income tax return automatically extends the due date of a gift tax return.

CONCEPT SUMMARY 17–1

Federal Gift Tax Provisions

1. The Federal gift tax applies to all gratuitous transfers of property made by U.S. citizens or residents. In this regard, it does not matter where the property is located.
2. In the eyes of the IRS, a gratuitous transfer is one not supported by full and adequate consideration. If the parties are acting in a business setting, such consideration usually exists. If, however, purported sales are between family members, a gift element may be suspected.
3. If one party lends money to another and intends some or all of the interest element to be a gift, the arrangement is categorized as a gift loan. To the extent that the interest provided for is less than the market rate, three tax consequences result. First, a gift has taken place between the lender and the borrower as to the interest element. Second, income may result to the lender. Third, an income tax deduction may be available to the borrower.
4. Property settlements can escape the gift tax if a divorce occurs within a prescribed period of time.

5. A disclaimer is a refusal by a person to accept property designated to pass to that person. The effect of a disclaimer is to pass the property to someone else. If certain conditions are satisfied, the issuance of a disclaimer will not be subject to the Federal gift tax.
6. Except for gifts of future interests, a donor is allowed an annual exclusion of $12,000. The future interest limitation does not apply to certain trusts created for minors.
7. The election to split a gift enables a married couple to be treated as two donors. The election doubles the annual exclusion and makes the nonowner spouse's unified tax credit available to the owner spouse.
8. The election to split gifts is not necessary if the property is jointly owned by the spouses. That is the case when the property is part of the couple's community.
9. In determining the tax base for computing the gift tax, all prior taxable gifts must be added to current taxable gifts. Thus, the gift tax is cumulative in nature.
10. Gifts are reported on Form 709. The return is due on April 15 following the year of the gift.

The Federal Estate Tax

The following discussion of the estate tax coincides with the formula that appeared earlier in the chapter in Figure 17–2. The key components in the formula are the gross estate, the taxable estate, the tax base, and the credits allowed against the tentative tax. This formula can be summarized as follows:

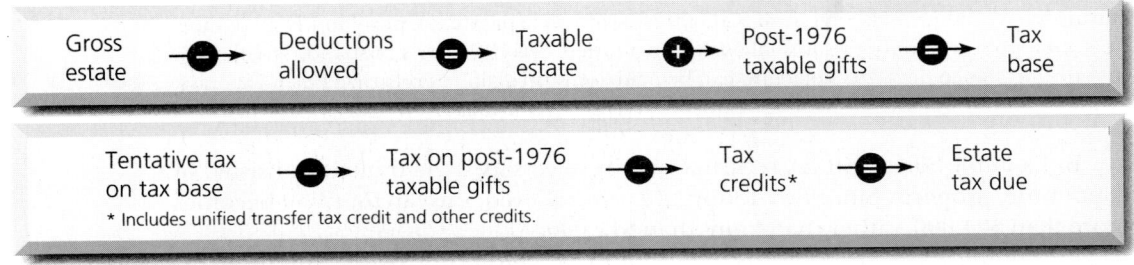

LO.6

Recognize the components of the gross estate.

Gross Estate

Simply stated, the **gross estate** includes all property subject to the Federal estate tax. This depends on the provisions of the Internal Revenue Code as supplemented by IRS pronouncements and the judicial interpretations of Federal courts.

In contrast to the gross estate, the **probate estate** is controlled by state (rather than Federal) law. The probate estate consists of all of a decedent's property subject to administration by the executor or administrator of the estate. The administration is supervised by a local court of appropriate jurisdiction (usually designated as a probate court). An executor (or executrix) is the decedent's personal representative

DEATH TAXES WORLDWIDE

As can be seen from the sample below, the maximum rate of the death tax levied in other countries varies considerably. Several countries impose no death tax at all.

Nation	Maximum Rate	Nation	Maximum Rate
Japan	70%	Austria	15%
Taiwan	50	Brazil	6
Korea	45	Argentina	0
United States	45	Australia	0
United Kingdom	40	India	0
France	40	Russia	0
Germany	30	Sweden	0
Chile	25	Switzerland	0
Ireland	20		

GLOBAL *Tax Issues*

appointed under the decedent's will. When a decedent dies without a will or fails to name an executor in the will (or that person refuses to serve), the local probate court appoints an administrator (or administratrix).

The probate estate is frequently smaller than the gross estate. It contains only property owned by the decedent at the time of death and passing to heirs under a will or under the law of intestacy (the order of distribution for those dying without a will). As noted later, such items as the proceeds of many life insurance policies and distributions from retirement plans become part of the gross estate but are not included in the probate estate.

All states provide for an order of distribution in the event someone dies *intestate* (i.e., without a will). After the surviving spouse, who receives some or all of the estate, the preference is usually in the following order: down to lineal descendants (e.g., children, grandchildren), up to lineal ascendants (e.g., parents, grandparents), and out to collateral relations (e.g., brothers, sisters, aunts, and uncles).

Property Owned by the Decedent (§ 2033). Property owned by the decedent at the time of death is included in the gross estate. The nature of the property or the use to which it was put during the decedent-owner's lifetime has no significance as far as the estate tax is concerned. Thus, personal effects (such as clothing), stocks, bonds, furniture, jewelry, works of art, bank accounts, and interests in businesses conducted as sole proprietorships and partnerships are all included in the deceased owner's gross estate. No distinction is made between tangible and intangible, depreciable and nondepreciable, business and personal assets. However, a deceased spouse's gross estate does not include the surviving spouse's share of the community property.

The application of § 2033 is illustrated as follows:

Handwritten margin notes: "Probate estate is frequently smaller than the gross estate" and "A Deceased spouse's gross estate does not include: surviving spouse's share of community property"

EXAMPLE 30

Irma dies owning some City of Denver bonds. The fair market value of the bonds plus any interest accrued to the date of Irma's death is included in her gross estate. Although interest on municipals is normally not taxable under the Federal income tax, it is property owned by Irma at the time of death. However, any interest accrued after death is not part of Irma's gross estate. ■

EXAMPLE 31

Sharon dies on April 8, 2008, at a time when she owns stock in Robin Corporation and Wren Corporation. On March 3 of this year, both corporations authorized a cash dividend payable on May 5. Robin's dividend is payable to shareholders of record as of April 3. Wren's date of record is April 11. Sharon's gross estate includes the following: the stock in Robin

Corporation, the stock in Wren Corporation, and the dividend on the Robin stock. It does not include the dividend on the Wren stock. ■

| EXAMPLE 32 | Ray dies holding some promissory notes issued to him by his son. In his will, Ray forgives these notes, relieving the son of the obligation to make any payments. The fair market value of these notes is included in Ray's gross estate. ■ |

| EXAMPLE 33 | At the time of his death on a business trip, Ray was a consulting engineer for Falcon Corporation. Ray's estate receives a distribution from Falcon's qualified pension plan of $1.1 million consisting of the following:

Falcon's contributions	$450,000
Ray's after-tax contributions	350,000
Income earned by the plan	300,000

Ray's estate also receives $150,000 from Hawk Insurance Company. The payment represents the maturity value of term life insurance from a group plan Falcon maintains for its employees. As to these amounts, Ray's gross estate includes $1,250,000 ($1,100,000 + $150,000). For income tax purposes, however, $750,000 ($450,000 + $300,000) is subject to tax, while $500,000 ($350,000 + $150,000) is not. ■ |

Regarding the result reached in Example 33, retirement plan benefits are invariably subject to estate tax. Besides the conventional qualified pension and profit-sharing plans involved in Example 33, retirement plans include those under § 401(k), § 403(b) for teachers, § 457 for government employees, Keogh (H.R. 10) for self-employed persons, and IRAs—both traditional and Roth. Inclusion in the gross estate occurs irrespective of income tax consequences. Thus, a benefit paid under a Roth IRA is fully subject to the estate tax even though it may not be taxable as income to the beneficiary. The possibility of an income tax deduction for estate taxes paid is covered in Chapter 19 in connection with the discussion of income in respect of a decedent.

Dower and Curtesy Interests (§ 2034).
In its common law (nonstatutory) form, dower generally gave a surviving widow a life estate in a portion of her husband's estate (usually the real estate he owned) with the remainder passing to their children. Most states have modified and codified these common law rules, and the resulting statutes often vary between jurisdictions. Curtesy is a similar right held by the husband in his wife's property that takes effect in the event he survives her.

Dower and curtesy rights are incomplete interests and may never materialize. Thus, if a wife predeceases her husband, the dower interest in her husband's property is lost.

| EXAMPLE 34 | Martin dies without a will, leaving an estate of $3.9 million. Under state law, Belinda (Martin's widow) is entitled to one-third of his property. The $1.3 million Belinda receives is included in Martin's gross estate. Depending on the nature of the interest Belinda receives in the $1.3 million, this amount could qualify Martin's estate for a marital deduction. (This possibility is discussed at greater length later in the chapter. For the time being, however, the focus is on what is or is not included as part of the decedent's gross estate.) ■ |

Adjustments for Gifts Made within Three Years of Death (§ 2035).
At one time, all taxable gifts made within three years of death were included in the donor's gross estate unless it could be shown that the gifts were not made in contemplation of death. The three-year rule has been retained for the following items:

- Inclusion in the gross estate of any gift tax paid on gifts made within three years of death. Called the *gross-up* procedure, it prevents the gift tax amount from escaping the estate tax.

- Any property interests transferred by gift within three years of death that would have been included in the gross estate by virtue of the application of § 2036 (transfers with a retained life estate), § 2037 (transfers taking effect at death), § 2038 (revocable transfers), and § 2042 (proceeds of life insurance). All except § 2037 are discussed later in the chapter.

EXAMPLE 35

Before her death in 2008, Jennifer made the following taxable gifts.

Year of Gift	Nature of the Asset	Fair Market Value		Gift Tax Paid
		Date of Gift	Date of Death	
1992	Hawk Corporation stock	$100,000	$ 150,000	$ –0–
2006	Policy on Jennifer's life	80,000	1,000,000	–0–
		(cash value)	(face value)	
2007	Land	800,000	810,000	16,000

Jennifer's *gross estate* includes $1,016,000 [$1,000,000 (life insurance proceeds) + $16,000 (gross-up for the gift tax on the 2007 taxable gift)] as to these transfers. Referring to the formula for the estate tax (see Figure 17–2), the other post-1976 taxable gifts are added to the *taxable estate* (at the fair market value on the date of the gift) in arriving at the tax base. Jennifer's estate is allowed a credit for the gift tax paid (or deemed paid) on the 2007 transfer. ■

The three-year rule also applies in testing for qualification under § 303 (stock redemptions to pay death taxes and administration expenses), § 2032A (special valuation procedures), and § 6166 (extensions of time to pay death taxes).[34] All these provisions are discussed in Chapter 18.

Transfers with a Retained Life Estate (§ 2036).

Code §§ 2036 through 2038 were enacted on the premise that the estate tax can be avoided on lifetime transfers only if the decedent does not retain control over the property. The logic of this approach is somewhat difficult to dispute. One should not be able to escape the tax consequences of property transfers at death while remaining in a position to enjoy some or all of the fruits of ownership during life.

Under § 2036, the value of any property transferred by the deceased during lifetime for less than adequate consideration must be included if either of the following was retained:

- The possession or enjoyment of, or the right to the income from, the property.
- The right, either alone or in conjunction with any person, to designate the persons who shall possess or enjoy the property or the income.

"The possession or enjoyment of, or the right to the income from, the property," as it appears in § 2036(a)(1), is considered to have been retained by the decedent to the extent that such income, etc., is to be applied toward the discharge of a legal obligation of the decedent. The term "legal obligation" includes a legal obligation of the decedent to support a dependent during the decedent's lifetime.[35]

The following examples illustrate the practical application of § 2036.

EXAMPLE 36

Carl's will passes all of his property to a trust, income to Alan for his life (Alan is given a life estate). Upon Alan's death, the principal goes to Melissa (Melissa is granted a remainder interest). On Alan's death, none of the trust property is included in his gross estate. Although Alan held a life estate, § 2036 is inapplicable because he was not the transferor (Carl was) of

---

[34]§§ 2035(c)(1) and (2).   [35]Reg. § 20.2036–1(b)(2).

the property. Section 2033 (property owned by the decedent) causes any income distributions Alan was entitled to receive at the time of his death to be included in his gross estate. ∎

EXAMPLE 37

By deed, Nora transfers the remainder interest in her ranch to Marcia, retaining for herself the right to continue occupying the property until death. Upon Nora's death, the fair market value of the ranch is included in her gross estate. Furthermore, Nora is subject to the gift tax. The amount of the gift is the fair market value of the ranch on the date of the gift less the portion applicable to Nora's retained life estate. (See Chapter 18 for the way this gift is determined.) ∎

Revocable Transfers (§ 2038).   Another type of lifetime transfer that is drawn into a decedent's gross estate is covered by § 2038. The gross estate includes the value of property interests transferred by the decedent (except to the extent that the transfer was made for full consideration) if the enjoyment of the property transferred was subject, at the date of the decedent's death, to any power of the decedent to *alter, amend, revoke, or terminate* the transfer. This includes the power to change the beneficiaries or the power to accelerate or increase any beneficiary's enjoyment of the property.

The Code and the Regulations make it clear that one cannot avoid inclusion in the gross estate under § 2038 by relinquishing a power within three years of death.[36] Recall that § 2038 is one of several types of situations listed as exceptions to the usual rule excluding gifts made within three years of death from the gross estate.

In the event § 2038 applies, the amount includible in the gross estate is the portion of the property transferred that is subject, at the decedent's death, to the decedent's power to alter, amend, revoke, or terminate.

The classic § 2038 situation results from the use of a revocable trust.

EXAMPLE 38

Maria creates a trust, life estate to her children, remainder to her grandchildren. Under the terms of the trust, Maria reserves the right to revoke the trust and revest the trust principal and income in herself. As noted in Example 10, the creation of the trust does not result in a gift because the transfer is not complete. However, if Maria dies still retaining the power to revoke, the trust is included in her gross estate under § 2038. ∎

Annuities (§ 2039).   Annuities can be divided by their origin into commercial and noncommercial contracts. Noncommercial annuities are issued by private parties and, in some cases, charitable organizations that do not regularly issue annuities. The two varieties have much in common, but noncommercial annuities present special income tax problems and are not treated further in this discussion.

Regulation § 20.2039–1(b)(1) defines an annuity as representing "one or more payments extending over any period of time." According to the Regulation, the payments may be equal or unequal, conditional or unconditional, periodic or sporadic. Annuity contracts that terminate upon the death of the person covered (i.e., annuitant) are designated as straight-life annuities. Other contracts provide for a survivorship feature (e.g., reduced payments to a surviving spouse).

In the case of a straight-life annuity, nothing is included in the gross estate of the annuitant at death. Section 2033 (property in which the decedent had an interest) does not apply because the annuitant's interest in the contract is terminated by death. Section 2036 (transfers with a retained life estate) does not cover the situation; a transfer made for full consideration is specifically excluded from § 2036 treatment. A commercial annuity is presumed to have been purchased for full consideration unless some evidence exists to indicate that the parties were not acting at arm's length.

[handwritten: except for payments received prior to death]

---

[36]§ 2038(a)(1) and Reg. § 20.2038–1(e)(1).

Annuities

EXAMPLE 39

Arnold purchases a straight-life annuity that will pay him $24,000 a month when he reaches age 65. Arnold dies at age 70. Except for the payments he received before his death, nothing relating to this annuity affects Arnold's gross estate. ■

In the case of a survivorship annuity, the estate tax consequences under § 2039(a) are usually triggered by the death of the first annuitant. The amount included in the gross estate is the cost from the same company of a comparable annuity covering the survivor at his or her attained age on the date of the deceased annuitant's death.

EXAMPLE 40

Assume the same facts as in Example 39, except that the annuity contract provides for Veronica to be paid $12,000 a month for life as a survivorship feature. Veronica is 62 years of age when Arnold dies. Under these circumstances, Arnold's gross estate includes the cost of a comparable contract that provides an annuity of $12,000 per month for the life of a female, age 62. ■

Full inclusion of the survivorship element in the gross estate is subject to an exception under § 2039(b). The amount includible is to be based on the proportion of the deceased annuitant's contribution to the total cost of the contract. This is expressed by the following formula:

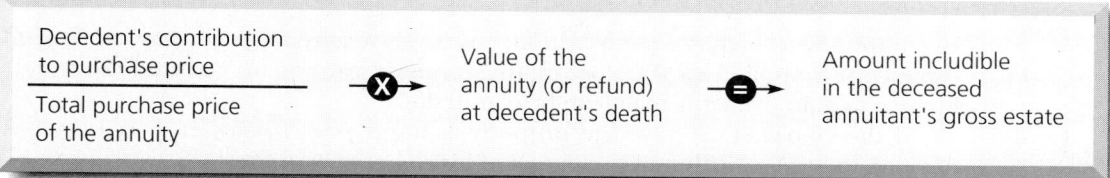

EXAMPLE 41

Assume the same facts as in Example 40, except that Arnold and Veronica are husband and wife and have always lived in a community property state. The premiums on the contract were paid with community funds. Since Veronica contributed half of the cost of the contract, only half of the amount determined under Example 40 is included in Arnold's gross estate. ■

The result reached in Example 41 is not unique to community property jurisdictions. The outcome would have been the same in a noncommunity property state if Veronica had furnished half of the consideration from her own funds.

In determining a decedent's contribution to an annuity contract, a special rule applies to employment-related retirement plans. In these cases, the employer's contribution to the plan is treated as having been made by the employee.

EXAMPLE 42

Under a noncontributory qualified retirement plan funded by his employer, Jim is entitled to an annuity for life. The plan also provides for a survivorship annuity for Jim's wife, Ellen, in the event he predeceases her. Upon Jim's prior death, the value of the survivorship annuity is included in his gross estate. Jim did not actually contribute to the cost of the annuity, but his employer's contributions are attributed to him. ■

Joint Interests (§§ 2040 and 2511).

Recall that joint tenancies and tenancies by the entirety are characterized by the right of survivorship. Thus, upon the death of a joint tenant, title to the property passes to the surviving tenant. None of the property is included in the *probate* estate of the deceased tenant. In the case of tenancies in common and community property, death does not defeat an ownership interest. Further, the deceased owner's interest is part of the probate estate.

The Federal *estate tax treatment* of tenancies in common or of community property follows the logical approach of taxing only the portion of the property included in the deceased owner's probate estate.

EXAMPLE 43

Homer, Wilma, and Thelma acquire a tract of land, ownership listed as tenants in common, each party furnishing $200,000 of the $600,000 purchase price. When the property is worth $900,000, Homer dies. If Homer's undivided interest in the property is 33⅓%, the gross estate *and* probate estate each include $300,000. This one-third interest is also the same amount that passes to Homer's heirs. ■

Unless the parties have provided otherwise, each tenant is deemed to own an interest equal to the portion of the original consideration he or she furnished. The parties in Example 43 could have provided that Homer would receive an undivided half interest in the property although he contributed only one-third of the purchase price. In that case, Wilma and Thelma have made a gift to Homer when the tenancy was created, and Homer's gross estate and probate estate each include $450,000.

For certain joint tenancies, the tax consequences are different. All of the property is included in the deceased co-owner's gross estate unless it can be proved that the surviving co-owners contributed to the cost of the property.[37] If a contribution can be shown, the amount to be *excluded* is calculated by the following formula:

$$\frac{\text{Surviving co-owner's contribution}}{\text{Total cost of the property}} \times \text{Fair market value of the property}$$

In computing a survivor's contribution, any funds received as a gift *from the deceased co-owner* and applied to the cost of the property cannot be counted. However, income or gain from gift assets can be counted.

If the co-owners receive the property as a gift *from another,* each co-owner is deemed to have contributed to the cost of his or her own interest.

The preceding rules can be illustrated as follows.

EXAMPLE 44

Keith and Steve (father and son) acquire a tract of land, ownership listed as joint tenancy with right of survivorship. Keith furnished $400,000 and Steve $200,000 of the $600,000 purchase price. Of the $200,000 provided by Steve, $100,000 had previously been received as a gift from Keith. When the property is worth $900,000, Keith dies. Because only $100,000 of Steve's contribution can be counted (the other $100,000 was received as a gift from Keith), Steve has furnished only one-sixth ($100,000/$600,000) of the cost. Thus, Keith's gross estate must include five-sixths of $900,000, or $750,000. This presumes Steve can prove that he did in fact make the $100,000 contribution. In the absence of such proof, the full value of the property is included in Keith's gross estate. Keith's death makes Steve the immediate owner of the property by virtue of the right of survivorship. None of the property is part of Keith's probate estate. ■

EXAMPLE 45

Francis transfers property to Irene and Martin as a gift, listing ownership as joint tenancy with the right of survivorship. Upon Irene's death, one-half of the value of the property is included in the gross estate. Since the property was received as a gift and the donees are equal owners, each is considered to have furnished half of the consideration. ■

To simplify the joint ownership rules for *married persons,* § 2040(b) provides for an automatic inclusion rule upon the death of the first joint-owner spouse to die. Regardless of the amount contributed by each spouse, one-half of the value of the property is included in the gross estate of the spouse who dies first. The special rule eliminates the need to trace the source of contributions and recognizes that any inclusion in the gross estate is neutralized by the marital deduction.

[37]§ 2040(a).

Hank purchases real estate for $300,000 using his separate funds and listing title as "Hank and Louise, joint tenants with the right of survivorship." Hank predeceases Louise 10 years later when the property is worth $900,000. If Hank and Louise are husband and wife, Hank's gross estate includes $450,000 (½ of $900,000) as to the property. ■

Assume the same facts as in Example 46, except that Louise (instead of Hank) dies first. Presuming the value at the date of death to be $900,000, Louise's gross estate includes $450,000 as to the property. In this regard, it is of no consequence that Louise did not contribute to the cost of the real estate. ■

In both Examples 46 and 47, inclusion in the gross estate of the first spouse to die is neutralized by the unlimited marital deduction allowed for estate tax purposes (see the discussion of § 2056 later in the chapter). Under the right of survivorship, the surviving joint tenant obtains full ownership of the property. The marital deduction generally is allowed for property passing from one spouse to another.

Whether a *gift* results when property is transferred into some form of joint ownership depends on the consideration furnished by each of the contributing parties for the ownership interest acquired.

Brenda and Sarah purchase real estate as tenants in common, each furnishing $400,000 of the $800,000 cost. If each is an equal owner in the property, no gift has occurred. ■

Assume the same facts as in Example 48, except that of the $800,000 purchase price, Brenda furnishes $600,000 and Sarah furnishes only $200,000. If each is an equal owner in the property, Brenda has made a gift to Sarah of $200,000. ■

Martha purchases real estate for $900,000, the title to the property being listed as follows: "Martha, Sylvia, and Dan as joint tenants with the right of survivorship." If under state law the mother (Martha), the daughter (Sylvia), and the son (Dan) are deemed to be equal owners in the property, Martha is treated as having made gifts of $300,000 to Sylvia and $300,000 to Dan. ■

Several important *exceptions* exist to the general rule that gift treatment is triggered by the creation of a joint ownership with disproportionate interests resulting from unequal consideration. First, if the transfer involves a joint bank account, there is no gift at the time of the contribution.[38] If a gift occurs, it is when the noncontributing party withdraws the funds provided by the other joint tenant. Second, the same rule applies to the purchase of U.S. savings bonds. Again, any gift tax consequences are postponed until the noncontributing party appropriates some or all of the proceeds for his or her individual use.

Cynthia deposits $400,000 in a bank account under the names of Cynthia and Carla as joint tenants. Both Cynthia and Carla have the right to withdraw funds from the account without the other's consent. Cynthia has not made a gift to Carla when the account is established. ■

Assume the same facts as in Example 51. At some later date, Carla withdraws $100,000 from the account for her own use. At this point, Cynthia has made a gift to Carla of $100,000. ■

Wesley purchases a U.S. savings bond that he registers in the names of Wesley and Harriet. After Wesley dies, Harriet redeems the bond. No gift takes place when Wesley buys the bond.

---

[38]Reg. § 25.2511–1(h)(4).

In addition, Harriet's redemption is not treated as a gift since the bond passed to her by testamentary disposition (Harriet acquired the bond by virtue of surviving Wesley) and not through a lifetime transfer. However, the fair market value of the bond is included in Wesley's gross estate under § 2040. ■

Powers of Appointment (§§ 2041 and 2514).

A **power of appointment** is a power to determine who shall own or enjoy, at the present or in the future, the property subject to the power. It must be created by another and does not include a power created or retained by the decedent when he or she transferred his or her own property.

Powers of appointment fall into one of two classifications: *general* and *special*. A general power of appointment is one in which the decedent could have appointed himself, his creditors, his estate, or the creditors of his estate. In contrast, a special power enables the holder to appoint to others but *not* to herself, her creditors, her estate, or the creditors of her estate. Assume, for example, that Don has the power to designate how the principal of the trust will be distributed among Edie, Frank, and Georgia. At this point, Don's power is only a special power of appointment. If Don is given the further right to appoint the principal to himself, what was a special power of appointment becomes a general power.

Three things can happen to a power of appointment: exercise, lapse, and release. Exercising the power involves appointing the property to one or all of the parties designated. A lapse occurs upon failure to exercise a power. Thus, if Don fails to indicate how the principal of a trust will be distributed among Edie, Frank, and Georgia, Don's power of appointment will lapse, and the principal will pass in accordance with the terms of the trust instrument. A release occurs if the holder relinquishes a power of appointment.

Powers of appointment have the following transfer tax consequences.

1. No tax implications result from the exercise, lapse, or release of a special power of appointment.
2. The exercise, lapse, or release of a general power of appointment created after October 21, 1942, during life or upon the death of the holder causes the fair market value of the property (or income interest) subject to the power to be a gift or to be included in the holder's gross estate.
3. In connection with (2), a holder is not considered to have had a general power of appointment if he or she had a right to consume or invade for his or her own benefit, as long as that right is limited by an ascertainable standard. The standard must relate to the holder's health, education, support, or maintenance. A power to use the property for the "comfort, welfare, or happiness" of the holder is not an ascertainable standard and therefore is a general power of appointment.

The following examples illustrate these rules.

EXAMPLE 54

Justin, Monica's father, leaves his property in trust, life estate to Monica and remainder to whichever of Monica's children she decides to appoint in her will. Monica's power is not a general power of appointment because she cannot exercise it in favor of herself. Thus, regardless of whether Monica exercises the power or not, none of the trust property subject to the power is included in her gross estate. ■

EXAMPLE 55

Assume the same facts as in Example 54. In addition to having the testamentary power to designate the beneficiary of the remainder interest, Monica is given a power to direct the trustee to pay to her from time to time as much of the principal as she might request "for her support." Although Monica now has a power that she can exercise in favor of herself, it is not a general power of appointment. The power is limited to an ascertainable standard. Thus, none of the property subject to these powers is subject to the gift tax or is included in Monica's gross estate at her death. ■

Life Insurance (§ 2042).

Under § 2042, the gross estate includes the proceeds of life insurance on the decedent's life if (1) they are receivable by the estate, (2) they are receivable by another for the benefit of the estate, or (3) the decedent possessed an incident of ownership in the policy.

Life insurance on the life of another owned by a decedent at the time of death is included in the gross estate under § 2033 (property in which the decedent had an interest) and not under § 2042. The amount includible is the replacement value of the policy.[39] Under these circumstances, inclusion of the face amount of the policy is inappropriate as the policy has not yet matured.

EXAMPLE 56

At the time of his death, Luigi owned a life insurance policy on the life of Benito, face amount of $500,000 and replacement value of $50,000, with Sofia as the designated beneficiary. Since the policy has not matured at Luigi's death, § 2042 is inapplicable. However, § 2033 (property in which the decedent had an interest) compels the inclusion of $50,000 (the replacement value) in Luigi's gross estate. If Luigi and Sofia owned the policy as community property, only $25,000 is included in Luigi's gross estate. ■

[handwritten: replacement value is included in estate if policy is not matured]

In the frequent situation where the beneficiary of the insurance is neither the insured nor the owner of the policy, no tax consequences ensue upon the beneficiary's death. Thus, in Example 56, if Sofia predeceases Benito, no transfer takes place because the policy has not matured. Sofia's interest as a beneficiary is a mere expectancy and not a property interest possessing any value.

The term *life insurance* includes whole life policies, term insurance, group life insurance, travel and accident insurance, endowment contracts (before being paid up), and death benefits paid by fraternal societies operating under the lodge system.[40]

As just noted, proceeds of insurance on the life of the decedent receivable by the executor or administrator or payable to the decedent's estate are included in the gross estate. The estate need not be specifically named as the beneficiary. Assume, for example, the proceeds of the policy are receivable by an individual beneficiary and are subject to an obligation, legally binding upon the beneficiary, to pay taxes, debts, and other charges enforceable against the estate. The proceeds are included in the decedent's gross estate to the extent of the beneficiary's obligation. If the proceeds of an insurance policy made payable to a decedent's estate are community assets and, under state law, one-half belongs to the surviving spouse, only one-half of the proceeds will be considered as receivable by or for the benefit of the decedent's estate.

Proceeds of insurance on the life of the decedent not receivable by or for the benefit of the estate are includible if the decedent at death possessed any of the incidents of ownership in the policy. In this connection, the term *incidents of ownership* means not only the ownership of the policy in a technical legal sense but also, generally speaking, the right of the insured or his or her estate to the economic benefits of the policy. Thus, it also includes the power to change beneficiaries, revoke an assignment, pledge the policy for a loan, or surrender or cancel the policy.[41]

[handwritten: so it will be included in the estate]

EXAMPLE 57

At the time of death, Broderick was the insured under a policy (face amount of $1 million) owned by Gregory with Demi as the designated beneficiary. Broderick took out the policy five years ago and immediately transferred it as a gift to Gregory. Under the assignment, Broderick transferred all rights in the policy except the right to change beneficiaries. Broderick died without having exercised this right, and the policy proceeds are paid to Demi. Under

---

[39]Reg. § 20.2031–8(a)(1).
[40]Reg. § 20.2042–1(a)(1). As to travel and accident insurance, see *Comm. v. Estate of Noel*, 65–1 USTC ¶12,311, 15 AFTR2d 1397, 85 S.Ct. 1238 (USSC,

1965). As to employer-sponsored group term life insurance, see Example 33 earlier in this chapter.
[41]Reg. § 20.2042–1(c)(2).

§ 2042(2), Broderick's retention of an incident of ownership in the policy (i.e., the right to change beneficiaries) causes $1 million to be included in his gross estate. ■

Assuming that the deceased-insured holds the incidents of ownership in a policy, how much is included in the gross estate if the insurance policy is a community asset? Only one-half of the proceeds becomes part of the deceased spouse's gross estate.

In determining whether a policy is *community property* or what portion of it might be so classified, state law controls. The states appear to follow one of two general approaches. Under the inception of title approach, the classification depends on when the policy was originally purchased. If purchased before marriage, the policy is separate property regardless of how many premiums were paid after marriage with community funds. However, if the noninsured spouse is not the beneficiary of the policy, he or she may be entitled to reimbursement from the deceased-insured spouse's estate for half of the premiums paid with community funds. The inception of title approach is followed in at least three states: Louisiana, Texas, and New Mexico.

Some community property jurisdictions classify a policy using the tracing approach: the nature of the funds used to pay premiums controls. Thus, a policy paid for 20 percent with separate funds and 80 percent with community funds is 20 percent separate property and 80 percent community property. The point in time when the policy was purchased makes no difference. Conceivably, a policy purchased after marriage with the premiums paid exclusively from separate funds is classified entirely as separate property. The tracing approach appears to be the rule in California and Washington.

Merely purchasing a life insurance contract with someone else designated as the beneficiary does not constitute a *gift*. As long as the purchaser still owns the policy, nothing has really passed to the beneficiary. Even on the death of the insured-owner, no gift takes place. The proceeds paid to the beneficiary constitute a testamentary and not a lifetime transfer. But consider the following possibility.

EXAMPLE 58

Kurt purchases an insurance policy on his own life that he transfers to Olga. Kurt retains no interest in the policy (such as the power to change beneficiaries). In these circumstances, Kurt has made a gift to Olga. Furthermore, if Kurt continues to pay the premiums on the transferred policy, each payment constitutes a separate gift. ■

Under certain conditions, the death of the insured may constitute a gift to the beneficiary of part or all of the proceeds. This occurs when the owner of the policy is not the insured.

EXAMPLE 59

Randolph owns an insurance policy on the life of Frank, with Tracy as the designated beneficiary. Up until the time of Frank's death, Randolph retained the right to change the beneficiary of the policy. The proceeds paid to Tracy by the insurance company by reason of Frank's death constitute a gift from Randolph to Tracy.[42] ■

EXAMPLE 60

Hubert and Carrie live in a community property state. With community funds, Hubert purchases an insurance policy with a face amount of $1 million on his own life and designates Ann as the revocable beneficiary. On Hubert's death, the proceeds of the policy are paid to Ann. If under state law Hubert's death makes the transfer by Carrie complete, Carrie has made a gift to Ann of $500,000. Since the policy is community property, Carrie is the owner of only one-half of the policy. Furthermore, one-half of the proceeds of the policy ($500,000) is included in Hubert's gross estate under § 2042. ■

---

[42]*Goodman v. Comm.*, 46–1 USTC ¶10,275, 34 AFTR 1534, 156 F.2d 218 (CA–2, 1946).

Taxable Estate

LO.7

Describe the components of the taxable estate.

After the gross estate has been determined, the next step is to compute the taxable estate. By virtue of § 2051, the **taxable estate** is the gross estate less the following: expenses, indebtedness, and taxes (§ 2053); losses (§ 2054); charitable transfers (§ 2055); the marital deduction (§§ 2056 and 2056A); and the deduction for state death taxes (§ 2058). As previously noted, the charitable and marital deductions also have gift tax ramifications (§§ 2522 and 2523).

→to calc gross estate

Expenses, Indebtedness, and Taxes (§ 2053).

A deduction is allowed for funeral expenses; expenses incurred in administering property; claims against the estate; and unpaid mortgages and other charges against property, whose value is included in the gross estate (without reduction for the mortgage or other indebtedness).

Expenses incurred in administering community property are deductible only in proportion to the deceased spouse's interest in the community.[43]

Exp.→proportion is deductible

Administration expenses include commissions of the executor or administrator, attorney's fees of the estate, accountant's fees, court costs, and certain selling expenses for disposition of estate property.

Claims against the estate include property taxes accrued before the decedent's death, unpaid income taxes on income received by the decedent before he or she died, and unpaid gift taxes on gifts made by the decedent before death.

Amounts that may be deducted as claims against the estate are only for enforceable personal obligations of the decedent at the time of death. Deductions for claims founded on promises or agreements are limited to the extent that the liabilities were contracted in good faith and for adequate and full consideration. However, a pledge or subscription in favor of a public, charitable, religious, or educational organization is deductible to the extent that it would have constituted an allowable deduction had it been a bequest.[44]

Deductible funeral expenses include the cost of interment, the burial plot or vault, a gravestone, perpetual care of the grave site, and the transportation expense of the person bringing the body to the place of burial. No deduction is allowed for cemetery lots that the decedent acquired before death for himself or herself and family, but the lots are not included in the decedent's gross estate under § 2033 (property in which the decedent had an interest).

cemetery lots
- not deducted
- not included in decedent's gross estate

ETHICAL and EQUITABLE *Considerations*   ## THE ADVANTAGE OF BEING PAID UP!

While in the hospital undergoing radical treatment for a terminal condition, Faith pays her medical expenses as they are incurred and satisfies her charitable pledges for the year.

Faith does not survive the medical treatment. What tax goals has Faith accomplished? Will her tax planning succeed?

Losses (§ 2054).

Section 2054 permits an estate tax deduction for losses from casualty or theft incurred during the period when the estate is being settled. As is true with casualty or theft losses for income tax purposes, any anticipated insurance recovery must be taken into account in arriving at the amount of the deductible loss. Unlike the income tax, however, the deduction is not limited by a floor ($100)

deduction not limited by a floor like the income tax is

---

[43]*U.S. v. Stapf*, 63–2 USTC ¶12,192, 12 AFTR2d 6326, 84 S.Ct. 248 (USSC, 1963).

[44]§ 2053(c)(1)(A) and Reg. § 20.2053–5.

or a percentage amount (the excess of 10 percent of adjusted gross income). If the casualty occurs to property after it has been distributed to an heir, the loss belongs to the heir and not to the estate. If the casualty occurs before the decedent's death, it should be claimed on the appropriate Form 1040. The fair market value of the property (if any) on the date of death plus any insurance recovery is included in the gross estate.

As is true of certain administration expenses, a casualty or theft loss of estate property can be claimed as an income tax deduction on the fiduciary return of the estate (Form 1041). But a double deduction prohibition applies, and claiming the income tax deduction requires a waiver of the estate tax deduction.[45]

Transfers to Charity (§§ 2055 and 2522). A deduction is allowed for the value of property in the decedent's gross estate that is transferred by the decedent through testamentary disposition to (or for the use of) any of the following.

1. The United States or any of its political subdivisions.
2. Any corporation or association organized and operated exclusively for religious, charitable, scientific, literary, or educational purposes.
3. Various veterans' organizations.

The organizations just described are identical to those that qualify for the Federal gift tax deduction under § 2522. With the following exceptions, they are also the same organizations that qualify a donor for an income tax deduction under § 170.

- Certain nonprofit cemetery associations qualify for income tax but not estate and gift tax purposes.
- Foreign charities may qualify under the estate and gift tax but not under the income tax.

No deduction is allowed unless the charitable bequest is specified by a provision in the decedent's will or the transfer was made before death and the property is subsequently included in the gross estate. Generally speaking, a deduction does not materialize when an individual dies intestate (without a will). The amount of the bequest to charity must be mandatory and cannot be left to someone else's discretion. It is, however, permissible to allow another person—such as the executor of the estate—to choose which charity will receive the specified donation. Likewise, a bequest may be expressed as an alternative and still be effective if the noncharitable beneficiary disclaims (refuses) the intervening interest before the due date for

---

[45]§ 642(g).

the filing of the estate tax return (nine months after the decedent's death plus any extensions of time granted for filing).

Marital Deduction (§§ 2056, 2056A, and 2523).

The **marital deduction** originated with the Revenue Act of 1948 as part of the same legislation that permitted married persons to secure the income-splitting advantages of filing joint income tax returns. The purpose of these statutory changes was to eliminate the major tax variations that existed between taxpayers residing in community property and common law states. The marital deduction was designed to provide equity in the estate and gift tax areas.

In a community property state, for example, no marital deduction generally was allowed, since the surviving spouse already owned one-half of the community and that portion was not included in the deceased spouse's gross estate. In a common law state, however, most if not all of the assets often belonged to the breadwinner of the family. When that spouse died first, all of these assets were included in the gross estate. Recall that a dower or curtesy interest (regarding a surviving spouse's right to some of the deceased spouse's property) does not reduce the gross estate. To equalize the situation, therefore, a marital deduction, usually equal to one-half of all separate assets, was allowed upon the death of the first spouse.

Ultimately, Congress decided to dispense with these historical justifications and recognize husband and wife as a single economic unit. Consistent with the approach taken under the income tax, spouses are considered as one for transfer tax purposes. By making the marital deduction unlimited in amount, neither the gift tax nor the estate tax is imposed on outright interspousal transfers of property. The unlimited marital deduction even includes one spouse's share of the community property transferred to the other spouse.

Passing Requirement. Under § 2056, the marital deduction is allowed only for property that is included in the deceased spouse's gross estate *and* that passes or has passed to the surviving spouse. In determining whether the parties are legally married, look to state law (see Example 1 earlier). Property that *passes* from the decedent to the surviving spouse includes any interest received as (1) the decedent's heir or donee; (2) the decedent's surviving tenant by the entirety or joint tenant; (3) the appointee under the decedent's exercise (or lapse or release) of a general power of appointment; or (4) the beneficiary of insurance on the life of the decedent.

[handwritten margin note: Marital deduction allowed for: - property included in the deceased spouse's gross estate & that passes or has passed to the surviving spouse]

EXAMPLE 61

At the time of his death in the current year, Matthew owned an insurance policy on his own life (face amount of $500,000) with Minerva (his wife) as the designated beneficiary. Matthew and Minerva also owned real estate (worth $600,000) as tenants by the entirety (Matthew had furnished all of the purchase price). As to these transfers, $800,000 ($500,000 + $300,000) is included in Matthew's gross estate, and this amount represents the property that passes to Minerva for purposes of the marital deduction.[46] ■

ETHICAL and EQUITABLE *Considerations*	IT'S THE THOUGHT THAT COUNTS

Joe (age 86) and Nicole (age 22) are married. Two days later they exchange wedding gifts. Joe's gift to Nicole is stock in IBM (valued at $2 million), while Nicole's gift to Joe is a bottle of cologne (value of $32). What tax goals are they trying to accomplish? Will their plan work?

---

[46]Inclusion in the gross estate falls under § 2042 (proceeds of life insurance) and § 2040 (joint interests). Although Matthew provided the full purchase price for the real estate, § 2040(b) requires inclusion of only one-half of the value of the property when one spouse predeceases the other.

Disclaimers can affect the amount passing to the surviving spouse. If, for example, the surviving spouse is the remainderperson under the will of the deceased spouse, a disclaimer by another heir increases the amount passing to the surviving spouse. This, in turn, will increase the amount of the marital deduction allowed to the estate of the deceased spouse.

A problem arises when a property interest passing to the surviving spouse is subject to a mortgage or other encumbrance. In this case, only the net value of the interest after reduction by the amount of the mortgage or other encumbrance qualifies for the marital deduction. To allow otherwise results in a double deduction since a decedent's liabilities are separately deductible under § 2053.

EXAMPLE 62

In his will, Oscar leaves real estate (fair market value of $500,000) to his wife. If the real estate is subject to a mortgage of $100,000 (upon which Oscar was personally liable), the marital deduction is limited to $400,000 ($500,000 − $100,000). The $100,000 mortgage is deductible under § 2053 as an obligation of the decedent (Oscar). ■

However, if the executor is required under the terms of the decedent's will or under local law to discharge the mortgage out of other assets of the estate or to reimburse the surviving spouse, the payment or reimbursement is an additional interest passing to the surviving spouse.

EXAMPLE 63

Assume the same facts as in Example 62, except that Oscar's will directs that the real estate is to pass to his wife free of any liabilities. Accordingly, Oscar's executor pays off the mortgage by using other estate assets and distributes the real estate to Oscar's wife. The marital deduction now becomes $500,000. ■

Federal estate taxes or other death taxes paid out of the surviving spouse's share of the gross estate are not included in the value of property passing to the surviving spouse. Therefore, it is usually preferable for the deceased spouse's will to provide that death taxes be paid out of the portion of the estate that does not qualify for the marital deduction.

Terminable Interest Limitation. Certain interests in property passing from the deceased spouse to the surviving spouse are referred to as **terminable interests**. Such an interest will terminate or fail after the passage of time, upon the happening of some contingency, or upon the failure of some event to occur. Examples are life estates, annuities, estates for terms of years, and patents. A terminable interest will not qualify for the marital deduction if another interest in the same property passed from the deceased spouse to some other person. By reason of the passing, that other person or his or her heirs may enjoy part of the property after the termination of the surviving spouse's interest.[47]

EXAMPLE 64

Vicky's will places her property in trust, life estate to her husband, Brett, remainder to Andrew or his heirs. The interest passing from Vicky to Brett does not qualify for the marital deduction. It will terminate on Brett's death, and Andrew or his heirs will then possess or enjoy the property. ■

EXAMPLE 65

Assume the same facts as in Example 64, except that Vicky created the trust during her life. No marital deduction is available for gift tax purposes for the same reason as in Example 64.[48] ■

---

[47]§§ 2056(b)(1) and 2523(b)(1).

[48]Both Examples 64 and 65 contain the potential for a qualified terminable interest property (QTIP) election discussed later in this section.

The justification for the terminable interest rule can be illustrated by examining the possible results of Examples 64 and 65. Without the rule, Vicky could have passed property to Brett at no cost because of the marital deduction. Yet, on Brett's death, none of the property would have been included in his gross estate. Section 2036 (transfers with a retained life estate) would not apply to Brett since he was not the original transferor of the property. The marital deduction should not be available in situations where the surviving spouse can enjoy the property and still pass it to another without tax consequences. The marital deduction merely postpones the transfer tax on the death of the first spouse and operates to shift any such tax to the surviving spouse.

The terminable interest rule can be avoided under a *power of appointment exception.*[49] Under the exception, a property interest passing from the deceased spouse to the surviving spouse qualifies for the marital deduction (and is not considered a terminable interest) if the surviving spouse is granted a general power of appointment over the property. Thus, the exercise, release, or lapse of the power during the survivor's life or at death will be subject to either the gift or the death tax.[50] If Examples 64 and 65 are modified to satisfy this condition, the life estate passing from Vicky to Brett is not a terminable interest and will qualify for the marital deduction.

As previously noted, the purpose of the terminable interest rule is to ensure that property not taxed to the transferor-spouse (due to the marital deduction) will be subject to the gift or estate tax upon disposition by the transferee-spouse.

Consistent with the objective of the terminable interest rule, another exception offers an alternative means for obtaining the marital deduction. Under this provision, the marital deduction is allowed for transfers of **qualified terminable interest property** (commonly referred to as QTIP). This is defined as property that passes from one spouse to another by gift or at death and for which the transferee-spouse has a qualifying income interest for life.

For a donee or a surviving spouse, a qualifying income interest for life exists under the following conditions:

- The person is entitled for life to all of the income from the property (or a specific portion of it), payable at annual or more frequent intervals.
- No person (including the spouse) has a power to appoint any part of the property to any person other than the surviving spouse during his or her life.[51]

If these conditions are met, an election can be made to claim a marital deduction as to the QTIP. For estate tax purposes, the executor of the estate makes the election on Form 706 (the Federal estate tax return). For gift tax purposes, the donor spouse makes the election on Form 709 (the Federal gift tax return). The election is irrevocable.

If the election is made, a transfer tax is imposed upon the QTIP when the transferee-spouse disposes of it by gift or upon death. If the disposition occurs during life, the gift tax applies, measured by the fair market value of the property as of that time.[52] If no lifetime disposition takes place, the fair market value of the property on the date of death (or alternate valuation date if applicable) is included in the gross estate of the transferee-spouse.[53]

E X A M P L E   66

In 1980, Clyde dies and provides in his will that certain assets (fair market value of $800,000) are to be transferred to a trust under which Gertrude (Clyde's wife) is granted a life estate with the remainder passing to their children upon Gertrude's death. Presuming all of the preceding requirements are satisfied and Clyde's executor so elects, his estate receives a marital deduction of $800,000. ∎

---

[49]For the estate tax, see § 2056(b)(5). The gift tax counterpart is in § 2523(e).   [52]§ 2519.
[50]§§ 2514 and 2041.   [53]§ 2044.
[51]§§ 2523(f) and 2056(b)(7).

| **EXAMPLE 67** | Assume the same facts as in Example 66, with the further stipulation that Gertrude dies in 2008 when the trust assets are worth $2.4 million. This amount is included in her gross estate. ■ |

Because the estate tax is imposed on assets not physically included in the probate estate, the law allows the liability for those assets to be shifted to the heirs. The amount to be shifted is determined by comparing the estate tax liability both with and without the inclusion of the QTIP. This right of recovery can be canceled by a provision in the deceased spouse's will.[54]

The major difference between the power of appointment and the QTIP exceptions to the terminable interest rules relates to the control the surviving spouse has over the principal of the trust. In the power of appointment situation, the surviving spouse can appoint the principal to himself or herself (or to his or her estate). Only if this power is not exercised will the property pass as specified in the deceased spouse's will. In the QTIP situation, however, the surviving spouse has no such control. If the QTIP election is made, the principal must pass as prescribed by the transferor (the donor in the case of a lifetime transfer or the decedent in the case of a death transfer).

Citizenship and Residency of Spouses. In the case of a nonresident alien whose spouse is a U.S. citizen, the marital deduction is allowed for estate and gift tax purposes. Property passing to a surviving spouse who is not a U.S. citizen is not eligible for the estate tax marital deduction.[55] Similarly, no gift tax marital deduction is allowed where the spouse is not a U.S. citizen. However, the annual exclusion for these gift transfers is $128,000 (up from $125,000 in 2007).[56]

For the estate tax, an exception exists for certain transfers to a surviving spouse who is not a U.S. citizen.[57] If the transfer is to a *qualified domestic trust,* the marital deduction is allowed.[58]

The requirements of a qualified domestic trust guarantee that the marital deduction property will not escape estate taxes on the death of the surviving spouse. This would be possible if the property and spouse are outside the jurisdiction of the U.S. tax laws.

State Death Taxes (§ 2058). The purpose of the § 2058 deduction is to mitigate the effect of subjecting property to multiple death taxes (i.e., both Federal and state). In this regard, however, it provides less relief than was available with the § 2011 credit it replaces. A credit results in a dollar-for-dollar reduction in tax, whereas the benefit of a deduction is limited by the effective tax bracket of the estate.

| **LO.8** | # Computing the Federal Estate Tax |
| Determine the Federal estate tax liability. | |

Once the taxable estate has been determined, post-1976 taxable gifts are added to arrive at the tax base. Note that pre-1977 taxable gifts do not enter into the computation of the tax base.

| **EXAMPLE 68** | Joyce dies in 2008, leaving a taxable estate of $2 million. During her life, Joyce made taxable gifts as follows: $50,000 in 1975 and $100,000 in 2000. For estate tax purposes, the Federal estate tax base becomes $2.1 million determined as follows: $2,000,000 (taxable estate) + $100,000 (taxable gift made in 2000). ■ |

Using the unified transfer tax rate schedule of § 2001(c), the tentative tax on the tax base is computed. Using the facts in Example 68, the tentative tax on

---

[54]§ 2207A(a).
[55]§ 2056(d)(1).
[56]§ 2523(i).

[57]§ 2056(d)(2).
[58]§ 2056A.

$2.1 million is $825,800 [$555,800 + 45%($2,100,000 − $1,500,000)]—see Appendix A, page A–7.

All available estate tax credits are subtracted from the tentative estate tax to arrive at the estate tax (if any) that is due.

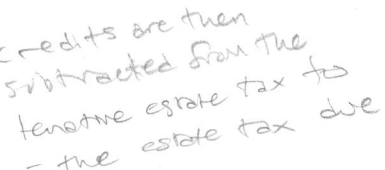

Estate Tax Credits

Unified Tax Credit (§ 2010). Recall from previous discussion of this credit that the amount of the credit allowed depends upon the year of the transfer. Returning to Example 68, the credit allowed on the gift in 2000 was $220,550. Since the exclusion amount was $675,000 (refer to Table 17–1), no gift tax was due on the transfer. On Joyce's death in 2008, however, the unified tax credit is $780,800, which is less than the tentative tax of $825,800 (refer to the discussion following Example 68). Disregarding the effect of any other estate tax credits, Joyce's estate owes a tax of $45,000 [$825,800 (tentative tax on a tax base of $2,100,000) − $780,800 (unified tax credit for 2008)].

Credit for State Death Taxes (§ 2011). The Code allowed a limited credit for the amount of any death tax actually paid to any state (or to the District of Columbia) attributable to any property included in the gross estate. Like the credit for foreign death taxes paid, this provision mitigated the harshness of subjecting the same property to multiple death taxes.

The credit allowed was limited to the lesser of the amount of tax actually paid or the amount provided for in a table contained in § 2011(b).

The Tax Relief Reconciliation Act of 2001 phased out § 2011 beginning in 2002 at the rate of 25 percent per year. Thus, by 2005, the credit was completely eliminated.[59] As previously noted, the *credit* for state death taxes paid has been replaced by a *deduction* under § 2058.

Credit for Tax on Prior Transfers (§ 2013). Suppose Nancy owns some property that she passes at death to Lisa. Shortly thereafter, Lisa dies and passes the property to Rita. Assuming both estates are subject to the Federal estate tax, the successive deaths result in a multiple effect. To mitigate the possible multiple taxation that might result, § 2013 provides relief in the form of a credit for a death tax on prior transfers. In the preceding hypothetical case, Lisa's estate may be able to claim as an estate tax credit some of the taxes paid by Nancy's estate.

The credit is limited to the lesser of the following amounts:

1. The amount of the Federal estate tax attributable to the transferred property in the transferor's estate.
2. The amount of the Federal estate tax attributable to the transferred property in the decedent's estate.

To apply the limitations, certain adjustments must be made that are not covered in this text.[60] However, it is not necessary for the transferred property to be identified in the present decedent's estate or for it to be in existence at the time of the present decedent's death. It is sufficient that the transfer of property was subjected to the Federal estate tax in the estate of the transferor and that the transferor died within the prescribed period of time.

If the transferor dies within two years after or before the present decedent's death, the credit is allowed in full (subject to the preceding limitations). If the transferor died more than two years before the decedent, the credit is a certain percentage: 80 percent if the transferor died within the third or fourth year preceding

---

[59]Section 2011 is reinstated as to decedents dying after 2010.   [60]See the instructions to Form 706 and Reg. §§ 20.2013–2 and –3.

CONCEPT SUMMARY 17–2

Federal Estate Tax Provisions

1. The Federal gift and estate taxes are both excise taxes on the transfer of wealth.
2. The starting point for applying the Federal estate tax is to determine which assets are subject to tax. Such assets comprise a decedent's gross estate.
3. The gross estate generally will not include any gifts made by the decedent within three years of death. It does include any gift tax paid on these transfers.
4. Based on the premise that one should not continue to enjoy or control property and not have it subject to the estate tax, certain incomplete transfers are included in the gross estate.
5. Upon the death of a joint tenant, the full value of the property is included in the gross estate unless the survivor(s) made a contribution toward the cost of the property. Spouses are subject to a special rule that calls for automatic inclusion of half of the value of the property in the gross estate of the first tenant to die. The creation of joint ownership is subject to the gift tax when a tenant receives a lesser interest in the property than is warranted by the consideration furnished.
6. A power of appointment is the right to determine who shall own or enjoy, at the present or in the future, the property subject to the power. The exercise, lapse, or release of a general power of appointment during the life of the holder is subject to the gift tax. If the exercise, lapse, or release occurs at death, the property subject to the power is included in the holder's gross estate. If, however, a special power of appointment is involved, no gift or estate tax consequences result.
7. If the decedent is the insured, life insurance proceeds are included in the gross estate if either of two conditions is satisfied. First, the proceeds are paid to the

estate or for the benefit of the estate. Second, the decedent possessed incidents of ownership (e.g., the right to change beneficiaries) over the policy.
8. In moving from the gross estate to the taxable estate, certain deductions are allowed. Under § 2053, deductions are permitted for various administration expenses (e.g., executor's commissions), funeral costs, debts of the decedent, and certain unpaid taxes. Casualty and theft losses incurred during the administration of an estate can be deducted in arriving at the taxable estate.
9. Charitable transfers are deductible if the designated organization holds qualified status with the IRS at the time of the gift or upon death.
10. Transfers to a spouse qualify for the gift or estate tax marital deduction. Except as noted in (11), such transfers are subject to the terminable interest limitation.
11. The terminable interest limitation will not apply if the transferee-spouse is given a general power of appointment over the property or the QTIP election is made. In the case of a lifetime transfer, the donor-spouse makes the QTIP election. In the case of a testamentary transfer, the executor of the estate of the deceased spouse has the election responsibility.
12. The tax base for determining the estate tax is the taxable estate plus all post-1976 taxable gifts. All available credits are subtracted from the tax.
13. Of prime importance in the tax credit area is the unified tax credit. Except for large taxable transfers, the unified tax credit varies and depends upon the year of death.
14. If due, a Federal estate tax return (Form 706) must be filed within nine months of the date of the decedent's death.

[handwritten marginal notes:] under 2 yrs 100% / 80% yr 3&4 / 60% yr 5 or 6 / 40% yr 7 or 8 / 20% yr 9 or 10

the decedent's death, 60 percent if within the fifth or sixth year, 40 percent if within the seventh or eighth year, and 20 percent if within the ninth or tenth year.

EXAMPLE 69

Under Nancy's will, Lisa inherits property. One year later Lisa dies. Assume the estate tax attributable to the inclusion of the property in Nancy's gross estate was $150,000 and the estate tax attributable to the inclusion of the property in Lisa's gross estate is $120,000. Under these circumstances, Lisa's estate claims a credit against the estate tax of $120,000 (refer to limitation 2). ■

EXAMPLE 70

Assume the same facts as in Example 69, except that Lisa dies three years after Nancy. The applicable credit is now 80% of $120,000, or $96,000. ■

Credit for Foreign Death Taxes (§ 2014). A credit is allowed against the estate tax for any estate, inheritance, legacy, or succession tax actually paid to a foreign country. For purposes of this provision, the term *foreign country* means not only

TREATY RELIEF IS NOT ABUNDANT!

One means of mitigating double taxation at the international level is to take advantage of treaty provisions. A treaty will determine which country has primary taxing rights, and this may depend on such factors as the domicile of the decedent or the nature of the property involved (e.g., personalty or realty). Unfortunately, the United States has death tax conventions with only 17 countries: Australia*, Austria*, Canada, Denmark*, Finland, France*, Germany*, Greece, Ireland, Italy, Japan*, the Netherlands, Norway, the Republic of South Africa, Sweden, Switzerland, and the United Kingdom*. In contrast, more than 50 countries have income tax treaties with the United States (see Exhibit 9–1 in Chapter 9). Thus, treaty relief in the estate tax area is not as widespread as with income tax situations.

*An asterisk indicates the existence of a gift tax treaty as well.

GLOBAL Tax Issues

states in the international sense but also possessions or political subdivisions of foreign states and possessions of the United States.

The credit is allowed for death taxes paid with respect to (1) property situated within the foreign country to which the tax is paid, (2) property included in the decedent's gross estate, and (3) the decedent's estate. No credit is allowed for interest or penalties paid in connection with foreign death taxes.

The credit is limited to the lesser of the following amounts:

1. The amount of the foreign death tax attributable to the property situated in the country imposing the tax and included in the decedent's gross estate for Federal estate tax purposes.
2. The amount of the Federal estate tax attributable to particular property situated in a foreign country, subject to death tax in that country, and included in the decedent's gross estate for Federal estate tax purposes.

Both of these limitations may require certain adjustments to arrive at the amount of the allowable credit. These adjustments are illustrated in the Regulations and are not discussed in this text.[61] In addition to the credit for foreign death taxes under the provisions of Federal estate tax law, similar credits are allowable under death tax conventions with a number of foreign countries. If a credit is allowed under either the provisions of law or the provisions of a convention, the credit that is most beneficial to the estate should be claimed.[62]

Procedural Matters

A Federal estate tax return, if required, is due nine months after the date of the decedent's death.[63] The time limit applies to all estates regardless of the nationality or residence of the decedent. Not infrequently, an executor will request and obtain from the IRS an extension of time for filing Form 706 (estate tax return).[64] Also available is an *automatic* six-month extension of time to file the estate tax return. To receive the extension, the executor must file Form 4768 [Application for Extension of Time to File a Return and/or Pay U.S. Estate (and Generation-Skipping Transfer) Taxes].

The filing requirements parallel the exclusion amounts of the unified tax credit available for each year (refer to Table 17-1). The filing requirements may be lower when the decedent has made taxable gifts after 1976.

---

[61]Reg. § 20.2014–2 illustrates the foreign death tax limitation, and Reg. § 20.2014–3 covers that applicable to the U.S. estate tax.

[62]Reg. § 20.2014–4 illustrates the selection process when both the § 2014 credit and a death tax convention are involved.

[63]§ 6075(a).

[64]§ 6081.

EXAMPLE 71

Carlos dies in 2008, leaving a gross estate of $2 million. If Carlos did not make any post-1976 taxable gifts, his estate need not file Form 706. But assume that Carlos made a taxable gift of $100,000 in 2000. Since the filing requirement now becomes $1.9 million [$2,000,000 (the regular filing requirement for 2008) − $100,000 (the post-1976 taxable gift)], Carlos's estate must file Form 706. ■

LO.9
Appreciate the role of the generation-skipping transfer tax.

The Generation-Skipping Transfer Tax

In order to prevent partial avoidance of Federal gift and estate taxes on large transfers, the tax law imposes an additional generation-skipping transfer tax.

The Problem

Previously, by structuring the transaction carefully, it was possible to bypass a generation of transfer taxes.

EXAMPLE 72

Under his will, Edward creates a trust, life estate to Stephen (Edward's son) and remainder to Ava (Edward's granddaughter) upon Stephen's death. Edward is subject to the Federal estate tax, but no tax results on Stephen's death. Stephen held a life estate, but § 2036 does not apply because he was not the grantor of the trust. Nor does § 2033 (property owned by the decedent) come into play because Stephen's interest disappeared upon his death. The ultimate result is that the property in trust skips a generation of transfer taxes. ■

EXAMPLE 73

Joshua dies at age 89 and leaves all of his property to a trust. Under the terms of the trust instrument, trust income and corpus are to be distributed equally over a 10-year period to Amber and Ethan. Amber is Joshua's 22-year-old third wife, while Ethan is his 30-year-old grandson. As a result of this arrangement, the following tax consequences ensue: the estate tax applies on Joshua's death; income earned by the trust will be subject to income tax (see Chapter 19); and normally no transfer tax results when distributions of trust income and corpus occur. ■

EXAMPLE 74

Amy gives assets to Eric (her grandson). Called a direct skip, the gift would circumvent any transfer taxes that would have resulted had the assets been channeled through Eric's parents. ■

The Solution

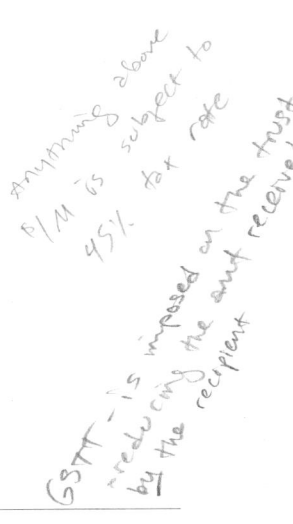

Anything above subject to E/M is tax rate 45%

GSTT – is imposed on the trust reducing the amount received by the recipient

The generation-skipping transfer tax (GSTT) is designed to preclude the avoidance of either the estate tax or the gift tax by making transfers that bypass the next lower generation. In the typical family setting, this involves transfers from grandparents to grandchildren. Such transfers, in effect, would skip any transfer tax that would result if the property were channeled through the children.

The GSTT is triggered by any of these three events: a taxable *termination* occurs; a taxable *distribution* takes place; or a *direct skip* is made.[65] Example 72 illustrates a termination event. Upon Stephen's death, the fair market value of the trust property that passes to Ava is subject to the GSTT (imposed on the trust). The GSTT will have the effect of reducing the amount Ava receives from the trust.

Example 73 illustrates a distribution event. When the trust makes a distribution to Ethan, the GSTT applies (imposed on Ethan). Any distribution to Amber is not subject to the GSTT because the spouse of the transferor (Joshua in this case) is deemed to be of the same generation.[66] The results reached in Example 73 show

---

[65]§ 2611.

[66]§ 2651(c)(1).

how ludicrous the application of the GSTT rules can be. Amber (age 22) is treated as being in the same generation as Joshua (age 89), while Ethan (age 30) is two generations removed!

Example 74 illustrates a lifetime version of the direct skip event.[67] In this situation, the GSTT is imposed upon Amy when the gift is made to Eric. Not only will Amy be subject to the GSTT but the amount of the tax represents an additional gift to Eric.[68] Thus, if a gift is a direct skip (such as Example 74), the total transfer tax (the GSTT plus the gift tax) may exceed what the donee receives.

imposed on Amy

EXAMPLE 75

In 2008, Norman makes a taxable gift of $1 million to his granddaughter Kristen. Norman, a widower, has made taxable gifts in the past and has exhausted his unified transfer tax credit. Norman's tax liability is computed as follows.

GSTT (45% × $1,000,000)	$ 450,000
Gift tax [45% × ($1,000,000 + $450,000)]	652,500
Total tax	$1,102,500

Note the disastrous consequences of the GSTT. To make the $1 million gift to Kristen, Norman's total outlay is $2,102,500 [$1,000,000 (gift) + $1,102,500 (tax incurred)]! ■

w/ GSTT, it is possible to pay more in taxes than what was actually given as a gift

A special provision provides relief from the GSTT when the parent of the skip person (e.g., a grandchild) is deceased. In such cases, the donee or heir is treated as being in the generation following that of the grantor.[69]

EXAMPLE 76

Assume the same facts as in Example 75, except that Kristen's father (i.e., Norman's son) is deceased. Now, Kristen is treated as being in the generation after Norman's (i.e., as his daughter rather than his granddaughter), and the GSTT does not apply. Norman's gift tax is $450,000 [45% (gift tax rate) × $1,000,000 (taxable gift)]. ■

If the parent inbetween is deceased then it skips the 2nd layer of taxation & the GSTT does not apply

The GSTT rate is the highest rate under the gift and estate tax schedule. Pursuant to transitional rules, these top rates are as follows: 45 percent (2007–2009) and 46 percent (2006). (The rates were 47 percent in 2005, 48 percent in 2004, and 49 percent in 2003.) To ameliorate the extra tax burden of the GSTT, an exemption is allowed equal to the exclusion amount applicable to the Federal estate tax (see Table 17–1).[70] For a donor who is married, the election to split the gift (under § 2513) will double the amount of the exemption.[71] For 2007, for example, the amount of the exemption could be $4 million ($2 million × 2). The exemption can be applied to whichever transfers the grantor (or personal representative of the grantor) chooses. Any appreciation attributable to the exempted portion of the transfer is not later subject to the GSTT.

EXAMPLE 77

Assume the same facts as in Example 72. Edward died in 2007, and the amount transferred to the trust was $2 million. Edward's executor elected to use the full $2 million exemption to cover the transfer. Stephen dies in 2008 when the trust is worth $2.7 million. None of this amount is subject to the GSTT. The $700,000 appreciation on the exclusion amount ($2,700,000 − $2,000,000) also escapes the GSTT. ■

Along with the estate tax, the GSTT is scheduled to be phased out by 2010.

Tax planning for the Federal gift and estate tax is discussed in Chapter 18 in connection with family tax planning.

TAX PLANNING
Considerations

---

[67]§ 2612(c)(1). A direct skip can also take place in a testamentary transfer.
[68]§ 2515.
[69]§ 2651(e).

[70]§ 2631(c).
[71]§ 2652(a)(2).

KEY TERMS

Alternate valuation date, 17–6

Annual exclusion, 17–13

Bypass amount, 17–6

Disclaimer, 17–12

Exclusion amount, 17–6

Exemption equivalent, 17–6

Future interest, 17–13

Gross estate, 17–18

Joint tenants, 17–9

Marital deduction, 17–31

Power of appointment, 17–26

Probate estate, 17–18

Qualified terminable interest property (QTIP), 17–33

Taxable estate, 17–29

Taxable gift, 17–4

Tenants by the entirety, 17–9

Tenants in common, 17–9

Terminable interests, 17–32

Totten trust, 17–11

Unified tax credit, 17–5

Unified transfer tax, 17–3

PROBLEM MATERIALS

DISCUSSION QUESTIONS

1. Why can the unified transfer tax be categorized as an excise tax? In this regard, how does it differ from an income tax?

2. Over the years, the tax treatment of transfers by gift and by death has not been consistent. In this regard, what was congressional justification for the rules applicable to:
   a. Pre-1977 transfers?
   b. Post-1976 and pre-2001 transfers?
   c. Current transfers?

3. In what manner does an inheritance tax differ from an estate tax?

4. Suppose that the person responsible for paying the Federal gift tax does not and cannot do so. Does the IRS have any recourse? Explain.

Issue ID

5. Kim, a wealthy Korean national, is advised by his physicians to have an operation performed at the Mayo Clinic. Kim is hesitant to come to the United States because of the possible tax consequences. If the procedure is not successful, Kim does not want his wealth to be subject to the Federal estate tax. Are Kim's concerns justified? Explain.

6. Carlos, a citizen and resident of Chile, would like to buy stock in General Electric and make gifts of the shares to his children. Will the Federal gift tax pose a problem for him? Explain.

7. The justification for a unified transfer tax is that it will eliminate the tax difference between transfers by gift and transfers by death. Does the current structure of the Federal gift and estate taxes accomplish this objective? In this regard, comment on the following aspects of the two taxes.
   a. Availability of the annual exclusion.
   b. Treatment of pre-1977 and post-1976 taxable gifts.
   c. Credit for gift taxes deemed paid.
   d. Amount of unified transfer tax credit allowed.
   e. Applicable tax rates.
   f. Applicability of the generation-skipping transfer tax.

Issue ID

8. During her life, Kelley makes many taxable gifts and, by using *all* of the unified transfer tax credit allowed, never paid any gift tax. Upon Kelley's death in 2008, her estate has a bypass amount available of $1 million.
   a. Are these statements plausible?
   b. Explain what happened.

9. As to the alternate valuation date of § 2032, comment on the following.
    a. The justification for the election.
    b. A Form 706 need not be filed for the estate.
    c. The main heir prefers the date of death value.
    d. An estate asset is distributed to an heir three months after the decedent's death.
    e. Some estate assets have appreciated in value since the death of the decedent.
    f. Effect of the election on income tax basis.
    g. Treatment of income accruing from the property from the date of death to the alternate valuation date.

10. The alternate valuation date cannot be used unless its election decreases the value of the gross estate *and* decreases the estate tax liability. Why are these conditions imposed?

11. An estate is eligible for the alternate valuation date of § 2032, but the executor does not make the election. Because the date of death valuation is used, more estate tax results.   **Issue ID**
    a. Is this proper procedure?
    b. Why might the § 2032 election not be made?

12. What type of ownership arrangement is appropriate to accomplish each of the following objectives?
    a. A grandmother wants her son to receive the income for his life and upon his death for the property to pass to his children.
    b. A married couple want co-ownership with right of survivorship.
    c. A parent wants co-ownership with his children with right of survivorship.
    d. A parent wants co-ownership with her children with no right of survivorship.

13. Why are transfers to political organizations exempt from the application of the Federal gift tax?

14. To provide his daughter, Sharon, with a sense of financial responsibility, Roy gives her the money needed to cover her estimated expenses for the first year of college. Has Roy needlessly made himself subject to the Federal gift tax by not sending these funds directly to the college involved? Explain.

15. Under Leon's will, all of his property is to pass to his son, Jody. Jody is a widower, and his only survivor is a daughter, Brenda. Jody has considerable wealth of his own and is in poor health. Do you recognize an attractive estate tax option for the parties?   **Issue ID**

16. The Randalls have a married daughter and three grandchildren (ages 17, 18, and 19). They establish a trust under which the income is to be paid annually to the grandchildren until the youngest reaches age 25. At that point, the trust terminates and the principal (corpus) is distributed to the daughter. What annual gift tax exclusions are allowed, if any, on the creation of the trust?   **Issue ID**

17. Qualified tuition programs under § 529 enjoy significant tax advantages. Describe these advantages with regard to the Federal:
    a. Income tax.
    b. Gift tax.
    c. Estate tax.

18. Regarding the gift-splitting provision of § 2513, comment on the following.
    a. What it was designed to accomplish.
    b. The treatment of any taxable gifts previously made by the nonowner spouse.
    c. How the election is made.
    d. The spouses are divorced during the year.
    e. The utility of the election in a community property jurisdiction.

19. In connection with the filing of a Federal gift tax return, comment on the following.
    a. No Federal gift tax is due.
    b. The gift is between spouses.
    c. The § 2513 election to split gifts is to be used.
    d. A gift of a future interest is involved.
    e. The donor uses a fiscal year for Federal income tax purposes.
    f. The donor obtained from the IRS an extension of time for filing his or her Federal income tax return.

20. In each of the following independent situations, indicate whether a transfer that is subject to the Federal gift tax has occurred.
    a. Martin creates a revocable trust, life estate to his children, remainder upon their death to his grandchildren.
    b. Ellen sells land to her son for one-third of what she paid for it 10 years ago.
    c. As part of a prenuptial marital settlement, Blake transfers to Andrea a portfolio of municipal bonds.
    d. As part of a property settlement, Floyd transfers to Inez income-producing real estate. Six months later, Floyd and Inez are divorced.
    e. Molly reimburses her 22-year-old son for the tuition he paid to attend medical school.
    f. Herman lends his adult daughter $200,000 to help her start a business.
    g. Marcie pays for her aunt's heart bypass operation. The money is sent directly to the medical service providers (i.e., hospital, doctors). The aunt does not qualify as Marcie's dependent.
    h. Taylor makes a substantial cash donation to the political campaign of a college classmate who is running for Congress.
    i. In his will, Corrine's father leaves her a valuable gun collection. As Corrine abhors firearms, she disclaims the bequest.

21. Distinguish between the following.
    a. The gross estate and the taxable estate.
    b. The taxable estate and the tax base.
    c. The gross estate and the probate estate.

22. Discuss the estate tax treatment of the following items.
    a. A surviving spouse's share of the community property.
    b. A dower interest claimed by the surviving spouse of the decedent.
    c. A dividend that has been declared but not paid on stock owned by the decedent.
    d. Interest accrued but unpaid on city bonds owned by the decedent.
    e. A note receivable due from a relative but forgiven in the decedent's will.
    f. A Roth IRA payable to the decedent's surviving spouse.
    g. A gift of stock made by the decedent prior to his death.
    h. In her will, the decedent exercised a special power of appointment.

23. Under what Code sections, if any, are the following transactions included in Mary's gross estate?
    a. A vested interest in her employer's contributory qualified pension plan with Jim, Mary's son, as the designated beneficiary.
    b. An insurance policy on her life, which Mary gave to Jim last year. Her grandson is the designated beneficiary of the policy.
    c. A CD at a local bank with ownership listed as "Mary, payable on proof of death to Jim."
    d. A revocable trust created by Mary, with a life estate to Jim, remainder to her grandson.
    e. In her will, Mary exercises a general power of appointment in favor of Jim. The power was granted to Mary by a trust created by her father.
    f. Mary paid a gift tax last year on a gift of real estate she made to Jim.
    g. Mary is the annuitant of a straight-life annuity policy that she purchased from an insurance company 10 years ago.

24. At the time of Emile's death, he was a joint tenant with Colette in a parcel of real estate. With regard to the inclusion in Emile's gross estate under § 2040, comment on the following independent assumptions:
    a. Emile and Colette received the property as a gift from Douglas.
    b. Colette provided all of the purchase price of the property.
    c. Colette's contribution was received as a gift from Emile.
    d. Emile's contribution was derived from income generated by property he received as a gift from Colette.

25. With regard to "life insurance," comment on the following.
    a. What the term includes (i.e., types of policies).
    b. The meaning of "incidents of ownership."
    c. When a gift occurs upon maturity of the policy.

    d.   The tax consequences when the owner of the policy predeceases the insured and the beneficiary.

    e.   The tax consequences when the beneficiary of the policy predeceases the insured.

26. Hal's residence is partially destroyed by fire. As a result of his burns, Hal dies shortly thereafter. One month after the fire and Hal's death, two antique automobiles are stolen from his garage. Do the fire and the theft have any Federal income or estate tax effects? Explain.

Issue ID

27. A qualified charity for estate and gift tax purposes is the same as one for Federal income tax purposes. Do you agree with this statement?

28. Sean's will creates a trust, life estate to his wife (Darcy), remainder to their children.
    a.   Will Sean's estate be allowed a marital deduction? Why or why not?
    b.   What course of action do you suggest to secure the deduction?
    c.   What are the consequences of any such course of action?

29. Tim and Ann are husband and wife. Tim dies first. Discuss the marital deduction result for each of the following situations.
    a.   In his will, Tim exercised a general power of appointment in favor of Ann.
    b.   Tim and Ann owned land (that Ann had purchased) as tenants by the entirety.
    c.   Tim is the owner of a policy on his life, and Ann is the beneficiary of the policy.
    d.   Tim is the owner of a policy on Ann's life with their children as the designated beneficiaries. Under Tim's will, the policy passes to Ann.
    e.   Ann is the designated beneficiary of IRAs held by Tim.
    f.   Tim is a nonresident alien, and Ann is a U.S. citizen.
    g.   Tim is a U.S. citizen, and Ann is a nonresident alien.

30. Using the legend provided, classify each of the following transactions.

Legend
NT = No transfer tax imposed
GT = Subject to the Federal gift tax
ET = Subject to the Federal estate tax

    a.   Hayden purchases a certificate of deposit listing title as "Hayden, payable on proof of death to Michele."
    b.   Same as (a). Hayden dies four years later, and Michele redeems the CD.
    c.   Using his funds, Marcus purchases real estate listing title as "Marcus and Kendal, joint tenancy with right of survivorship."
    d.   Same as (c). Kendal predeceases Marcus four years later.
    e.   Winston purchases insurance on the life of John and designates Sophia as the beneficiary.
    f.   Same as (e). Two years later, John dies first, and the insurance proceeds are paid to Sophia.
    g.   Pierce establishes a joint savings account listing ownership as "Pierce and Stella, joint tenants with right of survivorship."
    h.   Same as (g). One year later, Stella withdraws all of the funds from the account while Pierce is hospitalized.
    i.   Same as (h), except that Stella's withdrawal did not take place until after Pierce died while at the hospital.

31. Mary Beth Barksdale, age 70, is a widow in good health with an adult grandson, Marvin, and three great-grandchildren. Mary Beth's only son, Henry, died several years ago. Using securities worth $3 million, Mary Beth would like to create a trust, life estate to Marvin, remainder to his three children (Mary Beth's great-grandchildren). She is hesitant to do so because of the tax on generation-skipping transfers. Write a letter to Mary Beth advising her on this matter. Her address is 529 Magnolia Court, Meridian, MS 39307. (Note: Mary Beth's prior taxable gifts exhausted her unified transfer tax credit.)

Issue ID

Communications

32. In terms of the generation-skipping transfer tax, comment on the following.
    a.   A GSTT termination event and a GSTT distribution event look very similar.
    b.   A direct skip can occur only in gift situations, not in testamentary situations.

c.   Spouses may be of different generations if there is enough disparity in their ages.

d.   How the election to split a gift by a married donor can help avoid the tax.

PROBLEMS

33. Ima's estate includes the following assets.

	Fair Market Value	
	Date of Death	**Six Months Later**
Apartment building	$1,400,000	$1,380,000
Stock in Carmine Corporation	1,200,000	1,300,000
Stock in Garnet Corporation	900,000	700,000

Accrued rents on the apartment building are as follows: $50,000 (date of death) and $40,000 (six months later). In order to pay expenses, the executor of Ima's estate sells the Garnet stock for $600,000 eight months after her death.

a.   If the § 2032 election is made, how much is included in Ima's gross estate?

b.   As to part (a), assume the Garnet stock is sold for $600,000 five months (rather than eight months) after Ima's death. How does this change your answer, if at all?

c.   How much is included in the gross estate if the § 2032 election is not made?

34. In which, if any, of the following independent situations could the alternate valuation date *not be elected* in 2008? In all cases, assume that Bill and Nancy are husband and wife and that Nancy dies first.

a.   Nancy's will passes all of her property to Bill.

b.   Nancy's will passes half of her property to Bill and the other half to the First Christian Church of Ypsilanti, Michigan.

c.   The election would decrease the value of Nancy's gross estate but increase her estate tax liability.

d.   The election would increase the value of Nancy's gross estate but decrease her estate tax liability.

e.   Nancy's gross estate is $1,980,000. She made a taxable gift of $40,000 in January 1977.

f.   The executor of Nancy's estate sells or otherwise disposes of all of her assets within five months of her death.

Issue ID

35. In May 2007, Dudley and Eva enter into a property settlement preparatory to the dissolution of their marriage. Under the agreement, Dudley is to pay Eva $5 million in satisfaction of her marital rights. Of this amount, Dudley pays $2.5 million immediately, and the balance is due one year later. The parties are divorced in July. Dudley dies in December, and his estate pays Eva the remaining $2.5 million in May 2008. Discuss the tax ramifications of these transactions to the parties involved.

Issue ID

36. Jesse dies intestate (i.e., without a will) in May 2007. Jesse's major asset is a tract of land. Under applicable state law, Jesse's property will pass to Lorena, who is his only child. In December 2007, Lorena disclaims one-half of the property. In June 2008, Lorena disclaims the other half interest. Under state law, Lorena's disclaimer results in the property passing to Arnold (Lorena's only child). The value of the land (in its entirety) is as follows: $2 million in May 2007; $2.1 million in December 2007; and $2.2 million in June 2008. Discuss the transfer tax ramifications of these transactions.

37. In 2008, Alicia makes a gift of stock (basis of $900,000; fair market value of $1.2 million) to her son. She has made no prior taxable gifts. Alicia is married to Mitch, who made a taxable gift of $100,000 (gift tax paid was $23,800) in 2000 when he was single. How much gift tax is due on the 2008 transfer:

a.   If the § 2513 election to split the gift is not made?

b.   If the § 2513 election to split the gift is made?

38. At the time of his death on September 2, 2008, Brayden owned the following assets.

	Fair Market Value
City of Quincy bonds	$1,500,000
Stock in Taupe Corporation	900,000
Stock in Magenta Corporation	800,000
Promissory note issued by Hailey (Brayden's daughter)	300,000

In October 2008, the executor of Brayden's estate received the following: $60,000 interest on the City of Quincy bonds ($10,000 accrued since September 2); $7,000 cash dividend on the Taupe stock (date of record was September 3); and $8,000 cash dividend on the Magenta stock (date of record was September 1). The declaration date on both dividends was August 15. The $300,000 loan was made to Hailey in late 2006, and she used the money to create a very successful business. The note was forgiven by Brayden in his will. What are the estate tax consequences of these transactions?

39. At the time of Ronald's death in 2008, he was involved in the transactions described below.

- Ronald was a participant in his employer's contributory qualified pension plan. The plan balance of $1.8 million is paid to Brenda, Ronald's daughter and beneficiary. The distribution consists of the following.

Employer contributions	$800,000
Ronald's after-tax contributions	600,000
Income earned by the plan	400,000

- Ronald was covered by his employer's group term life insurance plan for employees. The $100,000 proceeds are paid to Brenda, the designated beneficiary.

a. What are the estate tax consequences?
b. The income tax consequences?
c. Would the answer to part (a) change if Brenda was Ronald's surviving spouse (not his daughter)? Explain.

40. Before her death in early 2008, Katie made the following transfers.

- In 2003, purchased stock in Green Corporation for $200,000 listing title as follows: "Katie, payable on proof of death to my son, Travis." Travis survives Katie, and the stock is worth $300,000 when Katie dies.
- In 2006, purchased an insurance policy on her life for $200,000 listing Paul, another of Katie's sons, as the designated beneficiary. The policy has a maturity value of $1 million and was immediately transferred to Paul as a gift.
- In 2007, made a gift of land (basis of $300,000; fair market value of $1.3 million) to Adriana, Katie's only daughter. As a result of the transfer, Katie paid a gift tax of $150,000. The value of the land is still $1.3 million at Katie's death.

As to these transfers, how much is included in Katie's gross estate?

41. In 2001, using $2 million in community property, Ernest creates a trust, life estate to his wife, Becky, and remainder to their children. Ernest dies in 2005 when the trust is worth $2.4 million, and Becky dies in 2008 when the trust is worth $2.6 million.

Issue ID

a. Did Ernest make a gift in 2001? Explain.
b. How much, if any, of the trust is included in Ernest's gross estate in 2005?
c. How much, if any, of the trust is included in Becky's gross estate in 2008?

42. At the time of his death, Garth was involved in the following arrangements.

- He held a life estate in the Myrtle Trust with the remainder passing to Garth's adult children. The trust was created by Myrtle (Garth's mother) in 1984 with securities worth $900,000. The Myrtle Trust had a value of $1.7 million when Garth died.

- Under the terms of the Myrtle Trust, Garth was given the power to provide for a disproportionate distribution of the remainder interest among his children. As Garth failed to exercise this power, the remainder interest is divided equally among the children.

Discuss the estate tax ramifications of these arrangements as to Garth.

43. In 2000, Alan purchases a commercial single premium annuity. Under the terms of the policy, Alan is to receive $120,000 annually for life. If Alan predeceases his wife, Katelyn, she is to receive $60,000 annually for life. Alan dies first at a time when the value of the survivorship feature is $900,000.
    a. How much, if any, of the annuity is included in Alan's gross estate? Taxable estate?
    b. Would the answers to part (a) change if the money Alan used to purchase the annuity was community property? Explain.

44. At the time of his death on June 6, 2008, Kirk was involved in the following real estate.

	Fair Market Value (on June 6, 2008)
Apartment building	$1,000,000
Tree farm	900,000
Pastureland	600,000
Residence	500,000

The apartment building was purchased by Eileen, Kirk's mother, and is owned jointly with her. The tree farm and pastureland were gifts from Eileen to Kirk and his two sisters. The tree farm is held in joint tenancy, and the pastureland is owned as tenants in common. Kirk purchased the residence and owns it with his wife as tenants by the entirety. How much is included in Kirk's gross estate based on the following assumptions?
    a. Kirk dies first and is survived by Eileen, his sisters, and his wife.
    b. Kirk dies after Eileen, but before his sisters and his wife.
    c. Kirk dies after Eileen and his sisters, but before his wife.
    d. Kirk dies last (i.e., he survives Eileen, his sisters, and his wife).

45. In 1982, Norman purchased real estate for $800,000 and listed title to the property as "Norman and Felicia, joint tenants with right of survivorship." Norman predeceases Felicia in 2008 when the real estate is worth $2.2 million. Norman and Felicia are brother and sister.
    a. Did a gift occur in 1982? Explain.
    b. What, if any, are the estate tax consequences in 2008?
    c. Under part (b), would your answer change if it was Felicia (not Norman) who died in 2008? Explain.

46. Assume the same facts as in Problem 45, except that Norman and Felicia are husband and wife (not brother and sister).
    a. What are the gift tax consequences in 1982?
    b. What are the estate tax consequences in 2008?
    c. Under part (b), would your answer change if it was Felicia (not Norman) who died in 2008? Explain.

Decision Making

Communications

47. Mike Edwards would like to make a lifetime transfer in trust of $1 million to his son, Keith, and accomplish the following objectives.

- Avoid any death tax on the deaths of Mike, Keith, and Bette (Keith's wife).
- Give Keith the right to determine what portion of the remainder should be allocated between Bette and their children.
- Give Keith some additional security by allowing him to reach the principal should the need materialize.
- Prevent Keith from squandering all of the principal to the detriment of Bette or her children.

Write a letter to Mike recommending a course of action making use of § 2041. Mike's address is 4320 Richmond Avenue, Syracuse, NY 13244.

48. In each of the independent situations below, determine the transfer tax (i.e., estate and gift) consequences of what has occurred. (In all cases, assume Gene and Mary are married and that Ashley is their daughter.)
    a. Mary purchases an insurance policy on Gene's life and designates Ashley as the beneficiary. Mary dies first, and under her will, the policy passes to Gene.
    b. Gene purchases an insurance policy on his life and designates Ashley as the beneficiary. Gene gives the policy to Mary and continues to pay the premiums thereon. Two years after the gift, Gene dies first, and the policy proceeds are paid to Ashley.
    c. Gene purchases an insurance policy on Mary's life and designates Ashley as the beneficiary. Ashley dies first one year later.
    d. Assume the same facts as in part (c). Two years later, Mary dies. Because Gene has not designated a new beneficiary, the insurance proceeds are paid to him.
    e. Gene purchases an insurance policy on his life and designates Mary as the beneficiary. Gene dies first, and the policy proceeds are paid to Mary.

49. Prior to his marriage to Alice, Ken took out an insurance policy on his life. The policy has a maturity value of $500,000 and designates Martha (Ken's mother) as the beneficiary. Twenty years later, Ken dies, and the insurance proceeds are paid to Martha. Premiums on the policy were paid as follows: 30% from Ken's separate property and 70% from community funds. Discuss the tax consequences of this situation if all of the parties live in:
    a. California.
    b. Texas.
    c. Suppose that prior to his death, Ken changed the designated beneficiary of the policy from Martha to Alice. How will this affect your answers to parts (a) and (b)?

50. In June 2008, Rudy died in an auto accident while vacationing in Maine. Discuss the tax ramifications of the following transactions involving the administration of Rudy's estate.
    a. The executor of the estate (Rudy's daughter) travels to Maine to pick up and transport the remains for burial in the family plot in Columbia, South Carolina. The expenses involved are paid by the estate.
    b. In early 2008, Rudy had promised to give his niece $10,000 if she passed the CPA exam. After Rudy's death, the niece passes the exam, and the executor of his estate pays her $10,000.
    c. In March 2008, Rudy had pledged $25,000 to the building fund of his church. The estate satisfies the pledge.
    d. Due to the accident, Rudy's auto (basis of $55,000; fair market value of $28,000) was completely destroyed. Insurance recovery of $27,000 is received by Rudy's estate.
    e. The local sheriff issued a ticket to Rudy for a moving traffic violation and leaving the scene of an accident. Rudy's estate paid the ticket, fine, and court costs of $3,500.
    f. Rudy's estate paid Federal ($72,000) and state ($6,100) income taxes when it filed his final (year of death) income tax return.
    g. The day after Rudy's death, his vacation cabin is burglarized and personal effects (e.g., laptop computer, Rolex watch) are stolen. The property taken cost Rudy $15,000 but had a value of $9,800 and was not insured.

51. At the time of his death in the current year, Bob owned the following assets.

    • Insurance policy on Bob's life (maturity value of $900,000) with Harriet (Bob's surviving spouse) as the designated beneficiary.
    • Personal residence (fair market value of $1.5 million) with ownership listed as: "Bob and Harriet, tenants by the entirety with right of survivorship." The residence was originally purchased by Harriet.
    • Undeveloped land (fair market value of $1.8 million) subject to a mortgage of $200,000.
    • Apartment building (fair market value of $1.5 million) owned by Bob and his two sisters as equal tenants in common.
    • Ten cemetery lots (valued at $6,000 each) purchased for family use.

    Under Bob's will, all of his property passes to Harriet. How much marital deduction is Bob's estate allowed?

52. In 1986, Bruce places in trust $900,000 worth of securities. Under the terms of the trust instrument, Wendy (Bruce's wife) is granted a life estate, and on Wendy's death, the remainder interest passes to Bruce and Wendy's children (as Wendy determines in her will). Upon Wendy's death in the current year, the trust assets are valued at $3 million.
    a. How much, if any, marital deduction will be allowed on the gift made in 1986?
    b. How much, if any, of the trust will be included in Wendy's gross estate upon her death?

53. Assume the same facts as in Problem 52, except that Bruce made the QTIP election when the trust was created. Further assume that Wendy has no choice as to which of her children will receive the remainder interest upon her death.
    a. How much, if any, marital deduction will be allowed on the gift made in 1986?
    b. How much, if any, of the trust will be subject to the Federal estate tax upon Wendy's later death?

54. Under Harrison's will, Dana (Harrison's brother) inherits his property. Three years later, Dana dies. Based on the following independent assumptions, what is Dana's credit for the tax on prior transfers?
    a. The estate tax attributable to the inclusion of the property in Harrison's gross estate is $900,000, and the estate tax attributable to the inclusion of the property in Dana's gross estate is $800,000.
    b. The estate tax attributable to the inclusion of the property in Harrison's gross estate is $1 million, and the estate tax attributable to the inclusion of the property in Dana's gross estate is $1.1 million.
    c. Would your answers to parts (a) and (b) change if Dana died five years (rather than three years) after Harrison?

55. In 2008, Loretta makes a taxable gift of $2 million to her granddaughter, Bertha. Presuming that Loretta used up both her unified transfer tax credit and her generation-skipping transfer tax credit, how much tax does Loretta owe as a result of the transfer?

56. In 2007, Marsha died, and her after-tax estate of $4 million passed to a trust. Under the terms of the trust, Wilma (Marsha's daughter) is granted a life estate with the remainder passing to Karl (Marsha's grandson) upon Wilma's death. The trustee elects to use $2 million of the generation-skipping transfer tax exemption. Wilma dies in 2008 when the trust is worth $6 million.
    a. Presuming the GSTT applies, is it caused by a termination event, a distribution event, or a direct skip?
    b. How much of the trust is subject to the GSTT?
    c. Who pays the tax?
    d. What is the GSTT rate that applies?

57. In each of the following independent situations, determine the decedent's final estate tax liability (net of any unified tax credit).

| | Decedent | | |
	Joyce	Lindsey	Ryan
Year of death	2002	2003	2008
Taxable estate	$800,000	$1,300,000	$1,400,000
Post-1976 taxable gifts—			
Made in 2000	800,000	—	—
Made in 2001	—	900,000	—
Made in 2003	—	—	1,100,000

TAX RETURN PROBLEMS

1. Warren S. and Hilda P. Harding (Social Security numbers 303–21–4678 and 304–84–3916) live at 110 Sycamore Drive, Richmond, IN 47374. Both Warren and Hilda are practicing oral surgeons and have been married for 20 years. They have three children (Corey, Ava, and Amanda). During 2007, they made the following transfers.

Transfer	Donor	
	Warren	Hilda
Purchased land in Henry County listing title as "Corey, Ava, and Amanda Harding, tenants in common"	$50,000	$50,000
Hilda paid for a heart bypass operation performed on her uncle (Charles Poe)—she paid $42,000 to the surgeons and reimbursed her uncle $38,000 for part of the hospital bill	—	80,000
Gave Hilda's parents (Don and Mary Poe) an RV on their 50th wedding anniversary	45,000	45,000
Purchased a $100,000 CD from Wayne State Bank listing title as "Hilda Harding, payable on proof of death to Corey, Ava, and Amanda Harding"	—	100,000
Warren and Hilda gave each other identical BMW automobiles as Christmas gifts	65,000	65,000
Donation to Salvation Army	1,500	1,500
Contribution to the mayor of Richmond reelection campaign	300	300
Paid the tuition to private schools for their three children (Corey, Ava, and Amanda)	30,000	30,000

By creating several trusts in 2006, the Hardings made taxable gifts of $2.2 million. As a consequence, they paid a gift tax of $82,000.

Prepare gift tax returns (Form 709) for the Hardings covering the taxable transfers made in 2007. As in the past, the Hardings make the § 2513 election to split the gifts.

2. Ernest P. Jackson (Social Security number 049–62–8105) is a widower who lives at 4322 Nutmeg Avenue, Danbury, CT 06810. During 2007, he made the following gifts to his four adult children.

    *   A tract of land in Tolland County (cost basis of $100,000 and fair market value of $600,000) to Jim Jackson and Camilla Paine as equal tenants in common.
    *   An apartment building in Manchester (CT) (cost basis of $320,000 and fair market value of $630,000) to George Jackson and Leona Hart as equal joint tenants with right of survivorship.

    Prepare a gift tax return (Form 709) for Ernest. He has not made any prior taxable gifts.

3. Michael (Mike) C. Harlan died on May 9, 2007, as a result of a single car accident. Relevant information regarding Mike's affairs is summarized below.

    *   Mike (age 66, born on March 10, 1941) resided at 135 Pine Lane, Pueblo County, Pueblo, CO 81003. He is survived by his wife, Carla R., and his adult children, Joshua and Jacob Harlan and Julia Peters.

- During his life, Mike developed several successful car dealerships that were incorporated under the name Rocky Motors Corporation. When Mike retired at age 60, he sold the stock in Rocky Motors to the children, all of whom are active in the business. The children issued promissory notes for the stock, and at the time of Mike's death, the following balances were outstanding.

Joshua	$300,000
Jacob	320,000
Julia	310,000

Because the notes are secured and no default is likely, they should be valued at face amount.

- During his working years, Mike participated in the Rocky Motors qualified pension plan administered by Falcon Benefit Fund of Colorado. Prior to death, Mike had taken no distributions from the plan and had not made any settlement options, but he had designated Carla as the beneficiary. Mike's accrued balance in the plan (as of May 9, 2007) was $980,000.

  - $400,000 (from Rocky Motors).
  - $200,000 (from Mike).
  - $380,000 (plan earnings).

On September 3, 2007, Falcon Benefit made $996,000 [$980,000 (plan balance) + $16,000 (interest accrued since May 9, 2007)] available to Carla.

- Mike was also covered by a group term life insurance policy sponsored by Rocky Motors with Peregrine Assurance as the carrier. Mike's policy, face amount of $100,000, contains a double indemnity provision. Since Mike had designated his mother as the beneficiary and she is deceased, Peregrine paid the $200,000 proceeds to Mike's estate.
- Mike and Carla owned whole life insurance policies on each other. Issued by Hawk Mutual Company, each policy has a maturity value of $600,000 and names the other spouse as the beneficiary. On Mike's death, Hawk pays Carla $600,000. The policy owned by Mike on Carla's life is worth $150,000 and passes to the executor of the estate. Later the estate sells the policy to the Harlan children.
- The Harlan residence on Pine Lane was purchased by Mike 10 years ago and is currently worth $840,000. Title to the property is listed as "Michael and Carla Harlan, tenants by the entirety with right of survivorship."
- In 2000, Mike purchased land in Crowley County for $150,000, financing part of the cost with a mortgage from Trinidad State Bank. On May 9, 2007, the land has a value of $220,000, and the mortgage balance is $40,000.
- In 1975, Mike, Carla, and Maxine (Carla's mother) acquired land in Otero County for $60,000. Mike furnished the purchase price, and title was registered as equal tenants in common. On May 9, 2007, the land is valued at $240,000.
- As a result of the accident, Mike's Escalade was totaled. The SUV cost $82,000 and had a fair market value of $64,000 at the time of the accident. After reducing the claim by a $500 deductible, the insurer (National Casualty) paid Mike's estate $63,500.
- Other assets not previously mentioned and owned by Mike at death (valued as of May 9, 2007) are listed below.

Joint checking account (with Carla) at Pueblo State Bank	$ 9,200
Certificate of deposit for $150,000 ($3,800 of interest accrued and included) at Countrywide Bank	153,800
Money market account ($600 of interest accrued and included) at Pueblo State Bank	44,600
City of Denver bonds ($9,000 of interest accrued and included)	189,000
Stock in Wyoming Coal Corporation (6,000 shares of common)	270,000
Personal and household goods (RV, clothing, furniture, fishing, camping, and hunting equipment, etc.)	81,000

- Amounts paid by the executor of Mike's estate are summarized as follows.

Credit card debt	$10,500
Unpaid bills (e.g., medical, dental, utilities, insurance, property taxes) as of May 9, 2007	18,000

Federal and state income taxes (January 1–May 9, 2007)	$41,000
Funeral expenses	12,000
Accountant's fees	8,200
Attorney's fees	21,000

Under Mike's will, his property is to be placed in trust, life estate to his grandchildren and remainder to their children. He also bequeaths $20,000 in cash to the First Methodist Church of Pueblo, CO. Julia Peters, Mike's daughter and a trained paralegal, is designated as the executor of his estate. Julia serves in this capacity and does not charge a fee for her services.

Prepare an estate tax return (Form 706) for the estate, making the following assumptions.

- Relevant Social Security numbers—Michael, 650–96–4571; Carla, 652–14–8462; Julia, 651–40–6194.
- No § 2032, § 2032A, and § 6166 elections are made.
- Disregard requests for information that is not available.
- Some deductions require a choice (Form 1040, Form 706, Form 1041) and cannot be claimed twice. Resolve all such choices in favor of deducting the item on Form 706.
- The Harlans have not made any *taxable* gifts in the past.

RESEARCH PROBLEMS

Note: Solutions to Research Problems can be prepared by using the **RIA Checkpoint®** **Student Edition** online research product, which is available to accompany this text. It is also possible to prepare solutions to the Research Problems by using tax research materials found in a standard tax library.

Communications

Research Problem 1. One of your clients, David Gorman, has been trying to convince his mother, Lorinda, to give him a tract of undeveloped land. Lorinda is willing to make the gift, but she is uncertain about the tax consequences involved. In any event, she wants David to pay any gift tax that would result.

The land was purchased by Lorinda 30 years ago for $30,000 and currently has a value of $200,000. Lorinda's only prior taxable gift occurred in 2004 and involved an apartment building worth $1 million. No gift tax resulted, due to the exemption equivalent.

Write a letter to David reviewing the tax consequences of a "net gift" of the land by his mother. As David was a business major in college, you can assume that he is knowledgeable as to basic tax concepts. David's address is 1480 Ash Street, Rolla, MO 65401.

Partial list of research aids:
Rev.Rul. 75–72, 1975–1 C.B. 310.
Diedrich v. Comm., 82–1 USTC ¶9419, 50 AFTR2d 82–5054, 102 S.Ct. 2414 (USSC, 1982).

Research Problem 2. In 2000, June, a 75-year-old widow, creates an irrevocable trust naming her five adult grandchildren as the beneficiaries. The assets transferred in trust consist of marketable securities (worth $800,000) and June's personal residence (worth $400,000). Bob, June's younger brother and a practicing attorney, is designated as the trustee. Other provisions of the trust are noted below.

- Bob is given the discretion to distribute the income to the beneficiaries based on their need or add it to corpus. He is also given the power to change trust investments and to terminate the trust.
- The trust is to last for June's lifetime or, if sooner, until termination by Bob.
- Upon termination of the trust, the principal and any accumulated income are to be distributed to the beneficiaries (June's grandchildren).

For 2000, June files a Form 709 to report the transfer in trust and pays a gift tax based on value of $1.2 million ($800,000 + $400,000).

After the transfer in trust and up to the time of her death, June continues to occupy the residence. Although she pays no rent, she maintains the property and pays the yearly property taxes. June never discussed the matter of her continued occupancy of the residence with either Bob or the beneficiaries of the trust.

On June's death in 2008, the value of the trust is $2.3 million, broken down as follows: marketable securities and cash ($1.6 million) and residence ($700,000). Shortly thereafter, Bob sells the residence, liquidates the trust, and distributes the proceeds to the beneficiaries.

What are the estate tax consequences of these transactions to June?

Partial list of research aids:
§ 2036.
Guynn v. U.S., 71–1 USTC ¶12,742, 27 AFTR2d 71–1653, 437 F.2d 1148 (CA–4, 1971).
Estate of Eleanor T. R. Trotter, 82 TCM 633, T.C.Memo. 2001–250.
Estate of Lorraine C. Disbrow, 91 TCM 794, T.C.Memo. 2006–34.

Research Problem 3.   Grace Tipton, a widow of considerable means, dies in February 2004. One month later, her designated executor is appointed by the probate court of appropriate jurisdiction, and the administration of the Tipton estate is initiated. Among the bequests in Grace's will is one that passes $10 million to the Christian Assisted Living Foundation (CALF), but only if it is a qualified charity for purposes of § 2055. Because the status of CALF has never been evaluated by the IRS, the executor feels compelled to postpone the satisfaction of the bequest. Instead, he files the Form 706 and pays the estate tax based on the charitable deduction being allowed. Further, he requests a "closing letter" from the IRS on the Form 706 that is filed. Since the issuance of a closing letter means acceptance of the deduction, it forces the IRS to investigate the charitable nature of CALF.

After investigating the activities of CALF, the IRS finds it to be a qualified charity. Consequently, in October 2006 the IRS issues a closing letter approving the charitable deduction claimed and accepting the Form 706 as filed. Shortly thereafter, the executor transfers $11 million to CALF. The amount transferred represents $10 million for the satisfaction of the bequest and $1 million for statutory interest accrued. Under state law, interest must be paid on any bequest that is not satisfied within a one-year period after the initiation of administration. The probate court sanctions the determination and payment of the $1 million interest amount.

Subsequent to the $11 million CALF distribution, the executor files an amended Form 706. The amended return claims a refund for the estate taxes attributable to the additional $1 million paid as interest. On the amended return, the interest is classified as an administration expense under § 2053, thereby reducing the taxable estate and resulting estate tax liability. The IRS denies the claim for refund on the grounds that the interest incurred was not necessary to the administration of the estate. If the executor had satisfied the CALF bequest earlier, the accrual of interest would have been avoided. The executor counters that the delay was necessary in order to maintain fiduciary integrity in complying with the terms of the decedent's will. Who should prevail?

Partial list of research aids:
§ 2053(a)(2).
Reg. § 20.2053–3(a).
Pitner v. U.S., 68–1 USTC ¶12,499, 21 AFTR2d 1571, 388 F.2d 651 (CA–5, 1967).
Turner v. U.S., 2004–1 USTC ¶60,478, 93 AFTR2d 2004–686, 306 F.Supp.2d 668 (D.Ct.Tex., 2004).

Research Problem 4.   In 1996, John Letts dies and is survived by his widow (Mildred) and two adult children. Under the terms of his will, most of his property passes to a trust, life estate to Mildred, remainder to their children. John designated Mildred and their children as executors of his estate.

The executors filed a Form 706 that reflected no taxes due because of the allowance of the marital deduction. On page 2 of Form 706, the executors indicated that the QTIP election of § 2056(b)(7) *was not* being made. John Letts's Form 706 was timely filed but never audited by the IRS.

In 2007, Mildred dies, and her will names her children as executors. Mildred's estate includes none of the trust created by John, as the QTIP election was not made. Mildred's life estate is not subject to inclusion under § 2036(a)(2), as she was not the grantor of the trust. The parties admit that John's estate should not have claimed a marital deduction, as what passed to Mildred was a terminable interest. The error, inadvertent as it was, cannot be corrected since the statute of limitations precludes filing an amended Form 706 for John Letts's estate.

Does the IRS have any recourse?

Partial list of research aids:
§ 2044.
Barry S. Glass, 87 T.C. 1087 (1986).
Estate of Mildred Geraldine Letts, 109 T.C. 290 (1997).

Use the tax resources of the Internet to address the following questions. Do not restrict your search to the World Wide Web, but include a review of newsgroups and general reference materials, practitioner sites and resources, primary sources of the tax law, chat rooms and discussion groups, and other opportunities.

 **Internet** *Activity*

Research Problem 5. What type of transfer tax, if any, does your home state impose? What about the state(s) contiguous to your home state? (For Alaska, use Washington; for Hawaii, use California.)

Research Problem 6. A considerable amount of material (e.g., magazine and newspaper commentaries, journal articles, books) is available on why the Federal estate tax should not be repealed. Identify three recent sources. Summarize them in an e-mail to your instructor, and include a list of citations.

Communications

Research Problem 7. What is the purpose of IRS Publication 950 (Rev. August 2007)? What does it contain?

Research Problem 8. Based on the most recent IRS data available, determine the following.
a. The number of estate tax returns (Form 706) filed in a year. What percentage of these returns did the IRS audit?
b. The number of estate tax returns filed that also included GSTT situations.
c. The number of gift tax returns (Form 709) filed in a year. What percentage of these returns did the IRS audit?

Family Tax Planning

LEARNING OBJECTIVES

After completing Chapter 18, you should be able to:

LO.1
Use various established concepts in carrying out the valuation process.

LO.2
Apply the special use valuation method in appropriate situations.

LO.3
Identify problems involved in valuing an interest in a closely held business.

LO.4
Compare the income tax basis rules applying to property received by gift and by death.

LO.5
Plan gifts so as to minimize gift taxes and avoid estate taxes.

LO.6
Make gifts so as to avoid income taxes for the donor.

LO.7
Reduce probate costs in the administration of an estate.

LO.8
Apply procedures that reduce estate tax consequences.

LO.9
Obtain liquidity for an estate.

Broadly speaking, *family tax planning* involves the use of various procedures that minimize the effect of taxation on transfers within the family unit. As such, planning involves a consideration not only of transfer taxes (i.e., gift and estate) but also of the income tax ramifications to both the transferor (i.e., donor or decedent) and the transferees (i.e., donees or heirs).

The valuation of the transferred property also is an essential element of family tax planning. The gift tax is based on the fair market value of the property on the date of the transfer. For the Federal estate tax, the fair market value on the date of the owner's death or the alternate valuation date (if available and elected) controls.

LO.1
Use various established concepts in carrying out the valuation process.

Valuation Concepts

The central focus of this chapter concerns the valuation of property involved in transfers by gift and by death.

Valuation in General

The Internal Revenue Code refers to "value" and "fair market value," but does not discuss these terms at length.[1] Section 2031(b) comes closest to a definition when it treats the problem of stocks and securities for which no sales price information (the usual case with closely held corporations) is available. In such situations, "the value thereof shall be determined by taking into consideration, in addition to all other factors, the value of stock or securities of corporations engaged in the same or similar line of business which are listed on an exchange."

Regulation § 20.2031–1(b) is more specific in defining fair market value as "the price at which property would change hands between a willing buyer and a willing seller, neither being under any compulsion to buy or to sell and both having reasonable knowledge of relevant facts." The same Regulation makes clear that the fair market value of an item of property is not determined by a forced sale price. Nor is the fair market value determined by the sale price of the item in a market other than that in which the item is most commonly sold to the public. Sentiment should not play a part in the determination of value. Suppose, for example, the decedent's daughter is willing to pay $500 for a portrait of her mother. If the painting is really worth $200 (i.e., what the general public would pay), then that should be its value.

---

[1]See, for example, §§ 1001(b), 2031(a), and 2512(a). Sections 2032A(e)(7) and (8) set forth certain procedures for valuing farms and interests in closely held businesses.

The item's location must also be considered. Thus, the fair market value of property that generally is obtained by the public in a retail market is the price at which the property (or comparable items) would be sold at retail.

EXAMPLE 1

At the time of his death, Don owned three automobiles. The automobiles are included in Don's gross estate at their fair market value on the date of his death or on the alternate valuation date (if elected). The fair market value of the automobiles is determined by looking at the price a member of the general public would pay for automobiles of approximately the same description, make, model, age, condition, etc. The price a dealer in used cars would pay for these automobiles is inappropriate, because an automobile is an item obtainable by the public in a retail market. ■

If tangible personalty is sold as a result of an advertisement in the classified section of a newspaper and the property is of a type often sold in this manner, or if the property is sold at a public auction, the price for which it is sold is presumed to be the retail sales price of the item at the time of the sale. The retail sales price is also used if the sale is made within a reasonable period following the valuation date, and market conditions affecting the value of similar items have not changed substantially.[2] Tangible personalty includes all property except real estate and intangible property.

Valuation of Specific Assets

Stocks and Bonds. If there is a market for stocks and bonds on a stock exchange, in an over-the-counter market, or otherwise, the mean between the highest and lowest quoted selling prices on the valuation date is the fair market value per unit. A special rule applies if no sales occurred on the valuation date but did occur on dates within a reasonable period before and after the valuation date. The fair market value is the weighted average of the means between the highest and the lowest sales prices on the nearest date before and the nearest date after the valuation date. The average is weighted *inversely* by the respective number of trading days between the selling dates and the valuation date.[3]

EXAMPLE 2

Carla makes a gift to Antonio of shares of stock in Green Corporation. The transactions involving this stock that occurred closest to the date of the gift took place two trading days before the date of the gift at a mean selling price of $10 and three trading days after the gift at a mean selling price of $15. The $12 fair market value of each share of Green stock is determined as follows.

$$\frac{(3 \times \$10) + (2 \times \$15)}{5} = \$12$$ ■

If no transactions occurred within a reasonable period before and after the valuation date, the fair market value is determined by taking a weighted average of the means between the bona fide bid and asked prices on the nearest trading dates before and after the valuation date. However, both dates must be within a reasonable period of time.

If no actual sales prices or bona fide bid and asked prices are available for dates within a reasonable period relative to the valuation date, the mean between the highest and lowest available sales prices or bid and asked prices on that date may be taken as the value.

In many instances, there are no established market prices for securities. This lack of information is typically the case with stock in closely held corporations. Problems unique to valuing interests in closely held businesses are discussed later in this chapter.

---

[2]Rev.Proc. 65–19, 1965–2 C.B. 1002.

[3]Reg. §§ 20.2031–2(b) and 25.2512–2(b).

Notes Receivable. The fair market value of notes, secured or unsecured, is the amount of unpaid principal plus interest accrued to the valuation date, unless the parties (e.g., executor, donor) establish a lower value or prove the notes are worthless. Factors such as a low interest rate and a distant maturity date are relevant in showing that a note is worth less than its face amount. Crucial elements in proving that a note is entirely or partially worthless are the financial condition of the borrower and the absence of any value for the property pledged or mortgaged as security for the obligation.[4]

EXAMPLE 3

At the time of his death, Ira held a note (face amount of $50,000) issued by his son, Kevin. Although Kevin is solvent, he is relieved of the obligation because Ira forgives the note in his will. Presuming the note is payable on demand, it is included in Ira's gross estate at $50,000 plus accrued interest. If the note is not due immediately and/or the interest provided for is under the current rate, a discount may be in order, and the fair market value of the note would be less than $50,000. The burden of proof in supporting a discount for the note is on the executor. ■

ETHICAL and EQUITABLE *Considerations*

ONE WAY TO HANDLE LOANS TO TROUBLESOME IN-LAWS

At the time of his death in 2008, Tim Landry held a note, payable on demand, in the amount of $40,000. The note had been issued by Roy Briggs, Tim's former brother-in-law, 10 years earlier. Roy used the funds to help pay the wedding and honeymoon expenses when he married Colleen Landry, Tim's sister. The couple have since separated, and Roy disappeared for parts unknown in 2002.

The executor of Tim's estate handled this matter as follows.

- Filed an amended income tax return for 2002 claiming a bad debt deduction. This set off a chain reaction, and several other amended returns had to be filed for years after 2002.
- Made no mention of the note on the Form 706 filed for Tim Landry's estate.

What, if any, could be the justification for the executor's actions? What caused the chain reaction? If an audit results, what position(s) might the IRS take?

Insurance Policies and Annuity Contracts. The value of a life insurance policy on the life of a person other than the decedent, or the value of an annuity contract issued by a company regularly engaged in selling annuities, is the cost of a comparable contract.[5]

EXAMPLE 4

Paul purchased a joint and survivor annuity contract from an insurance company (i.e., a commercial contract). Under the contract's terms, Paul is to receive payments of $120,000 per year for his life. Upon Paul's death, his wife (Kate) is to receive $90,000 annually for her life. Ten years after purchasing the annuity, when Kate is 40 years old, Paul dies. The value of the annuity contract on the date of Paul's death [and the amount includible in Paul's gross estate under § 2039(a)] is the amount the insurance company would charge in the year of Paul's death for an annuity that would pay $90,000 annually for the life of a female 40 years of age. ■

EXAMPLE 5

At the time of her death, Lana owns an insurance policy (face amount of $500,000) on the life of her son, Sam. No further payments need be made on the policy (e.g., it is a single premium policy or a paid-up policy). The value of the policy on the date of Lana's death (and the amount includible in her gross estate under § 2033 as property owned by the decedent) is the amount the insurance company would charge in the year of her death for a single premium contract (face amount of $500,000) on the life of someone Sam's age. ■

---

[4]Reg. §§ 20.2031–4 and 25.2512–4.

[5]Reg. §§ 20.2031–8(a)(1) and 25.2512–6(a).

Determining the value of an insurance policy by using the amount charged for a comparable policy is more difficult when, on the date of valuation, the contract has been in force for some time and further premium payments are to be made. In such a case, the value may be approximated by adding to the interpolated terminal reserve the proportionate part of the gross premium last paid before the valuation date that covers the period extending beyond that date.[6]

The valuation of annuities issued by parties *not regularly engaged in the sale of annuities* (i.e., noncommercial contracts) requires the use of special tables issued by the IRS.

Life Estates, Terms for Years, Reversions, and Remainders.

As with noncommercial annuities, the valuation of life estates, income interests for a term of years, reversions, and remainders involves the use of tables.

Because life expectancies change, the IRS is required to issue new tables at least every 10 years.[7] The current tables were issued in April 1999 and are effective for transfers beginning in May of that year.[8] The tables contain 50 different possible rates (ranging from 4.2 percent to 14 percent), but *only a portion of the tables is reproduced* in Appendix A.

The tables provide only the remainder factor. If the income interest (life estate) has also been transferred, the factor to be used is one minus the remainder factor.

Matt transfers $1 million in trust, specifying a life estate to Rita, remainder to Rick on Rita's death. The gift took place on January 4, 2008, when Rita was age 35. Assume that the appropriate rate is 6.8%. Using the table extract in Appendix A (Table S on page A–9) for a person age 35 under the 6.8% column, the value of the remainder interest is $96,380 (.09638 × $1,000,000). The life estate factor is .90362 (1.00000 − .09638). Thus, Matt has made a gift to Rita of $903,620 and a gift to Rick of $96,380. ■

EXAMPLE 6

In computing the value of an income interest for a term of years, a different table is used. Again, the table furnishes the remainder factor. To compute the factor for the income interest, subtract the remainder factor from one. *Only a portion of the tables is reproduced* in Appendix A.

On December 29, 2008, Julia transfers $200,000 by gift to a trust. Under the terms of the trust, income is payable to Paul for eight years. After the eight-year period, the trust terminates, and the trust principal passes to Sara. For the month in which the trust was created, the appropriate rate was 7.4%. The present worth of $1 due at the end of eight years is $0.564892 (Table B on page A–11). Thus, Julia has made a gift to Sara of $112,978.40 (.564892 × $200,000) and a gift to Paul of $87,021.60 (.435108 × $200,000). ■

EXAMPLE 7

What is the significance of dividing a gift into several distinct parts? This is important in determining the applicability of the annual exclusion and the marital deduction. Under the facts of Example 6, an annual exclusion probably would be allowed for the gift to Rita but not for the interest passing to Rick (because of the future interest limitation). If Rita is Matt's wife, no marital deduction is allowed because the life estate is a terminable interest. As noted in Chapter 17, however, this problem could be cured with a qualified terminable interest property (QTIP) election.

Why might a trust be arranged so that the income interest is limited to a term of years rather than the life of a beneficiary (compare Example 7 with Example 6)? Suppose in Example 7 that Paul is the 13-year-old son of Sara, a single parent. Julia, the grandmother, establishes the trust to assure that Paul's support needs (e.g., medical, educational) will be provided for until he reaches the age of majority.

---

[6]The terminal reserve value of a life insurance policy generally approximates the policy's cash surrender value. For an illustration on how to arrive at the interpolated terminal reserve value, see Reg. § 20.2031–8(a)(3) (Ex. 3).

[7]§ 7520.

[8]The valuation factors in the tables represent 120% of whatever the Federal mid-term rate is for the month of the valuation date.

Thereafter, the trust income will help maintain Sara. In this type of situation, however, caution is in order to avoid the possible application of the kiddie tax. Now applicable to children under the age of 19 (or under age 24 if the child is a full-time student, unless the child's earned income provides more than half of his or her support), the kiddie tax has the effect of taxing a child's net unearned income (i.e., unearned income in excess of $1,800) at the parents' income tax rate.

Real Estate and the Special Use Valuation Method

LO.2

Apply the special use valuation method in appropriate situations.

Proper valuation principles usually require that real estate be valued at its most suitable (i.e., "best" or "highest") use. Section 2032A, however, permits an executor to elect to value certain classes of real estate used in farming or in connection with a closely held business at its "current" use, rather than the most suitable use. The major objective of the **special use value** election is to provide a form of limited relief to protect the heirs against the possibility of having to sell a portion of the family farm to pay estate taxes.

EXAMPLE 8

At the time of his death, Rex owned a dairy farm on the outskirts of a large city. For farming purposes, the property's value is $1.5 million (the current use value).[9] As a potential site for a shopping center, however, the property is worth $2.2 million (the most suitable use value). The executor of Rex's estate can elect to include only $1.5 million in the gross estate. ∎

The special use valuation procedure permits a reduction of no more than $960,000 in estate tax valuation in 2008 ($940,000 for 2007). This amount is subject to indexation.

EXAMPLE 9

At the time of her death in 2008, Wanda owned a farm with a most suitable use value of $3.5 million but a current use value of $2.3 million. Assuming the property qualifies under § 2032A and the special use valuation election is made, Wanda's gross estate must include $2,540,000. Only $960,000 can be excluded under § 2032A. ∎

The special use valuation election is available if *all* of the following conditions are satisfied.

- At least 50 percent of the adjusted value of the gross estate consists of *real* or *personal* property devoted to a qualifying use (used for farming or in a closely held business) at the time of the owner's death.[10]
- The *real* property devoted to a qualifying use comprises at least 25 percent of the adjusted value of the gross estate.

  For purposes of satisfying both the 50 percent test (above) and the 25 percent test, the qualifying property is considered at its most suitable use value. Thus, in Example 8, the property would be treated as if it had a value of $2.2 million (not $1.5 million). The adjusted value of the gross estate is the gross estate less certain unpaid mortgages and other indebtedness.
- The qualifying property passes to a qualifying heir of the decedent. Qualifying heirs are certain family members as set forth in § 2032A(e)(2).
- The *real* property has been owned by the decedent or the decedent's family for five out of the eight years ending on the date of the decedent's death and was devoted to a qualifying use during that period.
- The decedent or a member of the decedent's family participated materially in the operation of the farm or business during the five-year period specified above.[11]

---

[9]Sections 2032A(e)(7) and (8) set forth various methods of valuation to be applied in arriving at current use value.

[10]§§ 2032A(b)(1)(A) and (b)(2). For a definition of "farm" and "farming," see §§ 2032A(e)(4) and (5).

[11]§ 2032A(b)(1)(C)(ii). "Material participation" is defined in § 2032A(e)(6).

TAX *in the News*

PITFALLS IN PLANNING FOR THE USE OF § 2032A

A number of variables need to be taken into account when planning to make the election under § 2032A. As noted below, some of these variables can have a negative impact on the parties involved.

- Meeting the percentage requirements of § 2032A (i.e., 50 and 25 percent tests) is a continuing challenge. What qualifies today may not do so 20 years from now when the owner dies. Recent significant fluctuations in the market value of farmland further complicate the planning. (These valuation problems are discussed on page 18–21 and illustrated in Examples 30 through 32 later in this chapter.)

- The participating heirs (i.e., those who continue to operate the farm or ranch) take a lower income tax basis in the property that is subject to the election. (See the discussion on pages 18–15 and 18–16 later in this chapter.)
- The participating heirs suffer the additional estate tax burden that results *if* recapture occurs. Perhaps the nonparticipating heirs should agree contractually to accept a portion of this burden.
- Making the § 2032A election gives the IRS a lien on the property. Will the existence of this lien affect the ability of the participating heirs to obtain loans against the property for operating purposes?

Section 2032A(c) provides that the estate tax savings derived from the special use valuation method are recaptured from the heir if he or she disposes of the property or ceases to use it as qualifying use property within a period of 10 years from the date of the decedent's death.

EXAMPLE 10

Assume the same facts as in Example 9. Further assume that by electing § 2032A, Wanda's estate tax liability was reduced by $245,000. Three years after Wanda's death, Otis (the qualifying heir) leases the farm to an unrelated party. At this point, Otis must pay the $245,000 additional estate tax liability that would have been imposed had § 2032A not been utilized. ■

In the event recapture occurs, the qualifying heir may *elect* to increase the income tax basis of the property by the amount of the recapture. If the election is made, however, interest on the additional estate tax due must be paid.[12]

In this regard, the Code gives the IRS security for compliance with the terms of § 2032A by placing a special lien on the qualifying property.[13]

Valuation Problems with a Closely Held Business

General Guidelines. Revenue Ruling 59–60 sets forth the approach, methods, and factors to be considered in valuing the shares of closely held corporations for gift and estate tax purposes.[14] The following factors, although not all-inclusive, are fundamental and require careful analysis in each case.

LO.3

Identify problems involved in valuing an interest in a closely held business.

- The nature of the business and the history of the enterprise from its inception.
- The economic outlook in general and the condition and outlook of the specific industry in particular.
- The book value of the stock and the financial condition of the business.
- The earning capacity of the company.
- The company's dividend-paying capacity.
- Whether the enterprise has goodwill or other intangible value.
- The prices and number of shares of the stock sold previously and the size of the block of stock to be valued.

---

[12]§ 1016(c).
[13]§ 6324B.

[14]1959–1 C.B. 237. See also Reg. § 20.2031–2(f).

  • The market price of stocks issued by corporations in the same or a similar line of business and actively traded in a free and open market, either on an exchange or over-the-counter.

Some of these factors are discussed in depth in the pages to follow.

Goodwill Aspects. If a closely held corporation's record of past earnings is higher than is usual for the industry, the IRS is apt to claim the presence of goodwill as a corporate asset.

EXAMPLE 11

Adam owned 70% of the stock of White Corporation, with the remaining 30% held by various family members. Over the past five years, White Corporation has generated average net profits of $200,000, and on the date of Adam's death, the book value of the corporation's stock was $500,000. If the IRS identifies 8% as an appropriate rate of return, one approach to the valuation of White stock would yield the following result.

Average net profit for the past five years	$ 200,000
8% of the $500,000 book value	40,000
Excess earnings over 8%	$ 160,000
Value of goodwill (5 × $160,000)	$ 800,000
Book value	500,000
Total value of the White stock	$1,300,000

Thus, the IRS might contend that the stock should be included in Adam's gross estate at 70 percent of $1,300,000, or $910,000. If the estate wishes to argue for a lower valuation, relevant factors might include any of the following.

  • The average net profit figure for the past five years ($200,000) may not be representative. Perhaps it includes some extraordinary gains that normally do not occur or are extraneous to the business conducted by the corporation. An example might be a windfall profit for a specific year because of an unusual market situation. The corporation may have recognized a large gain from an appreciated investment held for many years. The figure may fail to take into account certain expenses that normally would be incurred but for some justifiable reason have been deferred. In a family business during periods of expansion and development, it is not uncommon to find an unusually low salary structure. Profits might be considerably less if the owner-employees of the business were being paid the true worth of their services.
  • The appropriate rate of return for this type of business may not be 8 percent. If it is higher, there would be less goodwill because the business is not as profitable as it seems.
  • If Adam was a key person in the operation of White Corporation, could some or all of any goodwill developed by the business be attributed to his efforts? If so, is it not reasonable to assume that the goodwill might be seriously impaired by Adam's death?

Other Factors. Aside from the issue of goodwill, the valuation of closely held stock must take other factors into account. For example, consider the percentage of ownership involved. If the percentage represents a *minority interest* and the corporation has a poor dividend-paying record, a substantial discount is in order.[15] The justification for the discount is the general inability of the holder of the minority interest to affect corporate policy, particularly with respect to the distribution of dividends. At the other extreme is an interest large enough to represent control, either actual or effective. Considered alone, a controlling interest calls for valuation at a premium.[16]

---

[15]See, for example, *Jack D. Carr*, 49 TCM 507, T.C.Memo. 1985–19.

[16]*Helvering v. Safe Deposit and Trust Co. of Baltimore, Exr. (Estate of H. Walters)*, 38–1 USTC ¶9240, 21 AFTR 12, 95 F.2d 806 (CA–4, 1938), *aff'g* 35 B.T.A. 259 (1937).

A controlling interest may be so large, however, that the disposition of the stock within a reasonable period of time after the valuation date could have a negative effect on the market for such shares. The **blockage rule** recognizes what may happen to per-unit value when a large block of shares is marketed at one time.[17] Most often, the rule is applied to stock that has a recognized market. The rule permits a discount from the amount at which smaller lots are selling on or about the valuation date.[18] Although the blockage rule may have a bearing on the valuation of other assets, it is more frequently applied to stocks and securities.[19]

Because most stock in closely held corporations does not trade in a recognized market, a discount for *lack of marketability* may be in order. The discount recognizes the costs that would be incurred in creating a market for such shares to effect their orderly disposition.[20] The discount could be significant considering typical underwriting expenses and other costs involved in going public.

Closely related to the reasons that an asset's marketability might be impaired is the possibility of built-in income tax consequences. In one case, the value of stock in a holding company was significantly discounted because of the income tax that would ensue if the holding company distributed its major asset to its shareholders.[21]

Resolving the Valuation Problem for Stock in Closely Held Corporations. Since the valuation of closely held stock is subject to so many variables, planning should be directed toward bringing about some measure of certainty.

Polly wants to transfer some of her stock in Brown Corporation to a trust formed for her children. She would also like to make a substantial contribution to her alma mater, State University. At present, the Brown stock is owned entirely by Polly and has never been traded on any market or otherwise sold or exchanged. Brown's past operations have proved profitable, and Brown has established a respectable record of dividend distributions. Based on the best available information and taking into account various adjustments (e.g., discount for lack of marketability), Polly feels each share of Brown stock possesses a fair market value of $120. ■	*EXAMPLE 12*

If Polly makes a gift of some of the stock to the trust set up for the children and uses the $120 per share valuation, what assurance is there that the IRS will accept this figure? If the IRS is successful in increasing the fair market value per share, Polly could end up with additional gift tax liability.

Polly could hedge against any further gift tax liability. Concurrently with the gift of stock to the trust formed for the children, Polly could make an outright transfer of some of the shares to State University, thereby generating an income tax deduction. Polly would base the income tax deduction on the value used for gift tax purposes. If the IRS later raises the value and assesses more gift tax, Polly can file an amended income tax return, claim a larger charitable contribution deduction, and obtain an offsetting income tax refund. To carry out this hedge, Polly would derive the amount of her gift of Brown stock by comparing her prevailing gift tax and income tax brackets for the year of the transfers. By virtue of the charitable deduction allowed for gift tax purposes by § 2522 (discussed in Chapter 17), no gift tax liability is incurred for the stock transferred to State University.

---

[17]Reg. § 20.2031–2(e).

[18]See, for example, *Estate of Robert Damon*, 49 T.C. 108 (1967).

[19]In *Estate of David Smith*, 57 T.C. 650 (1972), the estate of a now-famous sculptor successfully argued for the application of the blockage rule to 425 sculptures included in the gross estate. See also *Estate of Georgia T. O'Keeffe*, 63 TCM 2699, T.C.Memo. 1992–210.

[20]See, for example, *Estate of Mark S. Gallo*, 50 TCM 470, T.C.Memo. 1985–363. In this case, the taxpayer also argued that a bad product image (i.e., the Thunderbird, Ripple, and Boone's Farm brands) would depress the value of the stock. Since the trend was toward better wines, association with cheaper products had a negative consumer impact. Not emphasized were the enormous profits that the sale of the cheap wines generated!

[21]*Estate of Artemus D. Davis*, 110 T.C. 530 (1998). The major asset held by the holding company was a considerable block of substantially appreciated stock in the Winn-Dixie supermarket chain.

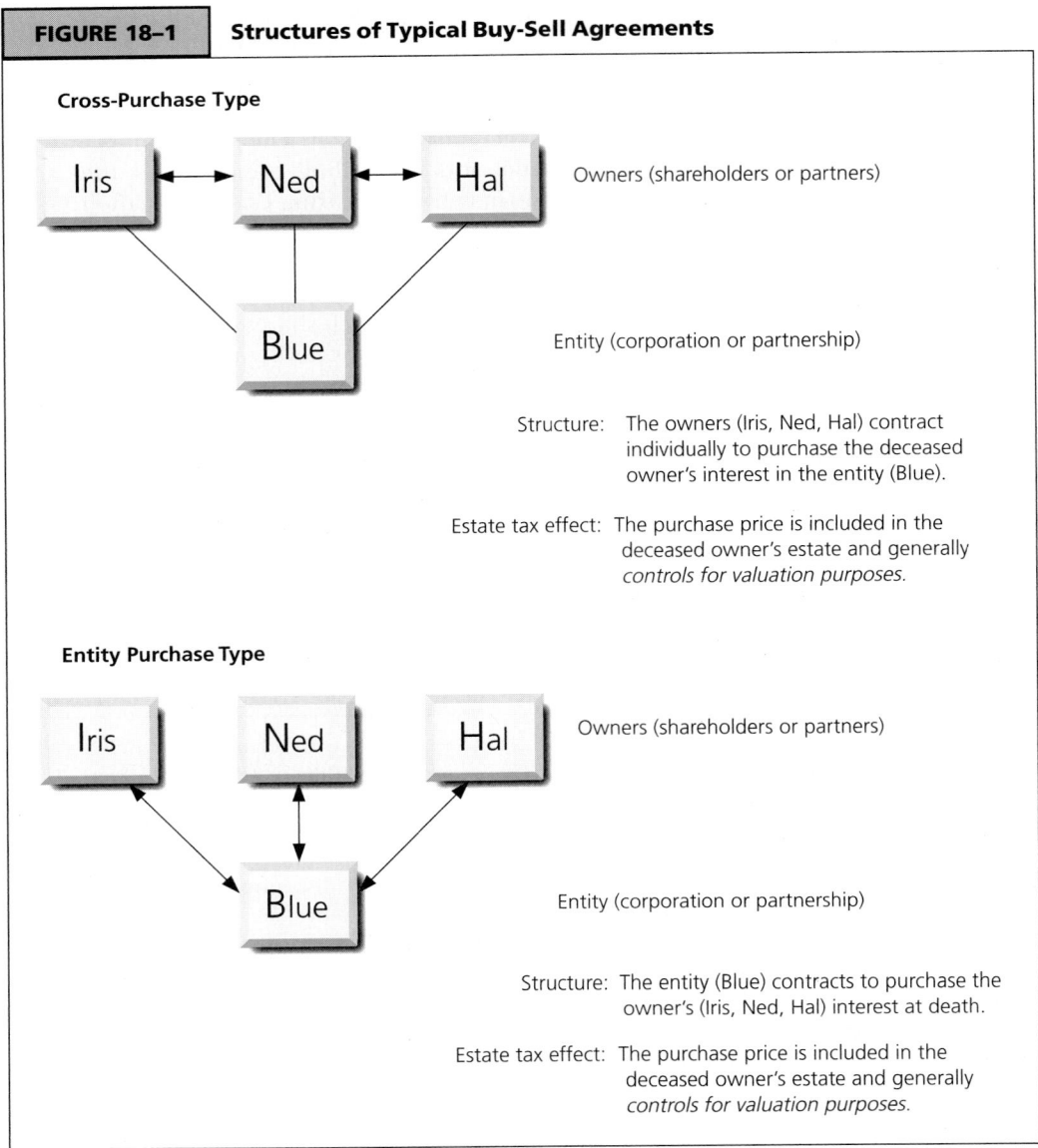

| FIGURE 18–1 | Structures of Typical Buy-Sell Agreements |

Cross-Purchase Type

Iris ↔ Ned ↔ Hal — Owners (shareholders or partners)

Blue — Entity (corporation or partnership)

Structure: The owners (Iris, Ned, Hal) contract individually to purchase the deceased owner's interest in the entity (Blue).

Estate tax effect: The purchase price is included in the deceased owner's estate and generally *controls for valuation purposes.*

Entity Purchase Type

Iris Ned Hal — Owners (shareholders or partners)

Blue — Entity (corporation or partnership)

Structure: The entity (Blue) contracts to purchase the owner's (Iris, Ned, Hal) interest at death.

Estate tax effect: The purchase price is included in the deceased owner's estate and generally *controls for valuation purposes.*

The Buy-Sell Agreement and Valuation. The main objective of a **buy-sell agreement** is to effect the orderly disposition of a business interest without the risk of the interest falling into the hands of outsiders. Moreover, a buy-sell agreement can ease the problems of estate liquidity and valuation.

Two types of buy-sell agreements exist: **entity** and **cross-purchase** arrangements. Under the entity type, the business itself (partnership or corporation) agrees to buy out the interest of the withdrawing owner (partner or shareholder). For a corporation, this normally takes the form of a stock redemption plan set up to qualify for income tax purposes under either § 302(b) or § 303. By making use of these provisions, corporate distributions can qualify for sale or exchange treatment rather than being treated as dividends (see Chapter 6). Under a cross-purchase agreement, the surviving owners (partners or shareholders) agree to buy out the withdrawing owner. The structures of the most typical buy-sell agreements are illustrated in Figure 18–1.

EXAMPLE 13

Iris, Ned, and Hal are equal and unrelated shareholders in Blue Corporation, and all three share in Blue's management. All agree to turn in their stock to the corporation for redemption at $100 per share if any one of them withdraws (by death or otherwise) from the business. Shortly thereafter, Hal dies, and the estate redeems the Blue stock at the agreed-upon price of $100 per share. ∎

EXAMPLE 14

Assume the same facts as in Example 13, except that the agreement is the cross-purchase type under which each shareholder promises to buy a portion of the withdrawing shareholder's interest. When Hal dies, the estate sells the Blue stock to Iris and Ned for $100 per share. ∎

Will the $100 per share paid to Hal's estate determine the amount to be included in his gross estate? The answer is *yes*, subject to the following conditions.

- The price is the result of a bona fide business agreement.
- The agreement is not a device to transfer property to family members.
- The agreement is comparable to other arrangements entered into by persons dealing at arm's length.[22]

Estate Freezes—Corporations. Over the years, owners of closely held businesses have searched for ways to transfer the major value of the business to their heirs while retaining some security interest. The typical approach with corporations has been for the owner to retain preferred stock and make gifts of common stock to the family. The approach freezes the amount that will be included in the owner's gross estate to the value of the preferred stock. Any post-gift appreciation in the business is attributed to the common stock and is *not* part of the owner's gross estate.

Under current law, some degree of the **estate freeze** is permitted.[23] Unfortunately, current law is designed to maximize the amount of the gift made by the donor upon the creation of the freeze. Generally, the retained interest is valued at zero, thereby resulting in the transfer of the *full* value of the business.

EXAMPLE 15

Quinn owns all of the stock in Robin Corporation valued as follows: $4 million common stock and $1 million preferred stock. The preferred stock is noncumulative, does not have a redemption date, and possesses no liquidation preference. Quinn gives the common stock to his adult children and retains the preferred stock. Quinn has made a gift to the children of $5 million. The $1 million worth of preferred stock Quinn retained is treated as having no value. ∎

The estate freeze does, however, allow any post-transfer appreciation that develops to escape later estate taxation.

EXAMPLE 16

Assume the same facts as in Example 15. Quinn dies 10 years after the gift when the Robin Corporation common and preferred stock are worth $10 million and $1 million, respectively. Quinn's estate includes only $1 million for the preferred stock. The $6 million appreciation on the common stock ($10 million − $4 million) has escaped a transfer tax. ∎

Estate Freezes—Partnerships. Due to the statutory limitations imposed on estate freezes using corporations, the adoption of a family limited partnership (FLP) to carry out an estate freeze has become popular. A common scenario is for grandparents to form an FLP to hold a closely held business or other assets that can be expected to appreciate (e.g., real estate). The grandparents make themselves general partners and over a period of years make gifts of limited partnership interests to their children and grandchildren.

---

[22]§ 2703.   [23]§ 2701.

In valuing gifts of limited partnership interests, generous discounts (from 25 to 60 percent) are made for lack of marketability and a minority interest. As the grandparents are the general partners, they remain in control of the business (i.e., the FLP). See the Tax in the News in Chapter 11 (page 11–32) of this text.

At one point, the IRS contended that a discount for a minority interest was not available as long as the business was held fully within the family unit (e.g., grandparents, children, grandchildren). After losing on the issue in several court cases, the IRS conceded that the valuation discount is available.[24]

The overall expectation underlying the FLP approach is that a lesser value of the business can be transferred by gift than would be the case if everything is passed by death. The key to success, however, is the acceptability of the discounts used to value the gifts. Overly generous discount percentages could result in vulnerability to the penalty for undervaluation.[25]

In light of what happened to the estate freeze of corporate stock previously discussed, it is not unlikely that Congress might enact statutory limitations on the use of FLPs.

Valuation concepts are reviewed in Concept Summary 18–1.

Income Tax Concepts

Family tax planning also involves an assessment of the income tax positions of the transferor (the donor or decedent) and the transferee (the donee or heir).

LO.4

Compare the income tax basis rules applying to property received by gift and by death.

Basis of Property Acquired by Gift

The income tax basis of property acquired by gift depends on whether the donee sells the property for a gain or for a loss and, in certain cases, on when the gift occurred.

- If the gift took place after 1920 and before 1977, the donee's basis for gain is the donor's adjusted basis plus any gift tax paid on the transfer (but not to exceed the fair market value on the date of the gift). The basis for loss is the lower of the basis for gain or the fair market value of the property on the date of the gift.

---

[24]Rev.Rul. 93–12, 1993–1 C.B. 202, rescinding Rev.Rul. 81–253, 1981–1 C.B. 187.

[25]§ 6662(b)(5). See the discussion of accuracy-related penalties in Chapter 16.

CONCEPT SUMMARY 18–1

Valuation Concepts

1. Fair market value is "the price at which property would change hands between a willing buyer and a willing seller, neither being under any compulsion to buy or to sell and both having reasonable knowledge of relevant facts."

2. Special rules govern the valuation of life insurance policies and annuity contracts. In the case of unmatured life insurance policies, value depends on whether the policies are paid up or not. Use of the IRS valuation tables is necessary when the annuities are issued by parties not regularly engaged in selling annuities.

3. The IRS valuation tables must be used to value multiple interests in property. Such interests include income for a term of years, life estates, and remainders.

4. Section 2032A provides valuation relief for the estates of persons who hold real estate used in farming or in connection with a closely held business. If the requirements of the provision are met and if the executor elects, the property can be valued at its *current use* rather than its *most suitable use*.

5. Determining the value of the stock in a closely held corporation presents unique problems. The presence or absence of *goodwill* at the corporate level has a direct bearing on the stock being valued. A discount may be in order for any of the following: a minority interest, lack of marketability, and the application of the blockage rule. The IRS will contend that a premium attaches to an interest that represents control of the corporation.

6. A properly structured buy-sell agreement will control the value to be assigned a deceased owner's interest in a partnership or a corporation.

7. An estate tax freeze is useful in avoiding post-transfer appreciation that develops on the partnership or corporate interest involved. However, the donor must consider the gift tax consequences that result when the freeze is created.

- If the gift took place after 1976, the donee's basis for gain is the donor's adjusted basis plus only the gift tax attributable to the appreciation of the property to the point of the gift. For this purpose, use the *taxable gift* amount (i.e., gift less annual exclusion). The basis for loss is the lesser of the basis for gain or the fair market value of the property on the date of the gift.[26]

EXAMPLE 17

In 1975, Norm receives stock as a gift from Lana. The stock cost Lana $20,000 and was worth $100,000 on the date of the gift. As a result of the transfer, Lana paid a gift tax of $10,000. Norm's income tax basis for gain or loss is $30,000 [$20,000 (Lana's basis) + $10,000 (gift tax paid by Lana)]. Norm does not have a different basis for loss; the fair market value of the property on the date of the gift ($100,000) is not less than the basis for gain ($30,000). ∎

EXAMPLE 18

Assume the same facts as in Example 17, except that the gift takes place in 2008. Only the portion of the gift tax that is attributable to the appreciation can be considered. This portion is determined as follows:

$$\frac{\$80,000 \text{ (appreciation)}}{\$88,000 \text{ (taxable gift)}} = 91\% \text{ (rounded)}$$

Consequently, Norm's income tax basis is $29,100.

Lana's basis	$20,000
Allowable gift tax adjustment (91% × $10,000)	9,100
Basis for gain and loss	$29,100

∎

The effect of the rule illustrated in Example 18 is to deny a donee any increase in basis for the gift tax attributable to the donor's adjusted basis.

---

[26]§§ 1015(a) and (d).

TAX *in the News*   **CARRYOVER BASIS—WILL IT EVER HAPPEN?**

Pursuant to the Tax Relief Reconciliation Act of 2001, the Federal estate tax is to be phased out by the end of 2009. If the phaseout takes place as planned, what will be the impact on the current "step-up" and "step-down" rules of § 1014? Different basis rules will come into play, and § 1014 will cease to apply.

Under Code § 1022, scheduled to become effective in 2010, an heir will receive a carryover basis from a decedent.

With certain exceptions, the basis determination rules governing property transferred by gift will also apply to transfers by death. For basis purposes, therefore, donees and heirs will be treated much the same.

As noted in Chapter 17, however, whether the estate tax will ever be entirely eliminated is an open political question.

Because the donee usually assumes the donor's basis in the property, transfers by gifts are considered carryover situations. Consistent with this approach, the donee's holding period includes that of the donor.[27]

Basis of Property Acquired by Death

General Rule. Except as otherwise noted in the following sections, the income tax basis of property acquired from a decedent is the fair market value on the date of death or, if elected, on the alternate valuation date. When property has appreciated in value between acquisition and date of death, a **step-up in** income tax **basis** occurs for the estate or heir of the deceased owner. A step-up in basis means that appreciation existing at death escapes the application of the Federal income tax.

EXAMPLE 19

Upon her death in 2008, Nancy owned real estate (adjusted basis of $200,000) worth $800,000 that she leaves to Jack. Assuming that the alternate valuation date is not elected, Jack's income tax basis in the property becomes $800,000. Thus, a subsequent sale of the real estate by Jack for $800,000 results in no gain or loss to him. ■

EXAMPLE 20

Assume the same facts as in Example 19, except that, shortly before her death, Nancy sells the real estate for $800,000. Nancy has a taxable gain of $600,000 for income tax purposes. ■

By contrasting Examples 19 and 20, one can see that the rules place a premium on holding appreciated property until death, to take advantage of the step-up in basis rule. The same cannot be said for property that has declined in value. Here, death causes a **step-down in basis.** This result should be avoided if selling the property would generate a deductible income tax loss.

EXAMPLE 21

Upon his death in 2008, Wes held stock as an investment with an adjusted basis of $200,000 and a fair market value of $120,000. Because only $120,000 is included in the gross estate, the basis of the stock to the estate or heir is this amount. Had Wes sold the stock before his death, a deduction for some or all of the $80,000 loss might have been available. ■

The holding period to the estate or heir of property acquired from a decedent is automatically treated as long term.[28]

If the property does not pass through a decedent's estate, there is no step-up (or step-down) in income tax basis.

---

[27]§ 1223(2).   [28]§ 1223(11).

EXAMPLE 22

In 1980, Aaron and Sandra (brother and sister) purchased land for $200,000, listing title as "joint tenants with the right of survivorship." Each furnished one-half of the purchase price. In 2008, when the land is worth $600,000, Aaron dies. Under § 2040 (see Chapter 17), Aaron's estate includes $300,000 as to the land. Sandra's income tax basis in the land is $400,000, determined as follows: $100,000 (Sandra's original cost basis) + $300,000 (amount passing through Aaron's estate). ∎

Community Property. Although there is usually no change in basis for property that is not part of a decedent's gross estate (see Example 22 above), a special exception applies to community property. In such situations, the surviving spouse's half of the community takes the same basis as the half included in the deceased spouse's gross estate.[29] The following examples illustrate the reason for and the effect of this special rule.

EXAMPLE 23

Leif and Rosa were husband and wife and lived in a common law state. At the time of Leif's death, he owned assets (worth $1.6 million with a basis to him of $200,000), which he bequeathed to Rosa. Presuming the transfer qualifies under § 2056, Leif's estate is allowed a marital deduction of approximately $1.6 million. As the property passes through Leif's estate, Rosa receives a step-up in basis to $1.6 million. ∎

EXAMPLE 24

Assume the same facts as in Example 23, except that Leif and Rosa had always lived in California (a community property state). If the $1.6 million of assets are community property, only one-half of this value is included in Leif's gross estate. Because the other half does not pass through Leif's estate (it already belongs to Rosa), is it fair to deny Rosa a new basis in it? Therefore, allowing the surviving spouse's share of the community to take on a basis equal to the half included in the deceased spouse's gross estate equalizes the income tax result generally achieved in common law states through the use of the marital deduction. By giving Rosa an income tax basis of $1.6 million ($800,000 for Leif's half passing to her plus $800,000 for her half) and including only $800,000 in Leif's gross estate, the tax outcome is the same as in Example 23. ∎

Effect of Special Valuation Provisions. The election of the special use valuation method under § 2032A (discussed earlier in the chapter) and the alternate valuation date under § 2032 (see Chapter 17) will have a direct impact on income tax basis. Since the election of either of these provisions reduces the value of the property for estate tax purposes, a lower income tax basis results. Thus, any estate tax saving should be contrasted with the income tax consequences (i.e., higher gain or lower loss) when the property is sold.

When community property is involved, the election of special valuation provisions can carry a double income tax penalty. This double impact comes about because the surviving spouse's half of the community property takes on the same basis as the half included in the deceased spouse's gross estate (see Example 24 above).

EXAMPLE 25

Christopher and Samantha are husband and wife and have always lived in Arizona, a community property state. Samantha dies before Christopher. At the time of her death, their community includes assets (mainly stock) worth $6.4 million that decline in value to $6.2 million six months later. Under Samantha's will, her share of the stock passes to her children. ∎

In Example 25, the election of § 2032 means that Samantha's estate includes only $3.1 million (50% of $6.2 million) as to the community property. But the estate tax saving on $100,000 [$3.2 million (date of death value) − $3.1 million (alternate

---

[29]§ 1014(b)(6).

valuation date)] must be compared with the $200,000 ($100,000 for the children + $100,000 for Christopher's share of the community property) loss in income tax basis.

Step-Up in Basis and the One-Year Rule. To understand the need for § 1014(e), consider the following situation.

EXAMPLE 26

Gary and Hazel are husband and wife and reside in a common law state. When the couple learns that Hazel has a terminal illness, Gary transfers property (basis of $100,000 and fair market value of $900,000) to her as a gift. Hazel dies shortly thereafter, and under the provisions of her will, the property returns to Gary. ■

If it were not for § 1014(e), what have the parties accomplished? No gift tax occurs on the transfer from Gary to Hazel because of the application of the marital deduction. Upon Hazel's death, her bequest to Gary does not generate any estate tax because the inclusion of the property in her gross estate is offset by the marital deduction. Through the application of the general rule of § 1014, Gary ends up with the same property, with its basis stepped up to $900,000. Thus, the procedure enables Gary to get a "free" increase in income tax basis of $800,000.

When applicable, § 1014(e) forces Gary (the original donor) to assume the property with the same basis it had to Hazel immediately before her death. Hazel's basis would have been determined under § 1015 (basis of property acquired by gift). The basis would have been $100,000 (donor's adjusted basis) plus any gift tax adjustment (none in this case) and any capital additions made by the donee (none in this case), or $100,000. If § 1014(e) applies to Example 26, Gary ends up where he started (with $100,000) in terms of income tax basis.

For § 1014(e) to be operative, the following conditions must be satisfied.

- The decedent must have received appreciated property as a gift during the one-year period ending with his or her death.
- The property is acquired from the decedent by the donor (or the donor's spouse).

Example 26 concerns a transfer between spouses, but the application of § 1014(e) is not so limited. The provision applies with equal effect when, for example, the donor-heir is a daughter of the donee-decedent. In such cases, moreover, the technique used in Example 26 might be susceptible to the imposition of gift or estate taxes, because of the unavailability of the marital deduction.

ETHICAL and EQUITABLE *Considerations*

WHEN DID THE SALE OCCUR?

At the time of her unexpected death, Leona was in the process of negotiating the sale of land to a real estate developer, Marcus Enterprises. Leona had purchased the land 20 years ago for $40,000 and held it as an investment. Leona and Marcus had agreed on a selling price ($900,000) and mode of payment ($100,000 in cash and four notes of $200,000 each). Not yet completed, however, were the rezoning of the property and the issuance of a title insurance policy.

After Leona's death, the executor of her estate completes the sale and distributes the proceeds to her heirs. The estate takes the position that the sale of the land occurred after Leona's death. Consequently, § 1014 applies and no gain from the sale results. Is this position sound? In what manner could it be vulnerable? With what result?

Income in Respect of a Decedent. Income in respect of a decedent (IRD) is income earned by a decedent to the point of his or her death but not reportable

CONCEPT SUMMARY 18–2

Income Tax Concepts

1. The income tax basis of property acquired by gift is the donor's basis with appropriate adjustment for any gift tax paid. With built-in loss situations, the income tax basis is the fair market value of the property on the date of the gift.

2. The income tax basis of property acquired through the death of the owner is its fair market value on the appropriate estate tax valuation date.

3. No step-up in basis is allowed if the property returns to the donor or donor's spouse within one year.

4. Items of income in respect of a decedent do not undergo a step-up or step-down in basis.

5. The value used for estate tax purposes is presumed to establish basis for income tax purposes. This presumption can be rebutted, but only with great difficulty.

on the final income tax return under the method of accounting used. IRD is most frequently applicable to decedents using the cash basis of accounting. IRD also occurs, for example, when a taxpayer at the time of death held installment notes receivable on which the gain has been deferred. For both cash and accrual taxpayers, IRD is increasingly including postdeath distributions from retirement plans [e.g., traditional IRA, § 401(k), H.R. 10 (Keogh), § 403(b)(1), qualified plan]. With the exception of Roth IRAs, distributions from retirement plans invariably contain an income component that has not yet been subject to income tax.

IRD is included in the gross estate at its fair market value on the appropriate valuation date. However, the income tax basis of the decedent transfers to the estate or heirs. Neither a step-up nor a step-down in basis is possible as is true of property received by death.[30] Furthermore, the recipient of IRD must classify it in the same manner (e.g., ordinary income, capital gain) as the decedent would have.[31]

How Conclusive Is the Value Used for Estate Tax Purposes?
Suppose a value is used for estate tax purposes and reflected on the estate tax return. At some future date, an heir to the property included in the gross estate believes the value used for estate tax purposes was incorrect. An heir might desire a change in value for countless reasons, including the following.

- The property is sold. Higher value leads to higher basis and less income tax gain.
- The property is depreciable. More basis means larger depreciation deductions.
- A home equity loan is obtained. With a higher value, a larger loan is allowed.
- If the heir is a charitable organization, higher value could improve its fund-raising potential.

Is there any chance of success in arguing for a different value and thereby changing the income tax basis? The answer is yes, but with definite reservations.

If the statute of limitations has not lapsed for the estate tax return, the heir may try for a higher income tax basis by having the estate tax valuation raised. Any new valuation, however, requires both cooperation from the decedent's executor and acceptance by the IRS.

If the statute of limitations has lapsed for the estate tax return, the success of the heir's challenge depends on the following factors.

---

[30]§ 1014(c).

[31]§ 691(a)(3). See Chapter 19 for a further discussion of IRD. Example 11 in Chapter 19 specifically deals with the IRD classification of distributions from retirement plans.

TAX *in the* News — KEEPING AN IRA ALIVE AFTER THE OWNER'S DEATH

One sizable asset of interest to the tax planner is the traditional IRA. Plan accumulations are characterized as income in respect of a decedent (IRD) and are subject to income tax when distributed to the beneficiary. But does the beneficiary have any flexibility as to when the distributions occur? Taking an immediate payout, the choice most frequently made, yields the worst result. Not only is the distribution fully taxable, but the bunching effect pushes the beneficiary into the top brackets. This horrendous tax result may occur because the parties involved are not aware that a more attractive tax alternative is available.

The deferral aspects of traditional IRAs need not terminate upon the owner's death. By following certain prescribed procedures, the distributions (and income recognition) can be "stretched" over the actuarial life expectancy of the beneficiary. The following rules apply to "inherited IRAs."

- Distributions to beneficiaries should be avoided. Any transfers between plans should be direct (i.e., from trustee to trustee) and not indirect (i.e., through beneficiaries).
- The IRA must be clearly designated as an inherited IRA. Records should indicate who the decedent was, who

the beneficiary is, and that the IRA is to continue in effect.
- The beneficiary must begin taking annual distributions from the IRA based on the beneficiary's life expectancy. In the case of a surviving spouse, the distributions need not start until the survivor reaches age 70½.
- Except in the case of a surviving spouse, the inherited IRA cannot be rolled over, added to, or combined with others—it must be kept separate.
- An income tax deduction is available to the beneficiary for any estate tax attributable to the IRA distribution. [See the discussion of § 691(c) in Chapter 19.]

Although the income tax rules dealing with lifetime IRA distributions are fairly well known, those relating to inherited situations are not. Needless to say, the tax planner needs to be aware of the "inherited IRA" and its role in postdeath distributions. [Note: The rules presented here also apply to testamentary distributions from § 401(k) plans; § 403(b) plans (retirement plans used by teachers); § 457 plans (retirement savings accounts for government workers); and Keogh plans (retirement plans for self-employed persons).]

- The value reflected on the estate tax return and accepted by the IRS is presumed to be correct.[32] The heir must rebut the presumption.
- To rebut the presumption of correctness, it is important to determine by what means the property was originally valued. Did the valuation result from a unilateral determination by the IRS, or was it the result of a carefully considered compromise between the estate and the IRS? The presumption is more difficult for the heir to overcome in the latter instance.
- Did the heir have a hand in setting the original value? If so, allowing the value to be changed now would seem to give the heir an unfair advantage. The heir used or influenced the use of a lower value for estate tax purposes (thereby eliminating estate taxes) and now wants a higher value for income tax purposes (thereby reducing a recognized gain).[33]
- Even if the concept of fairness is not applicable because the heir was not involved in setting the original value, justification for a new value must be produced.

<table>
<tr><td>**LO.5**

Plan gifts so as to minimize gift taxes and avoid estate taxes.</td><td>

Gift Planning

One of the ways to carry out family tax planning is to start a program of lifetime giving. The objectives of such a program are to minimize transfer taxes while keeping income tax consequences in mind.

</td></tr>
</table>

---

[32]Rev.Rul. 54–97, 1954–1 C.B. 113; *H. B. Levy*, 17 T.C. 728 (1951); and *Malcolm C. Davenport*, 6 T.C. 62 (1946).

[33]In *William A. Beltzer*, 74–1 USTC ¶9373, 33 AFTR2d 74–1173, 495 F.2d 211 (CA–8, 1974), *aff'g* 73–2 USTC ¶9512, 32 AFTR2d 73–5250 (D.Ct.Neb.,

1973), the concept of fairness was *invoked against the taxpayer* since, as the executor of the estate, he had been instrumental in setting the original value reported on the death tax return.

Minimizing Gift Taxes

The Federal gift tax can be avoided through proper use of the annual exclusion. Because a new annual exclusion is available each year, spacing gifts over multiple years increases the amount that can be transferred free of gift tax.

E X A M P L E   27

Starting in 2000, Cora makes gifts in the amount of the annual exclusion to each of her five grandchildren. Taking into account the changes in the amount of the annual exclusion allowed, Cora will have transferred $500,000 through 2008 with no gift tax consequences.

Years		Amount of Exclusion
2000–2001	$10,000 (annual exclusion) × 5 (number of donees) × 2 (number of years)	$100,000
2002–2005	$11,000 (annual exclusion) × 5 (number of donees) × 4 (number of years)	220,000
2006–2008	$12,000 (annual exclusion) × 5 (number of donees) × 3 (number of years)	180,000

■

For married donors, the § 2513 election to split gifts can double the amount of a tax-free transfer. Referring to Example 27, if Cora is married and her husband makes the § 2513 election, $1 million [$500,000 (amount allowed Cora) × 2 (number of donors)] can be transferred with no gift tax consequences.

From a practical standpoint, many donors who want to take advantage of the annual exclusion do not wish to give cash or near-cash assets (e.g., marketable securities). Where the value of the gift property substantially exceeds the amount of the annual exclusion, as is often the case with real estate, gifts of a partial interest are an attractive option.

E X A M P L E   28

Seth and Kate want to give a parcel of unimproved land to their three adult children and five grandchildren as equal owners. The land has an adjusted basis of $100,000, is held by Seth and Kate as community property, and has an appraised value of $384,000 as of December 19, 2008. On December 22, 2008, Seth and Kate convey a one-half undivided interest in the land to their children and grandchildren as tenants in common. This is followed by a transfer of the remaining one-half interest on January 5, 2009. Neither transfer causes gift tax because each is fully offset by annual exclusions of $192,000 [$24,000 (annual exclusion for two donors) × 8 (number of donees)]. Thus, in a period of less than two weeks, Seth and Kate transfer $384,000 in value free of any Federal tax consequences. ■

Further examination of Example 28 leads to the following observations.

- No income tax consequences ensue from the gift. However, had Seth and Kate first sold the land and made a gift of the cash proceeds, recognized gain of $284,000 [$384,000 (selling price) − $100,000 (adjusted basis)] would have resulted.

- The § 2513 election to split gifts is not necessary because the land was community property. If the land had been held by one of the spouses as separate property, the election would have been necessary to generate the same $384,000 of exclusions. The annual exclusion for 2009 is assumed to remain at $12,000.

GLOBAL Tax Issues

- Good tax planning generally dictates that sizable gifts of property be supported by reliable appraisals. In the case of successive gifts of partial interests in the same property, multiple appraisals should be obtained to cover each gift. This advice was not followed in Example 28 due to the short interval between gifts. Barring exceptional circumstances, the value of real estate will not change over a period of less than two weeks.

Minimizing Estate Taxes

Aside from the annual exclusion, do lifetime gifts offer any tax advantages over transfers at death? Someone familiar with the tax law applicable to asset transfers would answer "no" to this question. Under the unified transfer tax scheme, the tax rates are the same. However, as the following discussion shows, lifetime transfers may be preferable to those at death.

Avoiding a Transfer Tax on Future Appreciation. If property is expected to appreciate in value, a gift removes the appreciation from the donor's gross estate.

EXAMPLE 29

In 1986, Wilma transfers an insurance policy on her life to Karen, the designated beneficiary. At the time of the transfer, the policy had a fair market value of $50,000 and a face amount of $1 million. Wilma dies in 2008, and the insurance company pays the $1 million proceeds to Karen. By making the gift, Wilma has kept $950,000 in value from being subject to a transfer tax. ■

Besides life insurance, other assets that often appreciate in value include real estate, art objects, and special collections (e.g., rare books, coins, and stamps).

Providing for the Education of Family Members. Several different approaches can be taken to meet the educational needs of loved ones and still avoid any transfer taxes. One possibility is to pay tuition directly to an educational institution. As noted in Chapter 17, such payments are treated as excluded transfers under § 2503(e) and are not subject to the gift tax. In a private letter ruling, the IRS has indicated that the same treatment is available when the payment involves multiple years. Thus, grandparents can make tuition payments to a private school on behalf of their grandchildren for not only the current year but future years as well. Besides avoiding any gift tax, such payments are not subject to the estate tax on the later death of the donor.

Another approach to meeting family educational needs involves contributions to qualified tuition programs (i.e., "§ 529 plans"). Although usually touted for their income tax advantages, these plans can be structured so as to avoid transfer taxes. Like direct tuition payments, the contributions are not included in the gross estate on the later death of the contributor. Unlike direct tuition payments, however, the gift tax can apply and must be circumvented. This is done by judicious use of the annual exclusion. Extending contributions over several years and making the § 2513 election to split gifts are just two ways to maximize the availability of the annual exclusion. Moreover, for impatient donors, it is even possible to accelerate five years of annual exclusions into the current year (see Example 24 in Chapter 17).

Preparing for the Special Use Valuation Method. The § 2032A election is not available for valuing transfers by gift. Yet, if its use is planned in estate tax situations, gifts of nonqualifying property may aid in meeting the requirements of § 2032A. Recall that one of the requirements of § 2032A is that qualified use property must constitute at least 50 percent of the adjusted value of the gross estate.

EXAMPLE 30

In 2003, Floyd's estate includes the following.

	Fair Market Value
Farm operated by Floyd with current use value of $250,000	$2,000,000
Stock in a local bank	1,400,000
Marketable securities and cash	800,000

At this point, Floyd's estate does not qualify for the § 2032A election. The qualifying property [$2,000,000 (farm)] does not equal or exceed 50% of the adjusted gross estate [$2,000,000 (farm) + $1,400,000 (bank stock) + $800,000 (marketable securities and cash)]. ■

EXAMPLE 31

Continuing with the facts of Example 30, Floyd makes a gift of one-half of the bank stock in 2004. He dies in 2008 with no change in asset values. Floyd's estate now qualifies for § 2032A treatment since $2 million (farm) is 50% or more of $3.5 million [$2,000,000 (farm) + $700,000 (bank stock) + $800,000 (marketable securities and cash)]. The election enables the estate to value the farm at current use. As a result, the estate tax on $960,000 in value is saved. ■

Care must be taken to avoid gifts of property within three years of death. Though such gifts usually are not included in the gross estate of the donor for estate tax purposes, they are counted when testing for the percentage requirements of § 303 (stock redemptions to pay death taxes and administration expenses—refer to Chapter 6), § 2032A, and § 6166 (extension of time to pay estate taxes in installments—discussed later in this chapter).[34]

EXAMPLE 32

Assume the same facts as in Example 31, except that the gift occurs in 2007 (not 2004). Although only $700,000 of the bank stock is included in Floyd's gross estate for estate tax purposes, $1.4 million is used for the percentage requirements of the special use valuation provisions. As a result, the estate fails to qualify for the election. ■

Effect of Gift Taxes Paid. As to taxable gifts that generate a tax, consider the time value of the gift taxes paid. Since the donor loses the use of these funds, the predicted interval between the gift (and the imposition of the gift tax) and death (the imposition of the estate tax) may make the gift less attractive.

EXAMPLE 33

In 2003, Gail makes a gift that results in a gift tax of $100,000. She dies five years later. Presuming a 10% rate of return, the gift tax paid would have been worth $161,051 at Gail's death. Therefore, Gail has lost $61,051 by making the gift. ■

---

[34]§§ 2035(c)(1) and (2).

The analysis used in Example 33 requires refinement to yield a meaningful result. Variables that need to be questioned or interjected include the following.

- The life expectancy of the donor at the time of the gift. Actuarial tables can provide a start, but this kind of information must be adjusted for the general health and lifestyle of the donor. In any event, accurately predicting when a specific person will die is more chance than science.
- The interest factor used. Anticipating even short-rate changes, erratic at best, becomes mere guesswork as the time interval increases.
- Any change in the value of the property from the point of gift to the date of death. Appreciation in value during this interval makes the gift look like a wise choice. The opposite is true if value declines.
- The income tax ramifications of the gift. A donor escapes any post-transfer income yielded by the property. Thus, the income tax burden is shifted away from the donor to the donee.

Finally, a present value analysis must consider the estate tax effect of any gift tax paid. Except for gifts within three years of death (see Chapter 17), the gift tax paid itself is not subject to estate tax. Referring to Example 33, the $100,000 in gift taxes paid escapes inclusion in Gail's gross estate.

Income Tax Considerations

LO.6
Make gifts so as to avoid income taxes for the donor.

Income Shifting. One way to lower the overall tax burden on the family unit is to shift capital gain income from high-bracket taxpayers to lower-bracket family members. The maximum rates on dividends and net capital gain provide an excellent opportunity to take advantage of the 0 percent rate that normally would apply to certain younger donees. The maximum rate is 15%/0%, with the 0 percent rate being applicable to taxpayers below the 25 percent bracket (i.e., those in the 10 percent and 15 percent brackets).

The shifting is accomplished by giving capital assets (frequently securities) to others who make the sale and recognize the gain. If the donees are children, however, care must be taken to avoid the hazard of the kiddie tax. Under the kiddie tax, which currently applies to a child under age 19 (or to a full-time student under age 24 whose earned income is not more than 50 percent of his or her support), any gain is taxed at the parents' higher rate.[35]

EXAMPLE 34

The Martins have four daughters who are in graduate school. As each child reaches age 24, they give her enough appreciated stock to yield a gain of $30,000. The daughter sells the stock and uses the proceeds to pay for education loans. The daughter pays no tax on the recognized gain of $30,000 (0% × $30,000). Had the Martins sold the stock on their own instead of giving it, the tax would have been $4,500 (15% × $30,000). Thus, the Martins have saved $4,500 in capital gains taxes by making the transfer. If the same procedure is followed with the other three daughters, the total savings become $18,000 ($4,500 × 4). ■

In Example 34, note that the amount of the built-in gain transferred was controlled so as to keep the donee below the 25 percent income tax bracket (approximately $32,000 taxable income). Furthermore, no gift tax resulted from the transfer as the Martins are merely satisfying their obligation of support (providing an education for their child).

The procedure followed in Example 34 can be repeated with the same daughter in a later year with the same tax effect. It can also be used to shift capital gains to other family members. Furthermore, when the donees are not children, the kiddie tax problem will not be a hurdle.

If a gift of property is to shift income to the donee, the transfer must be *complete*.

---

[35]§ 1(g)(2)(A). Children who are married and file a joint return are exempted.

EXAMPLE 35

Gloria, subject to a 35% marginal income tax rate, owns all of the stock in Orange, an S corporation. Gloria transfers by gift 60% of the Orange stock to her three married children. The children range in age from 24 to 28 years and are all in the 10% income tax bracket. After the transfer, Gloria continues to operate the business. No shareholder meetings are held. Except for reporting 60% of the pass-through of Orange's profits, Gloria's children have no contact with the business. Aside from the salary paid to Gloria, Orange makes no cash distributions to its shareholders. ■

The situation posed in Example 35 occurs frequently and is fraught with danger. If the purported gift by Gloria lacks economic reality and Gloria is the true economic owner of all of Orange's stock, the pass-through to the children is disregarded.[36] The profits are taxed to Gloria at her 35 percent rate rather than to the children at their 10 percent rates. Consequently, the transfer has not accomplished the intended shifting of income.

What can be done to make the transfer in Example 35 tax-effective? First, a distribution of dividends would provide some economic benefit to the children. As the transfer is currently constituted, all that the children have received as a result of the gift is an economic detriment, because they must pay income taxes on their share of Orange's pass-through of profits. Second, some steps should be taken to recognize and protect the interests of the children as donees. Shareholder meetings should be held and attendance encouraged. That the children do not actively participate in the business of Orange is of no consequence, as long as they are given the opportunity to do so.

Income Tax Consequences to the Donor. Generally, a gift of property results in no income tax consequences to the donor. Two important exceptions, however, involve installment notes receivable and U.S. savings bonds.

A gift of an installment note receivable is a taxable disposition, and the donor is treated as if the note had been sold for its fair market value.[37] As a result, the donor recognizes the deferred profit.

EXAMPLE 36

In 2007, Adam sells real estate (basis of $200,000) to Norm (an unrelated party) for $800,000. Norm (the obligor) issues two notes of $400,000 each, one due in 2008 and one due in 2009. Adam (the obligee) does not elect out of the installment method. In 2008 and before the first note comes due, Adam gives both notes to his son, Sam. On this date, the notes have a fair market value of $760,000. As a result of the gift to Sam, Adam recognizes a gain of $560,000 [$760,000 (fair market value of the notes) − $200,000 (Adam's unrecovered basis)]. ■

A gift of U.S. savings bonds is not effective unless the bonds are re-registered in the donee's name.[38] This forces the donor to recognize any deferred income accrued on the bonds. The result may surprise donors who expect to postpone the recognition of interest income until the bonds are redeemed. Thus, the donor who desires to avoid income tax consequences should avoid gifts of installment notes receivable and U.S. savings bonds.

For purposes of contrasting tax results, what happens if these properties are passed by death?

• Installment notes receivable are taxed to whoever collects the notes (the estate or heirs).[39] If the notes are forgiven or canceled by the decedent's will, the income is taxed to the estate.

---

[36]*Donald O. Kirkpatrick*, 36 TCM 1122, T.C.Memo. 1977–281; *Michael F. Beirne*, 52 T.C. 210 (1969) and 61 T.C. 268 (1973).

[37]§ 453B(a).

[38]Reg. § 25.2511–1(h)(4).

[39]§ 453B(c). The deferred gain element of an installment note is income in respect of a decedent (see the discussion earlier in this chapter) and does not receive a step-up in basis at death.

- Deferred interest income on U.S. savings bonds is taxed to whoever redeems the bonds (the estate or heirs).
- Recapture potential disappears at death.[40] The estate or heirs take the property free of any recapture potential existing at the time of the owner's death.

Carryover Basis Situations. When considering the income tax effect of a transfer on the donee or heir, the basis rules of §§ 1014 and 1015 warrant close examination. When appreciated property is involved, receiving the property from a decedent is preferred to a lifetime transfer.

EXAMPLE 37	Keith plans to transfer unimproved real estate (basis of $200,000 and fair market value of $800,000) to his daughter, Esther. If the property passes by death, Esther's basis is $800,000. If the property passes by gift, her income tax basis (presuming no gift tax adjustment) is $200,000. The step-up effect of § 1014 provides Esther with an additional basis of $600,000. ■

EXAMPLE 38	Keith plans to transfer unimproved real estate (basis of $300,000 and fair market value of $150,000) to his daughter, Esther. If the property passes by death, Esther's basis is $150,000. If the property passes by gift, her income tax basis is $150,000 for losses and $300,000 for gains. Receiving the property as a gift, therefore, might be more advantageous to Esther than the complete step-down in basis under § 1014. ■

For Keith, the options posed by Example 38 are not attractive. By making a gift or passing the property by death, Keith sacrifices the potential loss deduction of $150,000. Presuming he holds the land as an investment, he can use the capital loss to offset capital gains or apply it against ordinary income to the extent of $3,000 per year. Unused capital losses can be carried over indefinitely but will not survive Keith's death.

ETHICAL and EQUITABLE *Considerations*   CAN A BUILT-IN LOSS SURVIVE DEATH?

Ethan and Isabella are husband and wife and live in a community property state. Their property includes the following.

Stock Investment	Nature of Ownership	Adjusted Basis	Fair Market Value
Grey stock	Separate property	$420,000	$70,000
White stock	Community property	680,000	80,000

The separate property was inherited by Ethan from his father. When Ethan learns that he has a terminal illness, he transfers by gift to Isabella his Grey stock and his community one-half interest in the White stock. When he dies shortly thereafter, Isabella is the sole owner of both the Grey and the White stock.

What has Ethan tried to accomplish? Will it succeed?

Estate Planning

Estate planning considers the nontax and tax aspects of death. In the nontax area are the various steps that can be taken to reduce the costs of probating an estate.

---

[40]§§ 1245(b)(1) and 1250(d)(1). Contrast this result with what happens when § 1245 or § 1250 property is transferred by gift. Here, the recapture potential carries over to the donee.

In the tax area, the focus is on controlling the amount of the gross estate and maximizing estate tax deductions.

Probate Costs

The probate estate consists of all properties subject to administration by an executor. The administration is conducted under the supervision of a local court, usually called a probate court. In certain states, probate functions are performed by county courts, surrogate courts, or orphan's courts.

Probate costs include attorney fees, accountant fees, appraisal and inventory fees, court costs, expenses incident to the disposition of assets and satisfaction of liabilities, litigation costs needed to resolve will contests, and charges for the preparation of tax returns. The total amount of probate costs cannot be accurately predicted because so many variables are involved. A conservative range might be from 5 to 15 percent of the amount of the probate estate.

Many procedures can be used to reduce the probate estate and thereby save probate costs, including the following.

- Owning property as joint tenants (or tenants by the entirety) with right of survivorship. Upon death, the property passes to the surviving tenant and generally is not subject to probate.
- Making life insurance payable to a beneficiary other than the estate.
- Utilizing a revocable trust. Upon the death of the creator, the trust becomes irrevocable and is not subject to probate. A revocable trust is often popularly referred to as a **living trust**.
- Listing bank accounts and title to securities by use of the Totten trust arrangement. As noted in Chapter 17, the designation "payable on proof of death" passes title to the property if the listed beneficiary survives the owner. A payable on death arrangement has the same effect as a revocable trust but avoids the need to create a formal trust.

Another advantage of bypassing the probate estate is that the beneficiary can obtain immediate possession and enjoyment of the property. The probate process can become prolonged, and the heir may have to await the final settlement of the estate before getting the property.

In terms of probate costs, the ownership of out-of-state real estate can cause horrendous problems. Out-of-state ownership is not uncommon with decedents who have relocated after retirement or who maintain vacation homes.

E X A M P L E 39

After retirement and five years before his death, Ted moved from Nebraska to Arizona. At death, Ted still owns a rental house in Nebraska and a vacation home in Idaho. To clear title to these properties, Ted's executor must institute ancillary probate proceedings in Nebraska and Idaho. This will result in additional attorney fees and court costs. ∎

The solution to the dilemma posed in Example 39 is to dispose of these properties before death. Although this may generate some legal fees, they will be far less than the cost of ancillary probate proceedings.

Controlling the Amount of the Gross Estate

Unlike the probate estate, the gross estate determines what property is subject to the Federal estate tax. In fact, many of the steps taken to reduce the probate estate will not have a similar effect on the gross estate—see the discussion of §§ 2036 and 2038 in Chapter 17.

Valuation procedures sometimes can be applied to control the amount of the gross estate. The special use valuation method of § 2032A can be elected when the estate consists of real estate used in farming or in connection with a closely held

---

TAX *in the News*   **HOW TO SAVE TAXES AND PROTECT THE ENVIRONMENT**

What do Ted Turner, Robert Redford, Clint Eastwood, and James Baker (former secretary of state) have in common? Besides being celebrities and financially well-to-do, all have issued **conservation easements** in some or all of the real estate they own. By this means, any "scenic view" that currently exists is preserved. The owner is precluded from obstructing the view by further development of the property. Allegedly, the transfer of the easement is motivated by the owner's desire to "conserve the environment." Realistically, the transfer is largely tax motivated.

The steps involved in creating a conservation easement and the tax consequences that ensue are as follows.

- After the easement is drafted, the owner transfers it to a conservation trust. Usually, the trust is already in existence, having been created by an environmental group,

and operates under the auspices of a local government agency.
- The owner obtains a generous appraisal as to the value of the easement transferred.
- The owner claims the value of the easement as an income tax deduction.
- The value of the property retained (e.g., residence, vacation home) is accordingly reduced by the value of the easement for ad valorem property tax purposes.
- Upon the owner's death, the gross estate includes the property at a discounted value due to the restrictions contained in the easement.

In summary, the conservation easement saves income, property, and estate taxes. The donor receives all of this plus the aura of being hailed as an environmentalist.[41]

---

business. When the estate comprises assets that have declined in value shortly after death, the use of the alternate valuation date of § 2032 (see Chapter 17) is advised.

Proper Handling of Estate Tax Deductions

Estate taxes can be reduced either by decreasing the size of the gross estate or by increasing the total allowable deductions. The lower the taxable estate, the less estate tax is generated. Planning with deductions involves the following considerations.

- Making proper use of the marital deduction.
- Working effectively with the charitable deduction.
- Taking advantage of the bypass amount.
- Optimizing other deductions and losses allowed under §§ 2053 and 2054.

Approaches to the Marital Deduction. When planning for the estate tax marital deduction, both tax and nontax factors are taken into account. Two major tax goals guide the planning. They are the *equalization* and *deferral* approaches.

- Attempt to equalize the estates of both spouses. Clearly, for example, the estate tax on $2 million is more than double the estate tax on $1 million [compare $780,800 with $691,600 ($345,800 × 2)].
- Based on the time value of taxes deferred, try to postpone estate taxation as long as possible. Also keep in mind the possible effect of the Tax Relief Reconciliation Act of 2001. If, as proposed, the estate tax is phased out, the exclusion amount (i.e., exemption equivalent) for the estate tax credit *increases*. The exclusion amount is $2 million for 2006 to 2008 and will increase to $3.5 million for 2009. See the discussion in connection with Table 17–1 in Chapter 17.

Barring certain circumstances, the deferral approach generally is preferable. By maximizing the marital deduction on the death of the first spouse to die, taxes are saved, and the surviving spouse can trim his or her future estate by entering into

---

[41]If the contribution of the conservation easement occurs postmortem (i.e., after the death of the owner), the estate can claim a § 2055(f) charitable contribution. It then can elect, under § 2031(c), to *exclude* up to 40% of the value of the land subject to the easement. In computing the amount of the exclusion, the value of the land must be reduced by the charitable contribution allowed.

a program of lifetime giving. By making optimum use of the annual exclusion, considerable amounts can be shifted without incurring *any* transfer tax.

Tax planning must remain flexible and be tailored to the individual circumstances of the parties involved. The equalization approach may be most attractive in the following situations.

- Both spouses are of advanced age and/or in poor health, and neither is expected to survive the other for a prolonged period of time.
- The spouse who is expected to survive has considerable assets of his or her own. Keep in mind that the transfer tax rate schedules are progressive in nature.
- Because of appreciation, property worth $1 million today when it passes to the surviving spouse may be worth $4 million five years later when the survivor dies.

Effectively Working with the Charitable Deduction. As a general guide to obtaining overall tax savings, lifetime charitable transfers are preferred over testamentary dispositions. For example, an individual who gives $20,000 to a qualified charity during his or her life secures an income tax deduction, avoids any gift tax, and reduces the gross estate by the amount of the gift. By way of contrast, if the $20,000 is willed to charity, no income tax deduction is available, and the amount of the gift is includible in the decedent's gross estate (though later deducted for estate tax purposes). In short, the lifetime transfer provides a double tax benefit (income tax deduction plus reduced estate taxes) at no gift tax cost (§ 2522). The testamentary transfer merely neutralizes the effect of the inclusion of the property in the gross estate (inclusion under § 2033 and then deduction under § 2055).

A lifetime transfer to charity, however, can have income tax implications when a bargain sale arrangement is involved. In a bargain sale, the taxpayer wants to make a charitable contribution as to the appreciation, while maintaining his or her investment in the property. The tax law treats these transactions as being part sale and part contribution.[42] Consequently, only a portion of the basis of the property can be utilized in determining the gain on the sale portion. This is calculated by applying the percentage resulting from dividing the sale price by the fair market value of the property.[43] Presuming that the transfer involves long-term capital gain property, the charitable deduction is the difference between its fair market value and the selling price.

EXAMPLE 40

Arthur transfers a tract of land to his church on which it will build a sanctuary. He acquired the land 20 years ago as an investment for $100,000, and it is currently worth $1 million. Because Arthur desires to recover his original investment, he sells the land to the church for $100,000. Arthur has a long-term capital gain of $90,000 [$100,000 (selling price) − $10,000 (allocated basis)] and a charitable contribution deduction of $900,000 [$1,000,000 (fair market value) − $100,000 (consideration received)]. ∎

To ensure that an estate tax deduction is allowed for a charitable contribution, the designated recipient must fall within the classifications set forth in § 2055 (or § 2522). For estate tax purposes, this is the status of the organization on the date the transfer becomes effective and not the status on the date the will authorizing the transfer was executed.

EXAMPLE 41

In 1982, Lisa drew up and executed a will in which she provided for $500,000 to pass to the Rose Academy, a nonprofit educational organization described in § 2055(a)(2) and, at that time, approved by the IRS as a qualified recipient. In 1984, the qualified status of the academy was revoked for practicing racial discrimination in the enrollment of its student body.[44]

---

[42]§ 1011(b).

[43]Reg. § 1.170(A)–4(c)(2)(i).

[44]Most of the organizations that are qualified recipients (which will permit the donor a charitable deduction) are listed in IRS Publication 78. This compila-

tion, revised and supplemented from time to time, addresses § 170 (income tax deduction) transfers. Publication 78, with the exceptions noted in Chapter 17, also applies to § 2055 (estate tax deduction) and § 2522 (gift tax deduction) transfers.

Lisa dies in 2008, and the executor of her estate, being compelled to satisfy the provisions of the will, transfers $500,000 to the academy. ■

Even though Lisa may have been unaware of the action taken by the IRS in 1984, her estate is not allowed a charitable deduction. The recipient was no longer qualified on the date of Lisa's death. It may be that Lisa, even if she had known about the probable loss of the charitable deduction, would still have wished the bequest carried out as originally conceived. If not, it is easy to see that the error was of Lisa's own making because of her failure to review her estate planning situation.

One way to circumvent the quandary posed by Example 41 (other than changing Lisa's will before her death) is to express the charitable bequest in more flexible terms. The transfer to the academy could have been conditioned on the organization's continued status as a qualified recipient at the time of Lisa's death. Alternatively, Lisa's will may grant her executor the authority to substitute a different, but comparable, charitable organization *that is qualified* in the event of the disqualification of the named group.

On occasion, a charitable bequest depends on the issuance of a disclaimer by a noncharitable heir.[45] Such a situation frequently arises with special types of property or collections, which the decedent may feel a noncharitable heir should have a choice of receiving.

E X A M P L E   42

Megan specified in her will that her valuable art collection is to pass to her son or, if the son refuses, to a designated and qualified art museum. At the time the will was drawn, Megan knew that her son was not interested in owning the collection. If, after Megan's death, the son issues a timely disclaimer, the collection passes to the museum, and Megan's estate takes a charitable deduction for its death tax value. ■

E X A M P L E   43

Dick's will specifies that one-half of his disposable estate is to pass to his wife and the remainder of his property to a specified qualified charitable organization. If the wife issues a timely disclaimer after Dick's death, all of the property passes to the charity and qualifies for the § 2055 charitable deduction. ■

Has the son in Example 42 acted wisely if he issues the disclaimer in favor of the museum? Although such a disclaimer will provide Megan's estate with a deduction for the value of the art collection, consider the income tax deduction alternative. If the son accepts the bequest, he can still dispose of the collection (and fulfill his mother's philanthropic objectives) through a lifetime donation to the museum. At the same time, he obtains an income tax deduction under § 170. Whether this saves taxes for the family depends on a comparison of the mother's estate tax bracket with the estimated income tax bracket of the son. If the value of the collection runs afoul of the percentage limitations of § 170(b)(1), the donations could be spread over more than one year. If this is done, and to protect against the contingency of the son's dying before the entire collection is donated, the son can neutralize any potential death tax consequences by providing in his will for the undonated balance to pass to the museum.

The use of a disclaimer in Example 43 would be sheer folly. It would not reduce Dick's estate tax; it would merely substitute a charitable deduction for the marital deduction. Whether the wife issues a disclaimer or not, no estate taxes will be due. The wife should accept her bequest and, if she is so inclined, make lifetime gifts of it to a qualified charity. In so doing, she generates an income tax deduction for herself.

---

[45]As noted in Chapter 17, a disclaimer is a refusal to accept the property. If the disclaimer is timely made, the property is not treated as having passed through the person issuing the disclaimer, and a gift tax is avoided.

Pursuant to the Pension Protection Act of 2006, a new provision permits, under very limited circumstances, a tax-free distribution from an IRA to a qualified charity. The provision does not generate a charitable deduction but allows the donor to avoid the recognition of income that normally results when a distribution occurs. An estate tax saving also takes place because the donor will no longer own the amount donated upon his or her later death. For the provision to apply, the donor must be age 70½ or older. The donation is limited to $100,000 per year and is available for distributions only in 2006 and 2007.

Taking Advantage of the Bypass Amount. The bypass amount, also known as the exclusion amount or the exemption equivalent, is the amount that can pass free of a transfer tax due to the unified credit. For a credit of $780,800, which is available for estate tax purposes for 2008, the bypass amount is $2 million.[46]

Use in Connection with the Marital Deduction. The availability of the bypass amount can be particularly useful in planning the marital deduction.

Ethan dies in 2008 and is survived by his wife, Hope, and their children. Ethan's will passes his entire estate of $5 million to Hope. ■

EXAMPLE 44

Assume the same facts as in Example 44, except that Ethan's will passes $2 million to the children and the remainder of his estate to Hope. ■

EXAMPLE 45

Although both situations avoid any estate taxes, Example 44 represents overkill in terms of the marital deduction. Not only does it unduly concentrate wealth in the surviving spouse's estate, but it fails to take advantage of the bypass amount. Example 45 remedies this shortcoming by permitting $2 million to pass to another generation free of any transfer tax.

In some cases, it may be possible to control the bypass amount by the judicious use of disclaimers.

Dylan dies in 2008 leaving an estate of $4.5 million. He is survived by his wife, Emma, and two adult children. His will passes $3 million to Emma and the remainder to the children. Emma disclaims $500,000 of her inheritance. ■

EXAMPLE 46

Assume the same facts as in Example 46, except that Dylan's will passes $2.5 million to the children and the remainder to Emma. The children disclaim $500,000 of their inheritance. ■

EXAMPLE 47

Both examples reflect the wise use of disclaimers. In Example 46, Emma's disclaimer has the effect of increasing the children's inheritance to $2 million, thereby optimizing the allowable bypass amount. In Example 47, the children avoid any estate tax on $500,000 (the excess over the $2 million bypass amount) by shifting it to the remainderperson. Since the remainderperson is the surviving spouse, the $500,000 is sheltered from estate tax by the marital deduction.

Choice of Property for the Bypass Amount. For the most effective use of the bypass amount, a choice of which assets to disclaim may be necessary. In marital deduction situations, the choice should consider the future estate tax consequences of the surviving spouse.

---

[46]The bypass amount is reduced if the decedent has made any post-1976 taxable gifts.

EXAMPLE 48

Rob dies in 2008 and is survived by his wife, Fran, and three adult children. At the time of his death, Rob owned the following major assets.

	Fair Market Value
Rental property	$1,500,000
Insurance policy on the life of Fran (maturity value of $500,000)	50,000
Vacation home (used by family)	450,000
Marketable securities	500,000

Under Rob's will, all assets except the rental property go to Fran. In the case of the rental property, Fran is granted a life estate with the remainder passing to the children. Based on the IRS valuation tables, the actuarial value of the remainder factor is approximately 0.5. Thus, the life estate and remainder interest each possess a value of $750,000. The executor of Rob's estate *does not* make a QTIP election as to the life estate passing to Fran. Under applicable state law, any inherited property Fran disclaims goes to the children. Fran has considerable assets of her own. ∎

Regarding Example 48, what are the options? Consider the following alternatives.

1. Fran does nothing and accepts the inheritance.
2. Fran disclaims all of the inheritance.
3. Fran disclaims the life estate in the rental property and ownership of the marketable securities.
4. Fran disclaims ownership of the insurance policy and vacation home.

Alternative 1 wastes $500,000 of Rob's $2 million bypass amount as only the rental property qualifies [$750,000 (Fran's life estate) + $750,000 (the children's remainder interest)].

Alternative 2 voids any marital deduction and overloads the bypass amount. This subjects Rob's estate to a tax on $500,000 [$1,500,000 (rental property) + $50,000 (insurance policy) + $450,000 (vacation home) + $500,000 (marketable securities) − $2,000,000 (bypass amount)].

In Alternative 3, Fran's renunciation of the life estate means that all of the rental property will go to the children. Consequently, the bypass amount of $2 million is reached [$1,500,000 (rental property) + $500,000 (marketable securities)]. Likewise, Rob's estate is not subject to tax since the property not sheltered by the bypass amount (i.e., the life insurance policy and the vacation home) passes to Fran and is covered by the marital deduction. Alternative 3, however, is not favorable to Fran for the following reasons.

- In disclaiming the life estate, Fran not only forgoes a source of income but also loses a potential valuable estate tax saving. The life estate is a terminable interest on which a QTIP election has not been made. Thus, none of the rental property would have been included in Fran's gross estate upon her later death. (See Examples 36 and 64 in Chapter 17.)
- In retaining the life insurance policy and the vacation home, Fran keeps "dry assets" (i.e., non-income-producing). Furthermore, Fran will have to use her funds to maintain these properties (e.g., pay insurance premiums).
- If Fran holds any of the incidents of ownership in the life insurance policy at her death, the $500,000 maturity value will be included in her gross estate. (See Example 57 in Chapter 17.)
- As is the case with most recreational realty, the vacation home can be expected to appreciate in value. Such appreciation will further aggravate any estate tax problems that materialize on Fran's death.

Alternative 4 clearly offers the best choice. The full $2 million bypass amount is reached [$1,500,000 (Fran's life estate and the children's remainder interest in the rental property) + $50,000 (life insurance policy) + $450,000 (vacation home)]. Rob's estate is insulated from any tax by virtue of the bypass amount and the marital deduction (covers the $500,000 of marketable securities Fran receives). Lastly, most of the unfavorable ramifications of Alternative 3, previously noted, have been corrected. Although Fran no longer owns the vacation home, it is hoped that her children will *invite* their mother to share in its use.

Avoid Losing the Bypass Amount. The bypass amount can also be used to advantage when there is a substantial difference in the amount of wealth owned by the spouses.

EXAMPLE 49

Valerie and Jordan are married and have adult children. Valerie has inherited considerable wealth (in excess of $4 million) from her family, while Jordan's net worth is negligible. Also, Jordan is older than Valerie and in poor health. Valerie transfers by gift $2 million to Jordan. In his will, Jordan designates the children as the beneficiaries of his estate. ∎

What have the parties accomplished if Jordan dies first? Of primary importance is the use of Jordan's bypass amount. This enabled Valerie to pass (through Jordan) an additional $4 million to the children free of any transfer tax. (Note that the original transfer from Valerie to Jordan is free of any gift tax due to the availability of the marital deduction.)[47] Had the transfer from Valerie to Jordan not been made, Jordan's bypass amount would have been wasted.

The procedure described in Example 49 does carry the possible disadvantage of subjecting Jordan's estate to extra probate cost. This factor should be taken into account by the parties in structuring Jordan's potential estate.[48]

Proper Handling of Other Deductions and Losses under §§ 2053 and 2054. Many § 2053 and § 2054 deductions and losses may be claimed either as estate tax deductions or as income tax deductions by the estate on the fiduciary return (Form 1041), but not both.[49] The income tax deduction is not allowed unless the estate tax deduction is waived. It is possible for these deductions to be apportioned between the two returns.

In situations where the taxpayer is terminal (i.e., death is imminent), it may be possible to shift the upcoming § 2053 expenses to obtain a lifetime income tax benefit. Thus, such items as accrued medical expenses, property taxes, and interest on home equity loans can be paid prior to death if they will be deductible on the decedent's final income tax return. Although this forgoes the § 2053 deduction that would have been available if the expenses had been paid by the estate, the estate tax saving still exists. As the funds that were used to pay these expenses are not part of the gross estate, the taxable estate is correspondingly reduced. The net result is the same estate tax saving, but with the added advantage of an income tax deduction.

Providing Estate Liquidity

LO.9

Obtain liquidity for an estate.

Recognizing the Problem. Even with effective predeath family tax planning directed toward a minimization of transfer taxes, the smooth administration of an estate necessitates a certain degree of liquidity. After all, probate costs will be incurred, and most important of all, death taxes must be satisfied. In the meantime, the

---

[47]For income tax purposes, the one-year rule of § 1014(e) does not apply to the children because they were not the donor or the donor's spouse. See the discussion in connection with Example 26 in this chapter.

[48]Jordan could virtually eliminate probate costs on the $2 million received from Valerie by placing it in a revocable trust. See the discussion on page 18–25 of this chapter.

[49]§ 642(g) and Reg. § 20.2053–1(d).

surviving spouse and dependent beneficiaries may need financial support. Without funds to satisfy these claims, estate assets may have to be sold at sacrifice prices, and most likely, the decedent's scheme of testamentary disposition will be defeated.

EXAMPLE 50

At the time of Myrtle's death, her estate was made up almost entirely of a large ranch currently being operated by Jim, one of Myrtle's two sons. Because the ranch had been in the family for several generations and was a successful economic unit, Myrtle hoped that Jim would continue its operation and share the profits with Bob, her other son. Unfortunately, Bob, on learning that his mother had died without a will, demanded and obtained a partition and sale of his share of the property. Additional land was sold to pay for administration expenses and death taxes. After all of the sales had taken place, the portion remaining for Jim could not be operated profitably, and he was forced to give up the family ranch activity. ■

What type of predeath planning might have avoided the result reached in Example 50? Certainly, Myrtle should have recognized and provided for the cash needs of the estate. Life insurance payable to her estate, although it adds to the estate tax liability, could have eased or solved the problem. This presumes that Myrtle was insurable or that the cost of the insurance would not be prohibitive. Furthermore, Myrtle made a serious error in dying without a will. A carefully drawn will could have precluded Bob's later course of action and perhaps kept much more of the ranch property intact. The ranch could have been placed in trust, life estate to Jim and Bob, remainder to their children. With such an arrangement, Bob would have been unable to sell the principal (the ranch).

Being able to defer the payment of death taxes may be an invaluable option for an estate that lacks cash or near-cash assets (e.g., marketable securities). In this connection, two major possibilities exist.

- The discretionary extension of time (§ 6161).
- The extension of time when the estate consists largely of an interest in a closely held business (§ 6166).

Discretionary Extension of Time to Pay Estate Taxes—§ 6161.
Currently, an executor or administrator may request an extension of time for paying the death tax for a period not to exceed 10 years from the date fixed for the payment. The IRS grants such requests whenever there is "reasonable cause." Reasonable cause is not limited to a showing of undue hardship. It includes cases in which the executor or administrator is unable to marshal liquid assets readily because they are located in several jurisdictions. It also includes situations where the estate is largely made up of assets in the form of payments to be received in the future (e.g., annuities, copyright royalties, contingent fees, or accounts receivable), or where the assets that must be liquidated to pay the estate tax must be sold at a sacrifice or in a depressed market.

Extension of Time When the Estate Consists Largely of an Interest in a Closely Held Business—§ 6166.
Congress always has been sympathetic to the plight of an estate that consists of an interest in a closely held business. The immediate imposition of the estate tax in such a situation may force the liquidation of the business at distress prices or cause the interest to be sold to outside parties.

A possible resolution of the problem is to use § 6166, which requires the IRS to accept a 15-payment procedure (5 interest-only payments, followed by 10 installment payments of the estate tax). This delay can enable the business to generate enough income to buy out the deceased owner's interest without disruption of operations or other financial sacrifice.

To meet the requirements of § 6166, the decedent's interest in a farm or other closely held business must exceed 35 percent of the decedent's adjusted gross estate.[50] The adjusted gross estate is the gross estate less the sum allowable as

---

[50]§ 6166(a)(1).

CONCEPT SUMMARY 18–3

Estate and Gift Planning

1. In reducing (or eliminating) gift taxes, one can take advantage of the annual exclusion and the election to split gifts. In the case of a single asset with high value (e.g., land), annual gifts of partial interests should be considered.

2. Gifts can reduce later estate taxes. This is accomplished by giving away assets that will appreciate in value (e.g., life insurance policies, art works, rare collections).

3. Timely gifts can help an estate qualify for § 2032A (special use valuation method), § 6166 (15-year payout of estate taxes), and § 303 (stock redemptions to pay death taxes). To be effective, the gift must avoid the three-year rule of § 2035.

4. Gifts can relieve the income tax burden on the family unit. This objective is accomplished by shifting the income from the gift property to family members who are in a lower income tax bracket. In this regard, make sure the gift is *complete* and circumvents kiddie tax treatment.

5. Avoid gifts of property that result in income tax consequences to the donor.

6. Potential *probate costs* can be an important consideration in meaningful estate planning. Some procedures that reduce these costs include joint tenancies with the right of survivorship, living trusts, and predeath dispositions of out-of-state real estate. Keep in mind that most of these procedures *do not reduce* estate taxes.

7. A program of lifetime gifts and proper use of valuation techniques will reduce a decedent's *gross* estate. Further planning can reduce the *taxable* estate by proper handling of estate tax deductions.

8. For a married decedent, the most important deduction is the *marital deduction*. The two major approaches to the marital deduction are the *equalization* and *deferral* approaches.

9. Whether the equalization approach or the deferral approach is emphasized, make use of the *bypass amount*.

10. Lifetime charitable contributions are preferable to transfers by death. The lifetime contributions provide the donor with an income tax deduction, and the amount donated is not included in the gross estate.

11. The *disclaimer* procedure can be used to control (either lower or raise) the amount of the marital deduction and to increase the amount of the charitable deduction.

12. Disclaimers can also be effective in taking full advantage of the available bypass amount. When spouses are involved, the choice of property to disclaim should take into account the estate tax consequences on the later death of the surviving spouse.

13. Gift planning can help ease potential *estate liquidity* problems (see item 3 above). After death, § 6166 can be useful if the estate qualifies. The provision allows installment payments of deferred estate taxes over an extended period of time.

deductions under § 2053 (expenses, indebtedness, and taxes) and § 2054 (casualty and theft losses during the administration of an estate).

An interest in a closely held business includes the following.[51]

- Any sole proprietorship.
- An interest in a partnership carrying on a trade or business, if 20 percent of the capital interest in the partnership is included in the gross estate *or* the partnership has 45 or fewer partners.
- Stock in a corporation carrying on a trade or business, if 20 percent or more of the value of the voting stock of the corporation is included in the gross estate *or* the corporation has 45 or fewer shareholders.

In meeting the preceding requirements, a decedent and his or her surviving spouse are treated as one owner (shareholder or partner) if the interest is held as community property, tenants in common, joint tenants, or tenants by the entirety. Attribution from family members is allowed.[52]

---

[51]§ 6166(b)(1).

[52]As described in § 267(c)(4).

EXAMPLE 51

Decedent Bonnie held a 15% capital interest in the Wren Partnership. Her son holds another 10%. Wren had 46 partners including Bonnie and her son. Since the son's interest is attributed to Bonnie, the estate is deemed to hold a 25% interest, and Wren (for purposes of § 6166) has only 45 partners. ∎

In satisfying the more-than-35 percent test for qualification under § 6166, interests in more than one closely held business are aggregated when the decedent's gross estate includes 20 percent or more of the value of each such business.[53]

EXAMPLE 52

Henry's estate includes stock in Green Corporation and Brown Corporation, each of which qualifies as a closely held business. If the stock held in each entity represents 20% or more of the total value outstanding, the stocks can be combined for purposes of the more-than-35% test. ∎

If the conditions of § 6166 are satisfied and the provision is elected, the following results transpire.

- No payments on the estate tax attributable to the inclusion of the interest in a closely held business in the gross estate need be made with the first five payments. Then, annual installments are made over a period not longer than 10 years.
- From the outset, interest at the rate of 2 percent is paid.[54] Originally, the 2 percent rate of interest applied only to the first $1 million of estate tax value. Since the estate tax value amount has been indexed for inflation, for 2008 it is $1.28 million (it was $1.25 million for 2007).
- Acceleration of deferred payments may be triggered upon the disposition of the interest or failure to make scheduled principal or interest payments.[55]

ETHICAL and EQUITABLE *Considerations*   IS IT TOO LATE?

Donald, who is suffering from a terminal illness, is advised by his CPA that his current estate needs an additional $180,000 in stock of Hawk Corporation to qualify for § 6166. Immediately thereafter, Donald purchases the stock. Upon Donald's death two months later, his executor elects to come under the provisions of § 6166. Presuming the percentage requirements are satisfied, is the election proper?

In qualifying for § 6166, prune the potential estate of assets that may cause the 35 percent test to be failed. In this regard, lifetime gifts of such assets as marketable securities and life insurance should be considered.[56]

Some of the estate planning procedures covered in the last part of this chapter appear in Concept Summary 18–3 on the previous page.

---

[53]§ 6166(c).
[54]§ 6601(j)(1).
[55]§ 6166(g).

[56]A gift within three years of death is not effective for this purpose. § 2035(c)(2).

KEY TERMS

Blockage rule, 18–9

Buy-sell agreement, 18–10

Conservation easements, 18–26

Cross-purchase buy-sell
agreement, 18–10

Entity buy-sell agreement, 18–10

Estate freeze, 18–11

Living trust, 18–25

Probate costs, 18–25

Special use value, 18–6

Step-down in basis, 18–14

Step-up in basis, 18–14

P R O B L E M   M A T E R I A L S

DISCUSSION QUESTIONS

1. Discuss the relevance of the following in defining "fair market value" for Federal gift
   and estate tax purposes.
   a. § 2031(b).
   b. The definition contained in Reg. § 20.2031–1(b).
   c. A forced sale price.
   d. The location of the property being valued.
   e. The sentimental value of the property being valued.
   f. The wholesale price of the property.
   g. Tangible personalty sold as a result of an advertisement in the classified section of a
      newspaper.
   h. Sporadic sales (occuring on other than the valuation date) of stocks traded in an
      over-the-counter stock exchange.

2. Marvin's daughter is a student at an exclusive private women's college. Each year that
   she attends, Marvin has her sign a note for $30,000 to cover books, tuition, and room
   and board. Ten years after the daughter graduates, Marvin dies without a will. The notes
   are found in his safe deposit box. Although the daughter has become a successful
   business executive, Marvin never discussed the notes with her or made any attempts at
   collection. What are the pertinent tax issues? [Note: In answering this question, a review
   of the earlier part of Chapter 17 might prove useful.]

   Issue ID

3. When Pierce dies, one of the assets of his estate is a note receivable from Geena in the
   amount of $50,000. In valuing this note, what effect, if any, do the following factors have?
   a. The interest on the note is 2%.
   b. The collateral for the note has become worthless.
   c. Geena is Pierce's daughter, and he forgave the note five years ago. (No gift tax
      return was filed.)
   d. Geena is Pierce's daughter, and Pierce forgives the note in his will.
   e. No one knows where Geena is.
   f. On his income tax return filed four years ago, Pierce claimed a bad debt deduction
      as to the loan.

4. Comment on the valuation of each of the following items.
   a. An annuity contract issued by a party not regularly engaged in issuing such contracts.
   b. An annuity contract issued by an insurance company.
   c. A single premium life insurance policy.
   d. A life insurance policy, not recently issued, on which future premiums need to be
      made.
   e. A trust that creates a life estate and remainder interests.
   f. A living trust.

5. Miles creates a trust, income payable to Nicole for six years, remainder to Laurie.
   a. What might be the justification for this type of trust?
   b. Has Miles made one or two gifts? What difference does it make?
   c. In terms of possible income tax consequences, is Nicole's age relevant? Explain.

6. In connection with § 2032A, comment on the following.
   a. The reason for the provision.
   b. Distinguish between "most suitable" and "special" use. Where do "best," "current," and "highest" use fit in?
   c. The amount of valuation that can be excluded under this provision.
   d. The relevance of the term "material participation."
   e. Satisfying the "qualified use" test.
   f. The income tax basis of the property subject to the election.
   g. The availability of the § 2032A election for gift tax purposes.

7. Eight years after the § 2032A election is made, the qualified heir sells the qualified property.
   a. What estate taxes result?
   b. What income taxes result?

8. A program of lifetime giving can help an estate qualify for the special use valuation election of § 2032A.
   a. Explain how this advice can succeed.
   b. What could go wrong?

9. In determining the value of goodwill attributable to stock in a closely held corporation, comment on the following factors.
   a. The corporation's average profit figure includes large gains from the sale of assets not related to the business conducted.
   b. The family members who own and run the business have not been paid salaries by the corporation.
   c. The operations of the corporation are largely financed with loans from its shareholders (rather than from outsiders).
   d. The rate of return used by the IRS for this type of business is too low.
   e. The deceased owner was active in the operation of the business.

10. What effect, if any, will each of the following factors have on the valuation of stock in a closely held corporation?
    a. The "blockage rule."
    b. A minority interest is involved.
    c. A majority interest is involved.
    d. The cost the corporation would incur in going public.
    e. The income tax consequences upon disposition of the stock.
    f. The existence of a buy-sell agreement between the shareholders.

Issue ID

11. A renowned artist dies. Explain what factors might have a bearing on the valuation of oil paintings included in her gross estate.

Issue ID

12. During the same year, a donor gives stock in a closely held corporation to family members and to a qualified charitable organization. In terms of tax planning, what might such a procedure accomplish?

13. In terms of buy-sell agreements, comment on the following.
    a. The type of agreement that envisions a stock redemption.
    b. The type of agreement that is to be carried out by using only the funds of the surviving owners.
    c. An agreement where the price set will control for estate tax purposes.

14. In terms of the income tax basis of property received by gift, comment on the following.
    a. The difference between pre-1977 and post-1976 gifts.
    b. When the donee's basis for gain and basis for loss will be the same.
    c. When the donee can take advantage of any gift tax paid by the donor.
    d. When the donee will have neither gain nor loss upon later disposition of the property.

15. As to the income tax basis of property acquired from a decedent, when does a step-up in basis occur? A step-down in basis?

16. In terms of a community property jurisdiction, comment on the following.
    a. How the death of one spouse affects the income tax basis of the surviving spouse's share of the community.

b. The advantages and disadvantages of this result.

c. How the disadvantages can be avoided.

17. Before electing certain valuation provisions such as § 2032 (alternate valuation date) and § 2032A (special use valuation), income tax consequences should be taken into account. Why?

18. Martina dies prior to her retirement. Among her assets is a traditional IRA (worth $800,000) with Spencer as the designated beneficiary. Advise Spencer as to his tax consequences, if he is Martina's:

a. Son.

b. Surviving spouse.

19. Jonathan Rand is distressed about the basis of some land he inherited five years ago and recently sold for a large gain. He feels that the value placed on the property is too low. Consequently, he requests your advice as to whether he is bound by this value.

a. Write a letter to Jonathan regarding this matter. Jonathan's address is 326 Wisteria Avenue, Charlotte, NC 28223.

b. Include in the letter a list of further information you will need before you can assess the probability of success in challenging the value used by the estate.

20. Cynthia and Norton Enright own all of the stock in Ibis Company, an S corporation. The Enrights are considering making gifts of some of the stock to their children (Addison, Tracy, Jordan, and Kirby) in order to shift income to them. Addison (age 20) is a high school graduate and does not intend to go to college. Tracy (age 21) is married and files a joint return with her husband. Jordan (age 23) and Kirby (age 24) are full-time college students. The Enrights request your advice on how to make these gifts effectively for tax purposes.

a. Write a letter to the Enrights on this matter. Their address is 1486 Garden Park, Elizabeth, NJ 07207.

b. Prepare a memo for your firm's tax research files.

21. Making gifts can save on estate taxes. Comment on the relevance of this statement to each of the following.

a. The amount of the annual exclusion utilized.

b. The amount of gift tax actually paid.

c. Subsequent appreciation of the property given.

d. Contributions to § 529 plans on behalf of family members.

e. Planning for the election of the special use valuation method of § 2032A.

f. The timely disclaimer of an inheritance. [Refer to Chapter 17 if necessary.]

22. For income tax purposes, what difference does it make to the parties (i.e., transferor and transferee) whether the following assets are transferred by gift or by death?

a. Installment notes receivable.

b. U.S. savings bonds.

c. Depreciable property that has § 1245 or § 1250 recapture potential.

23. Charles Horn wants his daughter Sharon to get stock that he owns in Crimson Corporation. He acquired the stock two years ago at a cost of $800,000, and it currently has a fair market value of $650,000. Charles has made prior taxable gifts and is in poor health. He seeks your advice as to whether he should gift the stock to Sharon or pass it to her under his will. Charles has a large capital loss carryover and has no prospect for any capital gains.

a. Write a letter to Charles regarding the tax implications of the alternatives he has suggested. His address is 648 Scenic Drive, Chattanooga, TN 37403.

b. Prepare a memo for your firm's files on this matter.

24. Several years ago, Heather retired and moved to Nevada from Wisconsin. She converted her former personal residence in Wisconsin to rental property. She owns several insurance policies on her life with her estate listed as the designated beneficiary. Heather is single, and her only heirs are two nieces. What can be done to ease any probate problems that might arise on Heather's later death? What if Heather wants to continue receiving the income stream from the rental property?

25. In deciding between the *deferral* and the *equalization* approaches to the marital deduction, comment on the following variables. In each case, the wife is expected to survive her husband's earlier death.
    a.   The wife has considerable wealth of her own.
    b.   The wife just won the championship (senior women's division) at her tennis club.
    c.   The wife is scheduled to undergo a triple bypass heart operation.
    d.   Most of the property that will pass to the wife is not expected to appreciate significantly in value.

26. Regarding charitable transfers, comment on the following issues.
    a.   A preference for lifetime, rather than testamentary, transfers.
    b.   Avoiding the danger that the designated recipient is no longer a "qualified" charity.
    c.   The charity receives the property only if the heir disclaims his or her interest.
    d.   Same as (c), except that the heir is the surviving spouse.

27. In connection with the *bypass amount*, comment on the following.
    a.   What is it?
    b.   How does it relate to the *exclusion amount?* The *exemption equivalent?*
    c.   How can it be utilized in the case of charitable bequests?
    d.   In the case of marital bequests?
    e.   Under what circumstances can a disclaimer by an heir increase the bypass amount and not change the amount of the taxable estate?
    f.   How can lifetime gifts between spouses prevent the bypass amount from being wasted?

Issue ID

28. The estate of Janet, currently still alive, almost qualifies for an election under § 6166. Janet is not concerned, however, because she plans on giving away her life insurance policy before her death. This, she believes, will allow her estate to meet the requirements of § 6166. Any comment?

29. Although not explicitly stated as such, certain Code provisions implicitly recognize that the owner-decedent of a small business may have a liquidity problem. How is this notion manifested in the following Code provisions?
    a.   Special use valuation election of § 2032A.
    b.   Stock redemptions under § 303 to pay death taxes and administration expenses.
    c.   Discretionary extension of time to pay estate taxes under § 6161.
    d.   Extension of time to pay estate taxes under § 6166.

PROBLEMS

30. When Kinsey died, she owned 1,000 shares of Blue Corporation. The stock is traded in an over-the-counter market. The nearest trades before and after the date of Kinsey's death are as follows.

	Per Share Mean Selling Price
Five days before Kinsey's death	$300
Six days after Kinsey's death	340

    Assuming the alternate valuation date is not elected, at what value should the Blue stock be included in Kinsey's gross estate?

31. Jackson creates a trust with securities worth $3 million. Under the terms of the trust, Courtney (age 52) receives a life estate, while Kara (age 24) receives the remainder interest. In the month the trust is created, the appropriate interest rate is 7.4%. Determine the value of Jackson's gifts.

32. Melissa creates a trust with securities worth $2 million. Under the terms of the trust, Jacob (age 17) receives the income for 10 years, remainder to Emily (age 40). In the month the trust is created, the appropriate interest rate is 8.2%. Determine the value of Melissa's gifts.

33. In 2003, Ethan (age 66) creates a trust worth $3.7 million. Under the terms of the trust, Ethan retains a life estate with the remainder passing to Marla (age 35) on his death. In the month the trust is created, the appropriate interest rate is 8%.
    a. Determine the amount of Ethan's gift. Of his taxable gift.
    b. Would your answer in part (a) change if Marla is Ethan's wife? Explain. [Refer to Chapter 17 if necessary.]

34. Assume the same facts as in Problem 33. Ethan dies five years later when the trust is worth $3.9 million. Marla is age 40 and the applicable interest rate is 7.8%.
    a. How much, if any, of the trust is included in Ethan's gross estate?
    b. Would your answer in part (a) change if Marla is Ethan's wife? Explain. [Refer to Chapter 17 if necessary.]

35. Regarding the special use valuation method of § 2032A, comment on the following independent statements.
    a. For purposes of meeting the requirements for making the election, the qualifying property may consist solely of real property and cannot include personal property.
    b. The election of § 2032A is made by the executor of the estate.
    c. For purposes of satisfying both the 50% and the 25% tests, the qualifying property is considered at its *current use* value (rather than at its *most suitable use* value).
    d. If the qualifying property has a most suitable use value of $3.5 million and a current use value of $3 million, the § 2032A election cannot reduce its estate tax value below $3 million.
    e. If the qualifying property has a most suitable use value of $4.6 million and a current use value of $3.4 million, the § 2032A election can reduce its estate tax value to $3.4 million.
    f. A qualifying heir could be the son of a deceased real estate broker who purchased the farm two years ago at a public auction.

36. Regarding the recapture provisions under the special use valuation method of § 2032A, comment on each of the following independent statements.
    a. If recapture occurs, any additional estate tax liability is imposed on the qualifying heir.
    b. If recapture occurs, an income tax basis adjustment to the qualifying property must take place.
    c. In the event of recapture, interest accrues on any additional estate tax that results.
    d. Recapture will not occur as long as the qualifying heir continues to own the property for at least 10 years.
    e. The § 2032A election can be made even if it is probable that the qualifying property will be disposed of within the 10-year recapture period.
    f. The IRS retains a measure of security to assure that taxpayers comply with the recapture provisions.

37. At her death, Paige owned 53% of the stock in Garnet Corporation, with the 47% balance held by family members. In the past five years, Garnet has earned average net profits of $800,000, and on the date of Paige's death, the book value of its stock is $2 million. An appropriate rate of return for the type of business Garnet is in is 7%.
    a. Assuming goodwill exists, what is the value of the Garnet stock?
    b. What factors could be present to reduce the value of such goodwill?

38. Philip owns all of the stock of Taupe Corporation. The stock has a value of $6 million for the common and $1.5 million for the preferred. The preferred is noncumulative, has no redemption value, and carries no preference as to liquidation. Philip gives the common stock to his children and retains the preferred stock. What are the tax consequences?

39. Assume the same facts as in Problem 38. Nine years after the gift, Philip dies. At that time, the Taupe stock is worth $8 million for the common and $1.6 million for the preferred. What are Philip's tax consequences?

40. Nolan gives stock (basis of $300,000; fair market value of $900,000) to Sarah. Determine Sarah's income tax basis for gain or loss under each of the following assumptions.
    a. The gift occurred in 1975, and Nolan paid a gift tax of $160,000.
    b. The gift occurred in 2008, and Nolan paid a gift tax of $250,000.

41. Margaret gives stock (basis of $800,000; fair market value of $700,000) to Leslie. As a result of the transfer, Margaret pays a gift tax of $150,000. Determine Leslie's gain or loss if he later sells the stock for:
    a. $650,000.
    b. $850,000.
    c. $750,000.

Decision Making

Communications

42. Ted and Marge Dean are married and have always lived in a community property state. Ted (age 92) suffers from numerous disorders and is frequently ill, while Marge (age 70) is in good health. The Deans currently need $500,000 to meet living expenses, make debt payments, and pay Ted's backlog of medical expenses. They are willing to sell any one of the following assets:

	Adjusted Basis	Fair Market Value
Wren Corporation stock	$200,000	$500,000
Gull Corporation stock	600,000	500,000
Unimproved land	650,000	500,000

The stock investments are part of the Deans' community property, while the land is Ted's separate property that he inherited from his mother. If the land is not sold, Ted is considering making a gift of it to Marge.
    a. Write a letter to the Deans advising them on these matters. Their address is 290 Cedar Road, Carson, CA 90747.
    b. Prepare a memo on this matter for your firm's client files.

43. In June 2007, Reba gives Julius a house (basis of $150,000; fair market value of $450,000) to be used as his personal residence. Due to the transfer, Reba incurs and pays a gift tax of $110,000. Before his death in May 2008, Julius installs a tennis court in the backyard at a cost of $25,000. The residence has a value of $465,000 when Julius dies. Determine the income tax basis of the property to the heir based on the following independent assumptions.
    a. The residence passes to Reba.
    b. The residence passes to Burl (Reba's husband).
    c. The residence passes to Tina (Reba's daughter).

Decision Making

44. Andy and Belle are husband and wife with five married children and nine grandchildren. Commencing in December 2008, they would like to transfer a tract of land (worth $912,000) equally to their children (including spouses) and grandchildren as quickly as possible and without making a taxable gift. What do you suggest?

45. At the time of her death, Hortense has an adjusted gross estate of $3.1 million. Her estate includes the family farm, with a most suitable use value of $1.6 million and a current use value of $800,000. The farm is inherited by Paul, Hortense's son, who has worked it for her since 1985. Paul plans to continue farming indefinitely.
    a. Based on the information given, is the § 2032A election available to Hortense's estate?
    b. If so, what value must be used for the farm?
    c. Suppose Hortense had made a gift of securities (fair market value of $150,000) to her cousin six months before her death. Does this fact affect your analysis? Explain.

46. Last year, Henry sold real estate (basis of $450,000) to Bill (an unrelated party) for $1.8 million, receiving $300,000 in cash and notes for the balance. The notes carry an 8.5% rate of interest and mature annually at $500,000 each over three years. Henry did not elect out of the installment method of reporting the gain. Before any of the

notes mature and when they have a fair market value of $1.3 million, Henry gives them to Jean.

    a.   Disregarding the interest element, what are the tax consequences of the gift?

    b.   Suppose that instead of making the gift, Henry died. The notes passed to his estate and were later sold by the executor. What is the tax result?

47. At the time of her death in the current year, Monica held the following assets.

	Fair Market Value
Personal residence (title listed as "Monica and Peter, tenants by the entirety with right of survivorship")	$800,000
Savings account (listed as "Monica and Rex, joint tenants with right of survivorship") with funds provided by Rex	40,000
Certificate of deposit (listed as "Monica, payable on proof of death to Rex") with funds provided by Monica	100,000
Unimproved real estate (title listed as "Monica and Rex, equal tenants in common")	400,000
Insurance policy on Monica's life, issued by Lavender Company (Monica's estate is the designated beneficiary)	300,000
Insurance policy on Monica's life, issued by Crimson Company (Rex is the designated beneficiary)	400,000
Living trust created by Monica five years ago (life estate to Peter, remainder to Rex)	700,000

Assuming Peter and Rex survive Monica, how much is included in Monica's *probate estate*? Monica's *gross estate*? [Refer to Chapter 17 if needed.]

48. During their marriage, Cory and Brooke have successfully operated the family business, and each has managed to accumulate investments worth approximately $2 million. Probabilities are that Cory will predecease Brooke, since he is almost 10 years older and is in poor health. Based on this premise, Cory is looking for a testamentary plan that will accomplish the following objectives.

Decision Making

- Provide Brooke with maximum financial security.
- Avoid concentrating wealth in Brooke's estate upon her subsequent death.
- Provide for an orderly transfer of property to their adult children upon the death of the survivor.
- Avoid (or minimize) estate (and gift) taxes as a result of whatever transfers Cory and Brooke make.

Neither Brooke nor Cory has made any prior taxable gifts.

    In making suggestions, you may find it helpful to review the discussion of §§ 2036 and 2041 in Chapter 17.

49. In terms of tax ramifications, comment on what is accomplished in the following disclaimer situations.

    a.   Lester dies intestate and is survived by a daughter, Nora, and a grandson, Nick. The major asset in Lester's estate is stock worth $2 million. Under the applicable state law of descent and distribution, children precede grandchildren in order of inheritance. As Nora is already well off and in ill health, she disclaims Lester's property.

    b.   Under her will, Audry's estate is to pass $2.5 million to her son, Raymond, and the $1 million remainder to her husband, George. Raymond disclaims $500,000 of his inheritance.

    c.   Under Isaac's will, $2 million is to pass to his wife, Brenda, and the $1.5 million remainder to his daughter, Sybil. Brenda disclaims $500,000 of her inheritance.

    d.   Under Tricia's will, her $3 million cubist art collection is to pass to her husband, Leroy. If Leroy declines, the collection is to pass to the San Francisco Museum of Modern Art. Leroy neither understands nor admires this type of art.

Decision Making

50. Cameron dies in 2008 and is survived by his wife, Kristen, and three adult children. Among the items included in his gross estate are the following.

	Fair Market Value
Apartment building	$1,400,000
Marketable securities	600,000
Lake cottage	300,000
Cabin cruiser	240,000
Insurance policy on Kristen's life (maturity value of $600,000)	60,000

As to the apartment building, Cameron's will grants Kristen a life estate (worth $800,000 under the IRS tables) with remainder (worth $600,000 under the IRS tables) to the children. Cameron's estate does not make a QTIP election regarding the life estate. Under Cameron's will, the rest of his property passes to Kristen. By applicable state law, whatever Kristen disclaims passes to the children. Kristen has considerable assets of her own. The children are self-supporting.
   a.   What needs to be done to maximize the bypass amount?
   b.   How can Kristen's potential estate tax consequences be minimized?

Issue ID

51. Brian (age 80 and in poor health) and Holly (age 70) have been married for many years and have adult children. Holly's net worth is approximately $4 million, while Brian's is negligible.
   a.   What happens for estate tax purposes if Brian dies first?
   b.   What tax planning procedures would avoid this result?
   c.   What if Holly predeceases Brian? What testamentary disposition would minimize estate tax consequences?

52. At the time of his death, Clint had an adjusted gross estate of $4.2 million. Included in the estate is a 15% capital interest in a partnership valued at $1.6 million. Except for Clint's daughter Phoebe, none of the other 48 partners are related to him. Phoebe holds a 10% capital interest.
   a.   Does Clint's estate qualify for the § 6166 election?
   b.   Suppose that one year prior to his death, Clint gave $400,000 cash to Phoebe. Does this change your analysis?

53. At the time of her death, June had an adjusted gross estate of $3 million. Included in the estate were the following business interests.

	Fair Market Value
A 30% capital interest in the JZ Partnership	$600,000
A 25% interest (i.e., 250 shares out of 1,000) in Silver Corporation	400,000
A catering service operated as a sole proprietorship	150,000

The JZ Partnership has 32 partners while Silver Corporation has a total of 30 shareholders. None of the other partners or shareholders are related to June. Can June's estate qualify for an election under § 6166? Explain.

RESEARCH PROBLEMS

Note: Solutions to Research Problems can be prepared by using the **RIA Checkpoint® Student Edition** online research product, which is available to accompany this text. It is also possible to prepare solutions to the Research Problems by using tax research materials found in a standard tax library.

Research Problem 1. Ruth Inman, age 88, is a widow with four married children, 11 grandchildren, and 20 great-grandchildren. When Ruth suffers a mild stroke in late November 2008, she begins building her cash position through the sale of nonappreciated assets. Prior to her scheduled surgery on December 28, Ruth makes out and mails 50 checks of $12,000 each to family members (including some in-laws). She also mails a check for $50,000 to Saint Anne's Church Building Fund in satisfaction of a pledge she had made earlier. Ruth dies one day after the surgery.

a. What was Ruth trying to accomplish?

b. Will it work?

Partial list of research aids:
Reg. §§ 20.2031–5 and 25.2511–2(b).
Estate of Gagliardi, 89 T.C. 1207 (1987).
Estate of Metzger, 100 T.C. 204 (1993), *aff'd* 94–2 USTC ¶60,179, 74 AFTR2d 94–7486, 38 F.3d 118 (CA–4, 1994).
Estate of Sarah H. Newman, 111 T.C. 81 (1998).

Research Problem 2. In 2006, Troy wins the Connecticut LOTTO grand prize of $15 million. The LOTTO contest is governed by the following rules.

- The prize money is to be paid in 20 equal annual installments (in this case, $750,000 per year) with no interest provided for.
- The rights to the prize award are not assignable. If a winner dies during the payout period, however, the remaining installment payments are to be made to the winner's duly appointed executor.
- The prize award is not specifically funded or guaranteed by any state agency. It constitutes a general obligation of the state of Connecticut.

Troy dies in 2008 after having received two payments of $750,000 each. Troy's estate includes the present value of the remaining $13.5 million prize award in the estate at $4.86 million. This is determined by using the IRS table amount of $6.75 million and discounting it for absence of security (i.e., no separate funding or guarantee of payment by a state agency) and lack of marketability (i.e., the award cannot be assigned). The table used is that issued by the IRS in Reg. § 20.2031–7 under the authority of § 7520. The table is to be used in valuing, among other income interests, private (i.e., noncommercial) annuity contracts.

Upon audit of the estate tax return, the IRS disputes the deviation from the table amount. The IRS argues that the absence-of-security discount is inappropriate because the state of Connecticut has never defaulted on any of its LOTTO obligations. Furthermore, the lack-of-marketability discount is inappropriately applied to annuity-type situations. Unlike stocks and bonds and other ownership interests, private annuities are not subject to marketplace valuation procedures.

Who should prevail? The taxpayer or the IRS?

Partial list of research aids:
§§ 2039 and 7520.
Reg. § 20.7520–3(b).
O'Reilly v. Comm., 92–2 USTC ¶60,111, 70 AFTR2d 92–6211, 973 F.2d 1403 (CA–8, 1992).
Shackleford v. U.S., 99–2 USTC ¶60,356, 84 AFTR2d 99–5902 (D.Ct.Calif., 1999), *aff'd* in 88 AFTR2d 2001–5658, 262 F.3d 1028 (CA–9, 2001).
Estate of Gribauskas, 116 T.C. 142 (2001), *rev'd* in 2003–2 USTC ¶60,466, 92 AFTR2d 2003–5914, 342 F.3d 85 (CA–2, 2003).
Estate of Donovan v. U.S., 2005–1 USTC ¶50,322, 95 AFTR2d 2005–2131 (D.Ct.Mass., 2005).

Research Problem 3. In late 2007, Gordon Clay unexpectedly suffered a stroke, and he died shortly thereafter. In his will, Gordon designated his sister, Loretta, as executor of his estate. Loretta was duly appointed executor, administered the estate, rendered a final accounting, and was discharged by the probate court in June 2008.

During the administration of the estate, Loretta satisfied a claim for $200,000 submitted by Raymond Clay, Gordon's older brother. Several years ago, Gordon had borrowed this amount from Raymond on open account. No note was issued or interest provided for. The loan was not a secret, and everyone in the immediate family was aware that it had been made and not repaid. When completing the Form 706 for Gordon's estate, Loretta deducted the $200,000 as a § 2053(a)(3) claim against the estate. Upon audit by the IRS, the deduction was disallowed on two grounds. First, the existence of the debt was not proved. Second, if the debt existed, it was barred by the statute of limitations.

The estate countered that the note existed and that its payment was sanctioned by the probate court. Further, the running of the statute of limitations does not invalidate a claim—it merely provides the creditor with a defense that may or may not be invoked. In the interest of family harmony, therefore, Loretta chose not to invoke the statute and bar a claim that was rightfully due and should be paid.

a. Who will prevail?

b. Has Loretta acted wisely? Answer also from the perspective of the remainderperson under Gordon's will.

Partial list of research aids:
Prop.Reg. §§ 20.2053–4(b)(4) and 4(d), Example 7. [Reg. § 143316–03
    published in I.R.B. No. 21, 1292 (May 21, 2007.)]

Internet
Activity

Use the tax resources of the Internet to address the following questions. Do not restrict your search to the World Wide Web, but include a review of newsgroups and general reference materials, practitioner sites and resources, primary sources of the tax law, chat rooms and discussion groups, and other opportunities.

Research Problem 4. Scheduled to become effective in 2010, § 1022 largely revokes the step-up and step-down in income tax basis that an heir gets in property received from a decedent. Using the Internet, locate and review § 1022. Are there any exceptions to the new rules that impose a "carryover basis" upon the heirs? Elaborate.

Communications

Research Problem 5. Identify the following forms issued by the IRS: Forms 706–NA, 706–CE, 712, 4768, and 4808. What purpose does each serve? Summarize your comments in an e-mail to your professor.

Communications

Research Problem 6. In your state, what is the designation of the court that handles the administration of an estate? What are the statutory guidelines on fees that an executor is allowed for probating an estate? Summarize your findings in a short PowerPoint presentation.

Communications

Research Problem 7. Review the data released by the IRS on the types of returns audited for fiscal years 2005 and 2006.

a. How many Forms 706 and 709 were selected for audit?

b. From 2005 to 2006, what was the percentage of increase or decrease in the annual audit rates?

c. Send an e-mail to your instructor with a table and graphs illustrating your findings.

Income Taxation of Trusts and Estates

LEARNING OBJECTIVES

After completing Chapter 19, you should be able to:

LO.1
Use working definitions with respect to trusts, estates, beneficiaries, and other parties.

LO.2
Identify the steps in determining the accounting and taxable income of a trust or estate and the related taxable income of the beneficiaries.

LO.3
Illustrate the uses and implications of distributable net income.

LO.4
Use the special rules that apply to trusts where the creator (grantor) of the trust retains certain rights.

An Overview of Subchapter J

Taxpayers create trusts for a variety of reasons. Some trusts are established primarily for tax purposes, but most are designed to accomplish a specific financial goal or to provide for the orderly management of assets in case of emergency.

Because a trust is a separate tax entity, its gross income and deductions must be measured, and an annual tax return must be filed. Similarly, when an individual dies, a legal entity is created in the form of his or her estate. This chapter examines the rules related to the income taxation of trusts and estates.

Table 19–1 lists some of the more common reasons for creating a trust, and Figure 19–1 illustrates the structure of a typical trust and estate.

The income taxation of trusts and estates is governed by Subchapter J of the Internal Revenue Code, §§ 641 through 692. Certain similarities are apparent between Subchapter J and the income taxation of individuals (e.g., the definitions of gross income and deductible expenditures), partnerships and limited liability entities (e.g., the pass-through principle), and S corporations (e.g., the pass-through principle and the trust or estate as a separate taxable entity). Trusts also involve several important new concepts, however, including the determination of *distributable net income* and the *tier system* of distributions to beneficiaries.

What Is a Trust?

LO.1

Use working definitions with respect to trusts, estates, beneficiaries, and other parties.

The Code does not contain a definition of a trust. However, the term usually refers to an arrangement created by a will or by an *inter vivos* (lifetime) declaration through which trustees take title to property for the purpose of protecting or conserving it for the beneficiaries.[1] Usually, trust operations are controlled by the trust document and by the fiduciary laws of the state in which the trust documents are executed.

Typically, the creation of a trust involves at least three parties: (1) The **grantor** (sometimes referred to as the settlor or donor) transfers selected assets to the trust entity. (2) The trustee, who usually is either an individual or a corporation, is charged with the fiduciary duties associated with the trust. (3) The beneficiary is designated to receive income or property from the trust.

[1]Reg. § 301.7701–4(a).

TABLE 19–1 **Common Motivations for Creating a Trust**

Type of Trust	Financial and Other Goals
Life insurance trust	Holds life insurance policies on the insured, removes the proceeds of the policies from the gross estate (if an irrevocable trust), and safeguards against receipt of the proceeds by a young or inexperienced beneficiary.
"Living" (revocable) trust	Manages assets, reduces probate costs, provides privacy for asset disposition, protects against medical or other emergencies, and provides relief from the necessity of day-to-day management of the underlying assets.
Trust for minors	Provides funds for a college education, shifts income to lower-bracket taxpayers, and transfers accumulated income without permanently parting with the underlying assets.
"Blind" trust	Holds and manages the assets of the grantor without his/her input or influence (e.g., while the grantor holds political office or some other sensitive position).
Retirement trust	Manages asset contributions as dictated by the terms of a qualified retirement plan.
Alimony trust	Manages the assets of an ex-spouse and assures they are distributed in a timely fashion to specified beneficiaries.
Liquidation trust	Collects and distributes the remaining assets of a corporation that is undergoing a complete liquidation.

In some situations, fewer than three persons may be involved, as specified by the trust agreement. For instance, an elderly individual who no longer can manage his or her own property (e.g., because of ill health) may create a trust under which he or she is both the grantor and the beneficiary. In this case, a family member or corporate trustee is charged with the management of the grantor's assets.

In another situation, the grantor might designate himself or herself as the trustee of the trust assets. For example, someone who wants to transfer selected assets to a minor child or elderly parent could use a trust entity to assure that the beneficiary does not waste the property. By naming himself or herself as the trustee, the grantor retains virtual control over the property that is transferred.

Under the general rules of Subchapter J, the **grantor trusts** just described are not recognized for income tax purposes. Similarly, when only one party is involved (when the same individual is grantor, trustee, and sole beneficiary of the trust), Subchapter J rules do not apply, and the entity is ignored for income tax purposes.

Other Definitions. When the grantor transfers title of selected assets to a trust, those assets become the **corpus** (body), or principal, of the trust. Trust corpus, in most situations, earns *income*, which may be distributed to the beneficiaries or accumulated for the future by the trustee, as the trust instrument directs.

In the typical trust, the grantor creates two types of beneficiaries: one who receives the accounting income of the trust and one who receives the trust corpus that remains at the termination of the trust entity. Beneficiaries in the former

| **FIGURE 19-1** | **Structure of a Typical Trust and Estate** |

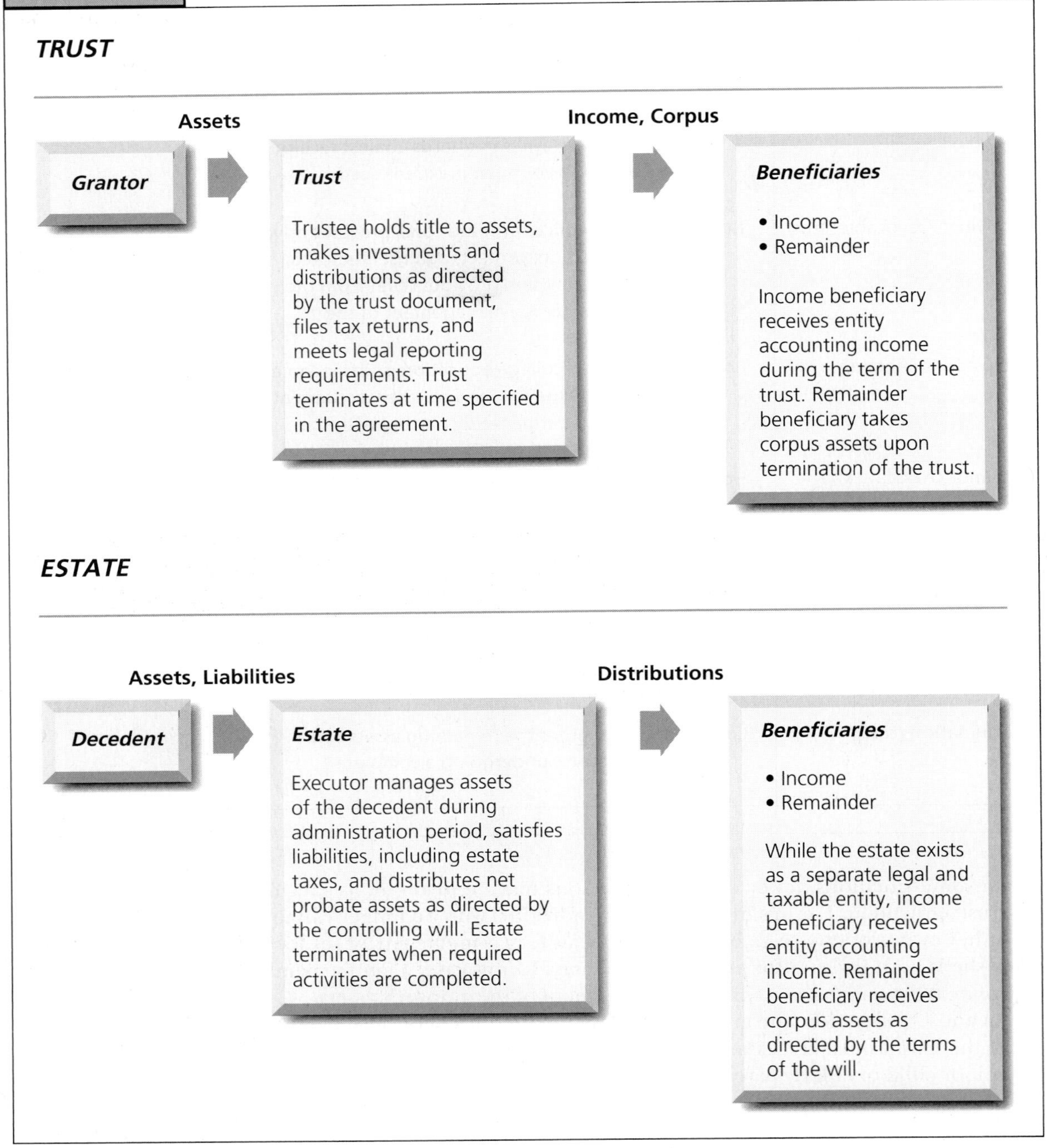

TRUST

Assets → Income, Corpus →

Grantor

Trust

Trustee holds title to assets, makes investments and distributions as directed by the trust document, files tax returns, and meets legal reporting requirements. Trust terminates at time specified in the agreement.

Beneficiaries

• Income
• Remainder

Income beneficiary receives entity accounting income during the term of the trust. Remainder beneficiary takes corpus assets upon termination of the trust.

ESTATE

Assets, Liabilities → Distributions →

Decedent

Estate

Executor manages assets of the decedent during administration period, satisfies liabilities, including estate taxes, and distributes net probate assets as directed by the controlling will. Estate terminates when required activities are completed.

Beneficiaries

• Income
• Remainder

While the estate exists as a separate legal and taxable entity, income beneficiary receives entity accounting income. Remainder beneficiary receives corpus assets as directed by the terms of the will.

category hold an *income interest* in the trust, and those in the latter category hold a *remainder interest* in the trust's assets. If the grantor retains the remainder interest, the interest is known as a **reversionary interest** (corpus reverts to the grantor when the trust entity terminates).

The trust document establishes the term of the trust. The term may be for a specific number of years (*term certain*) or until the occurrence of a specified event. For instance, a trust might exist (1) for the life of the income beneficiary, in which case the income beneficiary is known as a *life tenant* in trust corpus; (2) for the life of some other individual; (3) until the income or remainder beneficiary reaches the age of majority; or (4) until the beneficiary, or another individual, marries, receives a promotion, or reaches some specified age.

The trustee may be required to distribute the accounting income of the entity according to a distribution schedule specified in the agreement. Sometimes, however, the trustee is given more discretion with respect to the timing and nature of the distributions. If the trustee can determine, within guidelines that may be included in the trust document, either the timing of the income or corpus distributions or the specific beneficiaries who will receive them (from among those identified in the agreement), the trust is called a **sprinkling trust**. Here, the trustee can "sprinkle" the distributions among the various beneficiaries. As discussed in Chapters 17 and 18, family-wide income taxes can be reduced by directing income to those who are subject to lower marginal tax rates. Thus, by giving the trustee a sprinkling power, the income tax liability of the family unit can be manipulated by applying the terms of the trust agreement.

For purposes of certain provisions of Subchapter J, a trust must be classified as either a **simple trust** or a **complex trust**. A simple trust (1) is required to distribute its entire accounting income to designated beneficiaries every year, (2) has no beneficiaries that are qualifying charitable organizations, and (3) makes no distributions of trust corpus during the year. A complex trust is any trust that is not a simple trust.[2] These criteria are applied to the trust every year. Thus, every trust is classified as a complex trust in the year in which it terminates (because it distributes all of its corpus during that year).

What Is an Estate?

An estate is created upon the death of every individual. The entity is charged with collecting and conserving all of the individual's assets, satisfying all liabilities, and distributing the remaining assets to the heirs identified by state law or the will.

Typically, the creation of an estate involves at least three parties: the decedent, all of whose probate assets are transferred to the estate for disposition; the executor, who is appointed under the decedent's valid will (or the administrator, if no valid will exists); and the beneficiaries of the estate, who are to receive assets or income from the entity, as the decedent has indicated in the will. An estate's operations are controlled by the probate laws of the decedent's state of residence and by the terms of the will as interpreted by the probate court.

Recall that the assets that make up the probate estate are not identical to those that constitute the gross estate for transfer tax purposes (refer to Chapter 18). Many gross estate assets are not a part of the probate estate and thus are not subject to disposition by the executor or administrator. For instance, property held by the decedent as a joint tenant passes to the survivor(s) by operation of the applicable state's property law rather than through the probate estate. Proceeds of insurance policies on the life of the decedent, over which the decedent held the incidents of ownership, are not under the control of the executor or administrator. The designated beneficiaries of the policy receive the proceeds outright under the insurance contract.

An estate is a separate taxable entity. The termination date of the estate is somewhat discretionary, as it occurs when all of the assets and income of the decedent have been distributed, all estate and decedent liabilities have been satisfied, and all other business of the entity is completed. Thus, there may be an incentive to use the estate as part of an income-shifting strategy (e.g., where the income beneficiaries are subject to low marginal tax rates).

Maria dies, and her estate holds a high-yield investment portfolio. Paulo, the income beneficiary, is subject to a 15% marginal state and Federal income tax rate, while Julia, the remainder beneficiary, is subject to a 30% marginal rate. The tax adviser might suggest that Maria's estate delay its final distribution of assets by a year or more, to take advantage of the income tax reduction that is available before the entity terminates. ■	***E X A M P L E 1***

---

[2]Reg. § 1.651(a)–1.

TAX *in the News* **SHOULD YOUR TRUST BE ALL IN THE FAMILY?**

For decades, grantors have chosen a family member to be the trustee of the family savings, the children's education fund, or whatever other assets are placed into management by the trust. The relative chosen is often the most trusted but not always the one with the business sense. Now, however, as the financial work has become more complex, with wild stock market fluctuations, increased fiduciary standards, and potential conflicts of interest, some are questioning the wisdom of using a family member as the trustee.

Using a trust company or other financial institution as a trustee usually results in more stable investment returns, eliminating both the highs and the lows of the stock market cycle. Institutions also are more likely to be located in states that levy no income tax on trusts, preferring to attract such business with a friendly tax climate. (Delaware, South Dakota, and Alaska are known as being especially trust-friendly.) Institutions can also bring other advantages.

- They do not die, run away, develop a mental illness, or otherwise unexpectedly become unqualified for the position.
- They are not easily swayed by emotional appeals; nor do they react to family jealousies.
- They are prohibited by law from acting under a conflict of interest, such as might exist between family members when the related trustee is also a trust beneficiary.

On the negative side, human trustees often waive or discount their fiduciary fee, while institutions do not. Especially for trusts with a small corpus, institutional trustees can be prohibitively expensive. And the trust company most often is oriented toward expanding its customer base, rather than offering individual attention to existing clients.

Compromise solutions might be to:

- Appoint co-trustees. Aunt Grace or Uncle Roberto can provide the personal touch and ensure that trust decisions recognize family needs, while the trust company maximizes investment returns and furnishes professional management.
- Keep the family trustee, but hire needed professionals to provide advice only when needed, at an hourly rate. This approach avoids the fees based on asset values that trust companies usually charge.
- Use the advisory services of the mutual funds in which trust assets are invested, to manage and distribute the corpus and income. These services often are discounted from market rates and can be waived for well-to-do clients.

If an estate's existence is unduly prolonged, however, the IRS can terminate it for Federal income tax purposes after the expiration of a reasonable period for completing the duties of administration.[3]

Nature of Trust and Estate Taxation

In general, the taxable income of a trust or estate is taxed to the entity or to its beneficiaries to the extent that each has received the accounting income of the entity. Thus, Subchapter J creates a modified pass-through principle relative to the income taxation of trusts, estates, and their beneficiaries. Whoever receives the accounting income of the entity, or some portion of it, is liable for the income tax that results.

| EXAMPLE 2 | Adam receives 80% of the accounting income of the Zero Trust. The trustee accumulated the other 20% of the income at her discretion under the trust agreement and added it to trust corpus. Adam is liable for income tax only on the amount of the distribution, while Zero is liable for the income tax on the accumulated portion of the income. ∎ |

Table 19–2 summarizes the major similarities and differences between the taxation of trusts and estates and that of other pass-through entities—partnerships (including limited liability companies) and S corporations.

---

[3]Reg. § 1.641(b)–3(a).

TABLE 19–2	**Tax Characteristics of Major Pass-Through Entities**		
Tax Treatment	**Subchapter K (Partnerships, LLCs)**	**Subchapter S (S Corporations)**	**Subchapter J (Trusts, Estates)**
Taxing structure	Pure pass-through, only one level of Federal income tax.	Chiefly pass-through, usually one level of Federal income tax.	Modified pass-through, Federal income tax falls on the recipient(s) of entity accounting income.
Entity-level Federal income tax?	Never.	Rarely. See Chapter 12.	Yes, if the entity retains any accounting income amounts.
Form for reporting income and expense pass-through	Schedules K and K–1, Form 1065.	Schedules K and K–1, Form 1120S.	Schedules K and K–1, Form 1041.
Subject to entity-level AMT?	No, but preferences and adjustments pass through to owners.	No, but preferences and adjustments pass through to owners.	Yes, if the entity retains any AMT-related accounting income amounts.
Controlling documents	Partnership agreement, LLC charter.	Corporate charter and by-laws.	Trust document or will, state fiduciary or probate law.

Tax Accounting Periods and Methods

An estate or trust may use many of the tax accounting methods available to individuals. The method of accounting used by the grantor of a trust or the decedent of an estate need not carry over to the entity.

An estate has the same options for choosing a tax year as any new taxpayer. Thus, the estate of a calendar year decedent dying on March 3 can select any fiscal year or report on a calendar year basis. If the latter is selected, the estate's first taxable year will include the period from March 3 to December 31. If the first or last tax years are short years (less than one calendar year), income for those years need not be annualized.

To eliminate the possibility of deferring the taxation of fiduciary-source income simply by using a fiscal tax year, virtually all trusts (other than tax-exempt trusts) are required to use a calendar tax year.[4]

Tax Rates and Personal Exemption

Congress's desire to stop trusts from being used as income-shifting devices has made the fiduciary entity the highest-taxed taxpayer in the Code. The entity reaches the 35 percent marginal rate with only $10,700 of 2008 taxable income, so the grantor's ability to shift income in a tax-effective manner is nearly eliminated. Table 19–3, which lists the 2008 taxes paid by various entities on taxable income of $50,000, shows how expensive the accumulation of income within an estate or trust can be. Proper income shifting would move assets *out of* the estate or trust and into the hands of the grantor or beneficiary.

A fiduciary's dividend income and net long-term capital gain usually is taxed at a nominal rate of no more than 15 percent. In addition to the regular income tax, an estate or trust may be subject to the alternative minimum tax, as discussed below.[5]

---

[4] § 645.   [5] § 55.

TABLE 19–3	Comparative Tax Liabilities		
Filing Status/Entity	Taxable Income	Marginal Income Tax Rate (%)	2008 Tax Liability
Single	$50,000	25	$ 8,844
Married, filing jointly	50,000	15	6,698
C corporation	50,000	15	7,500
Trust or estate	50,000	35	16,519

Both trusts and estates are allowed a personal exemption in computing the fiduciary tax liability. All estates are allowed a personal exemption of $600. The exemption available to a trust depends upon the type of trust involved. A trust that is required to distribute all of its income currently is allowed an exemption of $300. All other trusts are allowed an exemption of $100 per year.[6]

The classification of trusts as to the appropriate personal exemption is similar but not identical to the distinction between simple and complex trusts. The classification as a simple trust is more stringent.

EXAMPLE 3

Three trusts appear to operate in a similar fashion, but they are subject to different Subchapter J classifications and exemptions.

Trust Alpha is required to distribute all of its current accounting income to Susan. Thus, it is allowed a $300 personal exemption. No corpus distributions or charitable contributions are made during the year. Accordingly, Alpha is a simple trust.

Trust Beta is required to distribute all of its current accounting income; it is allowed a $300 personal exemption. The beneficiaries of these distributions are specified in the trust instrument: one-half of accounting income is to be distributed to Tyrone, and one-half is to be distributed to State University, a qualifying charitable organization. Since Beta has made a charitable distribution for the tax year, it is a complex trust.

The trustee of Trust Gamma can, at her discretion, distribute the current-year accounting income or corpus of the trust to Dr. Chapman. As the trustee is not required to distribute current accounting income, only a $100 personal exemption is allowed. During the current year, the trustee distributed all of the accounting income of the entity to Dr. Chapman, but made no corpus or charitable distributions. Nonetheless, because it lacks the current-year income distribution requirement, Gamma is a complex trust. ∎

Alternative Minimum Tax

The alternative minimum tax (AMT) may apply to a trust or estate in any tax year. Given the nature and magnitude of the tax preferences, adjustments, and exemptions that determine alternative minimum taxable income (AMTI), however, most trusts and estates are unlikely to incur the tax. Nevertheless, they could be vulnerable, for example, if they are actively engaged in cashing out the stock options of a donor/decedent who was a corporate executive.

In general, derivation of AMTI for the entity follows the rules that apply to individual taxpayers. Thus, the corporate ACE adjustment does not apply to fiduciary entities, but AMTI may be created through the application of most of the other AMT preference and adjustment items discussed in Chapter 3.

The fiduciary's AMT is computed using Schedule I of Form 1041. Two full pages of the Form 1041 are dedicated to the computation of taxable income and

---

[6] § 642(b).

other items when the AMT applies to the trust or estate. A minimum tax credit might be available in future years through these computations.

The entity has a $22,500 annual AMT exemption, similar to that available to a married individual who files a separate return. The exemption phases out at a rate of one-fourth of the amount by which AMTI exceeds $75,000.

A 26 percent AMT rate is applied to AMTI, increasing to 28 percent when AMTI in excess of the exemption reaches $175,000. In addition, estimated tax payments for the entity must include any applicable AMT liability.

Taxable Income of Trusts and Estates

Generally, the taxable income of an estate or trust is computed similarly to that for an individual. Subchapter J does, however, include several important exceptions and provisions that make it necessary to use a systematic approach to calculating the taxable income of these entities. Figure 19–2 illustrates the procedure implied by the Code, and Figure 19–3 presents a systematic computation method to be followed in this chapter.

> **LO.2**
>
> Identify the steps in determining the accounting and taxable income of a trust or estate and the related taxable income of the beneficiaries.

Entity Accounting Income

The first step in determining the taxable income of a trust or estate is to compute the entity's accounting income for the period. Although this prerequisite is not apparent from a cursory reading of Subchapter J, a closer look at the Code reveals a number of references to the *income* of the entity.[7] Wherever the term *income* is used in Subchapter J without some modifier (e.g., *gross* income or *taxable* income), the statute is referring to the accounting income of the trust or estate for the tax year.

A definition of entity accounting income is critical to understanding the Subchapter J computation of fiduciary taxable income. Under state law, entity accounting income is the amount that the income beneficiary of the simple trust or estate is eligible to receive from the entity. More importantly, the calculation of accounting income is virtually under the control of the grantor or decedent (through a properly drafted trust agreement or will). If the document has been drafted at arm's length, a court will enforce a fiduciary's good faith efforts to carry out the specified computation of accounting income.

Entity accounting income generally is defined by state laws that are derived from the Uniform Principal and Income Act (latest major revision issued in 1997). Most states have adopted some form of the Uniform Act, which essentially constitutes generally accepted accounting principles (GAAP) in the fiduciary tax setting.

By allocating specific items of income and expenditure either to the income beneficiaries or to corpus, the desires of the grantor or decedent are put into effect. Table 19–4 shows typical assignments of revenue and expenditure items to fiduciary income or corpus.

Where the controlling document is silent as to whether an item should be assigned to income or corpus, state fiduciary law prevails. These allocations are an important determinant of the benefits received from the entity by its beneficiaries and the timing of those benefits.

The Arnold Trust is a simple trust. Mrs. Bennett is its sole beneficiary. In the current year, the trust earns $20,000 in taxable interest and $15,000 in tax-exempt interest. In addition, the trust recognizes an $8,000 long-term capital gain. The trustee assesses a fee of $11,000 for the year. If the trust agreement allocates fees and capital gains to corpus, trust accounting income is $35,000, and Mrs. Bennett receives that amount. Thus, the income beneficiary receives no immediate benefit from the trust's capital gain, and she bears none of the financial burden of the fiduciary's fees.

EXAMPLE 4

---

[7]For example, see §§ 651(a)(1), 652(a), and 661(a)(1).

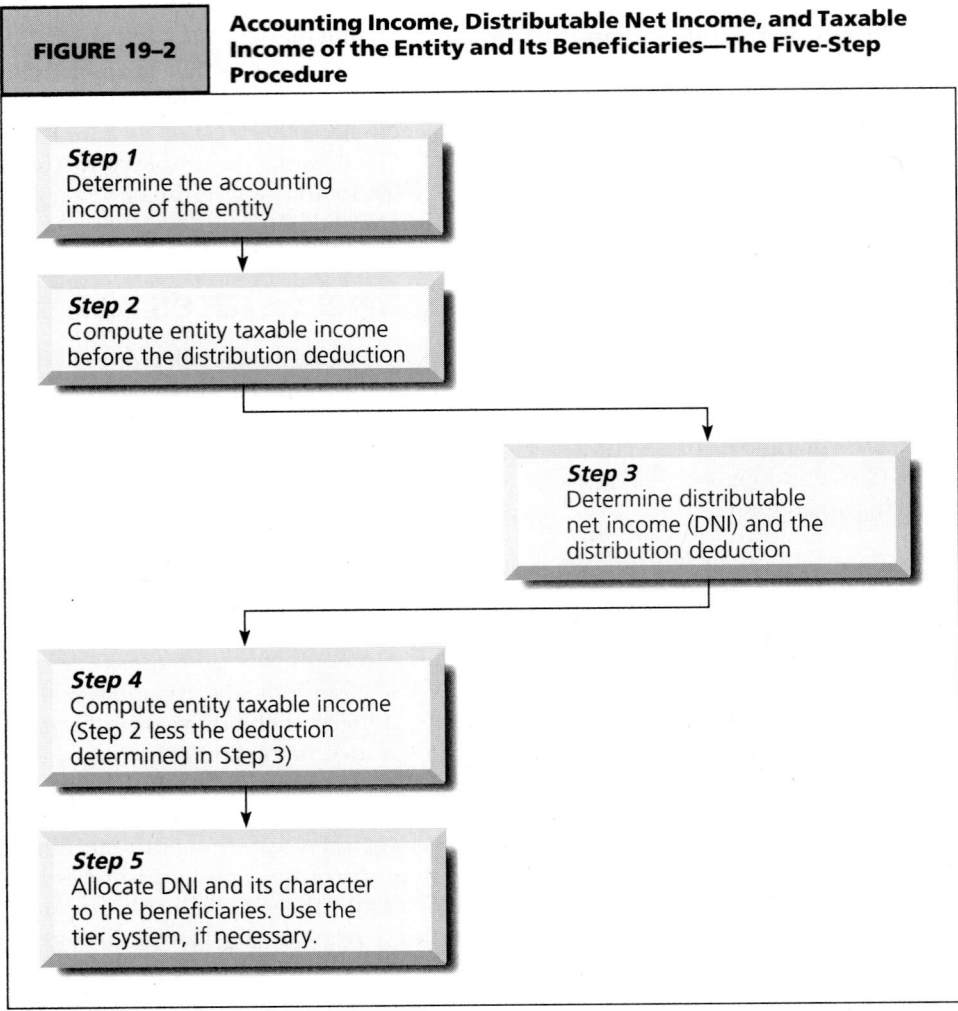

FIGURE 19–2   Accounting Income, Distributable Net Income, and Taxable Income of the Entity and Its Beneficiaries—The Five-Step Procedure

Interest income	$35,000
Long-term capital gain	± –0–*
Fiduciary's fees	± –0–*
Trust accounting income	$35,000

*Allocable to corpus.   ■

EXAMPLE 5

Assume the same facts as in Example 4, except that the trust agreement allocates the fiduciary's fees to income. The trust accounting income is $24,000, and Mrs. Bennett receives that amount.

Interest income	$35,000
Long-term capital gain	± –0–*
Fiduciary's fees	–11,000
Trust accounting income	$24,000

*Allocable to corpus.   ■

EXAMPLE 6

Assume the same facts as in Example 4, except that the trust agreement allocates to income all capital gains and losses and one-half of the trustee's commissions. The trust accounting income is $37,500, and Mrs. Bennett receives that amount.

FIGURE 19–3   **Computational Template Applying the Five-Step Procedure**

Item	Totals	Accounting Income	Taxable Income	Distributable Net Income/Distribution Deduction
Income				
Income	_____	_____	_____	
Expense	_____	_____	_____	
Expense	_____	_____	_____	
Personal exemption	_____	_____	_____	
			_____	
Accounting income/taxable income before the distribution deduction				
Exemption		_Step 1_	_Step 2_	
Corpus capital gain/loss				_____
Net exempt income				_____
Distributable net income				_____
Distribution deduction				_____
Entity taxable income			_____	_Step 3_
			_____	_Step 4_

Beneficiary taxable income is addressed in **Step 5.**

Interest income	$35,000
Long-term capital gain	+8,000
Fiduciary's fees	−5,500*
Trust accounting income	$37,500

*One-half allocable to corpus.

■

Gross Income

The gross income of an estate or trust is similar to that of an individual. In determining the gain or loss to be recognized by an estate or trust upon the sale or other taxable disposition of assets, the rules for basis determination are similar to those applicable to other taxpayers. Thus, an estate's basis for property received from a decedent is stepped up or stepped down to gross estate value (refer to Chapter 18 for a more detailed discussion). Property received as a gift (the usual case in trust arrangements) usually takes the donor's basis. Property purchased by the trust from a third party is assigned a basis equal to the purchase price.

Property Distributions. In general, the entity does not recognize gain or loss upon its distribution of property to a beneficiary under the provisions of the will or trust document. The distributed property has the same basis to the beneficiary of the distribution as it did to the estate or trust. Moreover, the distribution absorbs distributable net income (DNI) and qualifies for a distribution deduction (both of which are explained later in this chapter) to the extent of the lesser of the distributed asset's basis to the beneficiary or the asset's fair market value as of the distribution date.[8]

Estate's basis
• stepped up or down to gross estate value
• property received as gift takes the donor's AB
• purchased property = cost basis

Distributed Property
• no recognized gain or loss generally
• same basis
• absorbs DNI & qualifies for deduction
• lesser of AB or FMV of asset

---

[8] § 643(e).

[Handwritten margin notes: "DNI (Distributable net income) = basis of distributed asset" / "Beneficiary's basis = donor's basis (trust)"]

TABLE 19–4	Common Allocations of Items to Income or Corpus

Allocable to Income	Allocable to Corpus
Ordinary and operating net income from trust assets.	Depreciation on business assets.
Interest, dividend, rent, and royalty income.	Casualty gain/loss on income-producing assets.
Stock dividends.	Insurance recoveries on income-producing assets.
One-half of fiduciary fees/commissions.	Capital gain/loss on investment assets.
	Stock splits.
	One-half of fiduciary fees/commissions.

EXAMPLE 7

The Howard Trust distributes a painting, basis of $40,000 and fair market value of $90,000, to beneficiary Kate. Kate's basis in the painting is $40,000. The distribution absorbs $40,000 of Howard's DNI, and Howard claims a $40,000 distribution deduction relative to the transaction. ∎

EXAMPLE 8

Assume the same facts as in Example 7, except that Howard's basis in the painting is $100,000. Kate's basis in the painting is $100,000. The distribution absorbs $90,000 of Howard's DNI, and Howard claims a $90,000 distribution deduction. ∎

[Handwritten margin note: "If election is made to recognize gain or loss by the trustee or executor, beneficiary's basis = FMV."]

A trustee or executor can elect to recognize gain or loss with respect to all of its in-kind property distributions for the year. If the election is made, the beneficiary's basis in the asset is equal to the asset's fair market value as of the distribution date. The distribution absorbs DNI and qualifies for a distribution deduction to the extent of the asset's fair market value. However, § 267 can restrict an estate's or trust's deduction for such losses.

EXAMPLE 9

The Green Estate distributes an antique piano, basis to Green of $10,000 and fair market value of $15,000, to beneficiary Kyle. The executor elects that Green recognize the related $5,000 gain on the distribution. Accordingly, Kyle's basis in the piano is $15,000 ($10,000 basis to Green + $5,000 gain recognized). Without the election, Green would not recognize any gain, and Kyle's basis in the piano would be $10,000. ∎

EXAMPLE 10

Assume the same facts as in Example 9, except that Green's basis in the piano is $18,000. The executor elects that Green recognize the related $3,000 loss on the distribution. Accordingly, Kyle's basis in the piano is $15,000 ($18,000 − $3,000). Without the election, Green would not recognize any loss, and Kyle's basis in the piano would be $18,000.

The estate cannot deduct this loss, however. Because an estate and its beneficiaries are related parties, realized losses cannot be recognized immediately.[9] The loss could be recognized if Kyle later sells the piano to a stranger. ∎

[Handwritten margin note: "§ 267 — losses b/w an estate & its beneficiaries are not deductible until beneficiary sells loss asset to an unrelated 3rd party"]

Income in Respect of a Decedent.

The gross income of a trust or estate includes **income in respect of a decedent (IRD)** that the entity received.[10] For a cash basis decedent, IRD includes accrued salary, interest, rent, and other income items that were not constructively received before death. For both cash and accrual basis decedents, IRD includes, for instance, death benefits from qualified retirement plans and deferred compensation contracts.

---

[9]§ 267(b)(13).

[10]§ 691 and the Regulations thereunder. The concept of IRD was introduced in Chapter 18.

| TAX *in the News* | PICK THE HOME STATE FOR YOUR TRUST CAREFULLY |

In a continuing attempt to discourage tax-motivated income shifting among family members, steep income tax rates on estates and trusts are also being seen at the state level. Although a few states (e.g., Alaska, Nevada, Texas, and Washington) do not impose any income tax on fiduciary entities, those that do are tending to increase their rates as part of their efforts to solve budget deficit woes.

Legal, brokerage, and accounting fees to set up and operate a trust must be accepted as necessary administrative costs inherent to the trust arrangement. But careful selection of the state in which the trust is to be created and operated could allow for an annuity of tax savings and avoid unnecessary costs. Thus, the state chosen as the situs of a trust should offer trust-friendly rules regarding disclosure and asset protection as well as a favorable tax climate.

Individuals who attempt to move their state of residence upon retirement, perhaps from New York to Florida, usually must be prepared to spend time and effort in making the transition. In contrast, changing the location of a trust is con-

siderably simpler and may entail merely transferring assets from one trustee to another. Moving a trust after it is established, though, may draw unneeded attention to the parties involved.

The rewards for selecting a trust-friendly state can be great. A few states allow trusts to exist in perpetuity or for periods as long as 1,000 years (e.g., Alaska, Delaware, and Florida). When a grantor uses a "dynasty trust" to pass assets to later generations of the family, proper drafting of the trust language can result in various benefits.

- Deferral or avoidance of all Federal estate and generation-skipping taxes.
- Extended protection of assets from various hazards (e.g., lawsuits, creditors, bankruptcy).

A report by the Joint Committee on Taxation staff indicates that about $100 billion of assets have flowed into dynasty trusts in just the last few years.

The tax consequences of IRD can be summarized as follows.

- The fair market value of the right to IRD on the appropriate valuation date is included in the decedent's gross estate. Thus, it is subject to the Federal estate tax.[11]
- The decedent's basis in the property carries over to the recipient (the estate or heirs). There is no step-up or step-down in the basis of IRD items.

[handwritten note: no step up or down in the basis of IRD items]

- The recipient of the income recognizes gain or loss, measured by the difference between the amount realized and the adjusted basis of the IRD in the hands of the decedent. The character of the gain or loss depends upon the treatment that it would have received had it been realized by the decedent before death. Thus, if the decedent would have realized capital gain, the recipient must do likewise.
- Expenses related to the IRD (such as interest, taxes, and depletion) that properly were not reported on the final income tax return of the decedent may be claimed by the recipient. These items are known as **expenses in respect of a decedent**. Typically, such expenses also include fiduciary fees, commissions paid to dispose of estate assets, and state income taxes payable. They are deductible for both Federal estate and income tax purposes, *for* or *from* adjusted gross income (AGI) as would have been the case for the decedent.
- If the IRD item would have created an AMT preference or adjustment for the decedent (e.g., with respect to the collection of certain tax-exempt interest by the entity), an identical AMT item is created for the recipient.

Amanda died on July 13 of the current year. On August 2, the estate received a check (before deductions) for $1,200 from Amanda's former employer; this was Amanda's compensation for the last pay period of her life. On November 23, the estate received a $45,000 distribution from the qualified profit sharing plan of Amanda's employer, the full amount to which

EXAMPLE 11

---

[11]To mitigate the effect of double taxation (imposition of both the estate tax and the income tax), § 691(c) allows the recipient an income tax deduction for the incremental estate tax attributable to the net IRD. For individual recipients, this is an itemized deduction, not subject to the 2%-of-AGI floor.

TAX *in the News*   COORDINATE YOUR DEDUCTIONS

The deduction under § 691(c) may be one of the more obscure provisions of the tax law, but its benefits can add up fast. The deduction is allowed on the tax return of the recipient of income in respect of a decedent (IRD). IRD often is received by the estate of the decedent or a trust that he or she created under the will or during lifetime. The deduction is for the Federal estate tax attributable to the IRD item. For an individual, it is a miscellaneous itemized deduction *not* subject to the 2 percent-of-AGI floor.

Because IRD often includes the value of the survivorship feature on pensions and other retirement plans and assets, the amount subject to the estate tax can be quite high. On top of that, recall from Chapters 17 and 18 that the marginal estate tax rate can be as high as 45 percent. Thus, when computing the current-year income tax for the IRD recipient, the § 691(c) deduction can be extremely valuable in offsetting the IRD received.

For instance, suppose that a decedent's IRA balance generates $450,000 in attributable estate tax. If the recipient of the IRA takes the net-of-tax distribution in one year, the § 691(c) deduction shelters $450,000 in gross income and may be worth over $150,000 in Federal income taxes saved.

But taking the § 691(c) deduction is more complex than it looks. Because different tax advisers often prepare the Form 706 for the estate and the Form 1040 or 1041 for the IRD recipient, the § 691(c) deduction can get lost altogether or at least be miscomputed. When the IRD is paid out over several years, computing the § 691(c) deduction can become complex. And some tax professionals do not know the law well enough to track down the deduction, while tax software and IRS forms and publications say relatively little about it. One tax attorney believes that the omission or miscalculation of the deduction is "probably the most prevalent error today in respect to estate taxes."

As retirement assets become a larger portion of most gross estates, thanks to various rollovers from IRAs and qualified plans into the decedent's accounts, IRD and the § 691(c) deduction are likely to be encountered much more frequently in the future.

Amanda was entitled under the plan. Both Amanda and the estate are calendar year, cash basis taxpayers.

The last salary payment and the profit sharing plan distribution constitute IRD to the estate. Amanda had earned these items during her lifetime, and the estate had an enforceable right to receive each of them after Amanda's death. Consequently, the gross estate includes $46,200 with respect to these two items. However, the income tax basis to the estate for these items is not stepped up (from zero to $1,200 and $45,000, respectively) upon distribution to the estate.

The estate must report gross income of $46,200 for the current tax year with respect to the IRD items. The gain recognized upon the receipt of the IRD is $46,200 [$1,200 + $45,000 (amounts realized) − $0 (adjusted bases)]. ∎

Including the IRD in both the taxpayer's gross estate and the gross income of the estate may seem harsh. Nevertheless, the tax consequences of IRD are similar to the treatment that applies to all of a taxpayer's earned income. The item is subject to income tax upon receipt, and to the extent that it is not consumed by the taxpayer before death, it is included in the gross estate.

EXAMPLE 12

Assume the same facts as in Example 11, except that Amanda is an accrual basis taxpayer. IRD now includes only the $45,000 distribution from the qualified retirement plan. Amanda's last paycheck is included in the gross income of her own last return (January 1 through date of death). The $1,200 salary is already properly recognized under Amanda's usual method of tax accounting. It does not constitute IRD and is not gross income when received by the executor. ∎

EXAMPLE 13

Assume the same facts as in Example 11. Amanda's last paycheck was reduced by $165 for state income taxes that were withheld by the employer. The $165 tax payment is an expense in respect of a decedent and is allowed as a deduction on *both* Amanda's estate tax return *and* the estate's income tax return. ∎

[handwritten margin notes:]
° There is never step up or down of basis w/ IRD - items may be recognized as gain (income) or loss (expenses)

° Cash or accrual makes a difference as to the recognition of IRD

° state income taxes w/held are allowed on both a deduction on estate TR & estates income TR

Ordinary Deductions

As a general rule, the taxable income of an estate or trust is similar to that of an individual.[12] Deductions are allowed for ordinary and necessary expenses paid or incurred in carrying on a trade or business; for the production or collection of income; for the management, conservation, or maintenance of property; and in connection with the determination, collection, or refund of any tax.[13] Reasonable administration expenses, including fiduciary fees and litigation costs in connection with the duties of administration, also can be deductible.

Expenses attributable to the production or collection of tax-exempt income are not deductible.[14] The amount of the disallowed deduction is found by using a formula based upon the composition of the income elements of entity accounting income for the year of the deduction. The § 212 deduction is apportioned without regard to the accounting income allocation of such expenses to income or to corpus. The deductibility of the fees is determined strictly by the Code (under §§ 212 and 265), and the allocation of expenditures to income and to corpus is controlled by the trust agreement or will or by state law.

The Silver Trust operates a business and invests idle cash in marketable securities. Its sales proceeds for the current year are $180,000. Expenses for wages, cost of sales, and office administration are $80,000. Interest income recognized is $20,000 from taxable bonds and $50,000 from tax-exempt bonds. The trustee claims a $35,000 fee for its activities. According to the trust agreement, $30,000 of this amount is allocated to the income beneficiaries and $5,000 is allocated to corpus.

Sales income	$180,000
Cost of sales	−80,000
Interest income ($50,000 is exempt)	+70,000
Fiduciary's fees, as allocated	−30,000
Trust accounting income	$140,000

The sales proceeds are included in the gross income of the trust under § 61. The costs associated with the business are deductible in full under § 162. The taxable income is included in Silver's gross income under § 61, but the tax-exempt income is excluded under § 103. The fiduciary's fees are deductible by Silver under § 212, but a portion of the deduction is lost because § 265 prohibits deductions for expenses incurred in the generation of tax-exempt income.

Specifically, 50/250 of the fees of $35,000 can be traced to tax-exempt income, so $7,000 of the fees is nondeductible. For purposes of the computation, only the income elements of the year's trust accounting income are included in the denominator. Moreover, the allocation of portions of the fees to income and to corpus is irrelevant in the calculation. The disallowed deduction for fiduciary's fees is computed in the following manner.

$$\$35,000^*\text{ (total fees paid)} \times \frac{\$50,000^{**}\text{ (\textit{exempt} income elements of trust accounting income)}}{\$250,000^{**}\text{ (\textit{all} income elements of trust accounting income)}}$$

$$= \$7,000 \text{ (amount disallowed)}$$

*All of the fees, and not just those that are allocated to income, are deductible by the trust under § 212.

**The numerator and denominator of this fraction are *not* reduced by expense items allocable to income (e.g., cost of sales). ■

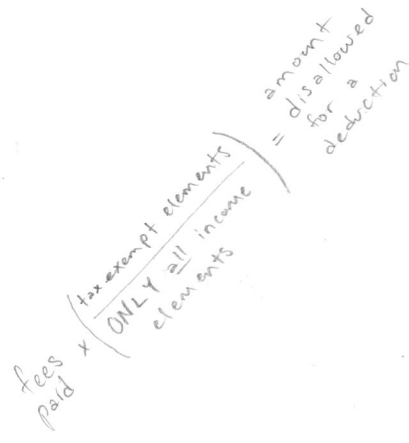

Under § 642(g), amounts deductible as administration expenses or losses for death tax purposes (under §§ 2053 and 2054) cannot be claimed by the estate for

---

[12]§ 641(b).

[13]§§ 162 and 212.

[14]§ 265.

income tax purposes, unless the estate files a waiver of the death tax deduction. Although these expenses cannot be deducted twice, they may be allocated as the fiduciary sees fit between Forms 706 and 1041; they need not be claimed in their entirety on either return.[15] As discussed earlier, the prohibition against double deductions does not extend to expenses in respect of a decedent.

Trusts and estates are allowed cost recovery deductions. However, such deductions are assigned proportionately among the recipients of the entity accounting income.[16]

EXAMPLE 15

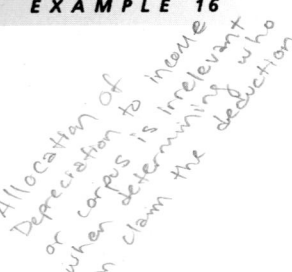

Lisa and Martin are the equal income beneficiaries of the Needle Trust. Under the terms of the trust agreement, the trustee has complete discretion as to the timing of the distributions from Needle's current accounting income. The trust agreement allocates all depreciation expense to income. In the current year, the trustee distributes 40% of the current trust accounting income to Lisa and 40% to Martin; thus, 20% of the income is accumulated. The depreciation deduction allowable to Needle is $100,000. This deduction is allocated among the trust and its beneficiaries on the basis of the distribution of current accounting income: Lisa and Martin each can claim a $40,000 deduction, and the trust can deduct $20,000. ∎

EXAMPLE 16

Assume the same facts as in Example 15, except that the trust agreement allocates all depreciation expense to corpus. Lisa and Martin both still claim a $40,000 depreciation deduction, and Needle retains its $20,000 deduction. The Code assigns the depreciation deduction proportionately to the recipients of entity accounting income. Allocation of depreciation to income or to corpus is irrelevant in determining which party can properly claim the deduction. ∎

When a trust sells property received by transfer from the grantor, the amount of depreciation subject to recapture includes the depreciation claimed by the grantor before the transfer of the property to the trust. However, depreciation recapture potential disappears at death.

EXAMPLE 17

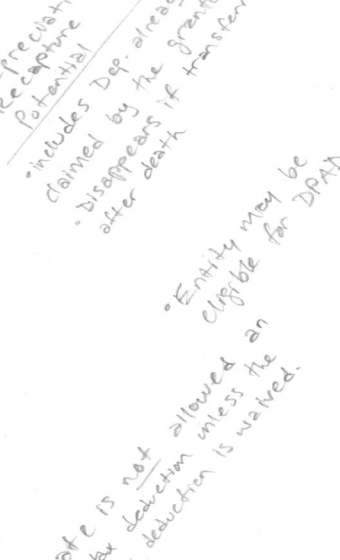

Jaime transferred an asset to the Shoulder Trust via a lifetime gift. The asset's total depreciation recapture potential was $40,000. If Shoulder sells the asset at a gain, ordinary income not to exceed $40,000 is recognized by the trust. Had Jaime transferred the asset after his death to his estate through a bequest, the $40,000 recapture potential would have disappeared. ∎

If a trust or estate operates a trade or business, the entity may be eligible for the domestic production activities deduction (DPAD).[17] Computation of qualified production activities income (QPAI) is made at the entity level. Each beneficiary receives, as a pass-through from the entity, his or her share of QPAI and the W–2 wages paid, based on the proportion of entity accounting income received. The DPAD then can be claimed at the beneficiary level. In the case of an individual beneficiary, the DPAD is subject to the modified AGI limitation. See Chapter 3 for further discussion of the DPAD.

Deductions for Losses

An estate or trust is allowed a deduction for casualty or theft losses that are not covered by insurance or other arrangements. Such losses may also be deductible by an estate for Federal death tax purposes under § 2054. As a result, an estate is not allowed an income tax deduction unless the death tax deduction is waived.[18]

The net operating loss (NOL) deduction is available for estates and trusts (i.e., where trade or business income is generated). The carryback of an NOL may

---

[15]Reg. § 1.642(g)–2.
[16]§§ 167(h) and 611(b)(3) and (4).
[17]§ 199(d)(1).

[18]See Reg. § 1.642(g)–1 for requirements as to the statement waiving the estate tax deduction. In addition, see Reg. §§ 1.165–7(c) and 1.165–8(b), requiring that a statement be filed to allow an income tax deduction for such losses.

reduce the distributable net income of the trust or estate for the carryback year and therefore affect the amount taxed to the beneficiaries for that year.

Certain losses realized by an estate or trust also may be disallowed, as they are for all taxpayers. Thus, the wash sale provisions of § 1091 disallow losses on the sale or other disposition of stock or securities when substantially identical stock or securities are acquired by the estate or trust within the prescribed 30-day period. Likewise, § 267 disallows certain losses, expenses, and interest with respect to transactions between related taxpayers. Generally, related parties include a trust, its trustee, its grantor, and its beneficiaries, as well as an estate, its executor, and its beneficiaries.

Except for the possibility of unused losses in the year of termination (discussed later in the chapter), the net capital losses of an estate or trust are used only on the fiduciary income tax return. The tax treatment of these losses is the same as for individual taxpayers.

Charitable Contributions

An estate or complex trust is allowed a deduction for contributions to charitable organizations under certain conditions.

- The contribution is made pursuant to the will or trust instrument, and its amount is determinable using the language of that document.
- The recipient is a qualified organization. For this purpose, qualified organizations include the same charities for which individual and corporate donors are allowed deductions, except that estates and trusts are permitted a deduction for contributions to certain foreign charitable organizations.
- Generally, the contribution is claimed in the tax year it is paid, but a fiduciary can treat amounts paid in the year immediately following as a deduction for the preceding year.[19] Under this rule, estates and complex trusts receive more liberal treatment than individuals or corporations.

Unlike the charitable contribution deductions of individuals and corporations, the deductions of estates and complex trusts are not limited (e.g., to a percentage of taxable or adjusted gross income). Nonetheless, an entity's charitable contribution may not be fully deductible.[20] Specifically, the deduction is limited to amounts included in the gross income of the entity in the year of the contribution. A contribution is deemed to have been made proportionately from each of the income elements of entity accounting income. Thus, if the entity has tax-exempt income, the contribution is deductible only to the extent that the income elements of entity accounting income for the year of the deduction are included in the entity's gross income.

This rule is similar to that used to limit the § 212 deduction for fiduciary fees and other expenses incurred to generate tax-exempt income. However, if the will or trust agreement requires that the contribution be made from a specific type of income or from the current income from a specified asset, the allocation of the contribution to taxable and tax-exempt income will not be required.

EXAMPLE 18

The Capper Trust has 2008 gross rent income of $80,000, expenses attributable to the rents of $60,000, and tax-exempt interest from state bonds of $20,000. Under the trust agreement, the trustee is to pay 30% of the annual trust accounting income to the United Way, a qualifying organization. Accordingly, the trustee pays $12,000 to the charity in 2009 (i.e., 30% × $40,000). The charitable contribution deduction allowed for 2008 is $9,600 [($80,000/$100,000) × $12,000]. ■

EXAMPLE 19

Assume the same facts as in Example 18, except that the trust instrument also requires that the contribution be paid from the net rent income. The agreement controls, and the allocation formula need not be applied. The entire $12,000 is allowed as a charitable deduction. ■

---

[19]§ 642(c)(1) and Reg. § 1.642(c)–1(b). [20]Reg. §§ 1.642(c)–3(b) and (c).

LO.3

Illustrate the uses and implications of distributable net income.

Deduction for Distributions to Beneficiaries

The modified pass-through approach of Subchapter J is embodied in the deduction allowed to trusts and estates for the distributions made to beneficiaries during the year. Some portion of any distribution that a beneficiary receives from a trust may be subject to income tax on the beneficiary's own return. At the same time, the distributing entity is allowed a deduction for some or all of the distribution. Consequently, the modified pass-through principle of Subchapter J is implemented. A good analogy is to the taxability of corporate profits distributed to employees as taxable wages. The corporation is allowed a deduction for the payment, but the employee receives gross income in the form of compensation.

A critical value that is used in computing the amount of the entity's distribution deduction is **distributable net income (DNI)**. As it is defined in Subchapter J, DNI serves several functions.

- DNI is the maximum amount of the distribution on which the beneficiaries can be taxed.[21]
- DNI is the maximum amount that the entity can use as a distribution deduction for the year.[22]
- The makeup of DNI carries over to the beneficiaries (the items of income and expenses retain their DNI character in the hands of the distributees).[23]

Subchapter J defines DNI in a circular manner, however. The DNI value is necessary to determine the entity's distribution deduction and therefore its taxable income for the year. Nonetheless, the Code defines DNI as a modification of the entity's taxable income itself. Using the systematic approach to determining the taxable income of the entity and its beneficiaries, as shown earlier in Figure 19–2, first compute *taxable income before the distribution deduction*, modify that amount to determine DNI and the distribution deduction, return to the calculation of *taxable income*, and apply the deduction that has resulted.

Taxable income before the distribution deduction includes all of the entity's items of gross income, deductions, gains, losses, and exemptions for the year. Therefore, to compute this amount, (1) determine the appropriate personal exemption for the year and (2) account for all of the other gross income and deductions of the entity.

The next step in Figure 19–2 is the determination of *distributable net income*, computed by making the following adjustments to the entity's *taxable income before the distribution deduction*.[24]

- Add back the personal exemption.
- Add back *net* tax-exempt interest. To arrive at this amount, reduce the total tax-exempt interest by charitable contributions and by related expenses not deductible under § 265.
- Add back the entity's *net* capital losses.
- Subtract any net capital gains allocable to corpus. In other words, the only net capital gains included in DNI are those attributable to income beneficiaries or to charitable contributions.

Since taxable income before the distribution deduction is computed by deducting all of the expenses of the entity (whether they were allocated to income or to corpus), DNI is reduced by expenses that are allocated to corpus. The effect is to reduce the taxable income of the income beneficiaries. The actual distributions to the beneficiaries exceed DNI because the distributions are not reduced by expenses allocated to corpus. Aside from this shortcoming of Subchapter J, DNI offers a good approximation of the current-year economic income available for distribution to the entity's income beneficiaries.

---

[21]§§ 652(a) and 662(a).
[22]§§ 651(b) and 661(c).

[23]§§ 652(b) and 662(b).
[24]These and other (less common) adjustments are detailed in § 643.

DNI includes the net tax-exempt interest income of the entity, so that amount must be removed from DNI in computing the distribution deduction. Moreover, for estates and complex trusts, the amount actually distributed during the year may include discretionary distributions of income and distributions of corpus permissible under the will or trust instrument. Thus, the distribution deduction for estates and complex trusts is computed as the lesser of (1) the deductible portion of DNI or (2) the taxable amount actually distributed to the beneficiaries during the year. For a simple trust, however, full distribution is always assumed, relative to both the entity and its beneficiaries, in a manner similar to the partnership and S corporation pass-through entities.

EXAMPLE 20

The Zinc Trust is a simple trust. Because of severe liquidity problems, its 2008 accounting income is not distributed to its sole beneficiary, Mark, until early in 2009. Zinc still is allowed a full distribution deduction for, and Mark still is taxable upon, the entity's 2008 income in 2008. ■

EXAMPLE 21

The Pork Trust is required to distribute its current accounting income annually to its sole income beneficiary, Barbara. Capital gains and losses and all other expenses are allocable to corpus. In the current year, Pork incurs the following items.

Dividend income	$25,000
Taxable interest income	15,000
Tax-exempt interest income	20,000
Net long-term capital gains	10,000
Fiduciary's fees	6,000

Item	Totals	Accounting Income	Taxable Income	Distributable Net Income/ Distribution Deduction
Dividend income	$25,000	$25,000	$ 25,000	
Taxable interest income	15,000	15,000	15,000	
Exempt interest income	20,000	20,000		
Net long-term capital gain	10,000		10,000	
Fiduciary fees	6,000		(4,000)	
Personal exemption			(300)	
Accounting income/ taxable income before the distribution deduction		$60,000	$ 45,700	$ 45,700
		Step 1	Step 2	
Exemption				300
Corpus capital gain/loss				(10,000)
Net exempt income				18,000
Distributable net income				$ 54,000
Distribution deduction			Step 3 (36,000)	
Entity taxable income			Step 4 $ 9,700	

Step 1. Trust accounting income is $60,000; this includes the tax-exempt interest income, but not the fees or the capital gains, pursuant to the trust document. Barbara receives $60,000 from the trust for the current year.

Step 2. Taxable income before the distribution deduction is computed as directed by the Code. The tax-exempt interest is excluded under § 103. Only a portion of the fees is deductible because some of the fees are traceable to the tax-exempt income. The trust claims a $300 personal exemption as it is required to distribute its annual trust accounting income.

Step 3. DNI and the distribution deduction reflect the required adjustments. The distribution deduction is the lesser of the distributed amount ($60,000) or the deductible portion of DNI ($54,000 − $18,000 net exempt income).

Step 4. Finally, return to the computation of the taxable income of the Pork Trust. A simple test should be applied at this point to assure that the proper figure for the trust's taxable income has been determined. On what is Pork to be taxed? Pork has distributed to Barbara all of its gross income except the $10,000 net long-term capital gains. The $300 personal exemption reduces taxable income to $9,700. ∎

EXAMPLE 22

The Quick Trust is required to distribute all of its current accounting income equally to its two beneficiaries, Faith and the Universal Church, a qualifying charitable organization. Capital gains and losses and depreciation expenses are allocable to income. Fiduciary fees are allocable to corpus. In the current year, Quick incurs various items as indicated.

Item	Totals	Accounting Income	Taxable Income	Distributable Net Income/ Distribution Deduction
Rent income	$100,000	$100,000	$100,000	
Expenses—rent income	30,000	(30,000)	(30,000)	
Depreciation—rent income	15,000	(15,000)		
Net long-term capital gain	20,000	20,000	20,000	
Charitable contribution			(37,500)	
Fiduciary fees	18,000		(18,000)	
Personal exemption			(300)	
Accounting income/ taxable income before the distribution deduction		$ 75,000	$ 34,200	$34,200
		Step 1	**Step 2**	
Exemption				300
Corpus capital gain/loss				
Net exempt income				
Distributable net income				$34,500
Distribution deduction			**Step 3** (34,500)	
Entity taxable income			**Step 4** ($ 300)	

Step 1. Trust accounting income of $75,000 reflects the indicated allocations of items to income and to corpus. Each income beneficiary receives $37,500.

Step 2. In the absence of tax-exempt income, a deduction is allowed for the full amount of the fiduciary's fees. Quick is a complex trust, but since it is required to distribute its full accounting income annually, a $300 exemption is allowed. The trust properly does not deduct any depreciation for the rental property. The depreciation deduction is available only to the recipients of the entity's accounting income for the period. Thus, the deduction is split equally between Faith and the church. The deduction probably is of no direct value to the church, as the church is not subject to the income tax. The trust's charitable contribution

[Handwritten margin notes:] • In absence of tax-exempt income, a deduction is allowed for the full amount of the fiduciary's fees. • Depreciation deduction is available only to the entity's recipients of accounting income.

deduction is based upon the $37,500 that the charity actually received (one-half of trust accounting income).

Step 3. As there is no tax-exempt income, the only adjustment needed to compute DNI is to add back the trust's personal exemption. Subchapter J requires no adjustment for the charitable contribution. DNI is computed only from the perspective of Faith, who also received $37,500 from the trust.

Step 4. Perform the simple test (referred to above) to assure that the proper taxable income for the Quick Trust has been computed. All of the trust's gross income has been distributed to Faith and the charity. As is the case with most trusts that distribute all of their accounting income, the Quick Trust "wastes" the personal exemption. ■

Tax Credits

An estate or trust may claim the foreign tax credit to the extent that it is not passed through to the beneficiaries.[25] Similarly, other credits are apportioned between the estate or trust and the beneficiaries on the basis of the entity accounting income allocable to each.

Taxation of Beneficiaries

The beneficiaries of an estate or trust receive taxable income from the entity under the modified pass-through principle of Subchapter J. Distributable net income determines the maximum amount that can be taxed to the beneficiaries for any tax year. The constitution of DNI also carries over to the beneficiaries (e.g., net long-term capital gains and dividends retain their character when they are distributed from the entity to the beneficiary).

The timing of any tax consequences to the beneficiary of a trust or estate presents a problem only when the parties involved use different tax years. A beneficiary includes in gross income an amount based upon the DNI of the trust for any taxable year or years of the entity ending with or within his or her taxable year.[26]

EXAMPLE 23

An estate uses a fiscal year ending on March 31 for tax purposes. Its sole income beneficiary is a calendar year taxpayer. For calendar year 2008, the beneficiary reports the income assignable to her for the entity's fiscal year April 1, 2007, to March 31, 2008. If the estate is terminated by December 31, 2008, the beneficiary also includes any trust income assignable to her for the short year. This could result in a bunching of income in 2008. ■

Distributions by Simple Trusts

The amount taxable to the beneficiaries of a simple trust is limited by the trust's DNI. However, since DNI includes net tax-exempt income, the amount included in the gross income of the beneficiaries could be less than DNI. When there is more than one income beneficiary, the elements of DNI are apportioned ratably according to the amount required to be distributed currently to each.

EXAMPLE 24

A simple trust has ordinary income of $40,000, a long-term capital gain of $15,000 (allocable to corpus), and a trustee commission expense of $4,000 (payable from corpus). The two income beneficiaries, Allie and Bart, are entitled to the trust's annual accounting income, based on shares of 75% and 25%, respectively. Although Allie receives $30,000 as her share (75% × trust accounting income of $40,000), she is allocated DNI of only $27,000 (75% × $36,000). Likewise, Bart is entitled to receive $10,000 (25% × $40,000), but he is allocated DNI of only $9,000 (25% × $36,000). The $15,000 capital gain is taxed to the trust. ■

---

[25]§§ 642(a)(1) and 901.　　　　　　　　　　　　　[26]§§ 652(c) and 662(c).

Distributions by Estates and Complex Trusts

A computational problem arises with estates and complex trusts when more than one beneficiary receives a distribution from the entity and the controlling document does not require a distribution of the entire accounting income of the entity.

EXAMPLE 25

The trustee of the Wilson Trust has the discretion to distribute the income or corpus of the trust in any proportion between the two beneficiaries of the trust, Wong and Washington. Under the trust instrument, Wong must receive $15,000 from the trust every year. In the current year, the trust's accounting income is $50,000, and its DNI is $40,000. The trustee pays $15,000 to Wong and $25,000 to Washington. ■

How is Wilson's DNI to be divided between Wong and Washington? Several arbitrary methods of allocating DNI between the beneficiaries could be devised. Subchapter J resolves the problem by creating a two-tier system to govern the taxation of beneficiaries in such situations.[27] The tier system determines which distributions will be included in the gross income of the beneficiaries in full, which will be included in part, and which will not be included at all.

Income that is required to be distributed currently, whether or not it is distributed, is categorized as a *first-tier distribution*. All other amounts properly paid, credited, or required to be distributed are *second-tier distributions*.[28] A formula is used to allocate DNI among the appropriate beneficiaries when only first-tier distributions are made and those amounts exceed DNI.

Only first tier distributions are made

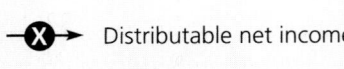

$$\frac{\text{First-tier distributions to the beneficiary}}{\text{First-tier distributions to all beneficiaries}} \quad \mathbf{X} \rightarrow \quad \text{Distributable net income} \quad \mathbf{=} \quad \begin{array}{l}\text{Beneficiary's share of} \\ \text{distributable net income}\end{array}$$

When both first-tier and second-tier distributions are made and the first-tier distributions exceed DNI, the above formula is applied to the first-tier distributions. In this case, none of the second-tier distributions are taxed, because all of the DNI has been allocated to the first-tier beneficiaries.

If both first-tier and second-tier distributions are made and the first-tier distributions do not exceed DNI, but the total of both first-tier and second-tier distributions does exceed DNI, the second-tier beneficiaries recognize income as shown below.

$$\frac{\text{Second-tier distributions to the beneficiary}}{\text{Second-tier distributions to all beneficiaries}} \quad \mathbf{X} \rightarrow \quad \begin{array}{l}\text{Remaining distributable net in-} \\ \text{come (after first-tier distributions)}\end{array} \quad \mathbf{=} \quad \begin{array}{l}\text{Beneficiary's share of} \\ \text{distributable net income}\end{array}$$

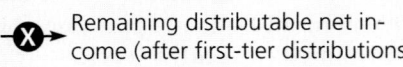
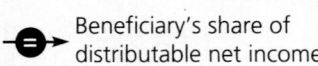

EXAMPLE 26

The trustee of the Gray Trust is required to distribute $10,000 per year to both Harriet and Wally, the two beneficiaries of the entity. In addition, he is empowered to distribute other amounts of trust income or corpus at his sole discretion. In the current year, the trust has accounting income of $60,000 and DNI of $50,000. However, the trustee distributes only the

---

[27]§§ 662(a)(1) and (2).   [28]Reg. §§ 1.662(a)–2 and –3.

required $10,000 each to Harriet and to Wally. The balance of the income is accumulated and added to trust corpus.

In this case, only first-tier distributions have been made, but the total amount of the distributions does not exceed DNI for the year. Although DNI is the maximum amount that is included by the beneficiaries for the year, they can include no more in gross income than is distributed by the entity. Thus, both Harriet and Wally may be subject to tax on $10,000 as their proportionate shares of DNI. ■

[handwritten margin note: beneficiaries can not be taxed in total on more than DNI]

EXAMPLE 27

Assume the same facts as in Example 26, except that DNI is $12,000. Harriet and Wally each receive $10,000, but they cannot be taxed in total on more than DNI. Each is taxed on $6,000 [DNI of $12,000 × ($10,000/$20,000 of the first-tier distributions)]. ■

EXAMPLE 28

Return to the facts in Example 25. Wong receives a first-tier distribution of $15,000. Second-tier distributions include $20,000 to Wong and $25,000 to Washington. Wilson's DNI is $40,000. The DNI is allocated between Wong and Washington as follows.

[handwritten margin note: Remaining DNI × Allocation % per beneficiary]

(1)	**First-tier distributions**	
	To Wong	$15,000 DNI
	To Washington	–0–
	Remaining DNI = $25,000	
(2)	**Second-tier distributions**	
	To Wong	$11,111 DNI [(20/45) × $25,000]
	To Washington	$13,889 DNI [(25/45) × $25,000] ■

EXAMPLE 29

Assume the same facts as in Example 28, except that accounting income is $80,000 and DNI is $70,000. DNI is allocated between Wong and Washington as follows.

(1)	**First-tier distributions**	
	To Wong	$15,000 DNI
	To Washington	–0–
	Remaining DNI = $55,000	
(2)	**Second-tier distributions**	
	To Wong	$20,000 DNI
	To Washington	$25,000 DNI ■

Separate Share Rule. For the sole purpose of determining the amount of DNI for a complex trust or estate with more than one beneficiary, the substantially separate and independent shares of different beneficiaries in the trust or estate are treated as *separate* trusts or estates.[29] An illustration shows the need for this special rule.

[handwritten margin note: complex trust or estate w/ >1 beneficiary: Separate share rule applies — substantially separate & independent shares of different beneficiaries in the trust or estate are treated as separate trusts or estates]

EXAMPLE 30

A trustee has the discretion to distribute or accumulate income on behalf of Greg and Hannah (in equal shares). The trustee also has the power to invade corpus for the benefit of either beneficiary to the extent of that beneficiary's one-half interest in the trust. For the current year, DNI is $10,000. Of this amount, $5,000 is distributed to Greg, and $5,000 is accumulated on behalf of Hannah. In addition, the trustee pays $20,000 from corpus to Greg. Without the separate share rule, Greg is taxed on $10,000 (the full amount of the DNI). With the separate share rule, Greg is taxed on only $5,000 (his share of the DNI) and receives the $20,000 corpus distribution tax-free. The trust is taxed on Hannah's $5,000 share of the DNI that is accumulated. ■

---

[29]§ 663(c); Reg. § 1.663(c)–1(a).

The separate share rule is designed to prevent the inequity that results if the corpus payments are treated under the regular rules applicable to second-tier beneficiaries. In Example 30, the effect of the separate share rule is to produce a two-trust result: one trust for Greg and one for Hannah, each with DNI of $5,000. The rule also results in the availability of extra entity personal exemptions and in a greater use of lower entity tax brackets.

Character of Income

Consistent with the modified pass-through principle of Subchapter J, various classes of income (e.g., dividends, passive or portfolio gain and loss, AMT preferences, and tax-exempt interest) retain the same character for the beneficiaries that they had when they were received by the entity. If there are multiple beneficiaries *and* if all of the DNI is distributed, a problem arises in allocating the various classes of income among the beneficiaries.

Distributions are treated as consisting of the same proportion as the items that enter into the computation of DNI. This allocation does not apply, however, if local law or the governing instrument specifically allocates different classes of income to different beneficiaries.[30]

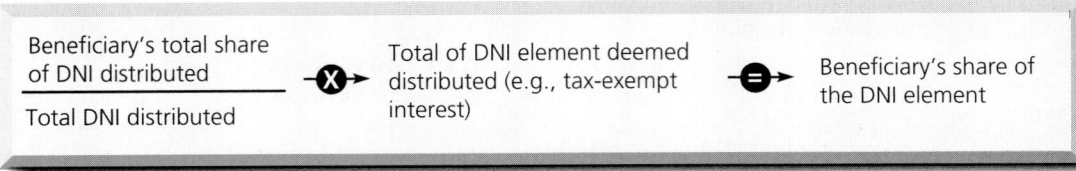

If the entity distributes only a part of its DNI, the amount of a specific class of DNI that is deemed distributed must first be determined.

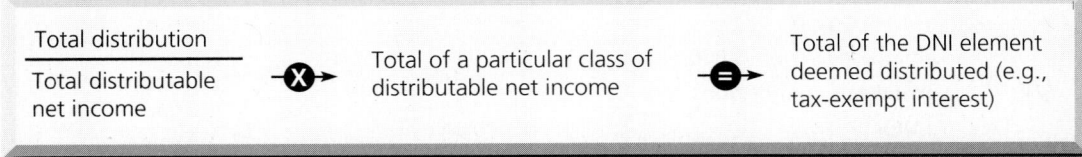

EXAMPLE 31

The Baron Trust has DNI of $40,000, including the following: $10,000 of taxable interest, $10,000 of tax-exempt interest, and $20,000 of passive activity income. The trustee distributes, at her discretion, $8,000 to Mike and $12,000 to Nancy.

Beneficiary	Amount Received	Income Type		
		Taxable Interest	Exempt Interest	Passive Income
Mike	$ 8,000	$2,000*	$2,000	$4,000
Nancy	12,000	3,000	3,000	6,000

*$8,000 distribution/$40,000 total DNI × $10,000 taxable interest in DNI.   ∎

EXAMPLE 32

Continue with the facts of Example 31. The character of the income that flows through to Mike and Nancy is effective for all other tax purposes. For instance, the $2,000 exempt interest allocated to Mike is used in computing the taxable portion of any Social Security benefits

---

[30]Reg. § 1.662(b)–1 seems to allow special allocations, but see *Harkness v. U.S.*, 72–2 USTC ¶9740, 30 AFTR2d 72–5754, 469 F.2d 310 (Ct.Cls., 1972).

Mike receives. If this exempt interest relates to nonessential activities of the issuing agency, Mike includes a $2,000 AMT preference on his current-year return.

The $4,000 passive activity income that is allocated to Mike is available for offset against passive losses that he has incurred from limited partnerships and rental activities for the year. Similarly, the $3,000 taxable interest income allocated to Nancy can be used to increase the amount of investment interest expense deductible by her in the year of the flow-through. The interest is treated as portfolio income to the same extent as that received directly by the taxpayer. ■

Special Allocations.

Under certain circumstances, the parties may modify the character-of-income allocation method set forth above. A modification is permitted only to the extent that the allocation is required in the trust instrument and only to the extent that it has an economic effect independent of the cash-flow and income tax consequences of the allocation.[31]

E X A M P L E   33

Return to the facts in Example 31. Assume that the beneficiaries are elderly individuals who have pooled their investment portfolios to avail themselves of the trustee's professional asset management skills. Suppose the trustee has the discretion to allocate different classes of income to different beneficiaries and that she designates $10,000 of Nancy's $12,000 distribution as being from the tax-exempt income. Such a designation *would not be recognized* for tax purposes, and the allocation method of Example 31 must be used.

Suppose, however, that the trust instrument stipulated that Nancy was to receive all of the income from the tax-exempt securities because she alone contributed the exempt securities to trust corpus. Under this provision, the $10,000 of the nontaxable interest is paid to Nancy. This allocation *is recognized*, and $10,000 of Nancy's distribution is tax-exempt. ■

Losses in the Termination Year

The ordinary net operating and capital losses of a trust or estate do not flow through to the entity's beneficiaries, as would such losses from a partnership or an S corporation. However, in the year in which an entity terminates its existence, the beneficiaries do receive a direct benefit from the loss carryovers of the trust or estate.[32]

Net operating losses and net capital losses are subject to the same carryover rules that otherwise apply to an individual. Consequently, NOLs can be carried back 2 years and then carried forward 20 years while net capital losses can be carried forward only, and for an indefinite period of time. However, if the entity incurs a negative taxable income in the last year of its existence, the excess of deductions over the entity's gross income is allowed to the beneficiaries (it will flow through to them directly). The net loss is available as a deduction *from* AGI in the beneficiary's tax year with or within which the entity's tax year ends. The amount allowed is in proportion to the relative amount of corpus assets that each beneficiary receives upon the termination of the entity, and it is subject to the 2-percent-of-AGI floor.

Any carryovers of the entity's other losses flow through to the beneficiaries in the year of termination in proportion to the relative amount of corpus assets that each beneficiary receives. The character of the loss carryover is retained by the beneficiary, except that a carryover of a net capital loss to a corporate beneficiary is always treated as short term. Beneficiaries who are individuals use these carryovers as deductions *for* AGI.

[handwritten margin note: • D' not flow through to beneficiaries]

[handwritten margin note: Net capital losses - carry forward only - in definitely]

E X A M P L E   34

The Edgar Estate terminates on December 31, 2008. It had used a fiscal year ending July 31. For the termination year, the estate incurred a $15,000 negative taxable income. In addition, the estate had an unused NOL carryover of $23,000 from the year ending July 31, 2004, and

---

[31]Reg. § 1.652(b)–2(b). This is similar to the § 704(b)(2) requirement for partnerships.

[32]Reg. §§ 1.642(h)–1 and –2.

an unused net long-term capital loss carryover of $10,000 from the year ending July 31, 2006. Dawn receives $60,000 of corpus upon termination, and Blue Corporation receives the remaining $40,000. Dawn and Blue are calendar year taxpayers.

Dawn can claim an itemized deduction of $9,000 [($60,000/$100,000) × $15,000] for the entity's negative taxable income in the year of termination. This deduction is subject to the 2%-of-AGI floor on her miscellaneous itemized deductions. In addition, Dawn can claim a $13,800 deduction *for* AGI in 2008 (60% × $23,000) for Edgar's NOL carryover, and she can use $6,000 of the estate's net long-term capital loss carryover with her other 2008 capital transactions.

Blue receives ordinary business deductions in 2008 for Edgar's NOLs: $6,000 for the loss in the year of termination and $9,200 for the carryover from fiscal 2004. Moreover, Blue can use the $4,000 carryover of Edgar's net capital losses to offset against its other 2008 capital transactions, although the loss must be treated as short term. ∎

The Sixty-Five-Day Rule

Amounts paid or credited to the beneficiaries in the first 65 days of the estate or trust's tax year may be treated as paid on the last day of the preceding taxable year.[33] This provision offers the trustee some flexibility in timing distributions so that entity-level accumulations can be avoided.

Grantor Trusts

LO.4

Use the special rules that apply to trusts where the creator (grantor) of the trust retains certain rights.

A series of special provisions applies when the grantor of the trust retains beneficial enjoyment or substantial control over the trust property or income.[34] In that event, the grantor is taxed on the trust income, and the trust is disregarded for income tax purposes. The person who is taxed on the income is allowed to claim, on his or her own return, any deductions or credits attributable to the income. Such taxes restrict the grantor's ability to redirect the income recognized from trust corpus to the trust or its beneficiaries. The trustee still files a Form 1041, but no dollar amounts are included on the mostly "blank" return. All income and deduction items are reported on the grantor's Form 1040.

Reversionary Trusts

Creation of virtually any new reversionary trust is subject to the Federal gift tax. If the grantor dies before the income interest expires, the present value of the reversionary interest is included in his or her gross estate; thus, a Federal estate tax could also result.

Powers Retained by the Grantor

Other restrictions apply concerning the extent of the powers over the trust that the grantor can retain without incurring grantor trust status.[35] If any of these provisions is violated, the income of the trust is taxed to the grantor, and the usual Subchapter J rules do not apply to the trust.

The grantor is taxed on the income if he or she retains (1) the beneficial enjoyment of corpus or (2) the power to dispose of the trust income without the approval or consent of any adverse party. An *adverse party* is any person having a substantial beneficial interest in the trust who could be affected adversely by the power the grantor possesses over the trust assets.[36]

A number of important powers, including the following, will *not* cause such income to be taxed to the grantor.[37]

---

[33]See Reg. § 1.663(b)–2 for the manner and timing of the election.
[34]§§ 671–679.
[35]§§ 674–677.

[36]§§ 672(a), (b), and 674. See Reg. § 1.672(a)–1 for examples of adverse party situations.
[37]§ 674(b).

TAX *in the News*   **DON'T TRUST YOUR DICTIONARY**

Today, the middle and upper classes are often including trusts in their estate plans. Usually, the purpose of the trust is to spare the survivors the time and effort required to work through a state's probate proceedings.

But planning for death can sometimes lead to confusion about terminology, especially between a living trust and a living will. A "living trust" is typically created to hold the assets of the decedent-to-be, including investments, homestead, and household goods. Assets are retitled in the name of the trustee, who periodically files a Form 1041 for the new entity. The idea underlying the living trust is to reduce the probate estate. This, in turn, lowers the fees for carrying out the probate process. Such fees often total 5 percent or so of the date of death value of the probate assets.

The living trust accomplishes virtually no Federal tax savings. The trust assets are included in the decedent's gross estate, as the living trust is an incomplete transfer under §§ 2036 and 2038. For the most part, the entity is treated as a grantor trust. Because of the retained investment and distribution powers, the donor is still liable for taxes on the taxable income of the fiduciary.

A "living will," on the other hand, is a document that conveys powers to relatives and third parties to make medical and financial decisions when the decedent-to-be can no longer do so. More appropriately referred to as a "medical power of attorney," the document expresses the person's wishes as to how and when to reduce specified medical treatments (including directives for removing life support systems).

Various states and estate planners use the terms *living trust* and *living will* differently, and sometimes interchangeably. Consequently, it is important that the *proper* document is used to accomplish the desired goals. Usually, it is "too late" to amend the document once a misunderstanding is discovered!

- To apply the income toward the support of the grantor's dependents (except to the extent that it actually is applied for this purpose).[38]
- To allocate trust income or corpus among charitable beneficiaries.
- To invade corpus on behalf of a designated beneficiary.
- To withhold income from a beneficiary during his or her minority or disability.
- To allocate receipts and disbursements between income and corpus.

The retention by the grantor or a nonadverse party of certain administrative powers over the trust causes the income to be taxed to the grantor. Such powers include those to deal with trust income or corpus for less than full and adequate consideration and to borrow from the trust without providing adequate interest or security.[39]

The grantor of a trust is taxed on the trust's income if he or she (or a nonadverse party) possesses the power to revoke the trust.[40] In addition, a grantor is taxed on all or part of the income of a trust when, without the consent of any adverse party, the income is or, at the discretion of the grantor or a nonadverse party (or both), may be:

- Distributed to the grantor or the grantor's spouse.
- Held or accumulated for future distribution to the grantor or the grantor's spouse.
- Applied to the payment of premiums on insurance policies on the life of the grantor or the grantor's spouse.[41]

EXAMPLE 35

Frank creates an irrevocable trust for his children with a transfer of income-producing property and an insurance policy on the life of Marion, his wife. During the year, the trustee uses $3,000 of the trust income to pay the premiums on the policy covering Marion's life. Frank is taxed on $3,000 of the trust's income. ∎

---

[38]§ 677(b).
[39]See Reg. § 1.675–1(b) for a further discussion of this matter.
[40]§ 676.
[41]§ 677(a).

Moreover, trust income accumulated for the benefit of someone whom the grantor is *legally obligated* to support is taxed to the grantor but only to the extent that it is actually applied for that purpose.[42]

EXAMPLE 36

Melanie creates an irrevocable accumulation trust. Her son, Sean, is the life beneficiary, and the remainder goes to any grandchildren. During the year, the trust income of $8,000 is applied as follows: $5,000 toward Sean's college tuition and other related educational expenses and $3,000 accumulated on Sean's behalf. If, under state law, Melanie has an obligation to support Sean, and if this obligation includes providing a college education, Melanie is taxed on the $5,000 that is so applied. ∎

Procedural Matters

The fiduciary is required to file a Form 1041 (U.S. Income Tax Return for Estates and Trusts) in the following situations.[43]

- For an estate that has gross income of $600 or more for the year.
- For a trust that either has any taxable income or, if there is no taxable income, has gross income of $600 or more.

The fiduciary return (and any related tax liability) is due, before extensions, no later than the fifteenth day of the fourth month following the close of the entity's taxable year. The IRS encourages electronic filing of the Form 1041 and schedules. A paper return is filed with the Internal Revenue Service in Cincinnati or Ogden, Utah, depending on the location of the fiduciary's principal place of business.

Many fiduciary entities recognize capital gains during the year, through sales of assets that are part of corpus. In that event, a Schedule D is filed with the Form 1041, and the fiduciary entity or its beneficiaries can qualify for the favorable 15 percent (or lower) tax rate on long-term capital gains.

The pass-through of income and deduction items to the beneficiary is accomplished through Schedule K–1 to Form 1041. This form is similar in format and function to the Schedule K–1 for partners and S corporation shareholders (see Chapters 10 and 12). Since the fiduciary entity usually has only a few transactions during the year, the Schedule K–1 for Form 1041 is less detailed than those for Forms 1065 and 1120S. See the specimen Form 1041 and schedules in Appendix B to this text.

Trusts and estates are required to make estimated Federal income tax payments using the same quarterly schedule that applies to individual taxpayers. This requirement applies to estates and grantor trusts only for tax years that end two or more years after the date of the decedent's death. Charitable trusts and private foundations are exempt from estimated payment requirements altogether.[44]

The two-year estimated tax exception for estates recognizes the liquidity problems that an executor often faces during the early months of administering the estate. The exception does not assure, however, that an estate in existence less than 24 months will never be required to make an estimated tax payment.

EXAMPLE 37

Juanita died on March 15, 2008. Her executor elected a fiscal year ending on July 31 for the estate. Estimated tax payments will be required from the estate starting with the tax year that begins on August 1, 2009. ∎

TAX PLANNING *Considerations*

Many of the tax planning possibilities for estates and trusts were discussed in Chapter 18. However, several specific tax planning possibilities are available to help minimize the income tax effects on estates and trusts and their beneficiaries.

---

[42]§ 677(b). The taxpayer's legal obligations vary according to state law, financial resources, and family expectations. See *Frederick C. Braun, Jr.*, 48 TCM 210, T.C.Memo. 1984–285, and *Cristopher Stone*, 54 TCM 462, T.C.Memo. 1987–454.

[43]§§ 6012(a)(3) and (4).
[44]§ 6654(l).

A Trust or Estate as an Income-Shifting Device

The compressed tax rate schedule applicable to Subchapter J entities may have reversed the traditional techniques by which families set aside funds for long-term activities, such as business startups, college education, and home purchases. When the tax rate schedules for trusts and estates were more accommodating, high-income individuals would shift income-producing assets to trusts to take advantage of the lower effective tax rate that would fall on the income accumulated within the trust. The target of the plan, usually a child, would receive the accumulated income (and, perhaps, trust corpus) at a designated age, and more funds would be available because a lower tax rate had been applied over the life of the investment in the trust.

Today, such an income shift would *deplete*, rather than shelter, the family's assets, as the rates falling on individuals are much more graduated than are those applicable to fiduciaries, and the kiddie tax also penalizes attempts to shift taxable income to children. Assuming that the objectives of the plan remain unchanged, possible strategies in view of these rate changes include the following.

- Trust corpus should be invested in growth assets that are low on yield but high on appreciation, so that the trustee can determine the timing of the gain and somewhat control the effective tax rate that applies.
- Trust corpus should be invested in tax-exempt securities, such as municipal bonds and mutual funds that invest in them, to eliminate the tax costs associated with the investment. If this approach is taken, a trust might be unnecessary—the parent should simply retain full control over the assets and invest in the exempt securities in his or her own account.
- The grantor should retain high-yield assets, so that control over the assets is not surrendered when the tax cost is too high.
- Use of trust vehicles should be reserved for cases where professional management of the assets is necessary for portfolio growth and the additional tax costs can be justified.
- An income-shifting strategy may require several steps to achieve the desired result. For instance, the grantor might increase contributions to his or her own qualified retirement plan, thereby sheltering the funds from all tax liabilities. Then the grantor could use the tax dollars saved from these contributions to purchase tax-deferred annuity contracts, savings bonds, exempt securities, or other assets where the tax liabilities are reduced or deferred. The grantor could then either retain these exempt securities as discussed above or transfer them to the trust at a later date.

Income Tax Planning for Estates

As a separate taxable entity, an estate can select its own tax year and accounting methods. The executor of an estate should consider selecting a fiscal year because this will determine when beneficiaries must include income distributions from the estate in their own tax returns. Beneficiaries must include the income for their tax year with or within which the estate's tax year ends. Proper selection of the estate's tax year can result in a smoothing out of income and a reduction of the income taxes for all parties involved.

Caution should be taken in determining when the estate is to be terminated. Selecting a fiscal year for the estate can result in a bunching of income to the beneficiaries in the year in which the estate is closed. Prolonging the termination of an estate can be effective income tax planning, but the IRS carefully examines the purpose of keeping the estate open. Since the unused losses of an estate pass through to the beneficiaries only in the termination year, the estate should be closed when the beneficiaries can enjoy the maximum tax benefit of the losses.

CONCEPT SUMMARY   19–1

Principles of Fiduciary Taxation

1. Estates and trusts are temporary entities created to locate, maintain, and distribute assets and to satisfy liabilities according to the wishes of the decedent or grantor as expressed in the will or trust document.

2. Generally, the estate or trust acts as a conduit of the taxable income that it receives. To the extent that the income is distributed by the entity, it is taxed to the beneficiary. Taxable income retained by the entity is taxed to the entity itself.

3. The entity's accounting income must first be determined. Accounting conventions that are stated in the controlling document or, lacking such provisions, in state law allocate specific items of receipt and expenditure either to income or to corpus. Income beneficiaries typically receive payments from the entity that are equal to the accounting income.

4. The taxable income of the entity is computed using the scheme in Figure 19–2. The entity usually recognizes income in respect of a decedent. Deductions for fiduciary's fees and for charitable contributions may be reduced if the entity received any tax-exempt income during the year. Cost recovery deductions are assigned proportionately to the recipients of accounting income. Upon election, realized gain or loss on assets that properly are distributed in kind can be recognized by the entity.

5. A distribution deduction, computationally derived from distributable net income (DNI), is allowed to the entity. DNI is the maximum amount on which entity beneficiaries can be taxed. Moreover, the constitution of DNI is preserved for the recipients of the distributions.

6. Additional taxes are levied under Subchapter J to discourage the retention of excessive administrative powers by the grantor of a trust when the gross income is taxed to a lower-bracket beneficiary.

The timing and amounts of income distributions to the beneficiaries also present important tax planning opportunities. If the executor can make discretionary income distributions, he or she should evaluate the relative marginal income tax rates of the estate and its beneficiaries. By timing the distributions properly, the overall income tax liability can be minimized. Care should be taken, however, to time the distributions in light of the estate's DNI.

EXAMPLE 38

For several years before his death on March 7, Don had entered into annual deferred compensation agreements with his employer. These agreements collectively called for the payment of $200,000 six months after Don's retirement or death. To provide a maximum 12-month period within which to generate deductions to offset this large item of income in respect of a decedent, the executor or administrator of the estate should elect a fiscal year ending August 31. The election is made simply by filing the estate's first tax return for the short period of March 7 to August 31. ■

EXAMPLE 39

Carol, the sole beneficiary of an estate, is a calendar year, cash basis taxpayer. If the estate elects a fiscal year ending January 31, all distributions during the period of February 1 to December 31, 2008, are reported on Carol's tax return for calendar year 2009 (due April 15, 2010). Thus, assuming estimated tax requirements have otherwise been met, any income taxes that result from a $50,000 distribution made by the estate on February 20, 2008, may be deferred until April 15, 2010. ■

EXAMPLE 40

Assume the same facts as in Example 39. If the estate is closed on December 15, 2009, the DNI for both the fiscal year ending January 31, 2009, and the final tax year ending December 15, 2009, is included in Carol's tax return for the same calendar year. To avoid the effect of this bunching of income, the estate should not be closed until early in calendar year 2010. ■

EXAMPLE 41

Review Examples 28 and 29 carefully. Note, for instance, the flexibility that is available to the executor or administrator in timing the second-tier distributions of income and corpus of the estate. To illustrate, if Washington is subject to a high tax rate, distributions to him should be minimized except in years when DNI is low. In this manner, Washington's exposure to gross income from the distributions can be controlled so that most of the distributions he receives will be free of income tax. ∎

In general, those beneficiaries who are subject to high income tax rates should be made beneficiaries of second-tier (but not IRD) distributions of the estate. Most likely, these individuals will have less need for an additional steady stream of (taxable) income while their income tax savings can be relatively large. Moreover, a special allocation of tax-favored types of income and expenses should be considered. For example, tax-exempt income can be directed more easily to beneficiaries in higher income tax brackets.

ETHICAL and EQUITABLE *Considerations*

SHOULD A TAX ADVISER ALSO BE A TRUSTEE?

Tax clients need to be counseled on the best use of the trust entity and the proper choice of beneficiary of the trust income. The objectives of the grantor typically will best be served by transferring more power to the trustee; sprinkling powers, in particular, enable the trustee to be sensitive to the short-term and ongoing needs of the various beneficiaries. The client, however, may not appreciate this suggestion when the trust document is drafted. Especially if the tax adviser is the trustee or a co-trustee, the client may balk at the professional's well-intended suggestion that future developments might favor one beneficiary over another in a manner that cannot be anticipated at the time.

Should the source of the estate plan—the tax adviser—also then be designated as the trustee by the grantor? When the adviser serves in that capacity, who is "the client"? Merely the grantor? How about the beneficiaries? And the trust itself? To avoid any potential for conflict with their clients, some professional firms have adopted a policy of refusing to serve as trustee of a client's trust (or executor of his or her estate). Certainly, surrendering a sprinkling power to a fiduciary who is less sensitive to the tax ramifications of Subchapter J may be costly to all of the parties, but these firms see the preservation of the client relationship as more valuable in the long term.

In creating a trust, the grantor must address critical issues: How much power and control over assets and income should be surrendered to "outsiders" through the trust? Which items lend themselves to such transfers of control?

Income Tax Planning with Trusts

The great variety of trusts provides the grantor, trustee, and beneficiaries with excellent opportunities for tax planning. Many of the same tax planning opportunities available to the executor of an estate are available to the trustee. For instance, the distributions from a trust are taxable to the trust's beneficiaries to the extent of the trust's DNI. If income distributions are discretionary, the trustee can time the distributions to minimize the income tax consequences to all parties.

Distributions of In-Kind Property

The ability of the trustee or executor to elect to recognize the realized gain or loss relative to a distributed noncash asset allows the gain or loss to be allocated to the optimal taxpayer.

EXAMPLE 42

The Yorba Linda Estate distributed some inventory, basis of $40,000 and fair market value of $41,500, to beneficiary Larry. Yorba Linda is subject to a 15% marginal income tax rate, and Larry is subject to a 33% marginal rate. The executor of Yorba Linda should elect that the entity recognize the related $1,500 realized gain, thereby subjecting the gain to the estate's lower marginal tax rate.

Tax without election, at Larry's 33% rate	$495
Tax with election, at trust's 15% rate	$225

∎

Deductibility of Fiduciary Expenses

Some deductions and losses may be claimed either on the estate tax return or as income tax deductions of the estate on the fiduciary return (Form 1041), at the taxpayer's choice.[45] In such a case, the deduction for income tax purposes is not allowed unless the estate tax deduction is waived. These deductions can be apportioned between the two returns.

EXAMPLE 43

Don's will named his surviving spouse, Donna, as the executor. The estate's assets total $5 million. The will includes bequests to pay various debts, make gifts to certain charities, and provide for the grandchildren through trusts. The will also allows for the payment of an executor's fee equal to 5% of the assets ($250,000).

Should Donna pay herself an executor's fee? If Donna is the estate's remainder beneficiary, a common occurrence, payment of the fee would result in the following.

- A deduction by the estate on the Form 706 (say, at the 45% marginal rate) or the estate's Form 1041 (probably at the 35% marginal rate).
- Gross income for services to Donna (say, at her individual 30% marginal tax rate).

If Donna waives the executor's fee, she will receive the $250,000 as the remainder beneficiary of the estate. Other results would be:

- An increased marital deduction on the Form 706 (deductible at the 45% tax rate).
- No income recognition to Donna, as the receipt of a bequest is nontaxable.

Almost certainly, a remainder beneficiary who is a surviving spouse would waive the fee.

If Donna is not the remainder beneficiary of the estate, the analysis becomes more difficult. Claiming the $250,000 as a fee will change the amounts that the charities and grandchildren receive, because the estate assets will have been reduced in Donna's favor. A surviving spouse, now perhaps the head of the family, will find this a difficult choice to make while fulfilling her executor duties. ■

An expense deductible for estate tax purposes may not qualify as an income tax deduction. Interest expense incurred to carry tax-exempt bonds is disallowed for income tax purposes. If this expense is not claimed for estate tax purposes, it is completely lost.

EXAMPLE 44

The executor of Dana's estate pays $5,000 in burial expenses (authorized under local law and approved by the probate court) from estate assets. The $5,000 expense should be claimed on the estate tax return, as it is not deductible at all for income tax purposes. ■

Medical expenses incurred by the decedent but unpaid at the time of the decedent's death are covered by a special rule. If paid by the estate during a one-year period beginning with the day after death, the expenses may be claimed as an income tax deduction in the year incurred or as an estate tax deduction, but not both.[46] The choice is between the decedent's appropriate Form 1040 and his or her estate tax return. The expenses may be divided in any way between Form 1040 and the estate tax return.

KEY TERMS

Complex trust, 19–5	Expenses in respect of a decedent, 19–13	Income in respect of a decedent (IRD), 19–12
Corpus, 19–3	Grantor, 19–2	Reversionary interest, 19–4
Distributable net income (DNI), 19–18	Grantor trusts, 19–3	Simple trust, 19–5
		Sprinkling trust, 19–5

---

[45]§ 642(g) and Reg. § 20.2053–1(d).   [46]§ 213(c).

PROBLEM MATERIALS

DISCUSSION QUESTIONS

1. Your firm is developing a brochure for clients who are considering the use of a trust to accomplish various tax and nontax objectives. Prepare a PowerPoint slide, with no more than four bullet points, that highlights some of the most common uses of the trust entity.

   Communications

2. How many parties are needed to create an estate? A trust? Identify the titles and responsibilities traditionally given to each party.

3. Define the following terms.
   a. Income interest.
   b. Remainder interest.
   c. Reversionary interest.
   d. Life tenant.

4. Comment on this statement: Unless certain requirements are met, every trust is a simple trust.

5. Is it more or less expensive in tax terms for a married couple to shift taxable income via a trust? What if they were to use a C corporation?

6. Evaluate this comment: A fiduciary entity such as a trust or an estate is not subject to the alternative minimum tax, but its beneficiaries are.

7. Illustrate the nature and operations of each of the following trusts by creating a fact pattern to match each result. Be specific.
   a. A simple trust.
   b. A complex trust with a $300 personal exemption.
   c. A complex trust with a $100 personal exemption.

8. Using Figure 19–2 as a guide, describe the computation of a fiduciary entity's accounting income, taxable income, and distributable net income.

9. The Lopez Trust is short of cash. It is required to distribute $120,000 to Judith every year, and that payment is due in six weeks. In its asset corpus, Lopez holds a number of investments that are valued at $120,000. One of them has a tax basis to the trust of $75,000. Assuming that the trust agreement allows, what are the Federal income tax consequences if Lopez distributes this stock to Judith?

10. In its first tax year, the Wittmann Estate generated $50,000 of taxable interest income and $25,000 of tax-exempt interest income. It paid fiduciary fees of $5,000. The estate is subject to a 45% marginal estate tax rate and a 33% marginal income tax rate. How should the executor assign the deductions for the payment of the fees?

    Decision Making

11. The Red Trust generated $50,000 in cost recovery deductions this year. Can Red claim this deduction in computing its entity taxable income?

12. In 2008, the Helpful Trust agreed to make a $50,000 contribution to Local Soup Kitchen, a charitable organization. Helpful's board agreed to the gift at a November 2008 meeting, but the check was not issued until February 20, 2009. Can the trust claim a charitable contribution deduction? If so, describe how Helpful should treat its gift.

13. The Flan Trust is scheduled to terminate in two years, when Amy Flan reaches age 30. The trust operated a business several years ago, and it generated a sizable NOL carryforward that the trust has not been able to use. In addition, due to a bearish stock market, the value of the entity's investment portfolio has declined 15% from its purchase price. What issues must you consider in advising Amy and the corporate trustee?

    Issue ID

14. Harriet wants to transfer some assets to a trust this year; the income beneficiaries will be her two grandchildren. The trust income and assets will be used to pay the grandchildren's

    Issue ID

tuition to private high schools and universities. Upon the younger grandchild's graduation, the trust assets will return to Harriet's ownership. Identify tax issues related to Harriet's plan to use a temporary fiduciary entity.

Decision Making

Communications

15. Carol has been promoted several times, and she may be named a partner next year. Thus, she will be subject to higher marginal income tax rates than in the past. Carol's colleague Isaiah has told her about a "college education trust" from which he pays tuition and fees for his children. He has implied that there are sizable tax advantages to setting up a trust for this purpose. Now Carol is considering establishing a similar trust to pay tuition for her own children. She believes that the trust will be able to deduct the tuition payments, something that she cannot currently do on her Form 1040. Write a memo to the tax research file addressing Carol's ideas.

16. The Winter Trust must file a Form 1041 for the first time, because it has recognized about $5,000 of gross income. Corpus assets are transferred to the trust on April 30. Considering only the Federal income effects of the creation of Winter:
   a.   What tax year should be used?
   b.   Where should the completed Form 1041 be sent?

17. For tax planning purposes, should an estate adopt a calendar or a fiscal tax year? Why?

18. To reduce taxes for a typical family, should income be shifted *to* a trust or *from* a trust? Why?

19. To reduce overall taxes, should a high-income, wealthy beneficiary be assigned to the first or second tier of trust distributions? Why?

20. To minimize taxes, how should a trust treat the distribution of an in-kind asset? Why?

PROBLEMS

21. Complete the following chart, indicating the comparative attributes of the typical simple trust and complex trust by answering yes/no or explaining the differences between the entities where appropriate.

Attribute	Simple Trust	Complex Trust
Trust could incur its own tax liability for the year	_____	_____
Trust generally distributes all of DNI	_____	_____
Trust can deduct its charitable contributions in the year of, or the year after, payment	_____	_____
Trust could claim a foreign tax credit	_____	_____
Maximum tax rate on net long-term capital gains = 15%	_____	_____
AMT preferences and adjustments flow through to beneficiaries ratably	_____	_____
Amount of personal exemption	_____	_____

22. Compute the Federal income tax liability for the Wren Estate. The executor reports the following transactions for the 2008 tax year.

Operating income from a business	$200,000
Dividend income, all from U.S. corporations	20,000
Interest income, City of San Antonio bonds	40,000
Fiduciary fees, deductible portion	(10,000)

23. The Purple Trust incurred the following items this year.

Taxable interest income	$35,000
Tax-exempt interest income, not on private activity bonds	50,000
Tax-exempt interest income, on private activity bonds	30,000

Compute Purple's tentative minimum tax for the year. Purple does not have any credits available to reduce the AMT liability.

24. The Grouper Trust will incur the following items next year, its first year of existence.

Decision Making

Interest income	$75,000
Rent income	12,000
Cost recovery expense	15,000
Capital gain income	40,000
Fiduciary and tax preparation fees	11,000

Betty, the grantor of the trust, is working with you on the language in the trust instrument relative to the derivation of annual accounting income for the entity. She will name Shirley as the sole income beneficiary and Benny as the remainder beneficiary.

a. Suggest language to Betty that will maximize the annual income distribution to Shirley.

b. Suggest language to Betty that will minimize the annual distribution to Shirley and maximize the accumulation on Benny's behalf.

25. Complete the following chart, indicating the comparative attributes of the typical trust and estate by answering yes/no or explaining the differences between the entities where appropriate.

Attribute	Estate	Trust
Separate income tax entity		
Controlling document		
Can have both income and remainder beneficiaries		
Computes entity accounting income before determining entity taxable income		
Termination date is determinable from controlling document		
Legal owner of assets under fiduciary's control		
Document identifies both income and remainder beneficiaries		
Separate share rules apply		
Generally must use calendar tax year		

26. Complete the chart below, indicating trust accounting income for each of the alternatives. For this purpose, use the following information.

Interest income, taxable	$100,000
Interest income, tax-exempt	30,000
Interest income, tax-exempt but AMT preference item	20,000
Long-term capital gain	25,000
Trustee fee	10,000

Trust Agreement Provisions	Trust Accounting Income
1 Fees and capital gains allocable to corpus	
2 Capital gains allocable to corpus, one-half of fees allocable to income	
3 Capital gains allocable to income, silent concerning allocation of fees	
4 Fees and exempt income allocable to corpus, silent concerning allocation of capital gain/loss	

27. Bob is one of the income beneficiaries of the LeMans Estate. This year, as directed by the will, Bob received all of the sales commissions that were earned and payable to LeMans (cash basis) at her death, as well as one of the remaining installment payments. Compute Bob's gross income attributable to LeMans's activities for the current year, given the following financial data.

Sales commissions receivable	$50,000
Deferred ordinary gain on installment sale, two payments remaining after this year	30,000

28. Brown incurred the following items.

Business income	$60,000
Tax-exempt interest income	40,000
Payment to charity from 2008 income, paid 3/1/2009	20,000

Complete the following chart, indicating how the Code treats charitable contributions under the various assumptions.

Assumption	2008 Deduction for Contribution
Brown is a cash basis individual.	_____
Brown is an accrual basis corporation.	_____
Brown is a trust.	_____

29. The Oliver Trust has generated $60,000 in depreciation deductions for the year. Its accounting income is $30,000. In computing this amount, pursuant to the trust document, depreciation was allocated to corpus. Accounting income was distributed at the trustee's discretion: $20,000 to Hernandez and $10,000 to Jackson.
    a. Compute the depreciation deductions that Hernandez, Jackson, and Oliver may claim.
    b. Same as (a), except that depreciation was allocated to income.
    c. Same as (a), except that the trustee distributed $10,000 each to Hernandez and to Jackson and retained the remaining accounting income.
    d. Same as (a), except that Oliver is an estate (and not a trust).

30. The Ricardo Trust is a simple trust that correctly uses the calendar year for tax purposes. Its income beneficiaries (Lucy and Ethel) are entitled to the trust's annual accounting income in shares of one-half each. For the current calendar year, the trust generates ordinary income of $50,000, a long-term capital gain of $25,000 (allocable to corpus), and a trustee commission expense of $10,000 (allocable to corpus). Use the format of Figure 19–3 to address the following items.
    a. How much income is each beneficiary entitled to receive?
    b. What is the trust's DNI?
    c. What is the trust's taxable income?
    d. How much gross income is reported by each of the beneficiaries?

31. Assume the same facts as in Problem 30, except that the trust instrument allocates the capital gain to income.
    a. How much income is each beneficiary entitled to receive?
    b. What is the trust's DNI?
    c. What is the trust's taxable income?
    d. How much gross income is reported by each of the beneficiaries?

32. Under the terms of the trust instrument, the trustee has discretion to distribute or accumulate income on behalf of Willie, Sylvia, and Doris in equal shares. The trustee also can invade corpus for the benefit of any of the beneficiaries to the extent of each person's respective one-third interest in the trust.

    In the current year, the trust has DNI of $75,000. Distributions were made as follows.

    • To Willie: $25,000 from DNI, $15,000 from corpus.
    • To Sylvia: $15,000. The remaining $10,000 DNI is accumulated.
    • To Doris: $0. The $25,000 DNI is accumulated.

a. How much income is taxed to Willie?
b. To Sylvia?
c. To Doris?
d. To the trust?

33. A trust is required to distribute $80,000 annually equally to its two income beneficiaries, Clare and David. If trust income is not sufficient to pay these amounts, the trustee can invade corpus to the extent necessary. During the current year, the trust generates only taxable interest income and has DNI of $100,000; the trustee distributes $40,000 to Clare and $75,000 to David.

a. How much of the $75,000 distributed to David is included in his gross income?
b. How much of the $40,000 distributed to Clare is included in her gross income?
c. Are these distributions first-tier or second-tier distributions?

34. An estate has $75,000 of DNI, composed of $30,000 in dividends, $20,000 in taxable interest, $15,000 passive activity income, and $10,000 in tax-exempt interest. The trust's two noncharitable income beneficiaries, Brenda and Del, receive $30,000 each. How much of each class of income is deemed to have been distributed to Brenda? To Del?

35. The trustee of the Purple Trust can distribute any amount of accounting income and corpus to the trust's beneficiaries, Lydia and Kent. This year, the trust incurred the following.

Taxable interest income	$40,000
Tax-exempt interest income	60,000
Long-term capital gains—allocable to corpus	30,000
Fiduciary's fees—allocable to corpus	10,000

The trustee distributed $40,000 to Lydia and $30,000 to Kent.

a. What is Purple's trust accounting income?
b. What is Purple's DNI?
c. What is Purple's taxable income?
d. How much is taxed to each of the beneficiaries?

36. Each of the following items was incurred by José, the cash basis, calendar year decedent. Under the terms of the will, Dora took immediate ownership in all of José's assets, except the dividend-paying stock. The estate received José's final paycheck.

Decision Making

Applying the rules for income and deductions in respect of a decedent, indicate on which return each item should be reported: Dora's income tax return (Form 1040); the estate's first income tax return (Form 1041); or the estate's estate tax return (Form 706). More than one alternative may apply in some cases.

	Item Incurred	Form(s) Reported on
a.	Wages, last paycheck	
b.	State income tax withheld on last paycheck	
c.	Capital gain portion of installment payment received	
d.	Ordinary income portion of installment payment received	
e.	Dividend income, record date was two days prior to José's death	
f.	Unrealized appreciation on a mutual fund investment	
g.	Depreciation recapture accrued as of date of death	
h.	Medical expenses of last illness	
i.	Apartment building, rents accrued but not collected as of death	
j.	Apartment building, property tax accrued and assessed but not paid as of death	

37. In each of the following independent cases, write a memo for the tax research file in preparation for a meeting with Gary. In each memo, explain whether the proposed plan meets his objective of shifting income and avoiding the grantor trust rules.

    a. Gary transfers property in trust, income payable to Winnie (his wife) for life, remainder to his grandson. Gary's son is designated as the trustee.

    b. Gary transfers income-producing assets and a life insurance policy to a trust, life estate to his children, remainder to his grandchildren. The policy is on Winnie's life, and the trustee (an independent trust company) is instructed to pay the premiums with income from the income-producing assets. The trust is designated as the beneficiary of the policy.

    c. Gary transfers property in trust. The trust income is payable to Gary's grandchildren, as Winnie sees fit. Winnie and an independent trust company are designated as trustees.

    d. Gary transfers property in trust, income payable to Winnie (Gary's ex-wife), remainder to Gary or his estate upon Winnie's death. The transfer was made in satisfaction of Gary's alimony obligation to Winnie. An independent trust company is designated as the trustee.

38. Determine the tax effects of the indicated losses for the Yellow Estate for both tax years. The estate holds a variety of investment assets, which it received from the decedent, Mrs. Yellow. The estate's sole income and remainder beneficiary is Yellow, Jr.

Tax Year	Loss Generated
2008 (first tax year)	Taxable income ($300)
	Capital loss ($10,000)
2009 (final tax year)	Taxable income ($30,000)

39. Woody wishes to transfer some of the income from his investment portfolio to his daughter, age 6. Woody wants the trust to be able to accumulate income on his daughter's behalf and to meet any excessive expenses associated with the daughter's prep school and private college education. Furthermore, Woody wants the trust to protect his daughter against his own premature death without increasing his Federal gross estate. Thus, Woody provides the trustee with the powers to purchase insurance on his life and to meet tuition, fee, and book expenses of his daughter's education. The trust is created in 1993. A whole life insurance policy with five annual premium payments is purchased during that year. The trustee spends $10,000 for the daughter's college expenses in 2008 (but in no other year). Woody dies in 2010. Has the trust been tax-effective?

40. Your client, Annie O'Toole (22 Beneficiary Lane, Bowling Green, KY 42101), has come to you for some advice regarding gifts of property. She has just learned that she must undergo major surgery, and she would like to make certain gifts before entering the hospital. On your earlier advice, she had established a plan of lifetime giving for four prior years.

    Build a spreadsheet, supplemented by a list of your assumptions, and write a cover letter to Annie, discussing each of the following assets that she is considering using as gifts to family and friends. In doing so, evaluate the income tax consequences of having such property pass through her estate to the designated heir.

    a. Annie plans to give a cottage to her son to fulfill a promise made many years ago. She has owned the cottage for the past 15 years and has a basis in it of $30,000 (fair market value of $20,000).

    b. Annie has $100,000 of long-term capital losses that she has been carrying forward for the past few years. Now she is considering making a gift of $200,000 in installment notes to her daughter. Her basis in the notes is $100,000, and the notes' current fair market value is $190,000.

    c. Annie has promised to make a special cash bequest of $25,000 to her grandson in her will. However, she does not anticipate having that much cash immediately available after her death. Annie requests your advice concerning the income tax consequences to the estate if the cash bequest is settled with some other property.

TAX RETURN PROBLEMS

1. Prepare the 2007 fiduciary income tax return (Form 1041) for the Blue Trust. In addition, determine the amount and character of the income and expense items that each beneficiary must report for 2007 and prepare a Schedule K–1 for Betty Blue. Omit all alternative minimum tax computations. The 2007 activities of the trust include the following.

Dividend income, all U.S. stocks	$20,000
Taxable interest income	30,000
Tax-exempt interest income	10,000
Fiduciary's fees	6,000

The trust and Betty both use the calendar tax year. Under the terms of the trust instrument, fiduciary's fees are allocated to income. The trustee must distribute all of the entity's accounting income to Betty Blue, by February 15 of the following year. The trustee followed this charge and made no other distributions during the year. Fiduciary's fees properly were assigned as an offset to taxable interest income.

The trust was created on July 8, 1990. There are no tax credits for the year, and none of the entity's income was derived from a personal services contract. The trust has no economic interest in any foreign trust. Its Federal identification number is 88–1122333.

The trustee, Hoover State Federal Bank, is located at 4959 Cold Harbor Boulevard, Mountain Brook, AL 35223. Its employer identification number is 88–4455666. Betty lives at 67671 Crestline Road, Birmingham, AL 35212. Her Social Security number is 399–00–1234.

2. Prepare the 2007 fiduciary income tax return (Form 1041) for the Green Trust. In addition, determine the amount and character of the income and expense items that each beneficiary must report for 2007 and prepare a Schedule K–1 for Marcus White. Omit all alternative minimum tax computations. The 2007 activities of the trust include the following.

Dividend income, all qualified U.S. stocks	$10,000
Taxable interest income	60,000
Tax-exempt interest income	30,000
Net long-term capital gain, incurred 11/1/07	15,000
Fiduciary's fees	5,000

Under the terms of the trust instrument, depreciation, net capital gains and losses, and any fiduciary's fees are allocable to corpus. The trustee is required to distribute $25,000 to Marcus every year. For 2007, the trustee distributed $50,000 to Marcus and $50,000 to Marcus's sister, Ellen Hayes. No other distributions were made.

In computing DNI, the trustee properly assigned all of the deductible fiduciary's fees to the taxable interest income.

The trustee paid $2,500 in estimated taxes for the year on behalf of the trust. Any 2007 refund is to be credited to 2008 estimates. The exempt income was not derived from private activity bonds.

The trust was created on December 14, 1953. It is not subject to any recapture taxes, nor does it have any tax credits. None of its income was derived under a personal services contract. The trust has no economic interest in any foreign trust. Its Federal identification number is 79–2635151.

The trustee, Wisconsin State National Bank, is located at 3100 East Wisconsin Avenue, Milwaukee, WI 53201. Its employer identification number is 66–7602487. Marcus lives at 9880 East North Avenue, Shorewood, WI 53211. His Social Security number is 498–98–8058. Ellen lives at 6772 East Oklahoma Avenue, St. Cecilia, WI 53204. Her Social Security number is 499–97–6531.

RESEARCH PROBLEMS

THOMSON
RIA

Note: Solutions to Research Problems can be prepared by using the **RIA Checkpoint®** **Student Edition** online research product, which is available to accompany this text. It is also possible to prepare solutions to the Research Problems by using tax research materials found in a standard tax library.

Communications

Research Problem 1.   Your client, Chuck Konkol, is a self-employed investment adviser who provides services to individuals and small investment clubs for an hourly fee. He is aware of the difficulty that his clients have in deducting payments to him, such as advisory fees, due to the 2%-of-AGI floor on miscellaneous itemized deductions.

His new client, the Ferguson Trust, wants to be certain that it can deduct such fees in computing entity taxable income. The Ferguson Trust operates in the jurisdiction of the Eighth Circuit Court of Appeals. Konkol asks you to make a presentation to the trust's officers on this subject. Provide a speaker's outline for this purpose, with citations to only the most important statutory and judicial law.

Research Problem 2.   For three generations, the Dexter family has sent its children to Private University, preparing them for successful professional careers. The Edna Dexter Trust was established in the 1950s by LaKeisha's late grandmother and has accumulated a sizable corpus. It makes distributions to Edna's descendants rarely and only when they need large capital amounts. For example, two years ago, the trust distributed $500,000 to DuJuan Dexter to aid him in starting a practice in retirement and elder law. In most years, the trust's income is donated to a single charity.

Under the terms of the trust, Bigby Dexter, LaKeisha's uncle and legal guardian, can specify the trust beneficiaries and the amounts to be distributed to them. He can also replace the trustee and designate the charity that will receive the year's contribution. Accordingly, the trust falls under the grantor trust rules of § 678, and Bigby reports the trust's transactions on his own Form 1040.

LaKeisha wants to attend the prestigious local Academy High School, which will require a four-year expenditure for tuition and fees of $100,000, payable in advance. She approaches the Edna Dexter trustee and requests a current-year distribution of this amount, payable directly to the Academy. Under the laws of the state, the parent or guardian has the responsibility to provide a child with a public school education (no tuition charge) until age 16.

If the payment to the Academy is made, how is it treated under the Subchapter J rules: as a charitable contribution to the Academy, as a corpus distribution to LaKeisha, or in some other manner?

Communications

Research Problem 3.   Laura is the executor of her mother's estate. She is collecting assets and paying off liabilities as she finds them, as she is required to do under the terms of the will. Three months after her mother died, Laura received for the estate a check from her father for back alimony payments that were due her mother at the date of death. The alimony payment was sizable, and Laura had sufficient cash with which to meet the rest of the obligations of the estate, so she distributed $100,000 of the total $300,000 check to herself this year, as the estate's sole beneficiary.

Laura, who lives in Charlotte, North Carolina, has come to you to help her determine the proper income tax treatment for the alimony. She maintains it is a tax-free inheritance from the estate. Summarize your analysis in a memorandum to the tax research file.

Partial list of research aids:
§§ 682(b), 691.
Holloway v. U.S., 70–2 USTC ¶9548, 26 AFTR2d 70–5034, 428 F.2d 140 (CA–9, 1970).

Internet Activity

Use the tax resources of the Internet to address the following questions. Do not restrict your search to the World Wide Web, but include a review of newsgroups and general reference materials, practitioner sites and resources, primary sources of the tax law, chat rooms and discussion groups, and other opportunities.

Communications

Research Problem 4.   Go to the IRS Web site. How many Form 1041s were filed last year? How many Form 1041s were audited last year, at various income levels? How much tax has been collected on Forms 1041 over the last three tax years? Summarize your findings in a series of graphs to share with your classmates.

Research Problem 5. Under the income tax laws of your state applicable to fiduciaries, how are the following items allocated? Put your findings in a PowerPoint presentation for your classmates.

Communications

- Capital gain.
- Cost recovery.
- Fiduciary fees.

Research Problem 6. The IRS's list of abusive tax shelters includes a "family residence trust," which attempts to create deductions for personal items such as utilities, furniture purchases, and swimming pool maintenance. Search the Web for current definitions of these trusts and descriptions of how they operate. Summarize your findings, as well as the litigation strategy of the government to curtail the use of these trusts, in an e-mail to your instructor.

Communications

Research Problem 7. Some states are allowing or encouraging the use of "dynasty trusts" that are based in their jurisdiction. In an e-mail to your instructor, define this term and discuss how your state and one of its neighbors tax a dynasty trust.

Communications

Research Problem 8. Find an example of a living trust and an example of a sprinkling trust on the Web. Using Word or Acrobat, mark up each specimen document with annotations highlighting how the terms of the trust make special allocations to certain income beneficiaries and how entity accounting income is defined. What powers does the trust document give to the trustee to change the definition of accounting income in later trust years?

Research Problem 9. Find the Web site of a law firm that seems to specialize in fiduciary entities, preferably a firm located in your state. Ask the firm to quote you a fee for (1) establishing a simple trust and (2) filing the annual Form 1041. Summarize your findings, and your communications with the firm, in an e-mail to your instructor.

Communications

TAX RATE SCHEDULES AND TABLES

2007 Tax Rate Schedules

Single—Schedule X

If taxable income is: Over—	But not over—	The tax is:	of the amount over—
$ 0	$ 7,825	........10%	$ 0
7,825	31,850	$ 782.50 + 15%	7,825
31,850	77,100	4,386.25 + 25%	31,850
77,100	160,850	15,698.75 + 28%	77,100
160,850	349,700	39,148.75 + 33%	160,850
349,700	....	101,469.25 + 35%	349,700

Head of household—Schedule Z

If taxable income is: Over—	But not over—	The tax is:	of the amount over—
$ 0	$ 11,200	........10%	$ 0
11,200	42,650	$ 1,120.00 + 15%	11,200
42,650	110,100	5,837.50 + 25%	42,650
110,100	178,350	22,700.00 + 28%	110,100
178,350	349,700	41,810.00 + 33%	178,350
349,700	....	98,355.50 + 35%	349,700

Married filing jointly or Qualifying widow(er)—Schedule Y–1

If taxable income is: Over—	But not over—	The tax is:	of the amount over—
$ 0	$ 15,650	........10%	$ 0
15,650	63,700	$ 1,565.00 + 15%	15,650
63,700	128,500	8,772.50 + 25%	63,700
128,500	195,850	24,972.50 + 28%	128,500
195,850	349,700	43,830.50 + 33%	195,850
349,700	....	94,601.00 + 35%	349,700

Married filing separately—Schedule Y–2

If taxable income is: Over—	But not over—	The tax is:	of the amount over—
$ 0	$ 7,825	........10%	$ 0
7,825	31,850	$ 782.50 + 15%	7,825
31,850	64,250	4,386.25 + 25%	31,850
64,250	97,925	12,486.25 + 28%	64,250
97,925	174,850	21,915.25 + 33%	97,925
174,850	....	47,300.50 + 35%	174,850

2008 Tax Rate Schedules

Single—Schedule X

If taxable income is: Over—	But not over—	The tax is:	of the amount over—
$ 0	$ 8,025	........10%	$ 0
8,025	32,550	$ 802.50 + 15%	8,025
32,550	78,850	4,481.25 + 25%	32,550
78,850	164,550	16,056.25 + 28%	78,850
164,550	357,700	40,052.25 + 33%	164,550
357,700	....	103,791.75 + 35%	357,700

Head of household—Schedule Z

If taxable income is: Over—	But not over—	The tax is:	of the amount over—
$ 0	$ 11,450	........10%	$ 0
11,450	43,650	$ 1,145.00 + 15%	11,450
43,650	112,650	5,975.00 + 25%	43,650
112,650	182,400	23,225.00 + 28%	112,650
182,400	357,700	42,755.00 + 33%	182,400
357,700	....	100,604.00 + 35%	357,700

Married filing jointly or Qualifying widow(er)—Schedule Y–1

If taxable income is: Over—	But not over—	The tax is:	of the amount over—
$ 0	$ 16,050	........10%	$ 0
16,050	65,100	$ 1,605.00 + 15%	16,050
65,100	131,450	8,962.50 + 25%	65,100
131,450	200,300	25,550.00 + 28%	131,450
200,300	357,700	44,828.00 + 33%	200,300
357,700	....	96,770.00 + 35%	357,700

Married filing separately—Schedule Y–2

If taxable income is: Over—	But not over—	The tax is:	of the amount over—
$ 0	$ 8,025	........10%	$ 0
8,025	32,550	$ 802.50 + 15%	8,025
32,550	65,725	4,481.25 + 25%	32,550
65,725	100,150	12,775.00 + 28%	65,725
100,150	178,850	22,414.00 + 33%	100,150
178,850	....	48,385.00 + 35%	178,850

Income Tax Rates—Estates and Trusts

Tax Year 2007

Taxable Income		The Tax Is:	Of the Amount
Over—	But not Over—		Over—
$ 0	$ 2,150	15%	$ 0
2,150	5,000	$ 322.50 + 25%	2,150
5,000	7,650	1,035.00 + 28%	5,000
7,650	10,450	1,777.00 + 33%	7,650
10,450	....	2,701.00 + 35%	10,450

Tax Year 2008

Taxable Income		The Tax Is:	Of the Amount
Over—	But not Over—		Over—
$ 0	$ 2,200	15%	$ 0
2,200	5,150	$ 330.00 + 25%	2,200
5,150	7,850	1,067.50 + 28%	5,150
7,850	10,700	1,823.50 + 33%	7,850
10,700	....	2,764.00 + 35%	10,700

Income Tax Rates—Corporations

Taxable Income		Tax Is:	Of the Amount
Over—	But not Over—		Over—
$ 0	$ 50,000	15%	$ 0
50,000	75,000	$ 7,500 + 25%	50,000
75,000	100,000	13,750 + 34%	75,000
100,000	335,000	22,250 + 39%	100,000
335,000	10,000,000	113,900 + 34%	335,000
10,000,000	15,000,000	3,400,000 + 35%	10,000,000
15,000,000	18,333,333	5,150,000 + 38%	15,000,000
18,333,333	....	35%	0

Unified Transfer Tax Rates

For Gifts Made and for Deaths After 1983 and Before 2002

If the Amount with Respect to Which the Tentative Tax to Be Computed Is:	The Tentative Tax Is:
Not over $10,000	18 percent of such amount.
Over $10,000 but not over $20,000	$1,800, plus 20 percent of the excess of such amount over $10,000.
Over $20,000 but not over $40,000	$3,800, plus 22 percent of the excess of such amount over $20,000.
Over $40,000 but not over $60,000	$8,200, plus 24 percent of the excess of such amount over $40,000.
Over $60,000 but not over $80,000	$13,000, plus 26 percent of the excess of such amount over $60,000.
Over $80,000 but not over $100,000	$18,200, plus 28 percent of the excess of such amount over $80,000.
Over $100,000 but not over $150,000	$23,800, plus 30 percent of the excess of such amount over $100,000.
Over $150,000 but not over $250,000	$38,800, plus 32 percent of the excess of such amount over $150,000.
Over $250,000 but not over $500,000	$70,800, plus 34 percent of the excess of such amount over $250,000.
Over $500,000 but not over $750,000	$155,800, plus 37 percent of the excess of such amount over $500,000.
Over $750,000 but not over $1,000,000	$248,300, plus 39 percent of the excess of such amount over $750,000.
Over $1,000,000 but not over $1,250,000	$345,800, plus 41 percent of the excess of such amount over $1,000,000.
Over $1,250,000 but not over $1,500,000	$448,300, plus 43 percent of the excess of such amount over $1,250,000.
Over $1,500,000 but not over $2,000,000	$555,800, plus 45 percent of the excess of such amount over $1,500,000.
Over $2,000,000 but not over $2,500,000	$780,800, plus 49 percent of the excess of such amount over $2,000,000.
Over $2,500,000 but not over $3,000,000	$1,025,800, plus 53 percent of the excess of such amount over $2,500,000.
Over $3,000,000*	$1,290,800, plus 55 percent of the excess of such amount over $3,000,000.

*For large taxable transfers (generally in excess of $10 million) there is a phaseout of the graduated rates and the unified tax credit.

Unified Transfer Tax Rates

For Gifts Made and for Deaths in 2002

If the Amount with Respect to Which the Tentative Tax to Be Computed Is:	The Tentative Tax Is:
Not over $10,000	18 percent of such amount.
Over $10,000 but not over $20,000	$1,800, plus 20 percent of the excess of such amount over $10,000.
Over $20,000 but not over $40,000	$3,800, plus 22 percent of the excess of such amount over $20,000.
Over $40,000 but not over $60,000	$8,200, plus 24 percent of the excess of such amount over $40,000.
Over $60,000 but not over $80,000	$13,000, plus 26 percent of the excess of such amount over $60,000.
Over $80,000 but not over $100,000	$18,200, plus 28 percent of the excess of such amount over $80,000.
Over $100,000 but not over $150,000	$23,800, plus 30 percent of the excess of such amount over $100,000.
Over $150,000 but not over $250,000	$38,800, plus 32 percent of the excess of such amount over $150,000.
Over $250,000 but not over $500,000	$70,800, plus 34 percent of the excess of such amount over $250,000.
Over $500,000 but not over $750,000	$155,800, plus 37 percent of the excess of such amount over $500,000.
Over $750,000 but not over $1,000,000	$248,300, plus 39 percent of the excess of such amount over $750,000.
Over $1,000,000 but not over $1,250,000	$345,800, plus 41 percent of the excess of such amount over $1,000,000.
Over $1,250,000 but not over $1,500,000	$448,300, plus 43 percent of the excess of such amount over $1,250,000.
Over $1,500,000 but not over $2,000,000	$555,800, plus 45 percent of the excess of such amount over $1,500,000.
Over $2,000,000 but not over $2,500,000	$780,800, plus 49 percent of the excess of such amount over $2,000,000.
Over $2,500,000	$1,025,800, plus 50 percent of the excess of such amount over $2,500,000.

Unified Transfer Tax Rates

For Gifts Made and for Deaths in 2003

If the Amount with Respect to Which the Tentative Tax to Be Computed Is:	The Tentative Tax Is:
Not over $10,000	18 percent of such amount.
Over $10,000 but not over $20,000	$1,800, plus 20 percent of the excess of such amount over $10,000.
Over $20,000 but not over $40,000	$3,800, plus 22 percent of the excess of such amount over $20,000.
Over $40,000 but not over $60,000	$8,200, plus 24 percent of the excess of such amount over $40,000.
Over $60,000 but not over $80,000	$13,000, plus 26 percent of the excess of such amount over $60,000.
Over $80,000 but not over $100,000	$18,200, plus 28 percent of the excess of such amount over $80,000.
Over $100,000 but not over $150,000	$23,800, plus 30 percent of the excess of such amount over $100,000.
Over $150,000 but not over $250,000	$38,800, plus 32 percent of the excess of such amount over $150,000.
Over $250,000 but not over $500,000	$70,800, plus 34 percent of the excess of such amount over $250,000.
Over $500,000 but not over $750,000	$155,800, plus 37 percent of the excess of such amount over $500,000.
Over $750,000 but not over $1,000,000	$248,300, plus 39 percent of the excess of such amount over $750,000.
Over $1,000,000 but not over $1,250,000	$345,800, plus 41 percent of the excess of such amount over $1,000,000.
Over $1,250,000 but not over $1,500,000	$448,300, plus 43 percent of the excess of such amount over $1,250,000.
Over $1,500,000 but not over $2,000,000	$555,800, plus 45 percent of the excess of such amount over $1,500,000.
Over $2,000,000	$780,800, plus 49 percent of the excess of such amount over $2,000,000.

For Gifts Made and for Deaths in 2004

(For amounts not over $2,000,000, see rates for 2003 above)	
Over $2,000,000	$780,800, plus 48 percent of the excess of such amount over $2,000,000

For Gifts Made and for Deaths in 2005

(For amounts not over $2,000,000, see rates for 2003 above)	
Over $2,000,000	$780,800, plus 47 percent of the excess of such amount over $2,000,000.

For Gifts Made and for Deaths in 2006

(For amounts not over $2,000,000, see rates for 2003 above)	
Over $2,000,000	$780,800, plus 46 percent of the excess of such amount over $2,000,000

Unified Transfer Tax Rates

For Gifts Made and for Deaths in 2007—2009

If the Amount with Respect to Which the Tentative Tax to Be Computed Is:	The Tentative Tax Is:
Not over $10,000	18 percent of such amount.
Over $10,000 but not over $20,000	$1,800, plus 20 percent of the excess of such amount over $10,000.
Over $20,000 but not over $40,000	$3,800, plus 22 percent of the excess of such amount over $20,000.
Over $40,000 but not over $60,000	$8,200, plus 24 percent of the excess of such amount over $40,000.
Over $60,000 but not over $80,000	$13,000, plus 26 percent of the excess of such amount over $60,000.
Over $80,000 but not over $100,000	$18,200, plus 28 percent of the excess of such amount over $80,000.
Over $100,000 but not over $150,000	$23,800, plus 30 percent of the excess of such amount over $100,000.
Over $150,000 but not over $250,000	$38,800, plus 32 percent of the excess of such amount over $150,000.
Over $250,000 but not over $500,000	$70,800, plus 34 percent of the excess of such amount over $250,000.
Over $500,000 but not over $750,000	$155,800, plus 37 percent of the excess of such amount over $500,000.
Over $750,000 but not over $1,000,000	$248,300, plus 39 percent of the excess of such amount over $750,000.
Over $1,000,000 but not over $1,250,000	$345,800, plus 41 percent of the excess of such amount over $1,000,000.
Over $1,250,000 but not over $1,500,000	$448,300, plus 43 percent of the excess of such amount over $1,250,000.
Over $1,500,000	$555,800, plus 45 percent of the excess of such amount over $1,500,000.

Valuation Tables (After April 30, 1999)

Table S Single Life Remainder Factors Interest Rate

Age	6.6%	6.8%	7.0%	7.2%	7.4%	7.6%	7.8%	8.0%
0	.02700	.02559	.02433	.02321	.02220	.02129	.02047	.01973
1	.01929	.01782	.01650	.01533	.01427	.01331	.01246	.01168
2	.01983	.01829	.01692	.01569	.01458	.01358	.01268	.01187
3	.02065	.01905	.01761	.01632	.01516	.01412	.01317	.01232
4	.02163	.01996	.01846	.01712	.01590	.01481	.01382	.01292
5	.02275	.02101	.01945	.01804	.01677	.01562	.01458	.01364
6	.02398	.02217	.02053	.01906	.01773	.01653	.01544	.01445
7	.02532	.02343	.02172	.02019	.01880	.01754	.01640	.01536
8	.02675	.02479	.02301	.02140	.01995	.01864	.01744	.01635
9	.02832	.02627	.02442	.02274	.02122	.01985	.01859	.01745
10	.03001	.02788	.02595	.02420	.02262	.02118	.01987	.01867
11	.03183	.02961	.02760	.02578	.02413	.02262	.02125	.02000
12	.03377	.03146	.02937	.02748	.02575	.02418	.02275	.02144
13	.03579	.03339	.03122	.02924	.02744	.02580	.02431	.02294
14	.03783	.03534	.03308	.03102	.02915	.02744	.02587	.02444
15	.03986	.03728	.03493	.03279	.03083	.02905	.02742	.02593
16	.04187	.03919	.03674	.03452	.03248	.03063	.02892	.02736
17	.04387	.04108	.03855	.03623	.03411	.03218	.03040	.02877
18	.04588	.04299	.04036	.03795	.03574	.03373	.03187	.03017
19	.04796	.04496	.04222	.03972	.03742	.03532	.03339	.03161
20	.05013	.04702	.04418	.04158	.03919	.03700	.03498	.03313
21	.05242	.04920	.04625	.04354	.04105	.03877	.03667	.03473
22	.05482	.05147	.04841	.04559	.04301	.04063	.03844	.03642
23	.05734	.05387	.05069	.04777	.04508	.04260	.04032	.03821
24	.06001	.05642	.05312	.05008	.04728	.04470	.04232	.04012
25	.06285	.05913	.05570	.05255	.04964	.04695	.04447	.04218
26	.06586	.06200	.05845	.05518	.05215	.04936	.04677	.04438
27	.06907	.06508	.06140	.05800	.05485	.05195	.04925	.04676
28	.07246	.06833	.06451	.06098	.05772	.05469	.05189	.04929
29	.07603	.07196	.06780	.06414	.06075	.05761	.05469	.05198
30	.07978	.07536	.07127	.06748	.06396	.06069	.05766	.05483
31	.08372	.07915	.07491	.07098	.06733	.06394	.06078	.05785
32	.08785	.08313	.07875	.07468	.07089	.06737	.06409	.06103
33	.09220	.08732	.08279	.07858	.07466	.07100	.06759	.06441
34	.09676	.09173	.08705	.08269	.07862	.07483	.07129	.06789

Valuation Tables (After April 30, 1999, *continued*)

Table S Single Life Remainder Factors Interest Rate

Age	6.6%	6.8%	7.0%	7.2%	7.4%	7.6%	7.8%	8.0%
35	.10157	.09638	.09155	.08704	.08283	.07890	.07522	.07179
36	.10662	.10127	.09628	.09162	.08726	.08319	.07938	.07581
37	.11193	.10641	.10126	.09645	.09194	.08772	.08377	.08006
38	.11751	.11183	.10652	.10155	.19689	.09253	.08843	.08459
39	.12338	.11753	.11206	.10693	.10212	.09761	.09337	.08938
40	.12955	.12355	.11791	.11262	.10766	.10299	.09860	.09447
41	.13606	.12989	.12409	.11864	.11352	.10870	.10417	.09989
42	.14291	.13657	.13061	.12500	.11972	.11475	.11006	.10564
43	.15010	.14360	.13747	.13171	.12627	.12115	.11631	.11174
44	.15764	.15098	.14469	.13876	.13317	.12789	.12290	.11819
45	.16550	.15867	.15223	.14615	.14040	.13496	.12982	.12496
46	.17370	.16671	.16011	.15387	.14796	.14238	.13708	.13207
47	.18220	.17505	.16830	.16190	.15584	.15010	.14466	.13950
48	.19102	.18373	.17682	.17027	.16406	.15817	.15258	.14727
49	.20018	.19274	.18568	.17898	.17262	.16658	.16084	.15539
50	.20969	.20210	.19490	.18805	.18155	.17536	.16948	.16388
51	.21955	.21182	.20448	.19749	.19084	.18452	.17849	.17275
52	.22973	.22186	.21438	.20726	.20047	.19400	.18784	.18196
53	.24022	.23222	.22461	.21735	.21043	.20383	.19753	.19151
54	.25101	.24290	.23516	.22777	.22072	.21399	.20756	.20140
55	.26212	.25389	.24604	.23853	.23136	.22450	.21793	.21166
56	.27355	.26522	.25725	.24963	.24233	.23535	.22867	.22227
57	.28529	.27686	.26879	.26106	.25365	.24656	.23976	.23324
58	.29731	.28878	.28061	.27278	.26528	.25807	.25116	.24453
59	.30956	.30095	.29269	.28477	.27716	.26986	.26284	.25610
60	.32202	.31334	.30500	.29699	.28929	.28190	.27478	.26794
61	.33473	.32598	.31757	.30948	.30170	.29422	.28701	.28007
62	.34772	.33892	.33044	.32229	.31443	.30687	.29958	.29255
63	.36101	.35216	.34363	.33542	.32750	.31986	.31250	.30539
64	.37456	.36568	.35711	.34884	.34087	.33317	.32574	.31857
65	.38838	.37947	.37087	.36257	.35455	.34681	.33932	.33208
66	.40249	.39357	.38496	.37663	.36858	.36079	.35326	.34597
67	.41694	.40803	.39941	.39107	.38299	.37518	.36761	.36028
68	.43170	.42281	.41419	.40585	.39777	.38994	.38235	.37499
69	.44672	.43786	.42927	.42094	.41286	.40503	.39743	.39006

Valuation Tables (After April 30, 1999, *continued*)

Table S Single Life Remainder Factors Interest Rate

Age	6.6%	6.8%	7.0%	7.2%	7.4%	7.6%	7.8%	8.0%
70	.46194	.45312	.44456	.43626	.42820	.42038	.41278	.40540
71	.47727	.46851	.46000	.45174	.44371	.43591	.42832	.42095
72	.49268	.48399	.47554	.46733	.45934	.45157	.44401	.43666
73	.50813	.49952	.49114	.48299	.47506	.46733	.45981	.45249
74	.52367	.51515	.50686	.49879	.49092	.48325	.47578	.46849
75	.53936	.53095	.52276	.51477	.50698	.49938	.49197	.48474
76	.55524	.54696	.53888	.53100	.52330	.51579	.50846	.50130
77	.57132	.56318	.55523	.54747	.53988	.53247	.52523	.51815
78	.58755	.57957	.57177	.56414	.55668	.54939	.54225	.53527
79	.60385	.59604	.58840	.58092	.57360	.56644	.55943	.55256
80	.62007	.61244	.60497	.59765	.59048	.58347	.57659	.56985
81	.63608	.62864	.62135	.61421	.60721	.60034	.59361	.58701
82	.65182	.64458	.63748	.63052	.62368	.61698	.61041	.60395
83	.66728	.66024	.65334	.64656	.63991	.63338	.62696	.62066
84	.68256	.67574	.66904	.66246	.65599	.64964	.64340	.63727
85	.69775	.69116	.68467	.67830	.67204	.66587	.65982	.65386
86	.71272	.70636	.70010	.69394	.68789	.68193	.67606	.67029
87	.72726	.72114	.71511	.70917	.70333	.69757	.69190	.68632
88	.74137	.73548	.72968	.72396	.71833	.71279	.70732	.70194
89	.75503	.74938	.74381	.73832	.73290	.72757	.72231	.71712
90	.76823	.76281	.75748	.75221	.74702	.74190	.73684	.73186
91	.78075	.77557	.77046	.76542	.76044	.75553	.75068	.74589
92	.79235	.78740	.78250	.77767	.77290	.76818	.76353	.75893
93	.80307	.79832	.79363	.78899	.78441	.77989	.77542	.77100
94	.81306	.80850	.80401	.79956	.79517	.79082	.78653	.78228
95	.82254	.81818	.81387	.80961	.80539	.80122	.79710	.79302
96	.83147	.82729	.82316	.81907	.81503	.81103	.80707	.80315
97	.83973	.83573	.83176	.82784	.82396	.82012	.81632	.81255
98	.84750	.84366	.83985	.83609	.83236	.82867	.82502	.82140
99	.85508	.85140	.84776	.84415	.84057	.83703	.83353	.83005
100	.86246	.85894	.85546	.85200	.84858	.84519	.84183	.83849
101	.86974	.86638	.86305	.85975	.85648	.85324	.85003	.84684
102	.87689	.87369	.87052	.86738	.86426	.86116	.85809	.85505
103	.88399	.88095	.87793	.87494	.87197	.86903	.86611	.86321
104	.89157	.88871	.88586	.88304	.88024	.87745	.87469	.87195

Valuation Tables (After April 30, 1989)

Table B Term Certain Remainder Factors Interest Rate

Years	7.4%	7.6%	7.8%	8.0%	8.2%	8.4%	8.6%	8.8%
1	.931099	.929368	.927644	.925926	.924214	.922509	.920810	.919118
2	.866945	.863725	.860523	.857339	.854172	.851023	.847892	.844777
3	.807211	.802718	.798259	.793832	.789438	.785077	.780747	.776450
4	.751593	.746021	.740500	.735030	.729610	.724241	.718920	.713649
5	.699808	.693328	.686920	.680583	.674316	.668119	.661989	.655927
6	.651590	.644357	.637217	.630170	.623213	.616346	.609566	.602874
7	.606694	.598845	.591111	.583490	.575982	.568585	.561295	.554112
8	.564892	.556547	.548340	.540269	.532331	.524524	.516846	.509294
9	.525971	.517237	.508664	.500249	.491988	.483879	.475917	.468101
10	.489731	.480704	.471859	.463193	.454703	.446383	.438230	.430240
11	.455987	.446750	.437717	.428883	.420243	.411792	.403526	.395441
12	.424569	.415196	.406046	.397114	.388394	.379882	.371571	.363457
13	.395316	.385870	.376666	.367698	.358960	.350445	.342147	.334060
14	.368078	.358615	.349412	.340461	.331756	.323288	.315052	.307040
15	.342717	.333285	.324130	.315242	.306613	.298236	.290103	.282206
16	.319103	.309745	.300677	.291890	.283376	.275126	.267130	.259381
17	.297117	.287867	.278921	.270269	.261901	.253806	.245976	.238401
18	.276645	.267534	.258739	.250249	.242052	.234139	.226497	.219119
19	.257584	.248638	.240018	.231712	.223708	.215995	.208561	.201396
20	.239836	.231076	.222651	.214548	.206754	.199257	.192045	.185107
21	.223311	.214755	.206541	.198656	.191085	.183817	.176837	.170135
22	.207925	.199586	.191596	.183941	.176604	.169573	.162834	.156374
23	.193598	.185489	.177733	.170315	.163220	.156432	.149939	.143726
24	.180259	.172387	.164873	.157699	.150850	.144310	.138065	.132101
25	.167839	.160211	.152943	.146018	.139418	.133128	.127132	.121416
26	.156275	.148895	.141877	.135202	.128852	.122811	.117064	.111596
27	.145507	.138379	.131611	.125187	.119087	.113295	.107794	.102570
28	.135482	.128605	.122088	.115914	.110062	.104515	.099258	.094274
29	.126147	.119521	.113255	.107328	.101721	.096416	.091398	.086649
30	.117455	.111079	.105060	.099377	.094012	.088945	.084160	.079640
31	.109362	.103233	.097458	.092016	.086887	.082053	.077495	.073199
32	.101827	.095942	.090406	.085200	.080302	.075694	.071358	.067278
33	.094811	.089165	.083865	.078889	.074216	.069829	.065708	.061837
34	.088278	.082867	.077797	.073045	.068592	.064418	.060504	.056835
35	.082196	.077014	.072168	.067635	.063394	.059426	.055713	.052238

Valuation Tables (After April 30, 1989, *continued*)

Table B Term Certain Remainder Factors Interest Rate

Years	7.4%	7.6%	7.8%	8.0%	8.2%	8.4%	8.6%	8.8%
36	.076532	.071574	.066946	.062625	.058589	.054821	.051301	.048013
37	.071259	.066519	.062102	.057986	.054149	.050573	.047239	.044130
38	.066349	.061821	.057609	.053690	.050045	.046654	.043498	.040560
39	.061778	.057454	.053440	.049713	.046253	.043039	.040053	.037280
40	.057521	.053396	.049573	.046031	.042747	.039703	.036881	.034264
41	.053558	.049625	.045987	.042621	.039508	.036627	.033961	.031493
42	.049868	.046120	.042659	.039464	.036514	.033789	.031271	.028946
43	.046432	.042862	.039572	.036541	.033746	.031170	.028795	.026605
44	.043233	.039835	.036709	.033834	.031189	.028755	.026515	.024453
45	.040254	.037021	.034053	.031328	.028825	.026527	.024415	.022475
46	.037480	.034406	.031589	.029007	.026641	.024471	.022482	.020657
47	.034898	.031976	.029303	.026859	.024622	.022575	.020701	.018986
48	.032493	.029717	.027183	.024869	.022756	.020825	.019062	.017451
49	.030255	.027618	.025216	.023027	.021031	.019212	.017552	.016039
50	.028170	.025668	.023392	.021321	.019437	.017723	.016163	.014742
51	.026229	.023855	.021699	.019742	.017964	.016350	.014833	.013550
52	.024422	.022170	.020129	.018280	.016603	.015083	.013704	.012454
53	.022739	.020604	.018673	.016925	.015345	.013914	.012619	.011446
54	.021172	.019149	.017322	.015672	.014182	.012836	.011620	.010521
55	.019714	.017796	.016068	.014511	.013107	.011841	.010699	.009670
56	.018355	.016539	.014906	.013436	.012114	.010923	.009852	.008888
57	.017091	.015371	.013827	.012441	.011196	.010077	.009072	.008169
58	.015913	.014285	.012827	.011519	.010347	.009296	.008354	.007508
59	.014817	.013276	.011899	.010666	.009563	.008576	.007692	.006901
60	.013796	.012339	.011038	.009876	.008838	.007911	.007083	.006343

TAX FORMS

(Tax forms can be obtained from the IRS web site: **http://www.irs.gov**)

Form **709**

Department of the Treasury
Internal Revenue Service

United States Gift (and Generation-Skipping Transfer) Tax Return

(For gifts made during calendar year 2007)

▶ **See separate instructions.**

OMB No. 1545-0020

2007

Part 1—General Information

1 Donor's first name and middle initial	2 Donor's last name	3 **Donor's social security number**

4 Address (number, street, and apartment number)	5 Legal residence (domicile)

6 City, state, and ZIP code	7 Citizenship (see instructions)

		Yes	No
8	If the donor died during the year, check here ▶ ☐ and enter date of death _____, _____		
9	If you extended the time to file this Form 709, check here ▶ ☐		
10	Enter the total number of donees listed on Schedule A. Count each person only once. ▶		
11a	Have you (the donor) previously filed a Form 709 (or 709-A) for any other year? If "No," skip line 11b		
11b	If the answer to line 11a is "Yes," has your address changed since you last filed Form 709 (or 709-A)?		
12	**Gifts by husband or wife to third parties.** Do you consent to have the gifts (including generation-skipping transfers) made by you and by your spouse to third parties during the calendar year considered as made one-half by each of you? (See instructions.) (If the answer is "Yes," the following information must be furnished and your spouse must sign the consent shown below. **If the answer is "No," skip lines 13–18 and go to Schedule A.**)		
13	Name of consenting spouse	14 SSN	
15	Were you married to one another during the entire calendar year? (see instructions)		
16	If 15 is "No," check whether ☐ married ☐ divorced or ☐ widowed/deceased, and give date (see instructions) ▶		
17	Will a gift tax return for this year be filed by your spouse? (If "Yes," mail both returns in the same envelope.) . . .		
18	**Consent of Spouse.** I consent to have the gifts (and generation-skipping transfers) made by me and by my spouse to third parties during the calendar year considered as made one-half by each of us. We are both aware of the joint and several liability for tax created by the execution of this consent.		

Consenting spouse's signature ▶ _____ Date ▶ _____

Part 2—Tax Computation

1	Enter the amount from Schedule A, Part 4, line 11	1	
2	Enter the amount from Schedule B, line 3	2	
3	Total taxable gifts. Add lines 1 and 2	3	
4	Tax computed on amount on line 3 (see *Table for Computing Gift Tax* in separate instructions) .	4	
5	Tax computed on amount on line 2 (see *Table for Computing Gift Tax* in separate instructions) .	5	
6	Balance. Subtract line 5 from line 4	6	
7	Maximum unified credit (nonresident aliens, see instructions)	7	345,800 00
8	Enter the unified credit against tax allowable for all prior periods (from Sch. B, line 1, col. C) .	8	
9	Balance. Subtract line 8 from line 7	9	
10	Enter 20% (.20) of the amount allowed as a specific exemption for gifts made after September 8, 1976, and before January 1, 1977 (see instructions)	10	
11	Balance. Subtract line 10 from line 9	11	
12	Unified credit. Enter the smaller of line 6 or line 11	12	
13	Credit for foreign gift taxes (see instructions)	13	
14	Total credits. Add lines 12 and 13	14	
15	Balance. Subtract line 14 from line 6. Do not enter less than zero	15	
16	Generation-skipping transfer taxes (from Schedule C, Part 3, col. H, Total)	16	
17	Total tax. Add lines 15 and 16	17	
18	Gift and generation-skipping transfer taxes prepaid with extension of time to file	18	
19	If line 18 is less than line 17, enter **balance due** (see instructions)	19	
20	If line 18 is greater than line 17, enter **amount to be refunded**	20	

Sign Here

Under penalties of perjury, I declare that I have examined this return, including any accompanying schedules and statements, and to the best of my knowledge and belief, it is true, correct, and complete. Declaration of preparer (other than donor) is based on all information of which preparer has any knowledge.

May the IRS discuss this return with the preparer shown below (see instructions)? ☐ **Yes** ☐ **No**

▶ _____
Signature of donor   Date

Paid Preparer's Use Only

Preparer's signature ▶	Date	Check if self-employed ▶ ☐
Firm's name (or yours if self-employed), address, and ZIP code ▶		Phone no. ▶ ( )

Attach check or money order here.

For Disclosure, Privacy Act, and Paperwork Reduction Act Notice, see page 12 of the separate instructions for this form.   Cat. No. 16783M   Form **709** (2007)

Form 709 (2007)   Page **2**

SCHEDULE A	**Computation of Taxable Gifts** (Including transfers in trust) (see instructions)

A Does the value of any item listed on Schedule A reflect any valuation discount? If "Yes," attach explanation . . . . . Yes ☐ No ☐

B ☐ ◄ Check here if you elect under section 529(c)(2)(B) to treat any transfers made this year to a qualified tuition program as made ratably over a 5-year period beginning this year. See instructions. Attach explanation.

Part 1—Gifts Subject Only to Gift Tax. Gifts less political organization, medical, and educational exclusions. See instructions.

A Item number	**B** • Donee's name and address • Relationship to donor (if any) • Description of gift • If the gift was of securities, give CUSIP no. • If closely held entity, give EIN	**C**	**D** Donor's adjusted basis of gift	**E** Date of gift	**F** Value at date of gift	**G** For split gifts, enter ½ of column F	**H** Net transfer (subtract col. G from col. F)
1							

Gifts made by spouse—*complete **only** if you are splitting gifts with your spouse and he/she also made gifts.*

Total of Part 1. Add amounts from Part 1, column H . . . . ►

Part 2—Direct Skips. Gifts that are direct skips and are subject to both gift tax and generation-skipping transfer tax. You must list the gifts in chronological order.

A Item number	**B** • Donee's name and address • Relationship to donor (if any) • Description of gift • If the gift was of securities, give CUSIP no. • If closely held entity, give EIN	**C** 2632(b) election out	**D** Donor's adjusted basis of gift	**E** Date of gift	**F** Value at date of gift	**G** For split gifts, enter ½ of column F	**H** Net transfer (subtract col. G from col. F)
1							

Gifts made by spouse—*complete **only** if you are splitting gifts with your spouse and he/she also made gifts.*

Total of Part 2. Add amounts from Part 2, column H . . . . ►

Part 3—Indirect Skips. Gifts to trusts that are currently subject to gift tax and may later be subject to generation-skipping transfer tax. You must list these gifts in chronological order.

A Item number	**B** • Donee's name and address • Relationship to donor (if any) • Description of gift • If the gift was of securities, give CUSIP no. • If closely held entity, give EIN	**C** 2632(c) election	**D** Donor's adjusted basis of gift	**E** Date of gift	**F** Value at date of gift	**G** For split gifts, enter ½ of column F	**H** Net transfer (subtract col. G from col. F)
1							

Gifts made by spouse—*complete **only** if you are splitting gifts with your spouse and he/she also made gifts.*

Total of Part 3. Add amounts from Part 3, column H . . . . ►

(If more space is needed, attach additional sheets of same size.)   Form **709** (2007)

Part 4—Taxable Gift Reconciliation

1	Total value of gifts of donor. Add totals from column H of Parts 1, 2, and 3	**1**	
2	Total annual exclusions for gifts listed on line 1 (see instructions)	**2**	
3	Total included amount of gifts. Subtract line 2 from line 1	**3**	

Deductions (see instructions)

4	Gifts of interests to spouse for which a marital deduction will be claimed, based on item numbers _____ of Schedule A . .	**4**			
5	Exclusions attributable to gifts on line 4	**5**			
6	Marital deduction. Subtract line 5 from line 4	**6**			
7	Charitable deduction, based on item nos. _____ less exclusions .	**7**			
8	Total deductions. Add lines 6 and 7		**8**	
9	Subtract line 8 from line 3		**9**	
10	Generation-skipping transfer taxes payable with this Form 709 (from Schedule C, Part 3, col. H, Total)		**10**	
11	**Taxable gifts.** Add lines 9 and 10. Enter here and on page 1, Part 2—Tax Computation, line 1 . . .		**11**	

Terminable Interest (QTIP) Marital Deduction. (See instructions for Schedule A, Part 4, line 4.)

If a trust (or other property) meets the requirements of qualified terminable interest property under section 2523(f), and:

a. The trust (or other property) is listed on Schedule A, and

b. The value of the trust (or other property) is entered in whole or in part as a deduction on Schedule A, Part 4, line 4, then the donor shall be deemed to have made an election to have such trust (or other property) treated as qualified terminable interest property under section 2523(f).

If less than the entire value of the trust (or other property) that the donor has included in Parts 1 and 3 of Schedule A is entered as a deduction on line 4, the donor shall be considered to have made an election only as to a fraction of the trust (or other property). The numerator of this fraction is equal to the amount of the trust (or other property) deducted on Schedule A, Part 4, line 6. The denominator is equal to the total value of the trust (or other property) listed in Parts 1 and 3 of Schedule A.

If you make the QTIP election, the terminable interest property involved will be included in your spouse's gross estate upon his or her death (section 2044). See instructions for line 4 of Schedule A. If your spouse disposes (by gift or otherwise) of all or part of the qualifying life income interest, he or she will be considered to have made a transfer of the entire property that is subject to the gift tax. See *Transfer of Certain Life Estates Received From Spouse* on page 4 of the instructions.

12 Election Out of QTIP Treatment of Annuities

☐ ◄ Check here if you elect under section 2523(f)(6) **not** to treat as qualified terminable interest property any joint and survivor annuities that are reported on Schedule A and would otherwise be treated as qualified terminable interest property under section 2523(f). See instructions. Enter the item numbers from Schedule A for the annuities for which you are making this election ► _____

SCHEDULE B   Gifts From Prior Periods

If you answered "Yes" on line 11a of page 1, Part 1, see the instructions for completing Schedule B. If you answered "No," skip to the Tax Computation on page 1 (or Schedule C, if applicable).

A Calendar year or calendar quarter (see instructions)	B Internal Revenue office where prior return was filed	C Amount of unified credit against gift tax for periods after December 31, 1976	D Amount of specific exemption for prior periods ending before January 1, 1977	E Amount of taxable gifts

1	Totals for prior periods **1**			
2	Amount, if any, by which total specific exemption, line 1, column D, is more than $30,000 . . . . **2**			
3	Total amount of taxable gifts for prior periods. Add amount on line 1, column E and amount, if any, on line 2. Enter here and on page 1, Part 2—Tax Computation, line 2 . . . . **3**			

(If more space is needed, attach additional sheets of same size.)

Form **709** (2007)

Form 709 (2007)

Page **4**

SCHEDULE C   Computation of Generation-Skipping Transfer Tax

Note. Inter vivos direct skips that are completely excluded by the GST exemption must still be fully reported (including value and exemptions claimed) on Schedule C.

Part 1—Generation-Skipping Transfers

A Item No. (from Schedule A, Part 2, col. A)	B Value (from Schedule A, Part 2, col. H)	C Nontaxable portion of transfer	D Net Transfer (subtract col. C from col. B)
1			
Gifts made by spouse (for gift splitting only)			

Part 2—GST Exemption Reconciliation (Section 2631) and Section 2652(a)(3) Election

Check here ″ ☐   if you are making a section 2652(a)(3) (special QTIP) election (see instructions)

Enter the item numbers from Schedule A of the gifts for which you are making this election ″ ----------------------

1	Maximum allowable exemption (see instructions)	**1**	
2	Total exemption used for periods before filing this return	**2**	
3	Exemption available for this return. Subtract line 2 from line 1	**3**	
4	Exemption claimed on this return from Part 3, column C total, below	**4**	
5	Automatic allocation of exemption to transfers reported on Schedule A, Part 3 (see instructions)	**5**	
6	Exemption allocated to transfers not shown on line 4 or 5, above. **You must attach a "Notice of Allocation."** (see instructions)	**6**	
7	Add lines 4, 5, and 6	**7**	
8	Exemption available for future transfers. Subtract line 7 from line 3	**8**	

Part 3—Tax Computation

A Item No. (from Schedule C, Part 1)	B Net transfer (from Schedule C, Part 1, col. D)	C GST Exemption Allocated	D Divide col. C by col. B	E Inclusion Ratio (subtract col. D from 1.000)	F Maximum Estate Tax Rate	G Applicable Rate (multiply col. E by col. F)	H Generation-Skipping Transfer Tax (multiply col. B by col. G)
1					45% (.45)		
					45% (.45)		
					45% (.45)		
					45% (.45)		
					45% (.45)		
					45% (.45)		
Gifts made by spouse (for gift splitting only)							
					45% (.45)		
					45% (.45)		
					45% (.45)		
					45% (.45)		
					45% (.45)		
					45% (.45)		
Total exemption claimed. Enter here and on Part 2, line 4, above. May not exceed Part 2, line 3, above		**Total generation-skipping transfer tax.** Enter here; on page 3, Schedule A, Part 4, line 10; and on page 1, Part 2—Tax Computation, line 16					

(If more space is needed, attach additional sheets of same size.)

Form **709** (2007)

Form **990**	**Return of Organization Exempt From Income Tax**	OMB No. 1545-0047
	Under section 501(c), 527, or 4947(a)(1) of the Internal Revenue Code (except black lung benefit trust or private foundation)	**2007**
Department of the Treasury Internal Revenue Service	▶ The organization may have to use a copy of this return to satisfy state reporting requirements.	**Open to Public Inspection**

A For the 2007 calendar year, or tax year beginning _____ , 2007, and ending _____ , 20 ____

B Check if applicable:	Please use IRS label or print or type. See Specific Instructions.	**C** Name of organization		**D** Employer identification number
☐ Address change				
☐ Name change		Number and street (or P.O. box if mail is not delivered to street address)	Room/suite	**E** Telephone number ( )
☐ Initial return				
☐ Termination		City or town, state or country, and ZIP + 4		**F** Accounting method: ☐ Cash ☐ Accrual
☐ Amended return				☐ Other (specify) ▶

☐ Application pending

● **Section 501(c)(3) organizations and 4947(a)(1) nonexempt charitable trusts must attach a completed Schedule A (Form 990 or 990-EZ).**

G Website: ▶

J Organization type (check only one) ▶ ☐ 501(c) ( ) ◀ (insert no.) ☐ 4947(a)(1) or ☐ 527

K Check here ▶ ☐ if the organization is not a 509(a)(3) supporting organization **and** its gross receipts are normally **not** more than $25,000. A return is not required, but if the organization chooses to file a return, be sure to file a complete return.

L Gross receipts: Add lines 6b, 8b, 9b, and 10b to line 12 ▶

H and I are not applicable to section 527 organizations.
H(a) Is this a group return for affiliates? ☐ Yes ☐ No
H(b) If "Yes," enter number of affiliates ▶ ....
H(c) Are all affiliates included? ☐ Yes ☐ No
(If "No," attach a list. See instructions.)
H(d) Is this a separate return filed by an organization covered by a group ruling? ☐ Yes ☐ No
I Group Exemption Number ▶
M Check ▶ ☐ if the organization is **not** required to attach Sch. B (Form 990, 990-EZ, or 990-PF).

Part I   Revenue, Expenses, and Changes in Net Assets or Fund Balances *(See the instructions.)*

1	Contributions, gifts, grants, and similar amounts received:		
a	Contributions to donor advised funds	**1a**	
b	Direct public support (not included on line 1a)	**1b**	
c	Indirect public support (not included on line 1a)	**1c**	
d	Government contributions (grants) (not included on line 1a)	**1d**	
e	**Total** (add lines 1a through 1d) (cash $_____ noncash $_____)	**1e**	
2	Program service revenue including government fees and contracts (from Part VII, line 93)	**2**	
3	Membership dues and assessments	**3**	
4	Interest on savings and temporary cash investments	**4**	
5	Dividends and interest from securities	**5**	
6a	Gross rents	**6a**	
b	Less: rental expenses	**6b**	
c	Net rental income or (loss). Subtract line 6b from line 6a	**6c**	
7	Other investment income (describe ▶)	**7**	
8a	Gross amount from sales of assets other than inventory	(A) Securities **8a** / (B) Other	
b	Less: cost or other basis and sales expenses.	**8b**	
c	Gain or (loss) (attach schedule)	**8c**	
d	Net gain or (loss). Combine line 8c, columns (A) and (B)	**8d**	
9	Special events and activities (attach schedule). If any amount is from **gaming,** check here ▶ ☐		
a	Gross revenue (not including $_____ of contributions reported on line 1b)	**9a**	
b	Less: direct expenses other than fundraising expenses	**9b**	
c	Net income or (loss) from special events. Subtract line 9b from line 9a	**9c**	
10a	Gross sales of inventory, less returns and allowances	**10a**	
b	Less: cost of goods sold	**10b**	
c	Gross profit or (loss) from sales of inventory (attach schedule). Subtract line 10b from line 10a	**10c**	
11	Other revenue (from Part VII, line 103)	**11**	
12	**Total revenue.** Add lines 1e, 2, 3, 4, 5, 6c, 7, 8d, 9c, 10c, and 11	**12**	
13	Program services (from line 44, column (B))	**13**	
14	Management and general (from line 44, column (C))	**14**	
15	Fundraising (from line 44, column (D))	**15**	
16	Payments to affiliates (attach schedule)	**16**	
17	**Total expenses.** Add lines 16 and 44, column (A)	**17**	
18	Excess or (deficit) for the year. Subtract line 17 from line 12	**18**	
19	Net assets or fund balances at beginning of year (from line 73, column (A))	**19**	
20	Other changes in net assets or fund balances (attach explanation)	**20**	
21	Net assets or fund balances at end of year. Combine lines 18, 19, and 20	**21**	

(left margin labels: Revenue, Expenses, Net Assets)

For Privacy Act and Paperwork Reduction Act Notice, see the separate instructions.   Cat. No. 11282Y   Form **990** (2007)

Form 990 (2007)   Page **2**

| **Part II** | **Statement of Functional Expenses** | All organizations must complete column (A). Columns (B), (C), and (D) are required for section 501(c)(3) and (4) organizations and section 4947(a)(1) nonexempt charitable trusts but optional for others. *(See the instructions.)* |

Do not include amounts reported on line 6b, 8b, 9b, 10b, or 16 of Part I.		**(A)** Total	**(B)** Program services	**(C)** Management and general	**(D)** Fundraising
22a	Grants paid from donor advised funds (attach schedule) (cash $ _____ noncash $ _____) If this amount includes foreign grants, check here ▶ ☐	**22a**			
22b	Other grants and allocations (attach schedule) (cash $ _____ noncash $ _____) If this amount includes foreign grants, check here ▶ ☐	**22b**			
23	Specific assistance to individuals (attach schedule)	**23**			
24	Benefits paid to or for members (attach schedule)	**24**			
25a	Compensation of current officers, directors, key employees, etc. listed in Part V-A . . .	**25a**			
b	Compensation of former officers, directors, key employees, etc. listed in Part V-B . . .	**25b**			
c	Compensation and other distributions, not included above, to disqualified persons (as defined under section 4958(f)(1)) and persons described in section 4958(c)(3)(B)	**25c**			
26	Salaries and wages of employees not included on lines 25a, b, and c	**26**			
27	Pension plan contributions not included on lines 25a, b, and c	**27**			
28	Employee benefits not included on lines 25a – 27	**28**			
29	Payroll taxes	**29**			
30	Professional fundraising fees	**30**			
31	Accounting fees	**31**			
32	Legal fees	**32**			
33	Supplies	**33**			
34	Telephone	**34**			
35	Postage and shipping	**35**			
36	Occupancy	**36**			
37	Equipment rental and maintenance	**37**			
38	Printing and publications	**38**			
39	Travel	**39**			
40	Conferences, conventions, and meetings . .	**40**			
41	Interest	**41**			
42	Depreciation, depletion, etc. (attach schedule)	**42**			
43	Other expenses not covered above (itemize):				
a	_____	**43a**			
b	_____	**43b**			
c	_____	**43c**			
d	_____	**43d**			
e	_____	**43e**			
f	_____	**43f**			
g	_____	**43g**			
44	**Total functional expenses.** Add lines 22a through 43g. (Organizations completing columns (B)–(D), carry these totals to lines 13–15)	**44**			

Joint Costs. Check ▶ ☐ if you are following SOP 98-2.

Are any joint costs from a combined educational campaign and fundraising solicitation reported in **(B)** Program services? . ▶ ☐ **Yes** ☐ **No**

If "Yes," enter **(i)** the aggregate amount of these joint costs $ _____ ; **(ii)** the amount allocated to Program services $ _____ ;

(iii) the amount allocated to Management and general $ _____ ; and **(iv)** the amount allocated to Fundraising $ _____

Form 990 (2007)

Part III   **Statement of Program Service Accomplishments** *(See the instructions.)*

Form 990 is available for public inspection and, for some people, serves as the primary or sole source of information about a particular organization. How the public perceives an organization in such cases may be determined by the information presented on its return. Therefore, please make sure the return is complete and accurate and fully describes, in Part III, the organization's programs and accomplishments.

What is the organization's primary exempt purpose? ▶ ---

	Program Service Expenses (Required for 501(c)(3) and (4) orgs., and 4947(a)(1) trusts; but optional for others.)

All organizations must describe their exempt purpose achievements in a clear and concise manner. State the number of clients served, publications issued, etc. Discuss achievements that are not measurable. (Section 501(c)(3) and (4) organizations and 4947(a)(1) nonexempt charitable trusts must also enter the amount of grants and allocations to others.)

a --

(Grants and allocations $) If this amount includes foreign grants, check here ▶ ☐

b --

(Grants and allocations $) If this amount includes foreign grants, check here ▶ ☐

c --

(Grants and allocations $) If this amount includes foreign grants, check here ▶ ☐

d --

(Grants and allocations $) If this amount includes foreign grants, check here ▶ ☐

e Other program services (attach schedule)
(Grants and allocations $) If this amount includes foreign grants, check here ▶ ☐

f **Total of Program Service Expenses** (should equal line 44, column (B), Program services).   .   .   .   . ▶

Form **990** (2007)

Form **990-EZ**

Department of the Treasury
Internal Revenue Service

Short Form
Return of Organization Exempt From Income Tax
Under section 501(c), 527, or 4947(a)(1) of the Internal Revenue Code
(except black lung benefit trust or private foundation)
▶ Sponsoring organizations, and controlling organizations as defined in section 512(b)(13) must file Form 990. All other organizations with gross receipts less than $100,000 and total assets less than $250,000 at the end of the year may use this form.
▶ *The organization may have to use a copy of this return to satisfy state reporting requirements.*

OMB No. 1545-1150

2007

Open to Public Inspection

A For the 2007 calendar year, or tax year beginning _____, 2007, and ending _____, 20___

B Check if applicable:	Please use IRS label or print or type. See Specific Instructions.	**C** Name of organization		**D** Employer identification number
☐ Address change				
☐ Name change		Number and street (or P.O. box, if mail is not delivered to street address)	Room/suite	**E** Telephone number ( )
☐ Initial return				
☐ Termination				
☐ Amended return		City or town, state or country, and ZIP + 4		**F** Group Exemption Number . . ▶
☐ Application pending				

• **Section 501(c)(3) organizations and 4947(a)(1) nonexempt charitable trusts must attach a completed Schedule A (Form 990 or 990-EZ).**

G Accounting method: ☐ Cash ☐ Accrual
Other (specify) ▶

I Website: ▶ _____

J Organization type (check only one)— ☐ 501(c) ( ) ◀ (insert no.) ☐ 4947(a)(1) or ☐ 527

H Check ▶ ☐ if the organization is **not** required to attach Schedule B (Form 990, 990-EZ, or 990-PF).

K Check ▶☐ if the organization is not a section 509(a)(3) supporting organization **and** its gross receipts are normally **not** more than $25,000. A return is not required, but if the organization chooses to file a return, be sure to file a complete return.

L Add lines 5b, 6b, and 7b, to line 9 to determine gross receipts; if $100,000 or more, file Form 990 instead of Form 990-EZ . ▶ $ _____

Part I Revenue, Expenses, and Changes in Net Assets or Fund Balances (See page 55 of the instructions.)

Revenue	**1** Contributions, gifts, grants, and similar amounts received.	**1**	
	2 Program service revenue including government fees and contracts	**2**	
	3 Membership dues and assessments	**3**	
	4 Investment income	**4**	
	5a Gross amount from sale of assets other than inventory ... **5a**		
	b Less: cost or other basis and sales expenses ... **5b**		
	c Gain or (loss) from sale of assets other than inventory. Subtract line 5b from line 5a (attach schedule)	**5c**	
	6 Special events and activities (attach schedule). If any amount is from **gaming,** check here ▶ ☐		
	a Gross revenue (not including $ _____ of contributions reported on line 1) ... **6a**		
	b Less: direct expenses other than fundraising expenses ... **6b**		
	c Net income or (loss) from special events and activities. Subtract line 6b from line 6a	**6c**	
	7a Gross sales of inventory, less returns and allowances ... **7a**		
	b Less: cost of goods sold ... **7b**		
	c Gross profit or (loss) from sales of inventory. Subtract line 7b from line 7a	**7c**	
	8 Other revenue (describe ▶ _____)	**8**	
	9 **Total revenue.** Add lines 1, 2, 3, 4, 5c, 6c, 7c, and 8. ▶	**9**	
Expenses	**10** Grants and similar amounts paid (attach schedule)	**10**	
	11 Benefits paid to or for members	**11**	
	12 Salaries, other compensation, and employee benefits	**12**	
	13 Professional fees and other payments to independent contractors	**13**	
	14 Occupancy, rent, utilities, and maintenance	**14**	
	15 Printing, publications, postage, and shipping	**15**	
	16 Other expenses (describe ▶ _____)	**16**	
	17 **Total expenses.** Add lines 10 through 16 ▶	**17**	
Net Assets	**18** Excess or (deficit) for the year. Subtract line 17 from line 9	**18**	
	19 Net assets or fund balances at beginning of year (from line 27, column (A)) (must agree with end-of-year figure reported on prior year's return)	**19**	
	20 Other changes in net assets or fund balances (attach explanation)	**20**	
	21 Net assets or fund balances at end of year. Combine lines 18 through 20 ▶	**21**	

Part II Balance Sheets—If Total assets on line 25, column (B) are $250,000 or more, file Form 990 instead of Form 990-EZ.

(See page 60 of the instructions.)		**(A)** Beginning of year		**(B)** End of year
22 Cash, savings, and investments			**22**	
23 Land and buildings			**23**	
24 Other assets (describe ▶ _____)			**24**	
25 **Total assets**			**25**	
26 **Total liabilities** (describe ▶ _____)			**26**	
27 **Net assets or fund balances** (line 27 of column (B) **must** agree with line 21)			**27**	

For Privacy Act and Paperwork Reduction Act Notice, see the separate instructions.   Cat. No. 10642I   Form **990-EZ** (2007)

Form 990-EZ (2007)   Page **2**

Part III	**Statement of Program Service Accomplishments** (See page 60 of the instructions.)	**Expenses** (Required for 501(c)(3) and (4) organizations and 4947(a)(1) trusts; optional for others.)

What is the organization's primary exempt purpose? _____
Describe what was achieved in carrying out the organization's exempt purposes. In a clear and concise manner, describe the services provided, the number of persons benefited, or other relevant information for each program title.

28 _____
_____
_____
(Grants $ _____) If this amount includes foreign grants, check here . . . . . ▶ ☐ | **28a** |

29 _____
_____
_____
(Grants $ _____) If this amount includes foreign grants, check here . . . . . ▶ ☐ | **29a** |

30 _____
_____
_____
(Grants $ _____) If this amount includes foreign grants, check here . . . . . ▶ ☐ | **30a** |

31 Other program services (attach schedule) . . . .
(Grants $ _____) If this amount includes foreign grants, check here . . . . . ▶ ☐ | **31a** |

32 Total program service expenses. Add lines 28a through 31a . . . . ▶ | **32** |

| **Part IV** | **List of Officers, Directors, Trustees, and Key Employees** (List each one even if not compensated. See page 61 of the instructions.) |

(A) Name and address	**(B)** Title and average hours per week devoted to position	**(C)** Compensation (If not paid, enter -0-.)	**(D)** Contributions to employee benefit plans & deferred compensation	**(E)** Expense account and other allowances

Part V	**Other Information** (Note the statement requirement in General Instruction V.)	**Yes**	**No**
33 Did the organization make a change in its activities or methods of conducting activities? If "Yes," attach a detailed statement of each change	**33**		
34 Were any changes made to the organizing or governing documents but not reported to the IRS? If "Yes," attach a conformed copy of the changes	**34**		
35 *If the organization had income from business activities, such as those reported on lines 2, 6, and 7 (among others), but **not** reported on Form 990-T, attach a statement explaining your reason for not reporting the income on Form 990-T.*			
a Did the organization have unrelated business gross income of $1,000 or more or 6033(e) notice, reporting, and proxy tax requirements?	**35a**		
b If "Yes," has it filed a tax return on **Form 990-T** for this year?	**35b**		
36 Was there a liquidation, dissolution, termination, or substantial contraction during the year? If "Yes," attach a statement.	**36**		
37a Enter amount of political expenditures, direct or indirect, as described in the instructions. ▶	37a			
b Did the organization file **Form 1120-POL** for this year?	**37b**		
38a Did the organization borrow from, or make any loans to, any officer, director, trustee, or key employee **or** were any such loans made in a prior year and still unpaid at the start of the period covered by this return? . . .	**38a**		
b If "Yes," attach the schedule specified in the line 38 instructions and enter the amount involved	38b			
39 *501(c)(7) organizations.* Enter:			
a Initiation fees and capital contributions included on line 9	39a			
b Gross receipts, included on line 9, for public use of club facilities	39b			

Form **990-EZ** (2007)

Form 990-EZ (2007)   Page **3**

Part V   **Other Information** (Note the statement requirement in General Instruction V.) *(Continued)*

40a *501(c)(3) organizations.* Enter amount of tax imposed on the organization during the year under:

section 4911 ▶ _____ ; section 4912 ▶ _____ ; section 4955 ▶ _____

		Yes	No
b *501(c)(3) and (4) organizations.* Did the organization engage in any section 4958 excess benefit transaction during the year or did it become aware of an excess benefit transaction from a prior year? If "Yes," attach an explanation	**40b**		
c Enter amount of tax imposed on organization managers or disqualified persons during the year under sections 4912, 4955, and 4958 ▶ _____			
d Enter amount of tax on line 40c reimbursed by the organization ▶ _____			
e *All organizations.* At any time during the tax year, was the organization a party to a prohibited tax shelter transaction?	**40e**		

41 List the states with which a copy of this return is filed. ▶ _____

42a The books are in care of ▶ _____ Telephone no. ▶ (_____) _____

Located at ▶ _____ ZIP + 4 ▶ _____

		Yes	No
b At any time during the calendar year, did the organization have an interest in or a signature or other authority over a financial account in a foreign country (such as a bank account, securities account, or other financial account)?	**42b**		
If "Yes," enter the name of the foreign country: ▶ _____			
See the instructions for exceptions and filing requirements for **Form TD F 90-22.1.**			
c At any time during the calendar year, did the organization maintain an office outside of the U.S.?	**42c**		
If "Yes," enter the name of the foreign country: ▶ _____			

43 *Section 4947(a)(1) nonexempt charitable trusts filing Form 990-EZ in lieu of Form 1041*—Check here ▶ ☐

and enter the amount of tax-exempt interest received or accrued during the tax year ▶ | **43** |

Please Sign Here	Under penalties of perjury, I declare that I have examined this return, including accompanying schedules and statements, and to the best of my knowledge and belief, it is true, correct, and complete. Declaration of preparer (other than officer) is based on all information of which preparer has any knowledge.
	▶ _____	_____
	Signature of officer	Date
	▶ _____
	Type or print name and title.

Paid Preparer's Use Only	Preparer's signature ▶		Date	Check if self-employed ▶ ☐	Preparer's SSN or PTIN (See Gen. Inst. X)
	Firm's name (or yours if self-employed), address, and ZIP + 4 ▶			EIN ▶	
				Phone no. ▶ ( )	

Form **990-EZ** (2007)

Form **1041**   Department of the Treasury—Internal Revenue Service
U.S. Income Tax Return for Estates and Trusts   **2007** | OMB No. 1545-0092

A Type of entity (see instr.):	For calendar year 2007 or fiscal year beginning , 2007, and ending , 20	
☐ Decedent's estate	Name of estate or trust (If a grantor type trust, see page 14 of the instructions.)	**C Employer identification number**
☐ Simple trust		
☐ Complex trust	Name and title of fiduciary	**D** Date entity created
☐ Qualified disability trust		
☐ ESBT (S portion only)	Number, street, and room or suite no. (If a P.O. box, see page 14 of the instructions.)	**E** Nonexempt charitable and split-interest trusts, check applicable boxes (see page 15 of the instr.):
☐ Grantor type trust		
☐ Bankruptcy estate–Ch. 7		☐ Described in section 4947(a)(1)
☐ Bankruptcy estate–Ch. 11	City or town, state, and ZIP code	☐ Not a private foundation
☐ Pooled income fund		☐ Described in section 4947(a)(2)

B Number of Schedules K-1 attached (see instructions) ▶	F Check applicable boxes:	☐ Initial return ☐ Final return ☐ Amended return ☐ Change in trust's name
		☐ Change in fiduciary ☐ Change in fiduciary's name ☐ Change in fiduciary's address

G   Check here if the estate or filing trust made a section 645 election . . . . . ▶ ☐

Income

1	Interest income	**1**	
2a	Total ordinary dividends	**2a**	
b	Qualified dividends allocable to: **(1)** Beneficiaries _____ **(2)** Estate or trust _____		
3	Business income or (loss). Attach Schedule C or C-EZ (Form 1040)	**3**	
4	Capital gain or (loss). Attach Schedule D (Form 1041)	**4**	
5	Rents, royalties, partnerships, other estates and trusts, etc. Attach Schedule E (Form 1040)	**5**	
6	Farm income or (loss). Attach Schedule F (Form 1040)	**6**	
7	Ordinary gain or (loss). Attach Form 4797	**7**	
8	Other income. List type and amount _____	**8**	
9	**Total income.** Combine lines 1, 2a, and 3 through 8 . . . . ▶	**9**	

Deductions

10	Interest. Check if Form 4952 is attached ▶ ☐	**10**	
11	Taxes	**11**	
12	Fiduciary fees	**12**	
13	Charitable deduction (from Schedule A, line 7)	**13**	
14	Attorney, accountant, and return preparer fees	**14**	
15a	Other deductions **not** subject to the 2% floor (attach schedule)	**15a**	
b	Allowable miscellaneous itemized deductions subject to the 2% floor	**15b**	
16	Add lines 10 through 15b . . . . ▶	**16**	
17	Adjusted total income or (loss). Subtract line 16 from line 9 . **17**		
18	Income distribution deduction (from Schedule B, line 15). Attach Schedules K-1 (Form 1041)	**18**	
19	Estate tax deduction including certain generation-skipping taxes (attach computation) . .	**19**	
20	Exemption	**20**	
21	Add lines 18 through 20 . . . . ▶	**21**	

Tax and Payments

22	Taxable income. Subtract line 21 from line 17. If a loss, see page 23 of the instructions	**22**	
23	**Total tax** (from Schedule G, line 7)	**23**	
24	**Payments: a** 2007 estimated tax payments and amount applied from 2006 return . . .	**24a**	
b	Estimated tax payments allocated to beneficiaries (from Form 1041-T)	**24b**	
c	Subtract line 24b from line 24a	**24c**	
d	Tax paid with Form 7004 (see page 23 of the instructions)	**24d**	
e	Federal income tax withheld. If any is from Form(s) 1099, check ▶ ☐	**24e**	
	Other payments: **f** Form 2439 _____ ; **g** Form 4136 _____ ; Total ▶	**24h**	
25	**Total payments.** Add lines 24c through 24e, and 24h . . . . ▶	**25**	
26	Estimated tax penalty (see page 24 of the instructions)	**26**	
27	**Tax due.** If line 25 is smaller than the total of lines 23 and 26, enter amount owed . .	**27**	
28	**Overpayment.** If line 25 is larger than the total of lines 23 and 26, enter amount overpaid	**28**	
29	Amount of line 28 to be: **a Credited to 2008 estimated tax** ▶ ; **b Refunded** ▶	**29**	

Sign Here ▶

Under penalties of perjury, I declare that I have examined this return, including accompanying schedules and statements, and to the best of my knowledge and belief, it is true, correct, and complete. Declaration of preparer (other than taxpayer) is based on all information of which preparer has any knowledge.

			May the IRS discuss this return with the preparer shown below (see instr.)? ☐ **Yes** ☐ **No**
▶ Signature of fiduciary or officer representing fiduciary	Date	▶ EIN of fiduciary if a financial institution	

Paid Preparer's Use Only

Preparer's signature ▶	Date	Check if self-employed ☐	Preparer's SSN or PTIN
Firm's name (or yours if self-employed), address, and ZIP code ▶		EIN	
		Phone no. ( )	

For Privacy Act and Paperwork Reduction Act Notice, see the separate instructions.   Cat. No. 11370H   Form **1041** (2007)

Form 1041 (2007)   Page **2**

Schedule A	**Charitable Deduction.** Do not complete for a simple trust or a pooled income fund.		
1	Amounts paid or permanently set aside for charitable purposes from gross income (see page 24)	**1**	
2	Tax-exempt income allocable to charitable contributions (see page 24 of the instructions)	**2**	
3	Subtract line 2 from line 1	**3**	
4	Capital gains for the tax year allocated to corpus and paid or permanently set aside for charitable purposes	**4**	
5	Add lines 3 and 4	**5**	
6	Section 1202 exclusion allocable to capital gains paid or permanently set aside for charitable purposes (see page 25 of the instructions)	**6**	
7	**Charitable deduction.** Subtract line 6 from line 5. Enter here and on page 1, line 13	**7**	

Schedule B	**Income Distribution Deduction**		
1	Adjusted total income (see page 25 of the instructions)	**1**	
2	Adjusted tax-exempt interest	**2**	
3	Total net gain from Schedule D (Form 1041), line 15, column (1) (see page 25 of the instructions)	**3**	
4	Enter amount from Schedule A, line 4 (minus any allocable section 1202 exclusion)	**4**	
5	Capital gains for the tax year included on Schedule A, line 1 (see page 25 of the instructions)	**5**	
6	Enter any gain from page 1, line 4, as a negative number. If page 1, line 4, is a loss, enter the loss as a positive number	**6**	
7	**Distributable net income.** Combine lines 1 through 6. If zero or less, enter -0-	**7**	
8	If a complex trust, enter accounting income for the tax year as determined under the governing instrument and applicable local law **8**		
9	Income required to be distributed currently	**9**	
10	Other amounts paid, credited, or otherwise required to be distributed	**10**	
11	Total distributions. Add lines 9 and 10. If greater than line 8, see page 26 of the instructions	**11**	
12	Enter the amount of tax-exempt income included on line 11	**12**	
13	Tentative income distribution deduction. Subtract line 12 from line 11	**13**	
14	Tentative income distribution deduction. Subtract line 2 from line 7. If zero or less, enter -0-	**14**	
15	**Income distribution deduction.** Enter the smaller of line 13 or line 14 here and on page 1, line 18	**15**	

Schedule G	**Tax Computation** (see page 27 of the instructions)		
1 Tax: a	Tax on taxable income (see page 27 of the instructions)	**1a**	
b	Tax on lump-sum distributions. Attach Form 4972	**1b**	
c	Alternative minimum tax (from Schedule I, line 56)	**1c**	
d	**Total.** Add lines 1a through 1c	**1d**	
2a	Foreign tax credit. Attach Form 1116	**2a**	
b	Other nonbusiness credits (attach schedule)	**2b**	
c	General business credit. Enter here and check which forms are attached:		
	☐ Form 3800 ☐ Forms (specify) ▶ _____	**2c**	
		2d	
d	Credit for prior year minimum tax. Attach Form 8801		
3	**Total credits.** Add lines 2a through 2d	**3**	
4	Subtract line 3 from line 1d. If zero or less, enter -0-.	**4**	
5	Recapture taxes. Check if from: ☐ Form 4255 ☐ Form 8611	**5**	
6	Household employment taxes. Attach Schedule H (Form 1040)	**6**	
7	**Total tax.** Add lines 4 through 6. Enter here and on page 1, line 23	**7**	

	Other Information	Yes	No
1	Did the estate or trust receive tax-exempt income? If "Yes," attach a computation of the allocation of expenses Enter the amount of tax-exempt interest income and exempt-interest dividends ▶ $ _____		
2	Did the estate or trust receive all or any part of the earnings (salary, wages, and other compensation) of any individual by reason of a contract assignment or similar arrangement?		
3	At any time during calendar year 2007, did the estate or trust have an interest in or a signature or other authority over a bank, securities, or other financial account in a foreign country?		
	See page 29 of the instructions for exceptions and filing requirements for Form TD F 90-22.1. If "Yes," enter the name of the foreign country ▶ _____		
4	During the tax year, did the estate or trust receive a distribution from, or was it the grantor of, or transferor to, a foreign trust? If "Yes," the estate or trust may have to file Form 3520. See page 29 of the instructions		
5	Did the estate or trust receive, or pay, any qualified residence interest on seller-provided financing? If "Yes," see page 29 for required attachment		
6	If this is an estate or a complex trust making the section 663(b) election, check here (see page 29) ▶ ☐		
7	To make a section 643(e)(3) election, attach Schedule D (Form 1041), and check here (see page 29) ▶ ☐		
8	If the decedent's estate has been open for more than 2 years, attach an explanation for the delay in closing the estate, and check here ▶ ☐		
9	Are any present or future trust beneficiaries skip persons? See page 29 of the instructions		

Form **1041** (2007)

Form 1041 (2007)   Page **3**

Schedule I   Alternative Minimum Tax (AMT) (see pages 29 through 37 of the instructions)

Part I—Estate's or Trust's Share of Alternative Minimum Taxable Income

1	Adjusted total income or (loss) (from page 1, line 17)	**1**	
2	Interest	**2**	
3	Taxes	**3**	
4	Miscellaneous itemized deductions (from page 1, line 15b)	**4**	
5	Refund of taxes	**5** ( )
6	Depletion (difference between regular tax and AMT)	**6**	
7	Net operating loss deduction. Enter as a positive amount	**7**	
8	Interest from specified private activity bonds exempt from the regular tax	**8**	
9	Qualified small business stock (see page 30 of the instructions)	**9**	
10	Exercise of incentive stock options (excess of AMT income over regular tax income) . . .	**10**	
11	Other estates and trusts (amount from Schedule K-1 (Form 1041), box 12, code A) . . .	**11**	
12	Electing large partnerships (amount from Schedule K-1 (Form 1065-B), box 6)	**12**	
13	Disposition of property (difference between AMT and regular tax gain or loss)	**13**	
14	Depreciation on assets placed in service after 1986 (difference between regular tax and AMT)	**14**	
15	Passive activities (difference between AMT and regular tax income or loss)	**15**	
16	Loss limitations (difference between AMT and regular tax income or loss)	**16**	
17	Circulation costs (difference between regular tax and AMT)	**17**	
18	Long-term contracts (difference between AMT and regular tax income)	**18**	
19	Mining costs (difference between regular tax and AMT)	**19**	
20	Research and experimental costs (difference between regular tax and AMT)	**20**	
21	Income from certain installment sales before January 1, 1987	**21** ( )
22	Intangible drilling costs preference	**22**	
23	Other adjustments, including income-based related adjustments	**23**	
24	Alternative tax net operating loss deduction (See the instructions for the limitation that applies.)	**24** ( )
25	Adjusted alternative minimum taxable income. Combine lines 1 through 24	**25**	

Note: *Complete Part II below before going to line 26.*

26	Income distribution deduction from Part II, line 44	**26**	
27	Estate tax deduction (from page 1, line 19)	**27**	
28	Add lines 26 and 27	**28**	
29	Estate's or trust's share of alternative minimum taxable income. Subtract line 28 from line 25	**29**	

If line 29 is:

• $22,500 or less, stop here and enter -0- on Schedule G, line 1c. The estate or trust is not liable for the alternative minimum tax.

• Over $22,500, but less than $165,000, go to line 45.

• $165,000 or more, enter the amount from line 29 on line 51 and go to line 52.

Part II—Income Distribution Deduction on a Minimum Tax Basis

30	Adjusted alternative minimum taxable income (see page 34 of the instructions)	**30**	
31	Adjusted tax-exempt interest (other than amounts included on line 8)	**31**	
32	Total net gain from Schedule D (Form 1041), line 15, column (1). If a loss, enter -0- . . .	**32**	
33	Capital gains for the tax year allocated to corpus and paid or permanently set aside for charitable purposes (from Schedule A, line 4)	**33**	
34	Capital gains paid or permanently set aside for charitable purposes from gross income (see page 34 of the instructions)	**34**	
35	Capital gains computed on a minimum tax basis included on line 25	**35** ( )
36	Capital losses computed on a minimum tax basis included on line 25. Enter as a positive amount	**36**	
37	Distributable net alternative minimum taxable income (DNAMTI). Combine lines 30 through 36. If zero or less, enter -0-.	**37**	
38	Income required to be distributed currently (from Schedule B, line 9)	**38**	
39	Other amounts paid, credited, or otherwise required to be distributed (from Schedule B, line 10)	**39**	
40	Total distributions. Add lines 38 and 39	**40**	
41	Tax-exempt income included on line 40 (other than amounts included on line 8)	**41**	
42	Tentative income distribution deduction on a minimum tax basis. Subtract line 41 from line 40	**42**	
43	Tentative income distribution deduction on a minimum tax basis. Subtract line 31 from line 37. If zero or less, enter -0-	**43**	
44	**Income distribution deduction on a minimum tax basis.** Enter the smaller of line 42 or line 43. Enter here and on line 26	**44**	

Form **1041** (2007)

Form 1041 (2007)   Page **4**

Part III—Alternative Minimum Tax

45	Exemption amount	**45**	$22,500	00

46 Enter the amount from line 29 — **46**

47 Phase-out of exemption amount — **47** $75,000 | 00

48 Subtract line 47 from line 46. If zero or less, enter -0- — **48**

49 Multiply line 48 by 25% (.25) — **49**

50 Subtract line 49 from line 45. If zero or less, enter -0- — **50**

51 Subtract line 50 from line 46 — **51**

52 Go to Part IV of Schedule I to figure line 52 if the estate or trust has qualified dividends or has a gain on lines 14a and 15 of column (2) of Schedule D (Form 1041) (as refigured for the AMT, if necessary). Otherwise, if line 51 is—
- $175,000 or less, multiply line 51 by 26% (.26).
- Over $175,000, multiply line 51 by 28% (.28) and subtract $3,500 from the result — **52**

53 Alternative minimum foreign tax credit (see page 35 of the instructions) — **53**

54 Tentative minimum tax. Subtract line 53 from line 52 — **54**

55 Enter the tax from Schedule G, line 1a (minus any foreign tax credit from Schedule G, line 2a) — **55**

56 **Alternative minimum tax.** Subtract line 55 from line 54. If zero or less, enter -0-. Enter here and on Schedule G, line 1c — **56**

Part IV—Line 52 Computation Using Maximum Capital Gains Rates

Caution: If you did not complete Part V of Schedule D (Form 1041), the Schedule D Tax Worksheet, or the Qualified Dividends Tax Worksheet, see page 36 of the instructions before completing this part.

57 Enter the amount from line 51 — **57**

58 Enter the amount from Schedule D (Form 1041), line 22, line 13 of the Schedule D Tax Worksheet, or line 4 of the Qualified Dividends Tax Worksheet, whichever applies (as refigured for the AMT, if necessary) — **58**

59 Enter the amount from Schedule D (Form 1041), line 14b, column (2) (as refigured for the AMT, if necessary). If you did not complete Schedule D for the regular tax or the AMT, enter -0- — **59**

60 If you did not complete a Schedule D Tax Worksheet for the regular tax or the AMT, enter the amount from line 58. Otherwise, add lines 58 and 59 and enter the **smaller** of that result or the amount from line 10 of the Schedule D Tax Worksheet (as refigured for the AMT, if necessary) — **60**

61 Enter the **smaller** of line 57 or line 60 — **61**

62 Subtract line 61 from line 57 — **62**

63 If line 62 is $175,000 or less, multiply line 62 by 26% (.26). Otherwise, multiply line 62 by 28% (.28) and subtract $3,500 from the result ▶ **63**

64 Maximum amount subject to the 5% rate — **64** $2,150 | 00

65 Enter the amount from line 23 of Schedule D (Form 1041), line 14 of the Schedule D Tax Worksheet, or line 5 of the Qualified Dividends Tax Worksheet, whichever applies (as figured for the regular tax). If you did not complete Schedule D or either worksheet for the regular tax, enter -0- — **65**

66 Subtract line 65 from line 64. If zero or less, enter -0- — **66**

67 Enter the **smaller** of line 57 or line 58 — **67**

68 Enter the **smaller** of line 66 or line 67 — **68**

69 Multiply line 68 by 5% (.05) ▶ **69**

70 Subtract line 68 from line 67 — **70**

71 Multiply line 70 by 15% (.15) ▶ **71**

If line 59 is zero or blank, skip lines 72 and 73 and go to line 74. Otherwise, go to line 72.

72 Subtract line 67 from line 61 — **72**

73 Multiply line 72 by 25% (.25) ▶ **73**

74 Add lines 63, 69, 71, and 73 — **74**

75 If line 57 is $175,000 or less, multiply line 57 by 26% (.26). Otherwise, multiply line 57 by 28% (.28) and subtract $3,500 from the result — **75**

76 Enter the **smaller** of line 74 or line 75 here and on line 52 — **76**

Form **1041** (2007)

661107

☐ Final K-1   ☐ Amended K-1   OMB No. 1545-0092

Schedule K-1
(Form 1041)

2007

Department of the Treasury
Internal Revenue Service

For calendar year 2007,
or tax year beginning _____ , 2007
and ending _____ , 20 _____

Beneficiary's Share of Income, Deductions, Credits, etc.

▶ See back of form and instructions.

Part I	**Information About the Estate or Trust**

A Estate's or trust's employer identification number

B Estate's or trust's name

C Fiduciary's name, address, city, state, and ZIP code

D ☐ Check if Form 1041-T was filed and enter the date it was filed
_____/_____/_____

E ☐ Check if this is the final Form 1041 for the estate or trust

Part II	**Information About the Beneficiary**

F Beneficiary's identifying number

G Beneficiary's name, address, city, state, and ZIP code

H ☐ Domestic beneficiary   ☐ Foreign beneficiary

Part III	**Beneficiary's Share of Current Year Income, Deductions, Credits, and Other Items**	
1 Interest income	**11** Final year deductions	
2a Ordinary dividends		
2b Qualified dividends		
3 Net short-term capital gain		
4a Net long-term capital gain		
4b 28% rate gain	**12** Alternative minimum tax adjustment	
4c Unrecaptured section 1250 gain		
5 Other portfolio and nonbusiness income		
6 Ordinary business income		
7 Net rental real estate income	**13** Credits and credit recapture	
8 Other rental income		
9 Directly apportioned deductions		
	14 Other information	
10 Estate tax deduction		

*See attached statement for additional information.

Note: A statement must be attached showing the beneficiary's share of income and directly apportioned deductions from each business, rental real estate, and other rental activity.

For IRS Use Only

For Paperwork Reduction Act Notice, see the Instructions for Form 1041.   Cat. No. 11380D   **Schedule K-1 (Form 1041) 2007**

Form 1065
Department of the Treasury
Internal Revenue Service

U.S. Return of Partnership Income

For calendar year 2007, or tax year beginning _____ , 2007, ending _____ , 20 _____ .
▶ **See separate instructions.**

OMB No. 1545-0099

2007

A Principal business activity	Use the IRS label. Other-wise, print or type.	Name of partnership	D Employer identification number
B Principal product or service		Number, street, and room or suite no. If a P.O. box, see the instructions.	E Date business started
C Business code number		City or town, state, and ZIP code	F Total assets (see the instructions) $

G Check applicable boxes: **(1)** ☐ Initial return **(2)** ☐ Final return **(3)** ☐ Name change **(4)** ☐ Address change **(5)** ☐ Amended return

H Check accounting method: **(1)** ☐ Cash **(2)** ☐ Accrual **(3)** ☐ Other (specify) ▶ _____

I Number of Schedules K-1. Attach one for each person who was a partner at any time during the tax year ▶ _____

J Check if Schedule M-3 attached . . . . ☐

Caution. *Include **only** trade or business income and expenses on lines 1a through 22 below. See the instructions for more information.*

Income	**1a** Gross receipts or sales **1a**		
	b Less returns and allowances **1b**	**1c**	
	2 Cost of goods sold (Schedule A, line 8)	**2**	
	3 Gross profit. Subtract line 2 from line 1c	**3**	
	4 Ordinary income (loss) from other partnerships, estates, and trusts *(attach statement)*. . .	**4**	
	5 Net farm profit (loss) *(attach Schedule F (Form 1040))*	**5**	
	6 Net gain (loss) from Form 4797, Part II, line 17 *(attach Form 4797)*	**6**	
	7 Other income (loss) *(attach statement)*	**7**	
	8 **Total income (loss).** Combine lines 3 through 7	**8**	
Deductions (see the instructions for limitations)	**9** Salaries and wages (other than to partners) (less employment credits)	**9**	
	10 Guaranteed payments to partners	**10**	
	11 Repairs and maintenance	**11**	
	12 Bad debts	**12**	
	13 Rent	**13**	
	14 Taxes and licenses	**14**	
	15 Interest	**15**	
	16a Depreciation *(if required, attach Form 4562)* **16a**		
	b Less depreciation reported on Schedule A and elsewhere on return **16b**	**16c**	
	17 Depletion **(Do not deduct oil and gas depletion.)**	**17**	
	18 Retirement plans, etc.	**18**	
	19 Employee benefit programs	**19**	
	20 Other deductions *(attach statement)*	**20**	
	21 **Total deductions.** Add the amounts shown in the far right column for lines 9 through 20 .	**21**	
	22 **Ordinary business income (loss).** Subtract line 21 from line 8	**22**	

Sign Here

Under penalties of perjury, I declare that I have examined this return, including accompanying schedules and statements, and to the best of my knowledge and belief, it is true, correct, and complete. Declaration of preparer (other than general partner or limited liability company member manager) is based on all information of which preparer has any knowledge.

▶ Signature of general partner or limited liability company member manager	▶ Date	May the IRS discuss this return with the preparer shown below (see instructions)? ☐ Yes ☐ No

Paid Preparer's Use Only	Preparer's signature		Date	Check if self-employed ▶ ☐	Preparer's SSN or PTIN
	Firm's name (or yours if self-employed), address, and ZIP code ▶			EIN ▶	
				Phone no. ( )	

For Privacy Act and Paperwork Reduction Act Notice, see separate instructions.   Cat. No. 11390Z   Form **1065** (2007)

Form 1065 (2007)   Page **2**

Schedule A	**Cost of Goods Sold** (see the instructions)		

1	Inventory at beginning of year	**1**	
2	Purchases less cost of items withdrawn for personal use	**2**	
3	Cost of labor	**3**	
4	Additional section 263A costs (attach statement)	**4**	
5	Other costs (attach statement)	**5**	
6	**Total.** Add lines 1 through 5	**6**	
7	Inventory at end of year	**7**	
8	**Cost of goods sold.** Subtract line 7 from line 6. Enter here and on page 1, line 2	**8**	

9a Check all methods used for valuing closing inventory:

   (i) ☐ Cost as described in Regulations section 1.471-3

   (ii) ☐ Lower of cost or market as described in Regulations section 1.471-4 ·

   (iii) ☐ Other (specify method used and attach explanation) ▶ ....

  b Check this box if there was a writedown of "subnormal" goods as described in Regulations section 1.471-2(c)   .   ▶ ☐

  c Check this box if the LIFO inventory method was adopted this tax year for any goods (if checked, attach Form 970)   ▶ ☐

  d Do the rules of section 263A (for property produced or acquired for resale) apply to the partnership?   .   .   ☐ **Yes** ☐ **No**

  e Was there any change in determining quantities, cost, or valuations between opening and closing inventory?   ☐ **Yes** ☐ **No**
    If "Yes," attach explanation.

Schedule B	**Other Information**

		Yes	No
1	What type of entity is filing this return? Check the applicable box:		

  a ☐ Domestic general partnership   **b** ☐ Domestic limited partnership

  c ☐ Domestic limited liability company   **d** ☐ Domestic limited liability partnership

  e ☐ Foreign partnership   **f** ☐ Other ▶ ....

2 Are any partners in this partnership also partnerships?

3 During the partnership's tax year, did the partnership own any interest in another partnership or in any foreign entity that was disregarded as an entity separate from its owner under Regulations section 301.7701-2 and 301.7701-3? If "Yes," see instructions for required attachment

4 Did the partnership file Form 8893, Election of Partnership Level Tax Treatment, or an election statement under section 6231(a)(1)(B)(ii) for partnership-level tax treatment, that is in effect for this tax year? See Form 8893 for more details .

5 Does this partnership meet all three of the following requirements?

  a The partnership's total receipts for the tax year were less than $250,000;

  b The partnership's total assets at the end of the tax year were less than $600,000; and

  c Schedules K-1 are filed with the return and furnished to the partners on or before the due date (including extensions) for the partnership return

    If "Yes," the partnership is not required to complete Schedules L, M-1, and M-2; Item F on page 1 of Form 1065; or Item L on Schedule K-1.

6 Does this partnership have any foreign partners? If "Yes," the partnership may have to file Forms 8804, 8805 and 8813. See the instructions .

7 Is this partnership a publicly traded partnership as defined in section 469(k)(2)? .

8 Has this partnership filed, or is it required to file, a return under section 6111 to provide information on any reportable transaction?

9 At any time during calendar year 2007, did the partnership have an interest in or a signature or other authority over a financial account in a foreign country (such as a bank account, securities account, or other financial account)? See the instructions for exceptions and filing requirements for Form TD F 90-22.1. If "Yes," enter the name of the foreign country. ▶ ....

10 During the tax year, did the partnership receive a distribution from, or was it the grantor of, or transferor to, a foreign trust? If "Yes," the partnership may have to file Form 3520. See the instructions .

11 Was there a distribution of property or a transfer (for example, by sale or death) of a partnership interest during the tax year? If "Yes," you may elect to adjust the basis of the partnership's assets under section 754 by attaching the statement described under *Elections Made By the Partnership* in the instructions .

12 Enter the number of Forms 8865, Return of U.S. Persons With Respect to Certain Foreign Partnerships, attached to this return ▶ ....

Designation of Tax Matters Partner (see the instructions)
Enter below the general partner designated as the tax matters partner (TMP) for the tax year of this return:

Name of designated TMP ▶		Identifying number of TMP ▶	
Address of designated TMP ▶			

Form 1065 (2007)   Page **3**

Schedule K	**Partners' Distributive Share Items**		**Total amount**	

<table>
<tr><td rowspan="20">Income (Loss)</td><td>1 Ordinary business income (loss) (page 1, line 22) . . . .</td><td></td><td>1</td><td></td></tr>
<tr><td>2 Net rental real estate income (loss) (attach Form 8825) . . . . . .</td><td></td><td>2</td><td></td></tr>
<tr><td>3a Other gross rental income (loss) . . . .</td><td>3a</td><td></td><td></td></tr>
<tr><td>b Expenses from other rental activities (attach statement) . . . .</td><td>3b</td><td></td><td></td></tr>
<tr><td>c Other net rental income (loss). Subtract line 3b from line 3a . . . . . .</td><td></td><td>3c</td><td></td></tr>
<tr><td>4 Guaranteed payments . . . .</td><td></td><td>4</td><td></td></tr>
<tr><td>5 Interest income . . . .</td><td></td><td>5</td><td></td></tr>
<tr><td>6 Dividends: a Ordinary dividends . . . .</td><td></td><td>6a</td><td></td></tr>
<tr><td>b Qualified dividends . . . .</td><td>6b</td><td></td><td></td></tr>
<tr><td>7 Royalties . . . .</td><td></td><td>7</td><td></td></tr>
<tr><td>8 Net short-term capital gain (loss) (attach Schedule D (Form 1065)) . . .</td><td></td><td>8</td><td></td></tr>
<tr><td>9a Net long-term capital gain (loss) (attach Schedule D (Form 1065)) . .</td><td></td><td>9a</td><td></td></tr>
<tr><td>b Collectibles (28%) gain (loss) . . . .</td><td>9b</td><td></td><td></td></tr>
<tr><td>c Unrecaptured section 1250 gain (attach statement) . . . .</td><td>9c</td><td></td><td></td></tr>
<tr><td>10 Net section 1231 gain (loss) (attach Form 4797) . . . .</td><td></td><td>10</td><td></td></tr>
<tr><td>11 Other income (loss) (see instructions) Type ▶ _____</td><td></td><td>11</td><td></td></tr>
</table>

<table>
<tr><td rowspan="5">Deductions</td><td>12 Section 179 deduction (attach Form 4562) . . . .</td><td></td><td>12</td><td></td></tr>
<tr><td>13a Contributions . . . .</td><td></td><td>13a</td><td></td></tr>
<tr><td>b Investment interest expense . . . .</td><td></td><td>13b</td><td></td></tr>
<tr><td>c Section 59(e)(2) expenditures: (1) Type ▶ _____ (2) Amount ▶</td><td></td><td>13c(2)</td><td></td></tr>
<tr><td>d Other deductions (see instructions) Type ▶ _____</td><td></td><td>13d</td><td></td></tr>
</table>

<table>
<tr><td rowspan="3">Self-Employ-ment</td><td>14a Net earnings (loss) from self-employment . . . .</td><td></td><td>14a</td><td></td></tr>
<tr><td>b Gross farming or fishing income . . . .</td><td></td><td>14b</td><td></td></tr>
<tr><td>c Gross nonfarm income . . . .</td><td></td><td>14c</td><td></td></tr>
</table>

<table>
<tr><td rowspan="6">Credits</td><td>15a Low-income housing credit (section 42(j)(5)) . . . .</td><td></td><td>15a</td><td></td></tr>
<tr><td>b Low-income housing credit (other) . . . .</td><td></td><td>15b</td><td></td></tr>
<tr><td>c Qualified rehabilitation expenditures (rental real estate) (attach Form 3468).</td><td></td><td>15c</td><td></td></tr>
<tr><td>d Other rental real estate credits (see instructions) Type ▶ _____</td><td></td><td>15d</td><td></td></tr>
<tr><td>e Other rental credits (see instructions) Type ▶ _____</td><td></td><td>15e</td><td></td></tr>
<tr><td>f Other credits (see instructions) Type ▶ _____</td><td></td><td>15f</td><td></td></tr>
</table>

<table>
<tr><td rowspan="13">Foreign Transactions</td><td>16a Name of country or U.S. possession ▶_____</td><td></td><td></td><td></td></tr>
<tr><td>b Gross income from all sources . . . .</td><td></td><td>16b</td><td></td></tr>
<tr><td>c Gross income sourced at partner level . . . .</td><td></td><td>16c</td><td></td></tr>
<tr><td>Foreign gross income sourced at partnership level</td><td></td><td></td><td></td></tr>
<tr><td>d Passive category ▶ _____ e General category ▶ _____ f Other ▶</td><td></td><td>16f</td><td></td></tr>
<tr><td>Deductions allocated and apportioned at partner level</td><td></td><td></td><td></td></tr>
<tr><td>g Interest expense ▶ _____ h Other . . . . ▶</td><td></td><td>16h</td><td></td></tr>
<tr><td>Deductions allocated and apportioned at partnership level to foreign source income</td><td></td><td></td><td></td></tr>
<tr><td>i Passive category ▶ _____ j General category ▶ _____ k Other ▶</td><td></td><td>16k</td><td></td></tr>
<tr><td>l Total foreign taxes (check one): ▶ Paid ☐ Accrued ☐ . . . . .</td><td></td><td>16l</td><td></td></tr>
<tr><td>m Reduction in taxes available for credit (attach statement) . . . .</td><td></td><td>16m</td><td></td></tr>
<tr><td>n Other foreign tax information (attach statement) . . . .</td><td></td><td></td><td></td></tr>
</table>

<table>
<tr><td rowspan="6">Alternative Minimum Tax (AMT) Items</td><td>17a Post-1986 depreciation adjustment . . . .</td><td></td><td>17a</td><td></td></tr>
<tr><td>b Adjusted gain or loss . . . .</td><td></td><td>17b</td><td></td></tr>
<tr><td>c Depletion (other than oil and gas) . . . .</td><td></td><td>17c</td><td></td></tr>
<tr><td>d Oil, gas, and geothermal properties—gross income . . . . .</td><td></td><td>17d</td><td></td></tr>
<tr><td>e Oil, gas, and geothermal properties—deductions . . . . .</td><td></td><td>17e</td><td></td></tr>
<tr><td>f Other AMT items (attach statement) . . . .</td><td></td><td>17f</td><td></td></tr>
</table>

<table>
<tr><td rowspan="9">Other Information</td><td>18a Tax-exempt interest income . . . .</td><td></td><td>18a</td><td></td></tr>
<tr><td>b Other tax-exempt income . . . .</td><td></td><td>18b</td><td></td></tr>
<tr><td>c Nondeductible expenses . . . .</td><td></td><td>18c</td><td></td></tr>
<tr><td>19a Distributions of cash and marketable securities . . . . . .</td><td></td><td>19a</td><td></td></tr>
<tr><td>b Distributions of other property . . . .</td><td></td><td>19b</td><td></td></tr>
<tr><td>20a Investment income . . . .</td><td></td><td>20a</td><td></td></tr>
<tr><td>b Investment expenses . . . .</td><td></td><td>20b</td><td></td></tr>
<tr><td>c Other items and amounts (attach statement) . . . .</td><td></td><td></td><td></td></tr>
</table>

Form **1065** (2007)

Form 1065 (2007)   Page **4**

Analysis of Net Income (Loss)

1 Net income (loss). Combine Schedule K, lines 1 through 11. From the result, subtract the sum of Schedule K, lines 12 through 13d, and 16l					**1**	

2 Analysis by partner type:	**(i)** Corporate	**(ii)** Individual (active)	**(iii)** Individual (passive)	**(iv)** Partnership	**(v)** Exempt organization	**(vi)** Nominee/Other
a General partners						
b Limited partners						

Schedule L Balance Sheets per Books	Beginning of tax year		End of tax year	
Assets	**(a)**	**(b)**	**(c)**	**(d)**
1 Cash				
2a Trade notes and accounts receivable				
b Less allowance for bad debts				
3 Inventories				
4 U.S. government obligations				
5 Tax-exempt securities				
6 Other current assets (attach statement) . . .				
7 Mortgage and real estate loans				
8 Other investments (attach statement)				
9a Buildings and other depreciable assets. . . .				
b Less accumulated depreciation				
10a Depletable assets				
b Less accumulated depletion				
11 Land (net of any amortization)				
12a Intangible assets (amortizable only)				
b Less accumulated amortization				
13 Other assets (attach statement)				
14 Total assets				
Liabilities and Capital				
15 Accounts payable				
16 Mortgages, notes, bonds payable in less than 1 year .				
17 Other current liabilities (attach statement) . . .				
18 All nonrecourse loans				
19 Mortgages, notes, bonds payable in 1 year or more .				
20 Other liabilities (attach statement)				
21 Partners' capital accounts				
22 Total liabilities and capital				

Schedule M-1   Reconciliation of Income (Loss) per Books With Income (Loss) per Return

Note. Schedule M-3 may be required instead of Schedule M-1 (see instructions).

1 Net income (loss) per books		**6** Income recorded on books this year not included on Schedule K, lines 1 through 11 (itemize):	
2 Income included on Schedule K, lines 1, 2, 3c, 5, 6a, 7, 8, 9a, 10, and 11, not recorded on books this year (itemize): _____		**a** Tax-exempt interest $ _____ _____	
3 Guaranteed payments (other than health insurance)		**7** Deductions included on Schedule K, lines 1 through 13d, and 16l, not charged against book income this year (itemize):	
4 Expenses recorded on books this year not included on Schedule K, lines 1 through 13d, and 16l (itemize):		**a** Depreciation $ _____ _____	
a Depreciation $ _____			
b Travel and entertainment $ _____		**8** Add lines 6 and 7	
_____		**9** Income (loss) (Analysis of Net Income (Loss), line 1). Subtract line 8 from line 5	
5 Add lines 1 through 4			

Schedule M-2   Analysis of Partners' Capital Accounts

1 Balance at beginning of year		**6** Distributions: **a** Cash	
2 Capital contributed: **a** Cash		**b** Property	
b Property . . .		**7** Other decreases (itemize): _____	
3 Net income (loss) per books		_____	
4 Other increases (itemize): _____			
_____		**8** Add lines 6 and 7	
5 Add lines 1 through 4		**9** Balance at end of year. Subtract line 8 from line 5	

Form **1065** (2007)

651107

☐ Final K-1	☐ Amended K-1

OMB No. 1545-0099

Schedule K-1
(Form 1065)

2007

Department of the Treasury
Internal Revenue Service

For calendar year 2007, or tax

year beginning _____ , 2007

ending _____ , 20____

Partner's Share of Income, Deductions, Credits, etc.

See back of form and separate instructions.

Part I	Information About the Partnership

A Partnership's employer identification number

B Partnership's name, address, city, state, and ZIP code

C IRS Center where partnership filed return

D ☐ Check if this is a publicly traded partnership (PTP)

Part II	Information About the Partner

E Partner's identifying number

F Partner's name, address, city, state, and ZIP code

G ☐ General partner or LLC member-manager   ☐ Limited partner or other LLC member

H ☐ Domestic partner   ☐ Foreign partner

I What type of entity is this partner? _____

J Partner's share of profit, loss, and capital:

	Beginning	Ending
Profit	_____ %	_____ %
Loss	_____ %	_____ %
Capital	_____ %	_____ %

K Partner's share of liabilities at year end:

Nonrecourse . . . . $_____

Qualified nonrecourse financing . $_____

Recourse . . . . $_____

L Partner's capital account analysis:

Beginning capital account . . . $_____

Capital contributed during the year . $_____

Current year increase (decrease) . $_____

Withdrawals & distributions . . $(_____)

Ending capital account . . . . $_____

☐ Tax basis   ☐ GAAP   ☐ Section 704(b) book
☐ Other (explain)

Part III	Partner's Share of Current Year Income, Deductions, Credits, and Other Items

1	Ordinary business income (loss)	**15**	Credits
2	Net rental real estate income (loss)		
3	Other net rental income (loss)	**16**	Foreign transactions
4	Guaranteed payments		
5	Interest income		
6a	Ordinary dividends		
6b	Qualified dividends		
7	Royalties		
8	Net short-term capital gain (loss)		
9a	Net long-term capital gain (loss)	**17**	Alternative minimum tax (AMT) items
9b	Collectibles (28%) gain (loss)		
9c	Unrecaptured section 1250 gain		
10	Net section 1231 gain (loss)	**18**	Tax-exempt income and nondeductible expenses
11	Other income (loss)		
		19	Distributions
12	Section 179 deduction		
13	Other deductions	**20**	Other information
14	Self-employment earnings (loss)		

*See attached statement for additional information.

For IRS Use Only

For Paperwork Reduction Act Notice, see Instructions for Form 1065.   Cat. No. 11394R   **Schedule K-1 (Form 1065) 2007**

SCHEDULE M-3
(Form 1065)

Department of the Treasury
Internal Revenue Service

Net Income (Loss) Reconciliation
for Certain Partnerships

Attach to Form 1065 or Form 1065-B.
See separate instructions.

OMB No. 1545-0099

20**07**

Name of partnership

Employer identification number

This Schedule M-3 is being filed because (check all that apply):

A ☐ The amount of the partnership's total assets at the end of the tax year is equal to $10 million or more.

B ☐ The amount of the partnership's adjusted total assets for the year is equal to $10 million or more. If box B is checked, enter the amount of adjusted total assets for the tax year _____ .

C ☐ The amount of total receipts for the taxable year is equal to $35 million or more. If box C is checked, enter the total receipts for the tax year _____ .

D ☐ An entity that is a reportable entity partner with respect to the partnership owns or is deemed to own an interest of 50 percent or more in the partnership's capital, profit, or loss, on any day during the tax year of the partnership.

Name of Reportable Entity Partner	Identifying Number	Maximum Percentage Owned or Deemed Owned

E ☐ Voluntary Filer

Part I	**Financial Information and Net Income (Loss) Reconciliation**

1a Did the partnership file SEC Form 10-K for its income statement period ending with or within this tax year?

   ☐ **Yes.** Skip lines 1b and 1c and complete lines 2 through 11 with respect to that SEC Form 10-K.

   ☐ **No.** Go to line 1b. See instructions if multiple non-tax-basis income statements are prepared.

b Did the partnership prepare a certified audited non-tax-basis income statement for that period?

   ☐ **Yes.** Skip line 1c and complete lines 2 through 11 with respect to that income statement.

   ☐ **No.** Go to line 1c.

c Did the partnership prepare a non-tax-basis income statement for that period?

   ☐ **Yes.** Complete lines 2 through 11 with respect to that income statement.

   ☐ **No.** Skip lines 2 through 3b and enter the partnership's net income (loss) per its books and records on line 4.

2 Enter the income statement period: Beginning ___/___/___   Ending ___/___/___

3a Has the partnership's income statement been restated for the income statement period on line 2?

   ☐ **Yes.** (If "Yes," attach an explanation and the amount of each item restated.)

   ☐ **No.**

b Has the partnership's income statement been restated for any of the five income statement periods preceding the period on line 2?

   ☐ **Yes.** (If "Yes," attach an explanation and the amount of each item restated.)

   ☐ **No.**

4	Worldwide consolidated net income (loss) from income statement source identified in Part I, line 1	**4**	
5a	Net income from nonincludible foreign entities (attach schedule)	**5a**	( )
b	Net loss from nonincludible foreign entities (attach schedule and enter as a positive amount) . .	**5b**	
6a	Net income from nonincludible U.S. entities (attach schedule)	**6a**	( )
b	Net loss from nonincludible U.S. entities (attach schedule and enter as a positive amount) . . .	**6b**	
7a	Net income (loss) of other foreign disregarded entities (attach schedule)	**7a**	
b	Net income (loss) of other U.S. disregarded entities (attach schedule)	**7b**	
8	Adjustment to eliminations of transactions between includible entities and nonincludible entities (attach schedule)	**8**	
9	Adjustment to reconcile income statement period to tax year (attach schedule)	**9**	
10	Other adjustments to reconcile to amount on line 11 (attach schedule)	**10**	
11	**Net income (loss) per income statement of the partnership.** Combine lines 4 through 10 . .	**11**	

For Paperwork Reduction Act Notice, see the Instructions for your return.   Cat. No. 39669D   **Schedule M-3 (Form 1065) 2007**

Schedule M-3 (Form 1065) 2007   Page **2**

Name of partnership	Employer identification number

Part II **Reconciliation of Net Income (Loss) per Income Statement of Partnership with Income (Loss) per Return**

Income (Loss) Items	(a) Income (Loss) per Income Statement	(b) Temporary Difference	(c) Permanent Difference	(d) Income (Loss) per Tax Return
1 Income (loss) from equity method foreign corporations				
2 Gross foreign dividends not previously taxed . .				
3 Subpart F, QEF, and similar income inclusions . .				
4 Gross foreign distributions previously taxed . . .				
5 Income (loss) from equity method U.S. corporations . .				
6 U.S. dividends				
7 Income (loss) from U.S. partnerships (attach schedule) .				
8 Income (loss) from foreign partnerships (attach schedule)				
9 Income (loss) from other pass-through entities (attach schedule)				
10 Items relating to reportable transactions (attach details)				
11 Interest income (attach Form 8916-A)				
12 Total accrual to cash adjustment				
13 Hedging transactions				
14 Mark-to-market income (loss)				
15 Cost of goods sold (attach Form 8916-A)	( )			( )
16 Sale versus lease (for sellers and/or lessors) . . .				
17 Section 481(a) adjustments				
18 Unearned/deferred revenue				
19 Income recognition from long-term contracts . .				
20 Original issue discount and other imputed interest				
21a Income statement gain/loss on sale, exchange, abandonment, worthlessness, or other disposition of assets other than inventory and pass-through entities				
b Gross capital gains from Schedule D, excluding amounts from pass-through entities				
c Gross capital losses from Schedule D, excluding amounts from pass-through entities, abandonment losses, and worthless stock losses				
d Net gain/loss reported on Form 4797, line 17, excluding amounts from pass-through entities, abandonment losses, and worthless stock losses				
e Abandonment losses				
f Worthless stock losses (attach details)				
g Other gain/loss on disposition of assets other than inventory				
22 Other income (loss) items with differences (attach schedule)				
23 **Total income (loss) items.** Combine lines 1 through 22				
24 **Total expense/deduction items** (from Part III, line 30)				
25 Other items with no differences				
26 **Reconciliation totals.** Combine lines 23 through 25 .				

Note. Line 26, column (a), must equal the amount on Part I, line 11, and column (d) must equal Form 1065, page 4, Analysis of Net Income (Loss), line 1.

Schedule M-3 (Form 1065) 2007

Page **3**

Name of partnership	Employer identification number

Part III **Reconciliation of Net Income (Loss) per Income Statement of Partnership With Income (Loss) per Return—Expense/Deduction Items**

	Expense/Deduction Items	(a) Expense per Income Statement	(b) Temporary Difference	(c) Permanent Difference	(d) Deduction per Tax Return
1	State and local current income tax expense				
2	State and local deferred income tax expense				
3	Foreign current income tax expense (other than foreign withholding taxes)				
4	Foreign deferred income tax expense				
5	Equity-based compensation				
6	Meals and entertainment				
7	Fines and penalties				
8	Judgments, damages, awards, and similar costs				
9	Guaranteed payments				
10	Pension and profit-sharing				
11	Other post-retirement benefits				
12	Deferred compensation				
13	Charitable contribution of cash and tangible property				
14	Charitable contribution of intangible property				
15	Organizational expenses as per Regulations section 1.709-2(a)				
16	Syndication expenses as per Regulations section 1.709-2(b)				
17	Current year acquisition/reorganization investment banking fees				
18	Current year acquisition/reorganization legal and accounting fees				
19	Amortization/impairment of goodwill				
20	Amortization of acquisition, reorganization, and start-up costs				
21	Other amortization or impairment write-offs				
22	Section 198 environmental remediation costs				
23a	Depletion—Oil & Gas				
b	Depletion—Other than Oil & Gas				
24	Intangible drilling & development costs				
25	Depreciation				
26	Bad debt expense				
27	Interest expense (attach Form 8916-A)				
28	Purchase versus lease (for purchasers and/or lessees)				
29	Other expense/deduction items with differences (attach schedule)				
30	**Total expense/deduction items.** Combine lines 1 through 29. Enter here and on Part II, line 24				

Schedule M-3 (Form 1065) 2007

Form 1120
Department of the Treasury
Internal Revenue Service

U.S. Corporation Income Tax Return

For calendar year 2007 or tax year beginning .... , 2007, ending .... , 20 ....
► See separate instructions.

OMB No. 1545-0123

2007

A Check if:

1a Consolidated return (attach Form 851) ☐
  b Life/nonlife consoli-dated return . ☐
2 Personal holding co. (attach Sch. PH) ☐
3 Personal service corp. (see instructions) . ☐
4 Schedule M-3 attached ☐

Use IRS label. Otherwise, print or type.

Name

Number, street, and room or suite no. If a P.O. box, see instructions.

City or town, state, and ZIP code

B Employer identification number

C Date incorporated

D Total assets (see instructions)
$

E Check if: (1) ☐ Initial return (2) ☐ Final return (3) ☐ Name change (4) ☐ Address change

Income	1a	Gross receipts or sales [____] **b** Less returns and allowances [____] **c** Bal ►	1c	
	2	Cost of goods sold (Schedule A, line 8)	2	
	3	Gross profit. Subtract line 2 from line 1c	3	
	4	Dividends (Schedule C, line 19)	4	
	5	Interest	5	
	6	Gross rents	6	
	7	Gross royalties	7	
	8	Capital gain net income (attach Schedule D (Form 1120))	8	
	9	Net gain or (loss) from Form 4797, Part II, line 17 (attach Form 4797)	9	
	10	Other income (see instructions—attach schedule)	10	
	11	**Total income.** Add lines 3 through 10 . . . . ►	11	

Deductions (See instructions for limitations on deductions.)	12	Compensation of officers (Schedule E, line 4)	12	
	13	Salaries and wages (less employment credits)	13	
	14	Repairs and maintenance	14	
	15	Bad debts	15	
	16	Rents	16	
	17	Taxes and licenses	17	
	18	Interest	18	
	19	Charitable contributions	19	
	20	Depreciation from Form 4562 not claimed on Schedule A or elsewhere on return (attach Form 4562)	20	
	21	Depletion	21	
	22	Advertising	22	
	23	Pension, profit-sharing, etc., plans	23	
	24	Employee benefit programs	24	
	25	Domestic production activities deduction (attach Form 8903)	25	
	26	Other deductions (attach schedule)	26	
	27	**Total deductions.** Add lines 12 through 26 . . . . ►	27	
	28	Taxable income before net operating loss deduction and special deductions. Subtract line 27 from line 11	28	
	29	**Less: a** Net operating loss deduction (see instructions).	29a	
		b Special deductions (Schedule C, line 20)	29b	29c

Tax and Payments	30	**Taxable income.** Subtract line 29c from line 28 (see instructions)	30	
	31	**Total tax** (Schedule J, line 10)	31	
	32 a	2006 overpayment credited to 2007 .	32a		
	b	2007 estimated tax payments . . .	32b		
	c	2007 refund applied for on Form 4466 .	32c ( ) **d Bal** ►	32d	
	e	Tax deposited with Form 7004	32e	
	f	Credits: (1) Form 2439 _____ (2) Form 4136 _____	32f	32g
	33	Estimated tax penalty (see instructions). Check if Form 2220 is attached . . . ► ☐	33	
	34	**Amount owed.** If line 32g is smaller than the total of lines 31 and 33, enter amount owed	34	
	35	**Overpayment.** If line 32g is larger than the total of lines 31 and 33, enter amount overpaid . . .	35	
	36	Enter amount from line 35 you want: **Credited to 2008 estimated tax** ► _____ **Refunded** ►	36	

Sign Here

Under penalties of perjury, I declare that I have examined this return, including accompanying schedules and statements, and to the best of my knowledge and belief, it is true, correct, and complete. Declaration of preparer (other than taxpayer) is based on all information of which preparer has any knowledge.

► _____ _____ ► _____
Signature of officer   Date   Title

May the IRS discuss this return with the preparer shown below (see instructions)? ☐ **Yes** ☐ **No**

Paid Preparer's Use Only

Preparer's signature ► _____ Date _____ Check if self-employed ☐ Preparer's SSN or PTIN _____

Firm's name (or yours if self-employed), address, and ZIP code ► _____ EIN _____ Phone no. ( )

For Privacy Act and Paperwork Reduction Act Notice, see separate instructions.   Cat. No. 11450Q   Form **1120** (2007)

Form 1120 (2007)   Page **2**

Schedule A   Cost of Goods Sold (see instructions)

1	Inventory at beginning of year	**1**
2	Purchases.	**2**
3	Cost of labor	**3**
4	Additional section 263A costs (attach schedule)	**4**
5	Other costs (attach schedule)	**5**
6	**Total.** Add lines 1 through 5	**6**
7	Inventory at end of year	**7**
8	**Cost of goods sold.** Subtract line 7 from line 6. Enter here and on page 1, line 2	**8**

9a Check all methods used for valuing closing inventory:

    (i) ☐ Cost

    (ii) ☐ Lower of cost or market

    (iii) ☐ Other (Specify method used and attach explanation.) ▶ --

  b Check if there was a writedown of subnormal goods . . . . ▶ ☐

  c Check if the LIFO inventory method was adopted this tax year for any goods (if checked, attach Form 970) . . . . ▶ ☐

  d If the LIFO inventory method was used for this tax year, enter percentage (or amounts) of closing inventory computed under LIFO **9d**

  e If property is produced or acquired for resale, do the rules of section 263A apply to the corporation? . . . . . ☐ Yes ☐ No

  f Was there any change in determining quantities, cost, or valuations between opening and closing inventory? If "Yes," attach explanation . . . . ☐ Yes ☐ No

Schedule C   Dividends and Special Deductions (see instructions)

		(a) Dividends received	(b) %	(c) Special deductions (a) ? (b)
1	Dividends from less-than-20%-owned domestic corporations (other than debt-financed stock)		70	
2	Dividends from 20%-or-more-owned domestic corporations (other than debt-financed stock)		80	
3	Dividends on debt-financed stock of domestic and foreign corporations		see instructions	
4	Dividends on certain preferred stock of less-than-20%-owned public utilities . . .		42	
5	Dividends on certain preferred stock of 20%-or-more-owned public utilities		48	
6	Dividends from less-than-20%-owned foreign corporations and certain FSCs . . .		70	
7	Dividends from 20%-or-more-owned foreign corporations and certain FSCs		80	
8	Dividends from wholly owned foreign subsidiaries		100	
9	**Total.** Add lines 1 through 8. See instructions for limitation			
10	Dividends from domestic corporations received by a small business investment company operating under the Small Business Investment Act of 1958		100	
11	Dividends from affiliated group members		100	
12	Dividends from certain FSCs		100	
13	Dividends from foreign corporations not included on lines 3, 6, 7, 8, 11, or 12 . . .			
14	Income from controlled foreign corporations under subpart F (attach Form(s) 5471) . .			
15	Foreign dividend gross-up			
16	IC-DISC and former DISC dividends not included on lines 1, 2, or 3			
17	Other dividends			
18	Deduction for dividends paid on certain preferred stock of public utilities			
19	**Total dividends.** Add lines 1 through 17. Enter here and on page 1, line 4 . . . ▶			
20	**Total special deductions.** Add lines 9, 10, 11, 12, and 18. Enter here and on page 1, line 29b . . . . ▶			

Schedule E   Compensation of Officers (see instructions for page 1, line 12)

Note: *Complete Schedule E only if total receipts (line 1a plus lines 4 through 10 on page 1) are $500,000 or more.*

	(a) Name of officer	(b) Social security number	(c) Percent of time devoted to business	Percent of corporation stock owned		(f) Amount of compensation
				(d) Common	(e) Preferred	
1			%	%	%	
			%	%	%	
			%	%	%	
			%	%	%	
			%	%	%	
2	Total compensation of officers					
3	Compensation of officers claimed on Schedule A and elsewhere on return					
4	Subtract line 3 from line 2. Enter the result here and on page 1, line 12					

Form **1120** (2007)

Schedule J   Tax Computation (see instructions)

1	Check if the corporation is a member of a controlled group (attach Schedule O (Form 1120)) ▶ ☐	
2	Income tax. Check if a qualified personal service corporation (see instructions) ▶ ☐	2
3	Alternative minimum tax (attach Form 4626).	3
4	Add lines 2 and 3	4

		5a	
5a	Foreign tax credit (attach Form 1118)	5a	
b	Credits from Forms 5735 and 8834	5b	
c	General business credit. Check applicable box(es): ☐ Form 3800 ☐ Form 5884 ☐ Form 6478 ☐ Form 8835, Section B ☐ Form 8844 ☐ Form 8846	5c	
d	Credit for prior year minimum tax (attach Form 8827)	5d	
e	Bond credits from: ☐ Form 8860 ☐ Form 8912	5e	

6	**Total credits.** Add lines 5a through 5e	6
7	Subtract line 6 from line 4	7
8	Personal holding company tax (attach Schedule PH (Form 1120))	8
9	Other taxes. Check if from: ☐ Form 4255 ☐ Form 8611 ☐ Form 8697 ☐ Form 8866 ☐ Form 8902 ☐ Other (attach schedule)	9
10	**Total tax.** Add lines 7 through 9. Enter here and on page 1, line 31	10

Schedule K   Other Information (see instructions)

Yes | No

1 Check accounting method: **a** ☐ Cash **b** ☐ Accrual **c** ☐ Other (specify) ▶ ....

2 See the instructions and enter the:

a Business activity code no. ▶ ....

b Business activity ▶ ....

c Product or service ▶ ....

3 At the end of the tax year, did the corporation own, directly or indirectly, 50% or more of the voting stock of a domestic corporation? (For rules of attribution, see section 267(c).)

If "Yes," attach a schedule showing: (a) name and employer identification number (EIN), (b) percentage owned, and (c) taxable income or (loss) before NOL and special deduction of such corporation for the tax year ending with or within your tax year.

4 Is the corporation a subsidiary in an affiliated group or a parent-subsidiary controlled group?

If "Yes," enter name and EIN of the parent corporation ▶ ....

5 At the end of the tax year, did any individual, partnership, corporation, estate, or trust own, directly or indirectly, 50% or more of the corporation's voting stock? (For rules of attribution, see section 267(c).)

If "Yes," attach a schedule showing name and identifying number. (Do not include any information already entered in 4 above.) Enter percentage owned ▶ ....

6 During this tax year, did the corporation pay dividends (other than stock dividends and distributions in exchange for stock) in excess of the corporation's current and accumulated earnings and profits? (See sections 301 and 316.)

If "Yes," file **Form 5452,** Corporate Report of Nondividend Distributions.

If this is a consolidated return, answer here for the parent corporation and on **Form 851,** Affiliations Schedule, for each subsidiary.

Yes | No

7 At any time during the tax year, did one foreign person own, directly or indirectly, at least 25% of **(a)** the total voting power of all classes of stock of the corporation entitled to vote or **(b)** the total value of all classes of stock of the corporation?

If "Yes," enter: **(a)** Percentage owned ▶ ....

and **(b)** Owner's country ▶ ....

c The corporation may have to file **Form 5472,** Information Return of a 25% Foreign-Owned U.S. Corporation or a Foreign Corporation Engaged in a U.S. Trade or Business. Enter number of Forms 5472 attached ▶ ....

8 Check this box if the corporation issued publicly offered debt instruments with original issue discount. ▶ ☐

If checked, the corporation may have to file **Form 8281,** Information Return for Publicly Offered Original Issue Discount Instruments.

9 Enter the amount of tax-exempt interest received or accrued during the tax year ▶ $ ....

10 Enter the number of shareholders at the end of the tax year (if 100 or fewer) ▶ ....

11 If the corporation has an NOL for the tax year and is electing to forego the carryback period, check here . . ▶ ☐

If the corporation is filing a consolidated return, the statement required by Regulations section 1.1502-21(b)(3) must be attached or the election will not be valid.

12 Enter the available NOL carryover from prior tax years (Do not reduce it by any deduction on line 29a.) ▶ $ ....

13 Are the corporation's total receipts (line 1a plus lines 4 through 10 on page 1) for the tax year **and** its total assets at the end of the tax year less than $250,000? . . . .

If "Yes," the corporation is not required to complete Schedules L, M-1, and M-2 on page 4. Instead, enter the total amount of cash distributions and the book value of property distributions (other than cash) made during the tax year. ▶ $ ....

Form 1120 (2007)   Page **4**

Schedule L	**Balance Sheets per Books**	Beginning of tax year		End of tax year	
	Assets	(a)	(b)	(c)	(d)
1	Cash				
2a	Trade notes and accounts receivable . . .				
b	Less allowance for bad debts	( )		( )	
3	Inventories				
4	U.S. government obligations				
5	Tax-exempt securities (see instructions) . .				
6	Other current assets (attach schedule) . .				
7	Loans to shareholders				
8	Mortgage and real estate loans . . .				
9	Other investments (attach schedule) . . .				
10a	Buildings and other depreciable assets . .				
b	Less accumulated depreciation	( )		( )	
11a	Depletable assets				
b	Less accumulated depletion	( )		( )	
12	Land (net of any amortization)				
13a	Intangible assets (amortizable only) . . .				
b	Less accumulated amortization	( )		( )	
14	Other assets (attach schedule)				
15	Total assets				
	Liabilities and Shareholders' Equity				
16	Accounts payable				
17	Mortgages, notes, bonds payable in less than 1 year				
18	Other current liabilities (attach schedule) .				
19	Loans from shareholders				
20	Mortgages, notes, bonds payable in 1 year or more				
21	Other liabilities (attach schedule)				
22	Capital stock: **a** Preferred stock . . .				
	b Common stock . . .				
23	Additional paid-in capital				
24	Retained earnings—Appropriated (attach schedule)				
25	Retained earnings—Unappropriated . . .				
26	Adjustments to shareholders' equity (attach schedule)				
27	Less cost of treasury stock		( )		( )
28	Total liabilities and shareholders' equity . .				

Schedule M-1	**Reconciliation of Income (Loss) per Books With Income per Return**
	Note: Schedule M-3 required instead of Schedule M-1 if total assets are $10 million or more—see instructions

1	Net income (loss) per books		7	Income recorded on books this year not included on this return (itemize):	
2	Federal income tax per books				
3	Excess of capital losses over capital gains .			Tax-exempt interest $ _____	
4	Income subject to tax not recorded on books this year (itemize): _____			_____	
	_____		8	Deductions on this return not charged against book income this year (itemize):	
5	Expenses recorded on books this year not deducted on this return (itemize):		a	Depreciation . . . . $ _____	
a	Depreciation . . . . $ _____		b	Charitable contributions $ _____	
b	Charitable contributions $ _____			_____	
c	Travel and entertainment $ _____			_____	
	_____		9	Add lines 7 and 8	
6	Add lines 1 through 5		10	Income (page 1, line 28)—line 6 less line 9	

Schedule M-2	**Analysis of Unappropriated Retained Earnings per Books (Line 25, Schedule L)**

1	Balance at beginning of year		5	Distributions: **a** Cash	
2	Net income (loss) per books			**b** Stock	
3	Other increases (itemize): _____			**c** Property	
	_____		6	Other decreases (itemize): _____	
			7	Add lines 5 and 6	
4	Add lines 1, 2, and 3		8	Balance at end of year (line 4 less line 7)	

Form **1120** (2007)

SCHEDULE M-3 (Form 1120) Department of the Treasury Internal Revenue Service	**Net Income (Loss) Reconciliation for Corporations With Total Assets of \$10 Million or More** ▶ Attach to Form 1120 or 1120-C. ▶ See separate instructions.	OMB No. 1545-0123 **2007**

Name of corporation (common parent, if consolidated return)

Employer identification number

Check applicable box(es): (1) ☐ Non-Consolidated return (2) ☐ Consolidated return (Form 1120 only)
(3) ☐ Mixed 1120/L/PC group (4) ☐ Dormant subsidiaries schedule attached

Part I **Financial Information and Net Income (Loss) Reconciliation** (see instructions)

1a Did the corporation file SEC Form 10-K for its income statement period ending with or within this tax year?
  ☐ **Yes.** Skip lines 1b and 1c and complete lines 2a through 11 with respect to that SEC Form 10-K.
  ☐ **No.** Go to line 1b. See instructions if multiple non-tax-basis income statements are prepared.
b Did the corporation prepare a certified audited non-tax-basis income statement for that period?
  ☐ **Yes.** Skip line 1c and complete lines 2a through 11 with respect to that income statement.
  ☐ **No.** Go to line 1c.
c Did the corporation prepare a non-tax-basis income statement for that period?
  ☐ **Yes.** Complete lines 2a through 11 with respect to that income statement.
  ☐ **No.** Skip lines 2a through 3c and enter the corporation's net income (loss) per its books and records on line 4.
2a Enter the income statement period: Beginning _____/_____/_____ Ending _____/_____/_____
b Has the corporation's income statement been restated for the income statement period on line 2a?
  ☐ **Yes.** (If "Yes," attach an explanation and the amount of each item restated.)
  ☐ **No.**
c Has the corporation's income statement been restated for any of the five income statement periods preceding the period on line 2a?
  ☐ **Yes.** (If "Yes," attach an explanation and the amount of each item restated.)
  ☐ **No.**
3a Is any of the corporation's voting common stock publicly traded?
  ☐ **Yes.**
  ☐ **No.** If "No," go to line 4.
b Enter the symbol of the corporation's primary U.S. publicly traded voting common
  stock . . . .
c Enter the nine-digit CUSIP number of the corporation's primary publicly traded voting
  common stock . . . .

4 Worldwide consolidated net income (loss) from income statement source identified in Part I, line 1	**4**	
5a Net income from nonincludible foreign entities (attach schedule)	**5a**	( )
b Net loss from nonincludible foreign entities (attach schedule and enter as a positive amount) . .	**5b**	
6a Net income from nonincludible U.S. entities (attach schedule)	**6a**	( )
b Net loss from nonincludible U.S. entities (attach schedule and enter as a positive amount) . . .	**6b**	
7a Net income (loss) of other disregarded entities (attach schedule)	**7a**	
b Net income (loss) of other includible entities (attach schedule)	**7b**	
8 Adjustment to eliminations of transactions between includible entities and nonincludible entities (attach schedule)	**8**	
9 Adjustment to reconcile income statement period to tax year (attach schedule)	**9**	
10a Intercompany dividend adjustments to reconcile to line 11 (attach schedule)	**10a**	
b Other statutory accounting adjustments to reconcile to line 11 (attach schedule)	**10b**	
c Other adjustments to reconcile to amount on line 11 (attach schedule)	**10c**	
11 **Net income (loss) per income statement of includible corporations.** Combine lines 4 through 10 .	**11**	

For Paperwork Reduction Act Notice, see the Instructions for Form 1120. Cat. No. 37961C **Schedule M-3 (Form 1120) 2007**

Schedule M-3 (Form 1120) 2007

Page **2**

| Name of corporation (common parent, if consolidated return) | Employer identification number |

Check applicable box(es): **(1)** ☐ Consolidated group **(2)** ☐ Parent corp **(3)** ☐ Consolidated eliminations **(4)** ☐ Subsidiary corp **(5)** ☐ Mixed 1120/L/PC group

Check if a sub-consolidated: **(6)** ☐ 1120 group **(7)** ☐ 1120 eliminations

| Name of subsidiary (if consolidated return) | Employer identification number |

Part II — Reconciliation of Net Income (Loss) per Income Statement of Includible Corporations With Taxable Income per Return (see instructions)

Income (Loss) Items (Attach schedules for lines 1 through 8)	(a) Income (Loss) per Income Statement	(b) Temporary Difference	(c) Permanent Difference	(d) Income (Loss) per Tax Return
1 Income (loss) from equity method foreign corporations				
2 Gross foreign dividends not previously taxed . .				
3 Subpart F, QEF, and similar income inclusions . .				
4 Section 78 gross-up				
5 Gross foreign distributions previously taxed . . .				
6 Income (loss) from equity method U.S. corporations . .				
7 U.S. dividends not eliminated in tax consolidation .				
8 Minority interest for includible corporations . . .				
9 Income (loss) from U.S. partnerships (attach schedule) .				
10 Income (loss) from foreign partnerships (attach schedule)				
11 Income (loss) from other pass-through entities (attach schedule)				
12 Items relating to reportable transactions (attach details)				
13 Interest income (attach Form 8916-A)				
14 Total accrual to cash adjustment				
15 Hedging transactions				
16 Mark-to-market income (loss)				
17 Cost of goods sold (attach Form 8916-A)	( )			( )
18 Sale versus lease (for sellers and/or lessors) . . .				
19 Section 481(a) adjustments				
20 Unearned/deferred revenue				
21 Income recognition from long-term contracts . .				
22 Original issue discount and other imputed interest				
23a Income statement gain/loss on sale, exchange, abandonment, worthlessness, or other disposition of assets other than inventory and pass-through entities				
b Gross capital gains from Schedule D, excluding amounts from pass-through entities				
c Gross capital losses from Schedule D, excluding amounts from pass-through entities, abandonment losses, and worthless stock losses				
d Net gain/loss reported on Form 4797, line 17, excluding amounts from pass-through entities, abandonment losses, and worthless stock losses .				
e Abandonment losses				
f Worthless stock losses (attach details)				
g Other gain/loss on disposition of assets other than inventory				
24 Capital loss limitation and carryforward used . . .				
25 Other income (loss) items with differences (attach schedule)				
26 **Total income (loss) items.** Combine lines 1 through 25				
27 **Total expense/deduction items** (from Part III, line 36) .				
28 Other items with no differences				
29a Mixed groups, see instructions. All others, add lines 26 through 28				
b PC insurance subgroup reconciliation totals . . .				
c Life insurance subgroup reconciliation totals . . .				
30 **Reconciliation totals.** Combine lines 29a through 29c .				

Note. Line 30, column (a), must equal the amount on Part I, line 11, and column (d) must equal Form 1120, page 1, line 28.

Schedule M-3 (Form 1120) 2007

Schedule M-3 (Form 1120) 2007   Page **3**

Name of corporation (common parent, if consolidated return)	Employer identification number

Check applicable box(es): **(1)** ☐ Consolidated group **(2)** ☐ Parent corp **(3)** ☐ Consolidated eliminations **(4)** ☐ Subsidiary corp **(5)** ☐ Mixed 1120/L/PC group

Check if a sub-consolidated: **(6)** ☐ 1120 group **(7)** ☐ 1120 eliminations

Name of subsidiary (if consolidated return)	Employer identification number

Part III **Reconciliation of Net Income (Loss) per Income Statement of Includible Corporations With Taxable Income per Return—Expense/Deduction Items** (see instructions)

Expense/Deduction Items	(a) Expense per Income Statement	(b) Temporary Difference	(c) Permanent Difference	(d) Deduction per Tax Return
1 U.S. current income tax expense				
2 U.S. deferred income tax expense				
3 State and local current income tax expense				
4 State and local deferred income tax expense				
5 Foreign current income tax expense (other than foreign withholding taxes)				
6 Foreign deferred income tax expense				
7 Foreign withholding taxes				
8 Interest expense (attach Form 8916-A)				
9 Stock option expense				
10 Other equity-based compensation				
11 Meals and entertainment				
12 Fines and penalties				
13 Judgments, damages, awards, and similar costs				
14 Parachute payments				
15 Compensation with section 162(m) limitation				
16 Pension and profit-sharing				
17 Other post-retirement benefits				
18 Deferred compensation				
19 Charitable contribution of cash and tangible property				
20 Charitable contribution of intangible property				
21 Charitable contribution limitation/carryforward				
22 Domestic production activities deduction				
23 Current year acquisition or reorganization investment banking fees				
24 Current year acquisition or reorganization legal and accounting fees				
25 Current year acquisition/reorganization other costs				
26 Amortization/impairment of goodwill				
27 Amortization of acquisition, reorganization, and start-up costs				
28 Other amortization or impairment write-offs				
29 Section 198 environmental remediation costs				
30 Depletion				
31 Depreciation				
32 Bad debt expense				
33 Corporate owned life insurance premiums				
34 Purchase versus lease (for purchasers and/or lessees)				
35 Other expense/deduction items with differences (attach schedule)				
36 **Total expense/deduction items.** Combine lines 1 through 35. Enter here and on Part II, line 27				

Schedule M-3 (Form 1120) 2007

Form 1120S

Department of the Treasury
Internal Revenue Service

U.S. Income Tax Return for an S Corporation

▶ Do not file this form unless the corporation has filed or is attaching Form 2553 to elect to be an S corporation.

▶ See separate instructions.

OMB No. 1545-0130

2007

For calendar year 2007 or tax year beginning , 2007, ending , 20

A S election effective date	Use IRS label. Otherwise, print or type.	Name	D Employer identification number
B Business activity code number (see instructions)		Number, street, and room or suite no. If a P.O. box, see instructions.	E Date incorporated
C Check if Sch. M-3 attached ☐		City or town, state, and ZIP code	F Total assets (see instructions) $

G Is the corporation electing to be an S corporation beginning with this tax year? ☐ Yes ☐ No   If "Yes," attach Form 2553 if not already filed

H Check if: (1) ☐ Final return   (2) ☐ Name change   (3) ☐ Address change
(4) ☐ Amended return   (5) ☐ S election termination or revocation

I Enter the number of shareholders in the corporation at the end of the tax year . . . . ▶

Caution. Include **only** trade or business income and expenses on lines 1a through 21. See the instructions for more information.

Income

1a	Gross receipts or sales	b Less returns and allowances	c Bal ▶	1c	
2	Cost of goods sold (Schedule A, line 8)		2	
3	Gross profit. Subtract line 2 from line 1c		3	
4	Net gain (loss) from Form 4797, Part II, line 17 (attach Form 4797)		4	
5	Other income (loss) (see instructions—attach statement)		5	
6	**Total income (loss).** Add lines 3 through 5. . . . . ▶		6	

Deductions (see instructions for limitations)

7	Compensation of officers	7	
8	Salaries and wages (less employment credits)	8	
9	Repairs and maintenance	9	
10	Bad debts	10	
11	Rents	11	
12	Taxes and licenses	12	
13	Interest	13	
14	Depreciation not claimed on Schedule A or elsewhere on return (attach Form 4562)	14	
15	Depletion (**Do not deduct oil and gas depletion.**)	15	
16	Advertising	16	
17	Pension, profit-sharing, etc., plans	17	
18	Employee benefit programs	18	
19	Other deductions (attach statement)	19	
20	**Total deductions.** Add lines 7 through 19 . . . . ▶	20	
21	**Ordinary business income (loss).** Subtract line 20 from line 6	21	

Tax and Payments

22a	Excess net passive income or LIFO recapture tax (see instructions) .	22a		
b	Tax from Schedule D (Form 1120S)	22b		
c	Add lines 22a and 22b (see instructions for additional taxes) . . .		22c	
23a	2007 estimated tax payments and 2006 overpayment credited to 2007	23a		
b	Tax deposited with Form 7004	23b		
c	Credit for federal tax paid on fuels (attach Form 4136)	23c		
d	Add lines 23a through 23c		23d	
24	Estimated tax penalty (see instructions). Check if Form 2220 is attached . . . . . ▶ ☐		24	
25	**Amount owed.** If line 23d is smaller than the total of lines 22c and 24, enter amount owed . .		25	
26	**Overpayment.** If line 23d is larger than the total of lines 22c and 24, enter amount overpaid .		26	
27	Enter amount from line 26 **Credited to 2008 estimated tax** ▶	Refunded ▶	27	

Sign Here

Under penalties of perjury, I declare that I have examined this return, including accompanying schedules and statements, and to the best of my knowledge and belief, it is true, correct, and complete. Declaration of preparer (other than taxpayer) is based on all information of which preparer has any knowledge.

▶ _____   _____   _____
Signature of officer   Date   Title

May the IRS discuss this return with the preparer shown below (see instructions)? ☐ Yes ☐ No

Paid Preparer's Use Only

Preparer's signature ▶		Date	Check if self-employed ☐	Preparer's SSN or PTIN
Firm's name (or yours if self-employed), address, and ZIP code ▶			EIN	
			Phone no. ( )	

For Privacy Act and Paperwork Reduction Act Notice, see separate instructions.   Cat. No. 11510H   Form **1120S** (2007)

Form 1120S (2007)   Page **2**

Schedule A   Cost of Goods Sold (see instructions)

1	Inventory at beginning of year	**1**	
2	Purchases	**2**	
3	Cost of labor	**3**	
4	Additional section 263A costs (attach statement)	**4**	
5	Other costs (attach statement)	**5**	
6	**Total.** Add lines 1 through 5	**6**	
7	Inventory at end of year	**7**	
8	**Cost of goods sold.** Subtract line 7 from line 6. Enter here and on page 1, line 2	**8**	

9a Check all methods used for valuing closing inventory: (i) ☐ Cost as described in Regulations section 1.471-3

    (ii) ☐ Lower of cost or market as described in Regulations section 1.471-4

    (iii) ☐ Other (Specify method used and attach explanation.) ▶ ------------------------------------

b Check if there was a writedown of subnormal goods as described in Regulations section 1.471-2(c) . . . . ▶ ☐

c Check if the LIFO inventory method was adopted this tax year for any goods (if checked, attach Form 970) . . . . . ▶ ☐

d If the LIFO inventory method was used for this tax year, enter percentage (or amounts) of closing inventory computed under LIFO . . . . **9d** | |

e If property is produced or acquired for resale, do the rules of section 263A apply to the corporation? . . . . ☐ Yes ☐ No

f Was there any change in determining quantities, cost, or valuations between opening and closing inventory? . . ☐ Yes ☐ No
If "Yes," attach explanation.

Schedule B   Other Information (see instructions)

		Yes	No
1	Check accounting method: **a** ☐ Cash **b** ☐ Accrual **c** ☐ Other (specify) ▶----------------------		
2	See the instructions and enter the:		
	a Business activity ▶---------------------------------- **b** Product or service ▶----------------------		
3	At the end of the tax year, did the corporation own, directly or indirectly, 50% or more of the voting stock of a domestic corporation? (For rules of attribution, see section 267(c).) If "Yes," attach a statement showing: **(a)** name and employer identification number (EIN), **(b)** percentage owned, and **(c)** if 100% owned, was a QSub election made?		
4	Has this corporation filed, or is it required to file, a return under section 6111 to provide information on any reportable transaction?		
5	Check this box if the corporation issued publicly offered debt instruments with original issue discount . . ▶ ☐		
	If checked, the corporation may have to file **Form 8281,** Information Return for Publicly Offered Original Issue Discount Instruments.		
6	If the corporation: **(a)** was a C corporation before it elected to be an S corporation **or** the corporation acquired an asset with a basis determined by reference to its basis (or the basis of any other property) in the hands of a C corporation **and (b)** has net unrealized built-in gain (defined in section 1374(d)(1)) in excess of the net recognized built-in gain from prior years, enter the net unrealized built-in gain reduced by net recognized built-in gain from prior years . . . . ▶ $----------------------		
7	Enter the accumulated earnings and profits of the corporation at the end of the tax year. $-----------		
8	Are the corporation's total receipts (see instructions) for the tax year **and** its total assets at the end of the tax year less than $250,000? If "Yes," the corporation is not required to complete Schedules L and M-1		

Schedule K   Shareholders' Pro Rata Share Items

				Total amount
Income (Loss)	**1** Ordinary business income (loss) (page 1, line 21)		**1**	
	2 Net rental real estate income (loss) (attach Form 8825)		**2**	
	3a Other gross rental income (loss)	**3a**		
	b Expenses from other rental activities (attach statement) . .	**3b**		
	c Other net rental income (loss). Subtract line 3b from line 3a		**3c**	
	4 Interest income		**4**	
	5 Dividends: **a** Ordinary dividends		**5a**	
	b Qualified dividends	**5b**		
	6 Royalties		**6**	
	7 Net short-term capital gain (loss) (attach Schedule D (Form 1120S))		**7**	
	8a Net long-term capital gain (loss) (attach Schedule D (Form 1120S))		**8a**	
	b Collectibles (28%) gain (loss)	**8b**		
	c Unrecaptured section 1250 gain (attach statement) . . .	**8c**		
	9 Net section 1231 gain (loss) (attach Form 4797)		**9**	
	10 Other income (loss) (see instructions) . . . Type ▶		**10**	

Form **1120S** (2007)

Form 1120S (2007)   Page **3**

	Shareholders' Pro Rata Share Items (continued)		Total amount	
Deductions	**11** Section 179 deduction (attach Form 4562)	**11**		
	12a Contributions	**12a**		
	b Investment interest expense	**12b**		
	c Section 59(e)(2) expenditures **(1)** Type ▶_____ **(2)** Amount ▶	**12c(2)**		
	d Other deductions (see instructions) . . . . Type ▶	**12d**		
Credits	**13a** Low-income housing credit (section 42(j)(5))	**13a**		
	b Low-income housing credit (other)	**13b**		
	c Qualified rehabilitation expenditures (rental real estate) (attach Form 3468)	**13c**		
	d Other rental real estate credits (see instructions) Type ▶ _____	**13d**		
	e Other rental credits (see instructions) . . . Type ▶ _____	**13e**		
	f Credit for alcohol used as fuel (attach Form 6478)	**13f**		
	g Other credits (see instructions) . . . . . .Type ▶	**13g**		
Foreign Transactions	**14a** Name of country or U.S. possession ▶_____			
	b Gross income from all sources	**14b**		
	c Gross income sourced at shareholder level	**14c**		
	Foreign gross income sourced at corporate level			
	d Passive category	**14d**		
	e General category	**14e**		
	f Other (attach statement)	**14f**		
	Deductions allocated and apportioned at shareholder level			
	g Interest expense	**14g**		
	h Other	**14h**		
	Deductions allocated and apportioned at corporate level to foreign source income			
	i Passive category	**14i**		
	j General category	**14j**		
	k Other (attach statement)	**14k**		
	Other information			
	l Total foreign taxes (check one): ▶ ☐ Paid ☐ Accrued	**14l**		
	m Reduction in taxes available for credit (attach statement)	**14m**		
	n Other foreign tax information (attach statement)			
Alternative Minimum Tax (AMT) Items	**15a** Post-1986 depreciation adjustment	**15a**		
	b Adjusted gain or loss	**15b**		
	c Depletion (other than oil and gas)	**15c**		
	d Oil, gas, and geothermal properties—gross income	**15d**		
	e Oil, gas, and geothermal properties—deductions.	**15e**		
	f Other AMT items (attach statement)	**15f**		
Items Affecting Shareholder Basis	**16a** Tax-exempt interest income	**16a**		
	b Other tax-exempt income	**16b**		
	c Nondeductible expenses	**16c**		
	d Property distributions	**16d**		
	e Repayment of loans from shareholders.	**16e**		
Other Information	**17a** Investment income	**17a**		
	b Investment expenses	**17b**		
	c Dividend distributions paid from accumulated earnings and profits	**17c**		
	d Other items and amounts (attach statement)			
Recon-ciliation	**18** **Income/loss reconciliation.** Combine the amounts on lines 1 through 10 in the far right column. From the result, subtract the sum of the amounts on lines 11 through 12d and 14l	**18**		

Form **1120S** (2007)

Form 1120S (2007)   Page **4**

Schedule L	Balance Sheets per Books	Beginning of tax year		End of tax year	
	Assets	**(a)**	**(b)**	**(c)**	**(d)**
1	Cash				
2a	Trade notes and accounts receivable . .				
b	Less allowance for bad debts	( )		( )	
3	Inventories				
4	U.S. government obligations.				
5	Tax-exempt securities *(see instructions)* .				
6	Other current assets *(attach statement)* .				
7	Loans to shareholders				
8	Mortgage and real estate loans . . .				
9	Other investments *(attach statement)* .				
10a	Buildings and other depreciable assets .				
b	Less accumulated depreciation. . . .	( )		( )	
11a	Depletable assets				
b	Less accumulated depletion.	( )		( )	
12	Land (net of any amortization)				
13a	Intangible assets (amortizable only) . .				
b	Less accumulated amortization. . . .	( )		( )	
14	Other assets *(attach statement)* . . .				
15	Total assets				
	Liabilities and Shareholders' Equity				
16	Accounts payable				
17	Mortgages, notes, bonds payable in less than 1 year .				
18	Other current liabilities *(attach statement)* .				
19	Loans from shareholders.				
20	Mortgages, notes, bonds payable in 1 year or more				
21	Other liabilities *(attach statement)* . . .				
22	Capital stock				
23	Additional paid-in capital.				
24	Retained earnings				
25	Adjustments to shareholders' equity *(attach statement)*				
26	Less cost of treasury stock		( )		( )
27	Total liabilities and shareholders' equity . .				

Schedule M-1	Reconciliation of Income (Loss) per Books With Income (Loss) per Return

Note: Schedule M-3 required instead of Schedule M-1 if total assets are $10 million or more—see instructions

1	Net income (loss) per books.		5	Income recorded on books this year not included on Schedule K, lines 1 through 10 (itemize):	
2	Income included on Schedule K, lines 1, 2, 3c, 4, 5a, 6, 7, 8a, 9, and 10, not recorded on books this year (itemize): _____		a	Tax-exempt interest $ _____	
3	Expenses recorded on books this year not included on Schedule K, lines 1 through 12 and 14l (itemize):		6	Deductions included on Schedule K, lines 1 through 12 and 14l, not charged against book income this year (itemize):	
a	Depreciation $ _____		a	Depreciation $ _____	
b	Travel and entertainment $ _____				
	_____		7	Add lines 5 and 6.	
4	Add lines 1 through 3.		8	Income (loss) (Schedule K, line 18). Line 4 less line 7	

Schedule M-2	Analysis of Accumulated Adjustments Account, Other Adjustments Account, and Shareholders' Undistributed Taxable Income Previously Taxed (see instructions)

		(a) Accumulated adjustments account	(b) Other adjustments account	(c) Shareholders' undistributed taxable income previously taxed
1	Balance at beginning of tax year	*Penalty and AMA ex*	*Tax Elept*	
2	Ordinary income from page 1, line 21. . .	*Cope Tax Example*		
3	Other additions.			
4	Loss from page 1, line 21	( )		
5	Other reductions	( )	( )	
6	Combine lines 1 through 5			
7	Distributions other than dividend distributions			
8	Balance at end of tax year. Subtract line 7 from line 6			

Form **1120S** (2007)

671107

☐ Final K-1 ☐ Amended K-1	OMB No. 1545-0130

Schedule K-1
(Form 1120S)
Department of the Treasury
Internal Revenue Service

2007

For calendar year 2007, or tax

year beginning _____ , 2007

ending _____ , 20 ___

**Shareholder's Share of Income, Deductions,
Credits, etc.**   ▶ **See back of form and separate instructions.**

Part III	Shareholder's Share of Current Year Income, Deductions, Credits, and Other Items

1	Ordinary business income (loss)	**13**	Credits
2	Net rental real estate income (loss)		
3	Other net rental income (loss)		
4	Interest income		
5a	Ordinary dividends		
5b	Qualified dividends	**14**	Foreign transactions
6	Royalties		
7	Net short-term capital gain (loss)		
8a	Net long-term capital gain (loss)		
8b	Collectibles (28%) gain (loss)		
8c	Unrecaptured section 1250 gain		
9	Net section 1231 gain (loss)		
10	Other income (loss)	**15**	Alternative minimum tax (AMT) items
11	Section 179 deduction	**16**	Items affecting shareholder basis
12	Other deductions		
		17	Other information

Part I   **Information About the Corporation**

A   Corporation's employer identification number

B   Corporation's name, address, city, state, and ZIP code

C   IRS Center where corporation filed return

Part II   **Information About the Shareholder**

D   Shareholder's identifying number

E   Shareholder's name, address, city, state, and ZIP code

F   Shareholder's percentage of stock
ownership for tax year .... _____ %

For IRS Use Only

* See attached statement for additional information.

SCHEDULE M-3 (Form 1120S) Department of the Treasury Internal Revenue Service	**Net Income (Loss) Reconciliation for S Corporations With Total Assets of \$10 Million or More** ▶ Attach to Form 1120S. ▶ See separate instructions.	OMB No. 1545-0130 20**07**

Name of corporation	Employer identification number

Part I **Financial Information and Net Income (Loss) Reconciliation**

1a Did the corporation prepare a certified audited non-tax-basis income statement for the period ending with or within this tax year? (See instructions if multiple non-tax-basis income statements are prepared.)

☐ **Yes.** Skip line 1b and complete lines 2 through 11 with respect to that income statement.

☐ **No.** Go to line 1b.

b Did the corporation prepare a non-tax-basis income statement for that period?

☐ **Yes.** Complete lines 2 through 11 with respect to that income statement.

☐ **No.** Skip lines 2 through 3b and enter the corporation's net income (loss) per its books and records on line 4.

2 Enter the income statement period: Beginning ____ / ____ / ____ Ending ____ / ____ / ____

3a Has the corporation's income statement been restated for the income statement period on line 2?

☐ **Yes.** (If "Yes," attach an explanation and the amount of each item restated.)

☐ **No.**

b Has the corporation's income statement been restated for any of the five income statement periods preceding the period on line 2?

☐ **Yes.** (If "Yes," attach an explanation and the amount of each item restated.)

☐ **No.**

4	Worldwide consolidated net income (loss) from income statement source identified in Part I, line 1	**4**	
5a	Net income from nonincludible foreign entities (attach schedule)	**5a**	( )
b	Net loss from nonincludible foreign entities (attach schedule and enter as a positive amount) . .	**5b**	
6a	Net income from nonincludible U.S. entities (attach schedule)	**6a**	( )
b	Net loss from nonincludible U.S. entities (attach schedule and enter as a positive amount) . . .	**6b**	
7a	Net income (loss) of other disregarded entities (except qualified subchapter S subsidiaries) (attach schedule)	**7a**	
b	Net income (loss) of other qualified subchapter S subsidiaries (QSubs) (attach schedule) . . .	**7b**	
8	Adjustment to eliminations of transactions between includible entities and nonincludible entities (attach schedule)	**8**	
9	Adjustment to reconcile income statement period to tax year (attach schedule)	**9**	
10	Other adjustments to reconcile to amount on line 11 (attach schedule)	**10**	
11	**Net income (loss) per income statement of the corporation.** Combine lines 4 through 10 . .	**11**	

**For Paperwork Reduction Act Notice,
see the Instructions for Form 1120S.**   Cat. No. 39666W   **Schedule M-3 (Form 1120S) 2007**

Schedule M-3 (Form 1120S) 2007   Page **2**

Name of corporation	Employer identification number

Part II Reconciliation of Net Income (Loss) per Income Statement of the Corporation With Total Income (Loss) per Return

Income (Loss) Items	(a) Income (Loss) per Income Statement	(b) Temporary Difference	(c) Permanent Difference	(d) Income (Loss) per Tax Return
1 Income (loss) from equity method foreign corporations				
2 Gross foreign dividends not previously taxed . . .				
3 Subpart F, QEF, and similar income inclusions . . .				
4 Gross foreign distributions previously taxed				
5 Income (loss) from equity method U.S. corporations				
6 U.S. dividends not eliminated in tax consolidation . .				
7 Income (loss) from U.S. partnerships (attach schedule)				
8 Income (loss) from foreign partnerships (attach schedule)				
9 Income (loss) from other pass-through entities (attach schedule)				
10 Items relating to reportable transactions (attach details)				
11 Interest income (attach Form 8916-A)				
12 Total accrual to cash adjustment				
13 Hedging transactions				
14 Mark-to-market income (loss)				
15 Cost of goods sold (attach Form 8916-A)	( )	( )		( )
16 Sale versus lease (for sellers and/or lessors)				
17 Section 481(a) adjustments				
18 Unearned/deferred revenue				
19 Income recognition from long-term contracts . . .				
20 Original issue discount and other imputed interest . .				
21a Income statement gain/loss on sale, exchange, abandonment, worthlessness, or other disposition of assets other than inventory and pass-through entities				
b Gross capital gains from Schedule D, excluding amounts from pass-through entities				
c Gross capital losses from Schedule D, excluding amounts from pass-through entities, abandonment losses, and worthless stock losses				
d Net gain/loss reported on Form 4797, line 17, excluding amounts from pass-through entities, abandonment losses, and worthless stock losses . .				
e Abandonment losses				
f Worthless stock losses (attach details)				
g Other gain/loss on disposition of assets other than inventory				
22 Other income (loss) items with differences (attach schedule)				
23 **Total income (loss) items.** Combine lines 1 through 22				
24 **Total expense/deduction items** (from Part III, line 30)				
25 Other items with no differences				
26 **Reconciliation totals.** Combine lines 23 through 25				

Note. Line 26, column (a), must equal the amount on Part I, line 11, and column (d) must equal Form 1120S, Schedule K, line 18.

Schedule M-3 (Form 1120S) 2007

Name of corporation	Employer identification number

Part III Reconciliation of Net Income (Loss) per Income Statement of the Corporation With Total Income (Loss) per Return—Expense/Deduction Items

Expense/Deduction Items	(a) Expense per Income Statement	(b) Temporary Difference	(c) Permanent Difference	(d) Deduction per Tax Return
1 U.S. current income tax expense				
2 U.S. deferred income tax expense				
3 State and local current income tax expense				
4 State and local deferred income tax expense				
5 Foreign current income tax expense (other than foreign withholding taxes)				
6 Foreign deferred income tax expense				
7 Equity-based compensation				
8 Meals and entertainment				
9 Fines and penalties				
10 Judgments, damages, awards, and similar costs				
11 Pension and profit-sharing				
12 Other post-retirement benefits				
13 Deferred compensation				
14 Charitable contribution of cash and tangible property				
15 Charitable contribution of intangible property				
16 Current year acquisition or reorganization investment banking fees				
17 Current year acquisition or reorganization legal and accounting fees				
18 Current year acquisition/reorganization other costs				
19 Amortization/impairment of goodwill				
20 Amortization of acquisition, reorganization, and start-up costs				
21 Other amortization or impairment write-offs				
22 Section 198 environmental remediation costs				
23a Depletion—Oil & Gas				
b Depletion—Other than Oil & Gas				
24 Depreciation				
25 Bad debt expense				
26 Interest expense (attach Form 8916-A)				
27 Corporate owned life insurance premiums				
28 Purchase versus lease (for purchasers and/or lessees)				
29 Other expense/deduction items with differences (attach schedule)				
30 **Total expense/deduction items.** Combine lines 1 through 29. Enter here and on Part II, line 24				

The words and phrases in this glossary have been defined to reflect their conventional use in the field of taxation. The definitions may therefore be incomplete for other purposes.

A

Accelerated cost recovery system (ACRS). A method in which the cost of tangible property is recovered over a prescribed period of time. The approach disregards salvage value, imposes a period of cost recovery that depends upon the classification of the asset into one of various recovery periods, and prescribes the applicable percentage of cost that can be deducted each year. The modified system is referred to as MACRS. § 168.

Accelerated depreciation. Various methods of depreciation that yield larger deductions in the earlier years of the life of an asset than the straight-line method. Examples include the double declining-balance and the sum-of-the-years' digits methods of depreciation.

Acceleration rule. Treatment of an intercompany transaction on a *consolidated return*, when a sold asset leaves the group.

Accounting method. The method under which income and expenses are determined for tax purposes. Important accounting methods include the cash basis and the accrual basis. Special methods are available for the reporting of gain on installment sales, recognition of income on construction projects (the completed contract and percentage of completion methods), and the valuation of inventories (last-in, first-out and first-in, first-out). §§ 446–474. See also *accrual basis, cash basis, completed contract method*, and *percentage of completion method*.

Accounting period. The period of time, usually a year, used by a taxpayer for the determination of tax liability. Unless a fiscal year is chosen, taxpayers must determine and pay their income tax liability by using the calendar year (January 1 through December 31) as the period of measurement. An example of a fiscal year is July 1 through June 30. A change in accounting periods (e.g., from a calendar year to a fiscal year) generally requires the consent of the IRS. Some new taxpayers, such as a newly formed corporation, are free to select either an initial calendar or a fiscal year without the consent of the IRS. §§ 441–443. See also *annual accounting period concept*.

Accrual basis. A method of accounting that reflects expenses incurred and income earned for any one tax year. In contrast to the cash basis of accounting, expenses need not be paid to be deductible, nor need income be received to be taxable. Unearned income (e.g., prepaid interest and rent) generally is taxed in the year of receipt regardless of the method of accounting used by the taxpayer. § 446(c)(2). See also *accounting method, cash basis*, and *unearned income*.

Accumulated adjustments account (AAA). An account that aggregates an S corporation's post-1982 income, loss, and deductions for the tax year (including nontaxable income and nondeductible losses and expenses). After the year-end income and expense adjustments are made, the account is reduced by distributions made during the tax year.

Accumulated earnings and profits. Net undistributed tax-basis earnings of a corporation aggregated from March 1, 1913, to the end of the prior tax year. Used to determine the amount of dividend income associated with a distribution to shareholders. See also *current earnings and profits* and *earnings and profits*. § 316 and Reg. § 1.316–2.

Accumulated earnings credit. A reduction allowed in arriving at accumulated taxable income, in determining the accumulated earnings tax. See also *accumulated earnings tax* and *accumulated taxable income*.

Accumulated earnings tax (AET). A special tax imposed on corporations that accumulate (rather than distribute) their earnings beyond the reasonable needs of the business. The accumulated earnings tax and related interest are imposed on accumulated taxable income in addition to the corporate income tax. §§ 531–537.

Accumulated taxable income. The base upon which the accumulated earnings tax is imposed. Generally, it is the taxable income of the corporation as adjusted for certain items (e.g., the Federal income tax, excess charitable contributions, the dividends received deduction) less the dividends paid deduction and the accumulated earnings credit. § 535.

Accumulating trust. See *discretionary trust*.

Accuracy-related penalty. Major civil taxpayer penalties relating to the accuracy of tax return data, including misstatements stemming from taxpayer negligence and improper valuation of income and deductions, are coordinated under this umbrella term. The penalty usually equals 20 percent of the understated tax liability.

Acquiescence. Agreement by the IRS on the results reached in some of the more significant decisions involving tax issues; sometimes abbreviated *Acq.* or *A.* See also *nonacquiescence.*

Acquisition. See *corporate acquisition.*

ACRS. See *accelerated cost recovery system.*

Ad valorem tax. A tax imposed on the value of property. The most common ad valorem tax is that imposed by states, counties, and cities on real estate. Ad valorem taxes can be imposed on personal property as well. See also *personalty.*

Adjusted basis. The cost or other basis of property reduced by depreciation allowed or allowable and increased by capital improvements. Other special adjustments are provided in § 1016 and the related Regulations. See also *basis.*

Adjusted current earnings (ACE). An adjustment in computing corporate alternative minimum taxable income (AMTI), computed at 75 percent of the excess of adjusted current earnings and profits over AMTI. ACE computations reflect restrictions on the timing of certain recognition events. Exempt interest, life insurance proceeds, and other receipts that are included in earnings and profits but not in taxable income also increase the ACE adjustment. See also *alternative minimum tax* and *earnings and profits.*

Adjusted gross estate. The gross estate of a *decedent* reduced by § 2053 expenses (e.g., administration, funeral) and § 2054 losses (e.g., casualty). Necessary in testing for the extension of time for installment payment of estate taxes under § 6166. See also *gross estate.*

Adjusted gross income (AGI). A tax determination peculiar to individual taxpayers. Generally, it represents the gross income of an individual, less business expenses and less any appropriate capital gain or loss adjustment. See also *gross income.*

Adjusted ordinary gross income (AOGI). A determination peculiar to the *personal holding company tax.* In ascertaining whether a corporation is a personal holding company, personal holding company income divided by adjusted ordinary gross income must equal 60 percent or more. Adjusted ordinary gross income is the corporation's gross income less capital gains, § 1231 gains, and certain expenses. §§ 541 and 543(b)(2). See also *personal holding company income.*

Administration. The supervision and winding up of an estate. The administration of an estate runs from the date of an individual's death until all assets have been distributed and liabilities paid.

Administrator. A person appointed by the court to administer (manage or take charge of) the assets and liabilities of a decedent (the deceased). See also *executor.*

Affiliate. A member of an *affiliated group.* See also *consolidated return.*

Affiliated group. A parent-subsidiary group of corporations that is eligible to elect to file on a consolidated basis. Eighty percent ownership of the voting power and value of all of the corporations must be achieved on every day of the tax year, and an identifiable parent corporation must exist (i.e., it must own at least 80 percent of another group member without applying attribution rules).

AFTR. *American Federal Tax Reports* contain all of the Federal tax decisions issued by the U.S. District Courts, U.S. Court of Federal Claims, U.S. Courts of Appeals, and the U.S. Supreme Court.

AFTR2d. The second series of the *American Federal Tax Reports,* dealing with 1954 and 1986 Code case law.

Aggregate concept. The theory of partnership taxation under which, in certain cases, a partnership is treated as a mere extension of each partner.

Alimony. Alimony deductions result from the payment of a legal obligation arising from the termination of a marital relationship. Payments designated as alimony generally are included in the gross income of the recipient and are deductible *for* AGI by the payer.

Allocable share of income. Certain entities receive conduit treatment under the Federal income tax law. This means the earned income or loss is not taxed to the entity, but is allocated to the owners or beneficiaries, regardless of the magnitude or timing of corresponding distributions. The portion of the entity's income that is taxed to the owner or beneficiary is the allocable share of the entity's income or loss for the period. The allocations are determined by (1) the partnership agreement for partners, (2) a weighted-average stock ownership computation for shareholders of an S corporation, and (3) the controlling will or trust instrument for the beneficiaries of an estate or trust.

Allocate. The assignment of income for various tax purposes. A *multistate corporation*'s nonbusiness income usually is allocated to the state where the nonbusiness assets are located; it is not *apportioned* with the rest of the entity's income. The income and expense items of an estate or trust are allocated between income and corpus components. Specific items of income, expense, gain, loss, and credit can be allocated to specific partners, if a substantial economic nontax purpose for the allocation is established. See also *apportion* and *substantial economic effect.*

Alternate valuation date. Property passing from a *decedent* by death may be valued for death tax purposes as of the date of death or the alternate valuation date. The alternate valuation date is six months from the date of death or the date the property is disposed of by the estate, whichever comes first. To use the alternate valuation date, the *executor* or *administrator* of the estate must make an affirmative election. Election of the alternate valuation date is not available unless it decreases the amount of the gross estate *and* reduces the estate tax liability.

Alternative minimum tax (AMT). AMT is a fixed percentage of alternative minimum taxable income (AMTI). AMTI generally starts with the taxpayer's adjusted gross income (for individuals) or taxable income (for other taxpayers). To this amount, the taxpayer (1) adds designated preference items (e.g., interest income on private activity bonds), (2) makes other specified adjustments (e.g., to reflect a longer, straight-line cost recovery deduction), (3) subtracts certain AMT itemized deductions for individuals (e.g., interest incurred on housing but not taxes paid), and (4) subtracts an exemption amount (e.g., $40,000 on a C corporation's return). The taxpayer must pay the greater of the resulting AMT (reduced by only the foreign tax credit) or the regular income tax (reduced by all allowable tax credits). The AMT does not apply to certain small C corporations. AMT preferences and adjustments are assigned to partners, LLC members, and S corporation shareholders.

Alternative minimum taxable income (AMTI). The base for computing a taxpayer's *alternative minimum tax*. Generally, the taxable income for the year, modified for AMT adjustments, preferences, and exemptions.

Amortization. The tax deduction for the cost or other basis of an intangible asset over the asset's estimated useful life. Examples of amortizable intangibles include patents, copyrights, and leasehold interests. Most intangible assets are amortized over 15 years. § 195. For tangible assets, see *depreciation.* For natural resources, see *depletion.* See also *estimated useful life* and *goodwill.*

Amount realized. The amount received by a taxpayer upon the sale or exchange of property. Amount realized is the sum of the cash and the fair market value of any property or services received by the taxpayer, plus any related debt assumed by the buyer. Determining the amount realized is the starting point for arriving at realized gain or loss. § 1001(b). See also *realized gain or loss* and *recognized gain or loss.*

Annual accounting period concept. In determining a taxpayer's income tax liability, only transactions taking place during a specified tax year are taken into consideration. For reporting and payment purposes, therefore, the tax life of taxpayers is divided into equal annual accounting periods. See also *accounting period* and *mitigation of the annual accounting period concept.*

Annual exclusion. In computing the taxable gifts for the year, each donor excludes the first $12,000 of a gift to each donee. Usually, the annual exclusion is not available for gifts of future interests. § 2503(b). See also *future interest* and *gift splitting.*

Annuitant. The party entitled to receive payments from an annuity contract. See also *annuity.*

Annuity. A fixed sum of money payable to a person at specified times for a specified period of time or for life. If the party making the payment (i.e., the obligor) is regularly engaged in this type of business (e.g., an insurance company), the arrangement is classified as a commercial annuity. A so-called private annuity involves an obligor that is not regularly engaged in selling annuities (e.g., a charity or family member).

Anticipatory assignment of income. See *assignment of income.*

Appellate court. For Federal tax purposes, appellate courts include the U.S. Courts of Appeals and the U.S. Supreme Court. If the party losing in the trial (or lower) court is dissatisfied with the result, the dispute may be carried to the appropriate appellate court. See also *Court of Appeals* and *trial court.*

Apportion. The assignment of the business income of a multistate corporation to specific states for income taxation. Usually, the apportionment procedure accounts for the property, payroll, and sales activity levels of the various states, and a proportionate assignment of the entity's total income is made, using a three-factor apportionment formula. These activities indicate the commercial domicile of the corporation, relative to that income. Some states exclude nonbusiness income from the apportionment procedure; they *allocate* nonbusiness income to the states

where the nonbusiness assets are located. See also *allocate, domicile, nonbusiness income, payroll factor, property factor,* and *sales factor.*

Appreciated inventory. In partnership taxation, appreciated inventory is a *hot asset,* and a partner's share of its ordinary income potential must be allocated. If a partner sells an interest in the partnership, ordinary income is recognized to the extent of the partner's share in the partnership's inventory and *unrealized receivables.* The definition of "inventory" is broad enough to include any accounts receivable, including unrealized receivables.

Arm's length concept. The standard under which unrelated parties would carry out a transaction. Suppose Bint Corporation sells property to its sole shareholder for $10,000. In determining whether $10,000 is an arm's length price, one would ascertain the amount for which the corporation could have sold the property to a disinterested third party.

Articles of incorporation. The legal document specifying a corporation's name, period of existence, purpose and powers, authorized number of shares, classes of stock, and other conditions for operation. The organizers of the corporation file the articles with the state of incorporation. If the articles are satisfactory and other conditions of the law are satisfied, the state will issue a charter recognizing the organization's status as a corporation.

Assessment. The process whereby the IRS imposes a tax liability. If, for example, the IRS audits a taxpayer's income tax return and finds gross income understated or deductions overstated, it will assess a deficiency in the amount of the tax that should have been paid in light of the adjustments made. See also *deficiency.*

Assignment of income. A taxpayer attempts to avoid the recognition of income by assigning to another the property that generates the income. Such a procedure will not avoid the recognition of income by the taxpayer making the assignment if the income was earned at the point of the transfer. In this case, the income is taxed to the person who earns it.

Assumption of liabilities. In a corporate formation, corporate takeover, or asset purchase, the new owner often takes assets and agrees to assume preexisting debt. Such actions do not create *boot* received on the transaction for the new shareholder, unless there is no *bona fide* business purpose for the exchange, or the principal purpose of the debt assumption is the avoidance of tax liabilities. Gain is recognized to the extent that liabilities assumed exceed the aggregated bases of the transferred assets. § 357.

At-risk amount. The taxpayer has an amount at risk in a business or investment venture to the extent that personal assets have been subjected to the risks of the business. Typically, the taxpayer's at-risk amount includes (1) the amount of money or other property that the investor contributed to the venture for the investment, (2) the amount of any of the entity's liabilities for which the taxpayer personally is liable and that relate to the investment, and (3) an allocable share of nonrecourse debts incurred by the venture from third parties in arm's length transactions for real estate investments.

At-risk limitation. Generally, a taxpayer can deduct losses related to a trade or business, S corporation, partnership, or investment asset only to the extent of the at-risk amount.

Attribution. Under certain circumstances, the tax law applies attribution rules to assign to one taxpayer the ownership interest of another taxpayer. If, for example, the stock of Tree Corporation is held 60 percent by Mary and 40 percent by Sam, Mary may be deemed to own 100 percent of Tree if Sam is her son. In that case, the stock owned by Sam is attributed to Mary. Stated differently, Mary has a 60 percent direct and a 40 percent indirect interest in Tree. It can also be said that Mary is the constructive owner of Sam's interest.

Audit. Inspection and verification of a taxpayer's return or other transactions possessing tax consequences. See also *correspondence audit, field audit,* and *office audit.*

Automobile expenses. Automobile expenses generally are deductible only to the extent the automobile is used in business or for the production of income. Personal commuting expenses are not deductible. The taxpayer may deduct actual out-of-pocket expenses (including depreciation and insurance), or a standard mileage rate for the tax year. For 2008, per-mile deduction amounts are 50.5 cents for business use of the auto, 14 cents if in support of charity, 19 cents for medical purposes, and 19 cents for a job-related move.

B

Bailout. Various procedures whereby the owners of an entity can obtain the entity's profits with favorable tax consequences. With corporations, for example, the bailout of corporate profits might be accomplished by using fringe benefit plans, or by paying salaries or interest. The alternative of distributing the profits to the shareholders as dividends generally is less attractive since dividend payments are not deductible. See also *preferred stock bailout.*

Bardahl **formula.** A formula approved in a Tax Court memorandum decision, used in the context of the accumulated earnings tax to compute the reasonable business needs of the corporation for working capital. Most appropriate where the corporation holds inventory.

Bargain sale or purchase. A sale or purchase of property for less than fair market value. The difference between the sale or purchase price and the fair market value of the property may have tax consequences. If, for example, a corporation sells property worth $1,000 to one of its shareholders for $700, the $300 difference probably represents a constructive dividend to the shareholder. Suppose, instead, the shareholder sells the property (worth $1,000) to his or her corporation for $700. The $300 difference probably represents a contribution by the shareholder to the corporation's capital. Bargain sales and purchases among members of the same family may lead to gift tax consequences. See also *constructive dividend.*

Basis. The acquisition cost assigned to an asset for income tax purposes. For assets acquired by purchase, basis is cost (§ 1012). Special rules govern the basis of property received by virtue of another's death (§ 1014) or by gift (§ 1015), the basis of stock received on a transfer of property to a controlled corporation (§ 358), the basis of the property transferred to the corporation (§ 362), and the basis of

property received upon the liquidation of a corporation (§ 334). See also *adjusted basis.*

Basis in partnership interest. The acquisition cost of the partner's ownership interest in the *partnership.* Includes purchase price and associated debt acquired from other partners and in the course of the entity's trade or business.

Beneficiary. A party who will benefit from a transfer of property or other arrangement. Examples include the beneficiary of a trust, the beneficiary of a life insurance policy, and the beneficiary of an estate.

Bequest. A transfer of personal property by will. To bequeath is to leave such property by will. See also *devise* and *personal property.*

Blockage rule. A factor to be considered in valuing a large block of stock. Application of this rule generally justifies a discount in the fair market value since the disposition of a large amount of stock at any one time may depress the value of the shares in the marketplace.

Bona fide. In good faith, or real. In tax law, this term often is used in connection with a business purpose for carrying out a transaction. Thus, was there a bona fide business purpose for a shareholder's transfer of a liability to a controlled corporation? § 357(b)(1)(B). See also *business purpose.*

Book value. The net amount of an asset after reduction by a related reserve. The book value of machinery, for example, is the amount of the machinery less the reserve for depreciation.

Boot. Cash or property of a type not included in the definition of a nontaxable exchange. The receipt of boot causes an otherwise nontaxable transfer to become taxable to the extent of the lesser of the fair market value of the boot or the realized gain on the transfer. For example, see transfers to controlled corporations under § 351(b) and like-kind exchanges under § 1031(b). See also *like-kind exchange* and *realized gain or loss.*

Branch profits tax. A tax on the effectively connected earnings and profits of the U.S. branch of a foreign corporation. The tax is levied in addition to the usual § 11 tax, in an amount equal to 30 percent of the dividend equivalent amount. Treaties can override the tax or reduce the withholding percentage. Earnings reinvested in the U.S. operations of the entity are not subject to the tax until repatriation. See also *dividend equivalent amount.*

Bribes and illegal payments. Section 162 denies a deduction for bribes or kickbacks, fines, and penalties paid to a government official or employee for violation of law, and two-thirds of the treble damage payments made to claimants for violation of the antitrust law. Denial of a deduction for bribes and illegal payments is based upon the judicially established principle that allowing such payments would be contrary to public policy.

Brother-sister controlled group. More than one corporation owned by the same shareholders. If, for example, Clara and Dan each own one-half of the stock in Top Corporation and Bottom Corporation, then Top and Bottom form a brother-sister controlled group.

B.T.A. The Board of Tax Appeals was a trial court that considered Federal tax matters. This court is now the U.S. Tax Court.

Built-in gains tax. A penalty tax designed to discourage a shift of the incidence of taxation on unrealized gains from a

C corporation to its shareholders, via an S election. Under this provision, any recognized gain during the first 10 years of S status generates a corporate-level tax on a base not to exceed the aggregate untaxed built-in gains brought into the S corporation upon its election from C corporation taxable years.

Built-in loss property. Property contributed to a corporation under § 351 or as a contribution to capital that has a basis in excess of its fair market value. An adjustment is necessary to step down the basis of the property to its fair market value. The adjustment prevents the corporation and the contributing shareholder from obtaining a double tax benefit. The corporation allocates the adjustment proportionately among the assets with the built-in loss. As an alternative to the corporate adjustment, the shareholder may elect to reduce the basis in the stock.

Burden of proof. The requirement in a lawsuit to show the weight of evidence and thereby gain a favorable decision. In cases of tax fraud, the burden of proof in a tax case is on the IRS. See also *fraud.*

Business bad debts. A tax deduction allowed for obligations obtained in connection with a trade or business that have become either partially or completely worthless. In contrast to nonbusiness bad debts, business bad debts are deductible as business expenses. § 166. See also *nonbusiness bad debt.*

Business purpose. A justifiable business reason for carrying out a transaction. Mere tax avoidance is not an acceptable business purpose. The presence of a business purpose is crucial in the area of corporate reorganizations and certain liquidations. See also *bona fide.*

Buy-sell agreement. An arrangement, particularly appropriate in the case of a closely held corporation or a partnership, whereby the surviving owners (shareholders or partners) or the entity agrees to purchase the interest of a withdrawing owner. The buy-sell agreement provides for an orderly disposition of an interest in a business and may aid in setting the value of the interest for death tax purposes. See also *cross-purchase buy-sell agreement* and *entity buy-sell agreement.*

Bypass amount. The amount that can be transferred by gift or death free of any unified transfer tax. For 2008, the by-pass amount is $2 million for estate tax (it is $3.5 million for 2009) and $1 million for gift tax. See also *exemption equivalent amount.*

Bypass election. In the context of a distribution by an *S corporation,* an election made by the entity to designate that the distribution is first from *accumulated earnings and profits,* and only then from the *accumulated adjustments account (AAA).*

C

C corporation. A separate taxable entity, subject to the rules of Subchapter C of the Code. This business form may create a double taxation effect relative to its shareholders. The entity is subject to the regular corporate tax and a number of penalty taxes at the Federal level.

Calendar year. See *accounting period.*

Capital account. The financial accounting analog of a partner's tax basis in the entity.

Capital asset. Broadly speaking, all assets are capital except those specifically excluded by the Code. Major categories of noncapital assets include property held for resale in the normal course of business (inventory), trade accounts and notes receivable, and depreciable property and real estate used in a trade or business (§ 1231 assets). § 1221. See also *capital gain* and *capital loss.*

Capital contribution. Various means by which a shareholder makes additional funds available to the corporation (placed at the risk of the business), sometimes without the receipt of additional stock. If no stock is received, the contributions are added to the basis of the shareholder's existing stock investment and do not generate gross income to the corporation. § 118.

Capital expenditure. An expenditure added to the basis of the property improved. For income tax purposes, this generally precludes a full deduction for the expenditure in the year paid or incurred. Cost recovery in the form of a tax deduction later comes in the form of depreciation, depletion, or amortization. § 263.

Capital gain. The gain from the sale or exchange of a capital asset. See also *capital asset.*

Capital interest. Usually, the percentage of the entity's net assets that a partner would receive on liquidation. Typically determined by the partner's capital sharing ratio.

Capital loss. The loss from the sale or exchange of a capital asset. See also *capital asset.*

Capital sharing ratio. A partner's percentage ownership of the entity's capital.

Capital stock tax. A state-level tax, usually imposed on out-of-state corporations for the privilege of doing business in the state. The tax may be based on the entity's apportionable income or payroll, or on its apportioned net worth as of a specified date.

Carryover basis. When a taxpayer exchanges one asset for another, many provisions in the tax law allow the basis assigned to the received asset to be precisely that of the traded asset. Thus, no step-up or -down of basis occurs as a result of the exchange. For instance, when an investor contributes an asset to a corporation or partnership, the entity generally takes a carryover basis in the property. § 723.

Cash basis. A method of accounting that reflects deductions as paid and income as received in any one tax year. However, deductions for prepaid expenses that benefit more than one tax year (e.g., prepaid rent and prepaid interest) usually are spread over the period benefited rather than deducted in the year paid. § 446(c)(1). See also *constructive receipt of income.*

Cash surrender value. The amount of money that an insurance policy would yield if cashed in with the insurance company that issued the policy.

CCH. Commerce Clearing House (CCH) is the publisher of a tax service and of Federal tax decisions (USTC series).

Cert. den. By denying the Writ of Certiorari, the U.S. Supreme Court refuses to accept an appeal from a U.S. Court of Appeals. The denial of *certiorari* does not, however, mean that the U.S. Supreme Court agrees with the result reached by the lower court.

Certiorari. Appeal from a U.S. Court of Appeals to the U.S. Supreme Court is by Writ of Certiorari. The Supreme Court need not accept the appeal, and it usually does not (*cert. den.*) unless a conflict exists among the lower courts that must be resolved or a constitutional issue is involved. See also *cert. den.*

Cf. Compare.

Charitable contributions. Contributions are deductible (subject to various restrictions and ceiling limitations) if made to qualified nonprofit charitable organizations. A cash basis taxpayer is entitled to a deduction solely in the year of payment. Accrual basis corporations may accrue contributions at year-end if payment is properly authorized before the end of the year and payment is made within two and one-half months after the end of the year. § 170.

Check the box Regulations. A business entity can elect to be taxed as a partnership, S corporation, or C corporation by indicating its preference on the tax return. Legal structure and operations are irrelevant in this regard. Thus, by using the check-the-box rules prudently, an entity can select the most attractive tax results offered by the Code, without being bound by legal forms. Not available if the entity is incorporated under state law.

Civil fraud. See *fraud*.

Closely held corporation. A corporation where stock ownership is not widely dispersed. Rather, a few shareholders are in control of corporate policy and are in a position to benefit personally from that policy.

Closing agreement. In a tax dispute, the parties sign a closing agreement to spell out the terms under which the matters are settled. The agreement is binding on both the IRS and the taxpayer.

Collapsing. To disregard a transaction or one of a series of steps leading to a result. See also *step transaction, substance vs. form concept,* and *telescoping*.

Commissioner of the IRS. The head of IRS operations, a presidential appointee.

Common law state. See *community property*.

Community property. Louisiana, Texas, New Mexico, Arizona, California, Washington, Idaho, Nevada, and Wisconsin have community property systems. The rest of the states are common law property jurisdictions. Alaska residents can elect community property status for assets. The difference between common law and community property systems centers around the property rights possessed by married persons. In a common law system, each spouse owns whatever he or she earns. Under a community property system, one-half of the earnings of each spouse is considered owned by the other spouse. Assume, for example, Hal and Wanda are husband and wife and their only income is the $50,000 annual salary Hal receives. If they live in New York (a common law state), the $50,000 salary belongs to Hal. If, however, they live in Texas (a community property state), the $50,000 salary is owned one-half each by Hal and Wanda. See also *separate property*.

Complete termination redemption. See *redemption (complete termination)*.

Completed contract method. A method of reporting gain or loss on certain long-term contracts. Under this method of accounting, gross income and expenses are recognized in the tax year in which the contract is completed. Reg. § 1.451–3. See also *percentage of completion method*.

Complex trust. Not a *simple trust*. Such trusts may have charitable beneficiaries, accumulate income, and distribute corpus. §§ 661–663.

Concur. To agree with the result reached by another, but not necessarily with the reasoning or the logic used in reaching the result. For example, Judge Ross agrees with Judges Smith and Tanaka (all being members of the same court) that the income is taxable but for a different reason. Judge Ross would issue a concurring opinion to the majority opinion issued by Judges Smith and Tanaka.

Condemnation. The taking of property by a public authority. The taking is by legal action, and the owner of the property is compensated by the public authority.

Conduit concept. An approach assumed by the tax law in the treatment of certain entities and their owners. Permits specified tax characteristics to pass through the entity without losing their identity. For example, long-term capital losses realized by a limited liability company are passed through as such to the individual members of the entity. Varying forms of the conduit concept apply for partnerships, trusts, estates, and S corporations. See also *aggregate concept*.

Consent dividend. For purposes of avoiding or reducing the penalty tax on the unreasonable accumulation of earnings or the personal holding company tax, a corporation may declare a consent dividend. No cash or property is distributed to the shareholders, although the corporation obtains a dividends paid deduction. The consent dividend is taxed to the shareholders and increases the basis in their stock investment. § 565.

Conservation easement. An interest in real property that maintains its natural or pristine condition. Most often it restricts the development of the property. Properly structured, the grant of such an easement can generate an income tax deduction for the donor. If the grant takes place after the owner's death, a § 2055 charitable deduction results, and a portion of the property's value is excluded from the gross estate. § 2031(c).

Consolidated return. A procedure whereby certain affiliated corporations may file a single return, combine the tax transactions of each corporation, and arrive at a single income tax liability for the group. The election to file a consolidated return usually is binding on future years. §§ 1501–1505 and related Regulations.

Consolidation. The combination of two or more corporations into a newly created corporation. Thus, Apt Corporation and Bye Corporation combine to form Cart Corporation. A consolidation may qualify as a nontaxable reorganization if certain conditions are satisfied. §§ 354 and 368(a)(1)(A).

Constructive dividend. A taxable benefit derived by a shareholder from his or her corporation that is not actually called a dividend. Examples include unreasonable compensation, excessive rent payments, bargain purchases of corporate property, and shareholder use of corporate property. Constructive dividends generally are found in closely held corporations. See also *bargain sale or purchase, closely held corporation,* and *unreasonable compensation*.

Constructive liquidation scenario. The means by which recourse debt is shared among partners in basis determination.

Constructive ownership. See *attribution*.

Constructive receipt of income. If income is unqualifiedly available although not physically in the taxpayer's possession, it is subject to the income tax. An example is accrued interest on a savings account. Under the constructive receipt of income concept, the interest is taxed to a depositor in the year available, rather than the year actually withdrawn. The fact that the depositor uses the cash basis of accounting for tax purposes is irrelevant. See Reg. § 1.451–2. See also *cash basis.*

Continuity of business enterprise. In a tax-favored reorganization, a shareholder or corporation that has substantially the same investment after an exchange as before should not be taxed on the transaction. Specifically, the transferee corporation must continue the historic business of the transferor or use a significant portion of the transferor's assets in the new business.

Continuity of interest test. In a tax-favored reorganization, a shareholder or corporation that has substantially the same investment after an exchange as before should not be taxed on the transaction. Specifically, the seller must acquire an equity interest in the purchasing corporation equal in value to at least 50 percent of all formerly outstanding stock of the acquired entity.

Continuity of life or existence. The death or other withdrawal of an owner of an entity does not terminate the existence of the entity. This is a characteristic of a corporation since the death or withdrawal of a shareholder does not affect the corporation's existence.

Contributions to the capital of a corporation. See *capital contribution.*

Contributory qualified pension or profit sharing plan. A plan funded with both employer and employee contributions. Since the employee's contributions to the plan are subject to income tax, a later distribution of the contributions to the employee generally is tax-free. See also *qualified pension or profit sharing plan.*

Control. Holding a specified level of stock ownership in a corporation. For § 351, the new shareholder(s) must hold at least 80 percent of the total combined voting power of all voting classes of stock. Other tax provisions require different levels of control to bring about desired effects, such as 50 or 100 percent.

Controlled foreign corporation (CFC). A non-U.S. corporation in which more than 50 percent of the total combined voting power of all classes of stock entitled to vote or the total value of the stock of the corporation is owned by "U.S. shareholders" on any day during the taxable year of the foreign corporation. For purposes of this definition, a U.S. shareholder is any U.S. person who owns, or is considered to own, 10 percent or more of the total combined voting power of all classes of voting stock of the foreign corporation. Stock owned directly, indirectly, and constructively is used in this measure.

Controlled group. A controlled group of corporations is required to share the lower-level corporate tax rates and various other tax benefits among the members of the group. A controlled group may be either a *brother-sister* or a *parent-subsidiary group.*

Corporate acquisition. The takeover of one corporation by another if both parties retain their legal existence after the transaction. An acquisition can be effected via a stock purchase or through a tax-free exchange of stock. See also *corporate reorganization* and *merger.*

Corporate liquidation. Occurs when a corporation distributes its net assets to its shareholders and ceases its legal existence. Generally, a shareholder recognizes capital gain or loss upon the liquidation of the entity, regardless of the corporation's balance in its earnings and profits account. However, the distributing corporation recognizes gain and loss on assets that it distributes to shareholders in kind.

Corporate reorganization. Occurs, among other instances, when one corporation acquires another in a merger or acquisition, a single corporation divides into two or more entities, a corporation makes a substantial change in its capital structure, or a corporation undertakes a change in its legal name or domicile. The exchange of stock and other securities in a corporate reorganization can be effected favorably for tax purposes if certain statutory requirements are followed strictly. Tax consequences include the nonrecognition of any gain that is realized by the shareholders except to the extent of *boot* received. See also *corporate acquisition* and *merger.*

Corpus. The body or principal of a *trust.* Suppose, for example, George transfers an apartment building into a trust, income payable to Wanda for life, remainder to Sam upon Wanda's death. Corpus of the trust is the apartment building.

Correspondence audit. An audit conducted by the IRS by mail. Typically, the IRS writes to the taxpayer requesting the verification of a particular deduction or exemption. The completion of a special form or the remittance of copies of records or other support is all that is requested of the taxpayer. See also *audit, field audit,* and *office audit.*

Court of Appeals. Any of 13 Federal courts that consider tax matters appealed from the U.S. Tax Court, a U.S. District Court, or the U.S. Court of Federal Claims. Appeal from a U.S. Court of Appeals is to the U.S. Supreme Court by *Certiorari.* See also *appellate court, Court of Federal Claims,* and *trial court.*

Court of Federal Claims. A trial court (court of original jurisdiction) that decides litigation involving Federal tax matters. Appeal is to the Court of Appeals for the Federal Circuit.

Credit for prior transfers. The death tax credit for prior transfers applies when property is taxed in the estates of different decedents within a 10-year period. The credit is determined using a decreasing statutory percentage, with the magnitude of the credit decreasing as the length of time between the multiple deaths increases. § 2013.

Criminal fraud. See *fraud.*

Cross-purchase buy-sell agreement. Under this type of arrangement, the surviving owners of the business agree to buy out the withdrawing owner. Assume, for example, Ron and Sara are equal shareholders in Tip Corporation. Under a cross-purchase buy-sell agreement, Ron and Sara would contract to purchase the other's interest should that person decide to withdraw from the business. See also *buy-sell agreement* and *entity buy-sell agreement.*

Current earnings and profits. Net tax-basis earnings of a corporation aggregated during the current tax year. A corporate distribution is deemed to be first from the entity's current earnings and profits and then from accumulated earnings and profits. Shareholders recognize dividend income to the extent of the earnings and profits of the corporation. A dividend results to the extent of current earnings and profits, even if there is a larger negative balance in accumulated earnings and profits. § 316 and Reg. § 1.316–2.

Current use valuation. See *special use value*.

Curtesy. A husband's right under state law to all or part of his wife's property upon her death. See also *dower*.

D

Death benefit. A payment made by an employer to the beneficiary or beneficiaries of a deceased employee on account of the death of the employee.

Death tax. A tax imposed on property transferred by the death of the owner. See also *estate tax* and *inheritance tax*.

Debt-financed income. Included in computations of the *unrelated business income* of an *exempt organization*, the gross income generated from debt-financed property.

Decedent. An individual who has died.

Deduction. The Federal income tax is not imposed upon gross income. Rather, it is imposed upon taxable income. Congressionally identified deductions are subtracted from gross income to arrive at the tax base, taxable income.

Deductions in respect of a decedent. Deductions accrued at the moment of death but not recognizable on the final income tax return of a decedent because of the method of accounting used. Such items are allowed as deductions on the estate tax return and on the income tax return of the estate (Form 1041) or the heir (Form 1040). An example of a deduction in respect of a decedent is interest expense accrued to the date of death by a cash basis debtor.

Deferred compensation. Compensation that will be taxed when received and not when earned. An example is contributions by an employer to a qualified pension or profit sharing plan on behalf of an employee. The contributions are not taxed to the employee until they are distributed (e.g., upon retirement). See also *qualified pension or profit sharing plan*.

Deferred tax asset. As determined under the rules of *FAS 109*, an item created on an enterprise's balance sheet by a temporary book-tax difference, such that a tax benefit will not be recognized until a later date, although it already has been reported in the financial statements, e.g., the carry-forward of a disallowed deduction.

Deferred tax liability. As determined under the rules of *FAS 109*, an item created on an enterprise's balance sheet by a temporary book-tax difference, such that a tax benefit is recognized earlier for tax purposes than it is in the financial accounting records, e.g., the use of an accelerated cost recovery deduction.

Deficiency. Additional tax liability owed by a taxpayer and assessed by the IRS. See also *assessment* and *statutory notice of deficiency*.

Deficiency dividend. Once the IRS has established a corporation's liability for the personal holding company tax in a prior year, the tax may be reduced or avoided by the issuance of a deficiency dividend under § 547. The deficiency dividend procedure does not avoid the usual penalties and interest applicable for failure to file a return or pay a tax.

Deficit. A negative balance, say in the earnings and profits account.

Demand loan. A loan payable upon request by the creditor, rather than on a specific date.

Depletion. The process by which the cost or other basis of a natural resource (e.g., an oil or gas interest) is recovered upon extraction and sale of the resource. The two ways to determine the depletion allowance are the cost and percentage (or statutory) methods. Under cost depletion, each unit of production sold is assigned a portion of the cost or other basis of the interest. This is determined by dividing the cost or other basis by the total units expected to be recovered. Under percentage (or statutory) depletion, the tax law provides a special percentage factor for different types of minerals and other natural resources. This percentage is multiplied by the gross income from the interest to arrive at the depletion allowance. §§ 613 and 613A.

Depreciation. The deduction for the cost or other basis of a tangible asset over the asset's estimated useful life. For intangible assets, see *amortization*. For natural resources, see *depletion*. See also *estimated useful life*.

Depreciation recapture. Upon the disposition of depreciable property used in a trade or business, gain or loss is measured by the difference between the consideration received (the amount realized) and the adjusted basis of the property. The gain recognized could be § 1231 gain and qualify for long-term capital gain treatment. The recapture provisions of the Code (e.g., §§ 291, 1245, and 1250) may operate to convert some or all of the previous § 1231 gain into ordinary income. The justification for depreciation recapture is that it prevents a taxpayer from converting a dollar of ordinary deduction (in the form of depreciation) into deferred tax-favored income (§ 1231 or long-term capital gain). The depreciation recapture rules do not apply when the property is disposed of at a loss or via a gift. See also *Section 1231 gains and losses*.

Determination letter. Upon the request of a taxpayer, the IRS will comment on the tax status of a completed transaction. Determination letters frequently are used to clarify employee status, determine whether a retirement or profit sharing plan qualifies under the Code, and determine the tax-exempt status of certain nonprofit organizations.

Devise. A transfer of real estate by will. See also *bequest*.

Disclaimers. Rejections, refusals, or renunciations of claims, powers, or property. Section 2518 sets forth the conditions required to avoid gift tax consequences as the result of a disclaimer.

Discretionary trust. A trust under which the trustee or another party has the right to accumulate (rather than distribute) the income for each year. Depending on the terms of the trust instrument, the income may be accumulated for future distributions to the income beneficiaries or added to corpus for the benefit of the remainderperson. See also *corpus* and *income beneficiary*.

Disguised sale. When a partner contributes property to the entity and soon thereafter receives a distribution from the partnership, the transactions are collapsed, and the distribution is seen as a purchase of the asset by the partnership. § 707(a)(2)(B).

Disproportionate. Not pro rata or ratable. Suppose, for example, Fin Corporation has two shareholders, Cal and Dot, each of whom owns 50 percent of its stock. If Fin distributes a cash dividend of $2,000 to Cal and only $1,000 to Dot, the distribution is disproportionate. The distribution would have been proportionate if Cal and Dot had received $1,500 each.

Disproportionate distribution. A distribution from a partnership to one or more of its partners in which at least one partner's interest in partnership hot assets is increased or decreased. For example, a distribution of cash to one partner and hot assets to another changes both partners' interest in hot assets and is disproportionate. The intent of rules for taxation of disproportionate distributions is to ensure each partner eventually recognizes his or her proportionate share of partnership ordinary income.

Disproportionate redemption. See *redemption (disproportionate)*.

Dissent. To disagree with the majority. If, for example, Judge Bird disagrees with the result reached by Judges Crown and Dove (all of whom are members of the same court), Judge Bird could issue a dissenting opinion.

Distributable net income (DNI). The measure that determines the nature and amount of the distributions from estates and trusts that the beneficiaries must include in income. DNI also limits the amount that estates and trusts can claim as a deduction for such distributions. § 643(a).

Distribution deduction. Used to compute an estate or trust's taxable income for the year. The lesser of the amount distributed to beneficiaries from income, or the deductible portion of distributable net income for the period.

Distributions in kind. Transfers of property "as is." If, for example, a corporation distributes land to its shareholders, a distribution in kind has taken place. A sale of land followed by a distribution of the cash proceeds would not be a distribution in kind of the land.

District Court. A Federal District Court is a trial court for purposes of litigating Federal tax matters. It is the only trial court in which a jury trial can be obtained. See also *trial court*.

Dividend. A nondeductible distribution to the shareholders of a corporation. A dividend constitutes gross income to the recipient if it is from the *current* or *accumulated earnings and profits* of the corporation.

Dividend equivalent amount (DEA). The amount subject to the *branch profits tax*, it is equal to the *effectively connected earnings and profits* of the U.S. branch of a foreign corporation, reduced/(increased) by an increase/(reduction) in U.S. net equity.

Dividends paid deduction. Relative to the *accumulated earnings* and *personal holding company taxes*, reductions in the tax base are allowed to the extent that the corporation made dividends payments during the year. Thus, this adjustment reduces *accumulated taxable income* and *personal holding company income*.

Dividends received deduction. A deduction allowed a corporate shareholder for dividends received from a domestic corporation. The deduction usually is 70 percent of the dividends received, but it could be 80 or 100 percent depending upon the ownership percentage held by the payee corporation. §§ 243–246.

Divisive reorganization. A corporate division: some of the assets of one corporation are transferred to another corporation in exchange for control of the transferee. Then, in a spinoff or split-off, stock of the transferee is distributed to the transferor's shareholders.

Dock sale. A purchaser uses its owned or rented vehicles to take possession of the product at the seller's shipping dock. In most states, the sale is apportioned to the operating state of the purchaser, rather than the seller. See also *apportion* and *sales factor*.

Domestic corporation. A corporation created or organized in the United States or under the law of the United States or any state. § 7701(a)(4). Only dividends received from domestic corporations qualify for the dividends received deduction (§ 243). See also *foreign corporation*.

Domestic production activities deduction (DPAD). A deduction allowed to sole proprietors, C corporations, partnerships, S corporations, cooperatives, estates, and trusts for certain production activities. The deduction rate is 6% of *qualified production activities income* for 2007 through 2009 and 9% for 2010 and thereafter. The deduction cannot exceed 50 percent of *W–2 wages*. § 199.

Domestic production gross receipts (DPGR). A key component in computing the *production activities deduction (PAD)*. Includes receipts from the sale and other disposition of qualified production property produced in significant part within the U.S. § 199(c)(4).

Domicile. A person's legal home.

Donee. The recipient of a gift.

Donor. The maker of a gift.

Double-weighted apportionment formula. A means by which the total taxable income of a *multistate corporation* is assigned to a specific state. Usually, the payroll, property, and sales factors are equally treated, and the weighted average of these factors is used in the apportionment procedure. In some states, however, the sales factor may receive a double weight, or it may be the only factor considered. These latter formulas place a greater tax burden on the income of out-of-state corporations. See also *apportion, payroll factor, property factor, sales factor,* and *UDITPA*.

Dower. A wife's right to all or part of her deceased husband's property; unique to common law states as opposed to community property jurisdictions. See also *curtesy*.

E

Earned income. Income from personal services. Distinguished from passive, portfolio, and other unearned income (sometimes referred to as "active" income). See §§ 469, 911, and the related Regulations.

Earnings and profits (E & P). Measures the economic capacity of a corporation to make a distribution to shareholders that is not a return of capital. Such a distribution results in dividend income to the shareholders to the extent of the corporation's current and accumulated earnings and profits.

Economic effect test. Requirements that must be met before a special allocation may be used by a partnership. The premise behind the test is that each partner who receives an allocation of income or loss from a partnership bears the economic benefit or burden of the allocation.

Effectively connected income. Income of a nonresident alien or foreign corporation that is attributable to the operations of a U.S. trade or business under either the asset-use or the business-activities test.

Electing large partnership. A partnership with 100 or more partners may elect to be subject to simplified tax reporting and audit procedures. The election allows the partnership to combine certain income and expense amounts and report net amounts to the partners. The result is fewer "pass-through" items to the partners, making the partners' tax returns easier to prepare. As an example, an electing large partnership with a long-term capital gain and a short-term capital loss would offset the two amounts and allocate the net amount among the partners.

Employee stock ownership plan (ESOP). A type of qualified profit sharing plan that invests in securities of the employer. In a noncontributory ESOP, the employer usually contributes its shares to a trust and receives a deduction for the fair market value of the stock. Generally, the employee does not recognize income until the stock is sold after its distribution to him or her upon retirement or other separation from service. See also *qualified pension or profit sharing plan.*

En banc. The case was considered by the whole court. Typically, for example, only one of the judges of the U.S. Tax Court will hear and decide on a tax controversy. However, when the issues involved are unusually novel or of wide impact, the case will be heard and decided by the full court sitting *en banc.*

Energy tax credit–business property. A 10 percent tax credit is available to businesses that invest in certain energy property. The purpose of the credit is to create incentives for conservation and to develop alternative energy sources. The credit is available on the acquisition of solar and geothermal property. §§ 46 and 48.

Enrolled agent (EA). A tax practitioner who has gained admission to practice before the IRS by passing an IRS examination.

Entity. An organization or being that possesses separate existence for tax purposes. Examples are corporations, partnerships, estates, and trusts.

Entity accounting income. Entity accounting income is not identical to the taxable income of a trust or estate, nor is it determined in the same manner as the entity's financial accounting income would be. The trust document or will determines whether certain income, expenses, gains, or losses are allocated to the corpus of the entity or to the entity's income beneficiaries. Only the items that are allocated to the income beneficiaries are included in entity accounting income.

Entity buy-sell agreement. An arrangement whereby the entity is to purchase a withdrawing owner's interest. When the entity is a corporation, the agreement generally involves a stock redemption on the part of the withdrawing shareholder. See also *buy-sell agreement* and *cross-purchase buy-sell agreement.*

Entity concept. Even in so-called flow-through entities, tax accounting elections are made (e.g., a tax year is adopted) and conventions are adopted (e.g., with respect to cost recovery methods) at the entity level. This may seem to violate the *conduit concept,* but such exceptions tend to ease the administration of such conduit taxpayers, especially in the context of a large number of shareholders/partners/members/beneficiaries.

Equity structure shift. A tax-free reorganization other than a *divisive reorganization* or *recapitalization.* If there is a more than 50 percent change in the ownership of a loss corporation in an equity structure shift, § 382 limits the use of net operating loss carryovers of the loss corporation. Specifically, the annual net operating loss carryover deduction is limited to the value of the loss corporation immediately before the equity structure shift times the *long-term tax-exempt rate.*

Escrow. Money or other property placed with a third party as security for an existing or proposed obligation. Cyd, for example, agrees to purchase Don's stock in Rip Corporation but needs time to raise the necessary funds. Don places the stock with Ernie (the escrow agent), with instructions to deliver it to Cyd when the purchase price is paid.

Estate. An entity that locates, collects, distributes, and discharges the assets and liabilities of a decedent.

Estate freeze. Procedures directed toward fixing and stabilizing the value of an interest retained in a business, while transferring the growth portion to family members. In the case of a closely held corporation, the estate freeze usually involves keeping the preferred stock and giving away the common stock. The ultimate objective is to reduce estate value when the original owner-donor dies.

Estate tax. A tax imposed on the right to transfer property by death. Thus, an estate tax is levied on the decedent's estate and not on the heir receiving the property. See also *death tax* and *inheritance tax.*

Estimated useful life. The period over which an asset will be used by the taxpayer. Assets such as collectible artwork do not have an estimated useful life. The estimated useful life of an asset is essential to measuring the annual tax deduction for depreciation and amortization.

Estoppel. The process of being stopped from proving something (even if true) in court due to a prior inconsistent action. It is usually invoked as a matter of fairness to prevent one party (either the taxpayer or the IRS) from taking advantage of a prior error.

Excess lobbying expenditure. An excise tax is applied on otherwise tax-exempt organizations with respect to the excess of total lobbying expenditure over *grass roots expenditure* for the year.

Excess loss account. When a subsidiary has generated more historical losses than its parent has invested in the entity, the parent's basis in the subsidiary is zero, and the parent records additional losses in an excess loss account. This treatment allows the parent to continue to deduct losses of the subsidiary, even where no basis reduction is possible, while avoiding the need to show a negative stock basis on various financial records. If the subsidiary stock is sold while an excess loss account exists, capital gain income usually is recognized to the extent of the balance in the account.

Excise tax. A tax on the manufacture, sale, or use of goods; on the carrying on of an occupation or activity; or on the transfer of property. Thus, the Federal estate and gift taxes are, theoretically, excise taxes.

Exclusion amount. The value of assets that is equal to the credit allowed for gifts or transfers by death. Thus, if the estate-tax unified transfer tax credit is $780,800, the exclusion amount is $2 million. The gift-tax exclusion amount is $1 million, based on its $345,800 unified credit. Often called the *exemption equivalent amount.* See also *bypass amount.*

Executor. A person designated by a will to administer (manage or take charge of) the assets and liabilities of a decedent. See also *administrator.*

Exempt organization. An organization that is either partially or completely exempt from Federal income taxation. § 501.

Exemption. An amount by which the tax base is reduced for all qualifying taxpayers. Individuals can receive personal and dependency exemptions, and taxpayers apply an exemption in computing their alternative minimum taxable income. Often, the exemption amount is phased out as the tax base becomes sizable.

Exemption equivalent. The maximum value of assets that can be transferred to another party without incurring any Federal gift or death tax because of the application of the unified tax credit.

Exemption equivalent amount. The taxable amount [currently $1 million for gift tax; for estate tax $2 million (2008) or $3.5 million (2009)] that is the equivalent of the unified transfer tax credit allowed. See also *bypass amount.*

Expanded affiliated group (EAG). For purposes of the *domestic production activities deduction (DPAD)*, all members of an expanded affiliated group (EAG) are treated as a single corporation. Thus, the activities of any member of the group are attributed to the other members. An EAG must meet the requirements for filing a *consolidated return* with ownership levels lowered to 50%. § 199(d)(4)(B).

Expenses in respect of a decedent. See *deductions in respect of a decedent.*

Extraterritorial income. A device by which the U.S. encouraged outbound (export) sales, services, and leases. An exclusion from gross income was computed under § 114 for certain transactions of U.S. taxpayers.

F

Fair market value. The amount at which property would change hands between a willing buyer and a willing seller, neither being under any compulsion to buy or to sell, and both having reasonable knowledge of the relevant facts. Reg. § 20.2031–1(b).

FAS 109. Guidance issued by the Financial Accounting Standards Board concerning how the tax expense of an enterprise is to be reported in the balance sheet, income statements, and associated footnotes. Permanent book-tax differences affect the enterprise's effective tax rate. Temporary book-tax differences create a *deferred tax asset* or a *deferred tax liability* on the balance sheet.

FASB. See *Generally accepted accounting principles (GAAP).*

Federal Register. The first place that the rules and regulations of U.S. administrative agencies (e.g., the U.S. Treasury Department) are published.

F.3d. An abbreviation for the third series of the *Federal Reporter*, the official series in which decisions of the U.S. Court of Federal Claims and the U.S. Court of Appeals are published. The second series is denoted F.2d.

F.Supp. The abbreviation for *Federal Supplement*, the official series in which the reported decisions of the U.S. Federal District Courts are published.

Feeder organization. An entity that carries on a trade or business for the benefit of an *exempt organization.* However, such a relationship does not result in the feeder organization itself being tax-exempt. § 502.

Fiduciary. A person who manages money or property for another and who must exercise a standard of care in the management activity imposed by law or contract. A *trustee,* for example, possesses a fiduciary responsibility to the *beneficiaries* of the *trust* to follow the terms of the trust and the requirements of applicable state law. A breach of fiduciary responsibility would make the trustee liable to the beneficiaries for any damage caused by the breach.

Field audit. An audit conducted by the IRS on the business premises of the taxpayer or in the office of the tax practitioner representing the taxpayer. See also *audit, correspondence audit,* and *office audit.*

FIN 48. An interpretation of *FAS 109* relating to when a tax benefit should be reported in an enterprise's financial statements. A tax benefit should be recorded for book purposes only if it is more likely than not that the taxpayer's filing position will be sustained after an audit, administrative appeal, and the highest applicable judicial review.

Financial Accounting Standards Board. See *Generally accepted accounting principles (GAAP).*

FIRPTA. Under the Foreign Investment in Real Property Tax Act, gains or losses realized by nonresident aliens and non-U.S. corporations on the disposition of U.S. real estate create U.S.-source income and are subject to U.S. income tax.

First-in, first-out (FIFO). An accounting method for determining the cost of inventories. Under this method, the inventory on hand is deemed to be the sum of the cost of the most recently acquired units. See also *last-in, first-out (LIFO).*

Fiscal year. See *accounting period.*

Flat tax. In its pure form, a flat tax would eliminate all exclusions, deductions, and credits and impose a one-rate tax on gross income.

Foreign corporation. A corporation that is not created in the United States or organized under the laws of one of the states of the United States. § 7701(a)(5). See also *domestic corporation.*

Foreign currency transaction. An exchange that could generate a foreign currency gain or loss for a U.S. taxpayer. For instance, if Avery contracts to purchase foreign goods, payable in a currency other than U.S. dollars, at a specified date in the future, any change in the exchange rate between the dollar and that currency generates a foreign currency gain or loss upon completion of the contract. This gain or loss is treated as separate from the underlying transaction; it may create ordinary or capital gain or loss.

Foreign earned income exclusion. The Code allows exclusions for earned income generated outside the United States to alleviate any tax base and rate disparities among countries. In addition, the exclusion is allowed for housing expenditures incurred by the taxpayer's employer with respect to the non-U.S. assignment, and self-employed individuals can deduct foreign housing expenses incurred in a trade or business.

Foreign sales corporation (FSC). An entity that qualified for a partial exemption of its gross export receipts from U.S. tax.

Foreign-source income. Income that is not sourced within the United States. Examples include earnings from the performance of a personal services contract outside the United States, interest received from a non-U.S. corporation, and income from the use of property outside the United States.

Foreign tax credit or deduction. A U.S. citizen or resident who incurs or pays income taxes to a foreign country on income subject to U.S. tax may be able to claim some of these taxes as a deduction or a credit against the U.S. income tax. §§ 27, 164, and 901–905.

Form 706. The U.S. Estate Tax Return. In certain cases, this form must be filed for a decedent who was a resident or citizen of the United States.

Form 709. The U.S. Gift Tax Return.

Form 870. The signing of Form 870 (Waiver of Restriction on Assessment and Collection of Deficiency in Tax and Acceptance of Overassessments) by a taxpayer permits the IRS to assess a proposed deficiency without issuing a statutory notice of deficiency (90-day letter). This means the taxpayer must pay the deficiency and cannot file a petition to the U.S. Tax Court. § 6213(d).

Form 872. The signing of this form by a taxpayer extends the applicable statute of limitations. § 6501(c)(4).

Form 1041. The U.S. Fiduciary Income Tax Return, required to be filed by estates and trusts. See Appendix B for a specimen form.

Form 1065. The U.S. Partnership Return of Income. See Appendix B for a specimen form.

Form 1120. The U.S. Corporation Income Tax Return. See Appendix B for a specimen form.

Form 1120–A. The U.S. Short-Form Corporation Income Tax Return. See Appendix B for a specimen form.

Form 1120S. The U.S. Small Business Corporation Income Tax Return, required to be filed by S corporations. See Appendix B for a specimen form.

Fraud. Tax fraud falls into two categories: civil and criminal. Under civil fraud, the IRS may impose as a penalty an amount equal to as much as 75 percent of the underpayment [§ 6651(f)]. Fines and/or imprisonment are prescribed for conviction of various types of criminal tax fraud (§§ 7201–7207). Both civil and criminal fraud involve a specific intent on the part of the taxpayer to evade the tax; mere negligence is not enough. Criminal fraud requires the additional element of willfulness (i.e., done deliberately and with evil purpose). In practice, it becomes difficult to distinguish between the degree of intent necessary to support criminal, rather than civil, fraud. In either situation, the IRS has the burden of proving fraud. See also *burden of proof.*

Free transferability of interests. The capability of the owner of an entity to transfer his or her ownership interest to another without the consent of the other owners. It is a characteristic of a corporation since a shareholder usually can freely transfer the stock to others without the approval of the existing shareholders.

Fringe benefits. Compensation or other benefits received by an employee that are not in the form of cash. Some fringe benefits (e.g., accident and health plans, group term life insurance) may be excluded from the employee's gross income and thus are not subject to the Federal income tax.

Functional currency. The currency of the economic environment in which the taxpayer carries on most of its activities and transacts most of its business.

Future interest. An interest that will come into being at some future time. Distinguished from a present interest, which already exists. Assume that Dora transfers securities to a newly created trust. Under the terms of the trust instrument, income from the securities is to be paid each year to Nan for her life, with the securities passing to Steve upon Nan's death. Nan has a present interest in the trust since she is entitled to current income distributions. Steve has a future interest since he must wait for Nan's death to benefit from the trust. The *annual exclusion* of $12,000 is not allowed for a gift of a future interest. § 2503(b). See also *annual exclusion* and *gift splitting.*

G

General business credit. The summation of various non-refundable business credits, including the energy credit, alcohol fuels credit, and research activities credit. The amount of general business credit that can be used to reduce the tax liability is limited to the taxpayer's net income tax reduced by the greater of (1) the tentative minimum tax or (2) 25 percent of the net regular tax liability that exceeds $25,000. Unused general business credits can be carried back 1 year and forward 20 years. §§ 38 and 39.

General partner. A partner who is fully liable in an individual capacity for the debts of the partnership to third parties. A general partner's liability is not limited to the investment in the partnership. See also *limited partner.*

General partnership. A partnership that is owned by one or more *general partners.* Creditors of a general partnership can collect amounts owed them from both the partnership assets and the assets of the partners individually.

General power of appointment. See *power of appointment.*

Generally accepted accounting principles (GAAP). Guidelines relating to how to construct the financial statements of enterprises doing business in the United States. Promulgated chiefly by the Financial Accounting Standards Board (FASB).

Gift. A transfer of property for less than adequate consideration. Gifts usually occur in a personal setting (such as between members of the same family). They are excluded from the income tax base but may be subject to a transfer tax.

Gift splitting. A special election for Federal gift tax purposes under which husband and wife can treat a gift by one of them to a third party as being made one-half by each. If, for example, Hal (the husband) makes a gift of $24,000 to Sharon, Winnie (the wife) may elect to treat $12,000 of the gift as coming from her. The major advantage of the election is that it enables the parties to take advantage of the nonowner spouse's (Winnie in this case) annual exclusion and unified credit. § 2513. See also *annual exclusion.*

Gift tax. A tax imposed on the transfer of property by gift. The tax is imposed upon the donor of a gift and is based on the fair market value of the property on the date of the gift.

Gifts within three years of death. Some taxable gifts automatically are included in the gross estate of the donor if death occurs within three years of the gift. § 2035.

Goodwill. The reputation and built-up business of a company. For accounting purposes, goodwill has no basis unless it is purchased. In the purchase of a business, goodwill generally is the difference between the purchase price and the value of the assets acquired. The intangible asset goodwill is amortized over 15 years. § 195. See also *amortization.*

Grantor. A transferor of property. The creator of a trust is usually referred to as the grantor of the trust.

Grantor trust. A trust under which the grantor retains control over the income or corpus (or both) to such an extent that he or she is treated as the owner of the property and its income for income tax purposes. Income from a grantor trust is taxable to the grantor, and not to the beneficiary who receives it. §§ 671–679. See also *reversionary interest.*

Grass roots expenditure. Exempt organizations are prohibited from engaging in political activities, but spending incurred to influence the opinions of the general public relative to specific legislation is permitted by the law. See also *excess lobbying expenditure.*

Green card test. Form I-551, received from a U.S. consul as a receipt showing that the holder has immigration status in the United States, and used to refute alien status for tax purposes.

Gross estate. The property owned or previously transferred by a *decedent* that is subject to the Federal estate tax. Distinguished from the *probate estate*, which is property actually subject to administration by the *administrator* or *executor* of an estate. §§ 2031–2046. See also *adjusted gross estate* and *taxable estate.*

Gross income. Income subject to the Federal income tax. Gross income does not include all economic income. That is, certain exclusions are allowed (e.g., interest on municipal bonds). For a manufacturing or merchandising business, gross income usually means gross profit (gross sales or gross receipts less cost of goods sold). § 61 and Reg. § 1.61– 3(a). See also *adjusted gross income* and *taxable income.*

Gross up. To add back to the value of the property or income received the amount of the tax that has been paid. For gifts made within three years of death, any gift tax paid on the transfer is added to the gross estate. § 2035.

Group term life insurance. Life insurance coverage provided by an employer for a group of employees. Such insurance is renewable on a year-to-year basis, and typically no cash surrender value is built up. The premiums paid by the employer on the insurance are not taxed to the employees on coverage of up to $50,000 per person. § 79 and Reg. § 1.79–1(b).

Guaranteed payment. Made by a partnership to a partner for services rendered or for the use of capital, to the extent that the payments are determined without regard to the income of the partnership. The payments are treated as though they were made to a nonpartner and thus are deducted by the entity.

Guardianship. A legal arrangement under which one person (a guardian) has the legal right and duty to care for another (the ward) and his or her property. A guardianship is established because the ward is unable to act legally on his or her own behalf (e.g., because of minority [he or she is not of age] or mental or physical incapacity).

H

Head of household. An unmarried individual who maintains a household for another and satisfies certain conditions set forth in § 2(b). This status enables the taxpayer to use a set of income tax rates that are lower than those applicable to other unmarried individuals but higher than those applicable to surviving spouses and married persons filing a joint return.

Heir. A person who inherits property from a decedent.

Hobby. An activity not engaged in for profit. The Code restricts the amount of losses that an individual can deduct for hobby activities so that these transactions cannot be used to offset income from other sources. § 183.

Holding period. The period of time during which property has been held for income tax purposes. The holding peri-

od is significant in determining whether gain or loss from the sale or exchange of a capital asset is long term or short term. § 1223.

Hot assets. Unrealized receivables and substantially appreciated inventory under § 751. When hot assets are present, the sale of a partnership interest or the disproportionate distribution of the assets can cause ordinary income to be recognized.

H.R. 10 plans. See *Keogh plans.*

I

Imputed interest. For certain long-term sales of property, the IRS can convert some of the gain from the sale into interest income if the contract does not provide for a minimum rate of interest to be paid by the purchaser. The seller recognizes less long-term capital gain and more ordinary income (interest income). § 483 and the related Regulations.

In kind. See *distributions in kind.*

Inbound taxation. U.S. tax effects when a non-U.S. person begins an investment or business activity in the U.S.

Incident of ownership. An element of ownership or degree of control over a life insurance policy. The retention by an insured of an incident of ownership in a life insurance policy places the policy proceeds in the insured's gross estate upon death. § 2042(2) and Reg. § 20.2042–1(c). See also *gross estate* and *insured.*

Income beneficiary. The party entitled to income from property. In a typical trust situation, Art is to receive the income for life with corpus or principal passing to Bev upon Art's death. In this case, Art is the income beneficiary of the trust.

Income in respect of a decedent (IRD). Income earned by a decedent at the time of death but not reportable on the final income tax return because of the method of accounting that appropriately is utilized. Such income is included in the gross estate and is taxed to the eventual recipient (either the estate or heirs). The recipient is, however, allowed an income tax deduction for the estate tax attributable to the income. § 691.

Income interest. The right of a beneficiary to receive distributions from the fiduciary income of a trust or estate.

Income shifting. Occurs when an individual transfers some of his or her gross income to a taxpayer who is subject to a lower tax rate, thereby reducing the total income tax liability of the group. Income shifting produces a successful assignment of income. It can be accomplished by transferring income-producing property to the lower-bracket taxpayer or to an effective trust for his or her benefit, or by transferring ownership interests in a family partnership or in a closely held corporation.

Incomplete transfer. A transfer made by a decedent during lifetime that, because of certain control or enjoyment retained by the transferor, is not considered complete for Federal estate tax purposes. Thus, some or all of the fair market value of the property transferred is included in the transferor's gross estate. §§ 2036–2038. See also *gross estate* and *revocable transfer.*

Indexation. Various components of the tax formula are adjusted periodically for the effects of inflation, so that the effects of the formula are not eroded by price level changes. Tax rate schedules, exemption amounts, and the standard deduction, among other items, are indexed in this manner.

Individual retirement account (IRA). Individuals with earned income are permitted to set aside up to 100 percent of that income per year (usually not to exceed $5,000) for a retirement account. The amount so set aside can be deducted by the taxpayer and is subject to income tax only upon withdrawal. The Code limits the amount of this contribution that can be deducted *for* AGI depending upon the magnitude of the taxpayer's AGI before the IRA contribution is considered. No deduction is allowed for a contribution to a Roth IRA, but withdrawals are completely tax-free. § 219.

Inheritance tax. A tax imposed on the right to receive property from a *decedent*. Thus, theoretically, an inheritance tax is imposed on the heir. The Federal estate tax is imposed on the estate. See also *death tax* and *estate tax*.

Inside basis. A partnership's basis in each of the assets it owns.

Installment method. A method of accounting enabling certain taxpayers to spread the recognition of gain on the sale of property over the collection period. Under this procedure, the seller arrives at the gain to be recognized by computing the gross profit percentage from the sale (the gain divided by the contract price) and applying it to each payment received. § 453.

Insured. A person whose life is the subject of an insurance policy. Upon the death of the insured, the life insurance policy matures, and the proceeds become payable to the designated beneficiary. See also *life insurance*.

Intangible asset. Property that is a "right" rather than a physical object. Examples are patents, stocks and bonds, goodwill, trademarks, franchises, and copyrights. See also *amortization* and *tangible property*.

Inter vivos transfer. A transfer of property during the life of the owner. Distinguished from testamentary transfers, where the property passes at death.

Interest-free loans. Bona fide loans that carry no interest (or a below-market rate). If made in a nonbusiness setting, the imputed interest element is treated as a gift from the lender to the borrower. If made by a corporation to a shareholder, a constructive dividend could result. In either event, the lender may recognize interest income. § 7872.

Intermediate sanctions. The IRS can assess excise taxes on disqualified persons and organization managers associated with so-called public charities engaging in excess benefit transactions. An excess benefit transaction is one in which a disqualified person engages in a non-fair market value transaction with the exempt organization or receives unreasonable compensation. Prior to the idea of intermediate sanctions, the only option available to the IRS was to revoke the organization's exempt status.

Internal Revenue Code. The collected statutes that govern the taxation of income, property transfers, and other transactions in the United States and the enforcement of those provisions. Enacted by Congress, the Code is amended frequently, but it has not been reorganized since 1954. However, because of the extensive revisions to the statutes that occurred with the Tax Reform Act of 1986, Title 26 of the U.S. Code is known as the Internal Revenue Code of 1986.

Internal Revenue Service (IRS). The Federal agency, a division of the Department of the Treasury, charged with administering the U.S. revenue enforcement and collection provisions.

Interpolated terminal reserve. The measure used in valuing insurance policies for gift and estate tax purposes when the policies are not paid up at the time of their transfer. Reg. § 20.2031–8(a)(3), Ex. (3).

Intestate. The condition when no will exists at the time of death. In such cases, state law prescribes who will receive the decedent's property. The laws of intestate succession generally favor the surviving spouse, children, and grandchildren, and then parents and grandparents and brothers and sisters.

Investment income. Consisting of virtually the same elements as portfolio income, a measure by which to justify a deduction for interest on investment indebtedness. See also *investment indebtedness* and *portfolio income*.

Investment indebtedness. Debt incurred to carry or incur investments by the taxpayer in assets that will produce portfolio income. Limitations are placed upon interest deductions that are incurred in connection with the debt (generally to the corresponding amount of investment income).

Investor losses. Losses on stock and securities. If stocks and bonds are capital assets in the hands of the holder, a capital loss materializes as of the last day of the taxable year in which the stocks or bonds become worthless. Under certain circumstances involving stocks and bonds of affiliated corporations, an ordinary loss is permitted upon worthlessness.

Involuntary conversion. The loss or destruction of property through theft, casualty, or condemnation. Any gain realized on an involuntary conversion can, at the taxpayer's election, be deferred for Federal income tax purposes if the owner reinvests the proceeds within a prescribed period of time in property that is similar or related in service or use. § 1033.

IRA. See *individual retirement account*.

Itemized deductions. Personal and employee expenditures allowed by the Code as deductions from adjusted gross income. Examples include certain medical expenses, interest on home mortgages, and charitable contributions. Itemized deductions are reported on Schedule A of Form 1040. Certain miscellaneous itemized deductions are reduced by 2 percent of the taxpayer's adjusted gross income. In addition, a taxpayer whose adjusted gross income exceeds a certain level (indexed annually) must reduce the itemized deductions by 3 percent of the excess of adjusted gross income over that level. Medical, casualty and theft, and investment interest deductions are not subject to the 3 percent reduction. The 3 percent reduction may not reduce itemized deductions that are subject to the reduction to below 20 percent of their initial amount.

J

Jeopardy assessment. If the collection of a tax appears in question, the IRS may assess and collect the tax immediately without the usual formalities. The IRS can terminate a taxpayer's taxable year before the usual date if it feels that the collection of the tax may be in peril because the taxpayer plans to leave the country. §§ 6851 and 6861–6864.

Joint and several liability. Permits the IRS to collect a tax from one or all of several taxpayers. A husband and wife who file a joint income tax return usually are collectively or individually liable for the full amount of the tax liability. The same rule applies to consolidated return partners. § 6013(d)(3).

Joint tenants. Two or more persons having undivided ownership of property with the right of survivorship. Right of survivorship gives the surviving owner full ownership of the property. Suppose Betty and Cheryl are joint tenants of a tract of land. Upon Betty's death, Cheryl becomes the sole owner of the property. For the estate tax consequences upon the death of a joint tenant, see § 2040. See also *tenants by the entirety* and *tenants in common*.

Joint venture. A one-time grouping of two or more persons in a business undertaking. Unlike a partnership, a joint venture does not entail a continuing relationship among the parties. A joint venture is treated like a partnership for Federal income tax purposes. § 7701(a)(2).

K

Keogh plans. Retirement plans available to self-employed taxpayers. They are also referred to as H.R. 10 plans. Under such plans, a taxpayer may deduct each year up to either 20 percent of net earnings from self-employment or $46,000 for 2008, whichever is less.

Kiddie tax. See *tax on unearned income of a child under age 19.*

L

Lapse. The expiration of a right either by the death of the holder or upon the expiration of a period of time. Thus, a power of appointment lapses upon the death of the holder if he or she has not exercised the power during life or at death (through a will).

Last-in, first-out (LIFO). An accounting method for valuing inventories for tax purposes. Under this method, it is assumed that the inventory on hand is valued at the cost of the earliest acquired units. § 472. See also *first-in, first-out (FIFO)*.

Leaseback. The transferor of property later leases it back. In a sale-leaseback situation, for example, Ron sells property to Sal and subsequently leases the property from Sal. Thus, Ron becomes the lessee and Sal the lessor.

Least aggregate deferral rule. A test applied to determine the allowable fiscal year of a *partnership* or *S corporation*. Possible year-ends are tested, and the fiscal year allowed by the IRS is the one that offers the least amount of income deferral to the owners on an individual basis.

Legacy. A transfer of cash or other property by will.

Legal age. The age at which a person may enter into binding contracts or commit other legal acts. In most states, a minor reaches legal age or majority (comes of age) at age 18.

Legal representative. A person who oversees the legal affairs of another; for example, the executor or administrator of an estate or a court-appointed guardian of a minor or incompetent person.

Legatee. The recipient of property that is transferred under a will by the death of the owner.

Lessee. One who rents property from another. In the case of real estate, the lessee is also known as the tenant.

Lessor. One who rents property to another. In the case of real estate, the lessor is also known as the landlord.

Letter ruling. The written response of the IRS to a taxpayer's request for interpretation of the revenue laws with respect to a proposed transaction (e.g., concerning the tax-free status of a reorganization). Not to be relied on as precedent by other than the party who requested the ruling.

LEXIS. An online database system through which a tax researcher can obtain access to the Internal Revenue Code, Regulations, administrative rulings, and court case opinions.

Liabilities in excess of basis. On the contribution of capital to a corporation, an investor recognizes gain on the exchange to the extent that contributed assets carry liabilities with a face amount in excess of the tax basis of the contributed assets. This rule keeps the investor from holding the investment asset received with a negative basis. § 357(c).

Life estate. A legal arrangement under which the beneficiary (the life tenant) is entitled to the income from the property for his or her life. Upon the death of the life tenant, the property is transferred to the holder of the remainder interest. See also *income beneficiary* and *remainder interest*.

Life insurance. A contract between the holder of a policy and an insurance company (the carrier) under which the company agrees, in return for premium payments, to pay a specified sum (the face value or maturity value of the policy) to the designated beneficiary upon the death of the insured. See also *insured.*

Like-kind exchange. An exchange of property held for productive use in a trade or business or for investment (except inventory and stocks and bonds) for other investment or trade or business property. Unless non-like-kind property (*boot*) is received, the exchange is fully nontaxable. § 1031.

Limited liability. The liability of an entity and its owners to third parties is limited to the investment in the entity. This is a characteristic of a corporation, as shareholders generally are not responsible for the debts of the corporation and, at most, may lose the amount paid for the stock issued.

Limited liability company (LLC). A form of entity allowed by all of the states. The entity is taxed as a partnership in which all owners of the LLC are treated much like limited partners. There are no restrictions on ownership, all partners may participate in management, and none of the owners has personal liability for the entity's debts.

Limited liability limited partnership (LLLP). A limited partnership for which the general partners are also protected from entity liabilities. An LLLP—or "triple LP"—can be formed in about 20 states. In those states, a limited partnership files with the state to adopt LLLP status.

Limited liability partnership (LLP). A form of entity allowed by many of the states, where a general partnership registers with the state as an LLP. Owners are general partners, but a partner is not liable for any malpractice committed by other partners. The personal assets of the partners are at risk for the entity's contractual liabilities, such as accounts payable. The personal assets of a specific partner are at risk for his or her own professional malpractice and tort liability, and for malpractice and torts committed by those whom he or she supervises.

Limited partner. A partner whose liability to third-party creditors of the partnership is limited to the amount he or she has invested in the partnership. See also *general partner* and *limited partnership.*

Limited partnership. A partnership in which some of the partners are *limited partners.* At least one of the partners in a limited partnership must be a *general partner.*

Liquidating distribution. A distribution by a partnership or corporation that is in complete liquidation of the entity's trade or business activities. Typically, such distributions generate capital gain or loss to the investors without regard, for instance, to the earnings and profits of the corporation or to the partnership's basis in the distributed property. They can, however, lead to recognized gain or loss at the corporate level.

Liquidation. See *corporate liquidation.*

Living trust. A revocable trust. Often touted as a means of avoiding some probate costs.

Lobbying expenditure. An expenditure made for the purpose of influencing legislation. Such payments can result in the loss of the exempt status and the imposition of Federal income tax on an exempt organization.

Long-term capital gain or loss. Results from the sale or other taxable exchange of a capital asset that had been held by the seller for more than one year or from other transactions involving statutorily designated assets, including § 1231 property and patents.

Long-term tax-exempt rate. Used in deriving net operating loss limitations in the context of an equity structure shift. The highest of the Federal long-term interest rates in effect for any of the last three months. § 382.

Low-income housing credit. Beneficial treatment to owners of low-income housing is provided in the form of a tax credit. The calculated credit is claimed in the year the building is placed in service and in the following nine years. § 42. See also *general business credit.*

Lump-sum distribution. Payment of the entire amount due at one time rather than in installments. Such distributions often occur from qualified pension or profit sharing plans upon the retirement or death of a covered employee.

M

MACRS. See *accelerated cost recovery system (ACRS).*

Majority. See *legal age.*

Malpractice. Professional misconduct; an unreasonable lack of due diligence in rendering a professional skill.

Marital deduction. A deduction allowed against the taxable estate or taxable gifts upon the transfer of property from one spouse to another.

Market value. See *fair market value.*

Matching rule. Treatment of an intercompany transaction on a *consolidated return,* when a sold asset remains within the group.

Meaningful reduction test. A decrease in the shareholder's voting control. Used to determine whether a redemption qualifies for sale or exchange treatment.

Merger. The absorption of one corporation by another with the corporation being absorbed losing its legal identity. Flow Corporation is merged into Jobs Corporation, and the shareholders of Flow receive stock in Jobs in exchange for their stock in Flow. After the merger, Flow ceases to exist as a separate legal entity. If a merger meets certain conditions, it is not currently taxable to the parties involved. § 368(a)(1)(A). See also *corporate acquisition* and *corporate reorganization.*

Minimum credit (AET). A fixed amount, $150,000 for personal service firms and $250,000 for all others, below which the *accumulated earnings credit* cannot be derived. Assures that small and start-up corporations can generate a minimum amount of earnings before being subject to the accumulated earnings tax (AET).

Minimum tax. See *alternative minimum tax.*

Minimum tax credit (AMT). When a corporation pays an alternative minimum tax (AMT), a minimum tax credit is created on a dollar-for-dollar basis, to be applied against regular tax liabilities incurred in future years. The credit is carried forward indefinitely, but it is not carried back. The effect of the credit for corporate taxpayers alternating between the AMT and regular tax models is to make the AMT liabilities a prepayment of regular taxes. Noncorporate AMT taxpayers are allowed the credit only with respect to the elements of the AMT that reflect timing differences between the two tax models.

Minority. See *legal age.*

Mitigate. To make less severe. See also *mitigation of the annual accounting period concept.*

Mitigation of the annual accounting period concept. Various tax provisions that provide relief from the effect of the finality of the annual accounting period concept. For example, the net operating loss carryover provisions allow the taxpayer to apply the negative taxable income of one year against a corresponding positive amount in another tax accounting period. See also *annual accounting period concept.*

Mortgagee. The party who holds the mortgage; the creditor.

Mortgagor. The party who mortgages the property; the debtor.

Most suitable use value. For gift and estate tax purposes, property that is transferred normally is valued in accordance with its most suitable or optimal use. Thus, if a farm is worth more as a potential shopping center, the value as a shopping center is used, even though the transferee (the donee or heir) continues to use the property as a farm. For an exception to this rule concerning the valuation of certain kinds of real estate transferred by death, see *special use value.*

Multistate corporation. A corporation that has operations in more than one of the states of the United States. Issues arise relative to the assignment of appropriate amounts of the entity's taxable income to the states in which it has a presence. See also *allocate, apportion, nexus,* and *UDITPA.*

Multistate Tax Commission (MTC). A regulatory body of the states that develops operating rules and regulations for the implementation of the *UDITPA* and other provisions that assign the total taxable income of a *multistate corporation* to specific states.

Multitiered partnerships. See *tiered partnerships.*

N

Necessary. Appropriate and helpful in furthering the taxpayer's business or income-producing activity. §§ 162(a) and 212. See also *ordinary.*

Negligence. Failure to exercise the reasonable or ordinary degree of care of a prudent person in a situation that results in harm or damage to another. Code § 6651 imposes a penalty on taxpayers who show negligence or intentional disregard of rules and Regulations with respect to the underpayment of certain taxes. See also *accuracy-related penalty.*

Net operating loss. To mitigate the effect of the annual accounting period concept, § 172 allows taxpayers to use an excess loss of one year as a deduction for certain past or future years. In this regard, a carryback period of 2 years and a carryforward period of 20 years currently are allowed. See also *mitigation of the annual accounting period concept.*

Net worth method. An approach used by the IRS to reconstruct the income of a taxpayer who fails to maintain adequate records. The IRS estimates gross income for the year as the increase in net worth of the taxpayer (assets in excess of liabilities), with appropriate adjustment for nontaxable receipts and nondeductible expenditures. The net worth method often is used when tax fraud is suspected.

Nexus. A *multistate corporation*'s taxable income can be apportioned to a specific state only if the entity has established a sufficient presence, or nexus, with that state. State law, which often follows the *UDITPA,* specifies various activities that lead to nexus in various states.

Ninety-day letter. See *statutory notice of deficiency.*

Nonacquiescence. Disagreement by the IRS on the result reached by selected tax decisions. Sometimes abbreviated *Nonacq.* or *NA.* See also *acquiescence.*

Nonbusiness bad debt. A bad debt loss that is not incurred in connection with a creditor's trade or business. The loss is classified as a short-term capital loss and is allowed only in the year the debt becomes entirely worthless. In addition to family loans, many investor losses are nonbusiness bad debts. § 166(d). See also *business bad debts.*

Nonbusiness income. Income generated from investment assets or from the taxable disposition thereof. In some states, the nonbusiness income of a *multistate corporation* is held out of the apportionment procedure and allocated to the state in which the nonbusiness asset is located. See also *allocate* and *apportion.*

Noncontributory qualified pension or profit sharing plan. A plan funded entirely by the employer with no contributions from the covered employees. See also *qualified pension or profit sharing plan.*

Nonliquidating distribution. A payment made by a partnership or corporation to the entity's owner is a nonliquidating distribution when the entity's legal existence does not cease thereafter. If the payor is a corporation, such a distribution can result in dividend income to the shareholders. If the payor is a partnership, the partner usually assigns a basis in the distributed property that is equal to the lesser of the partner's basis in the partnership interest or the basis of the distributed asset to the partnership. In this regard, the partner first assigns basis to any cash that is received in the distribution. The partner's remaining basis, if any, is assigned to the noncash assets according to their relative bases to the partnership.

Nonrecourse debt. Debt secured by the property that it is used to purchase. The purchaser of the property is not personally liable for the debt upon default. Rather, the creditor's recourse is to repossess the related property. Nonrecourse debt generally does not increase the purchaser's at-risk amount.

Nonresident alien. An individual who is neither a citizen nor a resident of the United States. Citizenship is determined under the immigration and naturalization laws of the United States. Residency is determined under § 7701(b) of the Internal Revenue Code.

Nonseparately stated income. The net income of an S corporation that is combined and allocated to the shareholders. Other items, such as capital gains and charitable contributions, that could be treated differently on the individual tax returns of the shareholders are not included in this amount but are allocated to the shareholders separately.

Not essentially equivalent redemption. See *redemption (not equivalent to a dividend).*

O

Obligee. The party to whom someone else is obligated under a contract. Thus, if Coop loans money to Dawn, Coop is the obligee and Dawn is the obligor under the loan.

Obligor. See *obligee.*

Offer in compromise. A settlement agreement offered by the IRS in a tax dispute, especially where there is doubt as to the collectibility of the full deficiency. Offers in compromise can include installment payment schedules, as well as reductions in the tax and penalties owed by the taxpayer.

Office audit. An audit conducted by the IRS in the agent's office. See also *audit, correspondence audit,* and *field audit.*

On all fours. A judicial decision exactly in point with another as to result, facts, or both.

Optimal use value. Synonym for most suitable use value.

Optional adjustment election. See *Section 754 election.*

Ordinary. Common and accepted in the general industry or type of activity in which the taxpayer is engaged. It comprises one of the tests for the deductibility of expenses incurred or paid in connection with a trade or business; for the production or collection of income; for the management, conservation, or maintenance of property held for the production of income; or in connection with the determination, collection, or refund of any tax. §§ 162(a) and 212. See also *necessary.*

Ordinary and necessary. See *necessary* and *ordinary.*

Ordinary gross income (OGI). A concept peculiar to personal holding companies and defined in § 543(b)(1). See also *adjusted ordinary gross income.*

Organizational expenditures. Items incurred early in the life of a corporate entity. Can be an immediate $5,000 amortization deduction, otherwise claimed over 180 months. Amortizable expenditures exclude those incurred to obtain capital (underwriting fees) or assets (subject to cost recovery). Typically, eligible expenditures include legal and accounting fees and state incorporation payments. Such items must be incurred by the end of the entity's first tax year. § 248.

Other adjustments account (OAA). Used in the context of a distribution from an *S corporation*. The net accumulation of the entity's exempt income (e.g., municipal bond interest) and nondeductible expenditures (e.g., fines and penalties).

Outbound taxation. U.S. tax effects when a U.S. person begins an investment or business activity outside the U.S.

Outside basis. A partner's basis in his or her partnership interest.

Owner shift. Any change in the respective ownership of stock by a 5 percent-or-more shareholder. Change is determined relative to a testing period of the prior three years. If there is a more-than-50 percent change in the ownership of a loss corporation, § 382 limitations apply to the use of net operating loss carryovers of the loss corporation.

Ownership change. An event that triggers a *Sec. 382 limitation* for the acquiring corporation.

P

Parent-subsidiary controlled group. A *controlled* or *affiliated group* of corporations, where at least one corporation is at least 80 percent owned by one or more of the others. The affiliated group definition is more difficult to meet.

Partial liquidation. A stock redemption where noncorporate shareholders are permitted sale or exchange treatment. In certain cases, an active business must have existed for at least five years. Only a portion of the outstanding stock in the entity is retired.

Partner. See *general partner* and *limited partner*.

Partnership. For income tax purposes, a partnership includes a syndicate, group, pool, or joint venture, as well as ordinary partnerships. In an ordinary partnership, two or more parties combine capital and/or services to carry on a business for profit as co-owners. § 7701(a)(2). See also *limited partnership* and *tiered partnerships*.

Passive foreign investment company (PFIC). A non-U.S. corporation that generates a substantial amount of personal holding company income. Upon receipt of an excess distribution from the entity or the sale of its shares, its U.S. shareholders are taxable on their pro rata shares of the tax that has been deferred with respect to the corporation's taxable income, plus an applicable interest charge.

Passive investment company. A means by which a *multistate corporation* can reduce the overall effective tax rate by isolating investment income in a low- or no-tax state.

Passive investment income (PII). Gross receipts from royalties, certain rents, dividends, interest, annuities, and gains from the sale or exchange of stock and securities. When E & P also exist, if the passive investment income of an *S corporation* exceeds 25 percent of the corporation's gross receipts for three consecutive years, S status is lost.

Passive loss. Any loss from (1) activities in which the taxpayer does not materially participate and (2) rental activities. Net passive losses cannot be used to offset income from non-passive sources. Rather, they are suspended until the taxpayer either generates net passive income (and a deduction of such losses is allowed) or disposes of the underlying property (at which time the loss deductions are allowed in full). Landlords who actively participate in the rental activities can deduct up to $25,000 of passive losses annually. However, this amount is phased out when the landlord's AGI exceeds $100,000. See also *portfolio income*.

Payroll factor. The proportion of a *multistate corporation*'s total payroll that is traceable to a specific state. Used in determining the taxable income that is to be apportioned to that state. See also *apportion*.

Pecuniary bequest. A bequest of money to an heir by a decedent. See also *bequest*.

Percentage depletion. See *depletion*.

Percentage of completion method. A method of reporting gain or loss on certain long-term contracts. Under this method of accounting, the gross contract price is included in income as the contract is completed. Reg. § 1.451–3. See also *completed contract method*.

Personal and household effects. Items owned by a decedent at the time of death. Examples include clothing, furniture, sporting goods, jewelry, stamp and coin collections, silverware, china, crystal, cooking utensils, books, cars, televisions, radios, and sound equipment.

Personal holding company (PHC). A corporation that satisfies the requirements of § 542. Qualification as a personal holding company means a penalty tax may be imposed on the corporation's undistributed personal holding company income for the year.

Personal holding company income. Income as defined by § 543. It includes interest, dividends, certain rents and royalties, income from the use of corporate property by certain shareholders, income from certain personal service contracts, and distributions from estates and trusts. Such income is relevant in determining whether a corporation is a personal holding company and is therefore subject to the penalty tax on personal holding companies. See also *adjusted ordinary gross income*.

Personal holding company tax. A penalty tax imposed on certain closely held corporations with excessive investment income. Assessed at the top individual tax rate on *personal holding company income*, reduced by dividends paid and other adjustments. § 541.

Personal property. Generally, all property other than real estate. It is sometimes referred to as personalty when real estate is termed realty. Personal property also refers to property not used in a taxpayer's trade or business or held for the production or collection of income. When used in this sense, personal property can include both *realty* (e.g., a personal residence) and *personalty* (e.g., personal effects such as clothing and furniture). See also *bequest*.

Personal service corporation (PSC). An entity whose principal activity is the providing of services by owner-employees. Subject to a flat 35 percent tax rate and limited to a calendar tax year.

Personalty. All property that is not attached to real estate (realty) and is movable. Examples of personalty are machinery, automobiles, clothing, household furnishings, inventory, and personal effects. See also *ad valorem tax* and *realty*.

Portfolio income. Income from interest, dividends, rentals, royalties, capital gains, or other investment sources. Net passive losses cannot be used to offset net portfolio income. See also *passive loss* and *investment income*.

Power of appointment. A legal right granted to someone by a will or other document that gives the holder the power to dispose of property or the income from property. When the holder may appoint the property to his or her own benefit, the power usually is called a general power of appointment. If the holder cannot benefit himself or herself but may only appoint to certain other persons, the power is a special power of appointment. Assume Gary places $500,000 worth of securities in trust granting Donna the right to determine each year how the trustee is to divide the income between Ann and Babs. Under these circumstances, Donna has a special power of appointment. If Donna had the further right to appoint the income to herself, she probably possesses a general power of appointment. For the estate tax and gift tax effects of powers of appointment, see §§ 2041 and 2514. See also *testamentary power of appointment.*

Precontribution gain or loss. Partnerships allow for a variety of *special allocations* of gain or loss among the partners, but gain or loss that is "built in" on an asset contributed to the partnership is assigned specifically to the contributing partner. § 704(c)(1)(A).

Preferences (AMT). See *alternative minimum tax (AMT)* and *tax preference items.*

Preferred stock bailout. A process where a shareholder used the issuance and sale, or later redemption, of a preferred stock dividend to obtain long-term capital gains, without any loss of voting control over the corporation. In effect, the shareholder received corporate profits without suffering the consequences of dividend income treatment. This procedure led Congress to enact § 306, which, if applicable, converts the prior long-term capital gain on the sale or redemption of the stock to dividend income. See also *bailout.*

Present interest. See *future interest.*

Presumption. An inference in favor of a particular fact. If, for example, the IRS issues a notice of deficiency against a taxpayer, under certain conditions a presumption of correctness attaches to the assessment. Thus, the taxpayer has the burden of proof to show that he or she does not owe the tax listed in the deficiency notice. See also *rebuttable presumption.*

Previously taxed income (PTI). Under prior law, the undistributed taxable income of an S corporation was taxed to the shareholders as of the last day of the corporation's tax year and usually could be withdrawn by the shareholders without tax consequences at some later point in time. The role of PTI has been taken over by the *accumulated adjustments account.*

Principal. Property as opposed to income. The term often is used as a synonym for the corpus of a trust. If, for example, Gil places real estate in trust with income payable to Ann for life and the remainder to Barb upon Ann's death, the real estate is the principal, or corpus, of the trust.

Private foundation. An *exempt organization* subject to additional statutory restrictions on its activities and on contributions made to it. Excise taxes may be levied on certain prohibited transactions, and the Code places more stringent restrictions on the deductibility of contributions to private foundations. § 509.

Pro rata. Proportionately. Assume, for example, a corporation has 10 shareholders, each of whom owns 10 percent of the stock. A pro rata dividend distribution of $1,000 means that each shareholder receives $100.

Pro se. The taxpayer represents himself or herself before the court without the benefit of counsel.

Probate. The legal process by which the estate of a decedent is administered. Generally, the probate process involves collecting a decedent's assets, liquidating liabilities, paying necessary taxes, and distributing property to heirs.

Probate costs. The costs incurred in administering a decedent's estate. See also *probate estate.*

Probate court. The usual designation for the state or local court that supervises the administration (*probate*) of a decedent's estate.

Probate estate. The property of a decedent that is subject to administration by the executor or administrator of an estate. See also *administration.*

Profit and loss sharing ratios. Specified in the partnership agreement and used to determine each partner's allocation of ordinary taxable income and separately stated items. Profits and losses can be shared in different ratios. The ratios can be changed by amending the partnership agreement. § 704(a).

Profits (loss) interest. A partner's percentage allocation of partnership operating results, determined by the *profit and loss sharing ratios.*

Property. Assets defined in the broadest legal sense. Property includes the *unrealized receivables* of a cash basis taxpayer, but not services rendered. § 351.

Property dividend. A dividend consisting of in-kind (noncash) assets of the payor, measured by the fair market value of the property on the date of distribution. Distribution of in-kind property causes the distributing corporation to recognize any underlying realized gain, but not loss.

Property factor. The proportion of a *multistate corporation*'s total property that is traceable to a specific state. Used in determining the taxable income that is to be apportioned to that state. See also *apportion.*

Property tax. An *ad valorem tax,* usually levied by a city or county government, on the value of real or personal property that the taxpayer owns on a specified date. Most states exclude intangible property and assets owned by exempt organizations from the tax base, and some exclude inventory, pollution control or manufacturing equipment, and other items to provide relocation or retention incentives for the taxpayer.

Proportionate distribution. A distribution in which each partner in a partnership receives a pro rata share of hot assets being distributed. For example, a distribution of $10,000 of hot assets equally to two 50 percent partners is a proportionate distribution.

Proposed Regulation. A *Regulation* may first be issued in proposed form to give interested parties the opportunity for comment. When and if a Proposed Regulation is finalized, it is known as a Regulation.

PTI. See *previously taxed income.*

Public Law 86–272. A congressional limit on the ability of the state to force a *multistate corporation* to assign income to that state. Under P.L. 86–272, where orders for tangible personal property are both filled and delivered outside the state, the entity must establish more than the mere solicitation of such orders before any income can be *apportioned* to the state.

Public policy limitation. A concept precluding an income tax deduction for certain expenses related to activities deemed to be contrary to the public welfare. In this connection, the Code includes specific disallowance provisions covering such items as illegal bribes, kickbacks, and fines and penalties. §§ 162(c) and (f).

Q

Qualified business unit (QBU). A subsidiary, branch, or other business entity that conducts business using a currency other than the U.S. dollar.

Qualified dividends. Distributions made by domestic (and certain non-U.S.) corporations to noncorporate shareholders that are subject to tax at the same rates as those applicable to net long-term capital gains. The dividends must be paid out of earnings and profits, and the shareholders must meet certain holding period requirements as to the stock. Qualified dividend treatment applies to distributions made after 2002 and before 2011. §§ 1(h)(1) and (11).

Qualified nonrecourse debt. Debt issued on realty by a bank, retirement plan, or governmental agency. Included in the *at-risk amount* by the investor. § 465(b)(6).

Qualified pension or profit sharing plan. An employer-sponsored plan that meets the requirements of § 401. If these requirements are met, none of the employer's contributions to the plan are taxed to the employee until distributed (§ 402). The employer is allowed a deduction in the year the contributions are made (§ 404). See also *contributory qualified pension or profit sharing plan, deferred compensation,* and *noncontributory qualified pension or profit sharing plan.*

Qualified production activities income. The base for computing the *domestic production activities deduction.* It comprises qualified production receipts less allocable cost of goods sold and other deductions. § 199.

Qualified small business corporation. A C corporation that has aggregate gross assets not exceeding $50 million and that is conducting an active trade or business. § 1202.

Qualified small business stock. Stock in a qualified small business corporation, purchased as part of an original issue after August 10, 1993. The shareholder may exclude from gross income 50 percent of the realized gain on the sale of the stock, if he or she held the stock for more than five years. § 1202.

Qualified terminable interest property (QTIP). Generally, the *marital deduction* (for gift and estate tax purposes) is not available if the interest transferred will terminate upon the death of the transferee spouse and pass to someone else. Thus, if Hannah places property in trust, life estate to Will, and remainder to their children upon Will's death, this is a terminable interest that will not provide Hannah (or her estate) with a marital deduction. If, however, the transfer in trust is treated as qualified terminable interest property (the QTIP election is made), the terminable interest restriction is waived and the marital deduction becomes available. In exchange for this deduction, the surviving spouse's gross estate must include the value of the QTIP election assets, even though he or she has no control over the ultimate disposition of the asset. Terminable interest property qualifies for this election if the donee (or heir) is the only beneficiary of the asset during his or her lifetime and receives income distributions relative to the property at least annually. For gifts, the donor spouse is the one who makes the QTIP election. As to property transferred by death, the *executor* of the estate of the deceased spouse has the right to make the election. §§ 2056(b)(7) and 2523(f).

R

RAR. A Revenue Agent's Report, which reflects any adjustments made by the agent as a result of an audit of the taxpayer. The RAR is mailed to the taxpayer along with the *30-day letter,* which outlines the appellate procedures available to the taxpayer.

Realistic possibility. A preparer penalty is assessed where a tax return includes a position that has no realistic possibility of being sustained by a court.

Realized gain or loss. The difference between the amount realized upon the sale or other disposition of property and the adjusted basis of such property. § 1001. See also *adjusted basis, amount realized, basis,* and *recognized gain or loss.*

Realty. Real estate. See also *personalty.*

Reasonable cause. Relief from taxpayer and preparer penalties often is allowed where there is reasonable cause for the taxpayer's actions. For instance, reasonable cause for the late filing of a tax return might be a flood that damaged the taxpayer's record-keeping systems and made difficult a timely completion of the return.

Reasonable needs of the business. A means of avoiding the penalty tax on an unreasonable accumulation of earnings. In determining base for this tax (*accumulated taxable income*), § 535 allows a deduction for "such part of earnings and profits for the taxable year as are retained for the reasonable needs of the business." § 537.

Rebuttable presumption. A presumption that can be overturned upon the showing of sufficient proof. See also *presumption.*

Recapitalization. An "E" reorganization, constituting a major change in the character and amount of outstanding equity of a corporation. For instance, common stock exchanged for preferred stock can qualify for tax-free "E" reorganization treatment.

Recapture. To recover the tax benefit of a deduction or a credit previously taken. See also *depreciation recapture.*

Recapture potential. A measure with respect to property that, if disposed of in a taxable transaction, would result in the recapture of depreciation (§§ 1245 or 1250), deferred LIFO gain, or deferred installment method gain.

Recognized gain or loss. The portion of realized gain or loss subject to income taxation. See also *realized gain or loss.*

Recourse debt. Debt for which the lender may both foreclose on the property and assess a guarantor for any payments due under the loan, even from personal assets. A lender may also make a claim against the assets of any general partner in a partnership to which debt is issued, without regard to whether that partner has guaranteed the debt.

Redemption. See *stock redemption.*

Redemption (complete termination). Sale or exchange treatment is available relative to this type of redemption. The shareholder must retire all of his or her outstanding shares in the corporation (ignoring family attribution rules) and cannot hold an interest, other than that of a creditor, for the 10 years following the redemption. § 302(b)(3).

Redemption (disproportionate). Sale or exchange treatment is available relative to this type of redemption. After the exchange, the shareholder owns less than 80 percent of his or her pre-redemption interest in the corporation and only a minority interest in the entity. § 302(b)(2).

Redemption (not equivalent to a dividend). Sale or exchange treatment is given to this type of redemption. Although various safe-harbor tests are failed, the nature of the redemption is such that dividend treatment is avoided, because it represents a meaningful reduction in the shareholder's interest in the corporation. § 302(b)(1).

Redemption to pay death taxes. Sale or exchange treatment is available relative to this type of redemption, to the extent of the proceeds up to the total amount paid by the estate or heir for death taxes and administration expenses. The stock value must exceed 35 percent of the value of the decedent's adjusted gross estate. In meeting this test, one can combine shareholdings in corporations where the decedent held at least 20 percent of the outstanding shares.

Regular corporation. See *C corporation.*

Regulations. The U.S. Treasury Department Regulations (abbreviated Reg.) represent the position of the IRS as to how the Internal Revenue Code is to be interpreted. Their purpose is to provide taxpayers and IRS personnel with rules of general and specific application to the various provisions of the tax law. Regulations are published in the *Federal Register* and in all tax services.

Related corporations. See *controlled group.*

Related parties. Various Code Sections define related parties and often include a variety of persons within this (usually detrimental) category. Generally, related parties are accorded different tax treatment from that applicable to other taxpayers who enter into similar transactions. For instance, realized losses that are generated between related parties are not recognized in the year of the loss. However, these deferred losses can be used to offset recognized gains that occur upon the subsequent sale of the asset to a nonrelated party. Other uses of a related-party definition include the conversion of gain upon the sale of a depreciable asset into all ordinary income (§ 1239) and the identification of constructive ownership of stock relative to corporate distributions, redemptions, liquidations, reorganizations, and compensation.

Remainder interest. The property that passes to a beneficiary after the expiration of an intervening income interest. If, for example, Greg places real estate in trust with income to Ann for life and remainder to Bill upon Ann's death, Bill has a remainder interest. See also *life estate* and *reversionary interest.*

Remand. To send back. An appellate court may remand a case to a lower court, usually for additional fact finding. In other words, the appellate court is not in a position to decide the appeal based on the facts determined by the lower court. Remanding is abbreviated *"rem'g."*

Reorganization. See *corporate reorganization.*

Research activities credit. A tax credit whose purpose is to encourage research and development. It consists of three components: the incremental research activities credit, the energy research credit, and the basic research credit. The incremental research activities credit is equal to 20 percent of the excess qualified research expenditures over the base amount. The basic research credit is equal to 20 percent of the excess of basic research payments over the base amount. § 41. The energy research credit is 20 percent of payments to an energy research consortium. See also *general business credit.*

Residential rental property. Buildings for which at least 80 percent of the gross rents are from dwelling units (e.g., an apartment building). This type of building is distinguished from nonresidential (commercial or industrial) buildings in applying the recapture of depreciation provisions. The term also is relevant in distinguishing between buildings that are eligible for a 27.5-year life versus a 31.5- or 39-year life for MACRS purposes.

Residual method. Used to allocate the new stepped-up basis of a subsidiary's assets among its property when a § 338 election is in effect. The purchase price that exceeds the aggregate fair market values of the tangible and identifiable intangible assets is allocated to goodwill or going-concern value. § 1060.

Return of capital. When a taxpayer reacquires financial resources that he or she previously had invested in an entity or venture, the return of his or her capital investment itself does not increase gross income for the recovery year. A return of capital may result from an annuity or insurance contract, the sale or exchange of any asset, or a distribution from a partnership or corporation.

Revenue Agent's Report. See *RAR.*

Revenue neutrality. A change in the tax system that results in the same amount of revenue. Revenue neutral, however, does not mean that any one taxpayer pays the same amount of tax as before. Thus, as a result of a tax law change, corporations could pay more taxes, but the excess revenue will be offset by lower taxes on individuals.

Revenue Procedure. A matter of procedural importance to both taxpayers and the IRS concerning the administration of the tax laws is issued as a Revenue Procedure (abbreviated Rev.Proc.). A Revenue Procedure is first published in an *Internal Revenue Bulletin* (I.R.B.) and later transferred to the appropriate *Cumulative Bulletin* (C.B.).

Revenue Ruling. A Revenue Ruling (abbreviated Rev.Rul.) is issued by the National Office of the IRS to express an official interpretation of the tax law as applied to specific transactions. It is more limited in application than a Regulation. A Revenue Ruling is first published in an *Internal Revenue Bulletin* (I.R.B.) and later transferred to the appropriate *Cumulative Bulletin* (C.B.).

Reversed (Rev'd.). An indication that a decision of one court has been reversed by a higher court in the same case.

Reversing (Rev'g.). An indication that the decision of a higher court is reversing the result reached by a lower court in the same case.

Reversionary interest. The property that reverts to the grantor after the expiration of an intervening income interest. Assume Gail places real estate in trust with income to Art for 11 years, and upon the expiration of this term, the property returns to Gail. Under these circumstances, she holds a reversionary interest in the property. A reversionary interest is the same as a remainder interest, except that, in the latter case, the property passes to someone other than the original owner (e.g., the grantor of a trust) upon the expiration of the intervening interest. See also *grantor trust* and *remainder interest.*

Revocable transfer. A transfer of property where the transferor retains the right to recover the property. The creation of a revocable trust is an example of a revocable transfer. § 2038. See also *incomplete transfer.*

Rev.Proc. Abbreviation for an IRS *Revenue Procedure.*

Rev.Rul. Abbreviation for an IRS *Revenue Ruling.*

Right of survivorship. See *joint tenants.*

S

S corporation. The designation for a small business corporation. See also *Subchapter S.*

Sales factor. The proportion of a *multistate corporation*'s total sales that is traceable to a specific state. Used in determining the taxable income that is to be apportioned to that state. See also *apportion.*

Sales tax. A state- or local-level tax on the retail sale of specified property. Generally, the purchaser pays the tax, but the seller collects it, as an agent for the government. Various taxing jurisdictions allow exemptions for purchases of specific items, including certain food, services, and manufacturing equipment. If the purchaser and seller are in different states, a *use tax* usually applies.

Schedule M-1. On the Form 1120, a reconciliation of book net income with Federal taxable income. Accounts for timing and permanent differences in the two computations, such as depreciation differences, exempt income, and nondeductible items. On Forms 1120S and 1065, the Schedule M-1 reconciles book income with the owners' aggregate ordinary taxable income.

Schedule M-3. An *expanded* reconciliation of book net income with Federal taxable income (see *Schedule M-1*). Required of C and S corporations and partnerships/LLCs, with total assets of $10 million or more.

Schedule PH. A tax form required to be filed by *personal holding companies.* The form is filed in addition to Form 1120 (U.S. Corporation Income Tax Return).

Section 306 stock. Preferred stock issued as a nontaxable stock dividend that, if sold or redeemed, would result in ordinary income recognition. § 306(c). See also *preferred stock bailout.*

Section 306 taint. The ordinary income that would result upon the sale or other taxable disposition of § 306 stock.

Section 338 election. When a corporation acquires at least 80 percent of a subsidiary in a 12-month period, it can elect to treat the acquisition of such stock as an asset purchase. The acquiring corporation's basis in the subsidiary's assets then is the cost of the stock. The subsidiary is deemed to have sold its assets for an amount equal to the grossed-up basis in its stock.

Section 382 limitation. When one corporation acquires another, the acquiror's ability to use the loss and credit carryovers of the target may be limited, in an anti-abuse provision specified in the Code. Generally, for instance, the maximum deduction available to the acquiror is the takeover-date value of the target times the tax-exempt interest rate on that date.

Section 754 election. An election that may be made by a partnership to adjust the basis of partnership assets to reflect a purchasing partner's outside basis in interest or to reflect a gain, loss, or basis adjustment of a partner receiving a distribution from a partnership. The intent of the election is to maintain the equivalence between outside and inside basis. Once the election is made, the partnership must make basis adjustments for all future transactions, unless the IRS consents to revoke the election.

Section 1231 assets. Depreciable assets and real estate used in a trade or business and held for the appropriate holding period. Under certain circumstances, the classification also includes timber, coal, domestic iron ore, livestock (held for draft, breeding, dairy, or sporting purposes), and unharvested crops. § 1231(b). See also *Section 1231 gains and losses.*

Section 1231 gains and losses. If the combined gains and losses from the taxable dispositions of § 1231 assets plus the net gain from business involuntary conversions (of both § 1231 assets and long-term capital assets) is a gain, such gains and losses are treated as long-term capital gains and losses. In arriving at § 1231 gains, however, the depreciation recapture provisions (e.g., §§ 1245 and 1250) are applied first, to produce ordinary income. If the net result of the combination is a loss, the gains and losses from § 1231 assets are treated as ordinary gains and losses. § 1231(a). See also *depreciation recapture* and *Section 1231 assets.*

Section 1244 stock. Stock issued under § 1244 by qualifying small business corporations. If § 1244 stock becomes worthless, the shareholders may claim an ordinary loss rather than the usual capital loss, within statutory limitations.

Section 1245 recapture. Upon a taxable disposition of § 1245 property, all depreciation claimed on such property is recaptured as ordinary income (but not to exceed recognized gain from the disposition).

Section 1250 recapture. Upon a taxable disposition of § 1250 property, accelerated depreciation or cost recovery claimed on the property may be recaptured as ordinary income.

Securities. Generally, stock, debt, and other financial assets. To the extent securities other than the stock of the transferee corporation are received in a § 351 exchange, the new shareholder realizes a gain.

Separate property. In a community property jurisdiction, property that belongs entirely to one of the spouses is separate property. Generally, it is property acquired before marriage or acquired after marriage by gift or inheritance. See also *community property.*

Separate return limitation year (SRLY). A series of rules limits the amount of an acquired corporation's net operating loss carryforwards that can be used by the acquiror. Generally, a *consolidated return* can include the acquiree's NOL carryforward only to the extent of the lesser of the subsidiary's (1) current-year or (2) cumulative positive contribution to consolidated taxable income.

Separately stated item. Any item of a partnership or S corporation that might be taxed differently to any two owners of the entity. These amounts are not included in ordinary income of the entity, but instead are reported separately to the owners; tax consequences are determined at the owner level.

Sham. A transaction without substance that will be disregarded for tax purposes.

Short-term capital gain or loss. Results from the sale or other taxable exchange of a capital asset that had been held by the seller for one year or less or from other transactions involving statutorily designated assets, including nonbusiness bad debts.

Simple trust. Simple trusts are those that are not complex trusts. Such trusts may not have a charitable beneficiary, accumulate income, or distribute corpus. See also *complex trust.*

Small business corporation. A corporation that satisfies the definition of § 1361(b), § 1244(c), or both. Satisfaction of § 1361(b) permits an S election, and satisfaction of § 1244(c) enables the shareholders of the corporation to claim an ordinary loss on the worthlessness of stock.

Small Cases Division of the U.S. Tax Court. Jurisdiction is limited to claims of $50,000 or less. There is no appeal from this court.

Special allocation. Any amount for which an agreement exists among the partners of a partnership outlining the method used for assigning the item among the partners.

Special power of appointment. See *power of appointment.*

Special use value. Permits the executor of an estate to value, for death tax purposes, real estate used in a farming activity or in connection with a closely held business at its current use value rather than at its most suitable or optimal use value. Under this option, a farm is valued for farming purposes even though, for example, the property might have a higher potential value as a shopping center. For the executor of an estate to elect special use valuation, the conditions of § 2032A must be satisfied. See also *most suitable use value.*

Spin-off. A type of reorganization where, for example, Ace Corporation transfers some assets to Bow Corporation in exchange for enough Bow stock to represent control. Ace then distributes the Bow stock to its shareholders.

Split-off. A type of reorganization where, for example, Arc Corporation transfers some assets to Bond Corporation in exchange for enough Bond stock to represent control. Arc then distributes the Bond stock to its shareholders in exchange for some of their Arc stock.

Split-up. A type of reorganization where, for example, Ally Corporation transfers some assets to Bar Corporation and the remainder to Zip Corporation. In return, Ally receives enough Bar and Zip stock to represent control of each corporation. Ally then distributes the Bar and Zip stock to its shareholders in return for all of their Ally stock. The result of the split-up is that Ally is liquidated, and its shareholders now have control of Bar and Zip.

Sprinkling trust. When a trustee has the discretion to either distribute or accumulate the entity accounting income of the trust and to distribute it among the trust's income beneficiaries in varying magnitudes, a sprinkling trust exists. The trustee can "sprinkle" the income of the trust.

Statute of limitations. Provisions of the law that specify the maximum period of time in which action may be taken on a past event. Code §§ 6501–6504 contain the limitation periods applicable to the IRS for additional assessments, and §§ 6511–6515 relate to refund claims by taxpayers.

Statutory depletion. See *depletion.*

Statutory notice of deficiency. Commonly referred to as the 90-day letter, this notice is sent to a taxpayer upon request, upon the expiration of the *30-day letter,* or upon exhaustion by the taxpayer of his or her administrative remedies before the IRS. The notice gives the taxpayer 90 days in which to file a petition with the U.S. Tax Court. If such a petition is not filed, the IRS will demand payment of the assessed deficiency. §§ 6211–6216. See also *deficiency.*

Step transaction. Disregarding one or more transactions to arrive at the final result. Assume, for example, that the shareholders of Clue Corporation liquidate the corporation and receive cash and operating assets. Immediately after the liquidation, the shareholders transfer the operating assets to newly formed Blue Corporation. Under these circumstances, the IRS may contend that the liquidation of Clue should be disregarded (thereby depriving the shareholders of capital gain treatment). What may really have happened is a reorganization of Clue with a distribution of boot (ordinary income) to Clue's shareholders. If so, there will be a carryover of basis in the assets transferred from Clue to Blue.

Step-down in basis. A reduction in the tax basis of property. See also *step-up in basis.*

Step-up in basis. An increase in the income tax basis of property. A step-up in basis occurs when a decedent dies owning appreciated property. Since the estate or heir acquires a basis in the property equal to the property's fair market value on the date of death (or alternate valuation date if available and elected), any appreciation is not subject to the income tax. Thus, a step-up in basis is the result, with no income tax consequences.

Stock attribution. See *attribution.*

Stock dividend. A dividend consisting of stock of the payor. Not taxable if a pro rata distribution of stock or stock rights on common stock. However, some stock dividends are taxable. § 305.

Stock redemption. A corporation buys back its own stock from a specified shareholder. Typically, the corporation recognizes any realized gain on the noncash assets that it uses to effect a redemption, and the shareholder obtains a capital gain or loss upon receipt of the purchase price.

Stock rights. Assets that convey to the holder the power to purchase corporate stock at a specified price, often for a limited period of time. Stock rights received may be taxed as a distribution of earnings and profits. After the right is exercised, the basis of the acquired share includes the investor's purchase price or gross income, if any, to obtain the right. Disposition of the right also can be a taxable event.

Subchapter S. Sections 1361–1379 of the Internal Revenue Code. An elective provision permitting certain small business corporations (§ 1361) and their shareholders

(§ 1362) to elect to be treated for income tax purposes in accordance with the operating rules of §§ 1363–1379. S corporations usually avoid the corporate income tax, and corporate losses can be claimed by the shareholders.

Subpart F. The subpart of the Code that identifies the current tax treatment of income earned by a controlled foreign corporation. Certain types of income are included in U.S. gross income by U.S. shareholders of such an entity as the income is generated, not when it is repatriated.

Substance vs. form concept. A standard used when one must ascertain the true reality of what has occurred. Suppose, for example, a father sells stock to his daughter for $1,000. If the stock is really worth $50,000 at the time of the transfer, the substance of the transaction is probably a gift to her of $49,000.

Substantial authority. Taxpayer understatement penalties are waived where substantial authority existed for the disputed position taken on the return.

Substantial economic effect. Partnerships are allowed to *allocate* items of income, expense, gain, loss, and credit in any manner that is authorized in the partnership agreement, provided that the allocation has an economic effect aside from the corresponding tax results. The necessary substantial economic effect is present, for instance, if the post-contribution appreciation in the value of an asset that was contributed to the partnership by a partner was allocated to that partner for cost recovery purposes.

Substituted basis. When a taxpayer exchanges one asset for another, many provisions in the tax law allow an assignment of basis in the received asset to be that of the traded asset(s) in the hands of its former owner. Thus, no step-up or -down of basis occurs as a result of the exchange. For instance, when an investor contributes an asset to a corporation or partnership, the partner generally takes a substituted basis in the partnership interest (i.e., the interest has a basis equal to the aggregated bases of the assets contributed by that partner). § 723.

Surviving spouse. When a husband or wife predeceases the other spouse, the survivor is known as a surviving spouse. Under certain conditions, a surviving spouse may be entitled to use the income tax rates in § 1(a) (those applicable to married persons filing a joint return) for the two years after the year of death of his or her spouse.

Survivorship. See *joint tenants.*

Syndication costs. Incurred in promoting and marketing partnership interests for sale to investors. Examples include legal and accounting fees, printing costs for prospectus and placement documents, and state registration fees. These items are capitalized by the partnership as incurred, with no amortization thereof allowed.

T

Tangible property. All property that has form or substance and is not intangible. See also *intangible asset.*

Tax benefit rule. Limits the recognition of income from the recovery of an expense or loss properly deducted in a prior tax year to the amount of the deduction that generated a tax saving. Assume that last year Tom had medical expenses of $3,000 and adjusted gross income of $30,000. Because of the 7.5 percent limitation, he could deduct only

$750 of these expenses [$3,000 − (7.5% × $30,000)]. If, this year, Tom is reimbursed by his insurance company for the $3,000 of expenses, the tax benefit rule limits the amount of income from the reimbursement to $750 (the amount previously deducted with a tax saving).

Tax Court. The U.S. Tax Court is one of four trial courts of original jurisdiction that decide litigation involving Federal income, death, or gift taxes. It is the only trial court where the taxpayer must not first pay the deficiency assessed by the IRS. The Tax Court will not have jurisdiction over a case unless a statutory notice of deficiency (90-day letter) has been issued by the IRS and the taxpayer files the petition for hearing within the time prescribed.

Tax haven. A country in which either locally sourced income or residents of the country are subject to a low rate of taxation.

Tax on unearned income of a child under age 19. Portfolio income, such as interest and dividends, that is recognized by such a child is taxed *to him or her* at the rates that would have applied had the income been incurred by the child's parents, generally to the extent that the income exceeds $1,800. The additional tax is assessed regardless of the source of the income or the income's underlying property. If the child's parents are divorced, the custodial parent's rates are used. The parents' rates reflect any applicable alternative minimum tax and the phase-outs of lower tax brackets and other deductions. A special rule applies if the child is a full-time student. § 1(g).

Tax preference items. Various items that may result in the imposition of the *alternative minimum tax.* §§ 55–58.

Tax treaty. An agreement between the U.S. State Department and another country, designed to alleviate double taxation of income and asset transfers and to share administrative information useful to tax agencies in both countries. The United States has income tax treaties with over 40 countries and transfer tax treaties with about 20.

Tax year. See *accounting period.*

Taxable estate. The *gross estate* of a *decedent* reduced by the deductions allowed by §§ 2053–2057 (e.g., administration expenses and marital and charitable deductions). The taxable estate is subject to the unified transfer tax at death. See also *adjusted taxable estate* and *gross estate.* § 2051.

Taxable gift. Amount of a gift that is subject to the unified transfer tax. Thus, a taxable gift has been adjusted by the annual exclusion and other appropriate deductions (e.g., marital and charitable). § 2503.

Taxable income. The tax base with respect to the prevailing Federal income tax. Taxable income is defined by the Internal Revenue Code, Treasury Regulations, and pertinent court cases. Currently, taxable income includes gross income from all sources except those specifically excluded by the statute. In addition, taxable income is reduced for certain allowable deductions. Deductions for business taxpayers must be related to a trade or business. Individuals can also deduct certain personal expenses in determining their taxable incomes. See also *gross income.*

Tax-free exchange. Transfers of property specifically exempted from income tax consequences by the tax law. Examples are a transfer of property to a controlled corporation under § 351(a) and a like-kind exchange under § 1031(a).

T.C. An abbreviation for the U.S. Tax Court used in citing a Regular Decision of the U.S. Tax Court.

T.C.Memo. An abbreviation used to refer to a Memorandum Decision of the U.S. Tax Court.

Technical advice memorandum. An interpretation of the tax law with respect to a disputed item, issued by the IRS, in response to a request from an agent, appellate conferee, or IRS executive. Often used to reconcile perceived differences in the application of the law among taxpayers or to identify an IRS position where no pertinent Regulations or rulings exist.

Technical termination of partnership. The entity is treated for tax purposes as though it has terminated, even though it continues in its activities. When there has been a sale or exchange of more than 50 percent of the capital interests of the partnership within 12 months, the partnership is deemed to have terminated when the 50 percent threshold is crossed. A new partnership immediately is formed through asset contributions by the partners. These activities can affect the entity's tax year and its bases in the assets it holds.

Telescoping. To look through one or more transactions to arrive at the final result. It is also referred to as the *step transaction* approach or the *substance vs. form concept.*

Temporary Regulation. The Treasury often issues Temporary Regulations to offer immediate guidance as to elections and other compliance matters after a change in the statute or a court ruling has been issued. Temporary Regulations carry the same precedential value as a final Regulation, and they should be followed as such for three years after issuance, after which they expire. Often a Temporary Regulation also is issued as a Proposed Regulation.

Tenants by the entirety. Essentially, a joint tenancy between husband and wife. See also *joint tenants* and *tenants in common.*

Tenants in common. A form of ownership where each tenant (owner) holds an undivided interest in property. Unlike a joint tenancy or a tenancy by the entirety, the interest of a tenant in common does not terminate upon that individual's death (there is no right of survivorship). Assume Brad and Connie acquire real estate as equal tenants in common, each having furnished one-half of the purchase price. Upon Brad's death, his one-half interest in the property passes to his estate or heirs, not to Connie. For a comparison of results, see *joint tenants* and *tenants by the entirety.*

Term certain. A fixed period of years used to determine the length of an income interest (i.e., prior to the termination of a trust or estate).

Terminable interest. An interest in property that terminates upon the death of the holder or upon the occurrence of some other specified event. The transfer of a terminable interest by one spouse to the other may not qualify for the marital deduction. §§ 2056(b) and 2523(b). See also *marital deduction.*

Testamentary disposition. The passing of property to another upon the death of the owner.

Testamentary power of appointment. A power of appointment that can be exercised only through the will (upon the death) of the holder. See also *power of appointment.*

Thin capitalization. When debt owed by a corporation to the shareholders becomes too large in relation to the corpora-tion's capital structure (i.e., stock and shareholder equity), the IRS may contend that the corporation is thinly capitalized. In effect, some or all of the debt is reclassified as equity. The immediate result is to disallow any interest deduction to the corporation on the reclassified debt. To the extent of the corporation's earnings and profits, interest payments and loan repayments are treated as dividends to the shareholders.

Thirty-day letter. A letter that accompanies an RAR (Revenue Agent's Report) issued as a result of an IRS audit of a taxpayer (or the rejection of a taxpayer's claim for refund). The letter outlines the taxpayer's appeal procedure before the IRS. If the taxpayer does not request any such procedure within the 30-day period, the IRS issues a *statutory notice of deficiency.*

Three-factor apportionment formula. A means by which the total taxable income of a *multistate corporation* is assigned to a specific state. Usually, the payroll, property, and sales factors are treated equally, and the average of these factors is used in the apportionment procedure. In some states, however, the sales factor may receive a double weight, or it may be the only factor considered. These latter formulas place a greater tax burden on the income of out-of-state corporations. See also *apportion, payroll factor, property factor, sales factor,* and *UDITPA.*

Throwback rule. If there is no income tax in the state to which a sale otherwise would be *apportioned*, the sale essentially is exempt from state income tax, even though the seller is *domiciled* in a state that levies an income tax. Nonetheless, if the seller's state has adopted a throwback rule, the sale is attributed to the *seller's* state, and the transaction is subjected to a state-level tax.

Tiered partnerships. An ownership arrangement wherein one partnership (the parent or first tier) is a partner in one or more partnerships (the subsidiary/subsidiaries or second tier). Frequently, the first tier is a holding partnership, and the second tier is an operating partnership.

Totten trust. A bank account or security that designates a survivor in the event the owner predeceases. As an example, Dan purchases a $50,000 CD and lists ownership as follows: "Dan, payable on proof of Dan's death to Nancy." The transfer is incomplete and can be revoked or changed by Dan as he sees fit. Once Dan dies, however, the CD belongs to Nancy. In effect, the Totten trust arrangement carries the same tax consequences as a revocable trust, with no *probate* required.

Trade or business. Any business or professional activity conducted by a taxpayer. The mere ownership of rental or other investment assets does not constitute a trade or business. Generally, a trade or business generates relatively little passive investment income.

Transfer pricing. The process of setting internal prices for transfers of goods and services among related taxpayers. For instance, what price should be used when Subsidiary purchases management services from Parent? Section 482 allows the IRS to adjust transfer prices when it can show that the taxpayers were attempting to avoid tax by, say, shifting losses, deductions, or credits from low-tax to high-tax entities or jurisdictions.

Transfer tax. A tax imposed upon the transfer of property. See also *unified transfer tax.*

Transferee liability. Under certain conditions, if the IRS is unable to collect taxes owed by a transferor of property, it may pursue its claim against the transferee of the property. The transferee's liability for taxes is limited to the extent of the value of the assets transferred. For example, the IRS can force a donee to pay the gift tax when such tax cannot be paid by the donor making the transfer. §§ 6901–6905.

Treasury Regulations. See *Regulations.*

Treaty shopping. An international investor attempts to use the favorable aspects of a tax treaty to his or her advantage, often elevating the form of the transaction over its substance (e.g., by establishing only a nominal presence in the country offering the favorable treaty terms).

Trial court. The court of original jurisdiction; the first court to consider litigation. In Federal tax controversies, trial courts include U.S. District Courts, the U.S. Tax Court, the U.S. Court of Federal Claims, and the Small Cases Division of the U.S. Tax Court. See also *appellate court, Court of Federal Claims, District Court, Small Cases Division of the U.S. Tax Court,* and *Tax Court.*

Trust. A legal entity created by a grantor for the benefit of designated beneficiaries under the laws of the state and the valid trust instrument. The trustee holds a fiduciary responsibility to manage the trust's corpus assets and income for the economic benefit of all of the beneficiaries.

Trustee. An individual or corporation that assumes the fiduciary responsibilities under a trust agreement.

U

UDITPA. The Uniform Division of Income for Tax Purposes Act has been adopted in some form by many of the states. The Act develops criteria by which the total taxable income of a *multistate corporation* can be assigned to specific states. See also *allocate, apportion, Multistate Tax Commission (MTC),* and *nexus.*

Undistributed personal holding company income. The tax base for the *personal holding company tax.* § 545.

Unearned income. Income received but not yet earned. Normally, such income is taxed when received, even for accrual basis taxpayers.

Unified tax credit. A credit allowed against any unified transfer tax. §§ 2010 and 2505.

Unified transfer tax. Rates applicable to transfers by gift and death made after 1976. § 2001(c).

Uniform Gift to Minors Act. A means of transferring property (usually stocks and bonds) to a minor. The designated custodian of the property can act on behalf of the minor without requiring a *guardianship.* Generally, the custodian possesses the right to change investments (e.g., sell one type of stock and buy another), apply the income from the custodial property to the minor's support, and even terminate the custodianship. During the period of the custodianship, the income from the property is taxed to the minor, although perhaps subject to *kiddie tax* rates. The custodianship terminates when the minor reaches *legal age.*

Unitary state. A state that has adopted the unitary theory in its apportionment of the total taxable income of a multistate corporation to the state.

Unitary theory. Sales, property, and payroll of related corporations are combined for *nexus* and apportionment purposes, and the worldwide income of the unitary entity is *apportioned* to the state. Subsidiaries and other affiliated corporations found to be part of the corporation's unitary business (because they are subject to overlapping ownership, operation, or management) are included in the apportionment procedure. This approach can be limited if a *water's edge election* is in effect.

Unrealized receivables. Amounts earned by a cash basis taxpayer but not yet received. Because of the method of accounting used by the taxpayer, these amounts have a zero income tax basis. When unrealized receivables are distributed to a partner, they generally convert a transaction from nontaxable to taxable or an otherwise capital gain to ordinary income.

Unreasonable compensation. A deduction is allowed for "reasonable" salaries or other compensation for personal services actually rendered. To the extent compensation is "excessive" ("unreasonable"), no deduction is allowed. Unreasonable compensation usually is found in closely held corporations, where the motivation is to pay out profits in some form that is deductible to the corporation.

Unrelated business income. Income recognized by an exempt organization that is generated from activities not related to the exempt purpose of the entity. For instance, the pharmacy located in a hospital often generates unrelated business income. § 511.

Unrelated business income tax. Levied on the *unrelated business income* of an *exempt organization.*

U.S.-owned foreign corporation. A foreign corporation in which 50 percent or more of the total combined voting power or total value of the stock of the corporation is held directly or indirectly by U.S. persons. A U.S. corporation is treated as a U.S.-owned foreign corporation if the dividend or interest income it pays is classified as foreign source under § 861.

U.S. real property interest. Any direct interest in real property situated in the United States and any interest in a domestic corporation (other than solely as a creditor) unless the taxpayer can establish that a domestic corporation was not a U.S. real property holding corporation during the five-year period ending on the date of disposition of such interest (the base period). See *FIRPTA.*

U.S. shareholder. For purposes of classification of an entity as a *controlled foreign corporation,* a U.S. person who owns, or is considered to own, 10 percent or more of the total combined voting power of all classes of voting stock of a foreign corporation. Stock owned directly, indirectly, and constructively is counted for this purpose.

U.S.-source income. Generally, income taxed by the United States, regardless of the citizenship or residence of its creator. Examples include income from sales of U.S. real estate and dividends from U.S. corporations.

U.S. Tax Court. See *Tax Court.*

U.S. trade or business. A set of activities that is carried on in a regular, continuous, and substantial manner. A non-U.S. taxpayer is subject to U.S. tax on the taxable income that is effectively connected with a U.S. trade or business.

Use tax. A sales tax that is collectible by the seller where the purchaser is domiciled in a different state.

USSC. An abbreviation for the U.S. Supreme Court, used in citing court opinions.

USTC. Published by Commerce Clearing House, *U.S. Tax Cases* contain all of the Federal tax decisions issued by the U.S. District Courts, U.S. Court of Federal Claims, U.S. Courts of Appeals, and the U.S. Supreme Court.

V

Value. See *fair market value.*

Vested. Absolute and complete. If, for example, a person holds a vested interest in property, such interest cannot be taken away or otherwise defeated.

Voluntary revocation. The owners of a majority of shares in an S corporation elect to terminate the S status of the entity, as of a specified date. The day on which the revocation is effective is the first day of the corporation's C tax year.

Voting trust. A trust that holds the voting rights to stock in a corporation. It is a useful device when a majority of the shareholders in a corporation cannot agree on corporate policy.

W

W–2 wages. The *domestic production activities deduction (DPAD)* cannot exceed 50% of the manufacturer's W–2 wages paid for the year. Several methods can be used to calculate the W–2 wages. The employee's work must be involved in the production process. § 199(b)(2).

Wash sale. A loss from the sale of stock or securities that is disallowed because the taxpayer has, within 30 days before or after the sale, acquired stock or securities substantially identical to those sold. § 1091.

Water's edge election. A limitation on the worldwide scope of the *unitary theory.* If a corporate water's edge election is in effect, the state can consider only the activities that occur within the boundaries of the United States in the *apportionment* procedure.

WESTLAW. An online database system, produced by the West Group, through which a tax researcher can obtain access to the Internal Revenue Code, Regulations, administrative rulings, and court case opinions.

Wherewithal to pay. A concept of tax equity that delays the recognition of gain on a transaction until the taxpayer has received means by which to pay the tax. The *installment method,* whereunder gain is taxed proportionately as installment proceeds are received, embodies the wherewithal to pay concept. See also *involuntary conversion* and *like-kind exchange.*

Writ of Certiorari. See *certiorari.*

[See Title 26 U.S.C.A.]

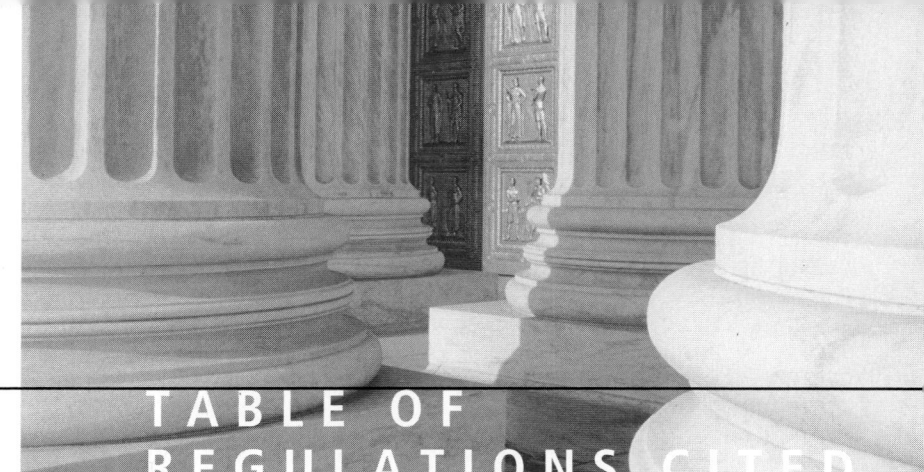

TABLE OF REGULATIONS CITED

Treasury Regulations

TABLE OF REVENUE PROCEDURES AND REVENUE RULINGS CITED

INDEX

B

C

E

G

S

U

Tax Return
Dr   Cr

1500

Unified Transfer Tax Rates

For Gifts Made and for Deaths in 2007–2009

If the Amount with Respect to Which the Tentative Tax to Be Computed Is:	The Tentative Tax Is:
Not over $10,000	18 percent of such amount.
Over $10,000 but not over $20,000	$1,800, plus 20 percent of the excess of such amount over $10,000.
Over $20,000 but not over $40,000	$3,800, plus 22 percent of the excess of such amount over $20,000.
Over $40,000 but not over $60,000	$8,200, plus 24 percent of the excess of such amount over $40,000.
Over $60,000 but not over $80,000	$13,000, plus 26 percent of the excess of such amount over $60,000.
Over $80,000 but not over $100,000	$18,200, plus 28 percent of the excess of such amount over $80,000.
Over $100,000 but not over $150,000	$23,800, plus 30 percent of the excess of such amount over $100,000.
Over $150,000 but not over $250,000	$38,800, plus 32 percent of the excess of such amount over $150,000.
Over $250,000 but not over $500,000	$70,800, plus 34 percent of the excess of such amount over $250,000.
Over $500,000 but not over $750,000	$155,800, plus 37 percent of the excess of such amount over $500,000.
Over $750,000 but not over $1,000,000	$248,300, plus 39 percent of the excess of such amount over $750,000.
Over $1,000,000 but not over $1,250,000	$345,800, plus 41 percent of the excess of such amount over $1,000,000.
Over $1,250,000 but not over $1,500,000	$448,300, plus 43 percent of the excess of such amount over $1,250,000.
Over $1,500,000	$555,800, plus 45 percent of the excess of such amount over $1,500,000.